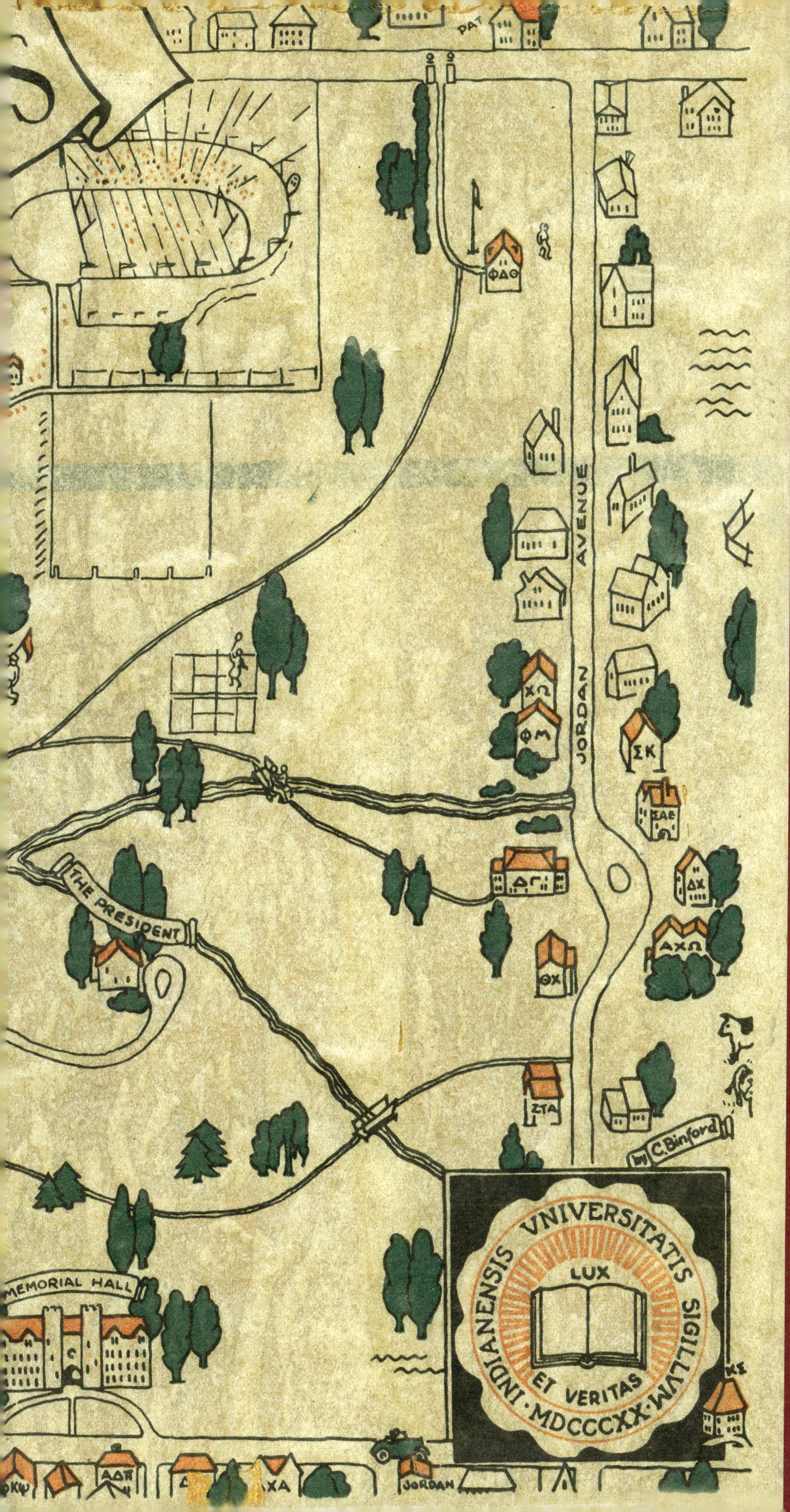

ΦΔΘ
JORDAN AVENUE
ΧΩ
ΦΜ
ΣΚ
ΔΓ
ΘΧ
ΔΧ
ΑΧΩ
ΖΤΑ
THE PRESIDENT
C. Binford
MEMORIAL HALL
INDIANENSIS UNIVERSITATIS SIGILLUM
LUX
ET VERITAS
MDCCCXX
JORDAN
ΑΔΠ
ΧΑ

INDIANA UNIVERSITY

BLOOMINGTON

To teach is to touch a life forever!

Congratulations Hannah!

We are so proud of you!

Love,

Mom, Dad and Kayt.

2020

A sense of something dear gone-by
Will stir, strange longings thrill the heart
For a small world embowered and close
Of which ye some time were a part.

EDWARD DOWDEN
"In the Cathedral Close"

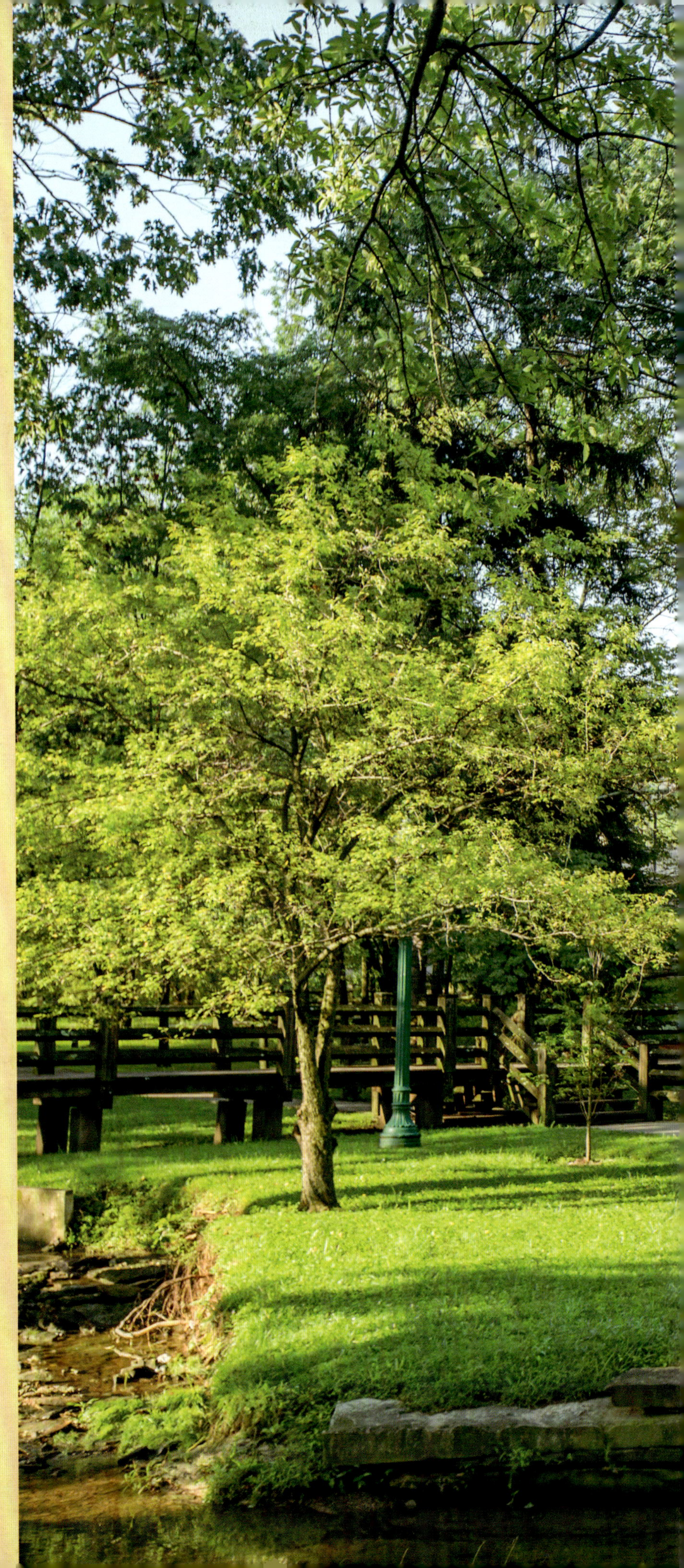

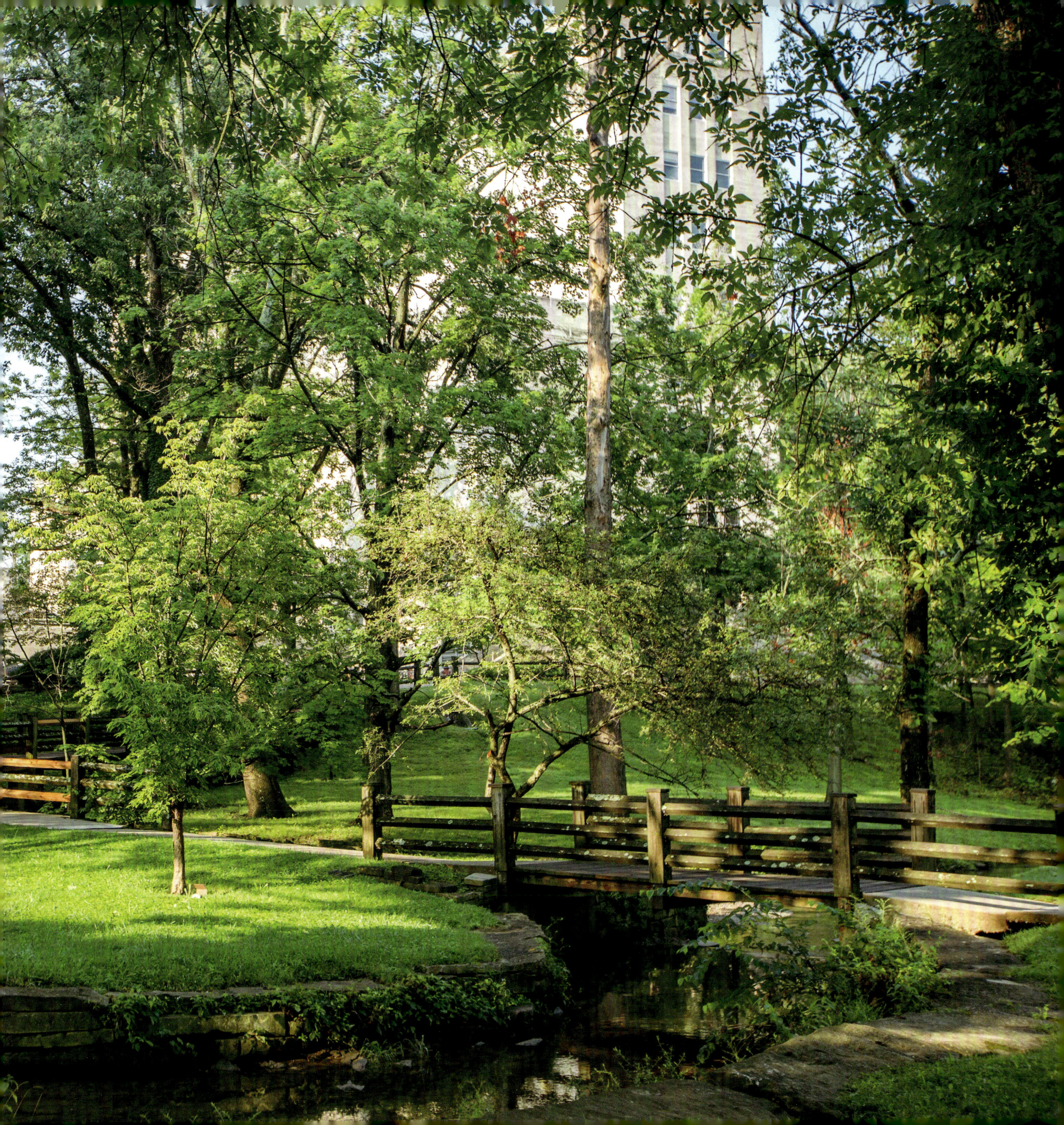

J. Terry Clapacs

With

SUSAN MOKE

DINA KELLAMS

AND

CARRIE SCHWIER

Edited by Linda Quigley

INDIANA UNIVERSITY PRESS

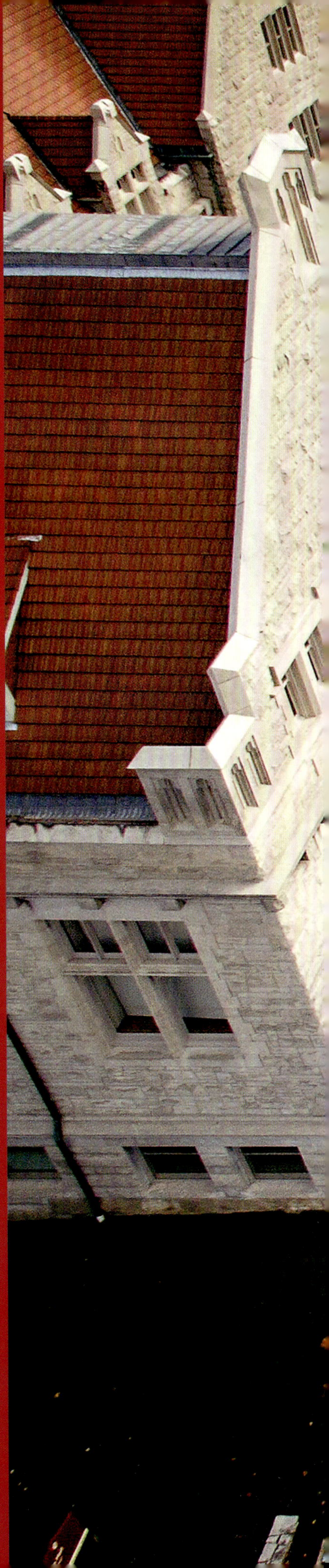

INDIANA UNIVERSITY

BLOOMINGTON

America's Legacy Campus

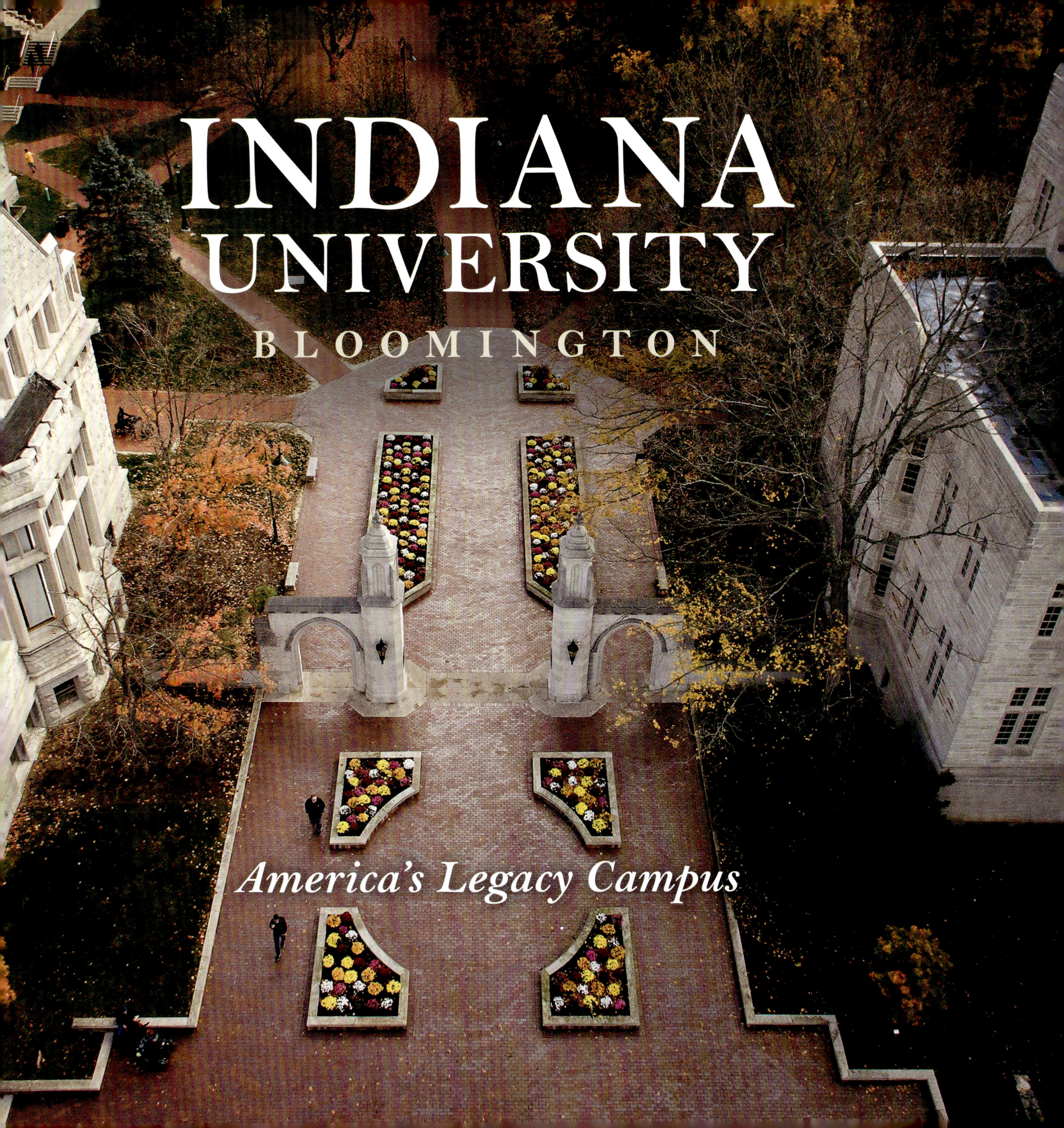

This book is a publication of

Indiana University Press
Office of Scholarly Publishing
Herman B Wells Library 350
1320 East 10th Street
Bloomington, Indiana 47405 USA

iupress.indiana.edu

Cover photo: Dunn's Woods just north of Swain Hall East, 1993. P0029530, IU Archives. Photo credit: Beverly Y. Sympson.

Front Endpaper illustration: Hand-drawn map of campus by student Charles Binford, circa 1929. P0034273, IU Archives.

Back Endpaper illustration: Photo credit: P0026037, IU Archives.

This book is printed on acid-free paper

Manufactured in China

Cataloging information is available from the Library of Congress.

ISBN 978-0-253-02903-4 (cloth)
ISBN 978-0-253-02928-7 (e-book)

1 2 3 4 5 22 21 20 19 18 17

CONTENTS

THE PROFESSIONS

THE SCIENCES

STUDENT HOUSING

COMMON FACILITIES

GREEN SPACES AND PUBLIC ART

CREAM AND CRIMSON SPIRIT

FOREWORD

Indiana University President Michael A. McRobbie

On January 20, 2020, Indiana University (IU) will celebrate its bicentennial—an event of the greatest importance in the life of any institution. For nearly two centuries, IU has served the people of Indiana and ascended to become one of the nation's and world's finest research universities. The bicentennial is truly an occasion for celebration and an opportunity to reflect with pride on all that Indiana University has achieved in the previous two hundred years.

Indiana University Bloomington: America's Legacy Campus is the first of several planned bicentennial publications by Indiana University Press, all of which will explore a wide variety of aspects of this university's rich history. This book focuses on the architectural heritage of the Bloomington campus—often cited as one of the most beautiful campuses in the country—and tells the story of its growth and development.

Many things characterize a great school like Indiana University—renowned faculty, dedicated administrators, a vibrant student body, distinguished academic and educational traditions, matchless heritage, highly engaged alumni, and a remarkable and inspiring history. In many ways, what unifies and brings all of this together is a beautiful campus and its extraordinary architecture. The impact of all of these has created the very essence of Indiana University. As Winston Churchill famously said, "We shape our buildings; thereafter they shape us."[1]

No one is better suited to tell the story of the architectural history of the Bloomington campus than Terry Clapacs. It is virtually impossible to look at any of the eight Indiana University campuses without seeing Terry's enormous impact. When he retired from the university in 2009 as vice president and chief administrative officer, Terry was one of the longest-serving vice presidents in Indiana University's history. Over the course of four decades, he worked for more than half a dozen IU presidents, and I am pleased to count myself among that number.

It is no exaggeration to say that over the years Terry has become a living archive of the transformations that have taken place across the university. During his years of dedicated service, Terry oversaw the development of approximately two-thirds of what is now Indiana University, including more than six hundred buildings throughout the IU system, as well as the construction of the Richmond and New Albany campuses.

Terry always understood that the first priority for any building or facility is that it serve as well as possible the needs of the faculty and students in pursuing education and research of the highest quality. He also understood that this could be done with structures of beauty and elegance. As the renowned art and social critic John Ruskin said, "We require from buildings two kinds of goodness: first, the doing their practical duty well: then that they be graceful and pleasing in doing it."[2]

Terry remained equally focused on preserving the natural beauty of IU's campuses. Like Herman B Wells, he understood that in order to cultivate the most productive intellectual environment, faculty and students need places to think, room to contemplate, space to debate and discuss. He understood that an inspiringly designed, well-built, and lovingly maintained environment could provide stimulation for these endeavors. Such an environment—the product of the "pleasing appearance and good taste of the whole" as the great Roman architect Vitruvius put it—leads to the kind of rich and lasting memories that continue to bring alumni back to the campus over and over again throughout their lives.[3] On the Bloomington campus and around the state, Terry oversaw the development of a physical environment that continues to encourage students and faculty alike to take on new intellectual challenges.

As deep and lasting an impact as Terry has had on the university, he would be the first to say that his achievements were due, in large part, to the efforts of a talented team of people. So, too, is this volume. Terry collaborated closely with the late Susan Moke, who worked as a writer for a number of Indiana University presidents and senior administrators, including myself. Terry also worked closely with Dina Kellams and Carrie Schwier of Indiana University Archives, whose extensive experience collecting, appraising, organizing, and preserving Indiana University's records will be as invaluable to future Bicentennial publications as it was to this volume. Linda Quigley, an IU alumna and longtime university employee, provided invaluable research and editorial guidance throughout the project.

During his time at Indiana University, one of Terry's greatest strengths was his ability to articulate to people his vision about the future landscape of the university, and to draw them in and inspire them to help build that landscape. This splendid book will draw readers in and help them to understand why and how the campus developed as it did. It will also introduce new members of the Indiana University community to the storied history of the Bloomington campus, and rekindle fond memories among those who have studied and taught in its iconic buildings or wandered its beautiful spaces.

Ultimately, *Indiana University Bloomington: America's Legacy Campus* tells the story of the development of a campus that has enjoyed tremendous success. Thus, it inspires all of us who care deeply about this great University to do all we can to ensure Indiana University's continued achievement during its third century and beyond.

ACKNOWLEDGMENTS

From the beginning it was clear a great deal of assistance and cooperation would be necessary to successfully complete this book. My acceptance of Indiana University President Michael McRobbie's suggestion to write a history of the Indiana University Bloomington campus—its buildings, grounds, and architectural styles—was conditioned on his "lending" the services of Susan Moke, a writer in his office, who would be a collaborator. Together Susan and I structured the book and began a monumental research effort that generated many file drawers of information for use as background material. Indiana University lost Susan way too early, and her passing left a broken circle of close friends as well as a large void in the project. Kelly Kish of IU's Office of the President, supportive in many ways throughout the progress of this book, came to the rescue by suggesting two outstanding IU archivists to help with the research and writing in their areas of special interest. Dina Kellams and Carrie Schwier proved to be delightful partners and now great friends. They are an essential component of the finished product. Our regular book meetings included hard work, history lessons, and side-splitting laughter, as both possess a keen sense of humor. Linda Quigley has been the editor since the outset, and her suggestions have consistently been right on target. Without question, the book would have never been finished without her editorial expertise and constant push to get things completed. I must thank Eli Molin for the valuable research material he provided as an intern in the formative years of the manuscript writing. The late former university architect and friend for more than fifty years, Ray Casati, answered many questions and revived old memories of our days together planning the campus. Another former university architect, Robert W. Meadows, and current senior associate university architect, Bob Richardson, were also very helpful in their willingness to share their professional knowledge. Dick Bishop, a longtime IU icon, Bloomington radio show host, and friend, provided background information and many amusing stories that found their way into the book. Unfortunately, Dick passed away before the book was completed. Patrick Murray and John Paflas, former colleagues, were instrumental in adding to the wealth of research and history, not only of the Indiana University campus but of the town of Bloomington, as well. Many of the wonderful photographs were taken by Tyagan Miller. I want to thank him for his amazing perception for just the right picture and his prodigious photography skills. Julie Stines, IU record keeper extraordinaire, was extremely gracious answering dozens of questions requiring her to consult age-old documents and photographs. This volume would not be complete without the contributions of Jim Madison, professor of history emeritus and the State of Indiana Historian; Jim wrote the essay "In the Beginning" and provided invaluable historical knowledge. A special thank you to Brian Keith, retired Senior Scientist from the Indiana Geological Survey, for his continuous support throughout the writing and his knowledgeable contributions toward the book's architectural narratives. I also want to thank Ken

Bikoff, media director for Peegs.com and former *Inside Indiana* editor-in-chief, who contributed his research and knowledge about IU athletic facilities, and also thank you to IU Athletics for sharing their photographs for use in this book. During the seven years of working on this book, I have been extremely fortunate to work with three outstanding editors from IU Press, Bob Sloane, who retired; Sarah Jacobi, who moved to another IU position; and finally Gary Dunham, who is not only editor for this book but director of IU Press. Many thanks to Nancy Lightfoot, IU Press project editor and manager, for her excellent direction and support. I also must thank Pam Rude, whose suggestions and artistic and technical skills have made possible the perfect combination and presentation of text and photographs. Peggy Solic of the IU Press staff has provided invaluable organizational skills as photographs and captions were selected and placed in appropriate sequence. Brad Cook of the Indiana University Archives provided substantial assistance in securing photographs and missing information. In addition, thank you to the two anonymous readers whose suggestions greatly improved the content of this book. Curt Simic, my close friend of fifty-five years and retired president of the Indiana University Foundation, and Ginger Winder, with whom our little band has shared office space since my retirement in 2009, tolerated many loud discussions and minor disruptions and for that I say "thank you." During our freshman year, more than half a century ago, I met Phyllis Wiseman while walking across this beautiful campus. We married upon graduation. Her love and support, along with that of our two boys, John Terry and Grantland, are the bedrock of my life and make it complete. They have been there for it all.

INTRODUCTION

Vice President Emeritus J. Terry Clapacs

In the midst of the gently rolling hills of southern Indiana is America's most beautiful college campus. Indiana University Bloomington, rich in architectural tradition, harmonious in building scale and materials, and comfortably nestled in a picturesque natural environment, stands today as a testimony to careful campus planning and committed stewardship. University administrators, trustees, and state leaders have preserved this treasure so that succeeding generations could enjoy the gifts found in this special place—an institution created to fulfill the promise of providing educational opportunity to every citizen of the state.

How Indiana University became a special combination of academic excellence and congruent beauty is a story filled with personalities and tradition. It is a story of two beginnings, sixty-five years apart at two separate campuses in Bloomington. It is a story of good fortune and profound leadership. It is a story that is also unique among major research universities in the United States. Planning principles adopted in the very early stages of campus development have been protected, enhanced, and faithfully preserved, resulting in an institution that can truly be called America's Legacy Campus. This book tells that story—a tale not only of the buildings, architecture, and growth, but of the people who brought the buildings to life. It is a story of academic achievement and scholarship advancement, a story of lives changed because students matriculated to IU and uncovered their dreams. Indiana University Bloomington has been a place for students from large cities and small towns across the state of Indiana, around the nation, and around the world to come and discover new interests, explore fresh ideas, and experience diverse peoples and cultures. A significant core value and institutional commitment at Indiana University is to provide an environment that is more than pleasant and comfortable—the campus is meant to inspire and to instill the idea that one's surroundings do make a difference.

For more than four decades I enjoyed the privilege of playing a role in the planning, building, and maintenance of the Indiana University Bloomington campus. For twenty-three of those years, I was the vice president and chief administrative officer, a position that included overseeing all of Indiana University's physical development (including Indiana University–Purdue University Indianapolis and the regional campuses). I had no idea in 1966 that my career would become a passion. Architecture quickly surfaced as an endless source of interest and pleasure, and I learned from many who were already making major contributions to Indiana University. Ray Casati, who served as IU's architect for more than fifty years, would top the list of tutors but there were others, too, like trustee Richard B. Stoner of Columbus, Indiana, who demonstrated through their work the importance of strong and thoughtful design. My on-the-job training resulted in an appreciation and commitment to ensuring that the architectural style and surrounding green space for each new building remained concordant with the past. The planning mantra was that every new

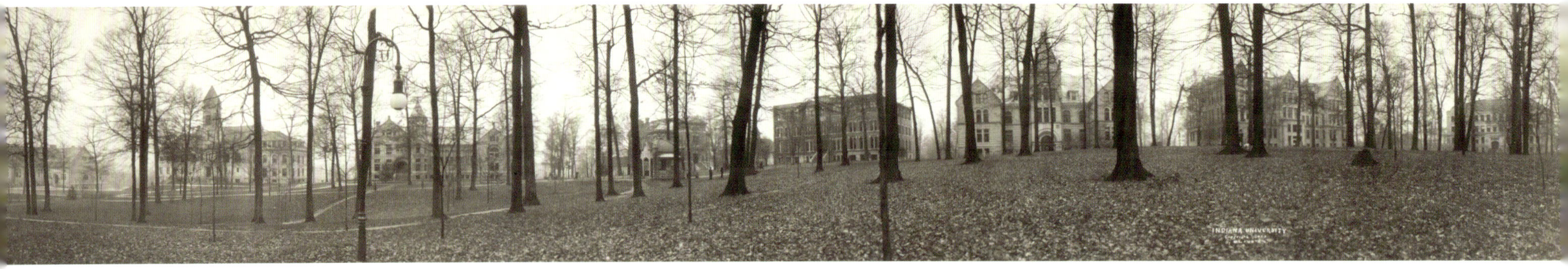

Black-and-white panorama of the Old Crescent, circa 1913. PAN US GEOG—Indiana no. 24, Library of Congress Prints and Photographs Division. Photo credit: O. L. Foster.

building should contribute to the campus as a whole, never stand on its own as a single architectural statement. Understanding and honoring historic places on campus, particularly the Old Crescent, provided a context for beginning each new building design. It was always clear to me that the best strategy for achieving these goals was to continue the master planning direction of the two longest-serving IU presidents, William Lowe Bryan and Herman B Wells. They have been guiding stars throughout my time at IU.

As retirement approached, it was obvious that stepping away from university responsibilities would leave a large void in my life. As discussions ensued about the transition with then president Michael McRobbie, he made a surprising suggestion: "Why don't you write a book about the history of IU's physical development?" The idea had never crossed my mind, but as I thought about his proposal, the more appealing it became. The next time we met I enthusiastically accepted his offer. We agreed work would begin following a short time away from the university. You are about to read the finished product.

LET'S COMMENCE WITH A LITTLE HISTORY . . .

Indiana University's beginnings took root from seeds planted by an 1816 act of the United States Congress that admitted Indiana into the Union as the nineteenth state. The Indiana Constitution, passed later in 1816 at Corydon, provided for the creation of a seminary (college). Eleven days after the constitutional convention adjourned, President James Madison, relying on survey maps prepared in 1812, designated a township in what would become Monroe County for the seminary's location. Madison couldn't have known the site he selected was directly over some of the purest limestone deposits in the world and that limestone would later be used as the primary exterior building material, helping give IU its distinctive uniform style and appearance. It is also unlikely that Madison understood the significance of the site selected in terms of its proximity to the terminal moraine of the last great glacial period in North America. The future site of Indiana University was just beyond the southernmost push of the Wisconsin Glacier, which had dramatically altered the landscape of the new state twelve thousand years earlier, creating an almost schizophrenic topography. The northern two-thirds of the state are basically flat, with rich soil suitable for agriculture, while the southern third of Indiana is more undulating and picturesque. The serendipitous location of the Indiana State Seminary—as it was then named—in the southern sector of the new state, provided a perfect setting for creating and nurturing what is now a campus wonderfully integrated with its natural environment.

The state of Indiana is unique in that the settlement pattern was primarily south to north, rather than the customary east to west pattern that took place in most states, particularly those west of the Appalachian Mountains. Individuals and families looking for a new place to call home generally traveled to Indiana by barge down the Ohio River or by wagon through the Cumberland Gap. They followed Indian trails and buffalo traces or made their own trails through the woods. Most were of English, Scottish, and Irish decent and brought with them the customs of those homelands. The movement of Abraham Lincoln's family was typical of settlement in the early 1800s: from Kentucky to Indiana and then north, in their case, to central Illinois. Those pioneers who stayed in Indiana cut farmland out of the heavily wooded countryside. It was a difficult life, and the settlers who came to Monroe County encountered many hardships. Still, they prospered and cultivated an educational system, so their children would have an opportunity to study and gain the advantage of a full education from township schools to a state university.

OLD COLLEGE CAMPUS, 1820–1883

In 1820 the state of Indiana consisted mainly of those counties located closest to the Ohio River, or about a third of what the state is today. In fact, just north of what is now Monroe County was land claimed by one or more of the thirteen Native American tribes that inhabited the region at the time of state admission to the Union. Indiana's population was counted at approximately a hundred thousand, and there were fewer than six hundred people living in the settlement of Bloomington. The site selected for the new seminary was as modest as the state it was to serve. It was located approximately a half mile south of the Bloomington Town Square on 11 acres of land. The site chosen was on high ground and conveniently close to a water source. Although authorization for the construction of the seminary was granted in 1820, work on the first building was not begun until 1822 and completed in 1824. The first seminary classes were held in 1825. The Seminary Square site, or the old college campus as it is now called, served the university for the next sixty years.

During the night of July 12, 1883, lightning struck Science Hall. In the resulting fire, the twelve thousand volumes constituting the school's entire library were lost. Also consumed by the fire were university records, the papers of David Starr Jordan (who became IU's seventh president), and the 85,000-specimen geological and archaeological cabinet assembled by the Owen brothers (David, Robert, and Dale) and Alexander and William Maclure. Following the fire, the university was in crisis, and soon newspapers around the state were running editorials calling for moving the campus to Indianapolis, the state capital.

The call to move the university was persuasive. The current site was compromised by the railroad to the west and the town of Bloomington just to the north. Railroad noise was a constant source of irritation to faculty and students. And then there were the fires. One in 1854 could be blamed on arson, but the 1883 fire was universally believed to be the result of lightning. This strike on Science Hall was seen as a sign from God to seek an improved, or at least different, setting for the university.

Furthermore, by the late 1800s, the country had changed and was continuing to evolve at a rapid pace. Indiana was

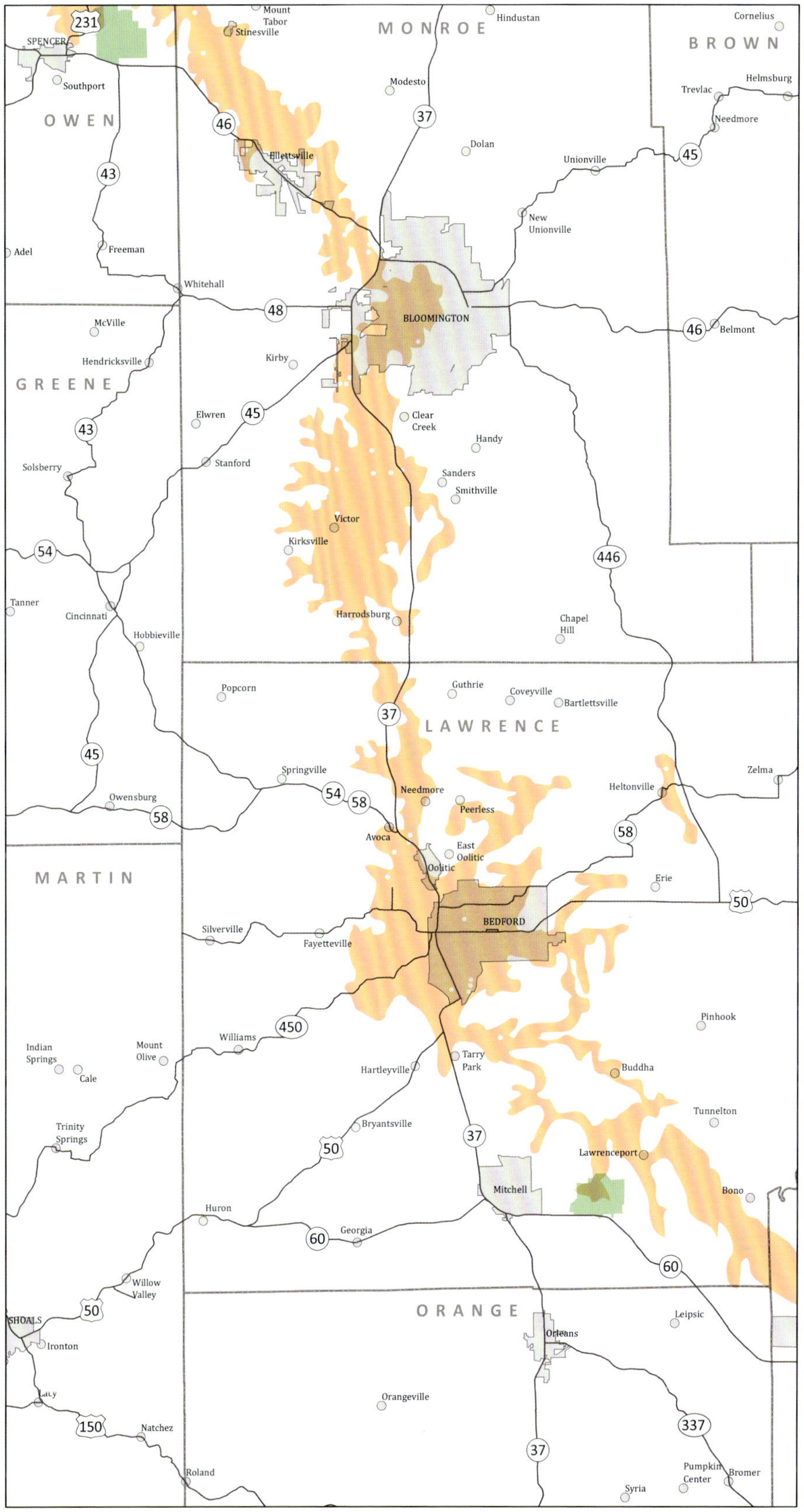

Map defining Salem limestone deposits in southern Indiana. Geological Survey.

no longer the frontier. Since its admission as the nineteenth state in 1816, Indiana was now joined by an additional nineteen states pushing the western boundary of the United States across the Mississippi River to the Pacific Ocean. Completion of the Transcontinental Railroad unified the states and made comfortable and reasonably safe travel possible from one end of the country to the other. The character of the United States was also shifting as a result of major discoveries and inventions that had taken place over the previous six decades. The coming of the telegraph, telephone, steam engine, internal combustion engine, and electric light bulb altered US life in startling ways, as did the transition from an agricultural to an industrial economy. Further, the social and economic changes brought about by the Civil War, during which some Indiana University students volunteered to fight for the Confederates and others for the Union, had permanently reshaped the country. The university would need room to grow if it were to fulfill its destiny. Banding together, the school and local community determined that Indiana University would remain in Bloomington, or at least close by.

Several sites in Monroe County were considered. In a close, five-to-three vote, IU trustees decided to move the university to a site on the eastern edge of Bloomington, a mile from the original seminary location. Hence, conceived in the afterglow of the American Revolution and established on land settled by the families of those who fought in that war and then crossed the Appalachian Mountains looking for a better life, Indiana University began a new chapter in its history. The old campus would be abandoned and the university would remake itself in a place that provided unlimited opportunity for growth and development. This place would attract the best faculty from around the world, and students would follow them to profit from their research and teaching. It became a place of great beauty and a testament to the importance of proper care and maintenance of the landscape and buildings. The trustees sold part of the old campus property to the city of Bloomington to be used for a high school and made plans to move immediately.

DUNN'S WOODS AND THE NEW CAMPUS

When Indiana University purchased 20 acres of lightly wooded ground from Moses Fell Dunn in 1883, it nearly doubled the size of the campus. Situated on a beautiful eminence, the new campus had the added advantage of not being hemmed in on any side by natural or manmade barriers. The university purchased the land using $20,000 of insurance proceeds from the Science Hall fire. The additional $50,000 raised by citizens of Monroe County made possible the construction of the first two permanent buildings on the new campus, Wylie Hall and Owen Hall. The selected architect, George W. Bunting of Indianapolis, designed the new buildings, prescribing red brick as cladding material (much of the brick used came from the remains of Science Hall). Bunting was one of Indiana's most prolific courthouse architects. He had completed successful projects in Montgomery County, Bartholomew County, Johnson County, and nearby Greene County, Indiana. Wylie Hall and Owen Hall were of similar style and feel as Bunting's courthouse work. Bunting would subsequently design other buildings for Indiana University, but Owen and Wylie would be the only two constructed of brick.

The original 20-acre purchase would provide sufficient land to support construction of what would become the Old Crescent. When Wylie and Owen were sited at a right angle to one another, an implied commitment was made to the lineal extension of those lines. All new buildings planned in the next twenty-five years would contribute to the L-shaped crescent configuration. The middle portion of the property was preserved as a natural wooded area. In 1883, future university president David Starr Jordan said to President Lemuel Moss regarding the land purchase, "I am glad to hear of the general brightness of the prospects of the institution . . . the location is certainly better among those great maples. I hope that you will let none be cut down, except when their removal is absolutely necessary."[1] Jordan's recommendation to practice restraint would become a campus management principle for the university and remains in place today.

David Starr Jordan's appointment as president in 1885 coincided with the opening of the new campus and the dedications of Owen and Wylie Halls. At thirty-four, Jordan became the country's youngest university president and the first president of IU who was not an ordained minister; he was a scientist and educator. Jordan was a member of the pioneer class of undergraduates at Cornell University and received graduate training in medicine at Indiana Medical College. He brought to the presidency a call to reform the curriculum by adding elective opportunity similar to what was offered at Cornell. His transformation of course work became the predecessor to the modern liberal arts education, and it required a new classroom environment. Mitchell Hall and Maxwell Hall, planned during Jordan's term in office, were both a response to that need, and

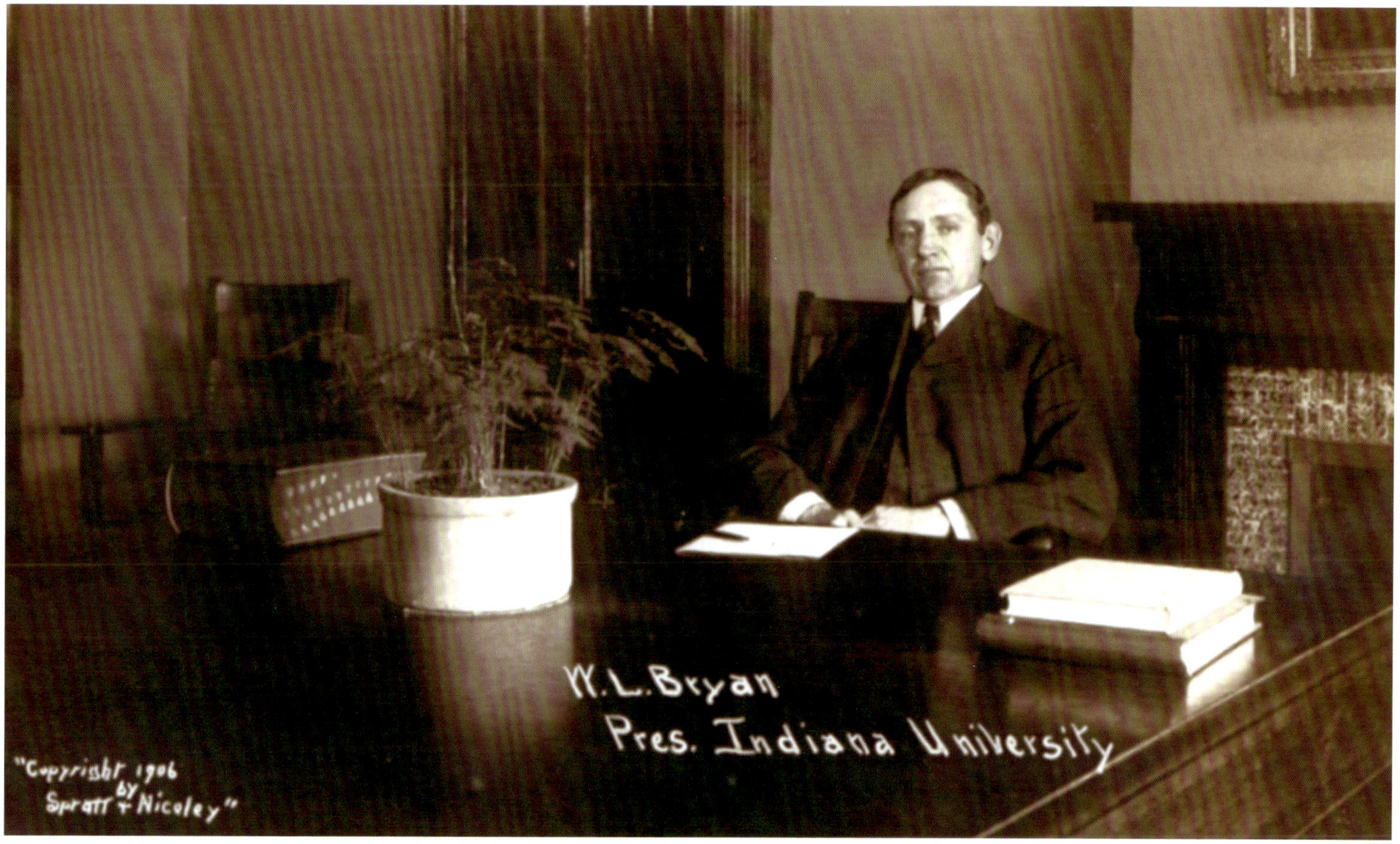

President William Lowe Bryan in his Maxwell Hall office, 1906. P0020474, IU Archives. Photo credit: Spratt and Niceley.

their completion continued the progression of the L-shaped Crescent.

The original 20-acre purchase of land from Moses Dunn was a significant move forward for Indiana University. However, the new campus, with its preserved wooded core of 10 acres, would need to expand soon if the site were to truly be a major improvement. Between 1883 and 1900, four additional parcels of property were acquired from the Dunn family, thus filling out the area that today is bounded by Indiana Avenue on the west, Seventh Street on the north, Third Street on the south and the drive that ran where Elisha Ballantine Hall sits today. With a total of 50 acres of ground, Indiana University was ready for the new century and the multitude of changes and development about to occur.

After serving Indiana University as president for six years, in 1891 David Starr Jordan accepted Leland and Jane Stanford's offer to become the first president of Stanford University. He took several prominent IU faculty members with him, including Professor of Mathematics Joseph Swain, who would return two years later to serve as IU's ninth president. The first native Hoosier to lead the university, Swain remained in that position until 1902. Indiana University was proving itself to be a fine training ground, as Joseph Swain departed to become president of Swarthmore College in 1902. At the time Joseph Swain left IU, William Lowe Bryan was a member of the faculty and vice president of the university. He succeeded Swain as president and remained in that position for thirty-five years. It is here, with President Bryan, that the modern story of Indiana University really begins.

WILLIAM LOWE BRYAN

When William Lowe Bryan moved into the president's office in 1902, seven buildings—Wylie Hall, Owen Hall, Mitchell Hall, Maxwell Hall, Kirkwood Hall, Kirkwood Observatory, and Lindley Hall (Science Hall)—comprised the new core campus. Each of the structures was an extension of the straight lines created by the right angle placement of Wylie and Owen. The L-shaped run of buildings surrounded a wooded area formally protected to give the campus a sense of place and recognition that there was value in the physical environment. The concept of mingling buildings and green areas was not new with Indiana University. Many universities had followed this model, notably used by Thomas Jefferson at the University of Virginia. Jefferson had designed that campus so that academic space, student living quarters, and faculty offices were sited around a tree-lined lawn, providing a pleasant and harmonious environment for teaching and scholarship—it was his "Academical Village." Thomas Jefferson had conceived a uniquely fashioned American college campus, establishing the first connection between learning and aesthetics.

President Bryan understood that his university was blessed in many ways. He saw that the natural setting provided by its southern Indiana location would require little in grounds alteration to be beautiful—the land was already forested, and the terrain gently rolling. Adhering to the simple principle that buildings should fit the landscape, rather than the other way around, would retain a natural feel on the campus.

Before William Lowe Bryan became president, campus planners had made one very important decision that would guide the university to this day. Limestone would be the primary building material used for its structures. Two phenomena influenced this decision. The country had witnessed massive structural destruction and loss of life as a result of fires in larger cities. The Great Chicago Fire of 1871, the Great Boston Fire of 1872, and the Seattle fire of 1889 were national calamities. One observation to come from the fires was that limestone buildings suffered less damage than brick buildings. In 1876, T. H. Oakshout of the US Office of Superintendent of Public Buildings declared Indiana limestone to be superior to any other stone quarried in the country. In addition, the rich limestone deposits found in Monroe and Lawrence counties supplied new markets as a result of transportation and shipping options provided by the completion of the north- and southgoing Monon Railroad that linked the town to major urban centers. The limestone industry began to flourish in the Bloomington area. Certainly Indiana University's new buildings would be, and should be, examples of how well limestone could serve as an exterior skin. All buildings constructed by the university after 1885 would be designed using limestone or would at least convey a stone appearance. That decision has become central to the unified look of the Indiana University campus. William Lowe Bryan endorsed and followed that direction during his entire thirty-five-year tenure as president.

Because President Bryan's administration is so far removed from today's generation, he is not usually given credit for the significant role he played in shaping the present-day Indiana University campus. But it was Bryan who commissioned the first two formal master plans for the campus. In 1915, George Kessler was hired to do the first fully comprehensive master plan, which laid the groundwork for much of the university's future expansion. Kessler was a city planner and landscape architect who believed "planning should be comprehensive. Even though a grand design could only be realized in bits and pieces, and over a long period of years, still, we should always know where we are going."[2] Kessler's plan established and created a naturalistic campus environment and celebrated the architectural building style found in the initial set of structures completed around the Crescent. Kessler presented Bryan with a master plan that would welcome strong building design and the continued use of a common building vocabulary. It's one thing to receive a new master plan and quite another to follow the plan. Bryan did both.

The university was growing rapidly. Enrollment at the beginning of President Bryan's term stood at 655, but by 1929 it had grown to 3,591 students. More importantly, the curriculum had changed and was no longer classically based but now included more student choice within various disciplines. Along with increasing student population, and the expanding curriculum, the campus itself—its buildings and its grounds—needed to grow as well. Bryan called on the eminent Olmsted Brothers firm to extend the Kessler master plan. The Olmsted Brothers carried on the work of their father, Frederick Law Olmsted, who is sometimes referred to as the father of landscape architecture. Frederick Law Olmsted is credited with many significant design projects involving public spaces, including Central Park in New York City and his portfolio featured master planning at Stanford University, the University of California at Berkeley, and the University of Chicago campus. The Olmsted Brothers earned a strong reputation on their own, particularly for the role they played in helping to establish the National Park Service. At Indiana University, the Olmsted Brothers refined George Kessler's master plan and identified several new building sites. Walkways, drives, and the orderly repetition of quads extending east and north were incorporated. Making Third Street a crisp southern edge of the campus and the placement of Wells Quad and Myers Hall site locations are examples of the legacy passed on from the plan created by the Olmsted Brothers.

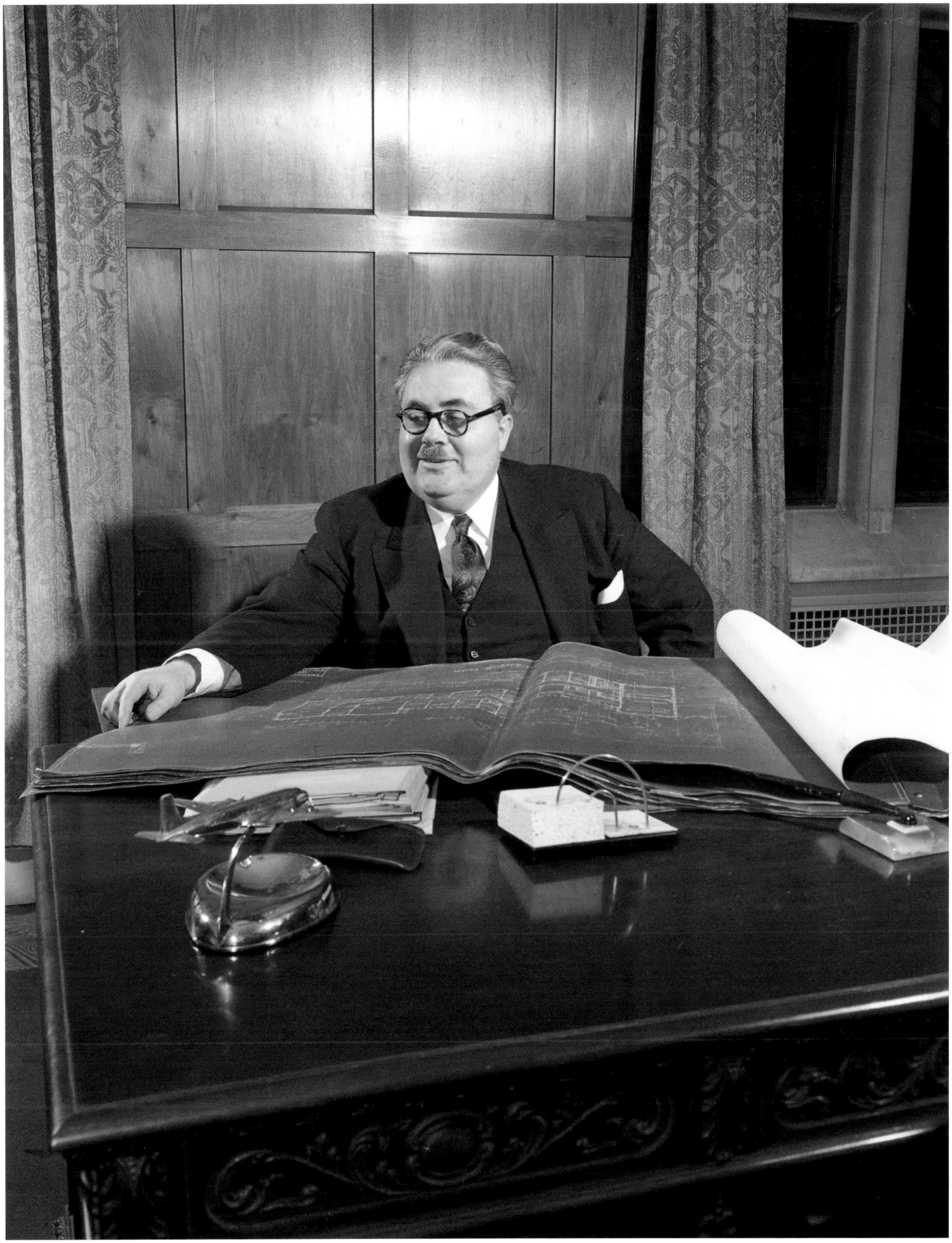

President Herman B Wells reviewing blueprints in his Bryan Hall office, 1950. P0035418, IU Archives.

In many ways, President William Lowe Bryan may be the most important figure in the Indiana University campus development story. He was the first to understand that Indiana University was changing dramatically as it moved into the twentieth century. He recognized how everyday campus life was changing, too, and why it was important to formally recognize those changes by commissioning a campus master plan and then updating that plan when warranted. Rather than insisting on a different style of architecture that would be more closely identified with his administration, Bryan embraced the Romanesque and traditional architectural styles established by his predecessors. The Student Building, Franklin Hall, and Swain Hall East demonstrate Bryan's commitment to those styles. As national architectural trends moved toward Collegiate Gothic, Bryan made sure that expression was blended with Romanesque detailing, thus allowing new structures such as the Memorial Union, Memorial and Louise A. Goodbody Halls, and Burton Dorr Myers Hall to harmonize with the rest of the campus and present a unified appearance. William Lowe Bryan gave the university a skeletal structure and a working palette consisting of limestone, slate roofs, and lush, natural landscape. His vision is still evident today.

HERMAN B WELLS

No other Indiana University leader is as highly respected and recognized as Herman B Wells, its president from 1938 to 1962. He is given the most credit for the success the university enjoys today both academically and aesthetically and he deserves much of that honor. Many present-day alumni had personal experience with Wells and tell stories of his incredible memory for names or the way he would walk across campus and interact with students. In many ways Wells and William Lowe Bryan are inextricably linked, and, from a historical point of view, Wells's administration is an extension of Bryan's. Both presidents were chosen from within the university, both were born in Indiana, and both brought to the office a genuine love for all things Hoosier, including southern Indiana, Bloomington, and the institution itself. Wells served as dean of the Commerce School under Bryan and endorsed Bryan's vision for what the university could and should become. Although Wells wasn't exactly a protégé of Bryan's, Wells nonetheless admired him greatly and publicly, and privately, called him one of the finest men he had ever met. The development of the campus barely missed a step in the transition between the two.

President Herman B Wells, or Hermie as he was often called on and off the campus, possessed a dynamic personality. He was smart, convivial, driven, and pragmatic. His natural charisma was gently muted by his small-town Indiana upbringing. He had the full confidence of the faculty and state political leaders, and all trusted him to always do what was best for the university. His quarter-century of leadership elevated Indiana University to national and international stature.

Herman Wells looked at campus planning a little differently than his predecessor Bryan, however. He thought planning should be an ongoing process, so he stayed away from printing and binding a master plan in finished presentation form. Wells preferred to keep master plans "loose-leaf," as he called it, and therefore fully accommodating to an ever-changing university. Wells adopted a practice still used by IU today of working with a master architect. Dr. Wells knew the university's thin planning staff would need assistance with key strategic issues as the campus continued to grow. Always pushing the notion of strong continuity and planning integrity, he thought it best to establish a working relationship with a highly experienced architect who was part of a national design firm. He found his man in Ted Young of the Eggers and Higgins firm, based in New York City. Young worked with the university for a number of years, providing schematic design solutions for new buildings and helping to keep the larger master plan in good order. As Young neared retirement, Bob Welz of that firm assumed his responsibility. President Wells always took care to pair Eggers and Higgins with an Indiana architectural firm. The customary fee arrangement was 20 percent of the fee to Eggers and Higgins for schematic design, and 80 percent of the fee to the Indiana firm for design development, construction documents, and construction administration. Wells insisted on this arrangement to satisfy the state chapter of the American Institute of Architects (AIA) and attendant political supporters.

Indiana University under the leadership of Herman B Wells prospered and grew. A particularly difficult but nonetheless welcome problem Wells confronted was the return of thousands of veterans following World War II. Student enrollment in the fall of 1945 was 4,498. By the following fall, enrollment more than doubled to 10,345. Space to support students was at a premium, and Wells was forced to allow temporary barracks to be placed on the campus. Some of those "temporary" structures remained until the early 1990s. As the university caught up with demands for space, Wells pushed his building program ahead, and for the most part he was able to remain true to the principles he inherited from Bryan in terms of building style and scale. A notable exception, and one Wells regretted, was Ballantine Hall, so unlike any other on campus at the time. Although the classroom and office space provided by Ballantine Hall was critically needed at the time, today the large, monolithic building is a reminder of how even the best-intended initiatives can sometimes have unfortunate consequences when it comes to nurturing a major research university.

Most memorable about Herman Wells and his campus planning is that he was a visionary who knew instinctively what to hold on to and what to let go of. He embraced change and new directions but, at the same time, retained the best of the old culture and traditions. Master planning to him was a continuous process requiring constant evaluation and maximum flexibility. He saw planning as a discipline that was always forward-looking. Wells never let his ego move to the forefront; he kept the decision-making process focused on the university.

THE UNIVERSITY TODAY

Indiana University Bloomington today spreads over almost 2,000 acres. Half of the university's property lies east and north of the Indiana 45/46 Bypass and stands ready to support further expansion. There are 550 structures now on campus, and most observers agree that the building fabric adheres together in a very cohesive way. Since President Wells first engaged a master architect, three additional planners have been selected to fill that role. Edward Larrabee Barnes of the Edward Larrabee Barnes Associates firm in New York City and John Belle of Beyer Blender Belle Architects & Planners, also of New York City, served in the planning capacity first defined by President Wells. Barnes was master architect from the early 1970s to the early 1990s, and Belle picked up the role from the 1990s to 2008. Each gave the university excellent advice that resulted in the continuation and protection of the harmonious look of the campus. A major contribution of Barnes was to define the Bloomington campus by functional zones beginning with an academic core bounded by Third Street, Tenth Street, Indiana Avenue, and Union Street. Additional zones fanned out to the east and north to include residential, recreational, athletic, and research areas. These defined zones are still valid today.

A number of projects were undertaken by the University during the tenure of Barnes and Belle that required special care to ensure a good match with the rest of the campus. The art museum, designed by the renowned architect I. M. Pei, was constructed with cast-in-place concrete rather than limestone. Pei, recognizing the need to create a structure synoptic with the adjacent buildings, added a buff coloring to his concrete. His solution worked well providing a unified appearance. The Musical Arts Center, Student Recreational Sports Center, and several athletic venues also were completed without the use of limestone. Yet, they all blend pleasingly with the rest of the campus.

In 2007, Michael A. McRobbie, eighteenth president of Indiana University, selected David King of SmithGroupJJR in Washington, DC, to serve as master architect and campus planner. King was commissioned to undertake a comprehensive new plan for the IU Bloomington campus, which was completed by the firm and adopted by the trustees in 2009. The planning process was bold in its vision and adopted clear themes that resulted in exciting new recommendations for the future growth of the Indiana University campus. A number of new structures were immediately placed on the drawing board by President McRobbie, and architects and engineers worked furiously to keep pace with his new direction. The result has been the completion of several important additions to the campus that strengthen long-held university planning principles.

GETTING STARTED

A major step in the writing process is to decide how the book will be arranged. This challenge and many more were thoughtfully addressed by our project team with the goal of creating a volume that would be both informative and enjoyable to read. An obvious layout alternative was to simply go through the development of the campus in linear chronology—that is, begin with the first Indiana University building constructed and follow with a narrative about each building thereafter. However, after much discussion, we decided that formatting in micro-chronologies would allow for the clearest picture of how and why the campus exists as it does today. The campus has grown in waves depending on enrollment in various disciplines, available funding, and other economic and social variables affecting Indiana and the nation. The need for classrooms, common facilities, residential housing, and athletic venues ebbed and flowed throughout the years from 1820 to the present. This book, except for the chapter on Seminary Square, deals with the IU Bloomington campus beginning in 1884. My goal was that *Indiana University Bloomington:*

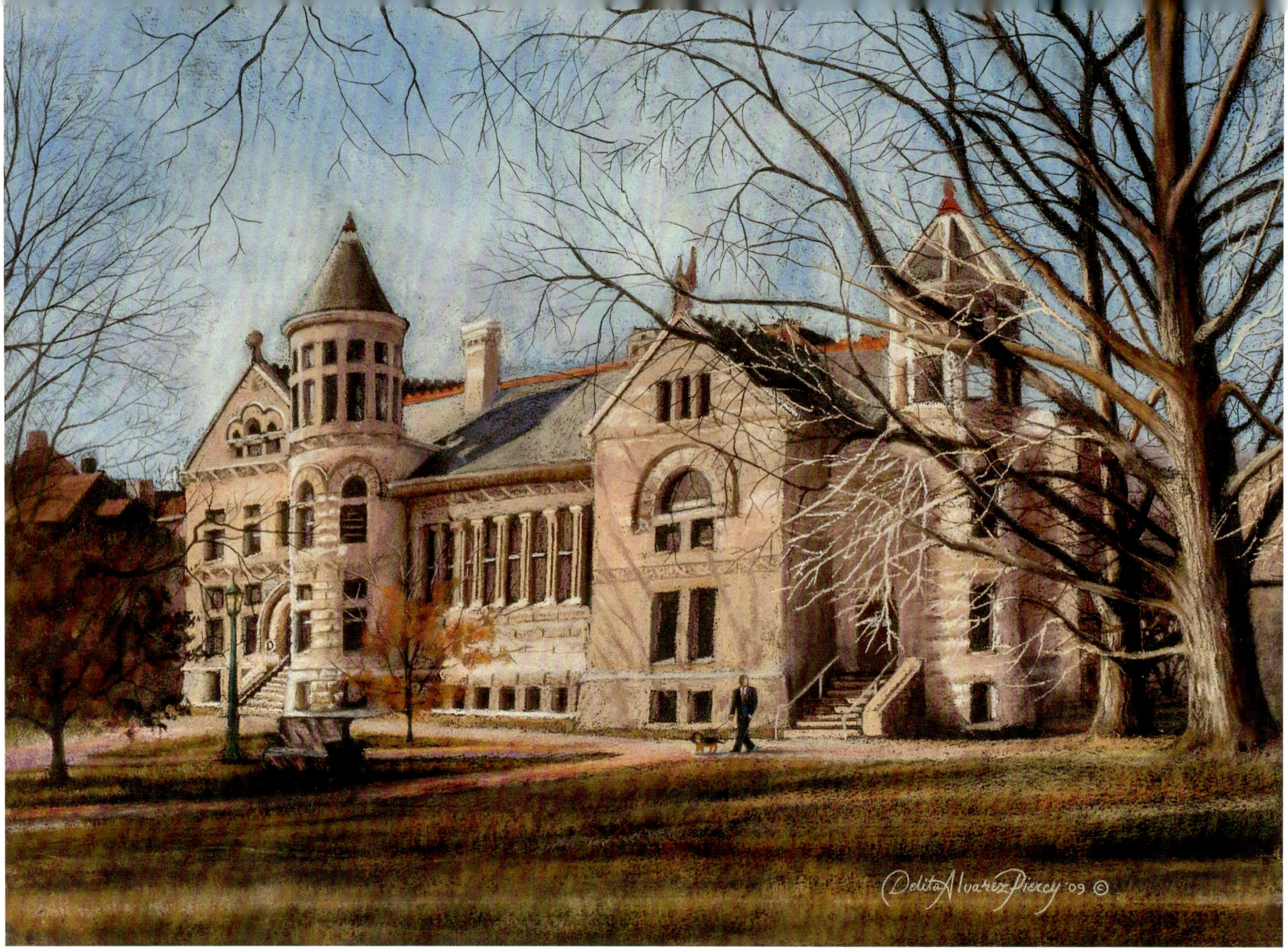

Painting of Maxwell Hall by Delita Piercy, 2009; note the author, J. Terry Clapacs, walking his beagle, Linus. Painting in author's private collection; photograph courtesy of Sidney and Lois Eskenazi Museum of Art.

America's Legacy Campus should reflect the evolution of the university, particularly its architecture, green spaces, and public art, since moving to the Dunn's Woods site.

Indiana University prior to 1884, the old Seminary Square campus, is described in the essay "In the Beginning" by Distinguished Professor of History James Madison, an expert on the old campus and Indiana state history. The opening chapters, covering buildings in the Old Crescent, set the tone for understanding why, in spite of embracing several architectural styles, the campus buildings relate to one another due to a common use of building materials and scale. Thereafter, the chapters are organized thematically according to discipline or function: "The Arts and Humanities," "The Professions," "The Sciences," "Student Housing," "Common Facilities," "Green Spaces and Public Art," "Cream and Crimson Spirit," and "The Way Things Might Have Been."

In the writing of this book, several themes anchored the intended framework.

The importance of master planning and IU's master planners

Presidential vision, particularly the roles of William Lowe Bryan and Herman B Wells, who successively served as Indiana University presidents for sixty years

The importance of landscaping and IU's woodland campus

The importance of philanthropy

How the curriculum drives the growth of the campus

My goal was to tell the story of Indiana University's growth from its original charter in 1820 to the present by describing the buildings and green spaces that comprise its historic, woodland campus. The university is more than buildings, of course. It is the people who conceive, construct, and inhabit them and the knowledge and experiences those individuals share. Thus, the narrative is replete with sketches about the buildings that provide insight into the lives of students, staff and administrators, whose stories are also the story of Indiana University.

IN THE BEGINNING

Although it was all very primitive, there was a definite recognition that there were great values in education, essential to the preservation of the democratic form of government [that the founders of the state of Indiana] had established. So here in the wilderness where Indian fires had but lately burned, they lighted the fire of Light and Truth which at times during sixty-five years flickered faintly but was never extinguished.

BURTON D. MYERS, Trustees and Officers of Indiana University 1820 to 1950

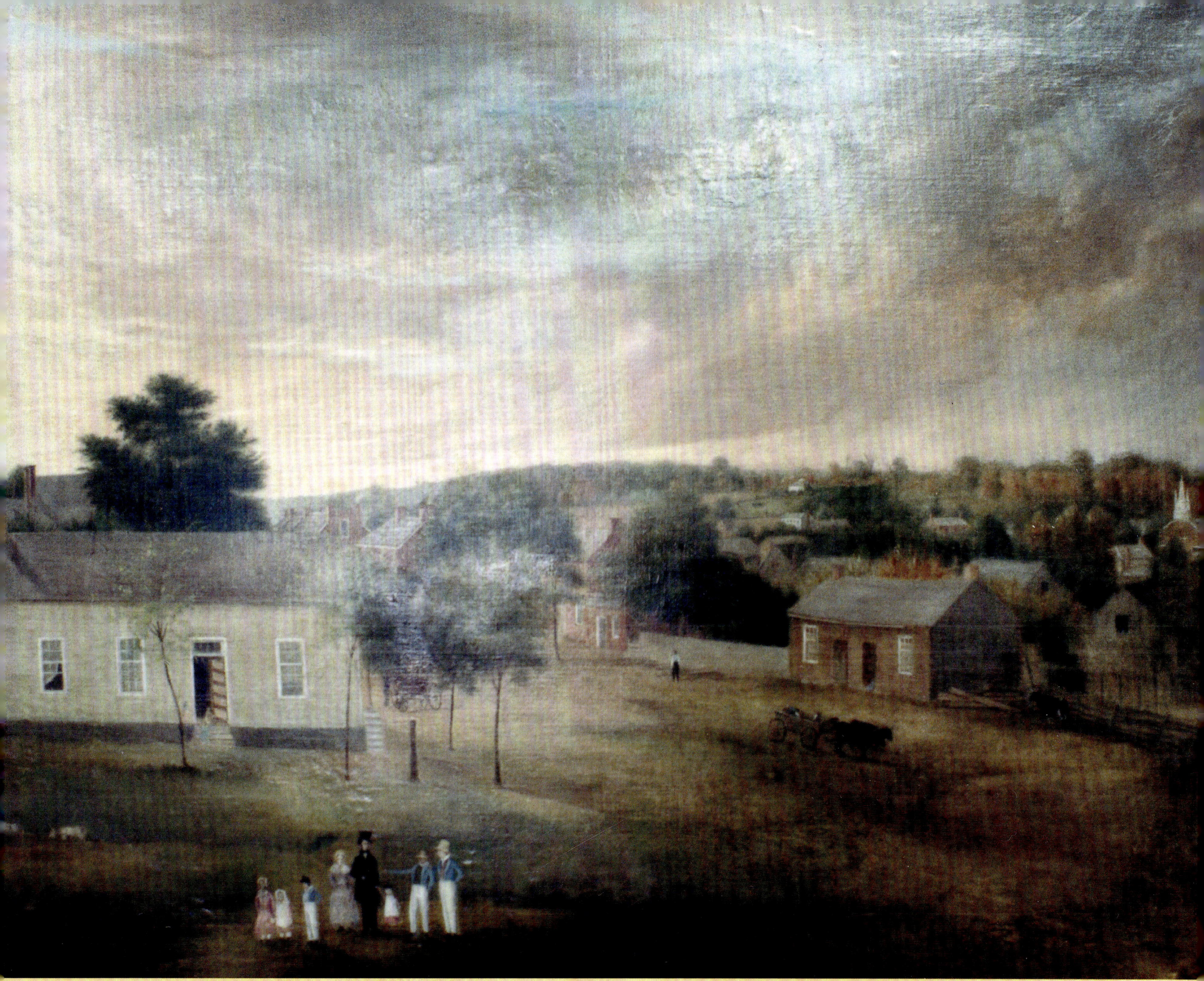

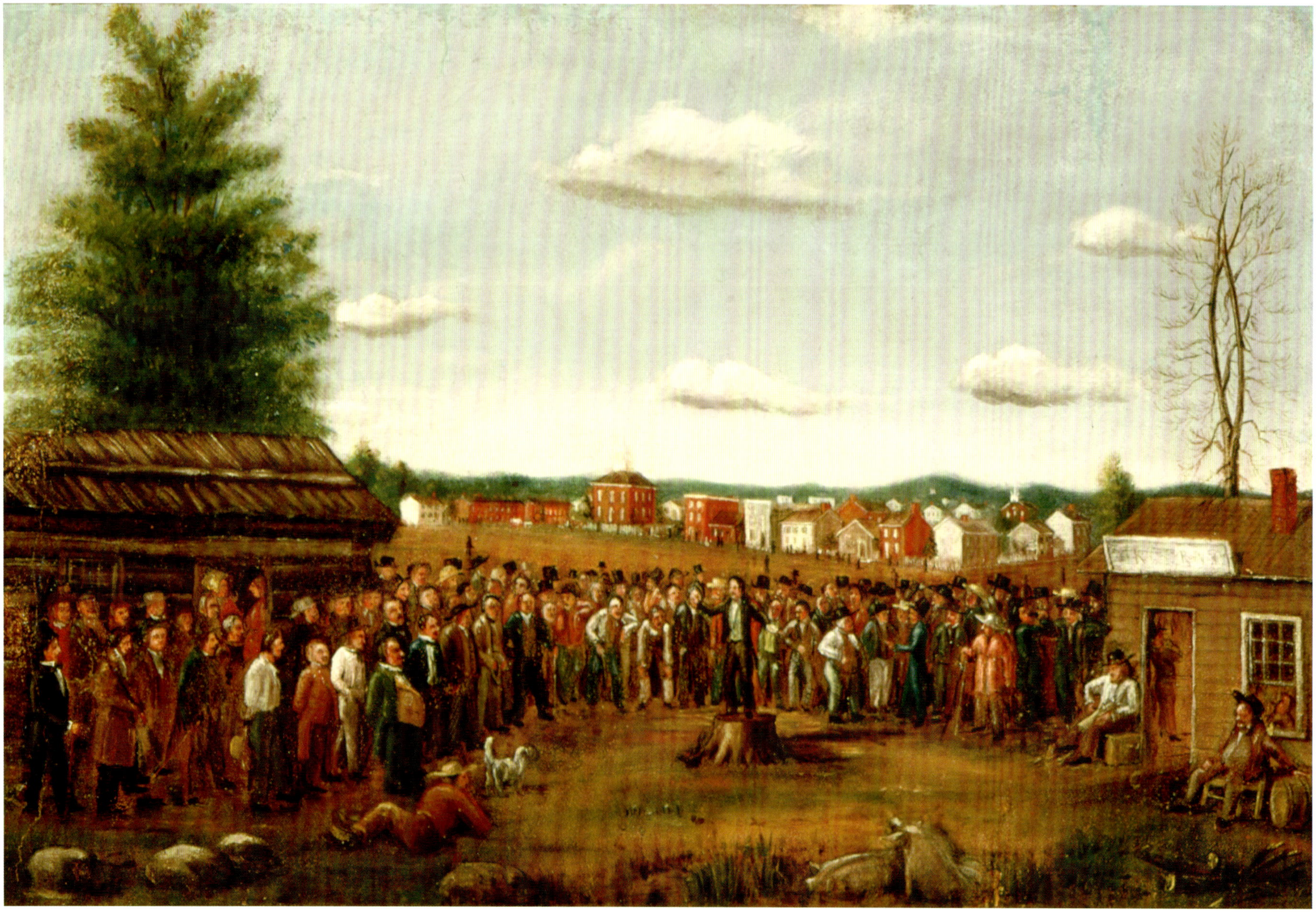

Glimpse of early Bloomington in *A Political Rally on the Square* by Theophilus A. Wylie, circa 1837. P0033916, IU Archives.

In the Beginning

The Seminary Square Campus

Professor James H. Madison

It was not a promising start. Why, after all, attempt to build a university in a frontier state with few books, newspapers, or schools? Abe Lincoln's family arrived on the Indiana frontier in 1816. He remembered: "We reached our new home about the time the State came into the Union. It was a wild region, with many bears and other wild animals, still in the woods. There I grew up. There were some schools, so called; but no qualification was ever required of a teacher beyond "readin, writin, and cipherin to the Rule of Three. If a straggler supposed to understand latin happened to sojourn in the neighborhood, he was looked upon as a wizzard [*sic*]."[1] In this wilderness some pioneers foretold the truth that an educated people might more readily become a democratic and prosperous people. Indiana's first Constitution (1816) contains words that are among the most important ever penned on Hoosier soil, committing the new state to create "a general system of education, ascending in a regular degradation from township schools to a state university, wherein tuition shall be gratis, and equally open to all."

In search of that future, state-appointed trustees in 1820 located a spot south of the Bloomington courthouse, a place with higher elevation and a spring for water. Work began on the Seminary Building and the professor's house in 1822, and both were completed by 1825. The Seminary Building was built of brick and locally cut timber, two stories high, 60 feet long and 31 feet wide, and topped by a bell. Some thought it pretentious, causing the trustees to explain to the legislature that they were wisely building for future growth. It housed classrooms, a chapel, administration office, some student bedrooms, and a janitor's room, where worked young Joseph A. Wright, who later would become governor of the state. A handful of students began meeting in the Seminary Building in 1825 to labor over Greek and Latin texts under the supervision of Professor Baynard Rush Hall. His house was of similar style as the Seminary Building, but much smaller; and Professor Hall, the school's only professor for a few years, brought a piano to the house, perhaps the first in Bloomington.

In 1836 a new three-story structure, sometimes called the First College Building, became the primary academic building. Construction began in 1829 but ran into obstacles along the way, such as faculty strife, an 1833 cholera outbreak, and lack of funding. The rectangular edifice had nineteen rooms, including a chapel, space for a library, and rooms for student literary societies. Believing an architect to be too costly, the trustees instead appointed a three-member committee to prepare a plan. The committee never reported its recommendations, and so, as one early writer, David D. Banta, claimed, the workers simply built upward until they ran out of bricks. The furnished structure was more functional in style than elegant, although it did have a belfry on top. A newly arrived faculty spouse recalled thinking at first sight that the Old College Building was a cotton mill.

Axes felled most of the trees on campus, but left stumps standing. Few called the place beautiful. A spring provided

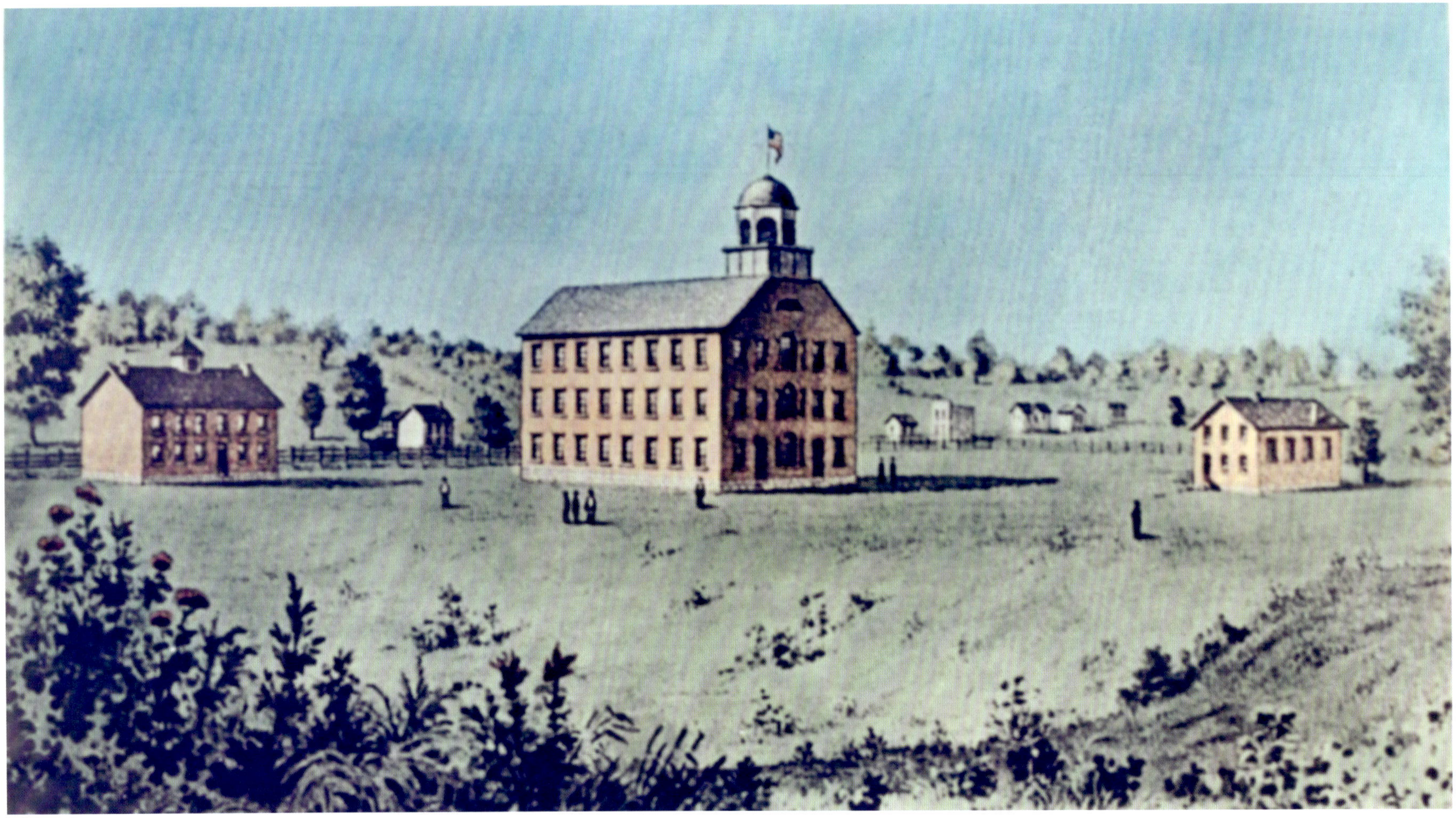

Seminary Square campus, 1890. *Left to right*: Seminary Building (circa 1825), First College Building (1836), and Laboratory (1840). P0022535, IU Archives. Artist: William B. Burford.

water, but became polluted—the beginning of decades of inadequate water supply. The town itself was isolated, as most Hoosiers lived along the rivers to the south, east, and west. Revenue from the sales of federal lands was intended to finance the new institution, but this was never adequate. The pioneer state had priorities more pressing than education. Trustees, faculty, and presidents struggled in the new college town to set a steady course toward a long-term mission. Andrew Wylie arrived as the first president in 1829. Six years later he began construction of his home, several blocks from the campus. Large and handsome, Wylie House stands today as a historic house museum at the corner of Second and Lincoln Streets.

Far more modest was the two-story boarding house, built as a reprieve for students struggling with boarding costs in town. Opened in 1838 and connected to the professor's house, it was a plain brick structure, 48 by 30 feet, with a gable roof. It was sold by the university in 1858 and razed in 1864. In the dining room and small bedrooms, young men found time to study, sleep, eat, and devise pranks, including stealing the bell clapper to prevent the call to morning chapel. Required chapel attendance brought out the best in student mischief. One lad once put a rooster inside the desk on the chapel rostrum so that when the presiding faulty member reached for the Bible he instead let free a cackling rooster. President Wylie was a firm Presbyterian, a clergyman like the five presidents who followed him. He insisted on daily chapel attendance and on disciplining students accused of cursing, chewing tobacco, drinking, and other immoral behaviors.

In 1840, a new laboratory building of three rooms provided space also for a lecture hall. In this modest brick structure, 48 by 32 feet, Professor Theophilus A. Wylie (the president's cousin) pursued his wide-ranging scientific interests. This building was sold in 1858. The university faced ongoing pressure to move to Indianapolis, the capital located in the center of the state.

And then there was fire. In the spring of 1854 a blaze turned the College Building to ashes, along with library books, school records, and the literary society collections. Insurance and contributions from local citizens enabled a hurried replacement and helped stay efforts to relocate the university to Indianapolis.

The fire pushed forward construction of the First University Building (also known as the Second College Building). Opened in 1855, it was a bit grander than its predecessor, fashioned of brick with limestone trim taken from a nearby quarry, and Collegiate Gothic in style that included gables, cornices, and a cupola. William Tinsley, an architect from Cincinnati, Ohio, designed it. The three stories included a chapel on the second floor with gas chandeliers to dispel the winter gloom. The chapel was also used for lecturers, including visitors such as the suffragist Elizabeth Cady Stanton, who much impressed Theophilus Wylie. Situated at the end of College Avenue, the building's main door looked north to the courthouse, connecting "town and gown" as the flagship building on campus. Later known as the Seminary Building, and although remodeled and repurposed, it stood into the 1960s.

In 1874, the seventh and last building was completed at Seminary Square; it was named Science Hall. This grand brick, Collegiate Gothic edifice, 130 by 50 feet and situated near the First University Building, enhanced the campus. It contained the massive collection of geological and zoological specimens gathered by David Dale Owen and his fellow New Harmony (Indiana) scientists, as well as laboratories, classrooms, and offices, and a room for the law department. The campus eventually included athletic grounds, beginning with a baseball diamond, a new sport brought to Bloomington by returning Civil War veterans. Playing with bases made of bags stuffed with straw, a team was formed in 1867, the start of organized sports at Indiana University. By the early 1880s other schools were coming to Bloomington to play the new game.

In later years, students would have fond memories of this first campus, and especially of their professors. Students knew the entire faculty, since there were so few. Especially remembered were the Big Four: Professors Theophilus A. Wylie, Daniel Kirkwood, Elisha Ballantine, and Richard Owen. It is fitting that buildings on the current campus are named for each of the four outstanding men. Professor Wylie was the longest serving. Beloved by students, he was a jack of all trades, teacher of numerous subjects, librarian, and sometimes superintendent of grounds. Professor Kirkwood, another favorite of the students, taught mathematics and specialized in astronomy. He was an old-style gentleman who wore a tall silk hat and carried a cane. Professor Ballantine was an erudite scholar, proficient in several languages. "Old Bally" struck fear in lackluster students and enduring respect from the more serious. Richard Owen cut his scientific teeth among the New Harmony scholars, eventually specializing in geology. As a colonel in the Civil War, Owen was in charge of an Indianapolis prisoner-of-war camp. Decades later, memories of Owen's humane treatment caused former Confederates to dedicate a monument to him—a most unusual honor in the nation's most brutal war. It stands in the Indiana State House, with a replica at the south entrance to the Indiana Memorial Union. Also on the faculty at Seminary Square were David Starr Jordan and James Albert Woodburn, whose names also have been immortalized on the new campus.

Into the 1880s there were still only two principal buildings, the First University Building and Science Hall. Inadequate for the expanding curriculum, the physical campus reflected the slow growth and uncertain future of Indiana University. Then on a stormy night in 1883, lightning struck Science Hall. The fire destroyed scientific labs and collections, including most of the Owen Cabinet, along with the library and university records. The disaster renewed calls to move the campus from Bloomington. However, local citizens and trustees resolved to rebuild, but not at the end of College Avenue. The site was too small and unappealing. At the western edge of the campus ran clanging trains, good for connections to the world beyond Monroe County, but not for learning; suitable land on which to expand was limited; and the water supply was insufficient. The search for a new site settled on an elevated piece of land known as Dunn's Woods to the east of the courthouse, and 20 acres were purchased from Moses Dunn in 1883. There two grand buildings rose quickly. The year 1885 saw not only the dedication of Owen Hall and Wylie Hall but also the inauguration of a new president, David Starr Jordan, the first non-clergyman in that office. Indiana University was moving in new directions, to brighter prospects than it ever had on the old campus.

The first campus was not forgotten. The First University Building was used for occasional lectures and commencement ceremonies in the late nineteenth century. The aged Professor Theophilus A. Wylie returned to the old campus in 1891 to watch the IU football team, though he did not much like "the rough and tumble game."[2] Eventually, in 1897, the First University Building was sold to the Bloomington High School Board for use as a high school, portions of which existed until 1965, when it was razed. Some of the land was later sold for business development, including a large grocery store and parking lot, under which likely still lies a time capsule buried in 1922 to commemorate the beginning of construction on the site. Special exercises were held to celebrate the one-hundredth anniversary of Indiana University's first building, construction of which began on April 17, 1822. The capsule was placed at the spot that marked the entrance to the chapel on the south side of the Seminary Building. More appealing to the eye was the dedication in 1976 of Seminary Park, a portion of the old campus, as a project of the university and the city.

The Seminary Square campus is mostly gone. There the university began, there it struggled mightily, there it endured, and from there it moved to Dunn's Woods to flourish. Some physical pieces of the first campus can be found on today's campus, including bricks reused to build Wylie Hall and Owen Hall, the limestone portals of the 1855 First University Building incorporated into the Rose Well House, and the Sundial, which stands outside Maxwell Hall.

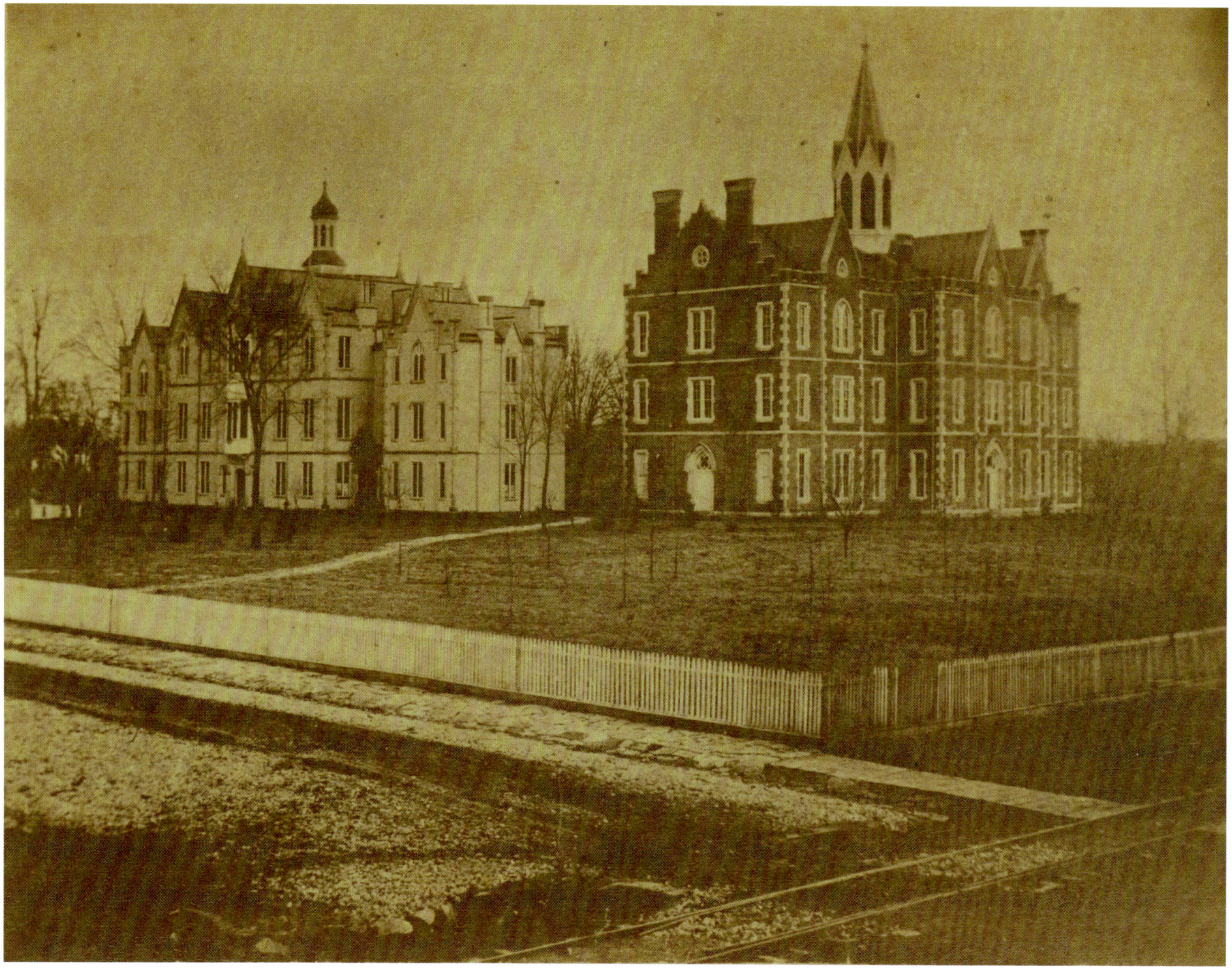

First University Building (*left*) and Science Hall (*right*) at Seminary Square shortly before the 1883 fire that destroyed Science Hall. P0022545, IU Archives. Photo credit: Barnes & Lewis, University Photograph Gallery.

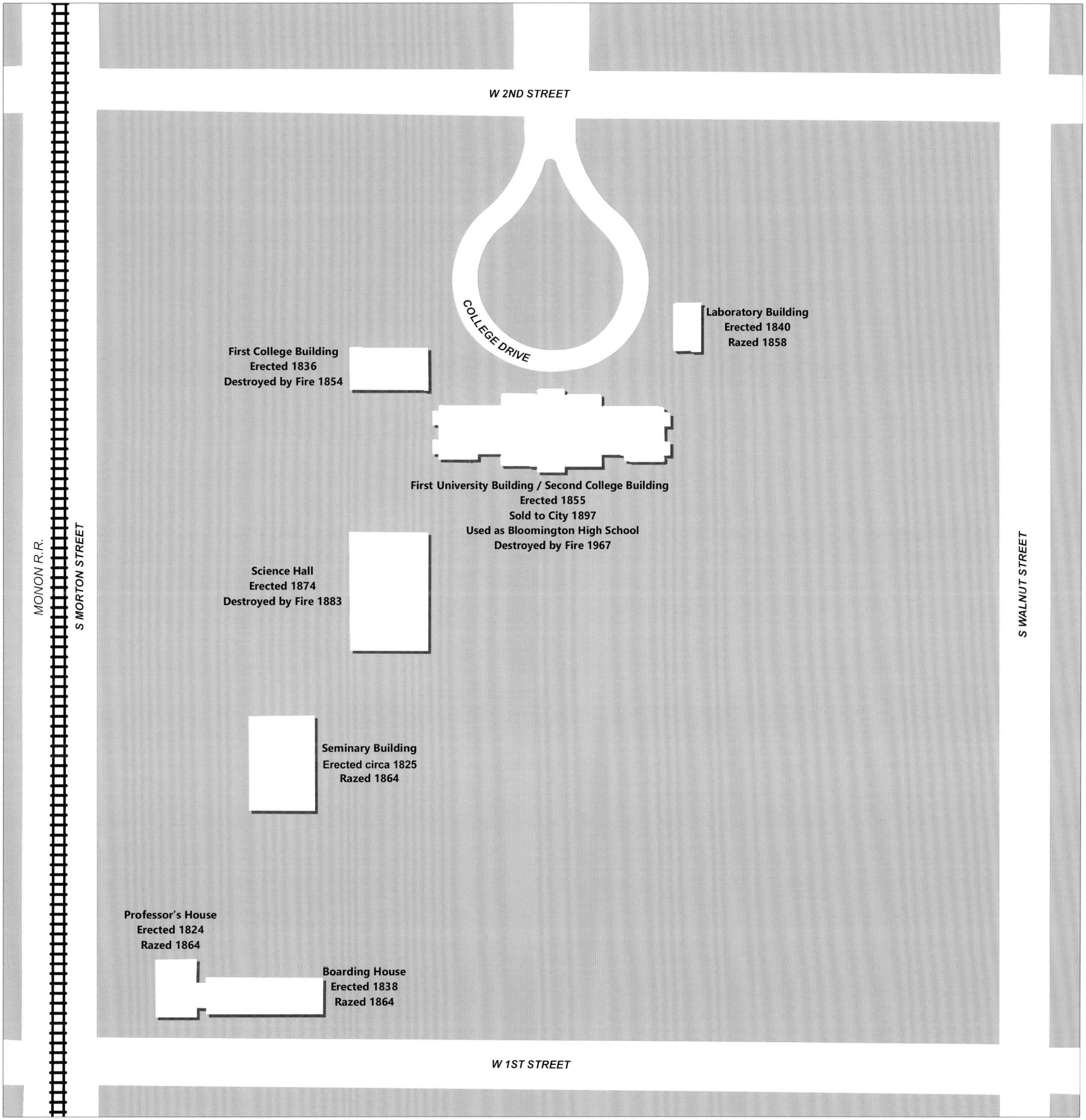
W 2ND STREET
COLLEGE DRIVE
Laboratory Building
Erected 1840
Razed 1858
First College Building
Erected 1836
Destroyed by Fire 1854
First University Building / Second College Building
Erected 1855
Sold to City 1897
Used as Bloomington High School
Destroyed by Fire 1967
MONON R.R.
S MORTON STREET
S WALNUT STREET
Science Hall
Erected 1874
Destroyed by Fire 1883
Seminary Building
Erected circa 1825
Razed 1864
Professor's House
Erected 1824
Razed 1864
Boarding House
Erected 1838
Razed 1864
W 1ST STREET

INDIANA UNIVERSITY

BLOOMINGTON

THE OLD CRESCENT

The new campus comprises twenty acres of elevated ground, on the eastern edge of the city, covered with a heavy growth of maple and beech timber. The commanding position of the land and the beauty of the natural forest which occupies it render this one of the most attractive college sites in the country.

College trustees on Dunn's Woods, 1883

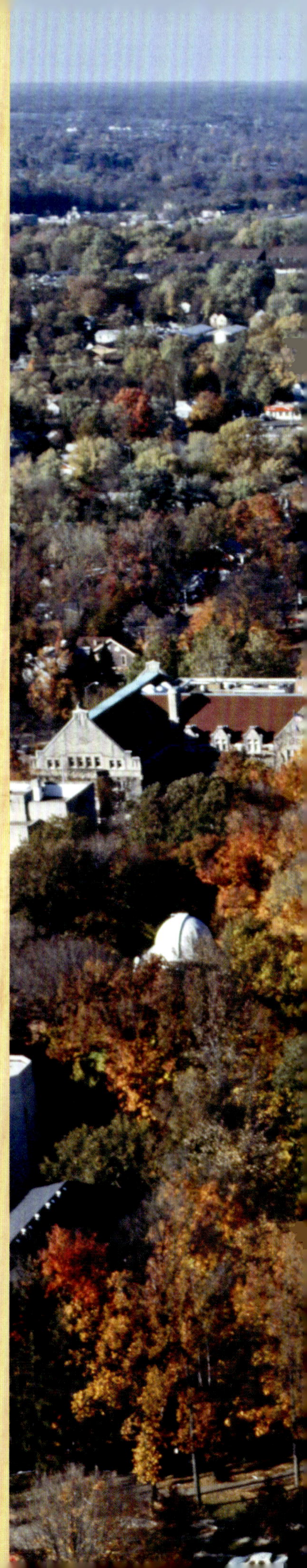

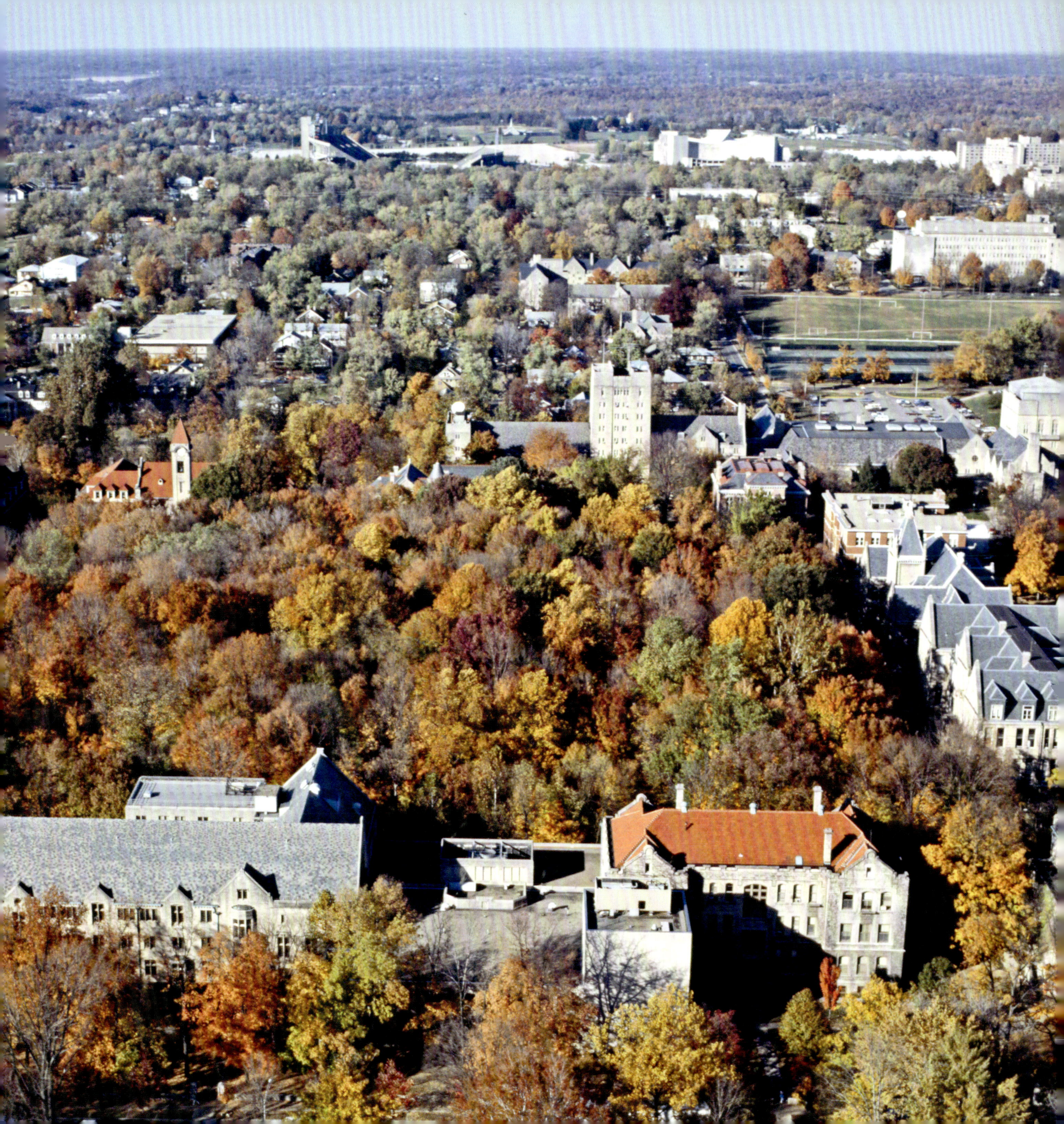

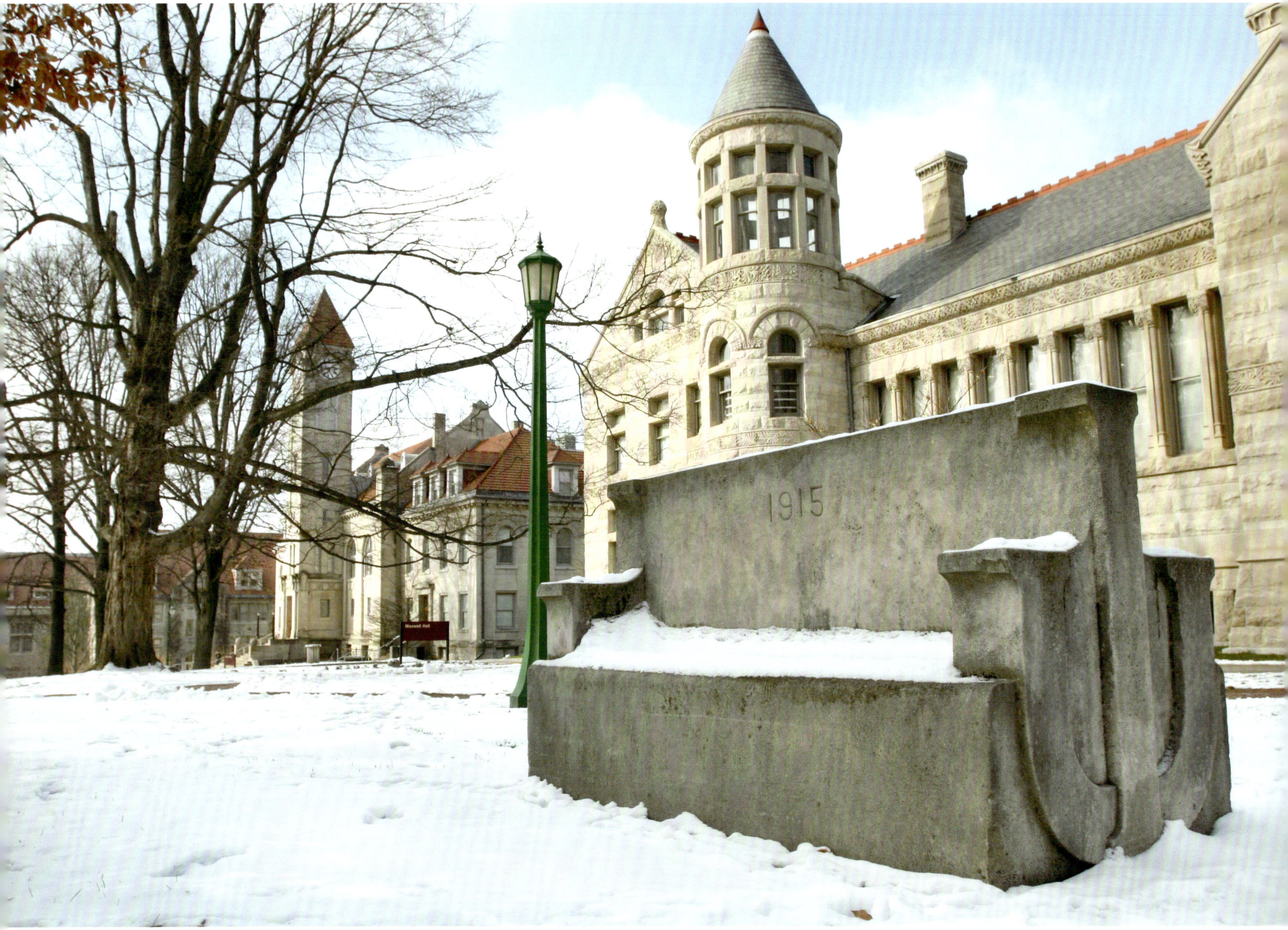

Stone bench, a gift from the class of 1915, in front of Maxwell Hall with the Student Building to the left, undated. Photo credit: Indiana University.

The Emergence of a Modern University

ON THE EVENING OF JULY 12, 1883, DURING A PARticularly violent lightning storm, the fate of Indiana University would forever be changed. The summer and fall of 1883 was a literal and metaphorical turning point in the history of the university. The fire in the "new" Science Hall set into motion a chain of events that would accelerate the university into the modern age, creating the Indiana University we know today.

By November 1883, 20 acres of land at the eastern edge of Bloomington had been purchased for a new campus from a local farmer, Moses Dunn; an architect, George Bunting, from Indianapolis, had been hired; and plans were underway to create a new home for Indiana University. By 1885, the first three buildings—Wylie, Owen, and Mitchell Halls—were erected on the newly acquired property.

The years between 1884 and 1910, when much of the Old Crescent was established, were a time of considerable growth and change for Indiana University, as well as for Bloomington and the nation. In the space of a quarter of a century, the course of Indiana University as the modern university we know today was charted, on a new site, in new buildings, with a new curriculum, and fresh energy. The new campus on the hill first became known as University Park, possibly due to the use of the grounds for picnics by the local townspeople. The name did not last, but what did endure was the commitment to preserve the parklike environment and maintain this district as the foundation of the campus. The Old Crescent is the historic core of the Bloomington campus, and its buildings are among the most distinctive and significant structures of Indiana University Bloomington.

By November 1885, the new campus opened its doors to 183 students and 19 instructors. That year also saw the installation of a new president, David Starr Jordan, a scientist and faculty member (1885–93). The student body doubled, curriculum was modernized, and faculty expanded and upgraded. The university continued to flourish, and by the end of William Lowe Bryan's thirty-five-year tenure as Indiana University president (1902–37), the campus area had nearly tripled in size and the student body had increased to 4,943.

The main buildings of the Old Crescent form an *L* (or crescent) on the crest of the campus proper, beginning with Wylie and Owen Halls (1884), forming the right angle of the *L*. They were compact structures, built of red brick with limestone accents and vertically proportioned openings in High Victorian style, reflecting the architectural trends of the time. The building sites allowed for generous space between the structures, in part to prevent flames from easily spreading should a fire occur. This spacing would become a common practice as the campus grew. With the completion of Wylie and Owen Halls, the university commenced the planning of Maxwell (1890) and Kirkwood (1894) Halls. These two structures flanked Owen Hall and Wylie Hall, respectively, and began to fill out the

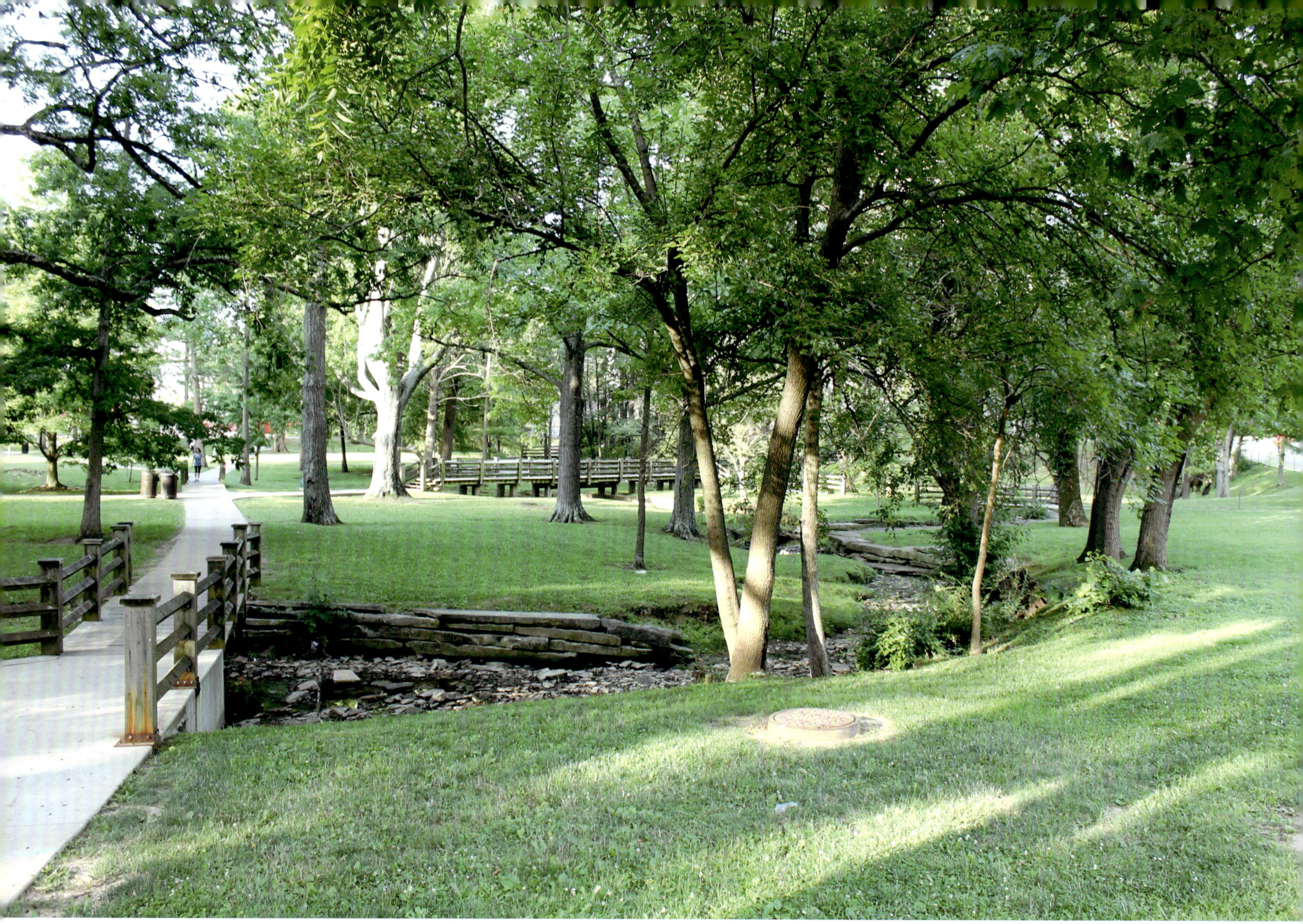

Wooden bridges span the Jordan River as it winds through the heart of campus, 2017. Photo credit: Indiana University.

crescent. This period of construction marked a shift in primary building materials and architectural style on campus. The new material used was limestone, quarried locally in Monroe and Lawrence Counties. This move to limestone signaled a change that would characterize Indiana University architecture from that time forward. The style also evolved with the times to represent a faithful Romanesque architecture with monumental towers, slate roofs, and arched openings.

Other structures that existed during the inaugural years of the new campus but that have since disappeared were Mitchell Hall (1885) and both early Men's Gymnasiums (1892 and 1896). Also, during the early days of the Old Crescent, in the tract of low ground northeast of Owen Hall, was Jordan Field, where football and baseball teams played and athletes participated in track and field competitions. On the contiguous ground to the west were a number of tennis courts for the male students. Two well-shaded courts for the women were on the south side of campus, near Mitchell Hall.[1]

As already mentioned, during the William Lowe Bryan administration (1902–37), the Bloomington campus experienced immense growth. Lindley Hall (1902), the Student Building (1906), and Franklin Hall (1907) were constructed during this period and continued the limestone and slate material palette and the Romanesque and Gothic architectural styles established by Maxwell and Kirkwood Halls. The Student Building's arched openings and central monumental tower represent a faithful interpretation of Romanesque architecture. Lindley Hall's facade is a more modern interpretation, while Franklin Hall expresses a more hybrid Romanesque Gothic style. "This Gothic expression was a harbinger of a stylistic shift that would define much of the new campus architecture in the coming decades."[2] The other buildings erected outside the crescent during this time were Kirkwood Observatory (1900) and the Rose Well House (1908), both within Dunn's Woods, and Swain Hall East (1910), to the south of Lindley Hall (1902).

The buildings of the Old Crescent were fabricated during a period of rapid changes in construction technology, which promoted safety and allowed new freedom in design. Following the catastrophic fires in Chicago in 1871 and Boston in 1872, the application of building codes became more prevalent in the construction industry. Architects employed by Indiana University were quick to adopt the new design standards. Furthermore, the use of iron as a building material became affordable, and the university employed it as the framework for new structures.

The Old Crescent was not, of course, important for just its buildings. Hired by William Lowe Bryan in 1915 as the university campus planner, George E. Kessler produced the first comprehensive campus master plan. He envisioned a natural campus that embraced its physical features along with a bold architectural infrastructure. "Many of his planning concepts live on today and form the basis of Bloomington's distinguished character and romantic imagery."[3] His visions were carried on by Frederick Law Olmsted's firm. In June 1929, the Olmsted Brothers presented a master plan with green spaces, walkways, quads, and well-sited buildings. They defined the Old Crescent district, including Dunn's Woods, preserving the plan that exists today. The district remains much the same as it was before World War I, as the Olmsted firm made official what had by then become a university tradition: "the exclusion of construction within the district that would alter its character or disturb its atmosphere." The Old Crescent stands distinct from its surroundings. The Sample Gates divide it from the town of Bloomington to the west and Dunn's Woods separates it from Third Street to the south; a north–south row of buildings borders it to the east and Jordan River and Dunn Meadow bound it to the north.[4]

The Old Crescent includes the distinguished and beautiful group of late nineteenth- and early twentieth-century buildings that surround it; Dunn's Woods, with its trees for all seasons, walking paths, and sculptures; and the expansive green space with Wells Plaza and vistas in all directions. This is the emotional core of Indiana University—if you stop for a moment, you can almost hear the heartbeats of all the past generations who have tread these rarified grounds.

Wylie Hall 1884

ARCHITECT George W. Bunting (original)

ARCHITECT Robert F. Daggett (reconstruction–1900)

ARCHITECTURAL STYLE Victorian Gothic/ Romanesque

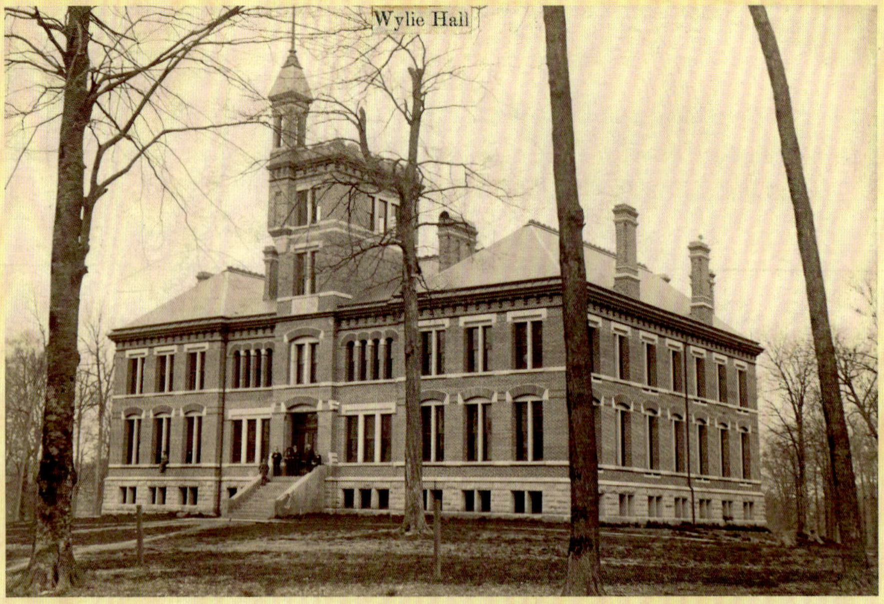

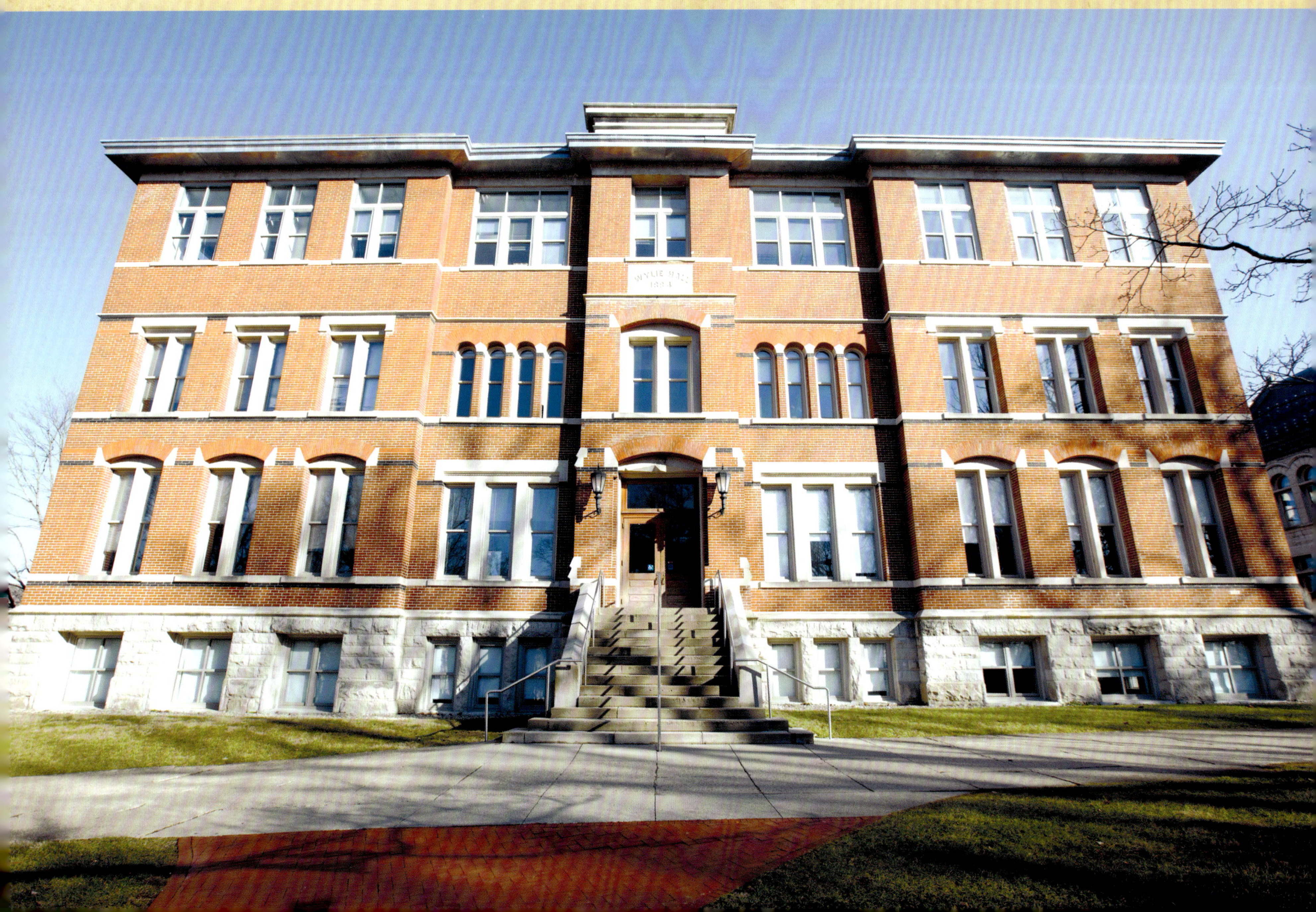

Wylie Hall

The First Building of the "New University"

The new university is no longer a bubble in the air, but by fall will be two grand buildings towering nearly two hundred feet above the city.

—Bloomington Telephone

After the destruction of Science Hall in 1883, there was talk of relocating Indiana University to a "more civilized" area of the state. The people of Monroe County were so opposed to the idea that they agreed to a landowner's tax to generate funds for reconstruction. The tax raised $50,000. With the addition of the $20,000 insurance benefit from Science Hall, reconstruction became possible. But where to rebuild? Some thought remaining at Seminary Square, half a mile southwest of the courthouse, was the best option. Others deemed the site both too noisy and inadequate to the university's continued growth, bordered as it was by the Louisville, New Albany, and Salem Railroad to the west; Second Street to the north; and Walnut Street to the east. After considerable debate, the trustees spent $6,000 on a 20-acre section of Dunn's Woods a mile northeast of Seminary Square. The land was accessed from Third Street and ran north slightly beyond Wylie and Owen Halls. The new site—3,000 feet from the courthouse—was connected to town by dirt roads that ran to mud in the rain.

The first university building constructed at Dunn's Woods is named for the Reverend Andrew Wylie, Indiana University's first president and third faculty member, and his cousin Theophilus A. Wylie, who taught natural philosophy, chemistry, and languages and also served as university librarian, historian, superintendent of grounds, vice president, and occasionally as acting president.

Lemuel Moss, Indiana University's sixth president, officiated at the laying of Wylie's cornerstone, in which artifacts from the Seminary Square campus are still held. These include a history of the university; the *IU Catalogue*; and scrolls inscribed with the names of local, state, and national officials, the building committee, architect, builder, and laborers. However, President Moss was not to guide the university's move from Seminary Square to Dunn's Woods. When scandal prompted his resignation in 1884, the trustees broke with the tradition of hiring "preacher presidents" and appointed professor of natural history David Starr Jordan (1885–91) as the institution's seventh and—at thirty-four years of age—youngest leader. In his inaugural address, Jordan spoke of Indiana University as "the most valuable of Indiana's possessions." He said it was "not yet a great university, not yet even a real university, but the germ of one, its growth being as certain as the progress of the seasons."[1] The construction of higher-education facilities would prove both an indicator and a facilitator of that growth.

George W. Bunting, a well-known courthouse architect from Indianapolis, was selected to design both Wylie and Owen Halls. They are built of brick with limestone footings and foundations, much of the brick salvaged from the ashes of Science Hall, and the limestone likely quarried on-site. Both buildings feature the low-pitched roof and rectangular shape typical of the Italian Renaissance style that was so popular in the late nineteenth-century United States. Wylie's tall,

Facing top, Wylie Hall, circa 1889, before the 1900 fire destroyed the cupola. P0020560, IU Archives. Photo credit: A. J. Summers.

Facing bottom, West elevation of Wylie Hall, 2017. Photo credit: Indiana University.

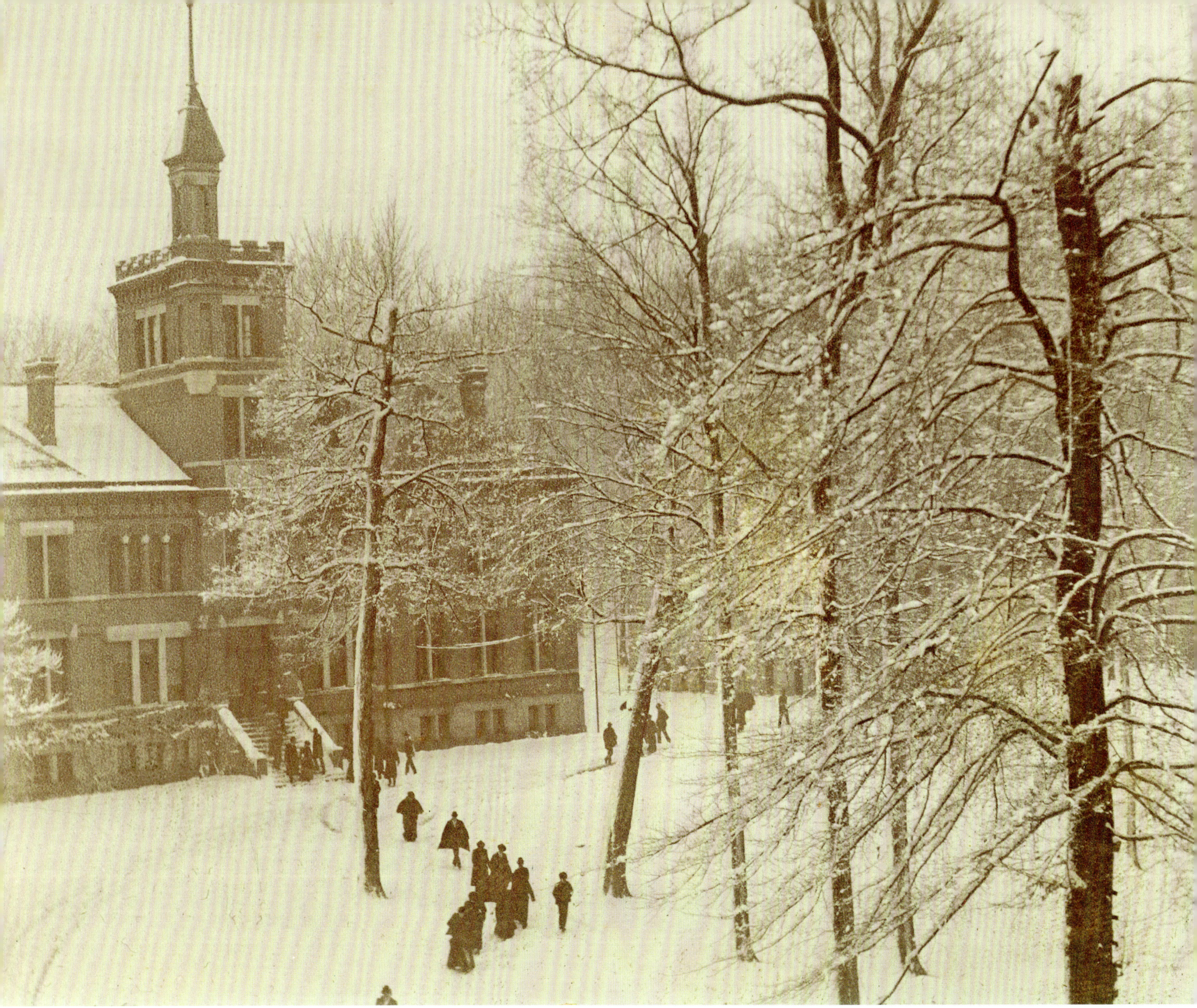

Wylie Hall on a snowy day, circa 1895. P0062501, IU Archives.

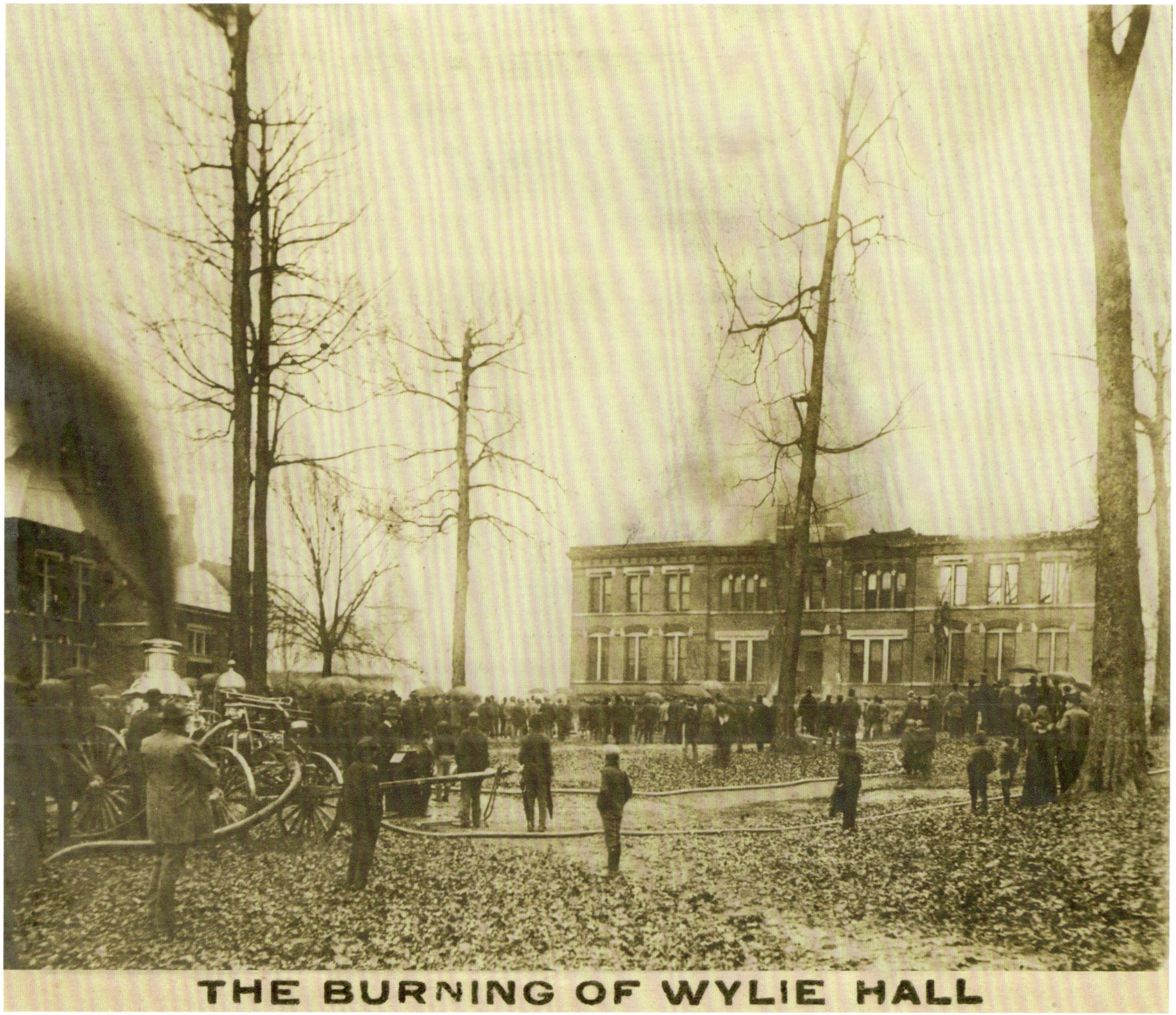

Only known photograph of the February 7, 1900, fire that destroyed the upper level of Wylie Hall, including the cupola; 1900 Arbutus. P0020563, IU Archives.

hooded windows and original high, square tower are reminiscent of Renaissance Italian villas, whereas the corner spire on the tower was a Gothic feature, and the belt coursings of black brick reflect the polychrome decoration typical of the High Victorian Gothic style. After the 1900 fire discussed just below, the remnants of the entry tower and its cupola were removed and a third story was added in a much simpler style than the rest of the building. Wylie Hall is the original home of the sciences on campus. Chemistry, complete with then state-of-the-art laboratories, occupied the first floor. The university library was on the second floor, along with physics and several other departments.[2]

Having thrice passed through flames, IU was again tried by fire in 1900. Two professors who were working late—William Lowe Bryan and Edward P. Morton—observed the blaze of a chemical fire in one of Wylie's laboratories. They rushed to the president's office in Owen Hall, which held the only telephone on campus, but found the door locked. Spying the open transom over the door, Bryan boosted Morton onto his shoulders. Morton wriggled inside to call in the alarm. Professor Bryan

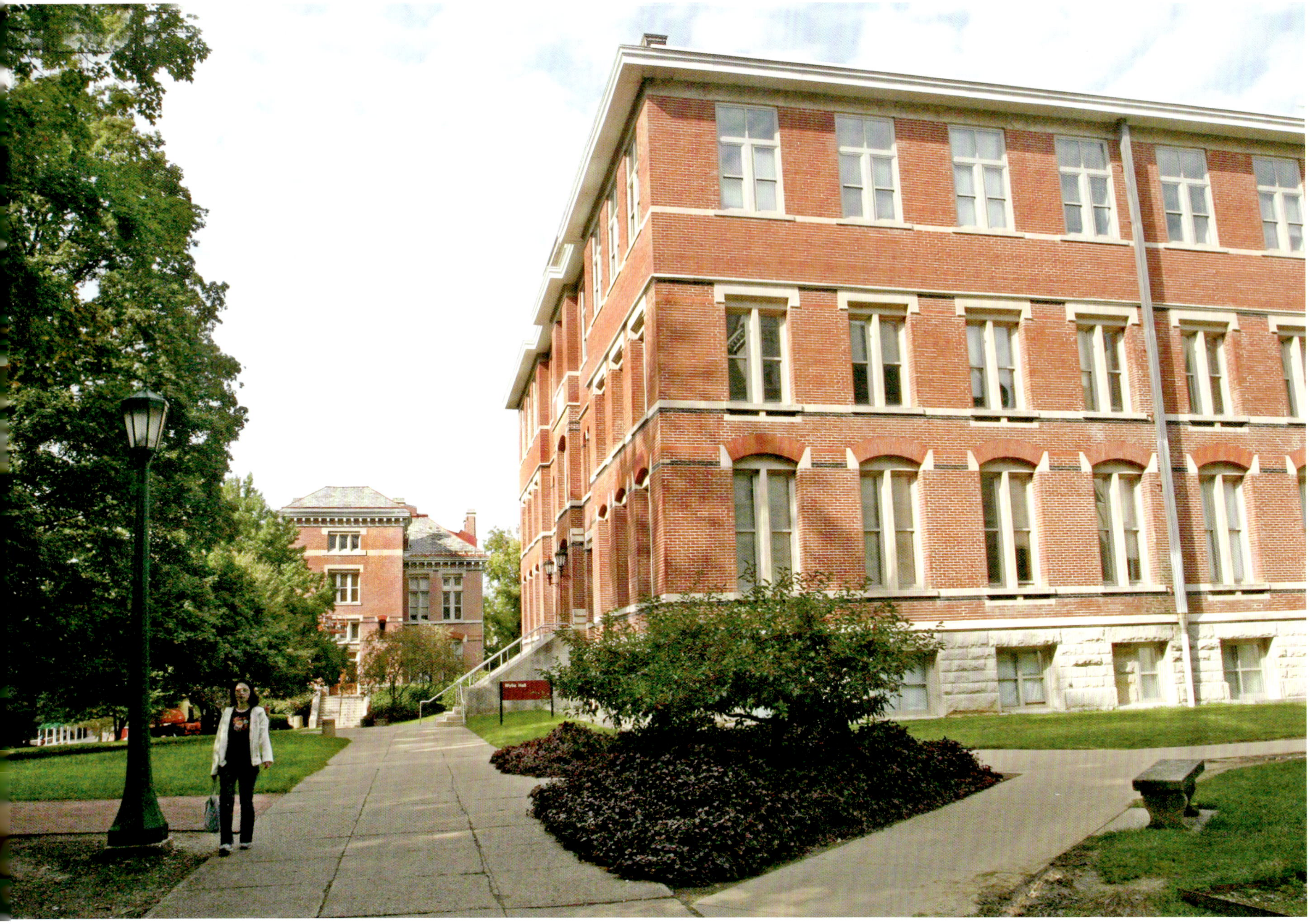

Wylie Hall, south facing facade; one of two red-brick buildings on Bloomington campus, undated. Photo credit: Indiana University.

would make a more dignified entry into that same office two years later when he was elected president of Indiana University—a position he held for thirty-five years.[3]

Wylie's two main floors were sound, but flames had ravaged the roof and the tower. The trustees turned disaster into opportunity and created badly needed classroom space by removing the tower and adding a new third floor and a flat roof.

In 1930 the building was again remodeled to refurbish it for the Department of Home Economics. Wylie has housed IU's women's gymnasium and its math, physics, French, German, Latin, Greek, English, law, and apparel merchandising departments. In the 1950s, it was home to Alfred Kinsey's Institute for Sex Research (now called the Kinsey Institute for Research in Sex, Gender, and Reproduction); one can imagine that at least some of the groundbreaking *Sexual Behavior in the Human Female* (1953) was written in Wylie's basement. In 1993 Wylie Hall was renovated to house IU's Department of Economics, which currently occupies the building.

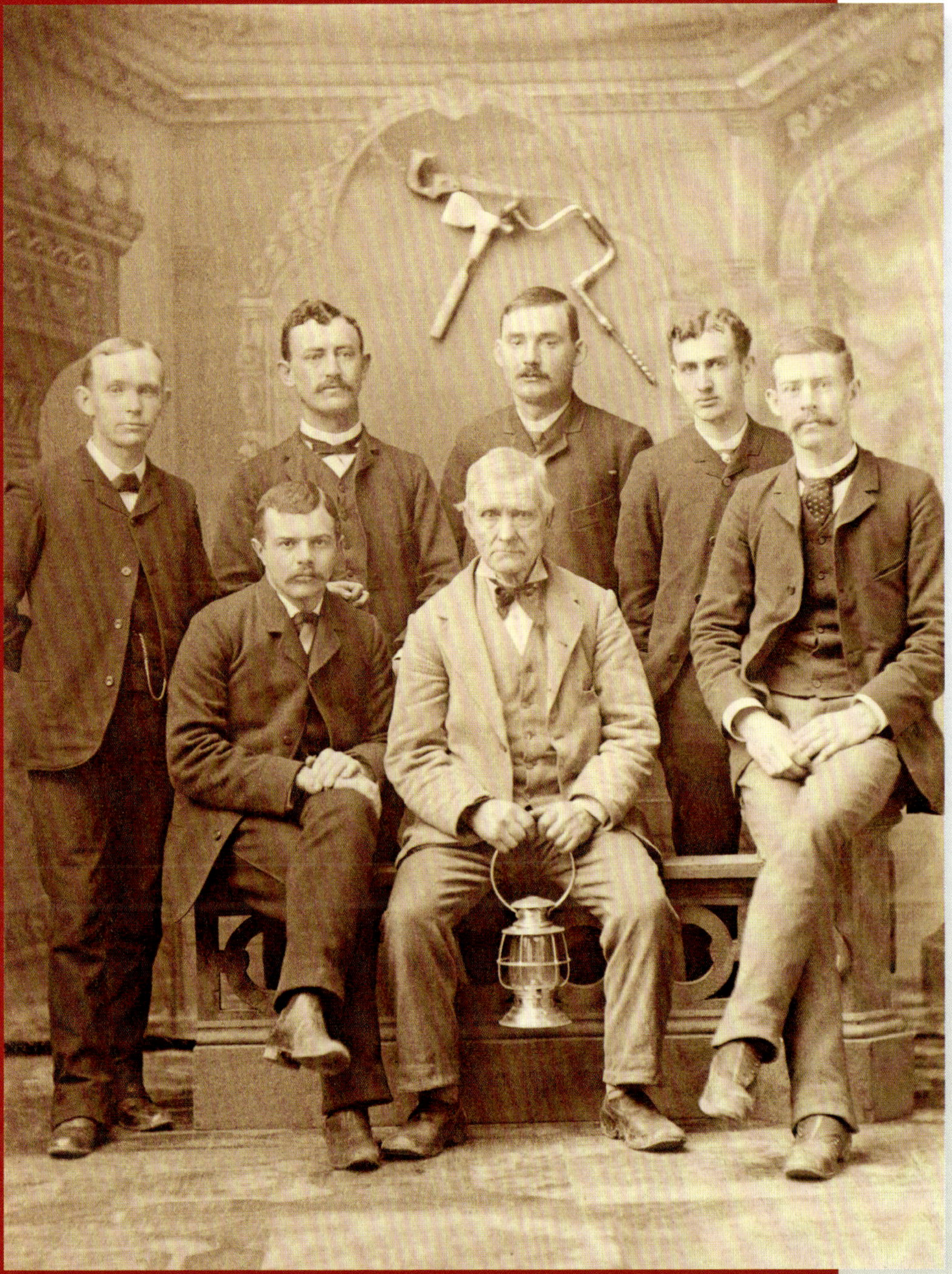

The vigilante Moss Killers; note the spying tools on the wall, 1884. P0024044, IU Archives. Photo credit: J. B. Allison.

Moss Killers

In the fall of 1884, rumors were afoot that President Lemuel Moss, who was married, had an overly fond relationship with a young instructor of Greek, Miss Katharine Graydon. Six university students and the school janitor, Tommy Spicer, took it upon themselves to verify or dispel the rumors. They drilled a hole in the ceiling of Miss Graydon's classroom. Spying on the classroom for several days, the group observed the president and Greek instructor exchanging gifts, endearments, and kisses. They made formal accusations to the trustees, after which both President Moss and Miss Graydon resigned. The group, which became known as the Moss Killers, is memorialized in this photograph. Note the saw, drill, and hatchet displayed on the wall behind them.

Owen Hall 1884

ARCHITECT George W. Bunting

ARCHITECTURAL STYLE Victorian Gothic / Romanesque

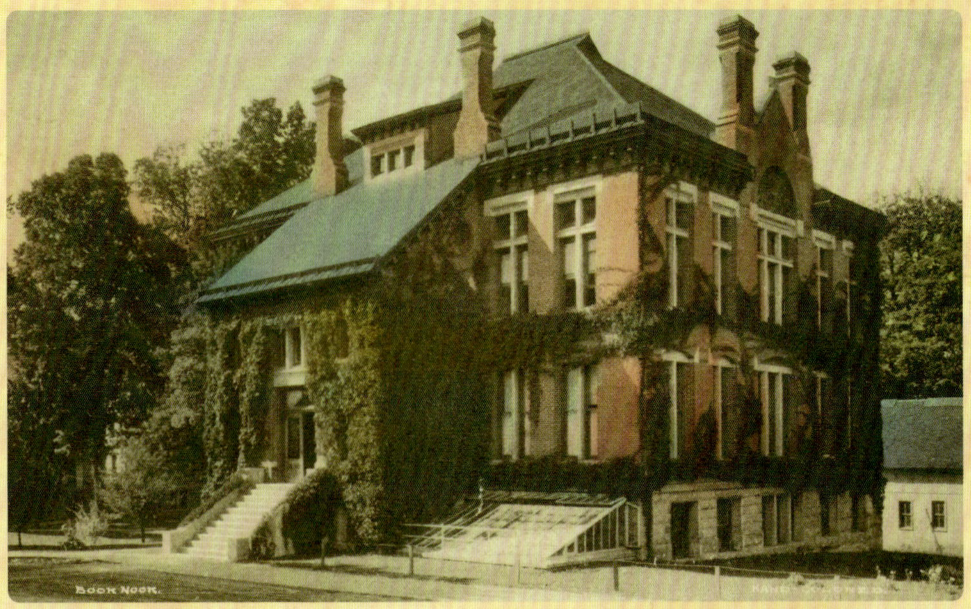

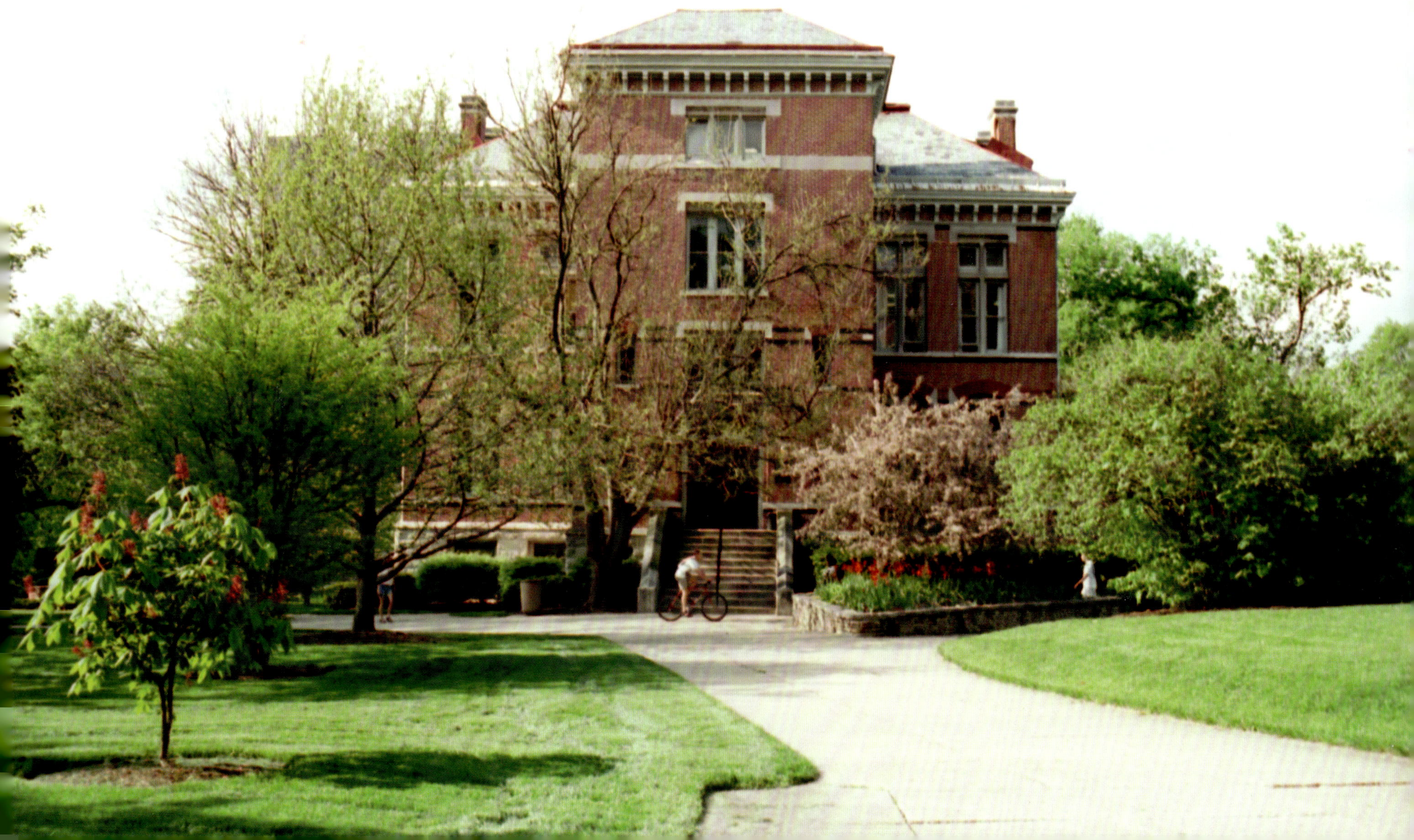

Owen Hall

A Citadel in the Woodlands

The commanding position of the land and the beauty of the natural forest which occupies it render this one of the most attractive college sites in the country.

—Indiana University Board of Trustees

While nearly all the trees had been felled on the original Seminary Square campus, the trustees were careful to avoid that mistake at Dunn's Woods, which greeted the new residents with a display of autumnal splendor. Two majestic gingko trees that were part of the original woods still stand—one in front of Owen Hall and the other in front of Wylie Hall—like leafy sentinels guarding the path to higher learning.

Sited at right angles to each other and both designed by architect George W. Bunting, Owen and Wylie Halls form the bend of IU's historic Old Crescent. Owen is a brick cube with heavy footings of limestone that was likely quarried on-site. Like those of Wylie Hall, its belt courses, sills, lintels, and other trim are limestone. Both buildings inspire a feeling of strength and stability that must have been reassuring after the university's travails with fire and a controversial president. Unlike Wylie, Owen's low-pitched, hipped roof features the wide cornices supported by decorative brackets that are typical of the Italianate style. The building's many ninety-degree angles are offset by two foliated terra-cotta fans adorning decorative gables. The fan on the east gable depicts Bacchus playing his flute amid peacocks and grape clusters, while on the west gable a cherub surveys the Old Crescent. Owen was extensively remodeled in 1909–10, with the addition of skylights and the opening up of the third-story attic. The shed roof of the entry tower was replaced with a higher hipped roof and cornice to match the Victorian Gothic style of the rest of the building. Remnants of the ornamentation below the original roof were preserved in the exterior walls of the new tower.

Owen Hall is named in honor of three brothers: David Owen, Indiana's first state geologist, who performed the pioneering geological surveys of Indiana, Kentucky, and Arkansas; Indiana University professor of natural science and chemistry Richard Owen, who was elected Purdue's first president but wisely resigned after two years and returned to IU; and Robert Owen, the eldest of the brothers, who was an Indiana University trustee, state and federal member of Congress, humane Civil War prison commandant, and champion of women's rights. Together the brothers assembled the Owen Cabinet, a collection of soils, minerals, rocks, fossils, and skeletons unrivaled in North America. Most of the collection went up in smoke when Science Hall at Seminary Square was struck by lightning in 1883.

Not everyone welcomed the progress heralded by a new location and a progressive new president. In September 1885, Professor Theophilus Wylie wrote in his diary: "College opened in the new building last Thursday. New arrangements, new studies, new teachers, new modes of teaching, give me much anxiety."[1] President David Starr Jordan reorganized the classics curriculum, giving new importance to anthropology,

Facing top, Postcard of Owen Hall featuring original shed roof over entry, circa 1912. P0029060, IU Archives.

Facing bottom, Early spring shot of Owen Hall, April 1993. P0046354, IU Archives. Photo credit: Beverly Y. Sympson.

Ornamental tree in spring bloom framing the main entry to Owen Hall, 2016. Photo credit: Tyagan Miller.

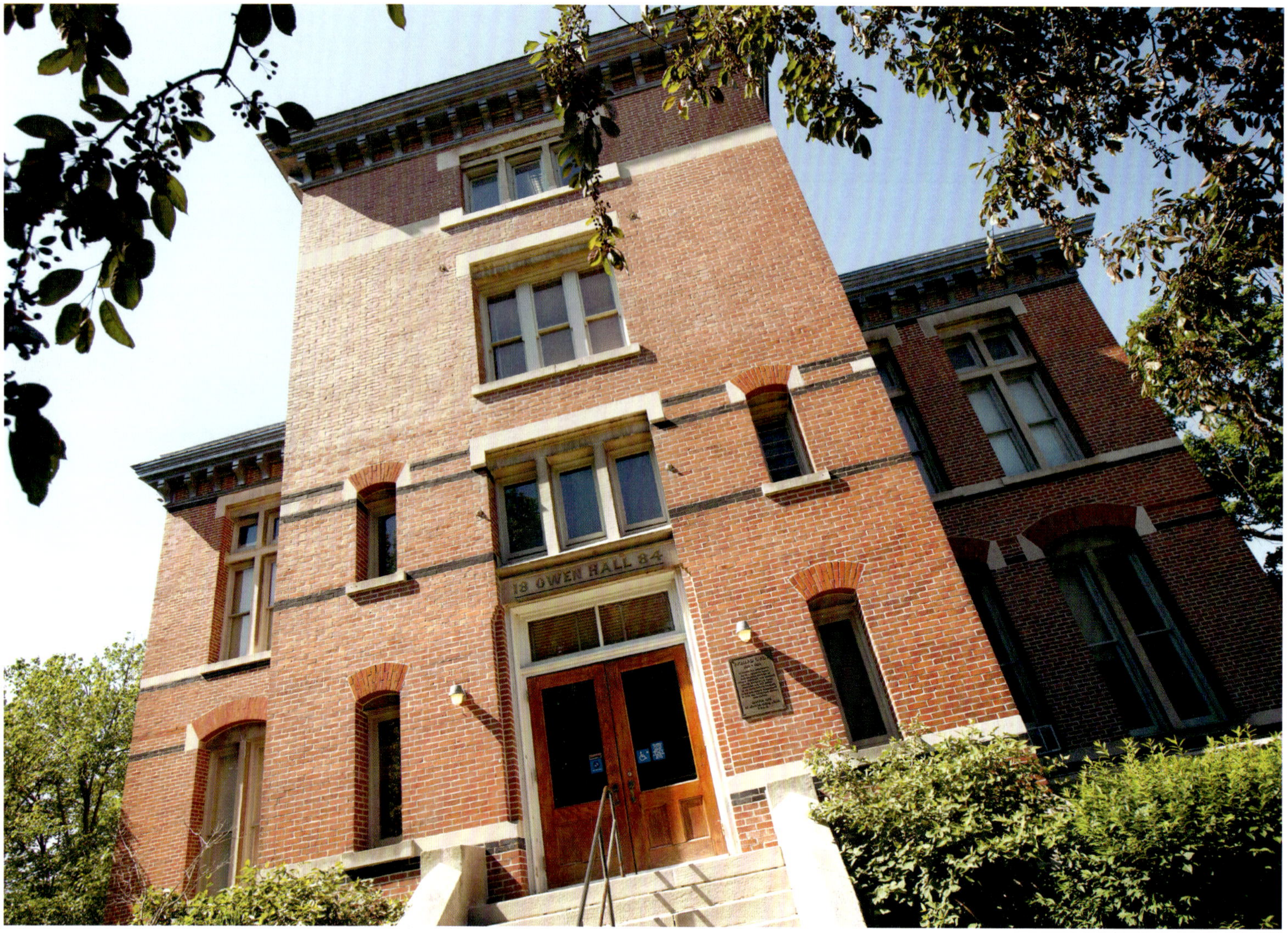

sociology, and psychology. He emphasized the study of modern languages over Greek and Latin and implemented the "majors" system that enabled students to choose a course of study. Jordan also led the university's first study-abroad ventures. At the turn of the century, as the state transformed itself from a rural to an industrial economy, IU was making the transition from an overgrown seminary to a modern university. Separate schools of education, medicine, music, commerce, and law were organized. A graduate school emerged in 1908.

Over the years, Owen Hall has housed the University Museum; the Departments of Mechanics and Astronomy, Zoology, Botany, and Geology; the School of Medicine; and the School of Continuing Studies. In 2014 as part of the master plan to reinvigorate the Old Crescent, the building was renovated to house the College of Arts and Sciences. Owen's most widely beloved resident was university chancellor and President Emeritus Herman B Wells. The large windows of his Owen Hall office gave him a panoramic view of campus activities and a front-row seat for the carillon concerts that issued daily from the Student Building's clock tower. Chancellor Wells's

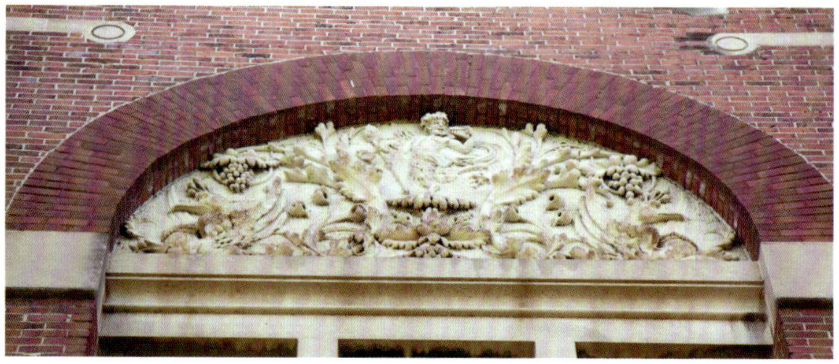

Foliated terra-cotta fan on east elevation of Owen Hall, 2016. Photo credit: Tyagan Miller.

door was always open to students, faculty, alumni, and administrators who frequently stopped by to enjoy a moment of his incomparable company or solicit his wise counsel.

One day Chancellor Wells and his staff received a visit from a retired physician who had done his medical training in Owen Hall. The aged gentleman walked through the halls sniffing and saying, "Can you smell it? I can still smell it. Can you?" Asked what he smelled, the man answered, "Formaldehyde, of course." He then explained how cadavers preserved by formaldehyde had been loaded into the dumbwaiter on the first floor (now a small elevator) and shuttled to the dissection room on the top floor, where skylights provided the illumination necessary for applied anatomy studies. Sometimes a foot, arm, or leg would fall off the dumbwaiter in transit, and a brave medical student would have to descend to the bottom of the shaft to retrieve it.[2]

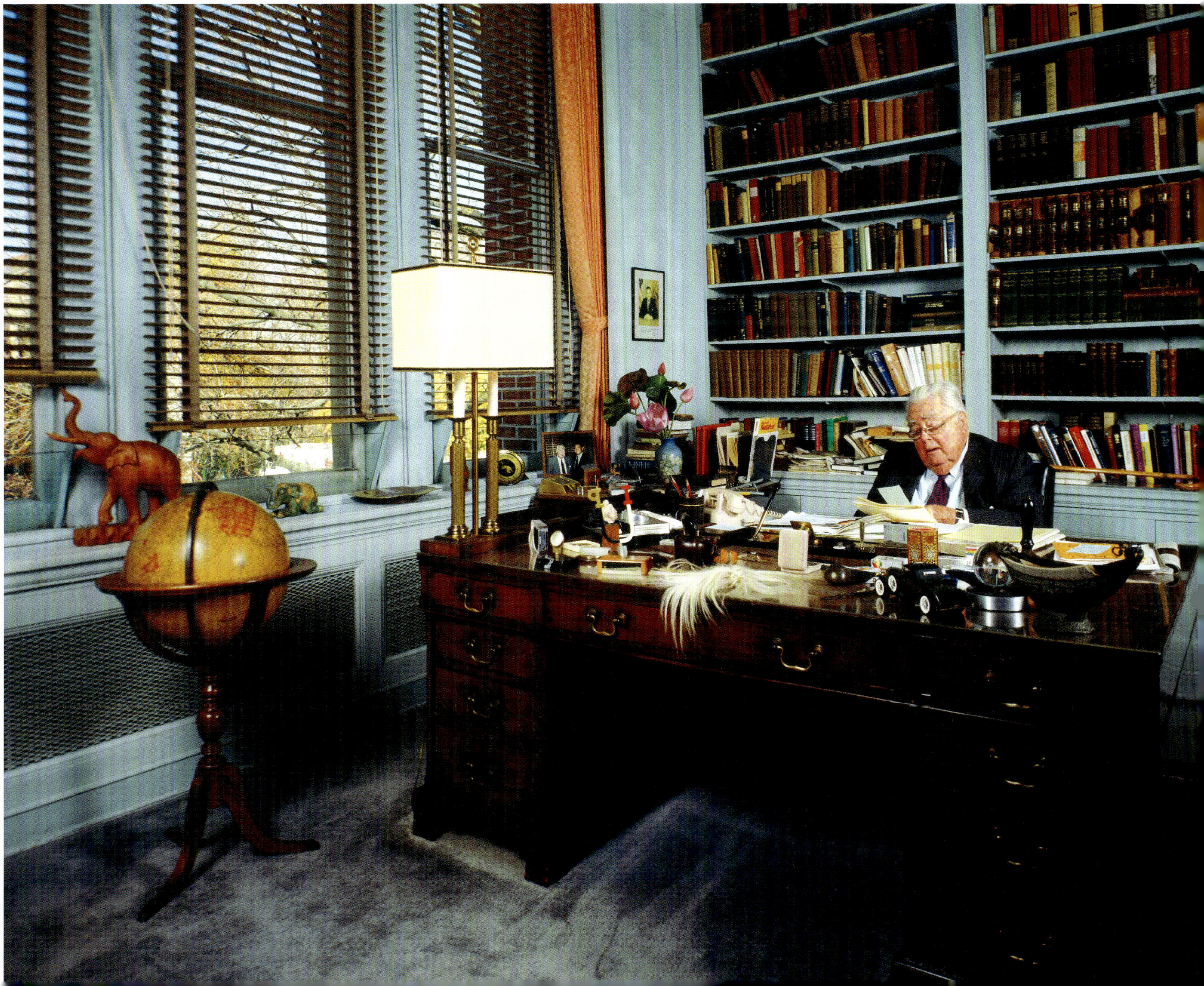

Herman B Wells in his Owen Hall office, 1988. P0033302, IU Archives.

Mitchell Hall 1885

ARCHITECT	George W. Bunting
ARCHITECTURAL STYLE	Prairie / Frame Building
ORIGINAL NAME	Maxwell Hall
RAZED	1991

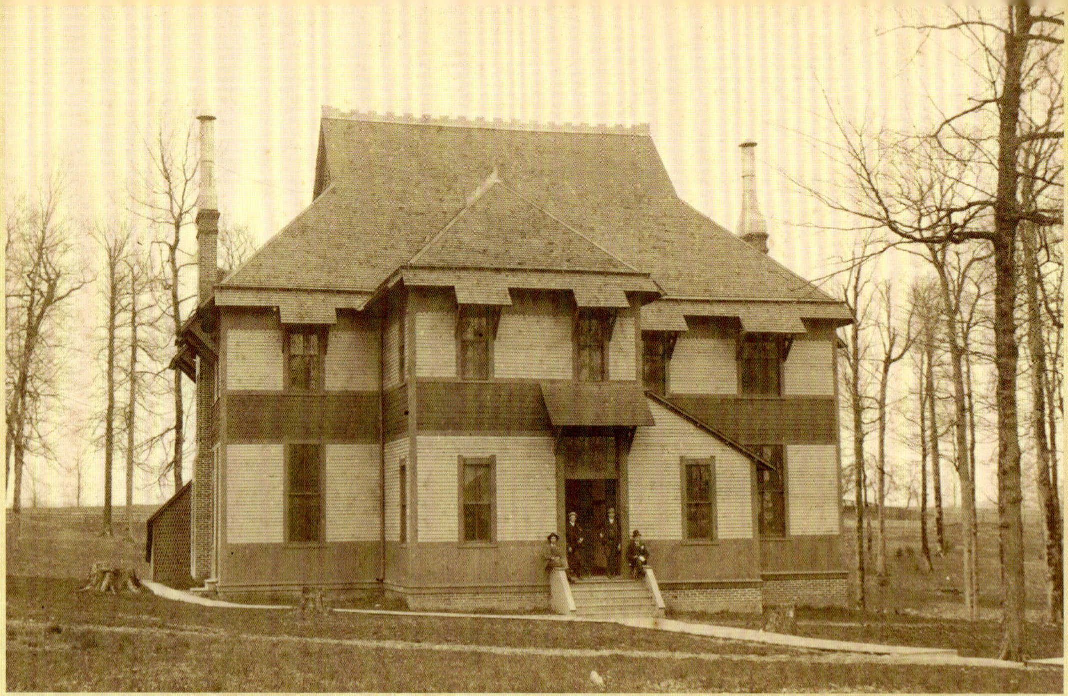

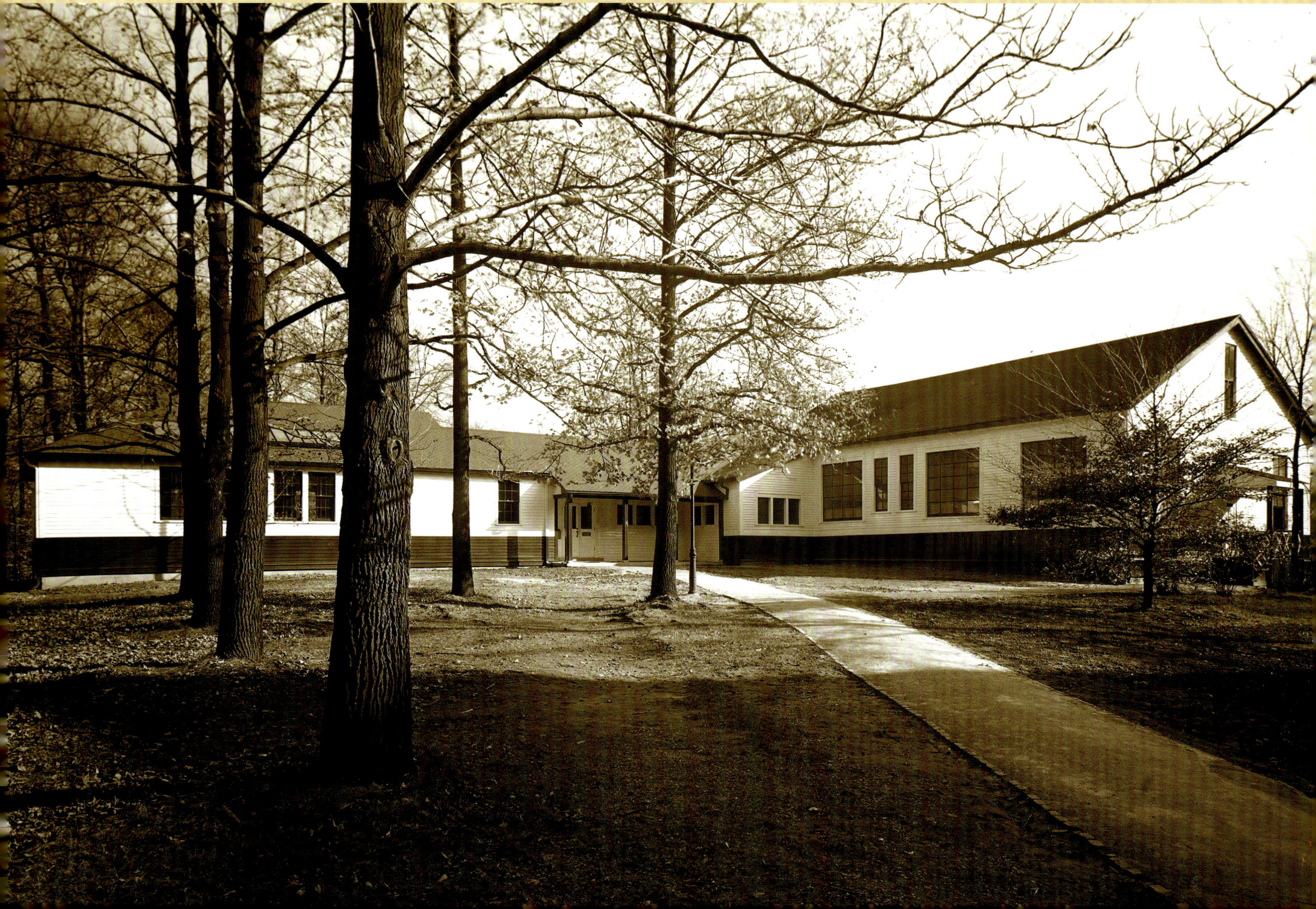

Mitchell Hall

A Building Lost in Time

> *Of the three new buildings, two—the larger and best equipped—are devoted to science. . . . There all the best modern apparatus and conveniences are supplied . . . the buildings heated with steam and lighted with gas. . . . The third, a poor little frame, is used for a chapel; and stored away in its attic are four or five little rooms, about 12 × 16, where the student must get his philosophy, political economy, literature, languages, etc. . . . It is clear that we are headed straight for science.*
>
> —Indiana Daily Student *editorial*

THE UNIVERSITY REQUIRED MORE CLASSROOM, administrative, and assembly space than Wylie and Owen Halls provided. One building remained at Seminary Park, but students and faculty could not be expected to trek a mile through muddy streets for the change of classes. The trustees solved the problem by appropriating some $4,000 that had been promised for science equipment to construct a third building, a two-story frame structure on the site where Lindley Hall currently stands. As were Wylie and Owen Halls, Mitchell Hall was constructed by George W. Bunting, but from its beginning it was considered a temporary building. Nevertheless, it housed a succession of IU schools and departments for more than a century.

On the first day of the fall 1885 term, 22 faculty members and 180 students gathered in the chapel of Mitchell Hall (also known as the literary building). The first floor also provided a recitation room and a women's room where female students (approximately one-third of the student body), could gather. The second floor held five classrooms for the teaching of Latin, Greek, German, rhetoric, and oratory.

Before it was six years old, the literary building was both renamed and relocated. Its original name—Maxwell Hall, in honor of trustees David Maxwell and his son James—was reassigned to the elegant new library building in 1894. The more humble frame structure then became Mitchell Hall, in honor of James L. Mitchell, an alumnus, trustee, and popular mayor of Indianapolis. In 1901, when the need for another science building became indisputable, Mitchell Hall was moved 210 feet east to make room for Lindley Hall, the fifth major building constructed in the Old Crescent.

The lover of art and literature who editorialized in 1886 that the university was "headed straight for science" would have been heartened to know IU's identity as a public liberal arts university was forged in Mitchell Hall, which became IU's first music hall and its first art museum. From 1906 to 1918 the sounds of trombones, cymbals, and flutes from the university band and melodies sung by the choir echoed through its shabby corridors. In 1918 the building's water-damaged upper story was removed. In 1921, the growing Department of Music (established in 1918) became a school, with B. Winfred Merrill as its founding dean. The Music Annex was then built on Mitchell's north side, providing badly needed classrooms, practice studios, and office space. A year later, Dean Merrill began campaigning for a new music building, a battle he would wage for fifteen years.

Facing top, Mitchell Hall following relocation from its original site to make room for Lindley Hall, circa 1889. P0045427, IU Archives.

Facing bottom, Mitchell Hall with wings added following removal of second story, 1941. P0030474, IU Archives.

After the music school moved to Merrill Hall in 1937, the Department of Sociology occupied Mitchell Hall until 1940. The following year, Henry Hope, chair of IU's Department of Fine Arts, the third-oldest art department at any college in the country, reluctantly moved his faculty and students from the upper floor of Maxwell Hall into Mitchell, which he thought looked more like a dilapidated Hoosier farmhouse than an academic building. He complained that Mitchell "was not safe for showing works of art" and that it had "no place for teaching sculpture." The summer before the move, two wings were added, one for a fireproof picture gallery and another to house a sculpture studio. The new department had barely settled in when Pearl Harbor was bombed. After the war, Mitchell, by then known only as the Art Center, grew more wings. Army hospitals and barracks were moved from northern Indiana and attached. The added space was desperately needed during the postwar flood of war veterans taking advantage of the GI Bill. President Wells and Department of Fine Arts chair Henry Hope agreed to mount an art exhibit a month, and many of these spilled out of the picture gallery into the library and hallways.

As Herman B Wells realized his vision of IU as a center of artistic as well as academic and scientific excellence, the Department of Fine Arts moved to the cultural sector of campus established by the Indiana University Auditorium and Lilly Library. From 1962 to 1986, Mitchell housed the Audio Visual Department and the Department of Instructional Systems Technology. When it was finally razed in 1991, Mitchell had been remodeled so many times that its threshold was the only remnant of the original building.

For all its leaking roofs and ramshackle glory, Mitchell Hall will live in memory as the birthplace of the arts at IU.

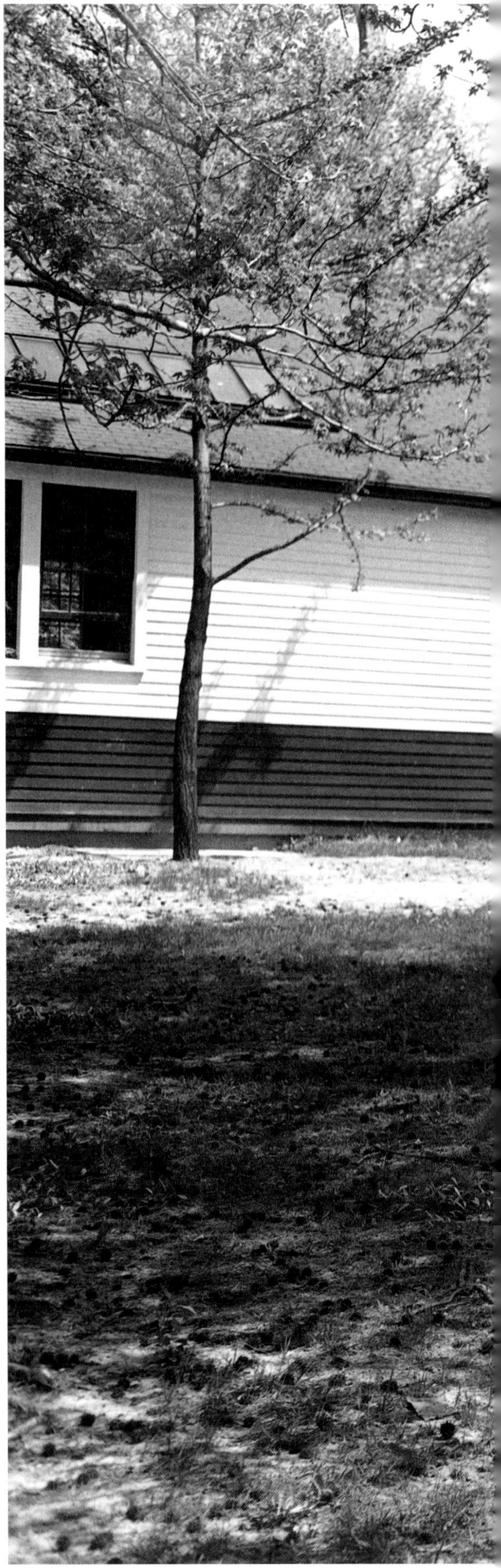

Students in front of Mitchell Hall Fine Arts Building, 1942. P0037691, IU Archives.

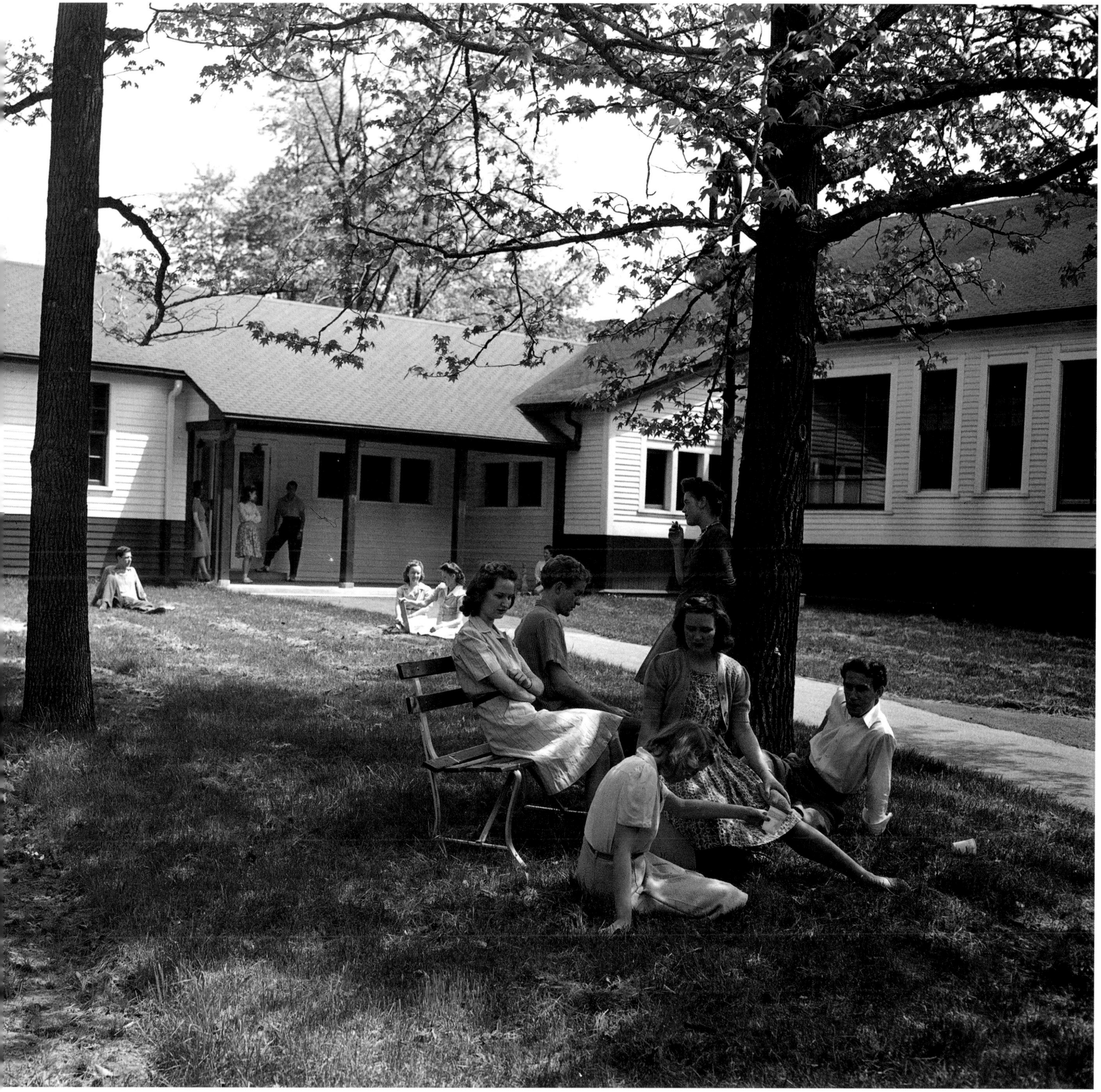

Maxwell Hall	1890
ARCHITECT	George W. Bunting
ARCHITECTURAL STYLE	Richardsonian Romanesque
ORIGINAL NAME	Library Building

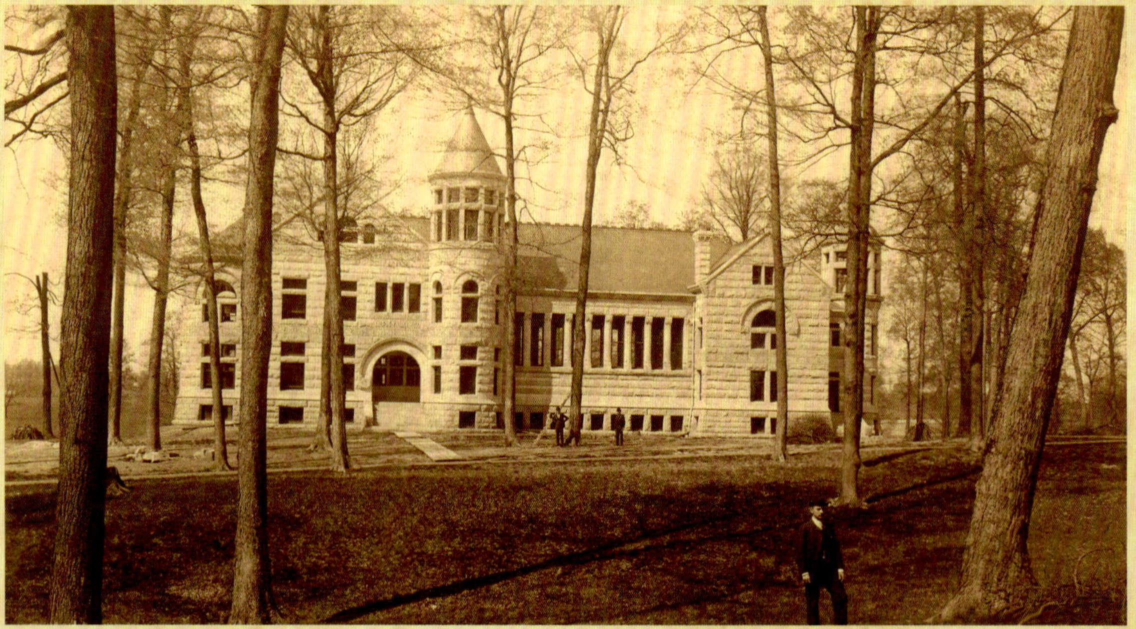

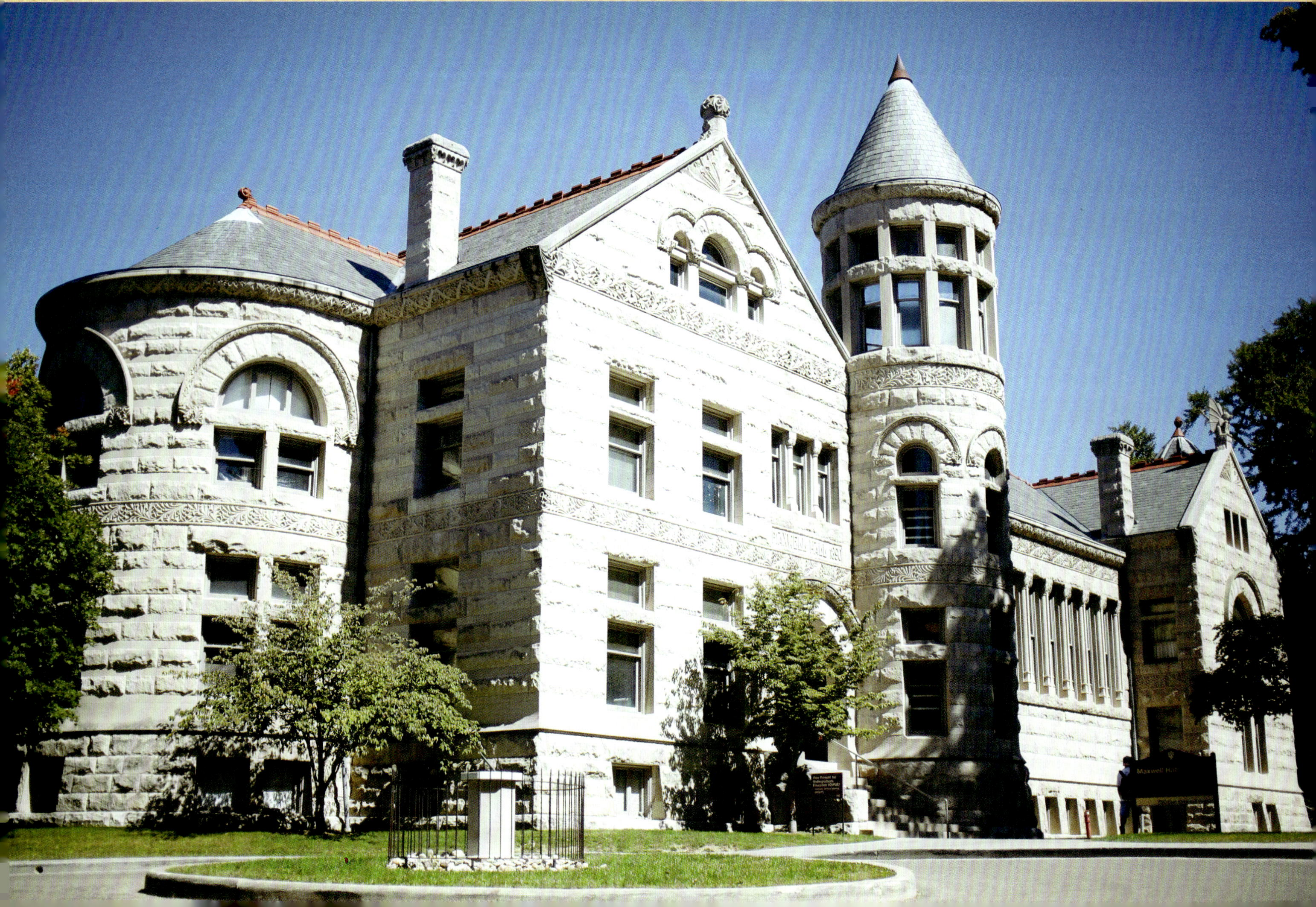

Maxwell Hall

A Medieval Castle in the Midwest

The handsomest building of all, and, from an architectural point of view, one of the finest in the state, is Library Hall.

—David Starr Jordan

ORIGINALLY CALLED LIBRARY HALL, THIS THREE-story, Richardsonian Romanesque castle is the first building on the Dunn's Woods campus constructed completely of limestone. It is also the first to be entirely underwritten with a legislative appropriation. In keeping with the work of U.S. architect H. H. Richardson (1838–86), a proponent of Romanesque Revival design, Maxwell features conspicuous arches, deeply recessed doors and windows, and a fantastical conical tower with a "witch's hat" roof. While the tower exaggerates Maxwell's height, alternating horizontal courses of smooth and rough-faced ashlar set off by wide belts of carved acanthus leaves give the building a massive appearance. By far the most ornate structure in the Old Crescent, Maxwell beautifully showcases the skill of Hoosier stonecutters. An intricately carved coiled serpent scrutinizes all those who enter. Whimsical, but fierce-looking, bat-like grotesques guard its roofline, one of them bearing an IU shield. Maxwell's windows and doors are decorated with wreaths that are repeated in the interior's ornate woodwork and cornices.

In 1894, Library Hall was renamed Maxwell Hall in honor of David Henry Maxwell, MD. Known as the Father of Indiana University, Dr. Maxwell actively petitioned the Indiana General Assembly to establish a state seminary and served as an IU trustee for more than three decades (1820–51). His son James Darwin Maxwell, an 1833 graduate, served as an IU trustee from 1860 to 1892.

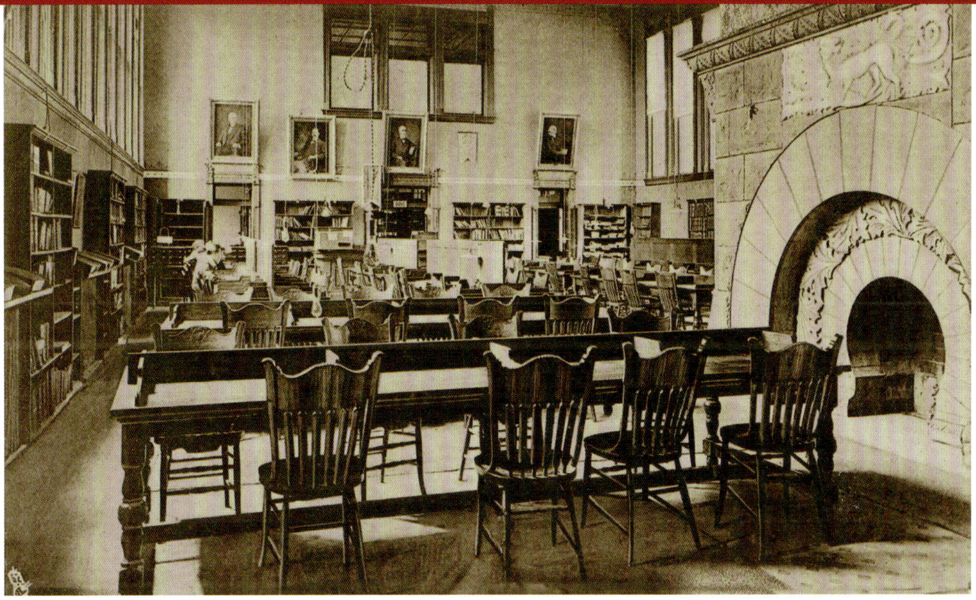

Maxwell Hall library reading room, undated. P0025758, IU Archives.

Architect George W. Bunting designed a fireplace of epic beauty and scale for the reading room of IU's first purpose-built library. It includes nine types of stone and echoes the arches and carvings on the building's exterior. Who wouldn't want to curl up with a book in front of such an inviting hearth? An arcade of tall lancet windows joins the building's two main sections and illuminates the reading room. When Maxwell Hall opened as Library Hall in 1890, the grand room dwarfed IU's library collection of fourteen thousand volumes. But the library had been conceived with room to grow. And grow it did. By the late 1900s, IU's library holdings had nearly quintupled, occupying all but the second floor of the building's east wing

Facing top, Maxwell Hall seen through Dunn's Woods shortly after completion, 1890. P0022217, IU Archives.

Facing bottom, Maxwell Hall with sundial in foreground on a summer day, 2014. Photo credit: Indiana University.

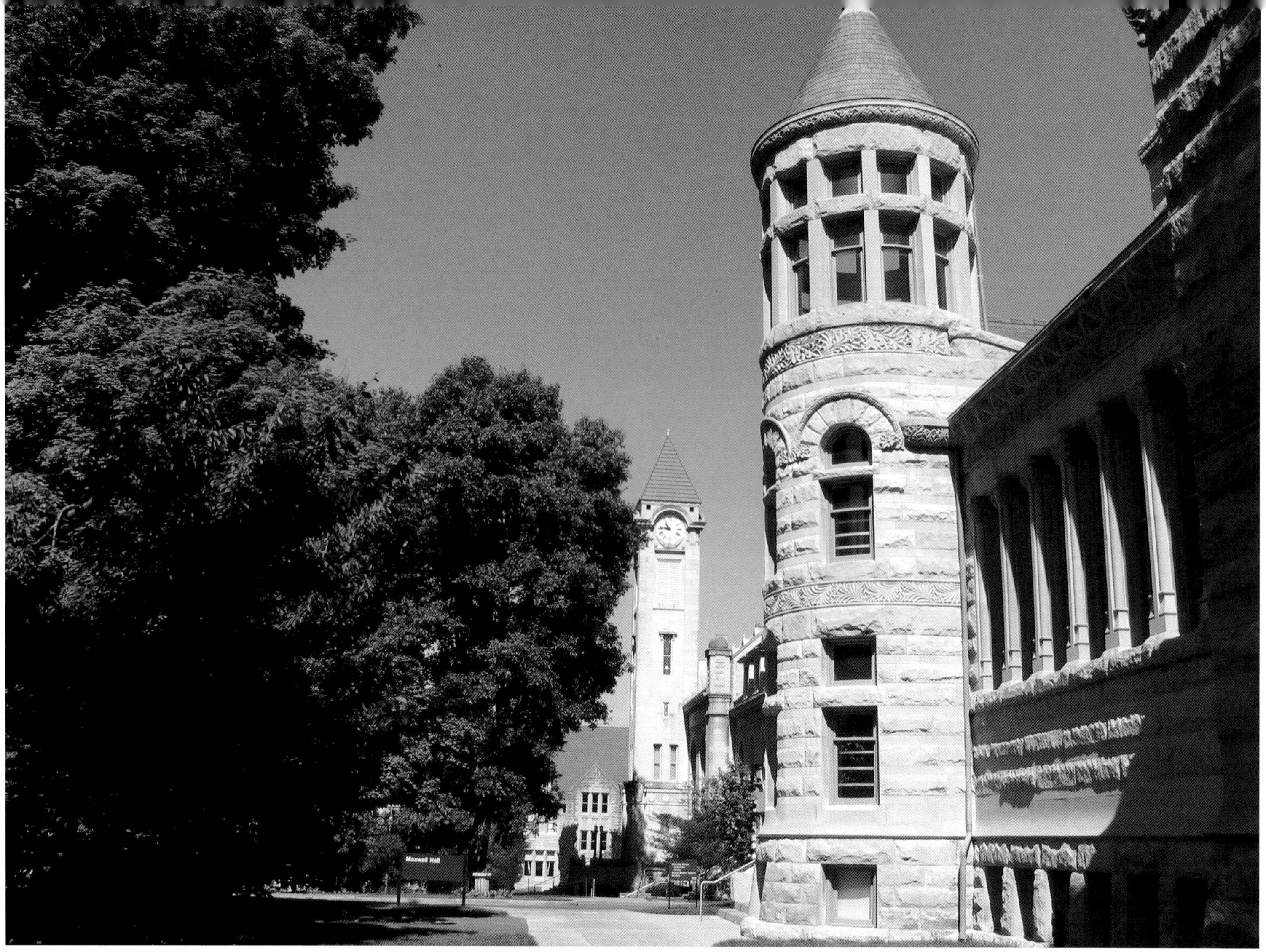

Maxwell Hall's turret and unique window colonnade, undated. Photo credit: Indiana University.

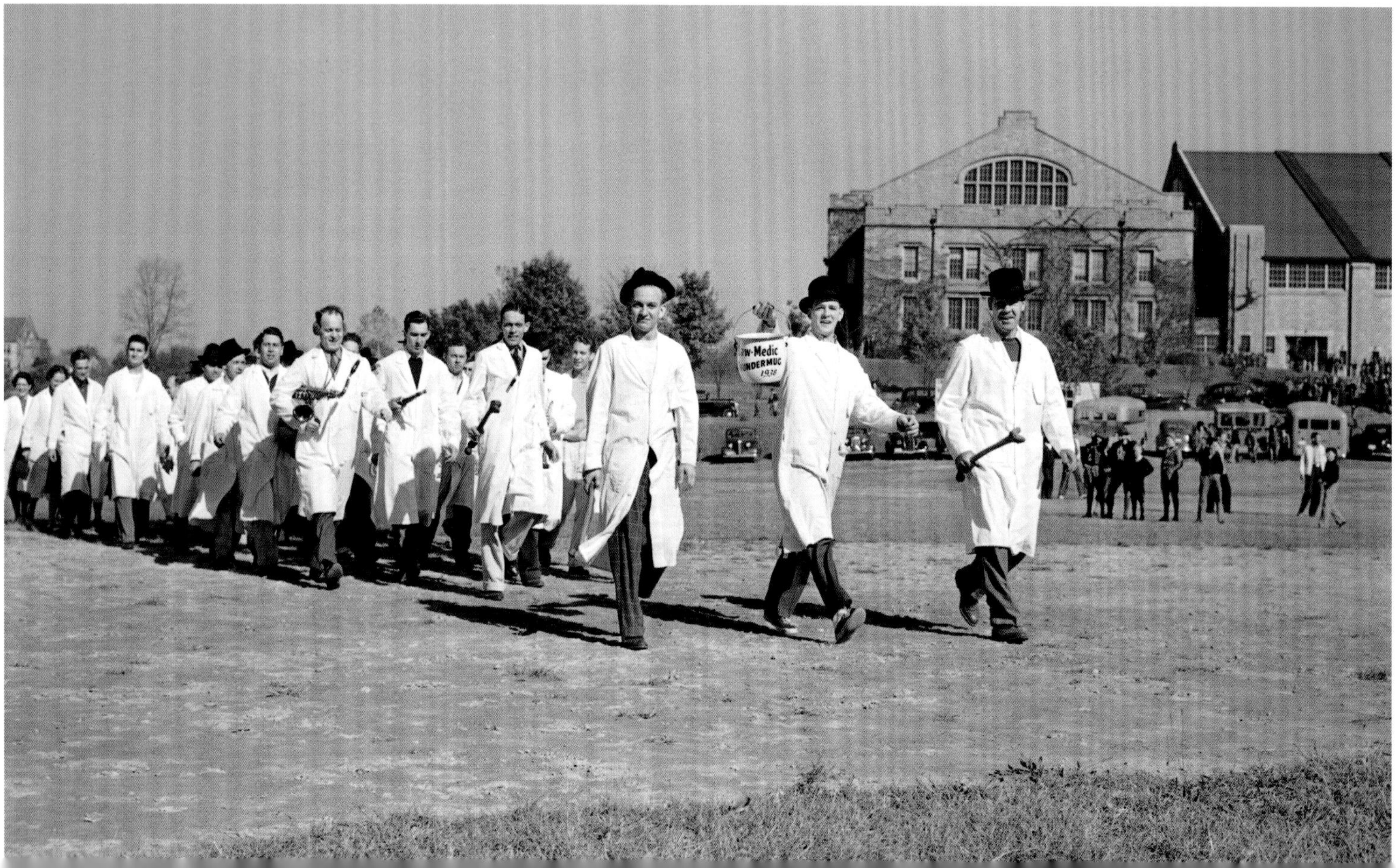

Medical and law students marching across Jordan Field during their annual Med-Law Boress for bragging rights and the Thundermug trophy, seen here in the hands of a freshman medical student, 1938. P0030996, IU Archives.

and eventually requiring the construction of another library building. Today, IU Bloomington's library holdings include over eight million books in more than nine hundred languages, as well as electronic journal titles, electronic books, maps, films, special collections, manuscripts, and sound recordings.

The IU School of Law, which for many years coexisted in Maxwell Hall with a succession of administrative and academic units, eventually colonized the entire building. In 1907 a three-story addition of recitation rooms and a small auditorium for the law school was built just north of the original building and connected to it by a short corridor. The university library moved to the newly constructed Franklin Hall, and the law library took over the old reading room. Indiana University historian Thomas Clark notes that by the 1950s, the law school would outgrow Maxwell Hall completely: "Out from [Maxwell's] maze of halls, chambers, attic nooks, and subterranean dungeons had gone the library, the central administration, the registrar, the deans of men and women, and of liberal arts. Law had pushed them out one by one, and now it was splitting the limestone cocoon and seeking new quarters."[1]

Oscar-winning songwriter Hoagy Carmichael studied in Maxwell, graduating with an LLB in 1926. He may well have taken part in the Med-Law Boress, an annual tradition in which the medical students challenged the law students to an athletic competition on Homecoming weekend. In the weeks leading up to the contests, medical students hung posters in Maxwell Hall, decrying the "lowly practice of shysterism." Law students declared "all medical students are nurtured on formaldehyde and had decided to become doctors only because they couldn't pass the entrance requirements of the plumbers' union."[2] Water hoses were wielded from rooftops, eggs were hurled, and songs full of insults and heckling speeches incited a mass Friday-night rally on the south steps of the Union. The white-coated "Medics" carried bones, and the derby-wearing "Laws" marched toward them armed with canes.

In the twentieth and twenty-first centuries, along with housing a library, administrative offices, and the law school, Maxwell has been home to the University Division, the Archives of Traditional Music, the Health Professions and Prelaw Center (HPPLIC), Continuing Studies, the Campus Writing Program, and the Groups Scholars Program, among other academic divisions.

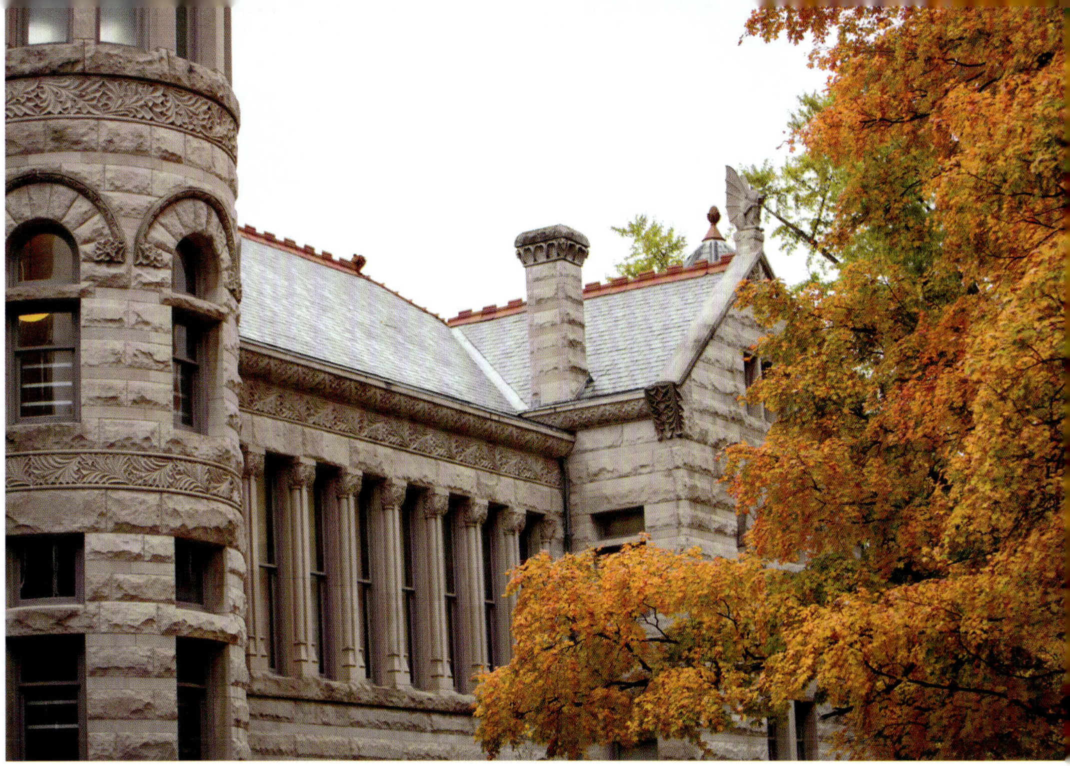

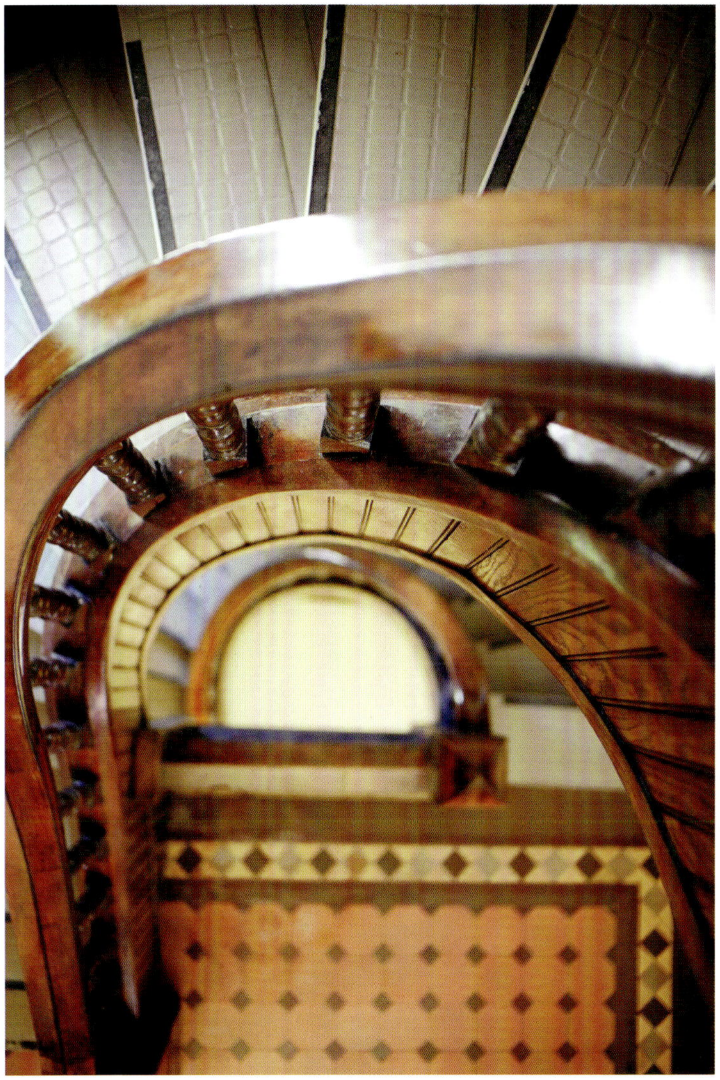

Above, Maxwell Hall with Richardsonian Romanesque architectural detail on full display, 2014. Photo credit: Indiana University.

Left, Maxwell Hall's nineteenth-century staircase craftsmanship, 2014. Photo credit: Indiana University.

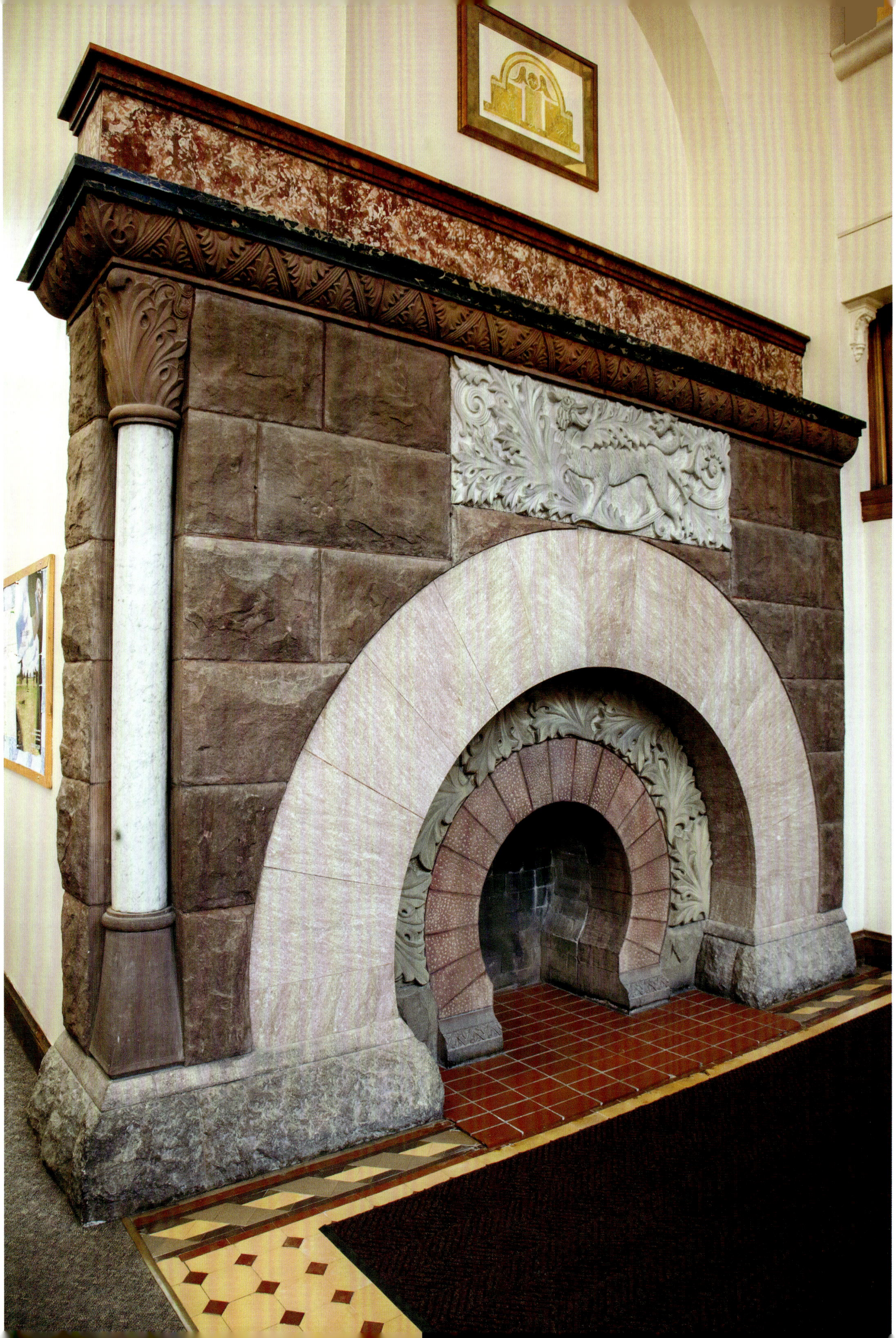

Nine types of stone and carvings of the monumental fireplace in the former Maxwell Hall library reading room echo the building exterior, 2016. Photo credit: Tyagan Miller.

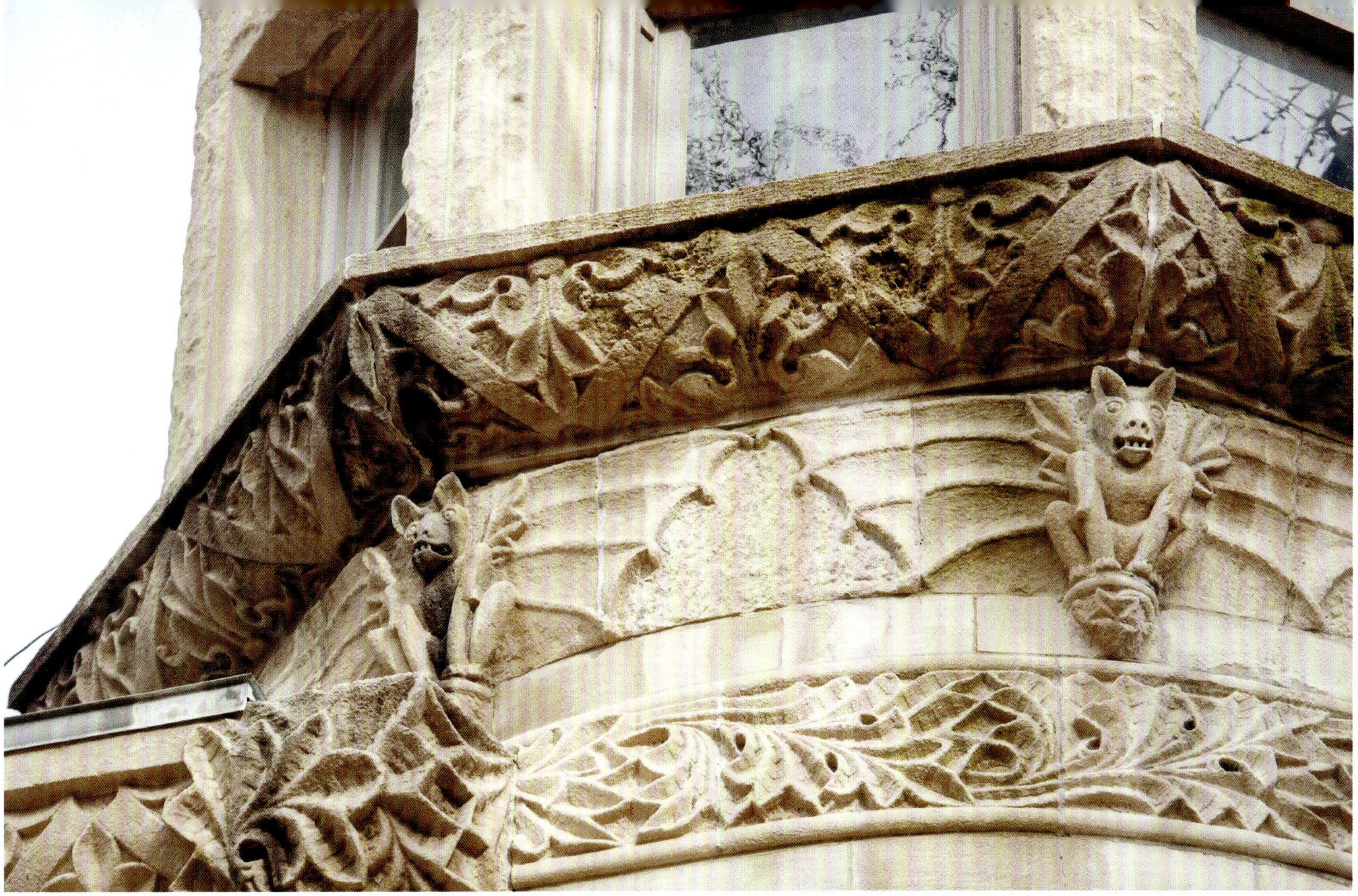

Bat-like grotesques guard Maxwell Hall roofline, 2016. Photo credit: Tyagan Miller.

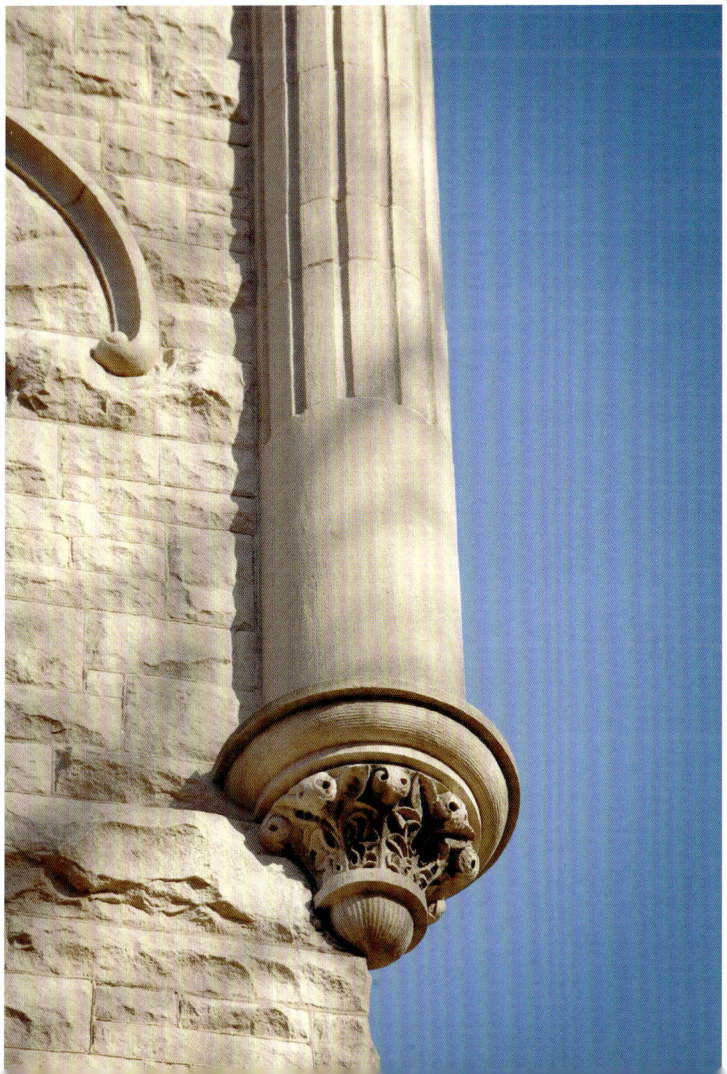

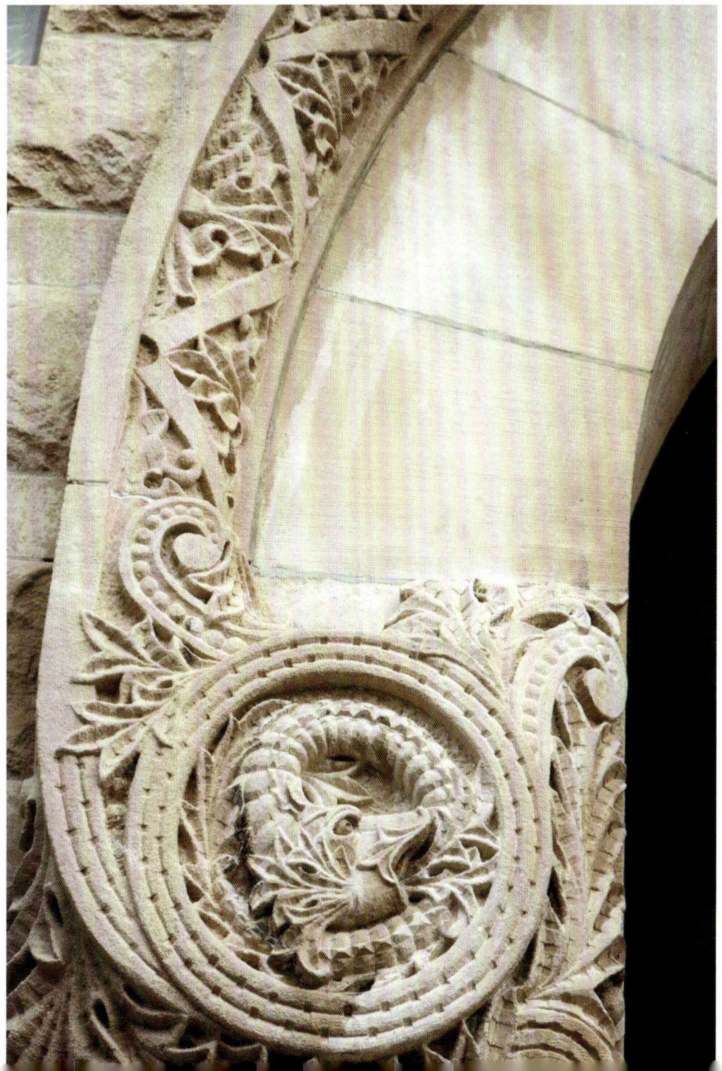

Left, Unique cornerpiece carving on Maxwell Hall, 2016. Photo credit: Tyagan Miller.

Right, Serpent coiled around Maxwell Hall entrance, 2016. Photo credit: Tyagan Miller.

Kirkwood Hall 1894

ARCHITECT Parker and Jeckel

ARCHITECTURAL STYLE Second Empire / Victorian / Romanesque

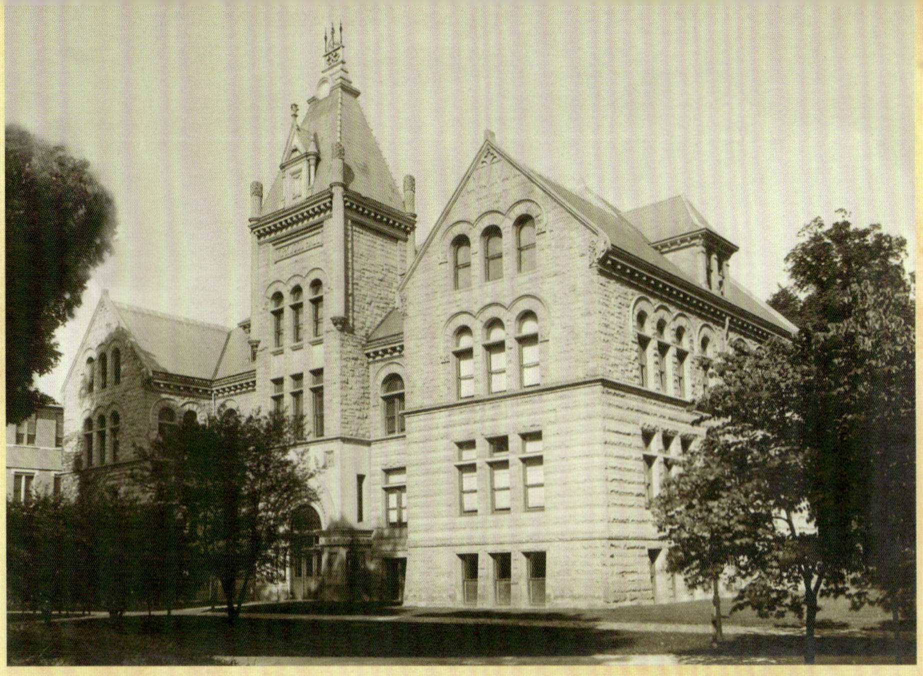

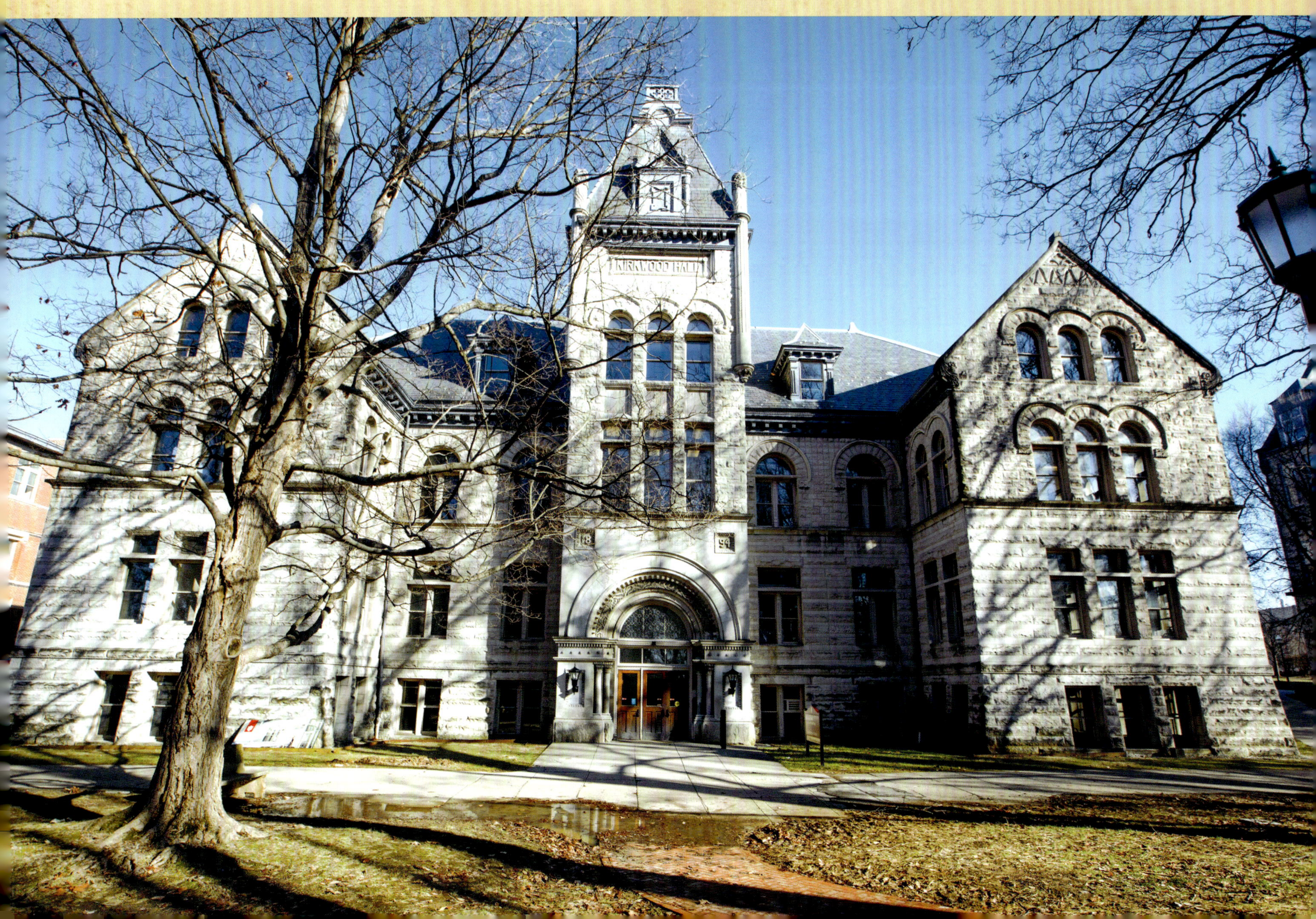

Kirkwood Hall

A Harbinger of Progress

Make no small plans for your institution; the small plans are very difficult to achieve. When you build, build for a long time. Build for a thousand years—do not build structures that will be cast away by tomorrow's fashion. Tradition has a role to play in our institutions, and traditions grow in part around physical symbols.

—Indiana University Chancellor Herman B Wells, Being Lucky

Identifying the lack of revenue as the main impediment to Indiana University's continued growth, President Joseph Swain, who served from 1893 to 1902, persuaded the state to provide a special appropriation for three new structures: a larger central heating plant, a new building for the humanities, and a new science building. He also advocated for more stable support of higher education. Hoosier lawmakers responded by imposing a tax equivalent to $0.00015 on each dollar of taxable property and dedicating the revenue stream to IU's maintenance and advancement.

On May 27, 1894, the *Bloomington Telephone* announced that the Anderson, Indiana, architectural firm of Parker and Jeckel would design Indiana University's fifth building on the new campus. Work would begin immediately, with a planned completion date just around the corner: January 1895. The building's name, already announced, was to be Kirkwood Hall in honor of professor Daniel Kirkwood. As described in the 1895 catalogue, the building was home to a great variety of university departments. The eight-room basement was occupied by laboratories for physics and experimental psychology, while physics and law laid claim to the first floor. The second floor was home to the language departments and finally, the Departments of History and Economics on the third.

Work was completed on time, and on January 25, 1895, dignitaries from around the state descended on Bloomington for the January festivities, which included a foxhunt for visiting newsmen. Indiana governor Claude Matthews and other elected officials traveled to Bloomington by train, and the town adorned itself in cream and crimson for the grand occasion. The dedication took place in Mitchell Hall. Governor Matthews congratulated the university for naming the new building after pioneering astronomer and Distinguished Professor of Mathematics Daniel Kirkwood, saying the name "pays a deserved tribute to a worthy man, expressing the affection he holds in thousands of hearts. Daniel Kirkwood may have been the 'Kepler of America'; he may have reached his hand among the stars and revealed their hidden secrets, yet withal he walked the earth a genial, companionable man, one of nature's gentlemen."[1]

Another among the day's many orators was Miss Edna Henry, who spoke on behalf of the student body. She compared the construction of the new building to the growth of a student's mind in the stimulating environment of the university. Although the text of Henry's remarks has not survived the years, perhaps she suggested that Kirkwood's thick walls of local limestone illustrate that great public universities are the bedrock foundation of a brighter future for Indiana's citizens. Maybe she compared the building's generous proportions to the broadening of horizons that study with great scholars inspires. She may have noted that Kirkwood's exceptionally wide staircases, central hall, and expansive landings provided open public spaces where faculty and students could engage

Facing top, Kirkwood Hall, 1907. P0020040, IU Archives.

Facing bottom, View of Kirkwood Hall from Dunn's Woods, 2017. Photo credit: Indiana University.

in the casual dialogue so essential to the educational process. She might even have compared the massive entry tower that soars a hundred feet skyward to the great heights an educated mind can reach.

Kirkwood Hall, the second IU building fully supported by state funds (Maxwell was the first), has four stories, including a basement and an attic. Following the lead of Maxwell Hall, its predecessor, Kirkwood is clad in rough and smooth courses of Indiana limestone, has rounded arches over the entry and second- and third-story windows, and an overall massive appearance. It is typical of the Second Empire style but has touches of Victorian and Richardsonian Romanesque, as well. While Kirkwood's main sections have gabled roofs, mansard treatments cap the tower and dormers; and the entry, windows, and gables are embellished with stone carvings. The Romanesque entrance surmounted by a large Second Empire tower is the most striking feature of the facade. Two Roman columns on either side of the entry frame the multiple bands of carved moldings on the door's arch. The tympanum (a semicircular or triangular decorative surface over an entrance bounded by the lintel and arch) features a beautiful leaded-glass window of beveled circles within circles.

Three of Indiana University's Nobel laureates collaborated in Kirkwood's attic. Then doctoral candidate James Watson worked there with faculty members Salvador Luria and Renato Dulbecco. Dulbecco's famous breakthrough concerning the interaction between tumor viruses and the genetic material of the cell had roots in his work with Luria, and Luria's signature discovery of the genetic structure of viruses laid the foundation for Watson's efforts to determine the structure of DNA.

Since its dedication, Kirkwood Hall has housed the Departments of French, Latin, Greek, German, Philosophy, Econom-

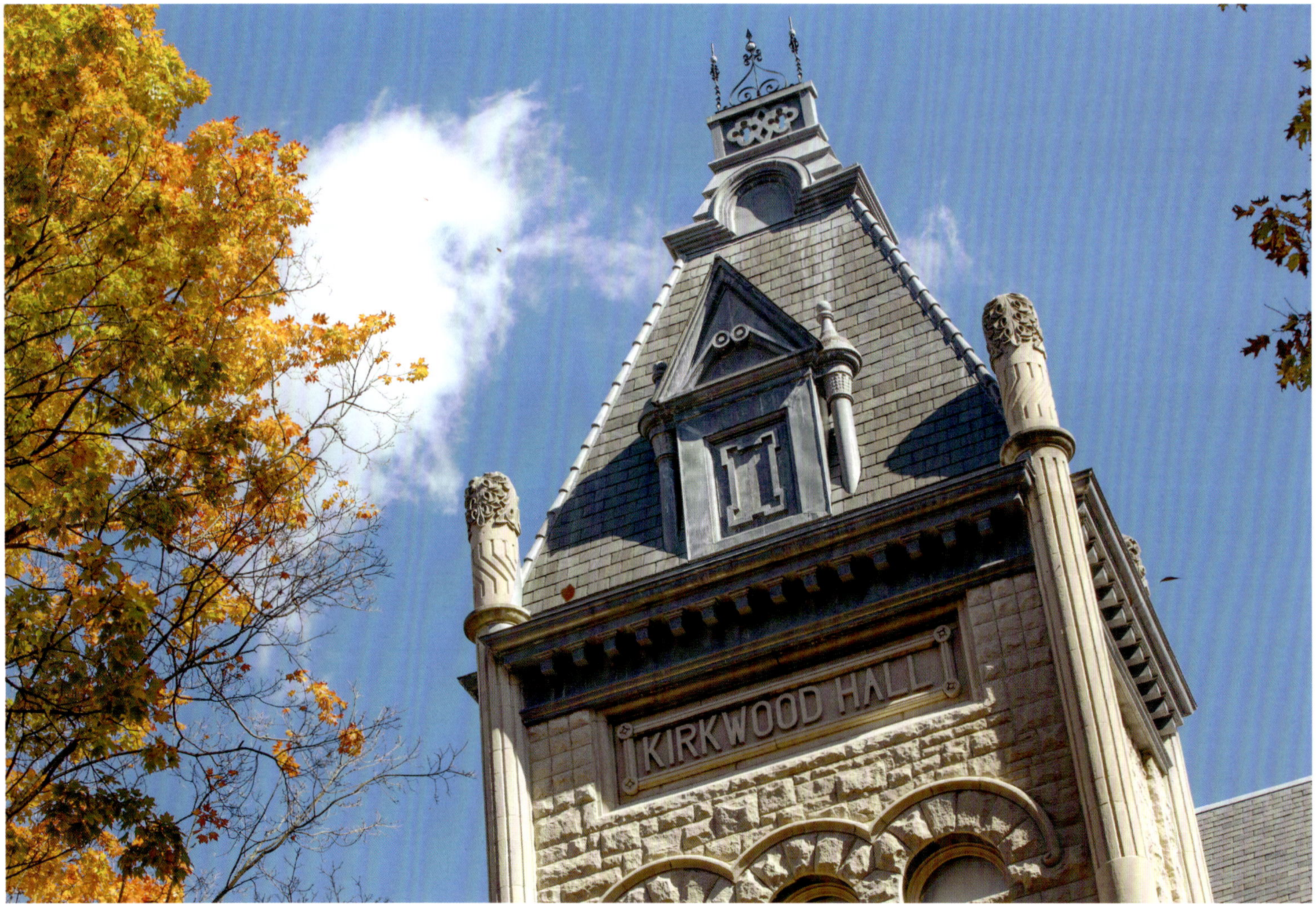

Kirkwood Hall's Second Empire tower topped with decorative lightning rods, 2014. Photo credit: Indiana University.

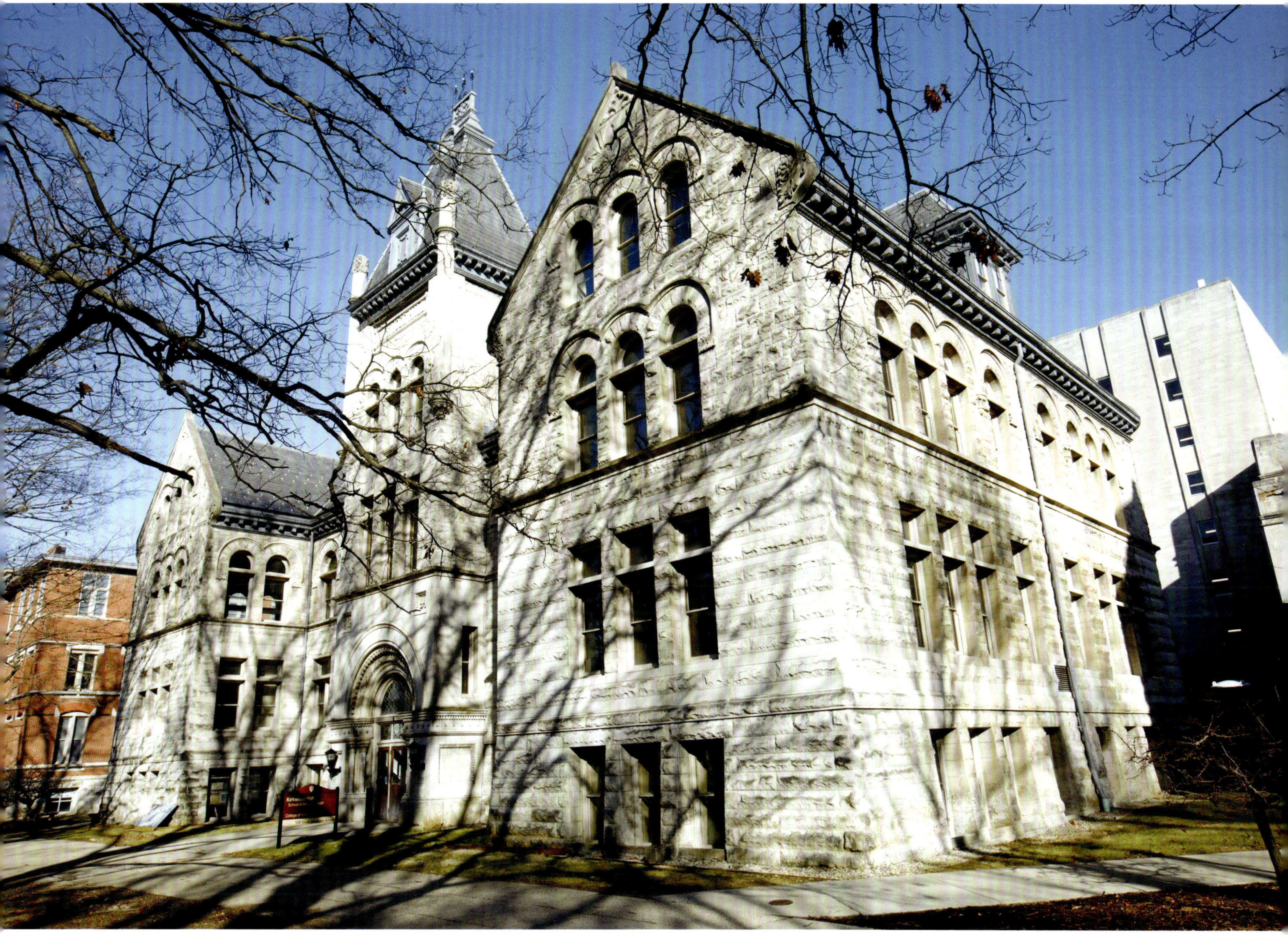

Winter shadows on Kirkwood Hall, 2017. Photo credit: Indiana University.

ics, Fine Arts, History, Political Science, Law, and Geography, and the administrative offices of the University Graduate School and the College of Arts and Sciences. The university is in the process of returning the Old Crescent, including Kirkwood Hall, to its original role housing academic departments, placing it once again at the center of academic vitality and student life. Accordingly, Kirkwood Hall has been renovated to accommodate offices and studio space for the new School of Art and Design (fine arts, interior design, and architecture).

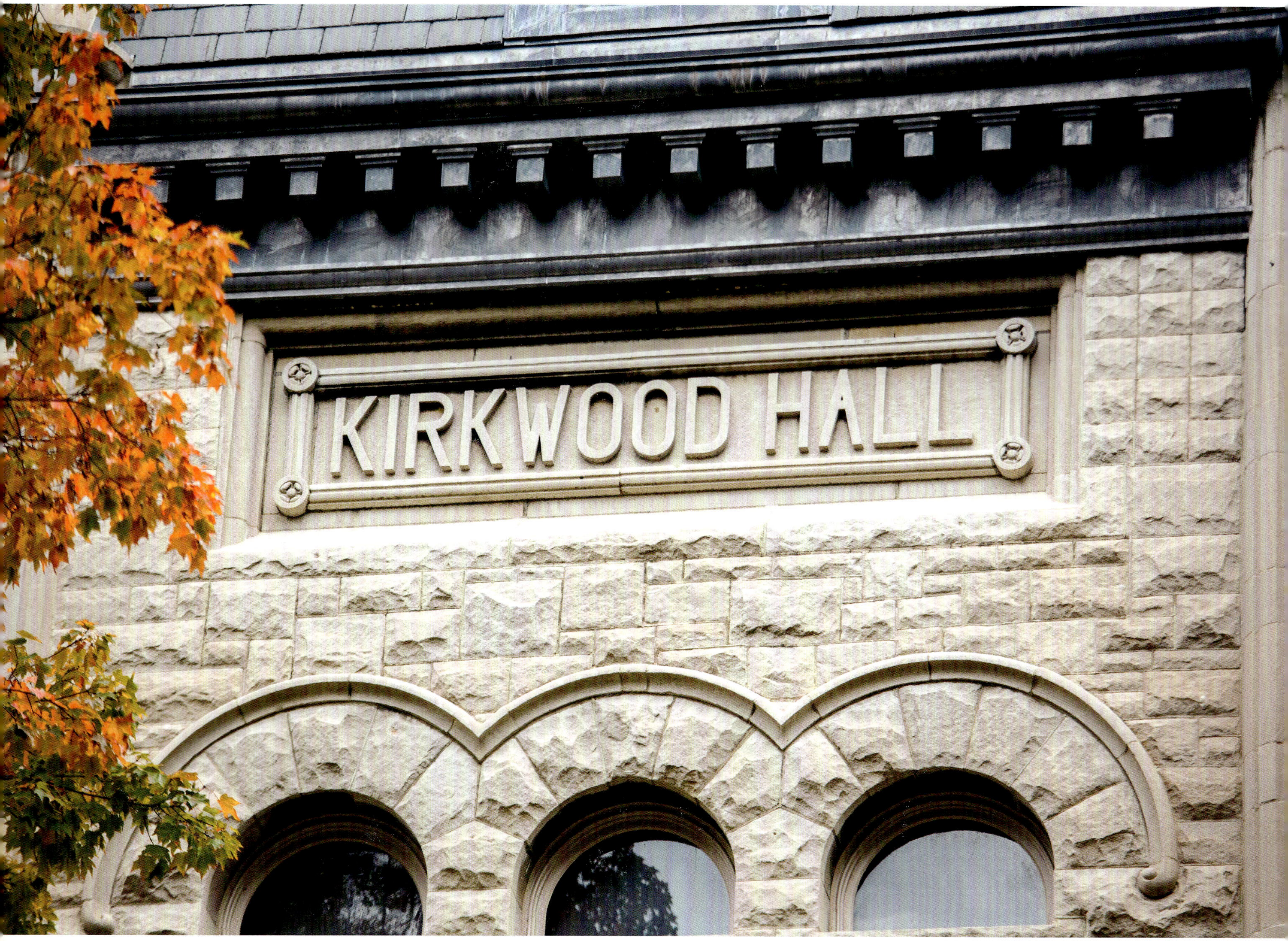

Decorative rounded window arches over Kirkwood Hall entry, 2016. Photo credit: Tyagan Miller.

Class Scraps

The class scraps began as a rebellion against classical poetry. In Indiana University's early years, sophomores were required to read the Roman poet Horace. In February 1830, on George Washington's birthday, several young men expressed their relief at having completed the course by setting their Horace texts ablaze. When the event became an annual occurrence, freshmen attempted to discover the time and place of the secret midnight ceremony in which their sophomore counterparts would eulogize Horace, burn books, and bury the ashes—all rituals the freshmen would forcibly try to prevent.

By the 1880s, the rivalry had left Horace behind, evolving into a capture-the-flag skirmish. Freshmen would display their colors on a triangular flag run up a pole or nailing it to a large tree in front of Kirkwood Hall. If the freshmen successfully defended their colors, they won the scrap. If the sophomores captured the flag, they flaunted it in victory marches around campus and the town. One evening in 1906, a freshman walking across campus detected fountains of dirt issuing from Kirkwood's basement windows. The sophomores had pried up the bricks of the furnace room floor and were digging a tunnel to the "scrap tree." Not to be thwarted, the next day the sophomores scaled Kirkwood's four stories bearing a parachute that would enable them to attack the flag from the air.

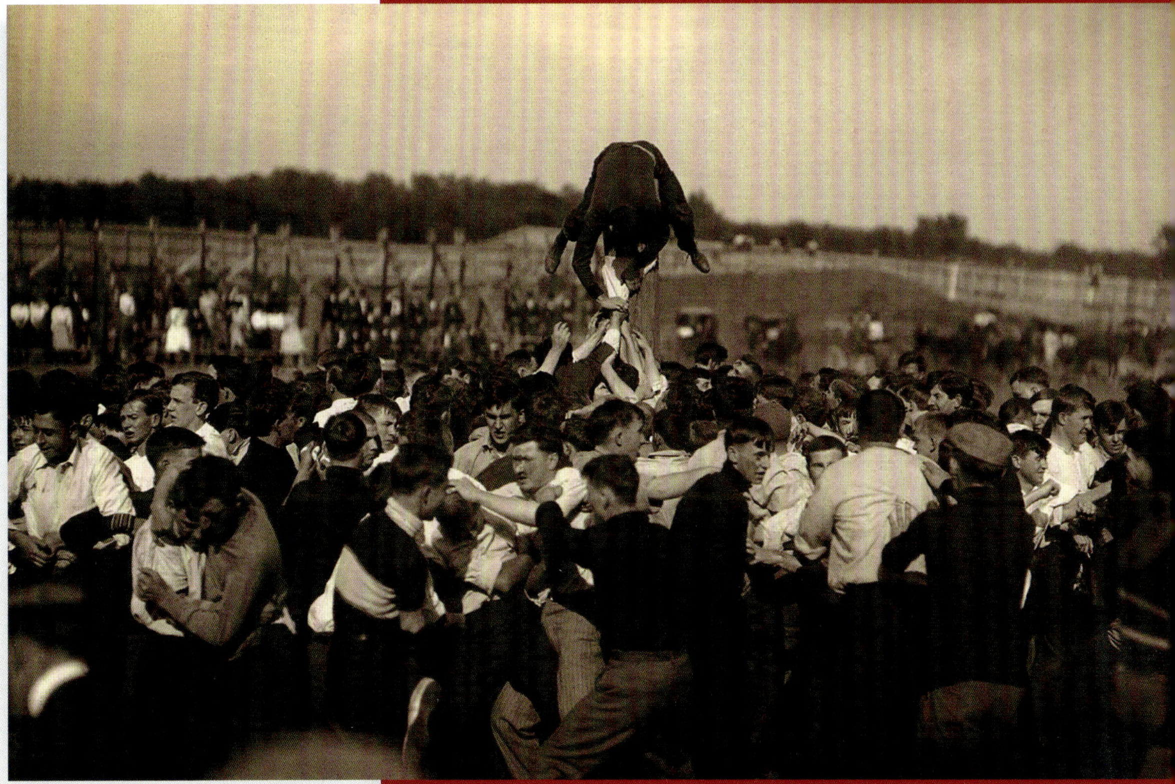

"Capture the Flag," a part of Class Scraps, 1909. P0023963, IU Archives.

An exclusively male pursuit, the class scraps sometimes involved black eyes, bloody noses, forced haircuts, and dunks in the Jordan River. Eventually the scraps occurred several times a year and lasted for weeks. Rules were developed, and juniors and seniors jumped into the fray. With the advent of anti-hazing rules in the late 1920s, the class spirit that motivated the scraps was transmuted to shuttle races, wrestling contests, and an annual football game pitting freshmen against sophomores. Many consider the class scraps precursors to the intramural sports that are so much a part of campus life today.

Kirkwood Observatory 1900

ARCHITECT John Nichols / Warner & Swasey

ARCHITECTURAL STYLE Victorian Gothic / Romanesque

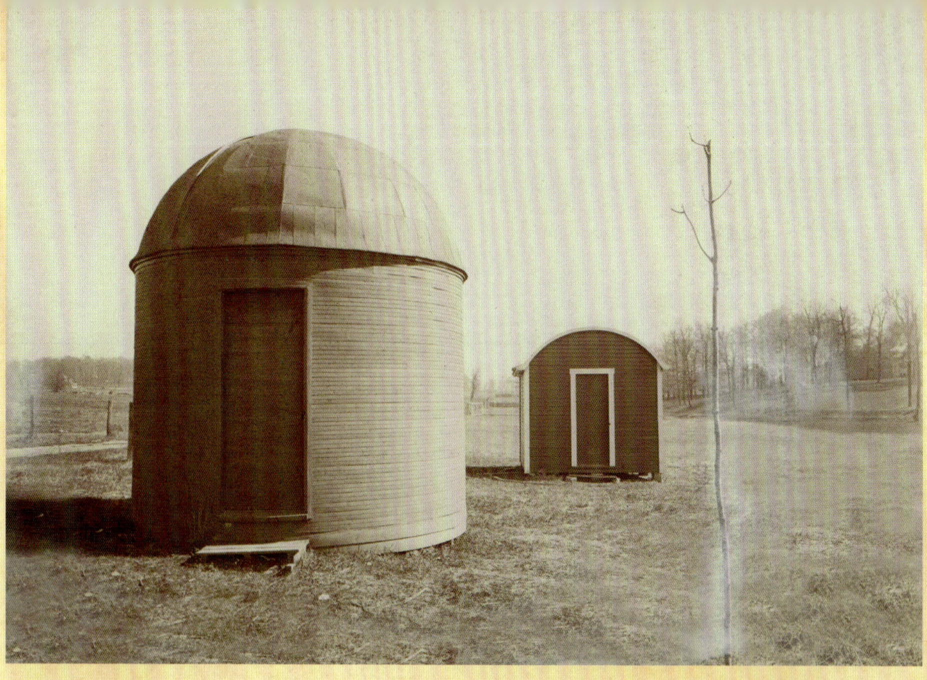

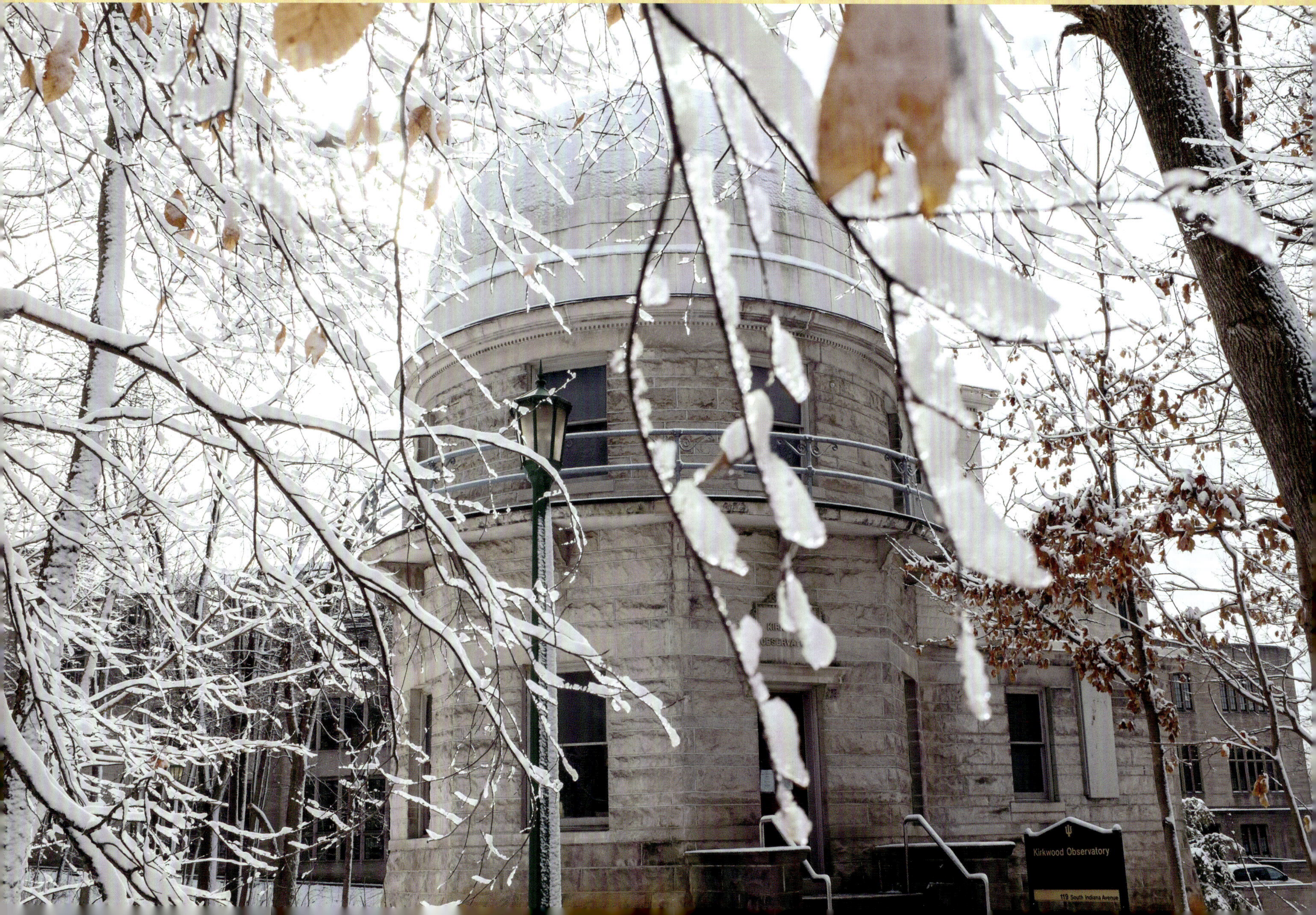

Kirkwood Observatory

Taking the Long View

In intellect he was keen, logical, and far-seeing. In integrity he was without reproach. He was "spotless before the world." In private character he was pure as an infant. He was in sympathy with humanity. He was as natural as a child and as free from self-conceit as the "lilies of the field." He saw and spoke the truth. The laws of Nature were to him the laws of God. The heavens indeed declared His glory. In revealing the secrets of the stars he revealed the beauty of his life. Kirkwood the scientist we admire, but Kirkwood the man we love. These characteristics made Daniel Kirkwood one of the greatest of Indiana's roll of heroes and one of the most lovable of men of any country or age.

—Indiana University President Joseph Swain, "Daniel Kirkwood"

A STUDY OF THE STARS HAS BEEN PART OF INDIana University's curriculum almost from the beginning. While IU was still the state seminary, professor of mathematics John Harney, our second faculty member, taught an astronomy class required for all juniors. Indiana University's first president, Andrew Wylie, shared Harney's interest in celestial science, as did the university's ninth president, Joseph Swain, whose mentor was the famous astronomer, Daniel Kirkwood. An authority on comets and meteors, "Daddy" Kirkwood, as he was called, chaired IU's Department of Mathematics from 1856 to 1886. This theoretical astronomer published more than a hundred books and articles during his fifty-year career. The spaces in the main asteroid belt created by gravitational interaction with Jupiter are known as Kirkwood gaps because of his calculations. He also identified a pattern relating the distances of the planets to their rotation periods. This theory became known as Kirkwood's Law and earned him an international reputation as the "Kepler of America."

Professor Kirkwood was universally admired and beloved. A former student offered the following tribute: "The specific lessons of the class room, the formulae and theorems of my college course have been forgotten, but there is one thing worth more than all else that will ever abide, the lesson in true life given me by my daily contact with the noble astronomer, Daniel Kirkwood."[1] Kirkwood Hall, Kirkwood Avenue, and the Kirkwood Observatory keep alive this remarkable man's contributions to the university, the community, and the science of astronomy.

Indiana University's establishment of the Department of Mechanics and Astronomy in the 1890s justified the purchase of a refracting telescope. Designed by John A. Bashear, the instrument had a 12-inch lens and state-of-the-art instrumentation. At that point, the university had just a small frame observatory that was insufficient to house the new telescope. Another frame observatory large enough to hold the new telescope could have been built for less than $1,000, but the faculty argued against housing such valuable equipment in a flammable wooden structure. By 1900 a site was identified on the southwest corner of campus, and construction began on a tri-level, six-room limestone structure. The observatory was designed to include a library and "computing-room," lecture room, darkroom, a dome room 26 feet in diameter, a ground-floor assembly room, and a transit room—complete with a Bamberg universal instrument, a chronograph by Fauth & Company, a Bond sidereal chronometer, and a sidereal clock.[2]

The observatory has a distinctive retracting dome, which houses the refracting telescope. Beneath the dome is a two-story structure. The upper story is round, with a limestone and steel balcony, whereas the lower story is hexagonal. Attached to the dome tower are several rectangular protrusions. The main structure has a limestone foundation, and the large rock face blocks are joined by mortar joints that are convex, with a

Facing top, The first observatory and transit house at the western end of Dunn Meadow, 1898; razed in 1928. P0022865, IU Archives.

Facing bottom, Kirkwood Observatory in winter, 2016. Photo credit: Indiana University.

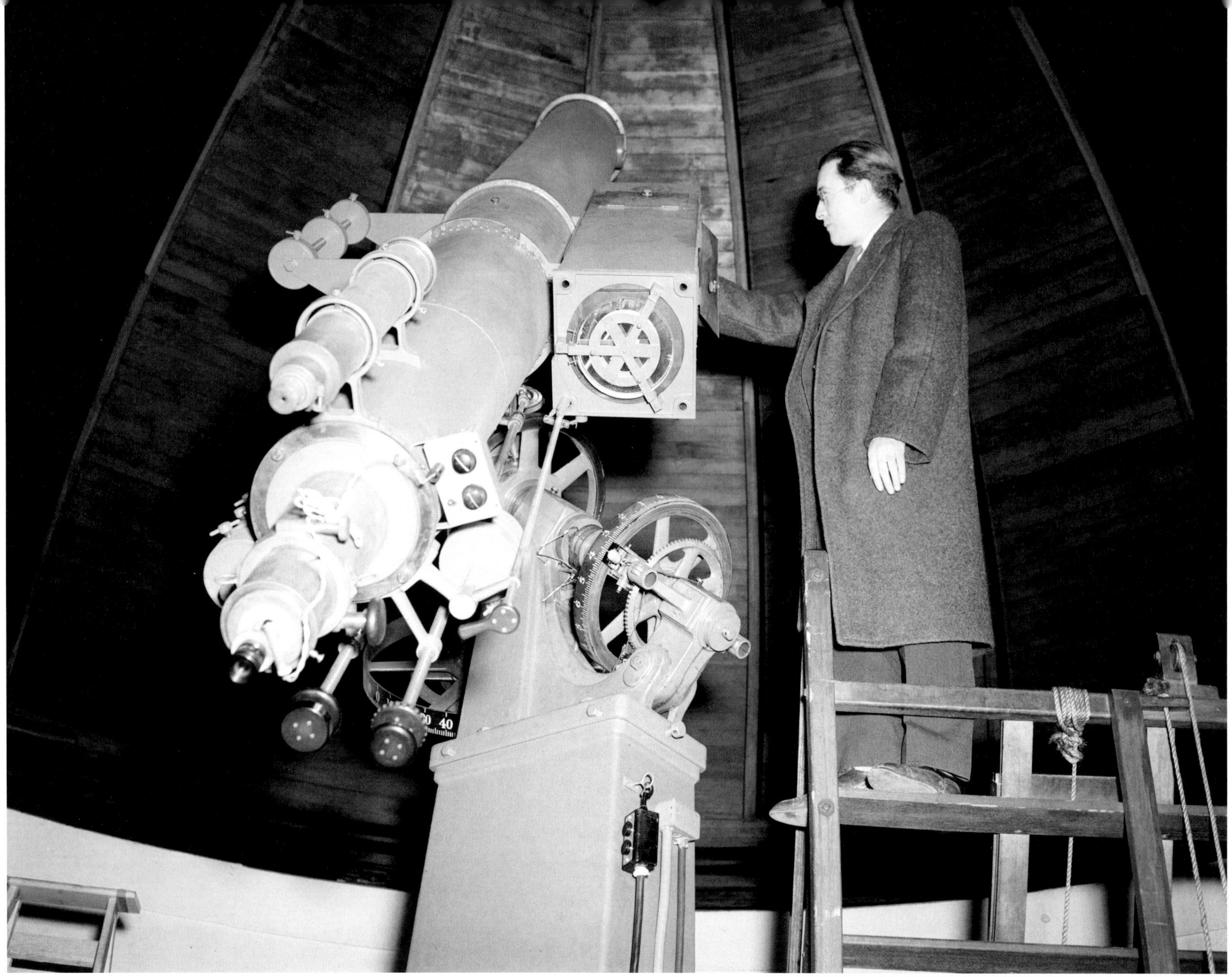

Professor Frank K. Edmondson with Kirkwood Observatory's Bashear refracting telescope, 1947. P0046835, IU Archives.

distinctive protruding profile not used on other buildings on campus.

In June 1901, a month after the building was dedicated, President Swain noted that the telescope and observatory had already justified their cost because they had "quickened immensely" students' interest in astronomy.[3] The first IU building dedicated in the twentieth century, the observatory was the largest in the state and the finest of its size in the country.

Indiana University conferred its first doctorate in astronomy in 1909 to Vesto Slipher. Dr. Slipher went on to identify an astronomical phenomenon concerning the velocity of recession in nebulae, a discovery that led to modern theories of the expanding universe. In 1914, the trustees established a separate Department of Astronomy. By 1920 the department had acquired instruments of such superior power and sensitivity that the original telescope was no longer used for research. Indiana University astronomers currently do most of their

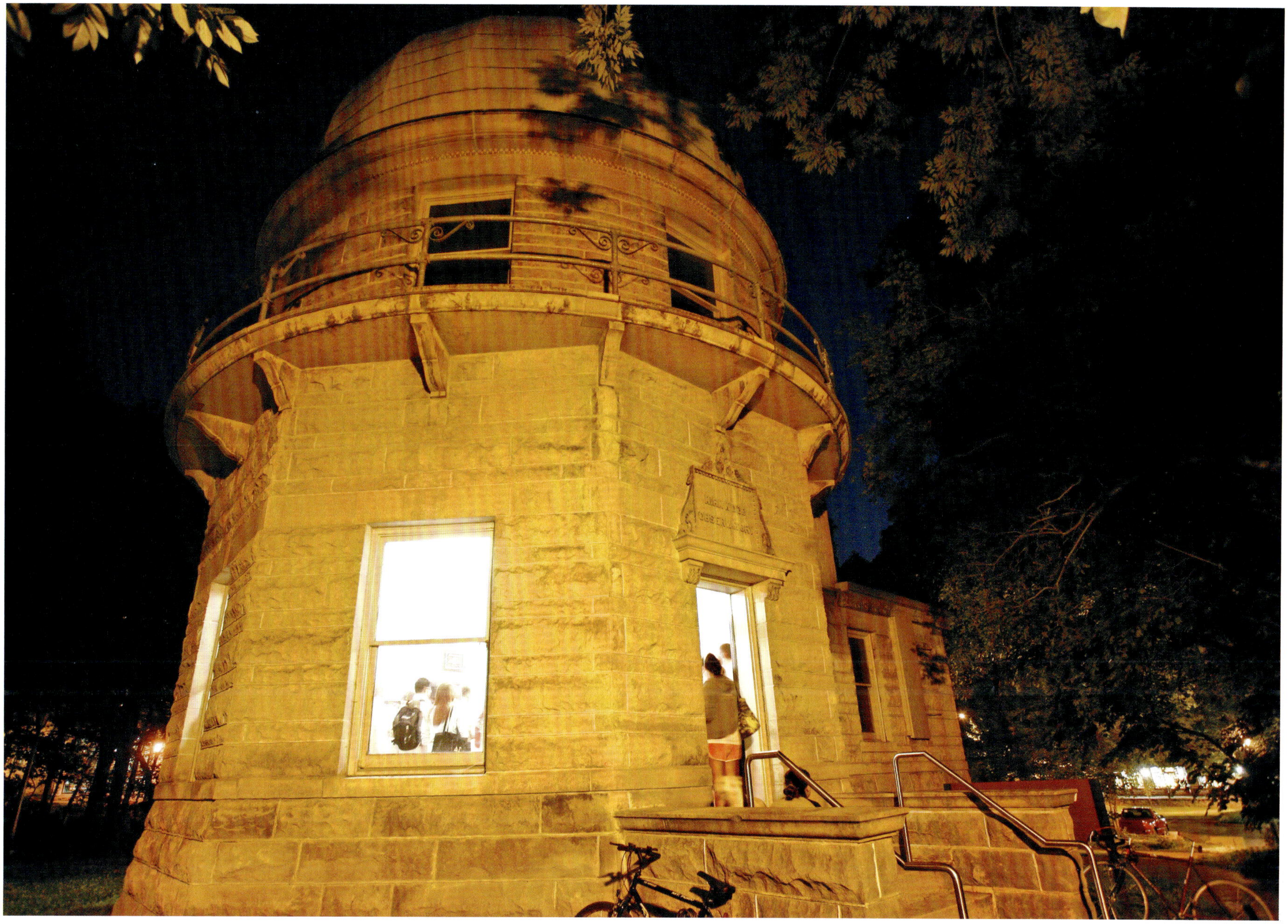

Kirkwood Observatory open seasonally at night to the public, undated. Photo credit: Indiana University.

direct research at the Morgan-Monroe Station of the Goethe Link Observatories, about 12 miles north of the Bloomington campus, and at the Kitt Peak National Observatory near Tucson, Arizona. But the observatory's on-campus convenience makes it an ideal facility for teaching introductory astronomy courses.

In 2001 the building was renovated and the equipment updated. The whitewashed wooden dome, which had begun to grate and stall as astronomy buffs followed the transit of stars and planets, was repaired—a copper skin replaced the original tin one—and a solar laboratory was installed. Each clear Wednesday evening from early spring to late fall, members of the campus and community flock to student-run open houses to explore the night sky. The historic Kirkwood Observatory is especially popular during celestial events such as eclipses, sunspots, and solar storms.

Ernest H. Lindley Hall 1902

ARCHITECT Lewis Gibson

ARCHITECTURAL STYLE Functional / Modern

ORIGINAL NAME Science Hall

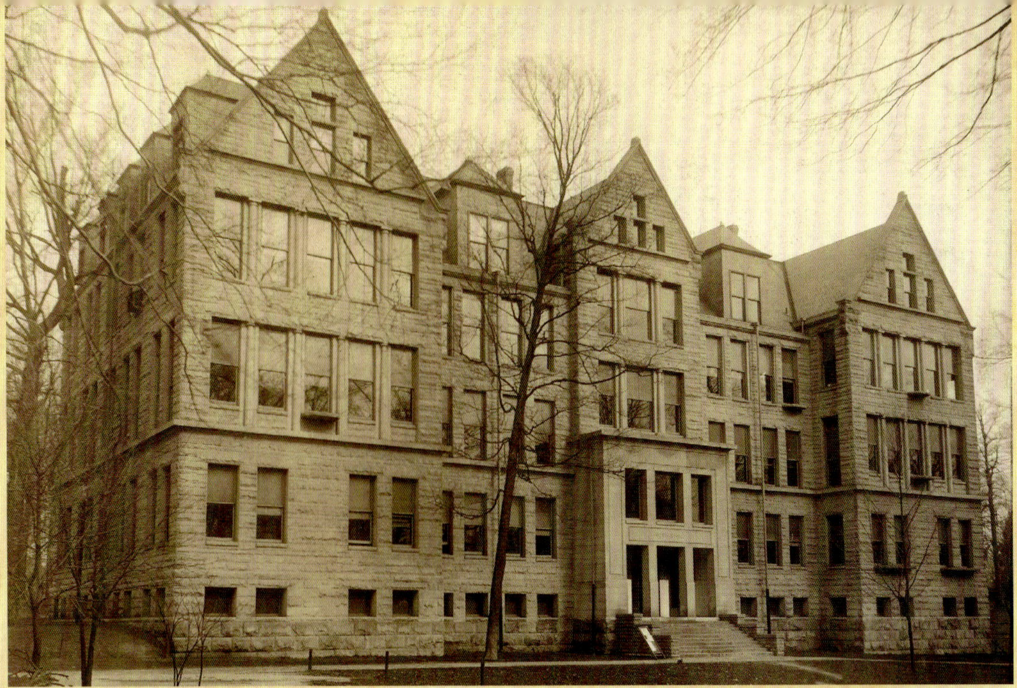

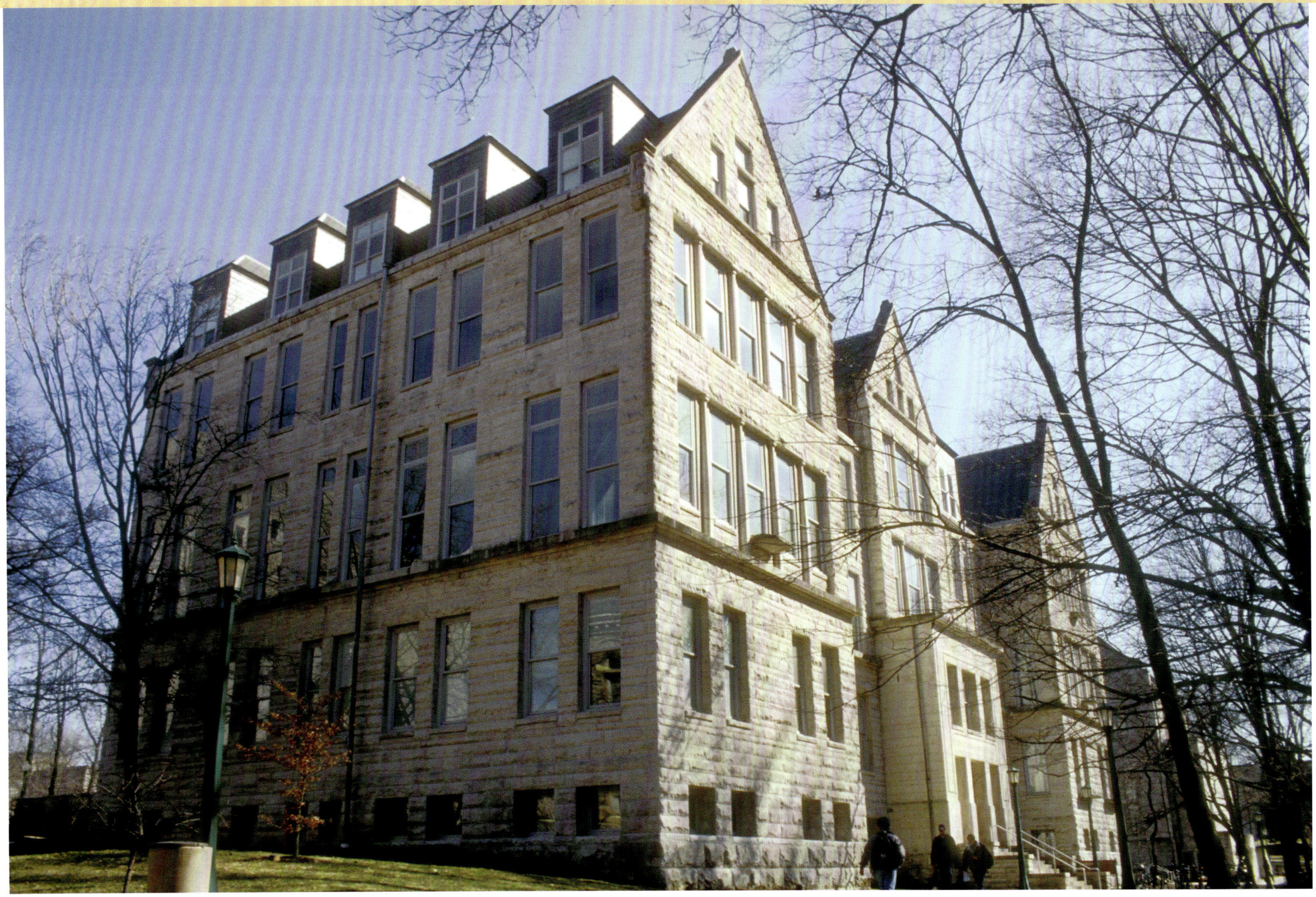

Ernest H. Lindley Hall

Faith in Education and *Research*

Everything about the University has a distinctive appearance. It is "Indiana-like." Once impressed upon the student it does not leave him. What we learn here may pass from our minds, even the images of familiar faces may grow dim, but the Indiana Campus, with its natural scenery, its loved retreats, and its well-remembered trysting places will not be forgotten.

—*1906* Arbutus

Between 1895 and 1899, Indiana University's enrollment increased from 488 to 629 students, raising the need for classrooms—particularly science facilities—to critical proportions. The science faculty lobbying for a new building consulted colleagues at the University of Chicago to develop specifications that would facilitate both instruction and research. After considerable debate over resources, Mitchell Hall, which originally occupied the southern tip of the crescent, was moved 210 feet to the east, and a four-story structure (plus basement) clad in local limestone was built in its place.

With the clean, vertical lines of the skyscrapers conceived by Chicago architects who took advantage of new steel-frame and cast-iron technology, the building was designed to be vibration free, fireproof, and temperature controlled, with a structural framework of heavy steel. Its first-floor laboratories were reinforced with piers of Portland cement that reached to the basement. All the laboratories had 14-foot ceilings to dissipate chemical fumes. The building was outfitted with darkrooms, the latest in scientific equipment, and an instrument fabrication shop. Stone shelves 6 inches thick, jutting out 2 feet from the window ledges, provided cooling platforms for chemical experiments and growing ledges for botanists' projects.

An example of form meeting function, Science Hall (as it was then called) has none of the ornamentation of its Old Crescent neighbors. Its austere facade could be called Modern Romanesque and reflects the pragmatism of data-driven science. The building's one concession to decoration is a grill in the bannister of the central steel staircase, suggesting the leaves and lilies of a William Morris print. At the time of its construction, Lindley Hall was the largest and most expensive building on campus.

The dedication occurred in January 1903 during a three-day Foundation Day celebration that included the installation of a new president, a basketball game against DePauw (IU won 43–9), and a performance of the annual play, which that year was Shakespeare's *Much Ado about Nothing* (hopefully *not* a comment on the celebration). William Lowe Bryan would become IU's longest-serving president (1902–37). Under his leadership, the Bloomington student body grew from 748 to 4,943 and the campus expanded from 50 to 1,137 acres.

Cornell University professor Edward Nichols spoke at the dedication, declaring that of the hundred physics laboratories in America, only twelve were used for special investigation, as the labs in this new building would be. He asserted that the

Facing top, Ernest H. Lindley Hall, 1907. P0020048, IU Archives.

Facing bottom, Lindley Hall, original home to sciences; note the cooling ledge for experiments, undated. Photo credit: Indiana University.

state should realize scientific research was as valuable as teaching science, if not more so, and should do more to foster individual investigation. The construction of Lindley Hall marked a new era for IU—one that acknowledged the university's vital role in providing educational opportunities *and* pushing forward the frontiers of scientific knowledge.

Originally, physics occupied the basement and first floor; pedagogy (which would become the School of Education in 1908) shared the second through fourth floors; philosophy, psychology, and university administrative offices the second and third floors; and geology and geography the third and fourth floors. Lindley Hall was the first home of the biology department and housed the School of Medicine until 1911.

In 1921, the university community gathered in Science Hall to hear physics professor Rollo Ramsey demonstrate a new sensation called radio. Famous behaviorist B. F. Skinner, chair of the Department of Psychology from 1945 to 1948, built rat mazes there to refine his theory of operant conditioning (more commonly known as behavior modification).

In 1957 the building was renamed Ernest H. Lindley Hall in honor of the Bloomington native, IU graduate, professor (1893–1917), and former chair of the Department of Philosophy/Psychology who later became president of the University of Idaho and chancellor of the University of Kansas. Among Professor Lindley's many duties as an IU faculty member was advising the then fledgling Union Board. When student J. T. Giles was writing the lyrics to IU's *Alma Mater*, he couldn't find a rhyme for "Indiana" and "gloriana." Professor Lindley suggested "frangipana," the brand name of a new soap and perfume that Lindley's father stocked in his downtown Bloomington drugstore.[1]

A year after the name change, the trustees considered razing the dilapidated building but instead opted for renovation, thus preserving the integrity of the Old Crescent and avoiding the mistake of many other universities that destroyed their architectural legacies. Another extensive renovation, completed in 1992, outfitted the building for the burgeoning Department of Computer Science (now part of the School of Informatics and Computing). Cable troughs cleverly disguised as attractive ceiling cornices enable quick wiring from any point in the building. Former chemistry and biology laboratories have become machine rooms filled with the blinks and hums of massive servers. But the jutting window ledges remain, reminding us of a simpler era.

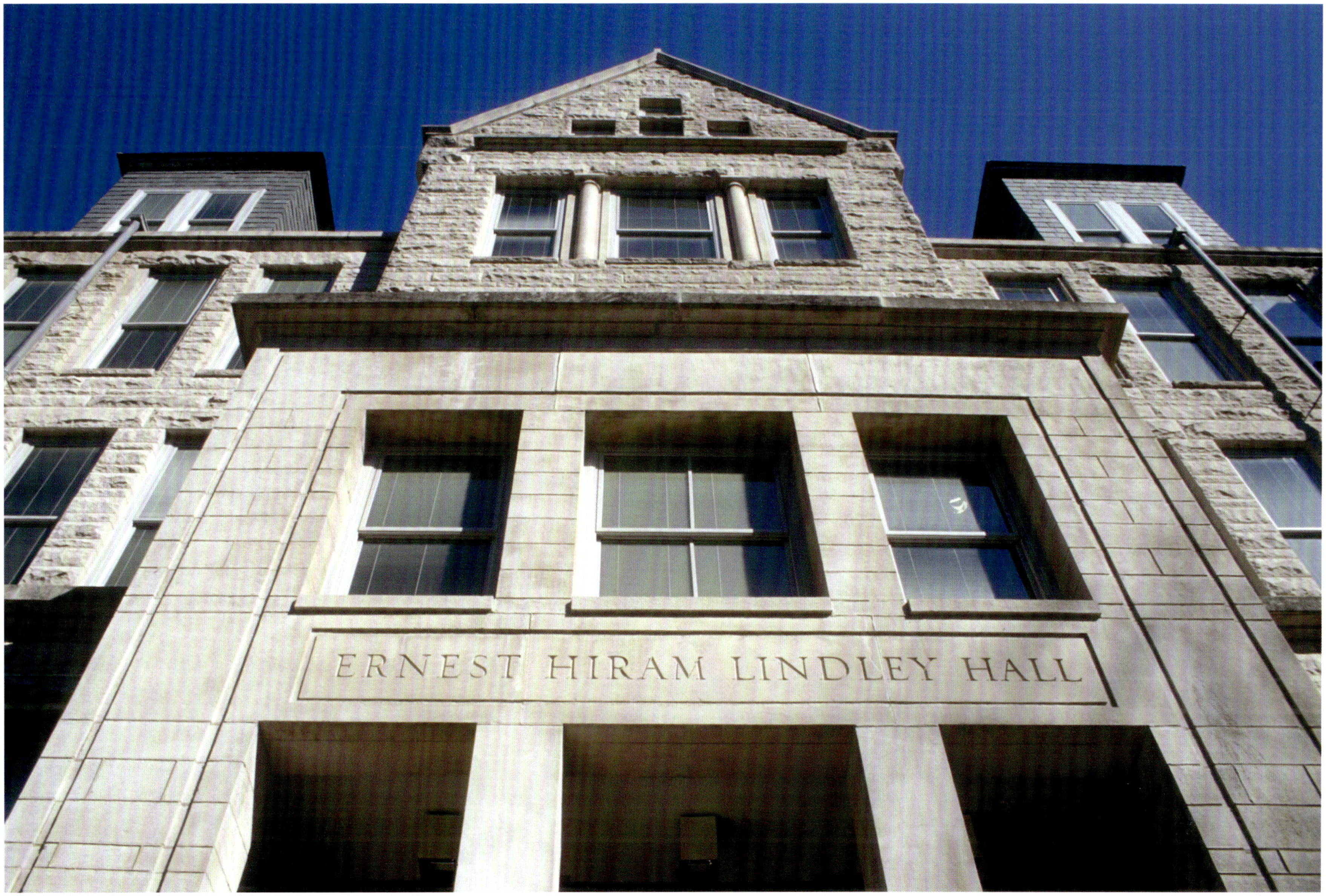

Austere Romanesque west elevation of Lindley Hall, undated. Photo credit: Indiana University.

Frances Morgan Swain Student Building 1906

ARCHITECT Vonnegut and Bohn

ARCHITECTURAL STYLE Romanesque Revival / Collegiate Gothic

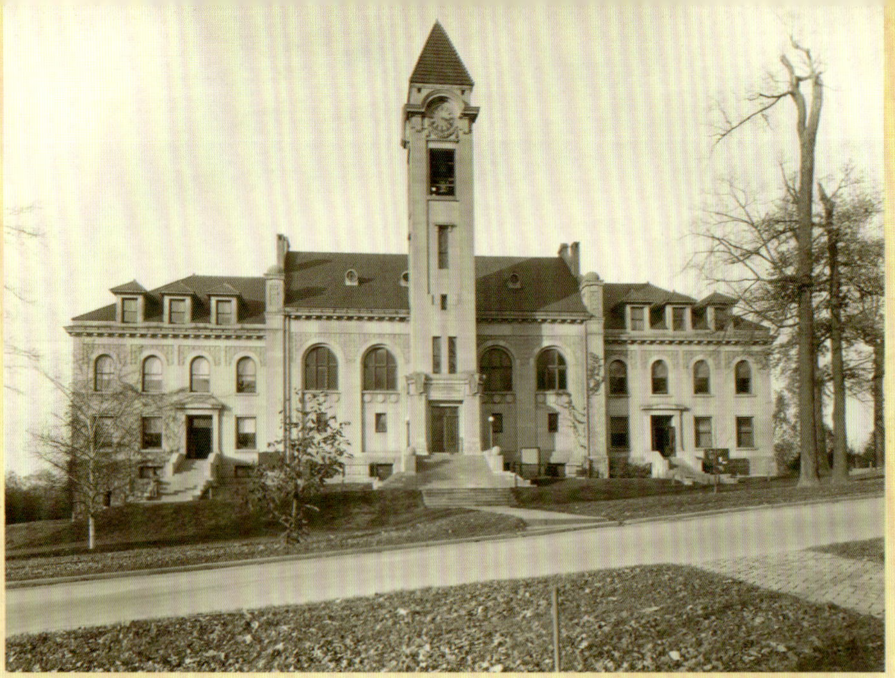

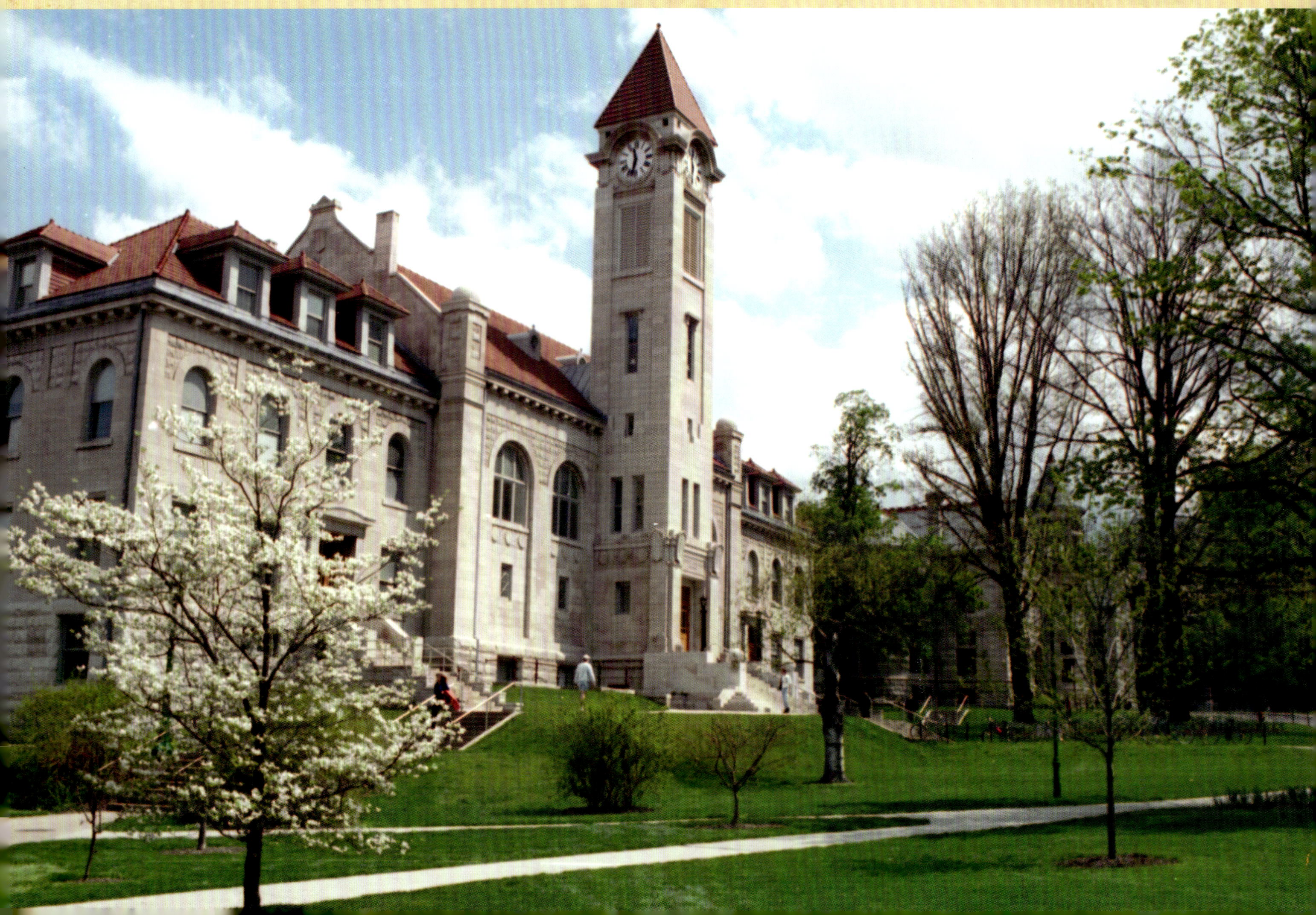

Frances Morgan Swain Student Building

IU's First Capital Campaign

For all who have lived and worked, studied and dreamed on this beautiful campus, the Student Building and its bell tower—risen again from the ashes—are symbols of Indiana University.

They hold a cherished place in our hearts and in our history.

—Indiana University President Thomas Ehrlich at rededication ceremony

In 1867 Indiana University became one of the nation's first public universities to admit women. By the turn of the century, women comprised nearly 30 percent of the student body, though the university had made few structural accommodations for its coeds. President and Mrs. Swain worried that the dullness of campus life and lack of proper facilities for women might prevent Hoosier parents from enrolling their daughters at IU. In 1901, First Lady Frances Morgan Swain made a presentation to the trustees advocating for a Women's Building that would contain "the woman's gymnasium, with all modern equipment, an auditorium, parlors, committee rooms, and greatly needed resting rooms."[1] Mrs. Swain had already raised $6,000 in support of her vision. The trustees assented, and IU launched its first capital campaign. To honor the then first lady, the Student Building was renamed Frances Morgan Swain Student Building in September 2016.

Nearly two thousand donors gave to the cause, contributing a total of $50,000, all but $438 of which was donated by Indiana residents.[2] In a final fund-raising push during the first two weeks of the 1902 fall term, IU's 758 students contributed $4,000, many of them sacrificing to do so. In his dedication speech, President Bryan noted the "ten dollars from a girl student who worked in a kitchen," noting her gift was "as sacred as the widow's mite."[3] Some community wives baked and sold cakes or crocheted borders on washcloths to pay their pledges.

In response to President Swain's solicitation, John D. Rockefeller Jr. agreed to match the $50,000 but requested that the building be expanded to include a wing for male students.

Construction began in 1904 on the Romanesque Revival building designed by the Indianapolis architectural firm Vonnegut and Bohn (the former was grandfather to Hoosier author Kurt Vonnegut Jr.). The building's two secondary wings flank a central three-story, eight-level structure, from which a tower reaches toward the sky. With its smooth-faced limestone and clean angles, the Student Building has a functional appearance, with contrasting motifs creating visual interest. The arched top-story windows—each crowned by rock-faced ashlar lintels—visually echo the stone spheres ornamenting the central entry. This circular motif is reiterated in bands of lozenges carved under the windows of the building's main body. While most of the building has sawed rectangular blocks, square rough- or rock-faced blocks surrounding the smooth, round lozenges provide another contrast. The Student Building was the first of IU's Old Crescent buildings to have a red-tile roof, rather than one of slate.

The finished building contained all that Frances Swain had envisioned, and more. The west wing housed women's facilities: a 40-by-80-foot swimming pool, parlors, restrooms, the women's gymnasium, and the YWCA headquarters. The east wing contained the YMCA headquarters, men's parlors, lounging rooms, clubrooms, billiard rooms (in which swearing

Facing top, Student Building, pre-1926. P0023146, IU Archives.

Facing bottom, Frances Morgan Swain Student Building, spring 1992. P0022916, IU Archives. Photo credit: Kevin Hutchison.

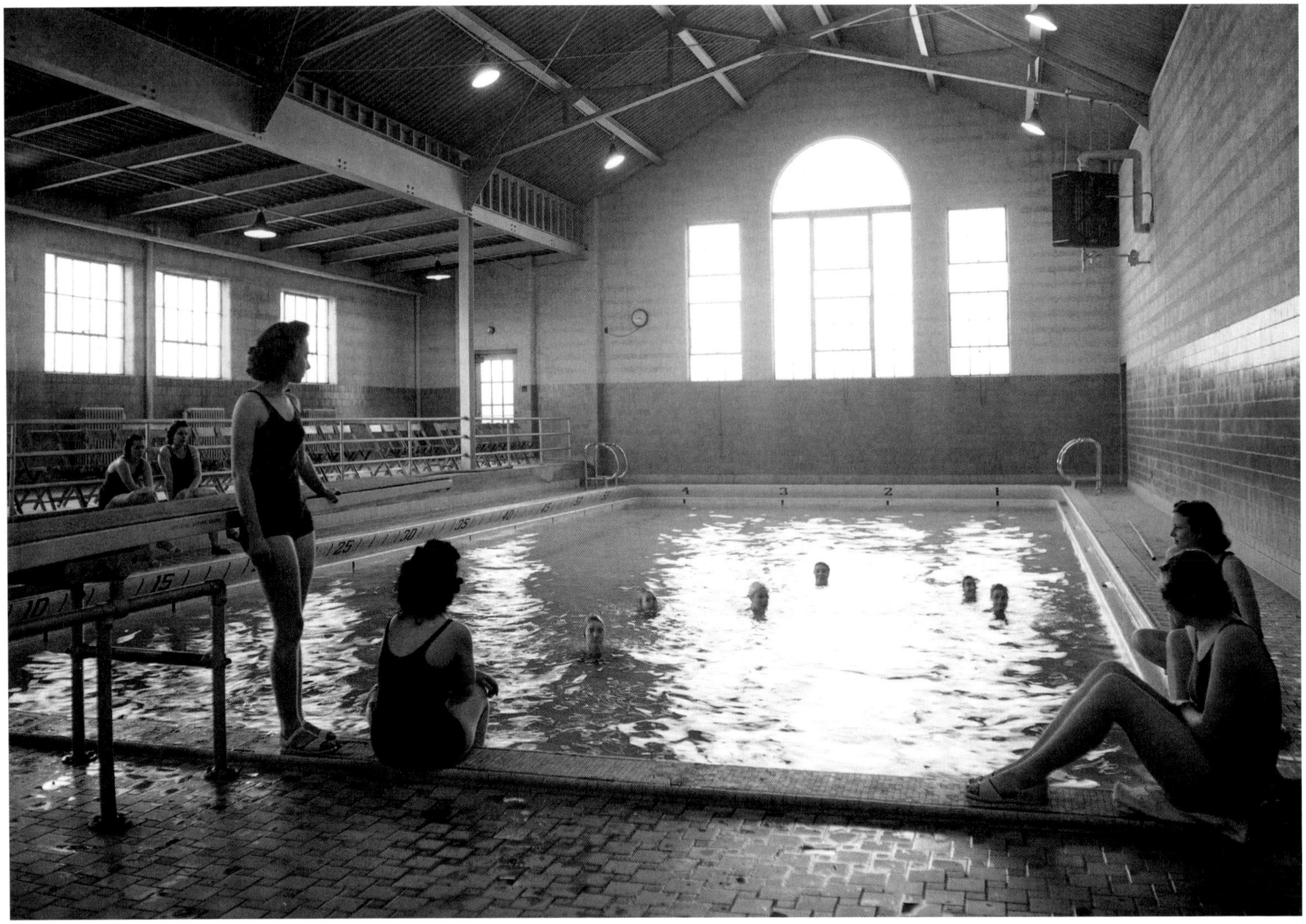

Women's swimming pool in the Student Building, circa 1939. P0030869, IU Archives.

and gambling were expressly prohibited), and a barber shop. The center of the structure held the auditorium and offices. In 1917 a cafeteria was added. During the influenza pandemic of 1918, the 600-seat auditorium was used as a hospital. In 1937 a new wing, financed by a state grant and WPA labor, was built to house a larger, deeper swimming pool for women.

The now-iconic clock tower—little more than a cupola in the original design—was added during construction. Thinking that a beautiful clock tower without chimes was "like ham without eggs," the classes of 1899, 1900, 1901, and 1902 mounted IU's first class campaign. Proceeds of the campaign purchased eleven bronze Westminster bells—the largest of them 4 feet wide.[4] Taken together, the Seth Thomas clock and bells weighed 5 tons and required that the tower be redesigned with its own foundation.

Each of the bells had two sets of clappers, an inner and outer set—the inner clappers were for playing music and the outer for keeping time.[5] Establishing an enduring tradition, President William Lowe Bryan asked that the IU "Alma Mater" be played every day at six o'clock. The custom has moved many an IU student, as this poignant statement from Charles Roll, class of 1909, illustrates: "I wondered if there really was such a thing as college spirit, and whether it would ever descend on me. Suddenly, the chimes pealed forth in the old college tune. My heart leaped up and as the tones of the last verse died away in the distance, I almost shouted, 'Dear old Indiana!'"[6]

For nearly a century, the bells marked the passing of the hours for the university community. They pealed out the victorious end of two world wars, tolled as we mourned the death of famous Hoosiers, celebrated hard-won athletic championships, and inspired Hoagy Carmichael to write "The Chimes of Indiana."

On the evening of December 17, 1990, a fire sparked by renovation work broke out in the Student Building's main hall. Although local fire fighters valiantly battled the blaze, flames consumed the heart of the structure and gutted the landmark clock tower. Onlookers watched in dismay as roof tiles snapped in the heat and windows popped from their frames. Shortly before midnight, the bells plummeted from the tower to lie melting in the grass. It was a sad day for IU, but not as sad as it might have been. Firewalls included in the original design confined the flames to the building's central section.

Demolition and reconstruction began immediately. The damaged building blocks served as patterns for the new ones. Insurance paid for reconstruction, a new clock, and the forging of eleven new bells. Donor contributions supported adding three more bells. A manual-play system similar to the old one was installed. At the rededication ceremony ten months later, President Tom Ehrlich held in his hand the same trowel that had been used to lay the building's cornerstone in 1904, thus emphasizing how fully the continuity of IU's traditions and spirit are embodied in the buildings of the Old Crescent.

The Student Building currently houses the Departments of Geography and Anthropology, Training in Global/Environmental Change, and a division of University Information Technology Services. The map room, another Old Crescent "grand space" (originally a swimming pool and then the Geography Library) has been transformed into a state-of-the-art classroom.

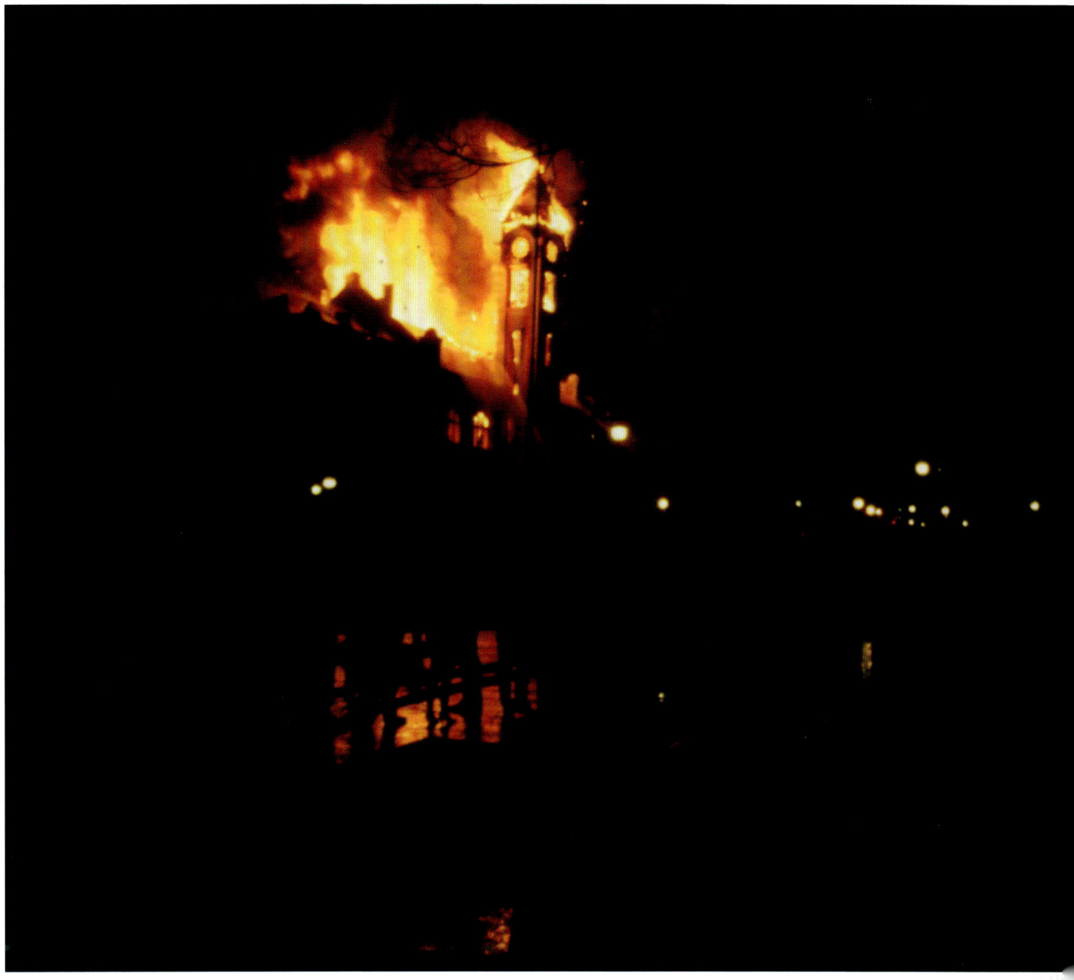

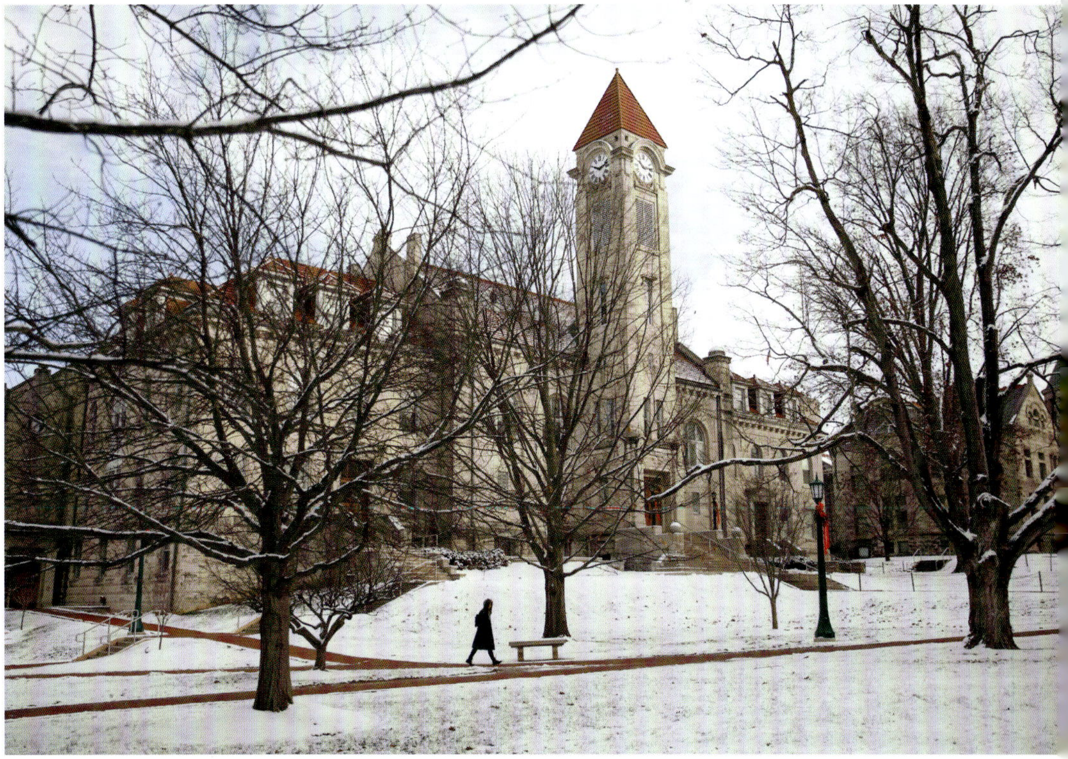

Top, Student Building fire, December 17, 1990. P0052303, IU Archives.

Right, Student Building's red-tile roof and surrounding brick walkways—a contrast on a snowy winter day, 2016. Photo credit: Indiana University.

The Boardwalk

Today red brick pathways traverse the Old Crescent area, but years ago, students and faculty used wooden boardwalks to travel from one place to the other. The first boardwalk on the current campus seems to have been constructed in the early 1890s to connect the houses on Forest Place (which ran north–south where Ballantine Hall now stands) to the central campus. Over the years the boardwalks multiplied until they crisscrossed throughout the Old Crescent, including Dunn's Woods. Bushes lined their borders and overhanging tree branches provided shade. The strands of wooden planks reached Third Street to the south, Indiana Avenue to the west, and Jordan Field to the north. Many early student publications, diaries, and letters bemoaned the decrepit conditions of Bloomington's muddy roads and walkways, including the boardwalks, which measured about 5 feet wide and cleared the ground by 6 or 7 inches. The wooden slats were uneven and sometimes difficult to navigate, but overall, many shoes and hemlines were saved from the mud, water, and snow that covered the ground from season to season. By the mid-twentieth century, the boardwalks had been replaced by paved and brick pathways, but alumni who hurried to class or strolled with their sweetheart in the moonlight remember the boardwalks fondly as a magical place.

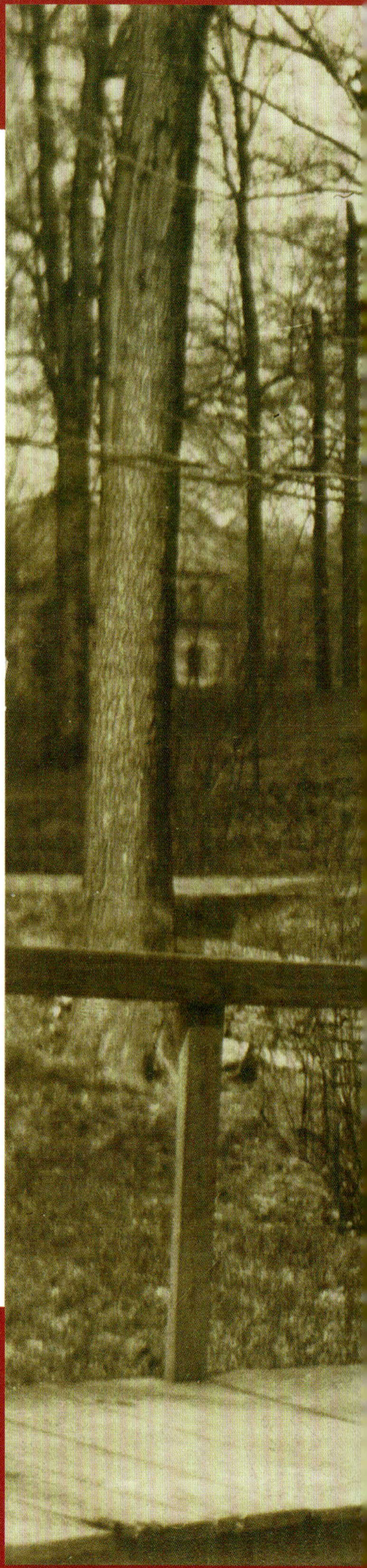

Indiana University students Dex Neal and George C. Hale on a boardwalk in Dunn's Woods, circa 1913; note the Student Building clock tower through the trees. P0039590, IU Archives.

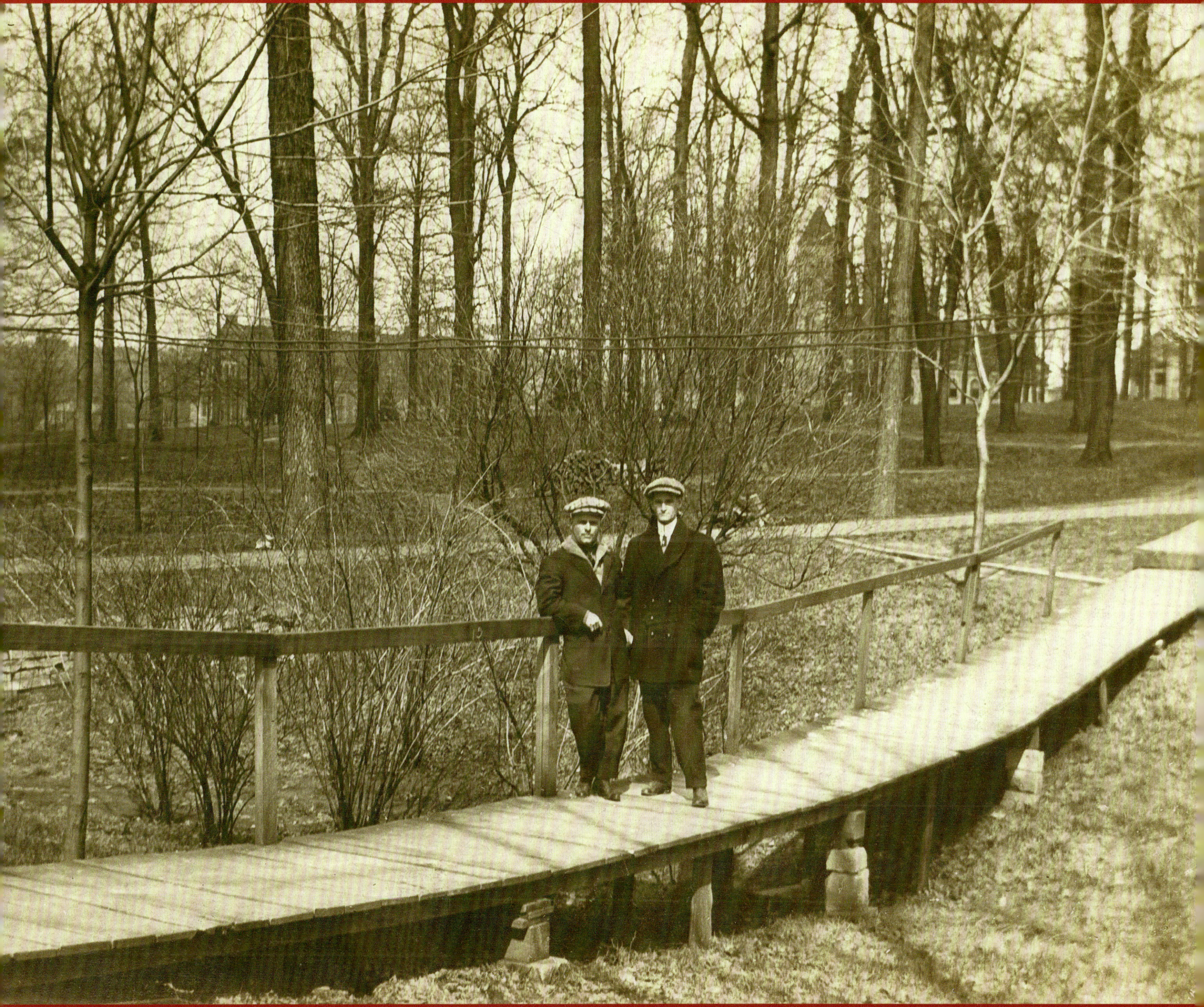

Joseph Amos Franklin Hall 1907

ARCHITECT Patton and Miller

ARCHITECTURAL STYLE English Gothic / Romanesque / Jacobean

ORIGINAL NAME Library Building

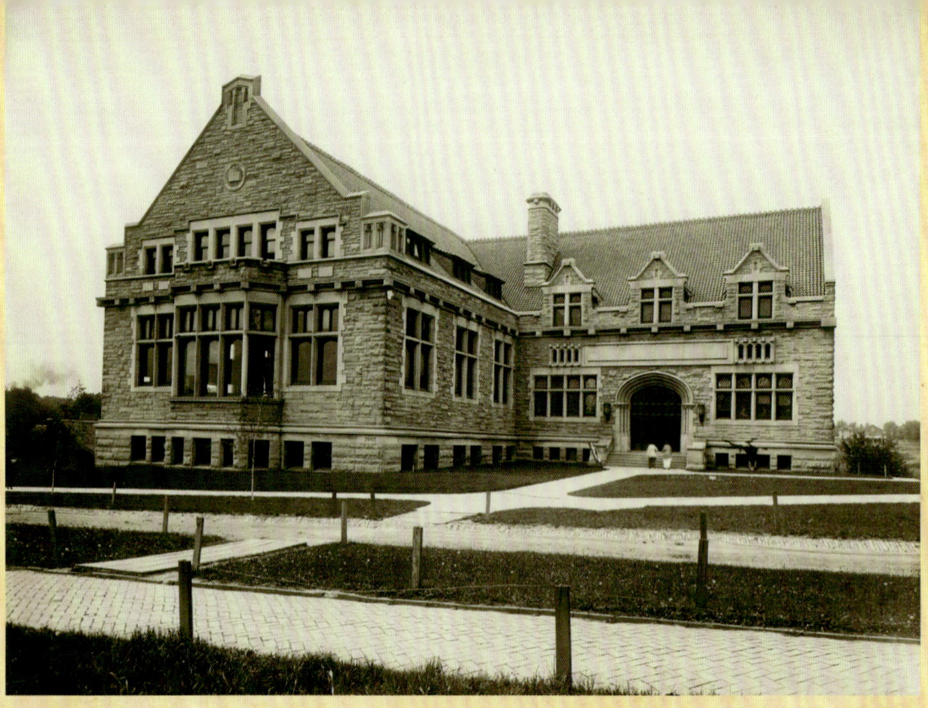

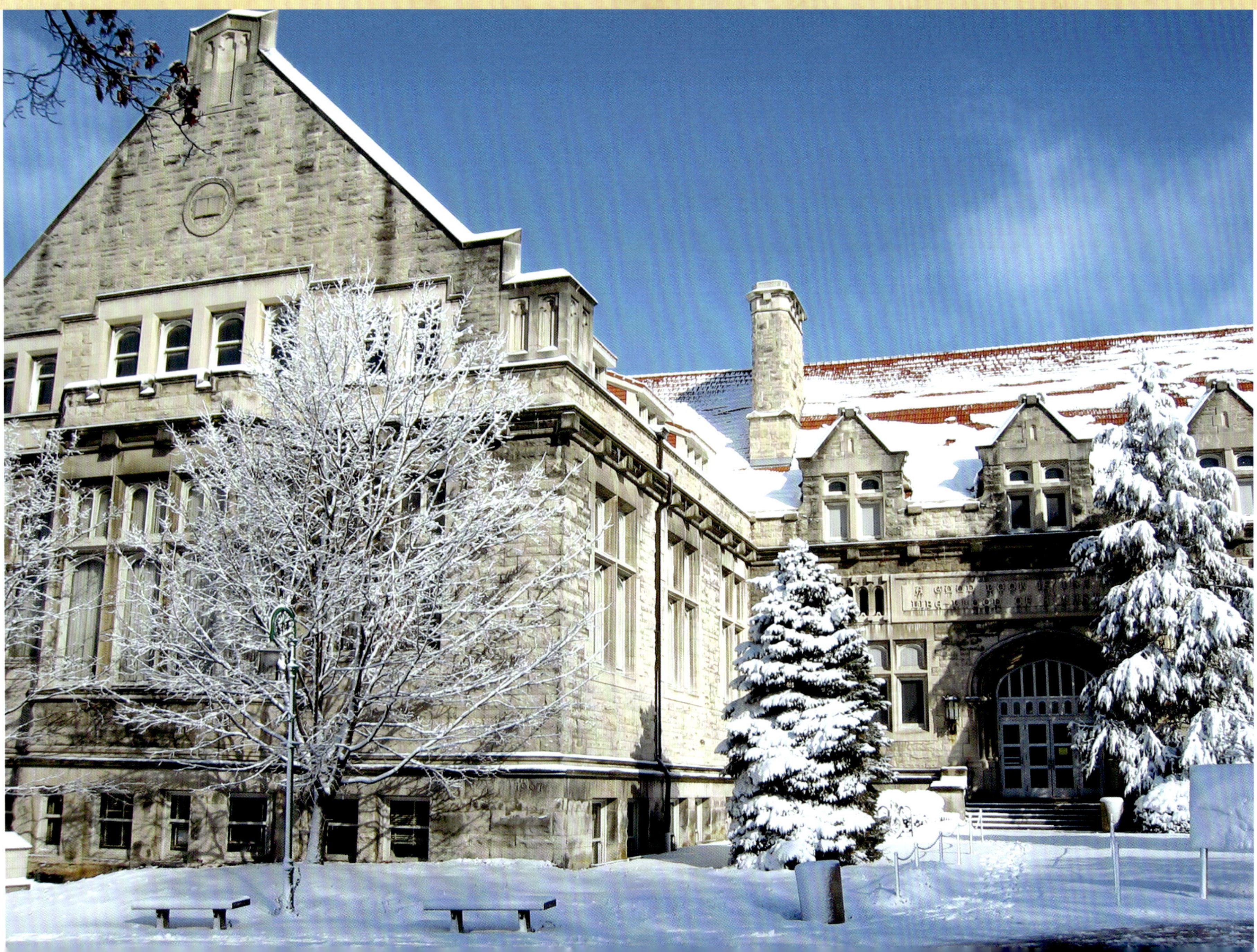

Joseph Amos Franklin Hall

A Monument to Light and Truth

I bring to you at these dedicating exercises a message of good will from a sister institution. All the pleasure and satisfaction that you feel is shared by Purdue. We forget the past rivalry between the two institutions, and in its place I bring to you the heartiest congratulations from Purdue. This library is important not only to Indiana University, but to the whole State as well. I rejoice to know that by reason of this enlargement the university is better able than ever before to serve the people of the State.

—Purdue University President Winthrop Stone at dedication ceremony

In the fifteen years from 1890 to 1905, IU's enrollment increased 500 percent. Library holdings grew apace, and Maxwell Hall was bursting at the seams. President Bryan assured the legislature that a new library twice the size of Maxwell Hall could be designed and built for $250,000. The legislature responded with $100,000.[1] Committed to meeting the university's needs, Bryan asked the university librarian, William Jenkins, to visit the nation's best libraries and develop a design for a building to which additions could be made over time. He then engaged Chicago architects Patton and Miller, builders of more than a hundred Carnegie libraries, instructing them to follow Jenkins's suggestions as closely as possible.

The project was beset by so many delays that the state auditor warned that the unused appropriation might revert to the state. One major hindrance was the architects' confusion over how to construct the ceiling of the grand reading room from a *single* concrete slab, which would ensure the building would be as safe as possible. After the architects' consultations with various outside engineers proved fruitless, President Bryan turned to more reliable experts: Indiana University faculty members in the Departments of Chemistry, Physics, and Analytical Mechanics. The scientists made the necessary calculations. The design was approved and the builders' contracts were signed. Construction proceeded, but by the winter of 1906, another $40,000 was required to complete the project. The legislature responded with $25,000, enough to install 60 percent of the planned book stacks.[2]

President Bryan praised the new library as a splendid addition to the university in a report to the governor and legislature: "[the] great reading room is the lightest and quietest reading room of the size I know of and compares favorably in attractiveness with any similar room in the country. . . . Use of the library jumped 25 percent almost from the day the new building was opened."[3] Students requested that library hours be extended past 11:00 p.m. on Saturday nights and that the library be open on Sundays. A degree in library science was added to the undergraduate curriculum. Below the 203-seat grand reading room were seminar rooms for economics, English, romance languages, education, Greek, Latin, and history classes. The Department of Fine Arts occupied the top floor. The east wing housed offices and staff work areas.

The largest of the original Old Crescent buildings, Franklin Hall completes the northern leg of the crescent. It is a four-story (two stories, an attic, and a basement), seven-level structure of Indiana limestone with a red-tile roof that visually connects it to the Student Building. The original building was constructed in an ell, with one wing parallel to Indiana Avenue. Its large windows feature the pointed arches and limestone tracery characteristic of the English Gothic style as represented in English manor houses and the monumental Salisbury Cathedral. The tall brick chimneys and straight bands on the gables

Facing top, Joseph Amos Franklin Hall, circa 1914; note blank panel above door. P0022446, IU Archives.

Facing bottom, South elevation of Franklin Hall, winter 2003. Photo credit: Indiana University.

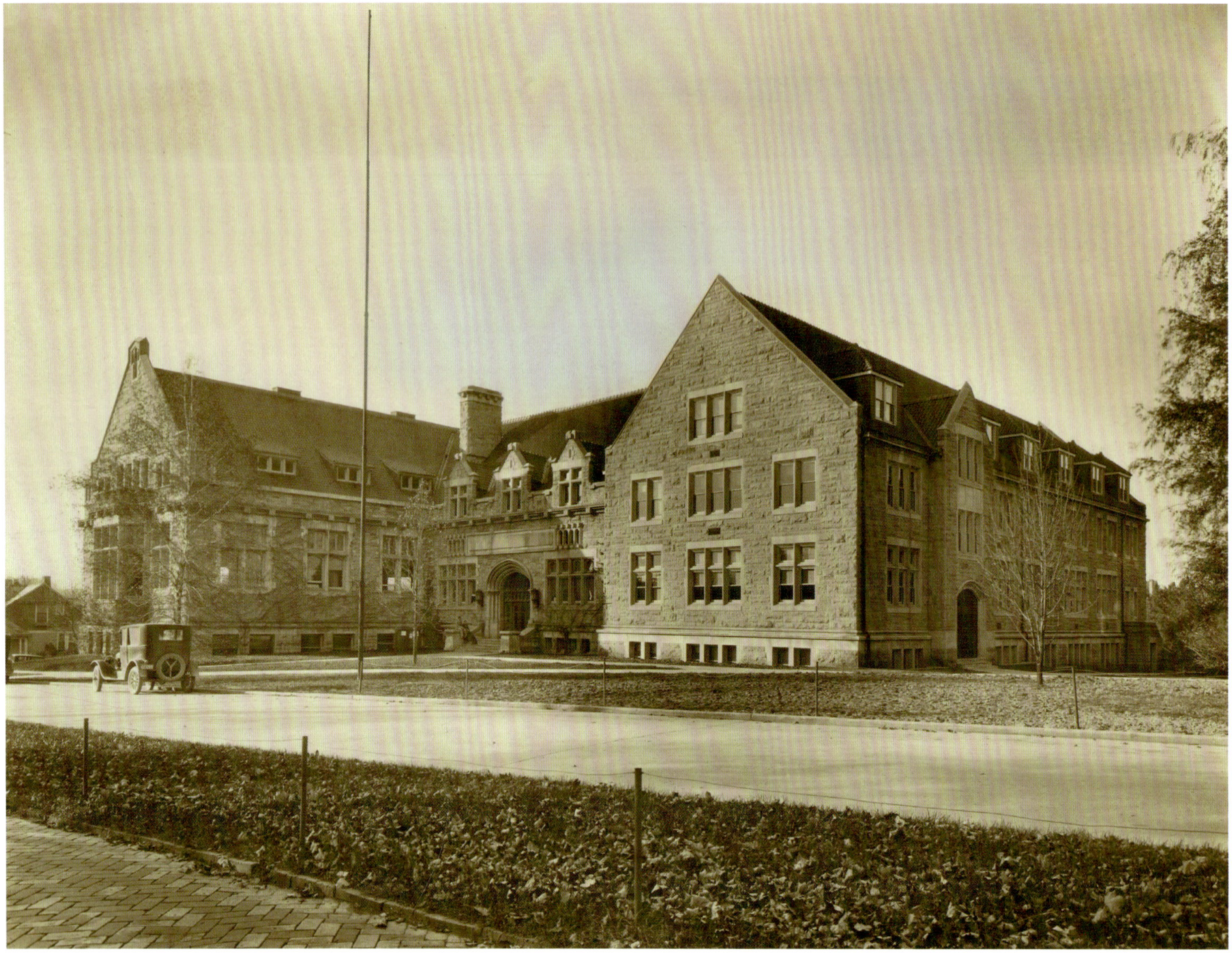

Franklin Hall with east wing addition completed, circa 1930. P0022448, IU Archives.

reflect the Jacobean style. Indiana University's seal is carved into the building's original south-facing gable, announcing the motto *Lux et Veritas*—light and truth—to all who pass. A quotation from John Milton caps the entry: "A good book is the precious life-blood of a master spirit." By 1925, the library held two hundred thousand volumes—nearly four times the holdings moved over from Maxwell.

A 1926 addition to the north end of the building completed the book stacks, and a legislative allocation provided for an eastern wing that would hold another large reading room for 180 students, a card catalog, a circulation desk, and a bindery. The Department of Mathematics cohabited with the library offices from 1929 to 1941. A rare books collection was added in 1942. In 1955, when burgeoning enrollments and growing library holdings demanded more space, a limestone-faced addition best described as Brutalist Modern in style was constructed on the building's north side.

In February 1969, fire broke out in the library basement but did little damage. In May that year, while student war protests surged in Dunn Meadow, smoke again billowed from the library. President Sutton praised the firefighters for saving the building, noting that their skill and quick response preserved IU's ability to "operate as a university." The fires destroyed or damaged a hundred thousand books and periodicals, in-

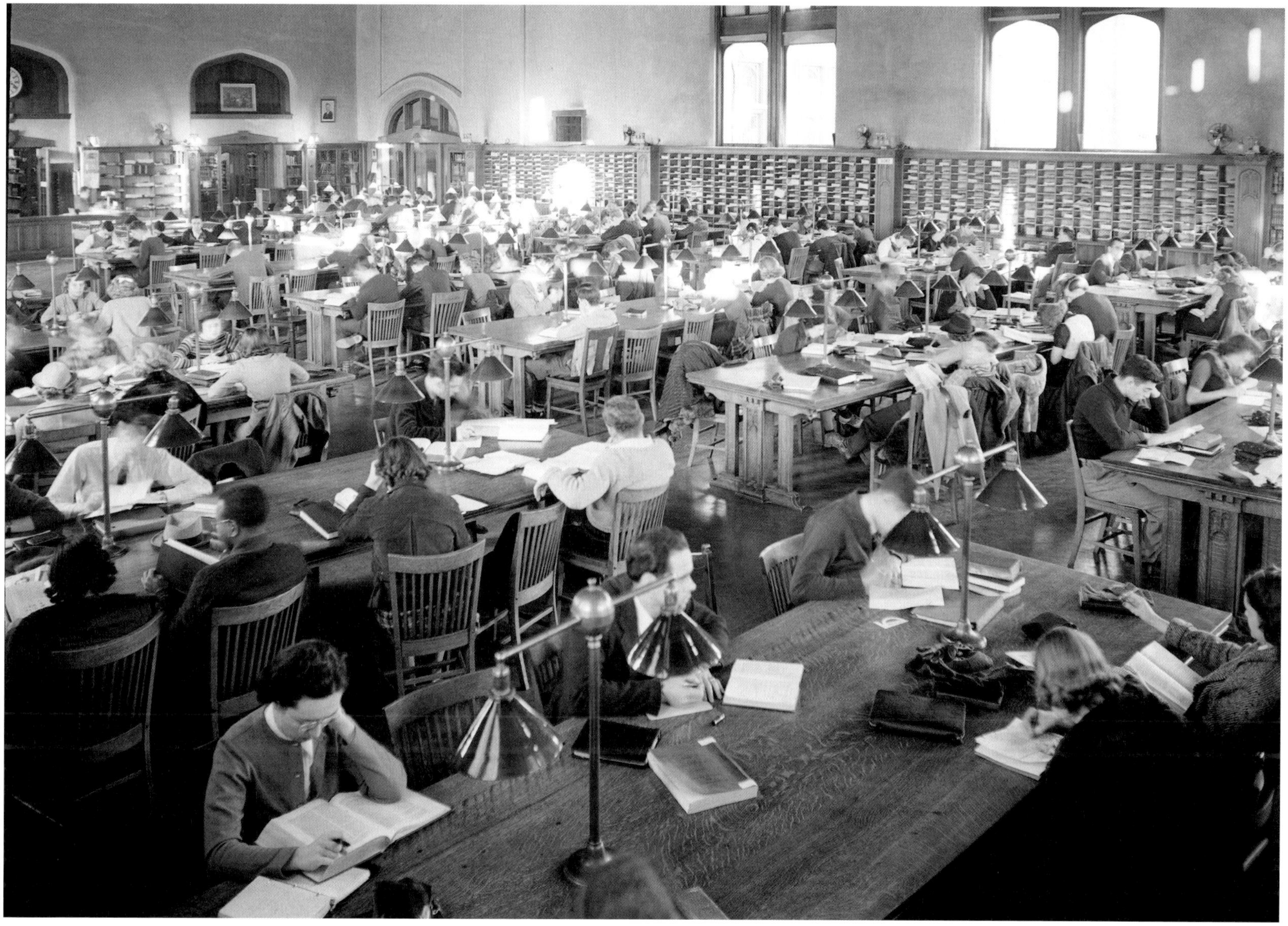

Franklin Hall main library reading room, 1939. P0030595, IU Archives.

cluding an archive of the *Times of London* dating back to 1835. Librarian Cecil Byrd noted that "there can be no worse act of vandalism on a college campus than setting fire to a library. This strikes at the very heart of the institution."[4] The arsonist, an IU graduate and library employee, was identified and successfully prosecuted. Fortunately, the move to the newly completed library building at Tenth and Jordan Streets was to begin within two months of the May fire.

In 1972 the old library was extensively renovated and repurposed to house administrative offices and renamed the Student Services Building. It was again renamed in 1988, this time Joseph Amos Franklin Hall, in honor of Indiana University alumnus, long-serving treasurer, and Vice President Joe Franklin. In 2013 Franklin Hall led the way in reinvigorating the Old Crescent for academic use and student life once again. After extensive renovations, it became the home of the new Media School (Journalism, Communication, and Film). Additionally, President's Hall, once the university library's reading room, is the first of the "grand spaces" to be restored to its original grandeur, with use for instruction, lectures, symposia, and other campus functions.

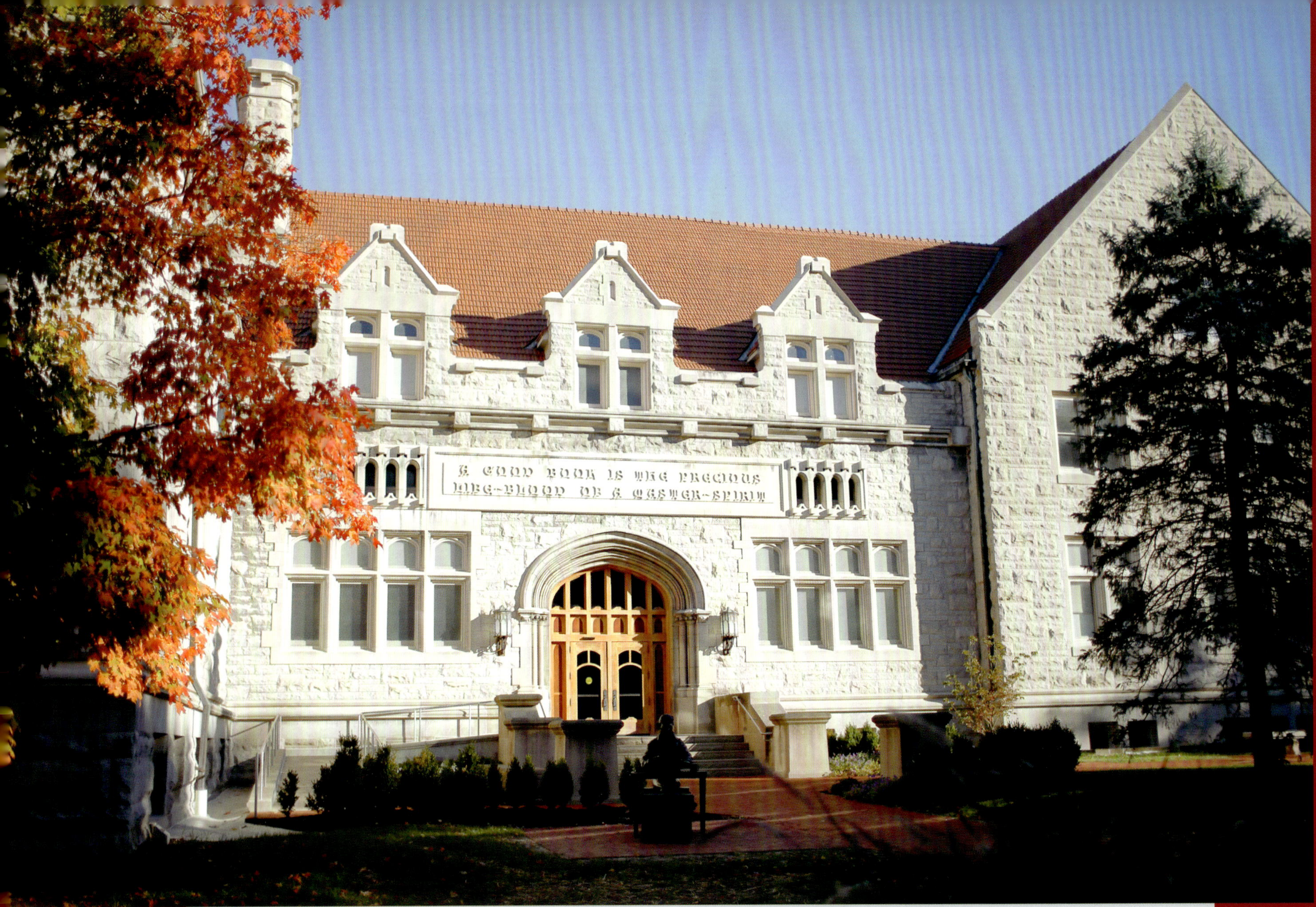

Words of Wisdom

The smooth limestone panel above the new library's main door, flanked on either side by four short lancet windows, remained blank until 1934. After years of contemplation, President Bryan, who was said to love a sentence packed with meaning and agreeable rhythm, decided the following words from John Milton's *Areopagitica* (1644) should be carved above the door: "A good book is the precious life-blood of a master spirit."[1] Bryan hoped that repeated contact with the inscription would help reinforce in students a deep respect for reading. The six stone carvers who did the work were part of a major, campus-wide refurbishment effort financed by Depression-era Civil Works Administration funds.

1. Statement about William Lowe Bryan by Selatie E. Stout (Dean Emeritus, College of Arts and Sciences)—The Late William Lowe Bryan, President Emeritus, Selects the Inscription for the Main Entrance to the Library, undated, Archives Reference file—Franklin Hall, Indiana University Archives, Indiana University, Bloomington.

T. C. Steele: IU Artist-in-Residence

In June 1922, while living in Brown County, Hoosier artist Theodore Clement Steele (1847–1926) received what is quite possibly the best job offer ever proffered by Indiana University President William Lowe Bryan: "I write on behalf of the Trustees of the University to invite you to be in residence at Indiana University next year. Your service would be what you choose to make it. We should by no means wish to interfere in the least with your continuing your work as a creative artist. You would have no prescribed duties. We would want you to do whatever you think most profitable for your art."[1]

President Bryan chose Steele because he was a local artist, born in Owen County. He studied in Germany but returned to the United States, becoming the first major artist to make a home in Brown County, Indiana. His paintings of southern Indiana were nationally acclaimed, earning him the highest honor a U.S. artist can achieve: appointment as an associate member of the National Academy of Design.

When Steele agreed to President Bryan's offer, he became IU's first honorary professor of painting, with a $2,500 honorarium—then a generous salary for the outlined expectations. Studio space was prepared for him on the uppermost floor of the Library Building (Franklin Hall). As Bryan had proposed, Steele continued to paint during his residency and turned some of his artistic attention to the Bloomington campus, completing several pieces, including *The Student Building on Campus,* which hangs in the Indiana Memorial Union. T. C. Steele became a much beloved figure on campus and would welcome students to his studio to observe him at work, or he could be seen surrounded—at a respectful distance—by students, faculty, and administrators if found painting outdoors. Steele served as artist-in-residence until his death in 1926.

1. William Lowe Bryan to Theodore R. Steele, letter June 9, 1922, "Steele, T. C." folder, collection C286, Indiana University Archives, Indiana University, Bloomington.

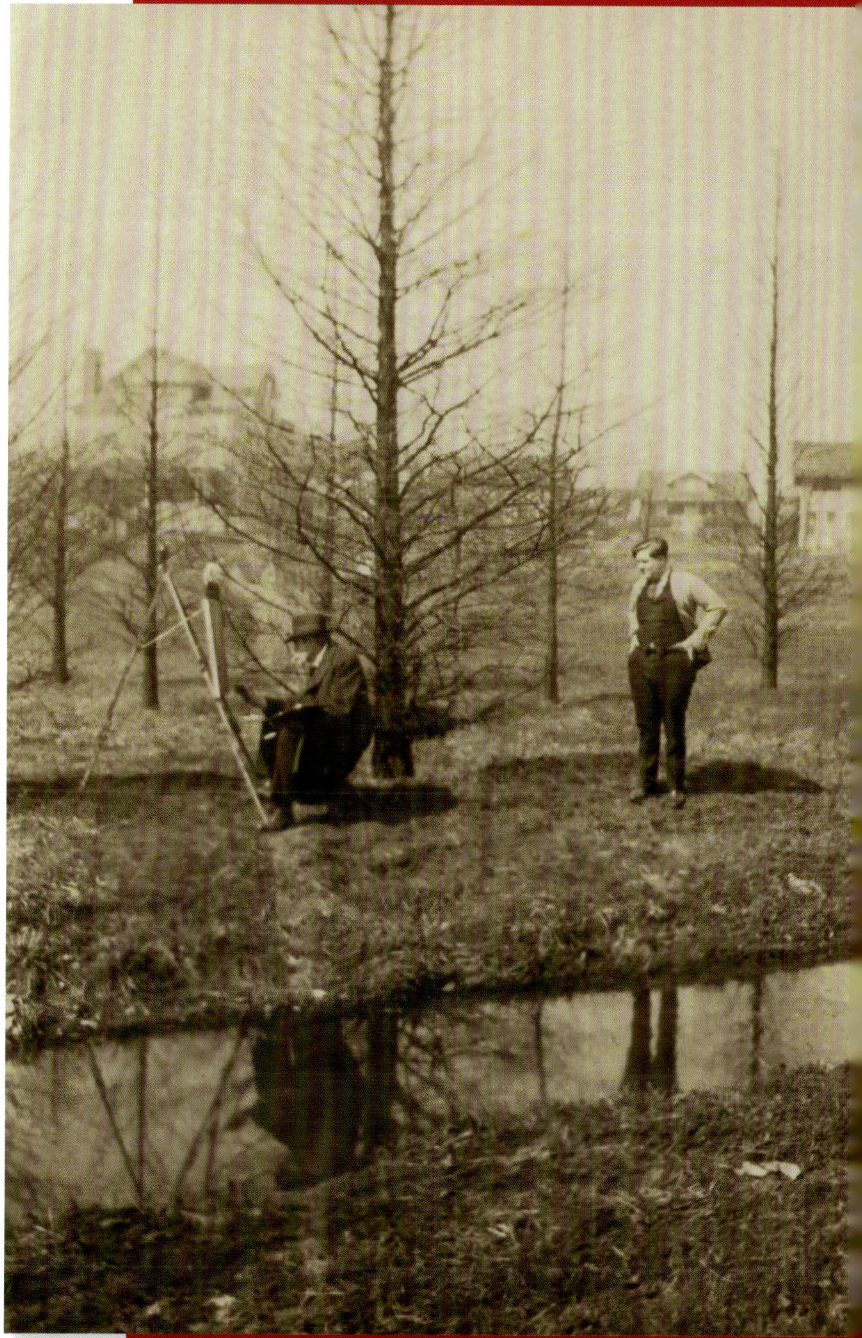

A young Herman B Wells—then an undergraduate—watching artist T. C. Steele at work, 1923. P0027137, IU Archives. Photo credit: Ralph H. Ogle.

Rose Well House 1908

ARCHITECT Arthur L. Foley

ARCHITECTURAL STYLE Open-Air Pavilion / Gothic Revival

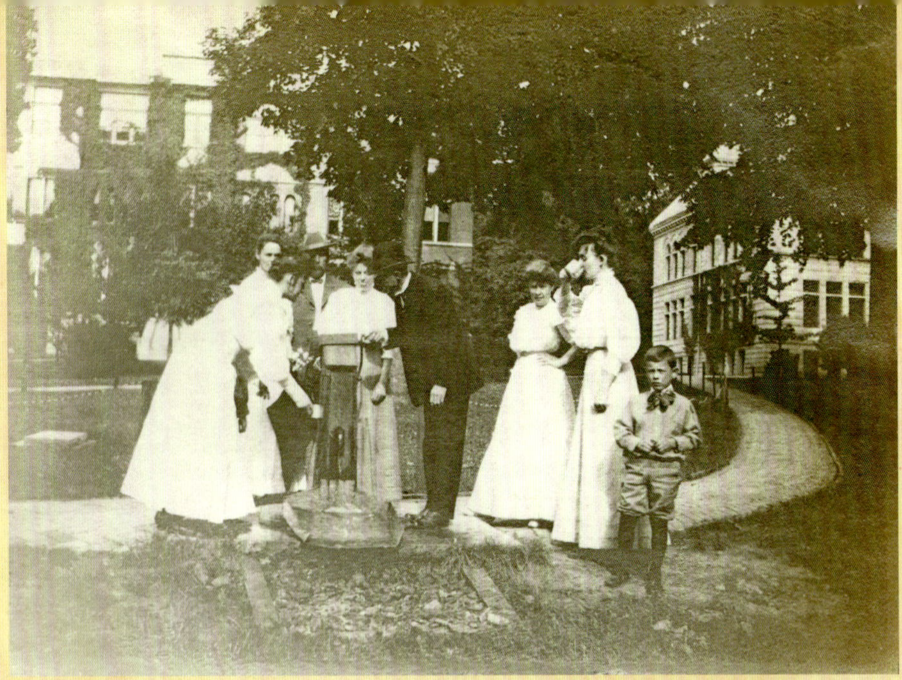

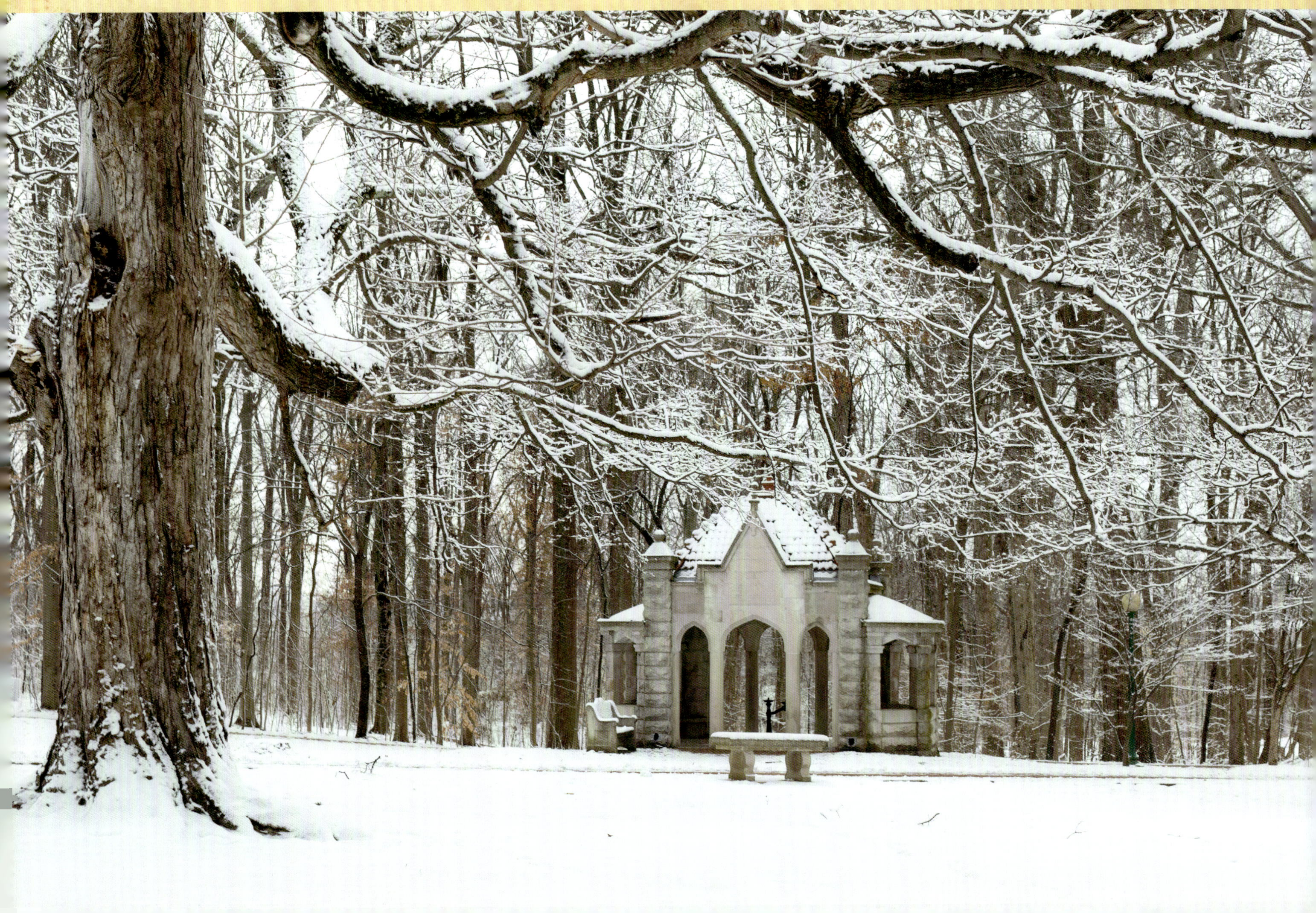

Rose Well House

Joining the Past to the Present

Among all the buildings which will ultimately adorn the University, there will be none so suggestive of sacred reminiscences to the old student and so pregnant of possibilities for the new as the beautiful new wellhouse which the trustees will erect on the site of the present cistern pump.

—Daily Student

"I HAD LEFT MY PLOW IN ITS FURROW THE NOON before. Once before that day I had been on railroad cars and made a trip of some forty miles from home," wrote John C. Robinson, describing his journey to enroll at IU in 1856. "I had never seen a building that would bear comparison with the frontispiece of the Catalogue of 1856–57. My conceptions of college life and of college students were entirely in harmony with that picture."[1] The structure that so impressed John Robinson—who later became a Hoosier teacher, attorney, and judge—was the First University Building at Seminary Square. The stone porticos that flanked its main section are now part of the Rose Well House, located in the center of the Old Crescent.

But that was not the original intent. After the university moved to Dunn's Woods, many envisioned a formal gateway at the Kirkwood Avenue entrance to campus. The classes of 1899, 1900, 1901, and 1902 established an Arch Fund for that purpose. In June 1904, the Indiana University trustees formed a committee chaired by board member and Muncie, Indiana, banker Theodore Rose "to secure the two porticos of the Old College Building, and [then] . . . confirm these for an entrance driveway for the campus at Kirkwood Avenue."[2] At that point, the Old College Building housed Bloomington High School. President Bryan was enthusiastic about the project, sending Rose blueprints of the old building, photographs of the porticos (one bears the university seal and the other a brief history of the institution), and measurements of the sidewalks and roadway into campus. However, it soon became clear the arches would block—rather than herald—the entrance to the university. They were too narrow for a carriage to pass through. The president and trustees went back to the drawing board.

At the turn of the twentieth century, water—or the lack of it—was on everyone's mind. A large cistern used for drinking water and fighting fires (including the 1900 blaze that consumed Wylie Hall's tower) was IU's only water source. Otherwise, the university relied on Bloomington for its water, and Bloomington was experiencing a "water famine." In December 1903, many feared IU would have to close for lack of water. A number of solutions were considered, including Trustee Rose's suggestion of damming the lower end of Dunn Meadow to create a lake. After fears of typhoid and other waterborne illnesses prevented the damming of Dunn Meadow, Trustee Rose offered a more viable suggestion: using the historical porticos to construct a well house over the campus cistern. The board

Facing top, Students drinking from campus cistern prior to construction of Rose Well House, circa 1906. P0025143, IU Archives. Photo credit: Floy Underwood.

Facing top, Rose Well House, winter 2016. Photo credit: Indiana University.

Right, Rose Well House featuring arches salvaged from the First University Building at Seminary Square, 2016. Photo credit: Tyagan Miller.

Below, Stained glass and ornate grillwork inside Rose Well House, 2016. Photo credit: Tyagan Miller.

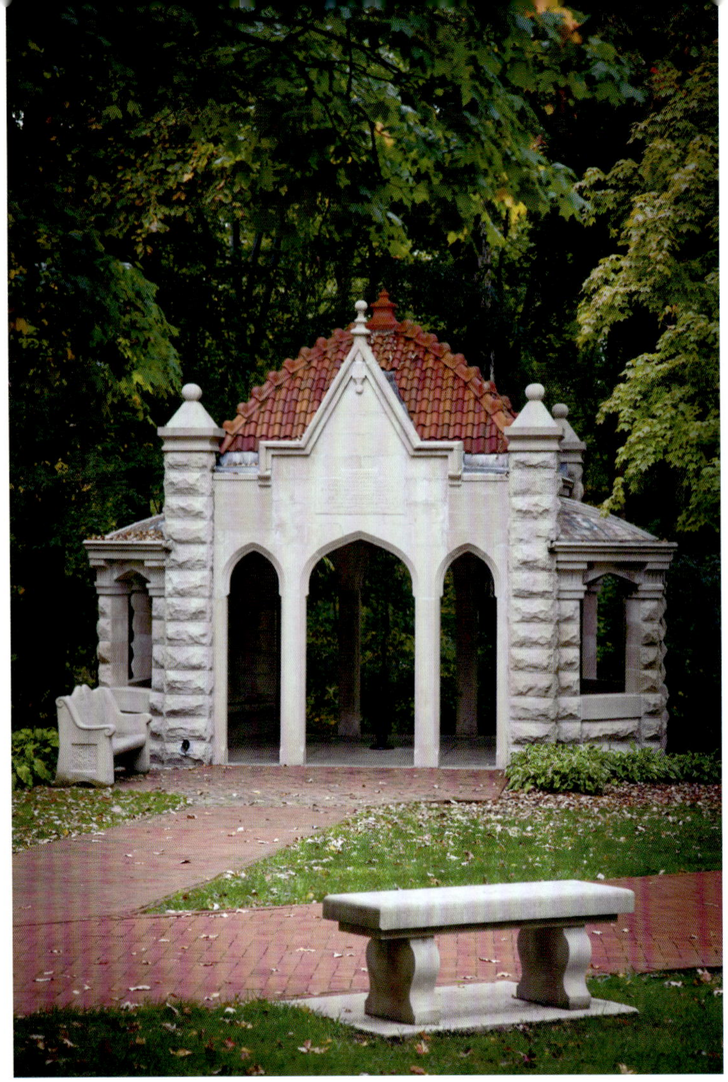

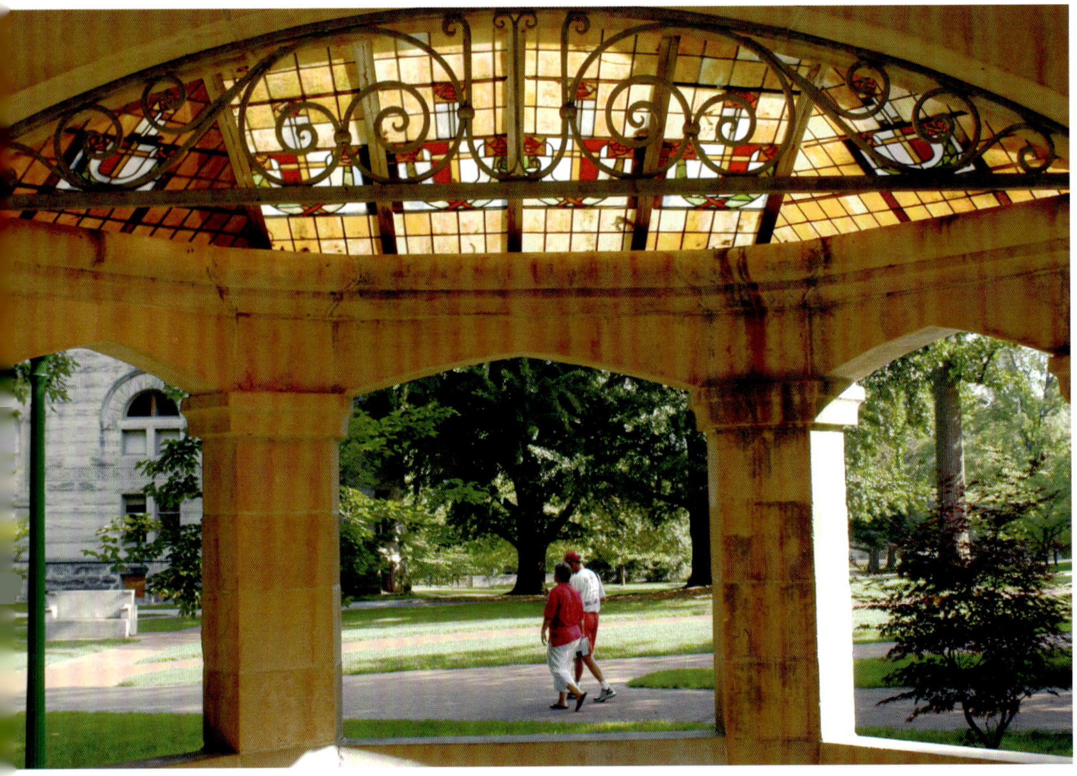

commissioned Patton and Miller, the architects designing what was then the new library (now Franklin Hall), and the Fort Wayne architects Wing and Mahurin to develop plans. Their vault-like designs, which featured flying buttresses and large stone columns, were deemed unsuitable. Arthur Foley, chair of the Department of Physics and Manual Training, was among those critical of the designs, saying they resembled a medieval arsenal or, worse yet, a mausoleum.

President Bryan asked Foley if he could do better. The professor conceived an open-air, octagonal building that salvaged nothing from the original design but the basic floor plan. He enlarged the windows to reflect the proportions of the Gothic arches from the porticos of the Old College Building; he added a domed, red-tile roof; and he affixed half domes to its north and south sides. The half-domes featured Tiffany-style, stained-glass windows and ornate grillwork. An arc-light chandelier made the entire structure glow.

Hoagy Carmichael's grandfather, Alex Robison, was among the local stonecutters who worked through the winter months to ensure the building was finished in time for the 1908 commencement.[3] Trustee Rose bore the cost of the building. He and his family presented it to the university in honor of the class of 1875, of which he was a member. Rose was also a member of the Beta Theta Pi fraternity, so it is perhaps no accident that the design closely resembles the shape of the Beta pin.

Today the first IU seal to ever adorn an Indiana University building welcomes all who enter the Rose Well House. That its legend—Lux et Veritas—is as readable and its arrises nearly as sharp as when they were carved in 1855 speaks to the quality of Indiana limestone and the skill of Hoosier stone carvers. Until 1953, when two drinking fountains were added, visitors to the pump customarily drank from a common cup, causing editors of the 1912 Arbutus to opine that the National Order of the Tin Cup Bacteria would be holding its grand convention in the well house.[4] In 1991 the cistern was filled in as part of an extensive renovation, but the fountain remains, inviting members of the campus community to slake their thirst, as IU students, professors, staff, and visitors have done over the course of two centuries.

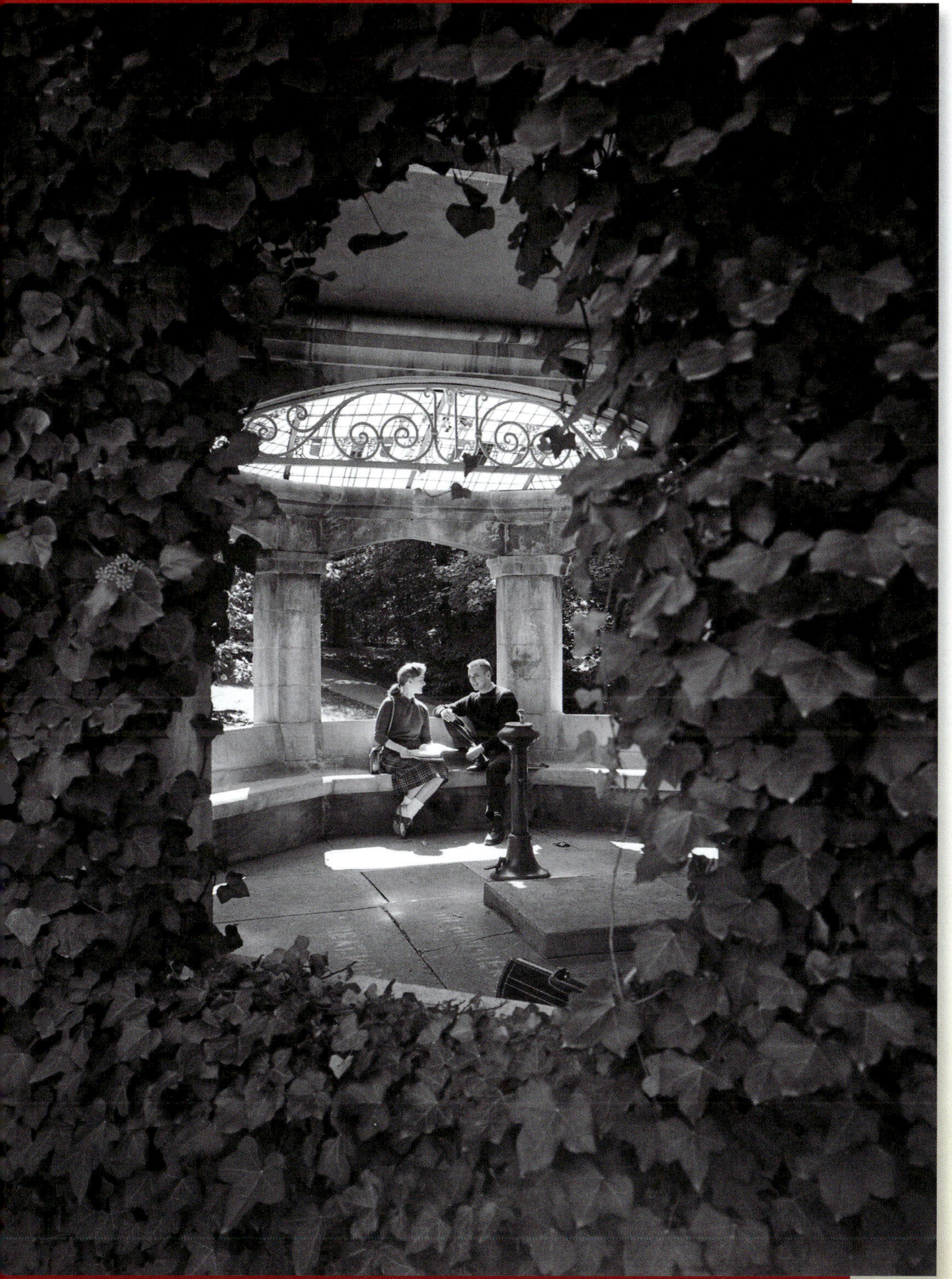

Students enjoying the Rose Well House, 1958. P0040640, IU Archives. Photo credit: Elwood Martin "Barney" Cowherd.

For Whom the Bells Toll

Here linger ghosts of old romance amid the calm cathedral of the trees.

DAISY WOODWARD BECK[1]

According to a time-honored tradition, a female student is not truly an IU coed until she has been kissed at midnight in the well house. And we're not talking a simple peck on the cheek. To officially transform a mere student into a coed, the kiss must last through the twelve peals of the Student Building bells.

Over the years, as the campus became better lit, more wattage was added to the well house, and this became cause for serious consternation among courting students. The 1959 Student Senate passed a resolution requesting that the Department of Buildings and Grounds "take the lights out of the Well-House [*sic*], or at least switch them off from 10 p.m. to 1 a.m.," unless they preferred that students continue to "knock them out with regularity." The resolution declares that "one of the institution's oldest and most cherished traditions is being endangered by a stern and unromantic administration."[2]

1. Opening quotation is from Daisy Woodward Beck, *Once Over Lightly: An Indiana University Story* (1962), Frank O. and Daisy Beck papers, collection C168, Indiana University Archives, Indiana University, Bloomington.

2. "A Mandate to the Executive Concerning the Lights in the Well House," Student Senate Resolution, September 12, 1959, "Well House Kissing Tradition" file, IU Student Senate records, collection C206, Indiana University Archives, Indiana University, Bloomington.

Swain Hall East 1910

ARCHITECT Robert Frost Daggett

ARCHITECTURAL STYLE Collegiate Gothic

ORIGINAL NAME Biology Hall

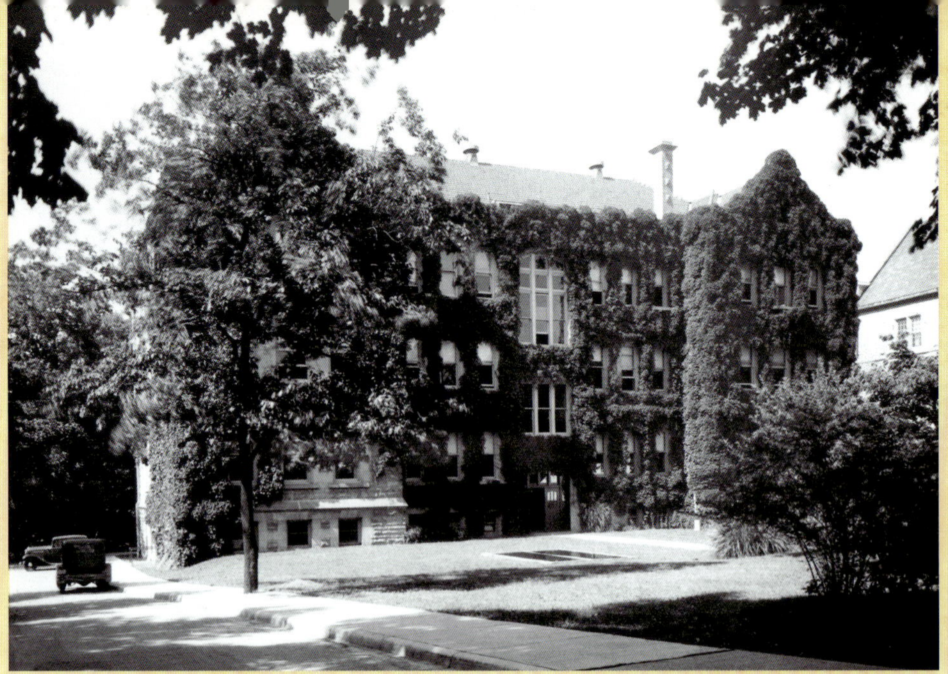

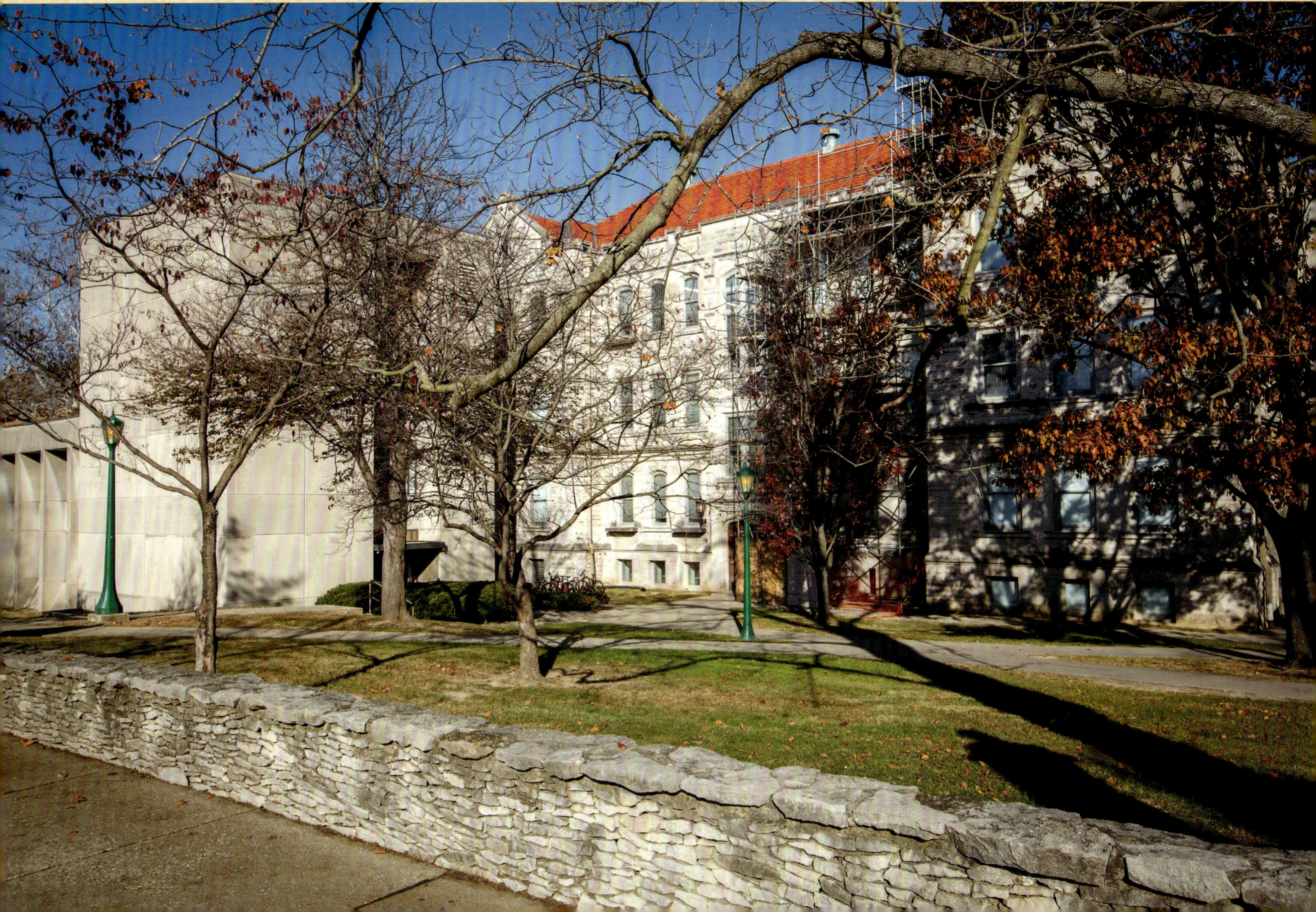

Swain Hall East

Home of IU Laureates

The Old Crescent . . . has significant associations with nationally prominent educators and alumni and, in its architecture, evokes the skills of Indiana architects, stone carvers, and masons and reflects changing national tastes as the United States entered the industrial age.

—National Register of Historic Places

In his 1908 report to the governor and legislative appropriation committee, Indiana University President William Lowe Bryan warned that IU could not continue to meet the state's evolving needs for educated citizens with the meager resources allotted to it: "We have been repeatedly obliged within the last few years to close certain classes . . . for lack of space or teachers or both," he said. "We have been obliged to tolerate classes which are too large. . . . We are at present obliged to deny books, laboratory facilities, and additional teachers where we know they are badly needed. . . . The most urgent need is in the sciences, which are utilizing all available space, including basements and attics, and are still unable to receive all the students who apply."[1]

To remedy the situation, the president requested funds to build a large science building modeled on a similar facility at Harvard.[2] When the state proffered only a third of the requested amount, an addition to Owen Hall was considered. That option was abandoned in favor of siting a small science building on the southern tip of the Old Crescent *L*. Interchangeably called the Physical Science Building, Biological Building, or Biology Hall, and later, Swain Hall, this was the first IU building to face Third Street. It features the pointed Gothic arches prevalent in its Old Crescent neighbors, as well as the red-tile roof of Franklin Hall, the Student Building, and the Rose Well House.

The building's main elements are expressed in threes, providing an appealing symmetry to a relatively unornamented design. Both vertically and horizontally, the windows of this three-story limestone structure align three to a panel. Two wings topped with simplified Flemish gables flank the building's main body. The gables terminate in arched finials that echo the curved heads of all but the middle row of windows. A sense of beauty-in-balance is further reinforced in the crenelated parapet wall that extends from the building's center to the corners of its gables. Both the main and secondary entries feature pointed English Gothic arches. The back entrance echoes the lancet windows of Franklin Hall and the lozenge ornamentation of the Student Building. Like those of Lindley Hall, several of Swain East's windowsills jut out into 2-foot-wide ledges used for botany experiments.

In the autumn of 1910, the Department of Botany moved into the first floor of Swain Hall. Zoology occupied the top floor, and the Department of English was sandwiched be-

Facing top, Swain Hall East, 1938. P0033321, IU Archives. Photo credit: Bob Hoff.

Facing bottom, South elevation of Swain Hall East, 2016. Photo credit: Tyagan Miller.

tween. Zoology has an eminent history at IU due to the discipline's esteemed faculty, one of whom was Alfred Kinsey, who joined the department in 1920. After he was asked to teach a class on sexuality for married and engaged students, Kinsey began gathering sexual histories from his students. Extending his taxonomist's approach to the study of human sexual behavior, he founded the Institute for Sex Research in 1947. *Sexual Behavior in the Human Male* was published a year later. The book generated both notoriety and funding for expanded research. In need of more space, the institute moved from Swain to Wylie Hall in 1950. From 1938 to 1963, when the initial two projects ended, the institute gathered more than eleven thousand sexual histories.

Several prominent scientists have claimed Swain East as their academic home. Geneticist Herman Muller came to IU in 1945 and won the Nobel Prize for Physiology or Medicine a year later for his research work in radiation-induced mutations—a timely topic in the wake of the atomic bombings of Hiroshima and Nagasaki. Associating with biologist Tracy Sonneborn, who was the world's expert in the genetics of the protozoa, and botanist Ralph Cleland, Muller established IU's reputation for doing cutting-edge work in the science of heredity among plants, animals, and humans. In 1943, Salvador Luria, an Italian bacteriologist, joined the department. Luria was awarded the Nobel Prize in Medicine in 1969 for discoveries concerning the replication mechanism and genetic structure of viruses. His research, which explained how bacteria develop resistance to antibiotics, paved the way for the field of molecular biology.

James Watson came to IU in 1947 to study with this remarkable group of geneticists. He finished his doctorate in zoology in 1950 at the age of twenty-two and then went on to earn the Nobel Prize for discovering the double helix structure of DNA, thus unlocking the secret of life and launching the genomics revolution. In a 1992 lecture given in Bloomington, Watson said "Bloomington was one of the places that made me." He noted that the exceptional scientists with whom he studied in Swain Hall helped him see the past and the future of genetics.[3]

Swain Hall East, constructed in 1910, was known as Biology Hall until 1957. At that time it was physically connected to Swain Hall, which had been built in 1940 and named in honor of former IU president and professor of mathematics, Joseph Swain.[4] Biology Hall then became Swain East, and the original Swain Hall was renamed Swain West. Swain East housed the Department of Mathematics until it moved to Rawles Hall in 1993, but it continues to be used as the site for numerous math and science classes. Swain West is home to the Department of Physics and its world-class faculty.

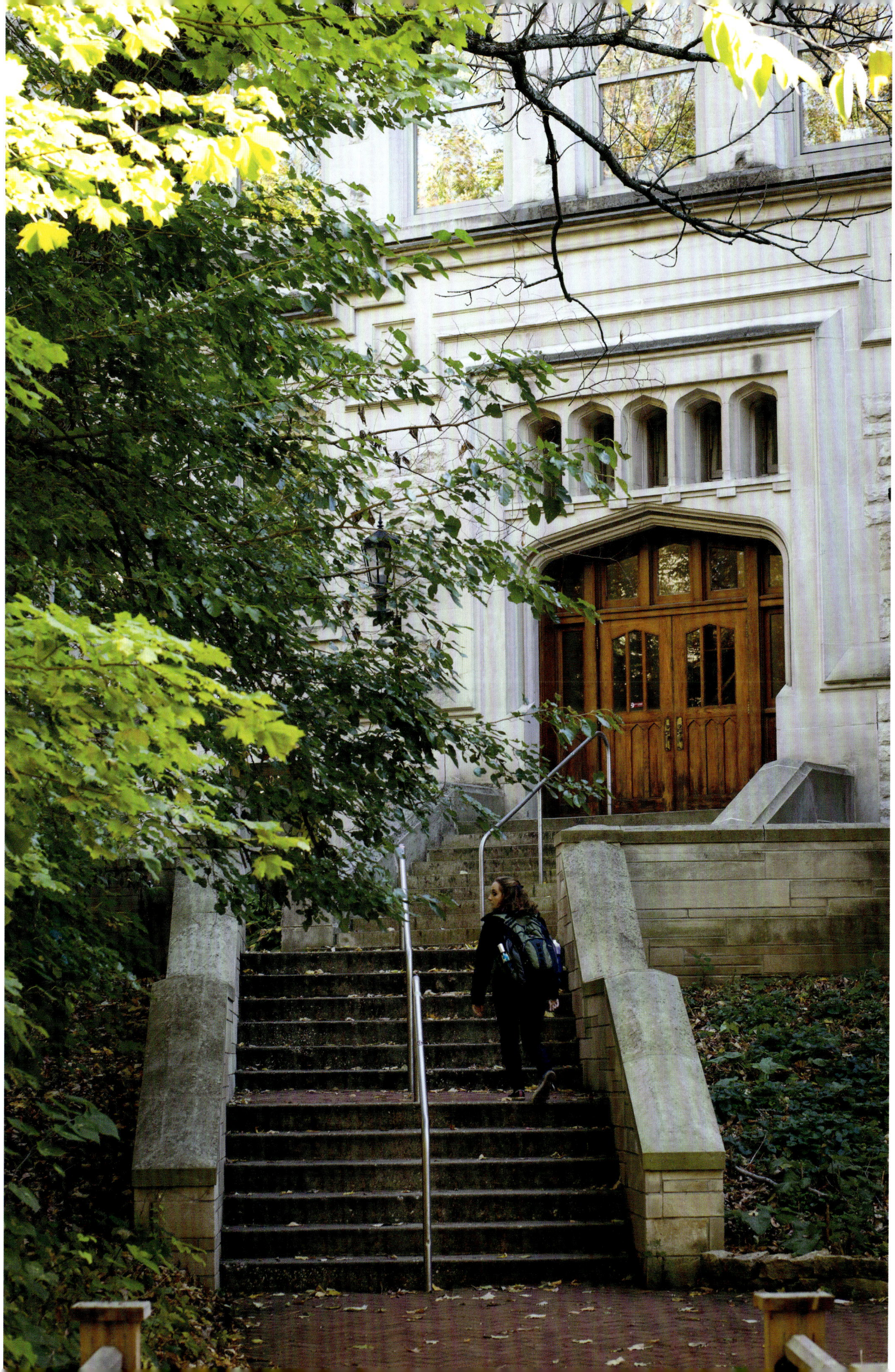

North entrance of Swain Hall East from Dunn's Woods, 2016. Photo credit: Tyagan Miller.

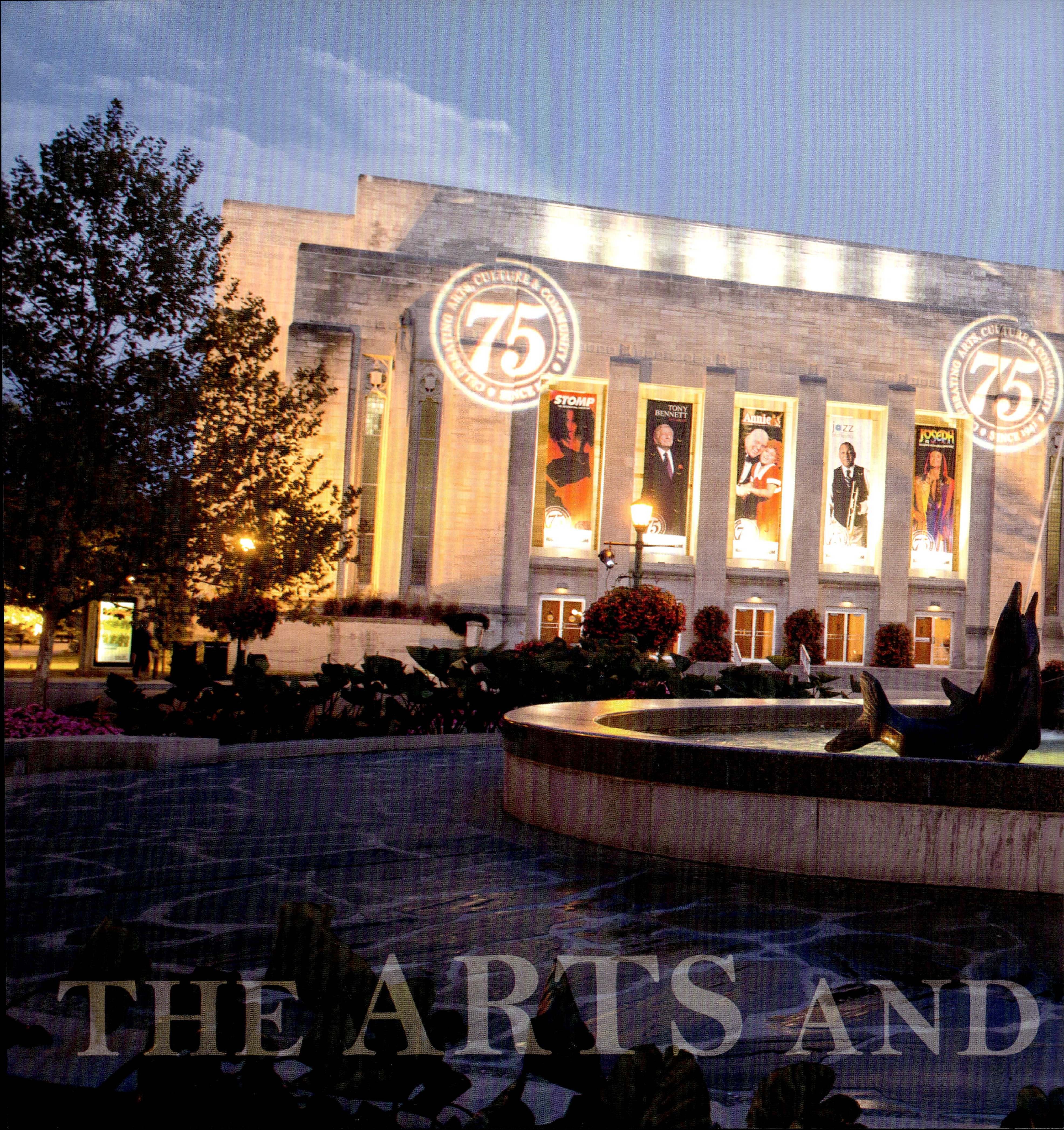
CELEBRATING ARTS, CULTURE & COMMUNITY
75
STOMP
TONY BENNETT
Annie
JOSEPH

THE ARTS AND

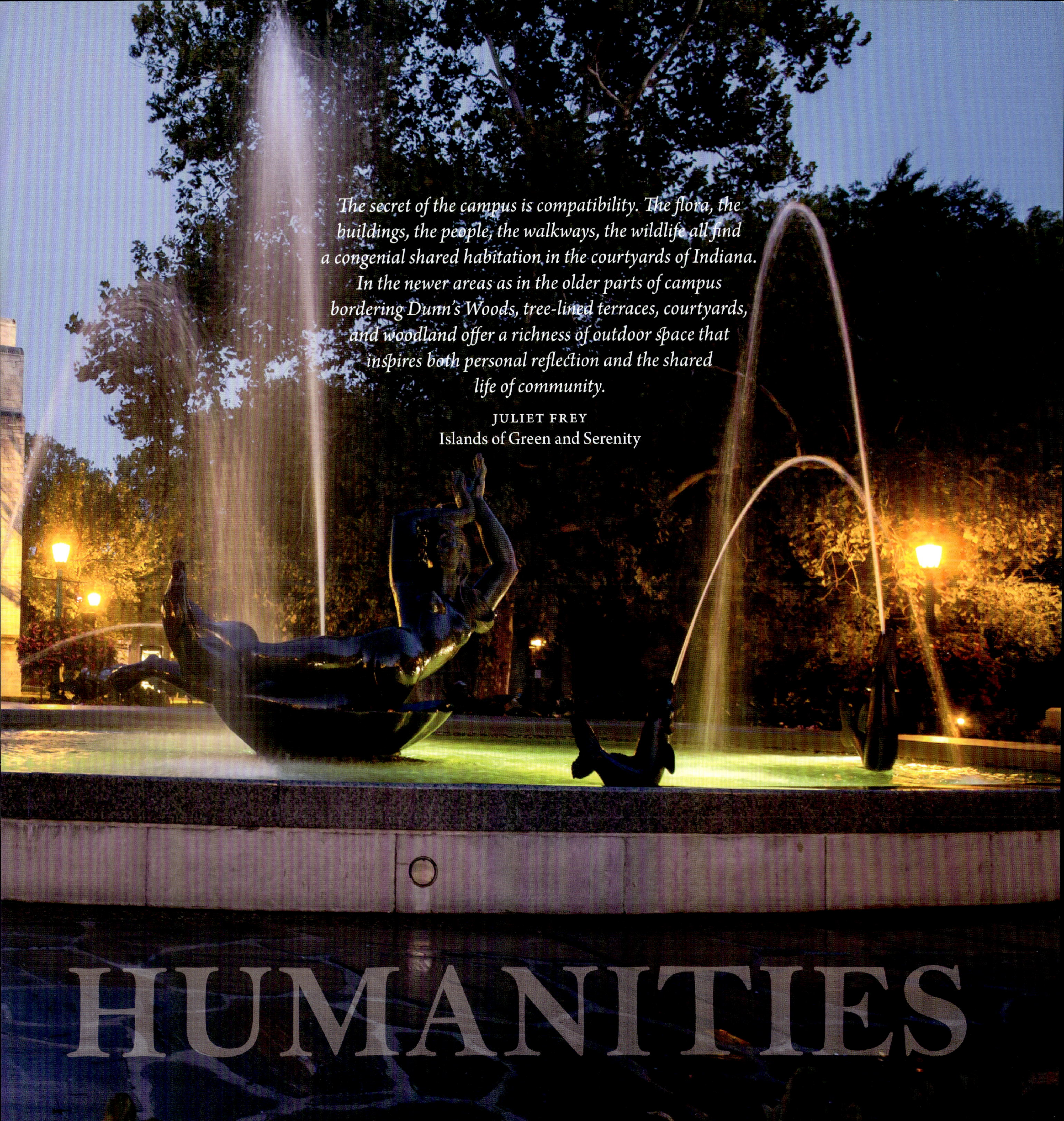

The secret of the campus is compatibility. The flora, the buildings, the people, the walkways, the wildlife all find a congenial shared habitation in the courtyards of Indiana. In the newer areas as in the older parts of campus bordering Dunn's Woods, tree-lined terraces, courtyards, and woodland offer a richness of outdoor space that inspires both personal reflection and the shared life of community.

JULIET FREY
Islands of Green and Serenity

HUMANITIES

B. Winfred Merrill Hall 1936

ARCHITECT Robert Frost Daggett

ARCHITECTURAL STYLE Art Deco / Moderne

ORIGINAL NAME Music Building

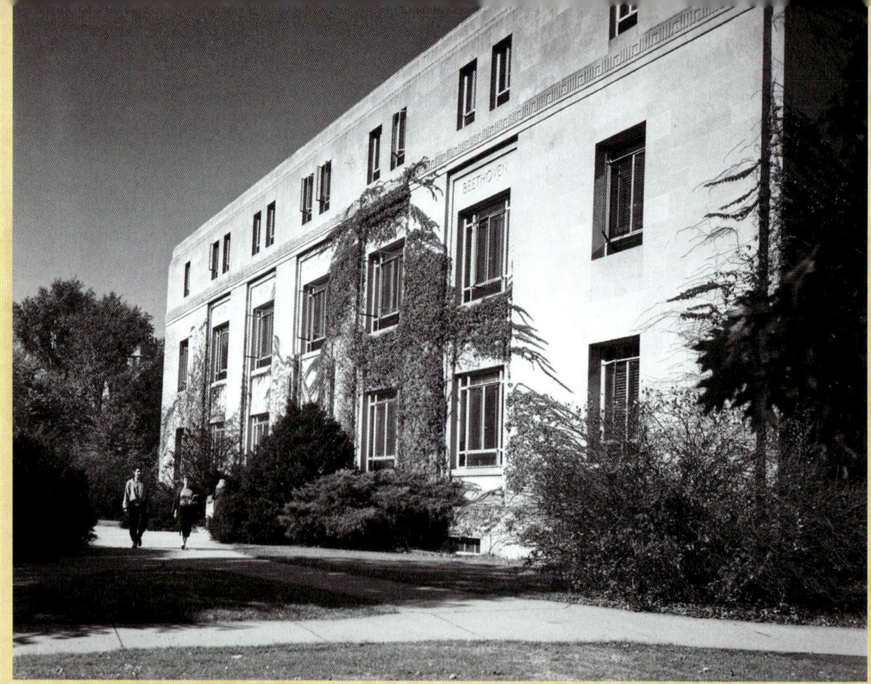

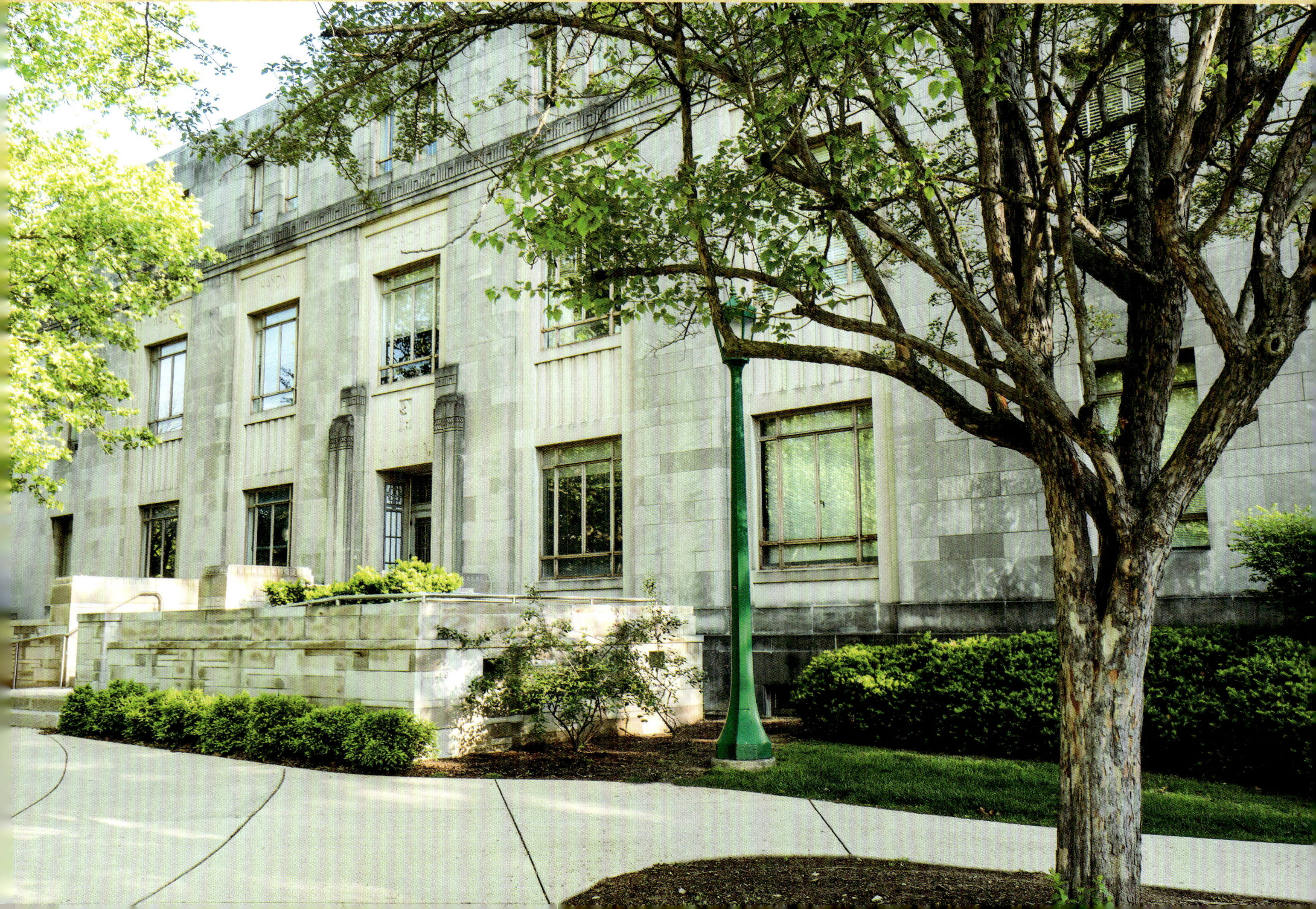

B. Winfred Merrill Hall

The Music Building

musicians, teachers, and amateurs, as heretofore, out of all proportion to the numbers, and—we conjure the authorities of this great University, present and to come, never to relax their thoughtful interest in this School, that its high ideals, maintained by strong characters at no small cost, may be safeguarded and preserved.

—Dean B. Winfred Merrill at dedication ceremony

When Indiana University President William Lowe Bryan lured Barzille Winfred Merrill to Indiana University in 1919 to head the Department of Music, it was a first step toward the growth and professionalization of the fledgling department. Unlike his predecessor, Charles Campbell, Merrill was a seasoned professional musician and administrator, fully prepared for the task of raising the status of the department—a task he immediately tackled. Although the university was in somewhat poor financial straits at the time, Merrill convinced the president and trustees to provide funding for an advertising campaign for the department. The campaign was almost too successful, as Merrill reported: "I have so many letters of inquiry from music students and prospective music students and we are so crowded for necessary rooms that it is worse than useless to advertise at present." While the facilities and equipment were inadequate (he claimed he had to find pianos in private homes on which his students could practice), Merrill focused on an area in which he thought he could succeed, that of additional faculty (he received approval for two).[1] He continued to pursue his goals for the department, and before the end of 1921, the Indiana University Board of Trustees had approved the establishment of a School of Music, with Merrill serving as its first dean.

In Merrill's view, one major hurdle remained—suitable space for the rapidly expanding discipline. Within three months of the school's establishment, he began campaigning

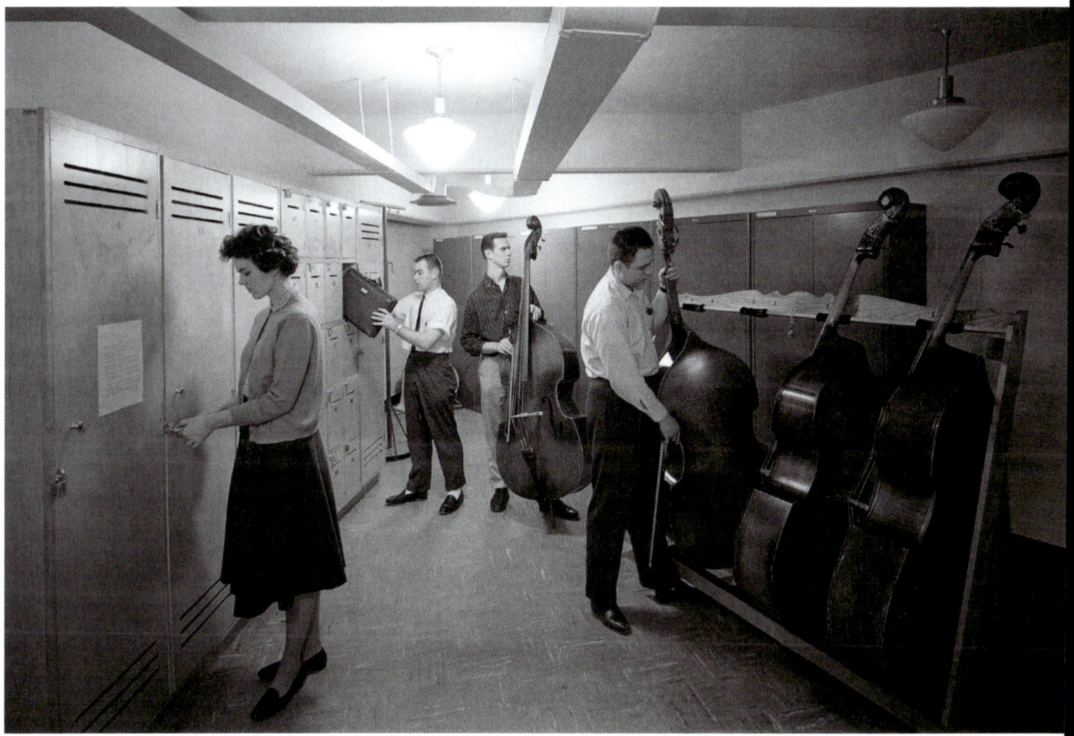

Above, Music students in B. Winfred Merrill Hall preparing for class, 1962. P0052996, IU Archives. Photo credit: John McGinnis.

Facing top, Merrill Hall, 1955. P0052988, IU Archives.

Facing bottom, Merrill Hall facing Third Street, 2016. Photo credit: Tyagan Miller.

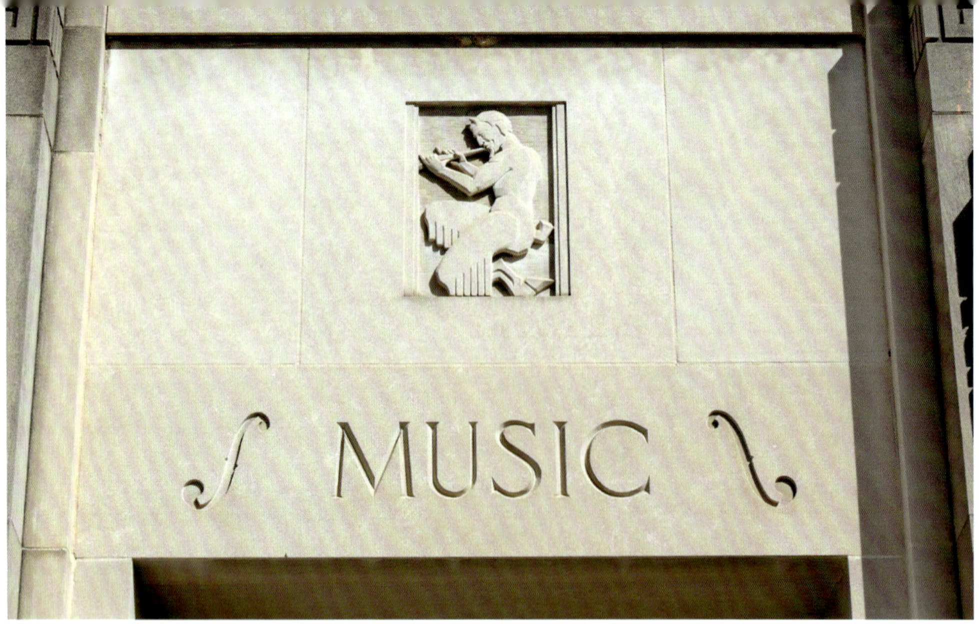

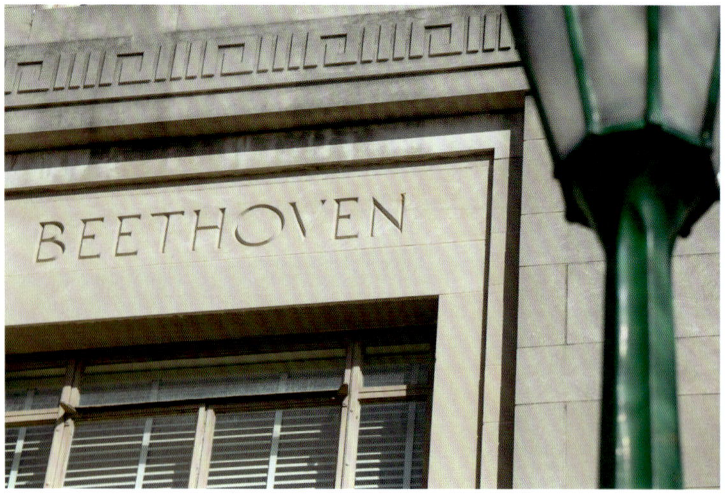

Above and facing, Names of renowned musicians and carving of Pan, the Greek god of music, above Merrill Hall windows, 2016. Photo credit: Tyagan Miller.

for relief from its overcrowded facilities. At the time, the school was occupying the run-down Mitchell Hall, where the hot, sticky conditions very much reduced the longevity of the instruments, where students had to get drinks from a shared cup in an old sink, and where, Merrill's daughter Winifred later remembered, the musician "fried his brain" as temperatures sometimes climbed to as high as 110 degrees.[2]

President Bryan and the trustees approved Merrill's request to reconfigure the space in Mitchell as well as to construct an annex to ease overcrowding. In the summer of 1921, the small annex, containing a classroom, two studios, and four practice rooms, was constructed to the north of Mitchell at a cost of $3,500. The two structures were later painted to provide some visual uniformity, but that, of course, did nothing to alleviate the continued sweltering and crowded conditions. Merrill promptly launched a new campaign for a purpose-built School of Music building.

Finally, with the establishment of the Works Progress Administration (WPA) and its federally subsidized construction projects in the 1930s, it seemed Merrill might have a real opportunity to realize his dream. It seems 1935 was Merrill's year. After the trustees visited and experienced the wretched conditions of Mitchell Hall on a hot June day, Merrill received approval to begin work on a building proposal. By October 1935, the federal government informed the trustees that WPA funding for 45 percent of the project had been approved.

Merrill, who had been collecting ideas for the building for fifteen years, worked with appointed architect Robert Frost Daggett to design a building unlike any other on the IU campus. Whereas the majority of buildings erected to this point could be described as Collegiate Gothic, the new music building, although faced with the traditional limestone, was Art Deco in style. There is a measure of simplicity in the overall design of the building, but that is not so with the stone carvings. In case there might be any doubt about the purpose of this building, the word *Music* is carved above the cast aluminum door (also designed with a musical motif) and flanked on each side with musical F holes. Above this is a bas-relief of Pan, the Greek god of music, seated with his flute. Large stacked windows flank the front and sides of the building, above which names of world-renowned musicians are carved (each name, it is said, was selected by the faculty member occupying the room within). A frieze designed from a motif of the musical staff and bar extends around the top of the building. Two unique features of this building are the completion date, carved in Roman numerals on the southwest corner, and the architect's name, Robert Frost Daggett, carved on the southeast corner.

Inside, the rooms were arranged around Merrill's pièce de résistance, Recital Hall, now IU's most historic performance space. Still used regularly, the first-floor auditorium with balcony was constructed with seats for more than four hundred

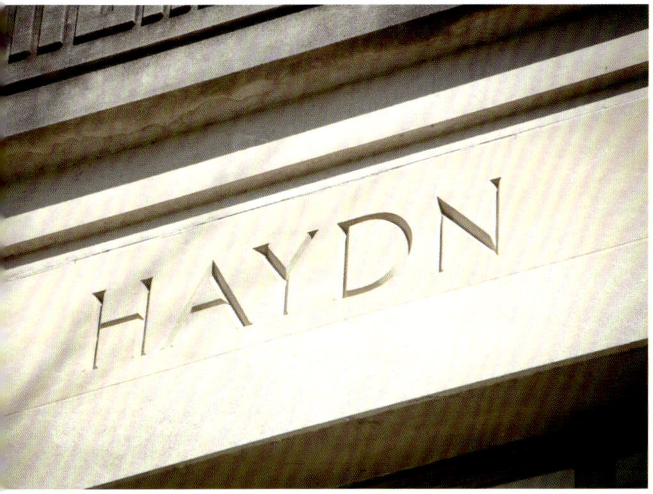

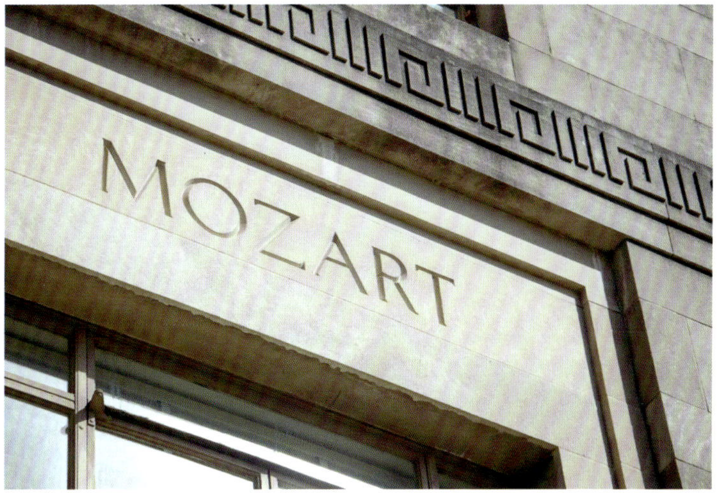

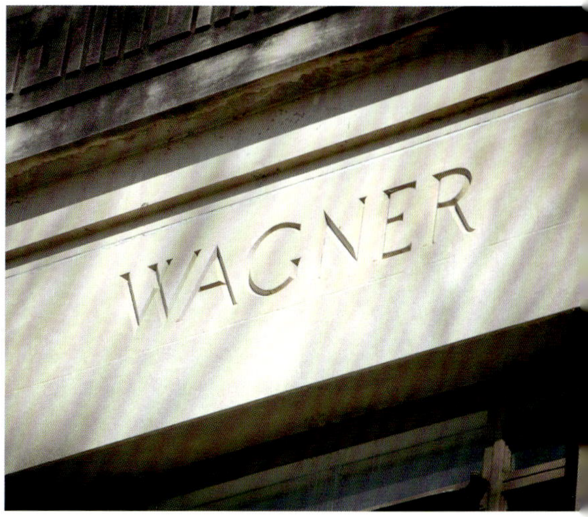

patrons as well as an orchestra pit that could accommodate over a hundred musicians and their instruments. Merrill told the student newspaper that the ceilings were "scientifically treated with acoustic devices to insure perfect tone reception."[3] A spacious student lounge, administrative offices, and studio space were housed on the first floor. On the second floor were recitation rooms, voice studios, a rehearsal room, listening room, and general and record libraries. The top floor had fifty soundproof practice rooms, complete with thick cork floors and walls made of double partitions separated by heavy felt layers, and ceilings suspended by insulated hooks so there were no connections to carry sound in or out of the rooms. Even the practice room doors were soundproof. Finally, the basement included locker rooms and a museum to hold musical rarities the university had received as gifts over the years.

The decorative touches throughout the building were elegant, with polished travertine from Wales and strips of Roman travertine and Pyrenees St. Anne marble on the floor and walls of the entry lobby, while the corridor floors were of white terrazzo. The windowsills glistened with Black Champlain marble, and the wainscoting on the walls featured contrasting Tennessee Tavernelle. The walls on the inside of the entry connecting Merrill Hall with the round Music Building Addition were finished in stunning polished green marble (serpentine).

Dean Merrill's dream may have taken years to achieve, but his long, thoughtful planning process and his perseverance have served Indiana University and what is now the Jacobs School of Music well. In 1989, the IU Board of Trustees approved naming the building for Dean Merrill to recognize his dedication and devotion to the university, the School of Music, and all lovers of music.

Throughout the early evolution of the School of Music at IU, the tenets of "the importance of the concept of a professional school or conservatory within a university; a focus on continually increasing enrollment; hiring professional performers as professors; public performance as a means of attracting positive attention for the institution; a pattern of moving ahead with or without adequate resources; and the continuing need for better physical facilities and adequate equipment" led to the world-renowned Jacobs School of Music that exists at Indiana University today.[4]

Bess Meshulam Simon Music Library and Recital Center

1938

ARCHITECT — McGuire and Shook Architects

ARCHITECTURAL STYLE — Art Moderne / Art Deco

ORIGINAL NAME — University School / Wendell W. Wright School of Education Building

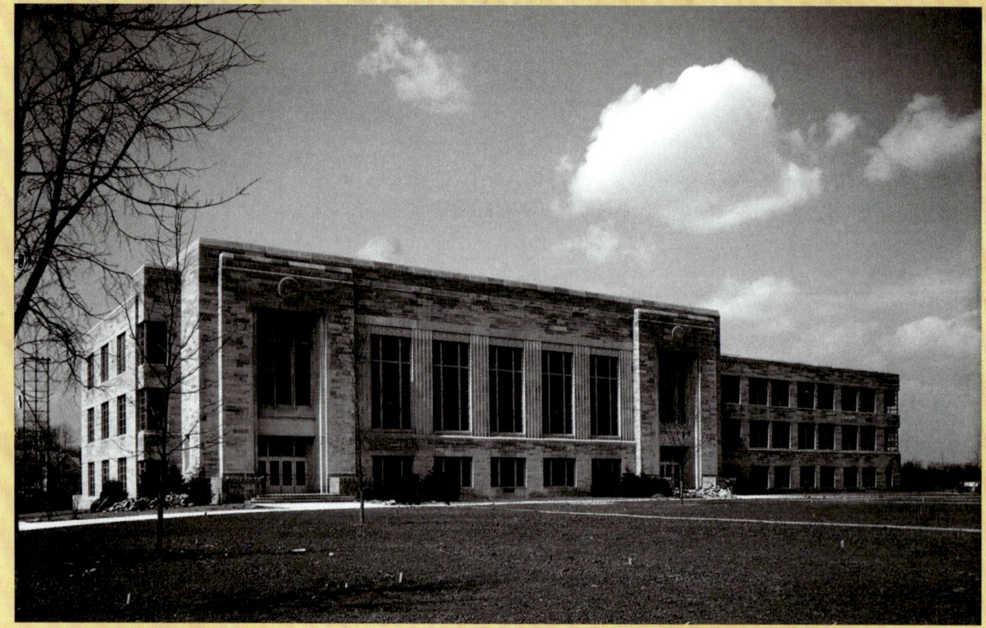

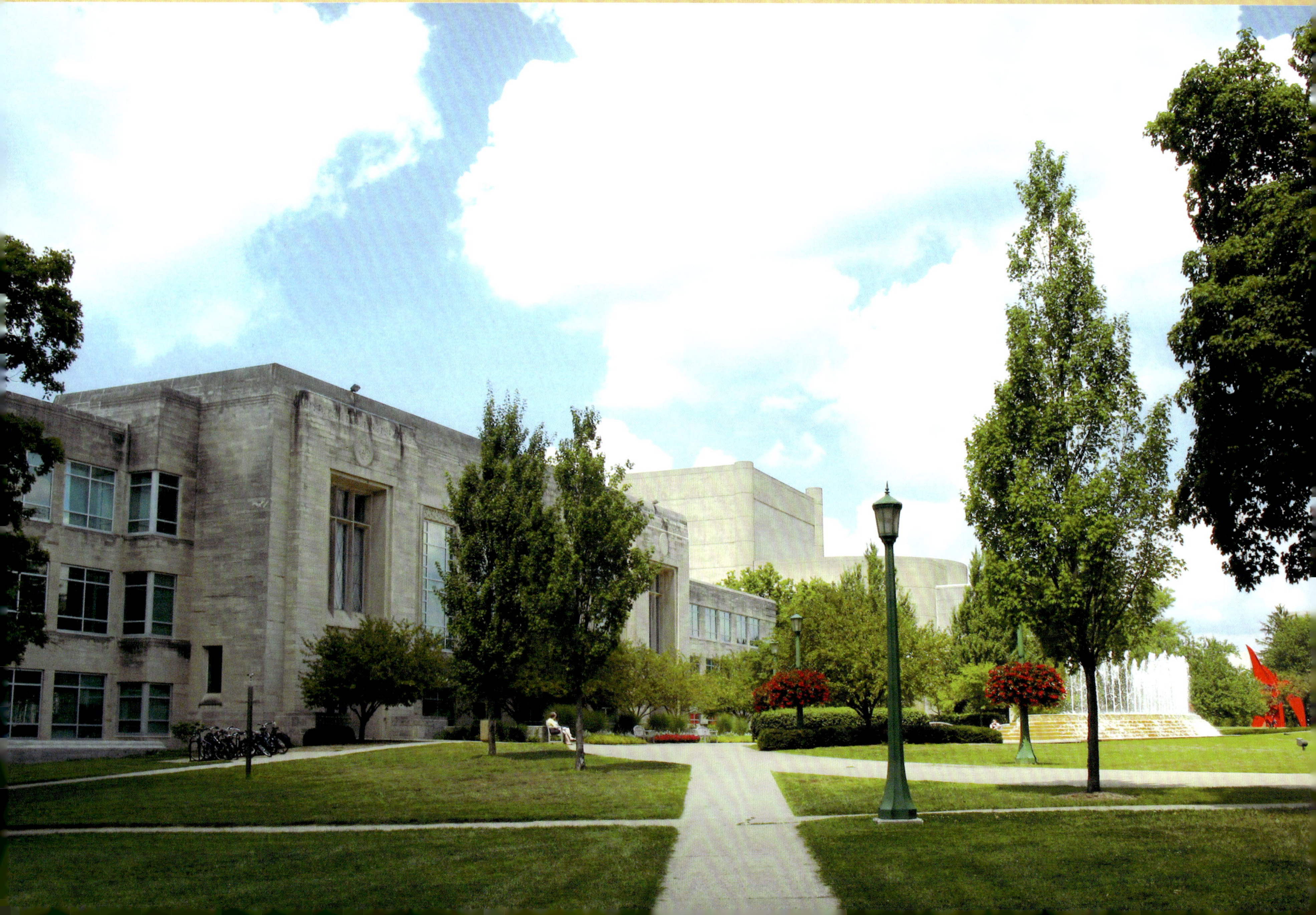

Bess Meshulam Simon Music Library and Recital Center

From Pedagogy to Music

Tonight we celebrate with tingling spirits and joyful hearts the realization of these dreams [great music library and concert halls]. As we build on a heritage that is a gift from those talented and devoted ones who have come before us, so we, in 1995, pledge that these magnificent new facilities dedicated tonight, will be used for the highest educational and artistic purposes, long into the next century.

—Dean of Indiana University School of Music Charles Webb at dedication ceremony

THE LARGE, ICONIC, ART DECO BUILDING STANDing on the northwest corner of Third Street and Jordan Avenue has served Indiana University as home to three important tenants since construction was completed in 1938. Federally funded through support from the Public Works Administration, and sited by a master plan created by the Olmsted Brothers in 1936, the structure was first a laboratory school under the auspices of the IU School of Education with classes from kindergarten through twelfth grade. The Olmsted Brothers firm, realizing the unique needs of a training facility for future teachers and the daily activity that would occur there, recommended a site for the building that was away from the central core of the campus: the school "should be somewhat removed from the main group of University buildings, so that children attending the Laboratory School would not have to pass through the Campus in reaching it."[1] McGuire and Shook Architects of Indianapolis was hired to formulate plans. The firm responded with a strong, functional, Art Moderne design clad in local limestone and of scale and mass typical of Indiana high schools in the early twentieth century. The architect purposely fashioned the school with a paucity of detail except for a stylized band around the stoops of the two main entries on the building's east side—a pattern duplicated in the design of the McKinney Fountain completed during the 1992–95 renovation.

By June 1938 the structure was ready to be occupied, and President Herman B Wells presided over the dedication ceremony that included formally naming the building University School: "I prefer to think of this model school building as a vast laboratory, where the staff of our School of Education can carry on scientific experimentation and research designed to yield a solution to many of the troublesome problems which confront educational administrators and teachers. Here there must be a willingness to re-examine traditional procedures fearlessly in the light of changed economic and social conditions."[2] Six hundred Bloomington schoolchildren attended the new school that first year and enjoyed an ultramodern educational facility.

Over the coming decades, thousands of Bloomington children received their early education at University School, with a wing added in 1950 to keep pace with the growing post–World War II population boom. By the 1960s, the Indiana University campus had expanded around the school, so when new classrooms and office space were necessary to handle the growing

Facing top, University School, later the Bess Meshulam Simon Music Library and Recital Center, circa 1945. P0030607, IU Archives.

Facing bottom, Bess Meshulam Simon Music Library and Recital Center with Frank E. McKinney Jr. Fountain and Alexander Calder's *Peau Rouge Indiana* in the background, undated. Photo credit: Indiana University.

IU student population in 1964, University School was moved to a new location east of the main campus, and the School of Education eagerly claimed the vacated space.

In 1968 an additional footprint was attached to the west side of the School of Education to accommodate the Speech and Hearing Clinic. In 1979 the building was renamed the Wendell W. Wright School of Education. The School of Education, with its mission to train teachers and discover new and more effective pedagogy, continued to prosper from the late 1960s through the 1980s, and ultimately, the school outgrew the building. Aware that the School of Education would continue to grow, Indiana University selected a site for a new home at the corner of East Seventh Street and Rose Avenue.

The move couldn't have made administrators in the Jacobs School of Music happier. Long suffering with crowded conditions, the school was the logical new occupant of the soon-to-be-vacated School of Education. A shortage of space to accommodate recital halls and the music library had been identified at least a decade earlier, but little had been achieved to alleviate the issue. Another factor made the School of Music the logical new occupant: the southeast quadrant of campus was home to several facilities serving the Jacobs School of Music, and the School of Education was directly in the middle of that district. A few advanced the idea of razing the structure and constructing anew on the cleared site, but the university had never removed one of its distinguished limestone buildings and wasn't about to begin that practice. Renovation was the agreed-upon direction.

The highly acclaimed architectural firm CRSS Inc. of Houston was hired to develop plans for a Jacobs School of Music facility that would provide an ultramodern music library and spacious, modern recital halls. RQAW of Indianapolis was chosen to partner with CRSS and provide construction administration services. The task of placing a new library in the structure was rather simple, but constructing recital halls with the volume required for musical performance was much more complicated. The design solution was to remove the north wing of the building and construct an addition in its place. The architect welcomed the chance to improve upon the previously existing wing with its dull, flat roof. The replacement wing would feature a pitched tile roof that would echo the shapes of the building's immediate neighbors. Another four-story addition to accommodate the library collections would be placed in the south courtyard area, giving the entire structure a new scale and prominence in the Jacobs School of Music's array of buildings, even though much of the exterior style remained the same as it was in the 1930s.

Constructed entirely from private funding, the final structure includes the three-story William and Gayle Cook Music Library, which initially housed the school's complete collection for the first time, including printed materials, scores, and recordings, as well as a music media center. It is one of the largest music libraries in the nation. Other spaces include the two-hundred-seat Elsie I. Sweeney Lecture Hall, with a state-of-the-art electronic multimedia system; the four-hundred-seat Ione B. Auer Concert Hall, which features side terraces and a beamed, coffered ceiling that can be retracted or released to adjust the acoustics; and the intimate one-hundred-seat Ford Recital Hall, designed specifically for solo recitals and chamber music performances. The renovation also included five classrooms, a recording center, and office space for the Departments of Music Theory, Musicology, and Music Education.

Although simple in basic design, some interesting carved details adorn the structure at every main entry. Tradition and former use history have been preserved above the entry doors facing the Musical Arts Center and the north entry facing Jordan Avenue, where the words *University School* remind all who enter that the structure was once home to hundreds of Bloomington schoolchildren. The IU official seal is displayed high above the north Jordan Avenue entry, and the Seal of the State of Indiana occupies a similar position above the south Jordan Avenue entry. The word *Education* is carved above the Third Street doorway, another reminder of the building's history as a school. On the left side of the doorway is a quotation from Caleb Mills, a prominent Indiana educator in the 1800s: "Teachers must inspire as well as instruct." On the right side of the doorway are words from a 1787 Indiana ordinance: "Education shall forever be encouraged."

This renovated 1938 building was named in honor of Melvin Simon's first wife, Bess Meshulam, an Indiana native with a lifelong love of music. Mrs. Simon's children provided the naming gift. The Bess Meshulam Simon Music Library and Recital Center was officially dedicated on November 17, 1995, as part of a four-day celebration filled with performances by luminaries of the music world, including Kurt Masur, music director of the New York Philharmonic; renowned sopranos Frederica von Stade and Sylvia McNair; tenor Jerry Hadley; violinist Joshua Bell; baritone Kurt Ollmann; and stage and film star Tyne Daly.

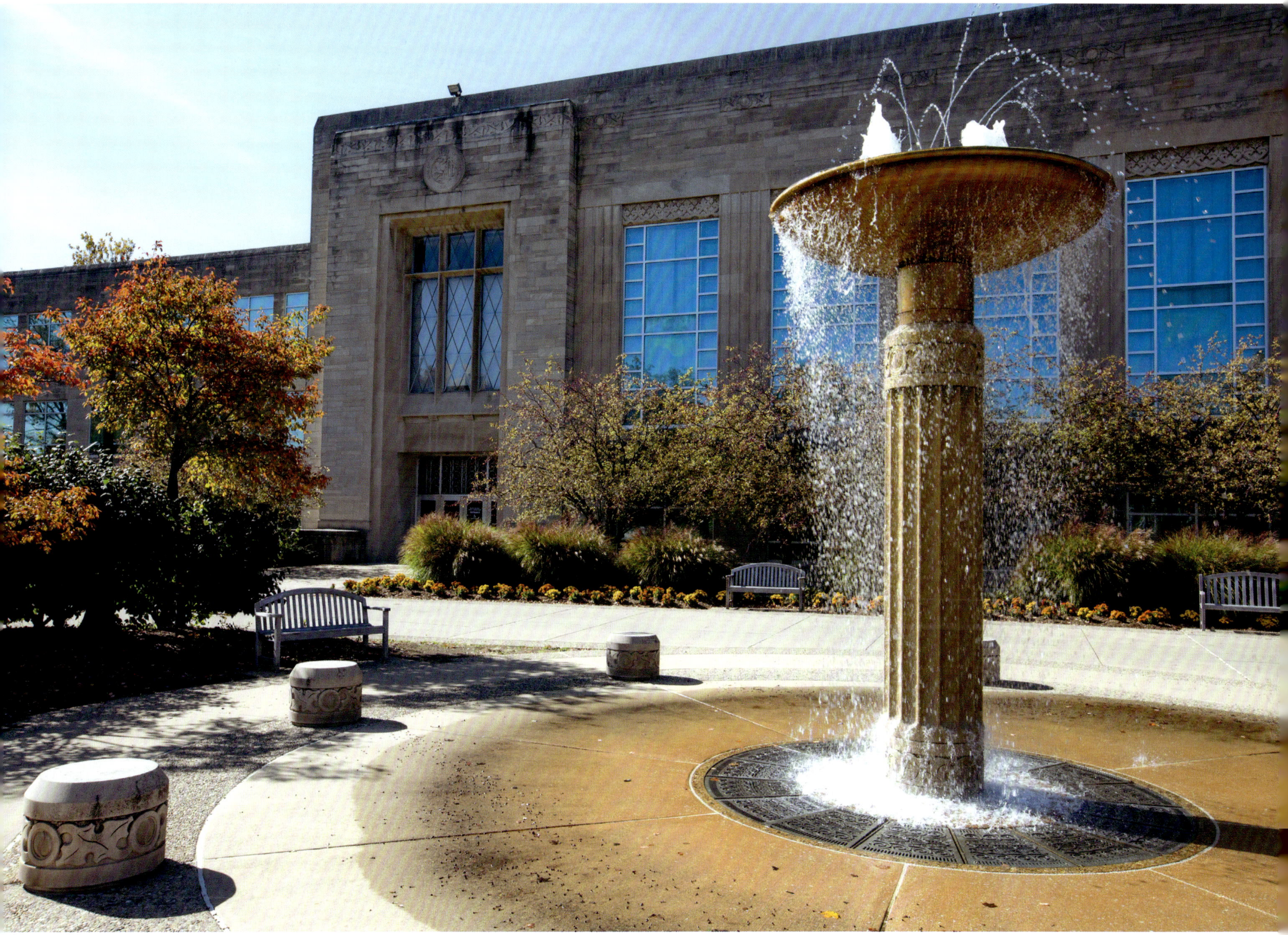

Frank E. McKinney Jr. Fountain at the entrance to the Simon Music Library and Recital Center, 2016. Photo credit: Tyagan Miller.

East Hall 1948

ARCHITECT Edward James and Associates

ARCHITECTURAL STYLE World War II Barracks

RAZED 1968

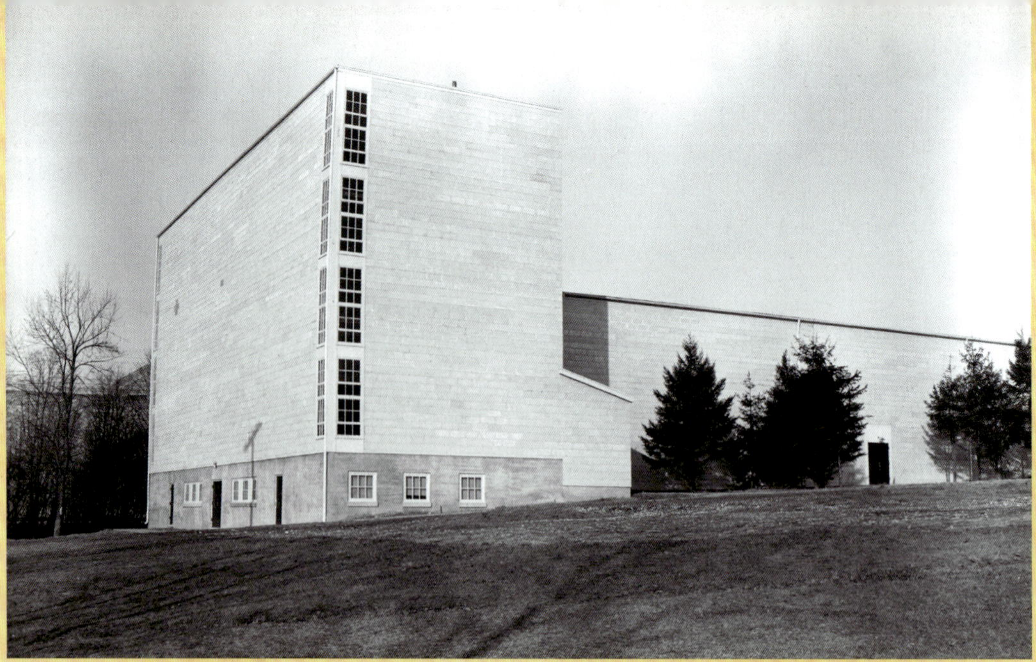

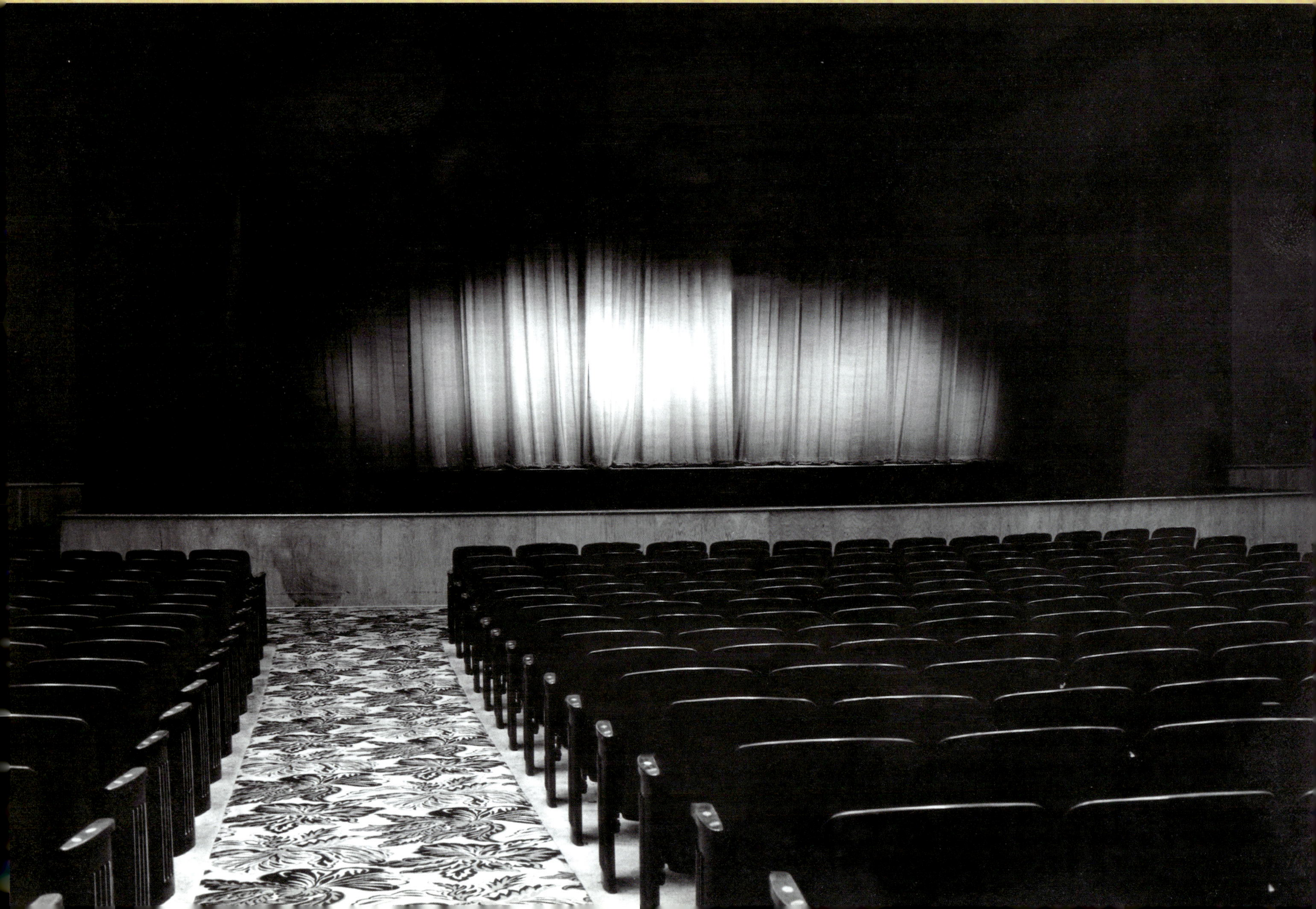

East Hall

The First Home of IU Opera

East Hall was an experiment. When, seventeen years ago, these primitive premises were entrusted to us, they reflected the administration's and the public's expectation of our raison d'être. In the course of these years we seem to have proven this right of existence in the pursuit of the musical theater as an integral and most notable expression of music and mankind's entire cultural heritage. . . . These drab and shaky walls have witnessed many joys and sorrows of our Opera Theater's growth from childhood to early youth.

—*Hans Busch, "Farewell to East Hall"*

AT THE END OF WORLD WAR II, WHILE THE UNIversity sought state funding for permanent structures such as new student housing and life sciences and education buildings, the trustees sought to fill other needs as rapidly and cheaply as possible by converting surplus military buildings for collegiate use. Faced with burgeoning enrollments, increasing campus musical productions, and ambitions for a full-scale opera, the School of Music was stretched well beyond capacity and using the relatively new Indiana University Auditorium to such an extent that it was beginning to interfere with other uses. On September 12, 1947, the university received an enabling notice from the Federal Works Administration for funds to cover a music practice building. Architect Edward James was authorized to proceed with the preparation of plans to place what would be named East Hall on a site approximately where the Musical Arts Center (MAC) sits today. Two military surplus buildings were moved from George Field in Lawrenceville, Illinois, and reerected at IU. The government paid for the move and reerection, but IU paid for the site work, utilities, and repurposing. The end product was a prefabricated, temporary structure with a main building and wing in an *L* shape. It was clad with white asbestos shingles.

With the opening of school in the fall of 1948, faculty and students moved into the office, classroom, and practice portions of the partially completed East Hall. The stage area was not finished until the beginning of 1950, and thus the 1948–49 opera season was again held in the auditorium. The interior of the main building featured a performance stage and seating capacity for more than one thousand people. The hall had a raked floor and was fully equipped for operatic productions, with a gridiron and stage hangings, a modern switchboard and lighting system, and an orchestra pit. Dressing rooms and a workshop were under the stage, and public spaces included a lobby and an exterior ticket booth. Practice rooms with pianos, a large instrument room for use by the orchestra, classrooms, opera departmental offices, and storage rooms were located in the wing.

March 2, 1950, marked the official opening of the building with the faculty and students of the School of Music presenting the four-act Puccini opera *La Bohème*, which, according to the *Indiana Daily Student*, closed to a full house of "'bravos' for singing and acting that has heretofore been seldom equaled on campus." That same year, new School of Music dean Wilfred Bain reported that the academic year "has without doubt been one of the most fruitful years of musical productivity in the long and distinguished history of the School of Music."[1]

Facing top, East Hall, destroyed in 1968 by fire, 1949. P0052699, IU Archives.

Facing bottom, East Hall auditorium, 1967. P0027400, IU Archives. Photo credit: George Murphy.

As the opera productions expanded, the inadequacies of the building became more apparent. The stage was shallow and had a low proscenium opening not conducive to the tall sets typical of opera. There was practically no side-stage space and thus a very limited capacity for housing scenery when it was not actually on stage. Furthermore, until 1954, the building was not air-conditioned, to the great discomfort of performers and patrons alike. By the 1960s it was apparent the "temporary" structure that had endured for well over a decade was not adequate, leading faculty member Hans Busch to suggest that "the termites who have taken possession of East Hall, might be our most dependable friends in our struggle for adequate facilities we so vitally need."[2]

The curtain fell for the final opera production of *Albert Herring* on Saturday, July 15, 1967, and on January 24, 1968, while already slated for demolition, East Hall, was destroyed by fire. The scenery, costumes, lighting, and forty-six pianos—including a 9-foot Steinway Concert Grand—were destroyed. Files documenting the annual productions of *Parsifal* and *The Nutcracker* were saved from the flames, however, allowing those traditions to continue.

Over the years, hundreds of students were involved in a total of 415 performances in East Hall. Productions of eighty-six works including *Die Fledermaus, La Traviata, Faust, Tosca,* and *Don Giovanni* gained IU Opera a reputation as one of the best collegiate operas in the country, as well as among the best in the world.[3] In a tribute to East Hall, even with its flaws, School of Music historian George M. Logan wrote that "the converted structure enormously facilitated the development of Bain's opera program, and thus the School as a whole."[4]

Students rehearsing in East Hall, 1950.
P0053009, IU Archives.

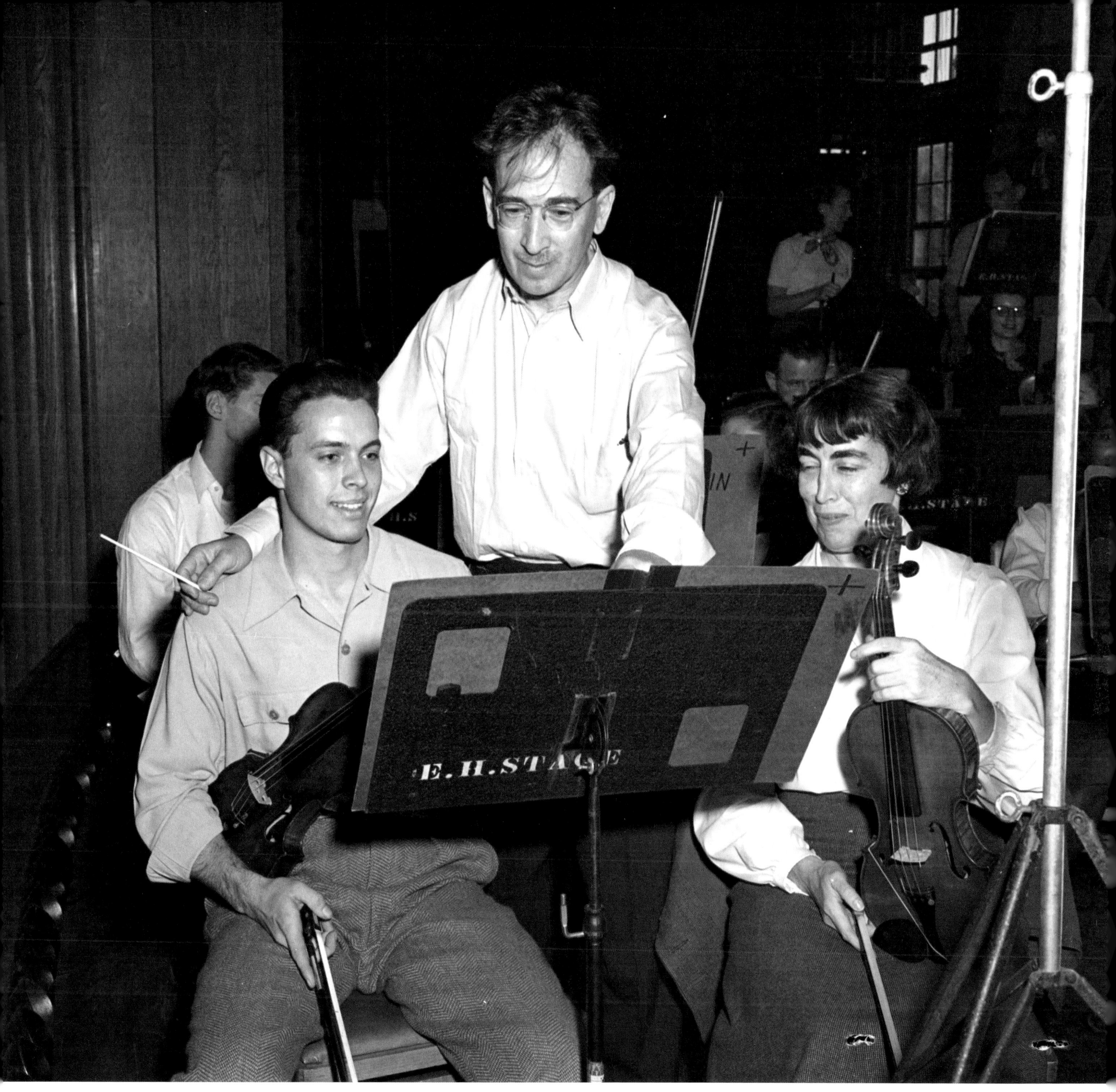
E.H.STAGE

Music Building Addition 1960

ARCHITECT Eggers and Higgins / Daggett, Naegele, and Daggett

ARCHITECTURAL STYLE 1950s Modern

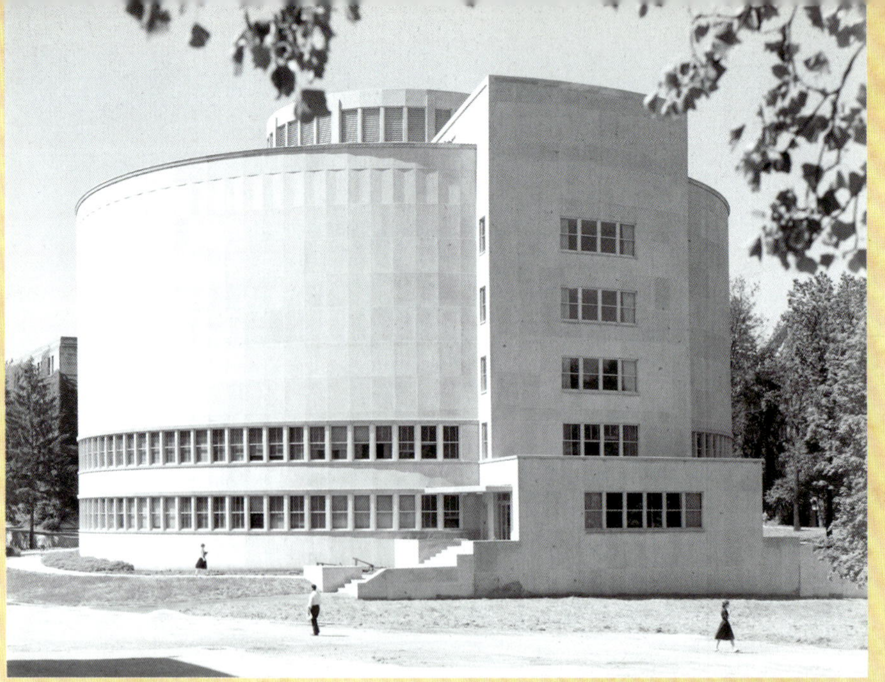

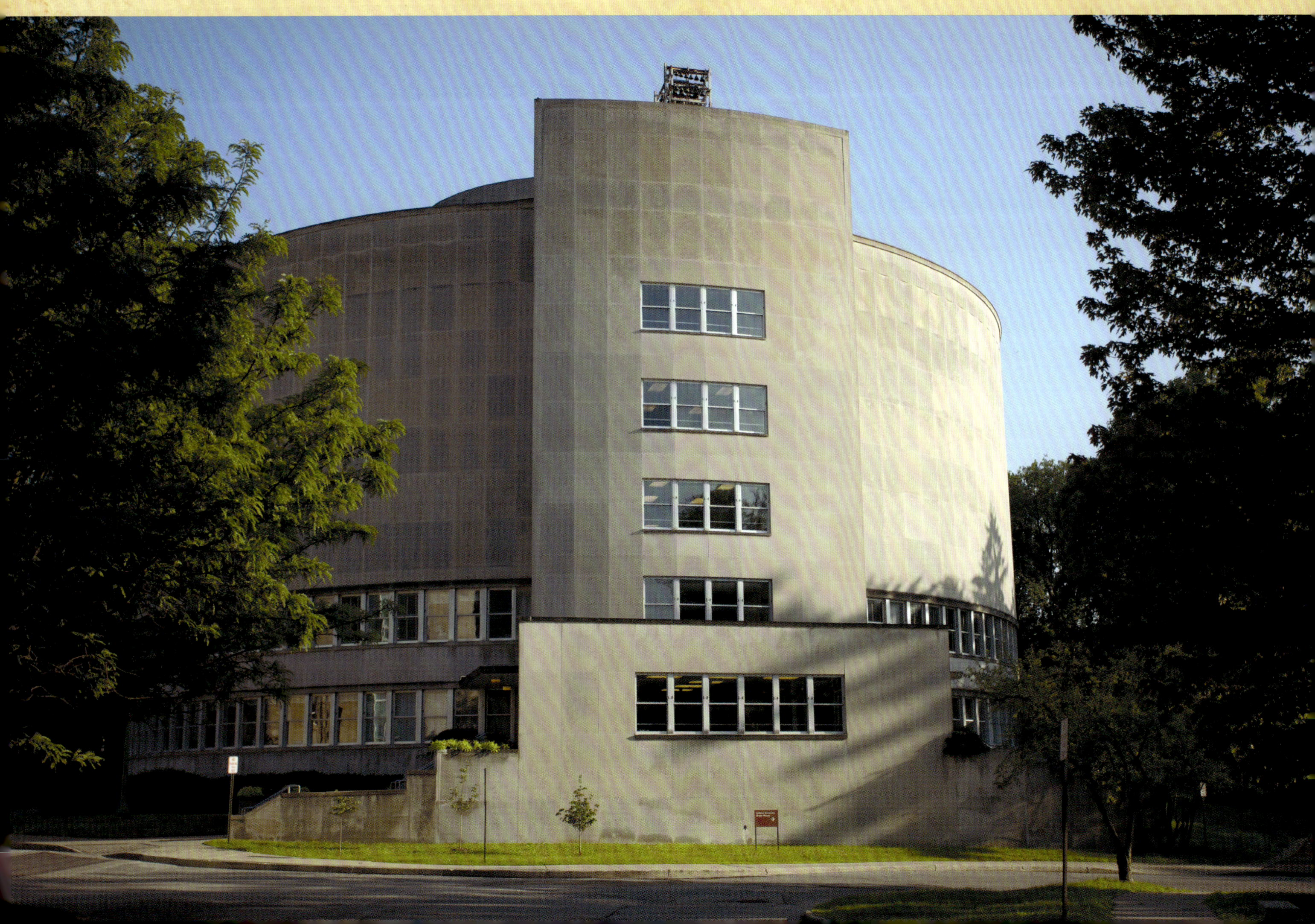

Music Building Addition

The "Round Building"

Music must be made the life of the entire nation. A responsibility lies with the faculty and student body to stimulate the country's awareness of music through the continued preparation of fine artists.

—Music critic Paul Hume at dedication ceremony

When Merrill Hall was dedicated in 1937, administrators in the young but successful School of Music undoubtedly breathed a great sigh of relief. For a while, at least, they would have sufficient space to house the school's expanding programs. "A while," as it turned out, was a very short while—within a few years, the school was once again bursting at the seams and its heavy reliance on the new Indiana University Auditorium, completed in 1941, caused interference with other events taking place there. In 1948, to alleviate the demands on the auditorium, the university added East Hall. The repurposed military buildings provided performance and practice space, classrooms, and departmental offices, and eased some of the overcrowding. The ever-growing School of Music required a long-term space solution, however.

By 1956 students, faculty, and staff from the School of Music were spread among seven buildings. In March of that year, the Board of Trustees approved a new addition to Merrill Hall. They believed that it would eliminate all temporary quarters with the exception of East Hall, which was then used by the IU opera program. The proposed addition included plans for a future second wing that would serve as an opera house with seating for a thousand. University favorites Eggers and Higgins of New York were selected as supervising architects for the project, scheduled to begin in the fall.

The Music Building Addition was to be unlike any other structure on the Bloomington campus, and a startling contrast to the elegance and classic design of Merrill Hall, the first home of the School of Music. Architect Theodore J. Young told the student newspaper, "in conceiving this building several solutions were considered, but the one that seemed to meet all requirements in the most direct way was a building of circular plan, easily permitting rooms of different widths and depths."[1] The anticipated circular structure would be joined to Merrill on the north side by lobbies on each floor; and to maintain favorable relations with its neighbors, all floors having practice rooms would be windowless to prevent the sound from carrying.

Work on the project did not commence in the fall as planned, and the call for bids was not issued until March 1958. The Indianapolis architectural firm Daggett, Naegele, and Daggett was chosen to partner with Eggers and Higgins, and the ground-breaking ceremony was finally held June 17, 1958. Apropos for a school for artists and performers, even the ground-breaking ceremony was an Event (with a capital E), with the Brass Choir performing "Fanfare for a New Music Building," composed

Facing top, Music Building Addition, or the "Round Building," 1961. P0025883, IU Archives. Photo credit: Ralph "Porky" Veal.

Facing bottom, North side of Music Building Addition, 2015. Photo credit: Indiana University.

specifically for the occasion by Professor Bernhard Heiden.[2] When the Music Addition Building opened in 1960, it was among the final buildings dedicated during the presidency of Herman B Wells. At the ceremony, President Wells told the crowd in attendance, "The building we dedicate today is admirable for its function and striking in design. It will in time become the central building of our music group."[3]

The "Round Building," as it is aptly known, is cylindrical in shape, with two concentric circular, windowless hallways lined with studios and offices. The six-story structure is faced with Indiana limestone, and the rooms within are trapezoidal in shape to provide a bit of soundproofing without the added expense of special acoustical treatment. The building provided an additional 106,000 square feet of classrooms (4), conference rooms (3), practice rooms (267), choral rehearsal rooms (4), a ballet room, several instrument storage rooms, and an orchestra repair room. The School of Music administrators told the student newspaper that, as a whole, the Music Building Addition was adequate but not spacious, and "designed for maximum efficiency with minimum cost."[4] While Dean of Music Wilfred Bain called the building "architecturally unique," a generation later, historian George Logan would express a different opinion: "Seldom in the annals of architecture can a building so unattractive have been grafted onto one so handsome."[5]

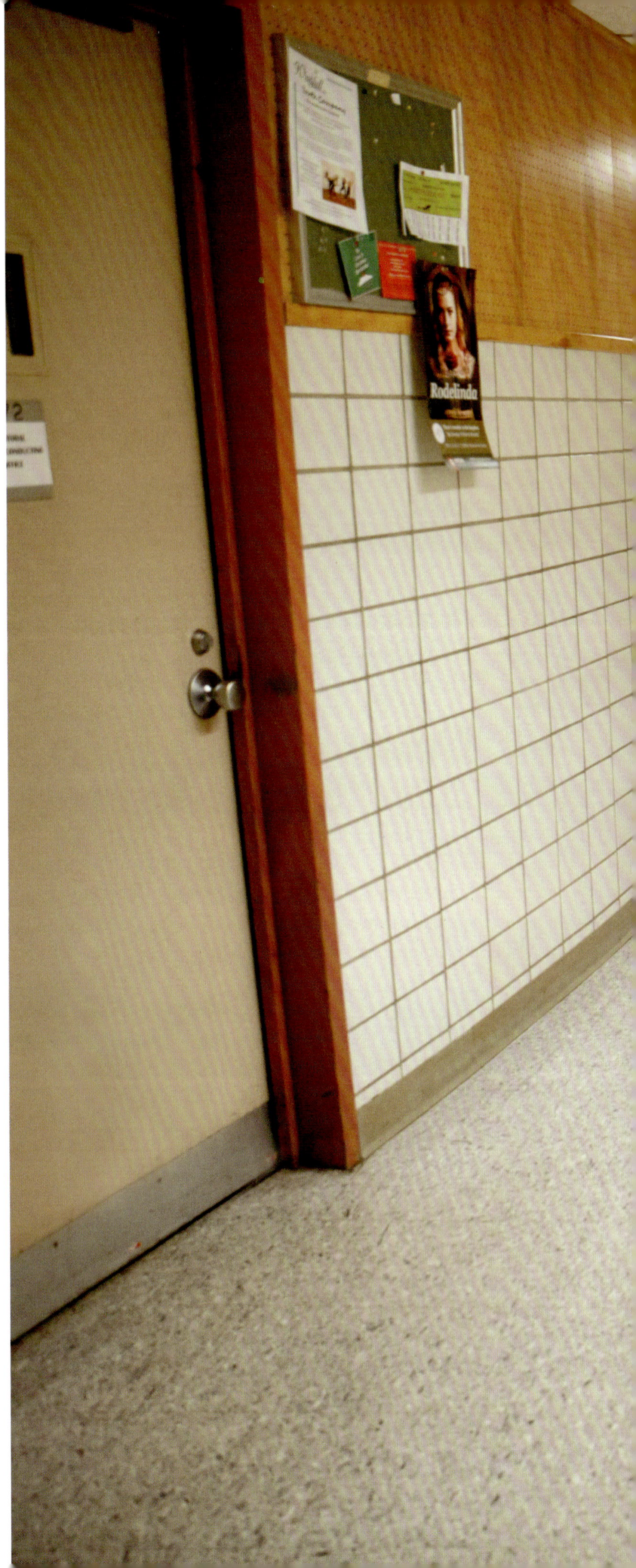

Hallway leading to offices and studios in Music Building Addition, 2017. Photo credit: Indiana University.

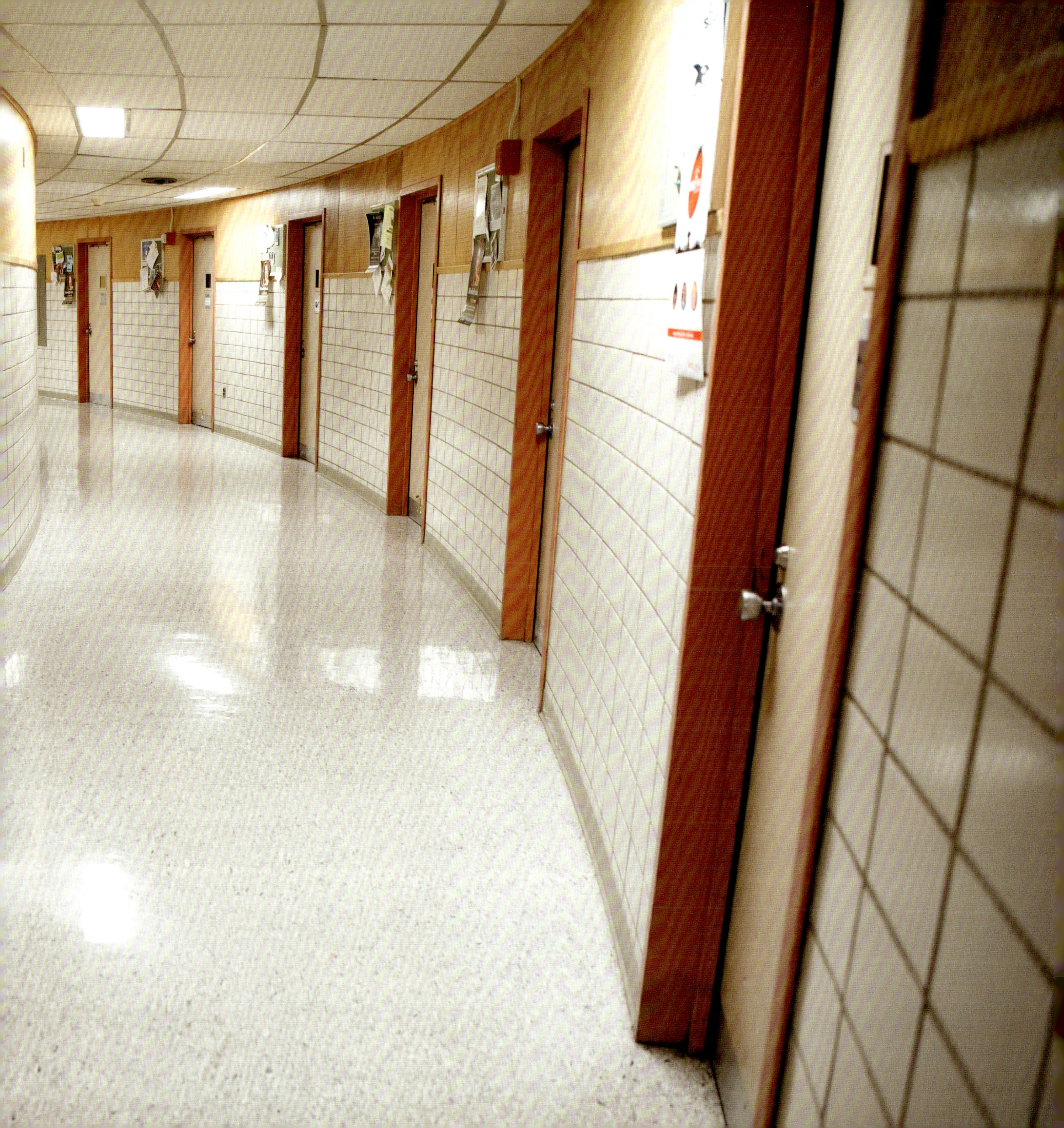

Musical Arts Center 1971

ARCHITECT Evans Woollen and Associates

ARCHITECTURAL STYLE 1960s Performance Modern

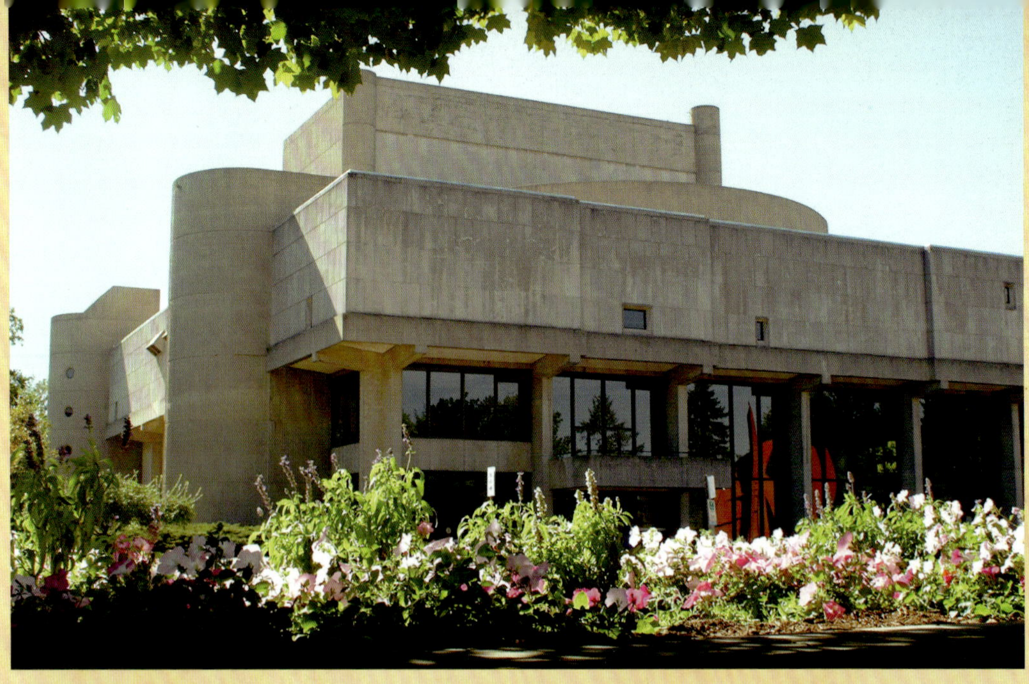

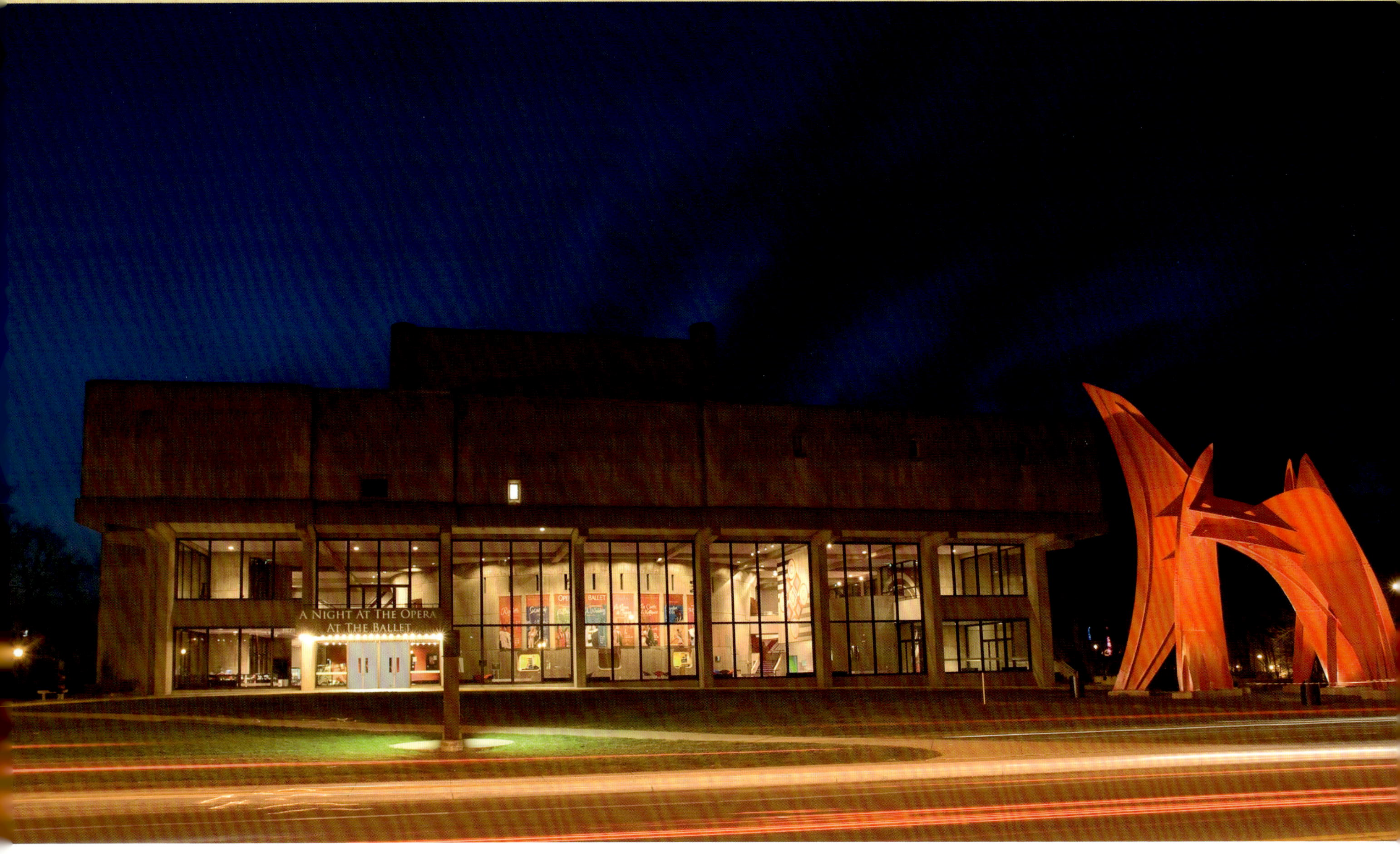

Musical Arts Center

Grand Performance Venue

We anticipate that this Center, with its flexibility, its tailoring to conceivable needs, its suitability for various forms of musical performance, and its advanced technical mechanisms designed to enhance training and production, will mark the beginning of a new era in the expression and appreciation of the divine art of music.

—Indiana University President John W. Ryan at dedication ceremony

SINCE ITS ESTABLISHMENT IN 1921, THE JACOBS School of Music has evolved into one of the leading institutions in the world for advanced music study. Yet, despite its prestige, the Jacobs School has continuously struggled with a lack of space. Even with Merrill Hall built in 1936, East Hall (the Opera House) in 1948, and the round Music Building Addition in 1960, which nearly tripled the available space, the school has continuously outgrown its physical capacity because of ballooning enrollments. As early as 1958, preliminary planning to remedy the problem was underway and in May 1960 the Board of Trustees added a new "Music Workshop and Laboratory Building" to replace East Hall on its list of construction priorities, and preliminary plans from the firm of Eggers and Higgins of New York were commissioned.

As plans for the building began to take shape, a massive fund-raising campaign for new construction projects to celebrate the university sesquicentennial commenced. President Elvis Stahr appointed a university committee to oversee the planning of a new music facility, and in 1964 the trustees hired the Indianapolis firm of Evans Woollen and Associates to carry out the final designs. In preparation for the construction of the building, a study was made of the new Metropolitan Opera House in Lincoln Center and several European opera houses, in particular those in Germany, that featured the most modern advances in acoustics and theater architecture. In October 1962, Dean Bain, his wife, and Ted Jones, a technical expert on music venues, embarked on the SS *Rotterdam* for a monthlong tour overseas for the purpose of seeing firsthand the finest opera houses in the world.

Although the architects hoped for a location more central to campus, ultimately the East Hall site west of Jordan Avenue and just north of Merrill Hall and the Music Addition won out for its "departmental convenience."[1] In June 1967, Governor Branigin and the Indiana State Budget Agency approved plans for the long-awaited Musical Arts Center. The project would be funded without the use of any state tax funds through a mix of federal grants under the Academic Facilities Act of 1963, bond sales authorized by the state legislature, insurance from the East Hall fire, and private gifts (notably major gifts from Herman C. and Ellnora Krannert of Indianapolis and Elsie Sweeney of Columbus, Indiana).

While East Hall was already slated for destruction, the January 24, 1968, fire resulted in the acceleration of the construc-

Facing top, Musical Arts Center in summer with Alexander Calder's *Peau Rouge Indiana* reflected in window, 2016. Photo credit: Indiana University.

Facing bottom, Nighttime view of Musical Arts Center from Jordan Avenue; *Peau Rouge Indiana* in foreground, undated. Photo credit: Indiana University.

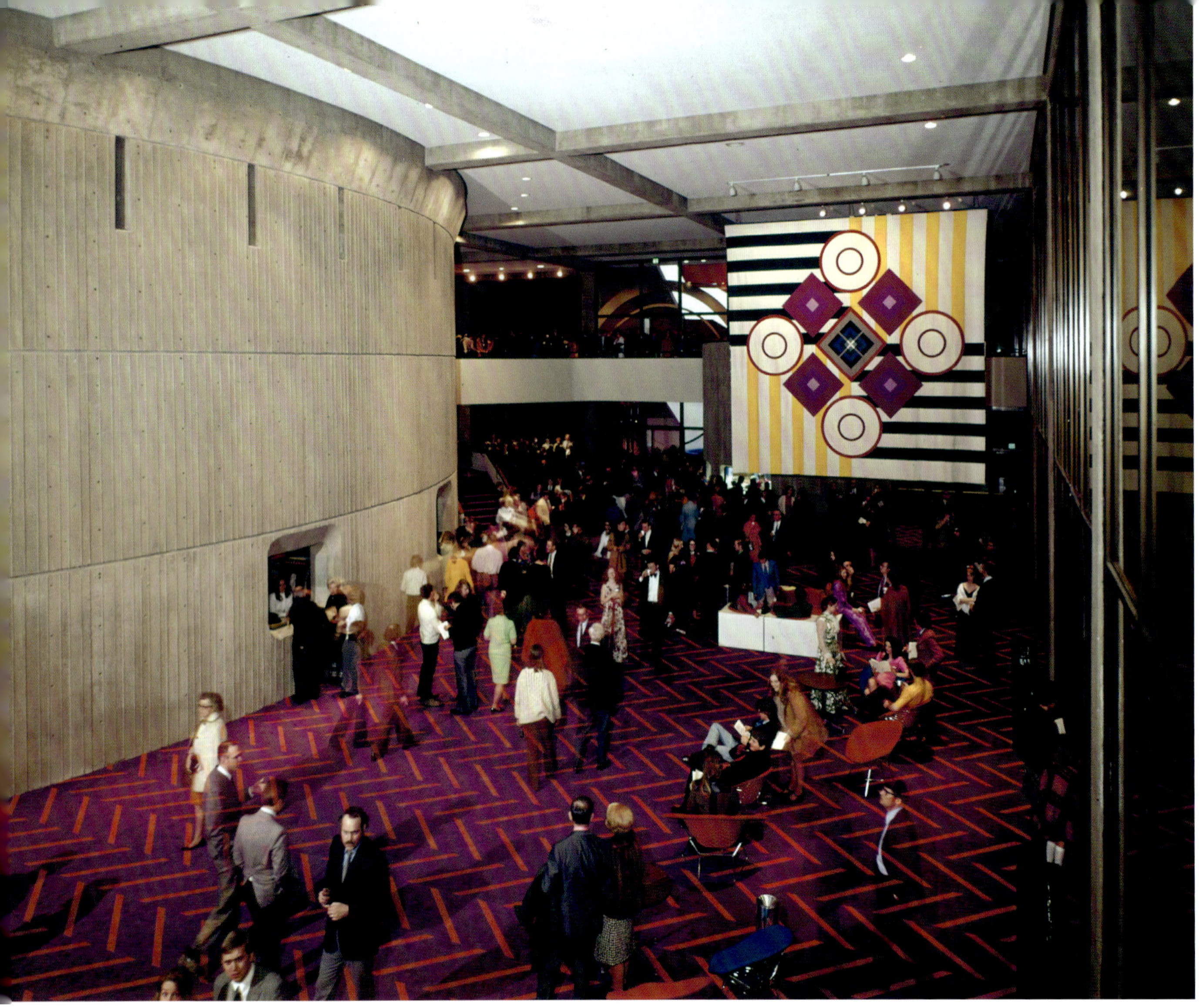

Crowd mingles below George Ortman banner in Musical Arts Center lobby on performance night, 1972. P0029867, IU Archives.

tion plans for the new Musical Arts Center; ground was broken on May 26, 1968.

The final design was 1960s Performance Modern in style and asymmetrical from all views, characteristic of Evans Woollen's emphasis on new architectural trends and viewpoints. He said in a 1967 *Architectural Record* article that "the pop artist has persuaded us to look again at the cityspace; to see that order and irrationality may exist happily, and that the whole raucous fabric may potentially be art. . . . The primary commitment seems to be the effective expression of use patterns, for such patterns stretch beyond the building into the fabric of the city. . . . Perfection is unobtainable, and the idea of it boring. Something incomplete, changing, and unknown is wanted in both buildings and men."[2]

Facing Jordan Avenue, the exterior is a graceful yet functional combination of concrete poured in rough-sawn-timber forms enhanced by glass and stone, reminiscent of a castle with its massive scale, turrets, and slit windows. The use of limestone is confined to rectangular panels on upper-level projections. The entrance is fronted by a spacious, glass-walled public foyer named for its benefactor, Hoagland "Hoagy" Carmichael, which at night glows like a beacon. The interior features a dramatic juxtaposition of contrasting colors, textures, and forms. Graceful, suspended ramps and spiral staircases lead to the upper levels, where a grand promenade offers a panoramic view of the scene below.

The lobby gives way to a majestic auditorium designed to accommodate an audience of 1,450 within a space that is wide yet shallow so as to maintain a feeling of intimacy in both sound and vision. Seating is nineteen rows deep arranged in the traditional German "continental style," with no center aisle, 900 seats on the main floor and 550 in three curving balconies. The main floor is steeply raked, similar to that at Bayreuth Festspielhaus in Germany, and provides an unobstructed view from every seat. The orchestra pit has two sections and can accommodate a hundred musicians and their instruments.

At the physical center of the building, the main stage has few rivals anywhere in the world; it is 90 by 60 feet, with a backstage area that occupies more than half the building, a space often compared to the Metropolitan Opera House. The stage is fully trapped, allowing for portions of the floor to be lifted out to add a layered effect to productions, and it includes a movable orchestra pit. The sides and top of the proscenium arch are completely movable so as to adjust the size of the stage for everything from a large-scale operatic production to a solo student performance. The technical capabilities of this performance venue are among the finest in the country. A state-of-the-art computerized light and sound system is supplemented ingeniously by a dramatic modern chandelier: the chandelier not only illuminates the hall, but allows for the adjustment of acoustics. Suspended from the ceiling, it consists of thirty-five

Top, Musical Arts Center house during opening night performance, 1971. P0025882, IU Archives. Photo credit: Ralph "Porky" Veal.

Bottom, Stairwell of Musical Arts Center reminiscent of the Op art and Pop art aesthetic period, 1972. P0025889, IU Archives.

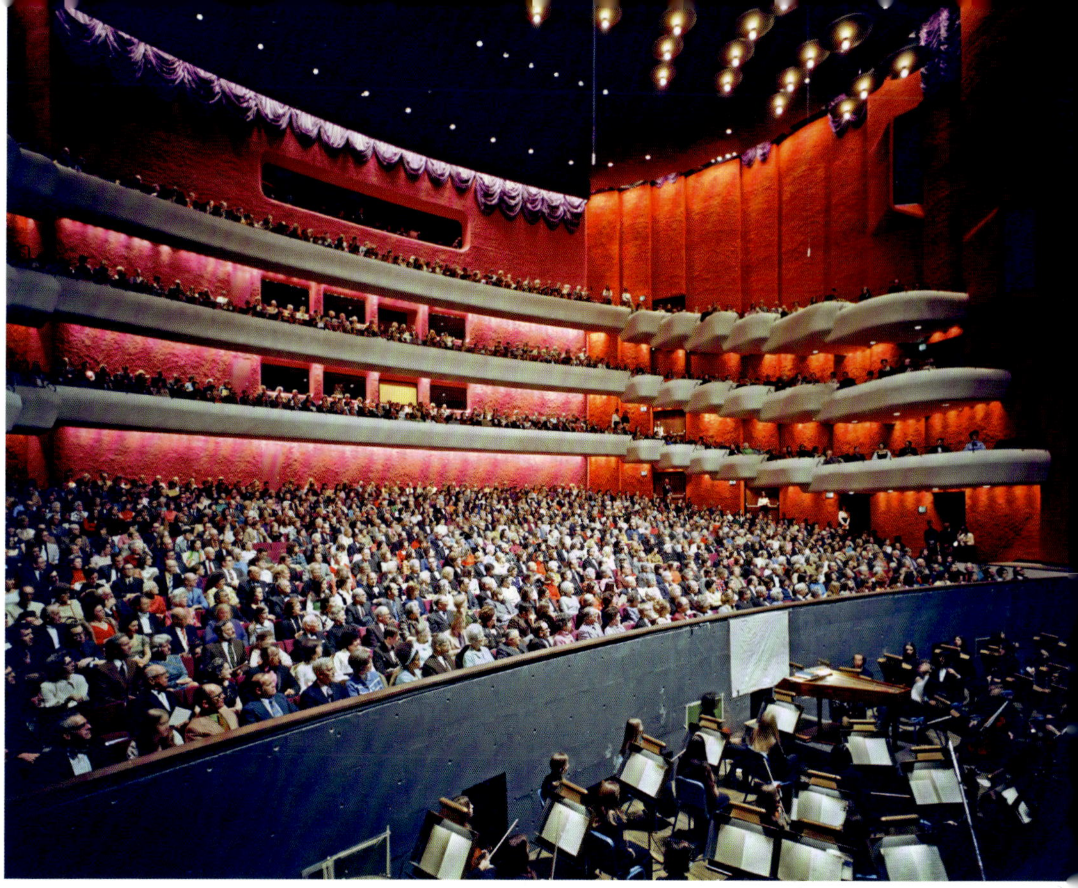

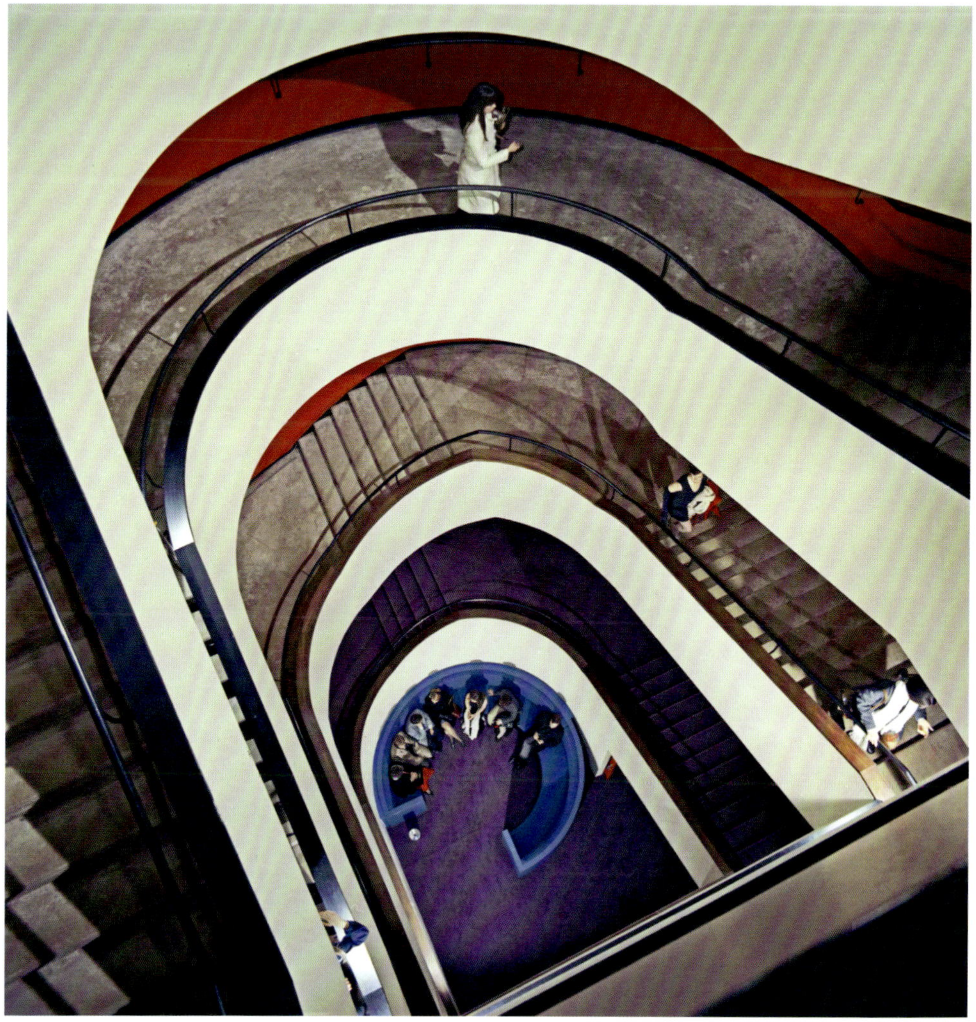

movable golden disks, each 3 feet in diameter. The rough texture of the side and back walls and the curving faces of the balcony disperse sound reflections.

Three soundproof rehearsal stages flank the main stage, each with motorized wagons (movable floors) allowing for rapid set changes, size adjustment for varying performances, and simultaneous rehearsals. Aside from the public facilities, a vast network of supporting accommodations forms a ring around the auditorium on the upper levels. These include several large rehearsal halls, three ballet studios, dressing rooms, scenery and costume studios, a carpentry and metal shop, and a state-of-the-art sound studio.

The interior decor of the auditorium is reminiscent of the Op art and Pop art aesthetic of the period. In the lobby, textured plaster walls painted in Spectrum Red rise in vivid contrast to the purple and gold striped carpet and boldly colored furniture. Two massive banners by U.S. artist and Guggenheim Award–winner George Ortman feature rich geometric designs, which add to the vibrant setting. The creamy white balconies stand out against the royal purple velour curtains and magenta rear walls, and even the stairwells at the north and south ends of the building are brightly colored.

The spectacular Musical Arts Center (MAC) opened its doors to the public on January 29, 1972, with Mozart's *Don Giovanni*; the facility wasn't officially dedicated until a few months later. A weeklong series of inaugural festivities began with the U.S. premiere of IU faculty member John Eaton's avant-garde opera *Heracles* on Saturday, April 15, 1972, and continued the rest of the week with ballet, solo recitals, symphony concerts, and even a jazz program with Hoagy Carmichael. In the days following, the MAC was lauded by critics around the country: it was described as "a winner" by the *New York Times,* "a staggeringly fine facility" by the *Louisville Courier-Journal,* "one of the major performing arts buildings in the land" by the *Dallas Morning News,* and "far superior to anything in Chicago" by the *Chicago Tribune.*[3]

East Studio Building 2013

ARCHITECT Browning, Day, Mullins, Dierdorf Architects / Flad Architects

ARCHITECTURAL STYLE Neo-Gothic / Contextual Modern

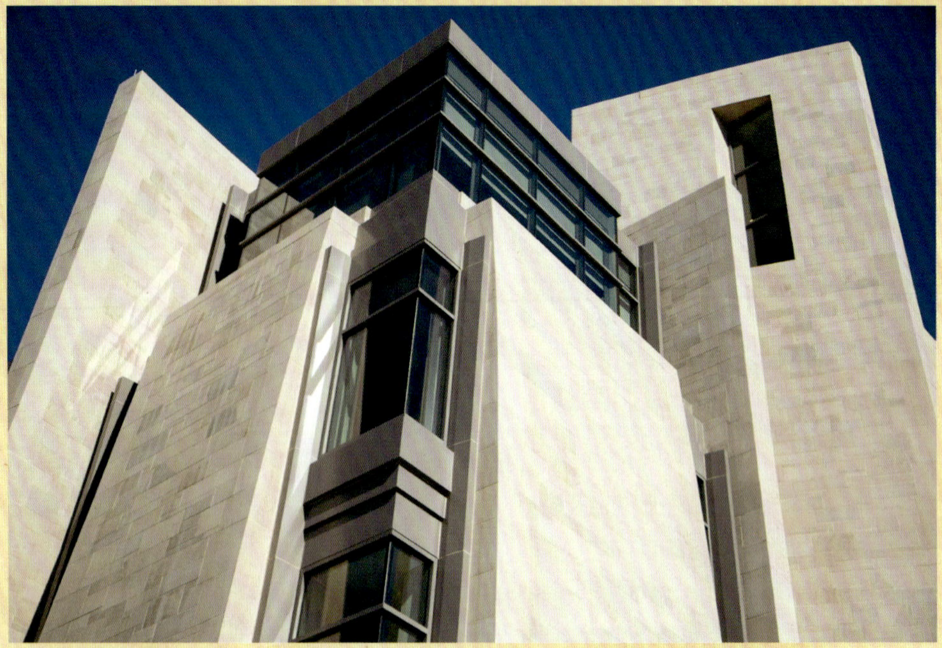

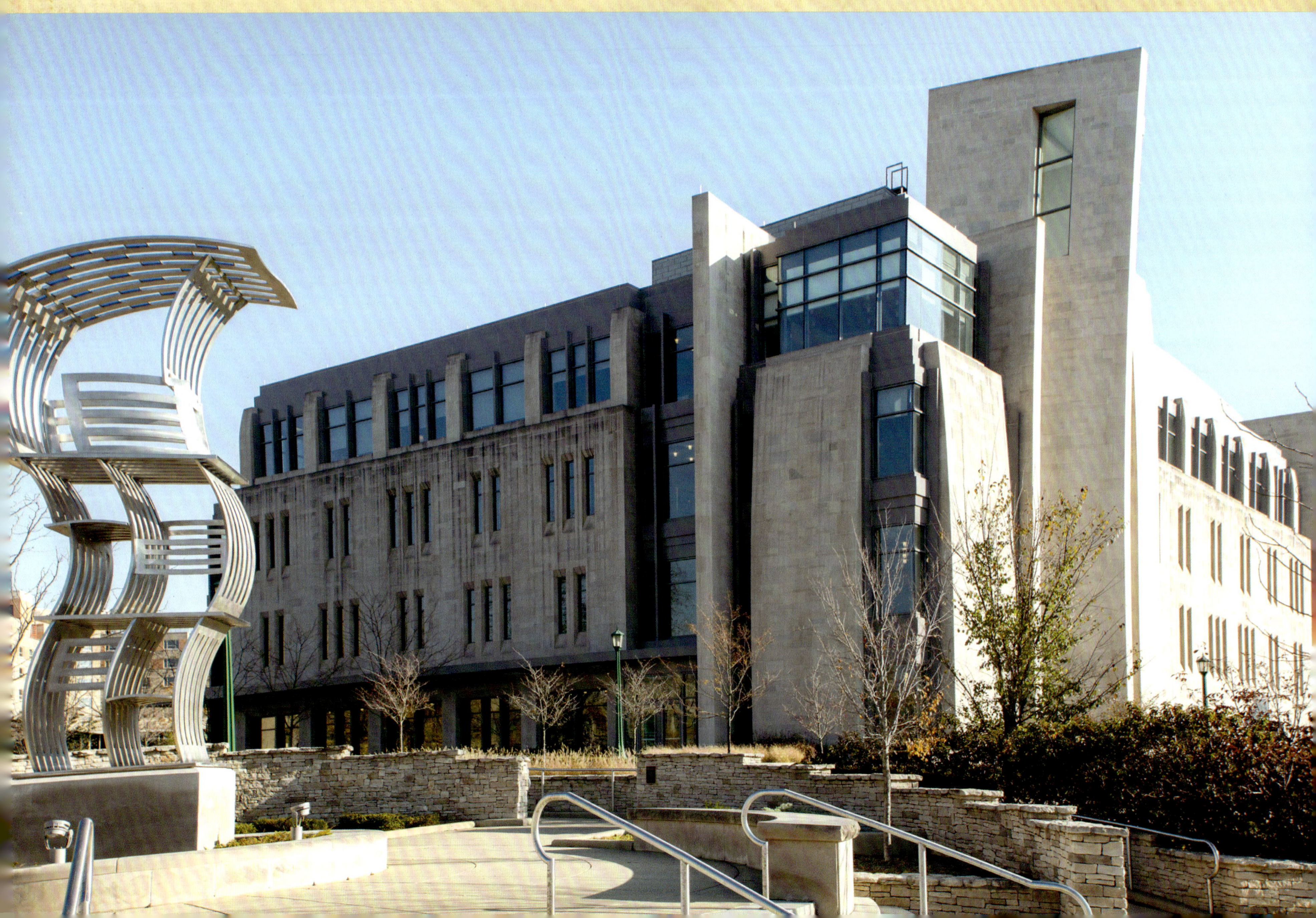

East Studio Building

A Testament to Excellence in the Musical Arts

The new building will give the Jacobs School a new soul and the strength to do remarkable things. The studio is where we teach, but also where we as artists create and think, where we do our most important work. A new faculty studio building gives us the lifeblood to make a real difference to the world of music.

—Professor Menahem Pressler

The Indiana University Jacobs School of Music is continuously among the top three music schools in the United States and one of the largest in the world. To accommodate this discipline, the university has constructed or renovated eight buildings throughout its history: Mitchell Hall (remodel 1921), Merrill Hall (1936), East Hall (1948–68), the Music Building Addition (the "Round Building" 1960), the Musical Arts Center (1971), the Music Practice Building (1979), the Bess Meshulam Simon Music Library and Recital Center (remodel, 1995), and finally the East Studio Building, finished in 2013.

For many years, the school was in dire need of more performance and composition studios. The addition of the Round Building in 1960 did provide more studios, but the acoustics were not ideal, as the sound would travel into the halls and other music rooms. After many years of cobbling together practice space, in 2007 the university was awarded a Lilly Endowment grant of $44 million for the new practice building.

Two architectural firms, Browning Day Mullins Dierdorf Architects (BDMD) of Indianapolis and Flad Architects of Madison, Wisconsin, were selected to design the new facility as joint venture partners. BDMD was an associate architect for the Student Recreational Sports Center (SRSC) on the Bloomington campus and the primary architect for both the Herron School of Art and Design at Indiana University–Purdue University Indianapolis and the Performing Arts Complex at Butler University. Flad Architects designed both the award-winning Simon Hall and the Multidisciplinary Science Building II in Bloomington.

The original plan was to remove the Round Building and construct the new music building on that site. Subsequently, a more favorable plan for the Jacobs School of Music was to erect a new building where the University West Apartments were located, at the corner of Jordan Avenue and Third Street. The apartments were torn down, and a contextual Modern limestone edifice adorned with Gothic detailing was built. The East Studio Building not only provides the Jacobs School with the quality space it needed but it also serves as the gateway to the university's music, fine arts, film, and performing arts district.

David Black, design principal at Flad Architects, described his firm's goal in working with BDMD as "[creating] a building that will be immediately identifiable as an IU building. It should look at home with the existing Indiana limestone structures on campus." He added that, when building on the

Facing top, Glass and stone detail of East Studio Building, 2016. Photo credit: Tyagan Miller.

Facing bottom, East Studio Building with Anniversary Plaza, added in 2015, in foreground, 2016. Photo credit: Tyagan Miller.

IU campus, "we've been able to interpret the character of the campus and make sure the rich history of the campus is represented. It's important to observe the features of a campus's open space, building forms and even the subtleties of the way the stone is worked."[1]

The dreams of the architectural team and university administrators were realized with a combination of exterior elegance and interior design and functionality. The 85,000-square-foot, L-shaped East Studio Building is contextual Modern in design. The four above-ground floors are clad in smooth-sawn, ashlar blocks of Indiana limestone with vertical recessed windows. As the building rises, the limestone transitions to matte-gray metal panels and glass on the top floor. The curving walls that border the walkways at the front create a pleasant effect and feature two carved panels, an atomic symbol and celestial bodies, both salvaged from the razed University West Apartments. On the south side is an exposed lower level that opens to a sunken landscaped area. The stone is ashlar but unique in that individual blocks have a rough face and project outward at diverse lengths. Picturesque stone walls, walkways, and landscaping were added to give the East Studio Building its finished and stunning presentation.

The first floor interior of the East Studio Building is appealing, with light-colored wood panels and hanging light fixtures that resemble Japanese paper lanterns. The space includes eighty-four studios, student services and administrative offices for the Jacobs School, and percussion spaces on the ground floor. One floor below ground level is a soundproof rehearsal space for large orchestral groups. The dean's office is located on the fourth floor, with a commanding view of the Jacobs School mini-campus. The East Studio Building provides superior technology and acoustics in teaching and practice facilities that rival any music school in the world. Soundproofing the practice rooms and studios was achieved by utilizing seventeen different wall treatments, extensive wrapping and insulations on the duct system, and a combination of concrete block and specialized drywall. In addition, the interior studio walls have a slight slope inward to discourage echoes, and each room has doors 2¼ inches thick that feature a bottom gasket and a perimeter gasket to further isolate the sound.[2] And finally, to extend the reach of the faculty expertise, each studio features high-definition videoconferencing capabilities that enable the faculty to teach interactively anywhere in the world.

The building was dedicated on October 31, 2013, to coincide with Cream and Crimson weekend. When bestowed in 2008, the $44 million gift from the Lilly Endowment was the largest to date to Indiana University in support of the arts. In 2015, through a generous donation from Cynthia and William Simon, a new plaza was added in front of the East Studio Building. Named Anniversary Plaza, it features a striking steel sculpture by nationally known artist Donald Gummer, who graduated from the Herron School of Art and Design at Indiana University–Purdue University Indianapolis. Combined with the gifts of the Jacobs, Cooks, and countless other donors, the East Studio Building is a powerful tool in bringing the Indiana University Jacobs School of Music to its next level of excellence.

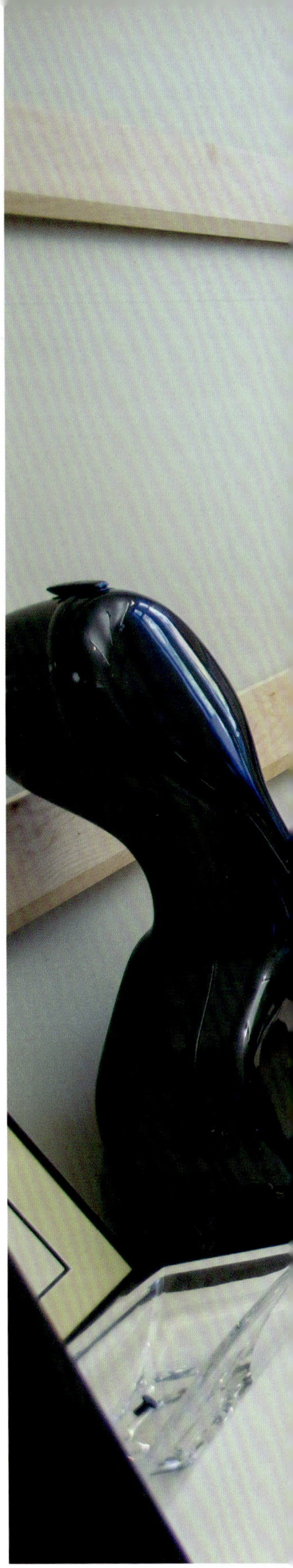

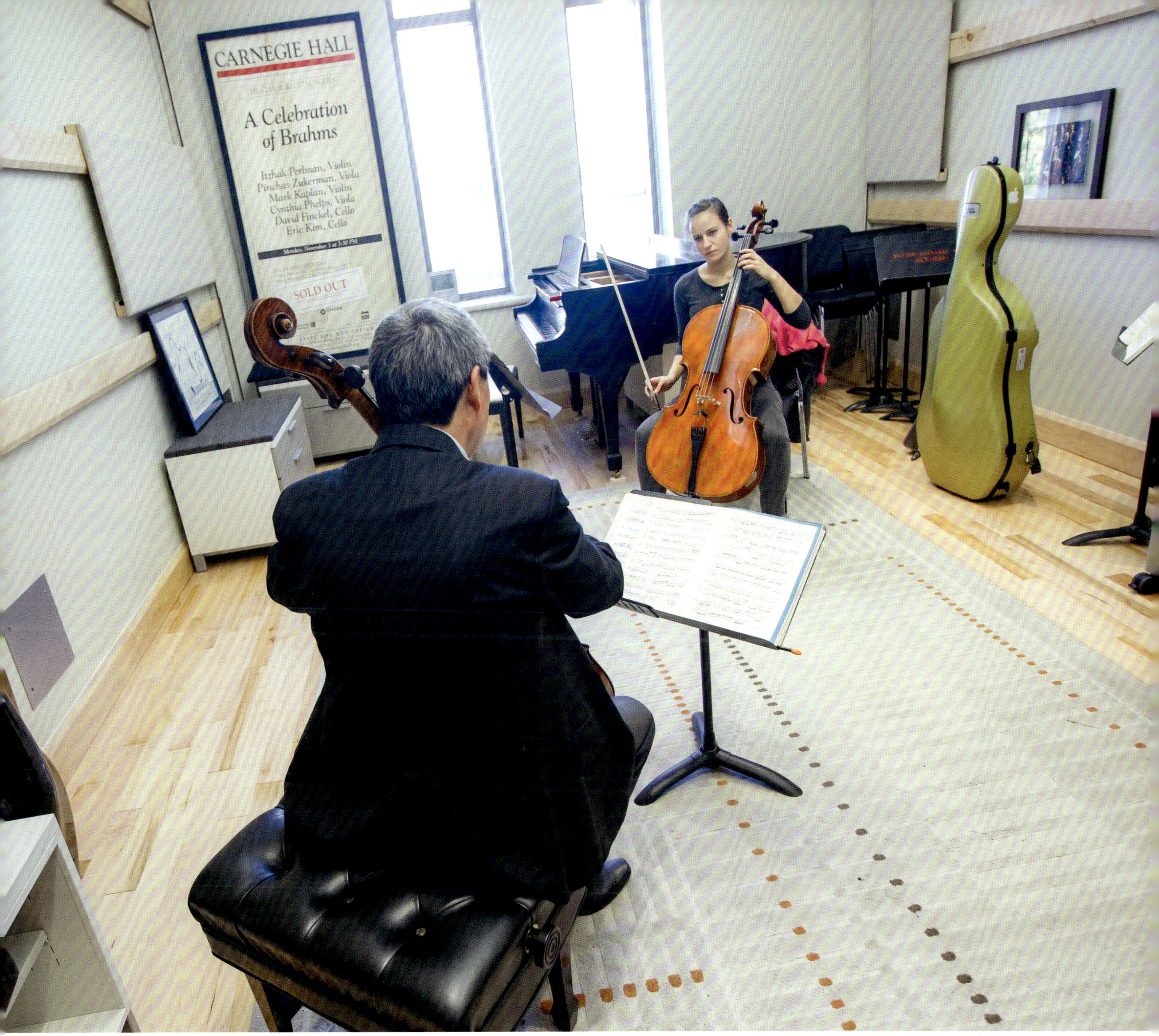

A faculty studio in East Studio Building, 2014. Photo credit: Indiana University.

Elisha Ballantine Hall 1959

ARCHITECT Eggers and Higgins / A. M. Strauss

ARCHITECTURAL STYLE 1960s Modern with Sparse Deco Detailing

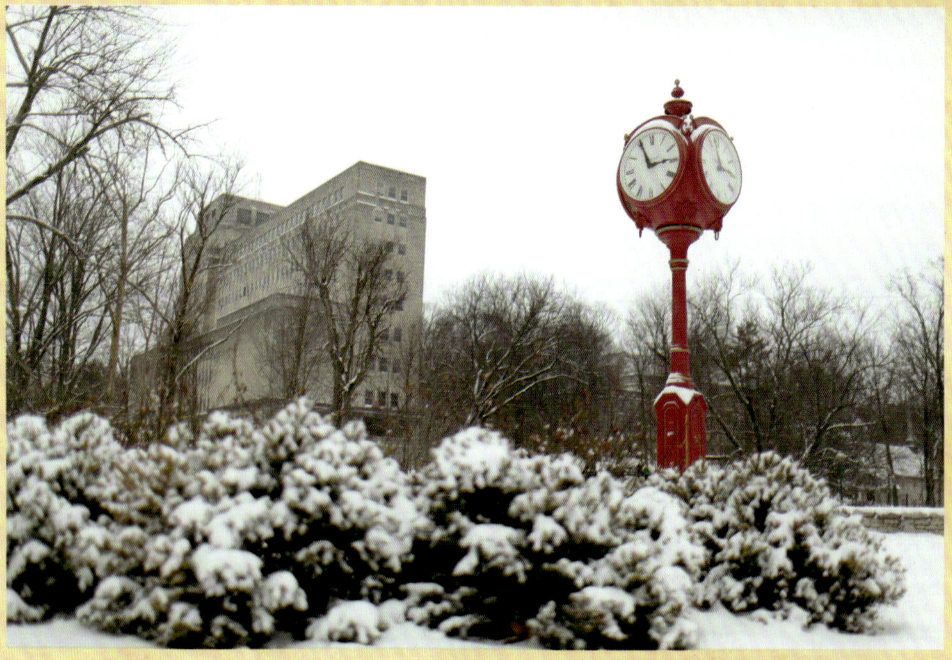

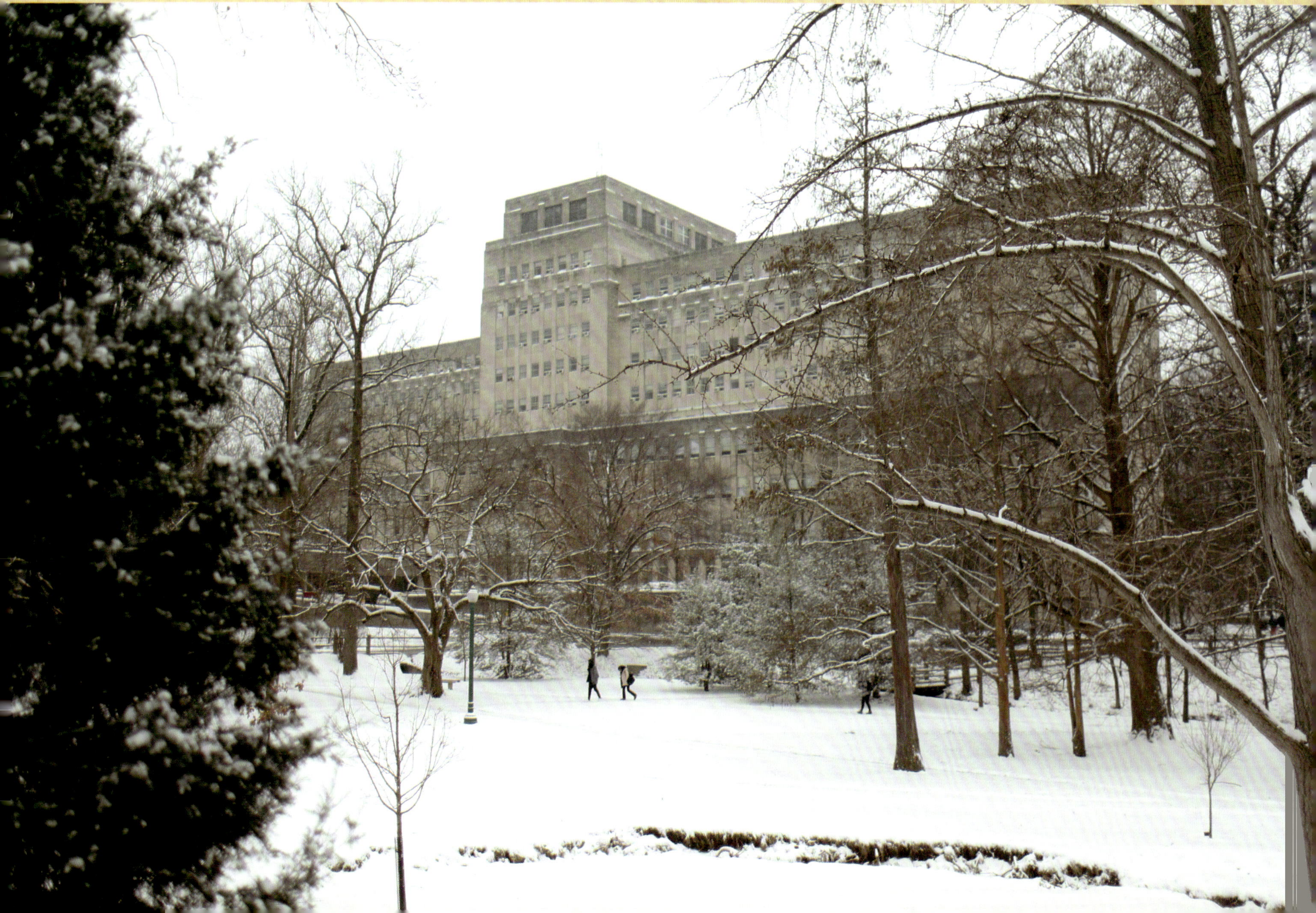

Elisha Ballantine Hall

The "White Giant"

More than stone and mortar, . . . it is a symbol of dedication to a most precious heritage; an expression of faith in the one hope for the future. Located in the very heart of this nation, its massive proportions, its graceful and simple lines, its solid and unadorned simplicity seem to embody the strength, the sincerity, the determination of a people much of whose history reveals through courage, hard labor, and sacrifice its faith in the worth and the dignity of man, its love for peace and justice, its hope for a better world.

—Professor Hulet H. Cook

FOLLOWING THE SECOND WORLD WAR THE UNIversity almost immediately found itself stretched precariously thin on classroom space. With the successful completion of several new housing structures, President Wells noted in his 1948–49 annual report, "The shortage of classroom and faculty and administrative office space still presents many acute and serious problems. . . . The space situation on the Bloomington campus is the worst it has been in the past 50 years."[1] While as early as 1945 the university had applied for and received funding through the state for the planning of a new general classroom building, state support for construction failed to materialize, and by 1950 Wells reported that the situation had become acute.

Finally, in 1954, the project received partial funding through the Indiana State Budget Committee for the 1955–57 biennium, with the rest allocated for the 1957–59 biennium. The architectural firm of Eggers and Higgins of New York was hired to design the new classroom building with the help of an academic committee chaired by Hulet H. Cook, professor of French and Italian. Eggers and Higgins partnered with the Fort Wayne firm of A. M. Strauss and Associates for local oversight of the project.

For Cook this was a lofty opportunity to benefit the future of the College of Arts and Sciences. He explained in a memo to university faculty and staff that "those who have had a share in the planning of this structure have sought to bring together

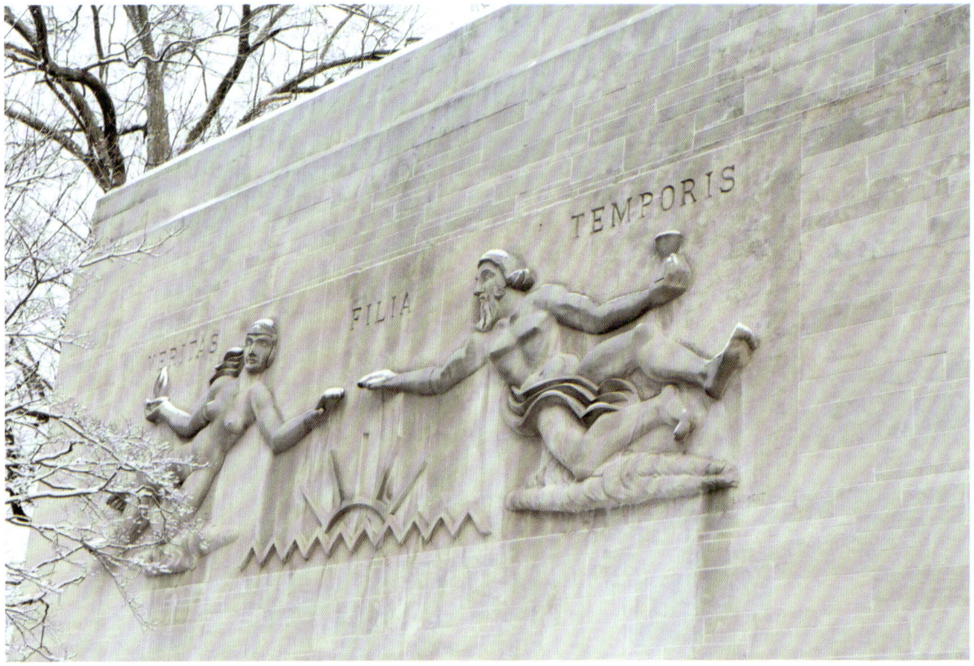

Facing top, North side of Elisha Ballantine Hall; with Beck Chapel on right and campus clock in foreground, 2015. Photo credit: Indiana University.

Facing bottom, East facade of Ballantine Hall, winter 2015. Photo credit: Indiana University.

Above, Robert Laurent's decorative bas-relief *Veritas Filia Temporis* (Truth Is the Daughter of Time) on northwest side of Ballantine Hall, 2016. Photo credit: Indiana University.

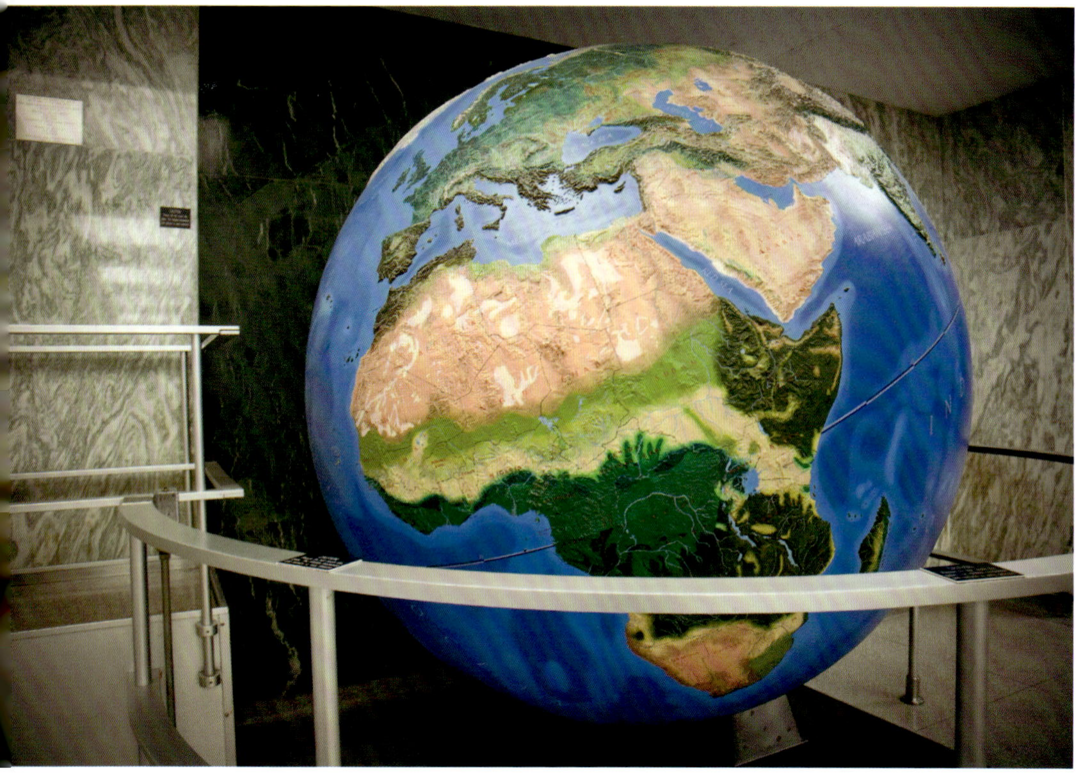

Six-foot geophysical globe in ground-floor foyer of Elisha Ballantine Hall, a gift of Stuart Wilson and Lucia Showalter Wilson in 1961, 2016. Photo credit: Tyagan Miller.

in strong co-operation all of those departments which are so intimately related in their effects upon the student's understanding of his social environment and that of the world in which he lives. Each feature and each facility (even the lounge and roof terrace) has been included for its particular contribution to this end."[2]

Originally referred to as the Humanities and Social Sciences Classroom Building, the unusually tall structure answered the demand for a considerable increase in classroom space for freshmen and sophomores in those fields of study without sacrificing a large segment of land. Wells reported later, however, that other significant compromises were made in order to cut costs that affected the functionality of the building and eventually required renovation. Following pressure from the faculty, two additional floors were added to the tower at the last minute, resulting in a drastically inadequate elevator and stairway system. Furthermore, because the additional two floors were completely exposed to the summer sun above the tree canopy, the elimination of air-conditioning in order to cut costs had an even more dramatic impact.[3] Other concerns included problems with the heating system and the bell system. Despite these pitfalls, Wells was able to report in his State of the University address in 1960 that "in a single year Ballantine Hall has become so integral a part of this University that it is difficult to understand how we operated before it was built. Not least among the advantages of this new building is the bringing together of people in a multitude of disciplines, with opportunities to meet and discuss common problems. Not only do students save time with classrooms, study areas, and faculty members' offices easily accessible to them, but they get a better idea of the interrelatedness of the academic disciplines."[4] Each of Ballantine's issues was later remedied through renovations: the north entrance was expanded, a stairway added, and air-conditioning installed throughout the first four floors. A university press release from 1960 reported that 1,064 different classes met in the new building, which at times held more than a fifth of the student population. Registrar Charles E. Harrell reported "the most important change effected by the opening of Ballantine was the reduction of the number of classes meeting in temporary buildings erected after World War II."[5]

Deemed the "new haven for the humanities" and the "white giant" by the *Indiana Daily Student*, Ballantine Hall, following two and a half years of construction, opened in September 1959. Named in honor of Elisha Ballantine, professor of mathematics, languages, and Greek from 1854 to 1886 as well as interim president in 1884, it was considered "one of the largest structures on an Indiana college campus."[6] The ground floor and the first three stories contained classrooms ranging in size from small seminar rooms to an auditorium capable of seating nearly four hundred, language laboratories, and faculty and student lounges. The upper floors house departmental and faculty offices. Shortly after its completion, the nine-story (with basement) Ballantine Hall was designated by the State of Indiana as the emergency statehouse in the event of a national invasion that would require the government to move to "less vulnerable" locations.[7]

Ballantine deviated dramatically from the Collegiate Gothic style of the old campus. Its monumental and modern towering facade of limestone is noticeably unadorned apart from a bas-relief on the northwest side of the building. It was designed by IU Fine Arts faculty member Robert Laurent (also known for his *Birth of Venus* sculpture in Showalter Fountain) and carved under his supervision by local stone masons directly onto the approximately 10 by 32 feet panel from a half-size-scale plaster model. With an inscription that reads *Veritas Filia Temporis* (truth is the daughter of time), the decorative panel depicts the mythological figure of Father Time and his daughter Truth in the clouds, representative of the fact that "truth is

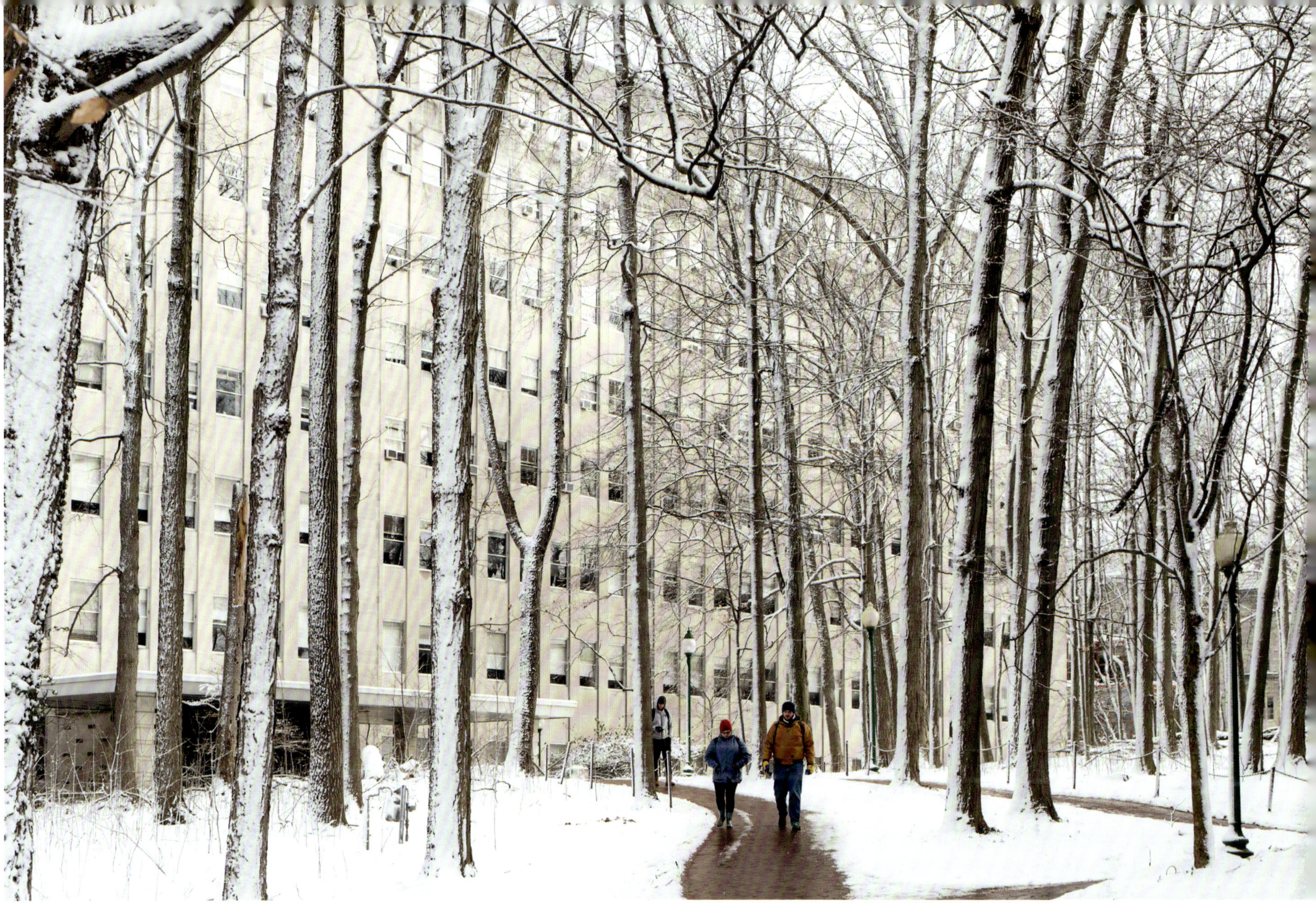

acquired only with the passage of time" and that "civilizations are the result of long history and the acquisition of truth."[8]

The interior of Ballantine Hall, while again rather unassuming and unadorned, features lobby walls on the ground floor in a banded white-and-green marble; first-floor walls in gray, red, and green Italian marble repurposed from a theater in France; and second- and third-floor walls in travertine.[9] Notably, the ground-floor foyer features a colorful, geophysical globe 6 feet in diameter. It was the gift of Stuart Wilson (AB 1920) and Lucia Showalter Wilson (AB 1922) in 1961. The raised-relief globe is cast of laminated reinforced plastic and motorized to revolve once every three minutes. The names of all the countries, major cities, major islands, water features, and longitudinal and latitudinal markings are hand-lettered. On the day that it was dedicated, it was the only known raised-relief globe of its kind.[10] Following the official ceremony, Dr. Walter H. C. Laves, chair of the Department of Government, elaborated on the gift, which serves as a "reminder of the interdependence of nations . . . people and the need for world community based on peace and advancement of human welfare."[11]

Elisha Ballantine Hall remains today an architectural aberration on the IU Bloomington campus. Its scale and height stand out, as does its austere style and sparse stone detailing. Yet, given the university's needs in the 1950s, it has served long and well. Some claim that former president Herman B Wells identified Ballantine Hall as one of his three major regrets, but no written record of this exists. Thousands of IU students would say that it was the epicenter of their classroom experience, particularly during their first two years on campus.

Walkway between Ballantine Hall and Chemistry Building, 2016. Photo credit: Indiana University.

Glenn A. Black
Laboratory of Archaeology /
William Hammond Mathers
Museum of World Cultures 1971 / 1982

ARCHITECT H. Roll McLaughlin of James Associates

ARCHITECTURAL STYLE Pavilion Modern

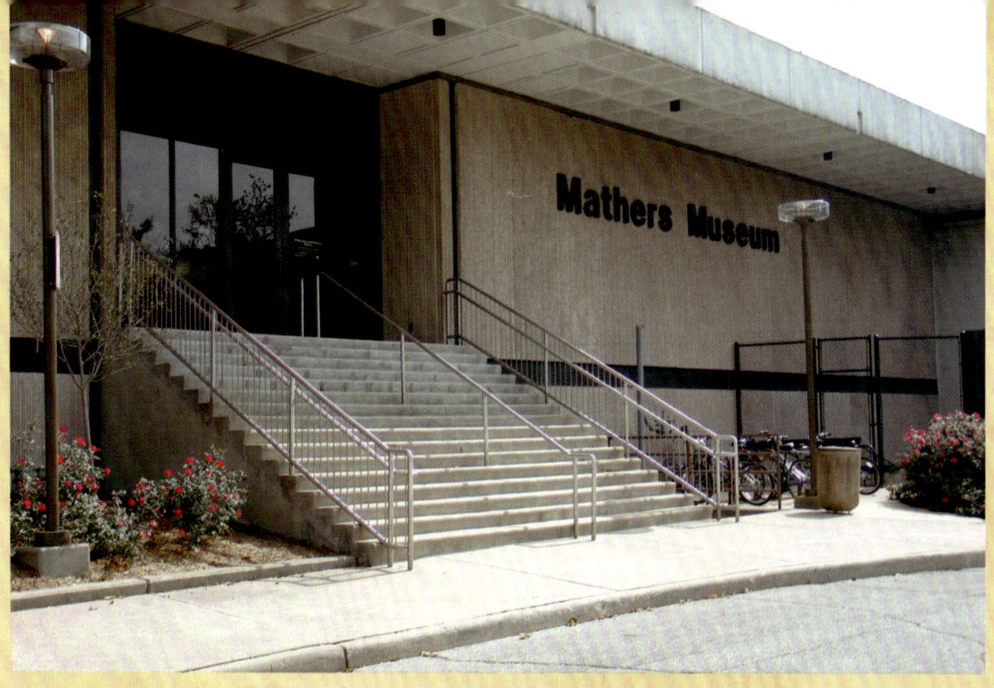

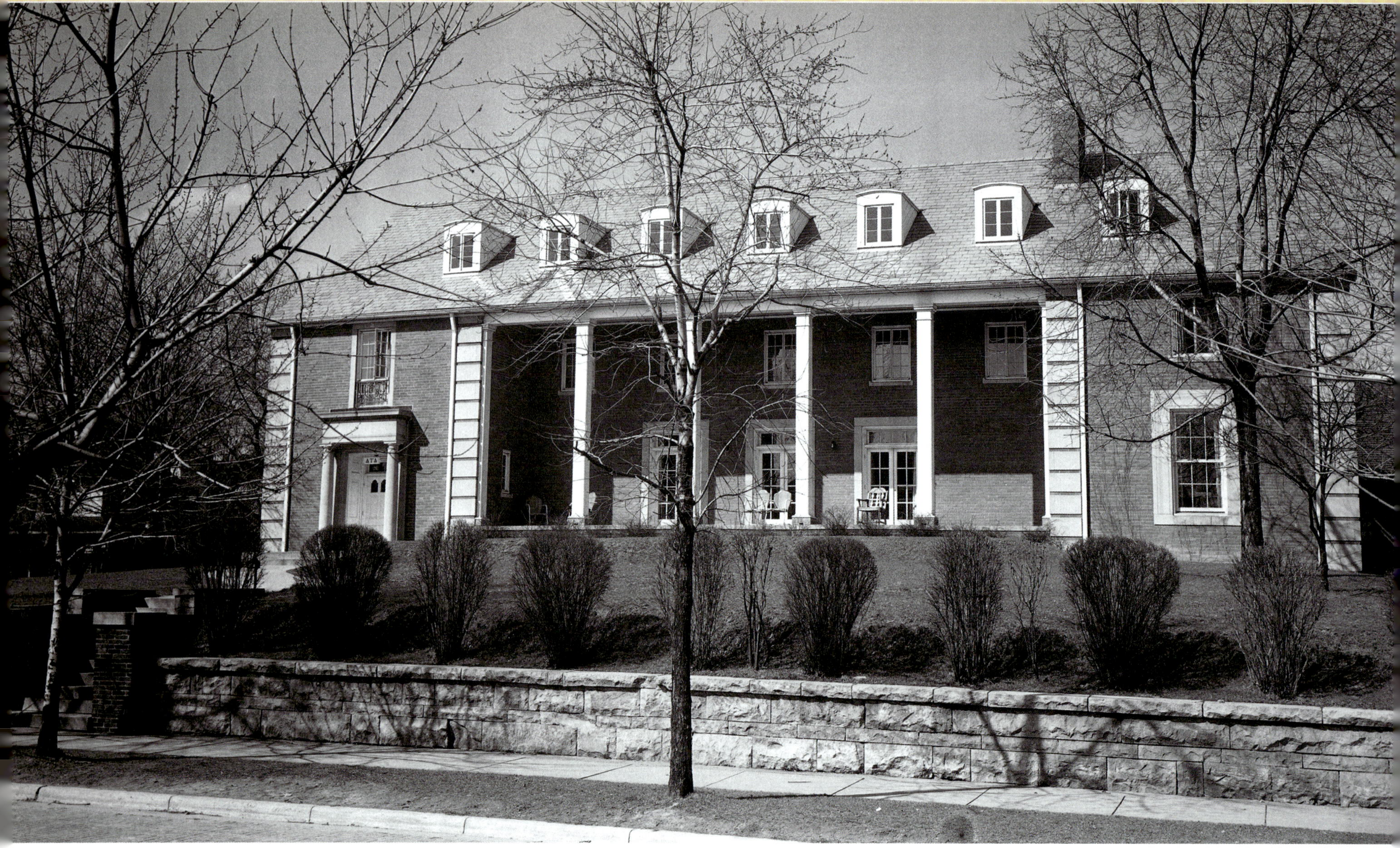

Glenn A. Black Laboratory of Archaeology / William Hammond Mathers Museum of World Cultures

Saving the Past

We are in danger of forgetting the value to be gained in exploring the past.

—Chancellor Herman B Wells at dedication ceremony of the Glenn A. Black Laboratory of Archaeology

MANY YEARS OF PREPARATION ENSURED THAT Indiana University's sesquicentennial in 1970 was appropriately commemorated. The celebration of IU's 150th year was the impetus for the university to construct and establish the Glenn A. Black Laboratory of Archaeology and the William Hammond Mathers Museum of World Cultures in order to preserve and study the histories of Hoosiers and peoples around the world. The Black Laboratory was intended to be the first building in the Hoosier Heritage Complex, a centerpiece of sesquicentennial plans and a pet project of then university chancellor Herman B Wells. Mathers Museum was to complete the project and be called Heritage Hall. (The name was changed to the William Hammond Mathers Museum, but the original name remains on a plaque in the hallway.)

At first glance, the Glenn A. Black Laboratory of Archaeology (1971) and William Hammond Mathers Museum (1982) appear to be one building. They are sited on the west edge of campus on a parcel of land enclosed by Eighth and Ninth Streets and Indiana and Fess Avenues. However, although now joined, they are two buildings with quite distinct purposes. The third component of this complex is the former Delta Tau Delta fraternity house, built in the 1930s in a brick, Jeffersonian style. Mathers Museum was attached to the old fraternity house at completion.

The facade of both laboratory and museum structures, now connected, consists of deeply grooved Salem limestone panels. A horizontal band of black metal runs through the center of the walls, providing a contrast to the vertical texture. As Brian Keith, retired senior scientist from the Indiana Geological Survey, described the exterior: "The panels along with the poured concrete flat roof and overhang give the building a massive and horizontal-dominated appearance that is similar to Prairie Style."[1]

With the 1964 death of its longtime archaeologist field director, Glenn A. Black, the Indianapolis-based Indiana Historical Society ultimately determined that its archaeological collection should be housed where it would get the most use, and, at the time, Indiana University had the only archaeology-anthropology program in the state. Indiana philanthropist and businessman Eli Lilly also decided to transfer his private archaeological collection to the university. However, proper facilities to house these collections were not available (the existing IU Museum had been moved around for years and shoehorned into spaces that were woefully inadequate for heritage

Facing top, Mathers Museum of World Cultures, 2017. Photo credit: Indiana University.

Facing bottom, Delta Tau Delta fraternity house before it was purchased by IU and repurposed for William Hammond Mathers Museum of World Cultures, 1942. P0037333, IU Archives. Photo credit: Herbert Radtke.

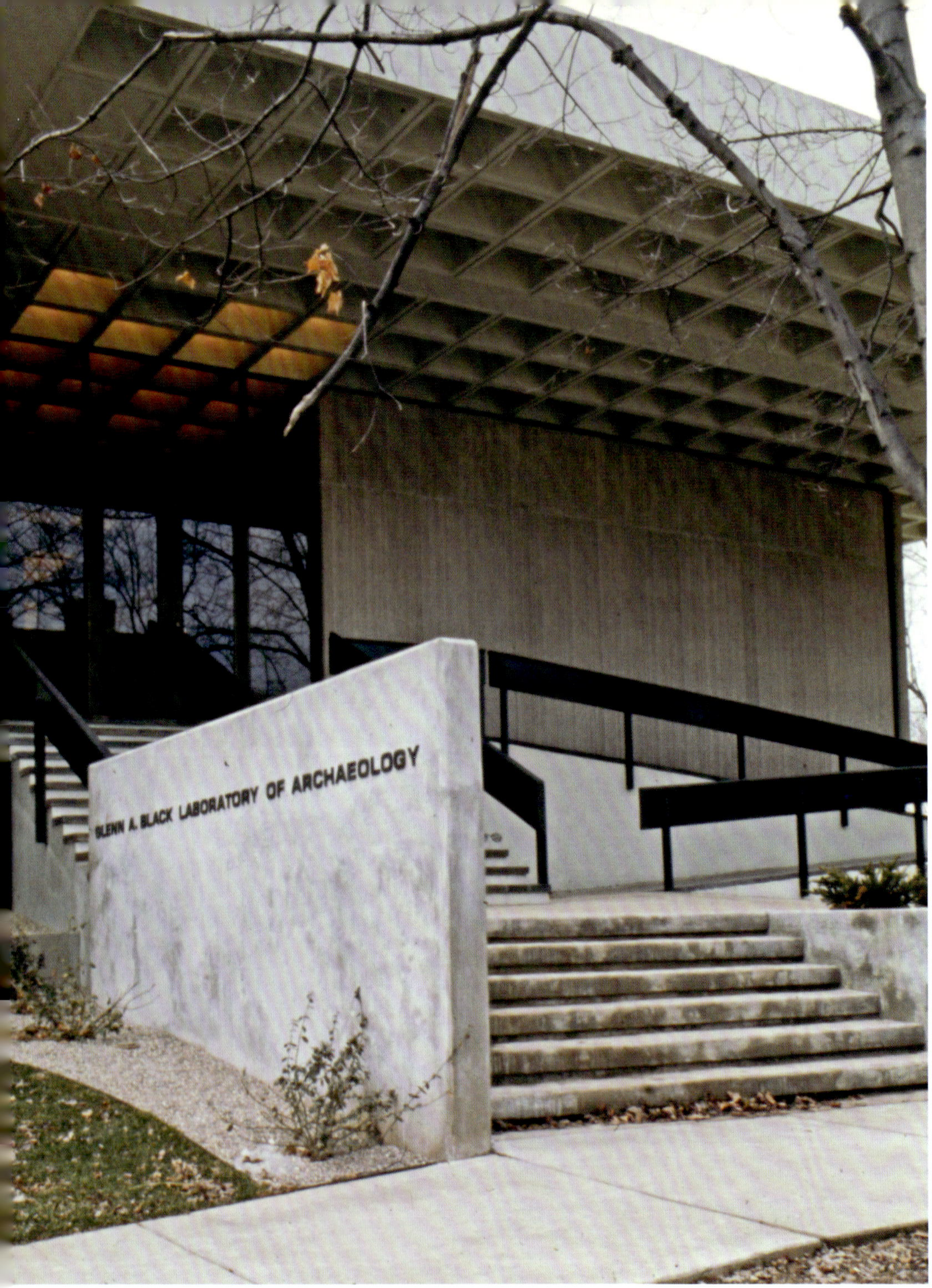

Glenn A. Black Laboratory of Archaeology, undated. P0025868, IU Archives.

collections). Thus, Lilly provided two sizable grants for a new campus space, which, together with money from the university's 150th birthday fund, permitted construction to commence on the Glenn Black Laboratory in 1969.

Architect H. Roll McLaughlin of James Associates Architects and Engineers of Indianapolis planned the laboratory. Its waffle-pattern ceiling extends outside over the entrance, providing a sense of design continuity. The floor-to-ceiling glass wall in the library-seminar room is one of the outstanding features of the laboratory, while throughout the interior the walls are paneled with glass and walnut, simple in design in order to highlight the collection.

The Glenn A. Black Laboratory was created to promote the study and preservation of, and education about, Indiana's rich archaeological heritage. This 17,000-square-foot, two-story structure contains an esteemed research library and seminar space, administrative offices, an auditorium, and exhibit and archival areas. The lower level was fashioned to accommodate the needs of archaeological processing and includes both wet and dry lab space, multimedia collection space, storage for field equipment, offices, and a curation and type collection repository housing millions of archaeological artifacts. The laboratory houses archaeological collections from Indiana, the Midwest, and beyond, including the archives of the Great Lakes–Ohio Valley Ethnohistory Research Project. Directed by Erminie Wheeler-Voegelin, IU professor emerita of history, the project researched and documented land rights for Native Americans throughout the Midwest.

The second building in the complex is the William Hammond Mathers Museum of World Cultures. James Associates Architects and Engineers also designed this building, which was completed in 1982 and dedicated on April 23, 1983. Connected to the Black Laboratory, this structure serves as a permanent home for the university museum, which had been in existence for years but had never had its own purpose-built space. Predecessors housing the museum were Owen Hall, Maxwell Hall, and the Student Building. The Mathers Museum was named for the youngest son of Frank C. Mathers (1881–1938), a professor of chemistry and research chemist at IU. The Mathers family donated the principle funds that supported bringing this building to life.

The footprint of the Mathers Museum was based on the existing layout of the Glenn Black Laboratory, which it then extended southward. The north wall of the Mathers lobby is formed by an old exterior wall of the Black Laboratory. In short, the first building shaped the second, not only in design but in their matching elevation, cladding (reinforced concrete with a limestone veneer), and roofline.

The architects strived to create an interior that would preserve the collections and allow for display and storage as well as provide a learning environment. Climate control was a primary focus, a quality sorely lacking in earlier venues. On the

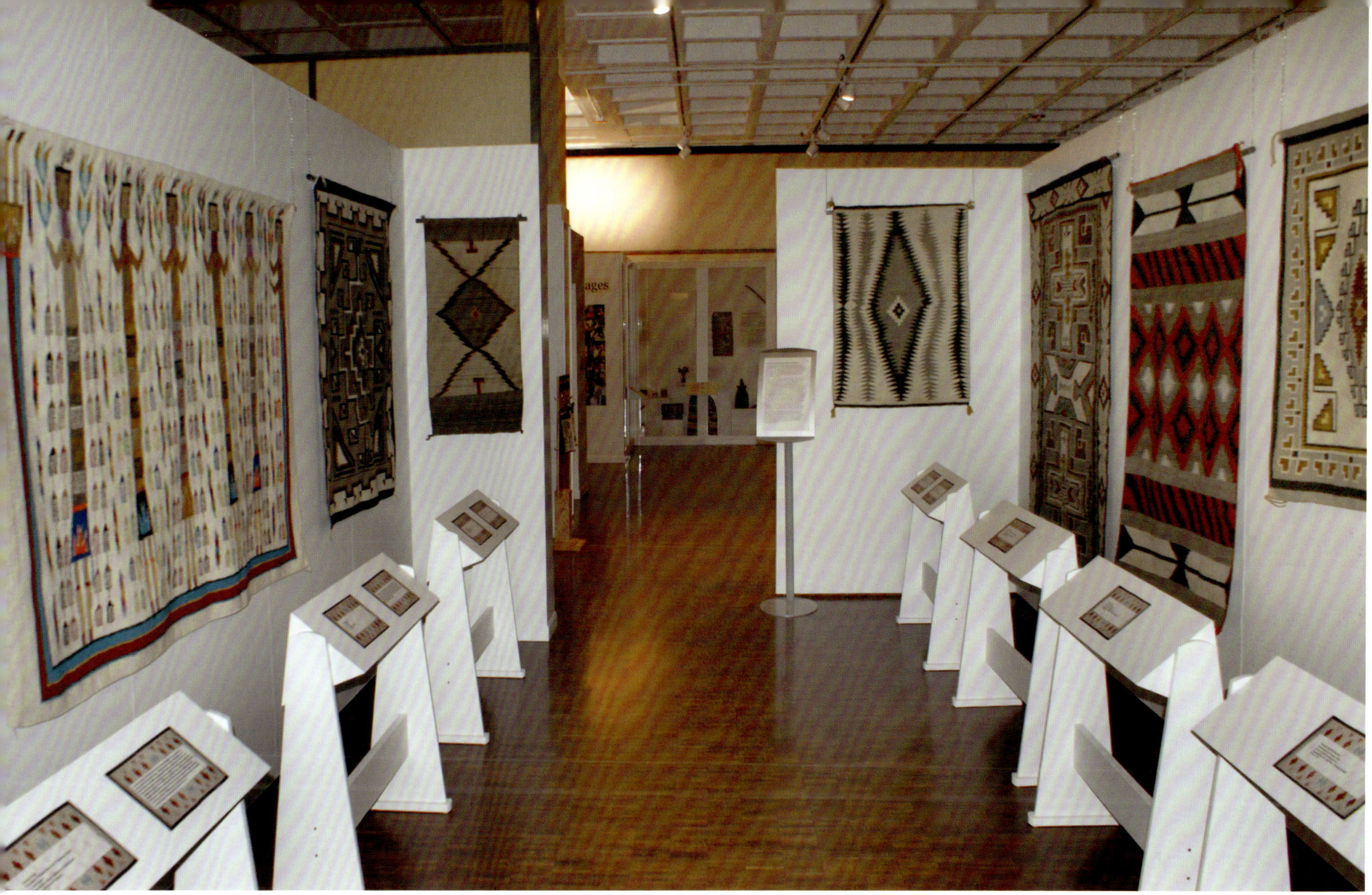

Mathers Museum of World Cultures exhibition *Hózhó: Navajo Beauty, Navajo Weavings*; hallmark waffle ceiling and open floor plan are apparent here, 2016. Photo credit: Mathers Museum, Indiana University.

lower level is a conservation laboratory, along with a catalog office and carpentry shop. The upper level is devoted primarily to a flexible L-shaped exhibit space that can be arranged as one large open room or three smaller galleries, and wide corridors planned to permit display of the collections. The largest area, Exhibition Hall, occupies more than 7,000 square feet of the 26,000-square-foot building. Also on the main level is the gift shop, the merchandise of which reflects the diverse collections within. The former Delta Tau Delta fraternity structure was completely renovated and connected to Mathers to provide offices, a darkroom, and a photo studio.

Intended as a museum of anthropology, history, and folklore, the Mathers Museum of World Cultures currently curates over thirty thousand objects and ten thousand photographs representing cultures around the world, including those of Bloomington and Indiana. Among its treasures are African, Native American, and Latin American exhibits; Indiana history collections; and musical instruments from around the world. The museum's compendium continues to grow, now including collections from the Middle East and Asia. Students with various interests can take advantage of the rotating and traveling exhibitions and regularly scheduled special events for scholars and families in this research and teaching museum. Jason Baird Jackson, appointed director in 2013, notes the strategic location of the museum: "It's at the edge of the university, connecting people between the community, state and world."[2]

Fine Arts Building	1962
ARCHITECT	Eggers and Higgins / A. M. Strauss
ARCHITECTURAL STYLE	Art Deco / Greco Deco

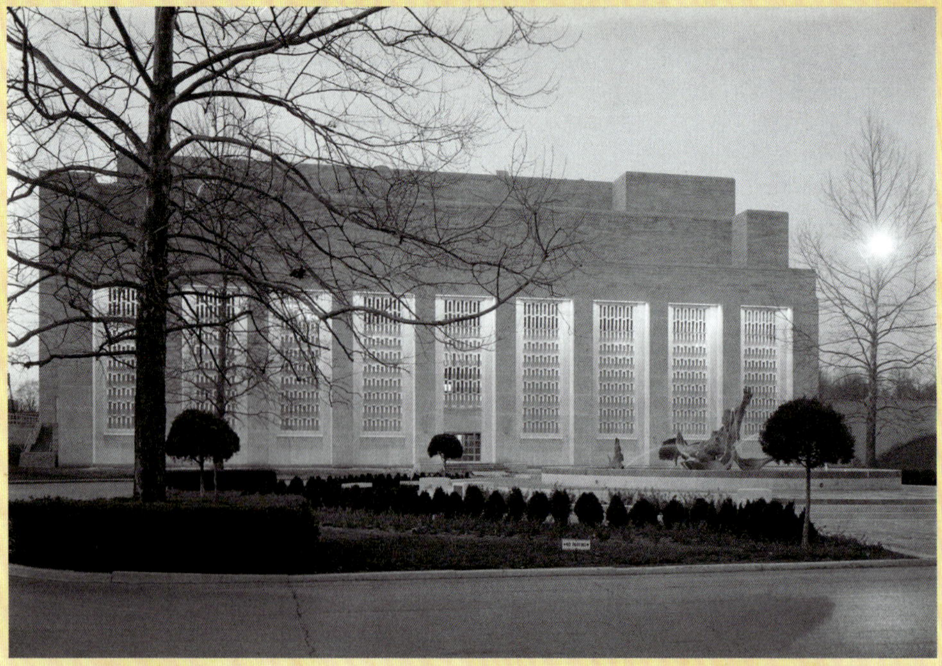

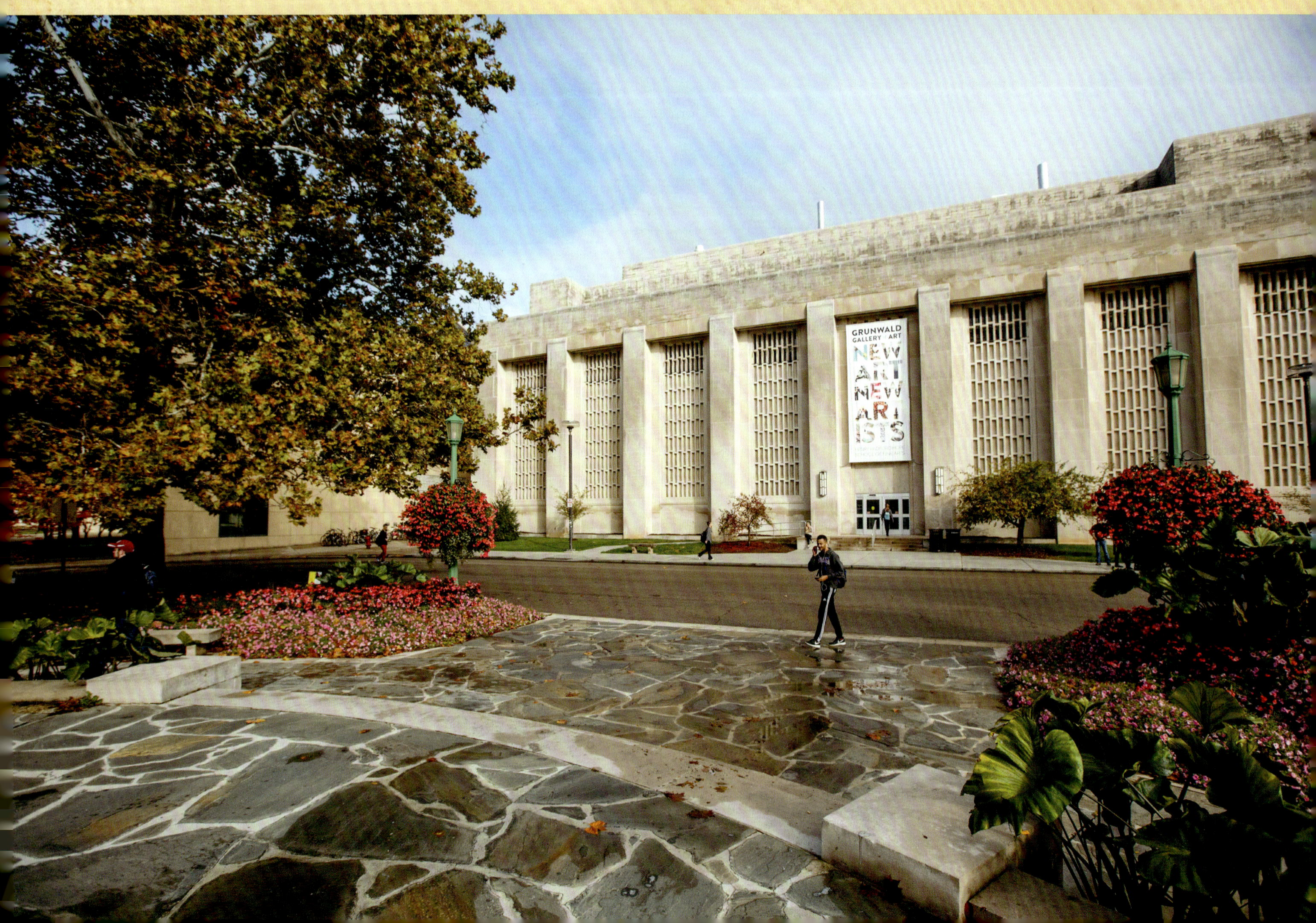

Fine Arts Building

Premier School of Art

Here are the things which differentiate man from animal, the things that in themselves give proof to the spark of divinity our creator placed in each of us. In an era when great forces for conformity press in upon the individual, it is especially gratifying to participate in an occasion which reaffirms the worth of the individual and exalts the expression of his creative talents.

—Indiana University President Elvis J. Stahr Jr. at dedication ceremony

In May 1941, during Henry Radford Hope's on-campus interview for chair of the Department of Fine Arts, President Herman B Wells unveiled a watercolor rendering for a new fine arts center to complete the north side of a plaza dedicated to the arts.[1] Meant to establish the university as the cultural crossroads of Indiana, the plaza, which was originally presented to the trustees in 1939, was a shared vision of campus planners, architects Eggers and Higgins, and President Wells that would bring together the four art forms of drama, music, sculpture, and painting. It called for an auditorium to the east (1941), a Greek open-air theater to the south (which became the Lilly Library 1960), a fine arts building to the north (1962), and a monumental fountain as the central focal point (Showalter Fountain 1961).

At the end of World War II, the visual arts at Indiana University were still in their relative infancy. Founded in 1895 as the Department of Freehand and Mechanical Drawing, the school was the third-oldest art department in the country. Prior to Hope's arrival in 1941, fine arts was housed in several rooms in the old library (Franklin Hall) and boasted only two faculty members. Months after his appointment, three faculty members were added to the department and a building to house the arts was in the plans. As with many other university initiatives, the outbreak of World War II interrupted those plans. Instead, the administration managed to find funds to move the growing department from the library to the newly renovated Mitchell Hall, which now included a small art gallery.

The end of the war and the influx of veterans to the campus caused the arts, along with other departments, to take second place to necessities such as student housing and general classroom space to manage an enrollment that had nearly tripled.[2] Henry Hope reminisced that "With the return of the G.I.'s in 1946, the departmental expansion spurted ahead both in studio and art history, and a lively program of loan exhibitions began to revive talk of a permanent collection. But the building facilities—three one-story frame structures salvaged from army camps and a cement-block gallery measuring 20 by 50 feet—provided neither space nor security, and the proposal for a new art building was at the bottom of the priority list."[3]

Hopes for a permanent structure waned until the mid-1950s, when a proposed fine arts building was again presented to the trustees. By 1954 the department employed sixteen full-time and seventeen part-time faculty and was the only major

Facing top, Southern facade of Fine Arts Building featuring three-story limestone piers with decorative screen detailing, 1962. P0049552, IU Archives. Photo credit: Herbert Hoeltke.

Facing bottom, Summer view of Fine Arts Building from Showalter Fountain, 2014. Photo credit: Indiana University.

Detail of decorative limestone screen on southern facade of Fine Arts Building, 2016. Photo credit: Tyagan Miller.

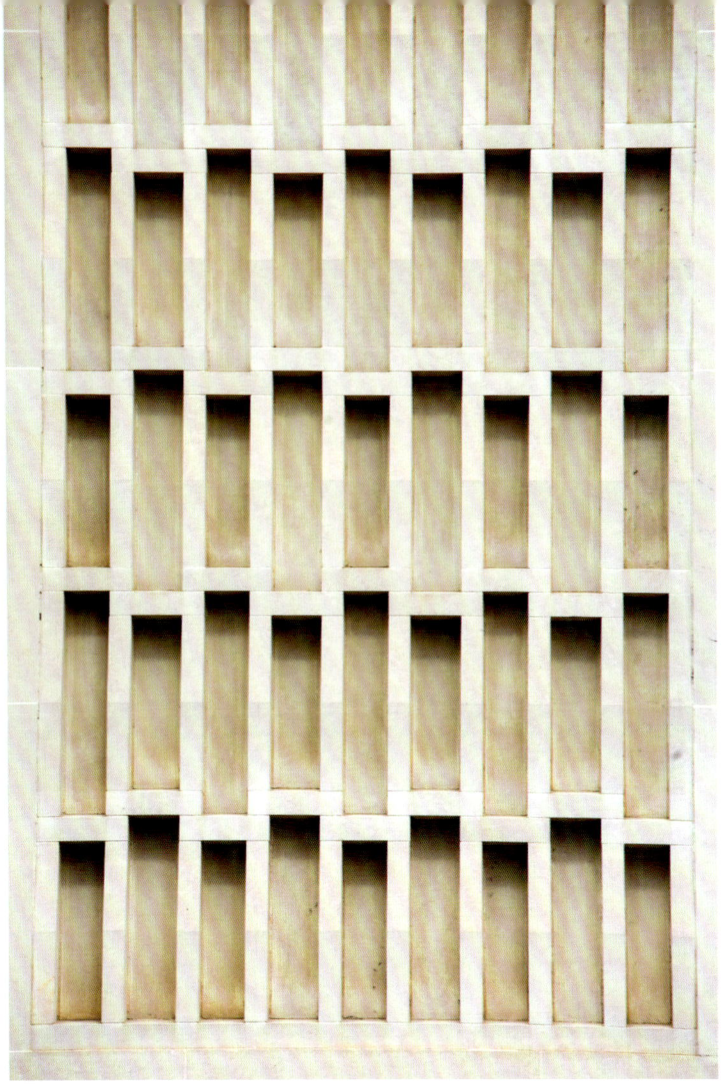

midwestern school without a dedicated art museum. Finally, in 1957, A. M. Strauss of Fort Wayne was hired as the local architect and Eggers and Higgins of New York was commissioned to serve as supervising architect. The external facade of the original plans, a U-shaped orientation with a monumental arcade, was simplified dramatically to a rectangular footprint. However, final construction contracts weren't awarded until 1960.

Constructed of limestone over a steel frame, the resulting five-story structure faces south toward the plaza and the Lilly Library, with Indiana University Auditorium to the east. The exterior facade to the south features a series of bold limestone piers, three stories high, in harmony with the Art Deco style and strong vertical elements of the Auditorium and the Lilly Library. According to the architect Eggers and Higgins, "though the rest of the architecture is dissimilar in each case; thereby harmony is obtained, without monotony."[4] The intervening bays are filled with a decorative limestone screen that shields the interior from excessive sunlight from the south. In contrast, the northern facade is largely glass, giving studios located on that side the advantage of northern light. The upper-level entrance on the east side has an ashlar stone facade and entry.

Once completed, the building housed all the functions of the School of Fine Arts as well as the first permanent university art museum, with more than 9,000 square feet of exhibition space and almost as much for storage. The first and second floors were dedicated predominantly to public space where visitors could view the extensive art collections. The first floor is slightly smaller than the one above, as it is set into the limestone bedrock of the building's sloping site, thus occupying a split level with a 4-foot elevation difference between the entrance and the rear. Directly inside the large front doors to the south is a stunning three-sided red-marble alcove and a marble sculpture, *Eve*, by Jean-Paul Darriau, an IU professor and nationally known sculptor. From this central point, a 260-seat auditorium opens to the left, while the rest of the floor originally included classrooms for art history and a small gallery for traveling exhibits, as well as storage and office space, a workshop, and a receiving dock.

From the marble entry, a divided stairway leads from the first to the second (main) floor. Here, the entire south side consisted of the museum art gallery with movable partitions, a library with stack room for thirty thousand volumes, departmental offices, a room for the slide collection, conference and seminar rooms, studios for ceramics and sculpture, and darkroom space for photography. The top three floors were functional and housed classrooms and studio space for design courses such as weaving and jewelry making, printmaking, drawing, graphic arts, and painting. The fourth and fifth floors are set back on the southern side, allowing for an open-roof terrace for outdoor drawing and painting classes.

The building was officially dedicated on October 21, 1962, with President Elvis J. Stahr Jr. presiding. Others on the program included Henry R. Hope, fine arts chair, and Peter Seltz, curator of painting and sculpture from the Museum of Modern Art, New York. By the time of Henry Hope's retirement in 1971, the museum and its rapidly expanding collections were outgrowing their space in the relatively new building, and with completion of the I. M. Pei–designed Sidney and Lois Eskenazi Museum of Art in 1982, all functions of the fine arts museum, including the art gallery and the library, moved to the new structure. In response, a renovation project at the close of

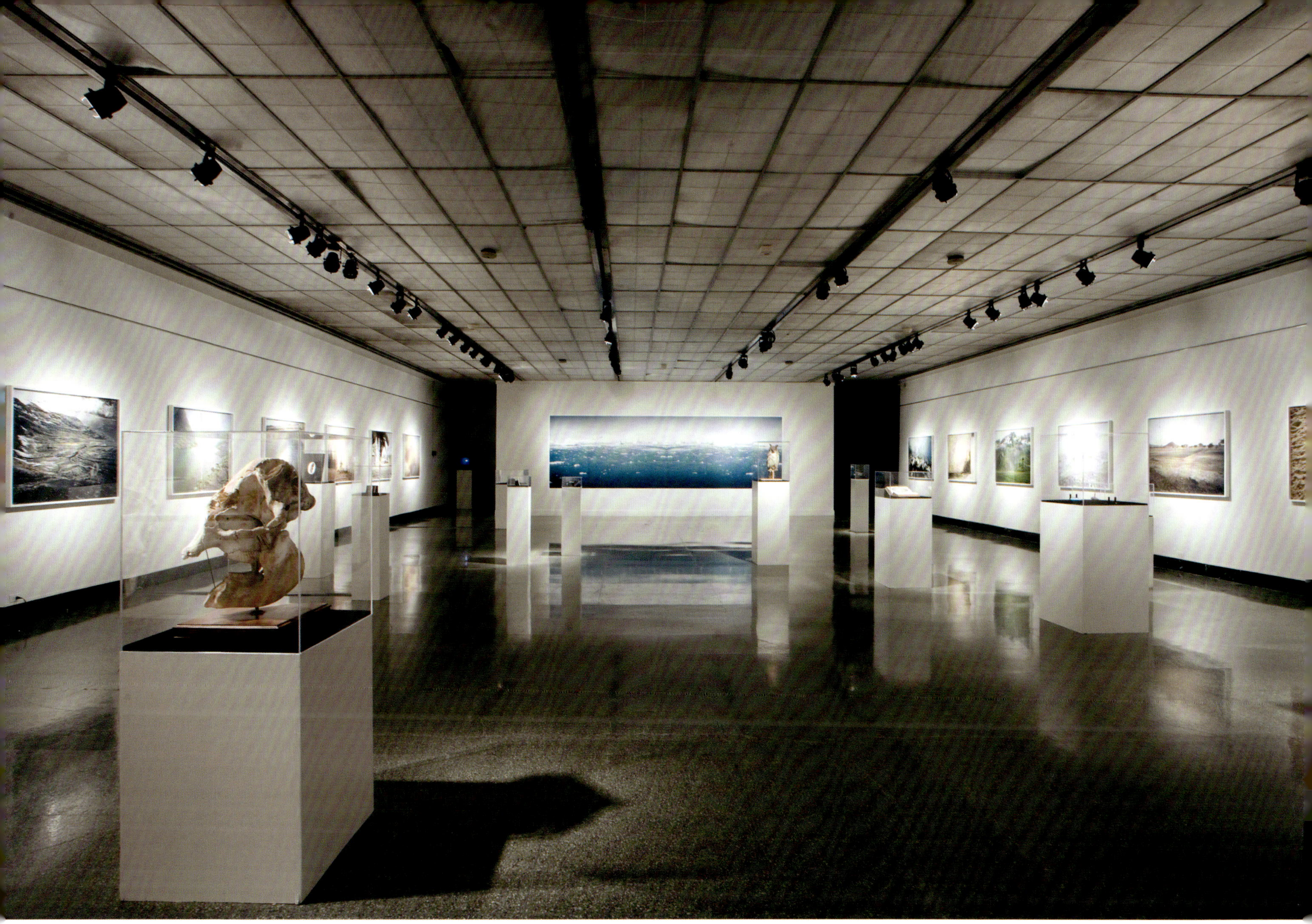

Interior view of Grunwald Gallery of Art, 2017. Photo credit: Kevin O. Mooney, Indiana University.

the decade updated and reconfigured the vacated space into further studio and classroom support. Also, the Grunwald Gallery of Art (formerly the School of Fine Arts Gallery) was added to the south end of the floor. This gallery features rotating exhibitions of contemporary art created by professional as well as student artists.

Following Henry Hope's death in 1989, the school was officially named in his honor. According to President Thomas Ehrlich, the School of Fine Arts was "the direct result of Henry Hope's vision, his determination, his skill as an administrator, his passion for art, and the extraordinary energy that charged his life. . . . Henry Hope never did anything by halves, or in the expected way, or in any way that meant waiting around. If something was worth doing, it was worth doing not only well, but worth doing immediately. As he knew so well, the creative energy of great artists continually drives back the frontiers of how we interpret the world, forcing us to see its new possibilities."[5]

Sidney and Lois Eskenazi Museum of Art 1981

ARCHITECT I. M. Pei

ARCHITECTURAL STYLE Geometric Modern

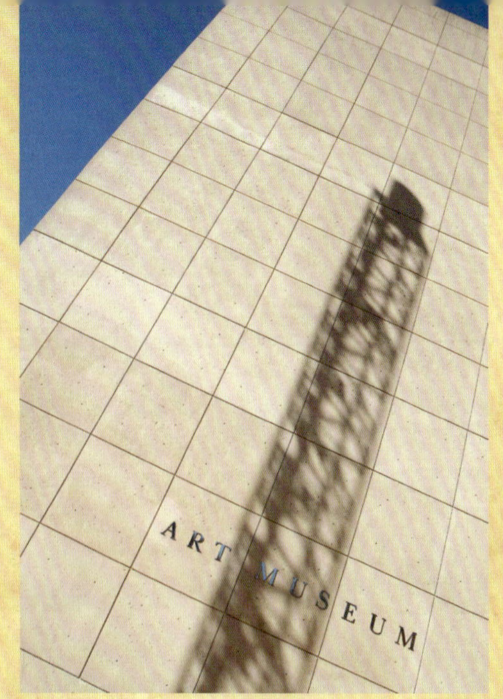

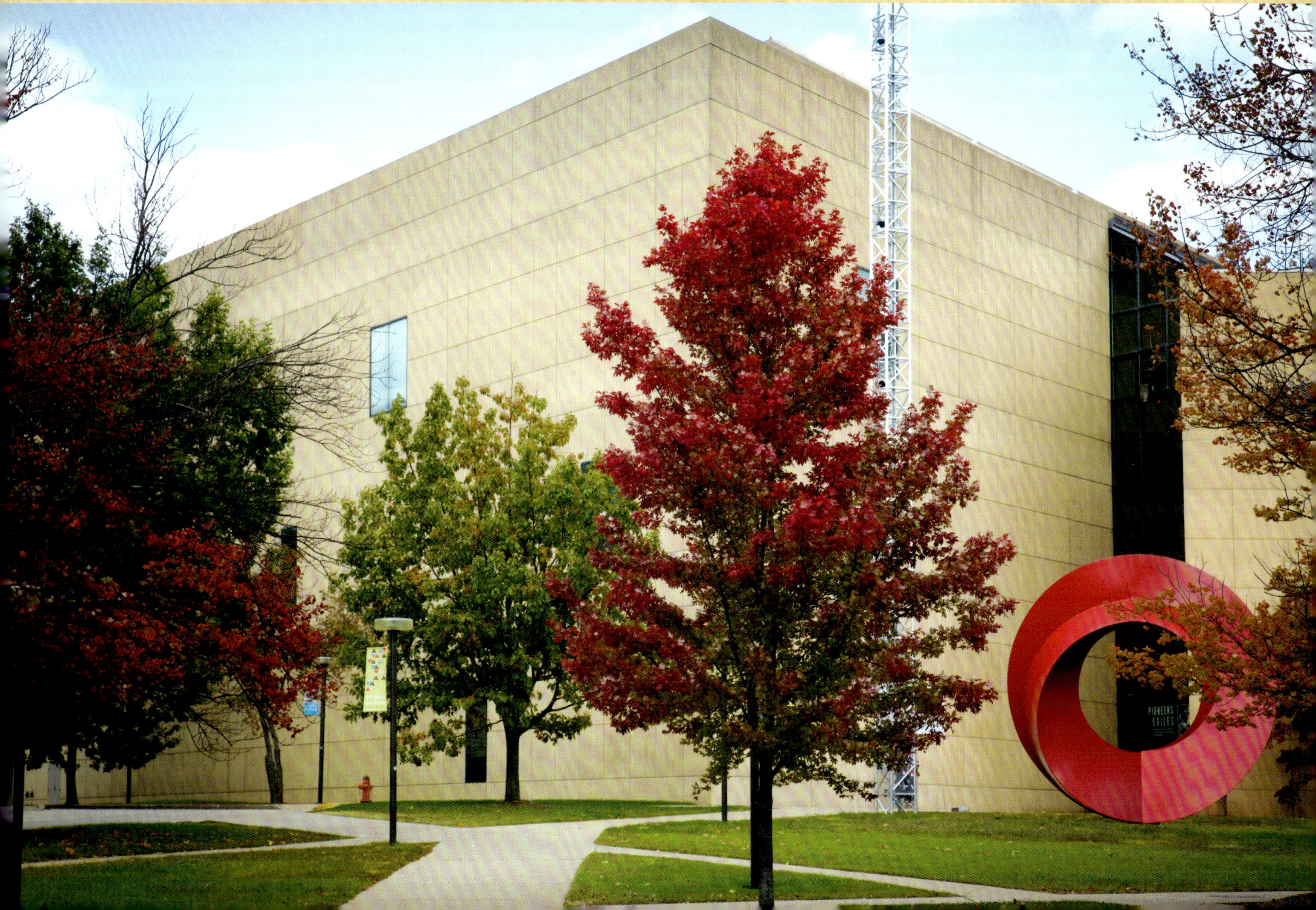

Sidney and Lois Eskenazi Museum of Art

Contemporary amid the Classics

Architecture is a building consisting of volumes, exterior and interior space pulled together so that it reaches the level of art. Functionally, it's not just shelter, it is more than shelter. It also has to reflect, it is a mirror of life. Architecture mirrors human conditions of that time.

—I. M. Pei

The first official art gallery space on the Indiana University campus opened in 1941 when an exhibit titled *Sixteen Brown County Painters* debuted in the small brick addition to Mitchell Hall, the first space designed solely for this purpose. Over the next forty years, first in Mitchell Hall and then in additional campus spaces, a variety of art exhibitions were presented, and the potential for the IU School of Fine Arts to become a major regional resource was apparent. All that was needed was a structure commensurate with the university's aspiration to have an exceptional exhibition space. From that early effort to display collections evolved a dream for Indiana University to have one of the finest university art museums in the United States.

The university had long planned for a major art museum and regional cultural resource center. In 1939, President Herman B Wells included a site for such a museum as part of the plan for a Fine Arts Plaza, which would eventually include the Indiana University Auditorium, Lilly Library, Fine Arts Building, and Showalter Fountain. Campus-wide excitement greeted IU trustee approval in April 1976 to commission I. M. Pei as architect for the $10 million project. Pei had recently completed the East Wing of the National Gallery of Art in Washington, DC, and several other highly visible projects around the world, and was actively sought after by major clients.

The selection of Pei had been an intricate matter involving consideration of several well-known architects with major museum design experience. Following discussions lasting well over a year, the selection committee, chaired by Chancellor Herman B Wells, narrowed its choices to two candidates: Louis Kahn and I. M. Pei. Both were internationally renowned and enjoyed outstanding design reputations, which would facilitate the necessary fund-raising campaign. As a nonacademic building, the proposed art museum did not qualify for customary state funding support and therefore required substantial gift funds if it were to become a reality. When Louis Kahn unexpectedly passed away, the selection was decided in favor of the Pei firm in New York, and the university was off on a great planning adventure, which included several site visits to successful art museums around the world.

Ground breaking took place in 1978, and the dedication, accompanied by prodigious accolades for the building's unique design, was celebrated on October 13, 1982. Prior to the opening, the Sidney and Lois Eskenazi Museum of Art was one of the most controversial structures ever designed at IU Bloom-

Facing top, Eskenazi Museum of Art, undated. Photo credit: Indiana University.

Facing bottom, Sidney and Lois Eskenazi Museum of Art, with Rob Shakespeare's Light Totem and *Indiana Arc* to the right, 2016. Photo credit: Tyagan Miller.

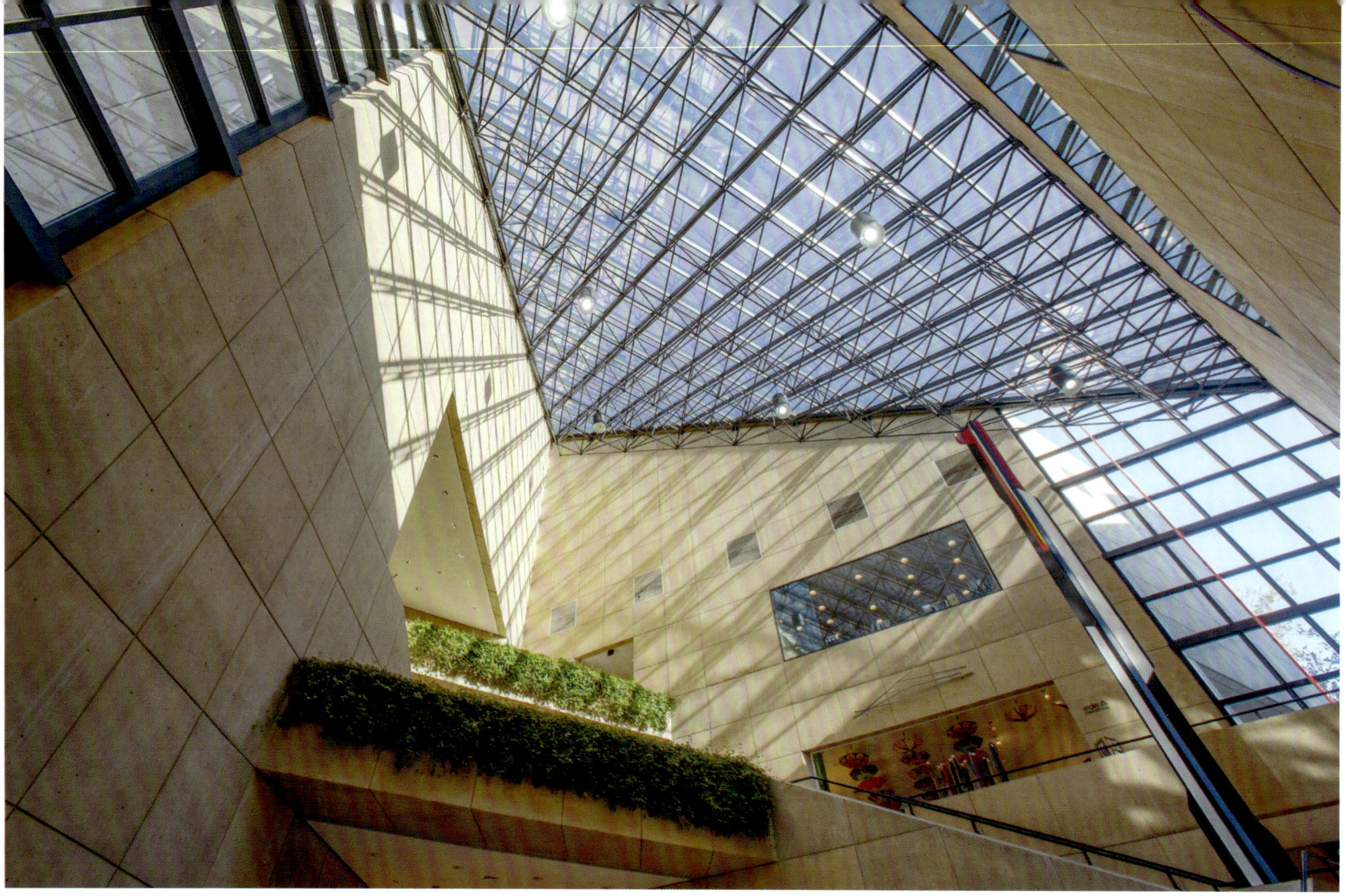

"The atrium is neither an outdoor space nor an indoor space. It's sort of mediating the space between the two."—I. M. Pei, 2016. Photo credit: Indiana University.

ington. On a college campus where traditional Collegiate Gothic architecture is expressed predominately in Indiana limestone, I. M. Pei designed a Modernist museum using cast-in-place concrete. Pei's concession to neighboring buildings, all constructed of limestone, was to add buff coloring to the art museum's concrete mix so the building would visually harmonize with its surroundings. Skeptics in the university community continue to debate the success of this sidestep from tradition, but most observers believe the museum fits in well with its environs and applaud its diverse contribution to the architectural fabric of the Bloomington campus.

The building was oriented on an axis that placed the museum not only as a destination in itself but on a walking path for students passing between the Indiana Memorial Union and the Wells Library. In that way, students could gain a passive exposure to the magnificent art collections of the university while making their way to class or to the library. Pei wanted this museum to be a "conduit," saying, "When you are designing an art museum, you want to expose the largest number of people possible. You want to put your building in the mainstream."[1] As hoped, students indeed pass through the Eskenazi Museum of Art all day long, as do the nearly one hundred thousand visitors who enter each year.

I. M. Pei chose the triangle as the primary building form. Pei's penchant for the triangular shape was reinforced by his great success with the triangle in the design of the East Wing of the National Gallery of Art, and he easily found a way to transition that concept to the building site on the Bloomington campus. Two massive triangular building blocks, one larger than the other, were connected by a taller, 110-foot triangular atrium featuring a monumental skylight that faced south toward the older, more established part of the IU campus. The skylight introduced natural light to the atrium's large entryway below. Pei made the following comment about the importance of the atrium to the building's design, "The atrium is neither an outdoor space nor an indoor space. It's a sort of mediating space between the two. And I think it makes the entrance into the building much less abrupt. Having entered the space, then you move."[2] Pei also placed a canted grand stairway to the upper floors from the atrium ground level, giving the building an overall appearance of a structure void of any right angles.

Three permanent collection gallery spaces of 10,200 square feet each were included in the west triangular building block, while a special collection gallery of 6,000 square feet, an art library of 13,500 square feet sufficient to hold 90,000 volumes, and various administrative offices and conservation laboratories were housed in the larger east triangular wing.

Today the Eskenazi Museum of Art ranks in the upper echelon of college and university museums. In 2015 it was named one of the "Best University Art Museums in America" by *Architectural Digest*. Its permanent collections include works by

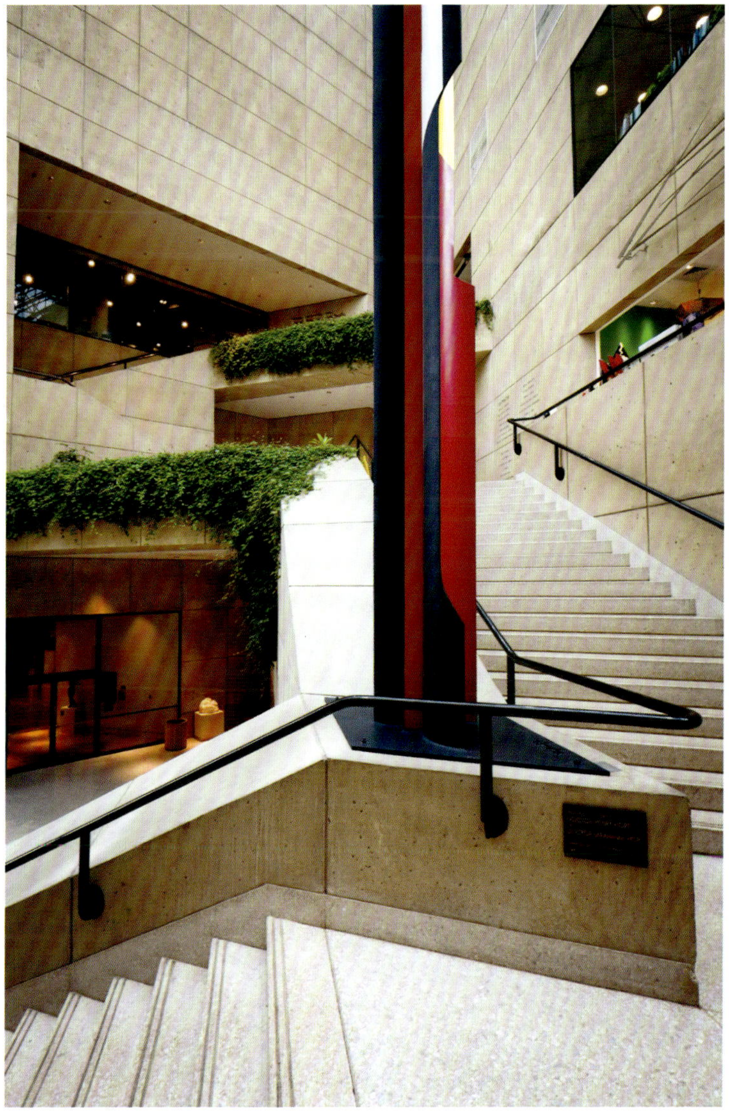

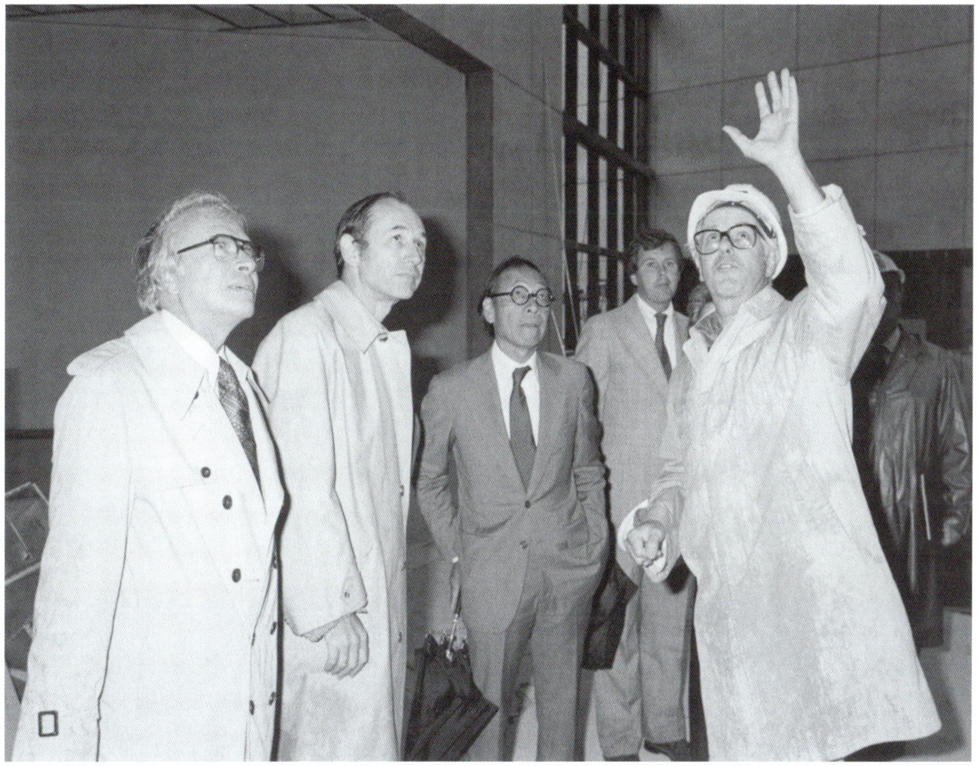

Above, University architect Ray Casati, I. M. Pei project manager Ted Musho, I. M. Pei, Vice President Terry Clapacs, and art museum director Tom Solley inspecting progress on the construction of the museum, 1980. Photo credit: Indiana University.

Left, Indiana Totem by Bernard Rosenthal (1989) on stairway leading from Eskenazi Museum of Art lobby, 2016. Photo credit: Tyagan Miller.

Pablo Picasso, Jackson Pollock, Henri Matisse, and Claude Monet, and its remarkable inventory features works of art from Africa, Oceania, the Americas, Ancient Greece, and Rome, all strengths of this outstanding museum. Building on the tradition of its first director Henry Radford Hope, the Eskenazi Museum of Art has enjoyed visionary leadership throughout its history. These leaders, including Thomas Solley and Heidi Gealt, have directed the art museum on an ever upward course of first-rate scholarship and wise investment in collecting.

In 2016, IU graduates Sidney and Lois Eskenazi presented the largest cash gift ever made to the IU Art Museum, the major contribution toward its renovation. They also bequeathed nearly a hundred works of art from their private collection. The Eskenazis live in Indianapolis and are philanthropists in the community as well as longtime IU benefactors.

Lee Norvelle Theatre and Drama Center 2002

ARCHITECT MGA Partners Architects

ARCHITECTURAL STYLE Contextual Modern / Neo-Classical

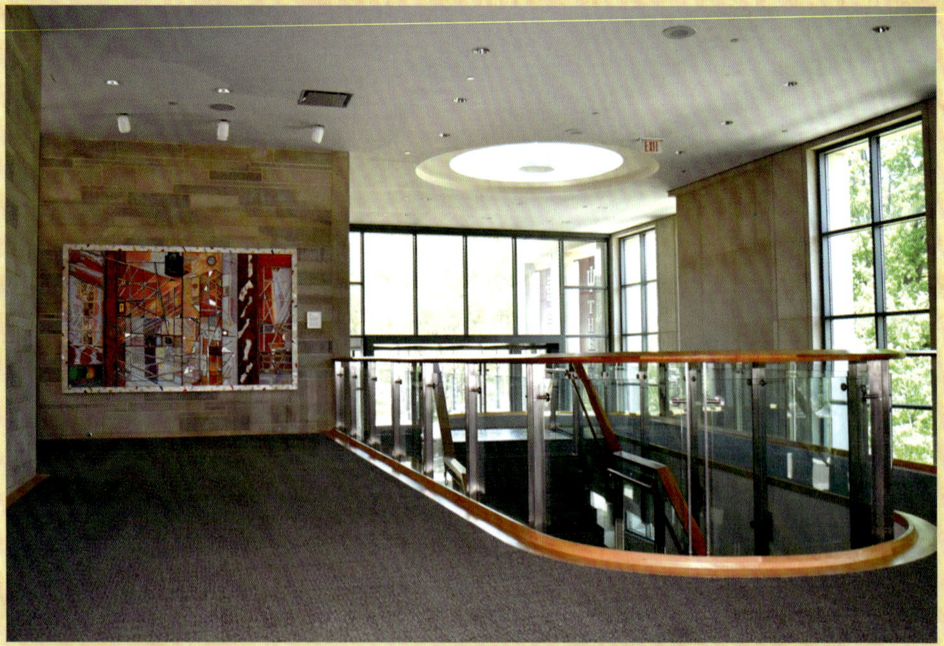

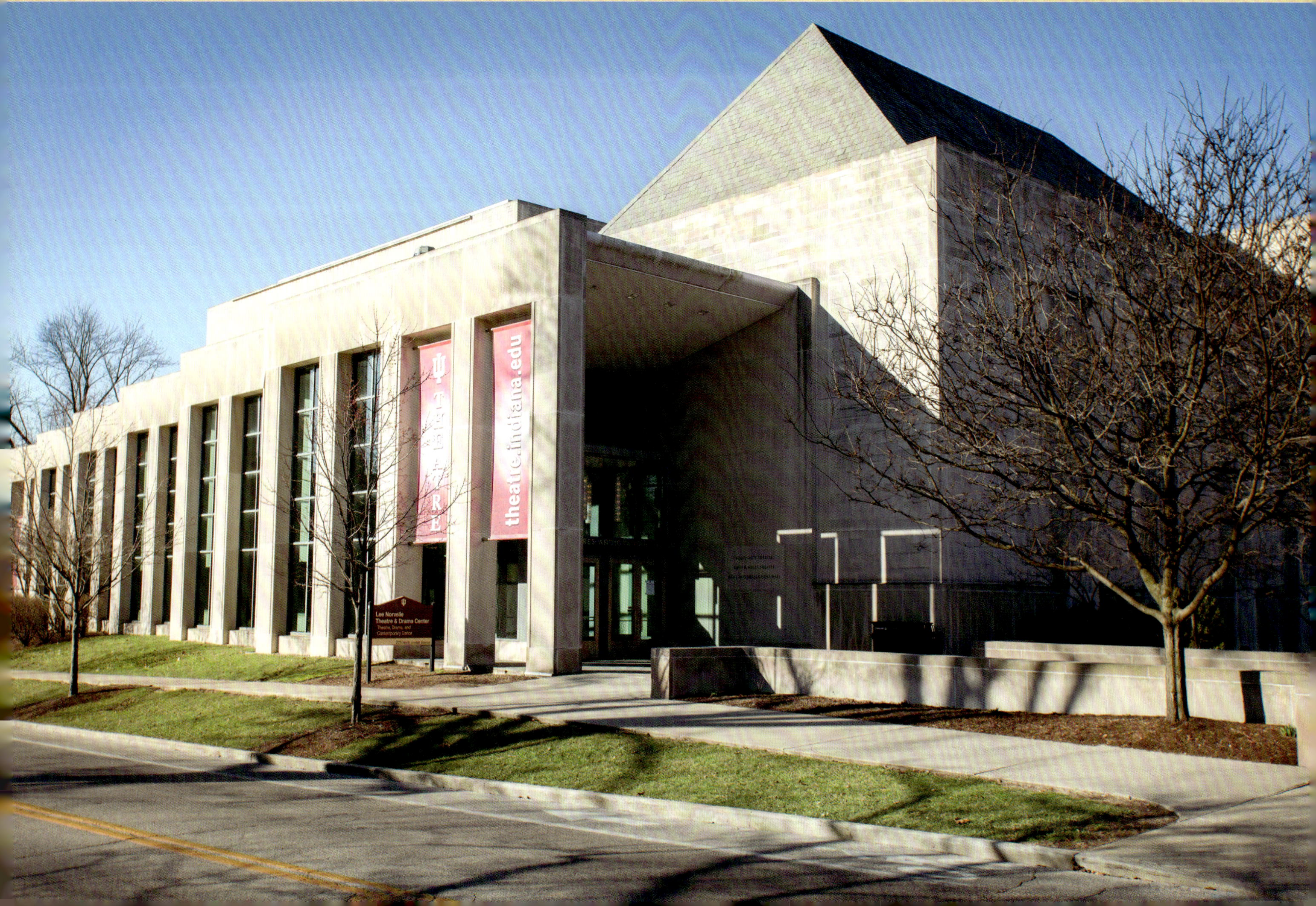

Lee Norvelle Theatre and Drama Center

Union of Art and Education

In conceiving the design of this building, it was our goal to create a unique vessel—a great pot from which the most savory flavors of art and education can simmer and be served. It is our hope that this building will occupy a special place on this beautiful campus and provide—through the years to come—beloved memories of the learning experiences and performances that occur here.

—Daniel O. Kelley of MGA Partners at dedication ceremony

WITH ROOTS DATING BACK TO THE CAMPUS AT Seminary Square, the study of theater and drama at Indiana University began with a student Shakespeare Club, which as early as February 1883 was meeting regularly at the home of Orrin B. Clark, professor of English language and literature. Over the coming decades, interest in theater and drama continued to grow; by 1915 there were several active drama groups on campus and Edgar Frazier offered the first theater course, the Staging of Plays, in the Department of English. Ten years later, the addition of Lee Norvelle to the English faculty shaped the path of the future program as he quickly began to expand the theater curriculum and organize student productions. He encouraged the university administration to provide additional resources and support for theater studies as he was aware that theater curriculum could be considered a frivolous luxury for a major state university. Norvelle quickly consolidated the disparate campus dramatic groups under a singular umbrella known as the University Players and sought a location for a dedicated performance space. After a few temporary homes, a theater wing opened on the east end of the new Indiana University Auditorium in 1941. For Norvelle the opening of the Little Theatre, as it was known, "was literally entering the 'Promised Land.'"[1]

By the mid-1960s, with advances in technology and increasing enrollment, faculty, and course offerings, the Department of Speech and Theatre was bursting at the seams and was forced to spread into nearby houses for additional space. While the Board of Trustees acknowledged the need for a home for the emergent department, funding was slow to materialize. Consistently ranked among the top theater education programs in the nation, in 1989 the need was further articulated when the National Association of Schools of Theatre called into question future accreditation of the department, noting that "the most serious problem confronting the Department of Theatre at Indiana University is its facilities. The program operates in a physical plant which is inappropriate for its stature."[2] Months later, a new proposal was submitted to the Board of Trustees for the construction of a multiuse complex connected to the existing Indiana University Auditorium to house the Neal-Marshall Black Culture Center and the Lee Norvelle Theatre and Drama Center, two disparate programs that nonetheless had significant program overlap and together would contribute to the reputation of IU as a center for arts and culture.

Facing top, View from second floor of the Lee Norvelle Theatre and Drama Center featuring *Opening Night,* a mixed media piece by Rudy Pozzatti, commissioned and presented by the Theatre Circle to the Department of Theatre and Drama. Photo credit: Indiana University.

Facing bottom, Northeast entrance and east facade of Lee Norvelle Theatre and Drama Center, 2017. Photo credit: Tyagan Miller.

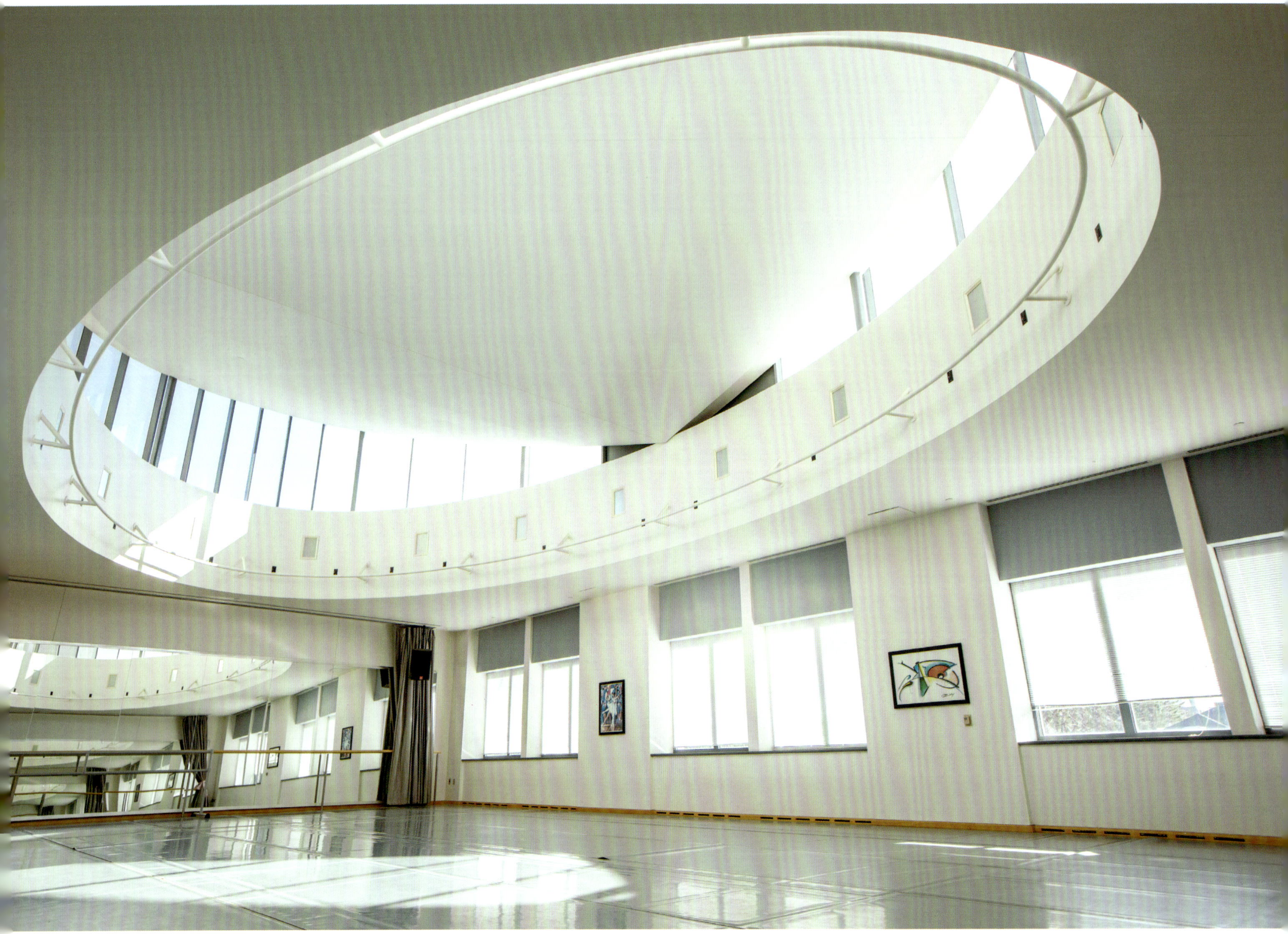

Elliptical ceiling above two-story dance studio in Lee Norvelle Theatre and Drama Center/
Neal-Marshall Black Culture Center, 2017. Photo credit: Tyagan Miller.

The project, which would extend east to Jordan Avenue and south to the Jordan River, allowed for more effective and cost-efficient use of a restrictive space through shared quarters, such as rooms for classes and services, and would present a new face in the heart of the arts district. While the design was to blend with the surrounding architecture of the campus, the proposal envisioned that "the Auditorium, Theatre and Drama Center, and the Neal-Marshall Center . . . must have clearly defined and distinctly separate architectural identities. The exterior . . . should promote a sense of 'occasion' when performances or special events are taking place."[3]

With funding from the state legislature and numerous private donations, the project moved forward and ground was broken in October 1998. The architectural firm of MGA Partners of Philadelphia delivered a sophisticated, linear building to the university that was unique but in harmony with the surrounding architecture. The entire complex is faced with Indiana limestone complemented by vertical elements and a custom ashlar pattern that blends well with the Indiana University Auditorium. The main entrance to the east features a long, folded limestone wall with windows facing Jordan Avenue and a dramatic arcade inside that creates an impressive public presence, especially when the interior is illuminated on performance nights. Distinctive roof shapes give each of the major venues an exterior identity behind the unifying facade. The south entrance is highlighted by an intimate courtyard and terrace opening out to the wooded campus and the pedestrian paths along Jordan River. The west side connects directly with the IU Auditorium.

The east end of the building houses the primary performances spaces, unified by a sleek, singular two-story lobby of limestone, wood, and glass facing Jordan Avenue. Toward the center, the 439-seat Ruth N. Halls Theatre—a more traditional venue—includes an orchestra pit capable of seating thirty musicians for large musical productions, high-end technical equipment, and limestone gallery walls accented by natural cherry and maple finishes native to Indiana along the side aisles. Fiber-optic lights dot the upper walls and ceiling, symbolic of the Indiana sky. Toward the north, the Wells-Metz Theatre is a 236-seat experimental venue with a flexible performance space for nontraditional performances. The room features movable audience seating so the theater can be customized to each performance as well as a full stage trap room and overhead suspension grid allowing for performer movement throughout the area. As the architects note, "in this theater, the emphasis is on engagement rather than comfort."[4] The Grand Hall for the Neal-Marshall Black Culture Center occupies a third space toward the south end. Facilities within the complex also include studios, high-tech classrooms, rehearsal rooms, and costume and scenery shops and storage, as well as the administrative offices of the department.

The Theatre and Drama Center opened in 2001, with dedication ceremonies on January 18, 2002. For Leon I. Brauner, chair of the Department of Theatre and Drama, it was a symbolic moment: "We live in a time in which hope often seems to be at a premium. In such a time, we look to the theatre to provide a voice of reason, joy, laughter, and inquiry. We come to the theatre to better understand our world, our lives, and our dreams. . . . More importantly, the Center's educational mission will serve another high purpose: To train young artists, to educate future scholars, to pass on the techniques of craft and tradition."[5] Lee Norvelle would be pleased that, with a masterful renovation in 2010, his "Little Theatre" evolved into the beautiful Indiana University Cinema, and the remaining space was remodeled to be part of the Lee Norvelle Theatre and Drama Center.

Neal-Marshall Black Culture Center 2002

ARCHITECT MGA Partners Architects

ARCHITECTURAL STYLE Contextual Modern

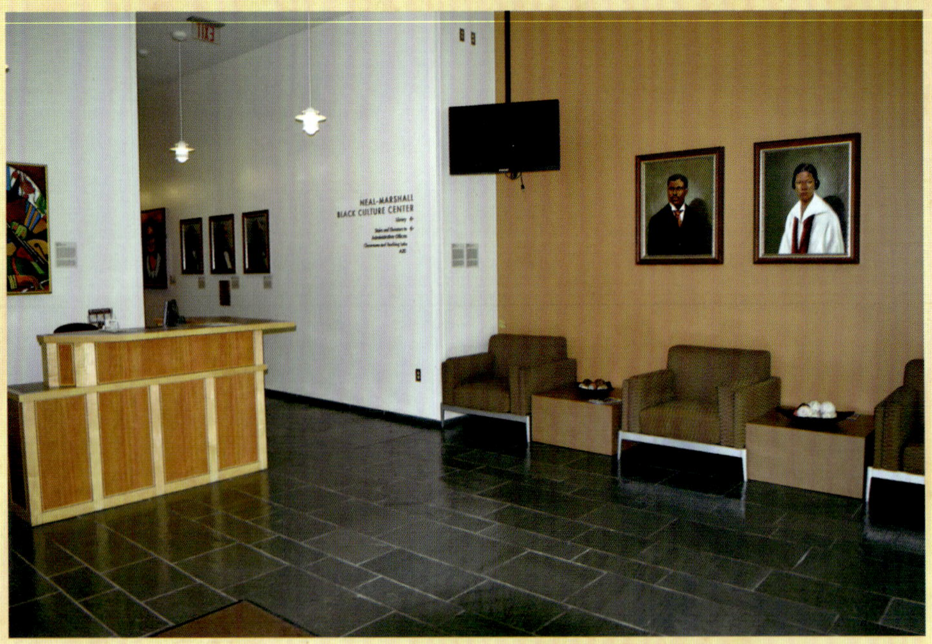

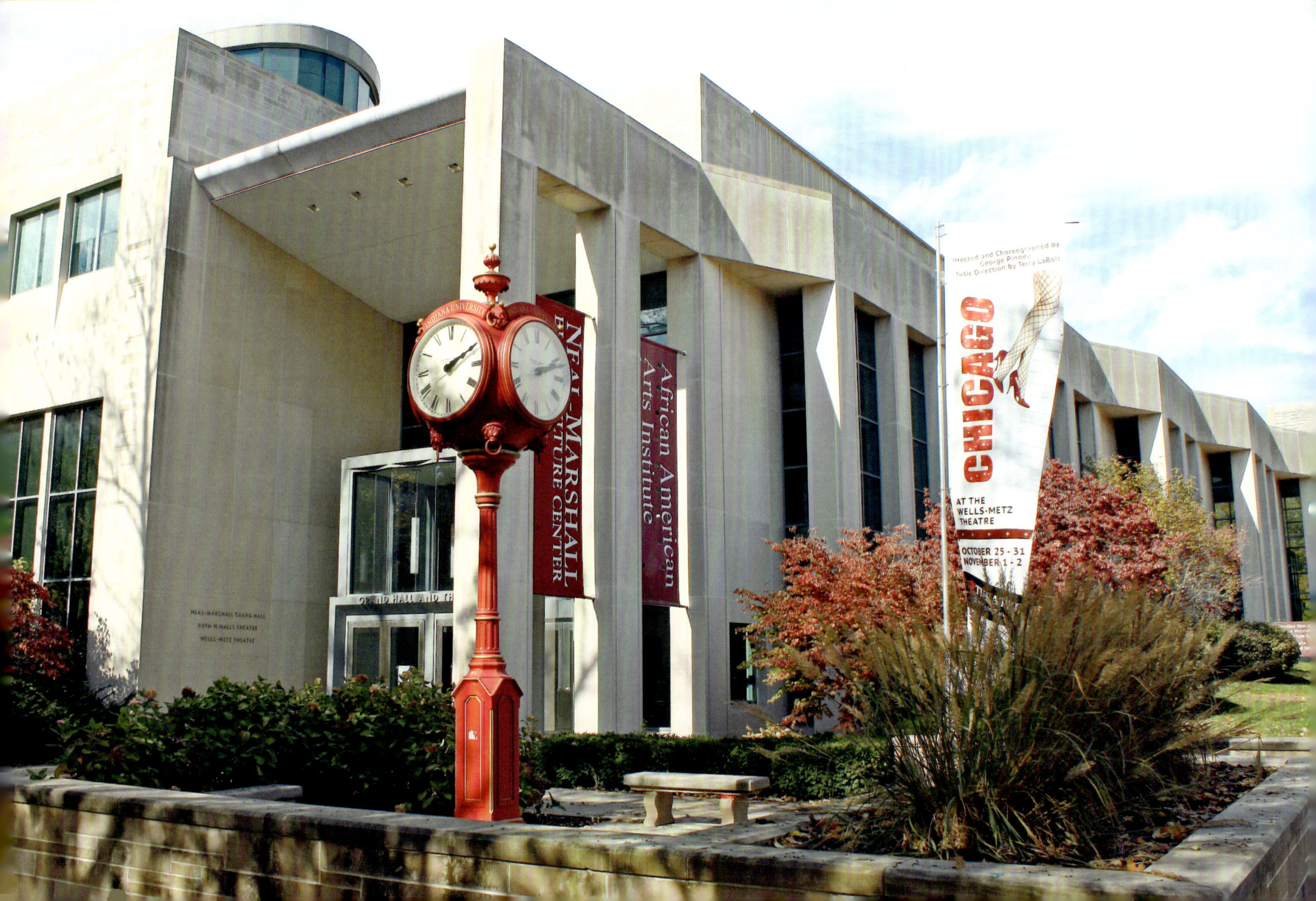

Neal-Marshall Black Culture Center

A Home for Diversity

We must be prepared to renounce prejudice of color, class and race. . . . Our renunciation must be personally implemented by deeds. Our activities will be the measure of the sincerity of the words.
—Indiana University President Herman B Wells

As an outgrowth of the political activism of the late 1960s, the Office of Afro-American Affairs was organized in 1968. After a series of demonstrations by African American students, President Joseph Sutton requested a document with their objectives. These goals included an increased number of black faculty, staff, and students; a black studies program; and a facility that "specializes in handling the economic, social and academic affairs of black students . . . for investigating, planning and implementing programs designed to correct the educational insufficiencies relating to black Americans at all levels."[1] The document, known as Circular 55, was presented to the Faculty Council in 1969 and upon approval Dr. Herman Hudson was named the first chair of Afro-American Studies (today the Department of African American and African Diaspora Studies). Three years later, following a series of relocations to dilapidated temporary locations, a three-story former fraternity house on North Jordan was renovated to accommodate the Black Culture Center. It opened in January 1973 to host student and community activities, to house a multimedia resource center and tutorial program, and to provide African American students with "a 'piece of turf' to call their own which could serve as a focal point of racial pride and identification."[2]

Although this new space was centrally located and nearly eight times larger than its previous home, the increasing enrollment of black students, growing use for academic purposes, demands from new and existing ethnic student and community organizations, and the success of the library and tutorial programs together encouraged Herman Hudson in his 1979–80 annual report to request that a new, larger facility receive the highest priority possible in the Capital Fund Drive. The proposed building, to be located on the site of the current center, would be named the Neal-Marshall Black Culture Center in honor of the first male and female African American graduates of the university—Marcellus Neal in 1894 and Frances Marshall in 1919.[3] The Indiana University Board of Trustees approved the project in 1984 for inclusion in the University's Ten-Year Capital Improvement Plan, and a fund-raising campaign was launched.[4]

While project plans continued to evolve over the next few years, funds were slow to materialize. In 1989, with the encouragement of President Thomas Ehrlich, a new proposal was submitted for the construction of a multiuse complex to house the

Facing top, Lobby of the Neal-Marshall Black Culture Center, featuring portraits of Frances Marshall and Marcellus Neal, 2017. Photo credit: Indiana University.

Facing bottom, Southeast entrance to Neal-Marshall Grand Hall, Ruth N. Halls Theatre, and Wells-Metz Theatre, 2016. Photo credit: Indiana University.

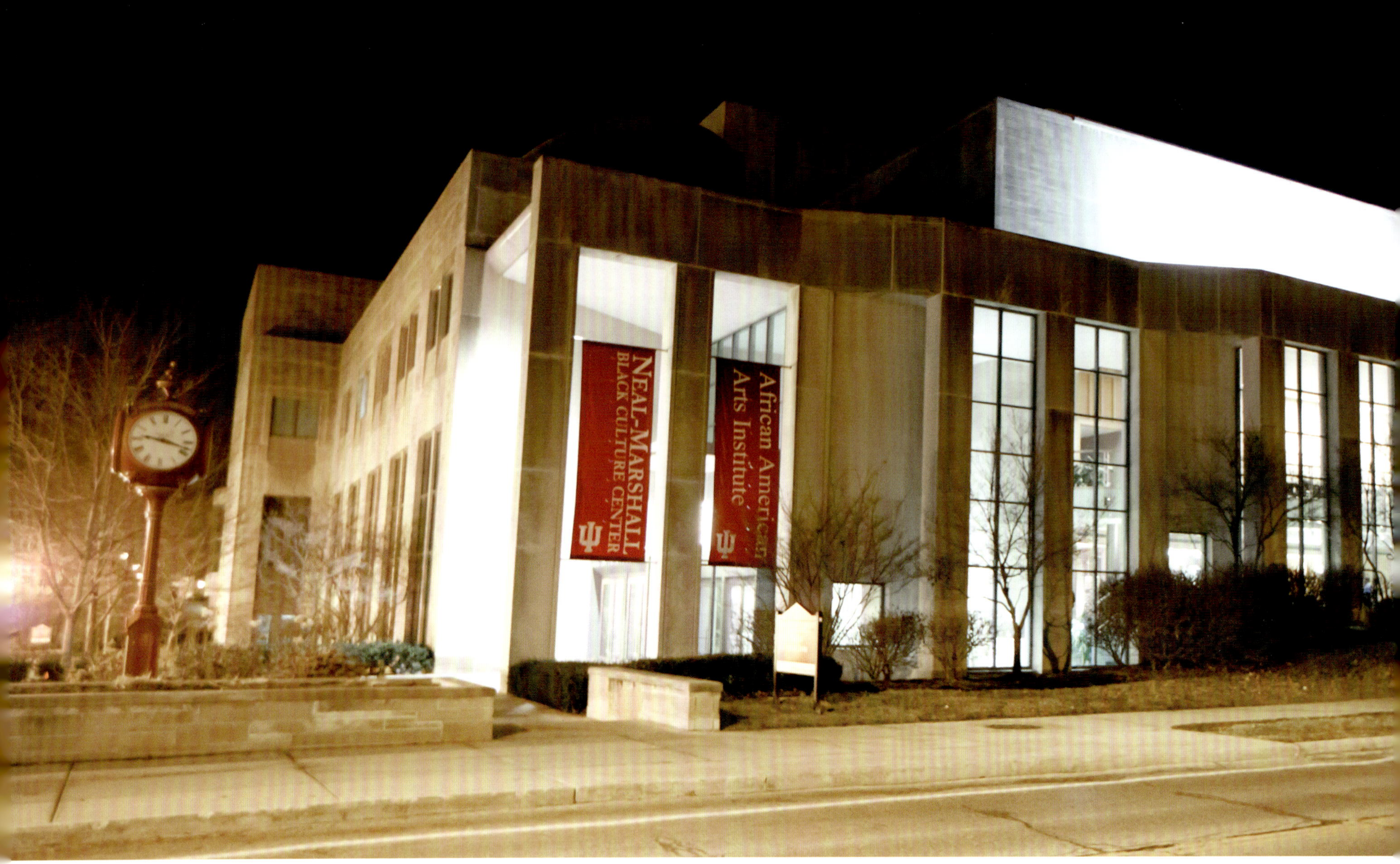

Nighttime view through the windows of Neal-Marshall Black Culture Center, undated. Photo credit: Indiana University.

Neal-Marshall Black Culture Center, the Lee Norvelle Theatre and Drama Center, and the IU Cinema (renovated in 2010), all connecting to the already existing Indiana University Auditorium. The project joined the old theater and extended east to Jordan Avenue and south to the Jordan River. It allowed for a more efficient and operative use of the limited space available: the design was fashioned to house two different venues in one structure, with each retaining its own distinctive architectural identity.

By 1997 the project was fully financed through a combination of funds from a state legislature appropriation and numerous private donations. The plans by the architectural firm MGA Partners in Philadelphia were approved, and ground was broken in October 1998. The result was a sophisticated building, linear in shape and clad in Indiana limestone set in a custom ashlar pattern, all of which harmonizes well with the surrounding architecture. The main entrance features a long wall with windows facing Jordan Avenue, exposing the stunning arcade inside. The south entrance includes a quiet courtyard and a terrace, which opens out to the wooded campus and Jordan River beyond.

Within the Neal-Marshall Black Culture Center is the Grand Hall, with tall windows framing the trees outside, as well as a state-of-the art library. Computer labs, administrative offices, dance and rehearsal studios, and seminar and study rooms fill the remaining space. According to then IU Foundation president Curt Simic, "When completed, the new Neal-Marshal Black Culture Center will represent a major milestone among Big Ten institutions and most colleges and universities in America. It will be the only structure of its kind built from the ground up for the express purpose of enhancing the appreciation and study of African-American culture."[5]

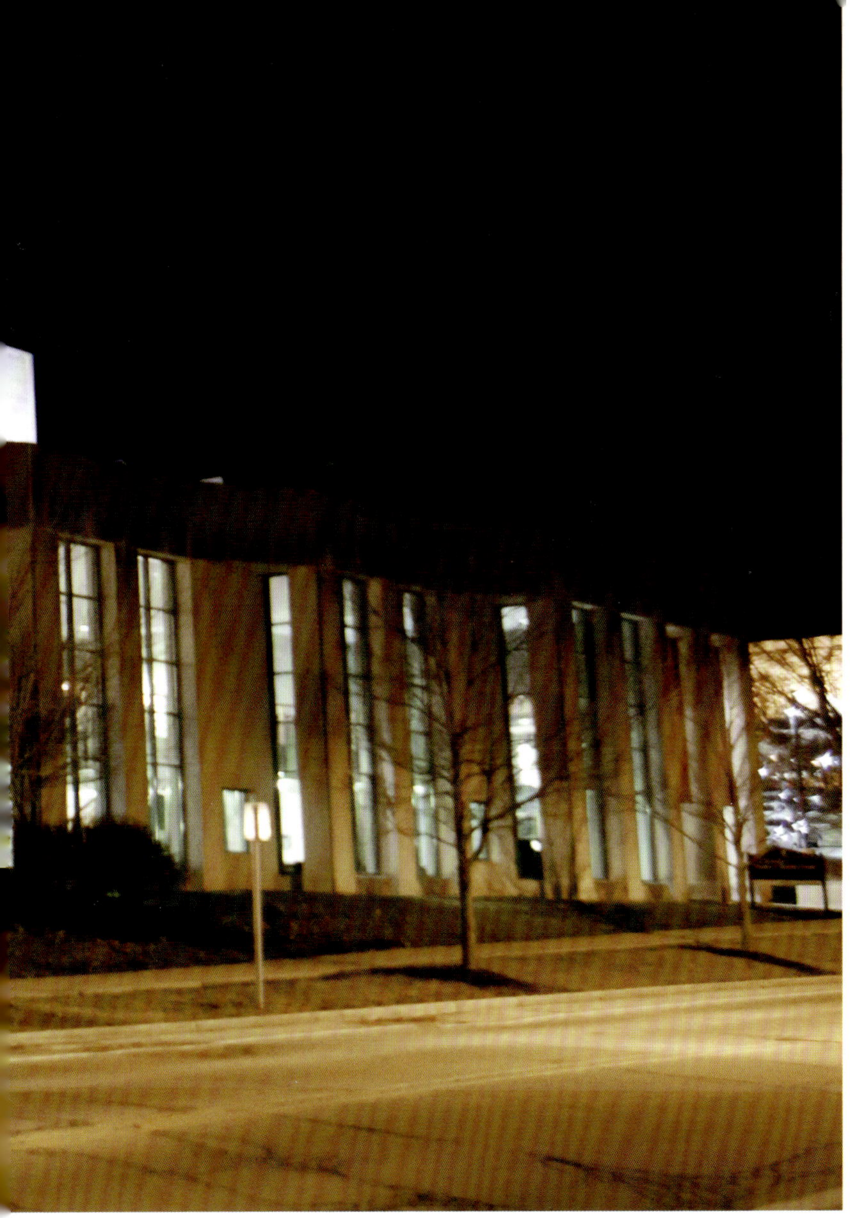

The center opened in 2001 and formal dedication ceremonies followed on January 18, 2002, with keynote addresses by Ossie Davis and Ruby Dee, noted authors, actors, and activist friends of Dr. Martin Luther King Jr., followed by remarks from President Myles Brand and others. In his comments, President Brand predicted that "the Neal/Marshall-Theatre Center will be a crucible for that mysterious alchemy in which creative minds and hearts transmute the common materials of life into gold. But if we are to participate in the alchemy of art and draw upon the richness of our diversity, we must all make maximum use of this exciting building. . . . This building and the programs it houses will help us move toward a greater understanding of ourselves, of one another, and of the obligations we all share to make the world a better place."[6]

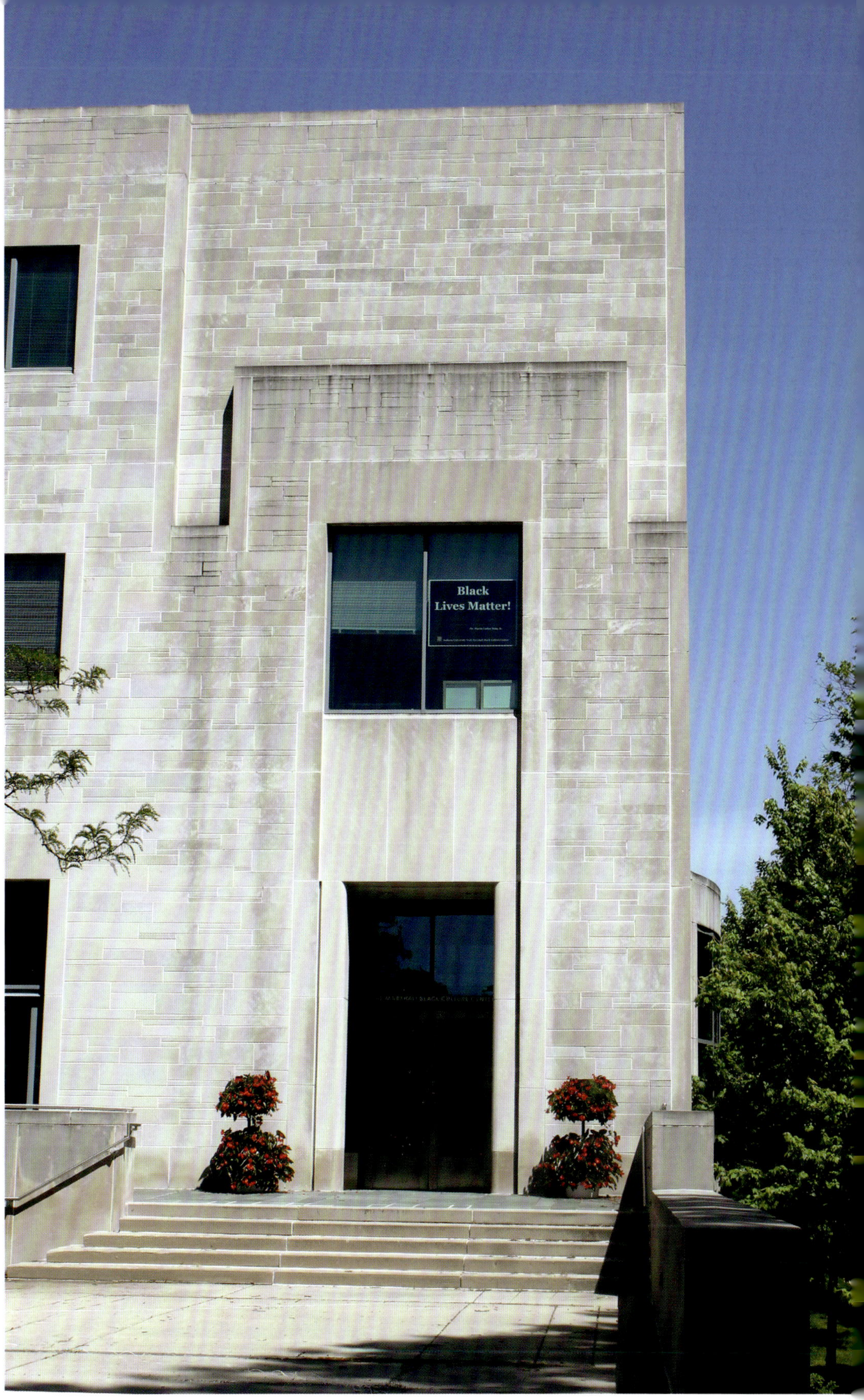

Main entrance of the Neal-Marshall Black Culture Center, 2017. Photo credit: Indiana University.

Indiana University Cinema 2010

ARCHITECT MGA Partners Architects / Roland Design

ARCHITECTURAL STYLE Art Deco

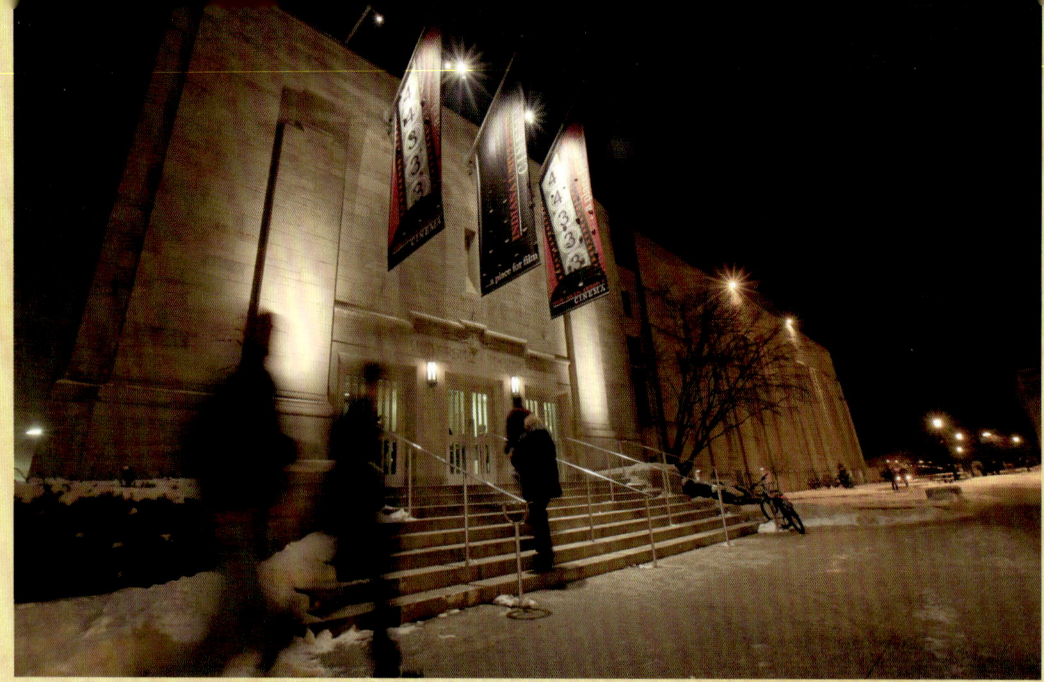

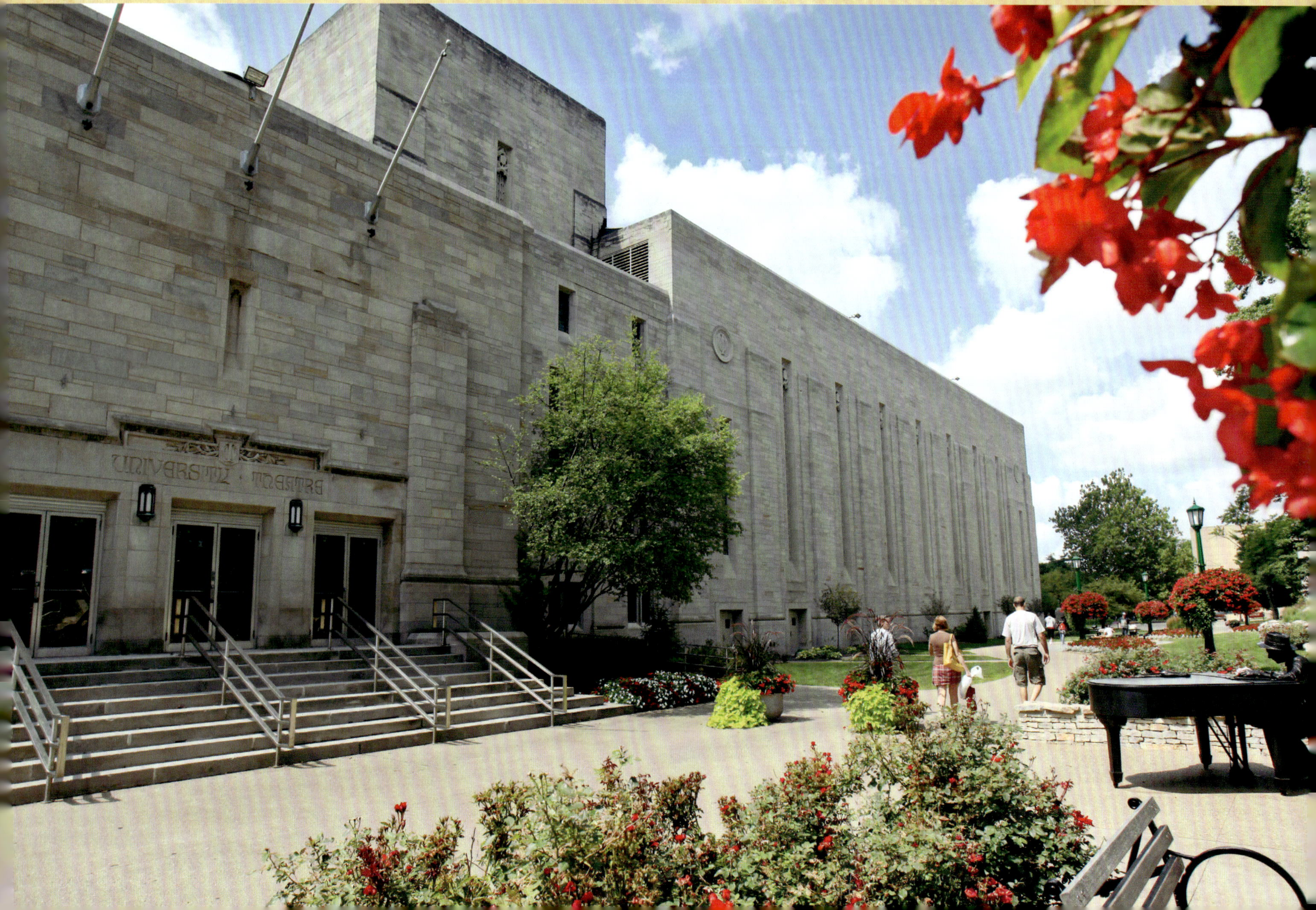

Indiana University Cinema

Where Film Is an Art Form

The very best cinema creates community. It brings people together from varied backgrounds to explore other worlds, to visit other times, and to suspend their own lives for that moment in the theatre. . . . To share that moment allows us to share the essence of our humanity: our passions and our fears; our greatest happiness and deepest sorrow. This quintessential art form of the twentieth century forges bonds between people and creates a shared cultural history that somehow transcends culture. This is the power that the cinema harnesses every time the lights dim and the curtain rises.

—Indiana University President Michael McRobbie at dedication ceremony

Use of the motion picture was in its infancy in November 1914 when Professor William A. Cogshall traveled to Chicago to buy a "moving picture machine" for use by the newly established Indiana Memorial Union Board film series.[1] A Simplex motion picture machine described as "one of the best of the American makes" was installed in the auditorium of the Student Building to show "the highest grade of popular films."[2] According to the *Indiana Daily Student*, it was the first time a motion picture was used on a college campus for entertainment. Four films, the Selig drama *The Tell-Tale Knife*, *The Mill of Life* with Maurice Costello, and two Vitagraph productions, *Wally Van* and *Thanks for the Lobster*, premiered at 7:00 p.m. on December 2, 1914, to a standing-room-only house. Admission was five cents, and the student newspaper reported that "the films are clear and have little or no 'rain' in them."[3] The series continued on Wednesday and Friday nights for the next few years, slowing only with the outbreak of World War I. The film series established an early tradition for film appreciation at Indiana University that would continue through the coming decades. One major problem persisted, however: while the university would become a leader in offering film curricula, the study of film had never enjoyed a dedicated space on campus.

The University Theatre, or Little Theatre, as it was called, was completed in 1941 as part of the larger auditorium complex. The theater served as a permanent performance space for the Department of Theatre and Drama and for productions not requiring the immense IU Auditorium. It offered a separate entrance, foyer, and ticket windows, and an interior featuring a fully equipped stage with orchestra pit, seating for four hundred on a raked floor, and excellent sight lines and acoustics. The Little Theatre debuted with an original variety show *Take the Day* by the Jordan River Review and over the decades witnessed the early steps of greats such as Academy Award–winner Kevin Kline, as well as Richard Jenkins, Charles Kimbrough, Claude Akins, and Jonathan Banks. The Little Theatre also witnessed the world premiere of William Saroyan's *Jim Dandy*. It was a vibrant center of activity until the opening of the Lee Norvelle Theatre and Drama Center in 2002, when all theater productions moved there.

For some time, the university had been interested in finding a venue for film viewing and study on campus, and President

Facing top, Art Deco facade of the old University Theatre—today the IU Cinema—with Indiana University Auditorium extending to the right, 2011. Photo credit: Indiana University.

Facing bottom, The plaza outside the Indiana University Cinema showcases Michael McAuley's sculpture of Hoagy Carmichael seated at his Steinway piano, 2009. Photo credit: Indiana University.

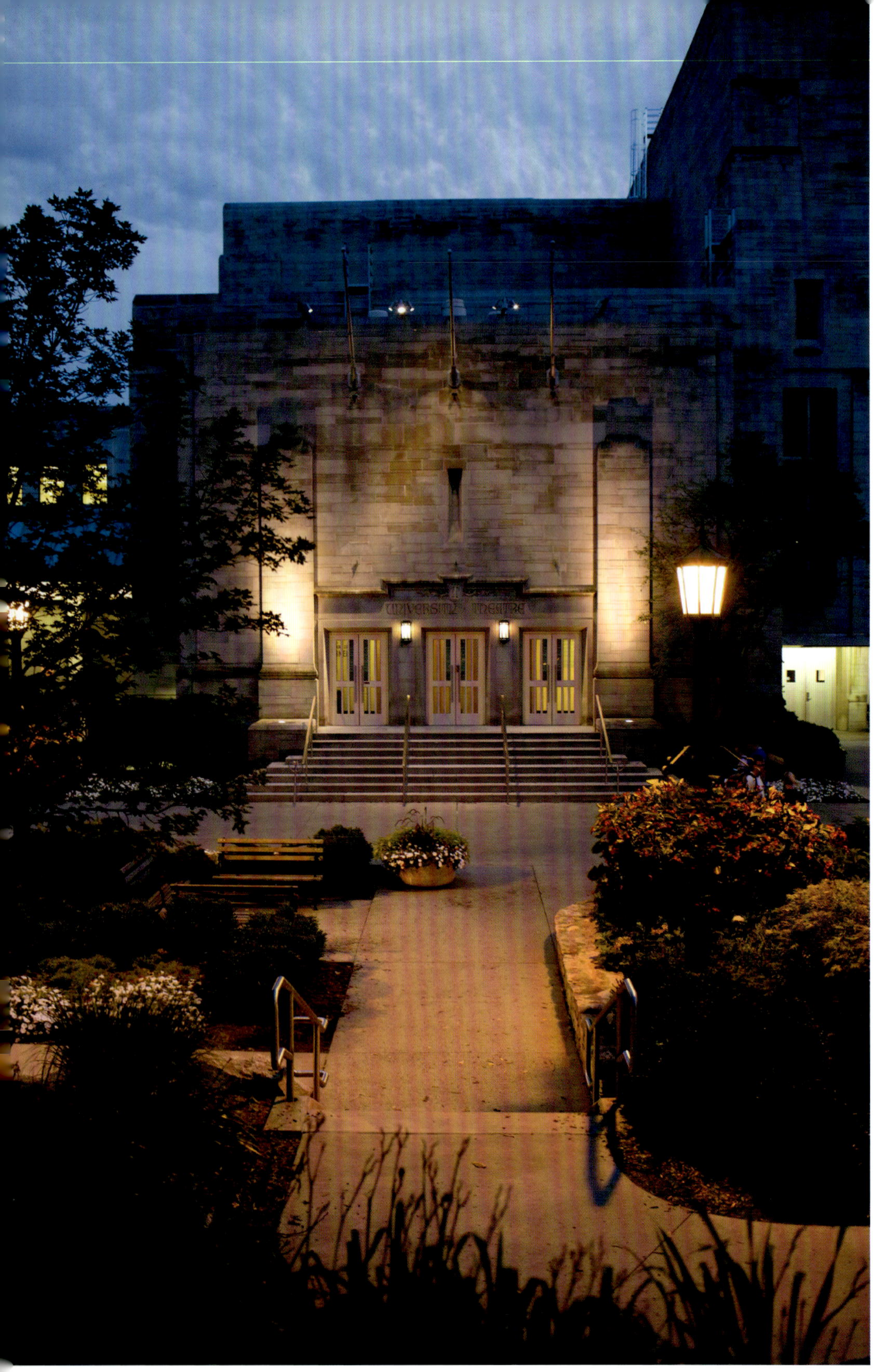

North view of Indiana University Cinema in the evening, 2016. Photo credit: Indiana University.

Myles Brand and the trustees found the now empty Little Theatre a promising space. In September 1997, the administration approved the conversion of "the vacated theatre space to an Advanced Technology Auditorium for campus use" as part of the theater and Neal-Marshall project.[4] MGA Architects of Philadelphia was hired to design the new theater, and ground was broken in October 2009. At the groundbreaking ceremony, President McRobbie stated that "this theater space will return to life, offering scholars, students, and the broader community an accessible dedicated facility that is vitally necessary to the cinematic experience. Once again they will be able to see the masterpieces of cinema as they were meant to be seen."[5] The Indiana University Cinema was officially dedicated on January 27, 2011.

The renovation retained the classic Art Deco–inspired lines and ornamentation of the exterior, mirroring that of the attached Indiana University Auditorium, while the interior kept the WPA-era movie-house feel. A decorative tray ceiling and plush, wine-colored curtains with matching seat upholstery add a sense of drama to the space, while bold geometric lighting sconces illuminate the sides. The original lighting booth converted easily into one for projection, and the orchestra pit was ideal for showing silent films with live music. The four Thomas Hart Benton murals from the 1941 installation were fully restored and reinstalled. At the time of its completion, the IU Cinema joined an elite group of university facilities in the United States that were THX certified. It features state-of-the art projection and sound, with the capability for reel-to-reel, 3-D, 35mm, 16mm, and 2K and 4K digital projection.[6]

The cinema provides an exhibition space for film courses, film festivals sponsored by various departments, campus cinema clubs, and annual viewings of 16mm films directed by Indiana University students. It also is a venue for major film conferences as well as visits by renowned filmmakers and scholars. Additionally, the cinema operates much like a film museum, offering programs and screenings of the university's massive film holdings, such as the David S. Bradley Film Collection, the Black Film Center/Archive, and the archives of the Kinsey Institute and the Lilly Library.

Since opening in 2011, the Indiana University Cinema has hosted a vast array of cinematic presentations: new local, national, and international films; the screening of rare prints from archives and museums around the world; and programs featuring eminent filmmakers, actors, directors, and authors.

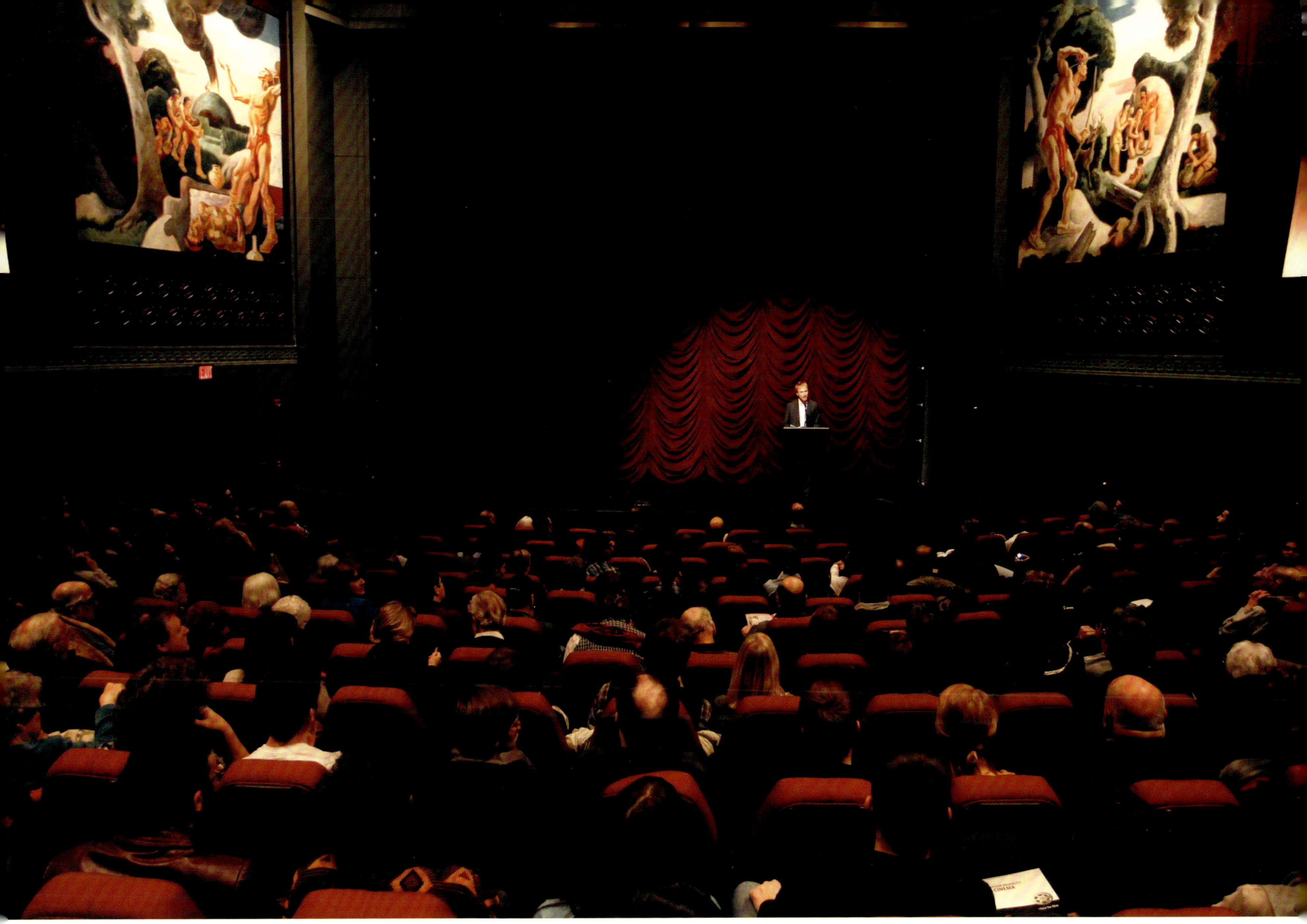

Interior view of the cinema during performance with Thomas Hart Benton's panels, *The Indians* and *Mound Builders*, from *The Cultural and Industrial History of Indiana* visible at top left and right, respectively, 2013. Photo credit: Indiana University.

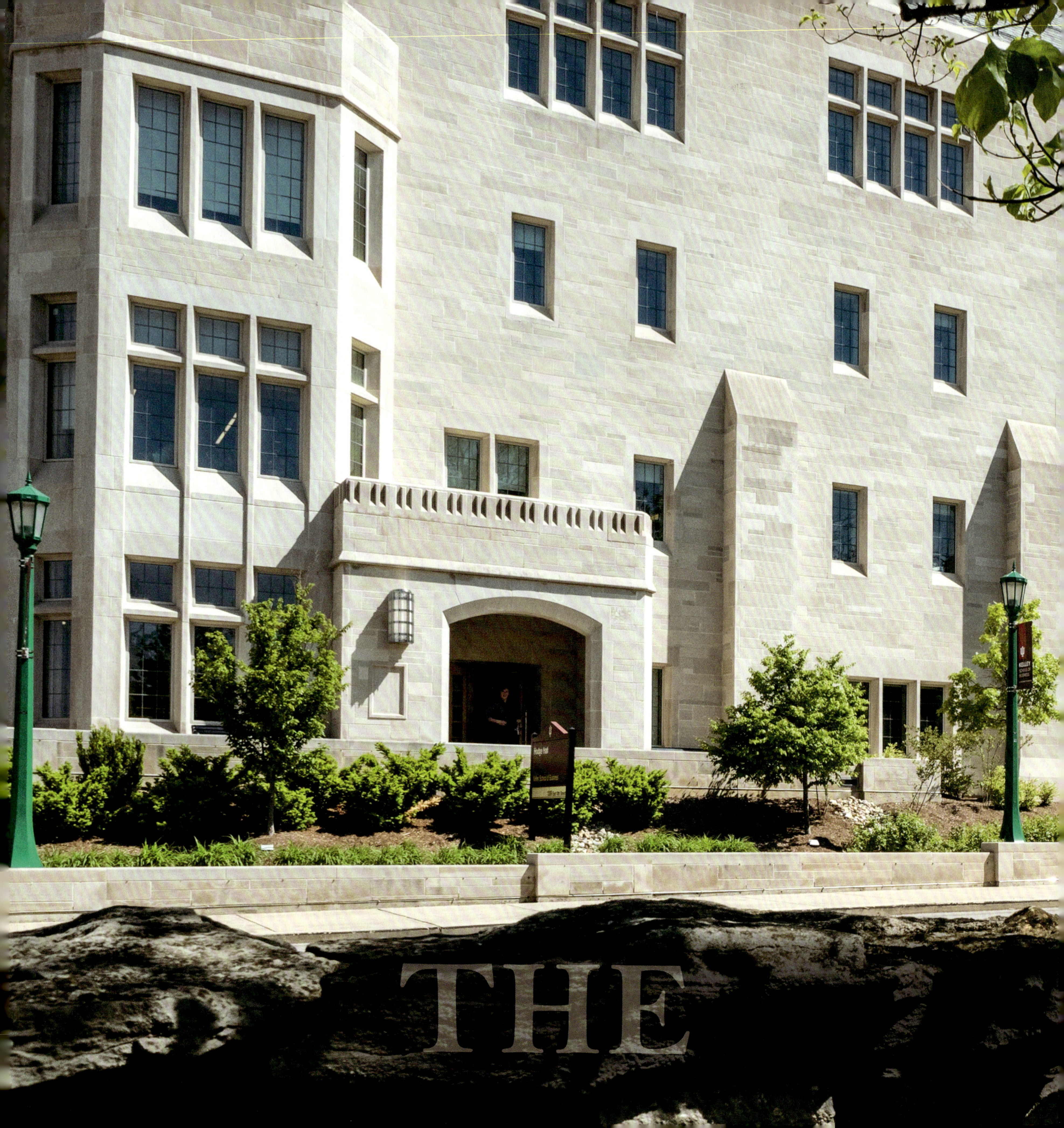
THE

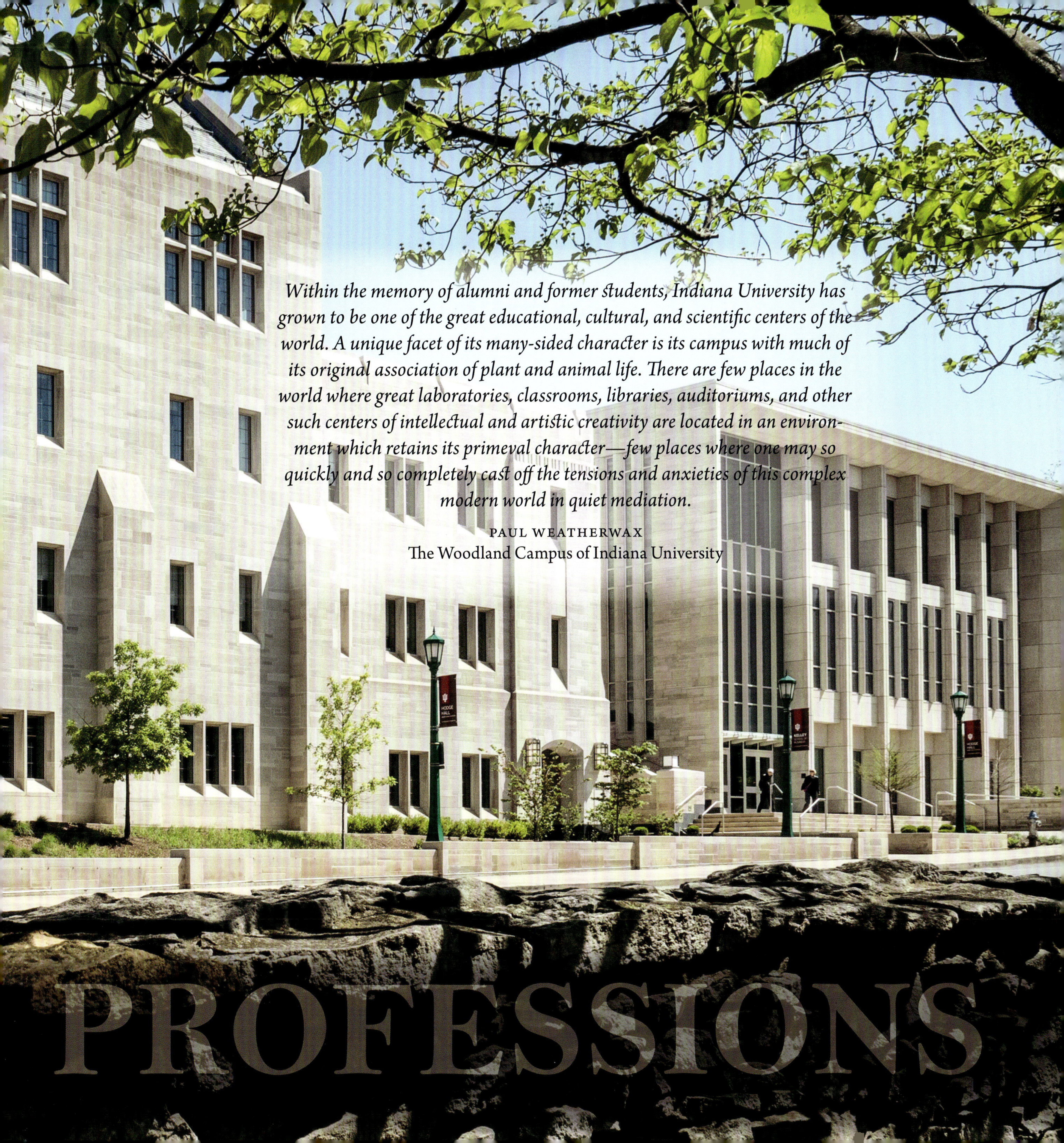

Within the memory of alumni and former students, Indiana University has grown to be one of the great educational, cultural, and scientific centers of the world. A unique facet of its many-sided character is its campus with much of its original association of plant and animal life. There are few places in the world where great laboratories, classrooms, libraries, auditoriums, and other such centers of intellectual and artistic creativity are located in an environment which retains its primeval character—few places where one may so quickly and so completely cast off the tensions and anxieties of this complex modern world in quiet mediation.

PAUL WEATHERWAX
The Woodland Campus of Indiana University

PROFESSIONS

William A. Rawles Hall 1936

ARCHITECT Robert Frost Daggett

ARCHITECTURAL STYLE Collegiate Gothic

ORIGINAL NAME Commerce Hall

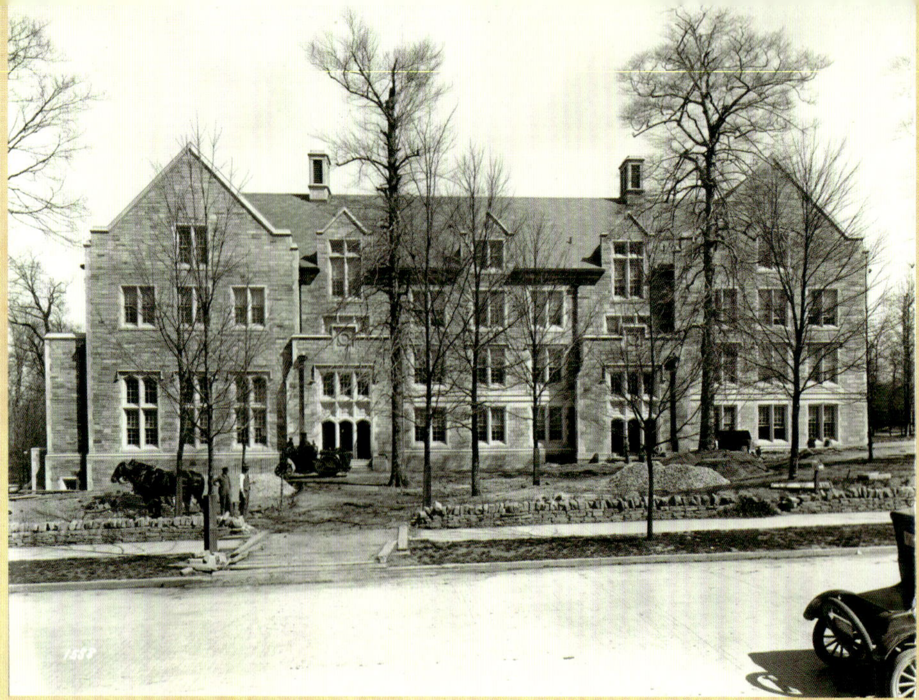

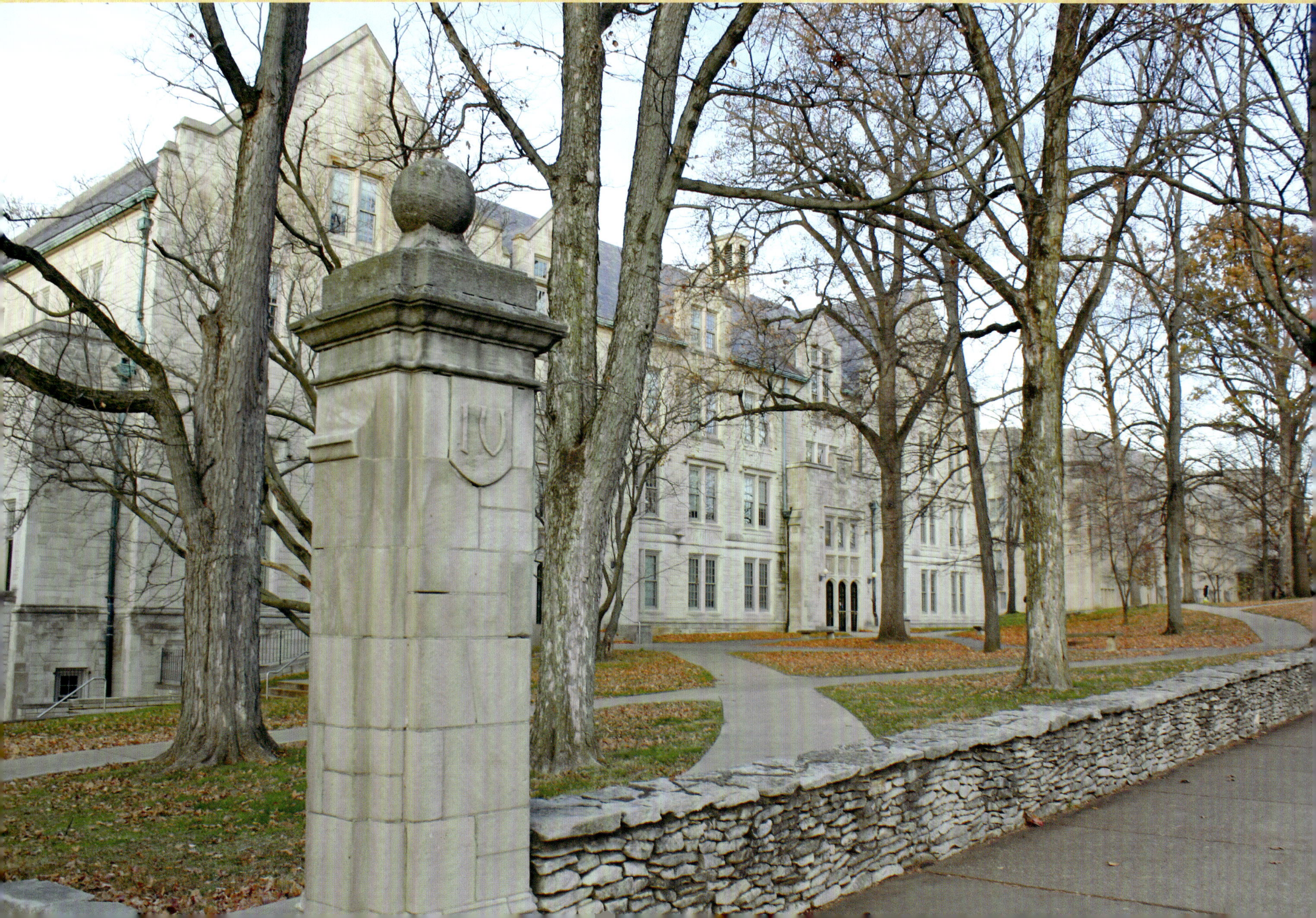

William A. Rawles Hall

At the Forefront of Business Education

Were I permitted to place a motto above your new building, it would be "In all thy getting, get understanding."

—Charles A. Lippincott at dedication ceremony

FROM ITS EARLIEST DAYS, INDIANA UNIVERSITY has offered a course on political economy, as the study of economics was called at the time. Over the years, such offerings multiplied and by 1916, Professor William A. Rawles, director of the "commercial courses," was urging the establishment of a School of Commerce. When demand was enough that additional business courses were introduced in 1919, it became clear that a school to oversee such studies was also needed. At its March 1920 meeting, the Board of Trustees moved to increase the number of business courses offered and to coordinate and organize them into a School of Commerce and Finance, with William Rawles serving as its first dean.

In that post, Rawles turned his attention to the physical needs of the school. His first report included a litany of complaints regarding the facilities used by the business students and faculty, which "greatly hampered" the school. Of Kirkwood Hall, he wrote that "the lighting and ventilation are wretched . . . it would be condemned by the State Board of Health for use as a school room," while the basement of Maxwell Hall, home to the Stenographic and Typewriting Department, not only had poor lighting and ventilation but was downright depressing.[1]

His entreaties did not fall on deaf ears. Early the next summer, Indiana University President William Lowe Bryan informed Rawles that the board had voted to proceed with construction of a building for the School of Commerce and Finance. Robert Frost Daggett of Indianapolis was named architect for the project. By fall 1921, the university had selected a site on Third Street that would allow for growth, if necessary, and construction commenced on April 27, 1922, right on schedule.

Daggett designed a structure with twenty-two classrooms (enough room for 700 students) as well as what would be the largest campus auditorium at the time. Plans also included a museum of commerce located in the attic—ultimately the fourth floor—that would feature "early implements, products of manufacture, and relics of value in commercial study."[2] At completion, the structure was one of only two buildings for the study of commerce in the Midwest.

In the early twentieth century, Indiana University was committed to the use of Collegiate Gothic style for its campus buildings, including Commerce Hall; this style had come to define its core campus. Following another IU tradition, the building is clad in locally sourced limestone. The smooth-faced stone from Oolitic, Indiana, is laid in a broken ashlar

Facing top, William A. Rawles Hall, circa 1923. IN2963_3, Indiana Geological Survey. Photo credit: Charles Gilbert Shaw.

Facing bottom, View from Third Street of Rawles Hall; note class gift gate and stone wall, undated. Photo credit: Indiana University.

pattern, or, as described in a 1923 *Indiana Daily Student* article, "the handsome edifice . . . is a distinctive though harmonious addition to the campus. Its difference consists in its crazy-quilt surface of smooth, variously shaded white and brown stones."[3] As with previous structures, the stone carvers left their marks on this campus building in a meaningful way. On the south side of Rawles Hall above the two sets of doors are mirror-image carvings with the Indiana University trident in the middle flanked by blank heraldic shields. Higher up the facade is a carving of the IU seal, symbolizing light and truth. On the north side of the building, the carvers took a more artistic approach. At each corner of the exterior doors, visitors will find depictions of an owl, a lamp of learning, an open book, and a caduceus—the staff carried by the Greek god Hermes, protector and patron of invention and trade.

Architectural plans called for a gray-slate roof, but when students learned of this they quickly circulated a petition in protest. They felt a red-tile roof would bring uniformity to that area of campus, and the sea of red roofs would create a stunning effect. Spearheaded by the Indiana Union Board, the petition acquired over a thousand signatures and was delivered to the Indiana University Board of Trustees. Upon consultation with the architect, however, the board learned that production of the slate roof was already underway and a change would have been prohibitively expensive. Besides, the board was told by Daggett, the slate roof was much more appropriate for the design of the building. The students did leave their touch on the building, however. The 1922 senior class presented a gift of ivy to be planted when the building was complete. (The university dutifully planted the ivy, but later removed it because the creepers damaged the building's copper drainpipes.)

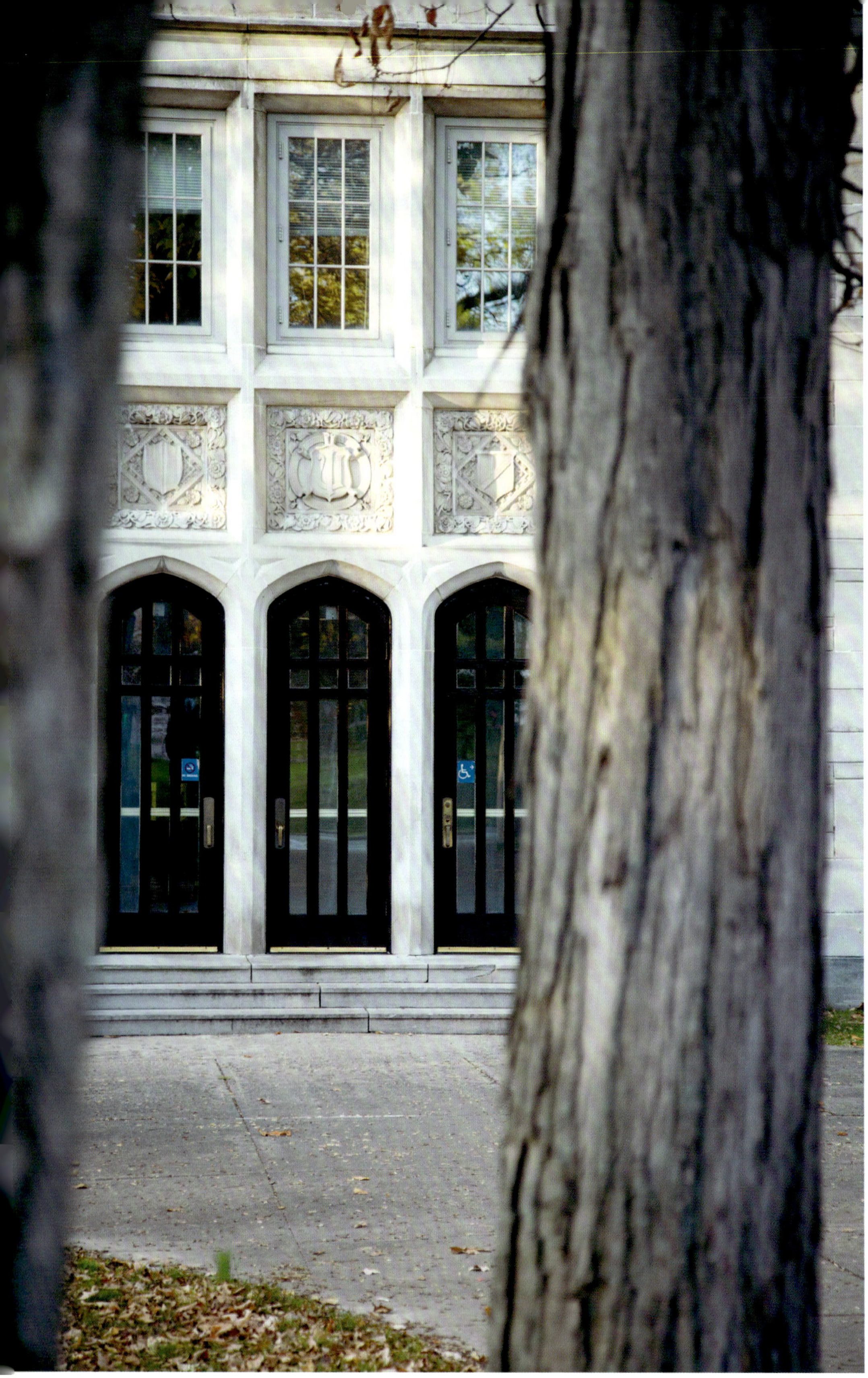

Main entrance to William A. Rawles Hall with ornate limestone carvings above arched doorways, 2016. Photo credit: Tyagan Miller.

The interior featured flat-finished, dark-oak panels on the walls of the first floor, and classroom furniture to match was purchased. French gray window shades complemented the woodwork and maple flooring. The terrazzo stairs and corridor baseboard were installed by the Santarossa Mosaic and Tile Company of Indianapolis. (The company continued to perform work at IU, including installing flooring in the Memorial Stadium North End Zone facility.) At the west end of Rawles is a 350-seat, two-story auditorium; there the dark-oak woodwork continues, running 4 feet up the walls and encasing the windows, stage, and box-beam ceiling.

The dedication ceremonies, reported to be among the finest ever held at the university, were held April 25–26, 1923. Speakers and attendees included major figures from the business and commerce world, among them General Herbert M. Lord, director of the U.S. Bureau of the Budget, and Dr. C. A. Lippincott, who helped establish one of the first departments of human resources at Indiana's Studebaker Company in South Bend.

Commerce Hall had several names over the years, including the Business Administration Building (1935) and the Social Science Building (1940). The IU Board of Trustees approved the name of William A. Rawles Hall in 1963, although the official naming ceremony was not held until 1971. Over the years Rawles Hall has housed many illustrious faculty, but it is perhaps most noteworthy as the first academic home of Herman B Wells when he became an instructor in economics and sociology at Indiana University in 1930. In more recent years, the Department of Mathematics has settled into its hallowed halls.

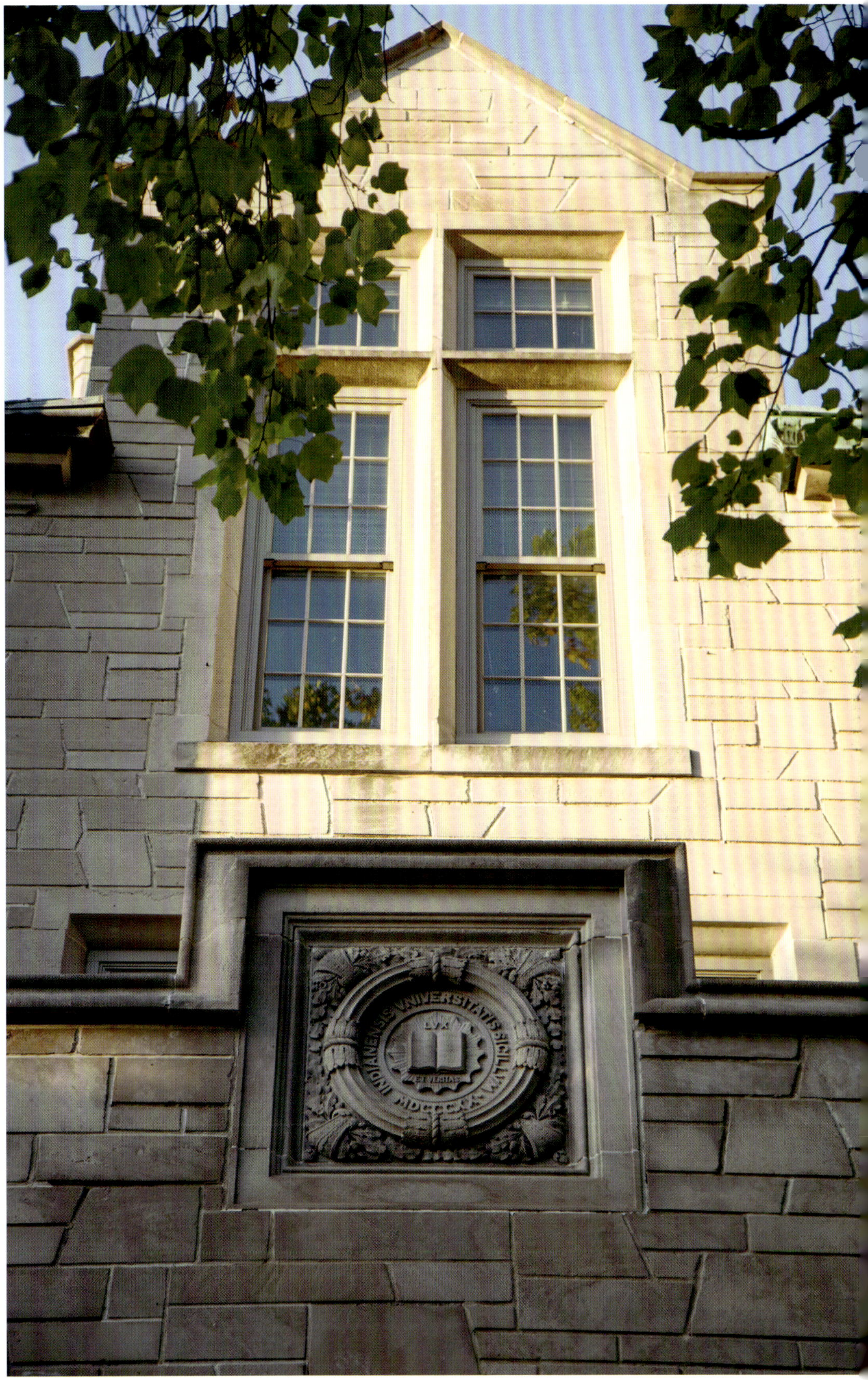

Indiana University seal, symbolizing light and truth, on south side of Rawles Hall above entry, 2016. Photo credit: Tyagan Miller.

Ernie Pyle Hall 1938

ARCHITECT A. M. Strauss

ARCHITECTURAL STYLE Collegiate Gothic

ORIGINAL NAME Stores and Services Building

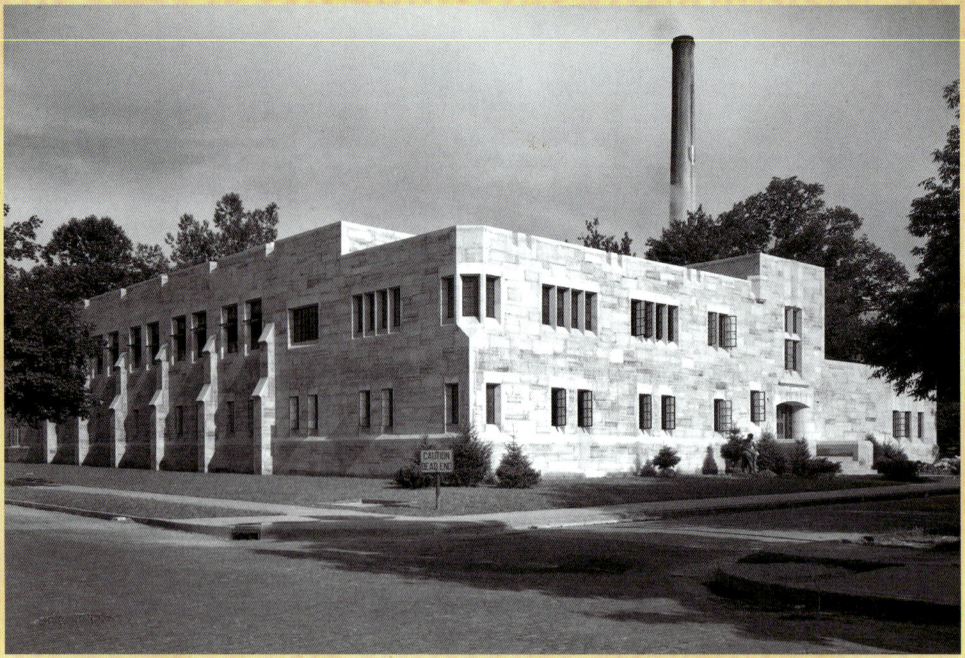

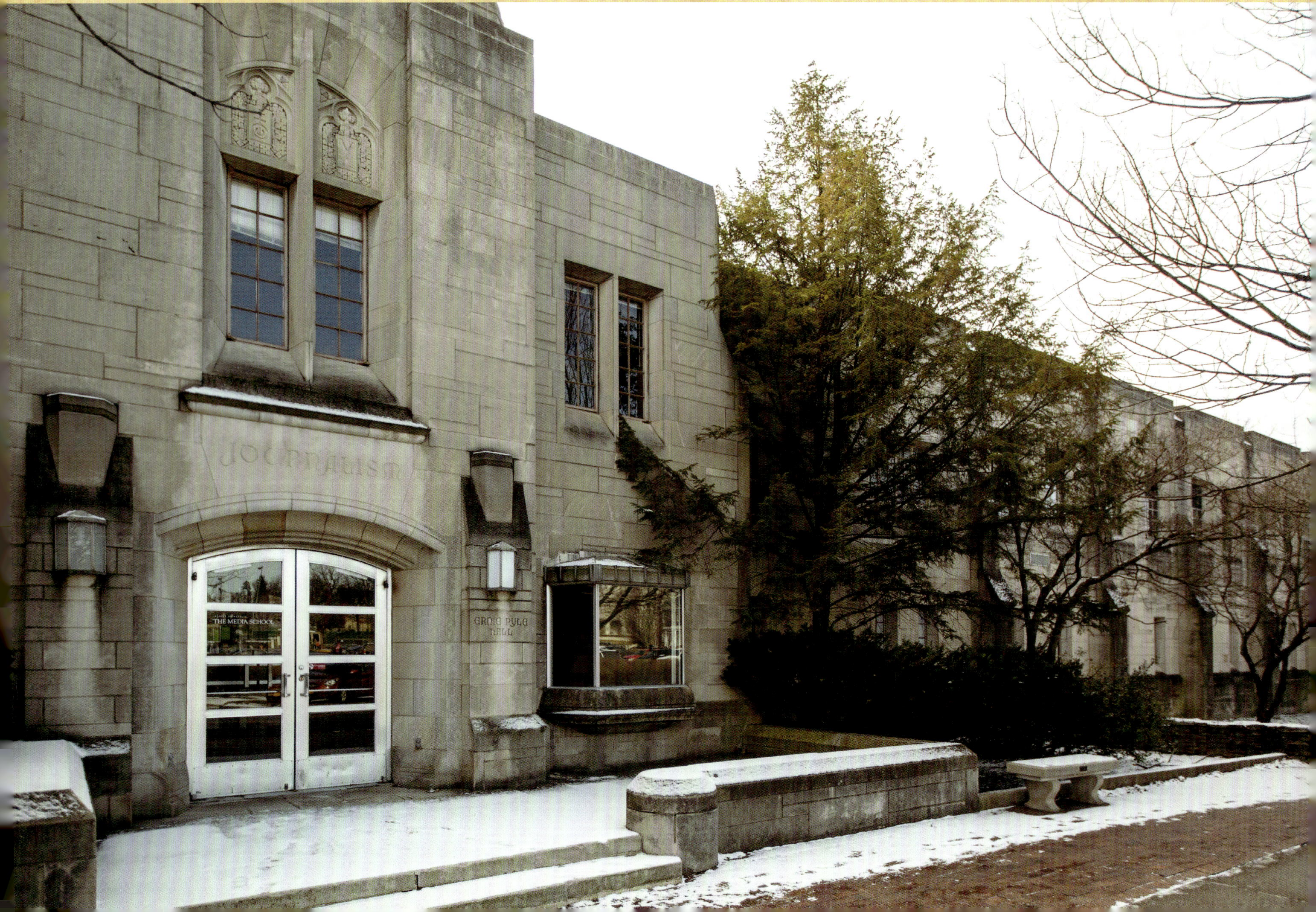

Ernie Pyle Hall

First Home of the School of Journalism

This building is a fitting home for a department of journalism which has long maintained the highest professional standards. It is even more than this. It has an even larger significance. A memorial it is, a monument and a school, but it is something more than any of these. It is, in a larger sense, a temple; a temple of no single cult, trade or profession; but a temple whose votaries have made vows to the common good.... This school will be a temple indeed if from its corridors young men and young women go forth dedicated not only to wisdom and to understanding, but to the defense of every American's right to seek it where he will.

—*J. R. Wiggins at dedication ceremony*

"THE FIRST NUMBER [ISSUE] OF THE *STUDENT* IS presented this morning, with the hope that it may in some degree supply what has seemed to be a real desideratum. The utility and practical benefit of an independent organ, conducted upon liberal principles and devoted to the interest of the students and the university, is conceded by all."[1] So began journalistic endeavors at Indiana University in the student newspaper, twenty-six years before the first journalism course was offered in 1893 by Professor Martin W. Sampson.

The Department of Journalism was established in 1911, and over the coming decades enrollment increased along with continuing growth of its related entities, such as the *Indiana Daily Student* and University Publications, which included the printing plant. Numerous locations scattered around campus were enlisted to house the budding discipline, such as Science Hall, the basement of the Student Building, a Quonset hut known as the Shack by journalism students, and former residences located on the periphery of campus.[2]

As early as 1942, new construction for the Department of Journalism appeared on the IU Board of Trustees' list of proposed projects. Although funds for a new building failed to materialize, in the early 1950s support for the renovation of an existing campus structure became available. The Stores and Services Building was converted to house the Department of Journalism, the *Indiana Daily Student* offices, and the printing plant. This service building was designed by A. M. Strauss and completed in 1938 for the Department of Buildings and Grounds to house the carpentry, plumbing, and electrical shops, and the department's offices and stores. The small rectangular structure's solid limestone exterior and leaded glass windows earned it the title of "the fanciest tool shed in the Big Ten."[3] It was sited adjacent to the original central heating plant for the campus, on Seventh Street, immediately in front of the Indiana Memorial Union.

In 1952 preliminary plans for the renovation and addition to both ends of the structure were completed by the building's original architect, A. M. Strauss, and contracts were awarded in 1953. The result, which nearly doubled the square footage of its predecessor, was "a dream realized for Hoosier newspapermen."[4] The newly renovated building was renamed Ernie Pyle Hall in July 1954 and dedicated in October of the same year. Dedication activities spanned three days to coincide with National Newspaper Week and the sesquicentennial of the Indiana Press.

Facing top, Stores and Service Building, 1938. The building would be renovated, designated home to the Department of Journalism, and renamed Ernie Pyle Hall in the fall of 1954. P0030726, IU Archives.

Facing bottom, Facing Seventh Street, Ernie Pyle Hall features recessed windows, an arched entry, and decorative sculptural reliefs, 2016. Photo credit: Tyagan Miller.

Ernie Pyle Hall was named for a renowned journalist, known for his rapport with soldiers in the trenches. Pyle was an IU graduate, *Indiana Daily Student* editor and columnist, and winner of the Pulitzer Prize for his World War II correspondence. Ernest Taylor Pyle (1900–1945) was killed by a sniper on Ie Shima (now known as Iejima) while reporting on the war in the Pacific. This building stands as a living memorial to the man President Herman B Wells described as "a homespun Hoosier, world traveler, discerning reporter, unexcelled interpreter of the minds and hearts of men in peace and in war."[5]

In harmony with the existing campus, Ernie Pyle Hall is Collegiate Gothic and clad in Indiana limestone. The exterior features vertical buttresses between the window groupings, notched crenellations along the roofline resembling a battlement, deeply recessed windows, and decorative sculptural reliefs above the arched entryway to the north. The flat roof is atypical of the campus architecture but a reminder of the building's original purpose. The first floor of the newly refurbished structure was occupied by University Publications, which housed the presses to print the *Indiana Daily Student*, course bulletins, and a range of university materials. The second floor was dedicated to the journalism program and included a spacious, well-lit "city room" for the *Indiana Daily Student*, with desks and typewriters for the staff, a specialized library, and photography print and dark rooms, as well as departmental offices, classrooms, and a large lecture hall named for alumnus Don Mellett. Mellett was a Canton, Ohio, editor who was killed in retaliation for his crusade against corruption in the local mob and police ranks. A lounge dedicated to Ernie Pyle, also on the second floor, featured a bust of Ernie Pyle above the fireplace and his portable typewriter along with a number of other personal belongings. The battered desk he used as an editor of the *Indiana Daily Student* found a home in the new offices of the student newspaper.

From late 1973 to 1976, Ernie Pyle Hall was closed for a massive interior redesign and reconfiguration under the direction of architect Edwin Gibson. University Publications moved into a space on the periphery of campus, making room for the Department of Journalism to occupy the building in its entirety. The "new" Ernie Pyle Hall was dedicated in 1977. While the exterior remained virtually untouched, the interior was nearly unrecognizable. During this period the Department of Journalism became an independent school within the College of Arts and Sciences. In 2014 the Media School was established, incorporating the School of Journalism, the Department of Telecommunications, and the Department of Communication and Culture. The Media School and all of its entities moved into Franklin Hall in 2016, initiating a new era for the disciplines at Indiana University.

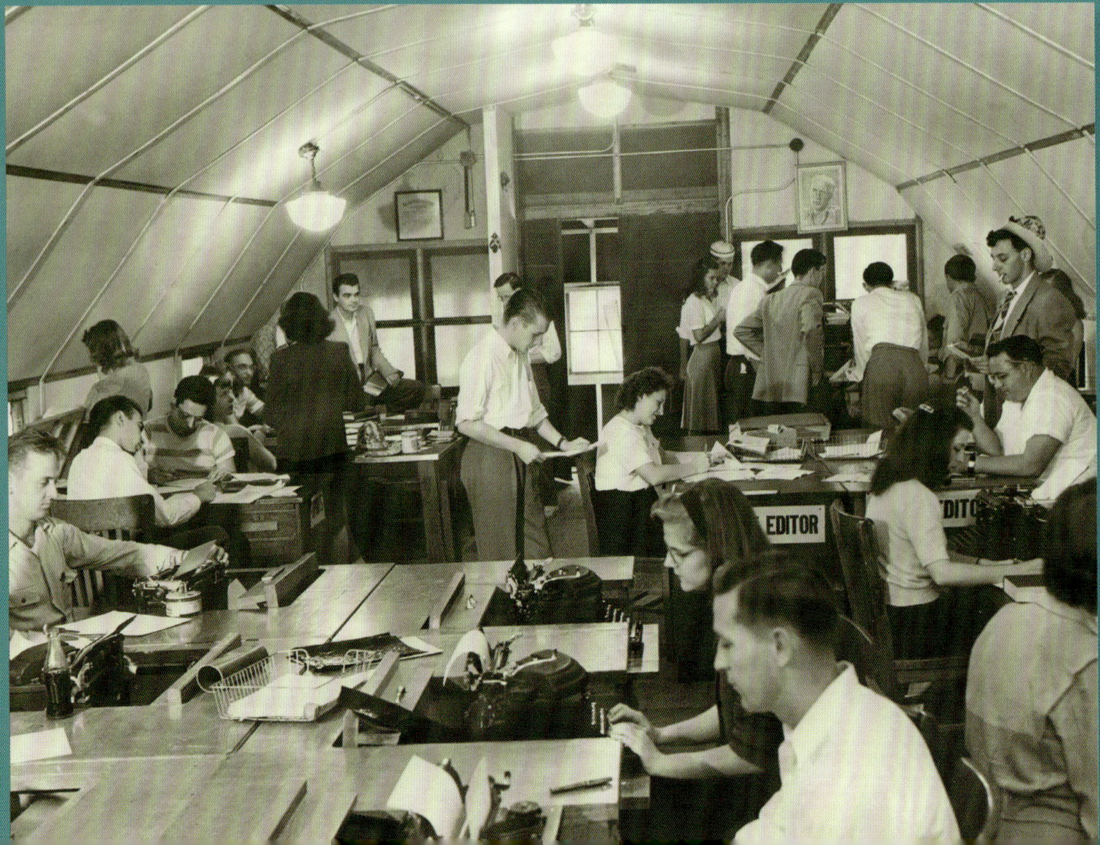

Below, Indiana Daily Student staff in the Quonset hut affectionately known as the Shack, 1947. P0024817, IU Archives.

Facing, Quonset hut serving as a dental research unit on IU's Bloomington campus, 1961. P0033188, IU Archives. Photo credit: John McGinnis.

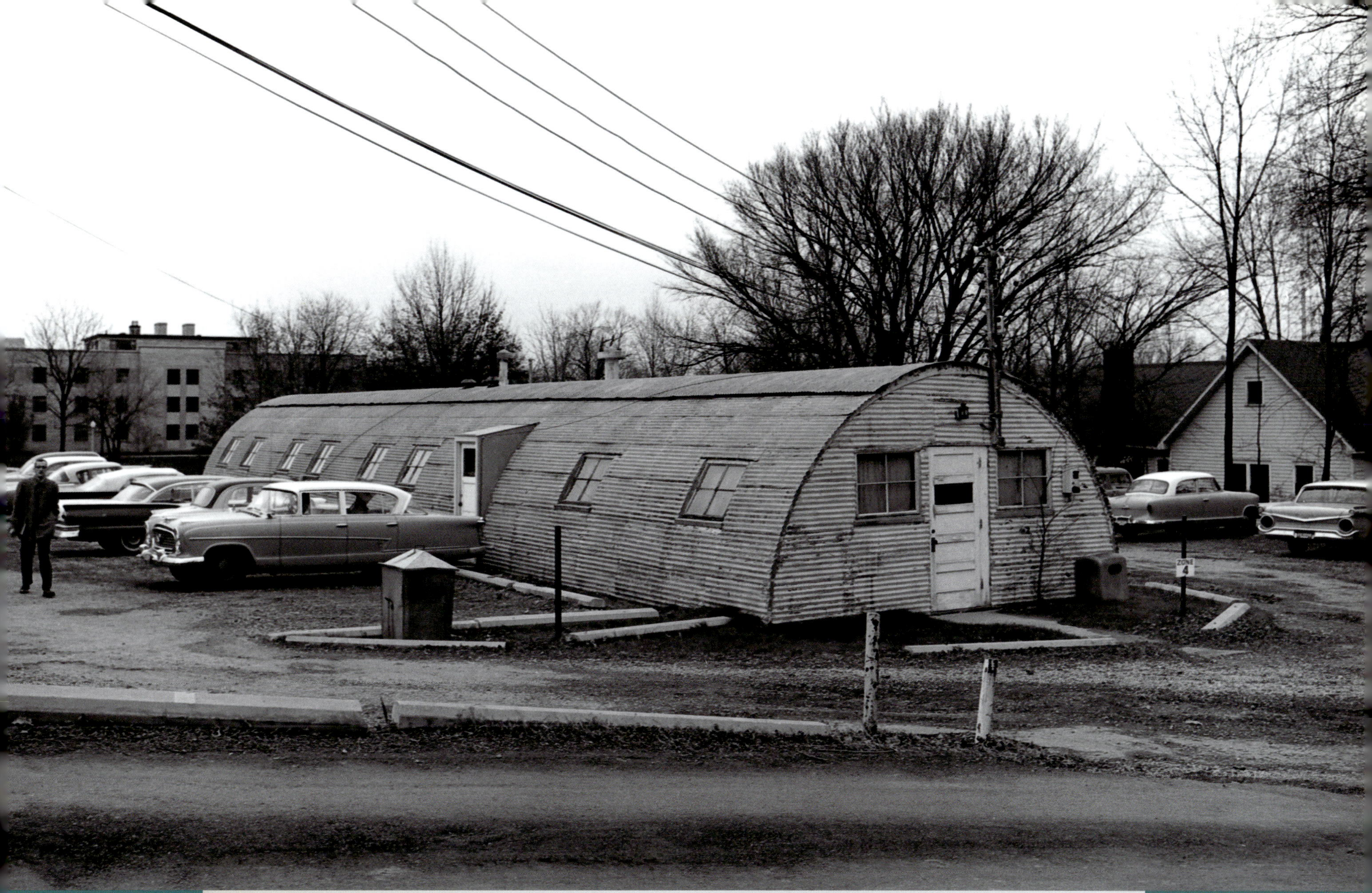

Quonset Huts

In addition to a housing crisis, the increased enrollment following World War II meant Indiana University administrators needed to find additional classroom and office space quickly. Enter once again to save the day—military surplus! By 1946 Quonset huts began appearing across campus for just about every imaginable use: classrooms, *Indiana Daily Student* office space (affectionately referred to as the Shack), and an animal house for the Zoology Department. One of the more noteworthy uses of the temporary structures was as a dental research unit in what is now the Herman B Wells Library parking lot. It was there that Bloomington children came to take part in clinical trials run by Joseph Muhler, Harry Day, and their team to develop the Crest toothpaste formula.

James Albert Woodburn Hall 1940

ARCHITECT Robert Frost Daggett

ARCHITECTURAL STYLE Collegiate Gothic with Characteristics of Romanesque Revival

ORIGINAL NAME Business and Economics Building

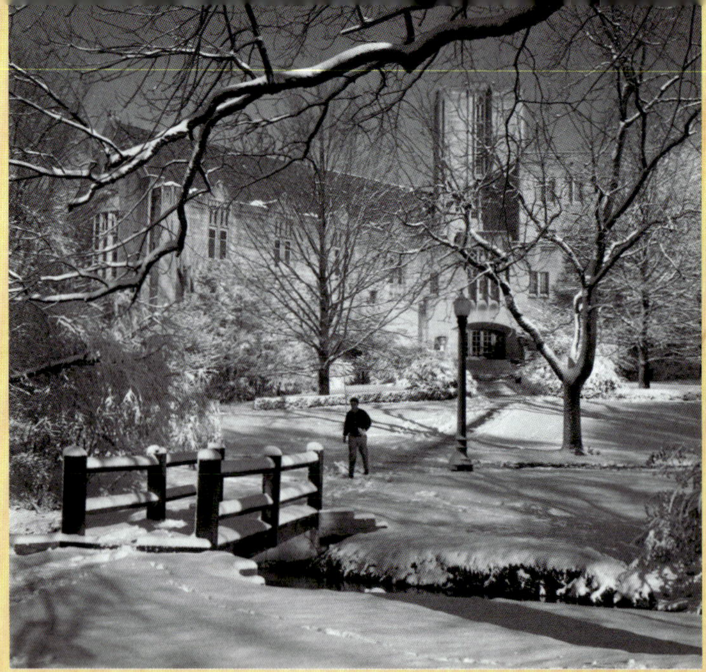

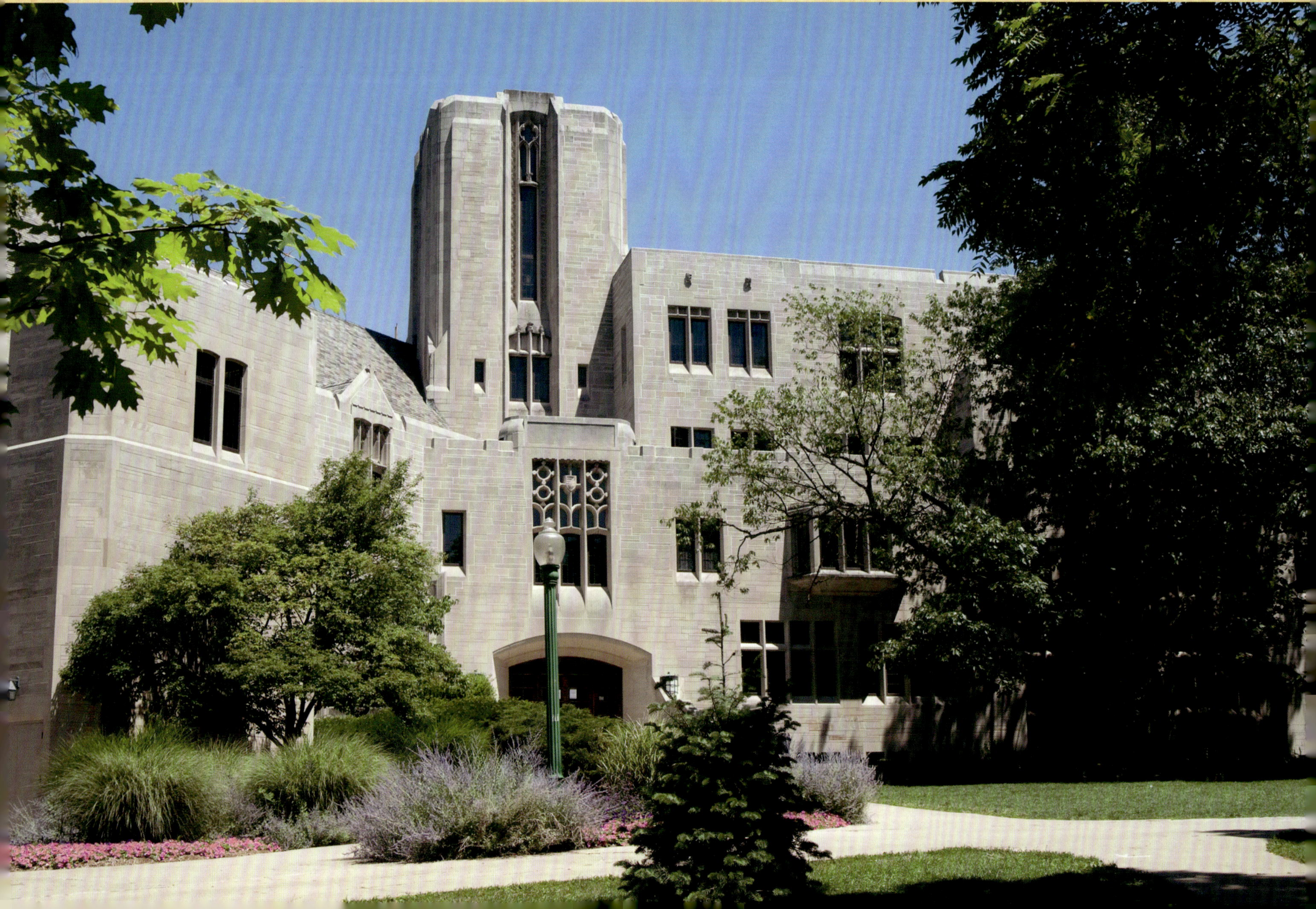

James Albert Woodburn Hall

An Edifice Forever Beautiful

It has proved to be admirably suited for the purposes it must serve. The completeness and quality of its facilities have contributed substantially to the further development of the School's functions, and its beauty has been a source of inspiration to students and faculty.

—Indiana University President Herman B Wells

FOLLOWING THE UNANIMOUS APPROVAL IN MAY 1938 to place a new building for the School of Business Administration at the top of the ten-year construction program, the Indiana University Board of Trustees applied for grant funding through the Public Works Administration (PWA) and employed architect A. M. Strauss of Fort Wayne to prepare plans and specifications. In the face of mounting enrollment, IU dean Burton D. Myers urged that "nothing should be left undone to maintain dominance of the University in this field of education." President Wells pressed the PWA, noting that "only one new classroom structure was erected on this campus from 1910 to 1930, a twenty-year period during which the Bloomington enrollment more than doubled."[1]

On July 26, 1938, news of approval by the PWA to fund 45 percent of the project arrived, and the remainder of the funding came from the State Educational Improvement Fund.[2] Strauss, in collaboration with the acting dean of the School of Business Administration, Clare W. Barker, and other departmental faculty, finalized plans for the new building with twenty-five classrooms and seating capacity for 1,700 students, plus offices for sixty faculty and a departmental library. In September the trustees approved a site on East Seventh Street opposite the Men's Gymnasium and just east of Jordan Field (today the Indiana Memorial Union parking lot). Additionally, with the retention of New York architectural firm Eggers and Higgins the same month to design the new Indiana University Auditorium nearby, Strauss drew on their consult, which

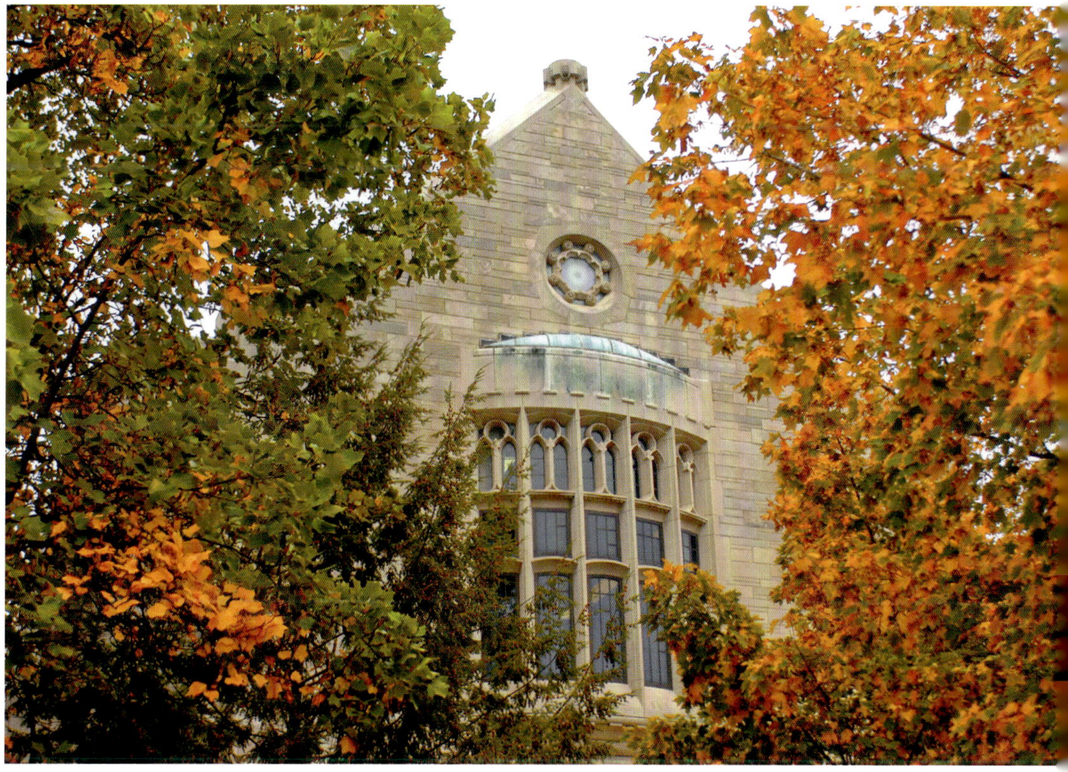

Above, West elevation of James Albert Woodburn Hall; note ornate bay window topped by rosette, 2016. Photo credit: Tyagan Miller.

Facing top, Woodburn Hall on a snowy day, 1958. P0052678, IU Archives. Photo credit: Elwood Martin "Barney" Cowherd.

Facing bottom, Collegiate Gothic south facade of Woodburn Hall displaying Art Deco influence, undated. Photo credit: Indiana University.

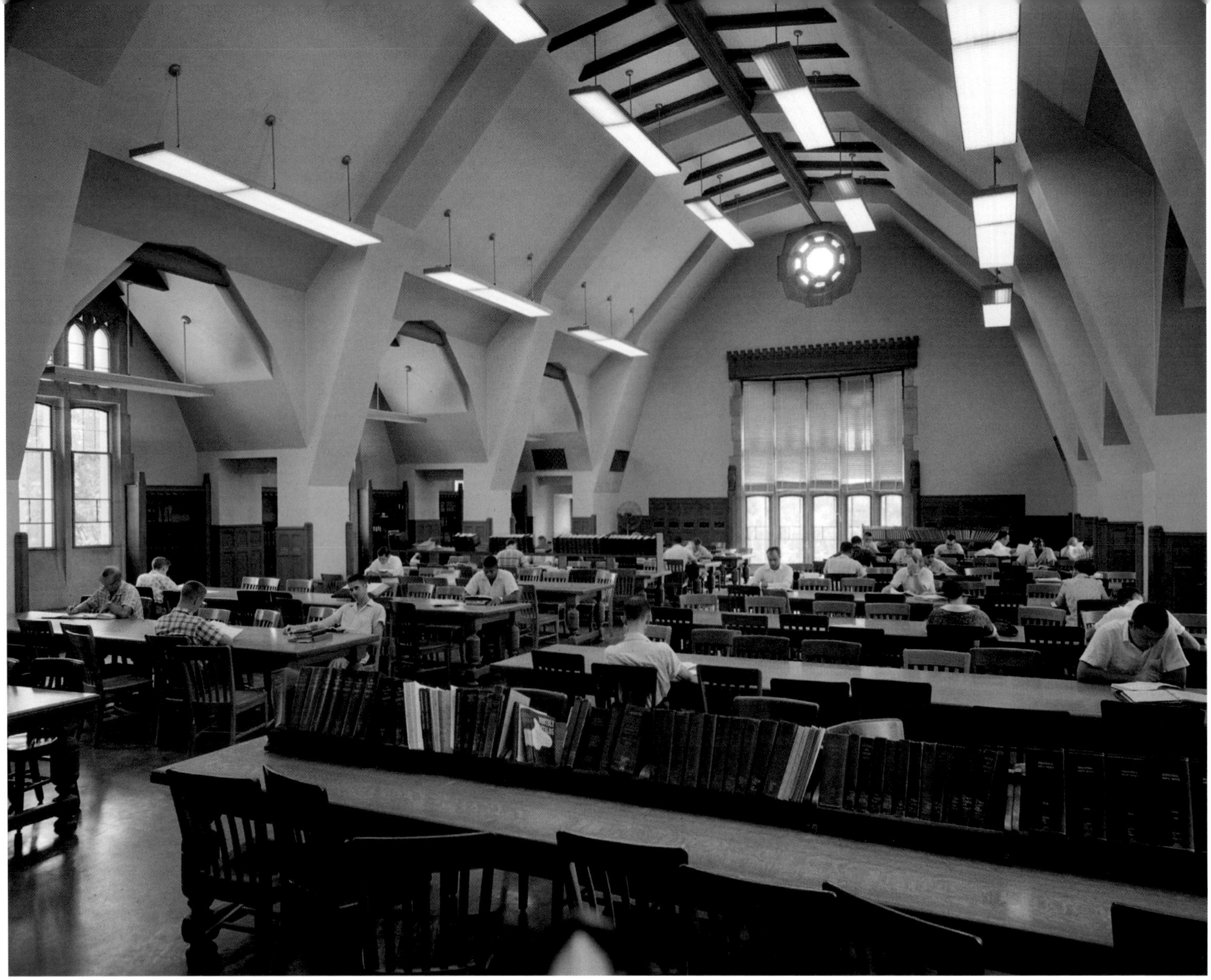

Woodburn Hall (Business and Economics Building) library featuring Gothic reading room with vaulted ceiling and arched bay window topped by rose window at apex, 1958. P0035102, IU Archives. Photo credit: Dave Curl.

resulted in some changes to the design. Primarily, the footprint of the building was modified from the originally planned rectangle to a Y-shaped design that would improve the functionality of the interior space and, according to Strauss, stylistically add "some interesting exterior possibilities" and an "improvement of the South elevation."[3]

Ground was broken that fall for the new Business and Economics building (or the B&E building, as it was affectionately known) and construction continued nearly congruently with a new physics building (now Swain Hall West). The two marked, according to university historian Thomas Clark, "the true beginning of the new academic era in Indiana University. . . . They served the more important function of symbolizing the opening of new approaches to the sciences and business."[4] The department faculty moved from eight separate buildings on campus into the new structure in January before it was fully finished. In June the building was completed with the addition of two panels from Thomas Hart Benton's *Social and Industrial History of Indiana* murals with business themes (*Electric Power, Motor Cars and Steel* and the controversial *Parks, the Circus, the Klan, the Press*) on the walls of the principal lecture hall. The official move occurred on July 5, 1940, bringing departmental classes and offices under one roof for the first time.

Woodburn can be described as modern Collegiate Gothic with Art Deco influences. The massing consists of five stories with a central tower rising above the main entrance and wings

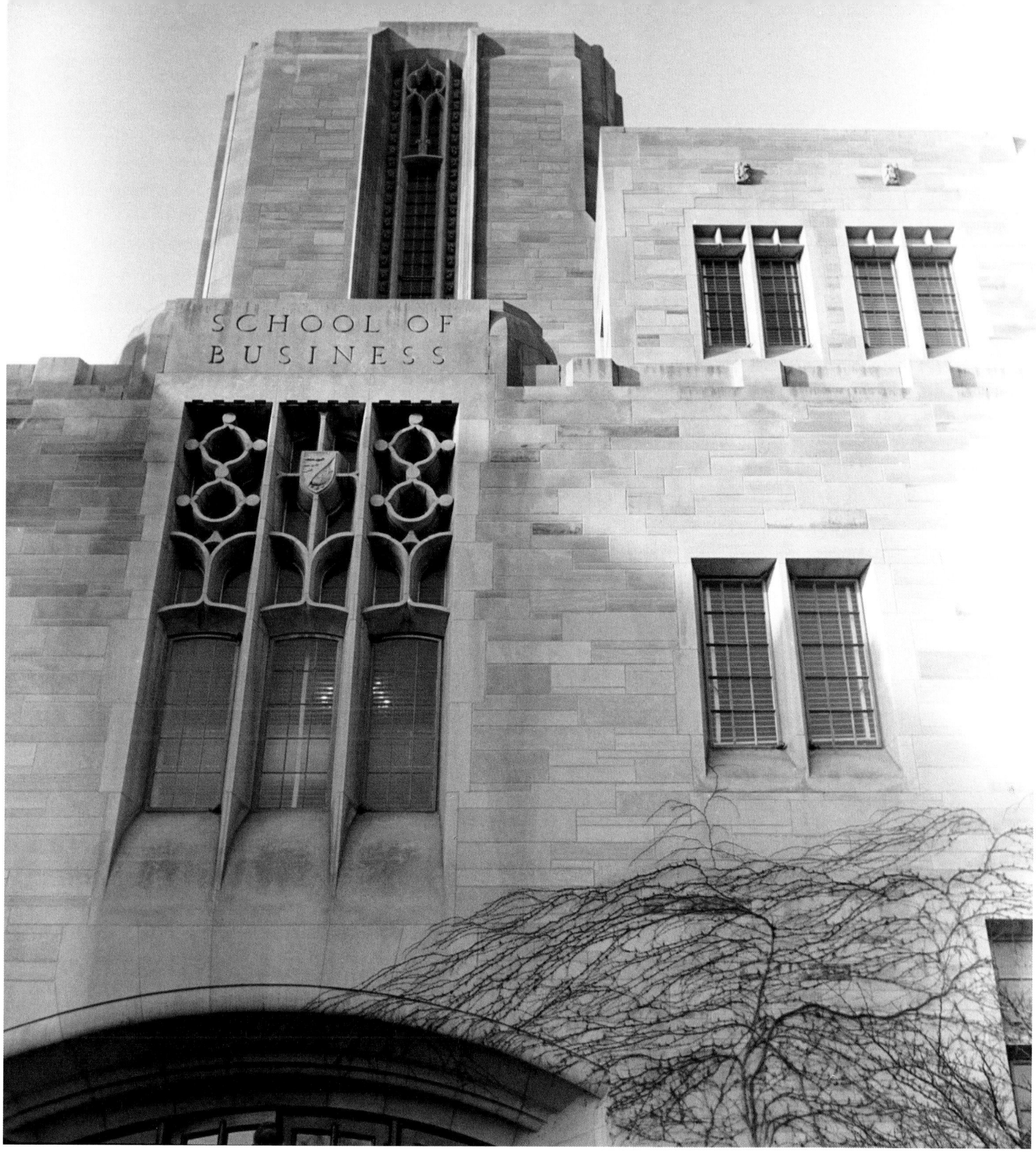

South elevation of Woodburn Hall tower embellished by decorative tracery, circa 1949.
P0049011, IU Archives.

extending to the east and west. There are three principal floors; a ground floor, which due to the elevated site has nearly full daylight lighting; and a small fourth floor that only extends across a portion of the elevation.[5] The exterior facade is mostly clad in sawn random ashlar Indiana limestone, with an overall sleek, linear appearance. Interestingly, the western wing and the tower seem more heavily influenced by the Collegiate Gothic, similar to the nearby Indiana Memorial Union and the older section of campus, while the eastern wing lacks much of this ornamentation, perhaps serving as a stylistic transition to Art Deco buildings such as the neighboring Indiana University Auditorium, which was planned for the Fine Arts Plaza. The eastern wing has a traditional rectangular footprint and features a flat roof and simple, unadorned windows. The western wing is arranged in a modified *Y* to fit the unusual concave shape of the site formed by the junction of Forest Place and Seventh Street. It features a steeply pitched roof accentuated with fleurs-de-lis, finial-topped gables, and simple parapets; a dramatic pointed arch over the main northern entry; a rose window; and rectilinear buttresses, which are accented by a stylized floral motif. The southern facade of the tower is embellished by decorative tracery, pointed arch windows, and vertical belt courses of a floral motif.

Inside the entrance on the western end, the semicircular lobby opens to two lecture halls. The lobby and remainder of the first floor are finished in limestone. The larger of the two lecture halls includes permanent seating and sloped floors to seat 450 students, while the smaller to the north seats 200. The two Benton Murals reside in the larger of the two spaces.

The second floor was dedicated to offices, research bureaus, and a library with a stunning Gothic reading room that utilized both parts of the modified *Y*. This room featured a vaulted ceiling 25 feet in height and on its west wall a spectacular arched bay window with decorative tracery and a rose window at the apex, the gift of former IU Trustee Robert Menke and his wife, Phyllis, in honor of Walter Laves, professor and chair of political science. The space was embellished with extensive woodwork and decorative carvings scattered throughout, most notably two carved owls symbolic of wisdom flanking the bay window. (Much of this architectural detail was retained in the 2014 conversion of this area into the Social Science Research Commons and its state-of-the-art Grand Hall.) Nearby, a small lounge, the Rawles Room, was dedicated to William A. Rawles, first dean of the School of Business.

On the eastern rectilinear end, the first and second floors were dedicated to classrooms, offices, and research bureaus. Of particular note, flexible partitions were used in the office spaces, presumably, according to Strauss, to "provide a practical demonstration of the use of this sort of thing in a business or industrial office and to assist in creating a typical business atmosphere in at least a portion of the building."[6] The second floor is now used primarily for office space.

The third and partial fourth floors on both the eastern and western ends housed a combination of classrooms and office space (now mostly offices), while the ground floor, in addition to containing the building's mechanical equipment, included classrooms and a student lounge with virtually full-daylight lighting. The student lounge is gone, but the classrooms remain.

In 1966, after the new home of the School of Business was completed at the corner of Tenth Street and Fee Lane, the Departments of Government, Social Sciences, and the Humanities became the primary occupants of Woodburn, and, more recently, the Departments of Political Science, African Studies, and the Social Science Research Commons. In 1971, with President John Ryan presiding, the building was renamed James Albert Woodburn Hall in honor of the notable "Chronicler of University History . . . Inspiring Teacher . . . Distinguished Historian . . . Wise Counselor and Warm Friend of Students . . . Leader in Community Affairs and Life-long Fighter Against Political and Electoral Corruption."[7]

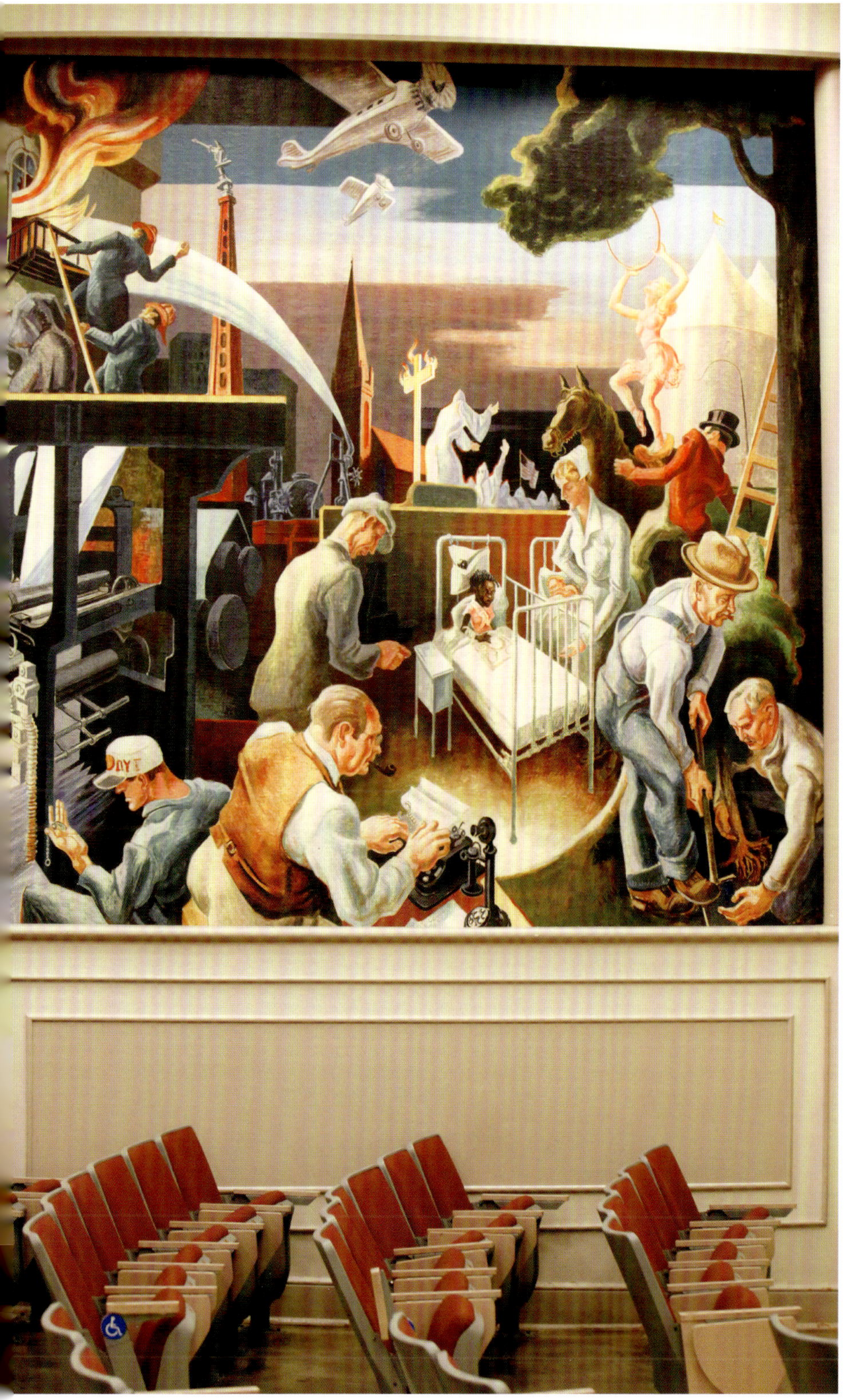

One of two Thomas Hart Benton mural panels found inside Woodburn Hall's main lecture room, *Parks, the Circus, the Klan, the Press,* referencing Indiana's darker history yet offering hope in the power of the free press, undated. Photo credit: Indiana University.

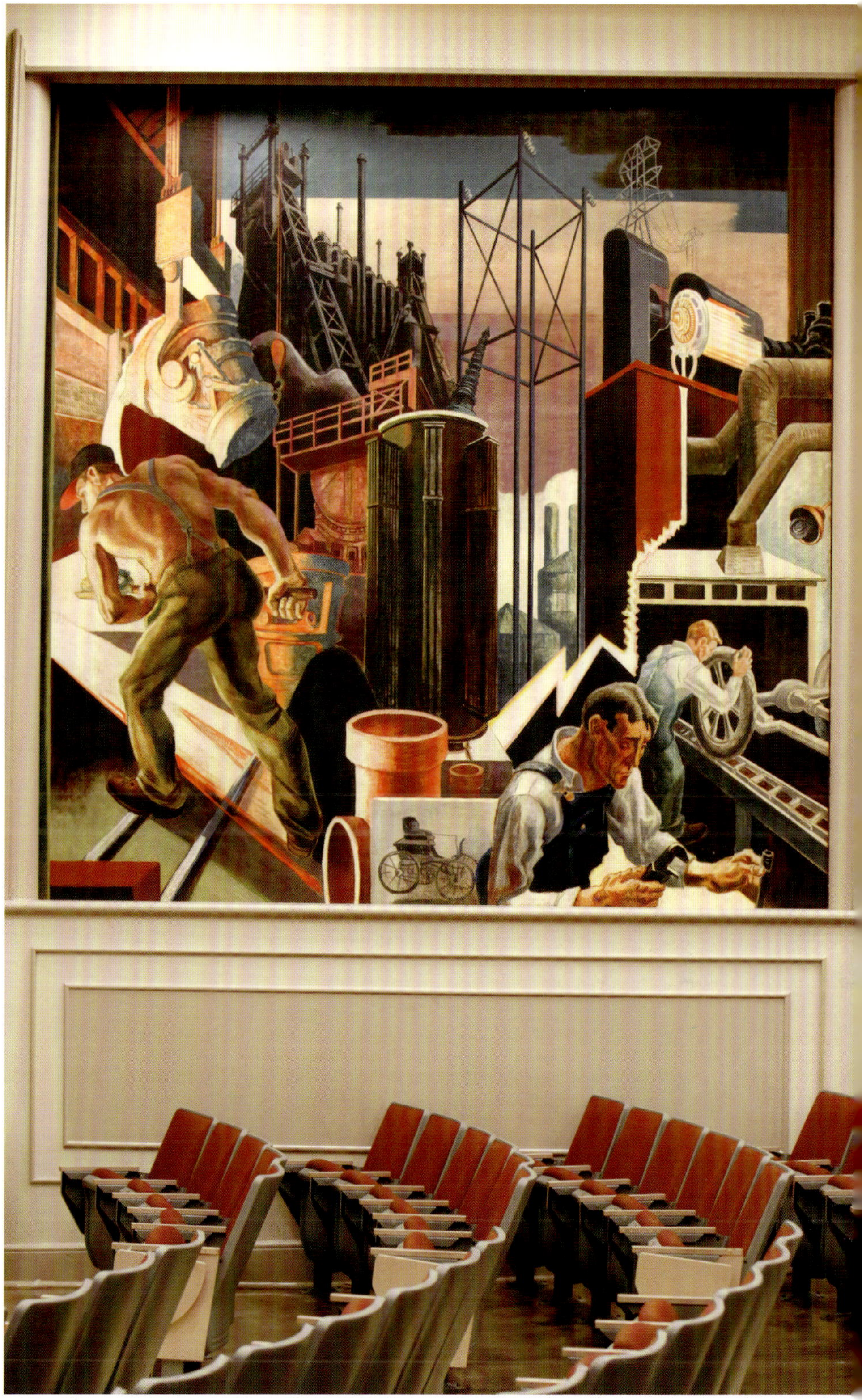

The second of two Thomas Hart Benton mural panels in Woodburn Hall, *Electric Power, Motor Cars, Steel,* representing Indiana's advances in manufacturing, undated. Photo credit: Indiana University.

Lowell E. Baier Hall 1956

ARCHITECT	Eggers and Higgins / A. M. Strauss
ARCHITECTURAL STYLE	Collegiate Gothic
ORIGINAL NAME	School of Law
ADDITION	1984, Eggers and Higgins / Odle-Burke Architects

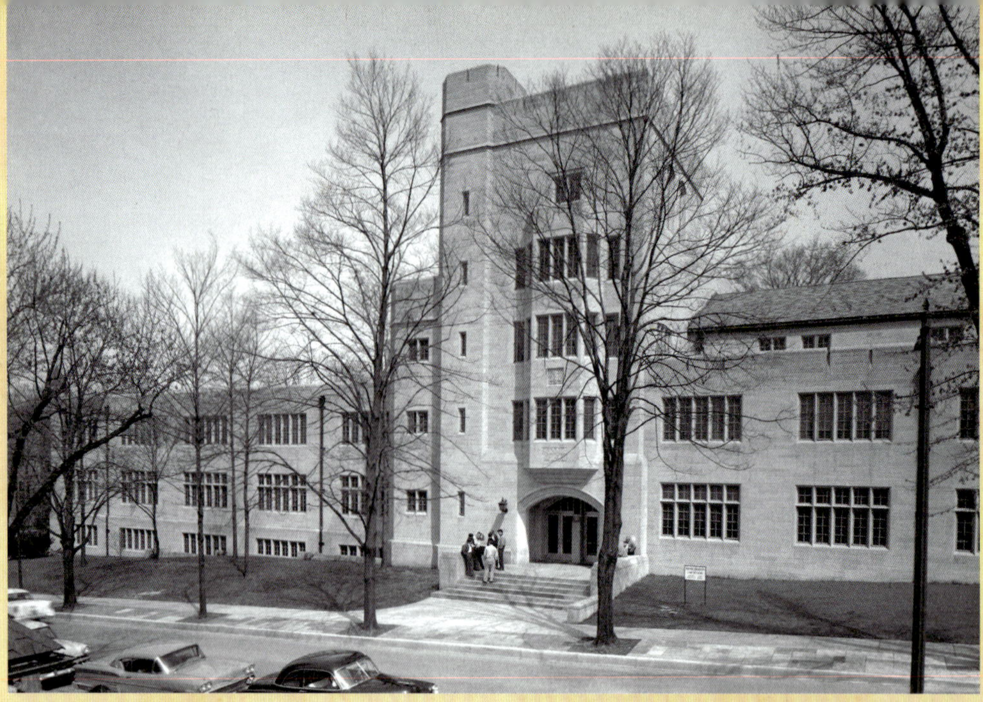

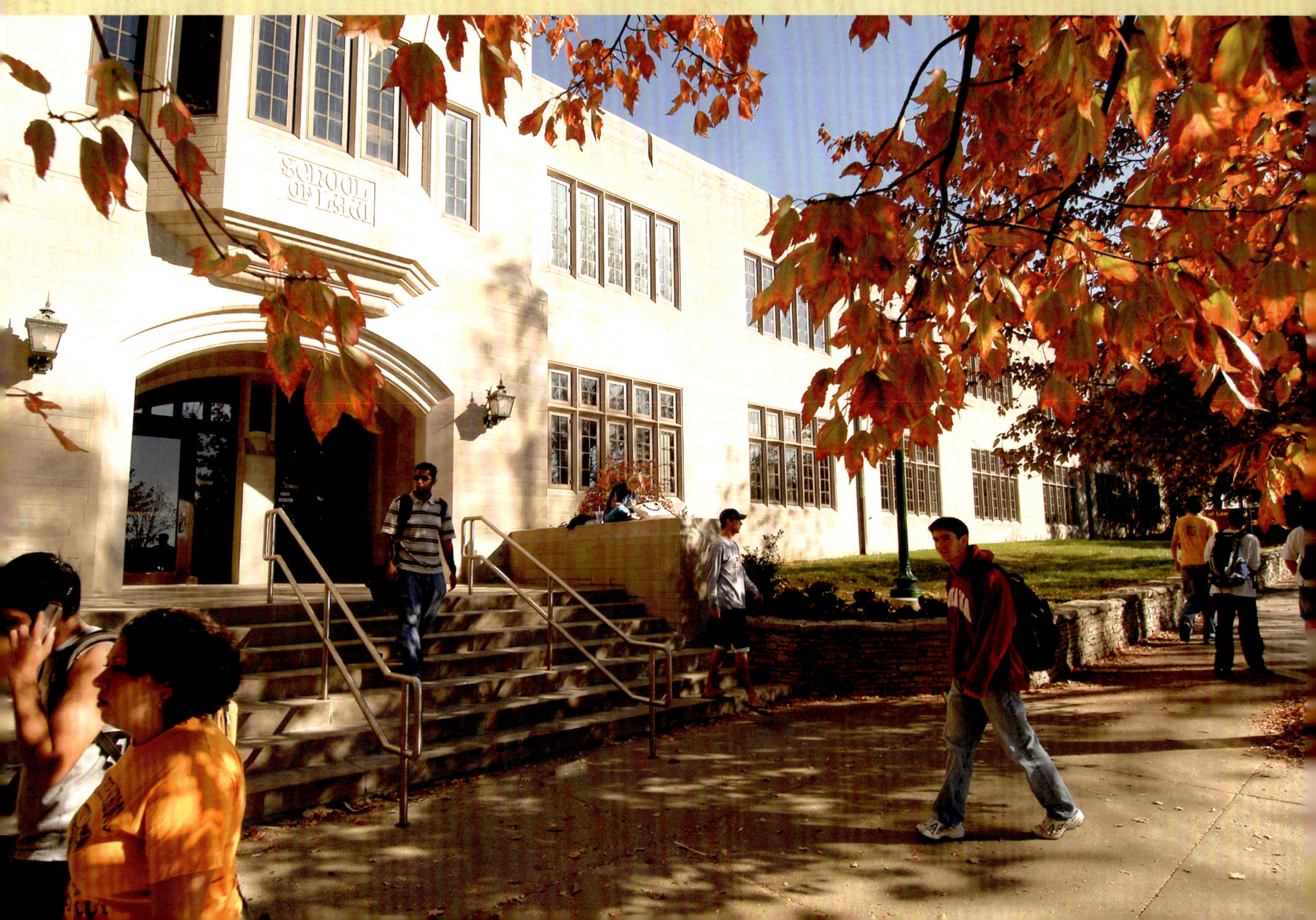

Lowell E. Baier Hall

Completing the Old Academic Quadrangle

We place our faith in government by law instead of the arbitrary rule of man. In the building which we are dedicating, young men and women shall be trained in this faith. They shall be jurists of a modern, dynamic democracy.

—Indiana University President Herman B Wells at dedication ceremony

IN 1957, IN HIS DEDICATION SPEECH FOR THE IU School of Law building, President Wells stated "we are dedicating a permanent home for our oldest professional school. It is the only one established before Dr. Bryan's administration."[1] In response to the Indiana General Assembly's direction that education be provided in the science of law, Indiana University offered its first law class on December 5, 1842. Due to lack of dedicated space, classes were held wherever room was available, both on and off the Seminary Square campus, until Science Hall opened in 1874.[2] Here the law students had a home, albeit a short-lived one, since in 1877 the state legislature cut support for the study of law to such a degree that it was necessary to cease instruction. Due in part to student demand, in 1889 the trustees reestablished the department as a school and named David Banta as its first dean.[3] The School of Law initially occupied the top floors of Kirkwood and Wylie Halls but then in 1908 moved to Maxwell Hall, where it remained until 1956.

The Indiana University School of Law was the first state law school in the Midwest and the ninth law school in the nation. By the early 1940s, as its student enrollment increased, the ensuing need for larger and better facilities became apparent. The Mad Monks of Maxwell, as law students were known, had outgrown their space. Law School dean Bernard C. Gavit began to campaign vigorously for a new purpose-built law building, an improved library, and increased faculty. But a nearly decadelong fight for new facilities seemed to take its toll, and poor health forced Gavit to resign before his dream became a reality. But in 1952 discussions finally began in earnest about construction of a building for the study of law with an eye toward future needs, prestige, and overall morale; in May 1954, the trustees approved preliminary plans, and ground was broken in early 1955.

The new Law School completed the old academic quadrangle near the corner of Third Street and Indiana Avenue. Designed by A. M. Strauss of Fort Wayne with supervising architectural firm Eggers and Higgins of New York, the building likely would have received Dean Gavit's full approval. The modified Gothic structure is built of Indiana limestone and exhibits an overall simplicity with a few decorative carvings. The words *School of Law* are inscribed above the arched doorway at the main entrance, and higher on the front wall the scales of justice can be seen within three tiers of stacked oriel windows. Gothic influence is particularly evident in the castle tower over the west entry and the subtle battlements at the peak of the

Facing top, Lowell E. Baier Hall, School of Law, 1959. P0052540, IU Archives.

Facing bottom, Lowell E. Baier Hall on a fall day, 2016. Photo credit: Tyagan Miller.

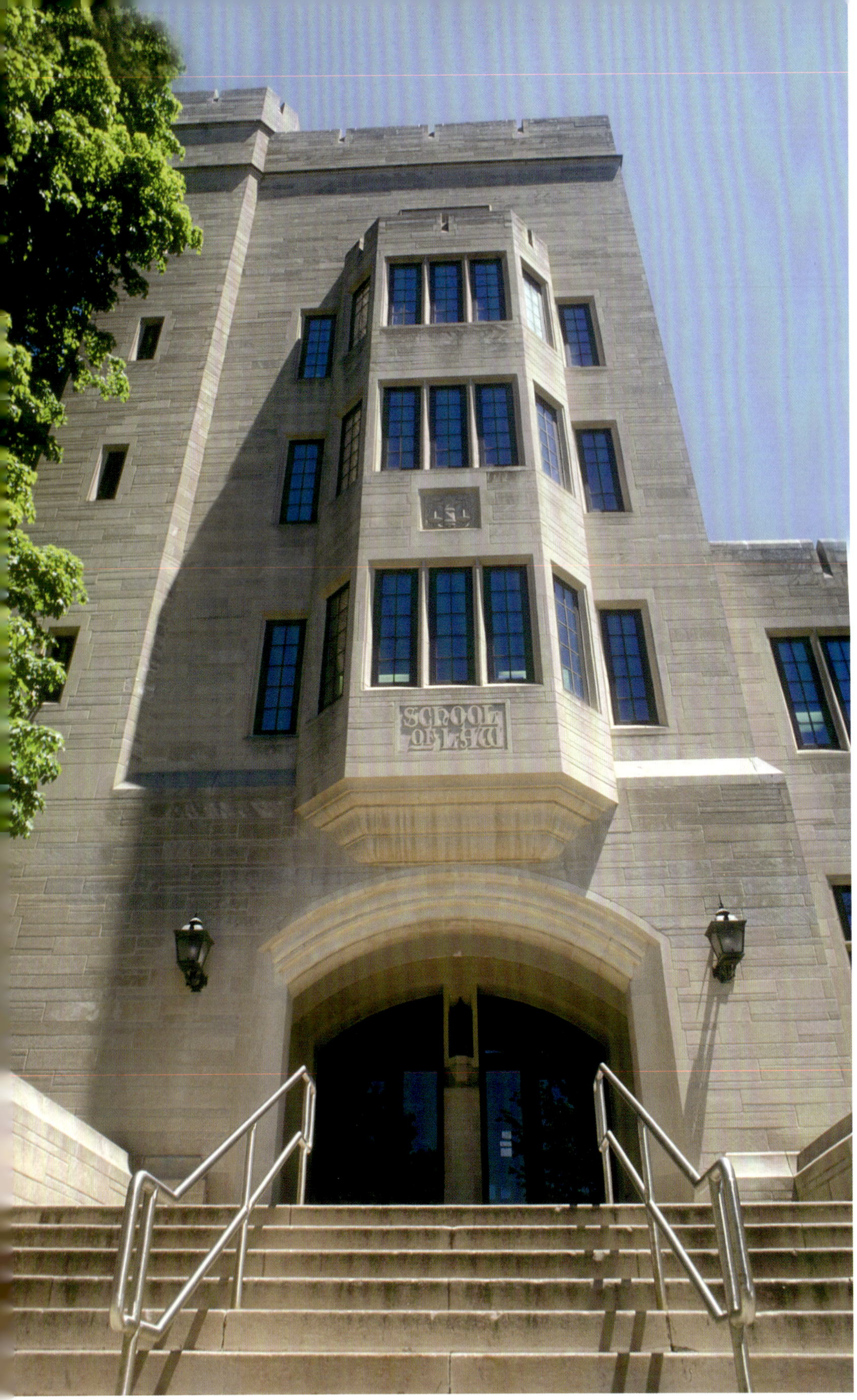

Stacked windows above main entrance to Baier Hall, undated. Photo credit: Indiana University.

windows and near the roofline. The interior included a library with shelving for 130,000 volumes covering 27,950 square feet on three floors. On the second floor was a student lounge with overstuffed furniture, and the ground floor had locker space for every student. Full-time faculty members each had their own private office with easy access to the library, and spare offices were available for expansion. The showplace, however, was the Moot Court Room on the first floor. With room for 272 attendees in auditorium-style seating, the practice courtroom included a judge's bench, a jury box for twelve, counsel tables, witness box, and a clerk and reporter's table.

The building fulfilled the needs of the law students for the next twenty-five years, but by the late 1970s, enrollment had exceeded the five hundred students for which the structure had been designed. As a result of the overcrowding, the American Bar Association accrediting team deemed the school not in compliance with national standards for major law schools. Sheldon Plager, then serving as dean, advised the Board of Trustees that doing nothing was not a viable option; they either needed a new building or they needed to proceed with expanding the existing one as soon as possible. After many discussions, in February 1980 the trustees approved going forward with a significant expansion, with most of the new space dedicated for the library.

Planning moved slowly, but by 1982 the university was ready to begin construction with designs from Eggers and Higgins Architects of New York. However, they found themselves up against a major obstacle. The law school addition was to go on the east side of the building. The approved plans included a small corner that encroached slightly across the brick walk bordering Dunn's Woods. In September 1980, the woods, along with the rest of the Old Crescent, had been added to the National Register of Historic Places, which made development in the area extremely difficult, if not impossible. And, even if the university were able to legally proceed with the expansion, it then faced protests from those intent on the protection of the woods, led on campus by the well-organized Save the Woods group.

The group found a crucial ally in their movement: Indiana University President John W. Ryan. Ryan requested other options and with that, plans were returned to the architects to see if they could be modified so the building would not impinge on the Old Crescent. The architects resubmitted a design that pushed the addition behind the existing walkway, alleviating opponents' concerns. To placate the astronomy department, provisions were implemented to minimize heat and light pollution that could interfere with nearby Kirkwood Observatory. Director of physical facilities J. Terry Clapacs remarked that the new plans as approved by the IU Architectural Committee resulted in "a better design for all parties concerned."[4] Construction moved forward in two phases, and by 1986, the law school gained one of the most beautiful library spaces on any college campus with multilevel windows that created rapport with the campus's historic legacy, Dunn's Woods. The addition added 60,000 square feet, and a library that is one of the premier research facilities and top law libraries in the nation. It also is one of the largest academic law libraries in United States.

In December 2008 the School of Law was renamed the Maurer School of Law in recognition of the longtime support of alumnus Michael Maurer and his wife, Janie, and their $35 million gift for law student scholarships—at the time, the largest donation ever received by a single donor. In March 2015, the building housing the Maurer School of Law was renamed Baier Hall for Lowell E. Baier, a 1964 alumnus, successful attorney, entrepreneur, and conservationist. At the dedication ceremony, Baier stated that "this gift will ensure the continuing integrity of the law school building and the law library, its very soul, inspiring the best in academic and scholastic achievement—remember, a sense of place creates a sense of purpose."[5]

The Maurer School of Law has many eminent alumni, including the Honorable Sherman Minton, associate justice of the Supreme Court; numerous state supreme court justices and federal appellate and district court judges; Wendell Willkie, 1940 candidate for U.S. president; composer and songwriter Hoagy Carmichael; Indiana governors George Craig and Frank O'Bannon; and several U.S. legislators, including William Jenner, Vance Hartke, Birch Bayh, and Lee Hamilton.

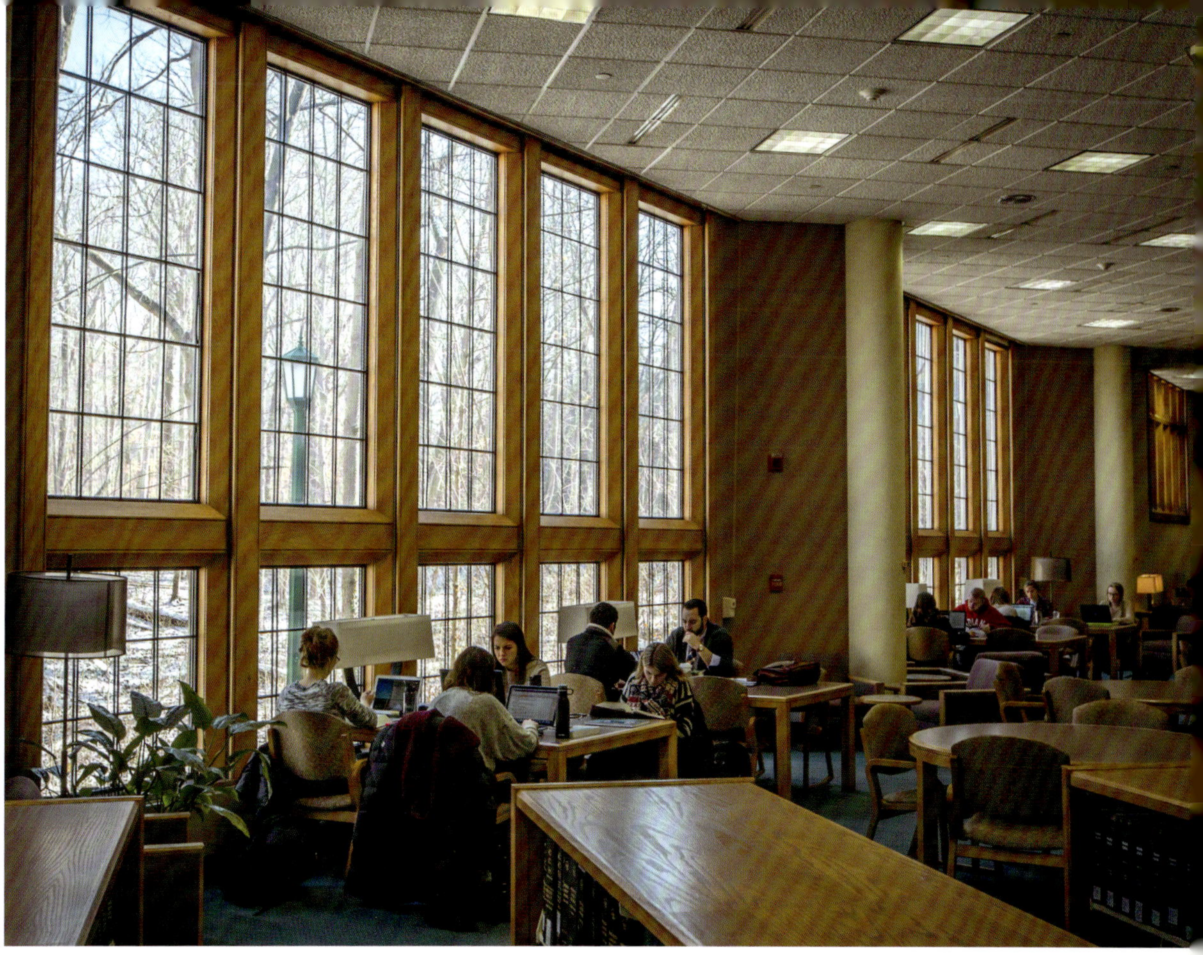

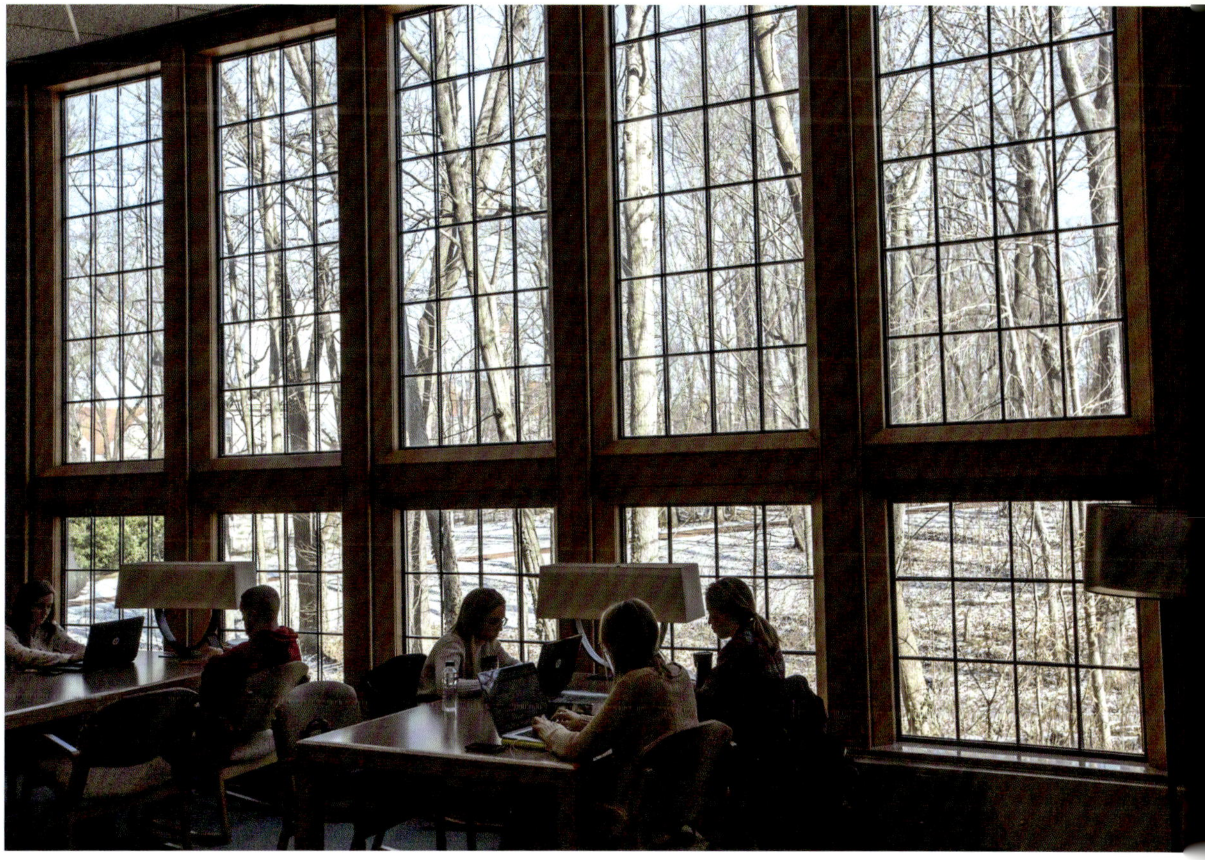

Window wall in law library overlooking historic Dunn's Woods, 2017. Photo credits: Tyagan Miller.

Radio and Television Building 1963

ARCHITECT	Eggers and Higgins / A. M. Strauss
ARCHITECTURAL STYLE	1950s Modern
ADDITION	1996
ARCHITECT	Ratio Architects

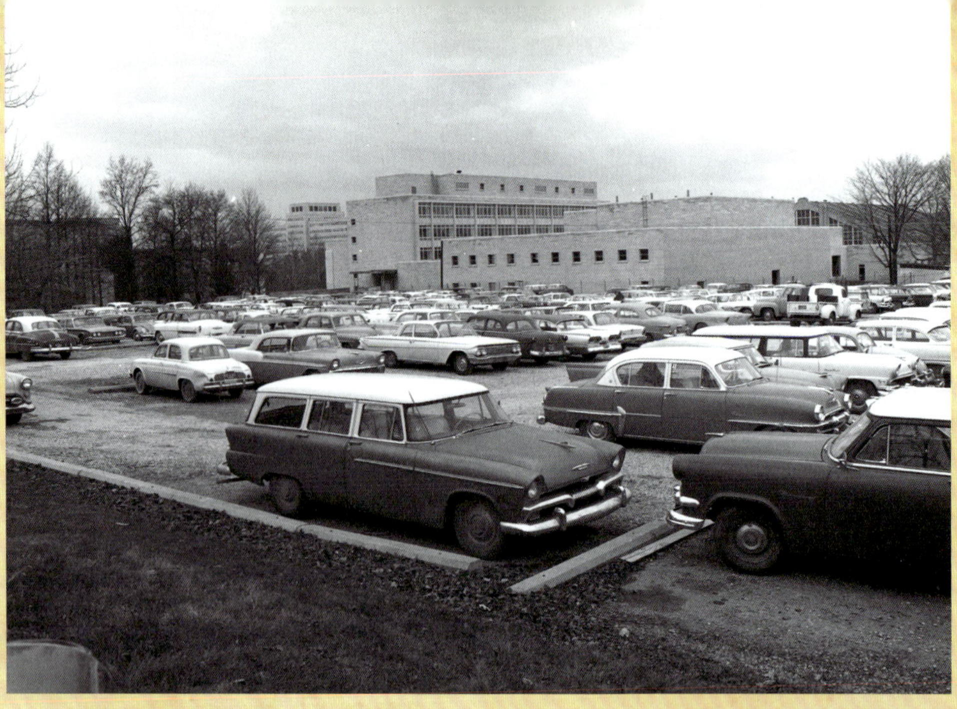

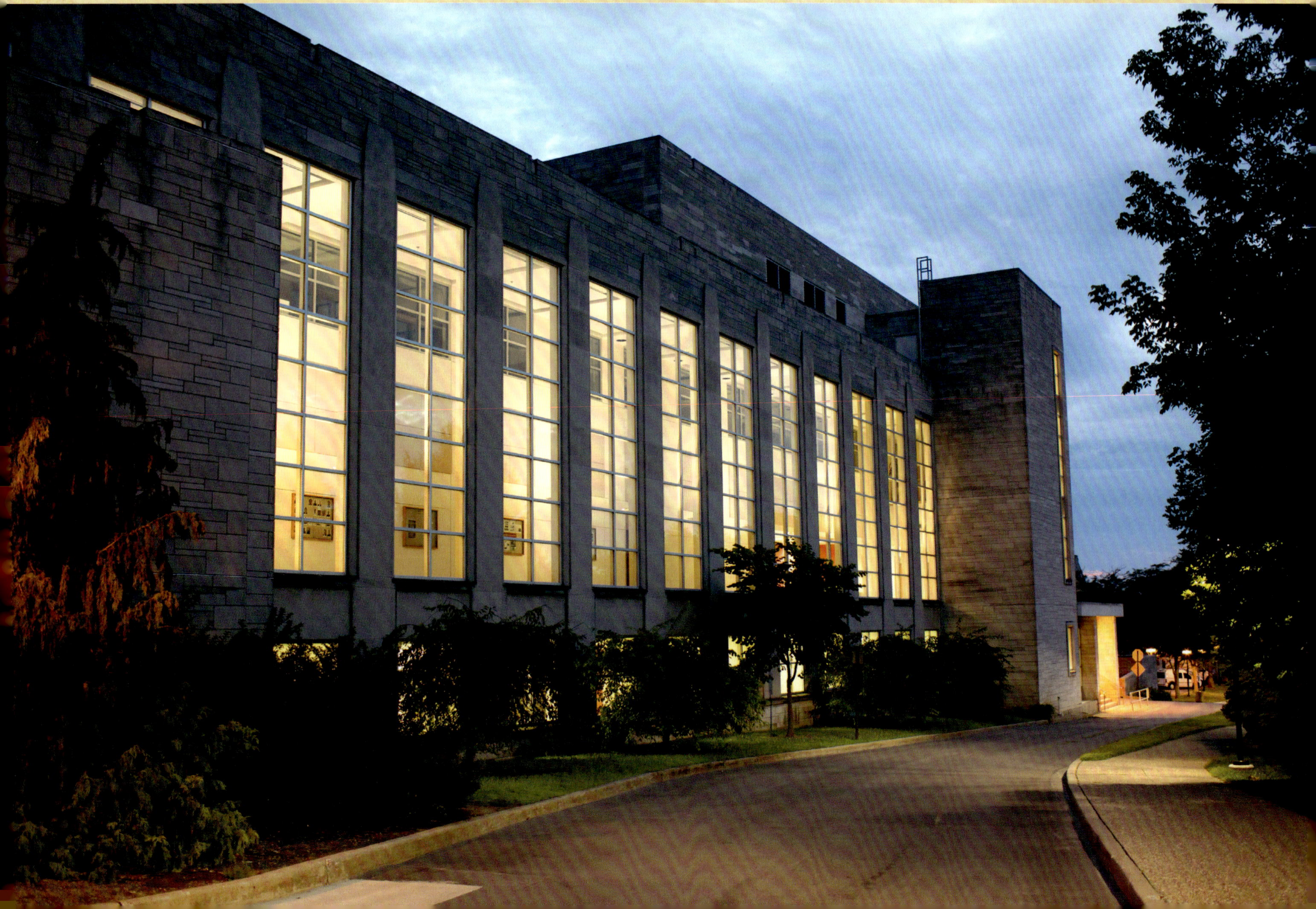

Radio and Television Building

Beaming WFIU and WTIU

The most complete structure of its kind to handle radio and television in the world.

—Elmer G. Sulzer, Chairman of the Department of Radio and Television

Indiana University was reportedly the first educational institution to utilize radio for educational purposes. Dr. Rolla Roy Ramsey of the Department of Physics had devoted much of his time to experimenting with the medium and teaching radio work to the men assigned to the U.S. Radio School in Bloomington during the First World War. On January 5, 1922, a group of seventy-five students and faculty packed the auditorium of Lindley Hall to listen to "flashes of speeches and music from points as far separated as Nebraska and New Jersey" in the first public demonstration of radio at the university.[1] Over the coming decades, faculty such as Harry Skornia (director of Radio Programs and later chair of the department, 1942–53) offered courses in radio production despite the fact that the Department of Radio was only established near the close of World War II in 1945. In 1953 the Department of Radio became the Department of Radio and Television within the College of Arts and Sciences, and in 1974 it was renamed the Department of Telecommunications. In 2014 the Departments of Telecommunications and Communications and Culture merged with the School of Journalism to become the Media School.

Although Indiana University was a leader in radio education early on, between 1922 and World War II other schools caught up and were surpassing the training offered at IU. University administrators understood that with the end of the war and the influx of returning GIs "we must meet the competition

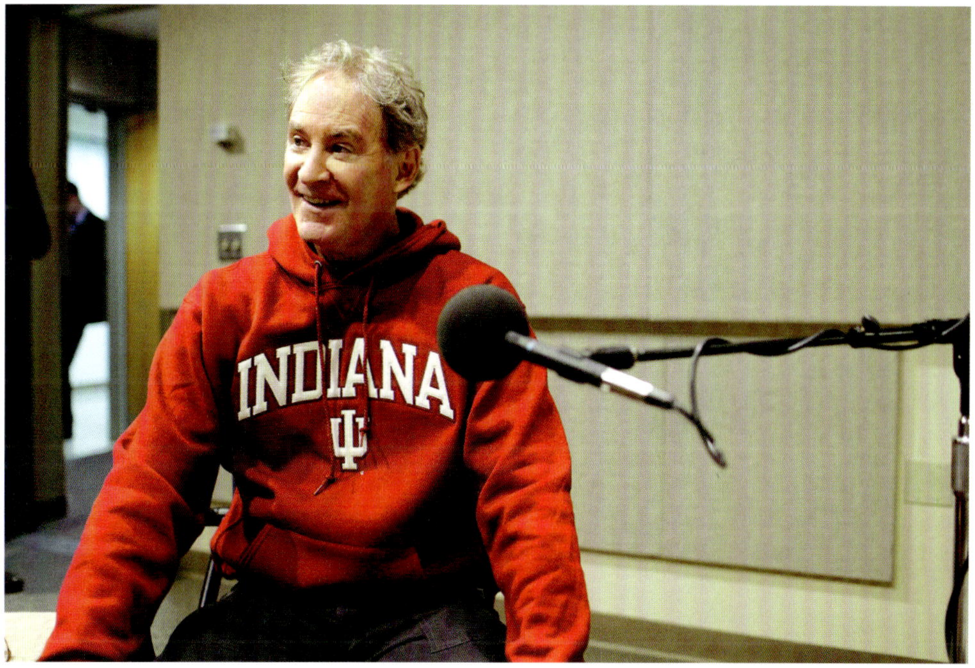

Above, IU alumnus Kevin Kline giving an interview in a Radio and Television Building studio, 2014. Photo credit: Indiana University.

Facing top, Radio and Television Building amid a sea of campus parking, 1961. P0033190, IU Archives.

Facing bottom, Nighttime view of the Radio and Television Building facing the Arboretum, 2016. Photo credit: Indiana University.

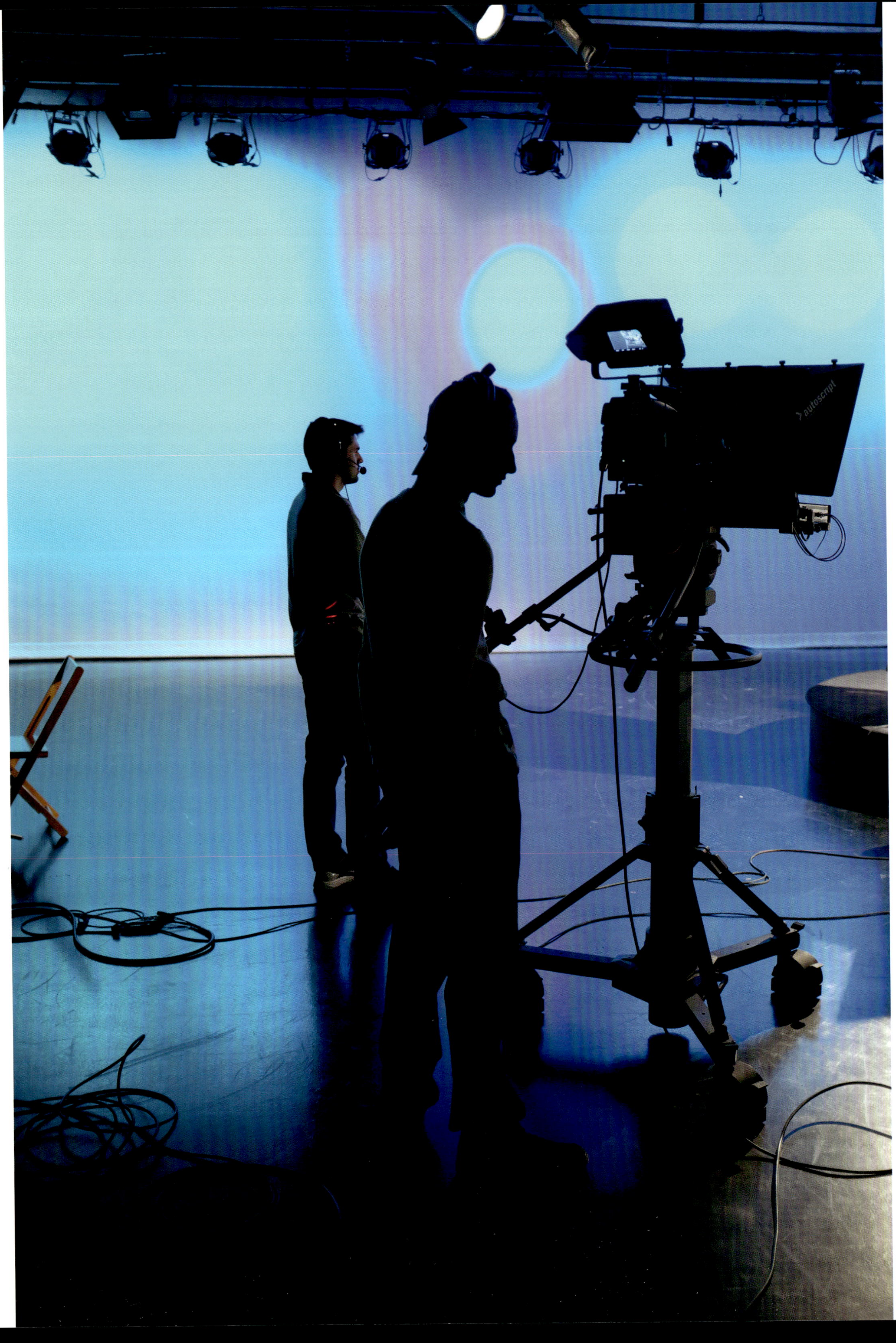

Students gaining practical experience in a Radio and Television Building studio, 2015. Photo credit: Indiana University.

or give up trying to attract to our institution students who are desirous of radio training . . . most of our sister institutions not only offer much more attractive work and opportunities than we do in radio, but are well on their way to post-war expansion on a scale not envisioned before the war."[2] Thus as early as 1944, a building for the new discipline appeared on the list of proposed construction projects. However, as with so many departments, the scramble to provide housing for the tidal wave of new students after World War II took precedence, so the classrooms and offices of the radio department were relegated to quarters in a Quonset hut east of Jordan Avenue near the site of the present-day Jordan parking garage.

In the mid-1950s the project again gained traction, and in February 1954 a preliminary proposal for a new structure to house both the fine arts and radio and television departments was presented to the Indiana University Board of Trustees. In 1957, the board approved proceeding with the preparation of plans and A. M. Strauss of Fort Wayne was selected as the local architect under the supervision of the New York firm of Eggers and Higgins. The two departments would be under one roof but separate, and connected by a north courtyard (enclosed in 1990) and a hallway on the ground floor. The section of the building facing the Fine Arts Plaza would be occupied by fine arts, while the section to the north would house radio and television. The contract for the entire steel frame was awarded in 1959, and work was completed before the end of the year; however, by the fall, while the fine arts section continued toward completion, construction of radio and television was delayed due to lack of funding.

The radio and television portion of the project was completed in 1963. Despite the new, state-of-the-art interior, the minimalist exterior was austere and according to Ray Casati (university architect) in 1995, it remained an "incomplete project," with the windowless north side of the structure (now facing the new Arboretum) reminiscent of "an emergency exit." The building had three aboveground floors and was clad in limestone in a random ashlar pattern. It was modern, with no ornamentation, small windows, and a flat roof. Both the radio and television and the psychology buildings were designed by the same architect, constructed by the same builder, and finished in the same year, so there was evident similarity in their appearance. However, the interior, according to Elmer Sulzer, department chair from 1954–1964, had "unusual facilities that are not duplicated in any other college broadcasting lay-out in the country."[3] In addition to superior acoustics and electrostatic air-conditioning (perfect air-quality environment), the building included classrooms to train students in programming and production, four radio studios, and four television studios, two of which were equipped for ordinary broadcasting and two for closed-circuit broadcasting that allowed for the simultaneous production of several programs. The largest studio could accommodate 150 individuals and was unique in that it combined the features of a theater stage with those of a television studio. This versatility rendered it widely usable for large ensemble productions by organizations such as the Indiana University Symphony Orchestra. The pride of the department was its WFIU radio station, which produced the notable *School of the Sky* program used by secondary schools in numerous Indiana counties and multiple states as well as Radio Free Europe and Voice of America.

In 1996, the university broke ground on a five-level limestone and glass addition for the north side of the building and a massive interior renovation designed by Ratio Architects of Indianapolis. The addition features vertical limestone panels in a random ashlar pattern as well as, according to Casati, "a nice rhythm of windows and columns" overlooking the Arboretum.[4] Interior renovations included the addition of a two-and-a-half-story atrium entryway to the east as well as updated facilities for the WFIU radio and WTIU television stations, advanced technology auditoriums, interactive classroom studios, video conferencing rooms, and faculty offices.

Hodge Hall Undergraduate Center 1966

ARCHITECT Hall-Kane Associates / Eggers and Higgins

ADDITION 2015, BSA LifeStructures

ARCHITECTURAL STYLE Collegiate Gothic

William Godfrey Graduate and Executive Education Center 2003

ARCHITECT Beyer Blinder Belle / BSA LifeStructures

ARCHITECTURAL STYLE Contextual Modern with Expressed Structural Patterns

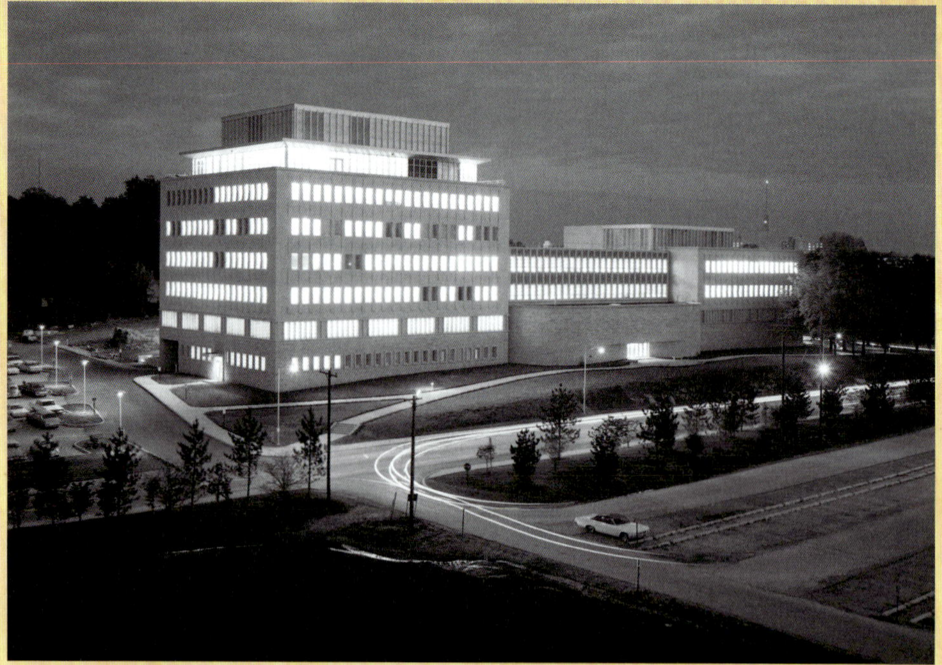

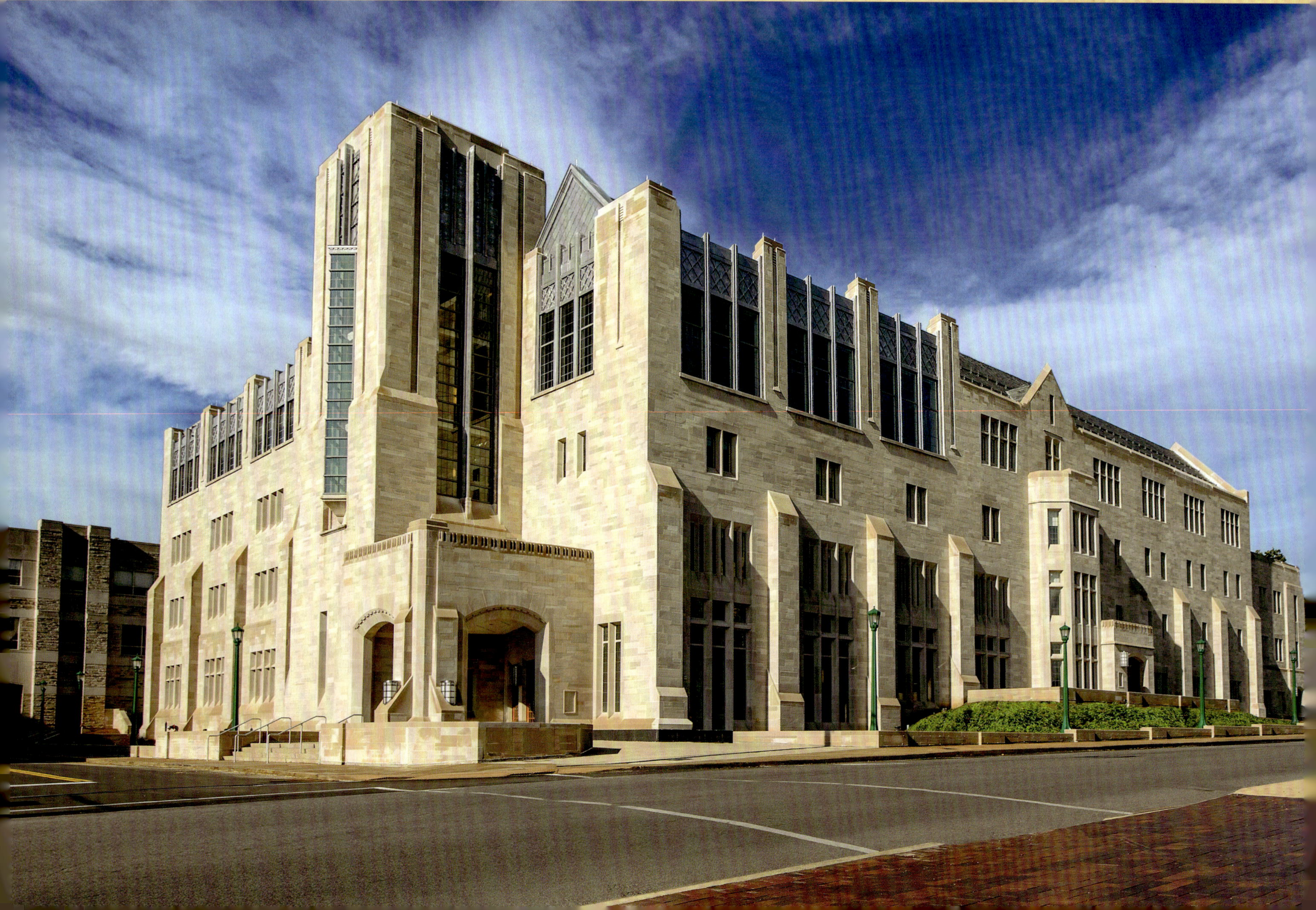

Hodge Hall Undergraduate Center / William Godfrey Graduate and Executive Education Center

A National Leader in Business Education

Enterprise, responsibility, work and usefulness—these are the foundation stones of business leadership. . . . A business career in modern America can be a path to the greatest realization of individual usefulness. It is just such sensitive, socially responsible leadership—whether in business, the professions, or the arts—that Indiana University upholds and honors for our young people.

—Indiana University President Elvis J. Stahr at dedication ceremony

The Indiana University Kelley School of Business, housed in a complex of two major structures at the corner of Tenth Street and Fee Lane, has had three permanent homes since its founding in 1920. Although the curricular origin of the school can be traced to a class in political economy taught by Andrew Wylie, IU's first president, the initial department was organized as the School of Commerce and Finance under founding dean William Rawles. The faculty and seventy students were primarily housed in Commerce Hall (renamed Rawles Hall in 1963), built as an extension of the Old Crescent in 1923. (In 1933 the School of Commerce and Finance became the School of Business Administration, in 1938 the School of Business, and in 1997 the Kelley School of Business.)

In July 1940, the School of Business moved into the Business and Economics Building (renamed Woodburn Hall in 1971) where it remained for twenty-five years. Although Woodburn Hall provided a central location and a beautiful edifice, eventually the success of the program, with its increasing enrollment, courses, and numbers of faculty, pushed the school to consider expansion. However, adding space at the Seventh Street site was not possible without broaching the protected wooded area to the south. Campus planners consequently looked north and identified a site on Tenth Street where the School of Business would have room for future growth and convenient parking.

The architectural firm Hall-Kane and Associates of Gary was commissioned to design the new building, with Eggers and Higgins of New York serving as supervising architect. Hall-Kane developed a unique structure with limestone-clad elevations that resembled a key punch card. Whether this was intentional or not is unknown, but the rhythm of window rows and openings was unmistakably in the image and spirit of the then innovative and life-changing role of computers systems in the nation. The building footprint consisted of two large wings connected by a smaller link that contained lecture halls, each with a capacity of 250 students. The seven-story north wing provided space for faculty offices, research rooms, and administrative staff. The four floors in the south wing contained modern, cutting-edge classrooms. University president Elvis J. Stahr presided over the dedication of the new building on November 18, 1966, and in his remarks traced the history of the school's leadership from Andrew Wylie to Herman B Wells, Art Weimer, and finally W. George Pinnell, all deans of the school. President Stahr claimed that the new home for the School of Business was the finest business academic building in the country.[1]

William Godfrey Graduate and Executive Education Center

William J. Godfrey enrolled at Indiana University in 1960. Of modest, small-town Indiana circumstances but blessed with

Facing top, The School of Business building resembled a keypunch card, especially at night, 1966. P0035106, IU Archives. Photo credit: Elwood Martin "Barney" Cowherd.

Facing bottom, Hodge Hall as viewed from the Arboretum, undated. Photo credit: Indiana University.

a strong work ethic, he earned a bachelor's degree in business. Three military tours of duty followed before Godfrey would return to Indiana University, complete his MBA, and then direct the School of Business's executive education program. Eventually Godfrey found great success in the pharmaceutical industry and as a real estate developer, but he never forgot his alma mater and the scholarship that made his education possible. He gifted $25 million to the School of Business: $20 million for scholarships for students who would not otherwise be able to attend the university, and $5 million toward a graduate education facility that would bear his name.

The William Godfrey Graduate and Executive Education Center was constructed directly across Fee Lane from the School of Business (Hodge Hall). Beyer Blinder Belle Architects (BBB) of New York teamed with BSA LifeStrucures of Indianapolis to design a new home for the overcrowded MBA program functions. BBB had recently completed a successful renovation of Grand Central Station in New York City and was gaining national distinction for its design work. A key project challenge for the architects was how to connect the two buildings separated by Fee Lane in a way that the undergraduate and graduate programs would remain integrated. John Belle, project architect for BBB, presented a controversial plan to the IU administration that included an overhead bridge between

William Godfrey Graduate and Executive Education Center and bridge to Hodge Hall, 2005. Photo credit: Indiana University.

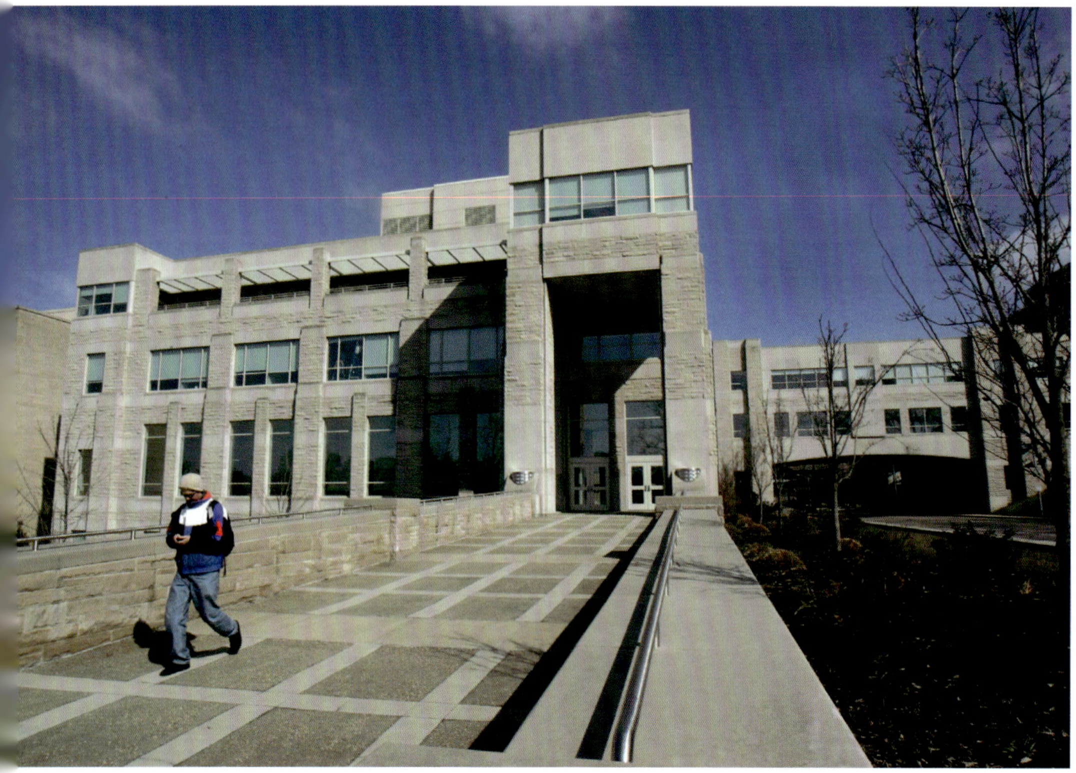

the buildings. The university architects had always believed that connecting links above grade was an urban solution not in keeping with the natural, bucolic environment of the campus. Nevertheless, Belle convinced IU administrators and trustees that the bridge was appropriate in that location and would be seen as a symbolic unifying element, particularly if the offices of the dean were placed there, thus bonding the two major components of the school.

BBB took inspiration for the Godfrey graduate center design from the Indiana Memorial Union. The firm honored campus tradition with a four-story Collegiate Gothic building and softened a large building mass with medium-scale bays of limestone and bay windows combined with a strong stone texture. Close examination reveals an architectural precedent found in prewar New York City buildings that ring Central Park, many of which had utilized Indiana limestone in their construction and possessed multiple setbacks affording terraces. Those same features can be seen in the detailing of the Godfrey center.

President Adam W. Herbert dedicated the William Godfrey Graduate and Executive Education Center on October 21, 2005, drawing reference to the circle of philanthropy that is the underpinning of many gifts received by the university—a student receives financial aid to make his or her education possible, and after the student achieves some success in life, he or she chooses to give back to the university, allowing other students to have the same opportunity.

HODGE HALL UNDERGRADUATE CENTER

Indiana University alumnus James R. Hodge (BS 1974) shared Bill Godfrey's desire to give back to the university. Combined with a $33 million Lilly Endowment grant and other smaller gifts, his $15 million gift allowed for the construction of a 90,000-square-foot wraparound addition to the 1966 School of Business building and a chance to change the key-punch-card design to a style more compatible with the Indiana University campus.

BSA LifeStructures of Indianapolis, led by designer Kalevi Huotilainen, was selected as architect for the project. The IU administration asked BSA LifeStructures to study Woodburn Hall, a prior home of the School of Business, as their architects moved through the schematic design phase of the project. More than an emblematic gesture, the university wanted to carry the feel of mature campus buildings over to those now on the drawing board. Woodburn Hall was rooted in the uni-

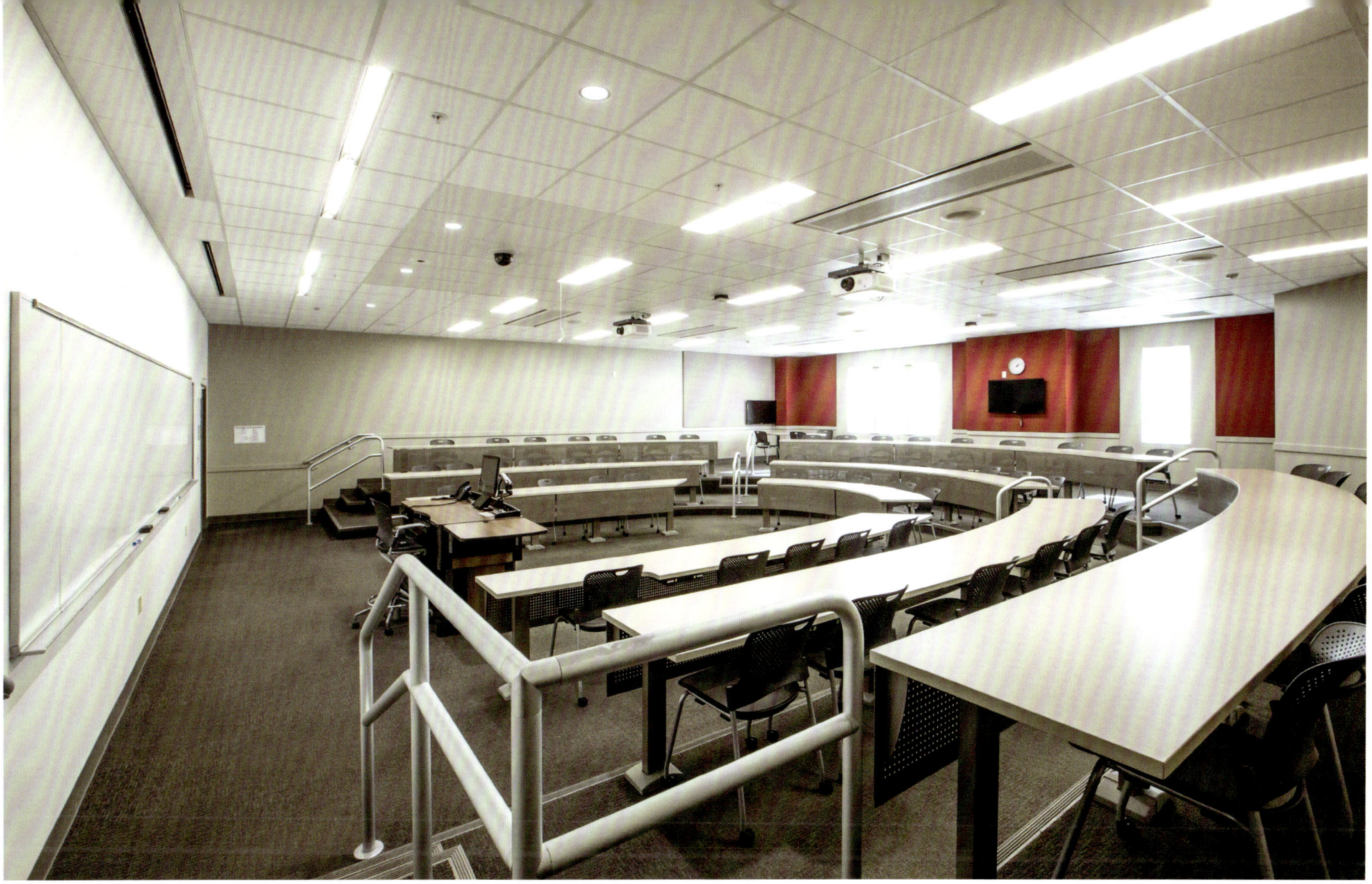

versity's well-established Collegiate Gothic tradition, with its buttressed stone walls, steep slate roof, and deeply recessed openings. Woodburn also has an attractive and interesting Art Deco–era overlay, which the university hoped to replicate.

BSA LifeStructures produced a design that met all of the goals with the wraparound addition, which now establishes a stronger Tenth Street presence and strengthens the visage of the Arboretum across the street with a more clearly defined northern edge. Thick smooth-cut ashlar limestone walls, multiple openings, buttresses, and prominent gables fashion the two main wings. The Indiana limestone is variegated in color, with smooth trim accenting and accentuating windows and doors. A corner tower connects the wings and anchors the building to the site, enhancing the sense of permanence. The tower steps inward as it rises and displays metal detailing, recalling older IU buildings.

The addition includes twenty classrooms, each with a sixty-person horseshoe configuration that fosters dialogue and interaction. Spacious meeting and multipurpose rooms provide areas where students can study, interact, and have room for teamwork. A fourth-level vaulted multipurpose room and terrace overlook the south campus.

In 2015 Hodge Hall received the annual AIA Indiana Honor Award for new construction design. The jury commented: "This project sensitively reinterprets its campus's traditional collegiate gothic language. In so doing, it successfully ties together the mid-century modern complex of which it is a part with the traditional campus core. Stone, metal and glass exteriors are beautifully and subtly composed in a delicate balance that is contemporary while clearly responding to context. This is carried into warm interiors, with well-articulated detailing, and generous natural light."[2]

Completion of Hodge Hall placed the physical plant of the Kelley School of Business in harmony with its reputation for academic excellence.

Hodge Hall classroom with horseshoe configuration, 2017. Photo credit: Tyagan Miller.

School of Public and Environmental Affairs 1982

ARCHITECT Ellerbe Associates

ARCHITECTURAL STYLE 1980s Modern

ADDITION 2017, BSA LifeStructures

ARCHITECTURAL STYLE Contextual Modern

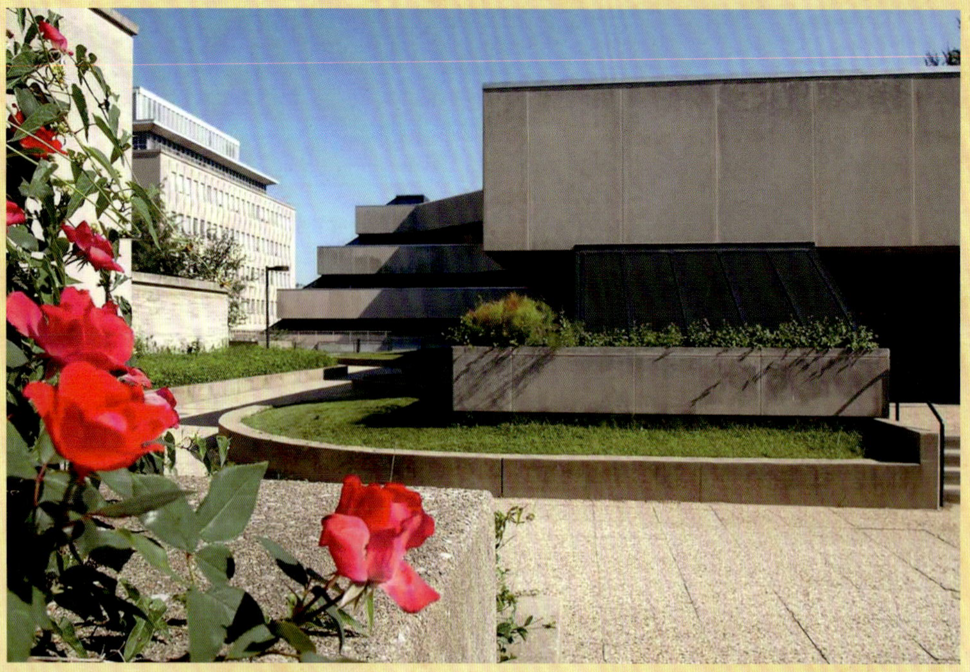

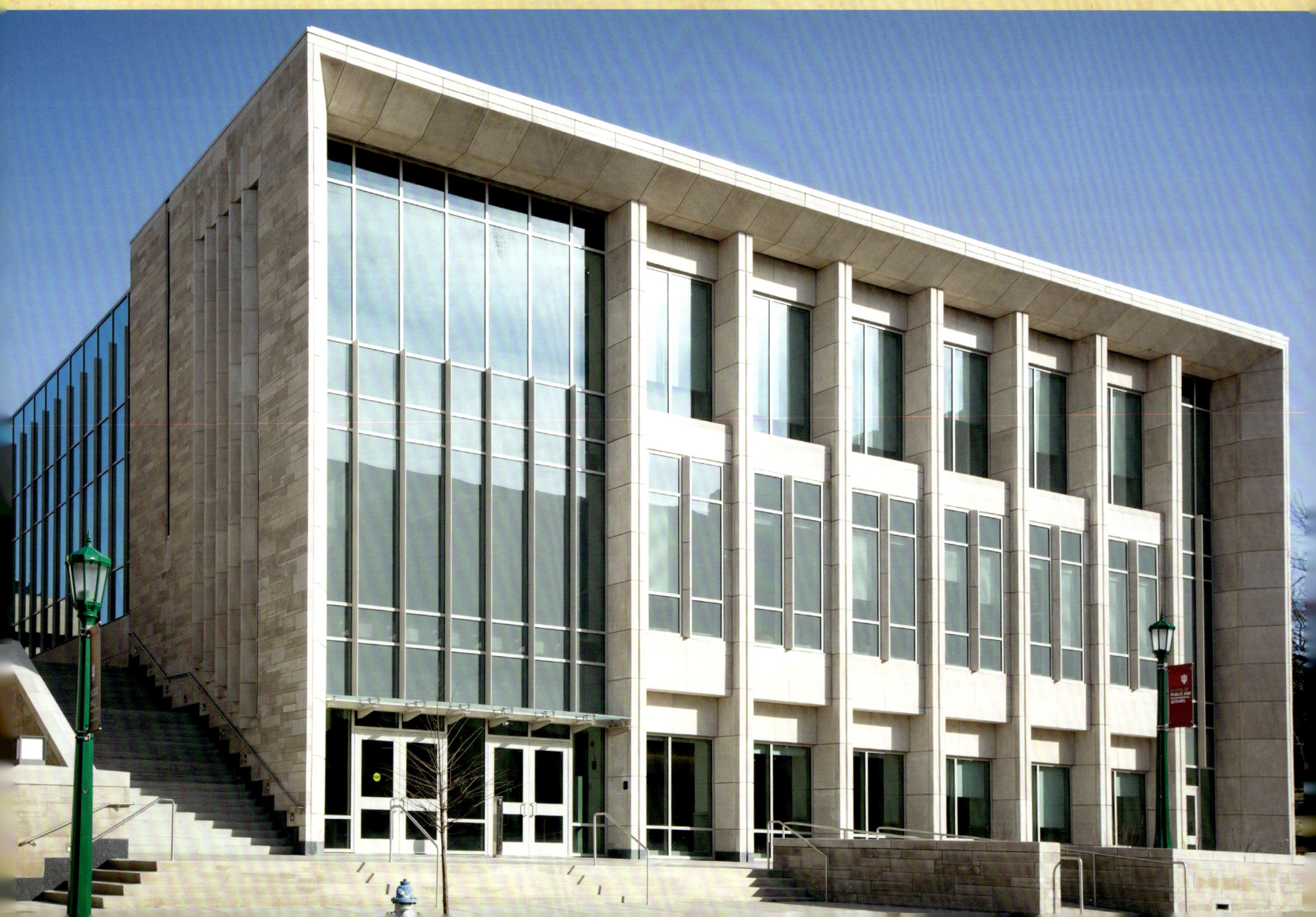

School of Public and Environmental Affairs

Leadership in Public Affairs and Environmental Science

It is doubtful that in the entire history of American higher education an institution had made proportionately greater efforts to serve a larger number of students in classroom, dormitories, and recreational facilities, scholars in libraries and laboratories, and to carry on a complexity of public functions. Every activity of the institution was influenced by this period of great expansion, but none so much as the image of Indiana University becoming a major American institution of higher education and assuming a significant degree of leadership in many fields.

—*Thomas D. Clark,* Indiana University, Midwestern Pioneer

INDIANA UNIVERSITY PRESIDENT JOHN W. RYAN created the School of Public and Environmental Affairs (SPEA) in 1972 against a backdrop of student unrest and civil turmoil generated by the Vietnam War and a period of national social change. Recognizing the need for offering coursework in the field of public policy, President Ryan selected Charles F. Bonser, highly respected School of Business faculty member, to serve as the first dean. SPEA quickly became a popular academic path for students and a clear alternative to pursuing a degree in the traditional School of Business programs.

By 1980, just eight years after its founding, the new school had outgrown its home in the Poplars on Seventh Street and plans were underway to provide a new building on campus. The IU Trustees placed the SPEA project at the top of the capital budget request sent to the Indiana General Assembly, which responded by appropriating half of the estimated cost. Undaunted, the university forged ahead and hired Ellerbe Architects of Minneapolis to begin work on design options. Although Ellerbe had extensive experience on college campuses, the SPEA project was his first IU commission. Given the reduced funding from the legislature, the university was faced with the decision to either build only half of what was needed or to construct the building in phases and go back to the state for additional funds. President Ryan elected to phase the project, and his insight turned out to be correct: the state legislature provided the second half of the necessary funding

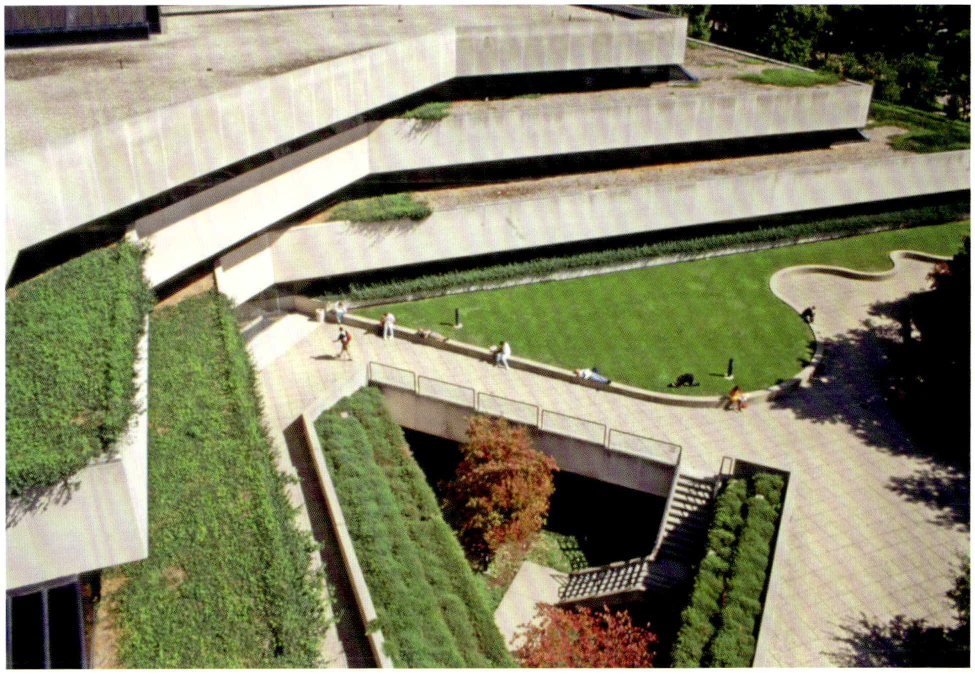

Above, Five levels of terraced gardens of the School of Public and Environmental Affairs, 1993. P0026021, IU Archives.

Facing top, Blend of minimalist angles, textures, and style of original SPEA building (Hodge Hall to the left), undated. Photo credit: Indiana University.

Facing bottom, South elevation of SPEA's Paul H. O'Neill Graduate Center, completed in 2017. Photo credit: Tyagan Miller.

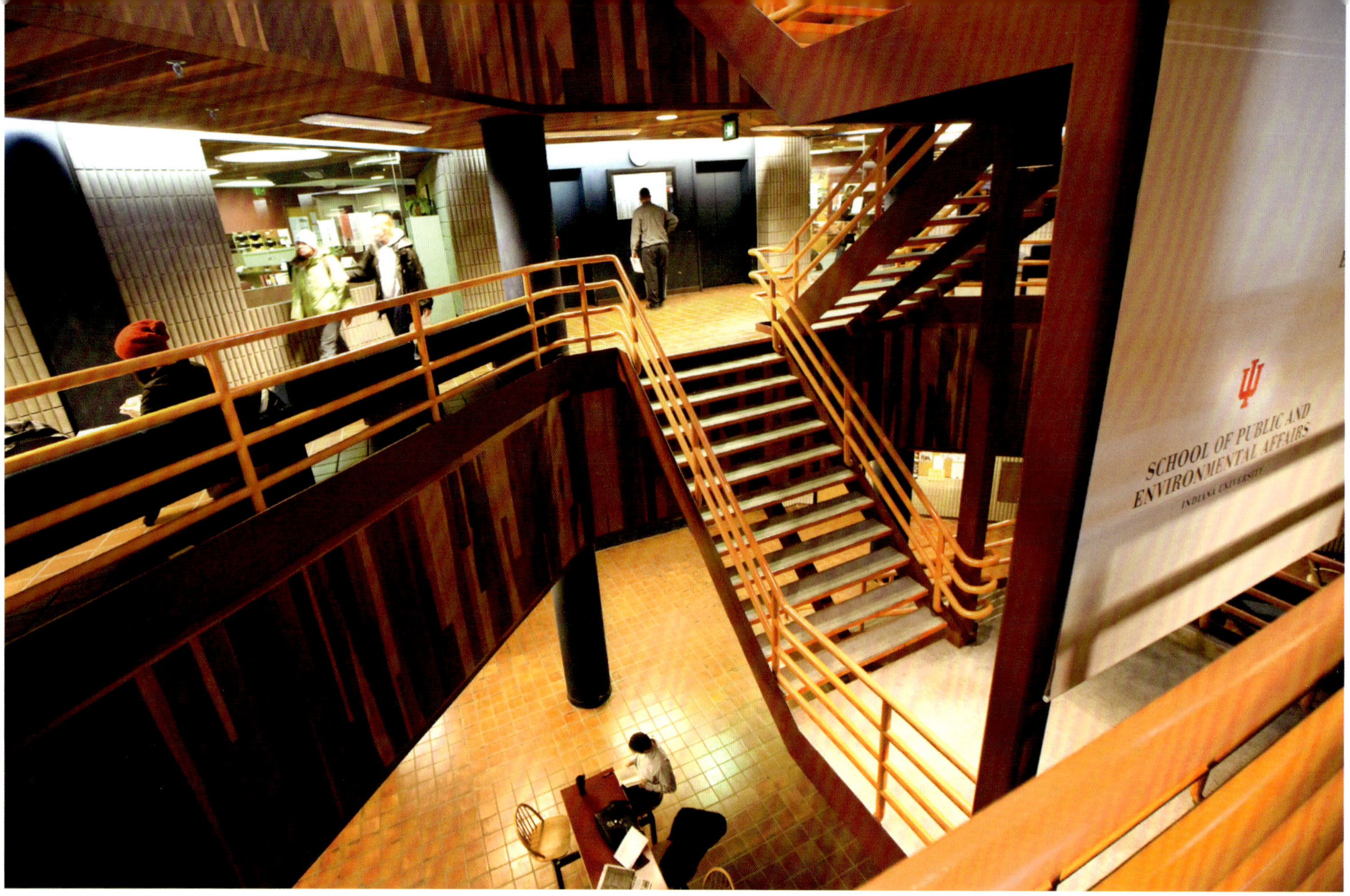

Interior atrium of SPEA showing controversial use of redwood finishing material in a building where environmental sensitivity is a core value, 2016. Photo credit: Tyagan Miller.

at the next session of the General Assembly, and construction of the entire project moved ahead seamlessly.

The building project actually benefited not only SPEA but also the School of Business, as an expanded business library was an important element of the plan. Ellerbe proposed connecting the two schools by placing a shared library space below grade and creating a separate configuration for SPEA above grade. The existing School of Business was completed in 1966, and its exterior elevation had a unique appearance that was impossible to match or even complement. Ellerbe instead gave SPEA a look all its own, both unique and distinctive. Respecting the setback line along Tenth Street, the new structure presented a stacked series of five floors that terraced back in deference to the huge mass of the Herman B Wells Library across the street. The exterior walls of the building are clad in smooth-faced limestone and the roofline is flat. To add to the singular presentation, Ellerbe specified lush landscaping on each terraced level, an embellishment that earned SPEA the nickname the Hanging Gardens of Babylon. A large atrium conveys an open and welcoming feeling for students and faculty as they enter the building; below ground, shared library space afforded School of Business and SPEA students then-state-of-the-art stacks, study carrels, and lighting.

President John W. Ryan presided over the dedication ceremony for the SPEA building on October 7, 1982. His remarks noted that the synergy created by the close juxtaposition of the School of Business and SPEA was Indiana University's response to the unsettled national mood that was threatening the vitality of the country. He observed that "higher education has an essential role to play in the recovery and the future welfare of the national economy. The flame from the lamp of knowledge which is a symbol of our research, instruction and service, must shine through the grim circumstances that threaten us."[1]

The School of Public and Environmental Affairs has continued to grow in student enrollment and reputation—national rankings place the graduate and undergraduate programs among the best in the nation. With this growth and to match the excellence of the school, the university determined that a significant addition and renovation were needed. The build-

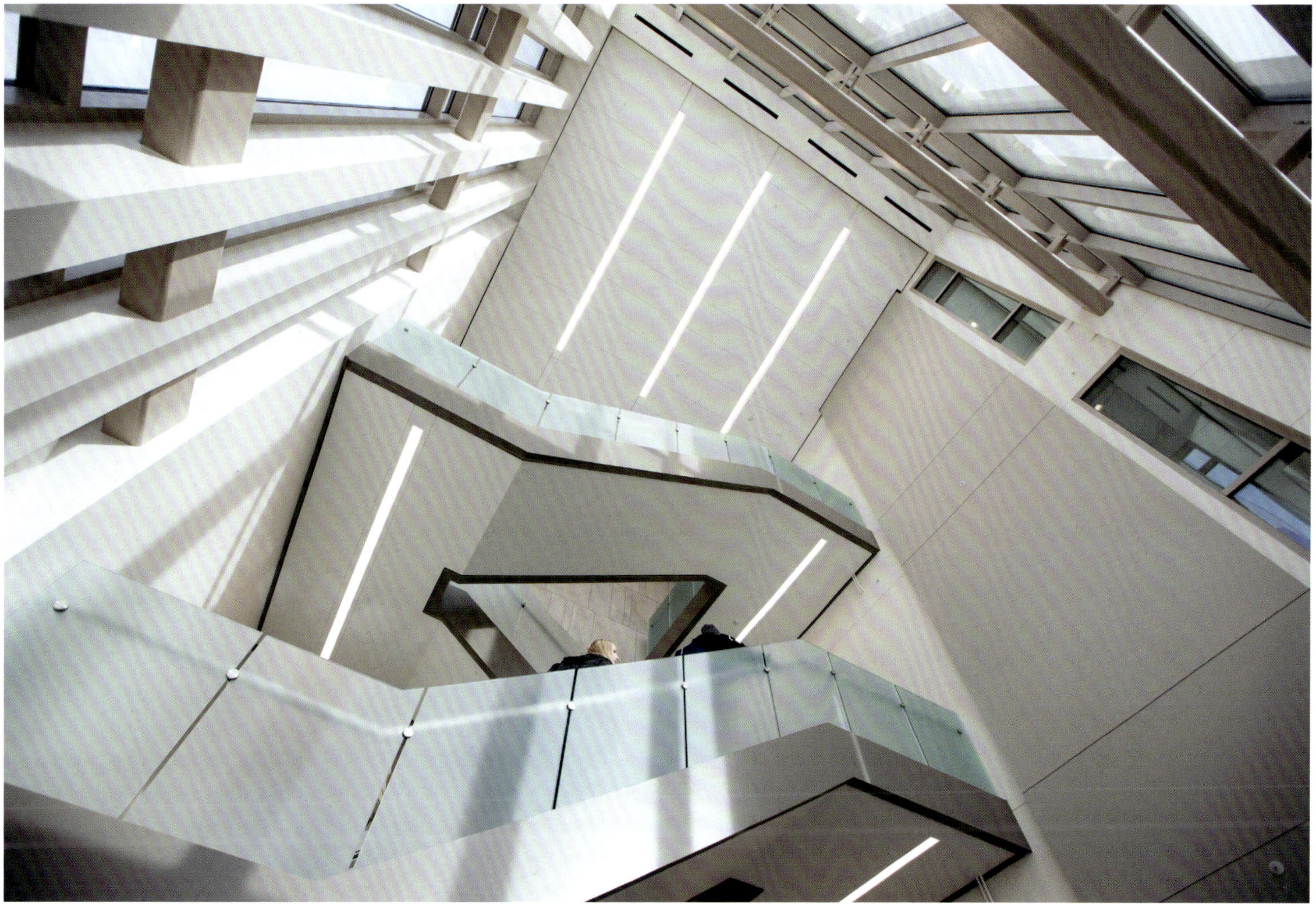

School of Public and Environmental Affairs interior stairwell, 2017. Photo credit: Indiana University.

ing completed in 1982 was no longer adequate in terms of office and classroom space nor did it contain the most current amenities.

BSA LifeStructures of Indianapolis was hired in 2014 to design a 34,000-square-foot addition to the existing SPEA building. A multilevel face was added on the south side of the current structure extending forward toward Tenth Street and connecting to Hodge Hall directly to the west. The space is a three-story rectangular limestone and glass structure, designed not to compete with the Gothic style of Hodge Hall. Architectural details have been purposely left minimal and unpretentious, but the overall scale of the building blends well with the surrounding streetscape. Respecting setback lines determined by immediate neighbors along the north side of Tenth Street, the clear glass curtain wall engenders a feeling of transparency and openness. The new addition's strong, vertical limestone colonnade recalls architectural features found on core campus buildings. The south-facing SPEA addition benefits from raised columns and spandrels that provide shade from the afternoon sun.

The new space is devoted to the graduate program and undergraduates occupy the original building. The new addition was completed in 2017 and named the Paul H. O'Neill Graduate Center. Indiana University alumnus Paul O'Neill was former secretary of the U.S. Treasury and chairman of ALCOA. O'Neill's $3 million gift helped fund the project and constituted the largest private donation in SPEA history.

The success of the School of Public and Environmental Affairs is a remarkable story. Seldom has any academic program anywhere in the country grown in size and stature in the way SPEA has at Indiana University. This new building addition and renovation provide an enhanced environment for the important work going on inside.

Wendell W. Wright Education Building 1992

ARCHITECT CRS Sirrine Inc.

ARCHITECTURAL STYLE Postmodern

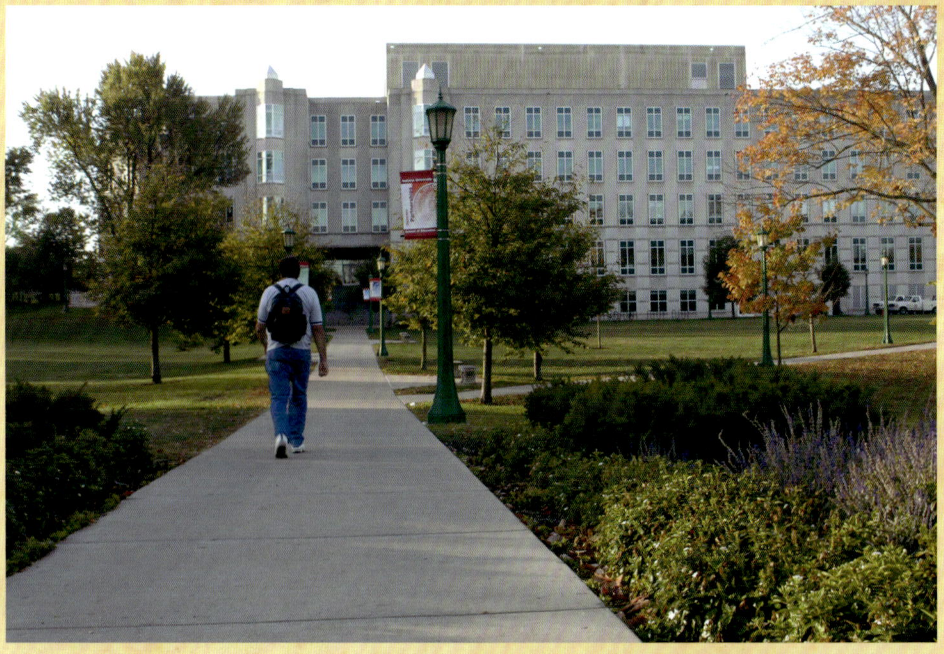

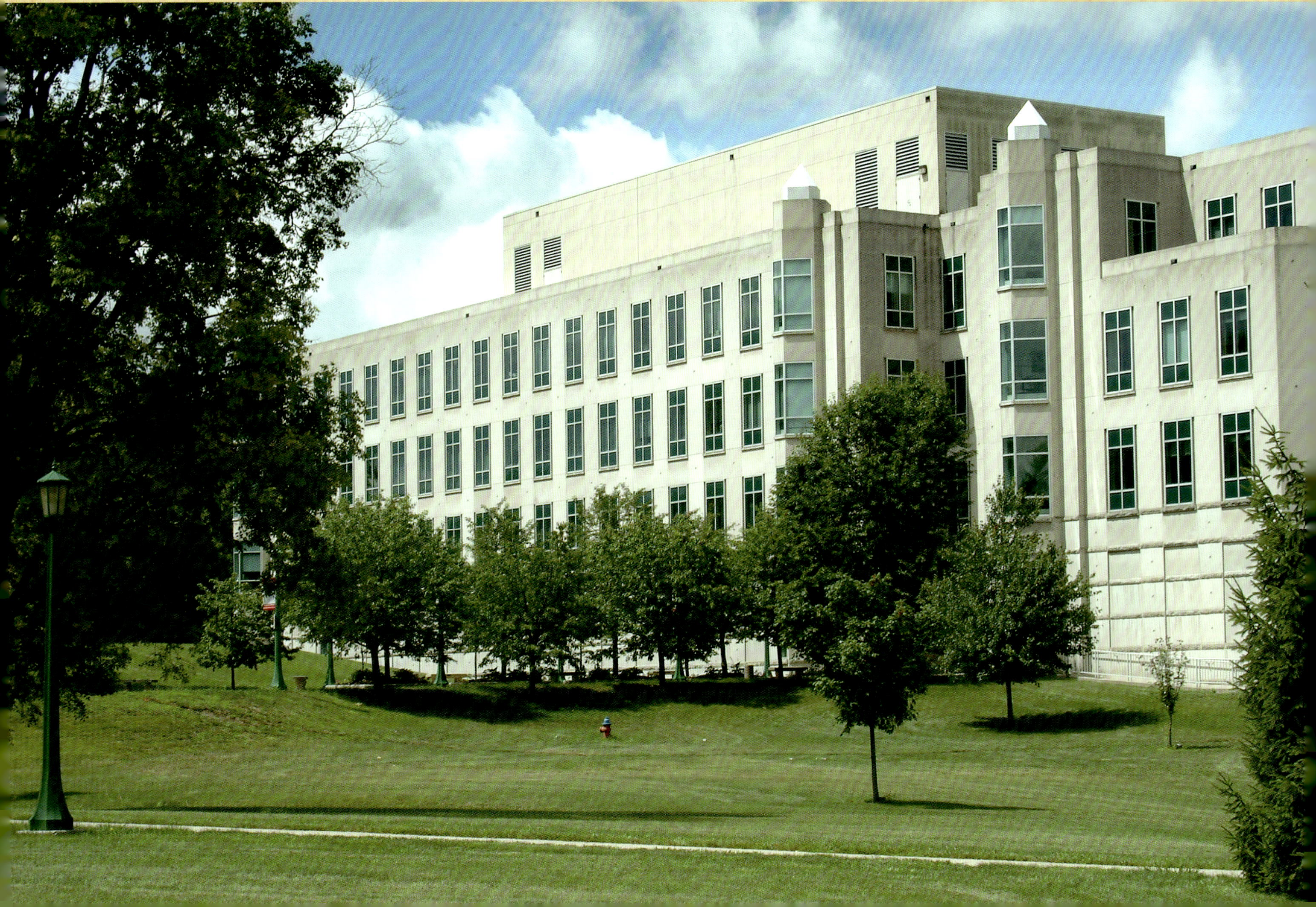

Wendell W. Wright Education Building

Teaching in the Information Age

This splendid facility and the equipment it contains fulfills a dream, a vision of what is required to prepare educators for work in the information age. . . . This building is dedicated to the proposition that the new information-age technology will someday have an effect on education equal to the printing press on earlier generations of teachers and students.

—Howard Mehlinger at dedication ceremony

IN CONSIDERATION OF HOWARD MEHLINGER'S acceptance of the position of dean of the School of Education in 1981, then president John Ryan agreed that a major renovation of the existing Wendell W. Wright School of Education building on Jordan Avenue would be given a high priority on the list of capital funding projects for 1983–85. However, despite these early intentions, funding opportunities for capital projects through the State of Indiana were slim and the administration was forced to begin a search for alternative funding. Fortunately in 1983, the Reagan administration's National Commission on Excellence in Education released the landmark report, *Nation at Risk: The Imperative for Educational Reform*, which called for collaboration between the public and private sectors to improve education in the country. Within months of its release, Mehlinger presented the first proposal for a newly envisioned Center for Excellence in Education (CEE) to the Board of Trustees. The proposal outlined the need to chart a transition in education from the industrial to the information age in an increasingly "scientific, technological, globally-interconnected, information processing, service-oriented society" and to "improve the quality and productivity of schooling throughout the state and region and provide a model for the nation."[1]

In the coming years, support streamed in through the U.S. Departments of Energy and Education, the State of Indiana, and major corporate benefactors such as AT&T and Thompson Consumer Electronics in the form of funding, grants, equipment, and technical expertise. Due to space constraints in the existing structure, the trustees ultimately decided against renovation and instead opted for a new building to house the new CEE as well as all the administrative and academic spaces of the School of Education, some of which were located in satellite locations on and near the campus. The existing structure would be renovated for use by the School of Music (today the Bess Meshulam Simon Music Library and Recital Center). The new School of Education building would assume the Wright name, given to the original structure in 1979 in honor of Wendell W. Wright, the second dean of the School of Education (1946–59) and a university vice president.

The trustees awarded the contract to the Houston-based architectural firm CRS Sirrine (CRSS), known nationally for its design excellence and integration of advanced technology. According to then university architect Raymond Casati, the firm understood the long-standing IU mission to preserve trees and thus, when a site for the new building was identified on a

Facing top, North view of Wendell W. Wright Education Building, 2016. Photo credit: Tyagan Miller.

Facing bottom, East elevation of Wendell W. Wright Education Building, undated. Photo credit: Indiana University.

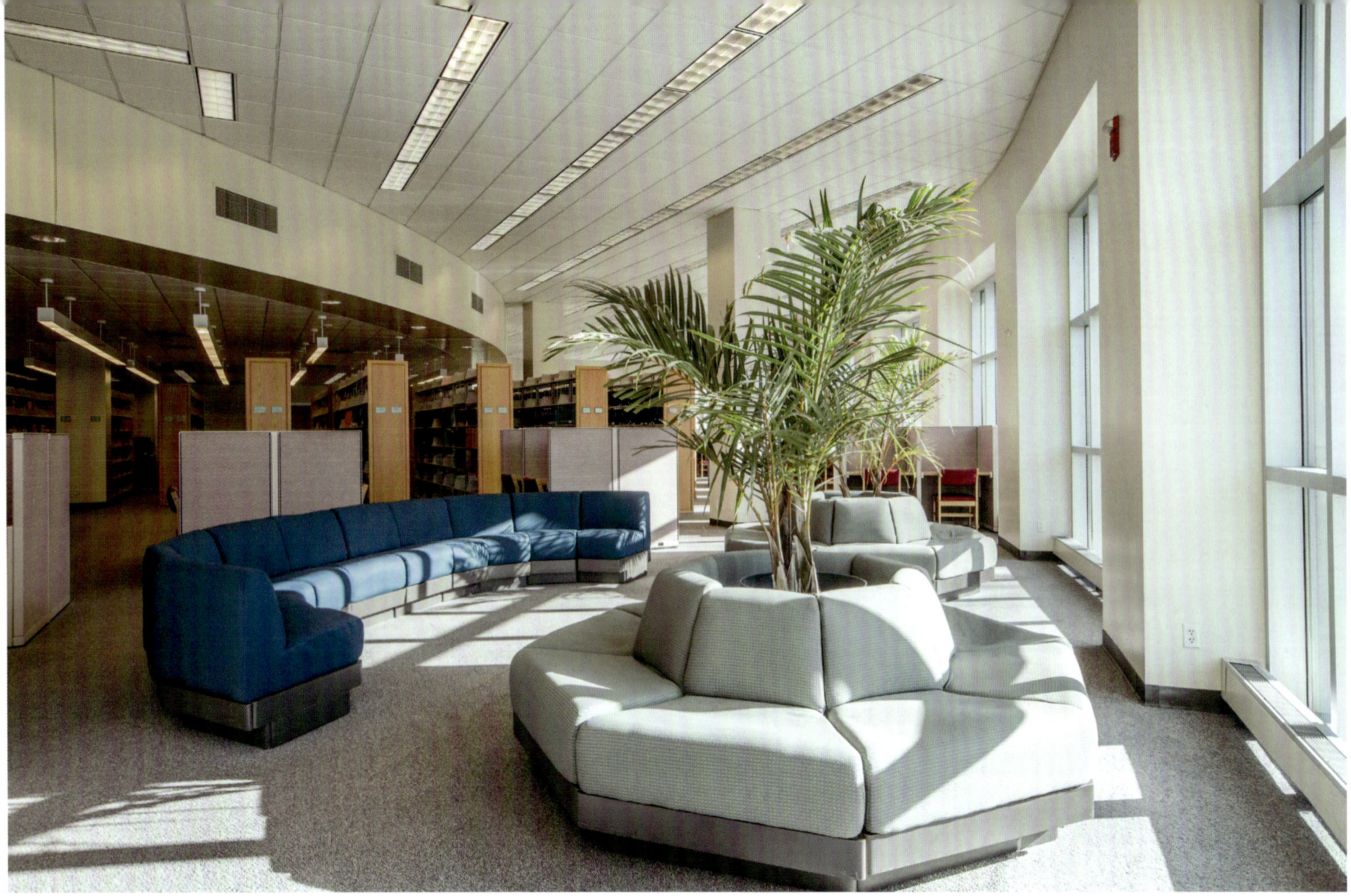

School of Education Library, 2017. Photo credit: Tyagan Miller.

wooded hilltop on Rose Avenue near East Seventh Street, the design retained the existing trees. The site established a new eastern edge to the academic campus, at the time only occupied by two remaining wooden barracks from Trees Center (Pine and Arbutus Halls), which served as housing during World War II. These were removed, along with a road that extended from Seventh Street, and the architects called for the return of the surrounding landscape to meadow and woods. On June 15, 1989, ground was broken on what Mehlinger called "one of the loveliest sites of the campus . . . for a human structure to add to, rather than detract from, its natural beauty."[2]

The CRSS design was featured in *American School and University Architectural Portfolio* as an outstanding architectural design for education. It stated that the CRSS design "looks to the future while retaining the sense of place and tradition that is so much a part of the university."[3] Built into the sloping site, the six-story building is L-shaped with a central lobby and library, and two wings. Completed in Modern style, the Wright building has smooth limestone panels and distinctive, sharp-angled towers with aluminum roofs. On the lower two stories, the panels are separated by single, thin courses of split-face limestone that give the building a horizontal feel. The panels between the limestone are alternately recessed as well, with a small circular indent in the center. These same circular indents appear on the panels between the windows on the upper stories. The combination of overall Modernist style with the towers and split-face limestone tie the building to both the modern and more traditional buildings on the rest of campus.

The building's wings project from a centralized multilevel lobby atrium that is the focal point of the structure and features a second-level balcony overlooking the common area. Horizontal striped tile detailing on the atrium walls adds interest. Nestled between the two wings of the building is the fan-shaped Education Library off the atrium, with a stunning glass wall to the southwest, which overlooks a wooded meadow. The remainder of the main level houses offices, multipurpose classrooms, and the main lecture hall. The below-ground floor is occupied by laboratories for research and development

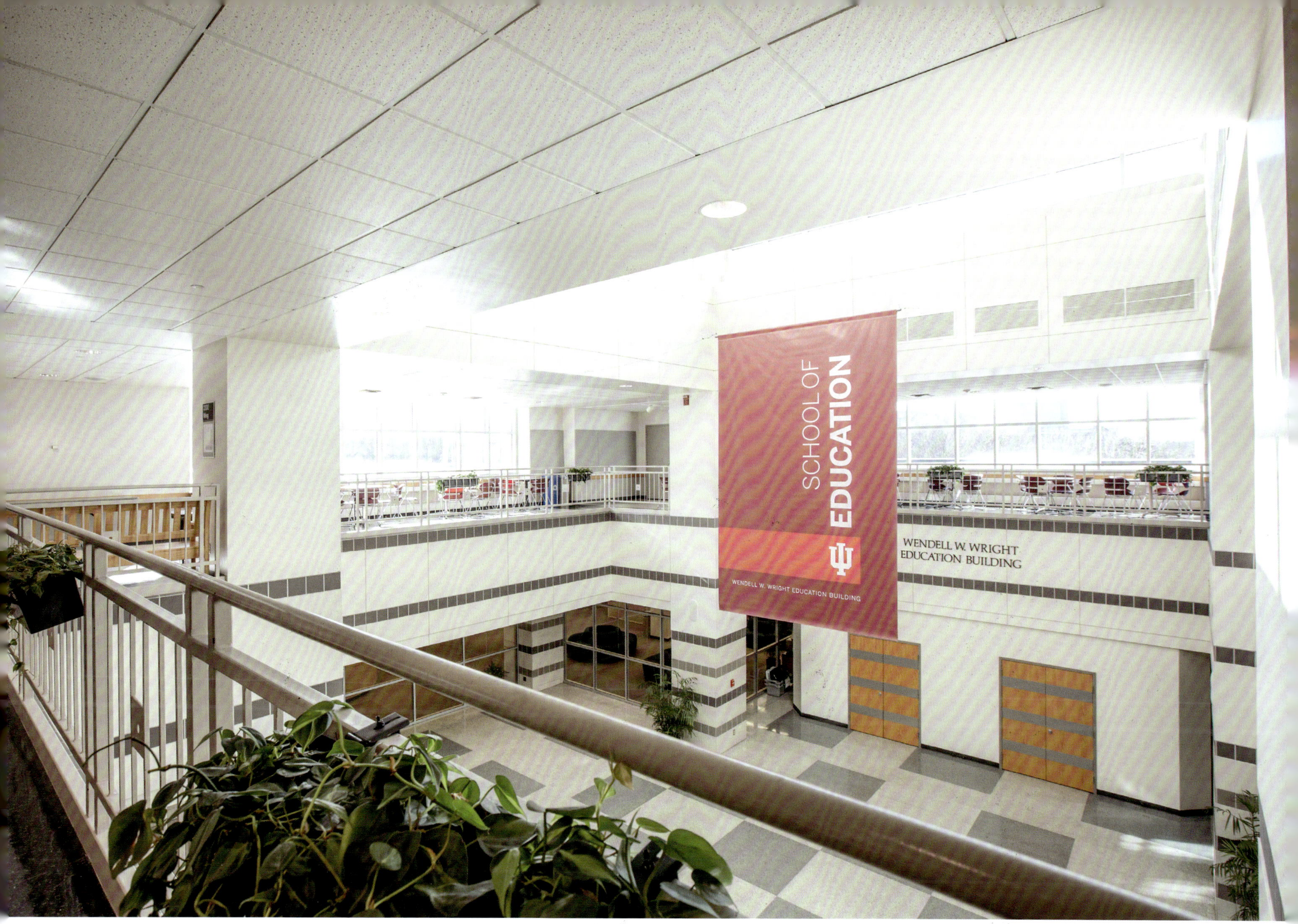

Multilevel lobby atrium with balcony overlooking common area, 2017. Photo credit: Tyagan Miller.

on teaching and learning. The second level features an advanced technology suite where educational technology and the research and development projects are showcased in research, computer, and graphics labs. The third floor consists primarily of classrooms and faculty offices, and the fourth, administrative offices.

Mehlinger envisioned the facility, among the first of its kind in the nation, as a "national demonstration center for the use of technology for instruction at all levels," with opportunities for students to learn through the simulation of real-world experience and self-paced instruction.[4] Moreover, the facilities expand the School of Education's reach through its abilities to link its experts with remote classrooms and to deliver course offerings both to the regional campuses and to students constrained by either geographic or physical limitations. The building officially opened in August 1992, with dedication ceremonies held in March 1993.

Global and International Studies Building 2015

ARCHITECT Ennead Architects / Browning Day Mullins Dierdorf

ARCHITECTURAL STYLE Contextual Modern

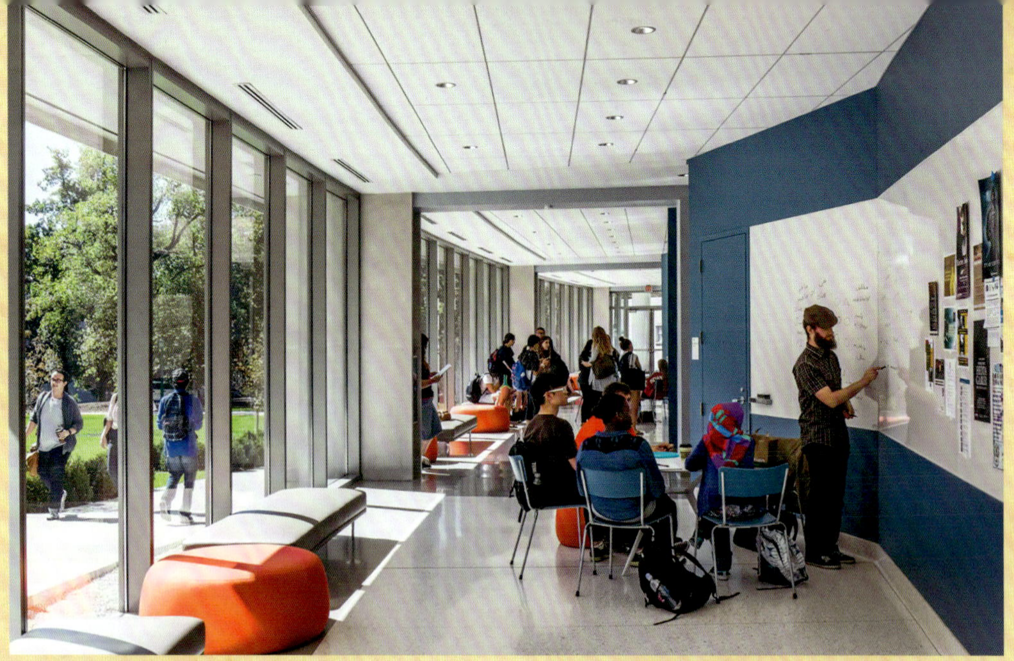

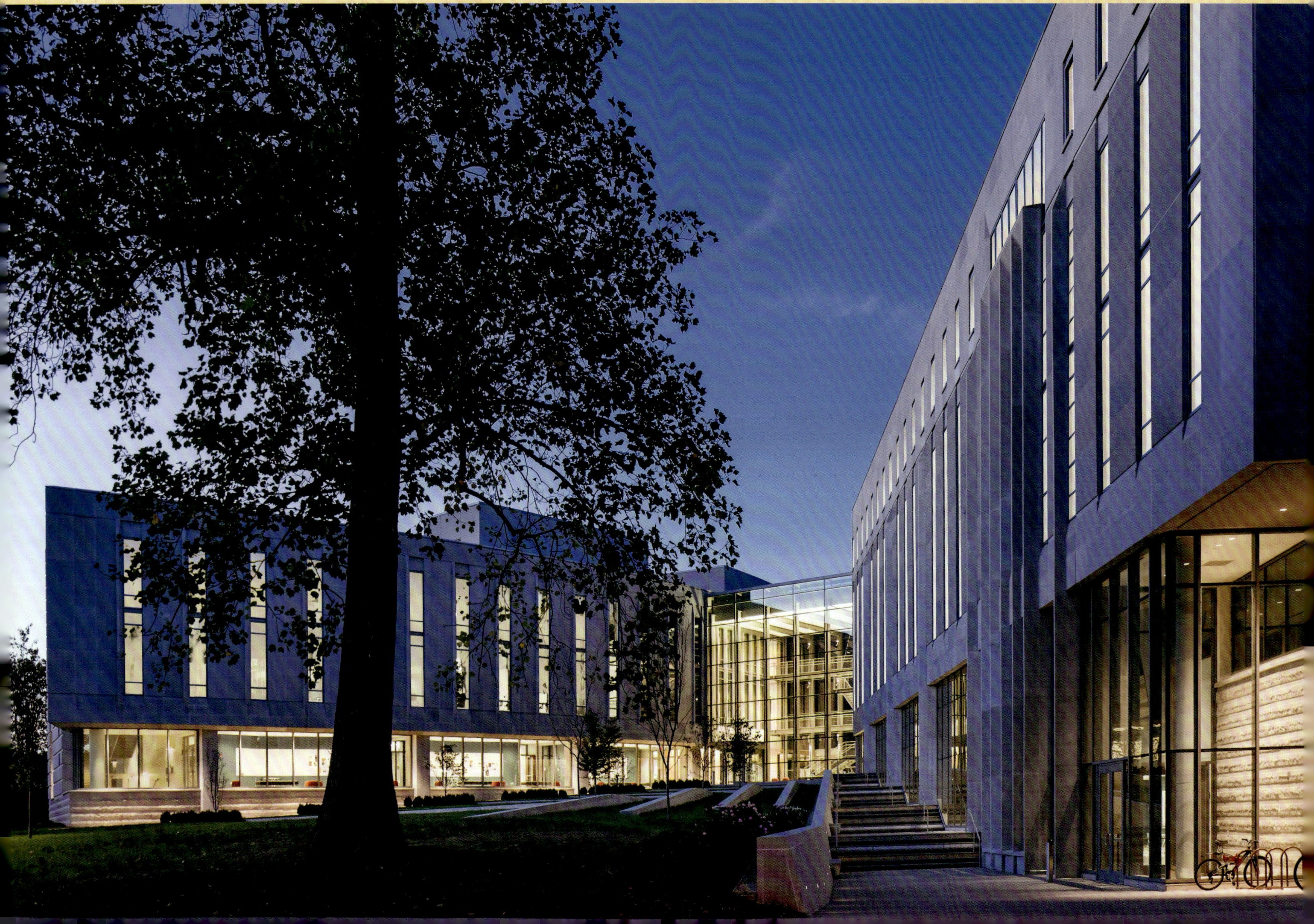

Global and International Studies Building

Understanding and Transforming the World

Beautiful and symbolic, the wall of stones evokes the green marble of the General Assembly of the United Nations and the aspirations of the UN Charter, alas imperfectly fulfilled, to save succeeding generations from the scourge of war . . . to reaffirm faith in fundamental human rights; in the dignity and worth of the human person; in the equal rights of men and women; and of nations large and small.

—Dean Lee Feinstein at dedication ceremony

Indiana University has had a long-standing commitment to international studies and related programs for students. Involvement in world events can be traced back to when Herman B Wells took a six-month leave of absence from his presidential duties in 1947 to lead the U.S. Education and Cultural Affairs Branch during the occupation of Germany. President John W. Ryan traveled to foreign countries extensively during his tenure, making new contacts for the university around the world. Michael McRobbie has made international outreach a hallmark of his presidency, opening doors and conduits between Indiana University and many foreign countries, with a substantial increase in the number of foreign students as one outcome.

Indiana University boasts more federally funded Title VI Area Study Program centers than any other university in the country. These centers have existed at IU since 1958, and they provide cultural and geopolitical research, educational opportunities and experiences, and resources to create a deeper understanding of regions deemed critical for national security. For many years the international studies departments and programs have been scattered across the Bloomington campus, taking space wherever that precious commodity could be found. The critical mass was in place but someone needed to assemble the parts in a way that comprehensive interaction could occur—enter President McRobbie and his idea for a new School of Global and International Studies. He asked the university trustees to move forward with a plan to "create a truly global research and educational environment where specialists in one part of the world might work side by side with scholars focusing on another part of the world, exploring common problems from diverse perspectives."[1] To implement his plan, a new building would be required that would physically bring together those groups that have international studies as a common denominator. University trustees enthusiastically endorsed President McRobbie's request.

Several eminent architectural firms were interviewed to provide site selection input and begin schematic designs for a new structure. Enneaud Architects of New York, then known as the Polshek Partnership, was chosen for the commission, and Susan T. Rodriguez of the Enneaud staff was assigned to work with the university. Browning Day Mullins Dierdorf of Indianapolis was engaged to provide local architectural representation. At the dedication of the Global and International Studies Building (GISB), Rodriguez stated it that it was always her goal to design a building that would "connect people with their place in the world and to each other—to open eyes to the context in which they live." She added that she "sought to create a building

Facing top, Student and faculty collaborative breakout space in Global and International Studies Building, 2016. Photo credit: © Jeff Goldberg / Esto.

Facing bottom, The Global and International Studies Building at night, 2016. Photo credit: © Jeff Goldberg / Esto.

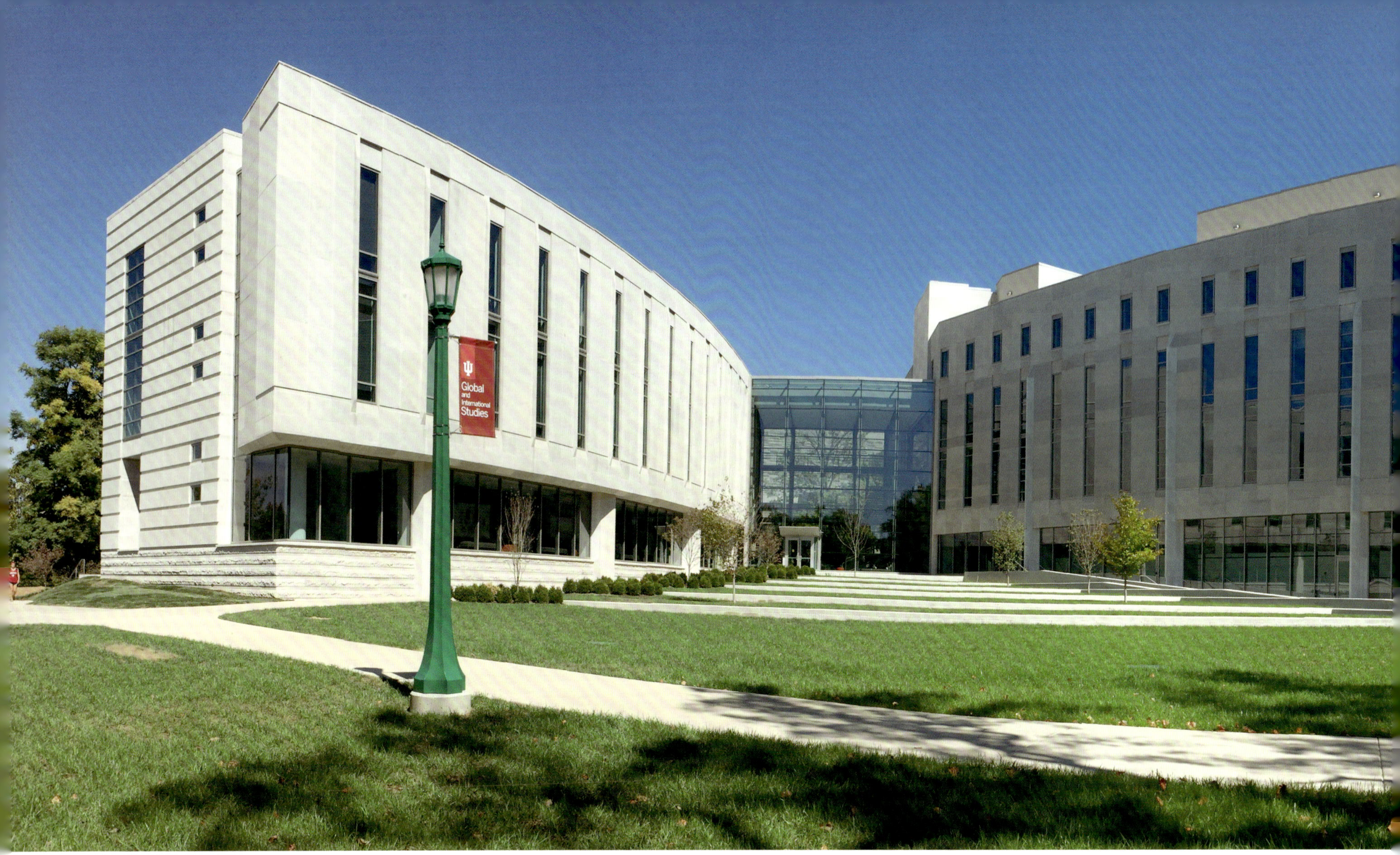

South view of Global and International Studies Building, 2016. Photo credit: Indiana University.

that would draw the community in both day and night—a place where campus life and the surrounding landscape become a natural extension of the spaces within the building."[2]

Planning for the Global and International Studies building began in 2008, but groundbreaking did not occur until April 2013. The $53 million budget was not funded in any part by the State of Indiana appropriation, causing the university to rely on gifts, support from IU Athletics, and proceeds from the real estate transaction that conveyed ownership of the university's Showers Complex to the City of Bloomington. The 165,000-square-foot structure is integrated in balanced proportion with the sloping topography between the Herman B Wells Library and the Radio and Television Building and borders the east edge of the Jesse H. and Beulah Chanley Cox Arboretum. Two wings are unified by a three-story glass atrium; the east wing lies parallel to the Wells Library parking lot, while the west wing gently curves around the Arboretum, hinting at the curvature of the Tenth Street Stadium grandstand that once stood on this site. Sustainable design principles guided the planning of the building, with strong emphasis placed on solar orientation and the integration of daylight and vistas throughout. Locally quarried limestone defines the building's exterior palette, but it also includes colored stones from around the world, referencing the school's mission of global study and understanding. The interior of the building echoes this design detail with a three-story wall of international stones in the central atrium. The stones represent ten countries on six continents and are intermingled with locally sourced limestone, thus connecting the university's local traditions to its global pursuits.

The entire building was designed to provide flexible teaching spaces and to foster collaboration and interdisciplinary

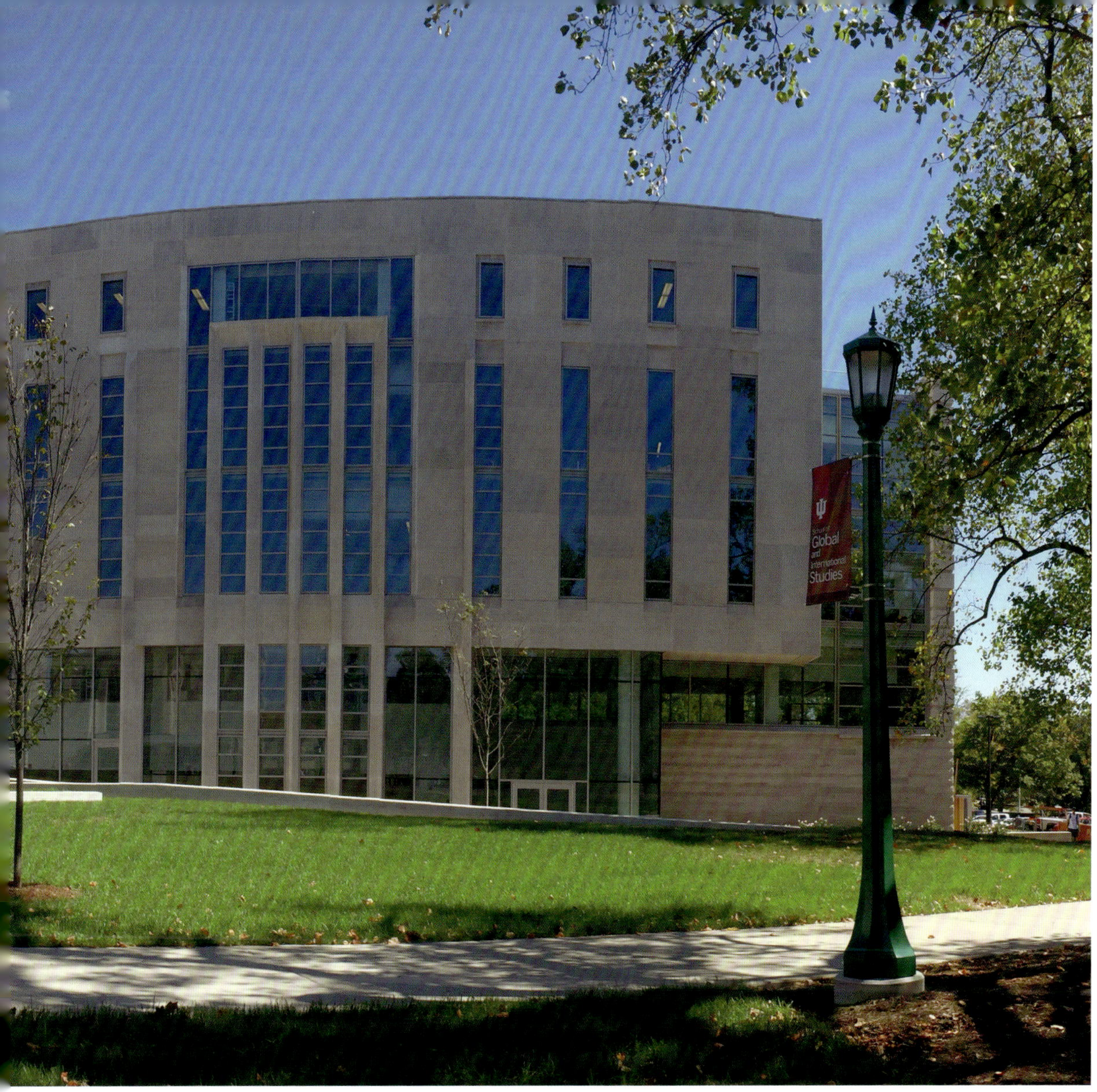

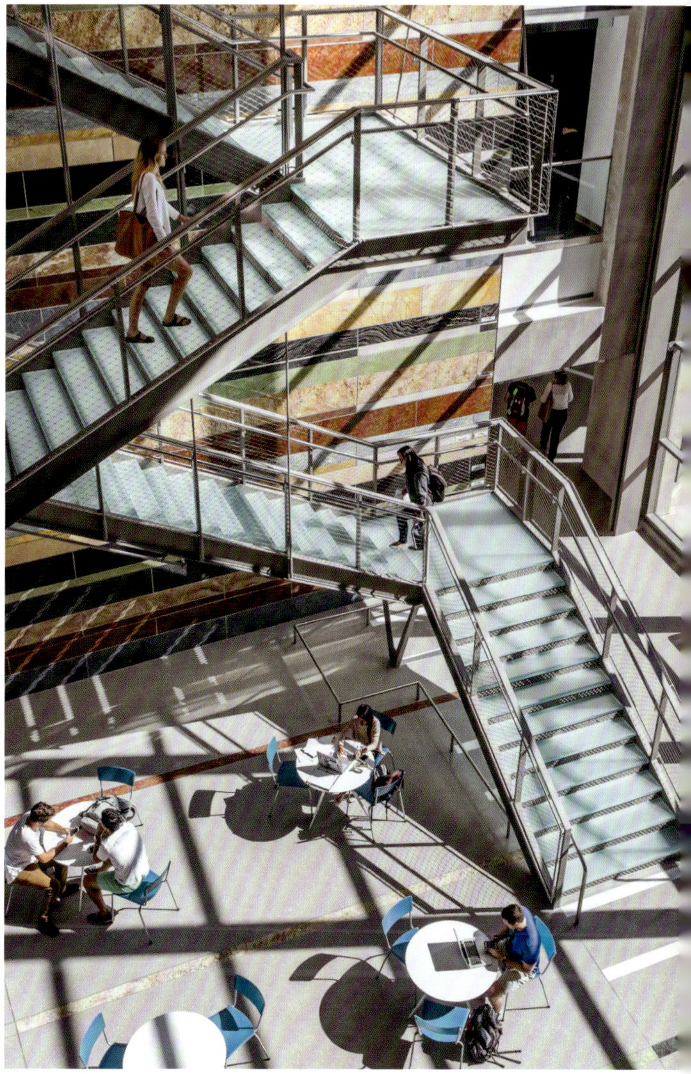

Global and International Studies Building atrium with three-story wall composed of stones from around the world, 2016. Photo credit: © Jeff Goldberg / Esto.

education. Many iterations of the array of academic programs to be located in the space were considered by the university. When the building opened it provided space for twenty academic programs in eight departments. Other elements include thirty classrooms and meeting rooms, 250 faculty offices, student and faculty collaborative spaces, research and language resource centers, an atrium that doubles as an event and function space, and open office space for graduate students.

The building is an impressive and contributing piece of the architectural fabric of the IU Bloomington campus. The university planning team, in partnership with Enneaud Architects, was committed to making the building fit with the neighborhood, particularly in its role as backdrop for the Arboretum, yet display its own identity in a form that would be a symbol of the work occurring inside the offices and classrooms. Rodriguez of Enneaud Architects expressed her support for meeting that challenge: "the design is grounded in the campus tradition of limestone buildings, but is ignited by the colorful accents of stones from around the world, which act as a visual reminder of the breadth and range of global studies at IU. It is a building that is from its place, yet one that extends its reach to distant lands."[3]

The Global and International Studies Building was dedicated on October 14, 2015, amid much excitement and expectation, not only for its beauty but for finally bringing together all of the pieces of the international studies puzzle and the hope that this collaboration inspires.

Luddy Hall 2018

ARCHITECT Ratio Architects / Pelli Clarke Pelli

ARCHITECTURAL Contextual Modern

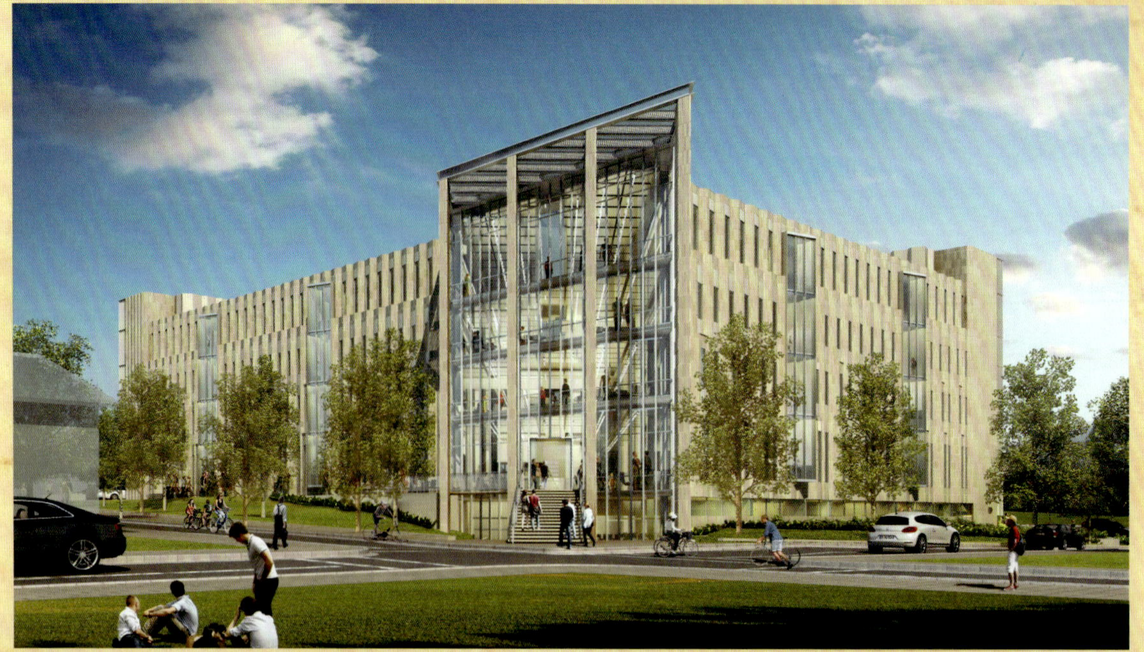

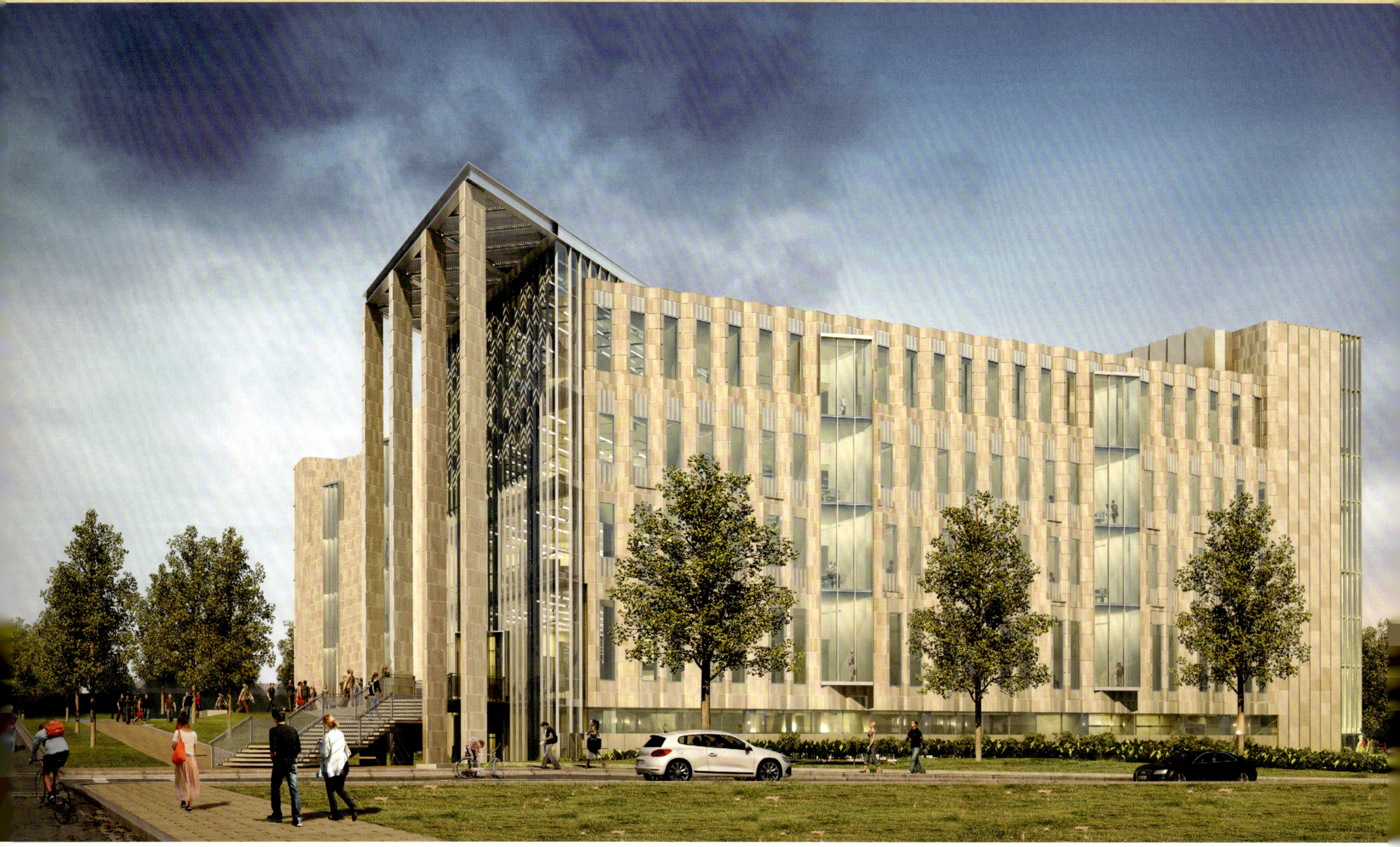

Luddy Hall

Home of the School of Informatics and Computing (SoIC)

This building is designed to encourage an atmosphere of both collaboration and community and a culture of innovation and entrepreneurship, combining the best qualities of academia and the tech sector.... So much of what happens at our school is predicated upon the right combination of people, technology and applications—this new building will give our entire school the proximity, environment and tools to collaborate and thrive.

—Dean Bobby Schnabel at ground-breaking ceremony

RESPONSIVE TO THE CHANGING NEEDS OF STUDENTS and society, Indiana University established the first School of Informatics in the country in 1999. Enrollment flourished in its first fifteen years, and informatics became one of the most popular majors on the Bloomington campus. In 2005 the Department of Computer Science moved from the College of Arts and Sciences to the School of Informatics, and in 2012 the School of Library and Information Science (SLIS) merged with the School of Informatics. This newly formed grouping was renamed the School of Informatics and Computing (SoIC); it was hoped the integration of the three departments would create a synergy that would benefit students, researchers, and employers. Of the merger, Indiana University President Michael A. McRobbie commented that "by placing these programs in a combined culture where rapid change is expected to be the norm, IU is provided with an excellent opportunity to contribute in a broader sphere at the confluence of information and computing."[1]

The immense success of the informatics program left the campus with a predicament, however. The school had operated out of two former Greek houses at the corner of Tenth Street and Woodlawn Avenue. With growing enrollment and the absorption of the Department of Computer Science and SLIS, it was evident that more space was needed, both to accommodate the increasing numbers of students and faculty and to encourage collaboration. Discussion about a new building gathered momentum, and at its April 17, 2015, meeting, the Board of Trustees approved a new structure for SoIC to be constructed at the northeast corner of Cottage Grove and Woodlawn Avenues, just one block north of the school's current facilities.

At their June 2015 meeting, the trustees were presented with design plans. Ratio Architects of Indianapolis and Pelli Clarke Pelli of Connecticut partnered to design the four-and-one-half-story building that will serve as the first step toward implementing the 2009 adapted master plan to expand the university north from the core campus. Somewhat reminiscent of the Collegiate Gothic style of architecture prevalent on IU's campus, Luddy Hall maintains a traditional look but with a contemporary flair, combining the traditional limestone facade with glass and textured metal.

From the outset, key words used to describe and plan Luddy Hall included *collaboration*, *cooperation*, and *innovation*, and the architects designed Luddy Hall with these objectives

Facing top, Architectural rendering of southwest elevation of Luddy Hall featuring glass portico, 2016. Photo credit: Architect César Pelli.

Facing bottom, Architectural rendering of south elevation of Luddy Hall featuring side view of southwest glass portico, 2016. Photo credit: Architect César Pelli.

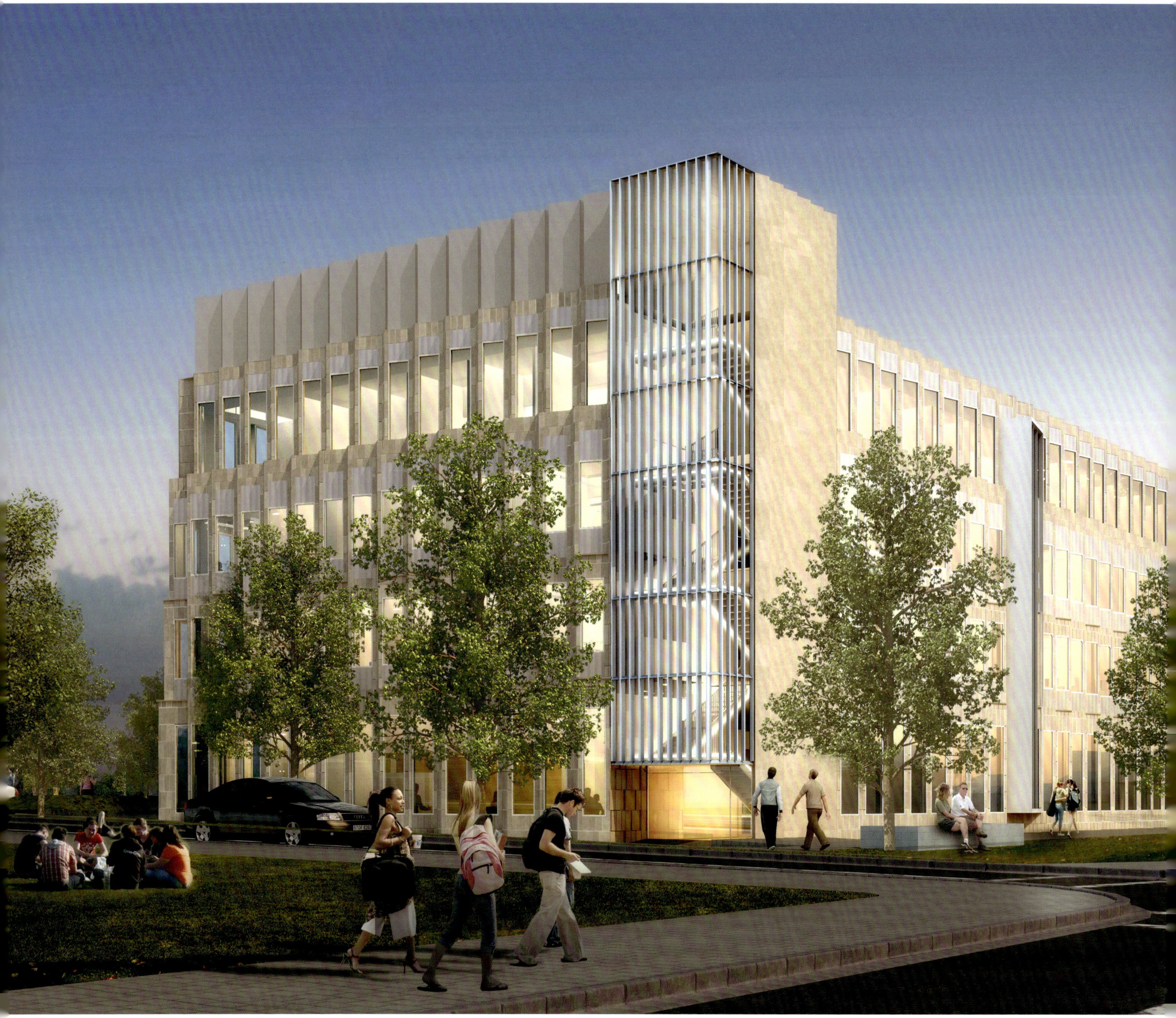

Architectural rendering of northwest elevation of Luddy Hall featuring one of two stair towers enclosed in frosted glass, 2016. Photo credit: Architect César Pelli.

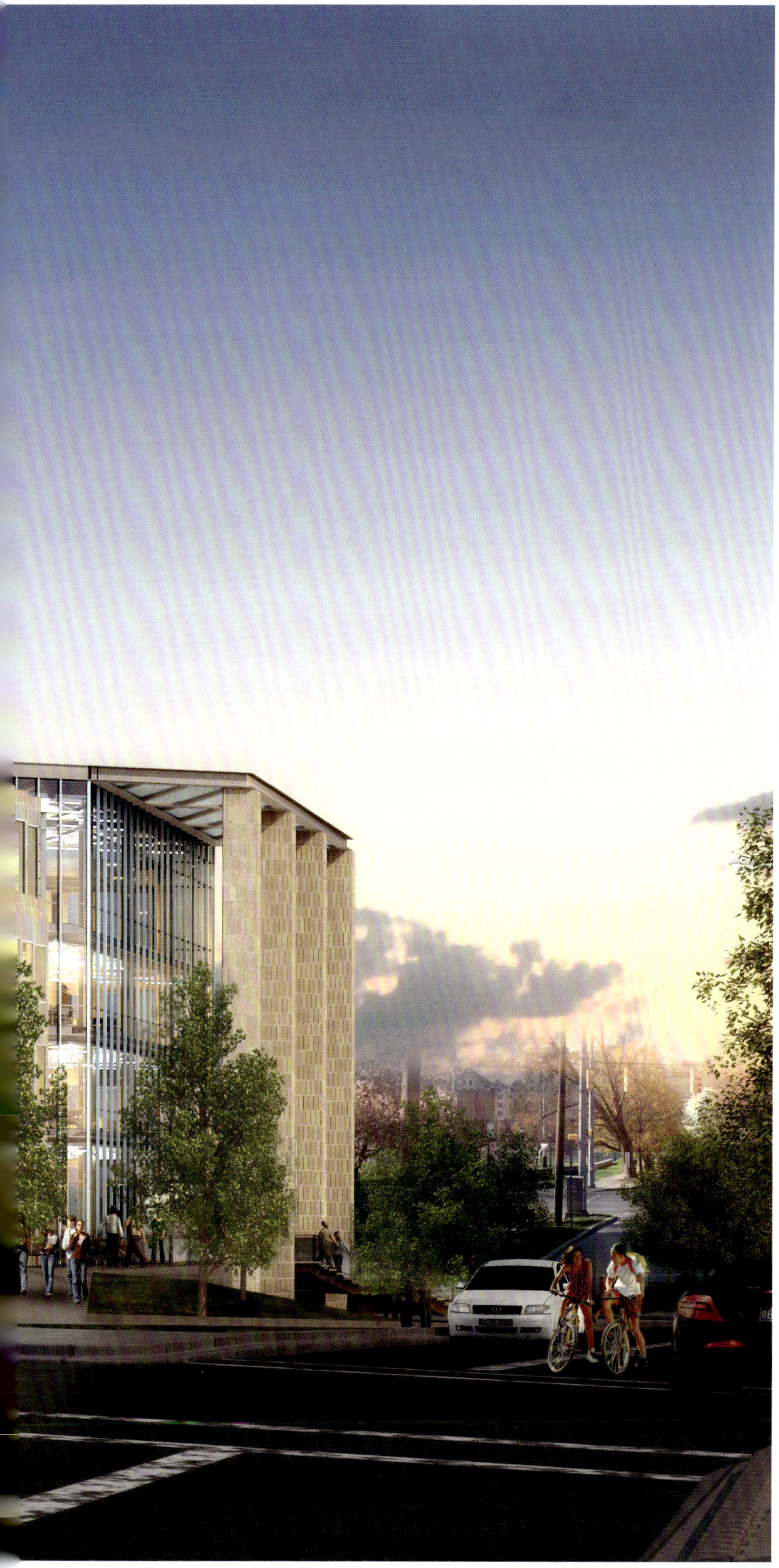

in mind. Their primary goal was to construct a building that would create a sense of community, foster interdisciplinary interaction, and extend learning outside the classroom. To that end, the large atrium, which has both open and enclosed collaborative spaces, runs through the core of the building, connecting all levels with an amphitheater-like staircase. This "central mixer" space is intended to be a social catalyst, promoting group exchange as well as independent research.[2]

Luddy Hall has two grand entrances; the northeast entrance features a stunning glass-paneled wall, and the southwest entrance features a large glass portico. Frosted glass encloses two stair towers on the other two corners of the building, providing more light during the day and appearing as lanterns at night. The exterior building facade is generally uniform, with pleated architectural detailing. The exterior elevations feature a series of stacked, diagonal, oriel windows, which are expressive and help define the overall character of the building.

The 124,000-square-foot L-shaped building abounds with natural light that is enhanced at every opportunity; faculty offices include interior glass doors and windows to allow the light to reach the interior of the building. Two wings, adjacent to the atrium on each level, accommodate classrooms, faculty offices, and open research clusters. On the lowest level resides the "fab lab" (fabrication laboratory), where students and faculty can create just about anything their imaginations can conceive of with 3-D printers and associated technologies. The ground floor features a 160-seat collaborative auditorium with expansive views of the eastern garden through its floor-to-ceiling windows. An innovation center with a flexible suite of rooms is on the second floor, while the third floor houses a multipurpose conference and board room. One of IU's newest programs, Intelligent Systems Engineering, occupies the fourth-floor space.

In honor of Luddy family members who are also Indiana University alumni, in 2015 alumnus Fred Luddy donated $8 million to the building as part of For All: The Indiana University Bicentennial Campaign. A programming student at IU in the 1970s, Luddy has since developed technology and innovations "used by thousands of corporations and millions of people worldwide." About the future of the program and its new home, whose name recognizes the Luddy family legacy, Luddy said, "This is a building where the future of the world is going to be crafted."[3]

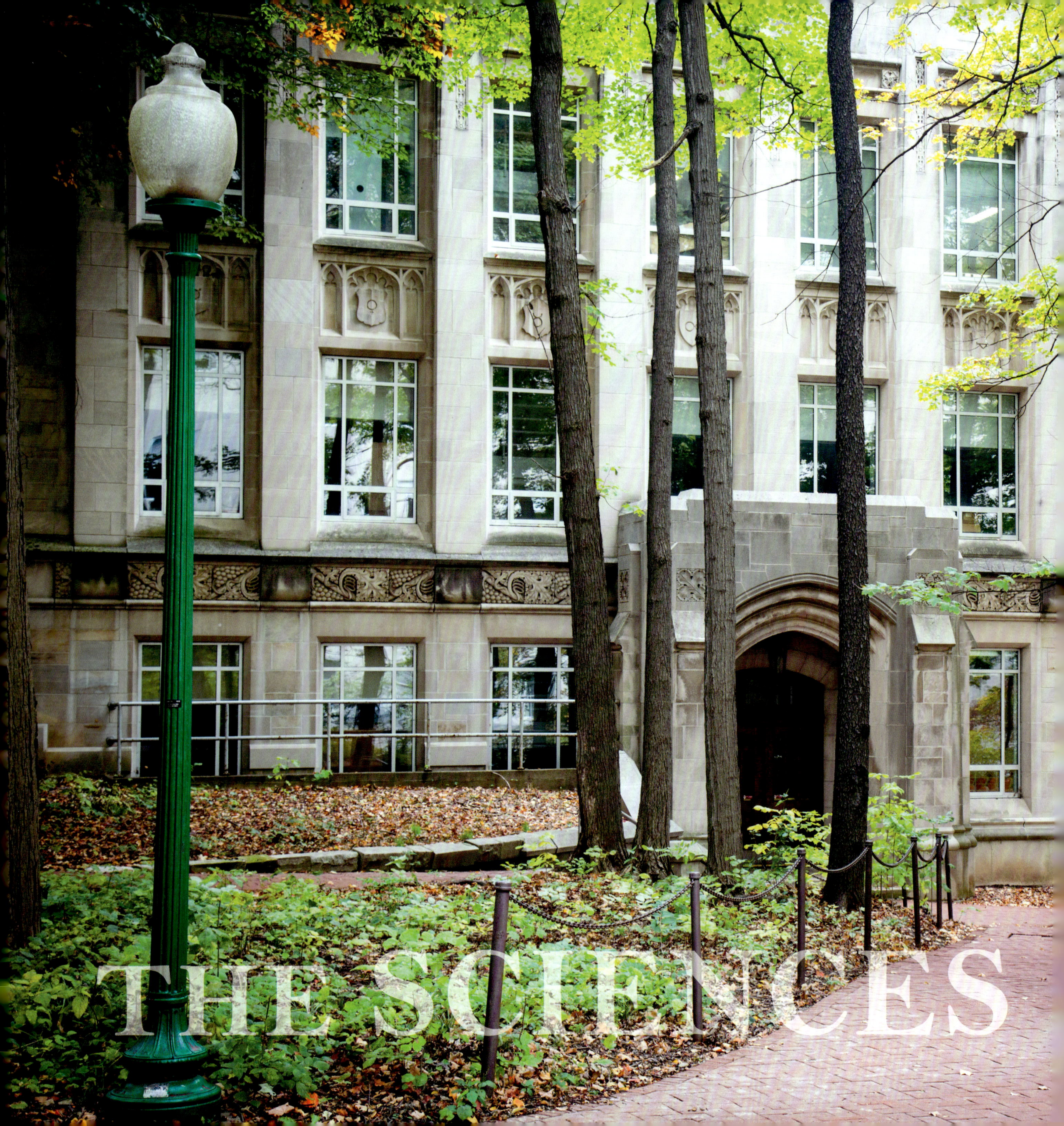
THE SCIENCES

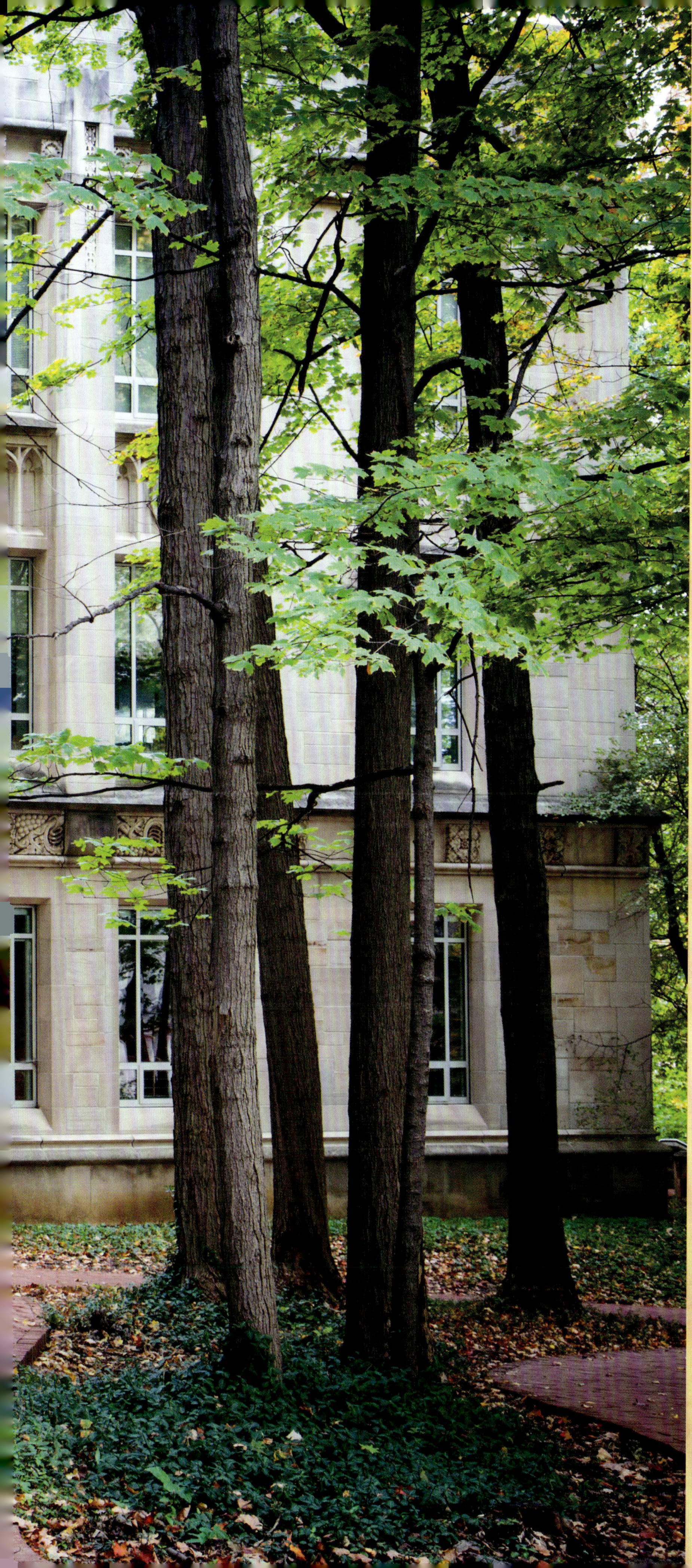

The University itself, though seemingly embodied in lovely acres and impressive buildings, is in truth far more spirit than stone, its beauty but a backdrop for its high endeavors.

ELVIS STAHR

Inaugural address, November 19, 1962

Chemistry Building 1931

ARCHITECT Robert Frost Daggett

ARCHITECTURAL STYLE Collegiate Gothic with Art Deco Characteristics

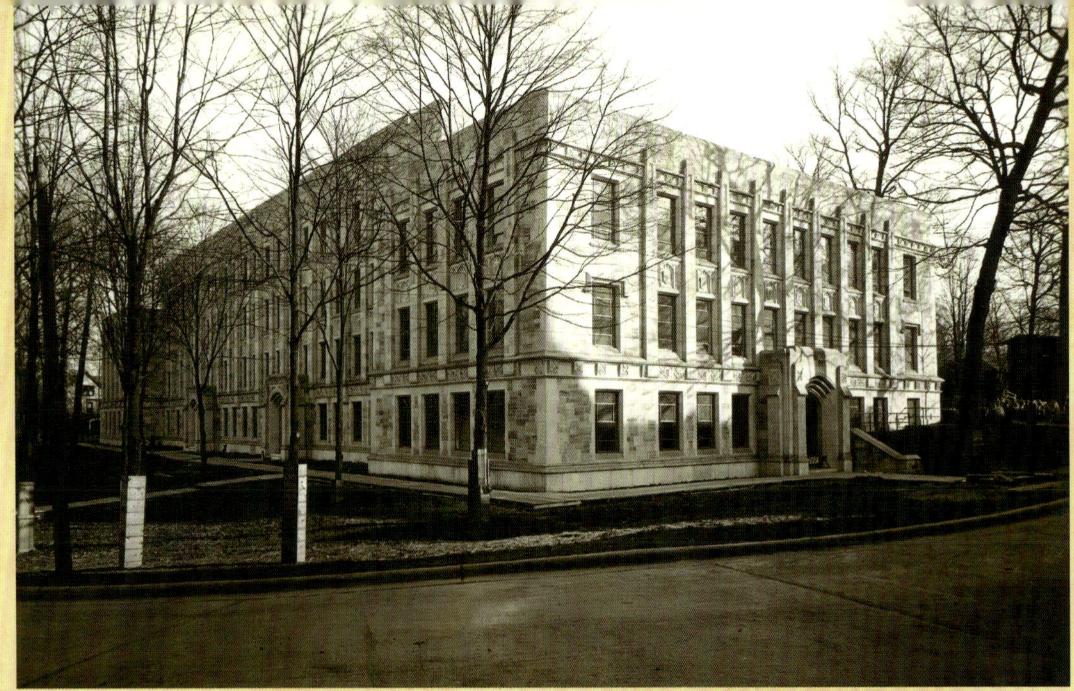

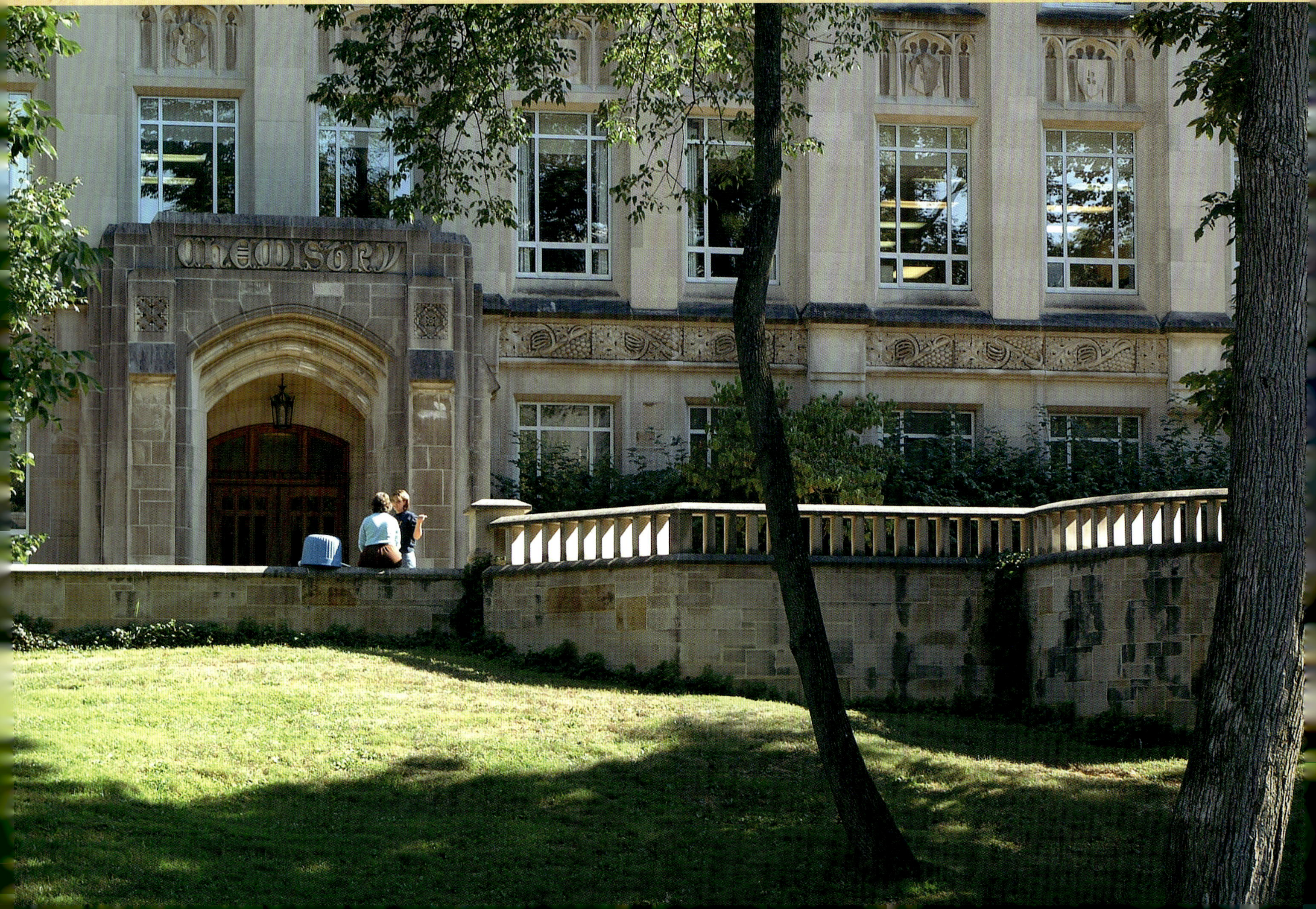

Chemistry Building

A Campus and Architectural Gem

And I want to say at the outset that I don't think I have ever been at a more beautiful university commencement than this. I shall always keep in mind this scene here in the open by the university buildings, a university which, in what we are apt to think of as a new nation, is approaching its centenary, here under these great trees, these maples and beeches, that have survived over from the primeval forest.

—Theodore Roosevelt at 1918 commencement

JOHN H. HARNEY WAS APPOINTED TO CHAIR mathematics, natural and mechanical philosophy, and chemistry at Indiana College in 1829, and so began the study of science at Indiana University. Laboratories for such purposes, however, were not added until more than a decade later. Still, instruction of chemistry and other sciences prospered, and in 1874, Indiana University (the college became a university in 1838) hired its first full-time professor of chemistry, Thomas Carlton Van Nuys. When the university moved to the present-day campus in 1884, it was Van Nuys who planned the arrangement of the first floor of Wylie Hall (1884) for the Department of Chemistry. Though it quickly outgrew that space, the department remained at Wylie Hall until the new purpose-built Chemistry Building opened nearly fifty years later in 1931.

To fulfill this significant project, Robert E. Lyons, head of the Chemistry Department, worked closely with architect Robert Frost Daggett. Ever aware of the steady growth of chemistry studies at the university, together Lyons and Daggett devised plans whereby harmonious additions could enlarge the building as needed.

The site selected for the new building was just east of Wylie Hall, slightly outside the Old Crescent. The footprint for the building forms the letter *E*, with the north side (the back of the *E*) four stories high, the auditorium in the middle two levels, and the east and west wings three stories each. The Chemistry Building is classic Collegiate Gothic in style and features buff Indiana limestone from the Monon Stone Company in Bloomington. The facade is enriched by carvings of ornamental shields bearing the symbols of the forty-six chemical elements known at the time of construction. Stone carvings continue to the wings and back of the original building with selected alchemistic symbols and a grape-and-leaf motif. On the north side rectangular pilasters with carved capitals extend to the fourth story. The location and landscaping were achieved with the natural beauty of the wooded site in mind, preserving as many of the trees and slopes as possible.

While many were impressed by the style and appearance of the Chemistry Building, the architectural feature Dr. Lyons particularly favored was the spacious auditorium with its seating for 475 and special acoustics, the discussion of which seemingly left no university stationery spared. The new building also included large laboratories in the central portion for each of the four major divisions of chemistry (general, analytical, physical, and organic), and smaller labs elsewhere for

Facing top, Chemistry Building shortly after completion, 1931. P0048171, IU Archives.

Facing bottom, North entrance to Chemistry Building, 2016. Photo credit: Indiana University.

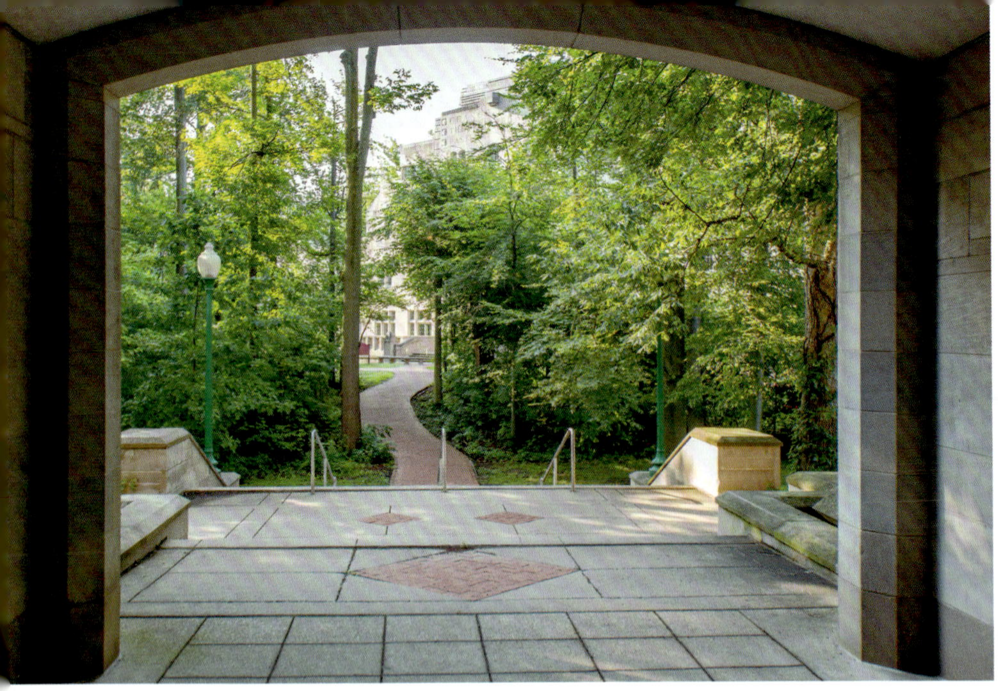

Jordan Hall visible beyond Chemistry Building archway, 2016. Photo credit: Tyagan Miller.

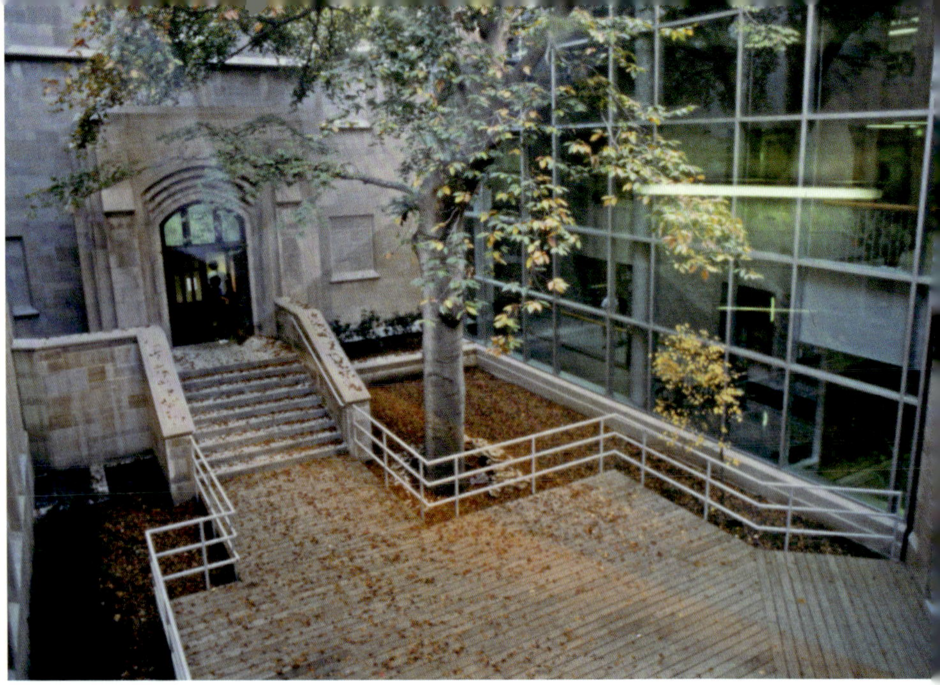

Beech tree preserved in Chemistry Building courtyard, 1989. P0025791, IU Archives.

the other branches. Faculty members were each provided with a laboratory and conference room, while graduate students shared twenty-three research rooms. For classroom work, three lecture rooms were provided, with space for a hundred students in each.

The dedication ceremony took place April 2, 1931, beginning with a luncheon and followed by a procession led by the university band from the Student Building to the auditorium in the Chemistry Building. Architect Daggett delivered the key to John W. Fesler, president of the Board of Trustees who in turn presented it to President William Lowe Bryan. He spoke a few words and was followed by guest speakers, the presentation of a portrait of Thomas C. Van Nuys, and conferral of honorary degrees to six prominent alumni of the Chemistry Department. The day ended with tours and tea in the library.

Planned for at the inception, additions both small and large have enhanced the Chemistry Building since 1931. In 1961, work began on an eight-story addition (the Annex) in order to better accommodate the growing discipline with additional research facilities and laboratories, including approximately 150 labs and offices for faculty and graduate research. The limestone addition was built onto the west side of the original building and was plain, with no exterior carvings or decorations.

After a 1979 external program review confirmed the years of complaints from faculty and students about the inadequate facilities for the Department of Chemistry, the university began planning for a three-stage remodeling project. Funding, however, was not approved, turning this into a two-stage project that broke ground in 1986. The project, designed by the architectural firm of Harley Ellington Pierce Yee Associates of Southfield, Michigan, began with a structure of approximately 80,000 square feet. The addition not only provided new space, but, wrapping around the Annex, it concealed what many had long considered a campus eyesore.

The seven-story addition is elegant, and its limestone facade and Collegiate Gothic style make it seem one with the original building. It features more of the shields, like those that adorn the original building, including one with the formula for stannous fluoride, the key ingredient of Crest toothpaste that was developed by IU professors Harry Day, Joseph Muhler, and William Nebergall. The addition housed twenty-eight laboratories for teaching and research and thirty-two offices for faculty, graduate students, and staff, as well as storage facilities. A two-day dedication ceremony was held in October 1988 and before the year was out, IU put out a call for bids for the second phase, which would focus on remodeling the interiors of the original building and 1964 addition, with a particular emphasis on addressing safety concerns.

While the original Chemistry Building is considered one of IU's campus treasures, the 1988 addition also has been recognized by those in the building and design industry. In January 1989, it was announced that, for its Chemistry Building

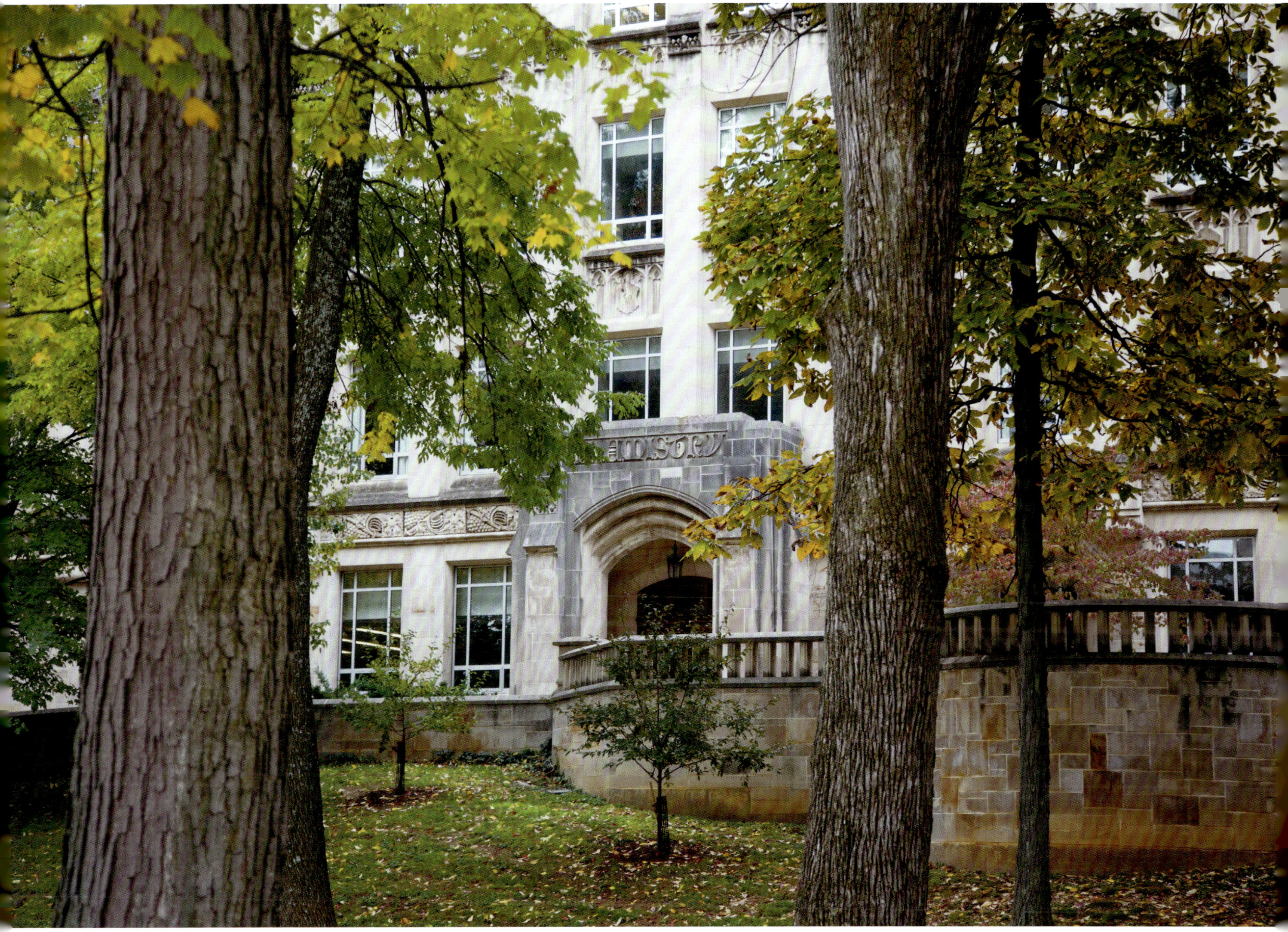

North side of Chemistry Building as seen from Indiana Memorial Union, 2016. Photo credit: Tyagan Miller.

renovation, Harley Ellington Pierce Yee Associates had been chosen by the Detroit Chapter of the American Institute of Architects to be honored for quality design, sensitivity to the architectural integrity of the existing building, and sensitivity to the surrounding campus—which included working its design around an existing large beech tree, now within the courtyard created by the addition. Additionally, the Indiana Mason Contractors Association and the Masonry Institute of Indiana recognized the firm for its "outstanding design with use of masonry."

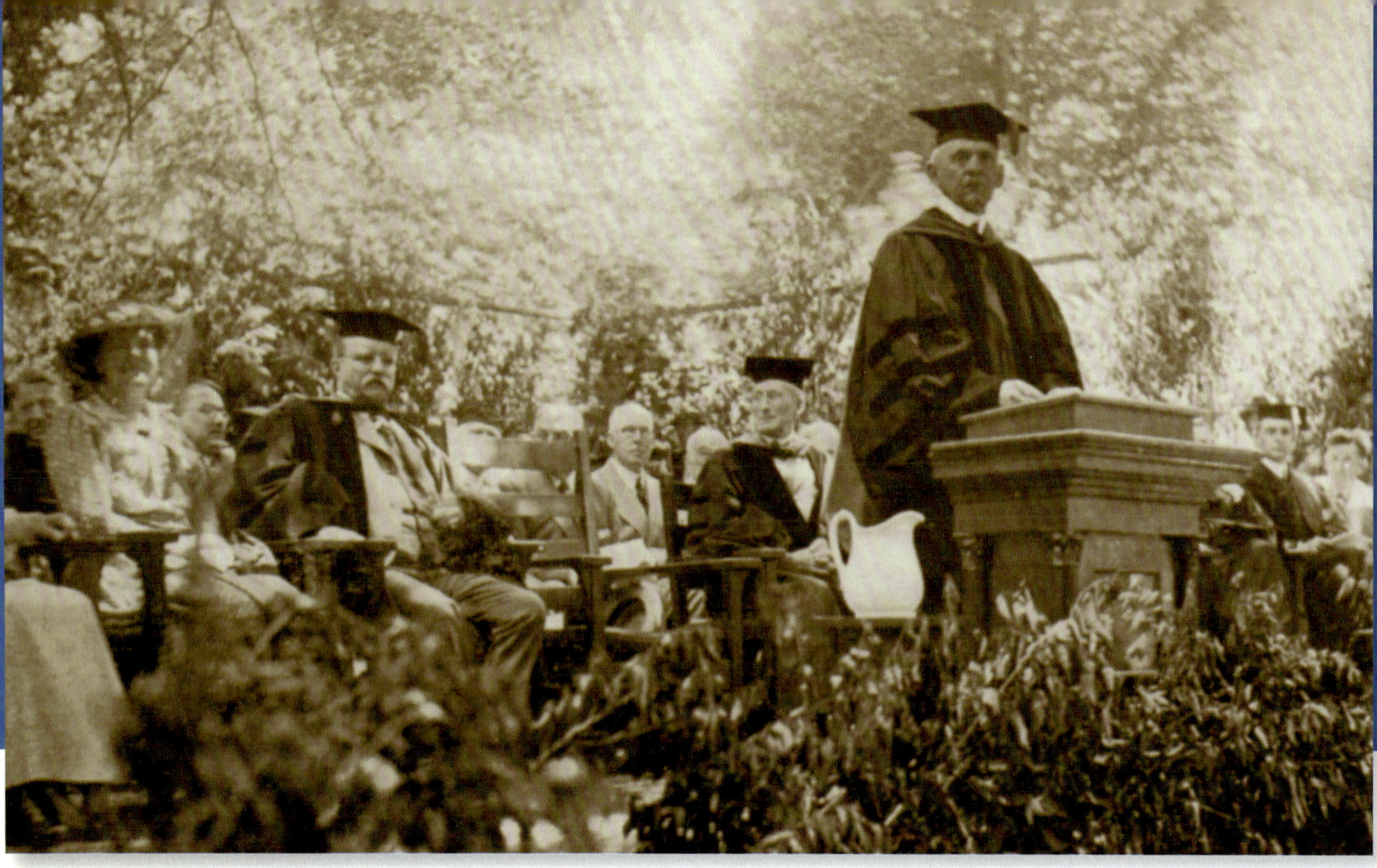

The Amphitheater

Before the construction of the Chemistry Building was completed in 1931, a Greek-style, open-air amphitheater graced a natural ravine directly behind Wylie and Kirkwood Halls. The amphitheater was a gift to the university from the classes of 1909 through 1912. In May 1909, the *Daily Student* reported that William E. Jenkins, the IU librarian and subsequently an English professor, had made a careful study of open-air theaters in the United States and Europe and created initial plans for the structure, designed to seat three to four thousand people. Indiana University was reportedly only the third institution of higher learning in the United States (after the University of California and the University of Syracuse) to possess such a structure.[1] The site was eventually equipped with a "stage, sounding board and lighting facilities" and later "enlarged and made suitable for a dance pavilion."[2] The amphitheater, with its natural beauty and abundance of shade, provided the venue for university commencements, convocations, lectures, orchestra performances, plays, and campus dances. Perhaps most notably, on June 12, 1918, former president Theodore Roosevelt spoke in the amphitheater as part of Commencement Day ceremonies.

1. "Plans Drawn for Big Amphitheatre: Librarian Jenkins Works on Specifications of Structure Adopted as Senior Memorial," *Daily Student*, May 26, 1909.

2. "Site of New Building Revered by Old Indiana Grads Who Danced, Attended Exercises Here in Bygone Days," *Indiana Daily Student*, April 2, 1931.

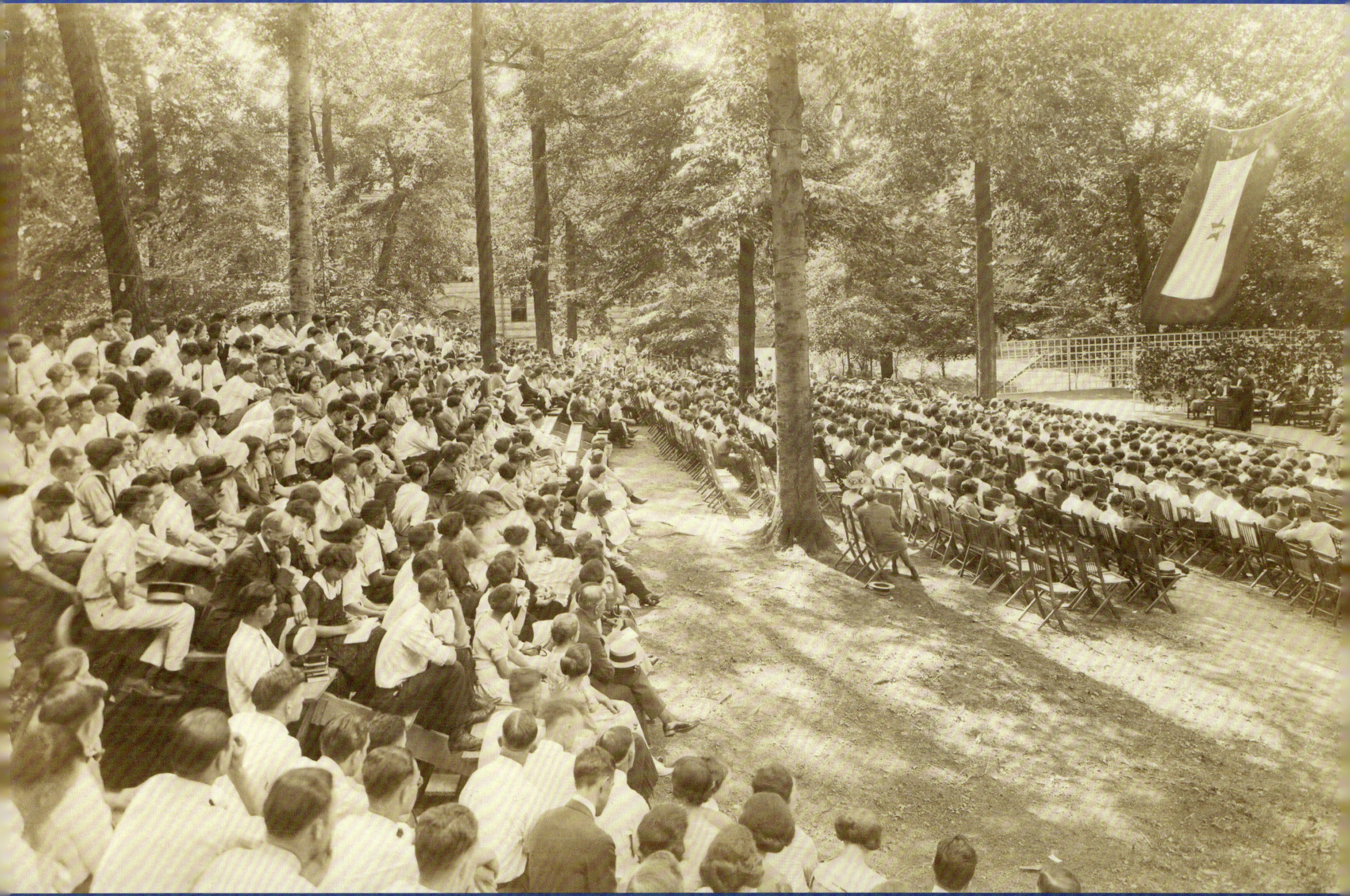

Facing, President William Lowe Bryan introducing former president Theodore Roosevelt (seated, left), guest speaker at the 1918 commencement in the amphitheater outside the Chemistry Building. P0021687, IU Archives. Photo credit: Charles Gilbert Shaw.

Above, Former Indiana governor Samuel M. Ralston addressing a crowd in the amphitheater outside the Chemistry Building, 1922. P0045005, IU Archives.

Burton Dorr Myers Hall 1937

ARCHITECT	A. M. Strauss
ARCHITECTURAL STYLE	Collegiate Gothic with Strong Art Deco Details
ORIGINAL NAME	Medical Building
MAJOR RENOVATION	1997
ARCHITECT	Frank M. Adams

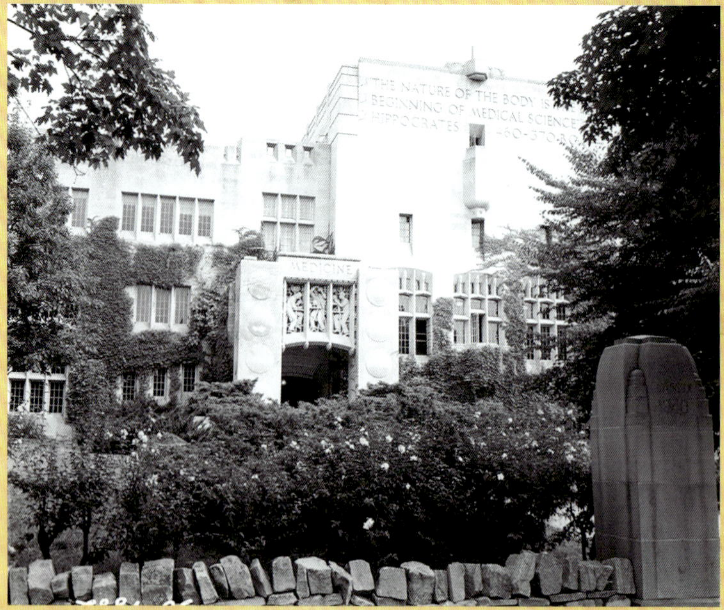

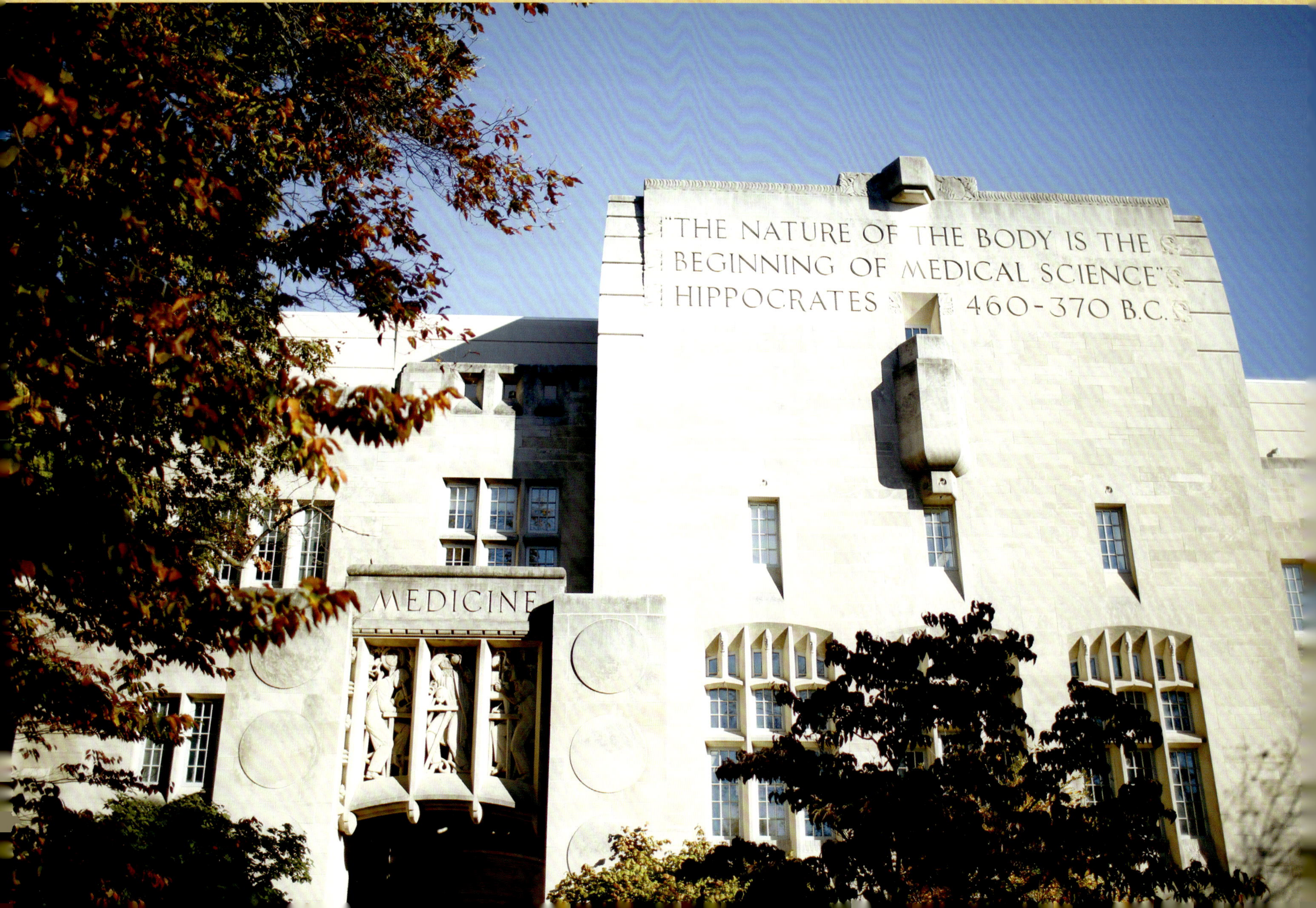

Burton Dorr Myers Hall

The Medical Building

Learning has blazed the way along which civilization has slowly and painfully moved forward. Progress has depended upon new ideas, new truth, and knowledge. In this structure, therefore, we can be certain that work will be done which will play a very real part in the slow and toilsome process by which society advances.

—Indian University President Herman B Wells at dedication ceremony

In 1926 Burton Dorr Myers, then serving as assistant dean of the IU School of Medicine, wrote to President William Lowe Bryan about the dire lack of space for the department. It was so bad, Myers claimed, that necessity had required them to place overflow students from the gross anatomy laboratory in the incinerator and animal room. Furthermore, the pressure was on to expand the program in order to meet the growing medical needs of Hoosiers and to replenish the number of Indiana doctors who were approaching retirement age.[1]

Despite these needs, IU was not able to proceed with construction of a new facility for the medical sciences until the 1930s. With the crash of the U.S. stock market in 1929 and the subsequent economic depression, the federal government turned its attention to creating jobs to alleviate the large-scale unemployment Americans felt throughout the country. In 1933 President Franklin D. Roosevelt's administration introduced a complex series of government-aid programs collectively known as the New Deal that focused on the three R's: Relief, Recovery, and Reform. The Works Progress Administration (WPA) was the largest New Deal agency, offering work to those in need by providing state grants for a variety of projects including highway and building construction, slum clearance, and reforestation.

Indiana University benefited from a number of WPA grants and used the funds for building projects, improvements to the campus grounds, library services, and research. In December 1935 the university was notified that $211,000 in federal funding was approved to support the construction of the much-needed medical sciences building and work began immediately.

Myers Hall, originally called the Medical Building, was named in 1958 for Burton Dorr Myers, who long served the School of Medicine as both professor and administrator. It is one of the best examples of the marriage of Art Deco and Collegiate Gothic architecture on the Bloomington campus. Arising from the gracefully sloping terrain, this stunning building commands attention with its elaborate limestone sculpture work. The eye is first drawn to the large carving of the Hippocratic quotation set in Indiana limestone just below the roofline: "The nature of the body is the beginning of medical science." While the building is rich in ornamentation throughout, the striking panels over the square portico serve as the centerpiece of its grandeur. Created by the artisans of Easton Studios (Bedford, Indiana), the three identical friezes portray the activities of medical research and practice, depicting a phar-

Facing top, South-facing facade of Burton Dorr Myers Hall showing frieze created by Easton Studios, 1950. P0051493, IU Archives.

Facing bottom, Hippocrates quotation, Myers Hall, 2016. Photo credit: Indiana University.

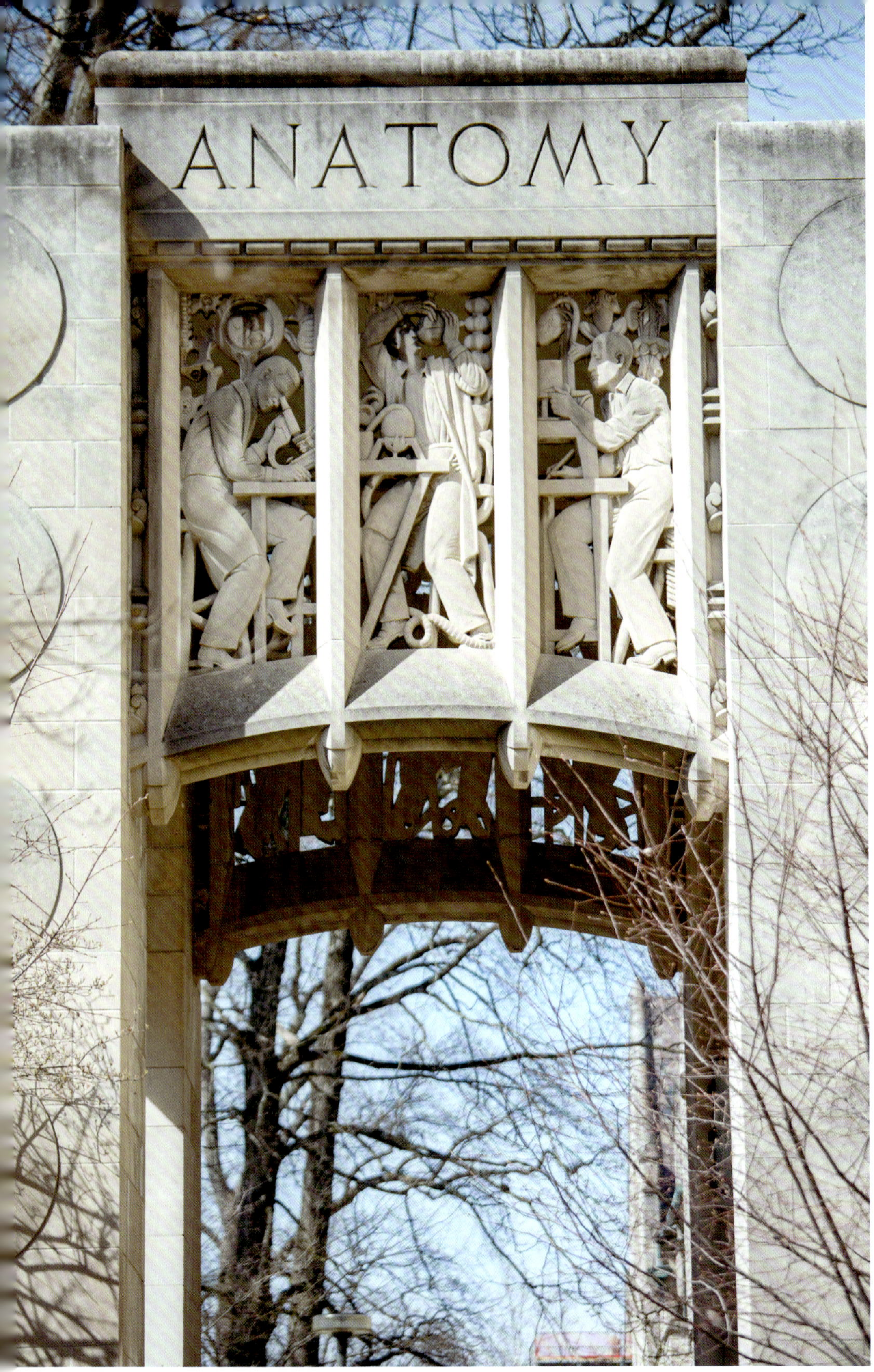

Above and facing, Over covered entry to Myers Hall, two of the three limestone friezes celebrating medical research and practice, 2012. Photo credit: Tyagan Miller.

macologist, anatomist, and physiologist. To obviate any remaining doubt about the activities taking place within the structure, above each panel are the single words *Medicine, Physiology,* and *Anatomy.* Continued reflection brings other details to light, such as the array of nautical-themed carvings, the battlements at the roofline, the Gothic-style faces that gaze down from the second-story windows on the south side, and below them, three stern-looking Art Deco owls, which look to the east.

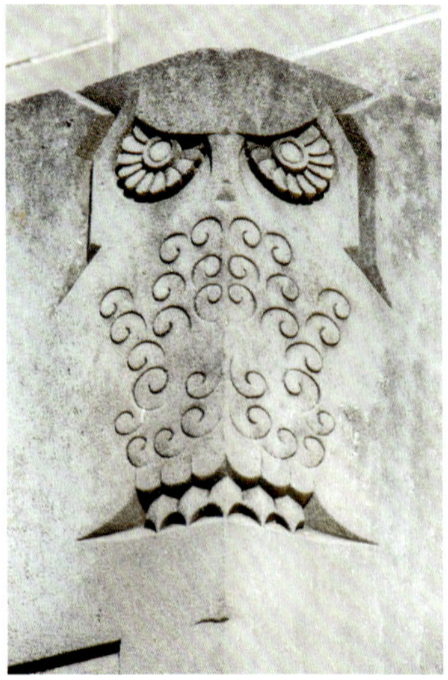

One of three Art Deco owls, Burton Dorr Myers Hall, 2012. Photo credit: Tyagan Miller.

Renowned landscape architects the Olmsted Brothers (Brookline, Massachusetts) worked closely with the architect A. M. Strauss (Fort Wayne, Indiana) on siting to ensure the best use of the land, to minimize excavation, and to save as many healthy mature trees as possible. (Indeed, many letters passed back and forth about moving the building in an attempt to preserve a beech tree with a 30-inch diameter that would have been directly in front of the entrance. Such steps, however, would have endangered two large maples, so in the end, the beech was sacrificed.) On February 24, 1936, Strauss sent a missive to the Olmsted firm: "In designing the entire building I have tried to conform to your thought of adjusting to the present terrain as much as possible both to secure the 'natural' effect and to reduce the destruction of the trees to the mimimum [*sic*]. . . . It has been our every effort to make the entire building 'nestle' close to the ground. The entire effect is rather informal and I believe well adapted to the character of this building which is after all simply one of the departments of the University and should not be too monumental in feeling."[2]

Although a labor strike delayed work in the summer of 1936, dedication ceremonies were held on November 20, 1937. The finished building housed the Departments of Physiology and Hygiene in the west wing and the Department of Anatomy and administrative offices in the east wing. The central portion of the building, one story higher than the wings, consisted of the common facilities such as the auditorium, library, locker room, and animal quarters.

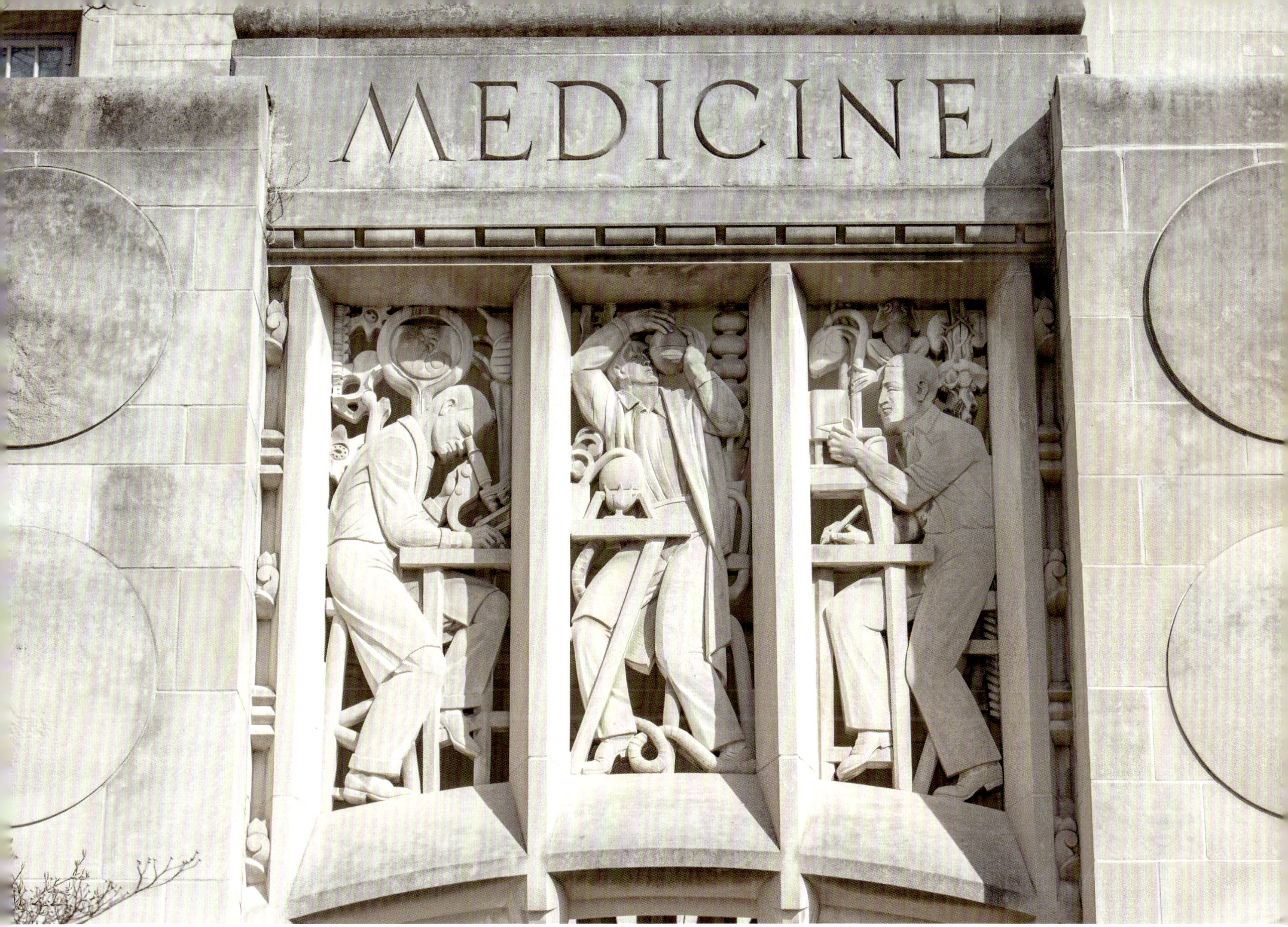

Myers Hall continues to serve as home to the medical sciences program but has been updated over the years. The first major project occurred in the early 1960s, when a 5,264-square-foot addition was constructed on the west end of the original structure. In the 1990s Myers underwent a multimillion-dollar facelift, with the main focus on providing new facilities for the Institute for Molecular and Cellular Biology, at the time housed in Jordan Hall. To accommodate the needs of the institute, extensive renovations were made under the direction of architect Frank M. Adams Jr. (Columbus, Indiana), which included lab space for fifteen research groups and facilities for DNA sequencing, advanced microscopy, crystallography, and plant genetics. At the 2002 Burton Dorr Myers Hall rededication, Indiana University Distinguished Professor Rudolf A. Raff echoed the words spoken by Interim President Wells in 1937: "In a very real sense this rededication lets us look at where we have been and where we are going, as biologists, as members of the university, and as members of the larger human community."[3]

Swain Hall West 1940

ARCHITECT A. M. Strauss

ARCHITECTURAL STYLE Collegiate Gothic

ADDITION 1960

ARCHITECT Eggers and Higgins

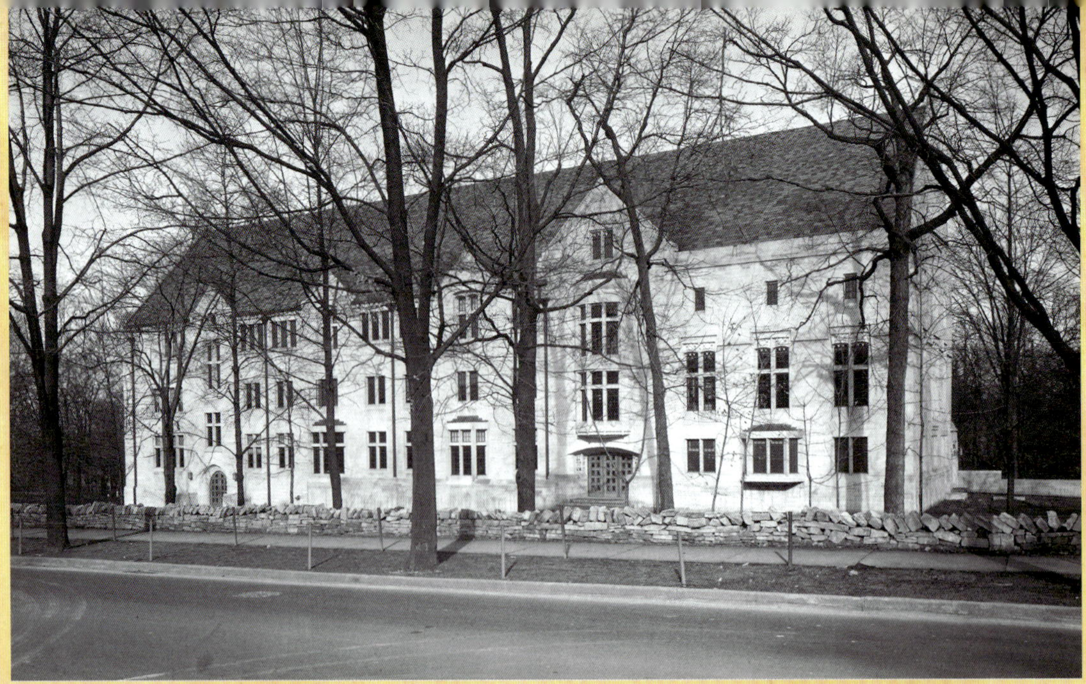

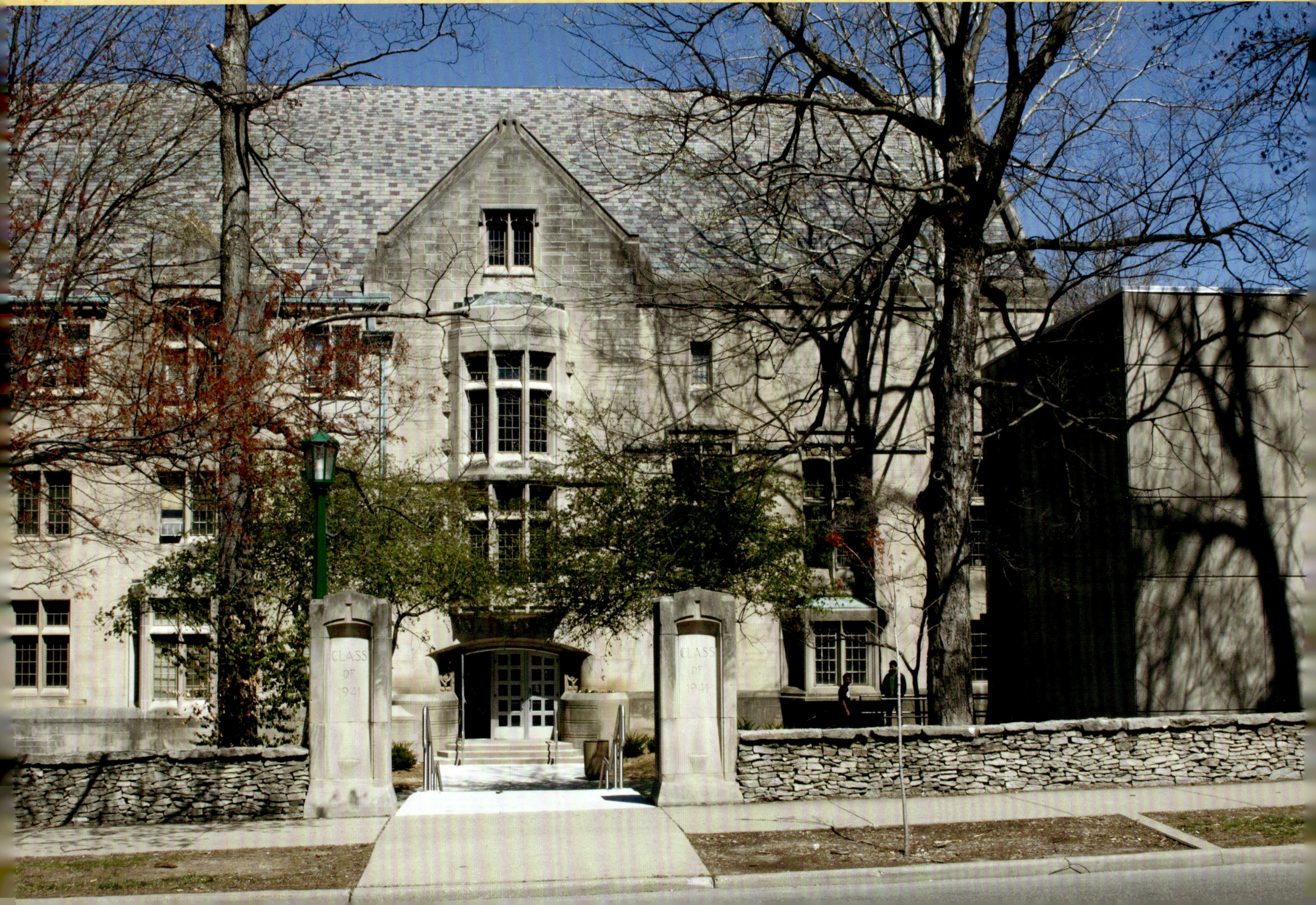

Swain Hall West

First Home of the Cyclotron

Swain Hall figured prominently in ushering in the new scientific age.
—*Thomas D. Clark,* Indiana University, Midwestern Pioneer

ON MAY 11, 1938, IU PRESIDENT HERMAN B WELLS wired New York University nuclear physicist Allan C. G. Mitchell to offer him a position as professor and head of the Physics Department with the enticement of a new building for the physical sciences. On an earlier visit, Mitchell had noted that "the rooms available for research were considerably too small for this purpose . . . the total space available to physics at present is not adequate." In his opinion, nuclear physics was "the most fundamental field in physics" and advised the construction of "a machine for generating high voltage ions."[1]

A new building (originally named the Physical Sciences Building) to house the Departments of Mathematics, Astronomy, and Physics and a cyclotron research laboratory shot to the top of the ten-year construction plan. The building site would be directly west of Biology Hall (today Swain East) and facing Third Street. Architect A. M. Strauss of Fort Wayne initiated preliminary plans, and the university submitted an application for a grant through the Public Works Administration. For his part, Mitchell assembled a team of talented nuclear physicists, including Lawrence M. Langer, one of his former doctoral students at New York University, who worked on various aspects of nuclear physics; Franz N. D. Kurie, a research associate in the radiation laboratory at UC Berkley under E. O. Lawrence who was directly involved with the building and operation of that institution's cyclotron facility; and Emil J. Konopinski, a research fellow from Cornell University known for his work on the theory of the atomic nucleus. Grant approval for the project finally arrived via telegraph from Washington, DC, on September 8, 1938, and contracts for construction were awarded in late January 1939.

Before its completion in June 1940, the trustees decided to name the new structure Swain Hall in honor of the university's ninth president, alumnus, and professor of mathematics and occasionally astronomy, Joseph Swain. As for the current names of the two-part building, the trustees decreed in their May 1957 minutes that the structures comprising "the Swain Hall–Biology Building complex . . . be designated respectively Swain Hall West and Swain Hall East."[2]

Clad in Indiana limestone with a slate roof, the structure was described at the time as "modified Gothic architecture," the Collegiate Gothic style visible in the window treatments, square rosettes, and a carved fleur-de-lis over the main entrance.[3] The building includes a subbasement and basement topped by three floors of research laboratories, classrooms,

Facing top, Swain Hall West from Third Street, 1941. P0035955, IU Archives. Photo credit: Indiana University.

Facing bottom, Swain Hall West from Third Street, 2016. Photo credit: Indiana University.

Professors L. Jackson Laslett, Franz N. D. Kurie, Lawrence M. Langer, and Allan C. G. Mitchell with Indiana University's first cyclotron, 1940. P0032291, IU Archives.

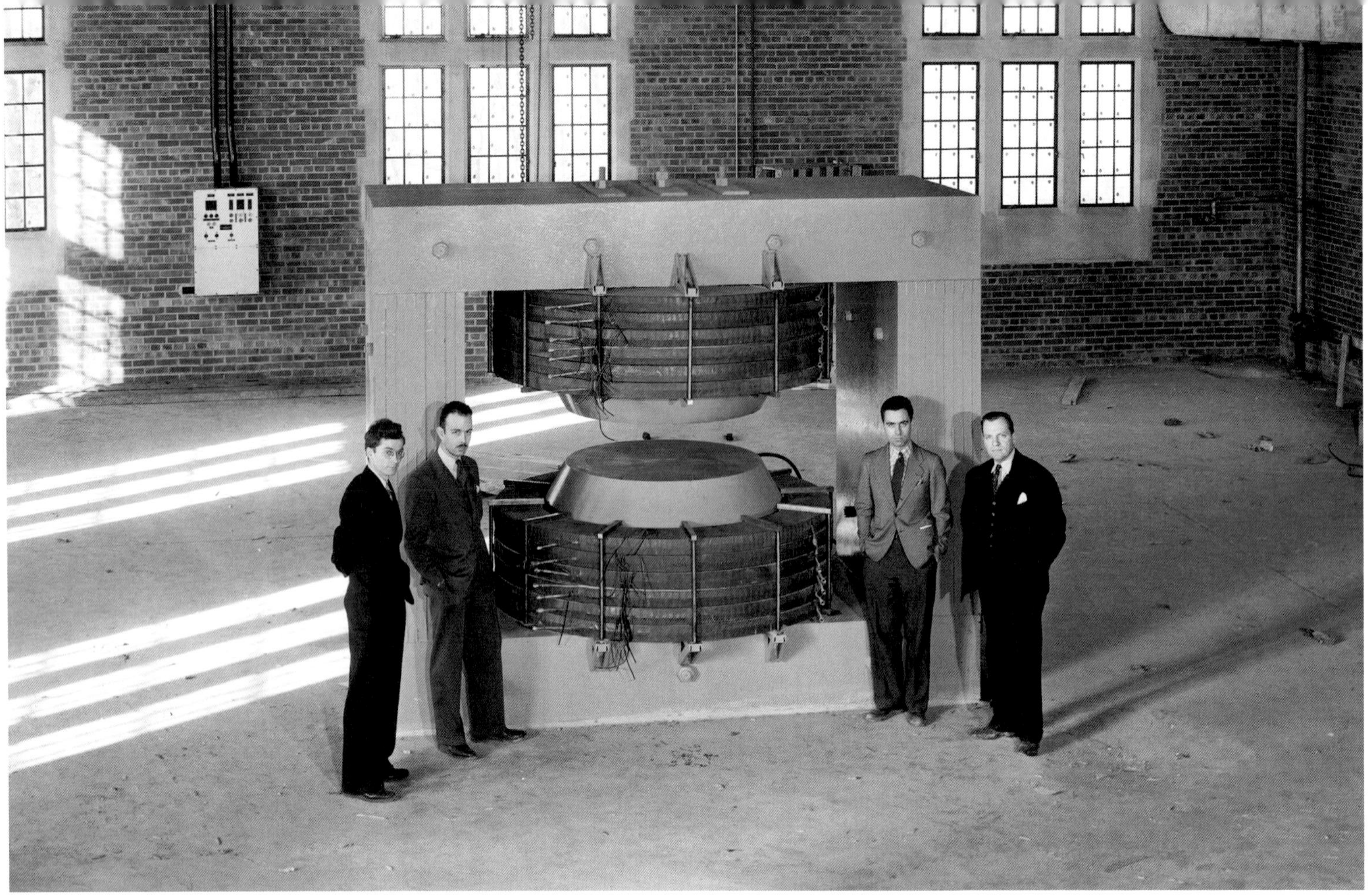

apparatus rooms, teaching laboratories, offices for the faculty of the departments, and a physical science library. At the time of completion, the subbasement was occupied by the cyclotron. The basement and first floors were used exclusively by the Physics Department. The second floor housed the science library, physics research and teaching laboratories, offices for the mathematics faculty, and a seminar room. Classrooms and offices for the Astronomy Department, research laboratories for physics, and a mathematics computing room occupied the third floor.

In August 1945, with the beginning of the atomic age and the subsequent end of World War II, Mitchell anticipated changes on the horizon, including the numbers of returning veterans. He noted in a memo to Wells that "we should immediately make plans for the development of our post war Physics Department. . . . Some imaginative planning now will put the Indiana University Physics Department among the top ranking Physics departments in the country. . . . What we must do now is to take as forward a looking policy to the future Physics department as we took to the present one in 1938."[4] Eggers and Higgins, the New York architectural firm, commenced plans for an addition to provide more classrooms and laboratories for physics, astronomy, and mathematics, as well as a connection between Swain Hall and Biology Hall (1910). The project was completed during the 1959–60 academic years but was not officially dedicated until November 1961. In 1965 a fourth floor was added atop the addition for the astronomy department, and a large classroom and faculty office addition was completed in 1972.

In conjunction with the design and construction of Swain Hall West, between 1939 and 1941, a team of faculty and graduate students worked for two and a half years to build the physics program's centerpiece, a nearly 100-ton cyclotron or "atom-smasher" capable of generating 17 million volts. At the time of completion, it was the third largest in the world, only behind those at the Universities of California and Tokyo.[5]

The massive cyclotron magnet was housed in a specially designed 50-by-75-foot room in the subbasement. The room featured an operator's station and a large, glass-enclosed observation booth overlooking the cyclotron room for occasional groups of visitors, but mainly for university classes to observe experiments. With little pomp and circumstance, the scien-

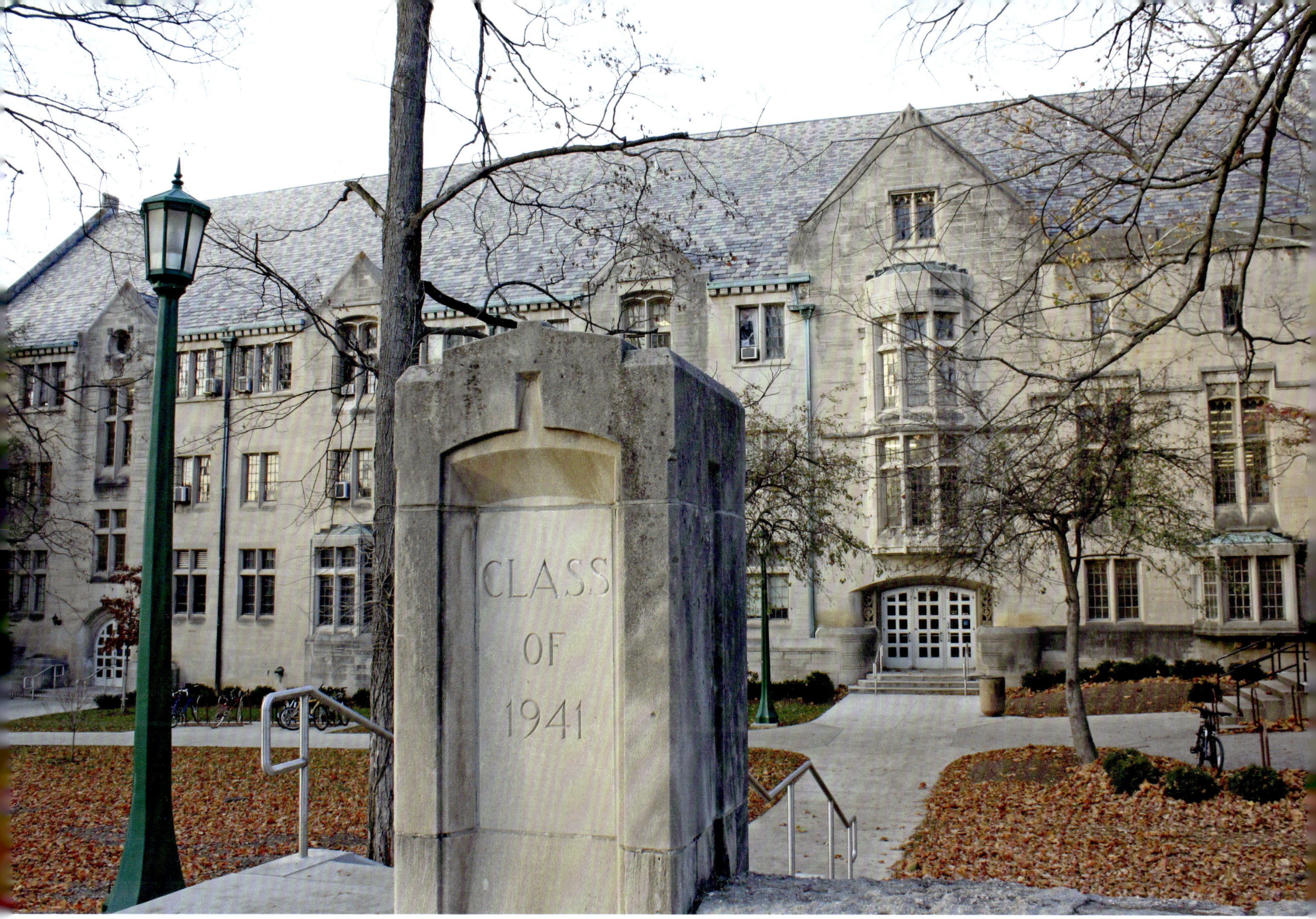

Swain Hall West; detail of gate from class of 1941 and stone wall, undated. Photo credit: Indiana University.

tists put the machine into operation on April 14, 1941 "in the exploration of a little known world in which conceivably may exist new sources of energy and new medical treatments for human ills."[6] However, after the bombing of Pearl Harbor, within months the faculty and most of the students in the department were drafted for war-related work, most notably the Manhattan Project, and research now took place in Swain Hall under the shelter of intense secrecy.[7] Even President Wells, during V-J Day celebrations, was forbidden from revealing the involvement, noting that "here at home, all the research facilities of the University have been distracted toward study of war problems. Even tonight, with hostilities ended, I am not permitted to tell you of many of the research contributions to our success that were originated and developed on this campus."[8]

By the 1960s, it was apparent that the Swain West cyclotron was nearing obsolescence, and it ceased operation in 1968. The following year, construction began on the new IU Cyclotron Facility, located north of campus; it was formally dedicated in April 1976. In 2011, the facility was rededicated as the Integrated Science and Technology Hall.

Jordan Hall 1955

ARCHITECT A. M. Strauss

ARCHITECTURAL STYLE Collegiate Gothic / 1950s Modern

ORIGINAL NAME Life Sciences Building

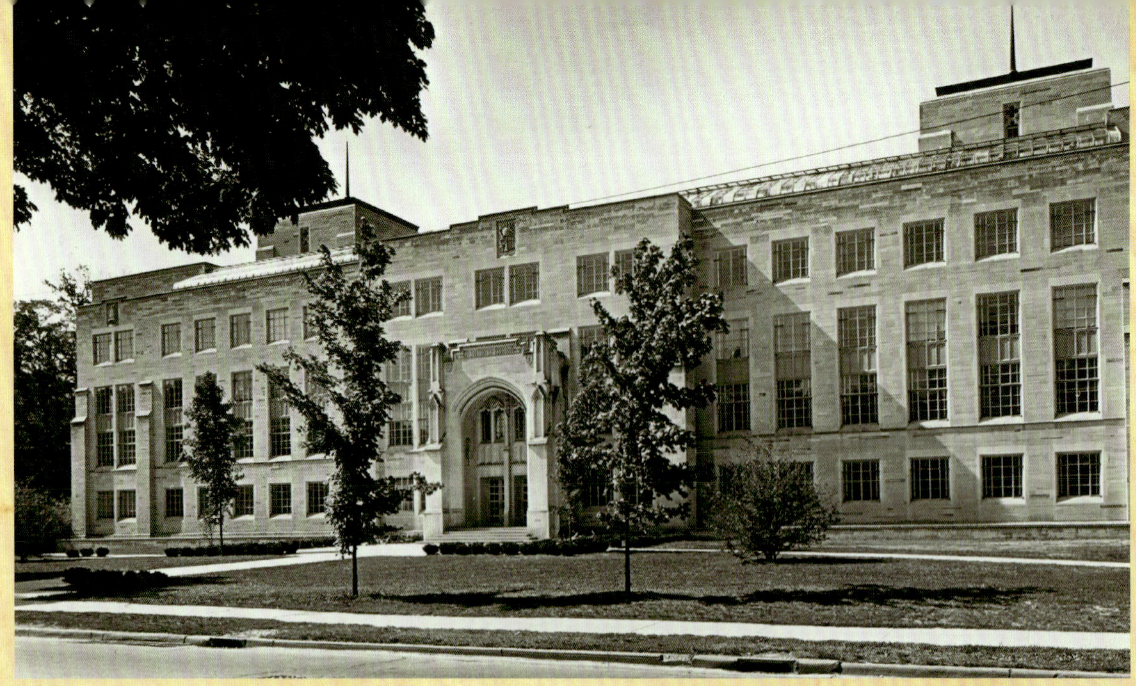

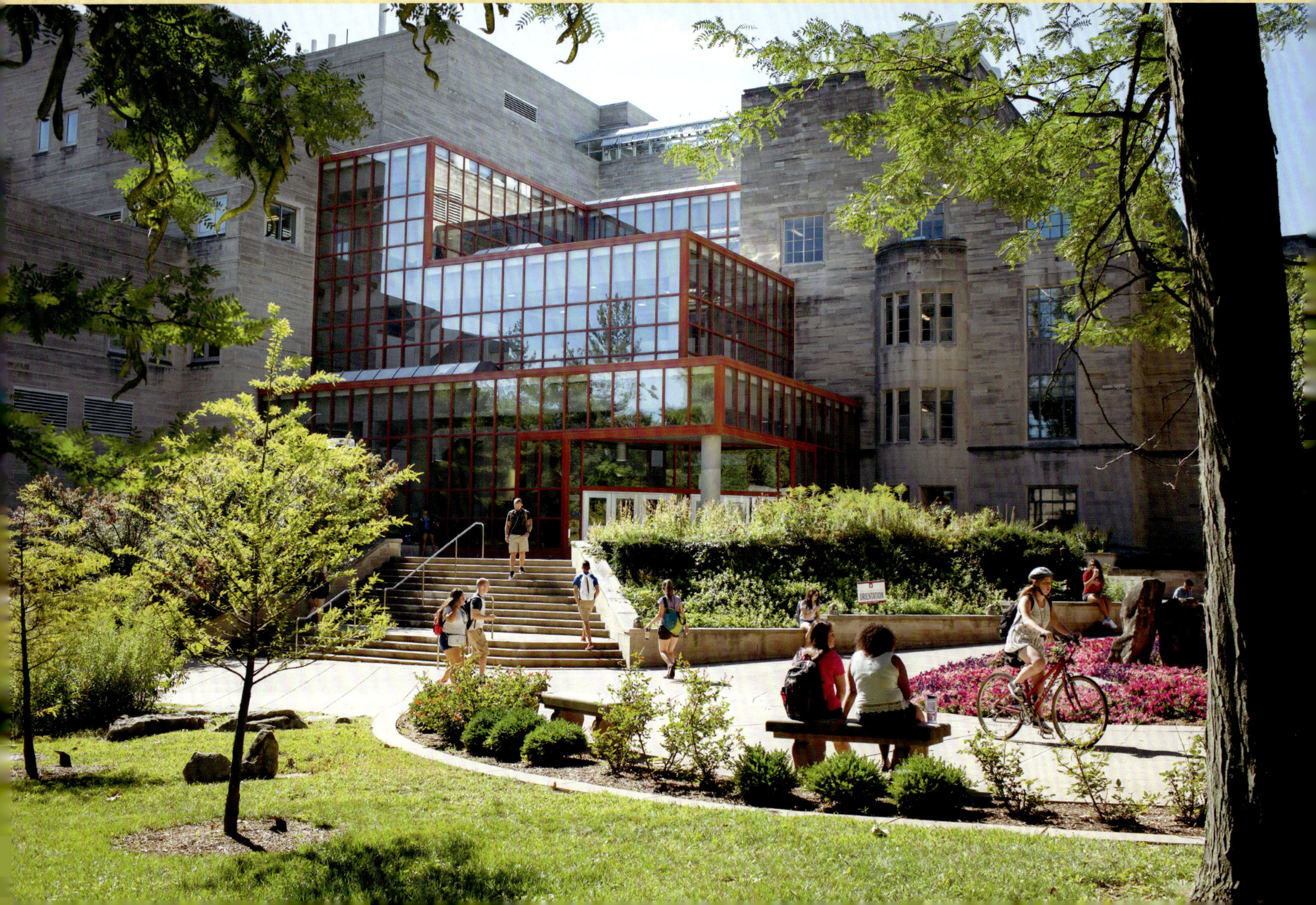

Jordan Hall

Alliance of the Life Sciences

This building, generously given by the people of Indiana, is not merely a monument of stone, steel and mortar, erected to beautify the campus, but a building within the walls of which are a multiplicity of rooms and laboratories adapted to the use of staffs and students for teaching and research in the biological sciences. Hence, we who work within Jordan Hall have an obligation to give our best efforts and to dedicate our lives to this end.

—Fernandus Payne at dedication dinner

Two years after the completion of the Indiana University Auditorium and before the end of World War II, the New York architectural firm of Eggers and Higgins was commissioned by the university to develop a comprehensive master plan for future development. Eggers and Higgins submitted a document that outlined proposed locations for a new library, an addition to the student union, and new housing structures and athletic facilities, in addition to a life sciences building to house the Departments of Bacteriology, Botany, and Zoology. President Wells later reminisced that "these departments had completely outgrown their former home, Biology Hall, and their work had to be scattered in six additional buildings and three Quonset huts wherever a few additional feet of space could be found. . . . More than 33 percent of our work has had to be carried on in attics, basements, Quonset huts, or temporary structures of one type of another."[1] The trustees placed the structure at the top of the priority list for postwar building, and in December 1944, Eggers and Higgins, teamed with A. M. Strauss of Fort Wayne, was asked to prepare detailed plans for use when funding became available.

The university received funding as part of the 1951–53 biennium state budget for the construction of Jordan Hall, the first new building financed by the state since the war. Site work began in July 1951, and the facility was completed in August 1955. The new Life Sciences Building, as it was originally called, became home to renowned faculty members such as botanist Ralph E. Cleland; geneticist and Nobel laureate Hermann J. Muller; biologist Tracy M. Sonneborn; zoologist and endocrinologist William R. Breneman; botanist Paul Weatherwax; limnologist David G. Frey; and biologist and director of the Institute for Sex Research, Alfred Kinsey.

Jordan Hall was designed to foster collaboration between the sciences. Theodore J. Young of Eggers and Higgins reported in a feature article in the *American School and University*: "The New Life Science Building soon to be constructed on the campus of Indiana University marks the abandonment of the notion that each of the biological sciences is a water-tight compartment of knowledge. Since the building will be the largest of its kind in the United States, and, perhaps, in the world, it will epitomize the synthesis of these sciences."[2]

Floor plans outlined a fully air-conditioned, five-story structure with an emphasis on common spaces and operational efficiency. It incorporated an amphitheater auditorium seating 350, a library, classrooms, greenhouses, animal rooms,

Facing top, Jordan Hall shortly after completion, circa 1955. P0020059, IU Archives. Photo credit: William Dellenback.

Facing bottom, North entrance to Jordan Hall, 2015. Photo credit: Indiana University.

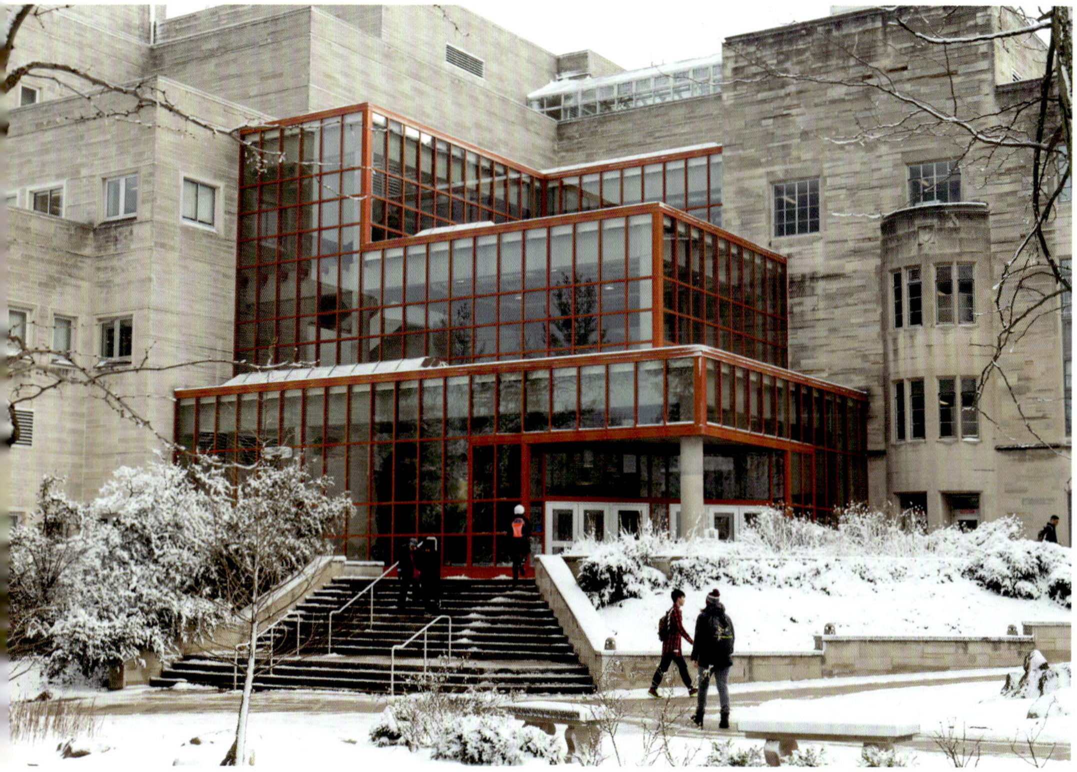

Five-story frame and glass atrium, north elevation Jordan Hall, 2016. Photo credit: Indiana University.

Jordan Hall facing Third Street, 2017. Photo credit: Tyagan Miller.

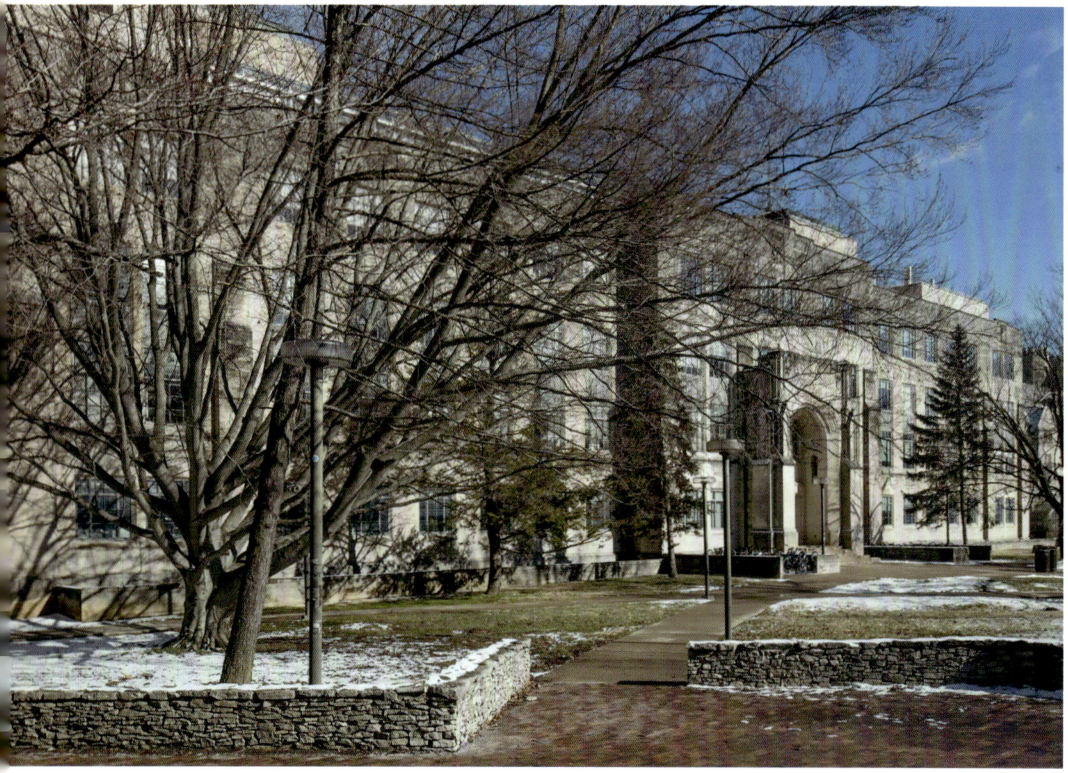

climate-controlled areas, dark rooms, laboratories for teaching and research, and offices. Young reported that the facilities "run through the alphabet from A to Z. The combination of facilities ranges from animal runs to a Geiger counter room where instruments measure radioactivity; from an herbarium and anthropological museum to photographic rooms and humidity-controlled X-ray laboratories."[3]

A site close to Myers Hall, parallel to Third Street, and in front of Alpha Hall (razed in 1961) was chosen for construction. To blend with the surrounding buildings and allow for the possibility of a future connection to Myers Hall, Jordan was designed in Collegiate Gothic style and clad in a smooth-faced Indiana limestone. Among the building's few embellishments are carvings of a microscope and other science instruments over the southern facade entry, carvings including an open book with the motto *Veritas* (Truth) above the southeast corner of the greenhouse, and various representations of the IU symbol. A pointed arch and Gothic windows, traditional Collegiate Gothic features, can be seen at the main entrance to the building.

Jordan Hall was named for David Starr Jordan, chairman of the Department of Natural Sciences and university president from 1885 to 1891. When the impressive new home for the biological sciences was completed, it was said to be "the most modern and best equipped structure of its kind on an American university campus."[4] Nearly a year later it was formally dedicated as part of commencement weekend events. On Friday, June 8, 1956, President Herman B Wells presided over the formal dedication, where he announced a massive $350,000 grant from the Rockefeller Foundation to continue the genetics research of the faculty. The optimistic tone shaped the course of the coming years, and it was reported in the university's September 1959 Construction Planning Report that "all phases of the activities of these departments have grown at a rate which would have been impossible in the old quarters. Enrollment in beginning courses in botany and bacteriology increased 60 percent between 1957 and 1958. The number of graduate students in training for the Ph.D. degree had almost doubled since the building was occupied. . . . Most striking has been the increased national recognition achieved by the three departments, much of which can be attributed to the stimulation of research programs provided by the new facilities. . . . The effect of this one structure on the academic prestige of Indiana University illustrates well the role of adequate facilities in modern educational programs."[5]

By the late 1970s, the departments housed within Jordan Hall were vying for space due to an enrollment that had more than doubled, and administrators began a push for an addition. Archonics Design Partnership of Indianapolis was hired for preliminary design work to increase the square footage by 33 percent. The final product completed in 1984 is "an ingeniously well-made puzzle piece" that fits between the east and west wings of the existing building. Built of reinforced concrete with a limestone veneer to blend with the existing building, the addition also features a dramatic five-story metal-and-glass atrium at the northwestern entrance.[6] The renovation included lecture halls, laboratories, offices, a biology library, research laboratories, dark rooms, and several greenhouses.

Indiana University continues its commitment to research and the life sciences with new construction, renowned faculty, and advanced programs.

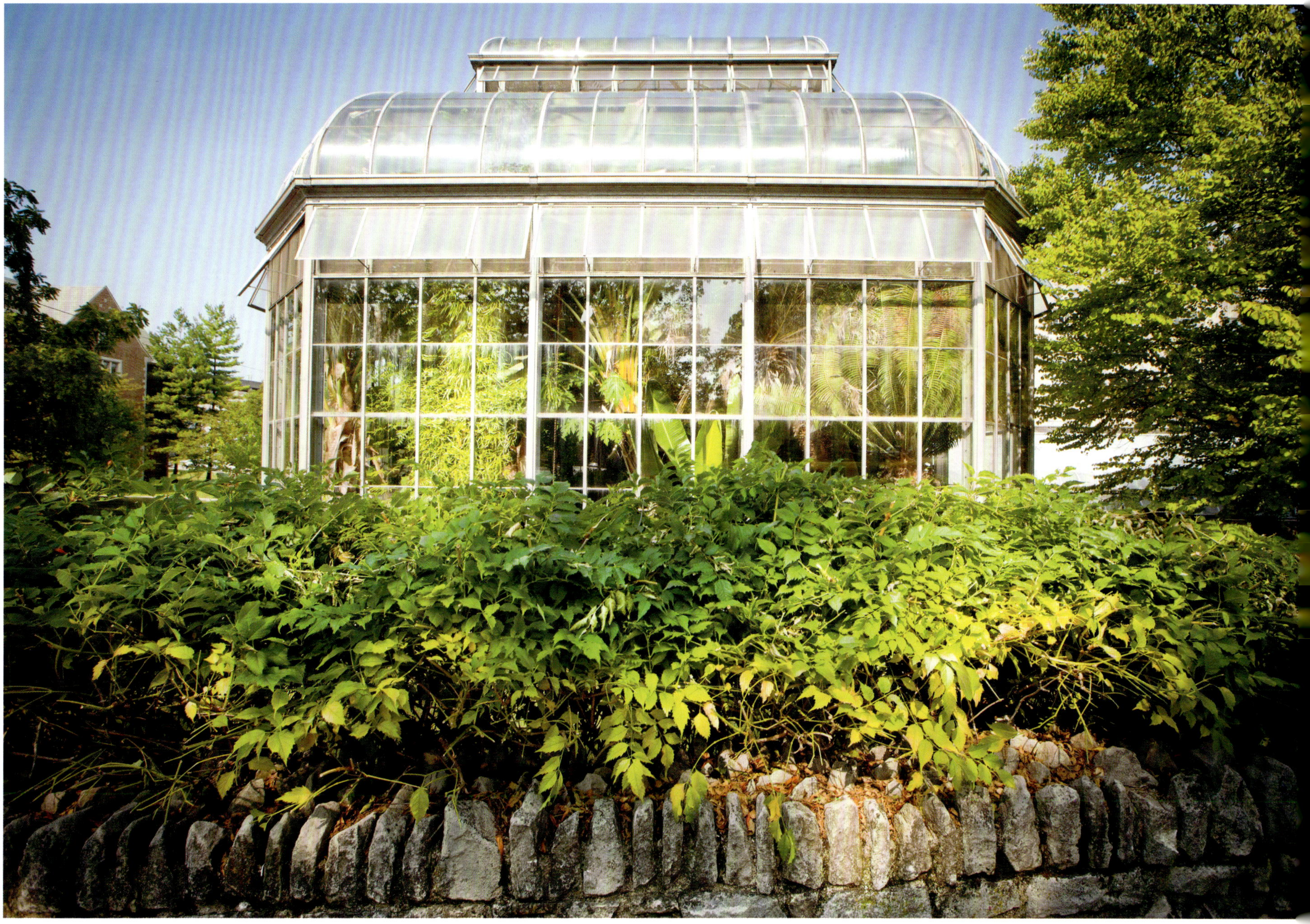

Jordan Hall greenhouse, 2011. Photo credit: Tyagan Miller.

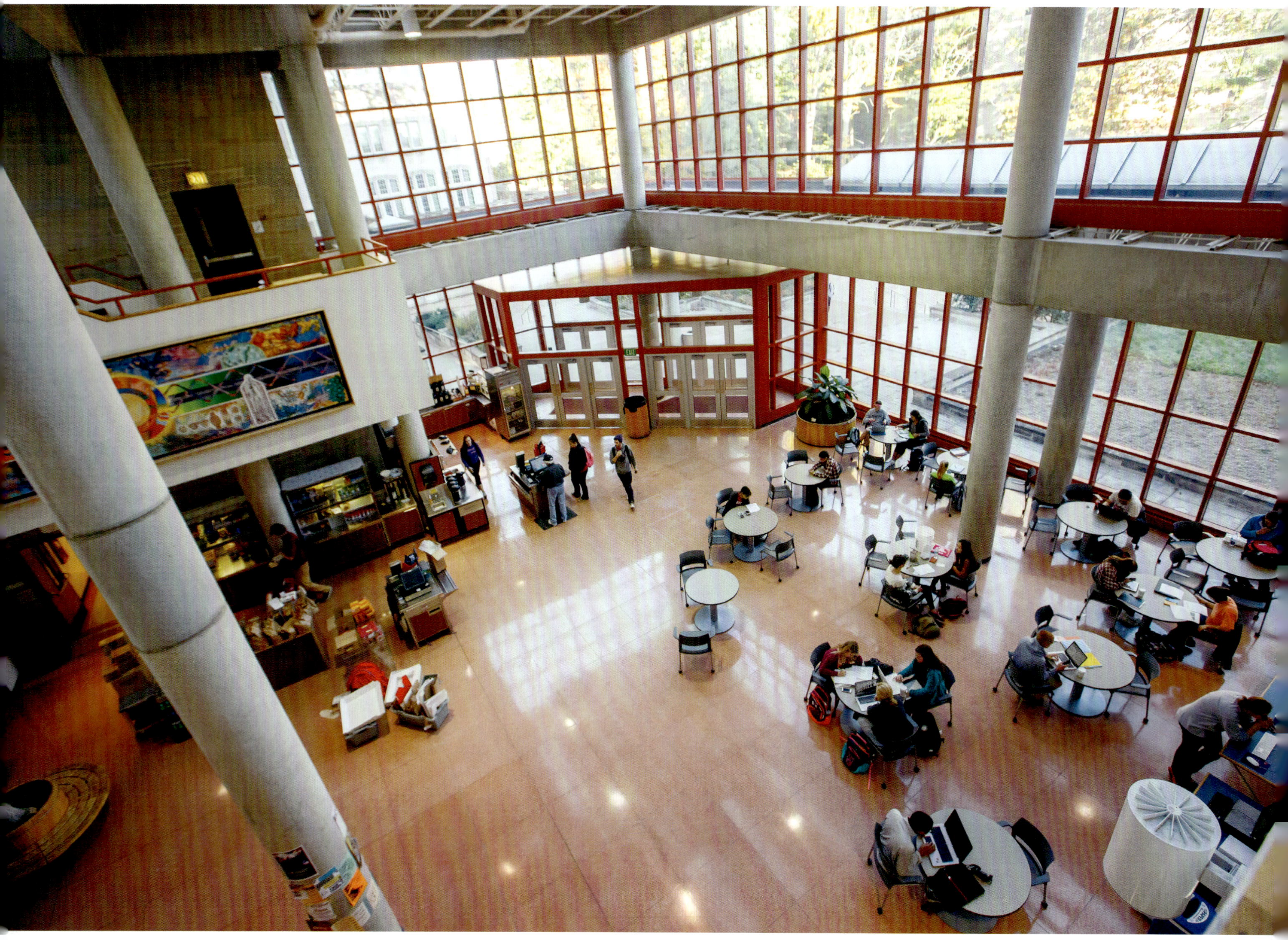

Above, Interior of Jordan Hall atrium, 2014; on left is *Phases of Biology,* painted by IU faculty member Rudy Pozzatti. Photo credit: Indiana University.

Facing, Postcard rendering of Sunken Gardens where Jordan Hall now stands, pre-1940. P0022923, IU Archives. Photo credit: Albertype Company published by the Indiana University Bookstore.

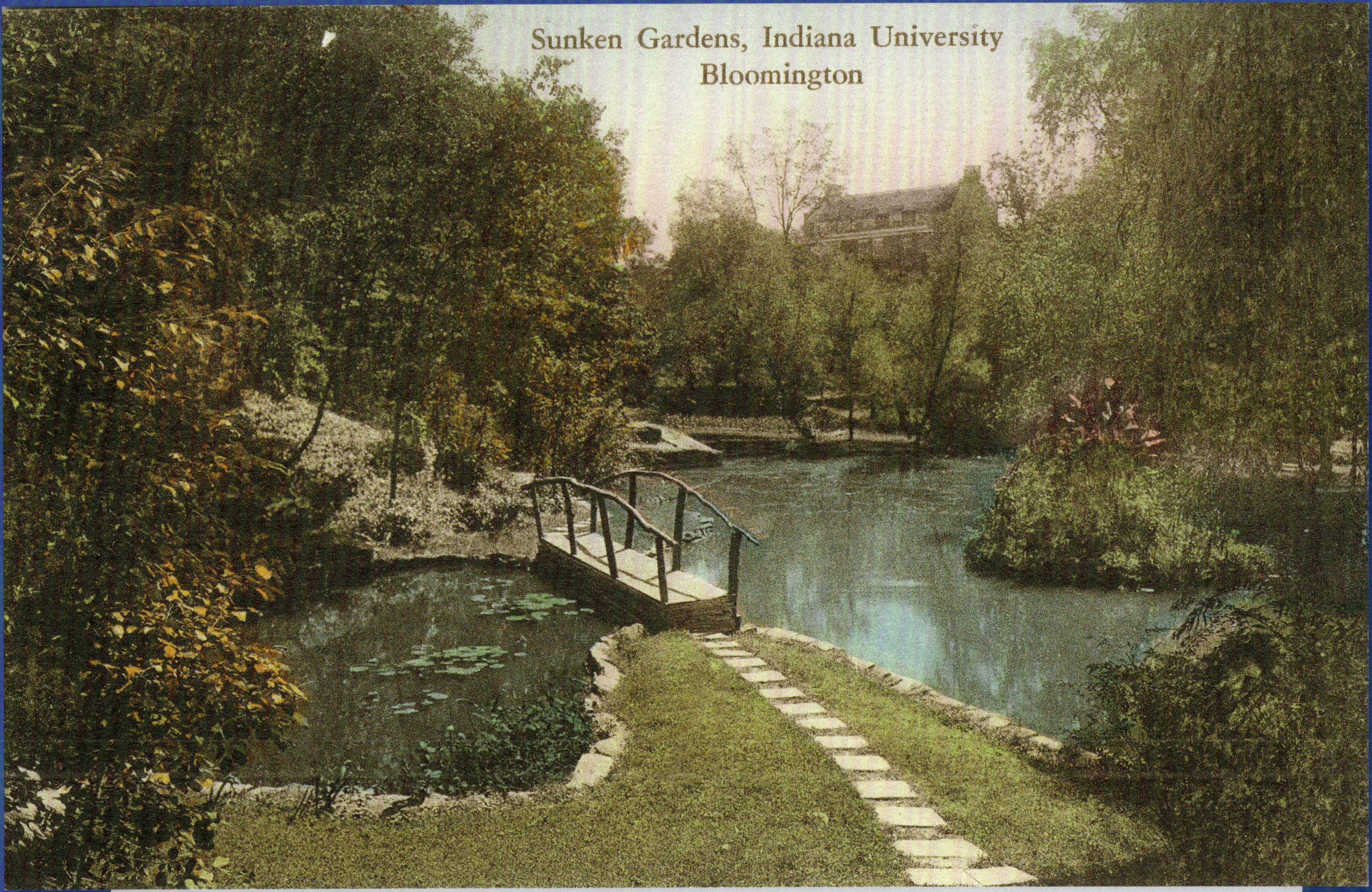

The Sunken Gardens

Spooners *are weeping gentle tears for the passing of the pit.*[1]

The sunken gardens were nestled in an area along Third Street between Memorial Hall and Alpha Hall in what was formerly Dunn Quarry in 1930. According to the *Indiana Alumni Magazine*, "the gardens were considered one of the most beautiful spots on campus."[2] For over two decades the tranquil spot was home to sunbathers and swimmers, artists, and college sweethearts. "Passion Pit" as it was called by the latter, was removed when site work began for Jordan Hall in 1952. The *Indiana Daily Student* lamented: "Last Spring the frogs and crickets serenaded the Women's Quad from their home in 'Passion Pit.' Flagstones, green grass, a small pond, and plentiful trees, painted patterns of beauty in the small hollow. But no longer."[3]

1. "The Memory Lingers," *Indiana Daily Student*, May 1, 1952.
2. *Indiana Alumni Magazine* 19, no. 7 (1957): 1.
3. "Life Science Building Moves in on 'Passion Pit,'" *IndianaDaily Student*, June 20, 1953.

Geology Building 1962

ARCHITECT Eggers and Higgins / Daggett, Naegele, and Daggett

ARCHITECTURAL STYLE 1950s Modern

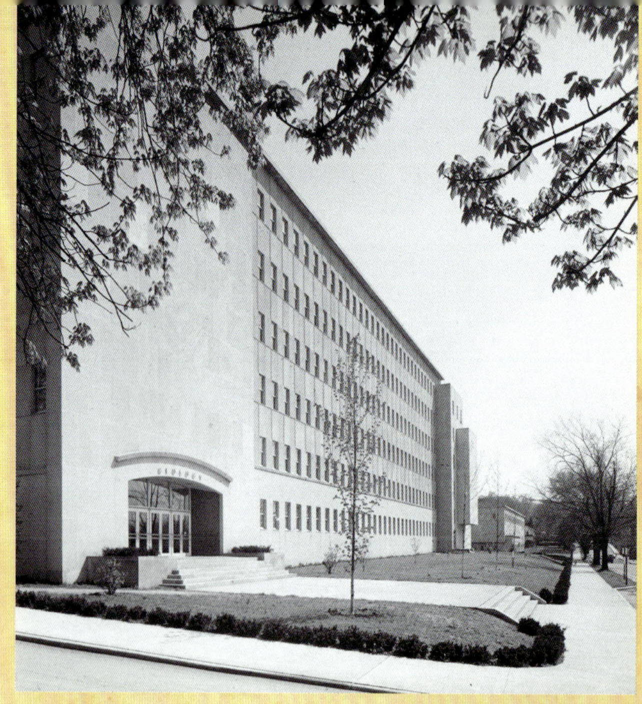

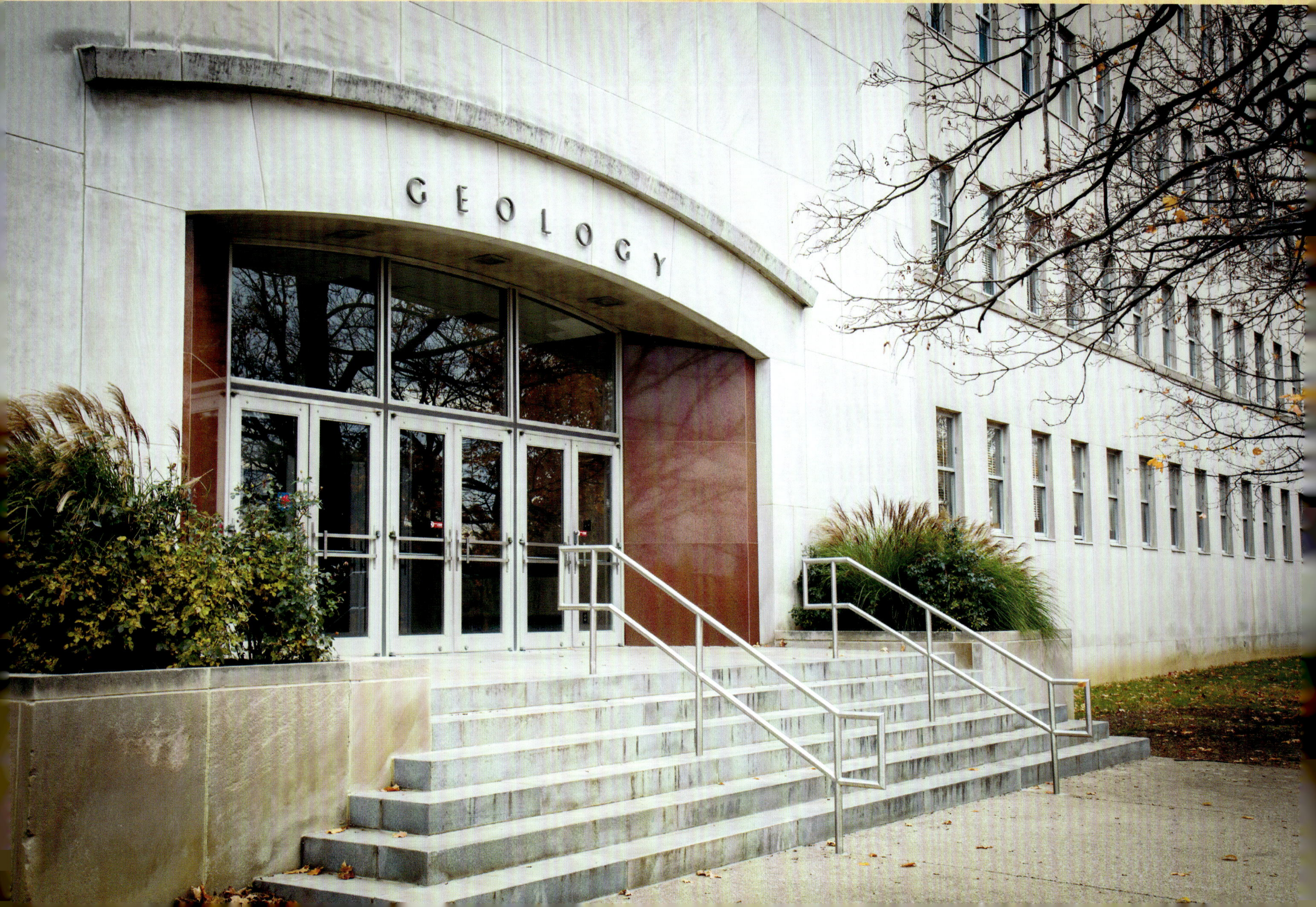

Geology Building

Academic Discipline and Geological Survey under One Roof

Our building in its greater size and the improved efficiency that its offers us is in itself a challenge to expand and improve our role in education, in research, and in service. . . . The building, if it inspires us to greater usefulness and accomplishment, thereby accelerating its own obsolescence, will thus have served its greatest purpose.

—John B. Patton at dedication ceremony

Established in 1885, the Department of Geology (now the Department of Earth and Atmospheric Sciences) was first housed in the newly completed Owen Hall, one of the first two buildings on IU's new Dunn's Woods campus. The department later occupied floors in Lindley Hall and parts of Wylie, Kirkwood, and Maxwell Halls. Training in the discipline had begun decades earlier, with the first course listed in the 1853–54 university catalog. The new building was named in honor of the three Owen brothers; the middle, David Dale, was considered to be Indiana's first state geologist (his younger brother, Richard, took over the position after David's death).

Established in 1869, the State Department of Geology and Natural Science (today the Indiana Geological Survey) was located in Indianapolis during its early years. With an agreement between the Indiana Department of Conservation and Indiana University in 1919, the office of state geologist would be held by a member of the IU Department of Geology faculty in Bloomington. In 1947, at the urging of President Herman B Wells, the chairmanship of the department and the state geologist/director of the Indiana Geological Survey (IGS) were combined into a single position, and all activities of the survey were to be carried out by geology faculty and students.

With the appointment of Charles F. Deiss as chair and state geologist in 1945, the department and the IGS began to flourish. The Indiana Geological Survey's duties expanded to such an extent that eventually the positions of chair and director were separated and it was given its own professional staff. In 1993, all administrative responsibility for the IGS was transferred fully to the university, although it continued to be funded directly by the state legislature.

As early as 1950, a new geology building appeared on the Board of Trustees' list of building priorities for the coming decade. Planning for the new structure began in 1955, and the New York firm of Eggers and Higgins was hired for the initial design, while Daggett, Naegele, and Daggett of Indianapolis was retained as the local architectural firm. The initial plans called for a large four-story structure of research laboratories, offices, and classrooms, but the rapidly increasing enrollments in the introductory courses necessitated building a much larger space for laboratory work and adding additional floors. In 1958 the Indiana Budget Committee approved funds to support a portion of the classroom and research wing of the new structure, while funding for a separate wing to house the IGS was temporarily deferred. With the reduction in funding, plans for a seven-story building were reduced to six and the trustees

Facing top, South facade of Geology Building, 1965. P0025888, IU Archives.

Facing bottom, Geology Building entrance framed by Cold Spring red granite, 2016. Photo credit: Tyagan Miller.

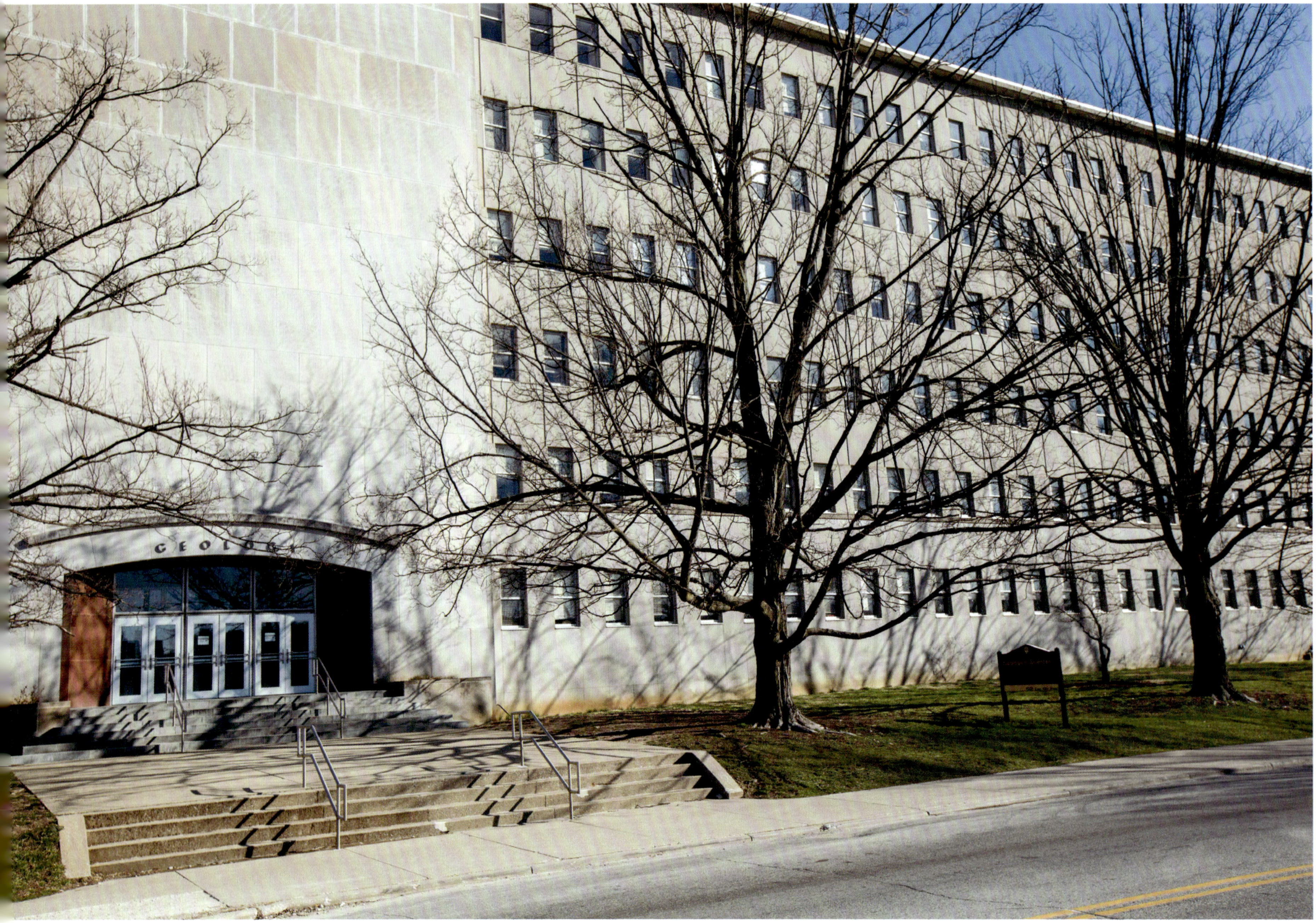

South elevation of Geology Building, 2017. Photo credit: Tyagan Miller.

advised "strict economy in decoration and finish."[1] Exterior carved stone ornamentation was eliminated along with interior decorative treatment, and only one of two planned elevators was actually installed.

The department moved into the new quarters in January 1962. The addition of the geological survey wing on the northeast corner was delayed until 1961, but finally opened in February 1964. A joint departmental and IGS dedication was held that April. The new structure, according to Richard K. Leininger, the building coordinator, would "put the two units under one roof and would make it possible for both to work together with little difficulty for the first time."[2]

Sited on the north side of the campus, the L-shaped Geology / Geological Survey Building occupies a block of ground bounded by East Tenth Street to the south, North Walnut Grove to the east, Cottage Grove Avenue to the north, and Forest Avenue to the west. The exterior facade of the structure still looks remarkably modern due to its lack of adornment and is clad predominately in large, plain panels of southern Indiana Salem limestone with a smooth-sawn finish. The two main entrances, on the west end facing Tenth Street (Department of Earth and Atmospheric Sciences) and the east end facing Walnut Grove (Geological Survey), are framed in Cold Spring red granite from Minnesota; the steps are Cold Spring gray granite. The entrance flagstones pavers are bluestone (sandstone) from New York.

The walls of the lobby in the IGS wing are spectacular gray-and-white marble from Belgium, with sills of polished fossiliferous limestone. The departmental lobby features a green Italian marble on the north wall, while the remaining walls are cream-colored fossiliferous limestone. Pink marble from Tennessee enhances the sills as well as the glass display cases used for mineral and rock exhibits throughout the building.

The remainder of the interior in the earth and atmospheric sciences wing is strictly functional, with concrete block walls and bare concrete floors in most areas. Planned to confine the heaviest traffic to the lower floors, the first floor contains large classrooms and most of the major departmental offices as well as a seismograph station and the geophysics drill hole (see sidebar). The second floor houses four large teaching labs for introductory courses as well as offices for faculty and associate instructors. On the second floor is a faculty lounge named for Richard Owen. It has yellow poplar flooring and is furnished in pieces contemporaneous with his lifetime. The next three floors house the various sections of the department—geochemistry, mineralogy, petrology, geophysics, hydrology, stratigraphy, and paleontology, each with its own facilities. The sixth floor was devoted entirely to the Geosciences Library, which in 1962 was considered one of the largest in the country. In December 2014 the library was closed and the collections absorbed by the rest of the university libraries to make way for an office suite for the Department of Psychological and Brain Sciences.

The four floors of the IGS wing house offices and laboratories along with maps, records, and rock collections from the state of Indiana integral to the IGS mission of data collection and applied research on Indiana geology. The first floor is shared by the IGS bookstore, where publications, maps, and teaching supplies are sold to the public, and a "subsurface section" housing well data and sample files from Indiana petroleum wells, which is also open to the public. The remaining floors are dedicated to coal and industrial minerals, geologic mapping, and data analysis and hydrology. Small extensions of the department's fifth and sixth floors connect with the IGS wing.

Seismograph Station and Drill Hole

Two technical features unique to the study of geology were included in the foundation of the earth and atmospheric sciences wing. Prior to construction, a drilling rig bored two holes below the foundation for use as a drill hole laboratory to study the rock below. The deeper hole extends to the Devonian strata 1,200 feet below the surface and is still occasionally used today to take readings. It is located in the east end of the wing. In addition, a seismograph station was set up in the far northwest corner, facing Forest Avenue. A series of concrete piers, reaching to the bedrock below, were poured beneath the building; they, too, are used for seismograph recordings. These piers avoid contact with the structure above so as to avoid vibration interference. When there is an earthquake in Indiana, or indeed any major seismic occurrence throughout the world, the geophysicists at the IU Department of Earth and Atmospheric Sciences can often provide details and further information.

Psychology Building 1963

ARCHITECT Eggers and Higgins / A. M. Strauss

ARCHITECTURAL STYLE 1950s Modern

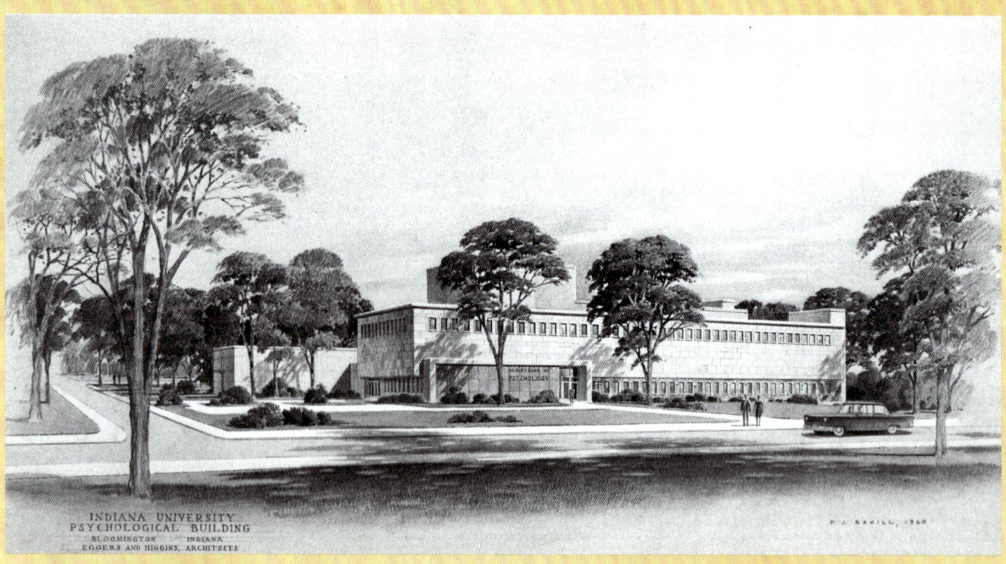

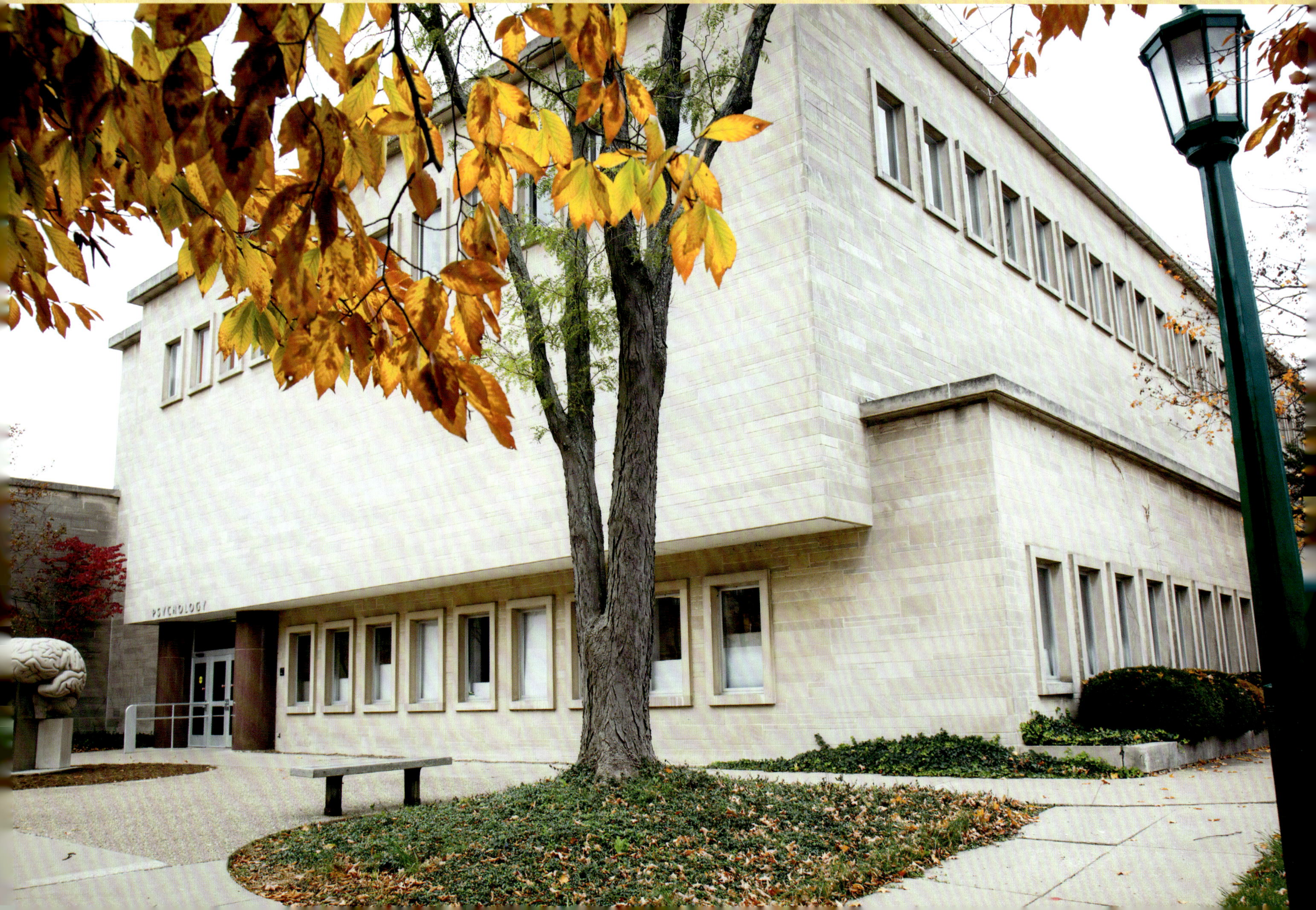

Psychology Building

A Bastion of Brain-Behavior Research

By whatever measure you wish to employ, the Department of Psychology at Indiana University Bloomington is one of the great psychology departments in the world. This new addition will make it possible for them to produce more of their particular kind of honey: well-educated students with knowledge that will change our view of humankind and strengthen our ability to help create more just and humane societies.

—Indiana University Chancellor Sharon Stephens Brehm

BLOOMINGTON NATIVE WILLIAM LOWE BRYAN began his work at Indiana University's Preparatory Department in 1876 and matriculated into the collegiate program the following year. After graduation, Bryan served as an instructor in the Prep Department for a few months before his unexpected appointment to the regular faculty, teaching Greek and English. During Bryan's time as a junior faculty member, IU hired its first non-clergy president, David Starr Jordan. Cut from a very different cloth compared with earlier presidents, Jordan focused on revamping the university curriculum as well as the mode of instruction. He found, however, that Bloomington's remote location made it difficult to retain faculty, so Jordan focused on developing local talent. One individual he identified was William Bryan, who later became IU's tenth president. Jordan encouraged Bryan's interest in psychology, and in 1886 Bryan traveled to the University of Berlin, where he worked with psychologist Hermann Ebbinghaus and learned how to operate a psychological laboratory.

On his return from Berlin the next year, Bryan was named a full professor. Invigorated by his work with Ebbinghaus, Bryan was eager to begin his own experimentation and developed plans to establish a psychological laboratory on the Bloomington campus. For his first piece of apparatus, Bryan requested funds to purchase a Hipp chronoscope, used to measure human reaction time. With the trustees' approval, in 1888 Bryan opened a psychology laboratory—now the oldest continuing psychological lab in the United States—with the chronoscope and plans to personally purchase or otherwise acquire additional equipment.

The Department of Psychology moved into Science Hall (now Lindley Hall) when it opened in 1902, remaining there for many years. As did other academic programs, it outgrew its space but continued to adapt as best it could. By the late 1950s, the Psychology Department had spread to three other campus locations, including W. N. Kellogg's dog laboratory in the basement of Alpha Hall. The construction had remedied only some of the post–World War II space issues, so university administrators continued to address the classroom and office needs of the Humanities and Social Sciences Departments.

In 1959 the university applied for and received a U.S. Public Health Service grant to expand its psychological research facilities. University planners then developed two location alternatives. One proposal seriously considered was to build a seven-story annex in the green space south of Lindley Hall that would connect with Rawles Hall. In this scenario, the

Facing top, Architectural rendering of the Psychology Building, 1960. P0043049, IU Archives. Photo credit: Elwood Martin "Barney" Cowherd.

Facing bottom, Psychology Building, 2016. Photo credit: Tyagan Miller.

Department of Psychology would eventually take over Rawles, and Lindley would be razed. A second proposal was to build a new facility on the north side of campus, at Tenth Street and Walnut Grove.

Ultimately, President Herman B Wells decided that building a new structure north of Tenth Street was the best option. The federal funds were to be used for the research wing, and IU would fund or seek state funds for the departmental wing, which would be divided into a psychology clinic, departmental office suite, classes and labs, and faculty offices. A. M. Strauss and Associates of Fort Wayne was tapped for the architectural work, with New York's Eggers and Higgins serving as supervising architect. The result was a decidedly modern design with a limestone exterior facade laid in the random ashlar pattern seen on many of the campus buildings. Two repeating rows of windows jut out slightly and wrap around the building near the base and roofline. The west entrance faces the Indiana Geological Survey wing of the Geology Building and is framed in the same red granite. The interior lobby has the polished limestone with embedded fossils common to some other buildings on campus, and houses 372 rooms and two auditoriums, one seating 255 and the other, 96.

The building was completed in spring 1963, but by 1965 department chair Roger Russell was already looking to the future. In a memo to Lynne Merritt Jr., chair of the campus's Science Advisory Committee, he told Merritt that, while the new building helped alleviate deficiencies, it provided just a temporary solution: "the new building was designed to reach a saturation point at 35 faculty members, 75 graduate students, and supporting staff." At the time of writing, they already had thirty-six faculty and one hundred graduate students and were using space in ways not intended by the federal grant.[1]

Discussions for an expansion did not begin in earnest, however, until the late 1990s. Vice President J. Terry Clapacs sought approval from the university trustees to build a four-story addition with research and teaching labs, offices, and animal quarters. Planning and funding moved slowly, but construction finally commenced in late 2000, with CSO Architects of Indianapolis hired to provide the plans. The new structure featured vertical style elements and both rock- and smooth-face textures. The new space included more than twenty psychology laboratories, office space for postdoctoral students and visiting scientists and researchers, and communal areas for personnel and a small meeting room. In his *Legacy of the Laboratory: Psychological and Brain Sciences at Indiana University, 1888–2013*, author James H. Capshew writes: "In contrast to the modern and unadorned façade of the existing building . . . the rear elevation echoed the predominant campus style of collegiate gothic. The addition was facing a grassy courtyard, with three other buildings filling in a traditional quadrangle design. Constructed of limestone, the addition boasted a handsome courtyard entrance, many windows, and precious new office and lab space."[2]

In 2013 the Department of Psychological and Brain Sciences (so renamed in 2005) celebrated 125 years with a series of lectures, career luncheons, and the unveiling of a large limestone brain sculpted by Bloomington artist Amy Brier and carved by Michael Donham. It was installed near the west entrance. At 10,000 pounds and 7 feet high, it is the largest anatomically accurate brain sculpture in the world.[3] The brain is indicative of the number of big thinkers who have walked the halls of the department, including J. F. Kantor (professor and author, 1920–59), B. F. Skinner (professor and department chair, 1945–48), William K. Estes (instructor and research professor, 1946–62; Distinguished Scholar 1999–2011), and Esther Thelen (developmental psychologist and professor, 1985–2005).

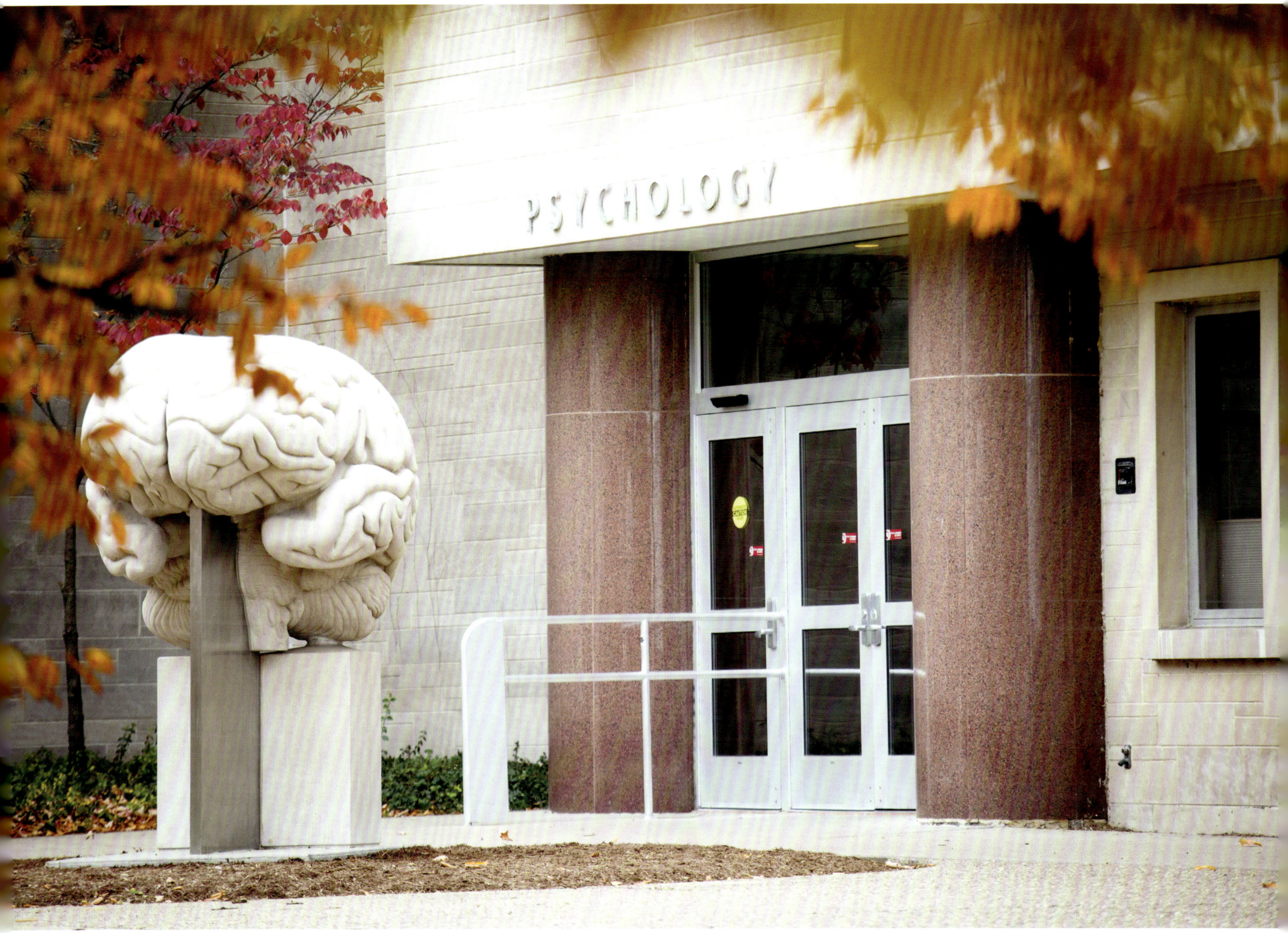

Limestone brain sculpture outside west entrance to Psychology Building, 2016. Photo credit: Tyagan Miller.

Simon Hall 2007

ARCHITECT Flad Architects

ARCHITECTURAL STYLE Neo-Gothic / Art Deco

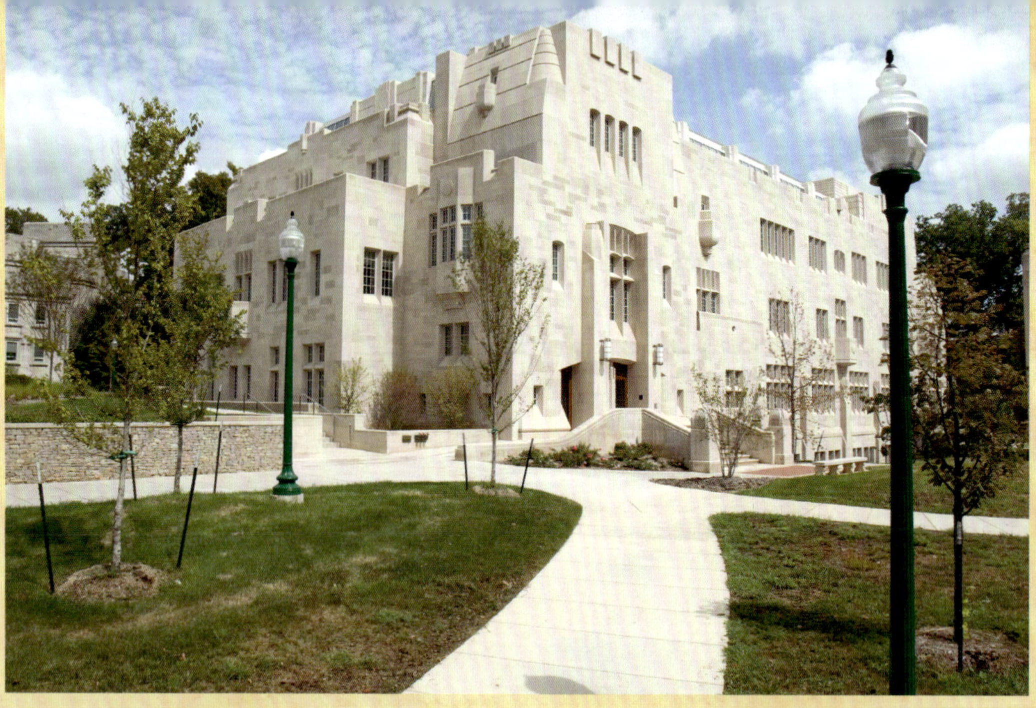

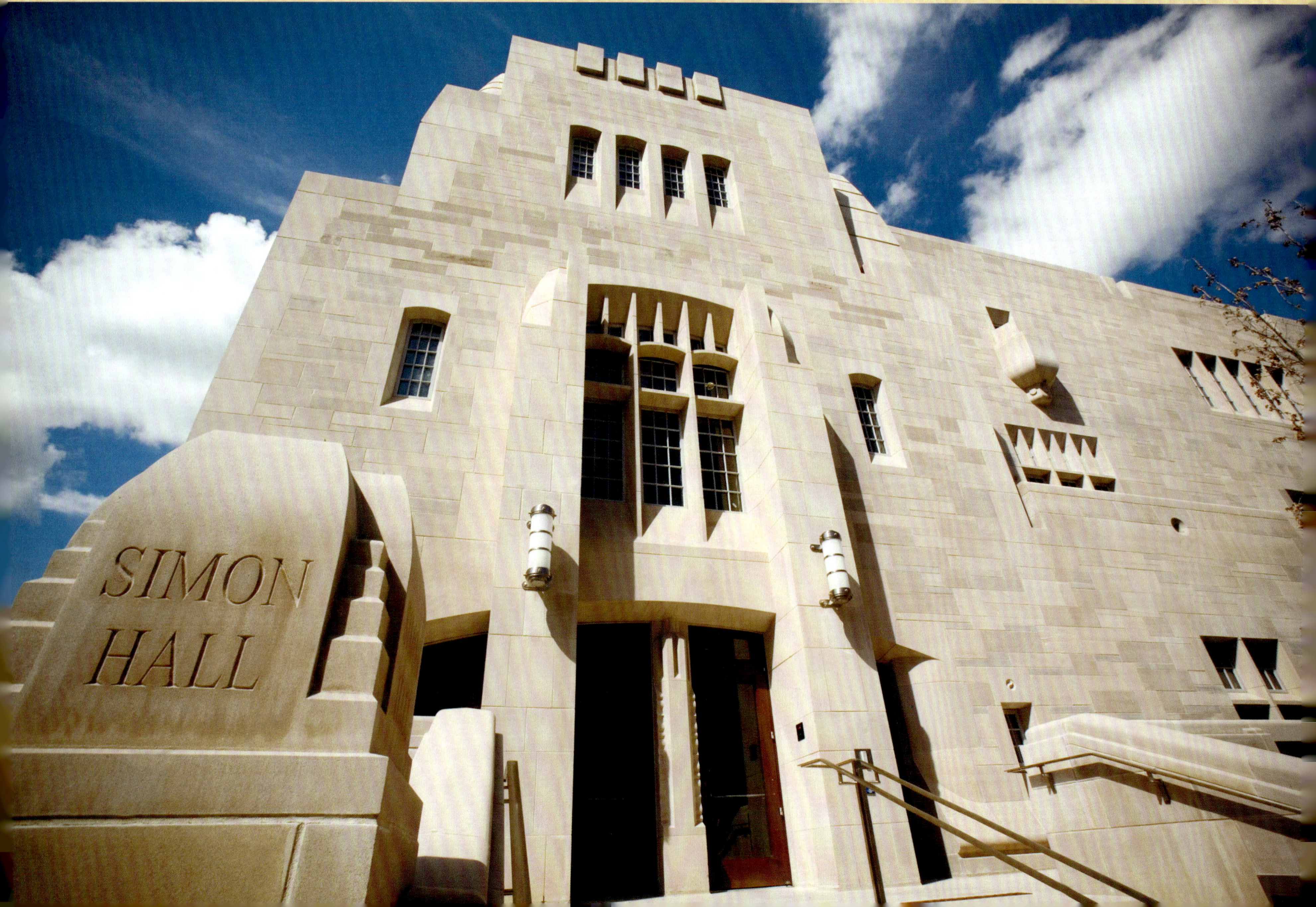

Simon Hall

Unifying Hub for Scientific Research

Simon Hall, beautifully designed for multi-disciplinary research, will make possible increased collaboration among our communities of scientists, including both faculty and students. The research space it provides is absolutely crucial. Simon Hall also sits beautifully on its site, and the entire campus can be grateful for this wonderful new building.

—Provost Karen Hanson

SIMON HALL—OR MULTIDISCIPLINARY SCIENCE I, as it was first called—was conceived as an inducement to promote overlapping research among science departments at Indiana University. The strategy was simple: provide research laboratories and equipment through a process that encouraged collaboration between scientists from the normally distinct disciplines of biology, mathematics, chemistry, physics, and psychology. To achieve this goal, it was important to not only juxtapose the new building close to existing science buildings, but, if possible, also connect the new space physically to existing laboratories. Given the small amount of available open space amid existing science buildings, and the university's overarching goal of protecting all precious green space on the campus, master planners were faced with a monumental task. It was clear early in the process that a sizable structure was needed if the university was going to continue to be a strong force in the academic science community. With peer institutions having made transformational investments in their science programs, IU was in danger of falling behind and losing key faculty to other research universities. The stakes were high. If Indiana University planned its first effort in collaborative research well, other opportunities for new laboratory and classroom buildings through gift and grant support would follow.

Following competitive interviews, Flad Architects of Madison, Wisconsin, was commissioned to design the new laboratory building. Flad was well known in university circles as a specialty architectural firm with confirmed strength in science facility design. The firm had completed a number of complex science buildings around the country, which gave Indiana University administrators confidence in Flad's ability to solve the site location problem. One option was to place the new building on the east edge of the campus, where space was plentiful. But science faculty supported placing the building in the interior of the campus, preferably between Myers Hall, Jordan Hall, and the Chemistry Building. That area had recently been cleared of an unattractive barracks-like structure, and the newfound open landscape provided breathing room in a densely built part of campus, presenting a second option. Trustees were reluctant to shoehorn in a new facility of significant scale, which might compromise IU planning standards that emphasized generous green space between major academic buildings. Flad Architects and Robert Meadows, university architect, responded by formulating a creative plan to mitigate the presence of the new building by depressing a significant

Facing top, Southwest elevation of Simon Hall, 2015. Photo credit: Indiana University.

Facing bottom, Simon Hall, home to faculty from many scientific disciplines, 2008. Photo credit: Tyagan Miller.

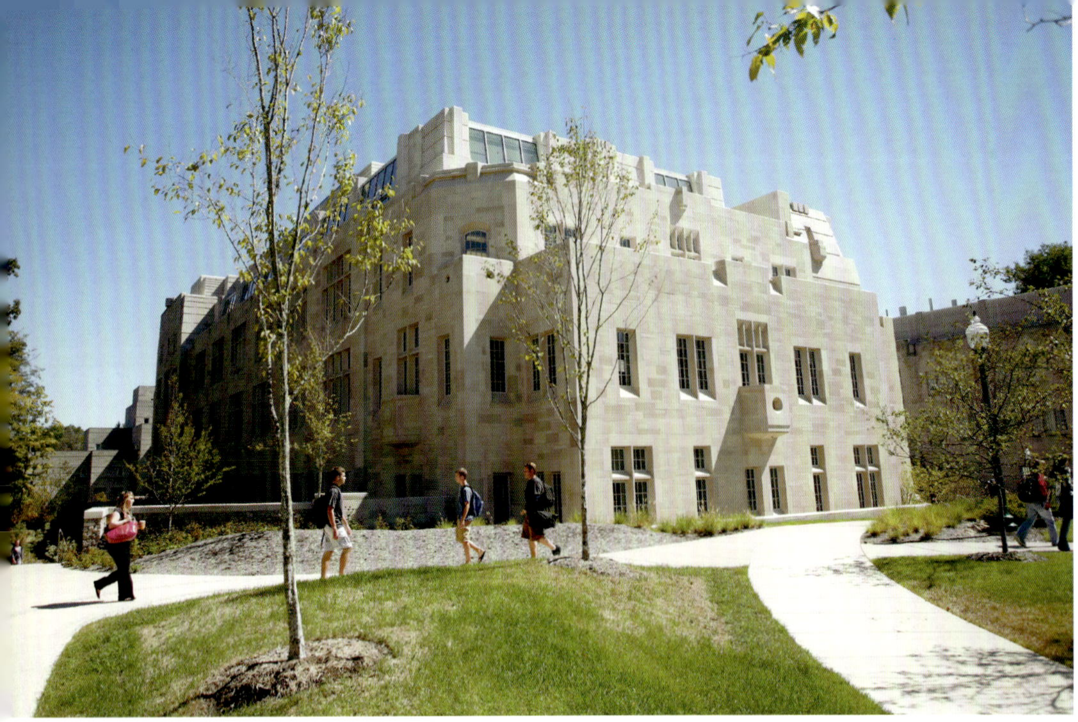

Northwest view of Simon Hall in midst of old campus, 2009. Photo credit: Indiana University.

amount of lab space below grade and then connecting the new science labs to existing labs in surrounding buildings through the use of contiguous space and tunnels.

The approach was feasible, but additional costs would be incurred. The entire site would require excavation due to limestone deposits found just below the surface; and, at completion, a vast amount of fill would be required to replace the overburden and allow for replanting a courtyard compatible with IU standards. University trustees, administrators, and faculty gathered to review the proposed design solution and consider the cost trade-offs in a memorable meeting at the Abe Martin Lodge in Brown County State Park. The end result was that the proposed building, although at a higher cost and with a third of the facility subgrade, would both comply with the IUB master planning principles *and* serve the research aspirations of its science community.

Because Simon Hall was to be constructed among some of the most historic buildings on campus, Flad Architects was instructed to develop a building design that fit seamlessly with the architectural style of the neighborhood. Flad responded with exterior elevations that mirrored the Art Deco look of Myers Hall as well as the Neo-Gothic feel of the Old Crescent buildings. Meyers was also used as a template to determine the mass and scale of Simon Hall. The end result was a seven-level, reinforced concrete building with smooth-face and buff-cut limestone cladding. Ornate limestone carvings were employed extensively on the exterior of the building. Of particular interest are the stone carvings by local sculptor and IU alumna Amy Brier on the east elevation. They depict six research organisms used by geneticists: a fruit fly, mouse, ear of maize, mushrooms, *E. coli* bacterium, and a paramecium. Approximately a third of the structure's 140,000 square feet was depressed below grade in accordance with the agreed-upon site plan, which achieved the master planning goal of fitting Simon Hall comfortably on the site without overwhelming adjacent buildings.

Inside Simon Hall, the architect specified glass walls throughout the floor plan to promote visual interaction among researchers. Laboratories were designed to meet the latest academic research standards, while non-laboratory space was positioned centrally to promote social community. The architect's interior designer chose elegant finishes of wood and stone coupled with earth-tone colors that complement the exterior feel of the building and the surrounding wooded area of the campus. Flad's unique building configuration and design was widely recognized, including by *R&D Magazine*, which named Simon Hall the 2008 best new research or laboratory facility in the country.

Today Simon Hall is a center of scientific research on the IUB campus. No single science department controls the assignment of space within the building. The building is "owned" by the College of Arts and Sciences, which assures professional collaboration. The Biocomplexity Institute, the Center for Genomics and Bioinformatics, and the Johnson Center for Entrepreneurship and Science Innovation are housed here. More than 750 scientists and support staff, including cell biologists, microbiologists, molecular biologists, geneticists, analytical chemists, biochemists, and biophysicists, all work together on various research projects. From its beauty and innovation to its state-of-the-art facilities and faculty, Simon Hall is the unifying hub of scientific research on the Indiana University Bloomington campus and an example for other universities to emulate.

Facing, Simon Hall stone carvings of research organisms by local sculptor and IU alumna Amy Brier: *E. coli* bacterium, mushrooms, fruit fly, ear of maize, mouse, and paramecium, 2017. Photo credit: Indiana University.

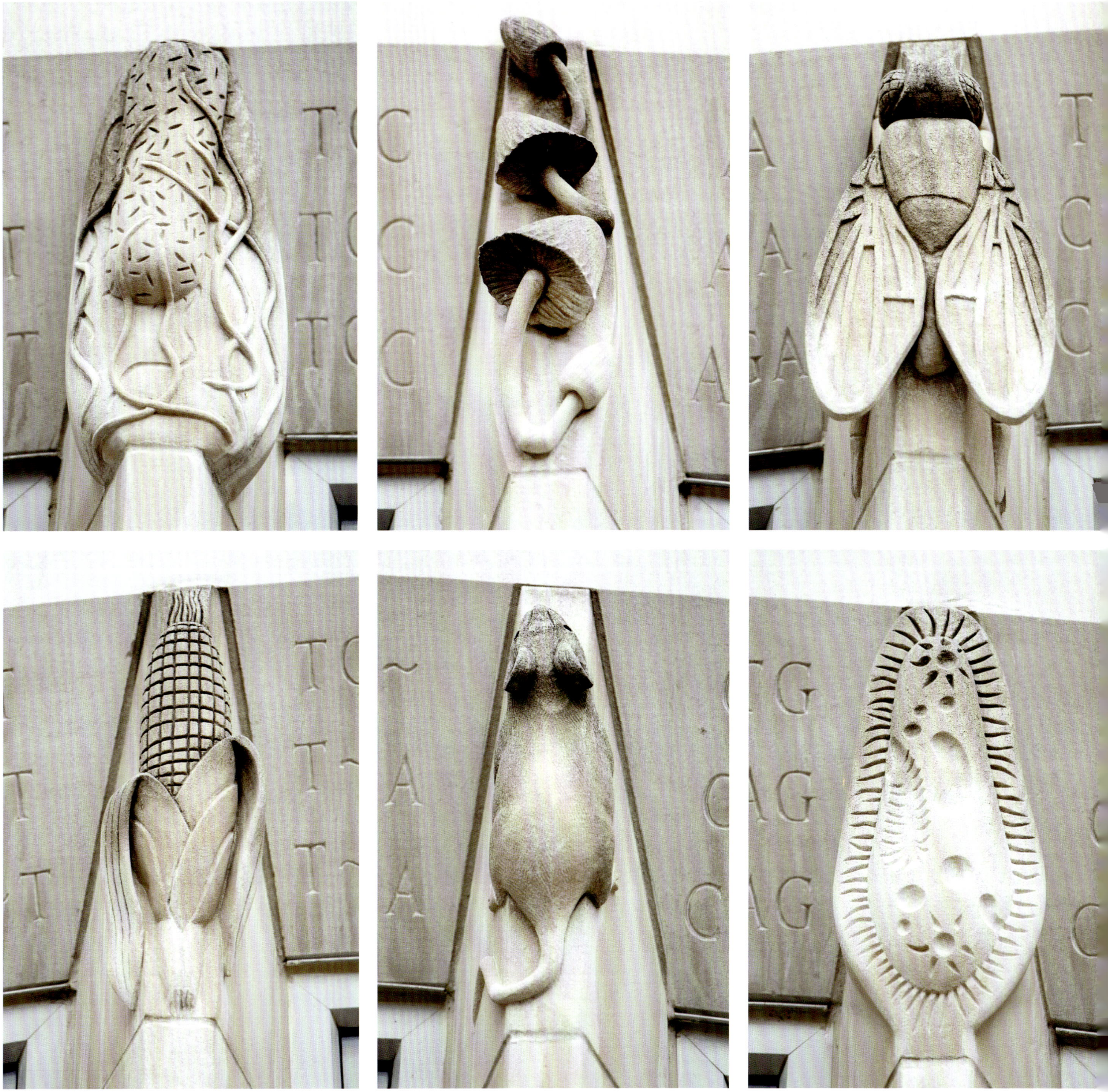

Multidisciplinary Science Building II 2009

ARCHITECT Flad Architects

ARCHITECTURAL STYLE Collegiate Gothic / Romanesque

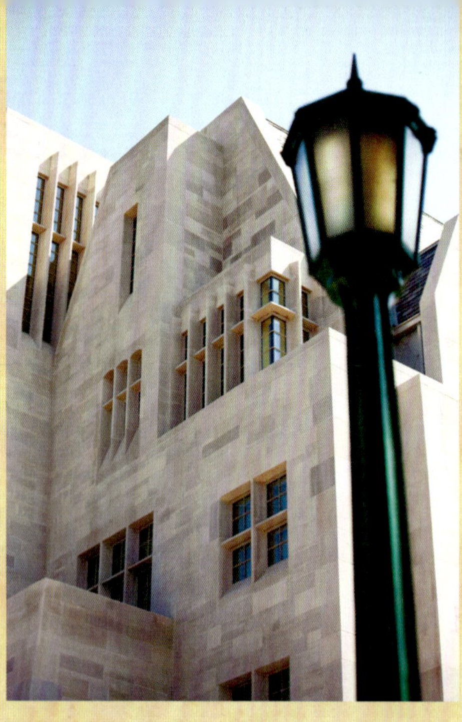

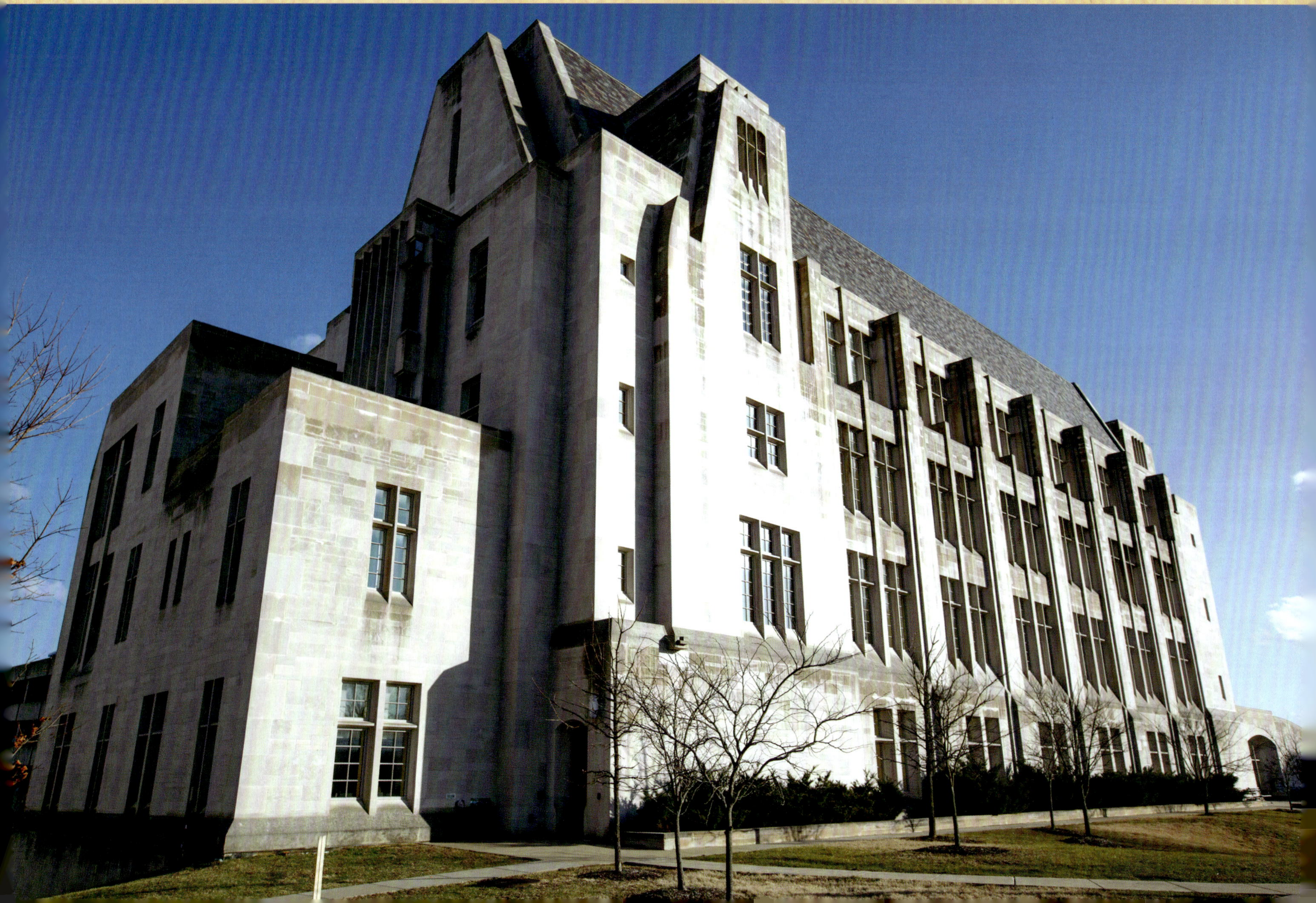

Multidisciplinary Science Building II

Gateway to a New Science District

Over time, may this building unfold—like the fern in its atrium—to reveal the great possibilities of collaborative interdisciplinary science.

—Indiana University President Michael A. McRobbie at dedication ceremony

Completed in 2009, the Multidisciplinary Science Building II (MSBII) represented the second phase—following Simon Hall in 2007—of a three-building project for advancing research and collaboration in the sciences on the IUB campus. MSBII's location on Walnut Grove (just north of Tenth Street) was selected to be a gateway to a science quad that includes the Geology and Psychology Buildings on Tenth Street. MSBII houses representative faculty and laboratories of the geological sciences, the psychological and brain sciences, geography and atmospheric sciences, and the School of Public and Environmental Affairs. The new facility offers limitless possibilities for cooperation and complimentary laboratory and field-based research in the geosciences and life sciences.

Flad Architects of Madison, Wisconsin, having completed the award-winning Simon Hall, was selected to design MSBII as an encore. In the late 1970s and early 1980s, the firm had expanded its practice into a more global science and technology lab specialization, including science and technology centers such as the Biochemical Sciences Complex at the University of Wisconsin, the Technological Institute at Northwestern University, and the Bindley Bioscience Engineering Center at Purdue University. In 1994, Flad became a member of the U.S. Green Building Council and played a part in developing the first LEED (Leadership in Energy and Environmental Design) rating system for buildings. The firm is among the top green design firms in the country.

The Multidisciplinary Science Building is a blend of the old and the new on campus. David Black, design partner at Flad Architects, told the *Indiana Daily Student* that, like Simon Hall, MSBII would reflect the Collegiate Gothic style of the main campus with "current modernist themes."[1] The Gothic influence can be seen in the sawed ashlar Indiana limestone facade; the slate roof; tall, slender recessed windows; and its entry arch. The lack of carvings and ornamentation add a more contemporary character. It also has a nonfunctional, limestone balcony on the south side nearly identical to those on Simon and Myers Halls. The building has seven levels, but floors five and six hold mechanical infrastructure only. MSBII was designed with the goal of achieving LEED status. Although this designation is unusual for a scientific research facility, in 2013 MSBII received the Silver LEED certification. Certain design

Facing top, Sawed ashlar Indiana limestone facade of the Multidisciplinary Science Building II, 2016. Photo credit: Tyagan Miller.

Facing bottom, Northwest view of MSBII, 2017. Photo credit: Indiana University.

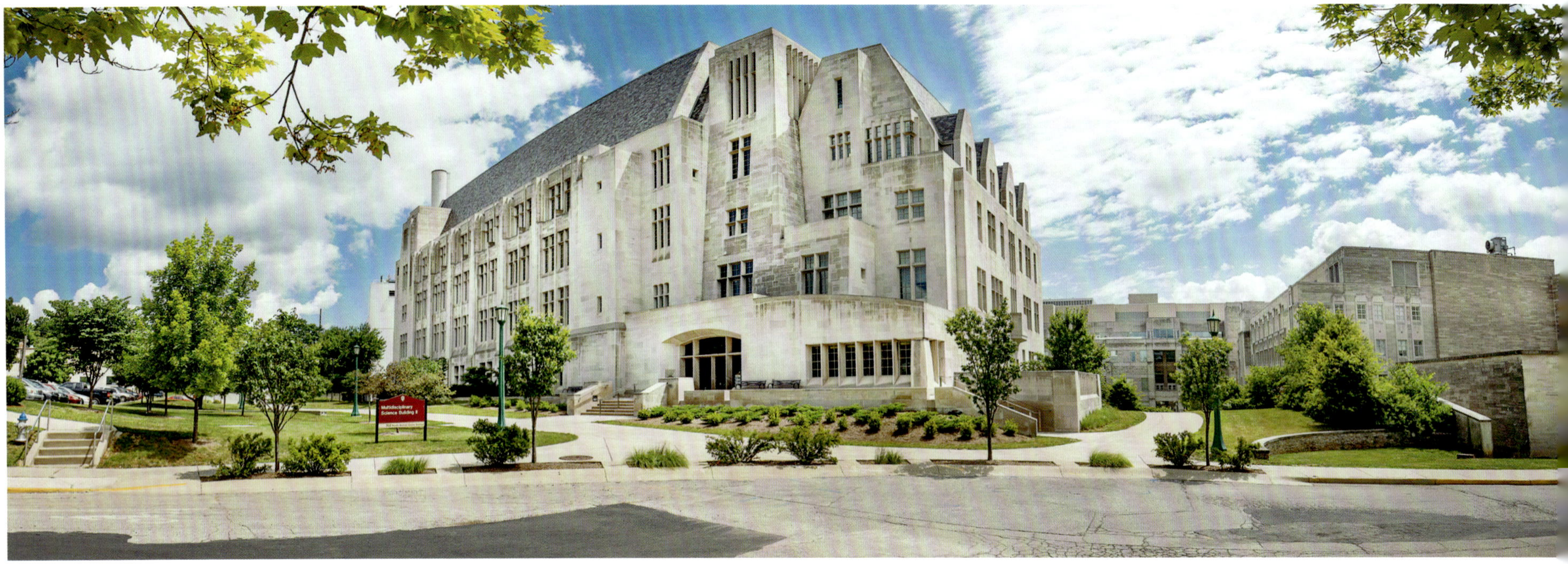

Southwest elevation of Multidisciplinary Science Building II, 2016. Photo credit: Indiana University.

details like the large, cathedral-like roof play a key role in the building's energy recovery system.

MSBII was dedicated in October 2009 as part of a monthlong "Celebrate IU" initiative. In his dedicatory address, university president Michael McRobbie noted that the range of research projects to be undertaken in the facility is reflected "in the changing colors of the building's interior—from the earthy greens and browns on the lower floors to the blues as the building ascends towards the sky. Highlighting the terrazzo floor of the atrium and visible from every level, an unfolding fern frond symbolizes the life and potential that fills this space."[2]

According to Blackburn Architects, the Indianapolis firm that partnered with Flad Architects on this project, "the interior concepts are based on the idea of moving from the earth to the heavens. The full story stair tower and atrium located at the main entrance link the building's interior to its exterior through the use of monumental scale and proportion."[3] The soaring spiral stairway rises up through the five-story atrium to connect lab space on the north end of the building with the office space on the south. About 65,000 square feet, or two-thirds of its space, are dedicated to laboratory space for research in neuroscience and brain imaging, atmospheric and environmental science, contaminant chemistry, and biogeochemistry. Three-quarters of the labs are shared by faculty and researchers in the College of Arts and Sciences, with the remainder allotted to SPEA. Open, transparent spaces foster interaction and collaboration among scientists as well as with students and staff. Along with its labs and offices, MSBII houses the Indiana Metabolomics and Cytomics Initiative (METACyt) instrumentation facility, an environmental scanning electron microscope and microscopy lab, a stable isotope research facility, and the Linda and Jack Gill Center for Biomolecular Science.

Multidisciplinary Building II represents one more step in fulfilling Indiana University's vision of becoming a leader in scientific research and collaboration among U.S. universities. The future is bright for constructing more buildings devoted to every genre of scientific research and bringing together scientists from all disciplines on the IUB campus.

Atrium linking the interior to the exterior of MSBII, 2016. Photo credit: Tyagan Miller.

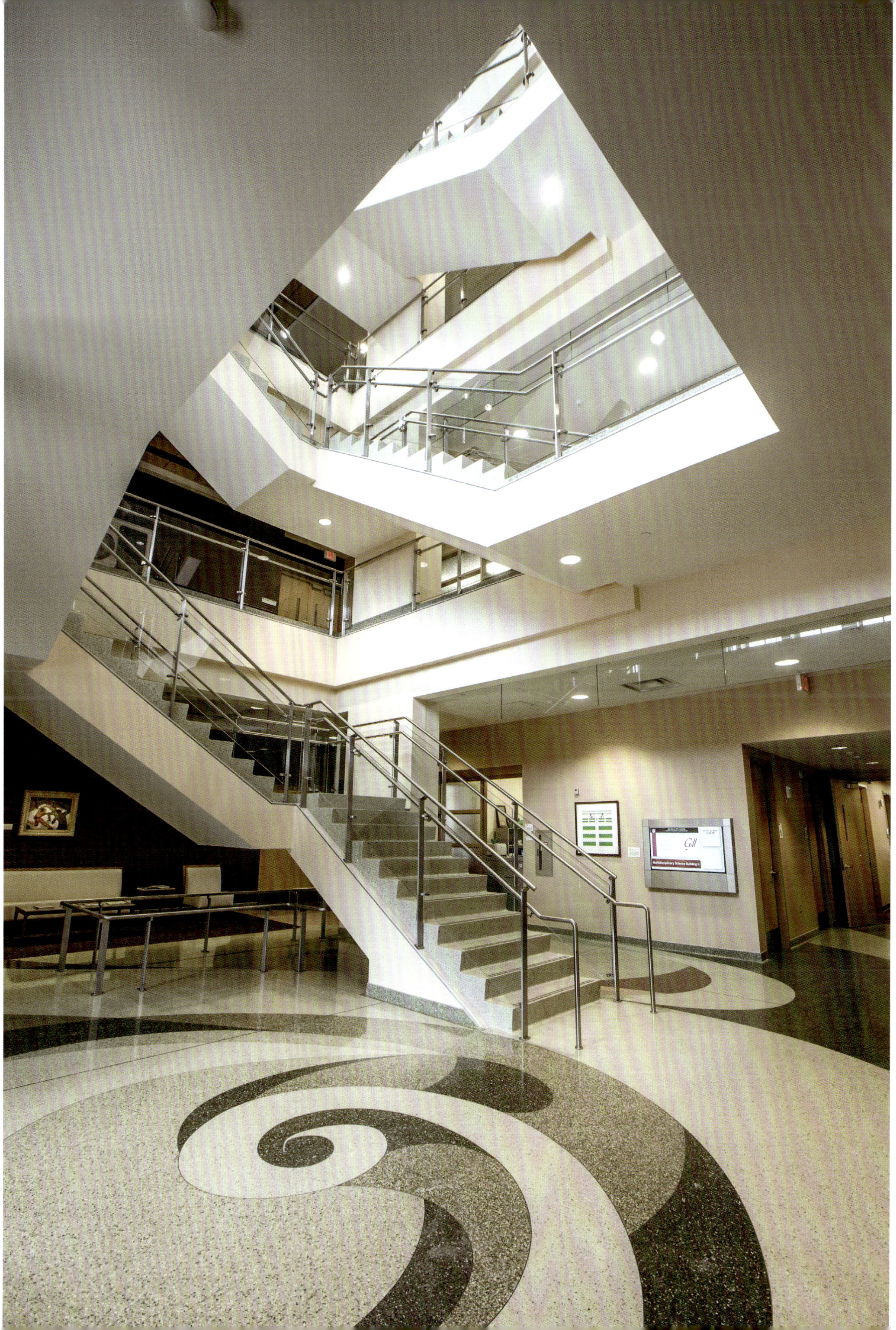
Gill
Multidisciplinary Science Building II

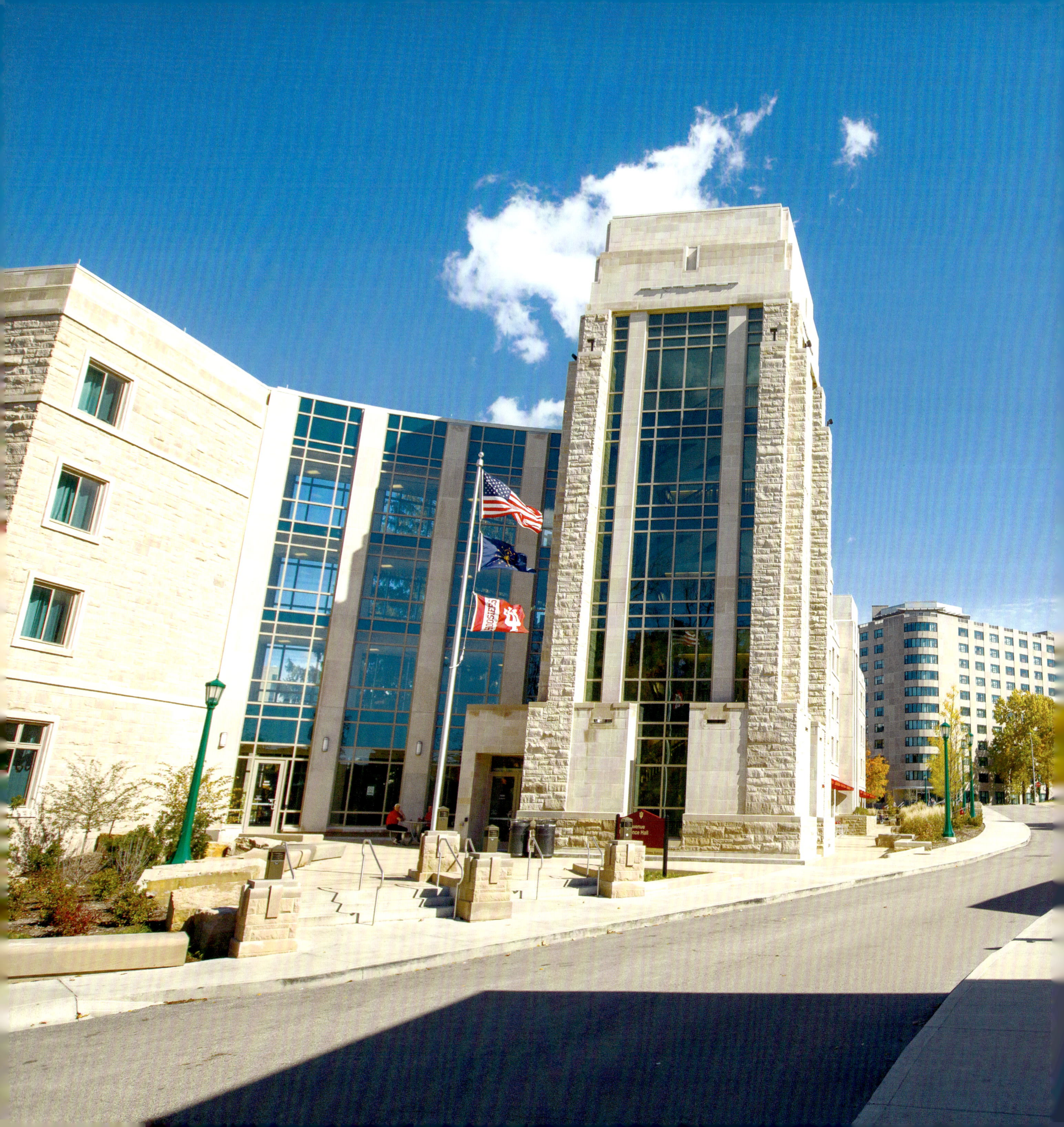

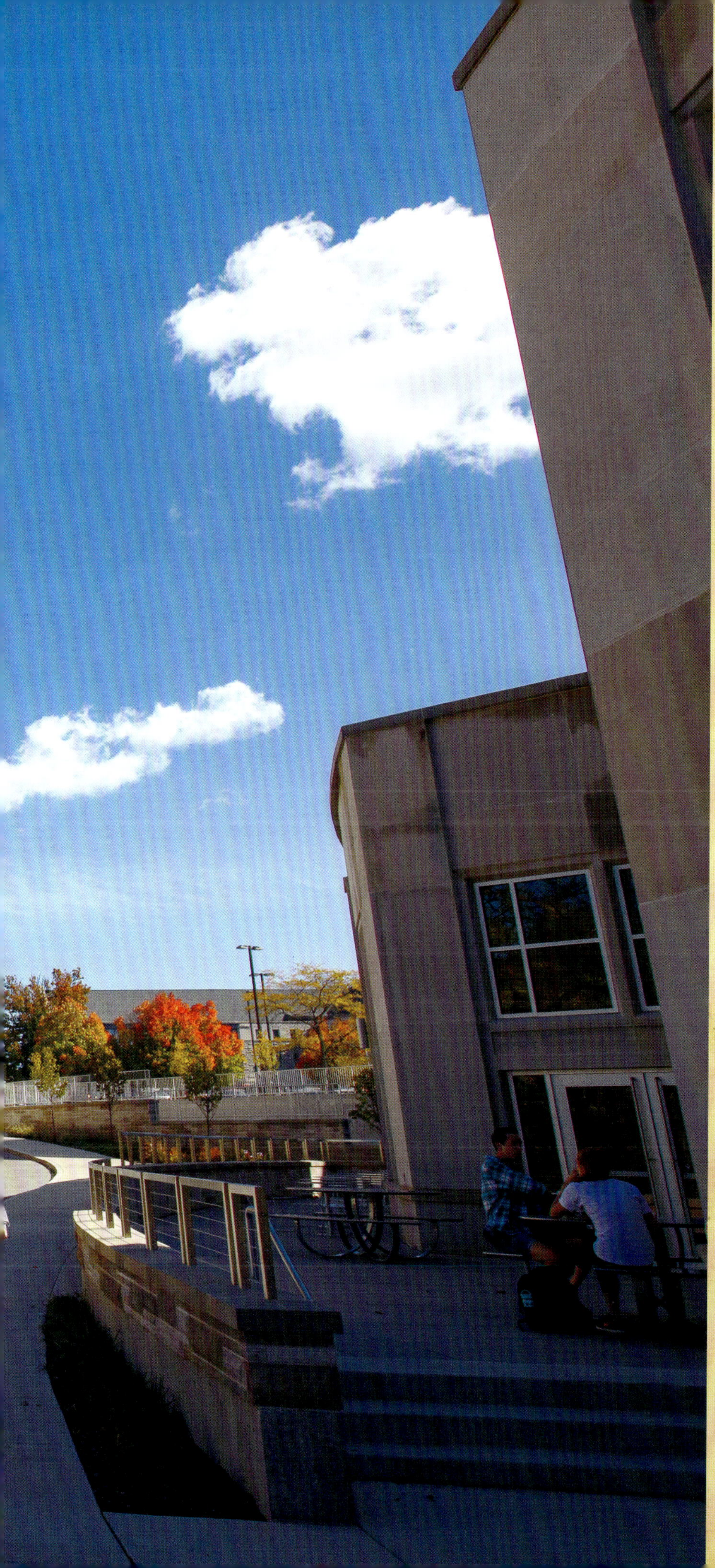

STUDENT HOUSING

Indiana's spirit is eternal! Long after the present buildings have crumbled away, and the great-grandchildren of the students of today have passed into history, the spirit of Indiana will survive! It is so mighty that mere words cannot express it. Indiana's sons and daughters will march forth into the life of the state and nation and perpetuate the work which has been so nobly performed in the past. Let us seek to be worthy bearers of the task which is so important to this splendid institution.

1926 Arbutus

Alpha Hall

Colonel Louden's Albatross

There was only that one place to live and frankly it wasn't a particularly attractive place.

—Lucia Showalter Wilson

When Sarah Parke Morrison entered Indiana University as its first female student in 1867, she, like the men of the university, had to find her own living arrangements at a boarding house or with a private family in town. The lack of university housing became a major source of concern for administrators and in particular the dean of women. Finally, an enterprising and well-placed alumnus and Bloomingtonian, Colonel Theodore J. Louden, launched plans to build a private women's dormitory. Assured of financial backing by several IU faculty members, including his father-in-law George Reinhard (vice president and dean of the law school), Louden proceeded with the planning and construction of the dormitory in the spring of 1906. After the untimely death of Reinhard that summer, the other faculty members informed Louden that they were no longer interested in his venture, which was scheduled to open in the fall. "Consequently," Louden later remembered, "I had the whole burden, the whole load to pay, and I sweat blood getting the money together to keep the bills paid."[1]

Located at the corner of Third Street and Forest Place (current site of Jordan Hall), Alpha Hall was designed by Thomas A. Winterrowd, an Indianapolis architect, who also designed residential homes in the now-historic Indianapolis Woodruff Place neighborhood. The rectangular exterior had a rough limestone veneer with a series of oriel (bay) windows on the south side; facing the street were three levels of porches for the women to enjoy, though by the 1950s the third porch had been removed. Inside, each sleeping room had a transom window above its door to aid in ventilation. Accommodating a hundred women, the dormitory included three floors of sleeping rooms, a living room and five parlors on the first floor, and a kitchen and dining room in the basement. The rooms came furnished with two large closets, a dresser, bookcase, and study table, as well as a stationary washstand to supplement the baths located on each sleeping floor.

While privately owned, Alpha Hall operated under university rules, which brought peace of mind to parents and helped fill the beds. Colonel Louden maintained regular communications with President Bryan and other university administrators, begging them to take this burden—what had become a financial albatross—off his hands. The hasty construction had not done Louden any favors; the women regularly complained of the conditions in Alpha Hall, and by 1912, just six years after its opening, the Indiana State Board of Health found the structure to be seriously lacking in many respects. Citing a

Facing top, Alpha Hall residents on front porch, 1914. P0043423, IU Archives.

Facing bottom, Alpha Hall, 1932. Photo credit: Courtesy of the National Park Service, Frederick Law Olmsted National Historic Site.

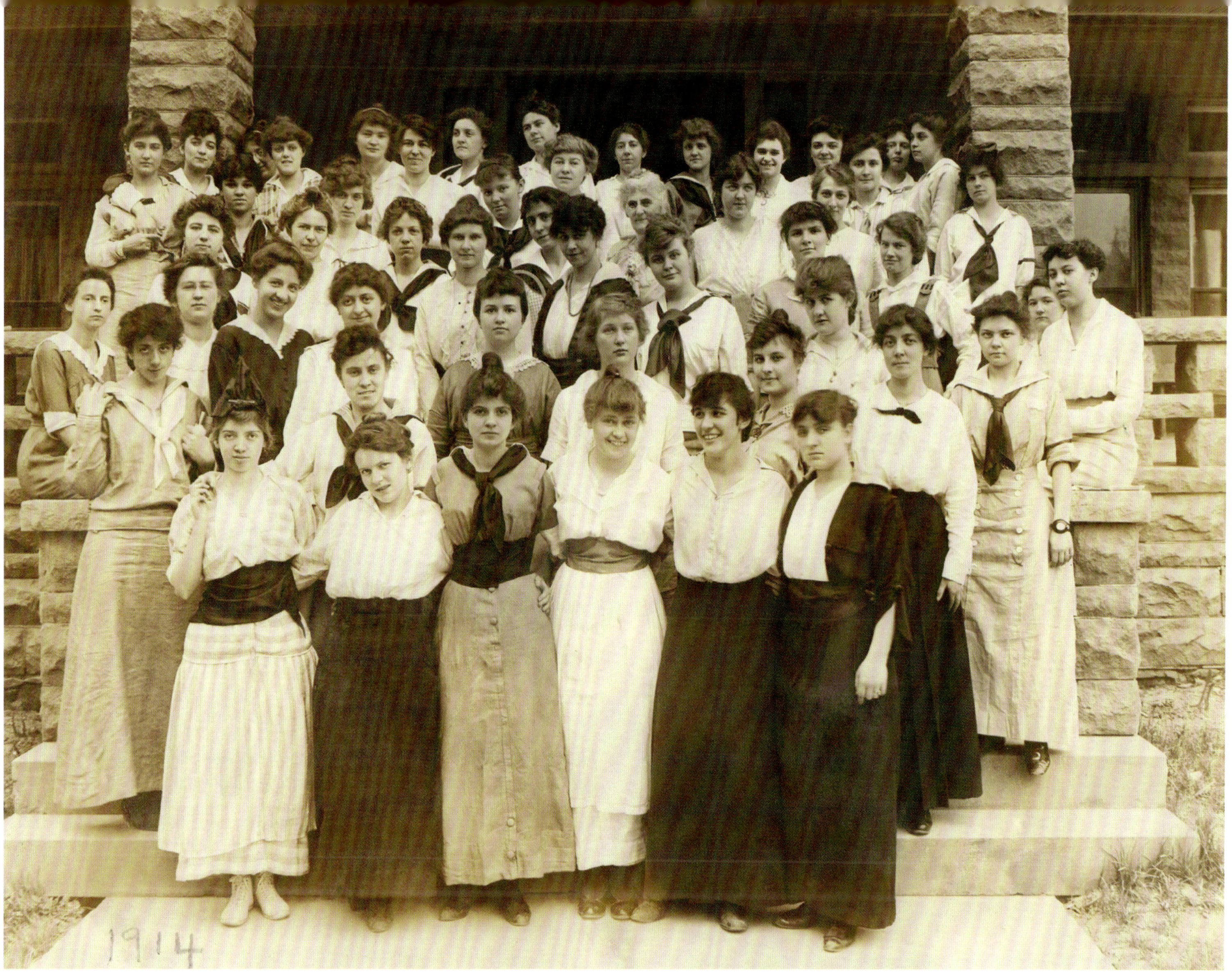
1914

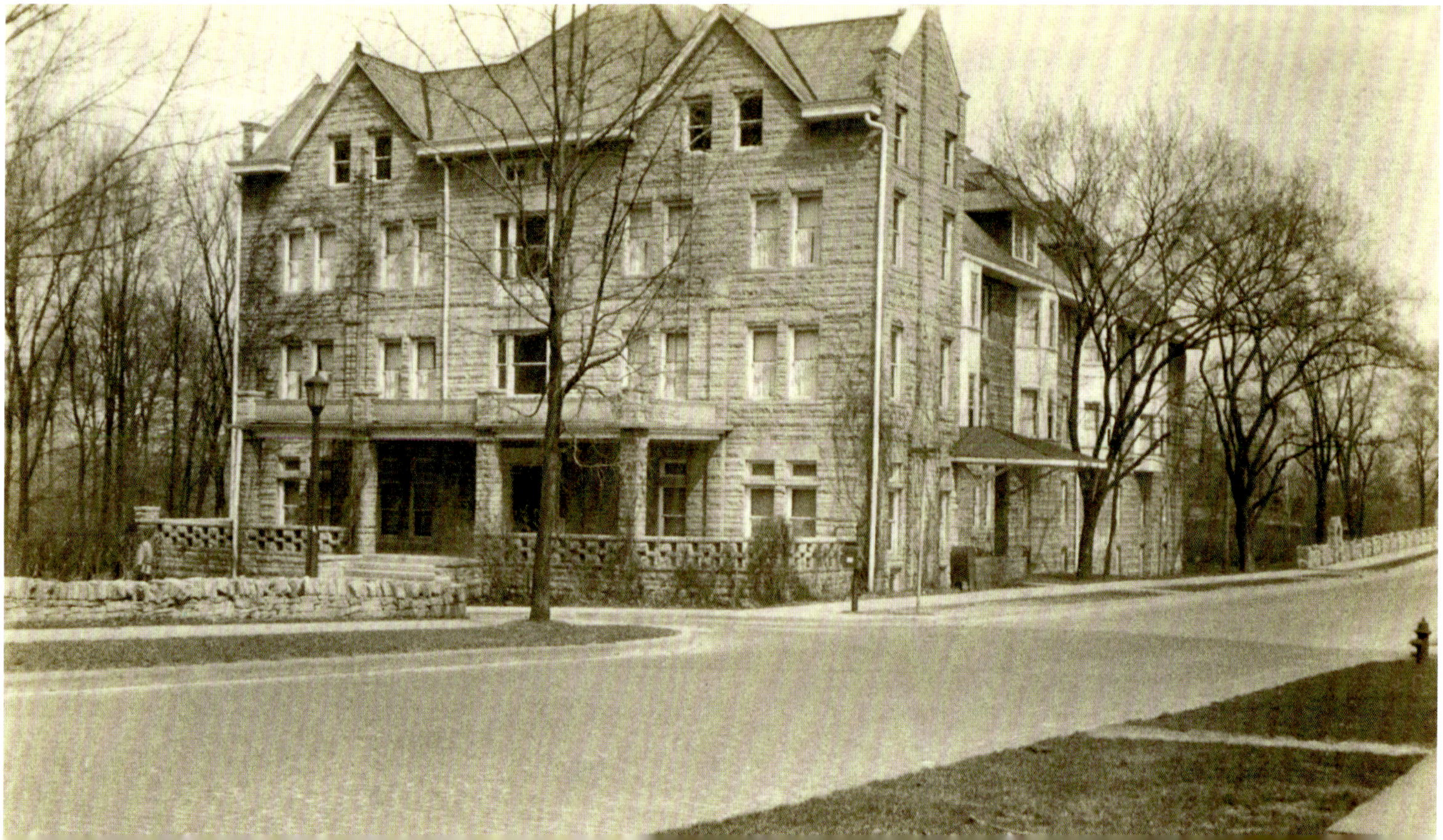

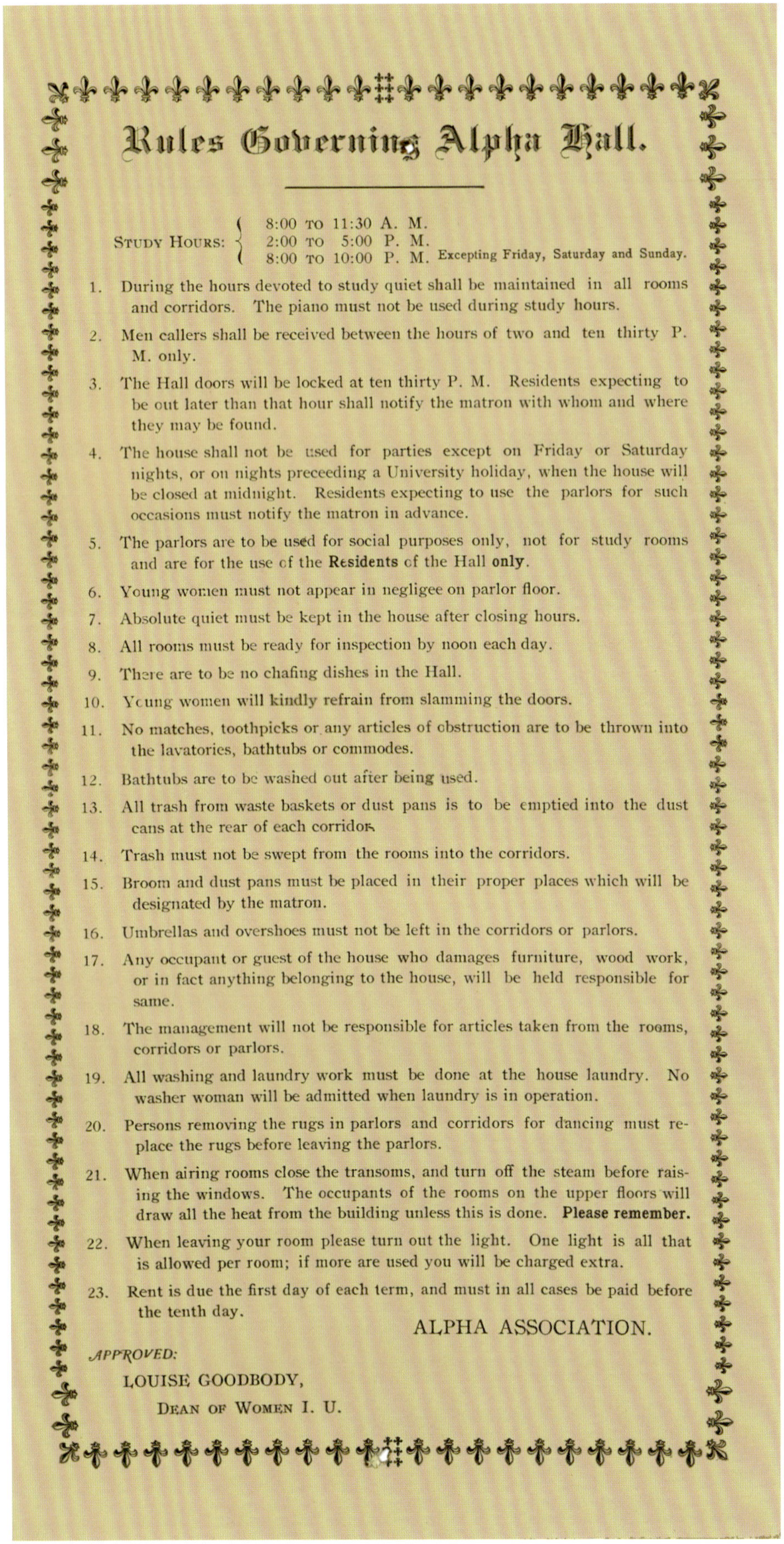

Rules Governing Alpha Hall.

STUDY HOURS: 8:00 TO 11:30 A. M.; 2:00 TO 5:00 P. M.; 8:00 TO 10:00 P. M. Excepting Friday, Saturday and Sunday.

1. During the hours devoted to study quiet shall be maintained in all rooms and corridors. The piano must not be used during study hours.
2. Men callers shall be received between the hours of two and ten thirty P. M. only.
3. The Hall doors will be locked at ten thirty P. M. Residents expecting to be out later than that hour shall notify the matron with whom and where they may be found.
4. The house shall not be used for parties except on Friday or Saturday nights, or on nights preceeding a University holiday, when the house will be closed at midnight. Residents expecting to use the parlors for such occasions must notify the matron in advance.
5. The parlors are to be used for social purposes only, not for study rooms and are for the use of the **Residents** of the Hall **only**.
6. Young women must not appear in negligee on parlor floor.
7. Absolute quiet must be kept in the house after closing hours.
8. All rooms must be ready for inspection by noon each day.
9. There are to be no chafing dishes in the Hall.
10. Young women will kindly refrain from slamming the doors.
11. No matches, toothpicks or any articles of obstruction are to be thrown into the lavatories, bathtubs or commodes.
12. Bathtubs are to be washed out after being used.
13. All trash from waste baskets or dust pans is to be emptied into the dust cans at the rear of each corridor.
14. Trash must not be swept from the rooms into the corridors.
15. Broom and dust pans must be placed in their proper places which will be designated by the matron.
16. Umbrellas and overshoes must not be left in the corridors or parlors.
17. Any occupant or guest of the house who damages furniture, wood work, or in fact anything belonging to the house, will be held responsible for same.
18. The management will not be responsible for articles taken from the rooms, corridors or parlors.
19. All washing and laundry work must be done at the house laundry. No washer woman will be admitted when laundry is in operation.
20. Persons removing the rugs in parlors and corridors for dancing must replace the rugs before leaving the parlors.
21. When airing rooms close the transoms, and turn off the steam before raising the windows. The occupants of the rooms on the upper floors will draw all the heat from the building unless this is done. **Please remember.**
22. When leaving your room please turn out the light. One light is all that is allowed per room; if more are used you will be charged extra.
23. Rent is due the first day of each term, and must in all cases be paid before the tenth day.

ALPHA ASSOCIATION.

APPROVED:
LOUISE GOODBODY,
DEAN OF WOMEN I. U.

Rules of Alpha Hall, circa 1910. IU Archives.

combination of poor construction and poor management, the report cataloged a slew of issues including cracked and falling plaster; grimy walls; and "stair-ways, window sills, wainscoting, base boards, book shelves and furniture, [which] generally, throughout the entire building, show a quantity of soot, dust and unclassifiable dirt that is not in harmony with good housekeeping or good sanitation."[2] It is not surprising that Indiana University did not jump at the prospect of ownership.

With the onset of World War I, universities and colleges across the country received the patriotic call to educate and train soldiers in the Student Army Training Corp (SATC). Indiana University was informed that two thousand soldiers would be heading its way, which left the administration scrambling to arrange suitable housing. After leasing the fraternity houses and putting men up on cots in the gymnasium, the university turned to Colonel Louden for help. They signed a lease with him to house and board 260 soldiers, who began moving into Alpha Hall in mid-September 1918.

Colonel Louden's property management skills, unfortunately, had not improved. The men complained of frigid temperatures throughout the dormitory and inedible food. Many of them, it was reported, spent their small incomes to eat elsewhere rather than face rotten meat and meal after meal of dried apricots and poor-quality coffee. By the end of 1918, World War I was wrapping up and the services of Alpha Hall were no longer needed by the U.S. military. The boys, it is said, demonstrated their "appreciation" for Colonel Louden's hospitality by purposely flooding the property on their way out.[3]

Although the university continued to take issue with Louden's management of the dormitory, upon fulfillment of a long list of required repairs and upgrades, IU officials finally signed a five-year lease with the colonel in 1919.[4] The university's management of the property alleviated some of the aforementioned problems, and the lease for Residence Hall (as it was called when IU began leasing it) was renewed a number of times until 1935. At that time, rather than continue to contend with landlord Louden, IU decided to build a second university-owned women's dormitory, Goodbody Hall, adjacent to Memorial Hall, which had opened in 1925.

Louden then began another campaign to persuade the university to purchase the building and his adjoining Forest Place property. Negotiations ensued and in September 1936, Louden and IU came to an agreement to purchase both prop-

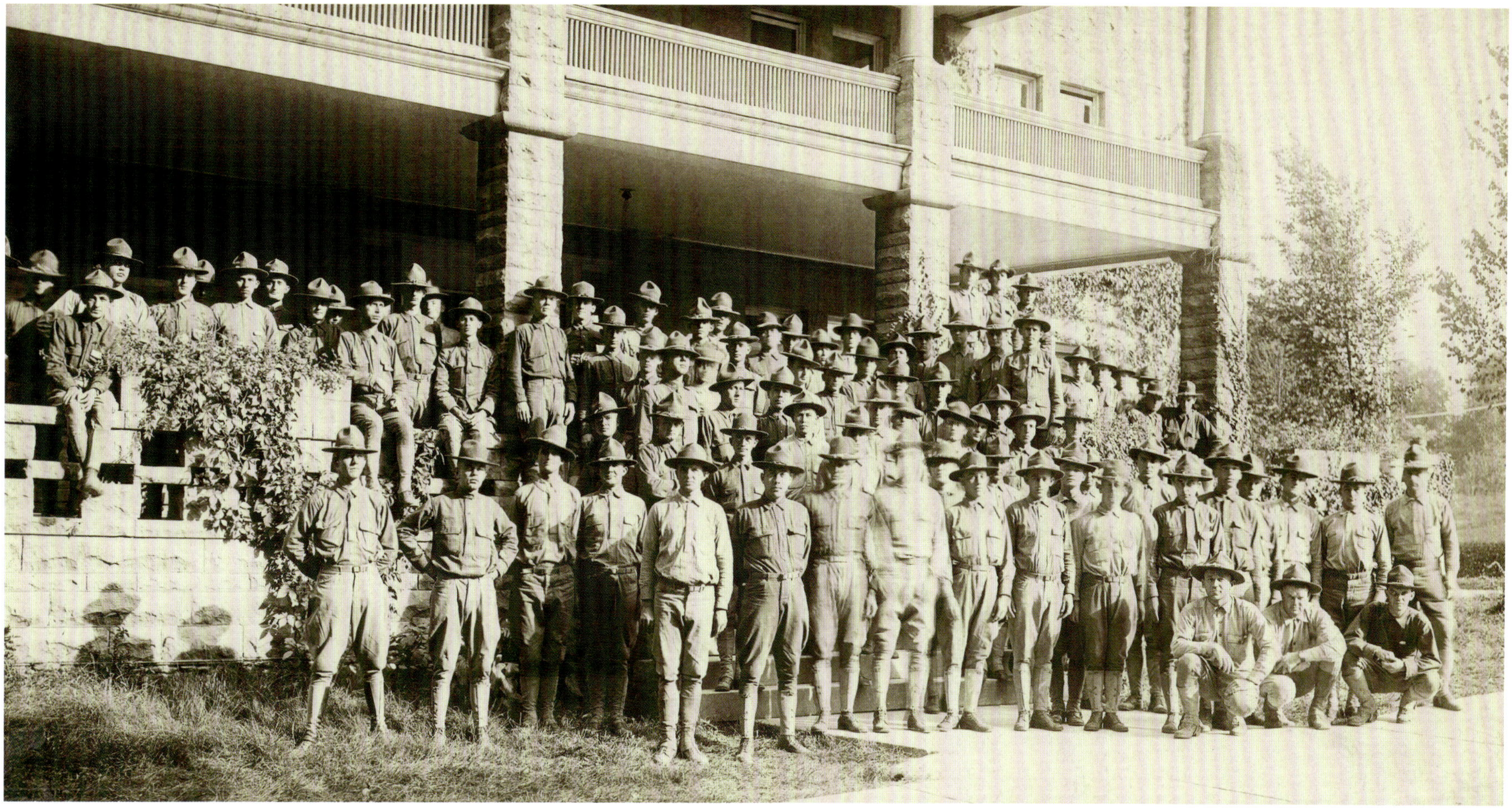

Company B of the Radio School quartered at Alpha Hall during World War I, circa 1918. P0043402, IU Archives. Photo credit: Henry Thew Stephenson.

erties for $70,000 and the Loudens headed to Florida for semiretirement.[5]

Rather than sink money into bringing the building up to housing standards, IU used Alpha Hall, as it was once again called, for offices and laboratories. Business Hall—now known as Rawles Hall—was bursting at the seams, so after minor renovations, several of its offices were moved to Alpha Hall, as was Professor Robert Milisen's Speech Clinic. Over the years, Alpha Hall continued to fill the needs of office and lab space, housing at various times the School of Education offices, Junior Division clinics and bureaus, Dr. Donald W. Lauer's dog laboratories (where he researched conditioning of the salivary response), and in its final years, the School of Health, Physical Education, and Recreation.

By the early 1960s, the administration decided to raze Alpha Hall, which had served the university in times of great need.

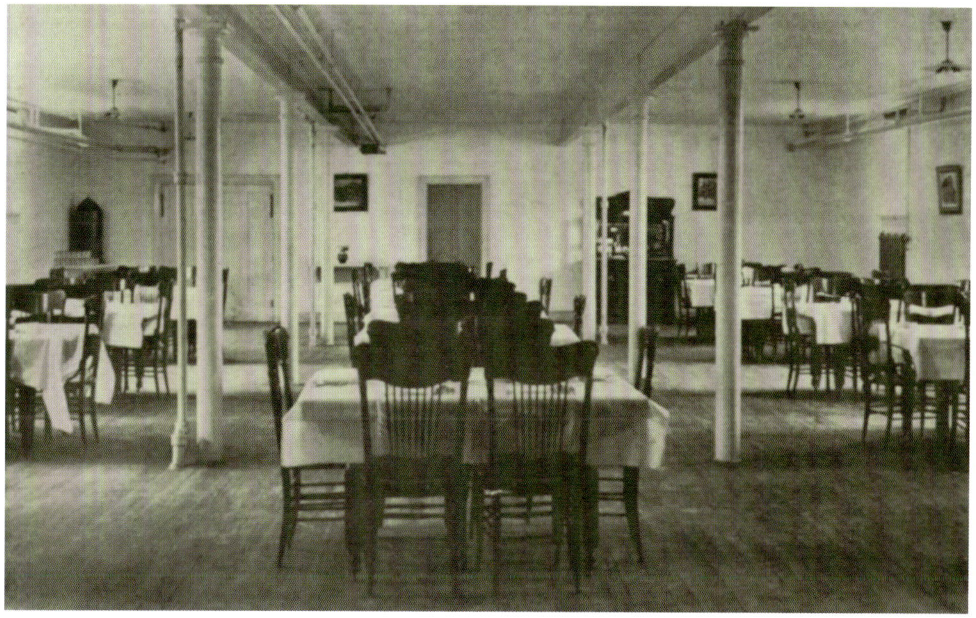

Alpha Hall dining room, 1907. P0031595, IU Archives. Photo credit: Spratt and Nicely.

Ralph L. Collins Living-Learning Center

Historic Dormitory

MRC has an atmosphere of tradition, a flavor of individuality, and an esprit de corps that might better serve the University now by producing stable students and in years to come as an indelible memory in the minds of a devoted and contributing alumni.

—Patricia Montgomery, IU parent

COLLINS BEGAN AS A SINGLE MEN'S DORMITORY building in 1924 and includes the oldest residence hall on IU's Bloomington campus, Smith Hall, which continues to house students nearly a century later. The building was originally named Washington Hall, but the Men's Dormitory Association petitioned the trustees to change the name to South Hall: "with all due reverence to our great American patriot we honestly believe that, were he alive at this time, he would not approve of having his name used in connection with our dormitory."[1]

Although not complete, South Hall opened to sixty-three incoming men on September 14, 1924. Alice McDonald Nelson, the business manager for university residences, feared it would be impossible to bring the men back if they were told to seek rooms elsewhere for the two to three weeks it would take to complete the dorm. She reported to President Bryan, "For the past two weeks the men have slept in the attic which is as fine a dormitory as any house possesses in Bloomington."[2]

In 1940 West and North Halls were built, and the three together were called the Men's Residence Center (MRC). At the request of its male residents, the center admitted women in 1970.[3] In 1959 the three were renamed Cravens (North), Smith (South), and Edmondson (West) Halls.

The three Collegiate Gothic buildings are constructed of Indiana limestone, which bears a distinctive random ashlar pattern. Other exterior details of note include a battlement near the roof peak on the east end of Smith Hall and hood molds over the original wood-paneled and leaded-glass doors adorned with iron lanterns. Smith has been damaged by fire twice in its long history, so while the exterior is similar to Cravens and Edmondson, the interior today has a more modern construction than the wood paneling of the other two. The interiors were designed with their male occupants in mind: an exposed beam ceiling and oversized fireplace with a floor-to-ceiling chimneypiece in Smith's lounge, while Cravens's lounge featured fielded wood paneling and a simple Tudor Revival stone fireplace. Architects Burns and James planned for an "English lodge feel" in the Edmondson dining hall, with 6-foot-high paneling on the walls, hardwood floors, and a soaring beamed ceiling.[4] Edmondson also has gnome stained-glass windows, a quirky detail that has remained in place for Collins residents to appreciate.

During World War II, university and fraternity housing were "enlisted" to house military men and women who came to IU for training. In July 1942, MRC became home for two hundred Navy yeomen and North Hall became known as the

Facing top, Colorized postcard, Men's Residence Center (later named Ralph L. Collins Living-Learning Center), circa 1941. P0043606, IU Archives.

Facing bottom, Colorized postcard of south elevation of South Hall, circa 1924. P0049305, IU Archives.

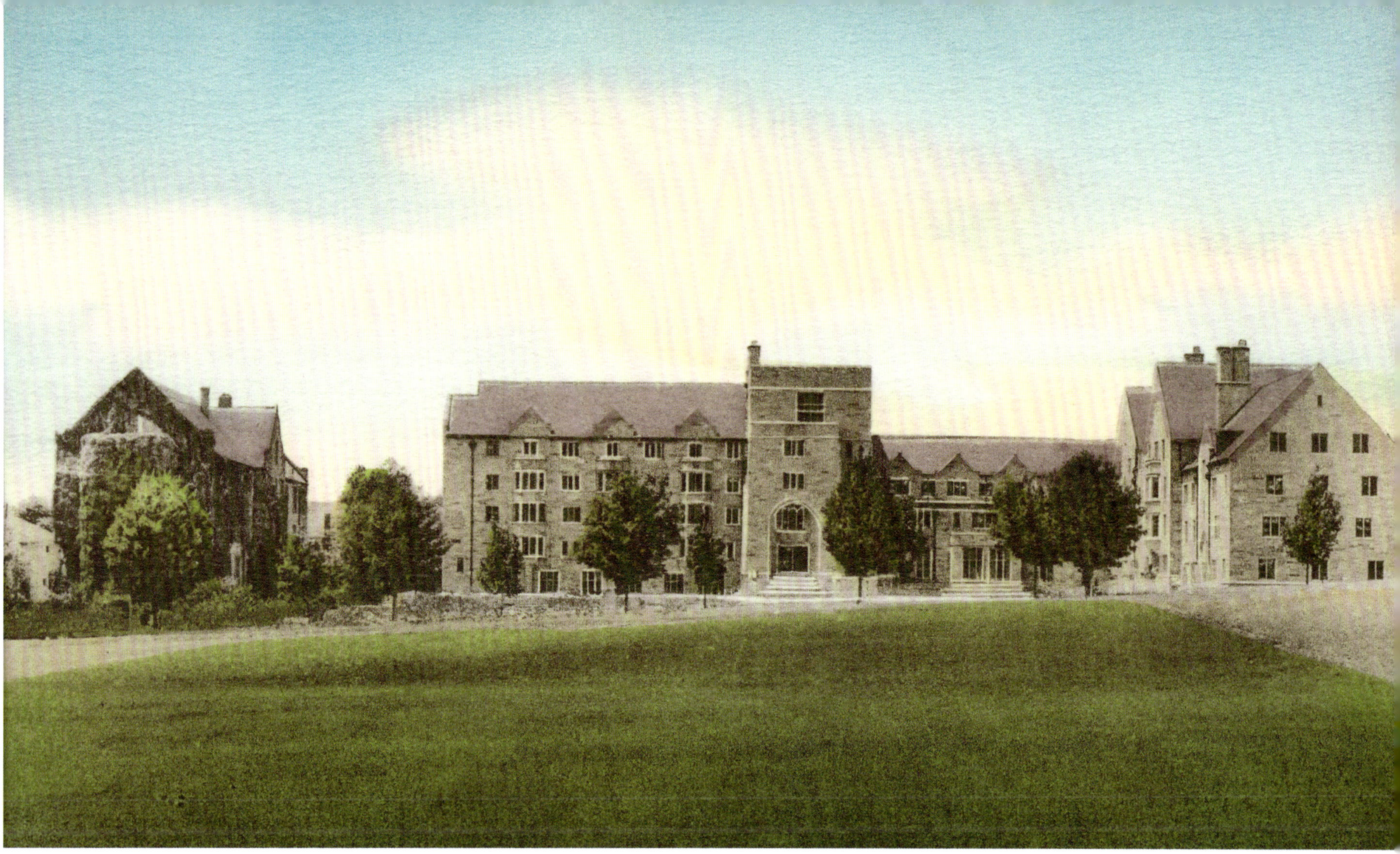

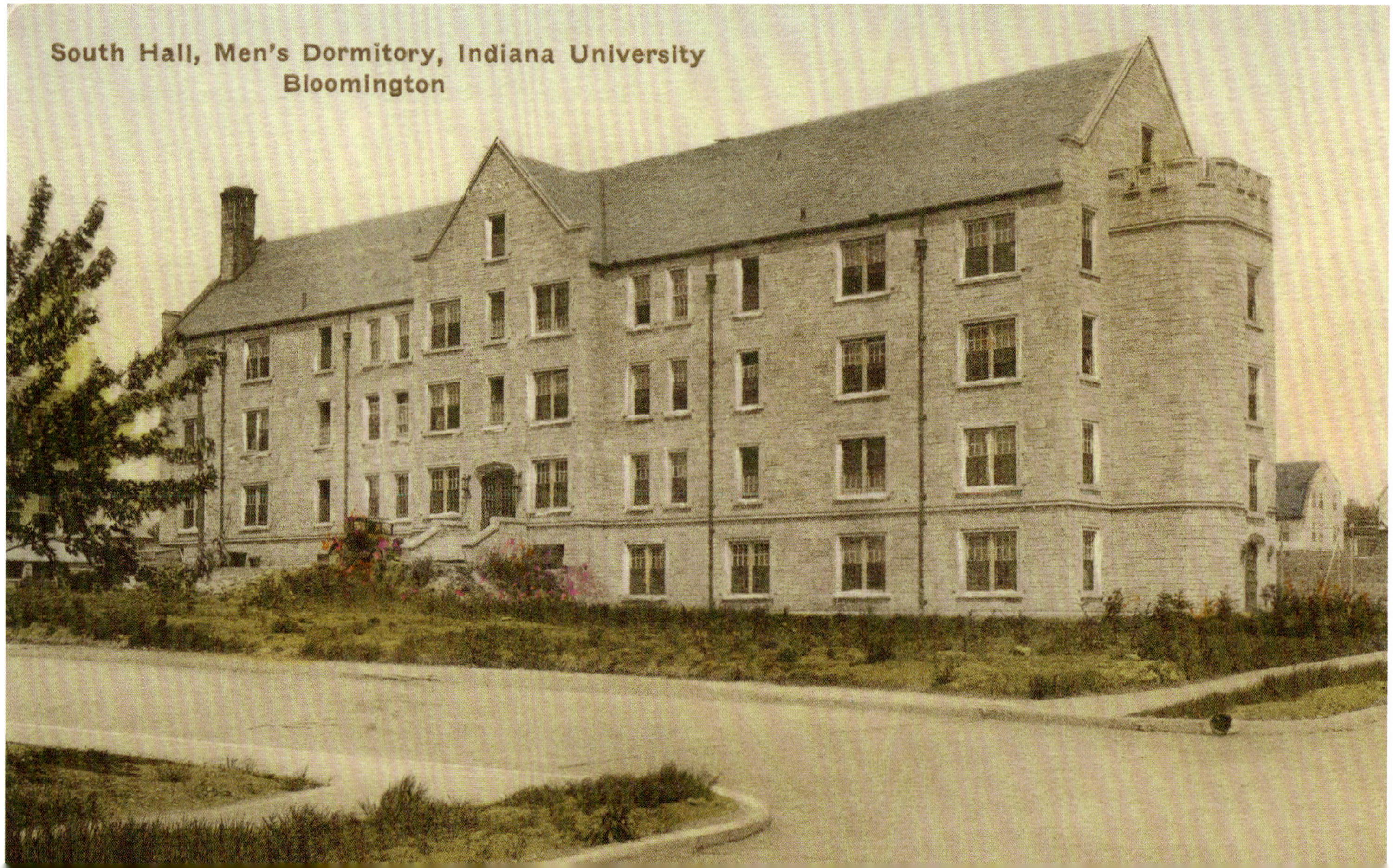
South Hall, Men's Dormitory, Indiana University
Bloomington

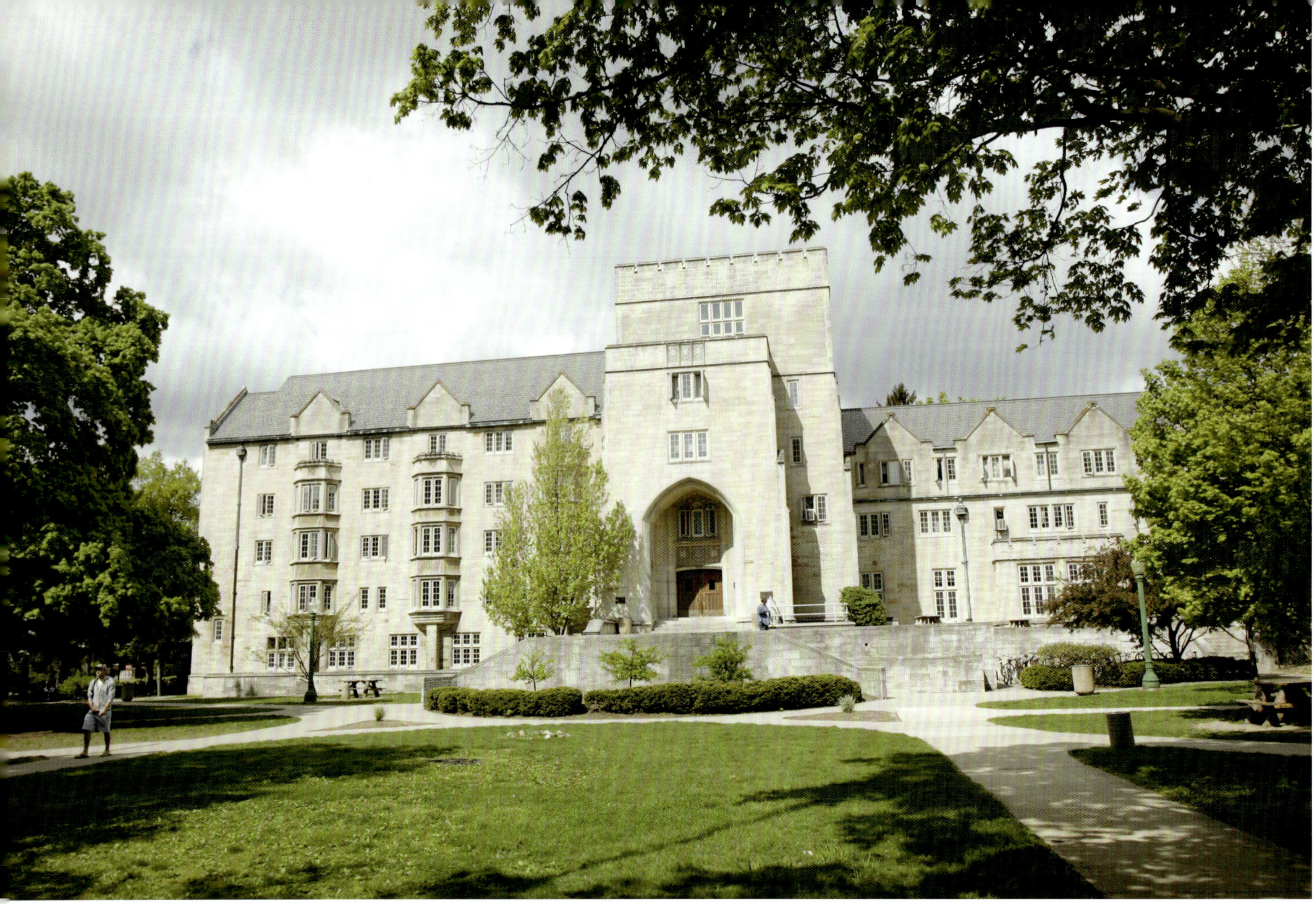

Ominous skies over Edmondson Hall, undated. Photo credit: Indiana University.

USS *Indiana*.[5] While on campus, the servicemen and women enjoyed a bit of campus life while taking courses on such skills as storekeeping, disbursement, and typewriting. MRC once again filled a military housing need during the Cold War of the 1950s and 1960s through federally funded intensive language and cultural education programs. The Air Force Language Training program, headed by IU's renowned linguist Thomas Sebeok, brought service personnel to IU—and specifically, to Collins—where they were immersed in such languages as Russian, Polish, Serbo-Croatian, and Hungarian. From these roots, Indiana University continues to have some of the strongest language programs in the country.

In 1971 the university needed more academic space and, as had been done with the Wells Quadrangle, the administration wanted to turn some of MRC into office and classroom space. Student residents banned together and began the "Save MRC" campaign. The students were successful but ultimately compromised with the administration; MRC became a living-learning center where unique educational programs could be offered within student housing. Foster Quad had created a living-learning center in 1967, but after just a few years the program was floundering. Establishing MRC Living-Learning Center permitted the university to try a different tack in a much smaller environment.

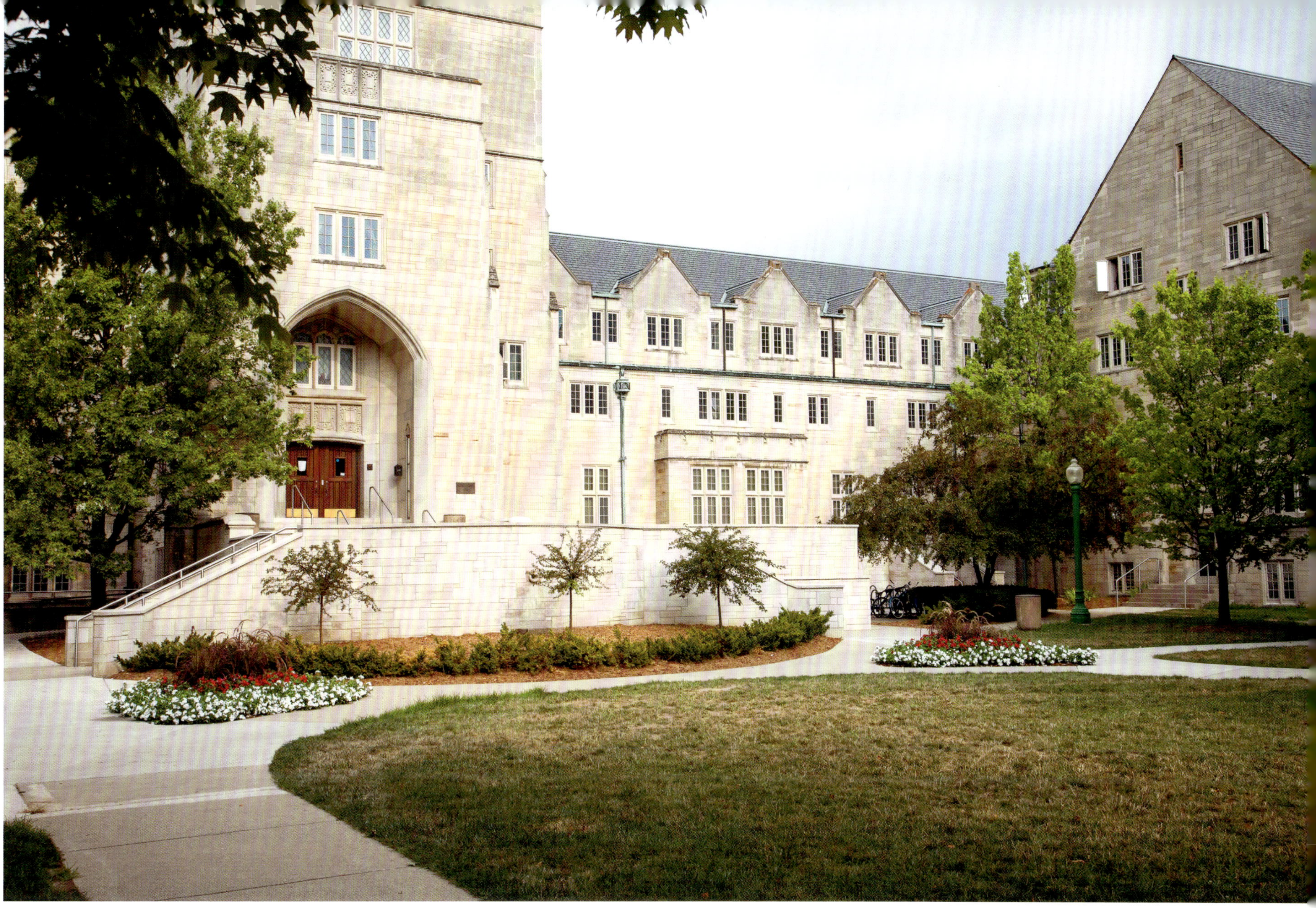

View across Collins courtyard, 2012. Photo credit: Tyagan Miller.

The Living-Learning Center (LLC) was created in 1972 and has since featured distinctive courses such as Marine Ecology (highlighted with a trip to the Florida Keys for research), Geology's Mobile Earth (or Commotion about the Notion of Motion in the Ocean), and The Psychology of Adornment, taught by one of the many visiting artists the LLC regularly hosts. In 1980 the center was named for Ralph L. Collins, an IU English professor and administrator who also served as MRC's first headmaster.

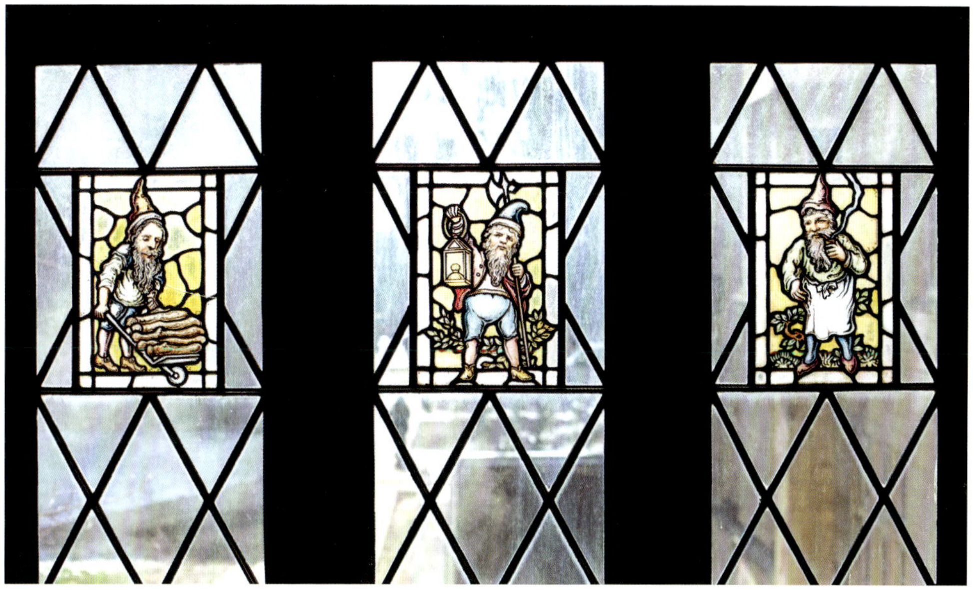

Iconic Edmondson Hall gnomes, 2017. Photo credit: Tyagan Miller.

Agnes E. Wells Quadrangle

IU's First Home for Women

We have dreamed many years of a dormitory. Now at last the dream of these years has become a reality. We are to have the actual house of stone, the house made with hands, the gift of our many friends.

—Charlotte Lowe Bryan at cornerstone-laying ceremony

THE AGNES E. WELLS QUADRANGLE, NAMED AFter the IU dean of women from 1918 to 1938, is the quintessence of how Indiana University insisted on superior planning and execution in its construction projects. Step inside the quad and the consistency of design among the buildings could lead one to believe they were all constructed at the same time; in truth, the quadrangle developed over fifteen years, following the campus plan prepared in 1936 by the world-renowned landscape architects the Olmsted Brothers.

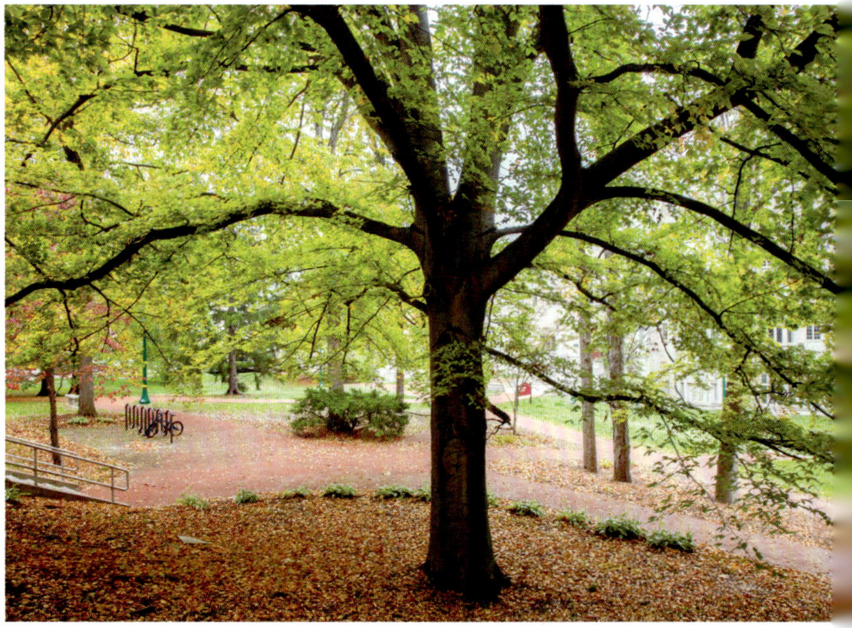

Agnes E. Wells Quadrangle courtyard, 2016.
Photo credit: Tyagan Miller.

MEMORIAL HALL

As women's enrollment continued to grow in the early 1900s, the problem of housing women grew along with it. For years, the university relied on private boarding houses and local families to assist with lodging students, but there came a time when the boarding houses and homes could no longer keep up. Theodore J. Louden's privately run dormitory, Alpha Hall, came along at the right time but, as described elsewhere, was not an ideal solution. It was time for the university to step in.

Dean of Women Agnes E. Wells is credited with pushing the university to build its first women's dormitory (1925). But perhaps even more credit should be given to the friends and alumni of Indiana University: Memorial Hall, the first building completed in the Wells Quad, was funded in large part by the Indiana Memorial Fund. The Memorial Fund campaign was approved by the IU Alumni Council in 1921 with the goal of raising $1 million for the construction of three buildings: a student union, a women's dormitory, and an athletic stadium, all honoring the university's men and women who served the country during World War I.

When the campaign commenced in 1922, dedicated Hoosiers stepped up to the challenge. Local quarries, including Hunter Brothers, Monroe County Oolitic, and B. G. Hoadley Quarries, donated limestone for the projects. Brick and tile

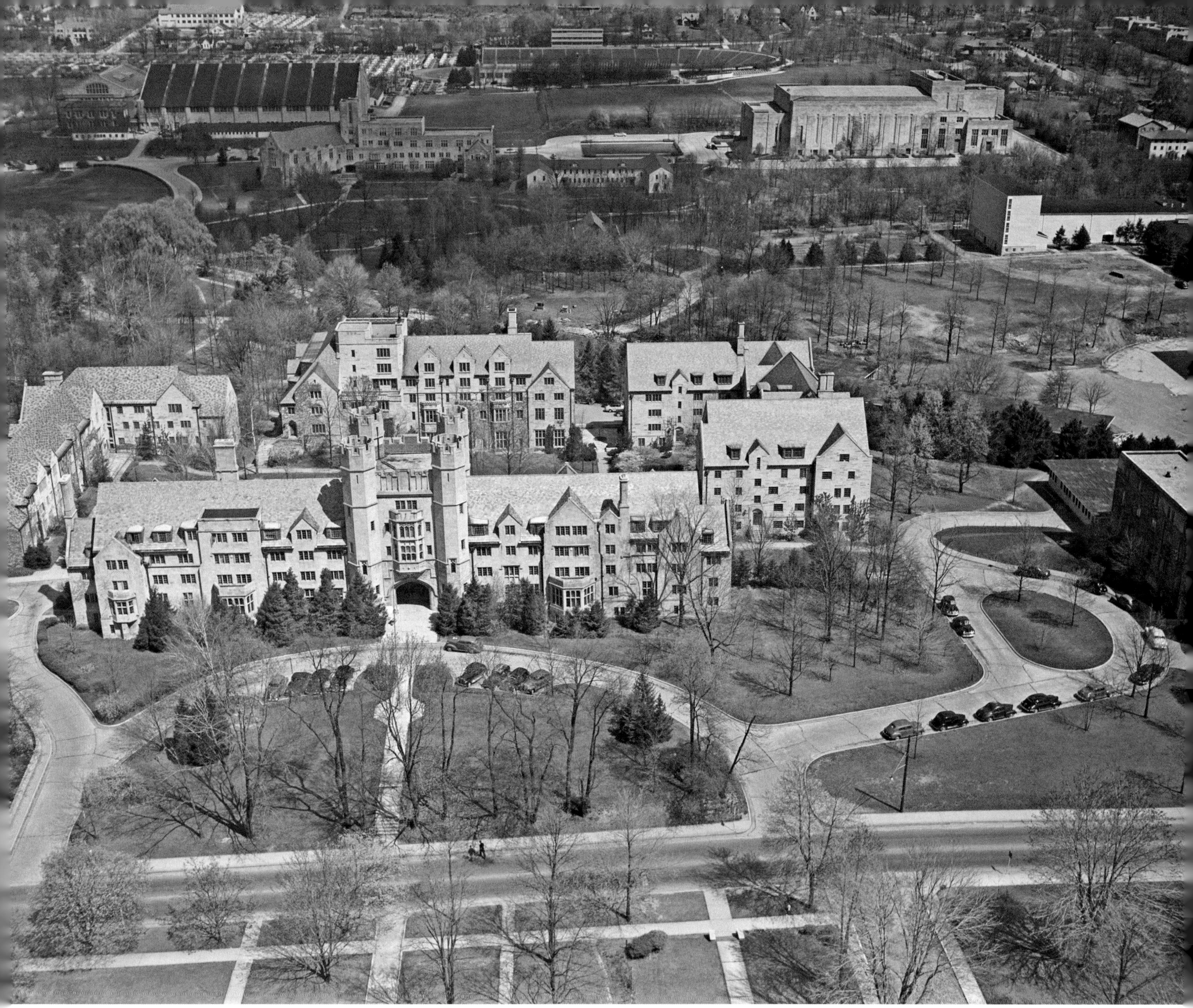

Aerial view of Agnes E. Wells Quadrangle, 1949. P0022953, IU Archives.

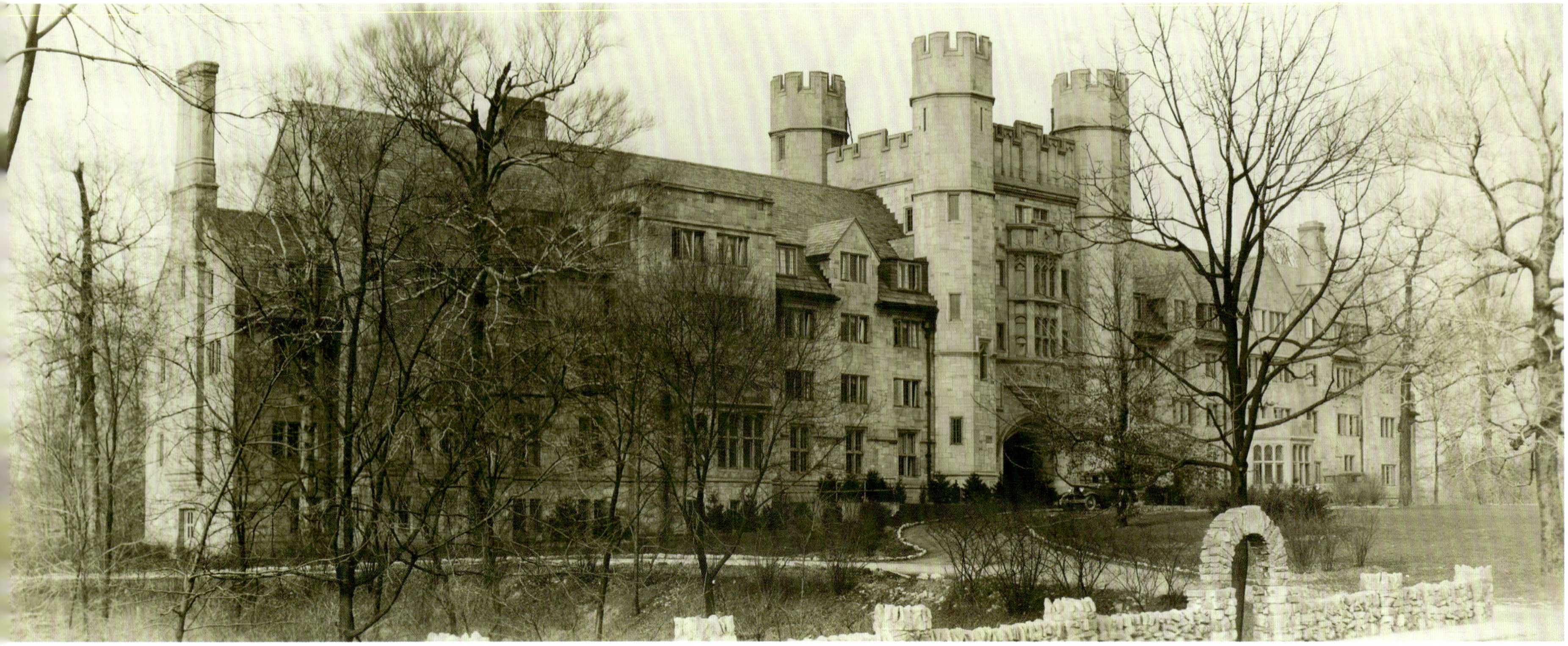

Above, Memorial Hall, IU's first women's dormitory, 1931. P0031160, IU Archives. Photo credit: Sinclair Studio, Bloomington, Indiana.

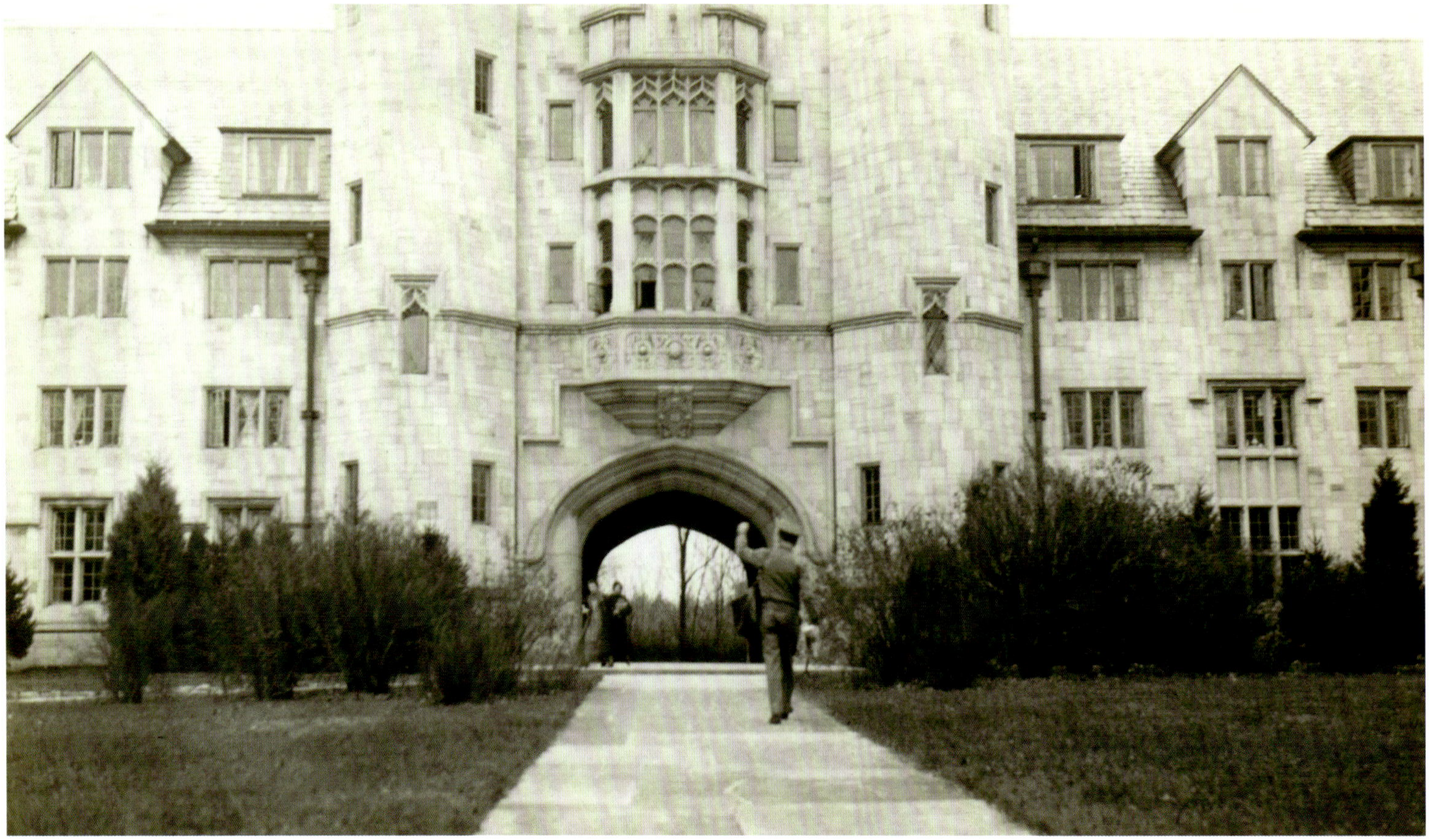

Right, Veteran returning to Memorial Hall, 1935. Courtesy of the National Park Service, Frederick Law Olmsted National Historic Site.

were secured from the state penal farm at a deeply discounted rate.[1] Current students and townspeople pledged $600,000 alone, so the committee raised its goal to $1.6 million, targeting alumni for the remaining million. Although the campaign was going well, in the midst of the fund-raising venture construction prices soared and the $250,000 intended for Memorial Hall was no longer sufficient. A loan was secured for the remainder and construction began.

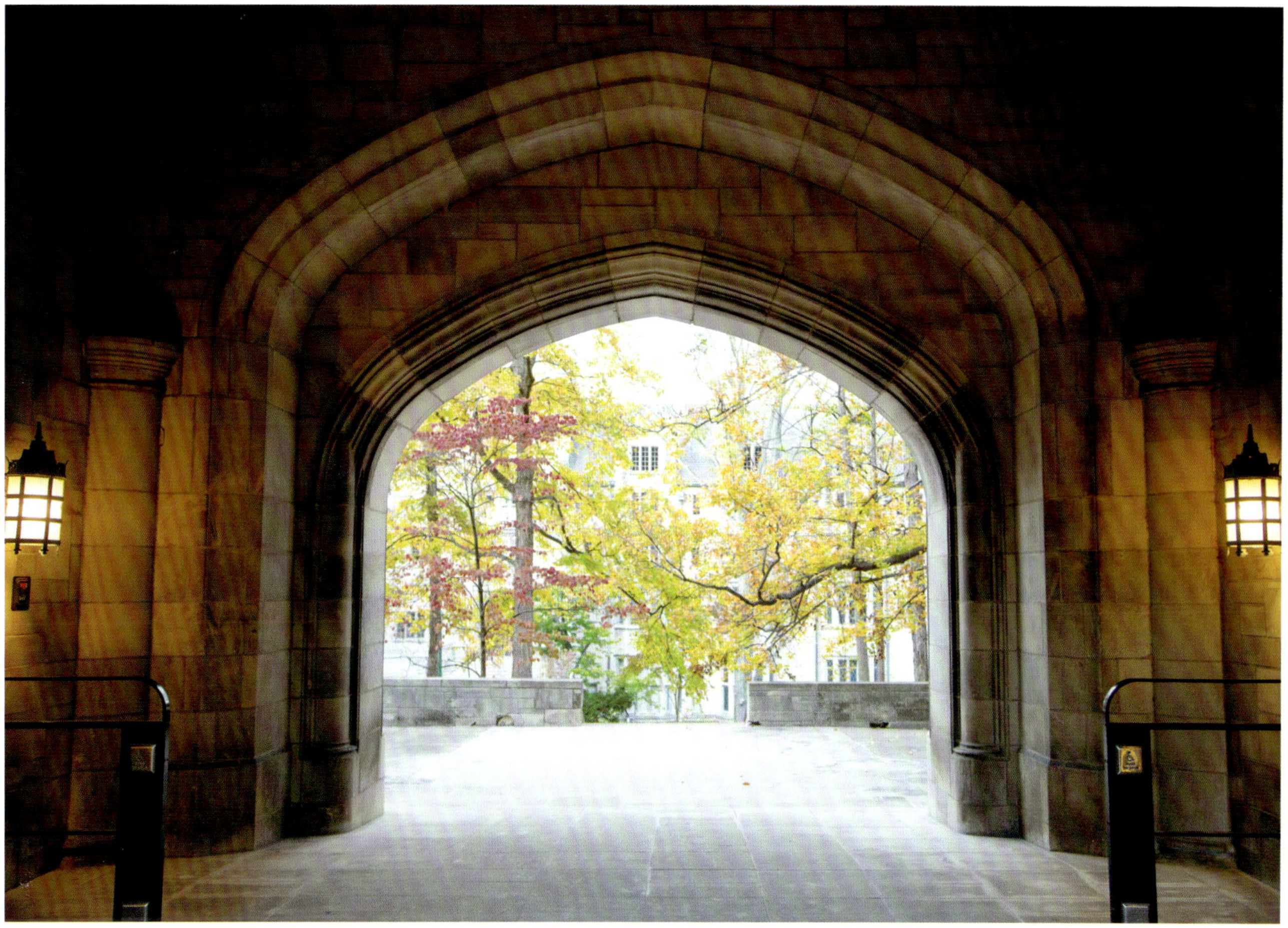

Courtyard as seen through Memorial Hall's Gothic archway, 2016. Photo credit: Tyagan Miller.

Memorial Hall is built of blue-and-gray Indiana limestone in the Collegiate Gothic style. Its striking exterior resembles a castle, including the four towers topped with decorative battlements. There are inconsistencies in the historical record relating to the meaning of Memorial Hall's four towers, but at the cornerstone laying ceremony on October 20, 1924, Dean Wells proffered this explanation: "The towers will be symbols of uplift, in health, scholarship, sports, and friendship."[2] The towers are flanked by two wings of equal size. Between the wings is an impressive Gothic arch, called Memorial Arch. Embedded in the flagstone under the arch is a bronze seal that honors the women of the university who served in World War I with the YMCA, Signal Corps, and Red Cross.

Imaginative carvings grace Memorial Hall, one of the many buildings on IU's campus that benefited from the artistry of local stonemasons over the years. Above the doors into each wing are four relief carvings of individuals praying, playing, reading, and serving, a balance of which the university hoped its female students would obtain. Beside the arch on the north side is a whimsical carving of a sleeping student and on the other side, a professor calling to him. Above the archway is a two-story oriel capped by a faux balcony wall, on which is carved a vertical sundial. As you enter the east wing, next to the door is an engraved Sir Walter Scott quote handpicked by President William Lowe Bryan: "Evil spirits cannot enter an inhabited house unless invited."

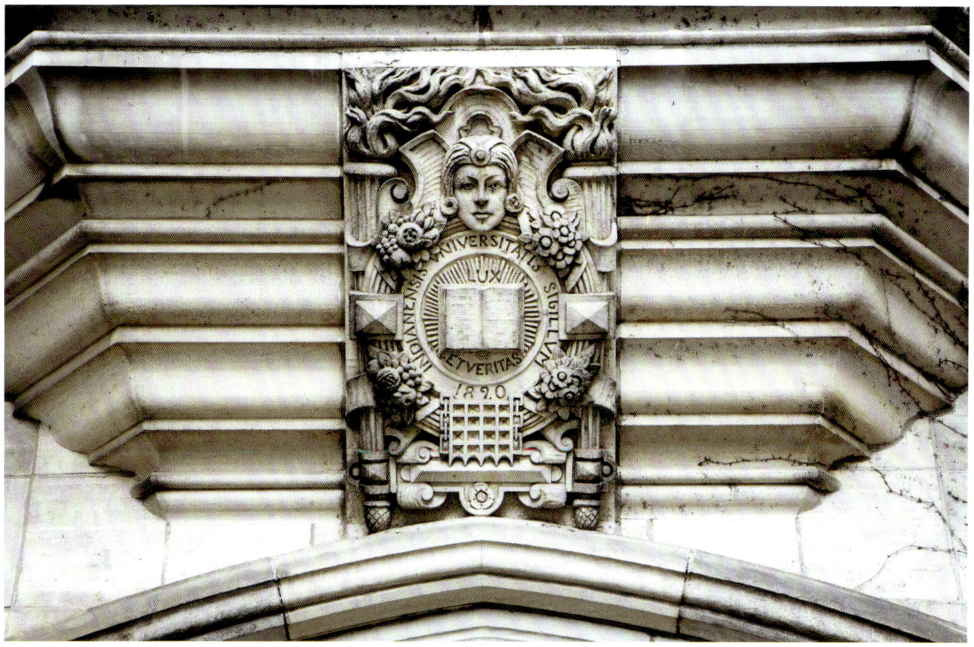

Detailed carving of Indiana University seal above Memorial Hall arch, 2016. Photo credit: Tyagan Miller.

Dean Wells met several times with architects to ensure that Memorial Hall's interior was designed to provide over two hundred of IU's women with the best possible dormitory facilities. On June 4, 1923, Wells sat down with architect and IU alumnus J. Carlisle Bollenbacher to recommend four pages of itemized changes in the preliminary sketches, focusing on the smallest details such as the necessity for an ice-cream room in the refrigerating space and a sewing room in the basement.[3] This attention to detail certainly would have been evident to the residents. Each wing had a living room, library, office, social director's suite, and resident faculty room. Unfortunately, each wing's dining facilities were in the basement with a central kitchen rather than the original design of a grand dining room complete with fireplace and musicians' balcony. The sleeping rooms were all doubles, but at the end of each hall was a sleeping porch available to residents and guests. The dormitory's floors were terrazzo, a result of the architect and builder having convinced the university to replace the cement floors originally planned.

The building opened to its first residents in the fall of 1925 at a cost of $190 for room and board per semester. Dedicatory exercises took place on November 20, 1925, before an audience of more than two thousand alumni, guests, faculty, and students. Dean Wells presided; President Bryan delivered an address titled "Spirit of a College Home."

GOODBODY, SYCAMORE, AND MORRISON HALLS

From the beginning, three additional women's dormitories had been planned for this area. When the federal government tried to inject life into the dying Depression-era economy by providing supplemental funds for large-scale public construction projects, university administrators were quick to apply in hopes of realizing building projects throughout the Bloomington campus. Forest Hall, renamed Louise A. Goodbody Hall in 1957, was built in 1936, situated perpendicular to Memorial Hall in the quad.

Designed by the Indianapolis architectural firm Burns and James, the three-story building was built to house an additional 140 women, although in 1959 it also became home to IU men. Goodbody, like all the buildings in the quad, features a limestone exterior in the Collegiate Gothic style, with stone of varying shades laid in a random ashlar pattern. The carvings of this and the other quad buildings pale in comparison to Memorial Hall's with one exception—perched atop the roof on

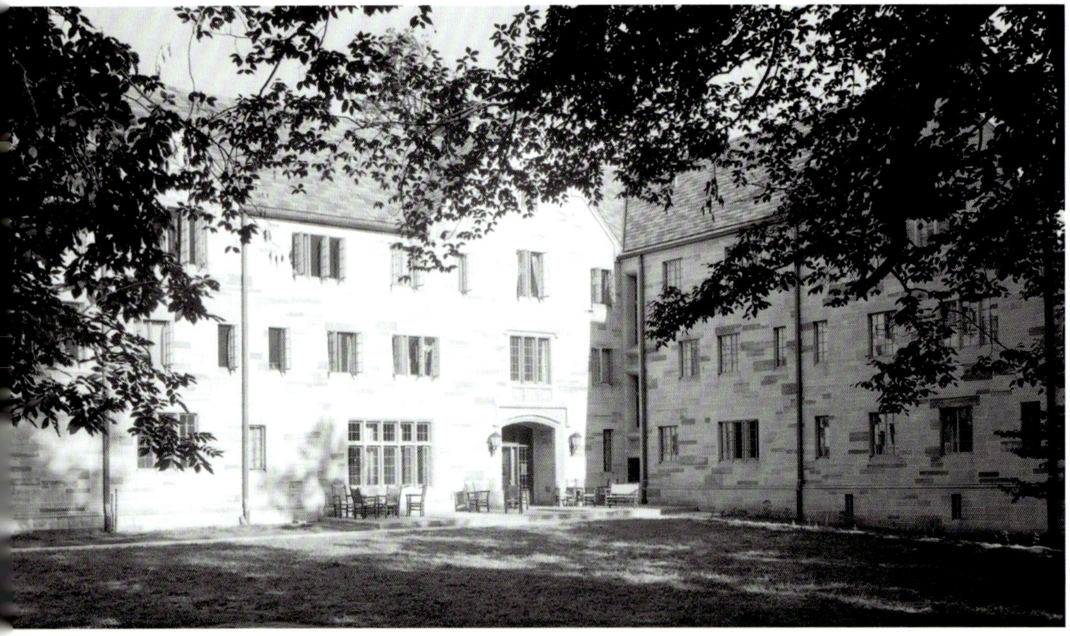

Above, Goodbody Hall, 1938. P0030604, IU Archives.

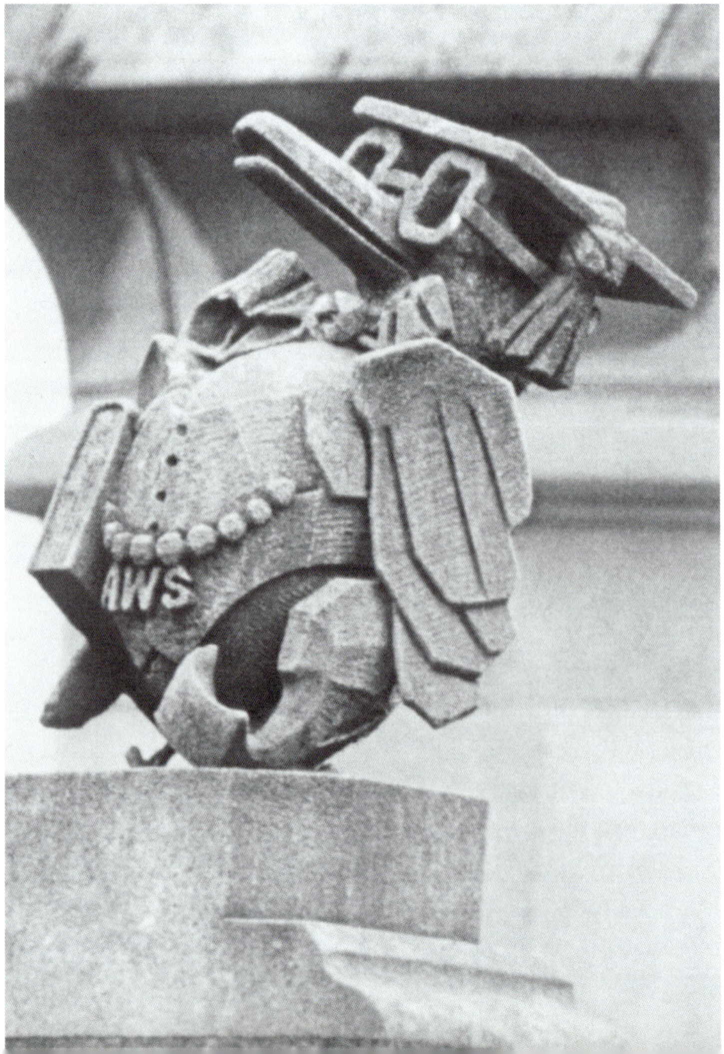

Right, Iconic Goodbody Hall duck as seen on west elevation roofline; watch fob initials "AWS" stand for Association of Women Students, undated. P0022769, IU Archives. Photo credit: James Capshew.

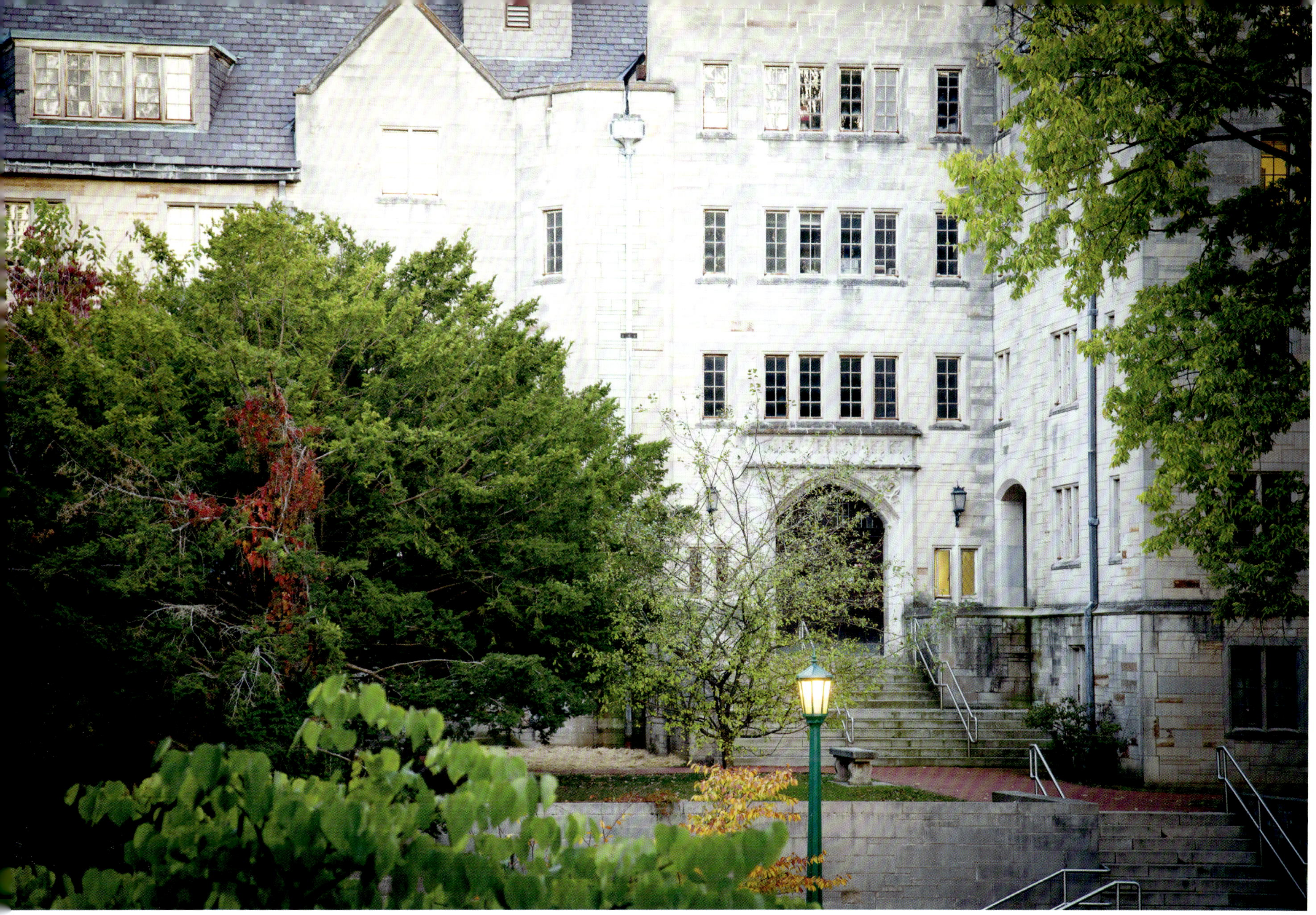

Sycamore Hall, 2016. Photo credit: Tyagan Miller.

the west side of Goodbody Hall is what has become known as the Goodbody Duck, a cartoonish bowtied duck dressed as a professor with mortarboard, glasses, vest, watch fob, and book. Below the fob is carved *AWS*, the Association of Women Students. While the names of the artisans of most of the campus stone carvings are lost, the Goodbody duck is said to have been hewn by Bloomington carver Albert McIlveen Sr. in 1940.

In 1940 Sycamore and Beech Halls were added to the site to complete the quadrangle and enclose the courtyard, and together housed nearly four hundred additional women. Both were also designed by architects Burns and James, and the two additions fit seamlessly into the quad, reflecting the Collegiate Gothic style of their predecessors.

In 1942 Beech Hall was renamed Sarah Parke Morrison Hall, in honor of IU's first female student and to commemorate seventy-five years of coeducation.[4] Morrison, on the north side of the quad, has variegated limestone laid in random ashlar design. The exterior echoes some of the castle-like features of its neighbor across the quad, Memorial Hall, with Gothic architecture's ever-popular decorative battlements enclosing the women's sundeck. Bay windows with leaded glass spread across the south side of the dormitory, facing the courtyard.

The interiors of Sycamore and Morrison, according to the architects, were to be styled "late Stuart" to give the buildings a homelike ambience. "We are trying to carry an atmosphere similar to the beautiful country homes of England."[5] Attention

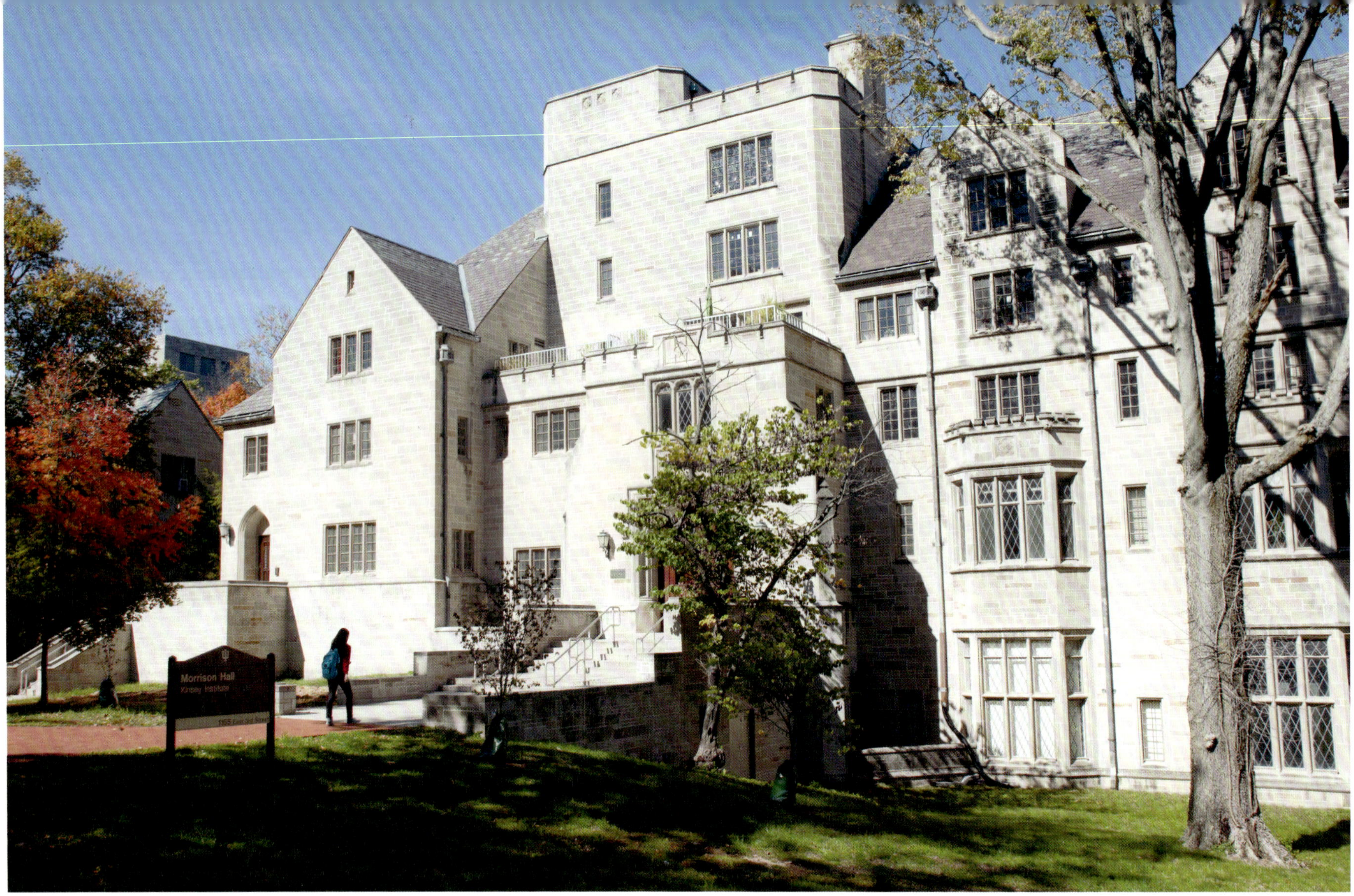

South view of Morrison Hall, undated. Photo credit: Indiana University.

to detail did not wane with these final two dormitories, as evidenced by the series of articles Dean of Women Kate Mueller wrote for the *Indiana Daily Student* describing the new structures. One of the "date" lounges featured wallpaper depicting a recently restored courthouse in Williamsburg, Virginia, while another was adorned with paper exhibiting a pastoral scene from the French Riviera coast. The new dining halls in Morrison were to have a "light and delicate treatment" with matte bone white woodwork, and the larger dining room would have a fireplace of Botticino marble.[6]

CONVERSION TO ACADEMIC SPACE

The dormitories served the students well, but by the early 1960s the university faced a serious need for academic space and in 1963 Goodbody Hall was converted to offices. It was thought this would be a temporary takeover, but necessity made it permanent. In quick succession, the other buildings were commandeered for administrative use, and by 1970 all student residents had been moved to other dormitories. (In 1975, a housing crunch forced the reversion of some of the rooms in Memorial Hall to men's housing, a situation that continued into the early 1980s.)[7] In carved-from-housing space, the world-famous Kinsey Institute found a home in Morrison Hall, while in Sycamore Hall, Robert Borkenstein, inventor of the Breathalyzer, hung his hat throughout the 1960s, '70s, and '80s. The Japanese Language Program and the Departments of Central Eurasian Studies and East Asian Languages and Cultures have all had quarters in Goodbody Hall, and for many years Memorial Hall once again served the women of IU housing the Office of Women's Affairs. As part of the master plan to return the historic core of campus to its past role as the focus of student life, Memorial and Goodbody Halls received extensive renovations and once again opened their doors to students in the fall of 2017.

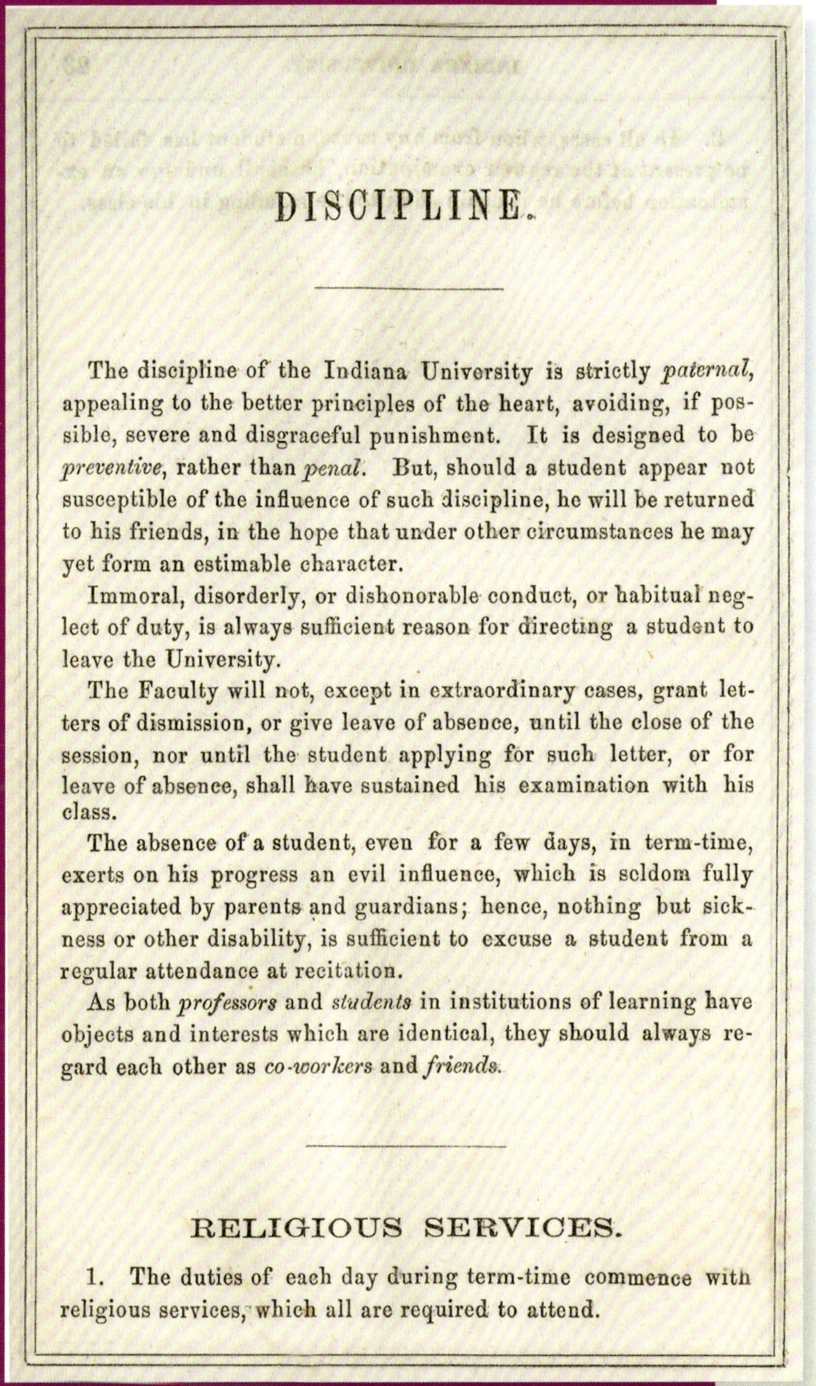

DISCIPLINE.

The discipline of the Indiana University is strictly *paternal*, appealing to the better principles of the heart, avoiding, if possible, severe and disgraceful punishment. It is designed to be *preventive*, rather than *penal*. But, should a student appear not susceptible of the influence of such discipline, he will be returned to his friends, in the hope that under other circumstances he may yet form an estimable character.

Immoral, disorderly, or dishonorable conduct, or habitual neglect of duty, is always sufficient reason for directing a student to leave the University.

The Faculty will not, except in extraordinary cases, grant letters of dismission, or give leave of absence, until the close of the session, nor until the student applying for such letter, or for leave of absence, shall have sustained his examination with his class.

The absence of a student, even for a few days, in term-time, exerts on his progress an evil influence, which is seldom fully appreciated by parents and guardians; hence, nothing but sickness or other disability, is sufficient to excuse a student from a regular attendance at recitation.

As both *professors* and *students* in institutions of learning have objects and interests which are identical, they should always regard each other as *co-workers* and *friends*.

RELIGIOUS SERVICES.

1. The duties of each day during term-time commence with religious services, which all are required to attend.

1862 Catalogue, Indiana University Archives.

In Loco Parentis

President Bryan was well known for his Victorian values and took very seriously the concept of *in loco parentis* (i.e., the idea that the university should act in place of the parents). Housing IU students must have been a tremendous burden on his mind, and he was determined to keep the men and women safe—from one another. On June 20, 1925, he wrote the following letter to Memorial Hall's architect, J. C. Bollenbacher:

> *My dear Mr. Bollenbacher:*
>
> *Some time ago you kindly suggested making plans for walks, et cetera, about the women's memorial dormitory. I wish to call your attention to the fact that fraternity men living on the south side of third street pass through the campus on an approximately straight line toward the men's gymnasium, and probably close to or through the archway of the women's dormitory.*
>
> *I suggest that you give careful consideration to the plans so that they may be provided with a walk which will not take them to or through the dormitory. It may be difficult to do this because their disposition would be to break through the shortest way.*
>
> *Sincerely yours,*
> *William Lowe Bryan*

The flummoxed architect took over a month to respond to this request.

> *The problem you mention to us of devising some way for the men students who live across the street to get* [to] *the main campus without going through the Memorial Archway has also been carefully considered and we have tried to suggest that they follow the west drive entrance and the path to the west of the building. It is impossible, of course, to force them to follow this path and to prevent them from going through Memorial Archway. However, the west path will be lower and will eliminate the clumb* [sic] *over the hill.*[1]

1. William Lowe Bryan to J. C. Bollenbacher, June 20, 1925, "Granger and Bollenbacher, 1924–1925" file, collection C286.110, Indiana University Archives, Indiana University, Bloomington. J. C. Bollenbacher to William Lowe Bryan, July 29, 1925, ibid.

Post–World War II Housing

A Tsunami of Students

Miracles have been performed, with the difficult done at once and the impossible taking just a little longer.

—Corridor

In his biography of Herman B Wells, *Herman B Wells: The Promise of the American University*, author James Capshew aptly describes the influx of students after World War II as a "tsunami" that left university administration scrambling.[1] This virtual flood of students was the result of the Serviceman's Readjustment Act (commonly known at the GI Bill of Rights), which was written into law by President Franklin Roosevelt in 1944. The law was created to benefit veterans to the United States and to invest in the nation's economic future.[2] It provided low-cost mortgages, low-interest loans to start a business, and tuition and living expenses to attend colleges or universities, along with funds for vocational schools and other training programs.

Thousands of veterans took advantage of the GI Bill to attend colleges and universities around the nation. In the peak year of 1947, veterans made up 49 percent of college admissions. By the end date of the original bill in 1956, 7.8 million World War II veterans had attended colleges and universities and other educational venues.[3]

When the fall semester of the 1946 school year began at Indiana University—three weeks late due to the housing shortage—student enrollment had doubled from the preceding year. Over ten thousand students converged on the campus, half of them World War II veterans.[4]

The university quickly improvised its housing options to accommodate this overwhelming number of new students, and existing housing on campus was not nearly adequate. IU put out a call to locals, begging them to assist by making any extra bedrooms available. Men fortunate enough to acquire a dorm room doubled up. Beds were shoved into the most unlikely of places—the Men's Gymnasium had 268 beds, the lounges and game rooms in the Men's Residence Center became sleeping quarters, and the Board of Trustees' meeting room in the Administration Building became home to a dozen men.[5] Fifty-seven rooms were secured for married couples 18 miles west of Bloomington at the Canyon Inn at McCormick's Creek State Park.[6] President Wells was called overseas for several weeks, but before leaving he turned his home over to Alice Nelson, director of the Halls of Residence, who divided it into three apartments for married couples. Despite the extraordinary steps IU administrators took to accommodate as many veterans and their families as possible with existing structures, it became necessary to turn to the U.S. government for help.

Trailer Courts

With the conclusion of World War II, the U.S. government had tremendous surpluses of all sorts, including trailers and barracks. Federal legislation was put into place to assist overburdened universities and colleges in acquiring this surplus property at a reasonable rate, resulting in something like a race as institutions scrambled to secure the goods before other universities and competing government agencies beat them to it.

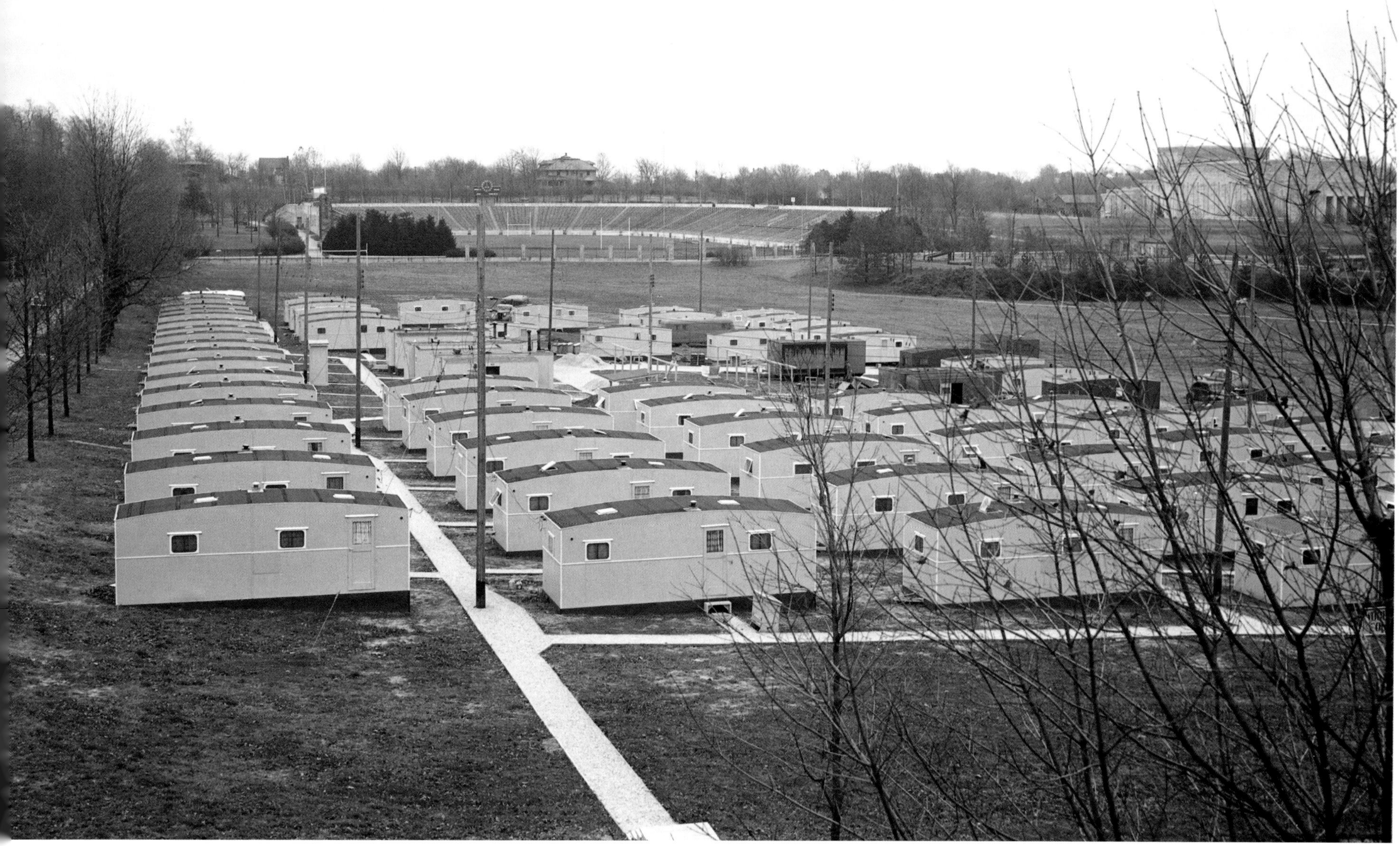

Woodlawn Courts trailer park, home to many Hoosier students and families from 1945 to 1957, 1945. P0030507, IU Archives.

The first supplemental housing units acquired by IU were trailers placed on Woodlawn Field at Tenth Street and Woodlawn Avenue for married veterans and their families. The small trailer court, known as Woodlawn Courts, opened in the fall of 1945 with a plan for seventy-five trailers. Over the next year, the number grew to three hundred Federal Public Housing Authority (FPHA) trailers brought in from all over the Midwest, including the local Crane Naval Surface Warfare Center (where commuting IU students also lived). Rental rates, regulated by the government, ranged from $25 to $32.50 per month, which included utilities. Additional units were secured for laundries, bathrooms, recreational facilities, and a nursery school. The enterprising families also established their own cooperative grocery store.

The trailers were far from glamorous—they were, after all, former military houses with no running water and few amenities. But for the veterans and families who had faced stressful separation during World War II, Woodlawn Courts trailers might have seemed like Shangri-la. On arrival in Bloomington, each trailer was cleaned, painted light tan, and set on wooden supports. Units came mostly furnished and had two studio couches, a table and chairs, kitchenette with kerosene

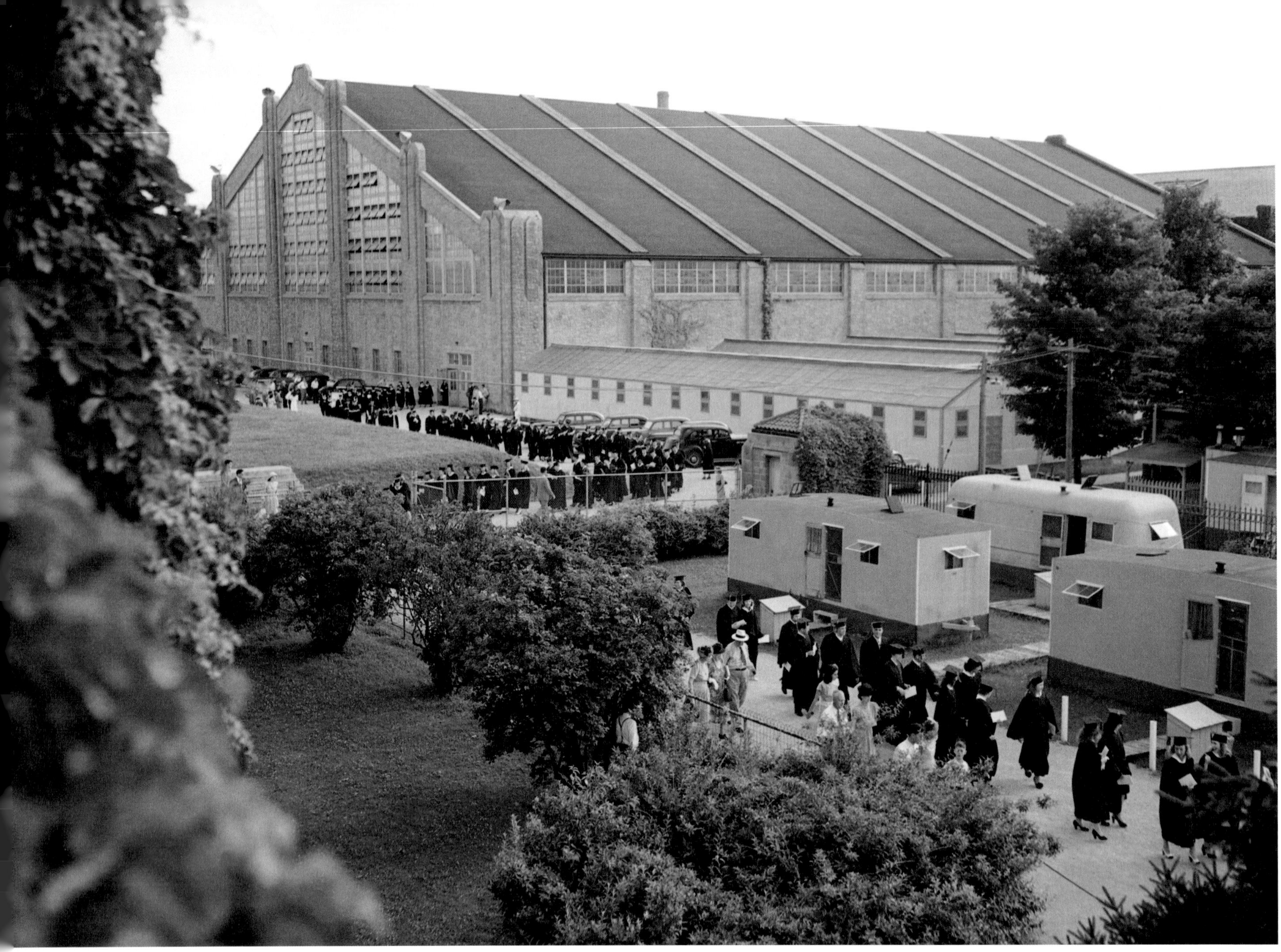

cookstove, icebox, sink, and built-in cabinets. It was difficult to maintain privacy with the trailers set close together, but as a result, the families bunking there evolved into a close-knit community and many turned down better housing options when they became available. Woodlawn Courts met the fate of most temporary housing, however, and was phased out. The last of the trailers were removed in 1957 and sold at auction, the debris was burned, and the field cleaned and relandscaped.

IU's student-veterans received $90 each month from the government, and for many, it was difficult or impossible to turn over a third of that for rent. The university began to receive letters from students asking to bring their own trailers, which for many was the only way they could afford a higher education. In response, in 1946 university-owned land was set aside on South Henderson for Hillcrest Trailer Park, where students could park their homes on wheels. Adding power lines and setting up the trailers for toilet and shower facilities was not without cost to the university, which in turn, charged tenants $12.50 a month for utilities. By 1953, the demand for space to park privately owned trailers had dissipated sufficiently that IU trustees voted to dismantle the trailer court and sell the property.

Facing, Graduating students parade past Men's Gymnasium and temporary trailers and barracks, 1946. P0033763, IU Archives.

Below, Hoosier Courts, repurposed and renovated military barracks, 1946. P0030543, IU Archives.

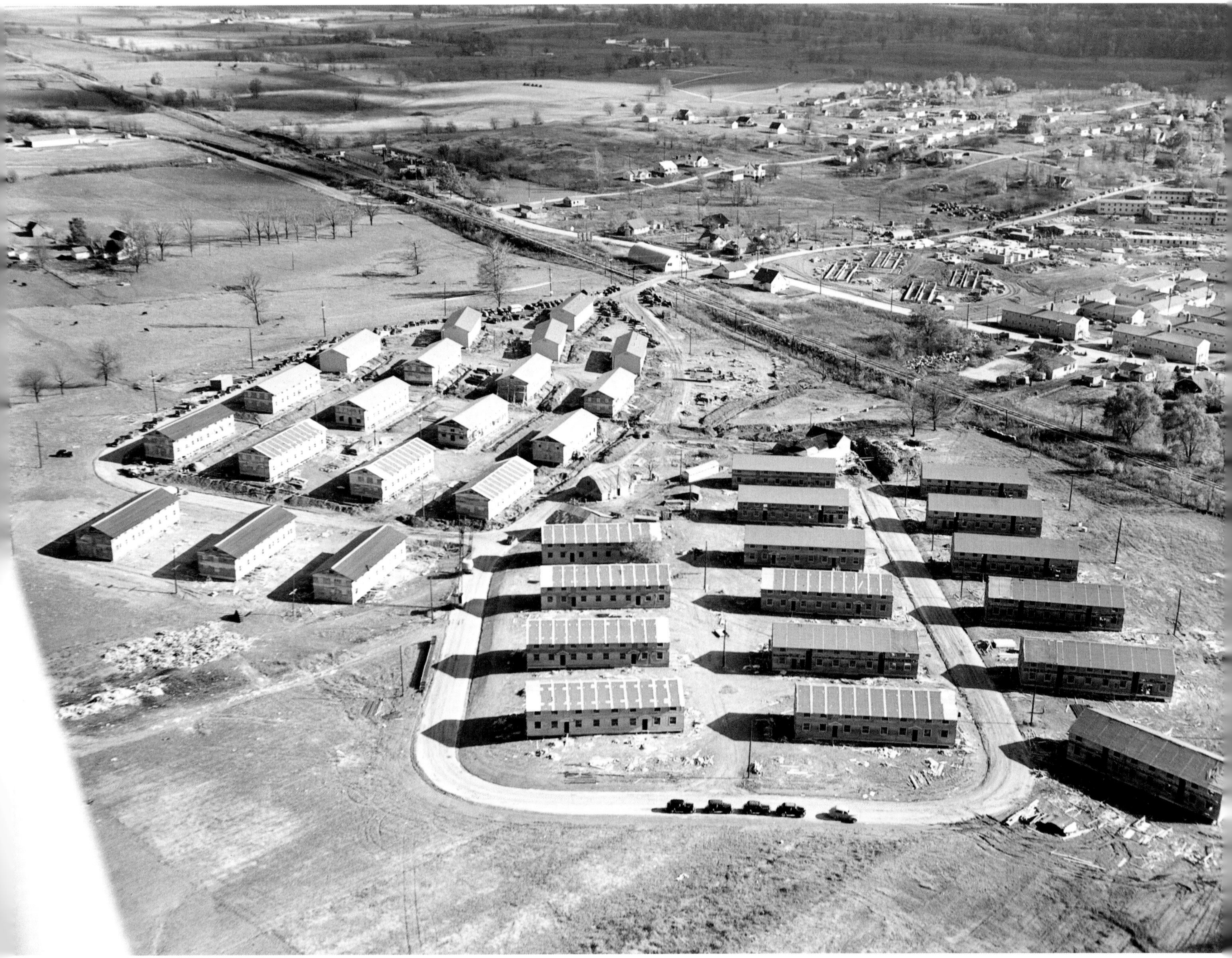

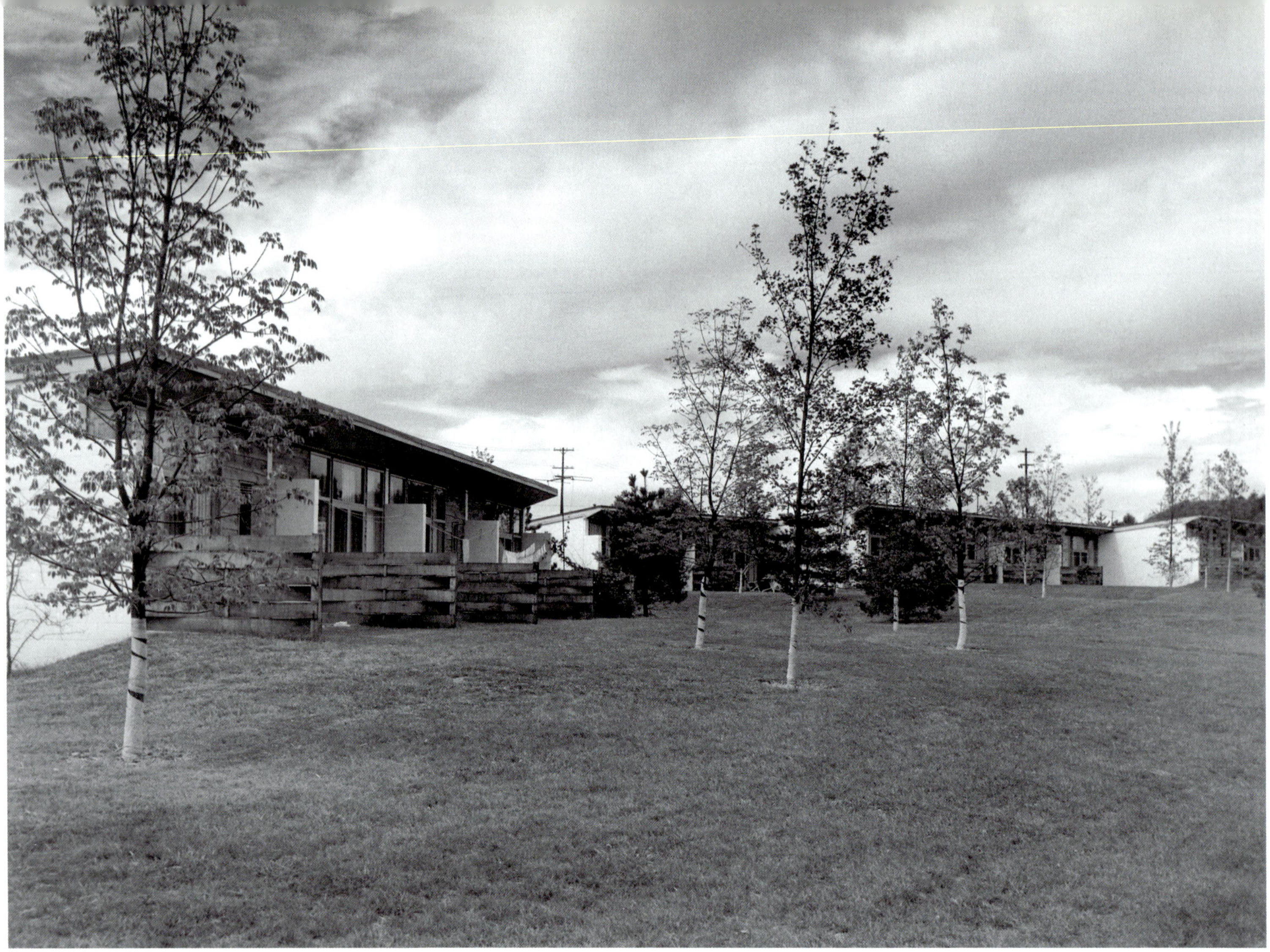

"New" Hoosier Courts, 1951. P0022776, IU Archives.

HOOSIER COURTS / UNIVERSITY APARTMENTS

The trailers went a long way to help provide for the influx of student-veterans with families, but more such accommodations were needed. In its search for suitable housing, IU found and quickly snapped up thirty-five barracks from Camp Grant, Illinois. Disassembled and transferred to the university farm north of Tenth Street and the Illinois Central Railroad, the barracks were remodeled into 280 apartments for married students and the site named University Apartments.[7] Opened in 1946, the apartments included a living room, kitchenette, bath, and two bedrooms, and were rented furnished for $42.50 per month. In 1948, the apartments were renamed Hoosier Courts, and the new permanent apartment buildings under construction on Third Street acquired the University Apartments name. Over the next decade, additional apartments—the "New" Hoosier Courts—were added to accommodate the change in the appearance of the national student body, many of whom were marrying before or during college.

One of the most notable features of Hoosier Courts was the cooperative nursery school established by residents in 1948. IU donated an old barn still standing on the former farmland and, in exchange, fathers and mothers toiled to ready the old structure for their children. Professional staff were hired to train the mothers to assist with teaching. While the "Old" Hoosier Courts began to come down in 1966, the school and the newer buildings remained. In the early 1970s the school, which was administratively under IU's School of Education, faced potential shutdown. With a budget of just over $20,000 and the only real income coming from parents paying $26 per semester per child, it was difficult for the School of Education to financially justify the support it continued to invest in the school.

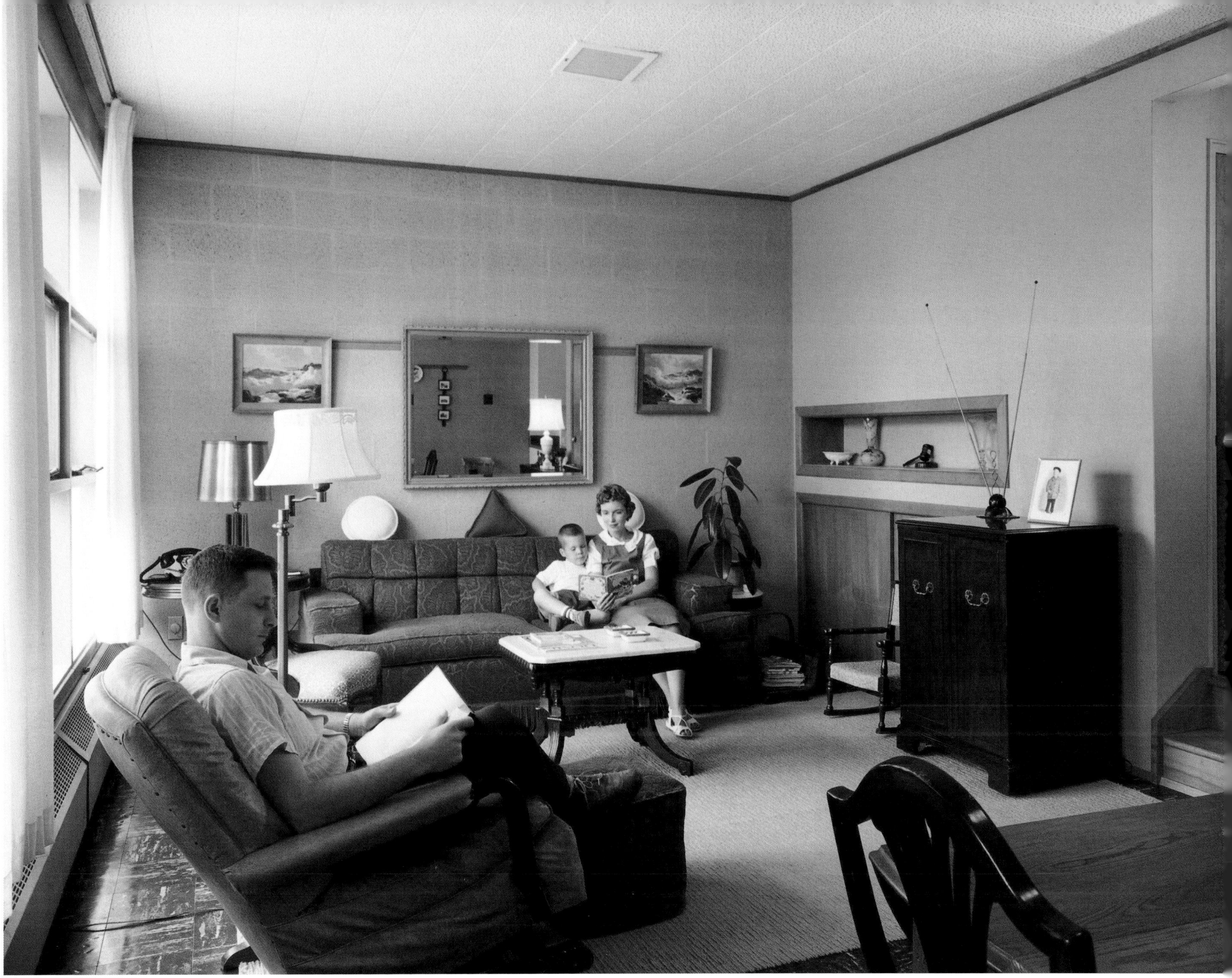

Law student Birch Bayh with wife, Marvella, and son, Evan, in their Hoosier Courts living room, 1959.
P0035976, IU Archives. Photo credit: Jack Welpott, Indiana University.

Fortunately for Hoosier Courts, U.S. Senator Birch Bayh had lived in Hoosier Courts in the 1950s and his son, Evan, was an alumnus of the preschool. Senator Bayh wrote to then chancellor Herman B Wells to ask if anything could be done to save what he saw as a valuable program. Chancellor Wells worked his magic and although the school continued to struggle in years to come, it was saved from closure.[8] Hoosier Courts Nursery School continues in operation today at North Union Court (the barn is long gone) as a cooperative with parental involvement and has often been recognized for its high-quality program.

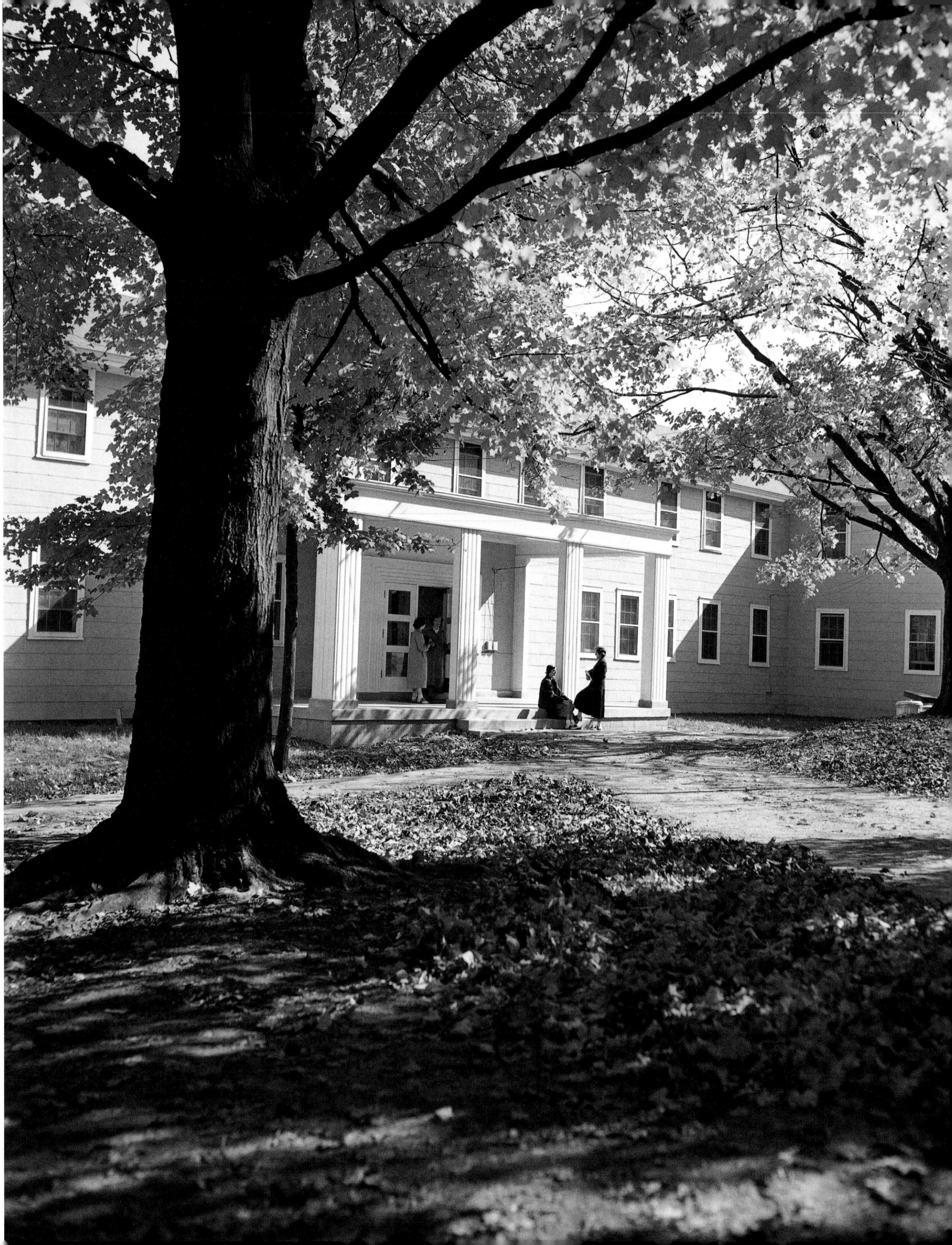

Walnut Hall, one of eight repurposed military barracks, Trees Center, 1948. P0032498, IU Archives. Photo credit: Allen Graham.

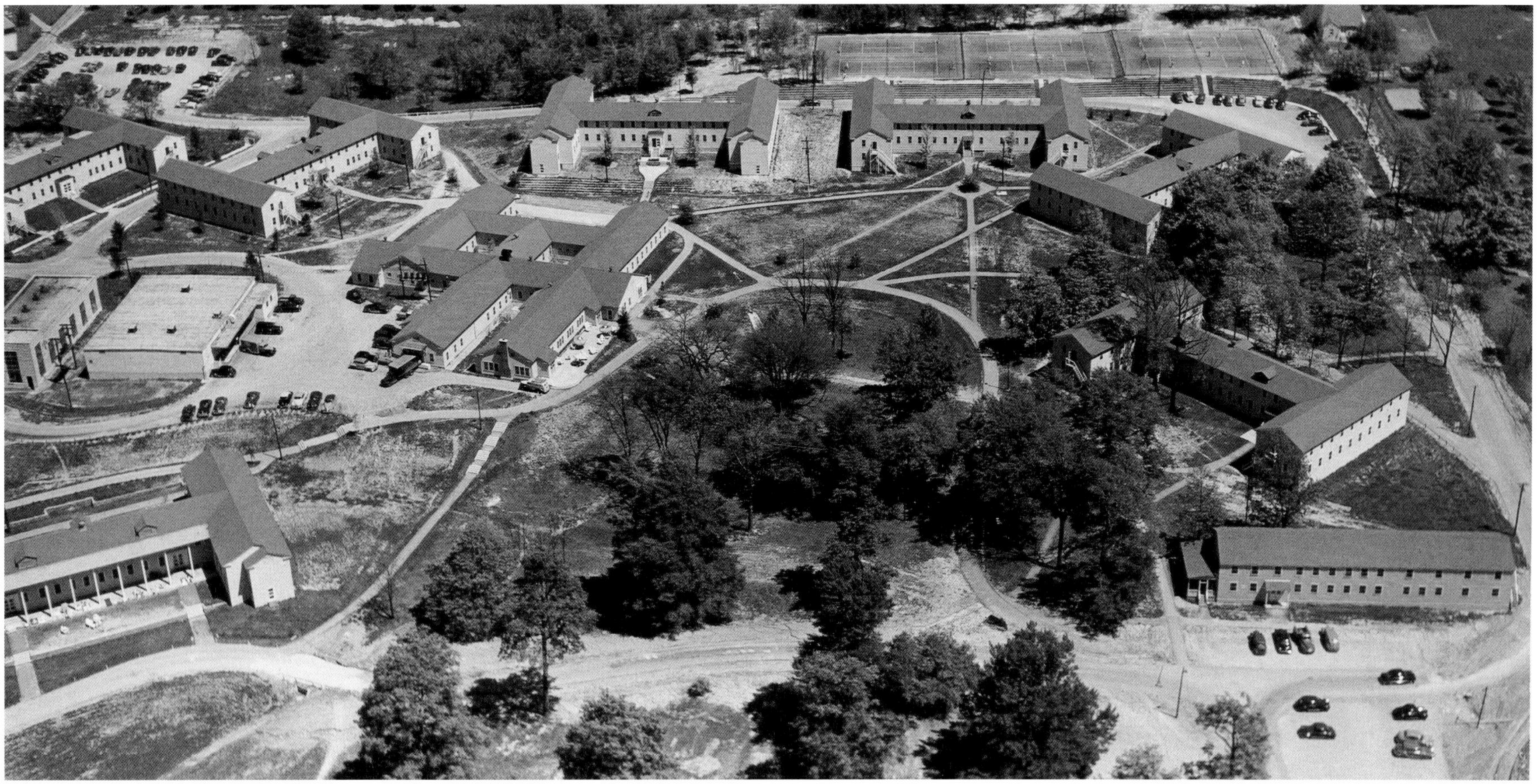

Aerial view of Trees Center, 1949. P0022939, IU Archives.

TREES CENTER

With the problem of housing married students somewhat solved, university administrators traveled throughout the country in search of suitable housing, goods, and service buildings for the remaining swell of student-veterans. On June 15, 1946, President Wells signed a contract on behalf of the university with the FPHA to acquire surplus military housing from the Naval Air Station at Bunker Hill, Indiana (now Grissom Air Reserve Base). Per the contract, IU was to remove the five-year-old structures, clean up the sites, and reerect them in Bloomington within ninety days. These eight buildings were set up in a wooded area of campus, which was previously part of the Smithwood family farm, and each christened with an arboreal name and collectively called Smithwood Center. When a new Smithwood Hall opened in the mid-1950s (now Daniel Read Hall), the name was changed to Trees Center.

Desirous of making the former barracks as homey as possible, Alice Nelson sent floor plans and her ideas to a designer at L. S. Ayres & Co.: "I had thought perhaps we would like to use some wall paper in some of them, in order to make them seem more feminine. The wood work in the halls is to be white and the hall ways are to be a cream color. Student rooms are in light shades of blue, green, and cream. . . . President Wells is very interested in these buildings and is anxious that they be most attractive, and if possible, a little unusual. He wants the students to forget that they have ever been army barracks and that they be as desirable as any of our regular dormitories."[9] In addition to creating lounges, several snack bars were constructed throughout the center's buildings, which exited out onto terraces with Adirondack chairs and shade umbrellas. Continuing with the exterior, architectural firm Burns and James did its best to dress up the buildings by bringing a touch of the Old South to Bloomington through the addition

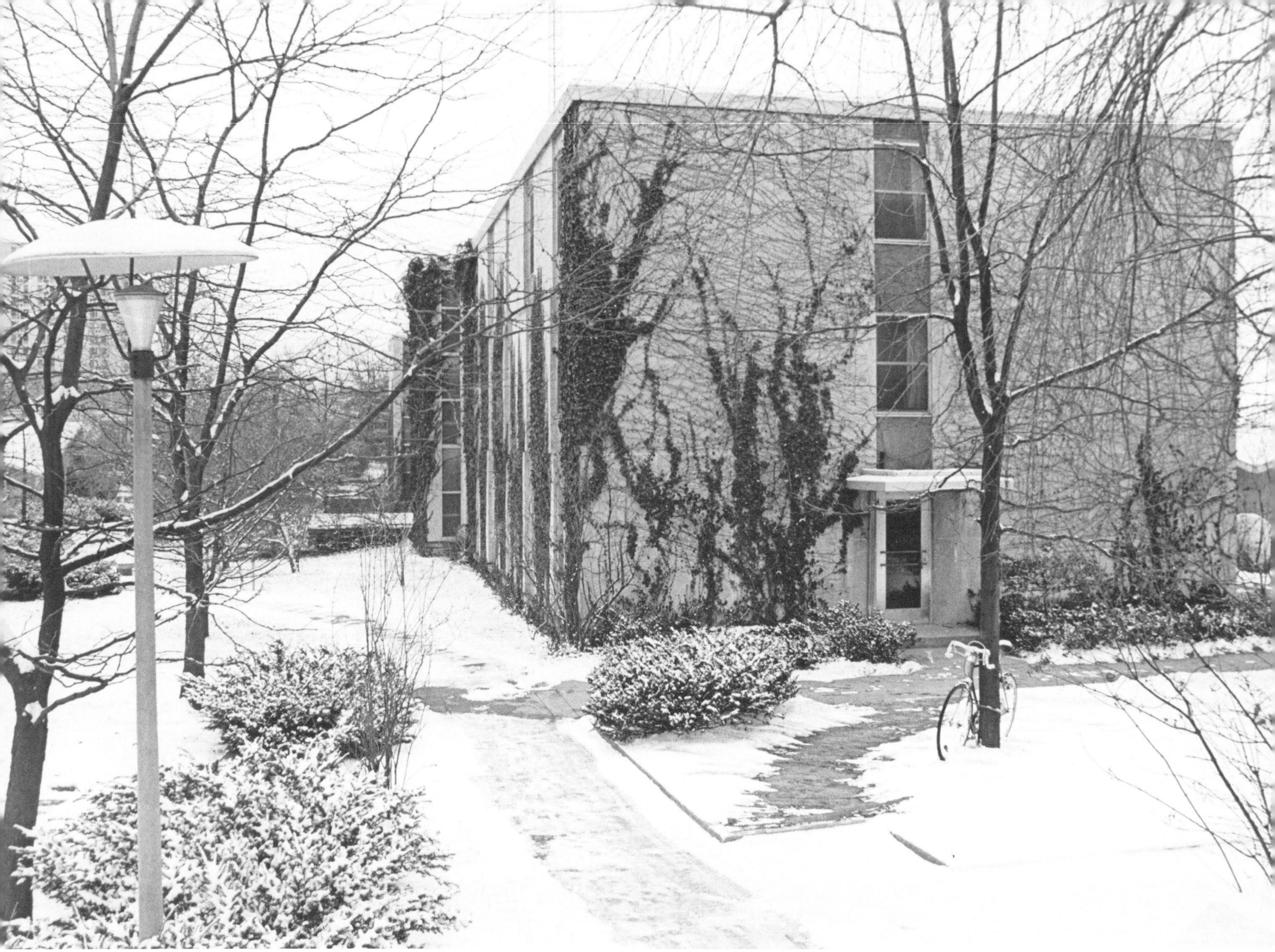

Residence hall in the complex first known as Rogers II, later John W. Ashton Center, undated. P0026094, IU Archives.

of columns to the porches of Oak and Walnut Halls. All told, some $125,000 was spent on remodeling and redecorating the buildings.[10]

Acquiring the barracks was a sound investment; they helped IU through a housing crunch and went on to serve the university for years despite their original temporary status. (As pointed out by the *IU Alumni Magazine* in January 1965, "there is nothing so permanent as a temporary building.") By the mid-1960s, however, it was time to begin decommissioning the structures, and students still living there were moved to more permanent housing at no increase in their fee. Still, Pine and Linden Hall held on, used by the Schools of Fine Arts and Music for studio and practice space, respectively. In 1979, Linden Hall, with its makeshift acoustic tiles of egg cartons and apple crates, was demolished. Pine Hall, as determined as the veterans it once housed, remained in place into the early

1990s, by then looking like it had been through a battle itself, with fallen chunks of siding, plywood covering what were once windows, and the sea-green roof bandaged with a motley assortment of leftover shingles.

ROGERS I AND II (JOHN W. ASHTON CENTER)

Many an alum has spent time at Rogers Center, residing in either the temporary Rogers I or in the more permanent Rogers II, which later became known as the Graduate Residence Center (GRC) and in 1980 as the John W. Ashton Center.

Rogers I consisted of eight two-story barracks buildings moved to Bloomington from Evansville, Indiana, and four one-story barracks from Walkerton, Indiana, which together provided for 698 unmarried men. Unlike the Trees Center, there were no attempts to disguise the buildings' origins as utilitarian barracks, as IU's contract with the FPHA stipulated that the buildings were to be removed within two years "after termination of the current national emergency, with provision for subsequent extensions of one year each if the housing emergency still exists."[11]

Rogers II included the first buildings the university erected with an eye to permanency—but also, economy—after World War II. Designed by the Indianapolis architectural firm Burns and James, the seven buildings were two stories high, 230 feet long, with dorm rooms designed for double occupancy. Student rooms had painted concrete block walls, asphalt tile floors, and painted precast concrete-slab ceilings. A separate one-story dining hall with a partial basement was constructed to serve the residents of both Rogers I and II. Exterior materials consisted of reinforced concrete and brick trimmed with Indiana limestone. When opened in 1946, the buildings were considered to be the pinnacle of dormitory modernity. Over the next decades, additions were made to the center, including two lounge buildings, a library, and residential facilities. By the time it was dedicated as the GRC in 1970, there were seventeen buildings. In the late 1990s and early 2000s IU began phasing out the buildings (then called Ashton Center) as dormitories, and in 2005, the Board of Trustees voted to raze several of them to make room for the Union Street Center.

FACULTY HOUSING

Given the influx of student-veterans, the university had to attract and house additional faculty, as well. President Wells received letters from faculty and department chairs begging that something be done. In the spring of 1946, IU history professor Oscar O. Winther wrote to President Wells from California, where he was doing research, that he would be among the "homeless faculty members" when he returned in the fall, as he had been wholly unsuccessful in securing housing. "I have tapped every source I can think of, and the most encouraging reply comes from a person who says, 'If I can get rid of my present undesirable tenant, then you will be eighth on my list.'" B. F. Skinner, then serving as chairman of the Psychology Department, wrote to President Wells in January 1946 describing the challenging Bloomington housing market and how the inflation rates put the properties out of reach of the average college professor. "I would not write you a letter of this sort if I had not given the matter serious thought and did not believe the situation to be very grave, indeed. A solution must be found, and it seems to be up to the University to find it."[12] Unknown to Skinner, the administration had already been quietly working to resolve the faculty housing situation, but a major obstacle was the postwar shortage of building materials. IU worked with several prefabricated housing companies to quickly erect thirtysome small prefab houses on the outskirts of campus. Additionally, the university converted large houses it already owned on Third Street and on the corner of Tenth Street and Jordan Avenue into faculty apartments, reaping about fifteen additional spaces.

Indiana University did everything in its power to make a home for returning veterans and their families, which President Herman B Wells clearly saw as a sound investment in Indiana's future and in the future of the nation.

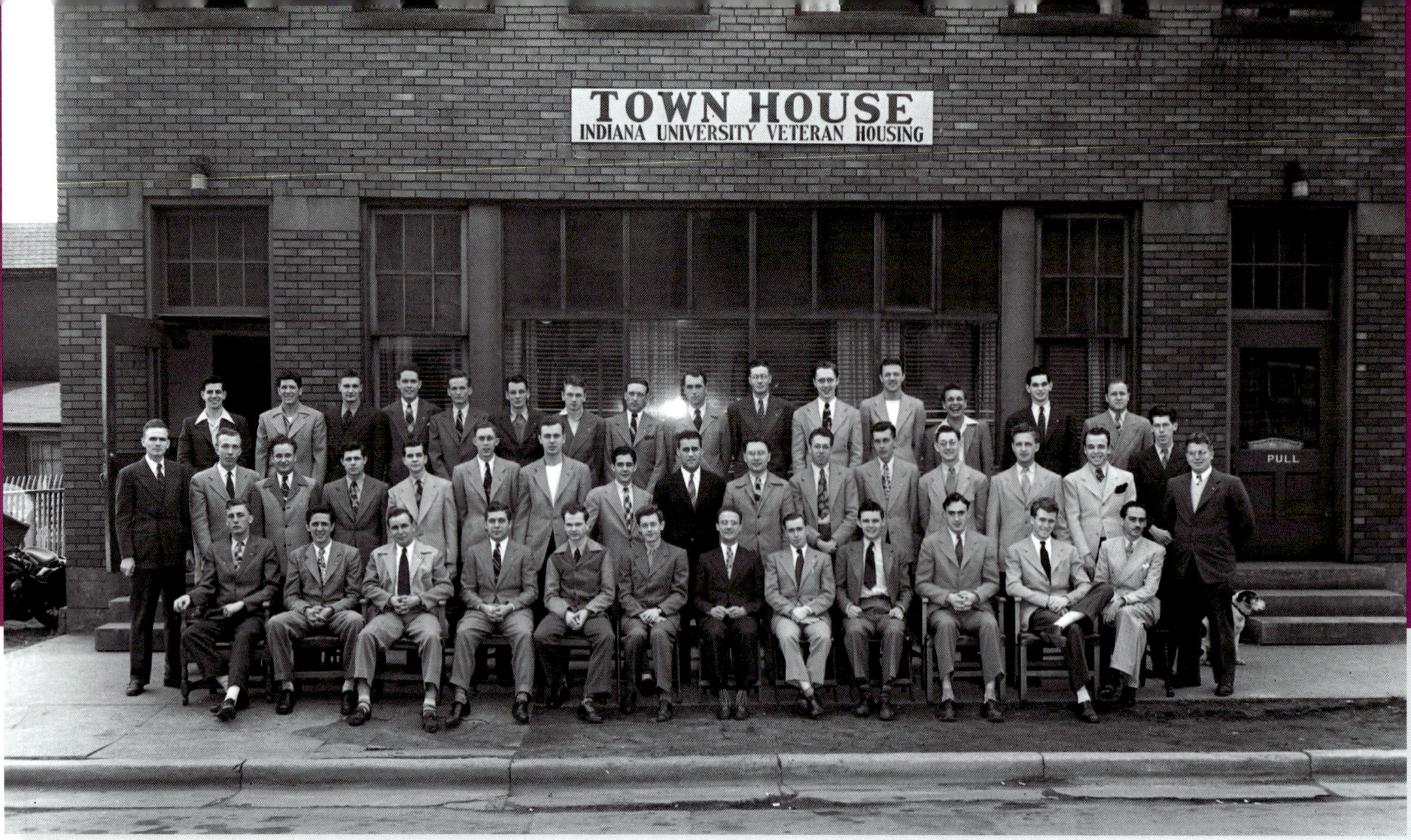

More Temporary Housing

Most of these facilities were instituted as answers to the housing shortage but later met academic needs:

Hoosier Halls North and South
(1946–73)
Former barracks dormitories north of the Fieldhouse boarded unmarried men.

Town House
(1946–47)
A former United Service Organizations (USO) building on Fourth Street housed approximately 115 unmarried men.

Cottage Grove Apartments (aka Cottage Grove North and South)
(1946–ca. 1993)
Two two-story barracks home to married couples and located on Cottage Grove Avenue one block north of Tenth Street.

Cottage Grove Trailers (aka Woodlawn Courts Annex)
(1946–57)
Forty-nine trailers from Nebraska provided married housing.

Campus Club (aka Union Club)
(ca. 1946–73)
Former officers' club at Bunker Hill at Seventh Street and Woodlawn Avenue housed campus visitors and male students. It contained eighty-nine sleeping rooms, lounges, offices, a solarium, bakery, dining room, kitchen, and storage facilities.

Above, Town House veteran housing located on the south side of Fourth Street between Walnut and College, 1946. P0034179, IU Archives.

Those Iconic Green Trailers

Alumni from the latter half of the twentieth century might remember the green trailers that made up the Walnut Grove Trailer Court stretching south for several blocks from Seventeenth Street to Fourteenth Street between Walnut Grove and Forest Avenue. Although they were not part of the flurry of new housing after World War II, these trailers, consisting of new, “modern” units, answered the university’s need for married housing in the later 1950s. The plan for the court was approved by the Board of Trustees in 1956, and before the initial forty-five units even arrived on campus, every one of them was reserved. The couples paid $35 a month plus utilities. Additional units were added over the years and the Walnut Grove trailers proved to be a popular and economic choice for both married and older students. They remained in place until the late 1980s.

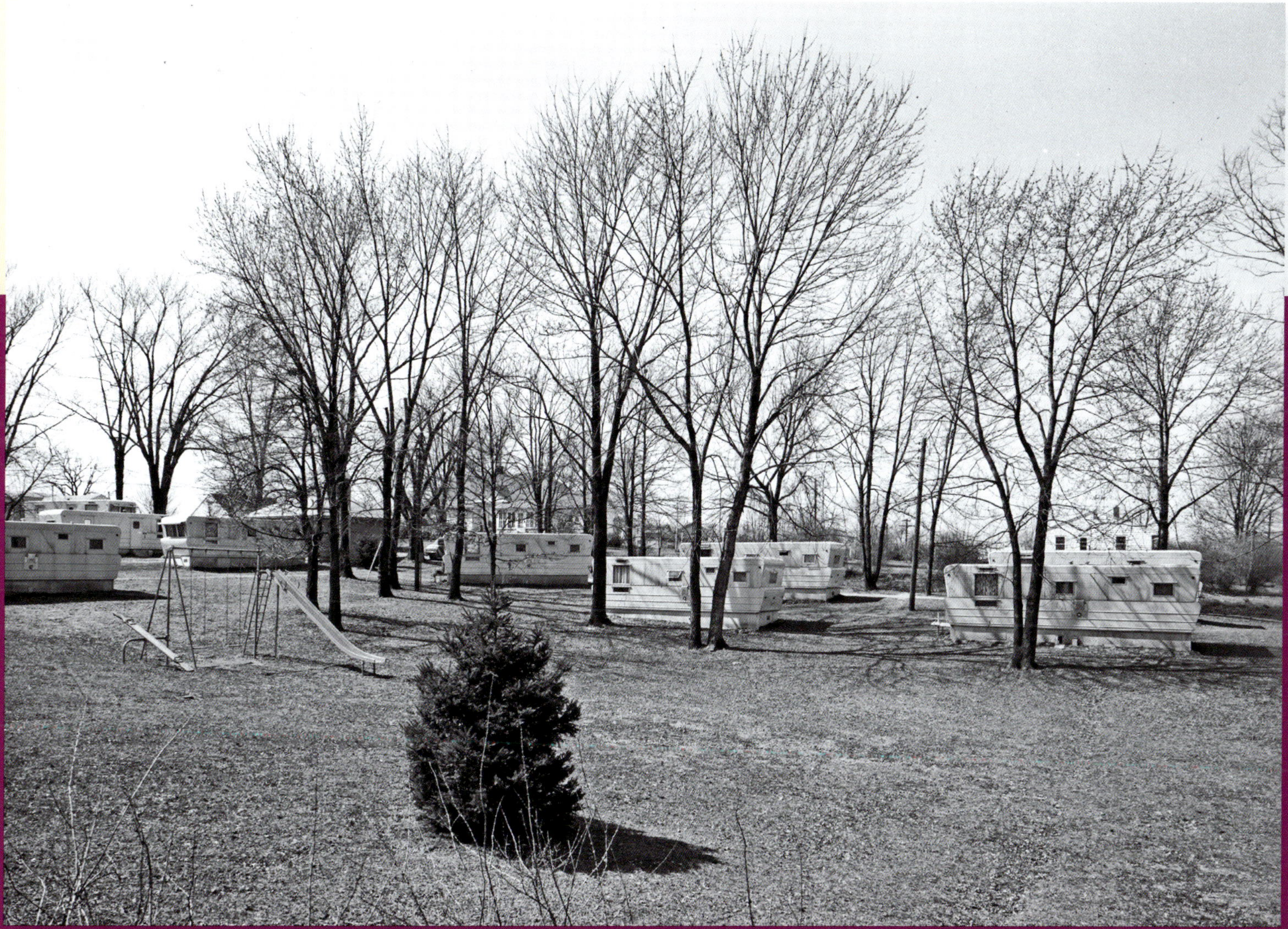

Walnut Grove Trailer Court, 1959. P0067216, IU Archives.

Joseph A. Wright Quadrangle

Home of Eighteen "Houses"

Getting together, eating together, and living together has strengthened social relations in all human activities. . . . When this closest contact of life comes in the college years, its vivifying power, its lasting influences are immeasurably increased.

—Indiana University President Herman B Wells

In the midst of their scrambling to secure temporary housing for the rush of students after World War II, administrators had the additional task of quickly devising plans for more permanent housing, as enrollment forecasts made clear that the number of incoming students would continue to climb. While discussions and plans for a new men's dormitory began in 1944, as of summer 1947, ground still had not been broken. At the June 1947 Board of Trustees meeting, President Herman B Wells was clearly exasperated by this lack of progress. He told the trustees that the crowded housing conditions could not continue and instructed Vice President Joseph Franklin to develop a financing proposal. In September, the trustees approved Franklin's plan, and construction commenced before the year was out.

For this project, Eggers and Higgins of New York was the consulting architect with Indianapolis-based Burns and James the supervising architect. One of the first considerations in the facility design was the site's topography at the corner of Tenth Street and Jordan Avenue. Rather than damage the rolling southern Indiana hills, the interconnected three-story buildings were placed at varying levels to take advantage of the land's natural terrain.

For the design of the buildings, the architects developed a new modern collegiate style. Theodore Young with Eggers and Higgins might have been influenced by what he heard at the 1947 Conference on Urban University Planning. Conference notes he shared with President Wells stated that university architecture "is veering away from buildings in romantic styles. All over the country the trend is toward a rationalized contemporary architecture that best serves the purpose of the building. It was felt that the important thing is what goes on the inside rather than its exterior and this should be the deciding factor, when the two are in conflict."[1]

Although the focus may have been on the interior, the exterior of the men's quad also received abundant attention and was, in fact, the subject of much discord between the architects and the Indiana University Board of Trustees. All agreed on Indiana limestone, but the architects proposed a controversial ochre-colored band of brick between the windows of the fourth floor to break the monotony of the limestone expanse. The buildings today are proof that the architects won that battle. Situated in an H-shaped configuration, the complex is constructed of rough-face limestone in a random ashlar pattern. The modern collegiate style gives a nod to both Art Deco and Art Moderne with the buildings' simple lines and forms and the hooded light fixtures with copper ornamentation. Relief panels by sculptor Joseph P. Pollia, depicting art, business, law, drama, science, football, track, basketball, and baseball further adorn the exterior.

Planned with a home-away-from-home feel, the large quad buildings were divided into eighteen "houses" connected by stairways, breezeways, and hallways, with each lodging some

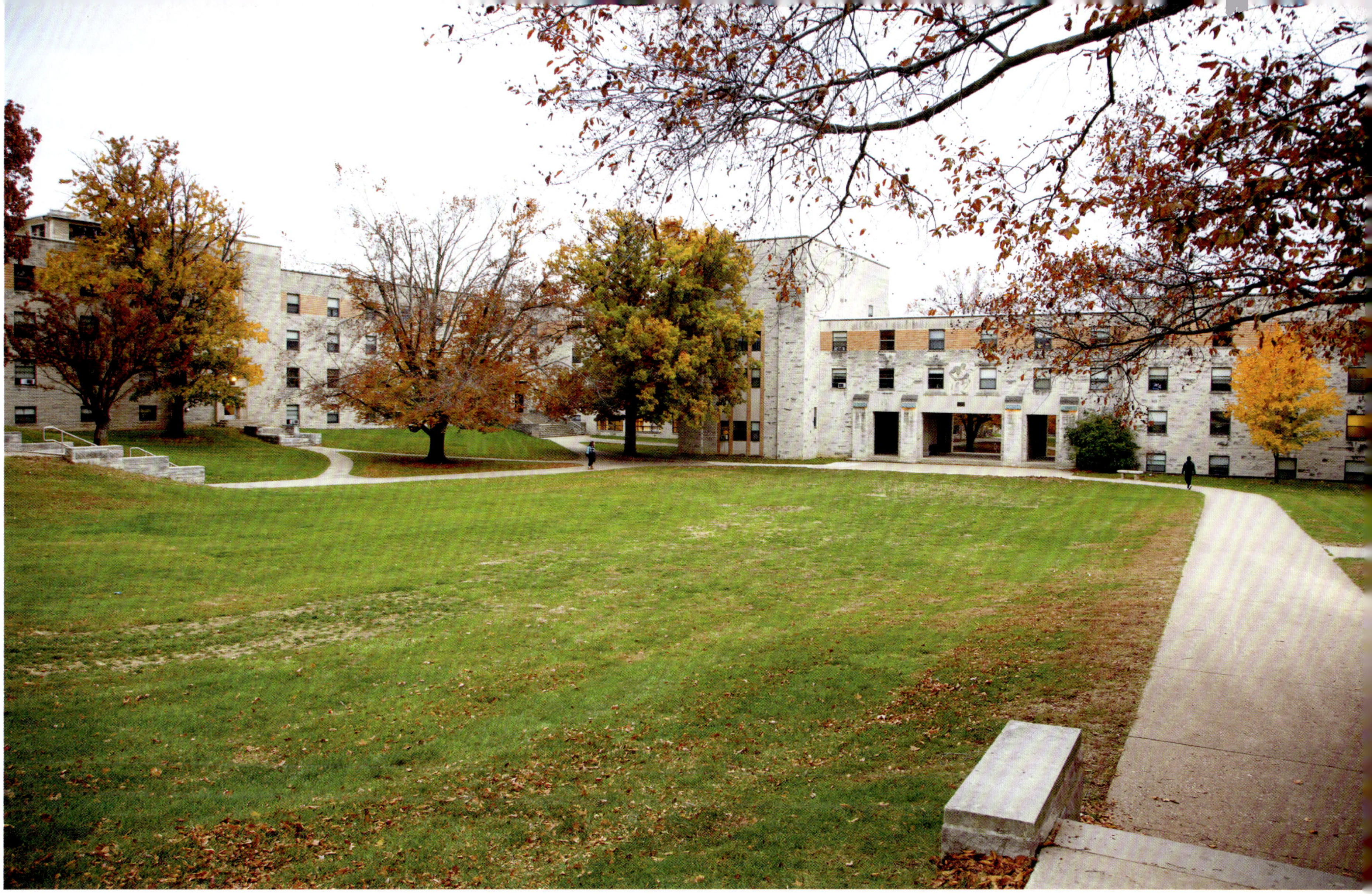

Joseph A. Wright Quadrangle as seen from Tenth Street, 2016. Photo credit: Tyagan Miller.

fifty-five men with a total capacity of 1,021 residents. The design included eighteen rooftop lounges, a large main lounge, a library, four recreation rooms, a party room, a snack bar, and a small nonsectarian chapel. When completed, the dining hall (the Wright Place Food Court) had a floor space of 16,000 square feet, the largest student dining facility and the largest single room on campus excluding the Indiana University Auditorium. The dining room served a second purpose—as a dance hall with capacity of five thousand guests. Massive black columns crowned by caps of bronze support the roof, and the room had two tiers of windows to endow the space with ample natural light. In 1957, the upper windows were covered with original murals depicting university history, created by visiting professor and artist Garo Antreasian (see sidebar).

Halls of Residence director Alice Nelson worked diligently to make the facilities warm, welcoming, and as practical as possible. Dorm rooms included desks recessed into the wall under a bookcase, two-door wardrobes with drawers and mirrors, and a new addition to student rooms: telephones. She took architect Edward James to task over what she viewed as glaring omissions on details. "I cannot understand why some of the most essential things such as four keys for every room, picture molding in student rooms and shelves in the bathrooms seem to cause so much difficulty. I have literally spent hours and weeks of my time trying to see that these three essentials are incorporated." She signed off on this missive with a postscript conveying her exhaustion with the housing situation she had been working on for nearly five years: "P.S.

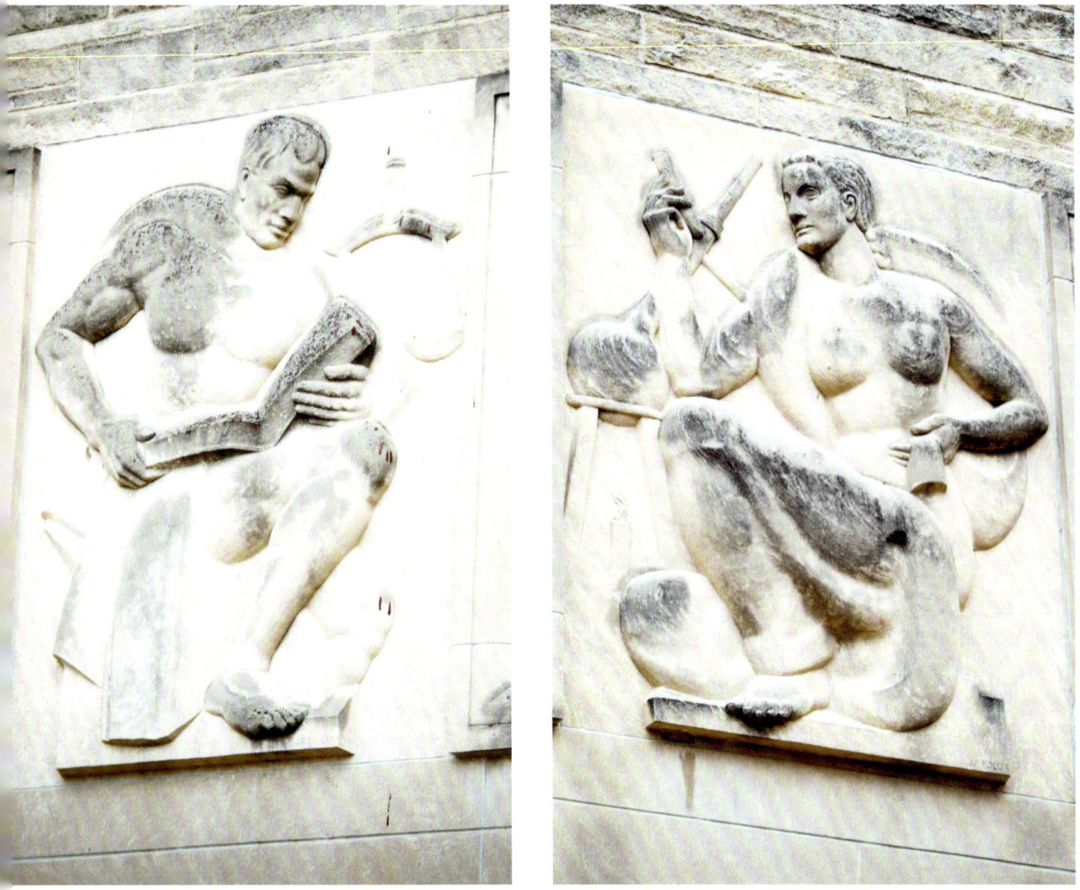

Study of law as depicted by sculptor Joseph P. Pollia, one of several disciplines and pastimes he completed throughout Wright Quad, 2016. Photo credit: Tyagan Miller.

I have about reached my limit. I hope at the present moment I shall never have to build another dormitory where Ed. James is the architect."[2] (Nelson did not get her way; James designed several more projects for the university, including Daniel Read Hall.)

In 1949 each "house" was given a name honoring a member of the first class of IU students, the first trustees, or first faculty. Over the years the houses have established their own identities and strengths, such as the Dodds House competitive Little 500 cycling team. In 1959 the complex was renamed the Joseph A. Wright Quadrangle. One of the first ten students admitted to IU, Wright enjoyed a career in politics, including serving as Indiana's governor from 1849 to 1857. In 1968 Wright Quad became coed to accommodate the growing female student population, and 250 women moved into four of the houses.

Today, Wright Quadrangle remains attractive to students for its central campus location and its proximity to Wells Library across the street.

The Wright Murals

Soaring high above the heads of diners in Wright dining hall are colorful murals that wrap around the room and tell the story of Indiana University. The original six murals were designed, painted, and installed in situ in 1957 by Hoosier muralist Garo Antreasian. He went on to be the first master printer of the Tamarind Lithography Workshop in Los Angeles, as well as the first technical director of the Tamarind Institute in Albuquerque.

The murals each portray distinct periods of the university's history, commencing with the *1820–1850* panel, which opens with the Corydon Statehouse, where state leaders set aside land in Monroe County for Indiana Seminary. Antreasian's subsequent panels are *1850–1900, 1900–1920, 1920–1938,* followed by *The Modern Concept* and *Mid-Twentieth Century*. In 1998 the murals were restored, and IU alumnus Mark Flickinger was selected to add a seventh mural focusing on student life and achievements spanning 1958–98.

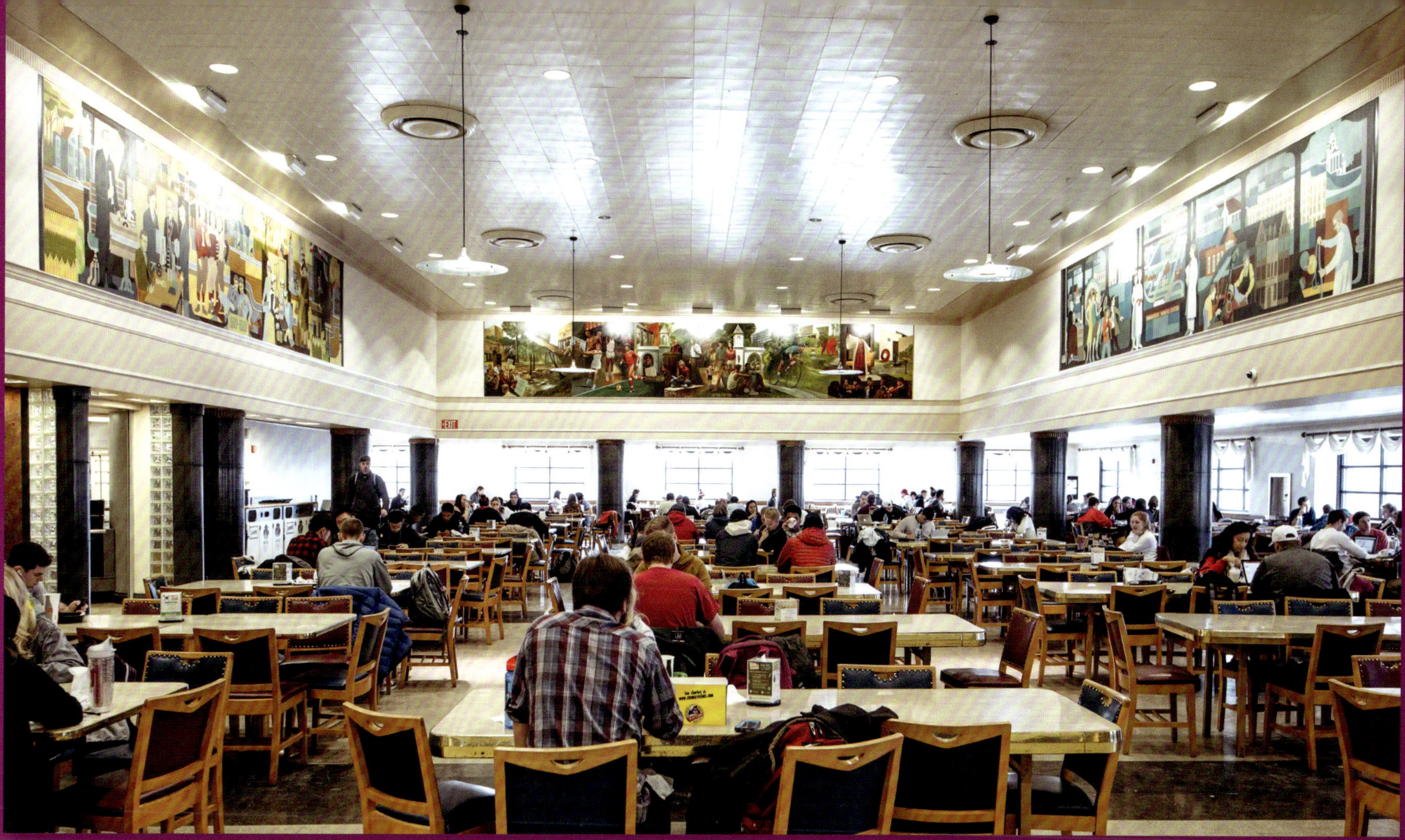

Garo Antreasian murals in Wright Quadrangle cafeteria, 2017. Photo credit: Tyagan Miller.

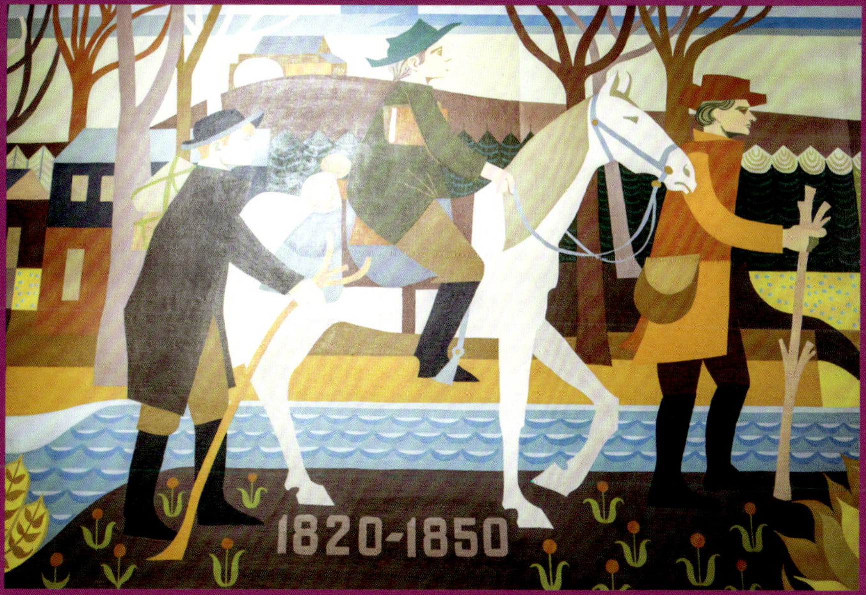

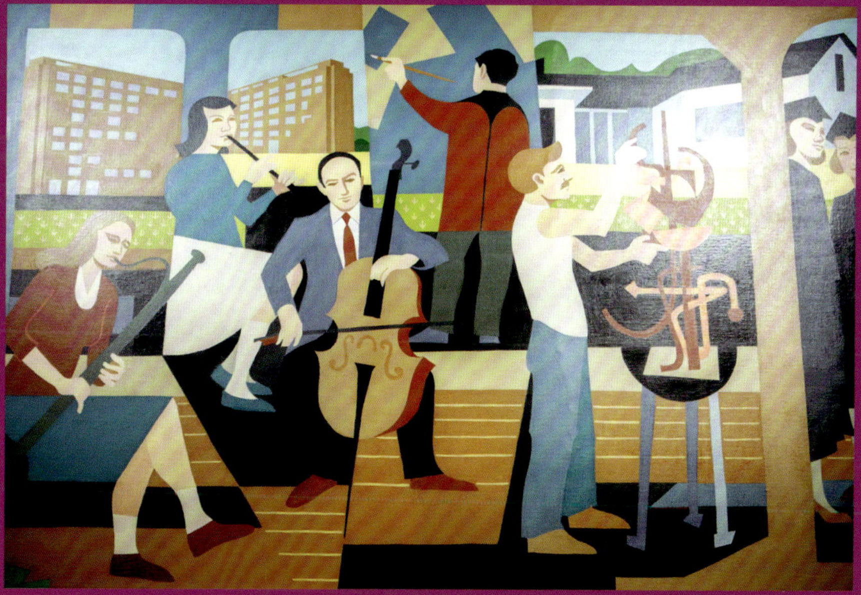

Left and right, Antreasian murals depicting early Indiana University life, 2017. Photo credit: Tyagan Miller.

Daniel Read Hall

The X Building

I really loved Smithwood. I thought it was just a beautiful place. I thought the design was very clever with the four wings. It was just fun to live there.

—Barbara Gordon Grande, Class of 1960

The rush of post–World War II campus housing developments continued throughout the 1950s (only to begin anew with the arrival of baby boomers on campus in the 1960s). In 1945 architects first presented drawings for the women's dormitory that came to be called Smithwood Hall (later Daniel Read Hall), but university administrators continued to focus on housing veterans—the majority male—and their families, as the needs of these groups were the most pressing. Once the veterans were settled into temporary and new permanent structures, attention returned to additional housing for IU women; at the time, the only permanent home for coeds was within the Wells Quadrangle.

Designed by architect Edward D. James of Indianapolis, with Eggers and Higgins (New York) serving as the consulting architect, Read Hall was completed in 1955. It was an exciting, new concept, considered state of the art at the time, featuring half baths shared by every two rooms rather than the typical common bathroom. The dormitory was built in an *X*, with four wings (Beck, Clark, Curry, and Landes) that connected in the center, called the hub.

Although Read now only has one dining room (designed with input from students), originally each seven-story wing included a dining room served from a central kitchen. Each wing also included its own recreation room and lounge with fireplaces, an elevator, and a redwood roof deck for sunbathing. Student rooms, mostly doubles, began on the second floor, with singles on the top floor. The four wings were connected by underground tunnels.

The exterior compliments that of its neighbor to the north, Wright Quadrangle, which was completed in 1949. Like Wright, Read was built in Modern style: the facade was Indiana limestone laid in a random ashlar pattern, with a salmon-colored band of brick toward the top of the building. Inside, the student rooms featured built-in wardrobes with sliding doors, sliding windows, two single beds and desks, a lounge chair, floor lamp, and telephone. When constructed, it housed nearly 1,100 women, making it the largest university dormitory in the Midwest. Its proximity to the School of Education (now Jacobs School of Music) made Read desirable housing for the many aspiring teachers attending the university.

Since the new women's dormitory had been placed on a tract of land purchased from the Smithwood family, university officials called it Smithwood Hall. As discussion ensued for a more permanent name, Arbutus Center and Alice Nelson Hall were among the suggestions. In May 1957, the All University Committee on Names proposed Daniel Read Hall in honor of Daniel Read, professor of ancient languages at IU from 1843 to 1856. Read was a proponent of women's education and permitted women from the Monroe County Female Seminary to

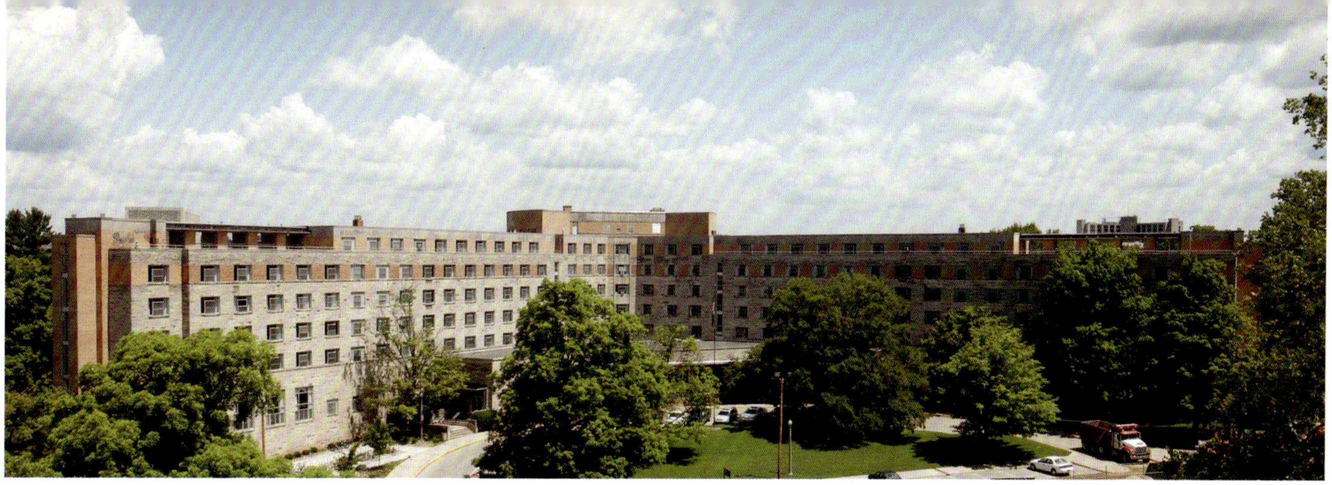

West elevation of Daniel Read Hall, undated. Photo credit: Indiana University.

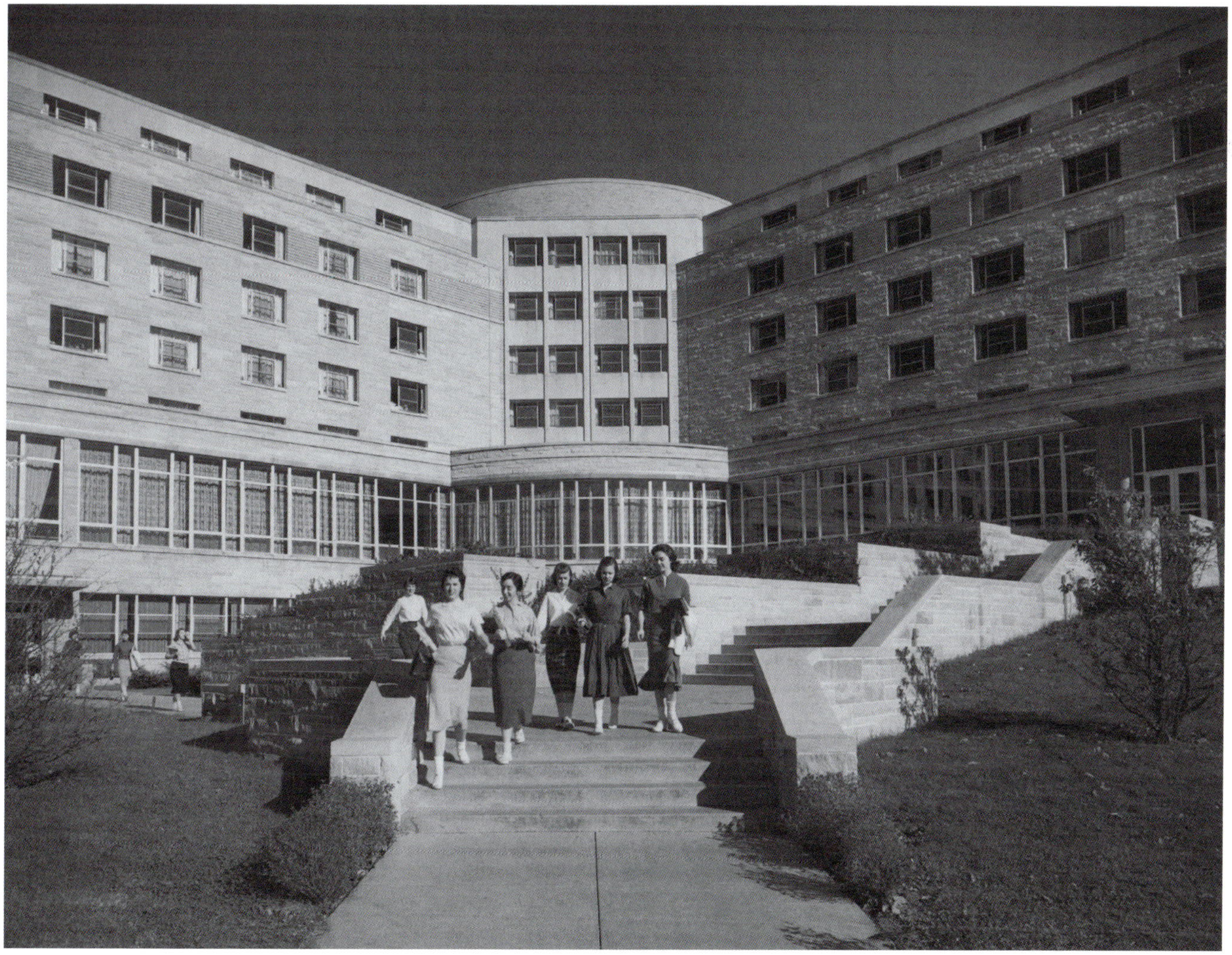

Read Hall (Smithwood), circa 1959. P0020014, IU Archives.

enroll in his courses. The naming discussion continued for the next few years. The Board of Trustees favored a woman's name, but the Committee on Names preferred Daniel Read Hall. Unexpectedly, on March 29, 1961, the *Indiana Daily Student* reported the announcement from Halls of Residence director Alice Nelson that Smithwood Hall would henceforth be known as Daniel Read Hall. Although its residents circulated a petition protesting the change, the new name remained and President Wells presided over the naming ceremony on May 13, 1962.

Today, Read is coed but offers residents single-gender floors. It is popular with Jacobs School of Music students due to its proximity to the music school's complex of buildings, but its campus location is favorable for all students.

Nellie S. Teter Quadrangle

A First in Housing

> *My love for Indiana University and all of the grand people connected with it is so great that I cannot tell you.*
>
> *—Nellie S. Teter*

As the continued growth of the student body after World War II meant housing became a perennial issue for Indiana University administrators. Upon completion of Read Hall, attention turned to developing the Tenth Street corridor with the addition of the Nellie S. Teter Quadrangle adjacent to the east of Wright Quadrangle.

Teter Quad has a place of distinction in IU's history as the first dormitory built specifically for coeducational undergraduate living. According to the 1960 *Arbutus*, the university had begun to recognize the important social education undergraduates of both sexes could gain by sharing dining facilities and planning activities together. As a result, administrators implemented this type of living arrangement in 1959 by opening Teter as a coed dorm and moving men into one building of the Agnes E. Wells Quadrangle, which previously housed only women.

What was first named Tower Quadrangle was designed by Edward James of Indianapolis and supervised by Eggers and Higgins of New York; construction began early in 1957, and the complex was fully ready for residents by fall 1959. Continuing the dormitory design trend of a central hub with separate wings, Teter included a central eight-story building (Rabb) to house three hundred women, with four outlying three- and four-story buildings (Boisen, Elkin, Thompson, and Wissler) to house nine hundred men, and a connected building (Hoffman) for dining facilities. The units were linked by arcades. Rabb also housed the library, central lounge with brick fireplace, office, and mail room. The dining building included a central kitchen with four large dining rooms where residents could congregate for study and socializing as well as meals. Interior design work for the public areas was directed by Francis Macomber of Indianapolis, who completed many other interior design commissions for Indiana University.

The facade features Indiana chat-sawn (rough-surface) limestone laid in a random ashlar pattern, with smooth panels below the windows. Overall, the exterior design is largely unassuming, in line with the simplicity of the Early Modern style that flourished after World War II. An exception is the large Indiana limestone relief to the left of the main doors of Rabb Hall created by African American sculptor Nathaniel Choate in 1959. It most likely depicts the Greek mythological twins Selene (Goddess of the Moon) and Helios (the Sun God) flanking their Titan father, Hyperion.

In 1959 the Board of Trustees approved the name of Tower Quadrangle for the dormitory but privately acknowledged future plans to name it after Nellie Showers Teter, IU's first female trustee, elected in 1924. Teter died in 1961 and the quad was renamed in May 1962 in honor of her focus on housing for women (IU's naming policy at the time specified that buildings could not be named for a person still living). Teter Quadrangle was one of the first IU buildings to be named after a woman.

Despite its size, Teter was already bursting at the seams by the 1961–62 school year, with bunk beds set up in the lounges

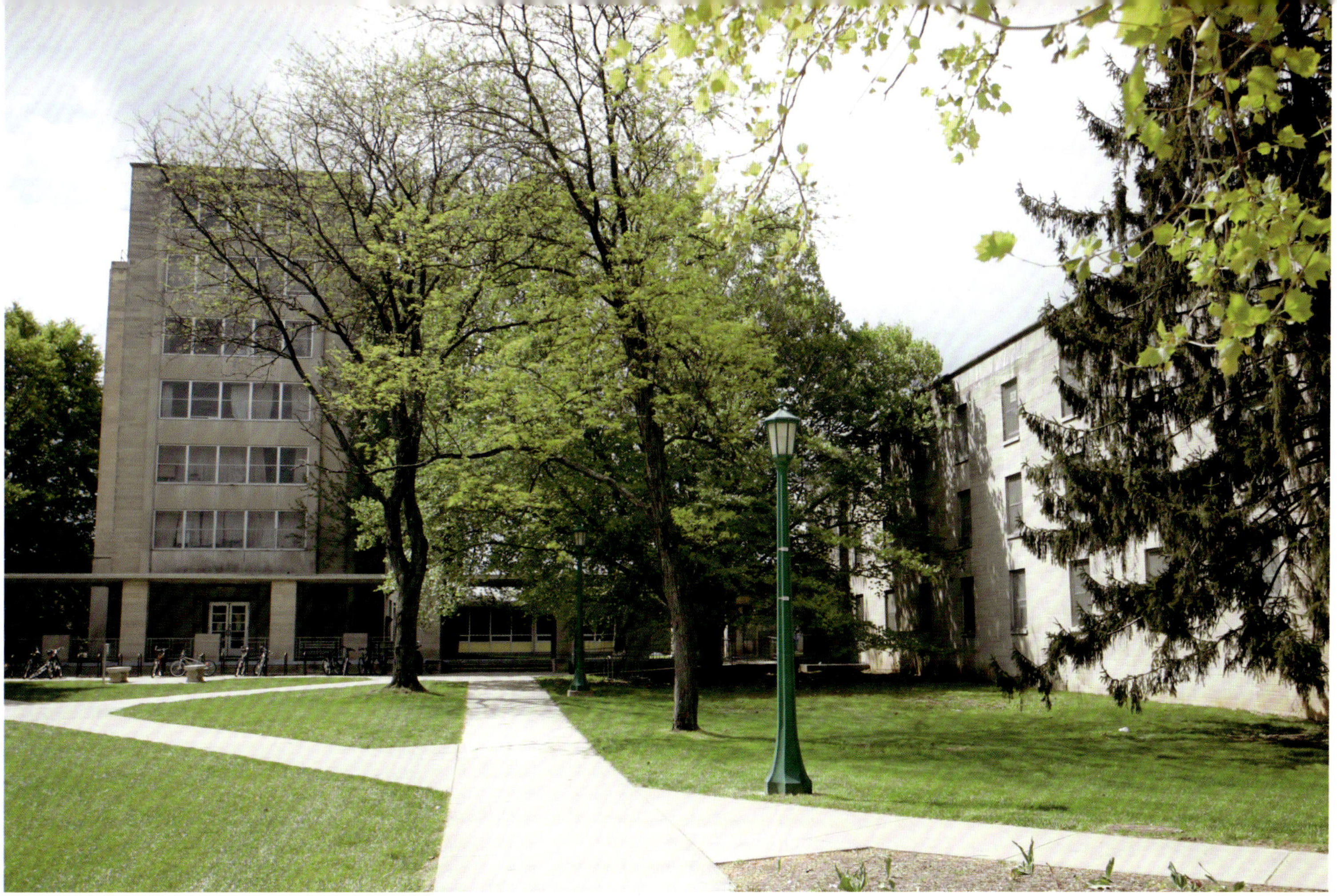

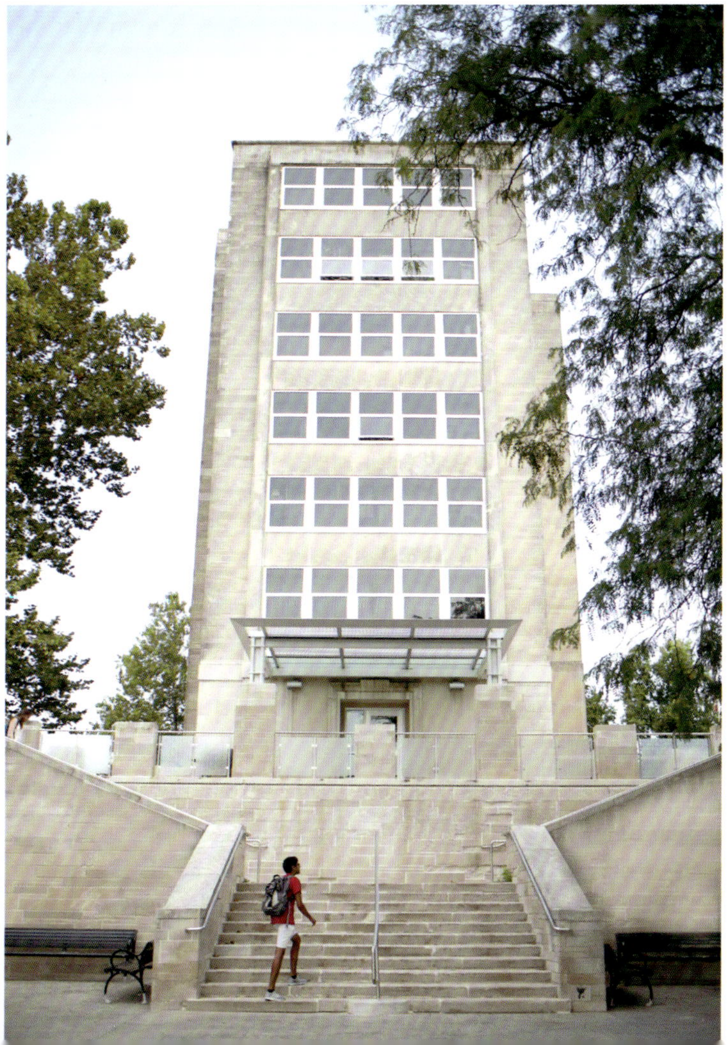

Above, Nellie S. Teter Quadrangle courtyard, undated. Photo credit: Indiana University.

Left, Teter Quadrangle, originally known as Tower Quad, 2015. Photo credit: Indiana University.

to accommodate overflow and three students bunking in rooms designed for two. By the following school year, there were fourteen hundred students residing in an area intended for twelve hundred. Fortunately, administrators recognized that the student population would only continue to grow and had already begun construction on the Fee Lane dormitories. While these housing units were far from complete, sleeping rooms in the still-under-construction Foster were far enough along that students could arrange a "room only" contract, giving them a place to study and lay their heads. (If they desired a bit more, they could also sign a dining contract with Wright Quad, an option two-thirds of the students accepted.)

Today Teter continues to be a highly desirable housing location for students due to its central location, with just a short walk to most locations around campus, including the Wells Library, School of Education, Kelley School of Business, and the Student Recreational Sports Center (SRSC).

Married Student Housing

Couples Flock to School

The most "marrying time in American history" was just after World War II.

—Peggy Fletcher Stack, "Marriage: What's Love Got to Do with It?"

The GI Bill, which provided U.S. veterans an opportunity for affordable education, sent those World War II veterans to the nation's universities in droves. Anxious to get on with their lives, young men returning from the war started families and brought their spouses with them to college campuses. Moreover, the GI benefits, coupled with the recovery of the economy after a harrowing depression, resulted in a surge of optimism among Americans, leading to the post–World War II baby boom. In 1949, nearly 3.6 million babies had been born in the United States, compared to 2.2 million in 1939.[1] In addition to finding housing for single veterans and married couples, universities now found themselves in need of housing and facilities for student-parents in numbers not previously seen.

University Apartments (1949)

Before the first GI stepped on campus, Indiana University administrators had already been scrambling to find suitable housing, which resulted in a large number of temporary structures throughout campus. The primary focus was on unmarried men and women, but the university was not unaware of the need for married housing. At the November 1945 Board of Trustees meeting, Vice President Ward Biddle pressed upon the trustees and officers the urgent need for apartments. He predicted that the increase in married student enrollment would be "tremendous" by the fall of 1946, and he felt confident that a building with efficiency apartments could be ready if they began immediately, meaning selection of an architect before adjournment that day.[2]

The site identified for this first permanent campus apartment building was on East Third Street, near Jordan Avenue. Joe H. Wildermuth of Gary was named the local architect, with Eggers and Higgins of New York performing supervisory services. Wildermuth was instructed to proceed immediately with plans and specifications for a hundred-unit efficiency apartment building. Instead, what resulted were two apartment buildings: University Apartments East and West, consisting of 236 units in total: 160 efficiencies and 76 one-bedroom apartments. Furnished units could be rented for between $70 and $90 a month, while the range for unfurnished was $60 to $75. Priority was given to veterans, but other students, faculty, and staff were all eligible to live in the apartments; the faculty housing situation was nearly as acute as the students'.

The two four-story buildings were faced with rough-hewn Indiana limestone but again incorporated the wide brick band featured on the other IU dormitories completed during the same time period, creating a look of continuity across the structures. Facing Third Street, a large vertical strip of glass block capped the entryway, providing architectural interest to the exterior and affording a stream of light into the interior hallway. Over the glass block could be seen a small limestone relief of an atomic symbol, one of the few decorative features of the exterior. Roller window awnings blocked some of the heat and glare of the Indiana sun.

Unfortunately, Biddle's expectation of a fall 1946 completion date turned out to be unachievable. Instead, the apartments were not ready for occupation until 1949, and while the two buildings helped tremendously with campus married housing, the need continued to grow. At the September 1949 IU Board of Trustees meeting, President Herman B Wells reported that the temporary trailers acquired after World War II were rapidly deteriorating and that the university needed to take immediate steps to generate low-cost housing for married students. It undoubtedly pained President Wells to inform the trustees that an estimated five hundred married students had been denied admission that semester simply for lack of housing. He proposed a pilot program, which would take up to $75,000 of unappropriated funds to erect ten to fifteen family units. Rather than temporary buildings, he envisioned something built of wood and concrete block to keep costs down, but of such quality that they would last at least twenty-five years. The board discussed the matter at length and authorized President Wells to begin work immediately on these new units.

"NEW" HOOSIER COURTS
(Student Row Housing Projects, 1951, and Married Housing II, 1955)

Within six months, Vice President and Treasurer Joseph Franklin was back with the trustees, armed with plans prepared by Indianapolis architect Edward James for a presentation on the pilot program of student row housing. The plans proposed six one-story buildings of ten apartments each. The one-room apartment dimensions would be 20 by 24 feet with built-in closets, desk, beds, and kitchen units. Although the estimated cost was well over the $75,000 previously recommended by President Wells, the trustees approved the plans and authorized advertising for construction bids. However, in the interim the university decided to go forward with a much smaller project than had been originally proposed by President Wells, announcing in May 1950 that it would build twenty units on a ridge overlooking the "old" (temporary) Hoosier Courts.

Construction of the twenty units moved swiftly. Before the end of the year, the university held an open house with a model apartment fully furnished by L. S. Ayres department store. Unfortunately, comment cards turned in after the open house, if not critical, were not overwhelmingly positive. Many pointed out that the apartments would be insufficient for families, had poor lighting, and one comment stated that the "external construction appears flimsy."[3]

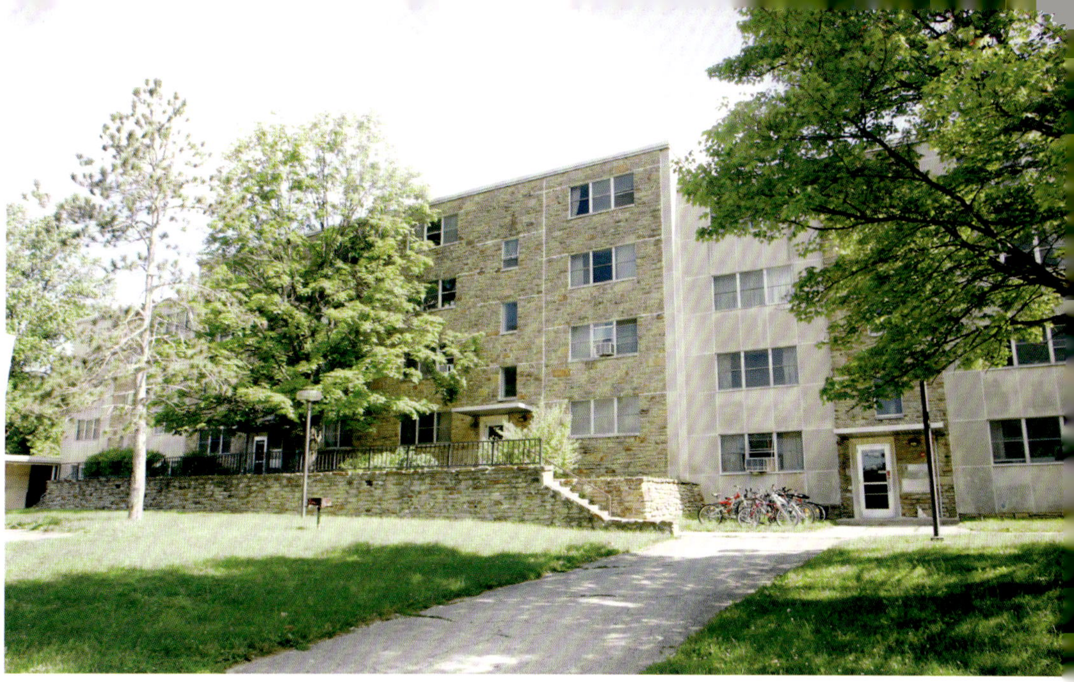

Redbud Hill Apartments, undated.
Photo credit: Indiana University.

Indeed, compared to the other permanent buildings on campus, the new row housing had a conspicuously no-frills design. The exterior was a mix of concrete block and wood. Each unit had a private entrance adjacent to a strip of small, high windows tucked up under an angled roof supported by narrow metal beams, which afforded the tenants a covered walk for a bit of protection. The backs of the units were more attractive, with floor-to-ceiling windows and double glass doors that opened onto a patio. Also included amid the units was a lounge with a limestone fireplace, rustic wood walls that mirrored the exterior facade, and the same strip of high windows. (The lounge, however, became a victim of the married housing shortage and was soon converted into additional units.)

Surveys conducted after residents had lived in the units were noticeably more positive, stating that the apartment was sufficient for families with one young child, the kitchen was fine for an efficiency unit, and general commendation to the university for providing "such excellent housing facilities."[4] Overall, this pilot program to provide married students with affordable housing that could be quickly constructed proved to be a success.

By late 1951, architect Edward James submitted a proposal to add even more efficiency apartments to the Hoosier Courts area. The plan was approved by the trustees in April 1952. Four

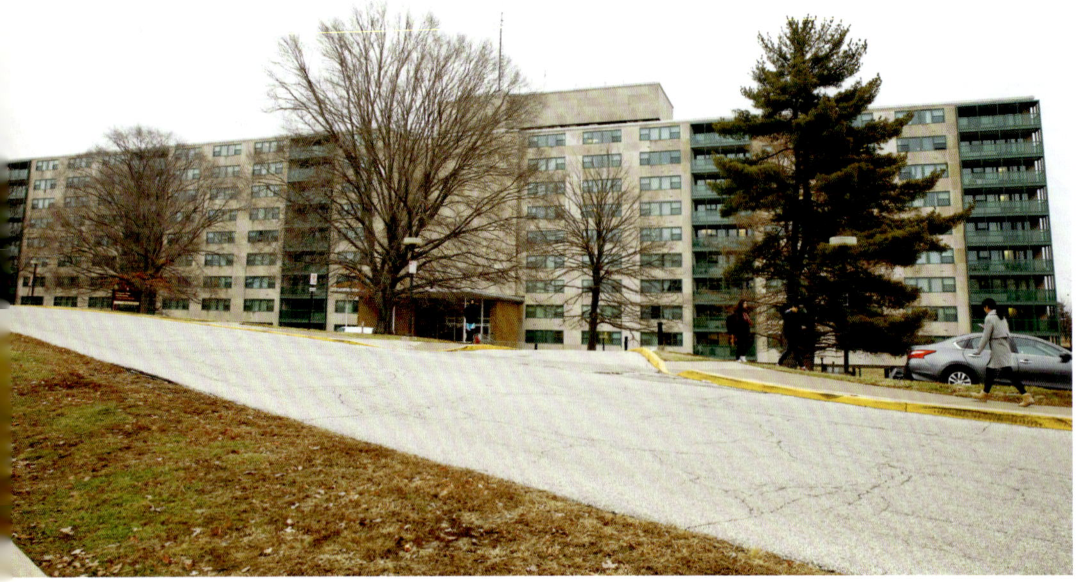

West elevation of Campus View Apartments, 2017. Photo credit: Indiana University.

one- and two-bedroom, ultramodern, two-story apartment buildings constituted Married Student Housing II. Opened in 1955, the units were a mixture of one and two stories, with families having two or more children given priority for the two-bedroom, two-story units to reduce the noise impact to tenants in other units. The exterior was a mix of rough-hewn limestone and asbestos siding in an assortment of colors, angled roofs, and an abundance of windows, including many high, long windows for privacy. The architects adapted to the topography of the land, siting the apartments on varying terrain.

In 1959, the four buildings were named the David D. Banta Apartments (trustee, 1877–89; Dean of the Law School, 1889–96), Ernest P. Bicknell Apartments (alumnus, 1887, LLD 1924; director of the American Red Cross), Charles M. Hepburn Apartments (dean of the Law School, 1918–25), and the Cyrus Nutt Apartments (president, 1860–75)—or collectively and commonly known as BBHN.

This new development with 144 apartments brought the total apartment units in the Hoosier Courts area to 445, which included the cheaply constructed one-story units opened in 1951 and the temporary structures brought to campus in 1946. A 1955 *Indiana Daily Student* article reported that there were still 393 applicants on a waiting list for the new apartments.[5] As before, fortunately, planning was already underway for another apartment project.

EVERMANN APARTMENT CENTER
(Married Student Apartments III), 1957

By the mid-1950s, Indiana University was well aware that there would be a continual need for married student housing. Construction of IU's Married Student Apartments III, designed by Edward James, began in May 1956 and was completed by fall 1957. The four-story building consists of three wings nestled into the contour of the southern Indiana hills. Evermann has 182 apartments, including both efficiency and one-bedroom units, with short hallways to minimize noise within the building. The interior features painted, lightweight concrete block and natural wood walls and trim. Laundry facilities and a computer lab, music practice room, and meeting room are provided for the residents' use. The exterior is finished in Indiana limestone in large chat-sawn panels with tooled joints. In 1957, the center was named for scientist Dr. Barton W. Evermann and his wife, Meadie Hawkins Evermann, the first married woman to graduate from IU (1887).

REDBUD HILL APARTMENTS
(Married Student Apartments IV), 1960

Across the way from Evermann are the Redbud Hill Apartments, completed in 1960. Another Edward James design, the two four-story buildings include 128 two-bedroom apartments divided into groups of eight that share a stairwell. The interior has painted, lightweight concrete block walls and painted, concrete slab ceilings. Like its neighbor, Evermann, the exterior is finished in large panels of Indiana limestone but Redbud is accented with large repeating vertical strips of Brown County sandstone.

CAMPUS VIEW APARTMENTS
(Married Student Apartments V), 1962

Also designed by Edward James, the next married housing unit to open had nine stories, the tallest campus building to date. Campus View further alleviated the married housing shortage with its more than two hundred two-bedroom apartments. Approximately half of the units have balconies. In 2002, the university began extensive renovations on the building, which included upgrading the bathrooms and kitchens and the plumbing, heating, and cooling systems. Each floor has laundry facilities, and centrally located within the building are a computer lab, music practice room, and library. The Campus View Child Care Center opened in 1990 and has since received accolades for its high-quality program, including an

Eco-Healthy Child Care Certification in 2013 in recognition of its work to implement environmentally healthy best practices.

TULIP TREE HOUSE
(Married Student Apartments VI), 1965

A distinctive landmark near State Road 45, Tulip Tree House (so named in 1963) rises eleven stories and is one of the most modern-looking buildings in Bloomington, with windows covering the east and west sides. The structure was positioned concavely on the lot in order to take full advantage of the reflection of the sun, according to H. H. Brooks, director of the IU Physical Plant. When it opened in 1965, Tulip Tree provided over two hundred additional housing units for married students. The Edward James design underwent major renovations in 2012 and now includes two- and three-bedroom apartments, a computer lab, music practice room, and activity room.

AND NOW?

All of the facilities described above are still in use, with the exception of University Apartments West (demolished in 2011 to make room for the new Jacobs School of Music Studio Building) and parts of Hoosier Courts. Demolition of the "Old" Hoosier Courts (aka the "temporary units") began in 1966 and extended into the 1970s, when the state fire marshal finally condemned them. The twenty one-story units that opened in 1951 were razed circa 1999.

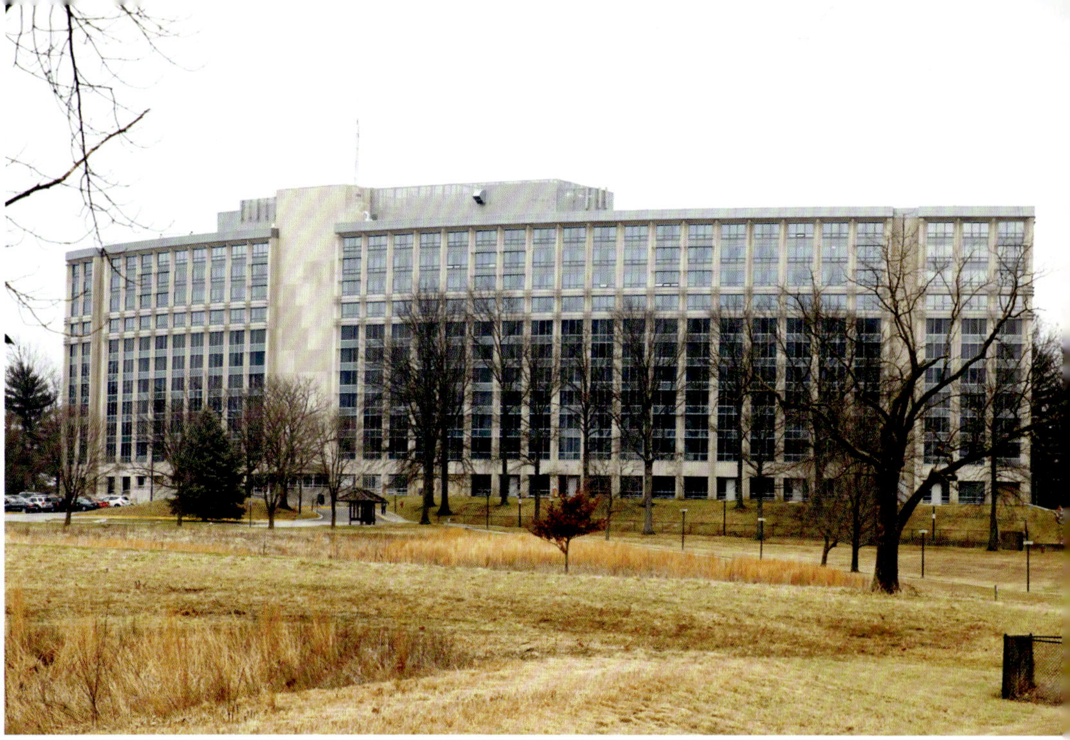

Top, West elevation of Tulip Tree Apartments, 2017. Photo credit: Indiana University.

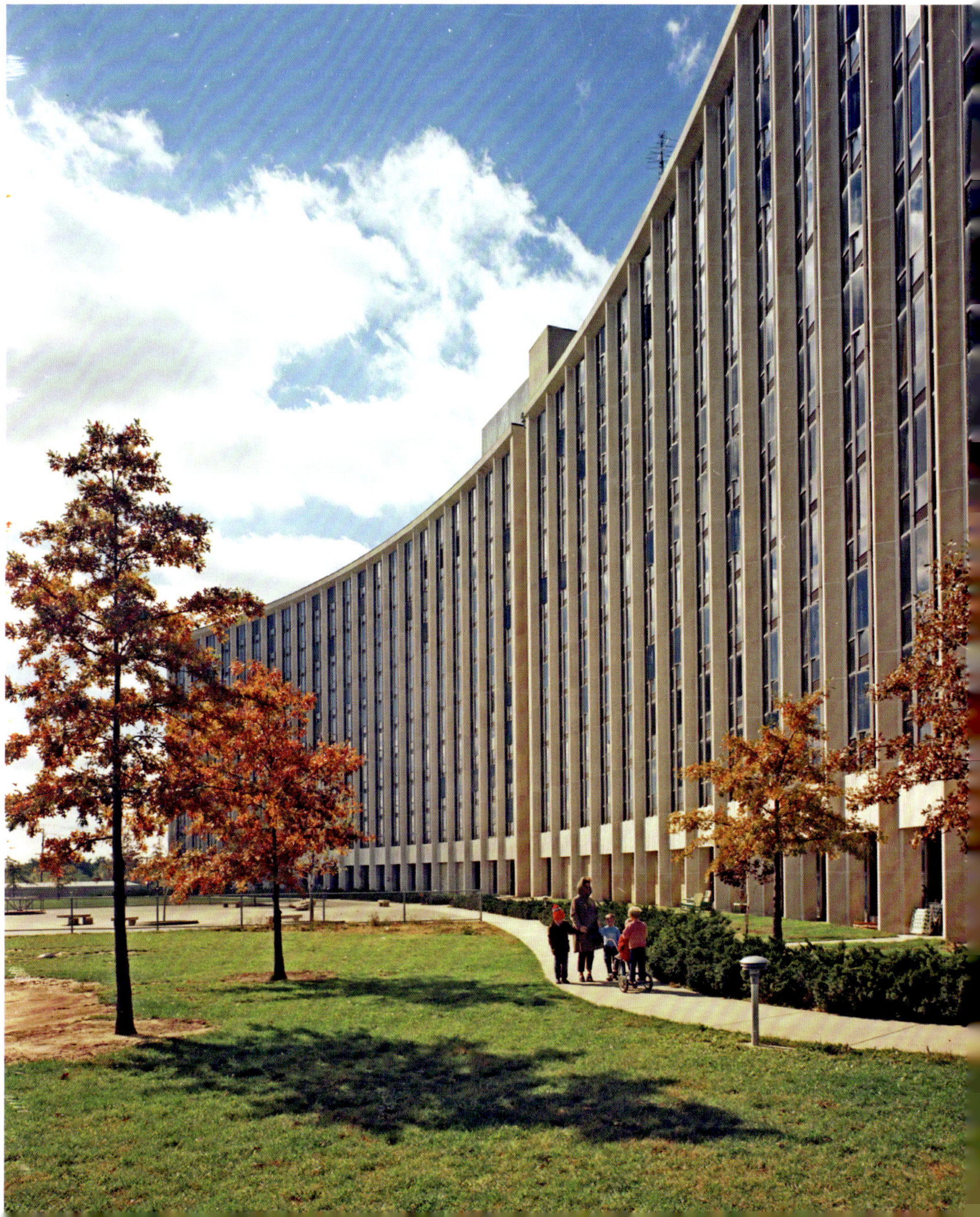

Right, Tulip Tree Apartments, 1969. P0026032, IU Archives. Photo credit: Ralph "Porky" Veal.

Fee Lane Dormitories

Northern Campus Gateway

Indiana University is exciting. You never know what is coming up next. You must walk through hilly gardens and woods to get to classes, to dorms, to the library, to the union. Surprise is surely a worthy goal of design.

—Thomas A. Gaines,
The Campus as a Work of Art

During the decade spanning 1960 to 1970, the IU Bloomington student population doubled, outgrowing the available campus housing. In response, the university constructed five undergraduate residence centers: Foster, McNutt, and Briscoe Quadrangles on the northwest side of campus; and Forest and Willkie Quadrangles on the southeast. Eigenmann Hall, east of central campus, was built to accommodate graduate students. Three housing units for married students also were constructed during the 1960s—Redbud, Campus View, and Tulip Tree.

North Fee Lane serves as the gateway to IUB's intercollegiate athletics complex and with John W. Foster Quadrangle (built 1963), Paul V. McNutt Quadrangle (1964), and Herman T. Briscoe Quadrangle (1965), is the second home to the most concentrated groups of freshmen on campus. Although the Fee Lane dormitories are farther from classes in the central part of campus and on Third Street, they are closest to all the campus sports arenas, the outdoor intramural facility (2015), the IU outdoor pool, tennis courts, fraternity and sorority row, the Student Recreational Sports Center (SRSC), the School of Public and Environmental Affairs (SPEA), and the Kelley School of Business.

These three Fee Lane dormitories are situated on either side of Fee Lane from Seventeenth Street to Law Lane; all were designed by Edward D. James Associates of Indianapolis, with Eggers and Higgins of New York consulting. Each displays a simple, Modernist style, with a facade of mostly smooth Indiana limestone panels, but there are some elevations of rough-faced ashlar as well. Near the entry to Foster-Harper is an allegorical stone carving of classic female figures, one holding a book and the other a lamp. Underneath the carving is a quotation from the Book of Psalms: "Open mine eyes that I may behold wondrous things."

Foster Quadrangle was named for John Watson Foster (1836–1917), a Hoosier diplomat, military officer, lawyer, and journalist. Construction began in January 1961 and was completed in July 1963. The housing crisis was so severe at that time that four hundred male students moved into Shea and Martin Halls at the start of the 1962 fall semester. The following January, nearly five hundred female students moved in when Harper Hall and Gresham Cafeteria were opened. It took another nine months for all of the lounges to be furnished and for the heating system to be installed and functional. During the Founders Day ceremonies on May 4, 1966, Foster was dedicated along with Briscoe, McNutt, and Willkie.[1]

Foster-Harper is the main nine-story building in the Foster complex. The four other Foster residences (Shea, Martin, Magee, and Jenkinson) are each four stories tall. Each consists mainly of double rooms, with a few singles. Within Foster are Foster International Living-Learning Center (Shea) and the Global Village Living-Learning Center (Martin). A perk for Foster residents is their proximity to the Gresham Food

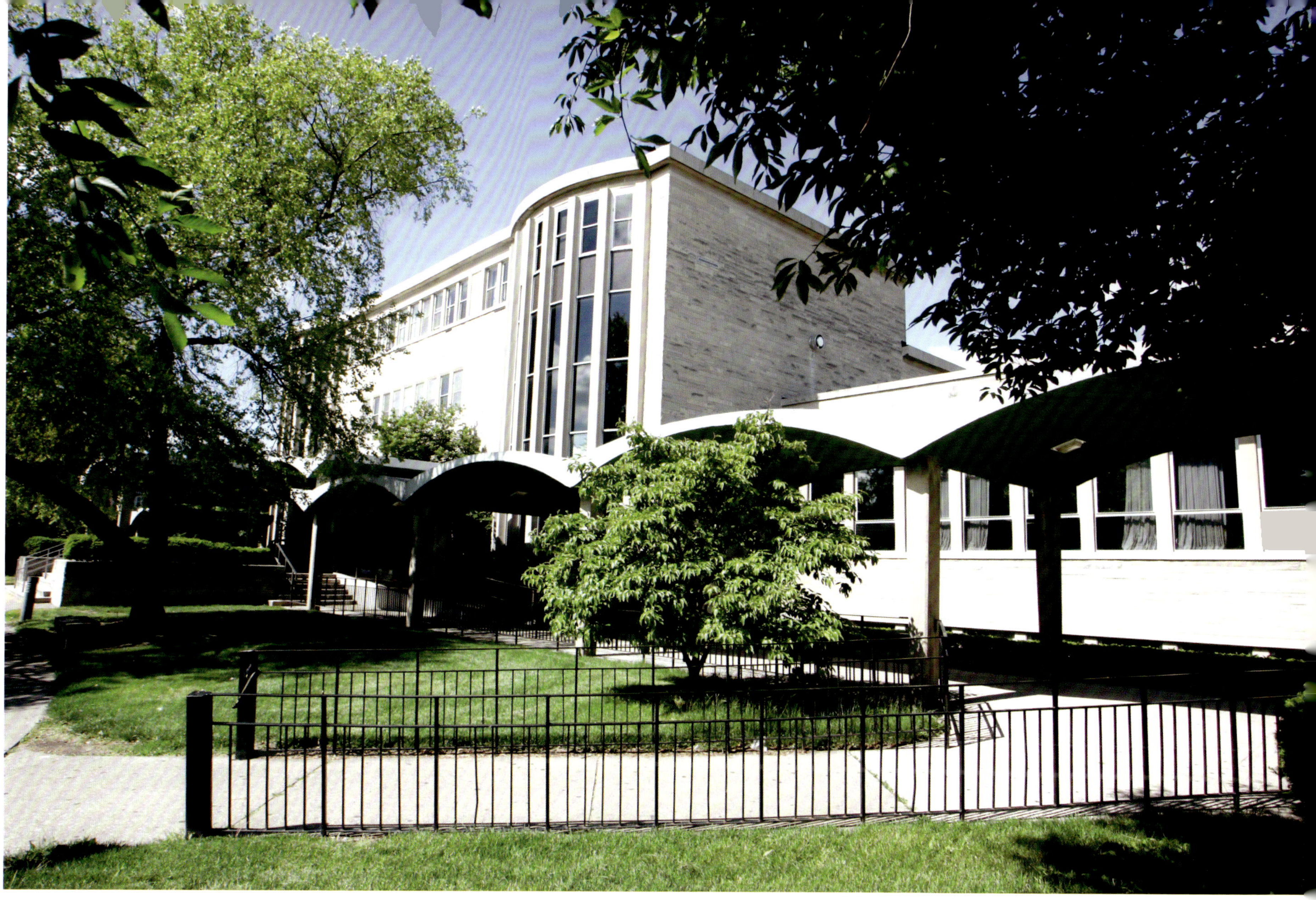

Above, Paul V. McNutt Quadrangle, undated. Photo credit: Indiana University.

Below, Foster-Harper, the central dormitory in the five-unit John W. Foster Quadrangle, 2017. Photo Credit: Indiana University.

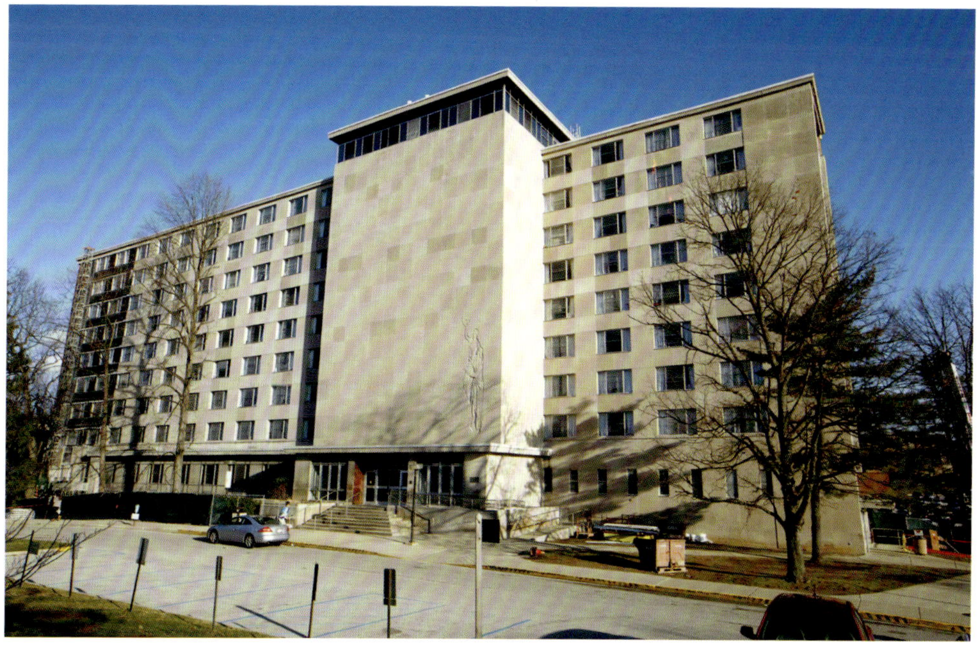

Court, where they can grab a bite to eat. Inside the lobby of Gresham is a wall of limestone panels depicting the life story of John Watson Foster. The newest space is a coffee shop. Rogers Cemetery, a tiny plot of ground surrounded by a stone wall, seems to be out of place in front of Harper. It dates from the early nineteenth century and is the burial site of some of Monroe County's earliest settlers.

McNutt Quadrangle was named for Paul Vories McNutt (1891–1955), an IU law professor, dean of the Law School, and governor of Indiana. The largest residence center at IU,

McNutt is made up of three buildings in the North Courtyard (Bordner, Bryan, Crone) and three in the South Courtyard (Bocobo, Dejoya, Delgado). Each building has five floors and contains mainly double rooms, with a few singles and triples. The courtyards provide a grassy area for students and visitors to mingle or just relax. The Kelley Living-Learning Center is located in McNutt, a bonus for business students; and the café and center offer a convenient place to satisfy hunger pangs.

Briscoe Quadrangle was named for Herman Thompson Briscoe (1893–1960), an IU vice president and its first dean of faculties. Briscoe is the smallest of the three dormitories. It consists of two V-shaped, eleven-story wings (Shoemaker and Gucker) connected by a two-story central unit containing the reception area, classrooms, a computer lab, and a movie room. It was remodeled in 2012–13. Briscoe is more hotel-like with its high-rise design, attractive central lobby, and double rooms with private baths. There are also single rooms with private baths, and doubles and singles that share a bath and a living room. Within Briscoe are the Hutton Honors College Community, the School of Public Health Living-Learning Center, and SPEA's Civic Leaders Living-Learning Center. Although Briscoe houses the smallest number of students of the Fee Lane dormitories, it boasts the largest percentage of returning women students.

Falling as it does in an "enhanced housing category," Briscoe is a bit more expensive than the other Fee Lane dorms but stands directly across the street from Assembly Hall and Memorial Stadium. In general, the Fee Lane residences tend to house the most freshmen athletes due to their proximity to the athletic facilities. Foster draws a number of Kelley students, and McNutt seems to attract the more social contingent, often earning a reputation as the most "active" dorm. Each building has its own personality, which naturally changes somewhat each year. All the halls are coeducational, but room assignments vary from year to year.

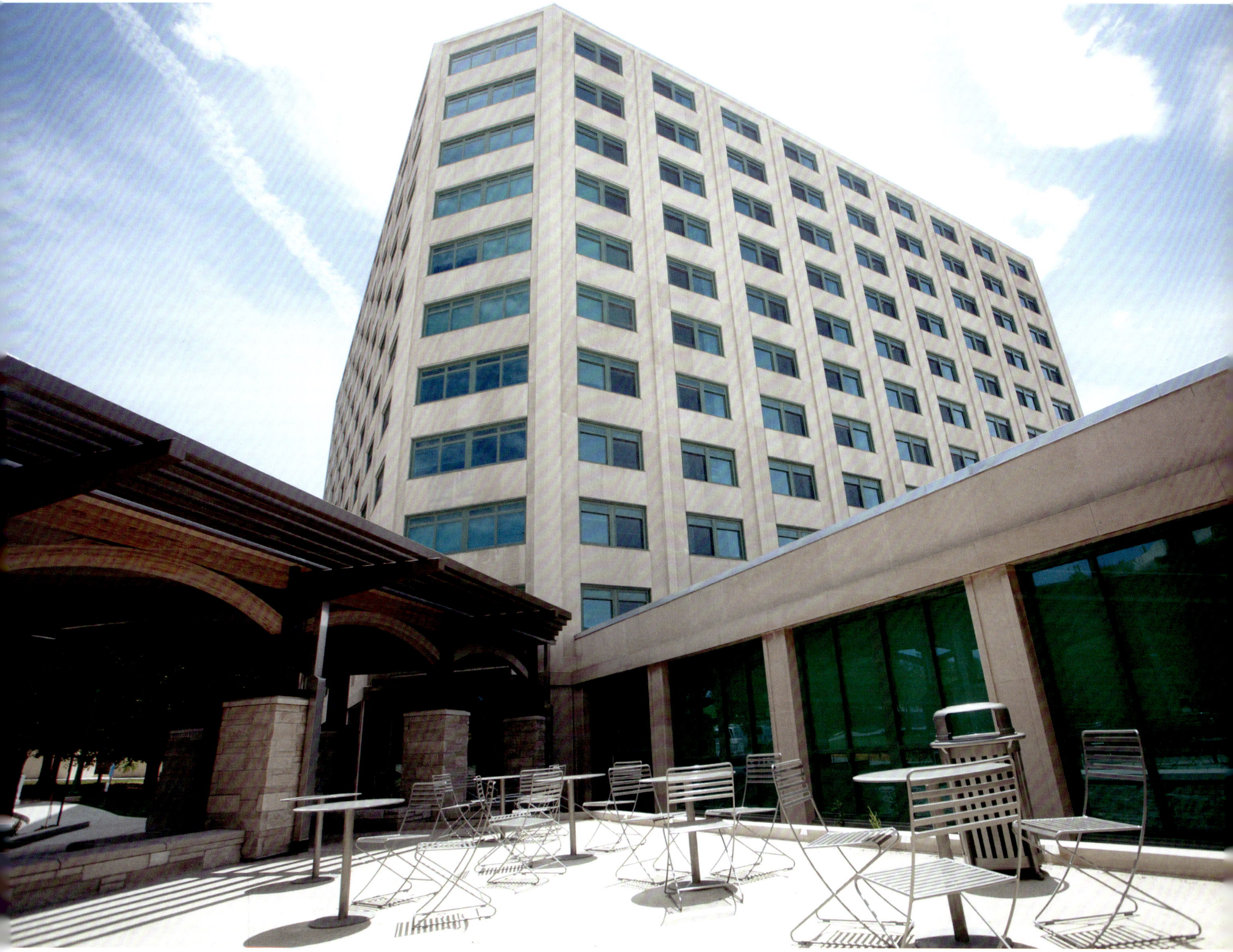

Herman T. Briscoe Quadrangle with patio, 2012. Photo credit: Indiana University.

Wendell L. Willkie Residence Center

Living in the Southeast Neighborhood

I believe in America because we have great dreams, and because we have the opportunity to make those dreams come true.

—Wendell L. Willkie

THE STUDENT POPULATION AT INDIANA UNIversity increased by nearly one-third between 1961 and 1965, leading to a construction boom in student housing from 1963 to 1966. In that period, all four Fee Lane residences went up, as did Forest Quadrangle, in the southeast part of campus. Willkie Residence Center was named after Wendell L. Willkie (1892–1944), an IU graduate, attorney, business executive, and politician, who was the Republican presidential nominee running against Franklin Delano Roosevelt in 1940.

The Willkie Residence Center is located on Rose Avenue between Third and Seventh Streets. Willkie is architecturally similar to Forest and Briscoe—all were built in the same time period and designed by the same architect, Edward James Associates, of Indianapolis. The three units that make up this complex are unattached and are modern in presentation and minimal in detail. Willkie's buildings include the north and south towers and a central unit. The north and south towers are V-shaped, each with an imposing thirteen floors. Like Forest, Willkie's towers are clad in limestone panels, broken only

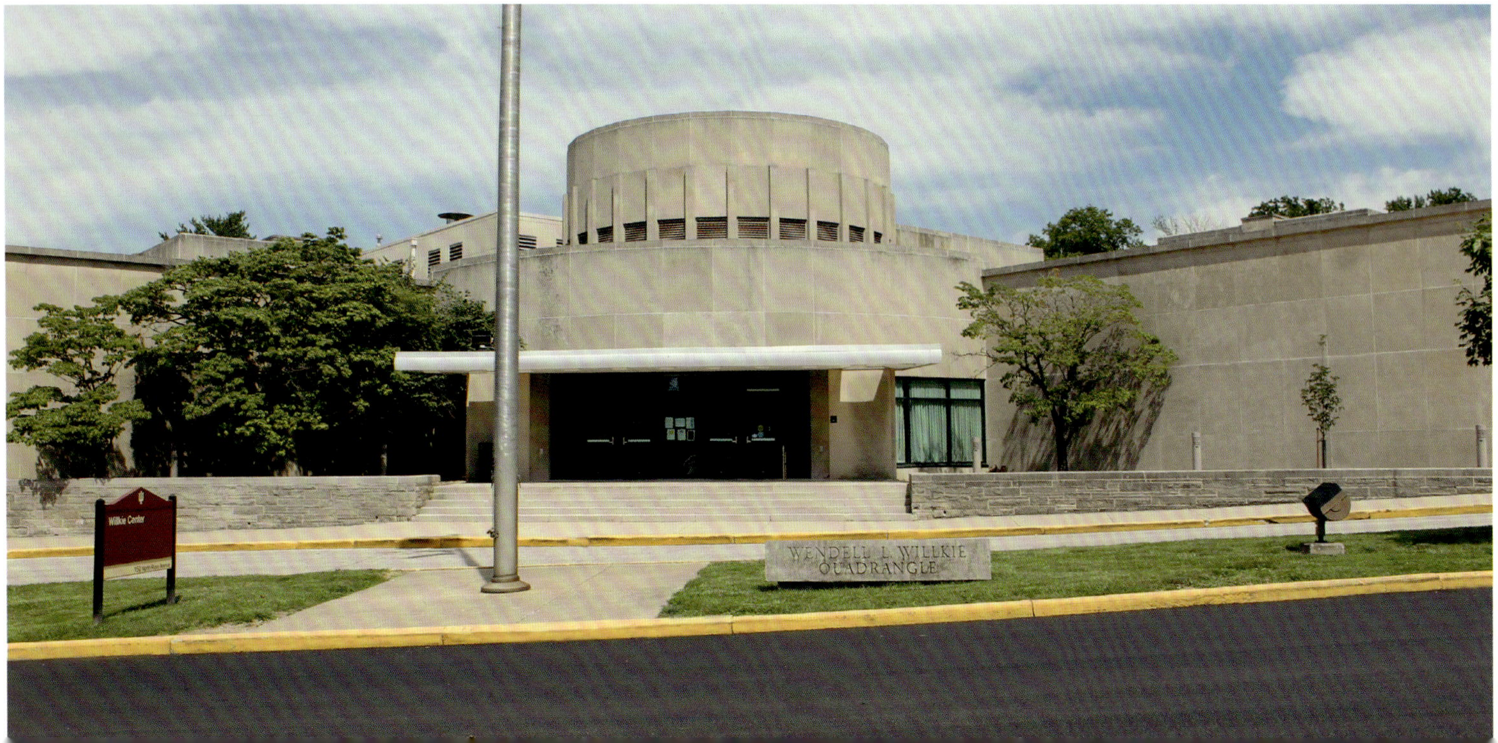

Central unit of Wendell L. Willkie Residence Center, 2017. Photo credit: Indiana University.

North Tower of Willkie Residence Center, 2017.
Photo credit: Indiana University

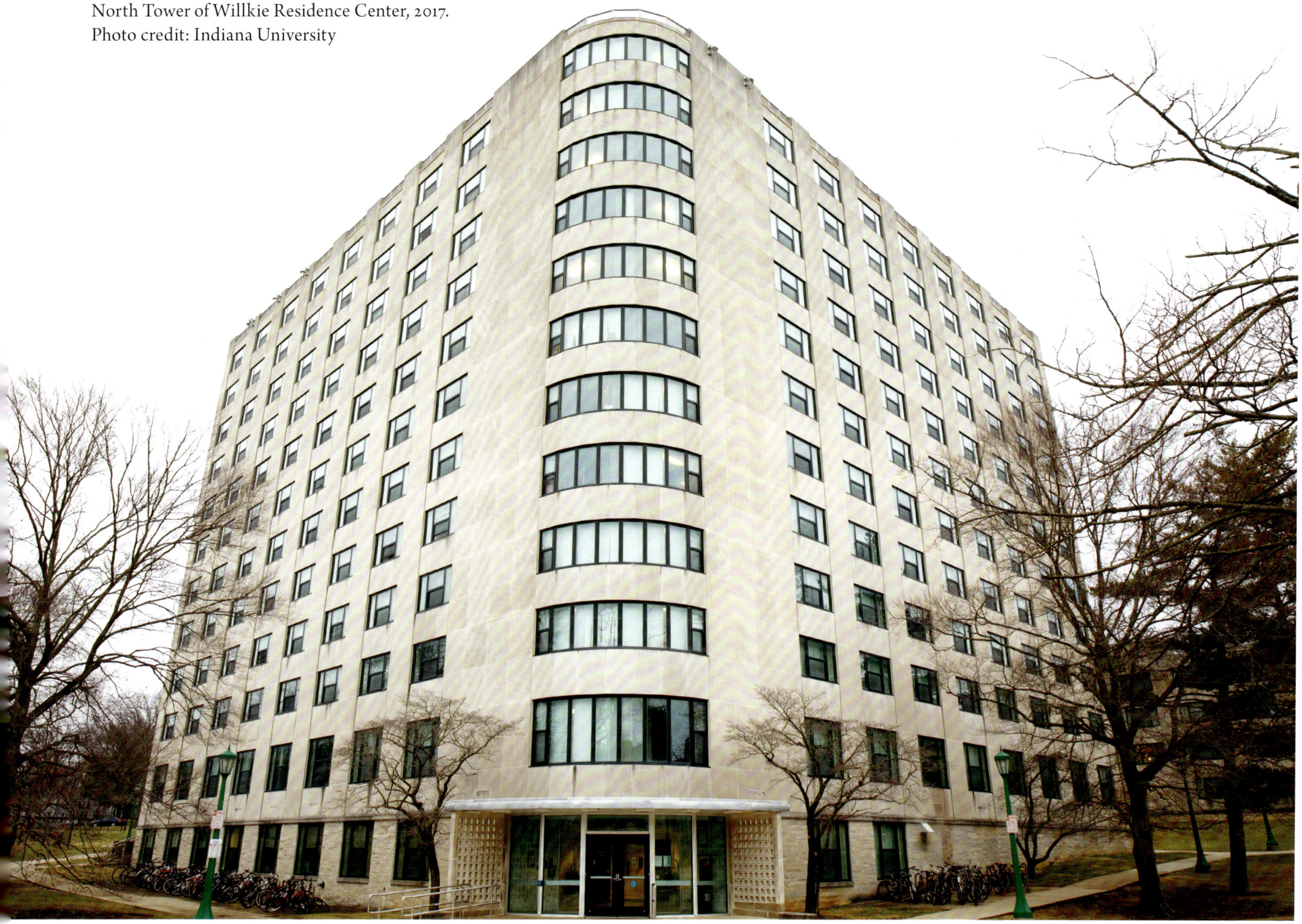

by their many windows, and have split-face ashlar over the ends of the wings where the stairwells are located. The central building also is faced with limestone panels with some smooth-face ashlar on the east side, but it is five levels with circular limestone tiers above its main entrance.

Freshmen were granted residence in Willkie for the first time in 2015, and this complex is unusual among residence centers in that the students may remain during university breaks. The Willkie complex includes single rooms, two- and three-bedroom suites, and four-bedroom apartments. The central building houses the common areas, including a lobby, the center café and store, and an auditorium, as well as additional student rooms. With a stage and capacity for over three hundred patrons, the auditorium is widely used. Weather permitting, students can enjoy Willkie's outdoor basketball court. Residents are a short walk from the Restaurants at Woodland in Forest Quadrangle, the Wendell W. Wright Education Building, and the restaurants and shops along Third Street.

Forest Quadrangle

A Gathering Place

It is doubtful that in the entire history of American higher education an institution had made proportionately greater efforts to serve a larger number of students in classroom, dormitories, and recreational facilities, scholars in libraries and laboratories, and to carry on a complexity of public functions.

—*Thomas D. Clark,* Indiana University, Midwestern Pioneer

FOREST QUADRANGLE WAS THE FOURTH DORMITORY constructed in the 1960s to address the ballooning student population: Foster, McNutt, and Briscoe on the north side of campus and Willkie and Forest on the southeast side. Forest was completed on Third Street in 1966, shortly after its neighbor, Willkie Quadrangle. The building was supposed to house both female and male students in its A and B towers, respectively. However, there were more women in need of housing at the time it opened, so Forest became an all-women residence hall. Forest became coed in 1996 but did not have split-gender floors until much later.

Edward D. James and Associates of Indianapolis designed Forest, along with the Fee Lane dorms, the Wendell L. Willkie Residence Center, Read Hall, and Teter Quadrangle. Forest was constructed with two eleven-story towers connected centrally by a common building. Its facade is unadorned and modern with a cladding of large, smooth, limestone panels and split-face ashlar over the ends of the wings where the stairwells are located. In 2013, a major renovation was completed, creating a path through the center of the building and transforming the central area into a culinary space, the Restaurants at Woodland, with a series of dining pavilions. The loading dock was replaced with a two-story glass and limestone facade, which harmonizes with the existing structure and the predominant campus architecture as well.

The Restaurants at Woodland is really "the icing on the cake," at Forest Quadrangle. "Creating a culinary-focused, presentation-style dining destination offering a variety of menu

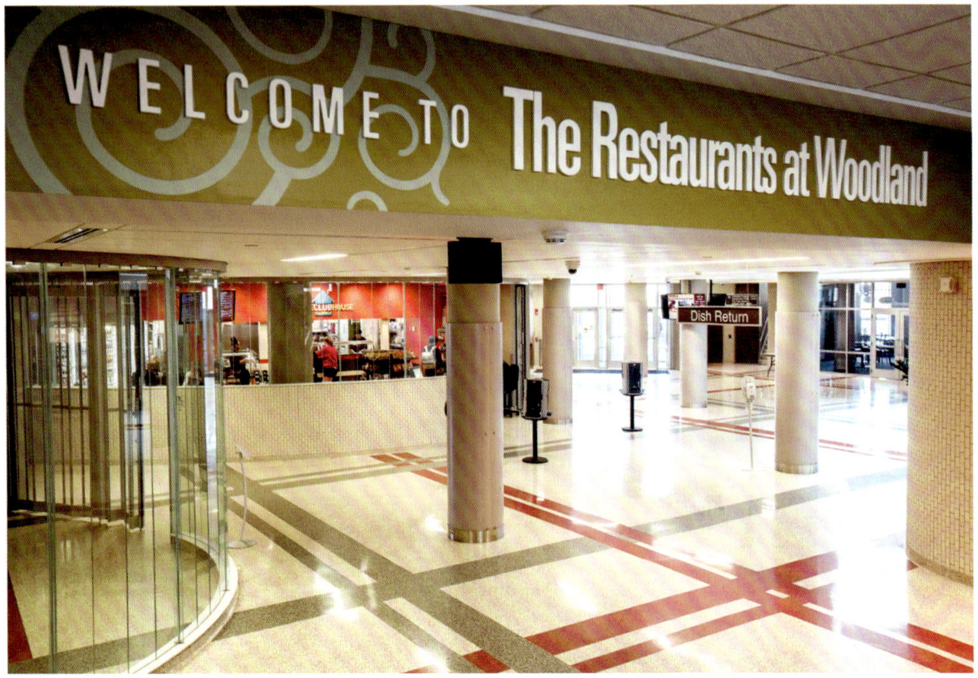

The Restaurants at Woodland, Forest Quadrangle, 2017. Photo credit: Tyagan Miller.

options was the goal for the residential neighborhood."[1] This outstanding venue features nine micro-restaurants that offer a wide variety of menu choices in four dining rooms and two outdoor terraces: the Stone Grill, a Cut Above, Romaine, Caliente, the Round, Bloomingberry, Fusion, Mangia, and the Clubhouse. The Restaurants at Woodland venue is open to all IU dormitory residents.

Students in Forest live in mainly double rooms, but there are some single rooms as well. A Tower includes an honors floor, and both the Atkins and Media Living-Learning Centers are housed here. Common areas include a computer lab, lounge, and conference and meeting rooms. This dormitory is close to Third Street restaurants and stores, such as Mother Bear's Pizza and TIS. It is next door to the Jacobs School of Music's East Studio Building and close to the Wendell W. Wright Education Building.

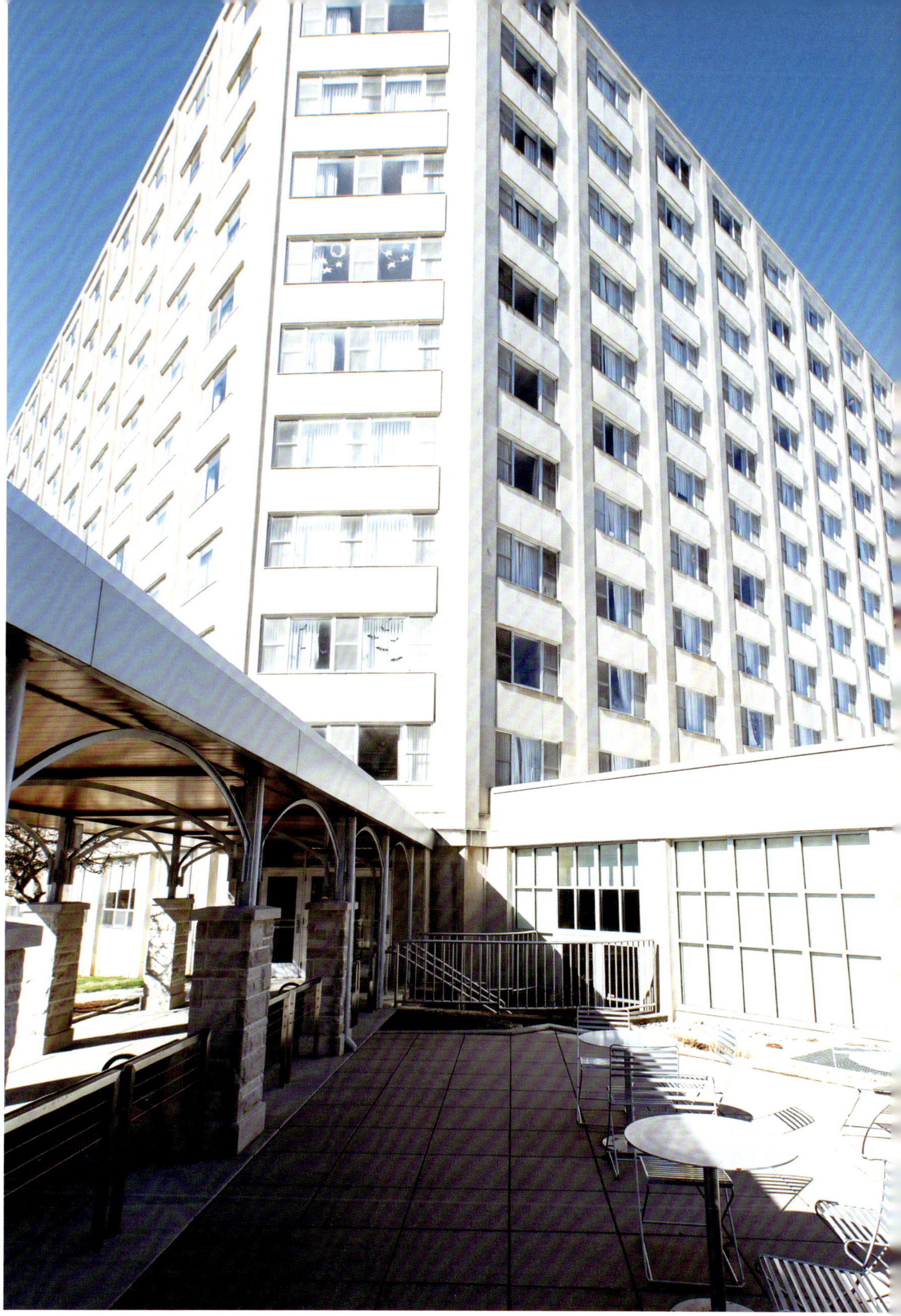

Forest Quadrangle, 2017. Photo credit: Tyagan Miller.

Eigenmann Hall

Once the Campus Melting Pot

Go where you will in the United States or the world today and identify yourself as a member of the Indiana University family, and you will find you are known, because a father or sister or husband has attended; or because a teacher or a Peace Corpsman or doctor has brought his education from Indiana to that place.

—Indiana University President John W. Ryan

EIGENMANN HALL WAS BUILT IN 1968 TO HOUSE graduate students, international students, and those undergraduates over twenty-one years of age. The firm of Edward James and Associates of Indianapolis was hired to plan the structure with the supervision of Eggers and Higgins of New York. Dedicated on November 15, 1970, it was named for Carl H. Eigenmann (1863–1927), known for his contributions in the field of ichthyology. At Indiana University he studied under David Starr Jordan and received his undergraduate degree in 1886 and his graduate degree in 1889. He then became a professor of zoology at IU in 1891, head of its department, and finally the first dean of IU's Graduate School in 1908. He also founded the Winona Lake Biological Station in northern Indiana, which afforded IU students valuable field experience in the study of biological sciences.

Like Ballantine Hall, Eigenmann Hall is another example of Brutalist Modern style, which stands out in stark contrast to the more classical and graceful design of the Collegiate Gothic buildings prevalent on the Bloomington campus. Eigenmann is one of the tallest buildings not only on campus but in all of Bloomington. The fourteen above-ground floors are clad in smooth panels of Indiana limestone with sawed ashlar on the stairway towers at the ends of each wing. Its four wings meet in the middle to form a central common area with four elevators. Eigenmann stands just east of central campus at the corner of Tenth and Union Streets.

Early on, Eigenmann Hall was the only residence center to stay open year-round, since it housed most of the international students living on campus. At one point, students speaking over forty languages and from over a hundred countries were represented among its residents. In 1998, under pressure from the university to use its vacant rooms, Eigenmann Hall joined the Residence Halls Association, which ended the era of it housing mostly graduate and international students. The room selection includes singles, doubles, and triples, all sharing community baths. There are study lounges, a library, and music practice rooms, and, for a snack, students can stop at Cool Beans Eigenmann or the center café and store. Additionally, half of Eigenmann Hall is currently used for offices and labs, such as the Center for Research on Learning and Technology, the Center for Postsecondary Research, and the Center for International Education, Development and Research.

Facing, Eigenmann Hall, undated.
Photo credit: Indiana University.

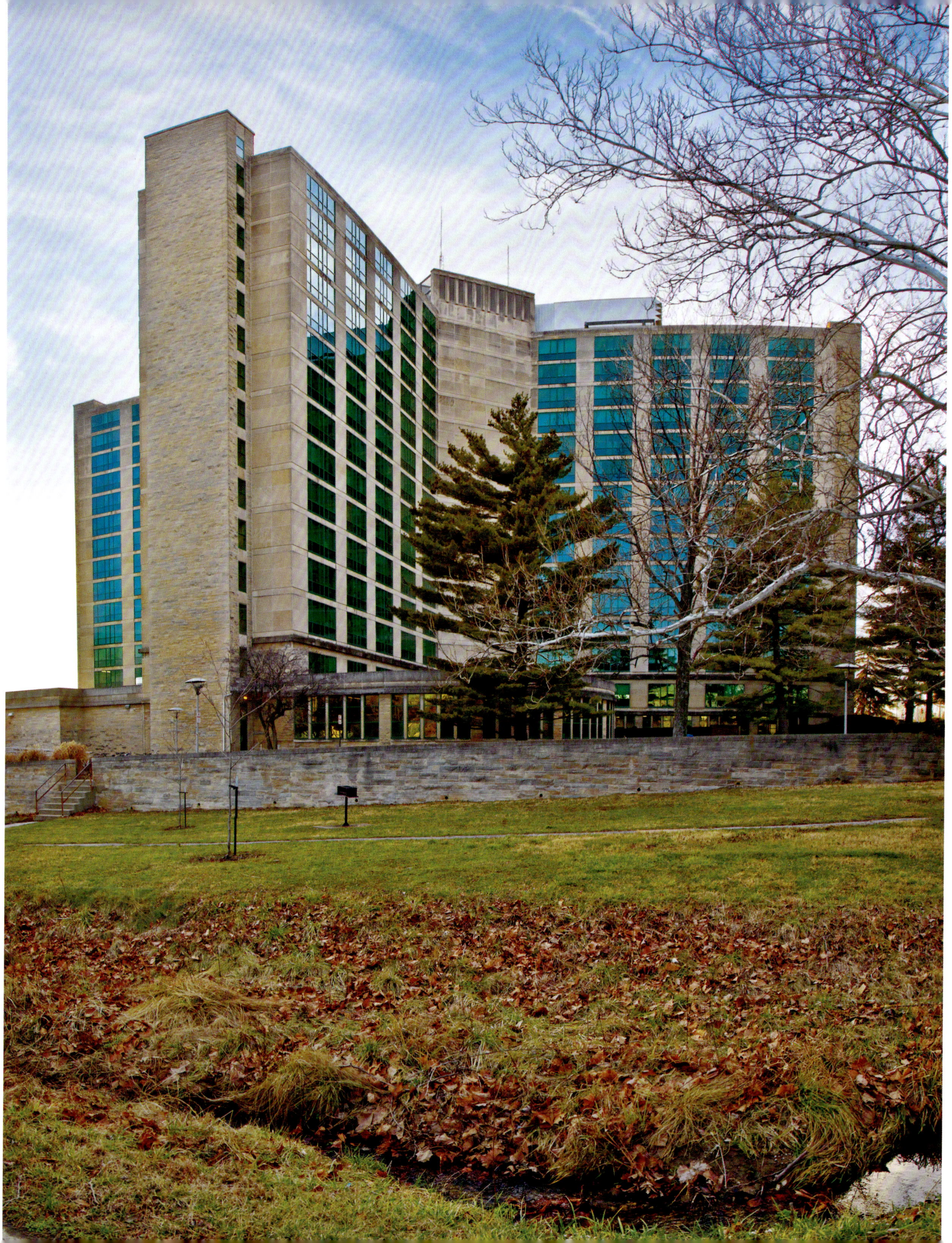

Union Street Center

Campus Apartment-Style Living

The landscape, rooted in the past, yet responsive to the present, provides not only the university but also all of Bloomington with an enduring and defining asset. For all who study, work, or visit, it is a magnificent composite of vistas and vignettes that inspire the soul and stimulate the mind and the senses.

—Moya Andrews, "The IU Campus in Spring"

ON THE SITE WHERE MOST OF THE OLD AND FORlorn Ashton dormitories once stood (some still remain) now stands an impressive example of the new era in university housing, Union Street Center. Recognizing the growing demand for more current campus housing and to compete with the lure of the off-campus market, Indiana University began construction in 2009 on the first new residential complex on the campus in forty years. Union Street Center was dedicated on October 26, 2010, on Union Street, one block south of Tenth Street.

Ratio architects of Indianapolis, selected by the university to create this new design for campus living, hoped to achieve not only architecture that blended well with the current campus but a complex that incorporated sustainable design principles and projected a village-like ambience. According to Ratio, the firm strove "to design environments where learning is supported, community is fostered, and the entire student life experience is enriched."[1]

Union Street Center consists of seven buildings. Cedar Hall, a multipurpose unit, ascends five levels, while the other six buildings each have four. The residence facility encircles two courtyards traversed by sidewalks and embellished with trees and other landscaping. The style is a modernized Collegiate Gothic accented with more contemporary sections of floor-to-ceiling glass walls. Cedar Hall has an extensive area on its west side faced with this same floor-to-ceiling glass. The cladding is mainly split-face limestone from Indiana quarries. Both tumbled blocks of stone and smooth panels appear in contrast on the walls and raised limestone bands surround the windows. Each of the buildings has one or more small peaked gables with slate roofs and flattened arches over passageways and entrances.

Union Street Center reinvented the living experience for its 827 non-freshmen residents by creating one-, two-, and, four-bedroom apartment-style suites with full kitchens, fully furnished living rooms and bedrooms, full baths, wireless Internet and cable, and washers and dryers. The structure also features state-of-the-art classrooms, fitness and recreation spaces, a café and store, a conference facility, and common areas and study lounges throughout. There is also a Hutton Honors College residential community. Union Street Center attracts students due to the twenty-first-century lifestyle it offers and its convenient location on the northeast side of campus.

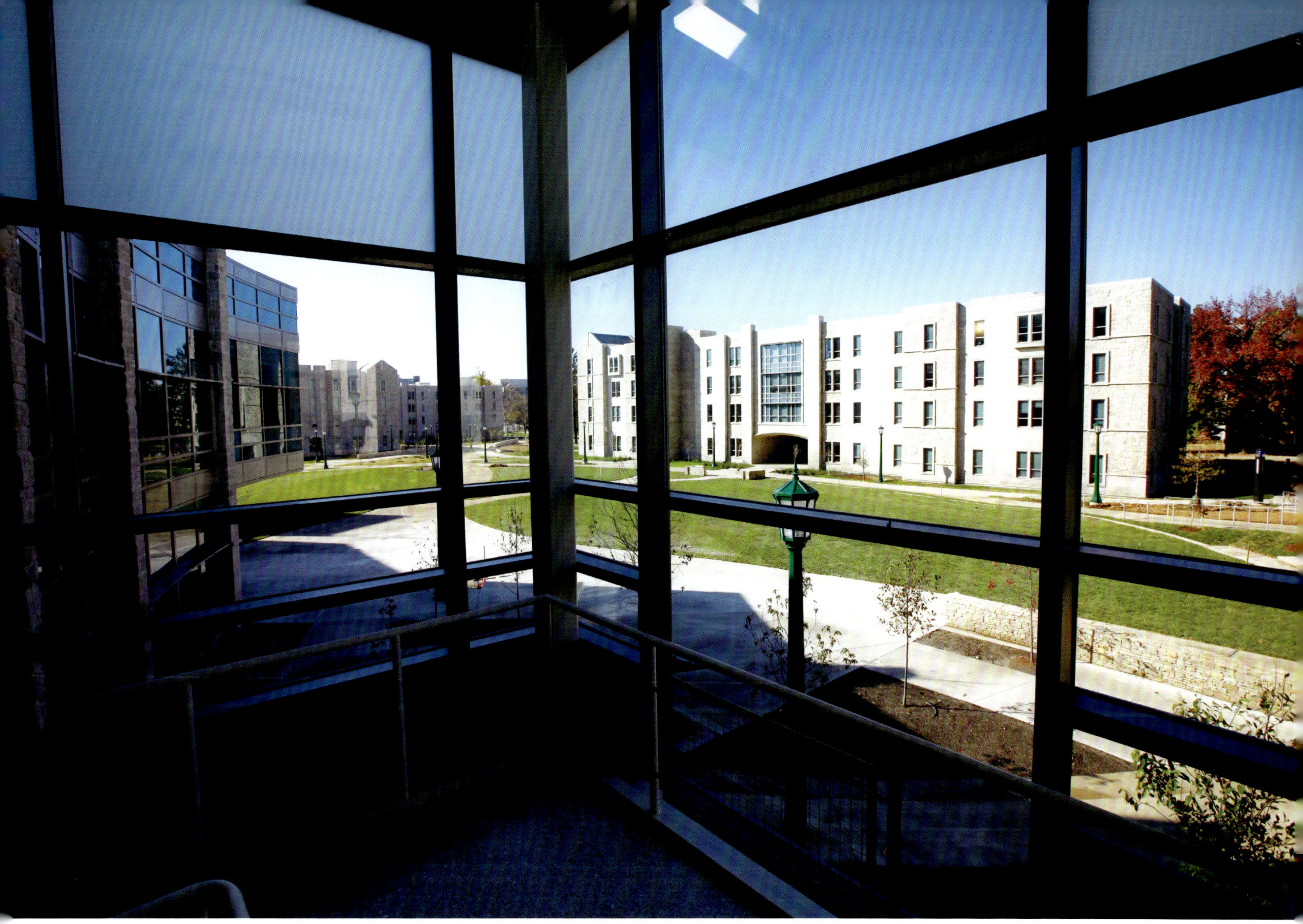

View of Union Street Center across courtyard, 2010. Photo credit: Indiana University.

Spruce Hall

A Twenty-First-Century Dorm

There are few places in the world where great laboratories, classrooms, libraries, and other beehives of intellectual and artistic activity are located so close to areas which retain the primeval character of midwestern America—few places where one may so quickly and so completely leave behind the tensions and anxieties of this complex modern world and find place for quiet meditation.

—*Paul Weatherwax,* The Woodland Campus of Indiana University

In step with the national trend to modernize university housing by making it less dorm-like and more in line with hotel accommodations, the university first constructed Union Street Center in 2010, renovated Briscoe in 2012–13, and built Spruce Hall (originally Rose Hall) in 2013. Spruce Hall is part of the Association of College and University Housing Officers–International 21st Century Project (ACUHO-I), a multiphase project to reinvent student housing on campuses. President McRobbie plans to have all residence halls upgraded or replaced by 2020, the university's bicentennial year.

Many of today's students arrive on campus accustomed to more personal space and modern amenities than, say, their parents' generation, and they have higher expectations for their surroundings. Spruce Hall was designed by MSKTD Architects of Fort Wayne and the plan was based on the four tenets of ACUHO-I's 21st Century Project: "community, sustainability, technology, and flexibility." IU students were involved in the ACUHO-I dialogue with MSKTD Architects and their consultants, Mackey Mitchell Architects of St. Louis, to create housing that would further student relationships and create a sense of community.[1]

The Spruce Hall Residence Center is located in the southeast section of campus near Third Street, neighboring Willkie, Forest, and Read residential centers and the Jacobs School of Music, and next door to the Wendell W. Wright Education Building. The style is trim and modern, with ground-to-roof windows drawing attention to the front of the building. The facade is clad in Indiana limestone to harmonize with the surrounding campus architecture. Most of the building is faced with an interesting quilt-like pattern of rough-faced ashlar, with accents of smooth-sawed panels. This is a spacious five-story building laid out in an angular C, with four above-ground floors, the top three housing students.

The well-appointed lobby is bathed in daylight from the expanse of glass. Spruce Hall accommodates 440 to 450 residents in clusters of four double rooms with a shared bath, double suites with shared baths, and single suites with a private bath.

For these new-generation students, each room has cable and wireless Internet, and each floor has a kitchenette. Study lounges are sprinkled throughout, along with practice rooms to accommodate the nearby Jacobs School of Music's students. Spruce Hall's café serves snacks and beverages, while meals can be taken in Forest Quadrangle or any other RPS facility. On-site are a fitness center and an outdoor basketball court. A School of Education Living-Learning Center was added to Spruce Hall in 2014.

Because it is newer construction and offers extra space and amenities (placing it in the "enhanced housing category"), Spruce Hall is somewhat more expensive than some of the other residence halls.

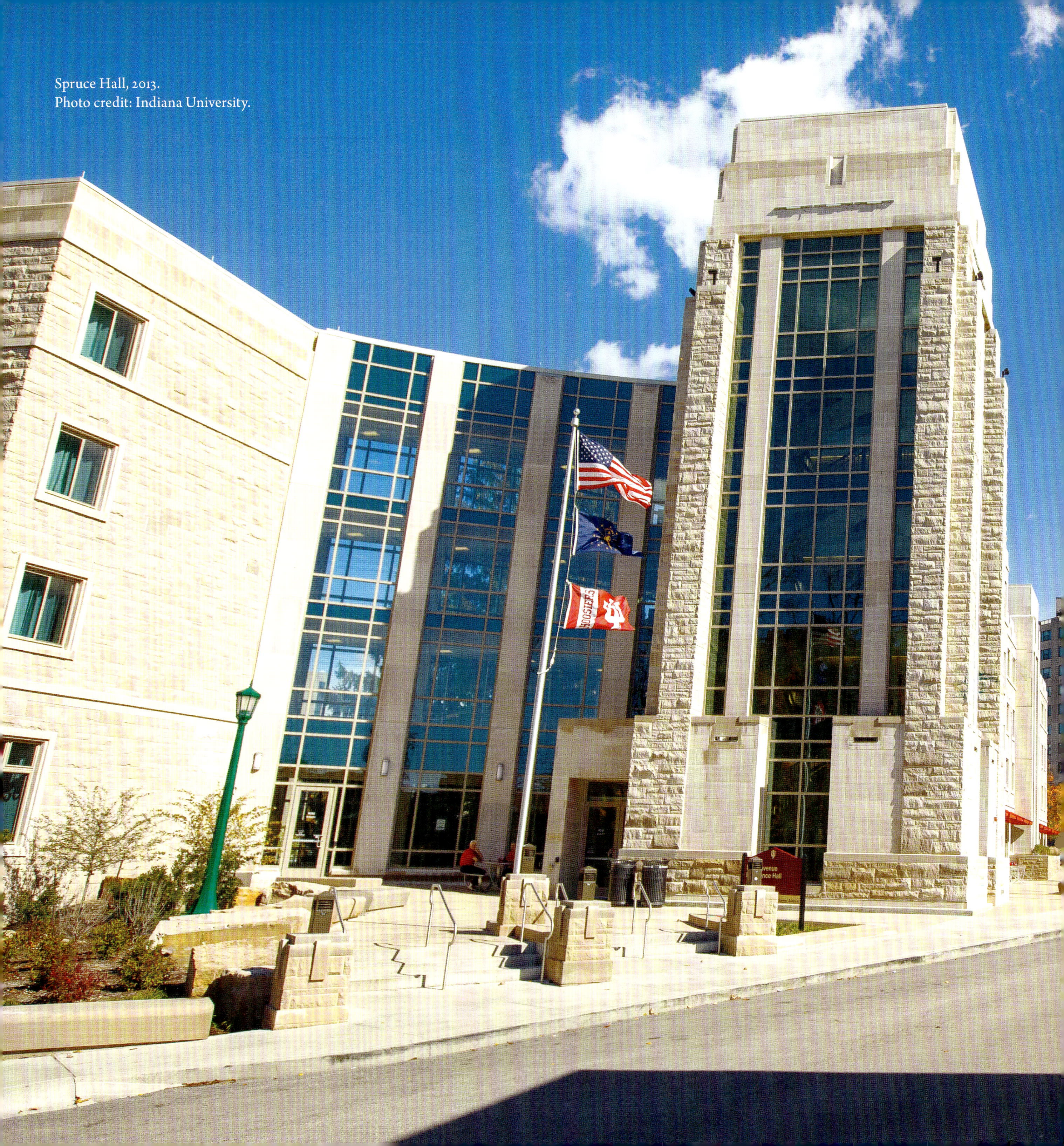

Spruce Hall, 2013.
Photo credit: Indiana University.

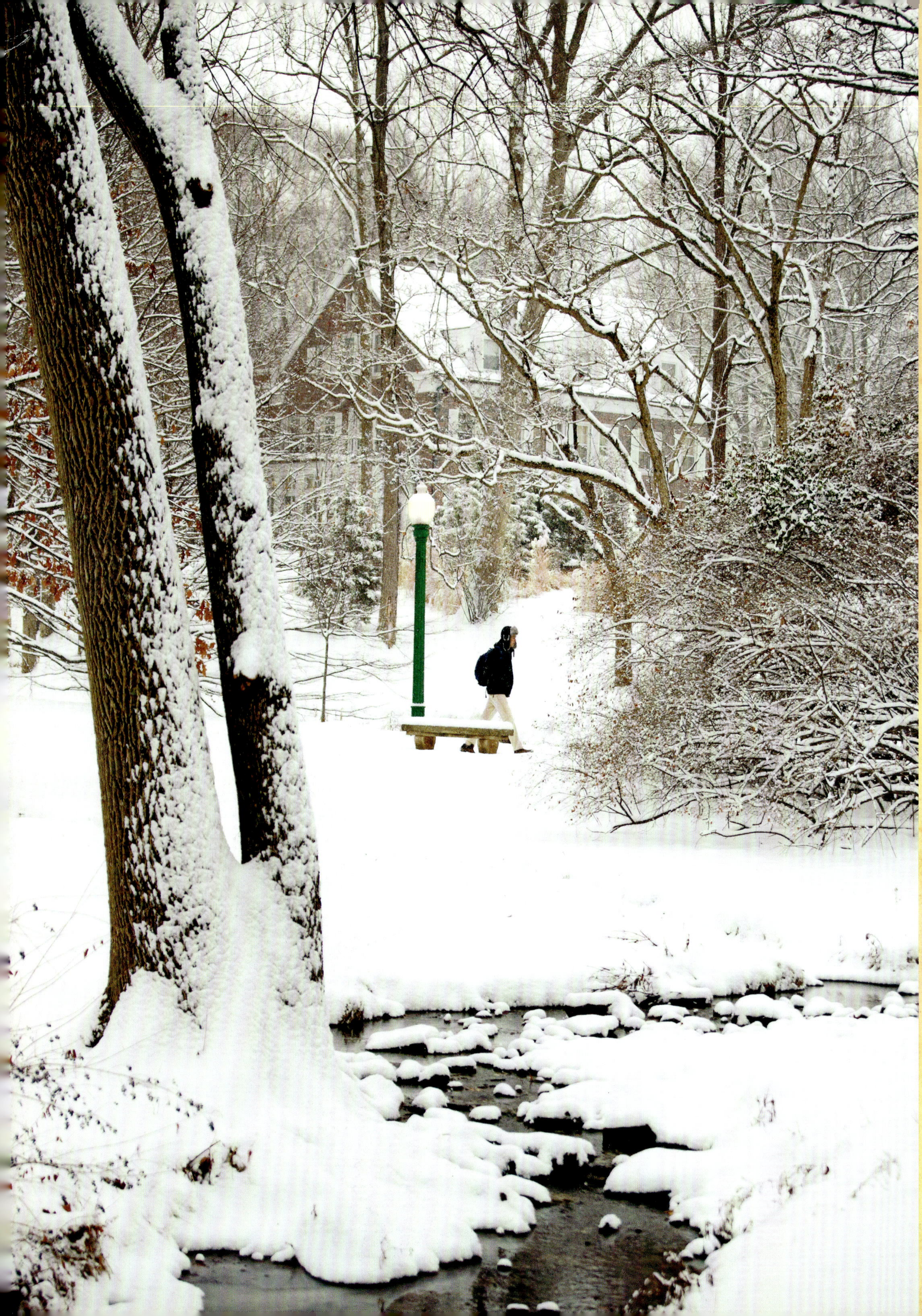

COMMON FACILITIES

It is more than a thing of beauty. Its trees are sanctuaries under which old men may dream dreams and young men may see visions. Certain scenes stamp themselves indelibly upon the mind: lingering shadows of tall trees creeping across the grass on long summer afternoons; masses of Forsythia bursting into sudden yellow bloom; and that loveliest of all Indiana springtime pictures, white dogwood and pink redbud blooming against a green background of maples.

EDITH HENNEL ELLIS
"The Trees on the I.U. Campus,"
Indiana University Alumni Quarterly, 1929

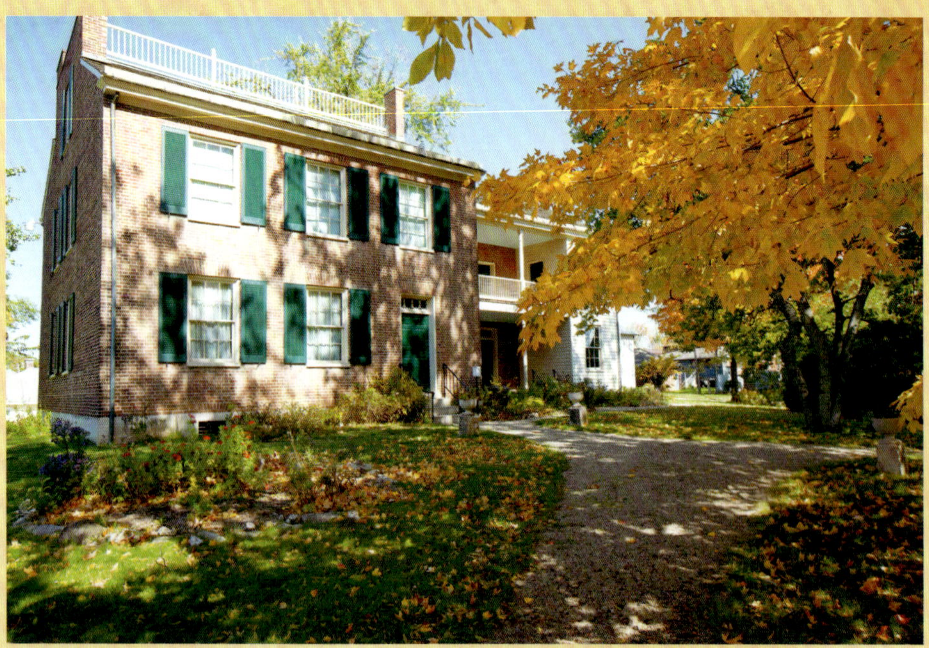

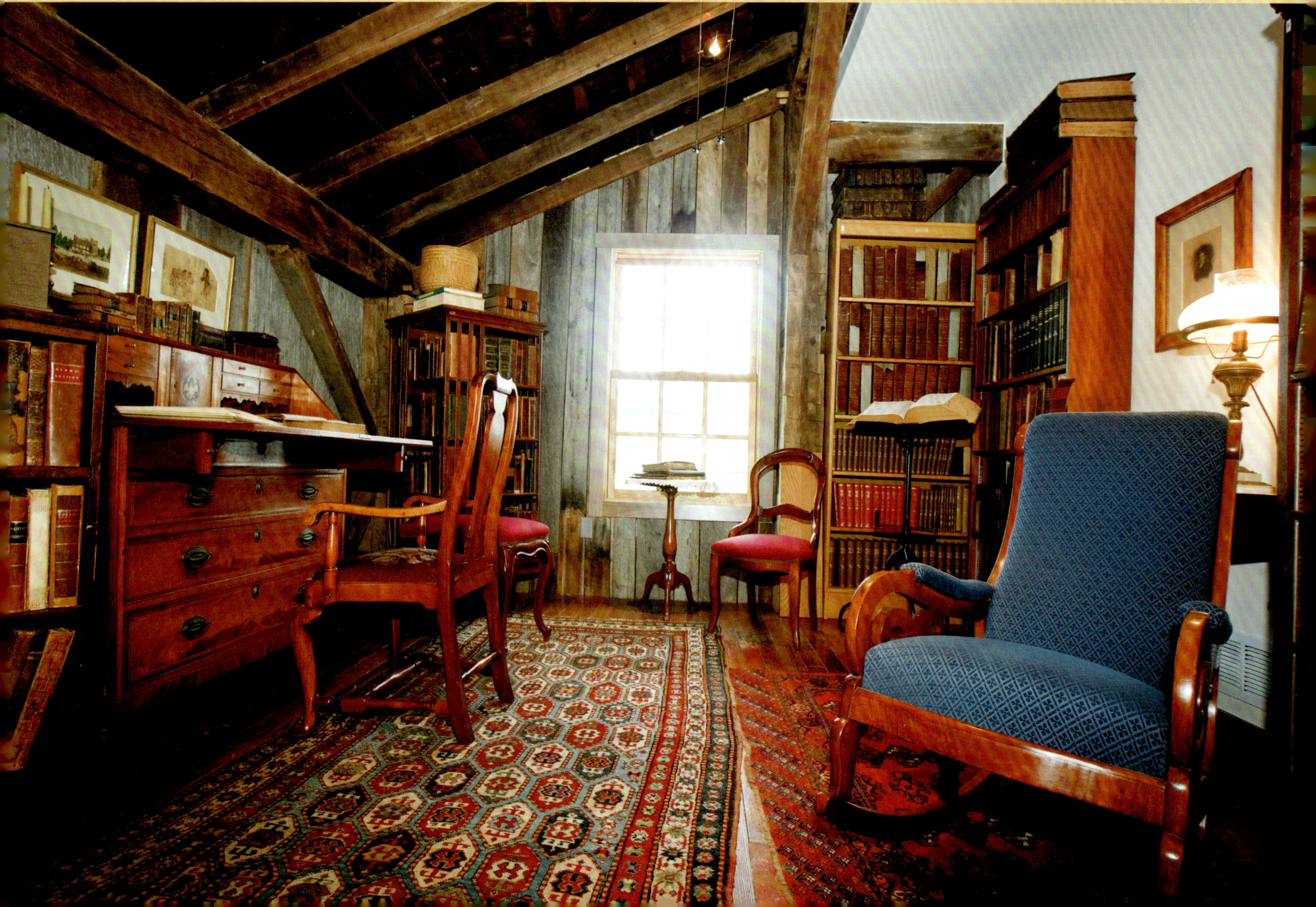

Wylie House Museum

Home of IU's First President

All of the materials of the best quality—the work to be neat and substantial. . . . All doors and windows to be arched, the arch reaching through four courses of brick work. The front to be done in Flemish bond.

—Construction contract

In 1835, Andrew Wylie, the first president of Indiana University, contracted with George L. Troop and John McDonald for the erection of his home in Bloomington. Situated at the center of a 20-acre farmstead—just east of the Indiana College campus (today the corner of Second and Lincoln Streets)—the stately structure was built with bricks made from clay removed during the cellar excavation. The home featured paired chimneys, a two-story porch, decorative brickwork, and a narrow widow's walk from which the Wylie family and students might stargaze. It was a blend of Federal and Georgian styles atypical for the period in southern Indiana, probably modeled after the Isaac Manchester House, a home in southwestern Pennsylvania where Andrew Wylie was born and raised.

The Wylie home was "the most stately mansion of its time and place," but despite the elegance and detail of his home, it was built without running water and heated only by fireplaces, as were all houses of the time. In fact, it was so cold in the winter that the inkwells would freeze.[1] On the large property, the family maintained a fully operational farm that included a smokehouse, barn, chicken house, vegetable garden, carriage house, and two-story utility building. Andrew and his wife, Margaret Ritchie Wylie, enjoyed plenty of help as they had twelve children, ten of whom lived in Bloomington. The home during this era was witness to times of great joy and tremendous sorrow. Their eldest child, Andrew Jr., had already finished a degree at Indiana College in 1832 and had moved back east to begin a law practice. Another son, William, died in the spring of 1835 from typhoid fever while a college senior. Family letters chronicle student boarders, hard work, cholera and typhoid epidemics, the college's precarious funding, the death of two more sons, and, in the parlor on May 17, 1849, the double wedding ceremony of daughters Maggie and Irene.

Following Andrew's death from an injury he sustained while chopping wood in 1851, Margaret remained in the house for the rest of her life. Her heirs then sold the home, along with 5 acres of the original homestead, to Andrew's half-cousin, Theophilus A. Wylie (1810–95), who moved into the house in 1859 along with his wife, Rebecca Dennis, and six of their eight children. Theophilus had come to Bloomington in 1837 to teach mathematics and science at the college. He also served as the librarian, and following Andrew's death he carried out the duties of president. The journals of prolific writer Theophilus chronicle a vivid portrait of a family and a sapling university during a dramatic period of U.S. history, which included the Civil War, the assassination of President Lincoln, the invention of the daguerreotype, the arrival of electricity in Bloomington, and, in 1883, the fire and devastation of Science Hall and the beginnings of the new university campus in 1884.[2]

The home was a regular stop for faculty and students alike. Faculty members Richard Owen and Daniel Kirkwood are regularly noted as dining with the family, and Sarah Parke

Facing top, Wylie House blends Federal and Georgian styles, 2012. Photo credit: Tyagan Miller.

Facing bottom, Cozy room in the Morton C. Bradley Education Center on Wylie House grounds, 2013. Photo credit: Tyagan Miller.

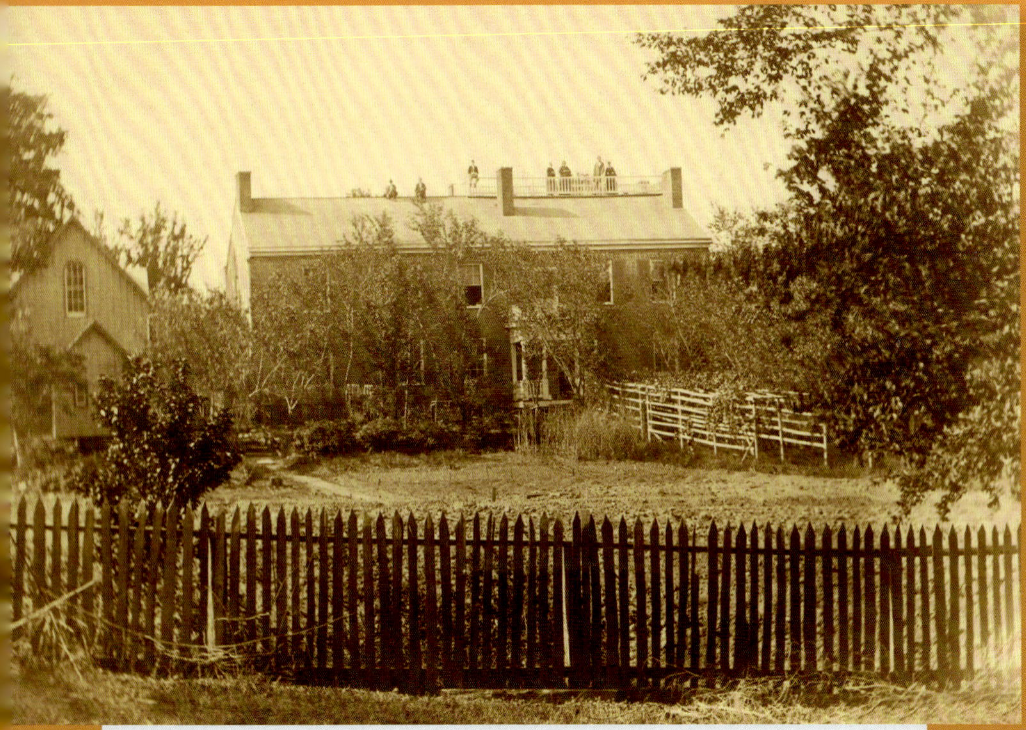

Stargazing from the Wylie House Widow's Walk

An amateur astronomer, T. A. Wylie and his family viewed celestial events from the widow's walk on the top of the house, documenting many in the pages of his diaries over the years. In 1863, he wrote to his daughter Louisa: "The weather has been mild, a little snow fell night before last. Thursday night before last, we had sixteen students sitting up by squads of 6 & 5 on the top of the house looking for meteors, they noticed about 250. The next night on which more were expected, proved cloudy & so we could not watch."[1]

1. T. A. Wylie to Miss E. Louise M. Wylie, received November 27, 1863, Theophilus Wylie Family Correspondence collection, Wylie House Museum, Indiana University Libraries, Bloomington, Indiana.

Morrison, a close family friend and the first female graduate of the university, stayed with the family for a time while attending classes.[3] The Wylie House also was often a target for lighthearted Senior Serenade shenanigans.

The Wylie family had owned the house for eighty years when in 1915 Amos Hershey, a well-known scholar in international politics, and his wife, Lillian, purchased the house, where she operated an antique and gift shop called the Old Treasure House in the front parlor. In 1947 at then president Herman B Wells's behest, Indiana University purchased the property, which housed the IU Press from 1951 to 1959. It subsequently went through extensive renovations to house a historic museum that re-created the Wylie home prior to 1860.

The Wylie House Museum opened to the public in 1965. One of the few extant pre-1840 structures in Bloomington, the home is filled with period furniture, including original Wylie family furnishings, many of which had been acquired by Herman B Wells. In 1977 Wylie House was placed on the National Register of Historic Places. In 2010 the Morton C. Bradley Education Center was added to the Wylie House grounds for education and outreach programs.

Above, North side of Wylie House; note people on the widow's walk, undated. P0043540, IU Archives.

Elizabeth "Lizzie" Breckenridge

At the age of thirteen, Elizabeth "Lizzie" Breckenridge joined the T. A. Wylie household as a cook.[1] She remained with the Wylies until her death fifty-five years later and was fondly described as "one of the family." Anton Boisen (T. A. Wylie's grandson) recalled in his memoir: "Lizzie came from a family of slaves who had been freed before the Civil War. Their presence in Bloomington was due to the Covenanter sympathy with the Negroes and she herself was a devout member of the Old Side Covenanter Church on South Walnut Street. She was a student of the stars, a study to which my grandfather had introduced her. She knew all the principal constellations and all the brighter stars, and no comet ever escaped her attention. A finer spirit there never was. We all looked upon her as one of the family."[2]

1. W. Bradfute, "In One Family for Nearly Forty-Five Years," *Indianapolis News*, February 3, 1903.
2. Anton T. Boisen, *Out of the Depths: An Autobiographical Study of Mental Disorder and Religious Experience* (New York: Harper & Brothers, 1960), 29–30.

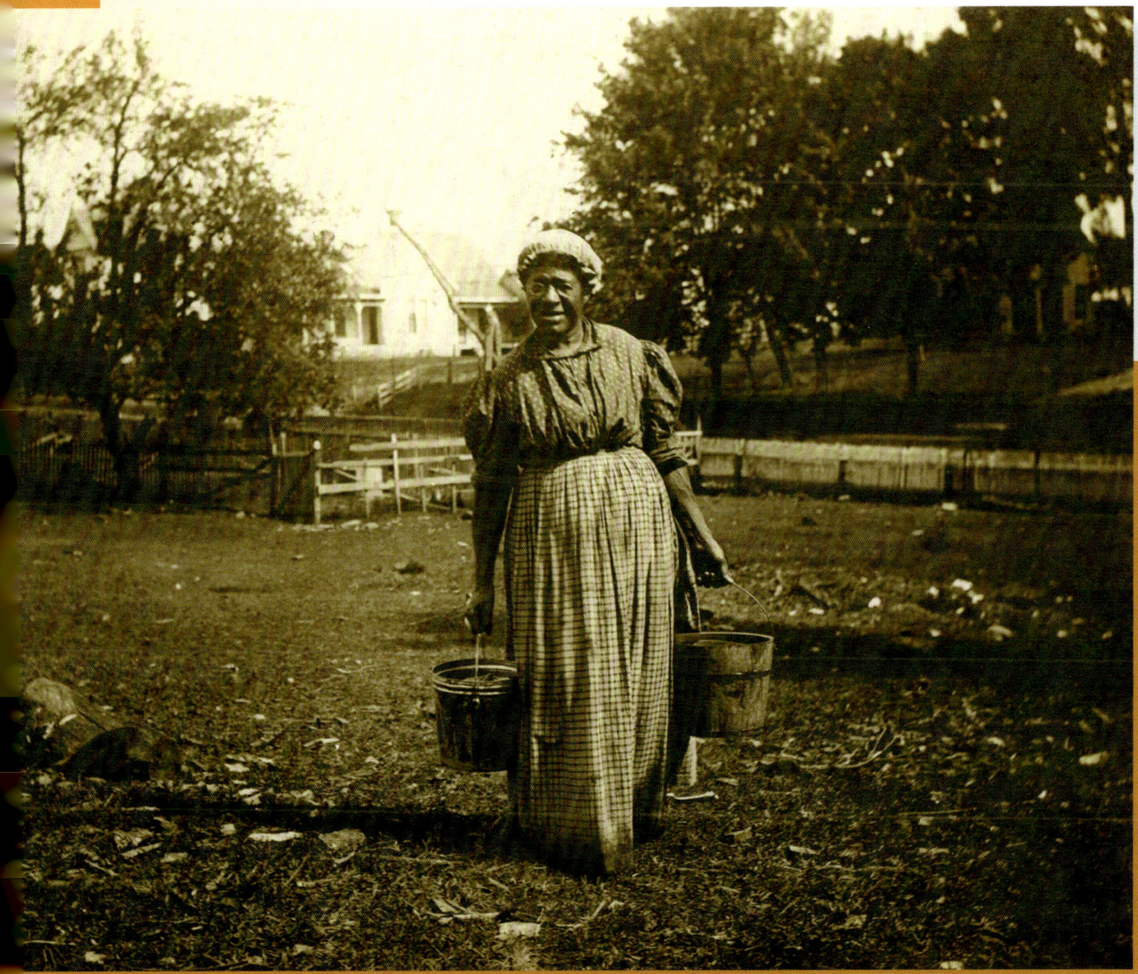

Elizabeth "Lizzie" Breckenridge, 1898. P0044406, IU Archives.

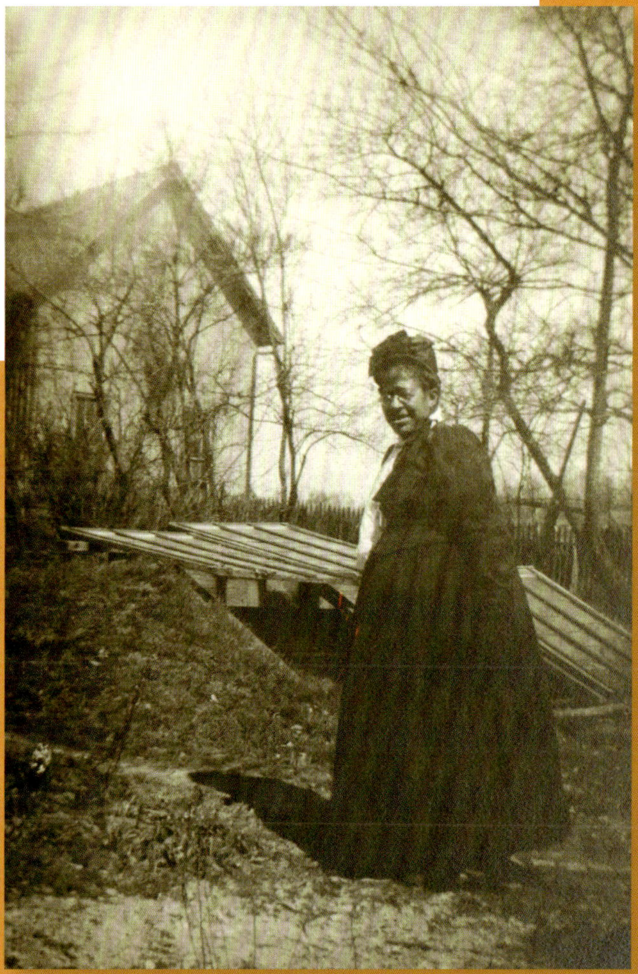

Elizabeth "Lizzie" Breckenridge, living with T. A. Wylie family in Wylie House, circa 1905. P0044405, IU Archives.

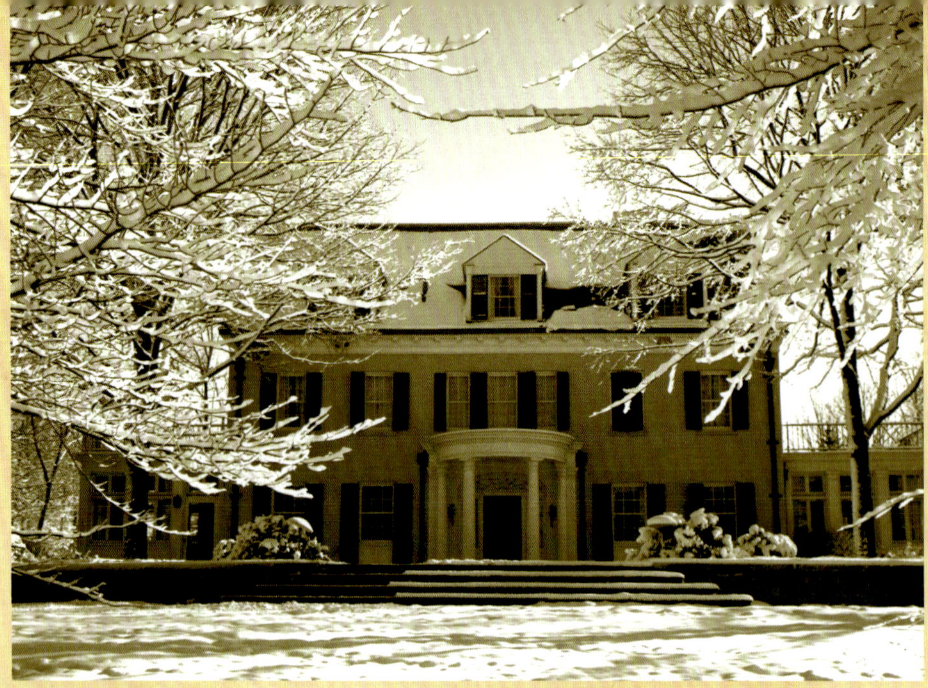

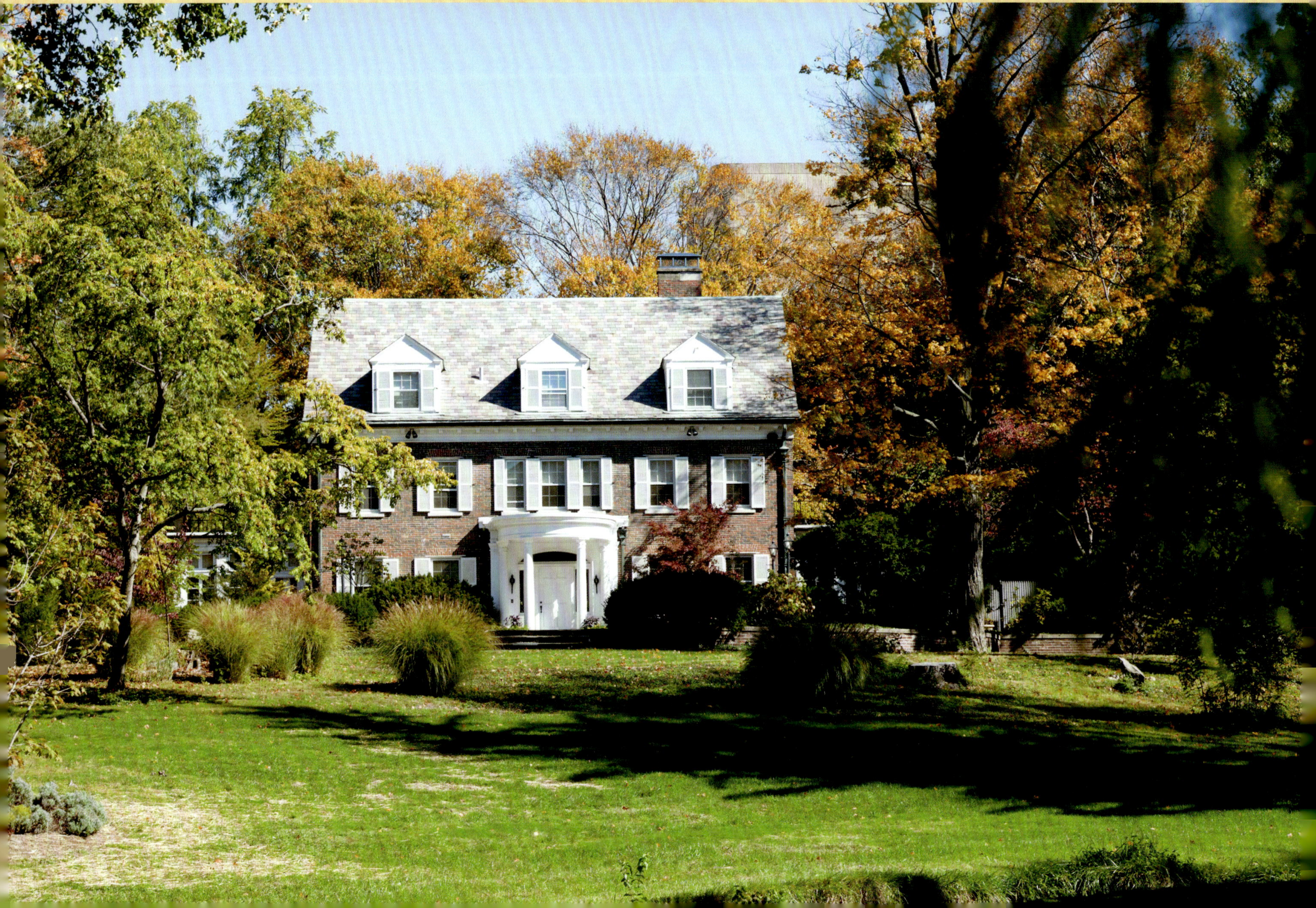

William and Charlotte Lowe Bryan House

The President's House

This house is, we think, a noble exemplification of domestic architecture and in some measure an expression, inadequate though it be, of [Dr. and Mrs. Bryan's] rank in work and worth in this University, this city and in the commonwealth of Indiana.

—Dedication Ceremony Program

On a grassy knoll near the banks of the Jordan River in what was then considered the extreme east side of campus, Bryan House was built in 1924 during the term of the university's tenth president, William Lowe Bryan, and his wife, Charlotte. The couple met while students at Indiana University and married on July 11, 1889. For much of his presidency, which extended from 1902 through 1937, the Bryans lived in a home off campus. Discussions concerning the need for a president's residence on campus, however, had been ongoing since early 1915.

Known as a prudent administrator, Bryan often returned a portion of his salary to the university in support of campus initiatives. Thus, in 1915 the *Indiana Daily Student* reported that "Daggett & Co. are working on plans for the President's new residence which Dr. Bryan is planning to erect on the campus, with the consent of the Board of Trustees. . . . Dr. Bryan has asked permission to build the home at his own expense and allow it eventually to become the property of the University."[1]

Although the trustees did not acquiesce to Bryan's wishes, in 1921 the board determined it was indeed time for the university president to have a home on campus. Bryan finally gave his consent in 1923, but with the stipulation that he would contribute $10,000 toward its cost. The eminent architect Robert Frost Daggett of Indianapolis was hired to design the home, and construction began. Campus lore suggests the Bryans chose the location for their home on the wooded hill where they would go for picnics throughout the year.

From the constant correspondence the Bryans conducted with architect Daggett during the design and construction of their home, the importance that they placed on their need for generous sunlight throughout the house is apparent. Correspondence ensued over matters such as the heating system, plaster, bathroom fixtures, cornice moldings, the marble on the hearth, slate for the roof, the color of the mortar between the brick, and the best glass for the windows. Known simply as the President's House until 1970, the home was patterned after Woodrow Wilson's private home in Washington, DC, and is a classic example of Colonial Revival architecture with its balanced brick facade, gabled roof, and centralized door enhanced by a portico, embellished cornice, and symmetrical windows.[2]

The original structure had a living room, dining room, kitchen, pantry, study, sun porch, and dining porch on the first floor; four bedrooms and two baths on the second floor; laundry and storeroom in the basement; and an attic that included plans for a maid's room and bath. The interior of the home was designed to be elegantly practical. In a 1950 *Indiana Daily Student* interview, Bryan credited his wife with the project: "[she] was at the house almost every day while it was being built. . . . Every room bears witness to the care and thoughtfulness with

Facing top, William and Charlotte Lowe Bryan House, 1958. P0052684, IU Archives. Photo credit: Elwood Martin "Barney" Cowherd, Indiana University.

Facing bottom, West elevation of William and Charlotte Lowe Bryan House, undated. Photo credit: Indiana University.

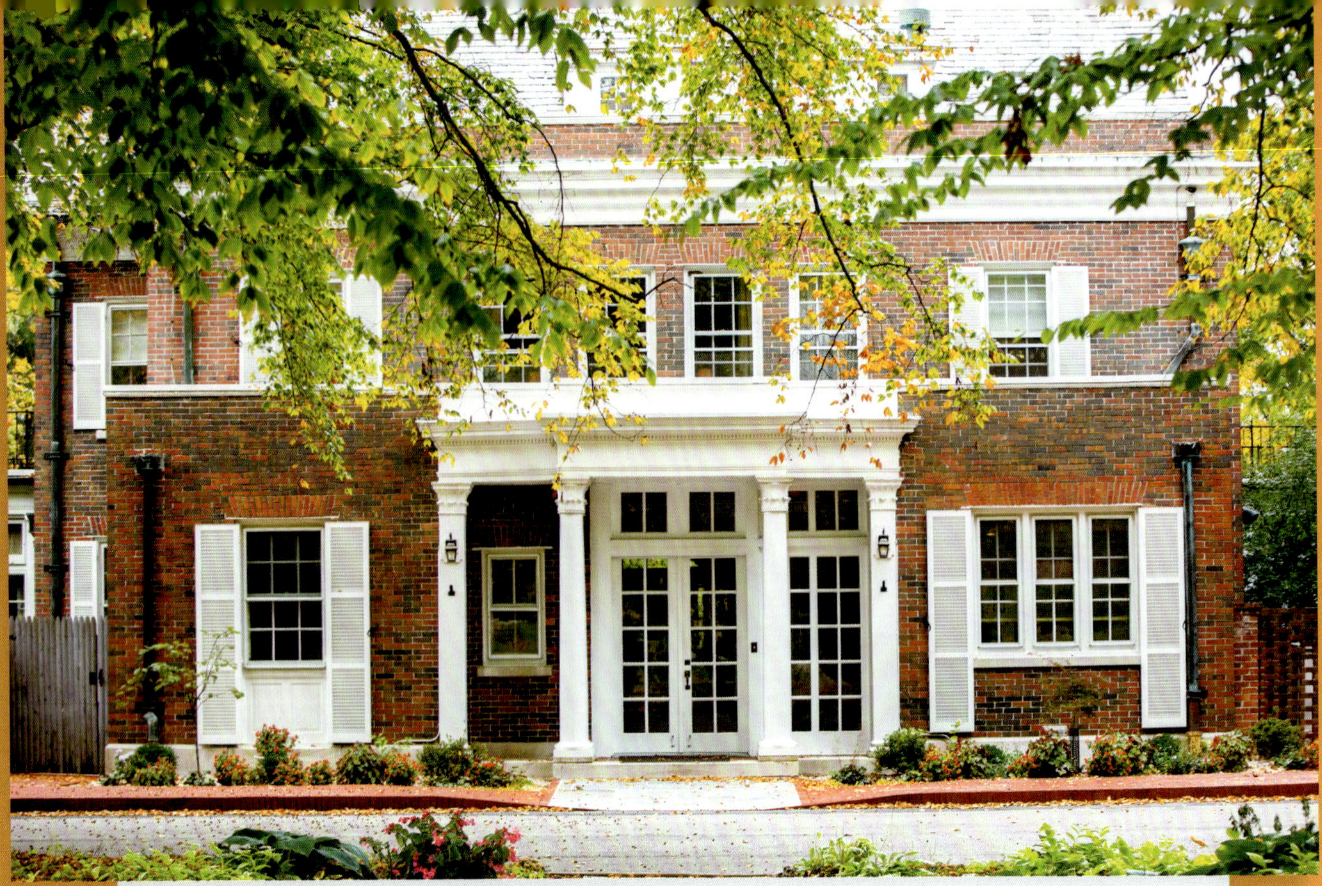

Famous Guests

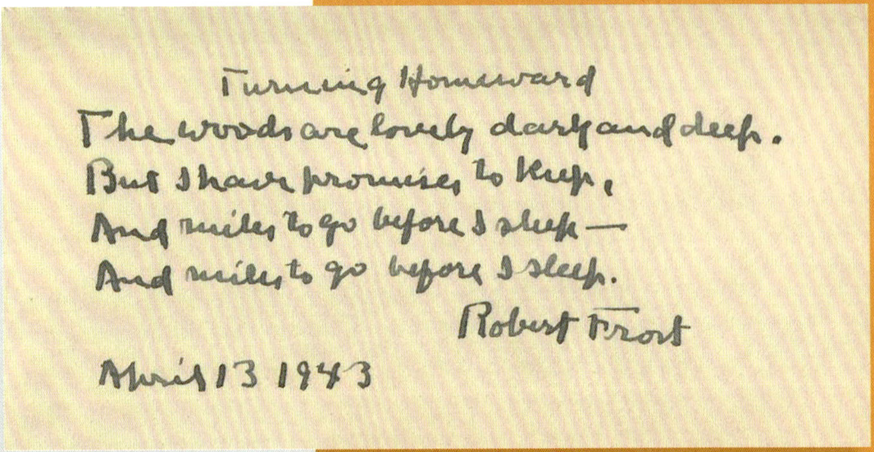
Turning Homeward
The woods are lovely dark and deep.
But I have promises to keep,
And miles to go before I sleep—
And miles to go before I sleep.
Robert Frost
April 13 1943

Upon the completion of their new home, the Bryans were presented with a guest book, which since has been filled with the names of numerous well-known individuals from Indiana and across the country. Authors, artists, government officials, and educators, as well as university faculty and students, have signed their names on the pages. A frequent caller to the Bryan's home was T. C. Steele; Bryan was instrumental in bringing Steele to the university as the first artist-in-residence. Carl Sandburg and Robert Frost signed the book with verses of poetry, while Eleanor Roosevelt signed it with "good wishes."[1] More recent additions to the guest book include Senator Birch Bayh, cellist Yo-Yo Ma, actress Meryl Streep, producer and director Spike Lee, and journalist and alumna Jane Pauley.

1. Carl Sandburg signature, March 31, 1942; final stanza of Robert Frost's "Stopping by Woods on a Snowy Evening," April 13, 1943; and Eleanor Roosevelt signature, January 14, 1950, all in Bryan House Guest Book, accession 9420, Indiana University Archives, Indiana University, Bloomington.

which she planned every detail. For instance, when the gently curving stairway leading from the main entrance hall was nearly finished, she had it dismantled and rebuilt. The original landing was too narrow for comfort and safety."[3]

Following William Lowe Bryan's retirement in 1937, the Bryans continued to live in the house until their passing. Charlotte died in 1948, followed by William seven years later. Since that time, the home has continued to serve as the residence for Indiana University presidents and their many guests.

Prior to President Herman B Wells's occupancy in 1957, the home underwent an extensive renovation. Changes included the modernization of the kitchen and the installation of an elevator, the addition of a catering kitchen in the basement, and the addition of three bedrooms and two baths on the third floor for staff and overnight guests, for which the roof was raised and dormer windows were added. Another extensive renovation project during the 1980s presidency of Thomas Ehrlich sought to return the interior of the home to its original appearance. The dark, quarter-sawn oak floors were uncovered, quarry tile was restored, and draperies were removed to reveal the detailed woodwork around the windows. The walls were repainted and recovered to emphasize the original simplicity of the home.

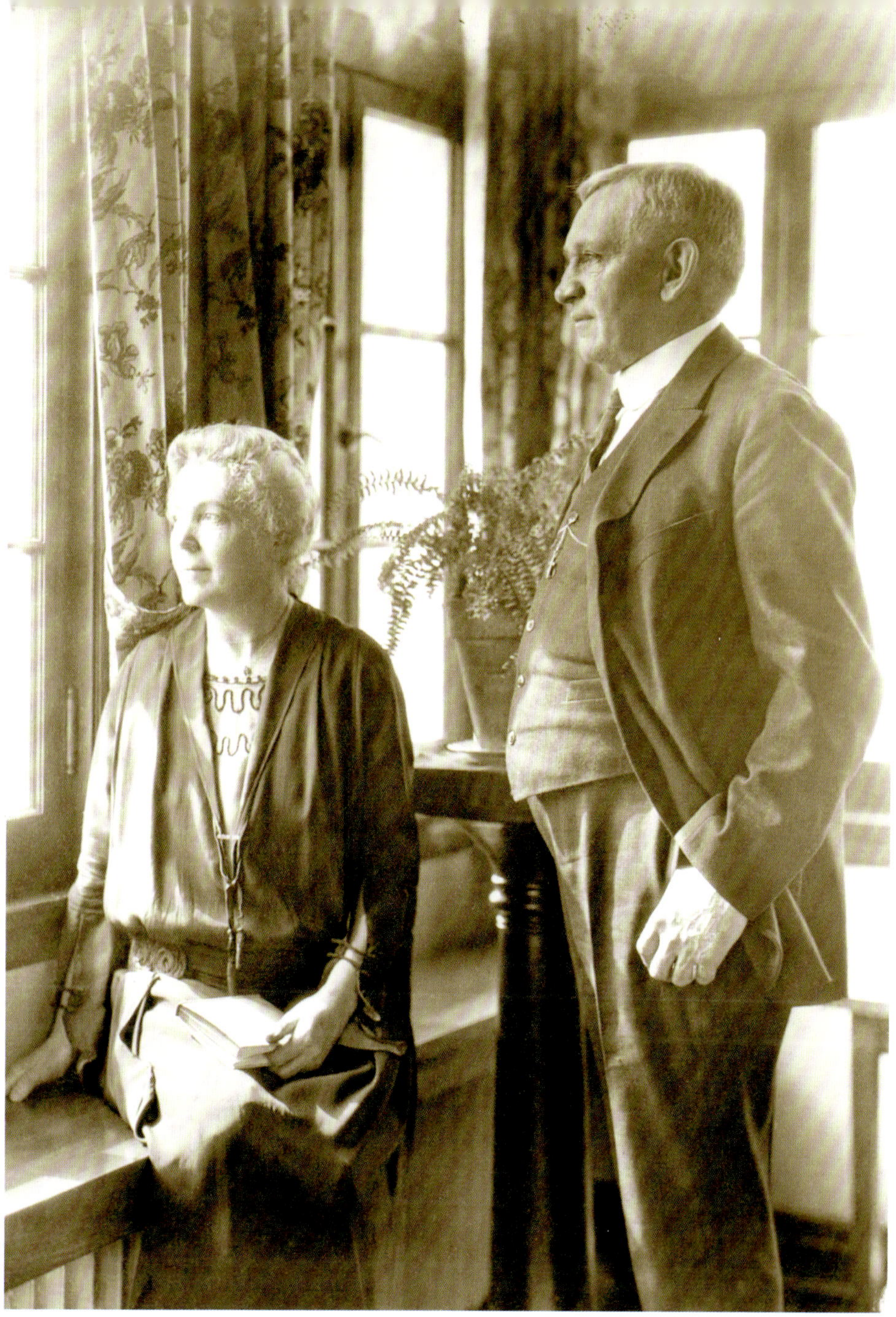

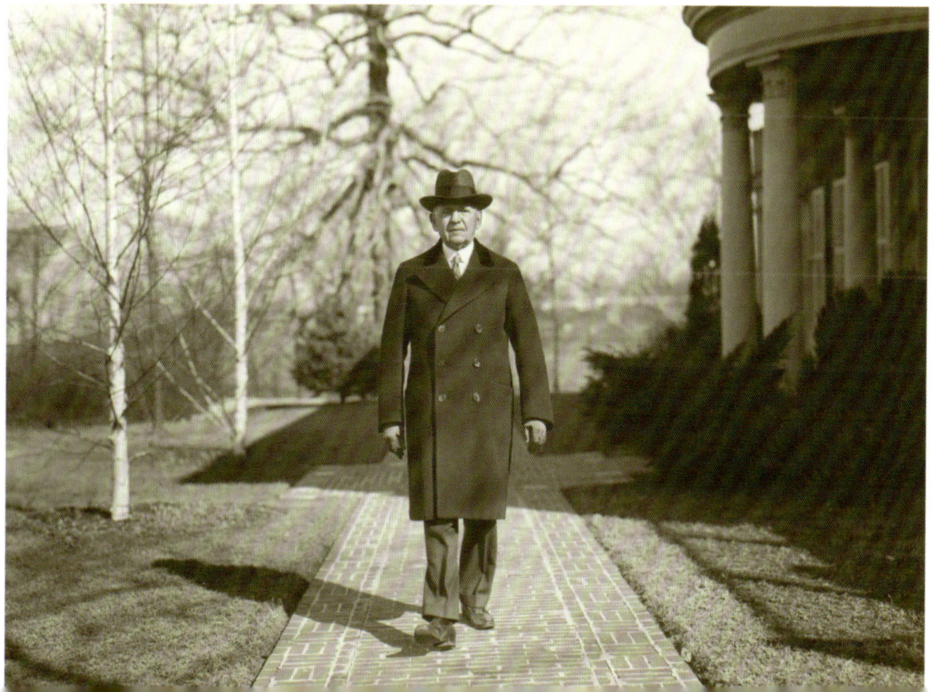

Facing top, East facade of Bryan House, a classic example of Colonial Revival architecture, 2016. Photo credit: Tyagan Miller.

Facing inset, Final stanza of Robert Frost's "Stopping by Woods on a Snowy Evening," scanned from a page in the Bryan House guestbook, 1943. P0038008, IU Archives.

Right above, William Lowe Bryan and Charlotte Lowe Bryan at home in the President's House, 1924. Photo credit: Mathers Museum of World Cultures, Indiana University.

Right below, William Lowe Bryan outside the President's House (later named Bryan House), undated. P0020487, IU Archives.

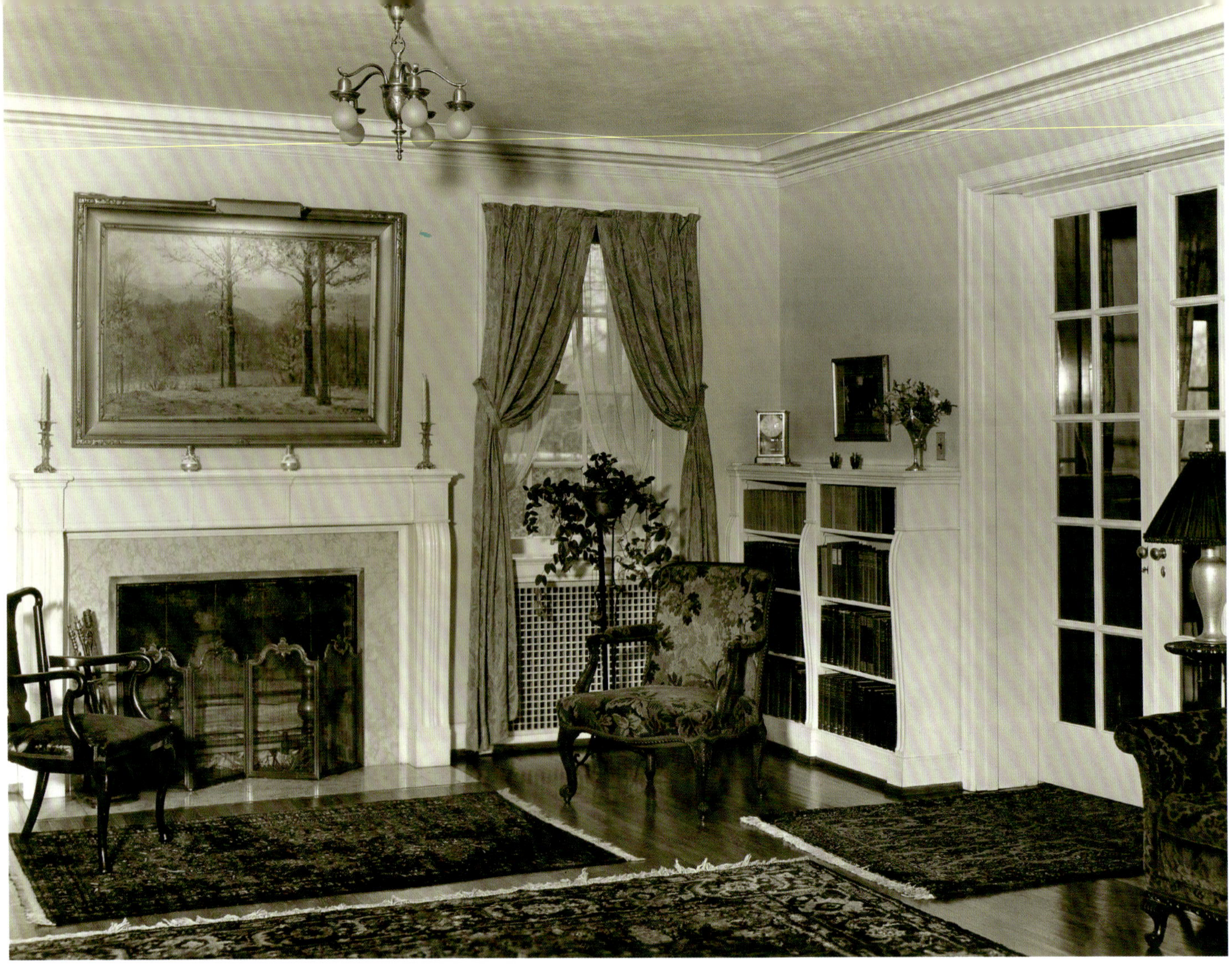

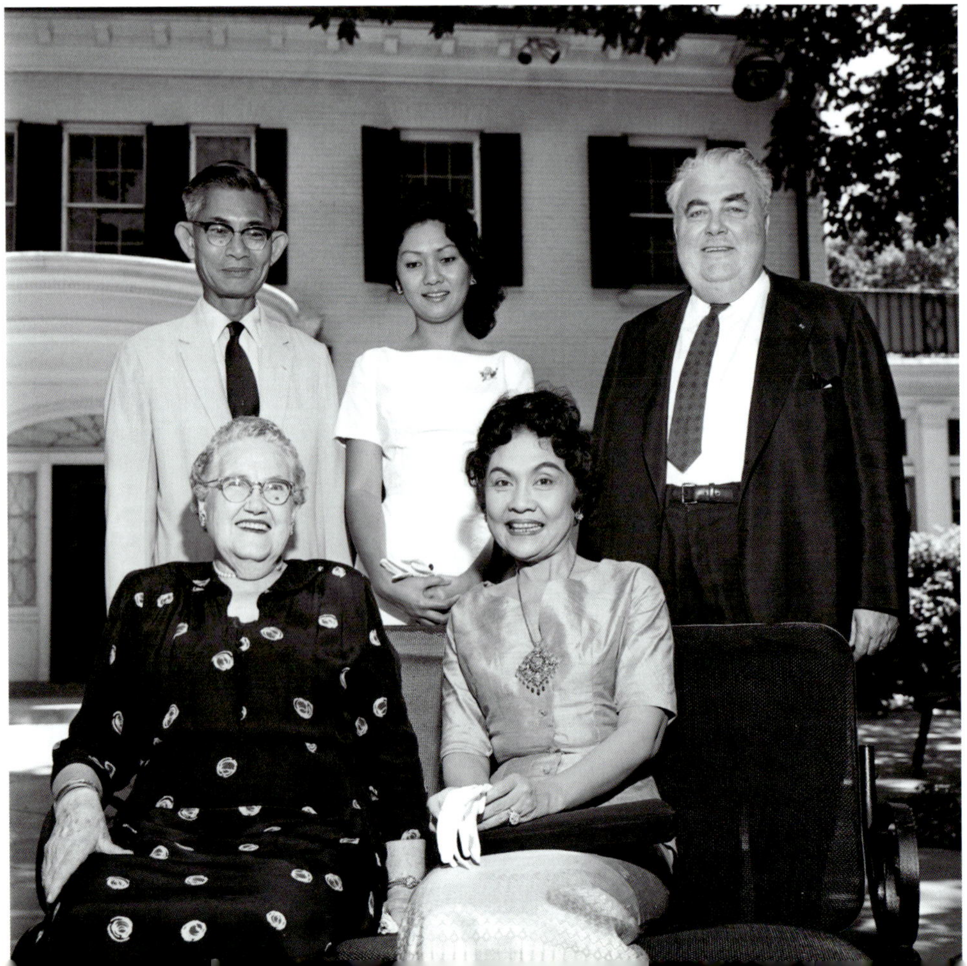

Above, Living room of President's House, circa 1935. P0037867, IU Archives. Photo credit: Sinclair Studio, Bloomington, Indiana.

Left, Herman B Wells and his mother, Mrs. Granville Wells, hosting Dr. Supachai Vanij-Yadahana, secretary-general of Chulalongkorn University, Bangkok, and his wife and daughter in the Bryan House gardens, 1960. P0033193, IU Archives. Photo credit: Elwood Martin "Barney" Cowherd.

Facing, Landscape study for Bryan House including formal gardens to the east, 1957. P0060929, IU Archives. Image credit: Fritz Loonsten.

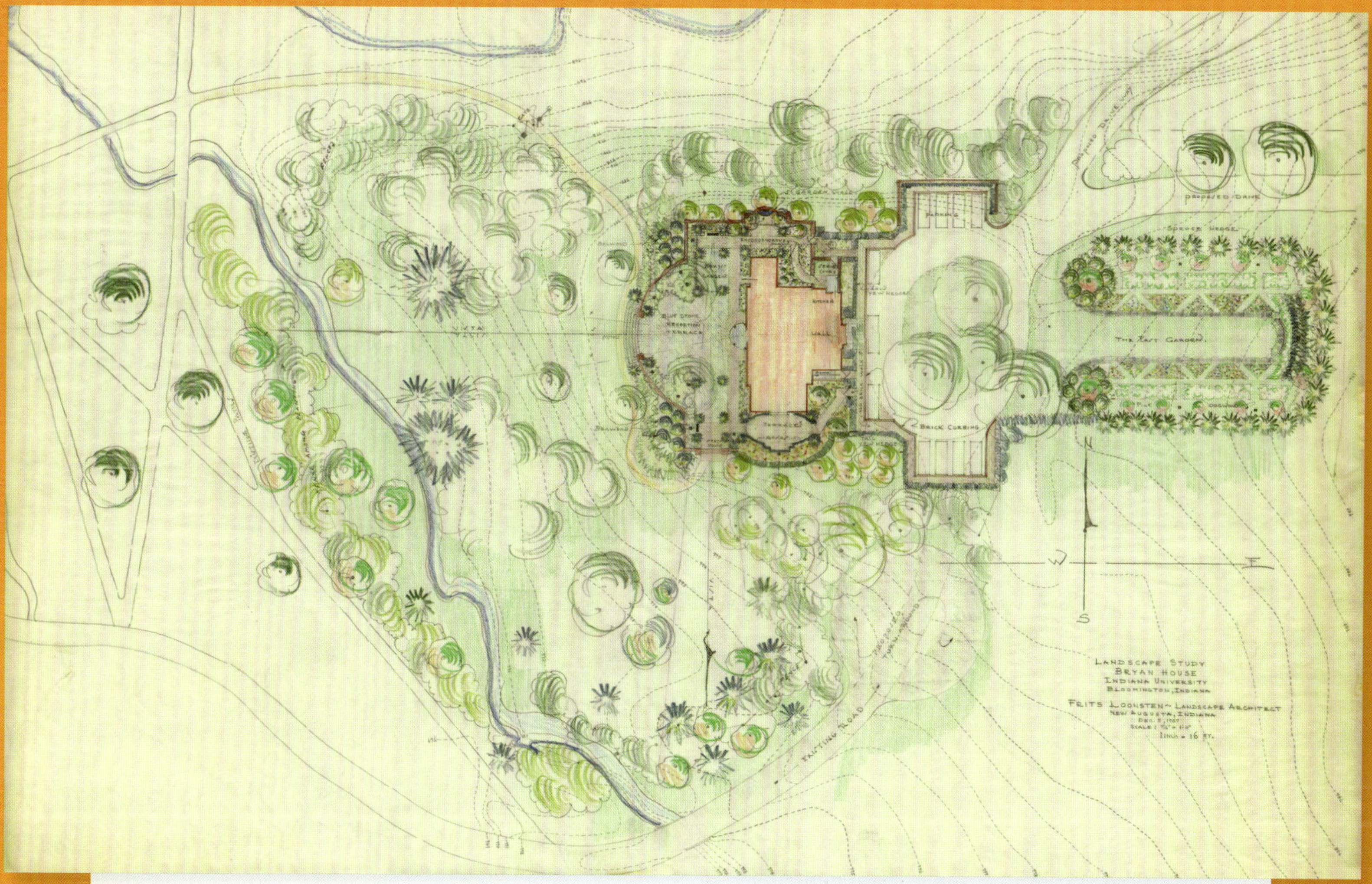

Landscape Design

With the arrival of spring every year, the grounds around Bryan House come alive, the result of William and Charlotte Lowe Bryan's vision as well as the careful planning by landscape architects over the years. George Kessler's initial designs proposed a circular drive to surround the house, leaving the landscape in its natural state. However, when construction on the structure began in 1923, the landscape designer Lawrence V. Sheridan designed front terrace areas to the west of the house and a narrow driveway coming from the south and ending in a circle at what would be the "carriage entrance" to the back of the house. Later landscape architects such as the Olmsted Brothers in 1936 and Fritz Loonsten in the 1950s made further suggestions for the grounds, including the formal gardens to the east of the home.[1]

1. Olmsted Study for Grounds around President's House, 1936, archives set 1444; and Fritz Loonsten Landscape Study, 1957, archives set 240, both in Indiana University Archives, Indiana University, Bloomington.

Indiana Memorial Union	1932
ARCHITECT	Granger and Bollenbacher
ARCHITECTURAL STYLE	Collegiate Gothic / Romanesque
ADDITION (N. MEN'S LOUNGE)	1939
Ward G. Biddle Hotel and Conference Center	1959
ARCHITECT	Edward D. James and Associates

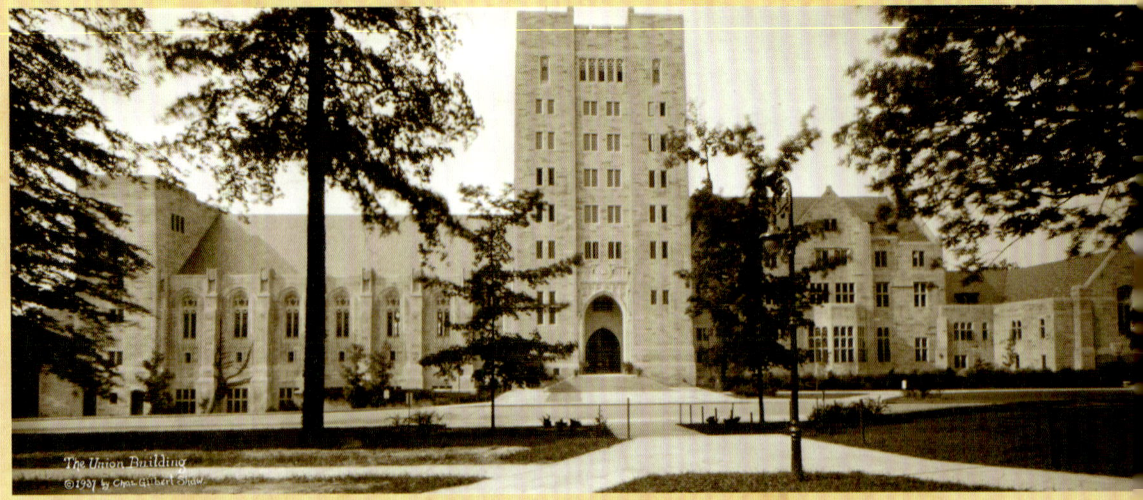

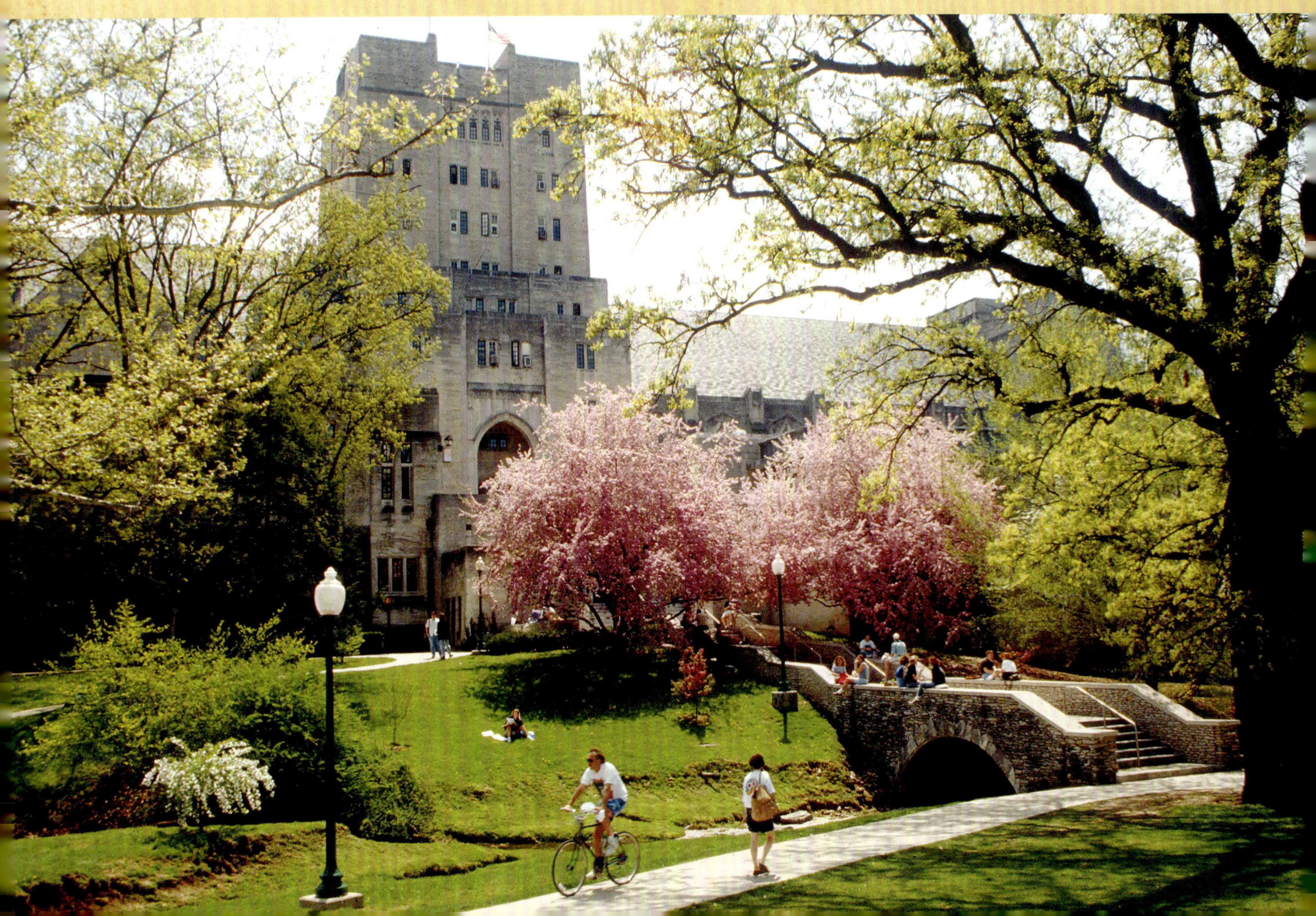

Indiana Memorial Union / Ward G. Biddle Hotel and Conference Center

The University's Living Room

A union building is the living room of a campus. It is the center of faculty and student life outside the classroom, library, and laboratory, and, in addition, fosters lectures, art festivals, and other cultural projects. It furnishes the one common meeting ground for all—for freshman and the distinguished professor, for the organized and the unorganized. All are welcome and all are a part of its life.

—Indiana University President Herman B Wells at the IMU addition dedication ceremony

JOHN WHITTENBERGER, AN INDIANA UNIVERSITY undergraduate in 1909, would be astonished if he walked through the Indiana Memorial Union (IMU) today. In his role as founder and first president of the newly formed Indiana Men's Union Club, Whittenberger voiced concern to President William Lowe Bryan about the lack of meeting space on campus for student groups. He encouraged President Bryan to establish a place for students to gather and pursue common interests in hopes of diminishing the intense rivalry that had developed between the freshmen and sophomore classes, which, at times, generated physical violence and bullying tactics.

President Bryan was receptive to Whittenberger's lobbying efforts, since he too was interested in easing tensions on campus. Bryan set aside space in the East Wing of the Student Building to support student activities, including a reading room, a smoking room, and a billiards room. Tragically, John Whittenberger died of typhoid fever in 1910 and thus missed knowing that the seeds he planted would grow into a magnificent campus edifice of 500,000 square feet, making it among the largest student unions in the United States.

The Indiana Memorial Union, built in three major phases, today includes a hotel, a bookstore, a bowling alley, restaurants, study areas, lounges, meeting rooms, and retail shops. The journey from three rooms in the Student Building to the largest structure on the IU Bloomington campus is remarkable and includes a healthy dose of student involvement and activism along the way.

THE MEMORIAL FUND

In 1921 President Bryan and the trustees kicked off the Memorial Fund drive, a capital campaign to fund construction of three new structures on the evolving Indiana University campus. The name of the student-run campaign was an homage to "the sons and daughters of Indiana University who had served in the wars of the Republic," including the recently ended Great War.[1]

More than $500,000 was pledged quickly, enabling the first two projects included in the fund, Memorial Stadium (built in 1925; later Tenth Street Stadium) and Memorial Hall, a dormitory for women, to be completed by 1925 on newly acquired campus property adjacent to Dunn's Woods.

The third project, a student activities building to include a large auditorium or what was to become the Union, was placed on hold due to slow fund-raising. However, by the late 1920s, fidelity to the "Chance for Loyalty" Memorial Fund prevailed, and, supplemented by student fees, sufficient funds were in place so that the new Union could move forward.

SITE CONTROVERSY

Architects Granger and Bollenbacher of Chicago were selected to craft plans and develop specifications for the new Union, but selecting a building site became a subject for campus-wide discussion. Initial ideas included removing Owen Hall and using that footprint. Another proposal placed the Union directly opposite the Book Nook, a well-known campus hangout

Facing top, Indiana Memorial Union, 1937. P0031159, IU Archives. Photo Credit: Charles Gilbert Shaw.

Facing bottom, Springtime view of Indiana Memorial Union, undated. Photo credit: Indiana University.

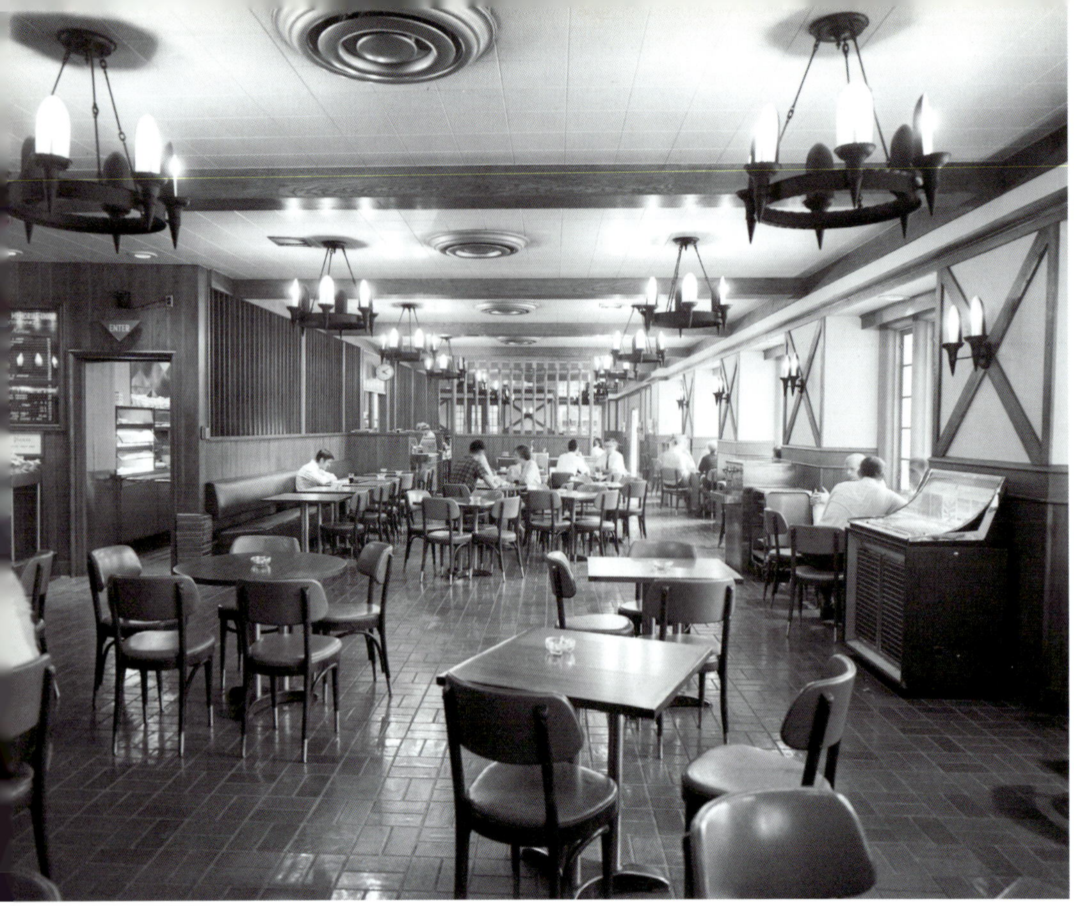

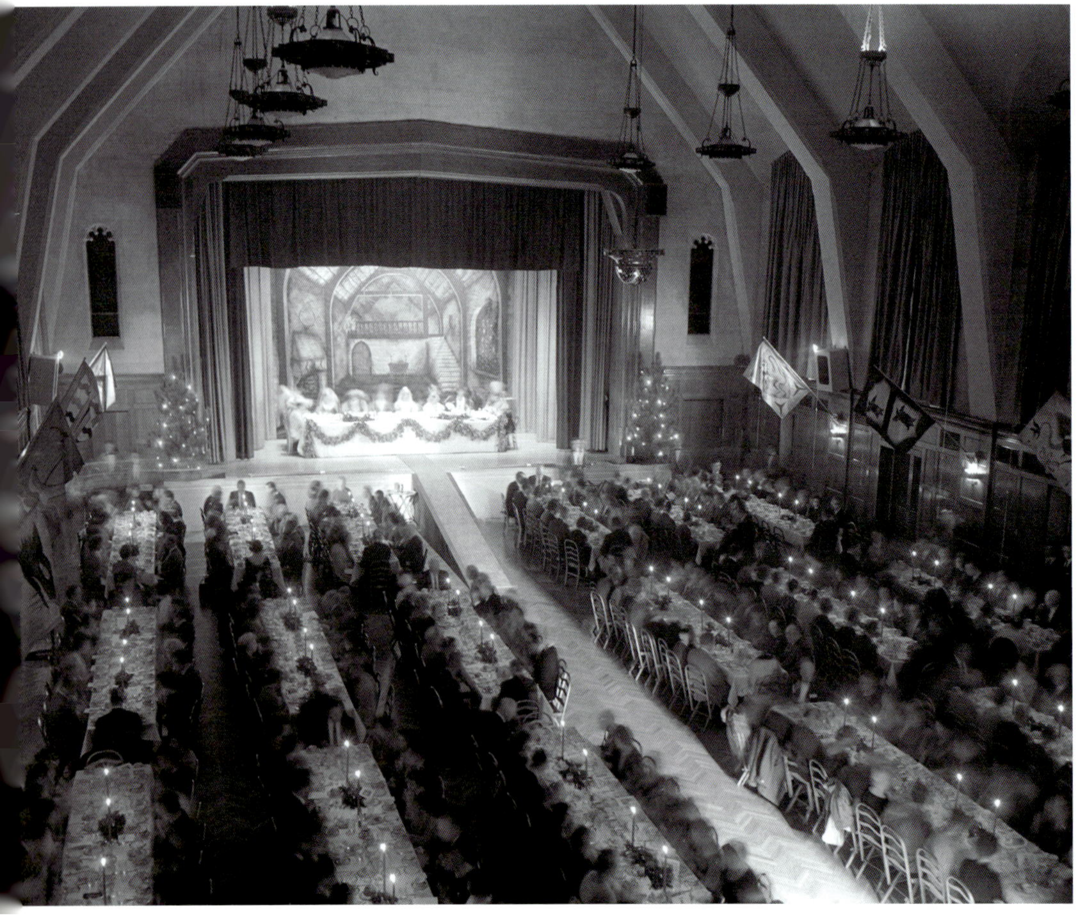

on Indiana Avenue, across the street from the Kirkwood Observatory.

Debate persisted. Even Artist in Residence and Professor T. C. Steele chimed in, stating that placing the Union along Indiana Avenue would greatly impair the beauty of the campus. His comment prompted the trustees to reconsider the location, choosing instead the current site along the Jordan River.

The result established a physical link between the Old Crescent campus and the newer buildings, such as the Men's Residence Hall, Men's Gymnasium, and the 1925 stadium.

THE GRAND EDIFICE

One aspect agreed on by all was that the building design should be faithful to true Collegiate Gothic architecture. Granger and Bollenbacher complied, producing a building of Romanesque design that featured a strong central tower seven stories high. The wings to the east and west of the tower were designed to highlight a massive and grand building worthy of its mission. The architects integrated the building design with the natural slope of the building site and blended the huge edifice into the mature trees flourishing in the surrounding landscape.

Granger and Bollenbacher generously embellished the Union exterior with many Gothic stone carvings: the university seal ornately over the entrance to the south tower, an owl standing guard over the bookstore entrance, and various other embellishments agreeably tucked under rooflines and windows. On the north side of the building, a monumental staircase flows down from the solarium to the Jordan River and Dunn Meadow.

Two major additions, both harmonizing architecturally with the original 1932 structure, were completed in 1939 (north men's lounge) and 1960 (Ward G. Biddle Hotel and Conference Center). They endowed the building with a uniform but massive presence as it relates to Owen Hall and Maxwell

Top, The Commons, a student hangout on the mezzanine of Indiana Memorial Union, 1967. P0024651, IU Archives. Photo Credit: Terry Weaver.

Left, One of the many Madrigal Dinners from 1947 to 2001, featuring strolling minstrels, jesters, and carolers in Alumni Hall, the largest banquet space in the IMU, 1961. P0027494, IU Archives. Photo Credit: Herbert Hoeltke.

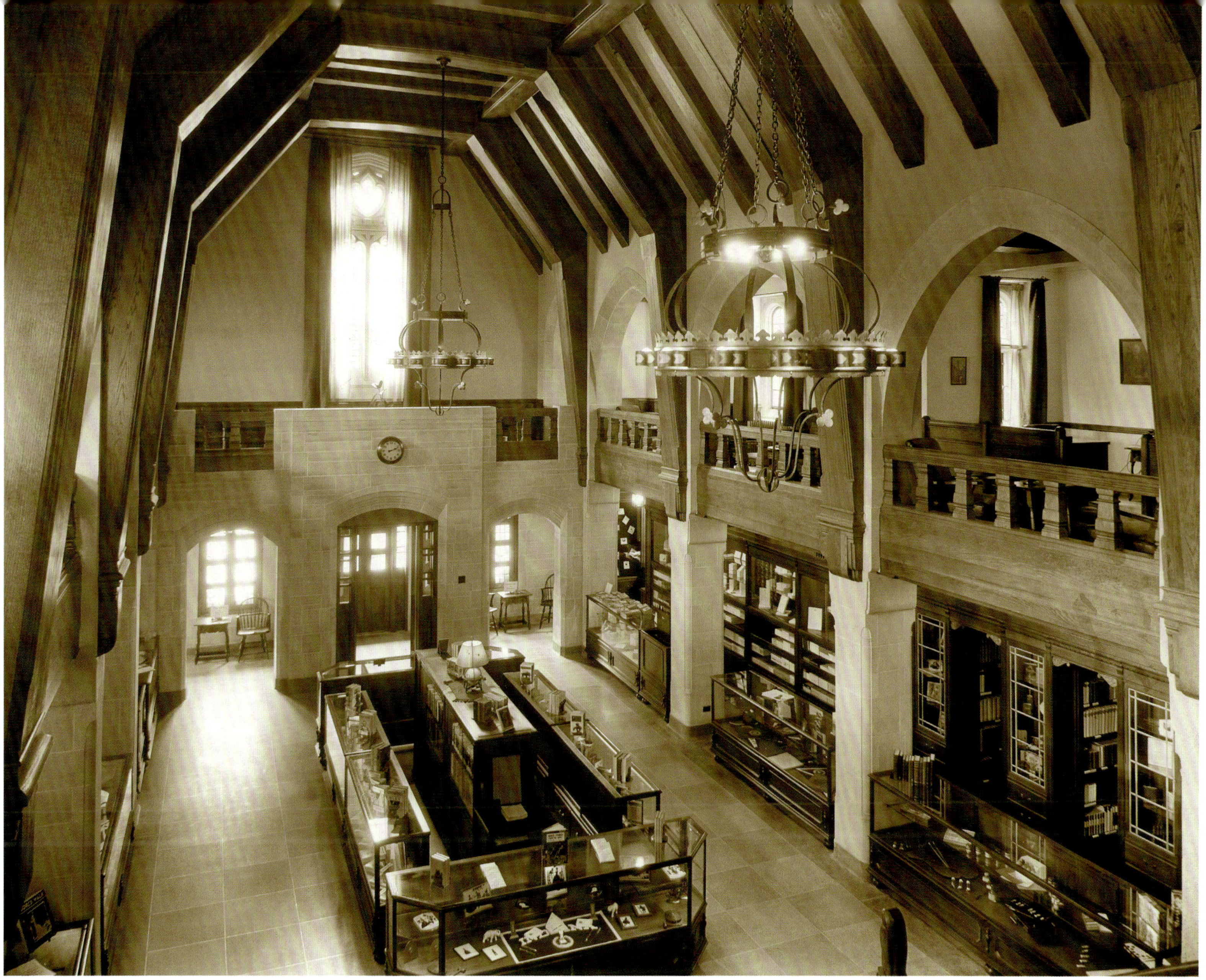

Above, Indiana Memorial Union Bookstore, 1932. P0034459, IU Archives. Photo Credit: Sinclair Studio, Bloomington, Indiana.

Right, Tudor Room, a popular dining room in the Union, 1975. P0024280, IU Archives. Photo Credit: Ralph "Porky" Veal.

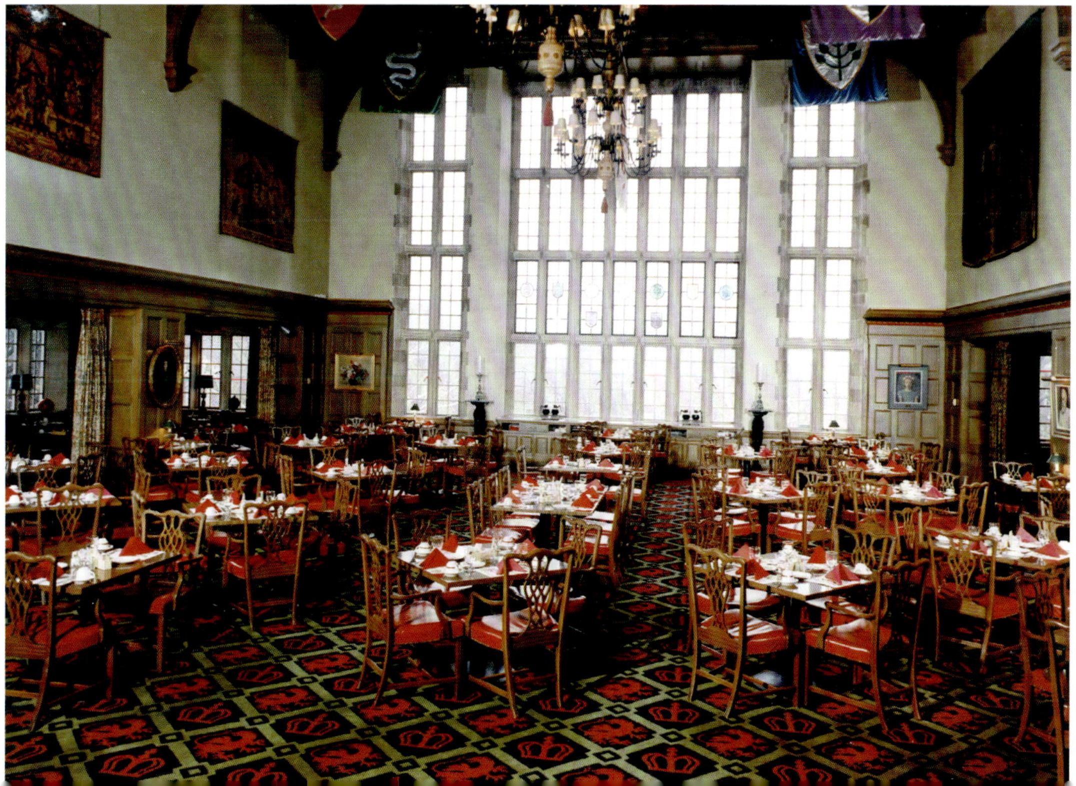

Entrance to Ward G. Biddle Hotel and Conference Center in the Indiana Memorial Union, 2016. Photo credit: Tyagan Miller.

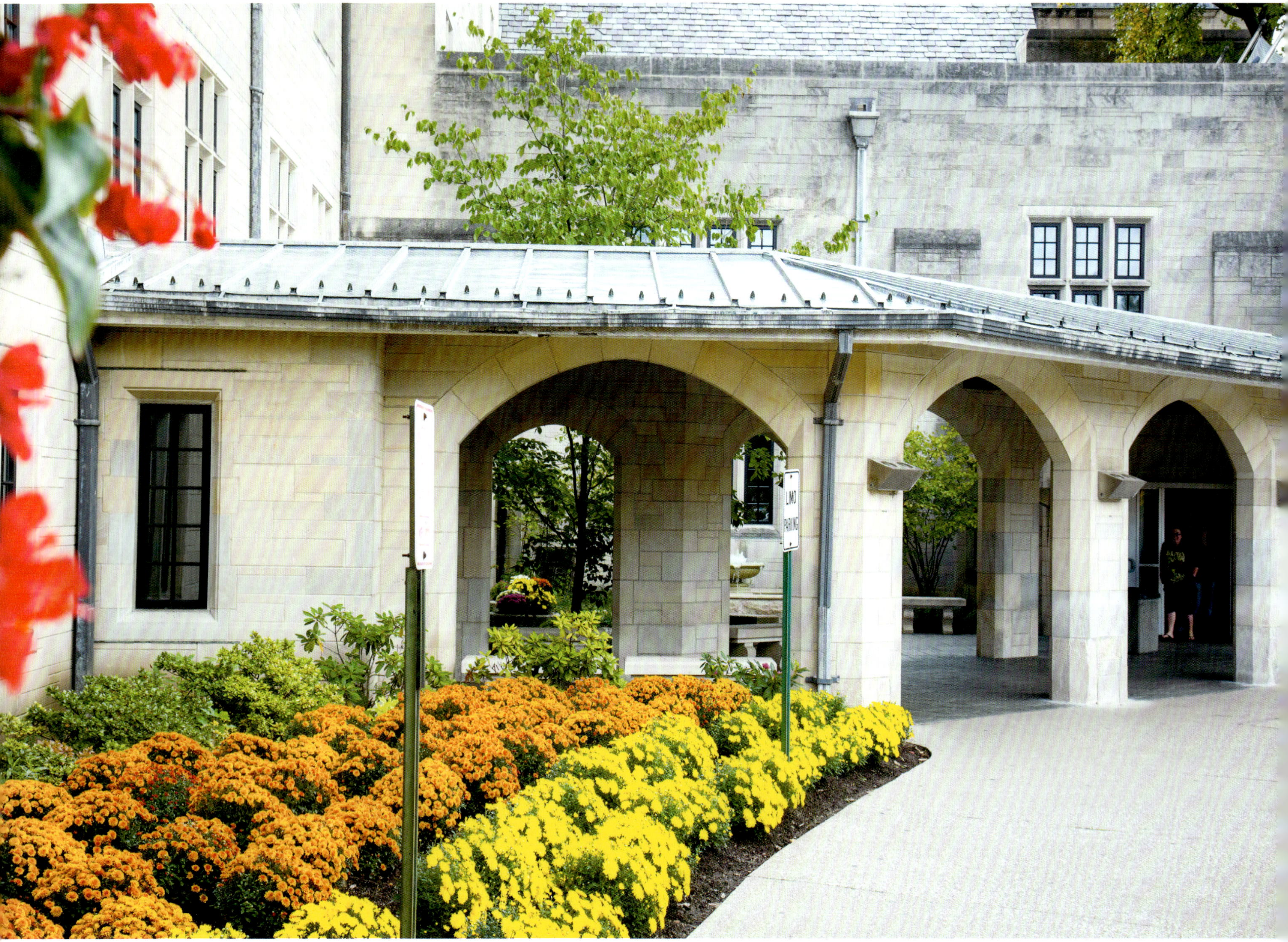

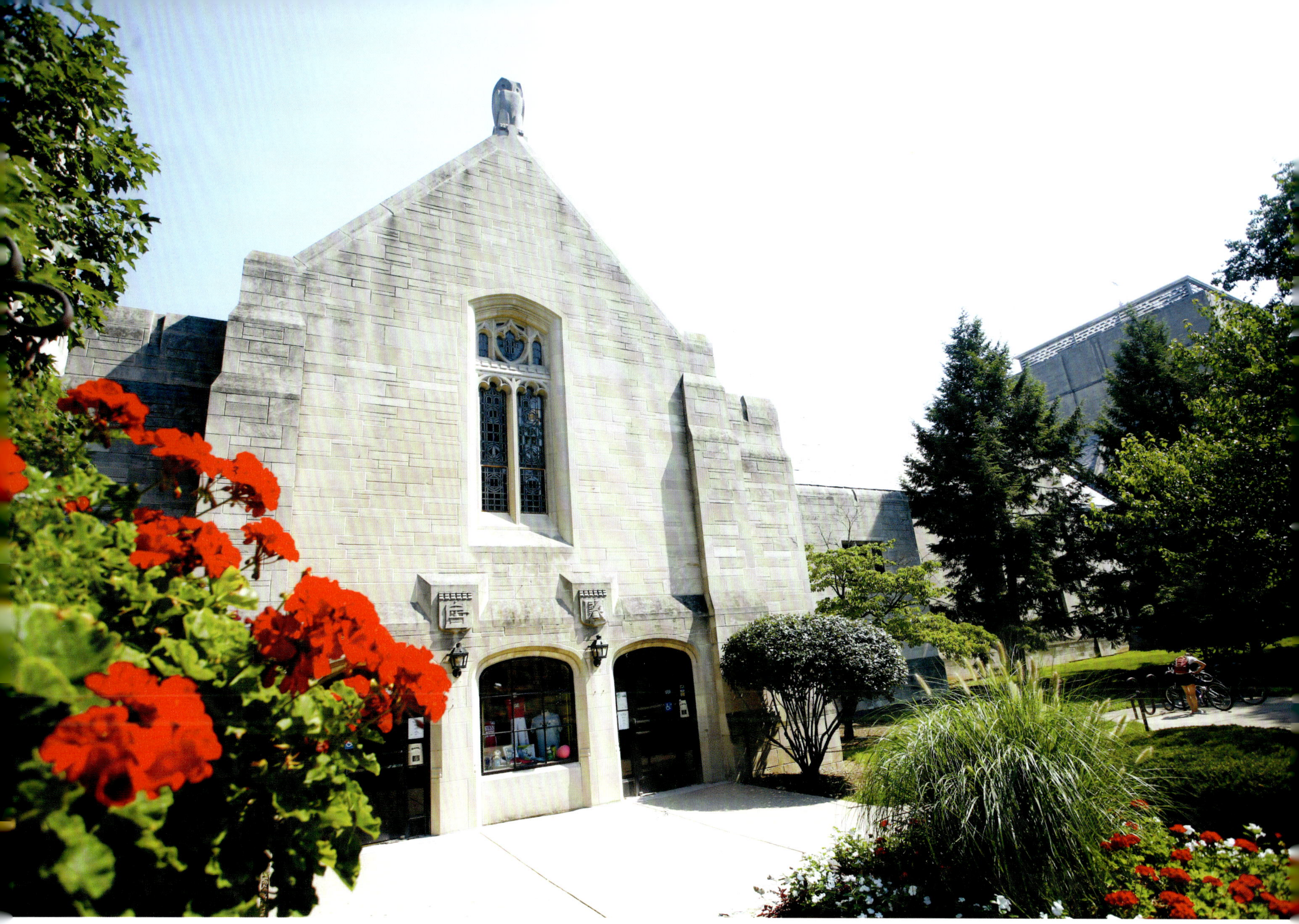

Bookstore entrance, Indiana Memorial Union, 2007. Photo credit: Indiana University.

Hall to the immediate south. The Indiana Memorial Union is an iconic structure appropriately holding the center of the Bloomington campus. Perhaps more than any other building, it is representative of the campus and the architecture, common building palette, scale, and landscape integration that make Indiana University Bloomington so beautiful.

From its simple beginning more than a century ago of one student's dream for a unifying place on campus, this massive but aesthetically pleasing building has become the heart not only of IUB student affairs but of the entire campus. Today one can find a place for almost every type of student service imaginable in the IMU. Even the Golden Book—a listing of IU's men and women who made the supreme sacrifice in the nation's wars, as well as the donors to the Memorial Fund—is preserved for viewing in the Memorial Room in IMU. The Union also is an active art museum, displaying works from the university's extensive collections.

William Lowe Bryan Hall 1936

ARCHITECT Granger and Bollenbacher

ARCHITECTURAL STYLE Collegiate Gothic with Art Deco influences

ORIGINAL NAME Administration Building

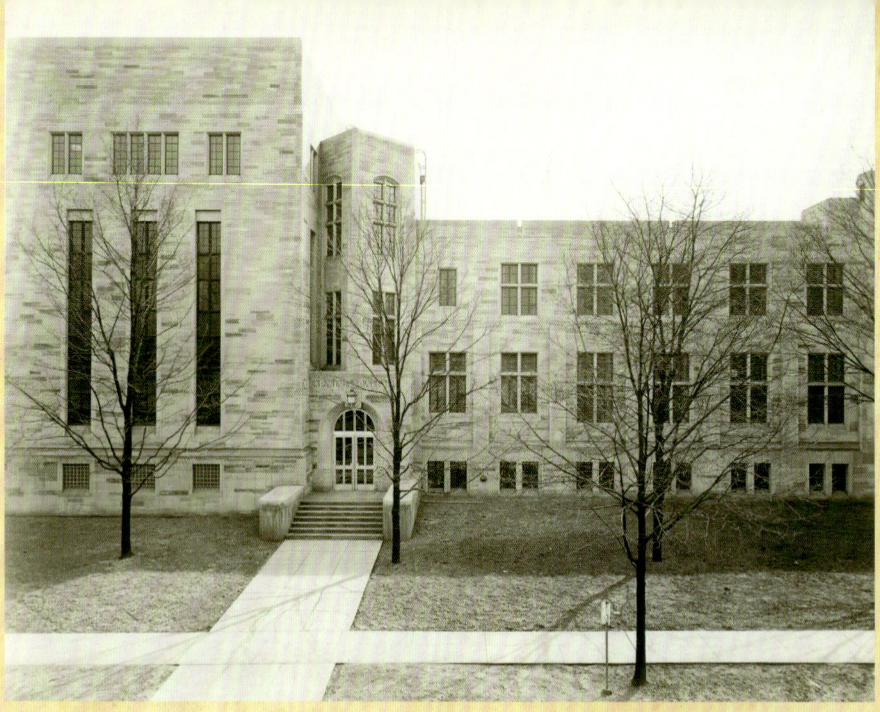

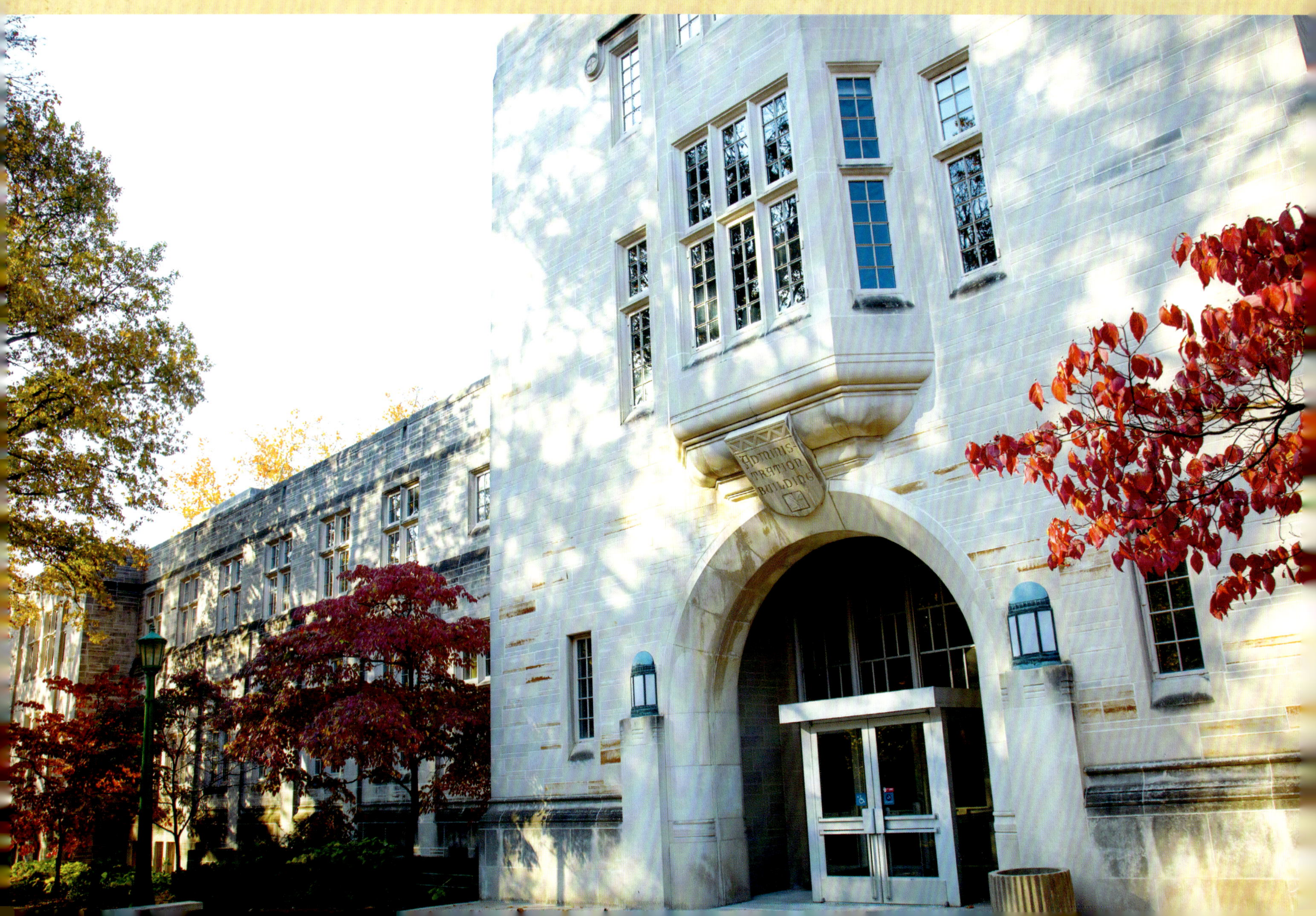

William Lowe Bryan Hall

Seat of the Administration

Whatever goes on elsewhere on the campus that which goes on here must be right if the life of the school as a whole is to be right.

—Indiana University President William Lowe Bryan at cornerstone laying

Even with university administrative offices overcrowded and scattered across campus, for years President Bryan and university trustees continued to defer construction of an administration building in the interest of other needs of the campus. In 1934 President Bryan described the conditions in comparison to the other major departments on campus as "grossly inconvenient, expensive, and in fact disgraceful."[1] However, when funds through the Depression-era Public Works Administration (PWA) for campus projects became available, the administration sought funding for an administration building, the first of several projects.

Months before the university received confirmation of funding for the project, intense controversy swirled around the location of the building. The early assumption was that the new building would be located on the site of the first Assembly Hall (built in 1896 and located directly east of Owen Hall), then described as a "campus eyesore," with that building to be relocated for use by the Theatre Department and to house handball courts. However on March 4, 1935, the Board of Trustees "ordered the new Administration Building to be located East of Kirkwood Observatory and north of Fourth Street," in the center of Dunn's woods. The university faculty, students, and alumni erupted in public opposition. A faculty zoologist, Alfred Kinsey, said that it would permanently destroy "our chief asset." However, the most poetic plea came from alumnus Alfred Kuntz: "There resides in this almost primitive forest, a mystical charm and a grandeur which makes it a classroom superior to any on the campus. Your piles of brick and limestone will pass with the years. . . . The forest campus grows more beautiful, more fitting and inspiring as a background for study, with the years. . . . Let us here in this one spot have less of man and more of God."[2]

Perhaps because of this public outcry—or because architect John Bollenbacher was an IU alumnus (1906) who valued the preservation of the campus woods—at their April 4 meeting the trustees reversed their decision and voted unanimously to locate the new building instead at the intersection of Indiana and Kirkwood Avenues with a north-to-south orientation. Finally in July of that year, the official approval from the PWA arrived via telegram that the university was approved for a $400,000 loan and grant.

Bryan Hall was designed by architects Granger and Bollenbacher in the Collegiate Gothic style to match the recently completed Indiana Memorial Union (1932), with a limestone facade in the random ashlar pattern, cut-stone trim, and a slate roof. The building also exhibits a strong Art Deco influence, which is characterized by an overall sleek, linear appearance. Additionally, it has a distinctive buff limestone finish and a stepped facade in front. Its low-relief carvings include the owl on the north side, the distinct presentation of the words *Administration Building* over the east entrance, and, inside that entrance, stone shields bearing the names of the various

Facing top, West elevation of William Lowe Bryan Hall, circa 1940. P0035957, IU Archives.

Facing bottom, East entrance to William Lowe Bryan Hall from Dunn's Woods, 2016. Photo credit: Tyagan Miller.

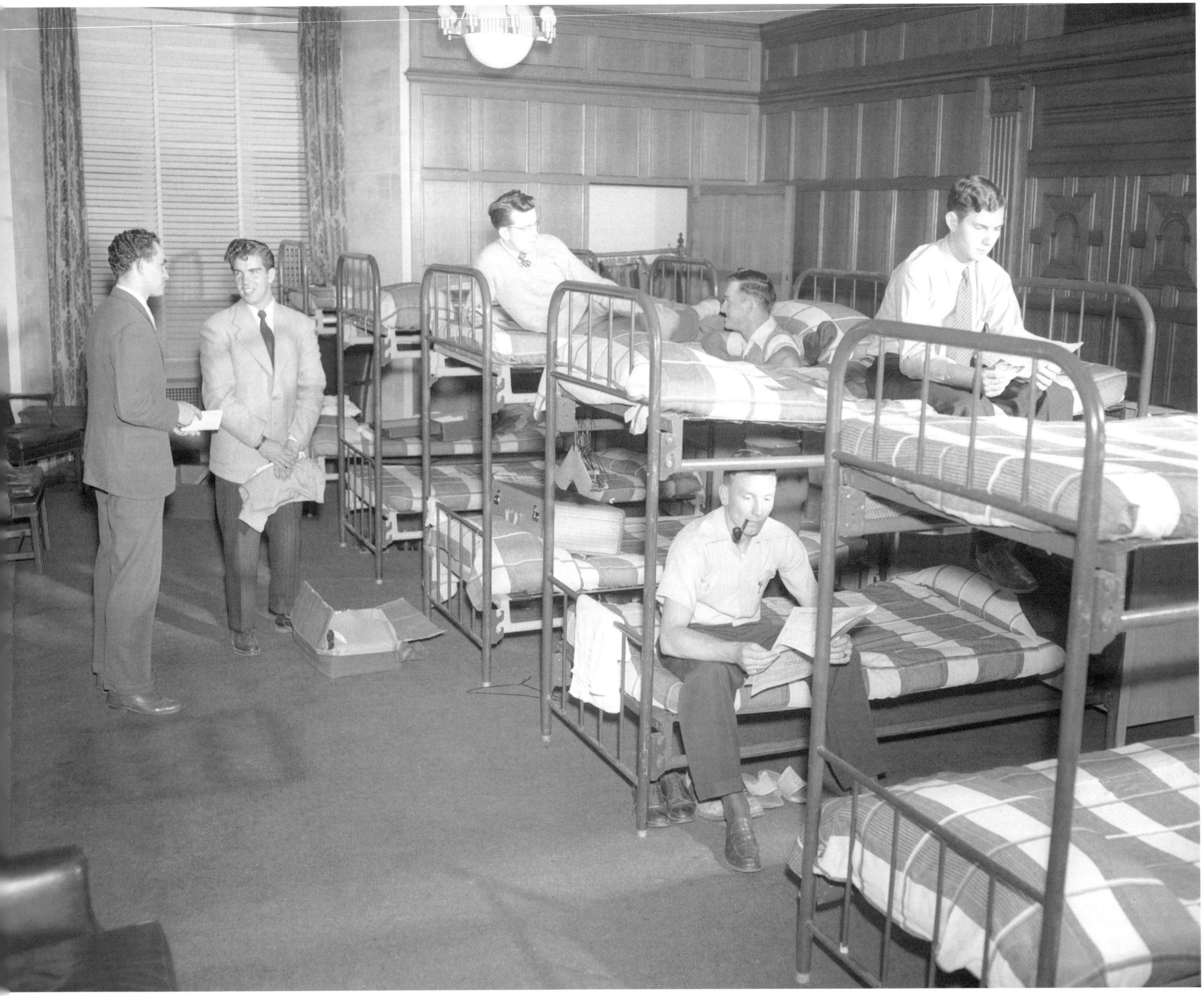

Bryan Hall "Dormitory": the president's conference room in Bryan Hall boarded overflow students during the post-World War II housing shortage, 1946. P0023889, IU Archives.

university schools. Also of note inside the building are the distinctive marble stairs and the wall of plaques honoring IU's Nobel laureates.

When President Bryan and his administration moved into their "magnificent Christmas gift" in December 1936,[3] the building housed the registrar, dean of men and women, and the deans of the College of Arts and Sciences on the first floor; the comptroller, the treasurer, the president, and the trustees on the second; and the publications and publicity office on the third floor. In the basement were the mailroom, telephone exchange, and storerooms. There was also a five-level, fireproof space to house the archives.

Originally christened the Administration Building due to a technicality that prevented federally funded buildings from being named after living individuals, it was finally renamed William Lowe Bryan Hall in 1957 for the tenth president of the university. In 1975 the building underwent a renovation designed by E. I. Brown and Associates of Indianapolis involving the basement, first and third floors, and an upgrade of all of the mechanical and electrical systems in the building.

Over the decades, the building bore witness to pivotal moments in the university's history. Here the Board of Trustees approved the applications for further construction funding from the PWA, including the Physical Science building (Swain Hall), School of Business building (Woodburn Hall), and the Indiana University Auditorium. Bryan Hall was the site of the first meeting of the Administration War Council after the bombing of Pearl Harbor, and the president's conference room later served as a temporary dormitory for veterans after the war. Numerous student demonstrations were held here through the 1960s and 1970s, and William Lowe Bryan Hall has housed the offices of IU presidents since 1936.

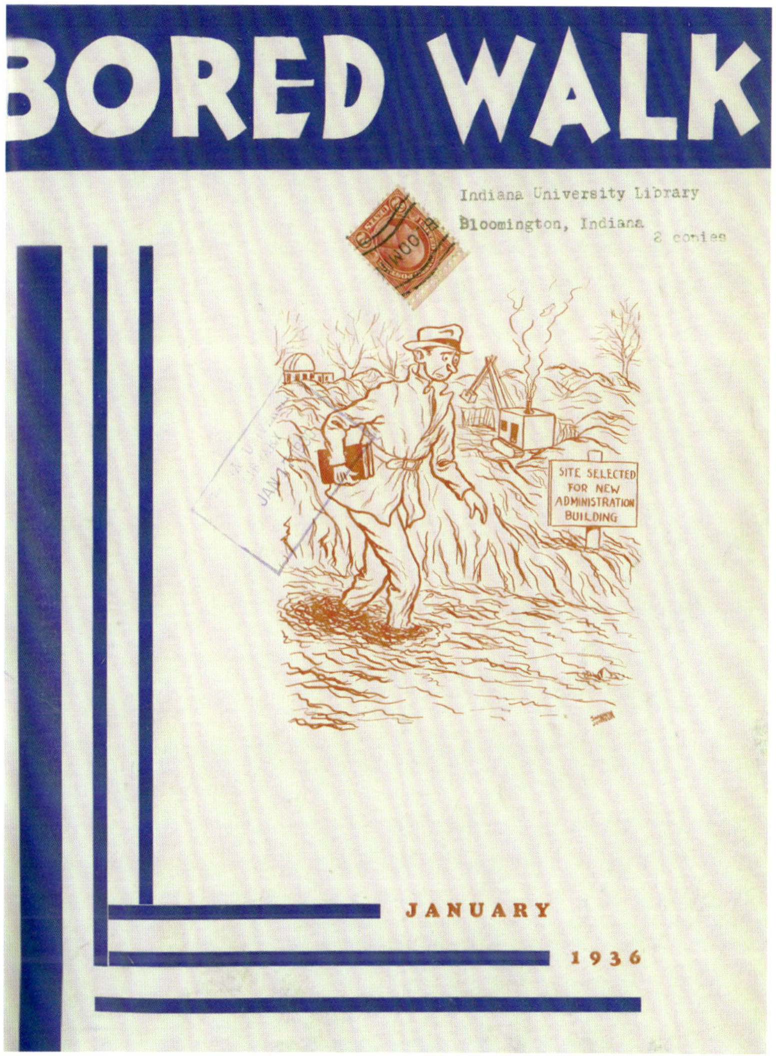

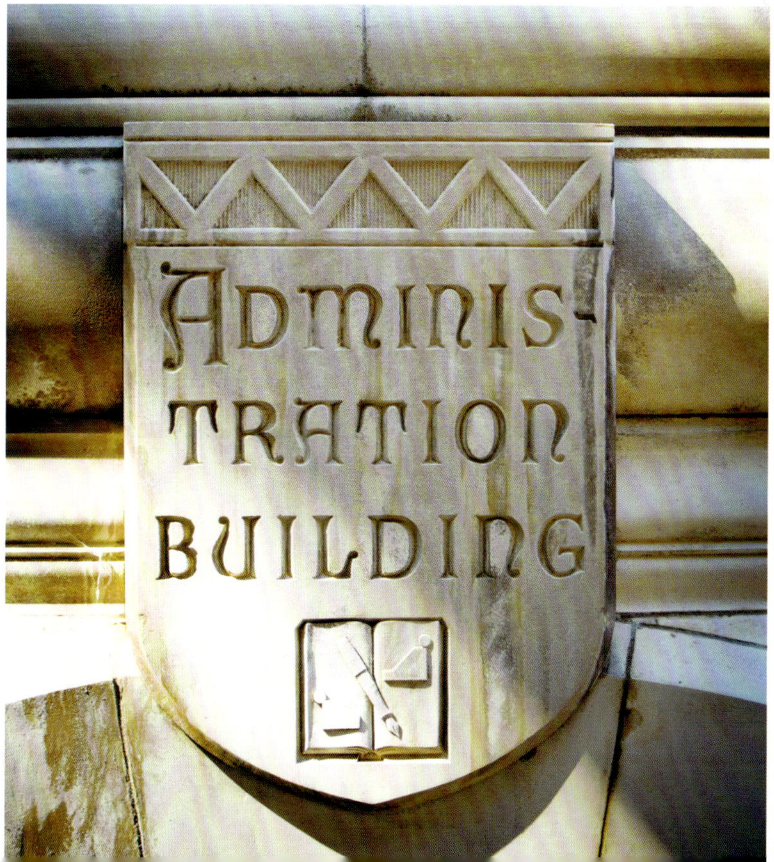

Top right, Cover of student magazine the *Bored Walk* protesting proposed site location for Bryan Hall, 1936. IU Archives.

Bottom right, Creative stone carving above east entrance to Bryan Hall, 2016. Photo credit: Tyagan Miller.

Indiana University Auditorium 1941

ARCHITECT Eggers and Higgins / A. M. Strauss

ARCHITECTURAL STYLE Art Deco / Greco Deco

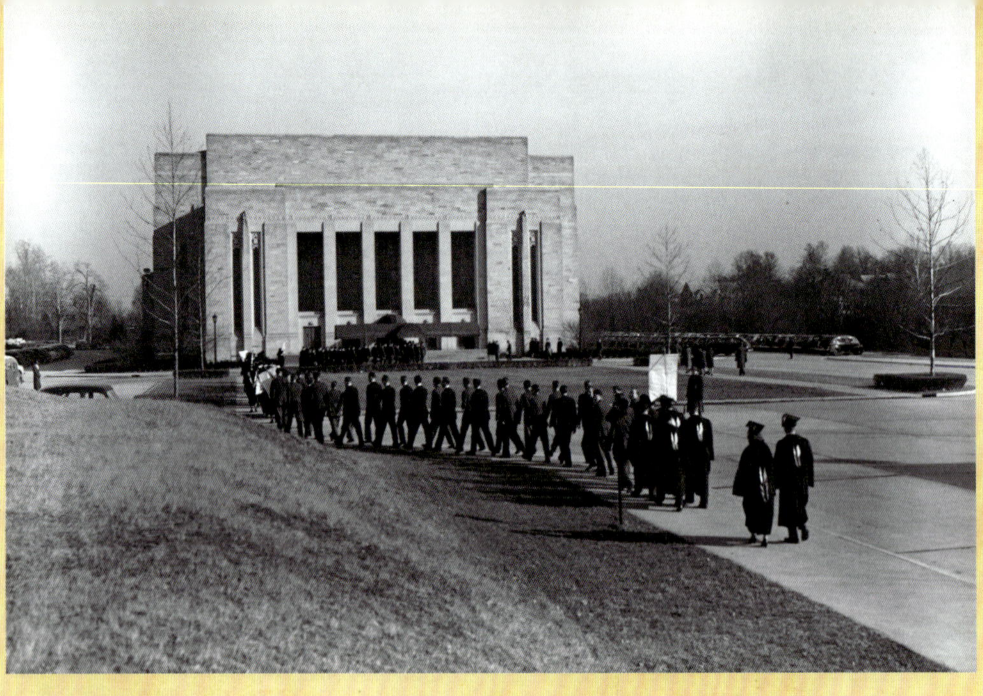

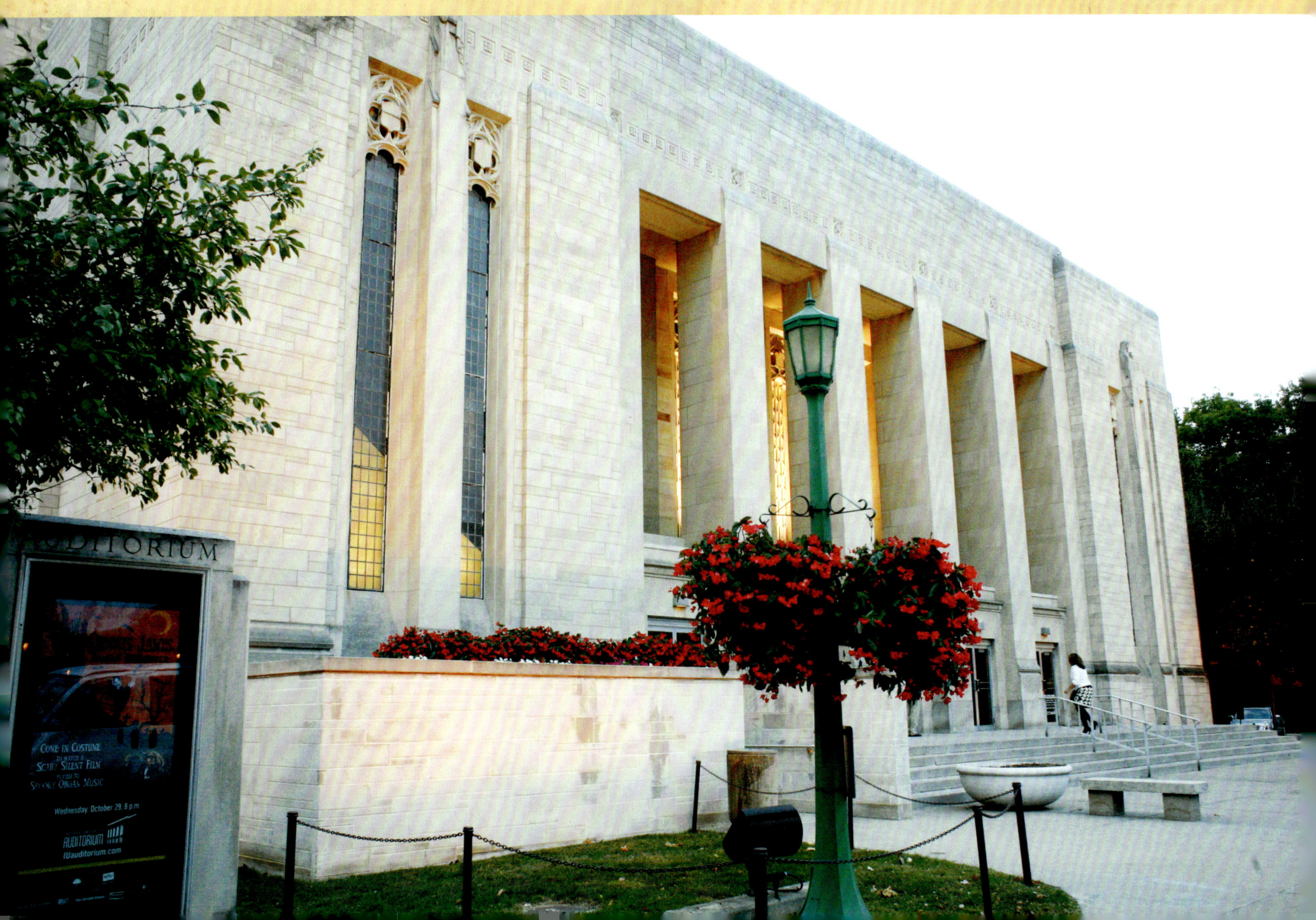

Indiana University Auditorium

Birthplace of the Arts

It is with our Hall of Music as with every first rate thing that men do—it is old and new. Builders of genius in Egypt, Babylon, Athens, and Canterbury were present within the man who conceived of this Home of Beauty.

—William Lowe Bryan at dedication ceremony

HERMAN B WELLS BROUGHT NEW DREAMS AND a fresh vision to the presidency when he assumed that office in 1938. Planning for the new business and economics building (Woodburn Hall) had begun under President Bryan, so Wells focused his attention on the orderly expansion of the campus and the selection of a site for an auditorium that would further expose IU students to the arts. Recognizing the need for campus planning assistance, Wells asked Ward Biddle, IU vice president and treasurer, to accompany him to New York so they could inform themselves about the leading architectural firms in the country.

They settled on Eggers and Higgins, a firm that had been involved in many outstanding building designs around the nation. The auditorium project would begin a partnership between Indiana University and the Eggers and Higgins firm that would last four decades and include schematic design work for almost every major building constructed at the university during that time. This project was also the first initiated and completed during the Wells presidency with the help of WPA (Works Progress Administration) funds.

Indiana University Auditorium was designated as the centerpiece of the Fine Arts Plaza, with future plans calling for a fine arts building and museum on one side and an open-air Greek theater on the other. A fountain was planned for the middle of the plaza, and compelling renderings were drawn and shared with prospective donors. University priorities changed as time passed and while the Fine Arts Building, art museum, and Showalter Fountain were eventually completed, the alfresco theater bowl was not. President Wells and campus master planners determined the site designated for the outdoor theater would better serve as the location for the Lilly Library.

When the IU Auditorium was dedicated on March 22, 1941, it was the largest building on campus and, as President Wells said at the dedication, "Here, the students, members of the staff and citizens of the state can receive the inspiration of the best in lectures, music, and drama." Indeed, the new auditorium would introduce students to the arts in a way not possible before. For example, the Metropolitan Opera Company of New York had long made annual tours to various cities in the Midwest but never to a small town or college campus. After much persuasion, the Met was convinced to make a stop at Indiana University. They performed Verdi's *Aida* on the auditorium stage on April 13, 1942. The spectacle was a resounding success on both sides. Met manager Edward Johnson gushed: "the Metropolitan likes Indiana University and Bloomington. So we are not saying 'goodbye' but only 'au revoir.'"[1]

True to Johnson's word, following the war years the Met began a series of annual campus appearances from 1946 through 1961. These and other performances, from Broadway plays to hometown favorites John Mellencamp and Straight No Chaser, have delighted audiences. The world of performance

Facing top, Commencement procession into Indiana University Auditorium, 1945. P0044889, IU Archives.

Facing bottom, Main entrance to IU Auditorium, undated. Photo credit: Indiana University.

Wells brought to the IU Auditorium, coupled with the amenities of the Fine Arts Plaza, supported his efforts to position Indiana University as a center for arts and culture.

The dedication of IU Auditorium was a five-day affair filled with performances, speeches, and dinner parties hosted by President Wells. Thomas Hart Benton, noted U.S. painter and muralist, attended the dedication. Herman B Wells had purchased Benton's narrative murals about Indiana history when he became university president in 1938, but finding a space large enough to house them was problematic (see Benton Murals entry). When the Indiana General Assembly authorized new music halls for both Indiana University and Purdue University, Wells knew he had his long-sought answer to the dilemma. He asked the architects to design the new auditorium in a way that would accommodate the Benton Murals, and they achieved the desired results. The murals were placed above the entrance in the foyer, thus establishing a Hall of Murals for patrons of the Auditorium to view.

Indiana University Auditorium also holds the famous Roosevelt Organ, which was first constructed and installed in the Chicago Auditorium Theatre by Hilborne L. Roosevelt of New York in 1889. The organ was sold at auction in 1942 and purchased by Dr. William H. Barnes, who subsequently donated it to IU. The organ was rebuilt and enlarged for its new location by Aeolian-Skinner in 1946–47 and dedicated in 1948. In 1961 water and then a small fire damaged the organ, rendering it unplayable. The Schantz Organ Company was hired to redesign and rebuild the organ and reinstall it in the Auditorium. The new organ was completed in 1969, an example of one of the finest installations of a large recital organ in the world.[2] Six ranks of the original organ were retained in the new installation. The organ can be played from four locations in the house—two on stage, in the orchestra pit, or from the first rows of the seating area.

The IU Auditorium is clad entirely in southern Indiana limestone. Eggers and Higgins, teaming with A. M. Strauss Associates of Fort Wayne, created a design that customized the international Art Moderne and Art Deco architectural style popularized in the 1920–1940s era to fit the building vocabulary of Indiana University. Often lumped in the general description of Collegiate Gothic, the building features a strong horizontal base that is articulated throughout the upper level by rhythmic vertical expression around the entire building. The west elevation features a colonnade clearly defining the building's entry and lobby area. The long north and south elevations, necessarily blank due to the intended absence of windows, is highlighted by engaged vertical piers. These give way on the east end to tripartite window treatments that emphasize vertical symmetry. Handsome stone carvings can be found around the entire building, including a tile course that delineates the top third of the structure. Two stone figures (never specifically identified in the plans), stand watch on either side of the entry doors on the west side of the building. The look and feel of the Auditorium is classical and monumental.

Taken as a whole, Indiana University Auditorium achieved the goal of establishing an architectural standard that would not only guide the procession of buildings to be constructed along Seventh Street, and, thus complete the Fine Arts Plaza, but would also influence the design of buildings as the campus expanded beyond Jordan Avenue to the east, and Seventh Street to the north.

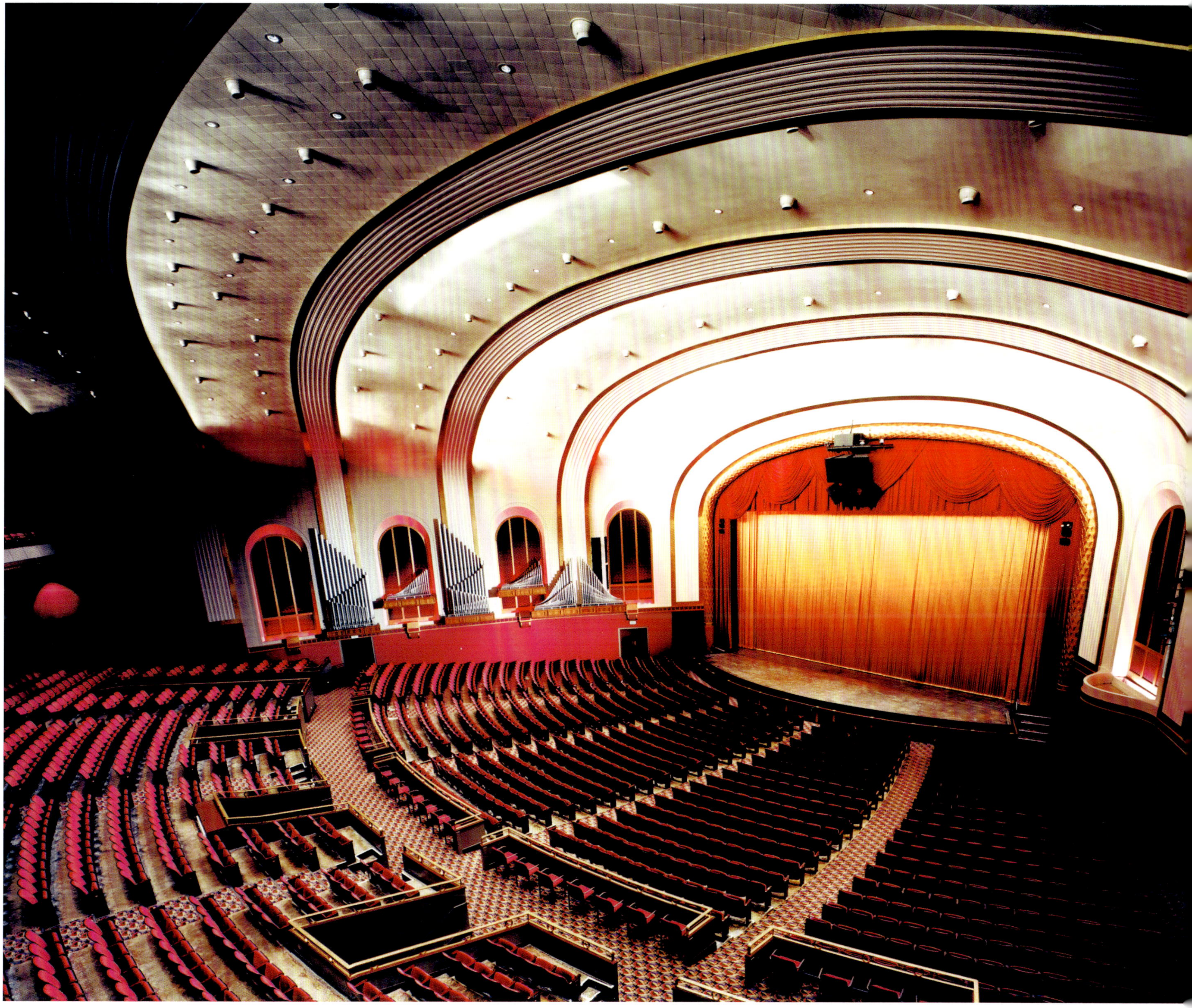

Auditorium performance space with tiered seating; note Roosevelt organ to the left, undated. Photo credit: Indiana University.

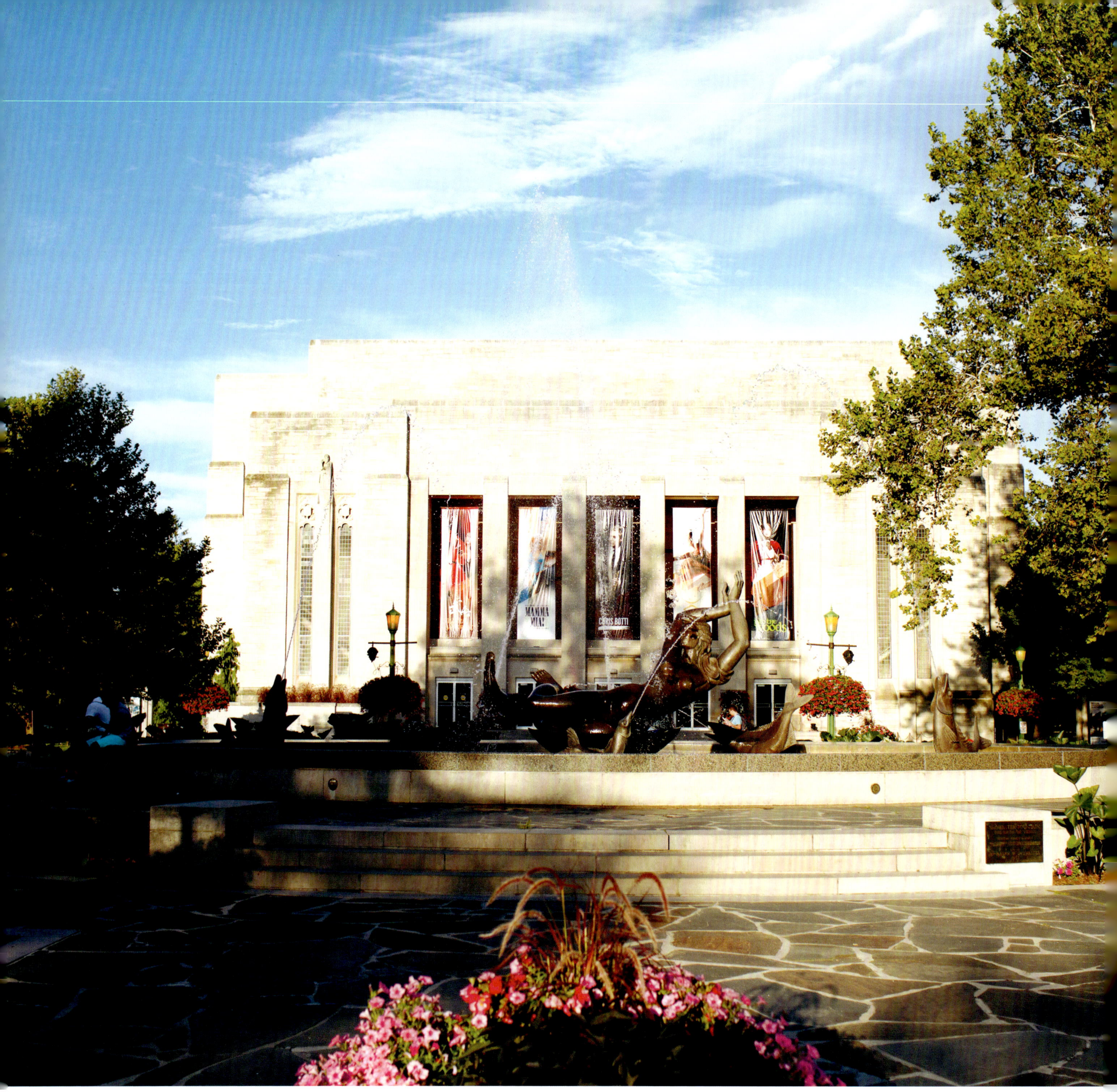

MAMMA MIA!
CHRIS BOTTI

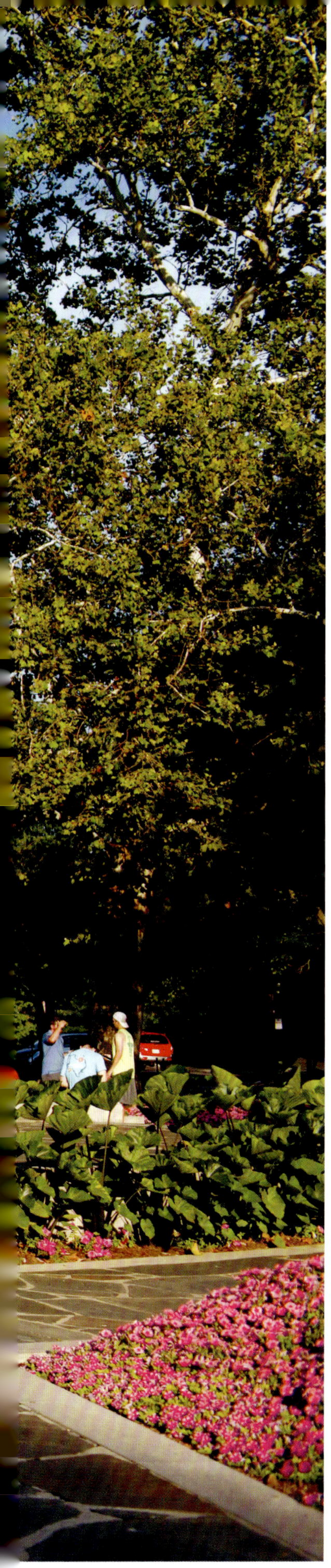

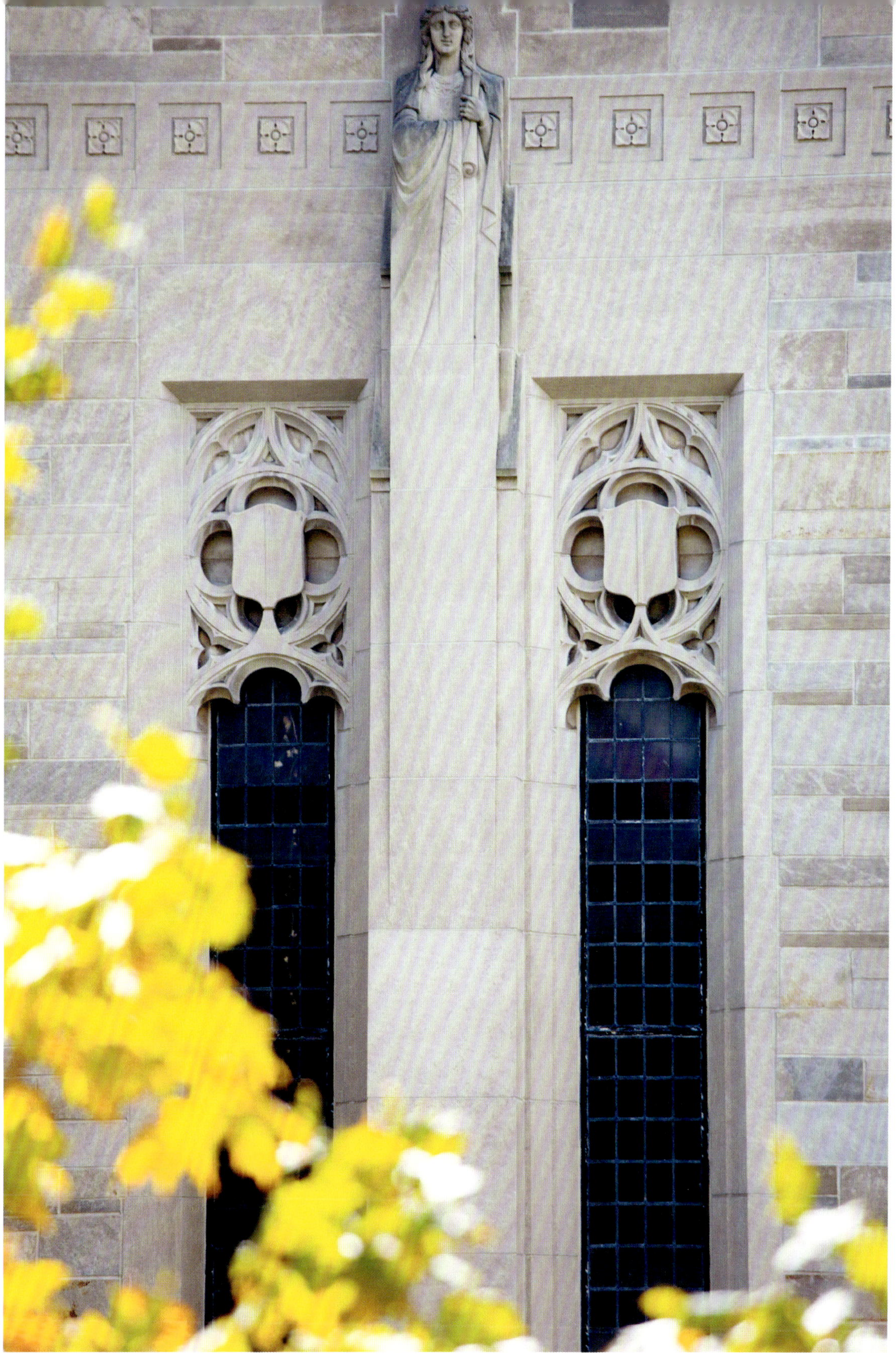

Above, Stone carvings on north auditorium facade, 2016.
Photo credit: Tyagan Miller.

Facing, IU Auditorium through Showalter Fountain, 2016.
Photo credit: Indiana University.

Beck Chapel 1956

ARCHITECT Edward D. James and Associates

ARCHITECTURAL STYLE Modified Tudor with Romanesque detailing

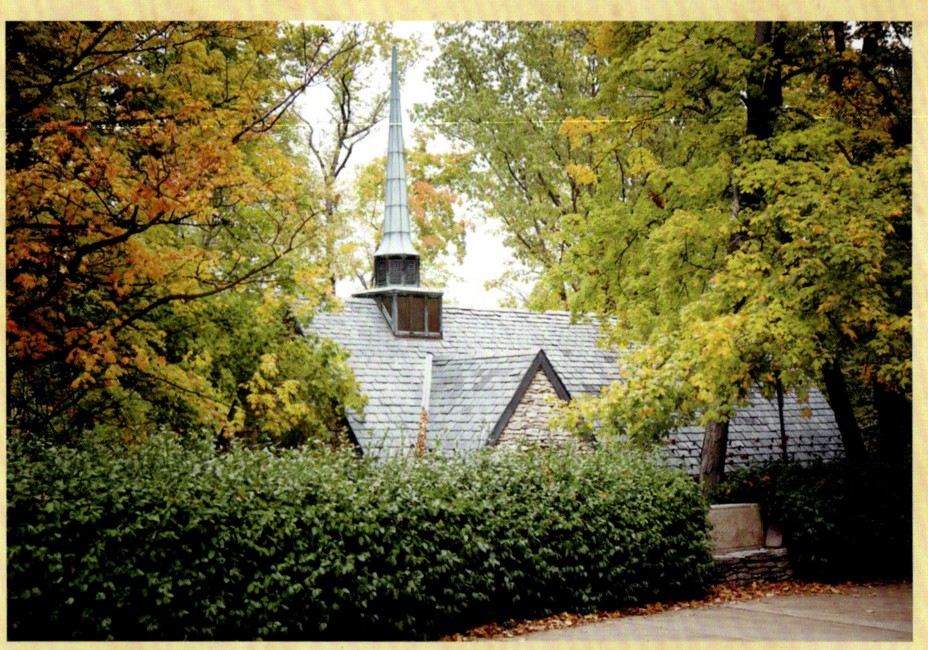

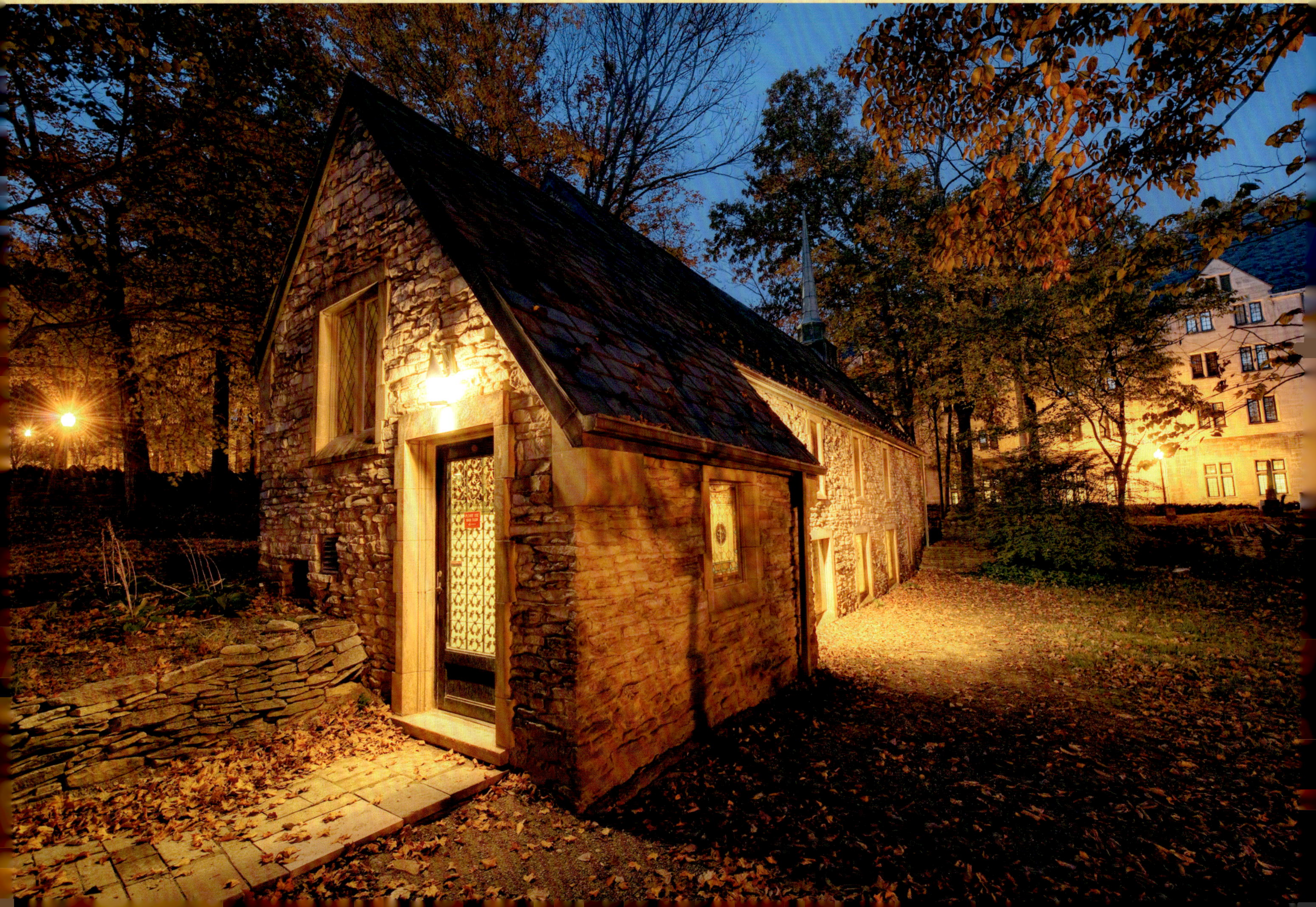

Beck Chapel

A Campus Sanctuary

Voices from this spot speak of vanishing years. They proclaim our everlasting link with the pioneer who gave us this spot and the ground about it. They remind us also of the inspiration from which stemmed our University and of the loving toil which nurtured its early growth. Where would one search for a spot more harmonious as a location for a Chapel of Prayer and Meditation.

—Frank Beck on chapel location

DESPITE THE FACTS THAT THE FIRST SEMINARY building contained a chapel and that for decades students were "required to assemble every morning shortly after daybreak for prayers," for nearly a century and a half a building did not exist at Indiana University that was devoted exclusively to religion.[1] By the end of the First World War, the university had buildings dedicated to law, science, medicine, music, business, health, and living facilities, but no chapel.

In 1934 two university alumni, Frank Orman Beck (AB 1894, AM 1895) and Daisy Woodward Beck (AB 1899), returned to their alma mater after more than twenty-five years in Chicago, where Frank served as a teacher, minister, and social worker in places such as the Wabash Avenue Methodist Church in the infamous First Ward, in Hull House with Jane Addams, and in the missions along Skid Row. Back in Bloomington, the Becks became unofficial counselors to the student body and the administration and sought to build a religious program on the campus that would ease prejudice and promote tolerance and understanding. As the programs grew, the Becks began a nearly twenty-year campaign to build a place of worship for those of all faiths.

On January 29, 1941, during a banquet in Alumni Hall sponsored by the Committee on Religion and the Student Religious Cabinet, Nobel laureate Dr. Arthur Compton gave a talk titled "A Scientist's Conception of God." Following the lecture, university president Herman B Wells stood before more than four hundred members of the faculty, student body, and public to announce a generous gift from Frank and Daisy Beck to construct a chapel for those of all faiths on the campus. The Board of Trustees accepted the gift, and the Indianapolis architect Edward D. James soon thereafter presented a conceptual drawing for the proposed structure (although the final product was dramatically different).

In the words of Frank Beck, the chapel

> does not aim to resolve religious differences, or to seek religious compromise, or to reduce faiths to the lowest common denominator. On the other hand it holds a sensitive regard to the rights of varying religious opinions and seeks to encourage respect for the ethical and religious values of each of the historic faiths represented in the student body and faculty.
>
> The Chapel would, however, represent a sense of unity in this rich diversity. It will not become a Chapel of a universal religion but a Chapel that recognizes the claims of all religions—a Chapel that avows that "light is good in whatever lamp it burns. . . ." Thus, the Chapel will not become the Chapel of a common creed, but the Chapel of a common quest, granting free and full expression to each faith represented on the campus.[2]

The wartime scarcity of building materials delayed construction of the chapel. Finally, as part of commencement activities on June 12, 1954, the ground was dedicated. Two years later the cornerstone was laid, and the official dedication ceremony took place during commencement activities the following year, on June 9, 1957.

Facing top, Beck Chapel in its wooded setting, 2016. Photo credit: Tyagan Miller.

Facing bottom, Twilight view of Beck Chapel looking toward Indiana Memorial Union, undated. Photo credit: Justin Kern, wwwthegolden sieve.com.

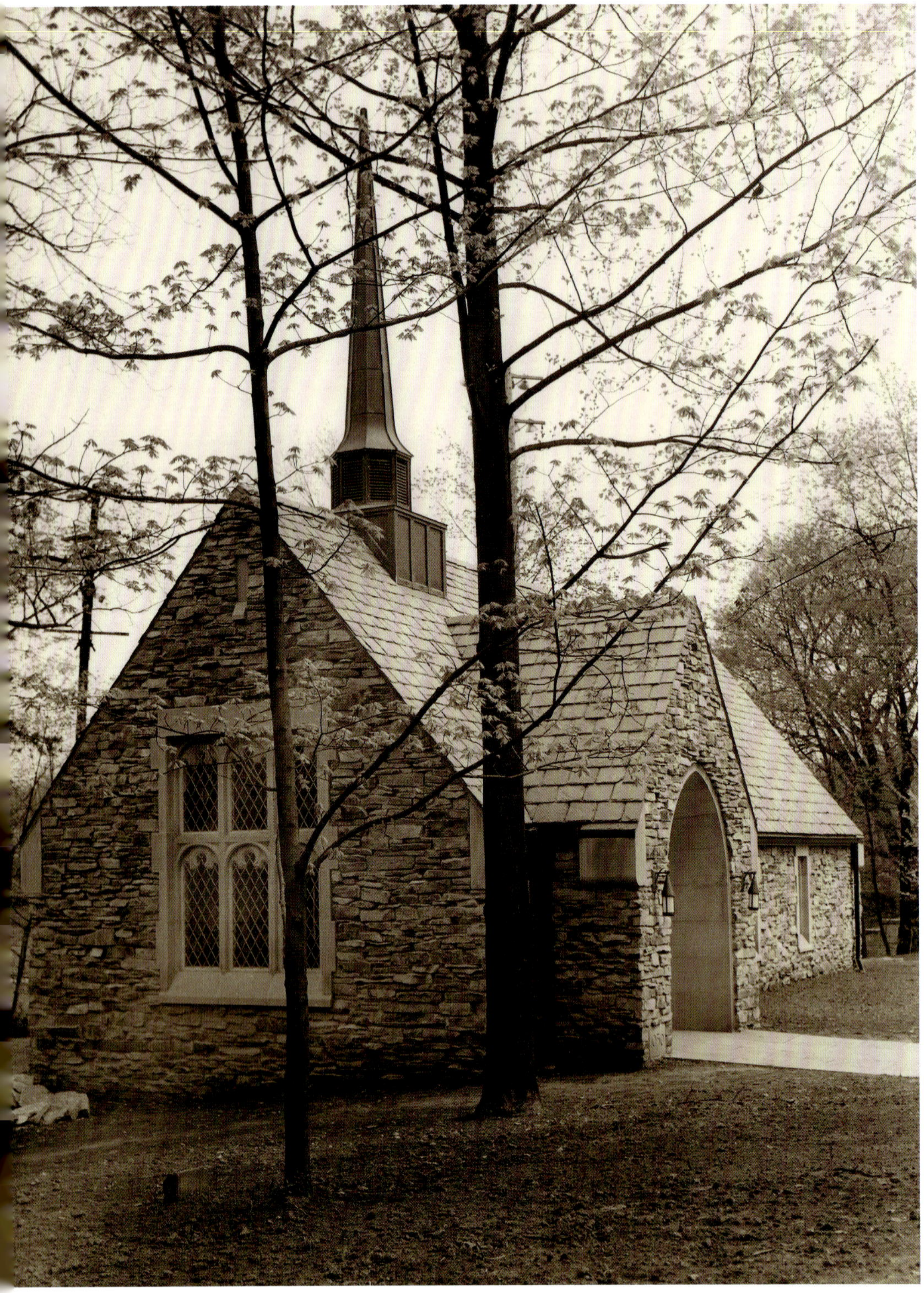

Beck Chapel, featuring a modified Tudor style with steeply pitched slate roof, 1957. P0020420, IU Archives.

The chapel is nestled in a wooded setting, east of Indiana Memorial Union and north of Ballantine Hall, adjacent to Dunn Cemetery. It is built in a modified Tudor style with a steeply pitched slate roof with prominent gables, copper spire, gabled entryway with a four-centered arch, tall narrow windows with small panes arranged in sets of three, and an interior that features richly wood-paneled walls in the entryway. The exterior walls, which blend with the adjoining Dunn Cemetery stone walls, were built with local Indiana limestone. The interior is small and intimate, permitting space for only sixty to seventy people on sixteen golden oak pews. The north side's two stories take advantage of the slope of the land. As is traditional in many religions, the chapel is situated on a longitudinal axis, with the altar facing east so that the morning sun streams through the high six-pointed rose widow symbolic of the star of creation.

Beck Chapel reflects the unity of the IU community. The IU Men's Club donated the spire as a memorial to the men who lost their lives in World Wars I and II; the bronze doors were a gift from the wife of the chapel architect; the rose window was a gift of Mark and Luta Shrum; Robert R. Sturgeon gave the lych-gate in memory of his wife; and the stained-glass windows, designed by Rudy Pozzatti, professor emeritus of the IU School of Fine Arts, were a gift from Mark and Linda Wisen in celebration of their twenty-fifth wedding anniversary.

Within the chapel sacristy are housed the holy symbols and scriptures of the world's major religions, including rare copies of the Torah and Koran, hand-painted in gold; the Book of Genesis written in Hebrew and printed in 1578 from woodcuts in Rome; the Dahamapada, the canonical scriptures of Buddhism; and a Bible. Today Beck Chapel continues to be the campus home for those of all faiths, with services held representing the Christian (Catholic and Protestant), Jewish, Buddhist, Confucian, Hindu, Muslim, Shinto, Sikh, Zoroastrian, Taoist, Coptic, and Baha'i faiths.

In addition, numerous ceremonies take place in the sanctuary, including christenings, memorials, and weddings. The latter can range from strictly formal affairs to a humorous 1987 wedding in which the bride reached the altar to find all of the groomsmen sporting goggles.[3] Noteworthy events have included the 1971 wedding of Gary Atwood and Angela DeAngelis (future member of the Symbionese Liberation Army), a 1982 prenuptial service for Robert F. Kennedy Jr. and Emily Black, the 2005 wedding of IU President Michael McRobbie and Laurie Burns, and in 2009 the filming of John Mellencamp's music video for "A Ride Back Home."

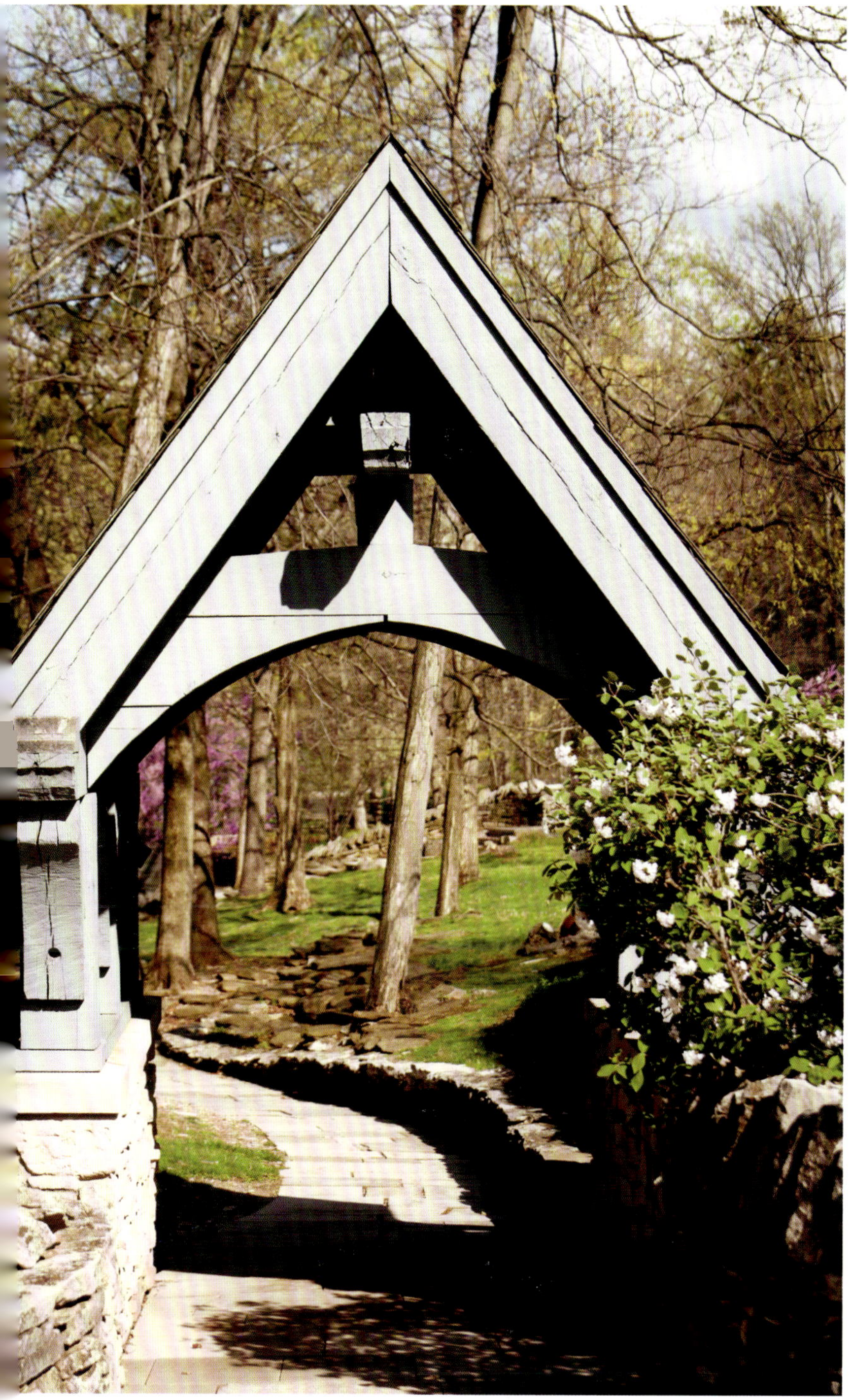

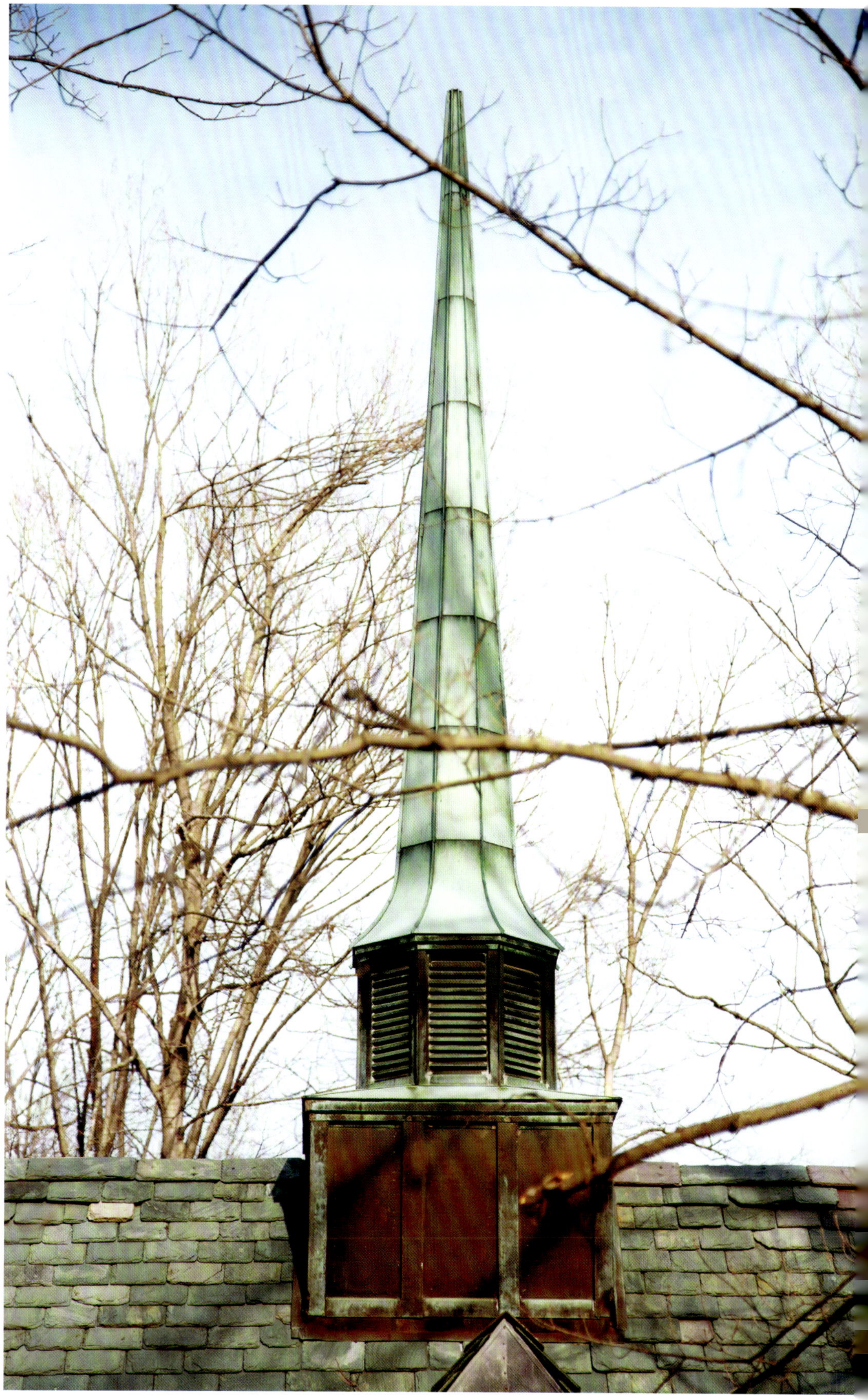

Above, Lych-gate at entrance to Beck Chapel, a gift from Robert R. Sturgeon in memory of his wife, 2016. Photo credit: Tyagan Miller.

Right, Copper spire on Beck Chapel, a gift from the IU Men's Club as a memorial to the men who lost their lives in World Wars I and II, 2016. Photo credit: Tyagan Miller.

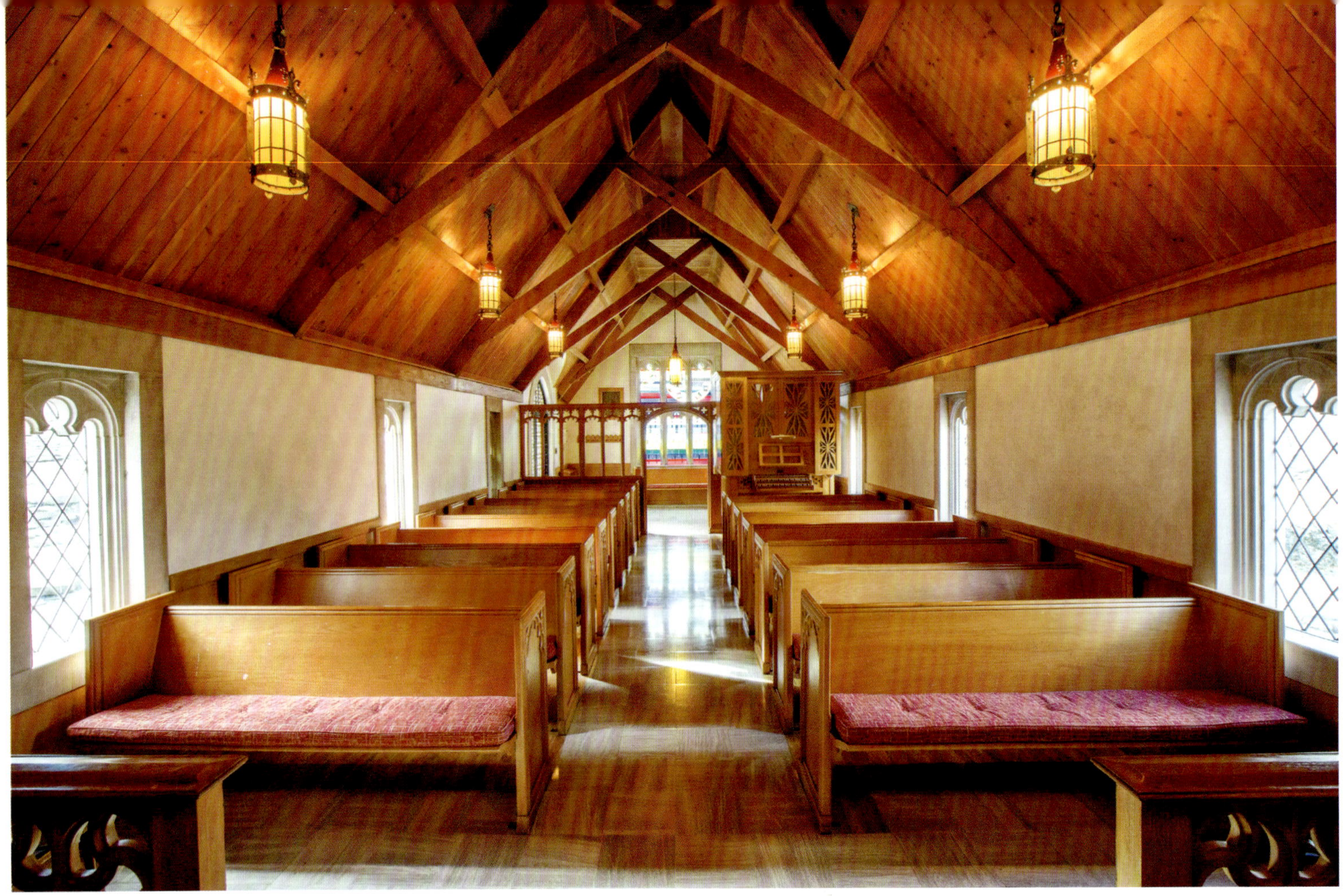

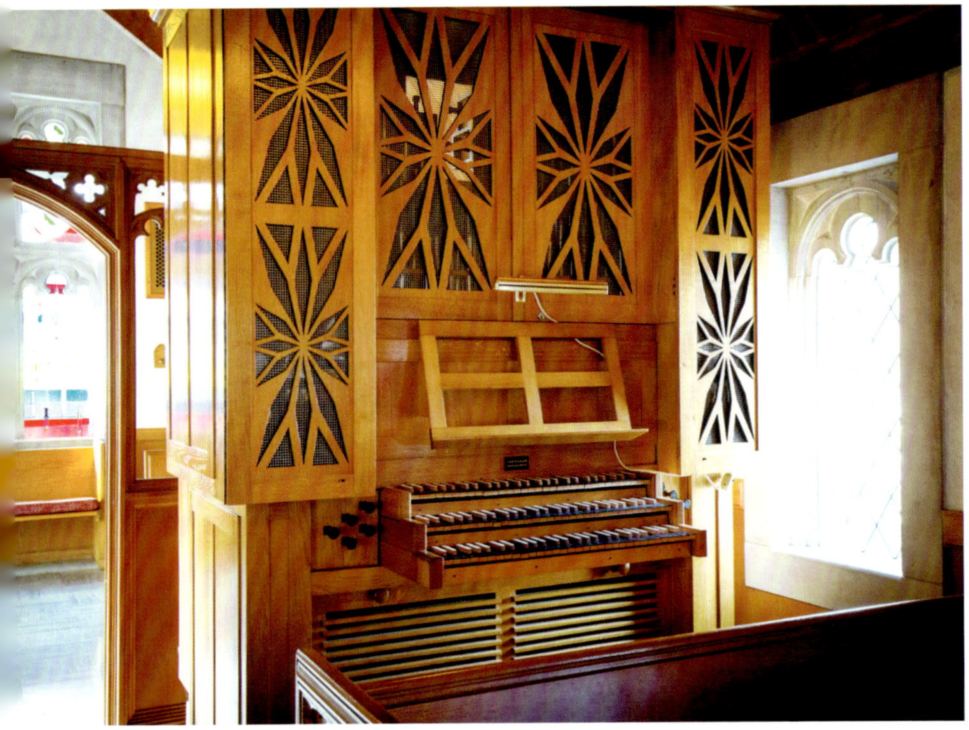

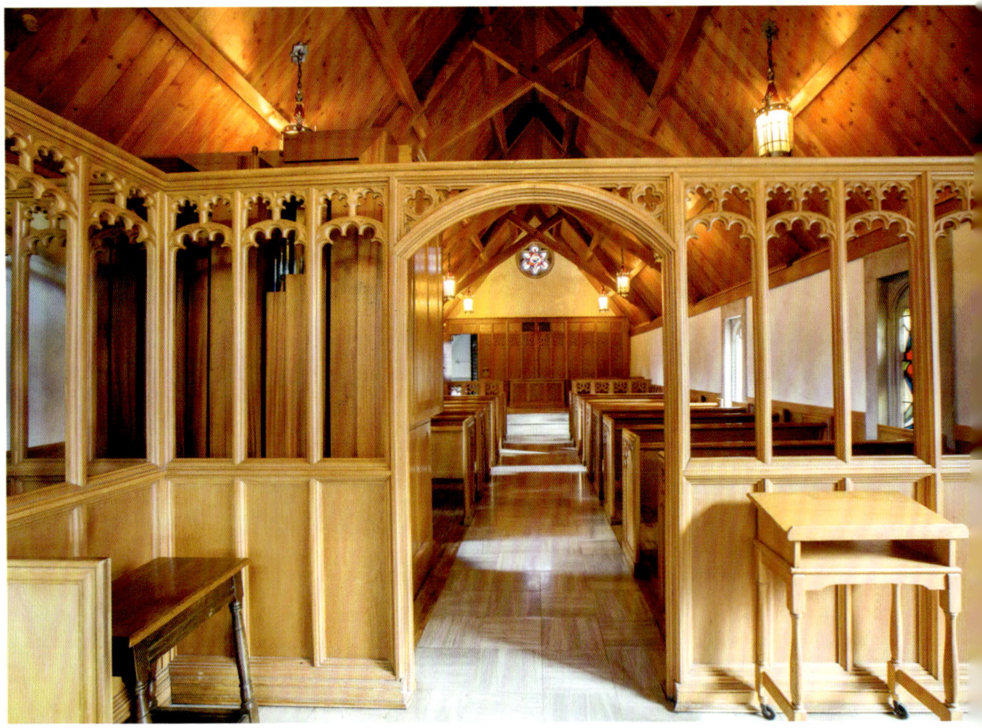

Top, Intimate space of Beck Chapel with sixteen oak pews and a rustic vaulted ceiling, 2016. Photo credit: Tyagan Miller.

Above, Richly carved oak organ at back of Beck Chapel, 2016. Photo credit: Tyagan Miller.

Beck Chapel looking from vestibule toward altar; note six-pointed rose window, 2016. Photo credit: Tyagan Miller.

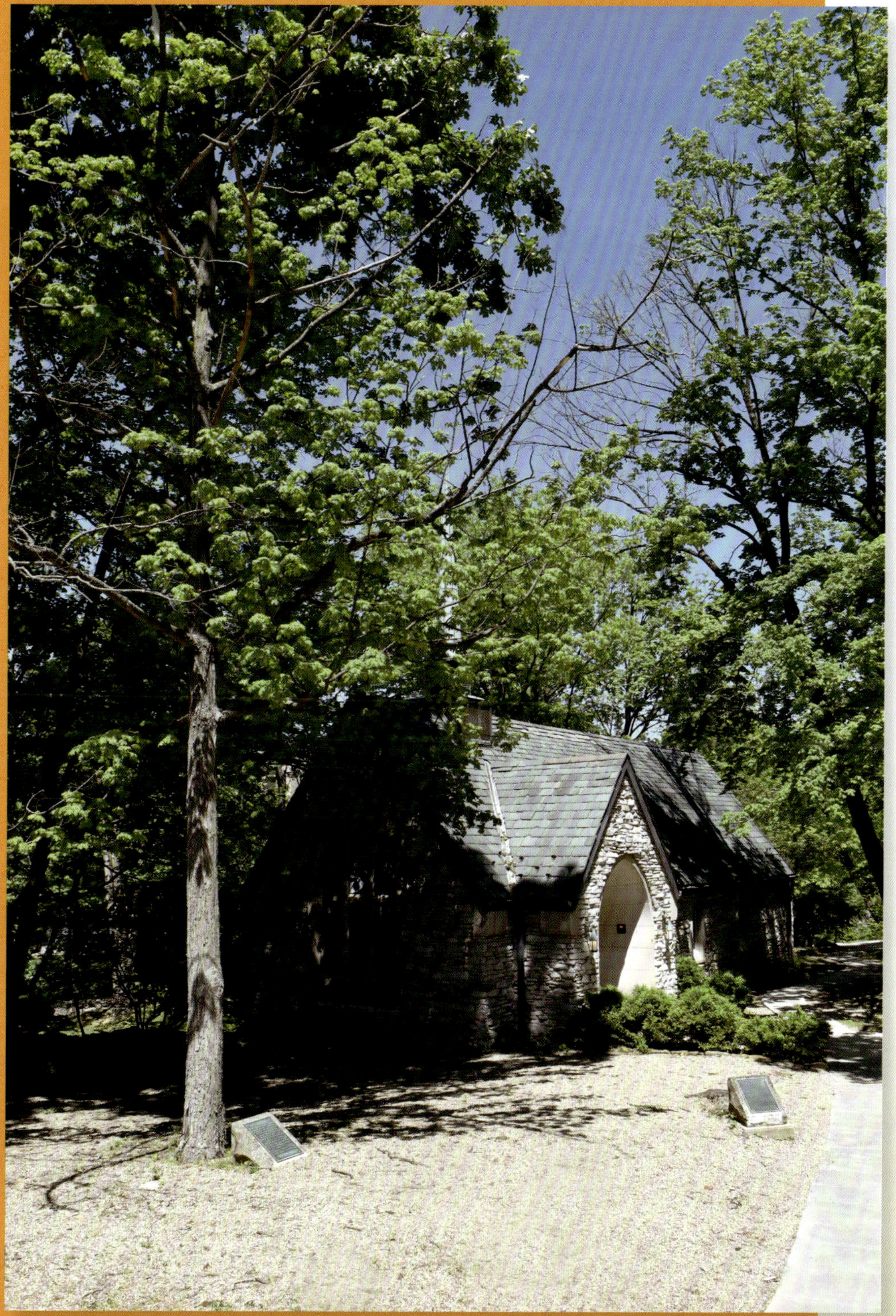

Beck Chapel in its wooded setting, 2016. Photo credit: Indiana University.

The Grove of All Faiths

On February 10, 1942, President Wells, Dr. Frank Beck, representatives from a hundred student organizations, and three religious leaders—Rabbi Cronbach, professor at the Hebrew Institute of Cincinnati; Dr. James Gillis, editor of the *Catholic World*; and Dr. Charles C. Morrison, editor of the *Christian Century*—gathered on the proposed site of the new chapel to plant three trees representing Judaism, Catholicism, and Protestantism. Those present recited in unison the dedication: "Planted in a Triangle, may these trees ever symbolize to us the harmony and unity that should dwell among us, and, above all the divisions, of our imperfect society, assert the Brotherhood of man."[1]

Over the coming years, trees symbolizing the other religions of the world joined the initial three, including Christian Science and those described at the time as the "Religions of the Orient."

1. Script for reciting: "For the Planting of Three Trees on the Indiana University Campus," February 10, 1942, Frank O. and Daisy Beck papers, collection C168, Indiana University Archives, Indiana University, Bloomington.

Lilly Library 1960

ARCHITECT Eggers and Higgins / A. M. Strauss

ARCHITECTURAL STYLE Art Deco / Greco Deco

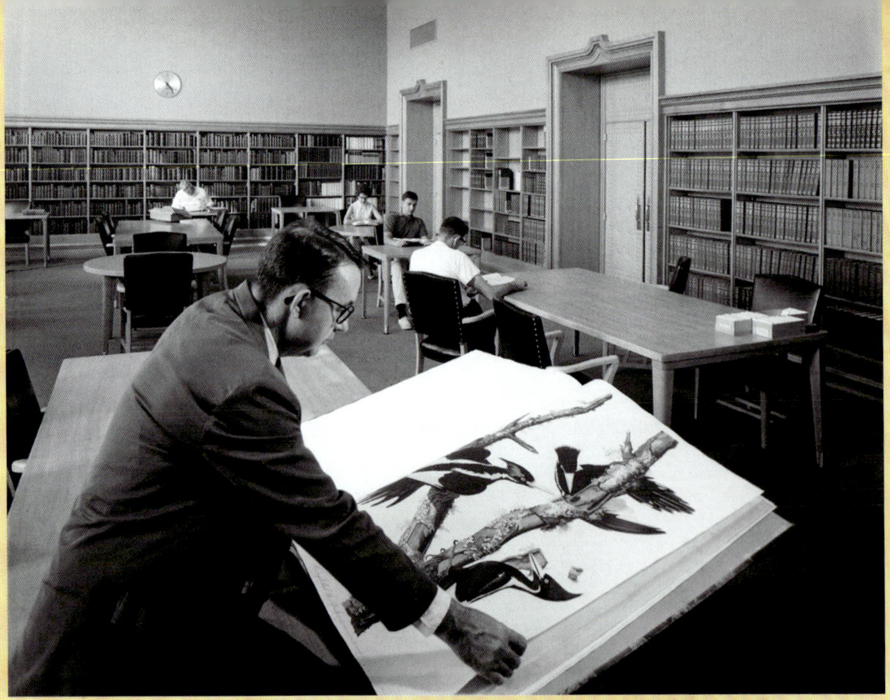

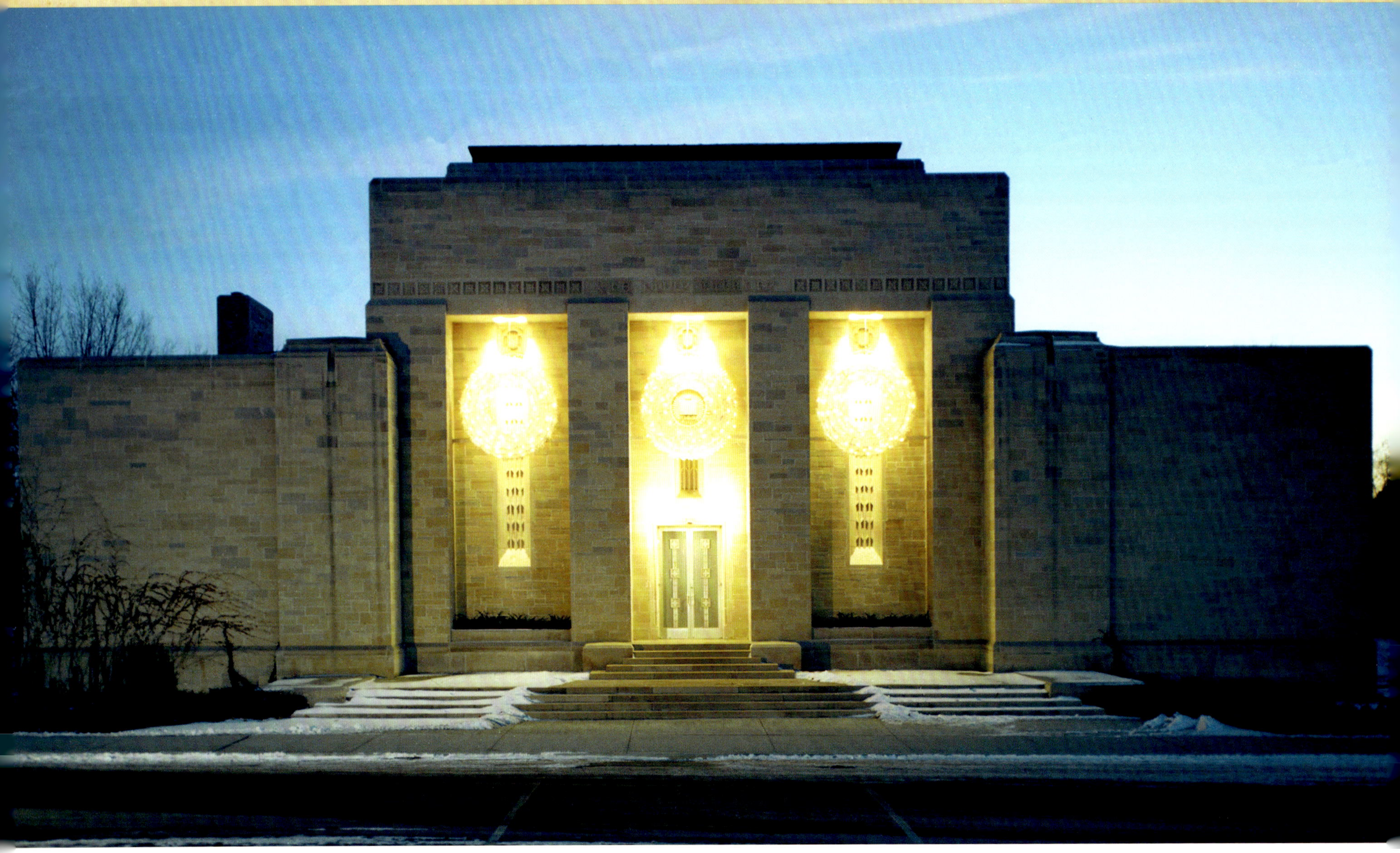

Lilly Library

Repository of Rare Works

As ideas are the fruit of the university and scholars the blood that give her life, so books are the university's sustenance. . . . The presence on this Midwestern campus of these special collections of books and manuscripts has regional and indeed national significance. Their presence here is a proof again of our determination in America to bring to all of our people, wherever they may live, the inspiration and sense of creative excitement which derive from personal acquaintanceship with the original evidence of man's highest intellectual achievements.

—Indiana University President Herman B Wells

By the first part of the twentieth century, according to university historian Thomas Clark, Indiana University "had built a solid regional library with certain areas of better than ordinary strength, but its holdings were undistinguished because there was not a single strong research collection." This changed in President Herman B Wells's special announcement to the Board of Trustees in December 1954 of a significant donation of rare books and manuscripts from Josiah Lilly, a pharmaceutical industrialist and president of Eli Lilly and Company from 1948 to 1953. Wells described the gift as a collection of "tremendous cultural significance . . . representing an addition of inestimable value to our Library. . . . It includes originals of most of the significant publications relating to the beginnings of American history." With the formal announcement of the gift in January 1956, Wells reported to the trustees that "the concept of the Library as a local service was expanded to include its new responsibility of national scholarship . . . and to lay the foundation for a wider scholarly use of its rare books and special collections."[1]

As the collections began to arrive on campus for deposit in the five-story archives located in Bryan Hall, the need for a separate structure to house them became apparent. Wells had long dreamed of a cultural arts plaza that would be centrally located on campus. With Wells's vision in mind, a plan by Eggers and Higgins back in 1939 had called for an auditorium to serve as the focal point to the east, a fine arts building to the north, a sculptural fountain as the centerpiece, and on the sloping site to the south an open-air Greek theater reminiscent of those on the Athenian Acropolis. In 1954, with the need to house Lilly's generous donation, these plans changed. According to Wells, "By the time we were ready to build the theater, the public had become so accustomed to air-conditioning that there was little desire for outdoor performances and assemblages. It seemed appropriate to use that site for the Lilly Library since it would contribute its share to the fine arts."[2]

Designed by Eggers and Higgins of New York and A. M. Strauss Inc. of Fort Wayne, the new library building was clad with Indiana limestone with a combination Art Deco and Art Moderne style that blended well with the nearby Indiana University Auditorium. The flattened vertical columns on the north entrance reveal a heavy Greek influence, and the building as a whole is simple and streamlined, with rectilinear lines and forms and stylized yet repetitive decorative bands of carving. To protect the rare collections, the interior was constructed with fireproof walls and outfitted with constant humidity and temperature controls. The stacks occupy seven floors, with a basement that includes two separate "bombproof" vaults.

On the main level, a large centralized display hall with walnut floor and walls opens up into a reading room as well as several interior exhibit rooms, each designed to represent the collections they house. In the Lincoln Room, which contains items from the Joseph B. Oakleaf collection, furnishings are representative of those in the White House during the Civil War; the Elisabeth W. Ball Room is Georgian in style, influenced

Facing top, John F. Schrodt Jr. perusing Audubon's Birds of America in Lilly Library reading room, 1960. P0056012, IU Archives.

Facing bottom, Lilly Library shortly after dedication, 1960. P0051690, IU Archives. Photo credit: Indiana University.

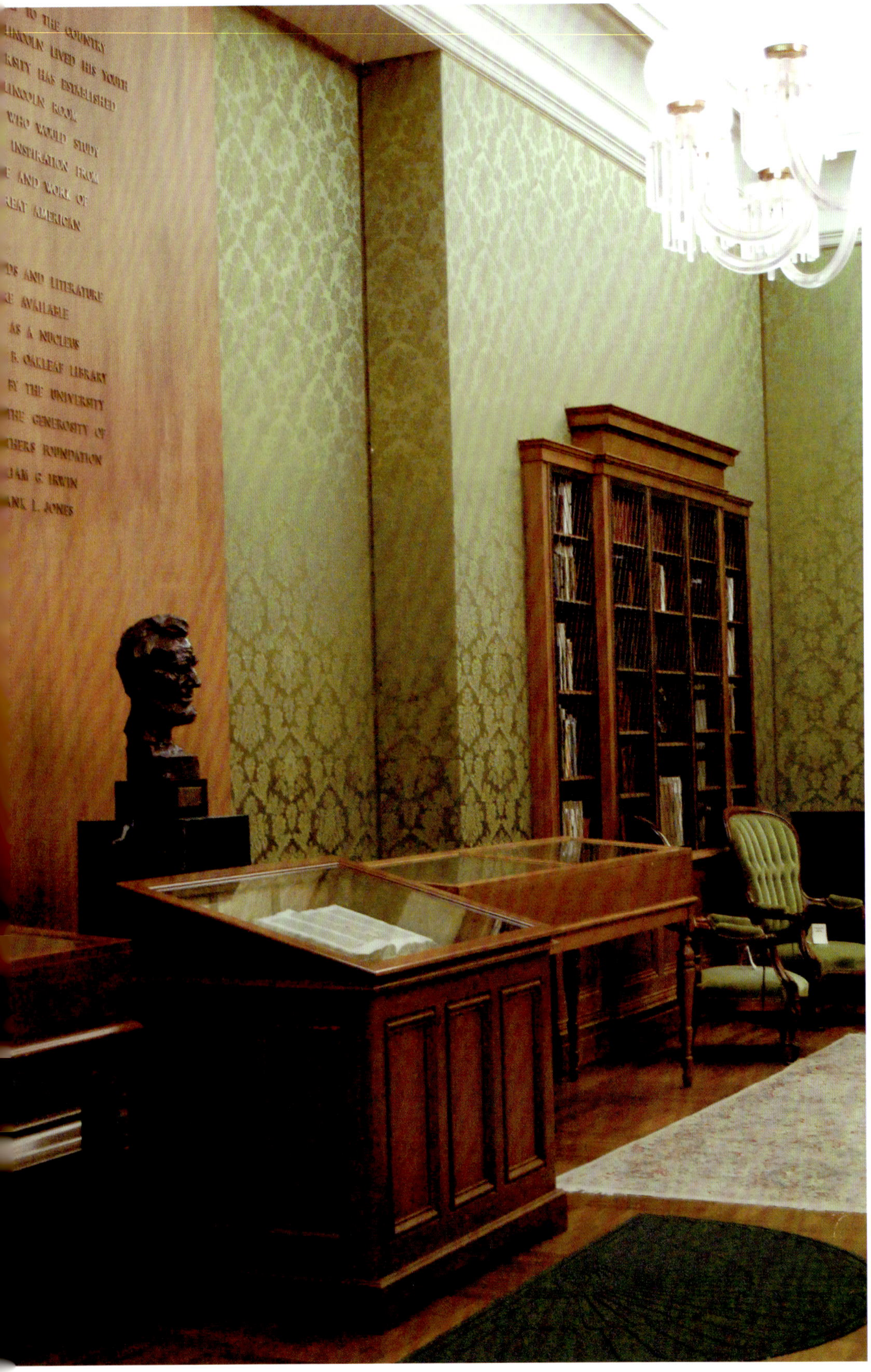

by an eighteenth-century English library; the Ellison Room of Western Americana is in a frontier genre; and the Slocum Puzzle Room contains examples from Jerry Slocum's collection of over thirty-five thousand mechanical puzzles. The mezzanine level includes a gallery, a seminar room, and the Bernardo Mendel Room, furnished in the style of fifteenth-century Spain and holding portions of his extensive book collection.

The official opening and dedication of the building on October 3, 1960, brought national and international publicity. Before beginning his prepared talk, speaker Frederick B. Adams Jr., director of the Piermont Morgan Library in New York, delighted the audience by presenting as a dedication gift twenty-seven long-thought-missing leaves of Hoosier General Lew Wallace's manuscript for *Ben-Hur*. Adams prophesized: "We cannot foretell the far destinies of this building and its collections. We can only stand at the threshold of its progress. . . . A great library never stops growing."[3] President Wells remarked that "in America we have never sought to construct a capital of culture. Instead we have attempted to distribute across our land the rich fruit of man's mental effort in the same way as we share among all of our people the wealth of our farms and factories."[4]

With completion of the Showalter Fountain (1961) and Fine Arts Building (1962), by 1970, according to Thomas Clark, "the cultural and creative potential of the university had assumed global distinction, and the long standing objective of extending the intellectual impulse of the institution well beyond its immediate campus had become a reality."[5] The final building in the arts plaza, the Sidney and Lois Eskenazi Museum of Art, was added in 1981.

Today the Lilly Library includes many significant collections, which can be seen by appointment or during scheduled hours. Highlights include a copy of the first printing of the Declaration of Independence, printed on July 4, 1776, in Philadelphia; a first edition of Geoffrey Chaucer's Canterbury Tales, printed in the 1470s; the Gutenberg Bible New Testament; a four-volume double elephant folio edition of John James Audubon's *The Birds of America* (a new folio is on display each week); the First Folio of William Shakespeare's works printed in 1623; a rare first edition of John Bunyan's *Pilgrim's Progress*; and the first editions of compositions by George Frideric Handel. The works of such celebrated artists as directors Orson Welles and John Ford; poets Ezra Pound, Sylvia Plath, and James Whitcomb Riley; and authors Ian Fleming, Edith Wharton, and Upton Sinclair can be viewed at the Lilly Library.

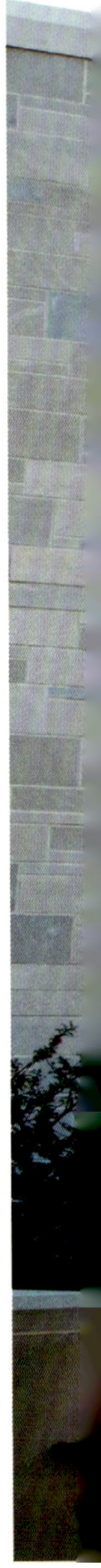

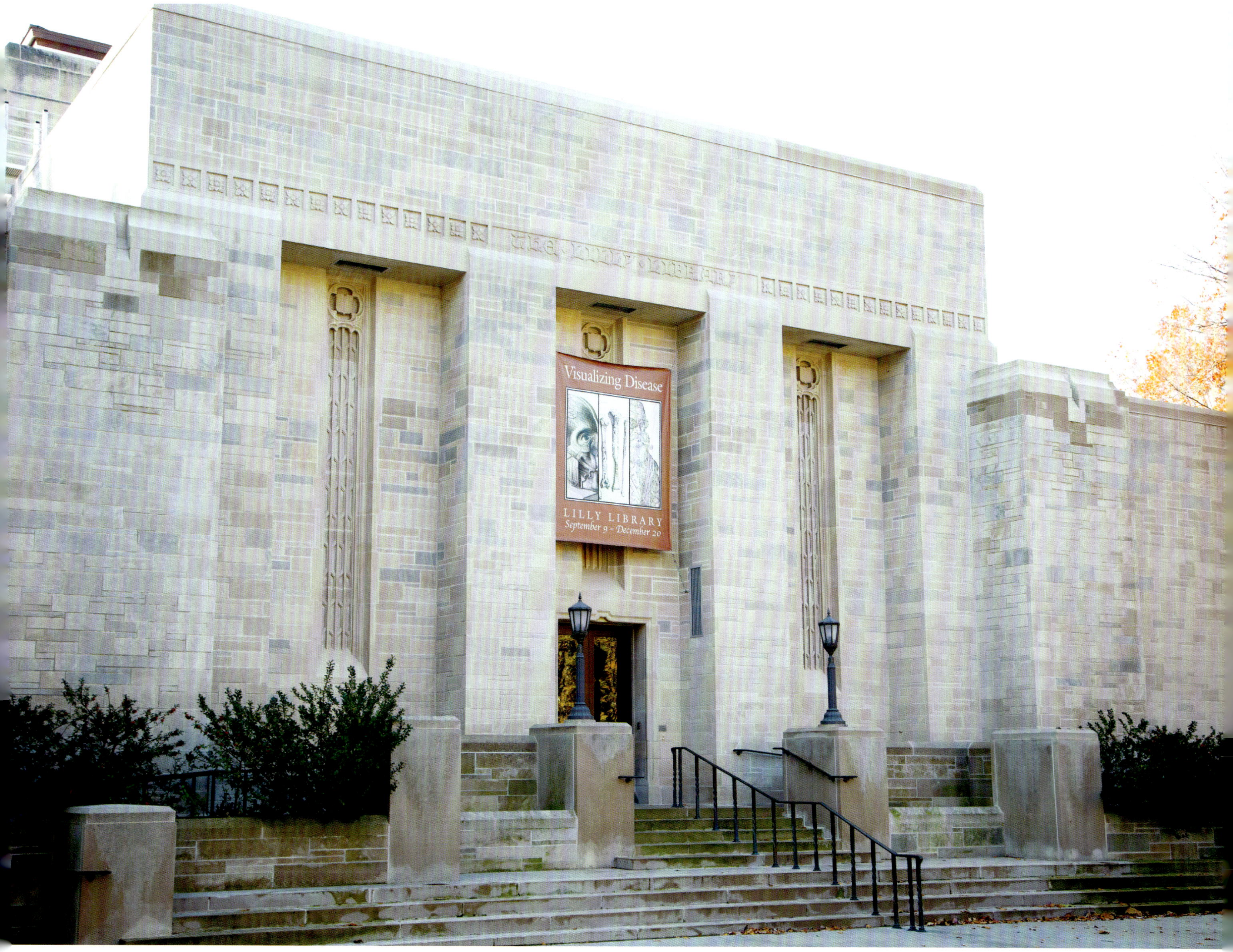

Facing, Lincoln Room in Lilly Library with furnishings representative of those in White House during Civil War, undated. Photo credit: Indiana University.

Above, North facade of Lilly Library featuring Art Deco and Greek influences, 2015. Photo credit: Tyagan Miller.

Virgil T. DeVault Alumni Center 1963

ARCHITECT	William Strain
ORIGINAL NAME	Administrative Services Building
MAJOR RENOVATION	1997, Schmidt Associates
ARCHITECTURAL STYLE	Collegiate Gothic

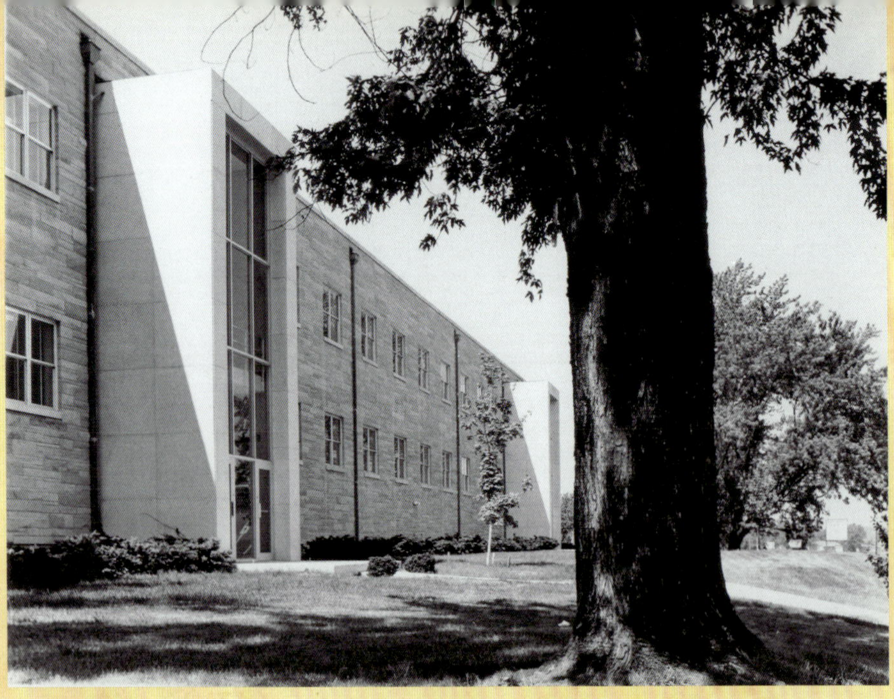

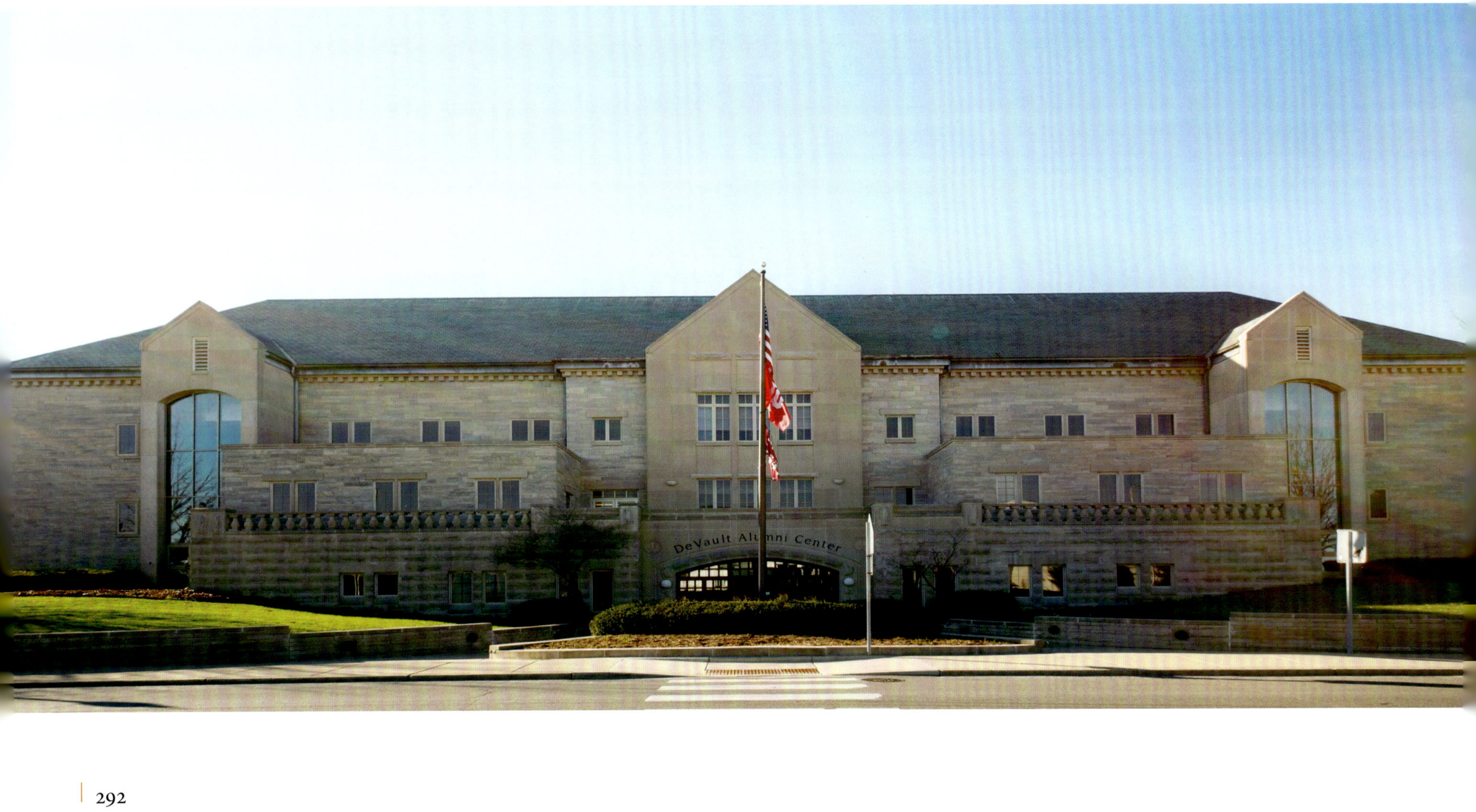

Virgil T. DeVault Alumni Center

From Ugly Duckling to Alumni Home

Indiana University would not be the extraordinary institution that it is without you, our alumni. You are our extended family, our role models, our best friends. . . . This is your building, a bustling center for today's activities, a monument to those who have gone before and a beacon for tomorrow's alumni who will carry on the traditions of caring and compassion that enrich Indiana University every day.

—Indiana University President Myles Brand at dedication ceremony

BY THE EARLY 1960S, STUDENT ENROLLMENT had nearly tripled since the construction of Bryan Hall in 1936. Indiana University's administrative support departments were strained for space and scattered about the campus. A report on space issues to the Board of Trustees mentioned that the director of Campus Stores "will now occupy a closet 7' wide (which became available on the death of another staff member)" and that "the hallway is being used as work space by at least seven employees."[1]

With cost efficiency in mind, the trustees considered various proposals: to renovate space for several of these departments in Alpha Hall shortly before it was razed; to complete the third floor of Bryan Hall, which at that time was only partially occupied; and even to build a steel "Butler-type building, perhaps modified with some use of conventional materials" at Seventeenth Street near Faculty Avenue. The last site was selected because it would permit easy employee parking in the athletic lots across the street and allow for "a functional, inexpensive style of architecture." The use of a steel Butler building, however, was not approved. Vice President Joseph Franklin suggested that another building proposal from local Bloomington architect William J. Strain "seems to have greater beauty and dignity, more fitting to a University campus, than the steel buildings, which do not look like permanent structures and which seem better adapted to warehouse or factory use."[2]

Strain's proposal won out, and the resulting utilitarian two-story limestone Administrative Services Building was completed in 1963 to house departments such as accounting, personnel, payroll, data processing, and purchasing. It was renamed the Information Services Building in 1987 when most of the administrative departments moved to Poplars, leaving University Computing Services as the building's primary occupant.

The Indiana University Alumni Association (IUAA), home to the alumni associations on all IU's campuses, had never resided in its own building. The IUAA was in the Indiana Memorial Union (IMU) for nearly sixty years, moving to Fountain Square Mall in downtown Bloomington when the massive IMU renovation project began in 1991. Although construction of a new building would be too expensive, remodeling an existing campus building was deemed feasible. When the Information Services Building became available, Jerry Tardy, the Alumni Foundation director, thought its size and location were perfect.

The location on a hill on the north side of campus across from Memorial Stadium and Assembly Hall had potential, since it would be inviting to alumni as they arrived for sporting and other university events. With the decision to use this building as the first on-campus alumni center, the "Coming Home" campaign, a massive fund-raising endeavor, was initiated to transform the utilitarian "ugly duckling . . . forgettable

Facing top, Original Administrative Services Building (later Information Services Building) before conversion to Virgil T. DeVault Alumni Center, 1964. P0022628, IU Archives. Photo credit: David Repp.

Facing bottom, North view of DeVault Alumni Center, 2017. Photo credit: Tyagan Miller.

limestone rectangle . . . into a gracious and hospitable home away from home" for alumni.[3] In 1993 distinguished alumnus, doctor, and philanthropist Virgil T. DeVault of Washington, DC, stepped forward with a $1.5 million lead gift for the project. The architectural firm Schmidt Associates of Indianapolis was hired to plan the renovations.

The interior renovation included the addition of offices and the reconfiguration of several interior areas to house all of the administrative functions of the association as well as facilities for public use. For the architectural style of the new alumni center, IU administrators visited several universities for ideas, but in the end, elements from the Collegiate Gothic architecture of the Old Crescent buildings in the center of campus were incorporated into the design. According to architect Wayne S. Schmidt, "We thought about what it means for alumni to visit campus and determined that it often meant going to the heart of campus, to those original buildings or to the Well House." Vice President for Administration Terry Clapacs added that "it extends the aesthetics of the old part of campus out to the new part."[4] The finished renovation has many features reminiscent of IU's early buildings such as Kirkwood and Maxwell Halls, with a tiered northern facade of textured limestone that rises to a second-floor balcony; a pitched, gabled slate roof; arched windows; and a broad, arched doorway.

The entrance opens into the spacious, high-ceilinged, poplar- and oak-paneled Carlton Foyer, which features an open stairway and a brass IU seal, moved from the walkway in front of the Sample Gates and inlaid in the lobby's slate floor. The remainder of the main level is appointed in an elegant yet comfortable style and includes the Metz Board Room, Inskeep Library, Dutton Living Room, and ninety-seat Kelley Dining Room. Outside the south doors is Haugh Plaza, paved with bricks bearing the name of donors to the center's fund-raising campaign; a fountain, which was a gift of the IU Foundation; and terraced risers that lead up to the sloping green space behind the building. While the first floor serves primarily as an inviting public space, the second and third floors house almost exclusively administrative offices. Numerous alumni and campus activities are held here, including board meetings, seminars, catered dinners, and homecoming and reunion events.

Photographs of the original Administrative Services Building are hard to reconcile with the stately Virgil T. DeVault Alumni Center today.

Main entryway to DeVault Alumni Center, 2017.
Photo credit: Tyagan Miller.

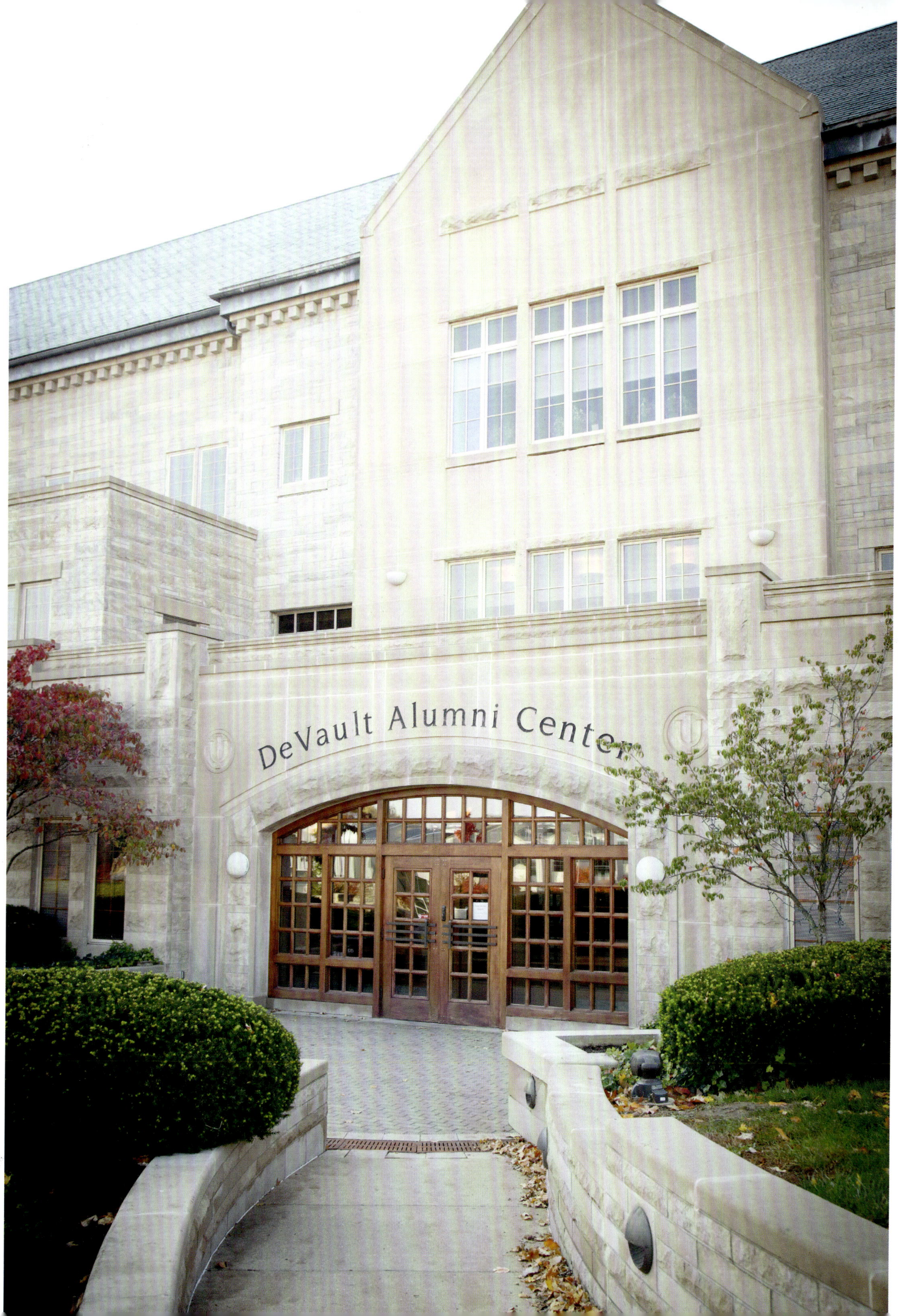
DeVault Alumni Center

Herman B Wells Library 1969

ARCHITECT Eggers and Higgins

ARCHITECTURAL STYLE Brutalist Modern

ORIGINAL NAME Main Library

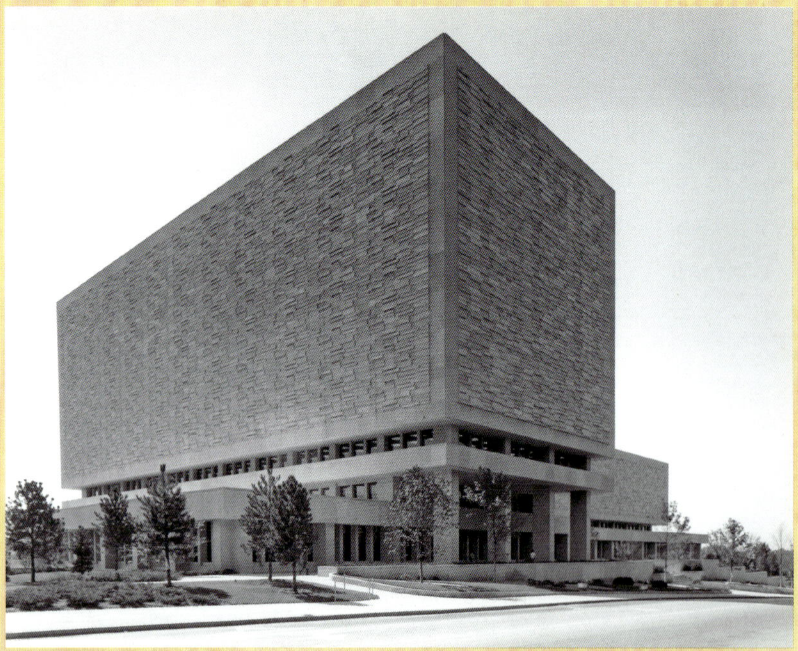

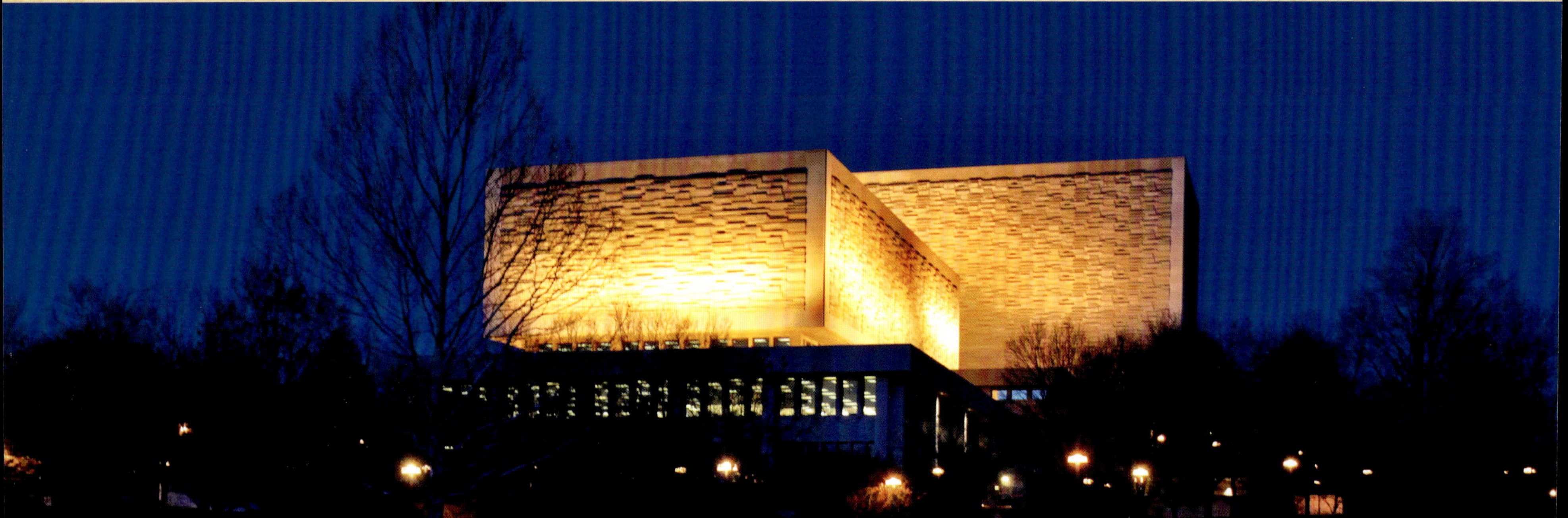

Herman B Wells Library

The Towers of Silence

A University library is a large and complicated organism. . . . It is a living storehouse of the accumulated knowledge and wisdom of the ages, and it is unlike most other organs and institutions in that its value and utility grow with age.

—Section Committee on the University Library

As with so many classrooms on campus, the library in Franklin Hall was bursting at the seams with the influx of new students following World War II. The problem was twofold. Not only was there a lack of study carrels, but the library collections had outgrown the available stacks. By 1950 a new undergraduate library was second on the university's list of capital priorities behind the Life Sciences Building.[1] The State of Indiana issued a grant to the university for the preparation of plans for a new building, and the architectural firm Eggers and Higgins of New York was commissioned to design it. Despite these early planning efforts, the project was set aside in 1953 over the objection of Director of Libraries Robert Miller, who insisted that Franklin Hall was over capacity. To remedy the situation, an addition to the library stack area of Franklin Hall was completed in 1956 and the Student Building was remodeled to serve as an undergraduate library in 1961.

In 1961 Joseph Sutton, political science instructor (and future IU president), along with Robert F. Byrnes, professor of history, emphasized the importance of a new library during the faculty input phase of the university's forthcoming ten-year plan. Byrnes stressed that he "could not conceive of a project that should supersede the library as the no. 1 item in our building program. The only major dissatisfaction with the University among faculty and, even so, among students [is] the library. . . . We are now behind and shall lose valuable faculty members if we don't get going right now."[2] President Wells was not entirely convinced, deeming the university had greater priorities at the time. Miller, however, continued to press the issue, and with the support of the Board of Trustees the firm of Eggers and Higgins was released to continue planning the new library.

In February 1962, the Library Review and Planning Committee (LRPC) submitted its report outlining the desired space needs, location (at the corner of Tenth Street and Jordan Avenue), and architecture for the new structure: "The architects should be under no obligation to reproduce the architectural style of other buildings on the campus. On the contrary, a new departure would be most appropriate. The site itself encourages independence in this respect. . . . As the heart of the University, the library, we hope, will combine genuine functionalism with aesthetic imagination."[3]

Facing top, Early photograph of the Main Library, now the Herman B Wells Library, 1969. P0027307, IU Archives. Photo credit: Ralph "Porky" Veal.

Facing bottom, Herman B Wells Library as reflected in the Jesse H. and Beulah Chanley Cox Arboretum pond, 2010. Photo credit: Indiana University.

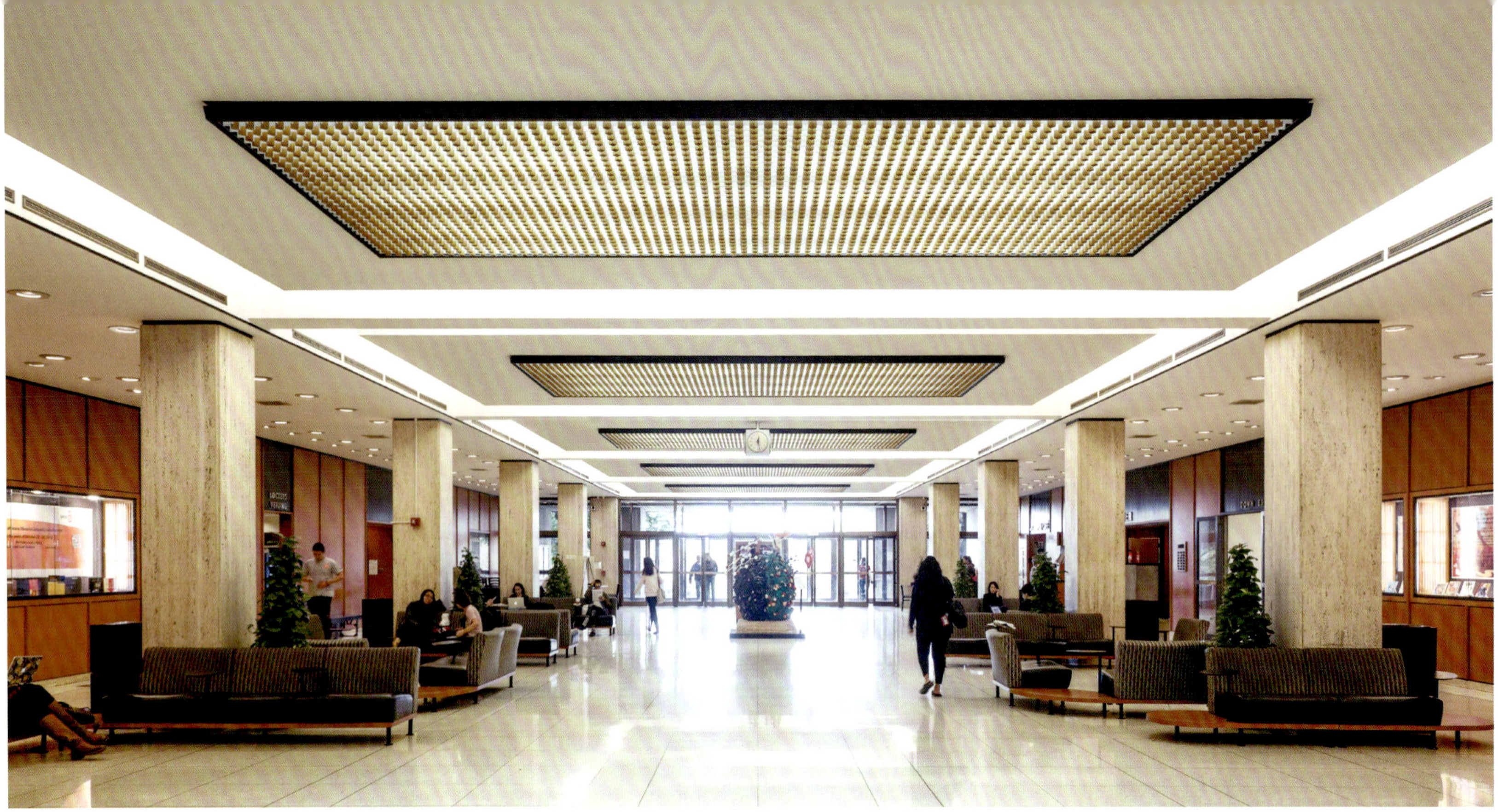

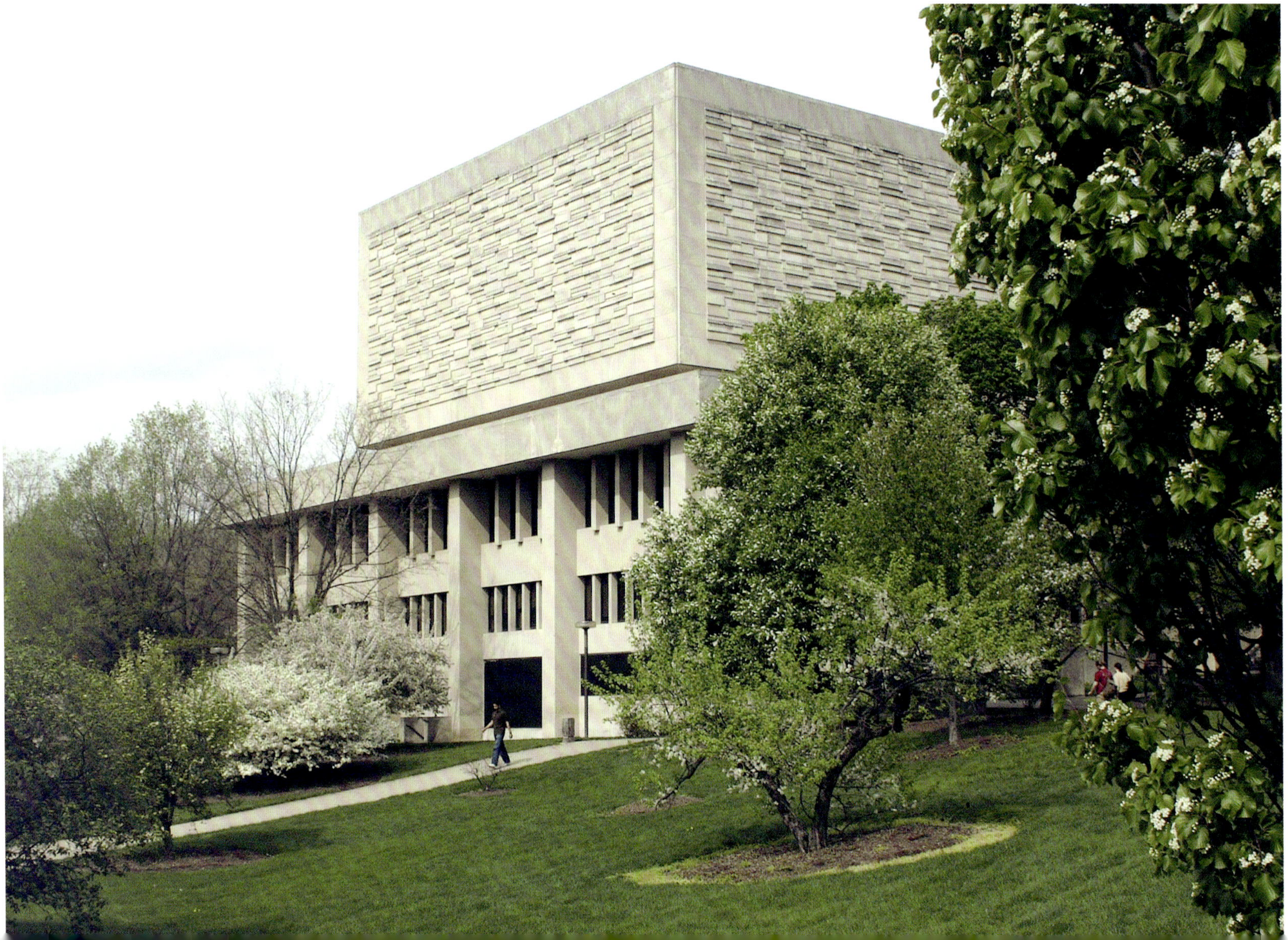

By November, the LRPC reported that "a new library building enjoys the position of first priority on the list of new construction" and furthermore "that the undergraduate library and research libraries shall rise separately but from a common base of two or three floors. The common floors will provide access to both libraries, as well as space for jointly used services. . . . Yet each library shall also have its own independence."[4] In 1964 during President Elvis Stahr's administration, the university submitted a budget request to the state for the construction of the new building, and in 1966 approval was received and final planning for IU's library was underway.

Designs for the structure evolved and, in the end, the Eggers and Higgins schematic alternative affectionately known as the "Towers of Silence" was approved. Construction began in 1966 and the building was completed in the summer of 1969. The library was located in the heart of campus, as envisioned by Herman B Wells, and set on a slight hill overlooking what is now the Jesse H. and Beulah Chanley Cox Arboretum. Thomas Gaines, author of *The Campus as a Work of Art*, described the edifice as "a strong cubist statement of stone," whose "long approach relieves the enormity of the building, thus avoiding an otherwise overbearing presence."[5] Brutalist Modern in style, it was constructed of a reinforced concrete frame with prefabricated concrete panels faced with irregular Indiana limestone blocks that allowed for rapid construction, durability, and cost savings. The three-story base features windows with an aluminum sash, while the upper floors are windowless.

The Main Library, as it was originally named, would unify the library system, both graduate and undergraduate libraries, under one roof. It encompassed eleven floors in the graduate tower and five floors in the undergraduate tower, and a general commons area below, with public services used by both. The Wells Library now houses the undergraduate library and Information Commons (a fully integrated technology center) in the West Tower. The East Tower is home to the Scholars' Commons; the Department of Government Information, Maps, and Microfilm Services; Indiana University Archives; and eleven floors of research collections. In 2013, Indiana University Press moved into offices on the third floor.

The main entrance of the library opens on a massive teak paneled lobby with travertine marble columns. The lobby stretches the entire width of the building and is oriented to follow the pedestrian traffic pattern between the classroom and dormitory sections of campus. Windows span the north and south entrances, which were designed to accommodate twenty thousand entrances and exits a day. The lobby opens onto the Information Commons in the West Tower and the Scholars' Commons in the East Tower. The eight stack floors (floors four through eleven) feature seminar rooms, hundreds of study carrels for graduate students and faculty, and offices for library subject specialists. The shared ground floor under both towers contains the cafeteria, classrooms, offices, and the film archives.

Following more than a year of occupancy, the library was formally dedicated on October 10, 1970, as the first in a series of events during IU's Sesquicentennial Academic Festival. Alumnus and president of the John Simon Guggenheim Foundation, Gordon N. Ray, delivered the dedication address before a large crowd, challenging those present to remember that "libraries are massive reminders of the long view, of the degree to which the past controls the present. Their very existence constitutes a denial that society is bankrupt, that our current problems are so urgent as to be possibly terminal, that the four-horsemen of the apocalypse will shortly ride us down. In society's balance sheet they represent the capital funds of the mind."[6] In June 2005, five years after the death of Herman B Wells, the library was renamed in his honor.

Facing top, Herman B Wells Library lobby featuring travertine marble columns and teak paneled walls, 2014. Photo credit: Tyagan Miller.

Facing bottom, West elevation of Herman B Wells Library from the Jesse H. and Beulah Chanley Cox Arboretum, undated. Photo credit: Indiana University.

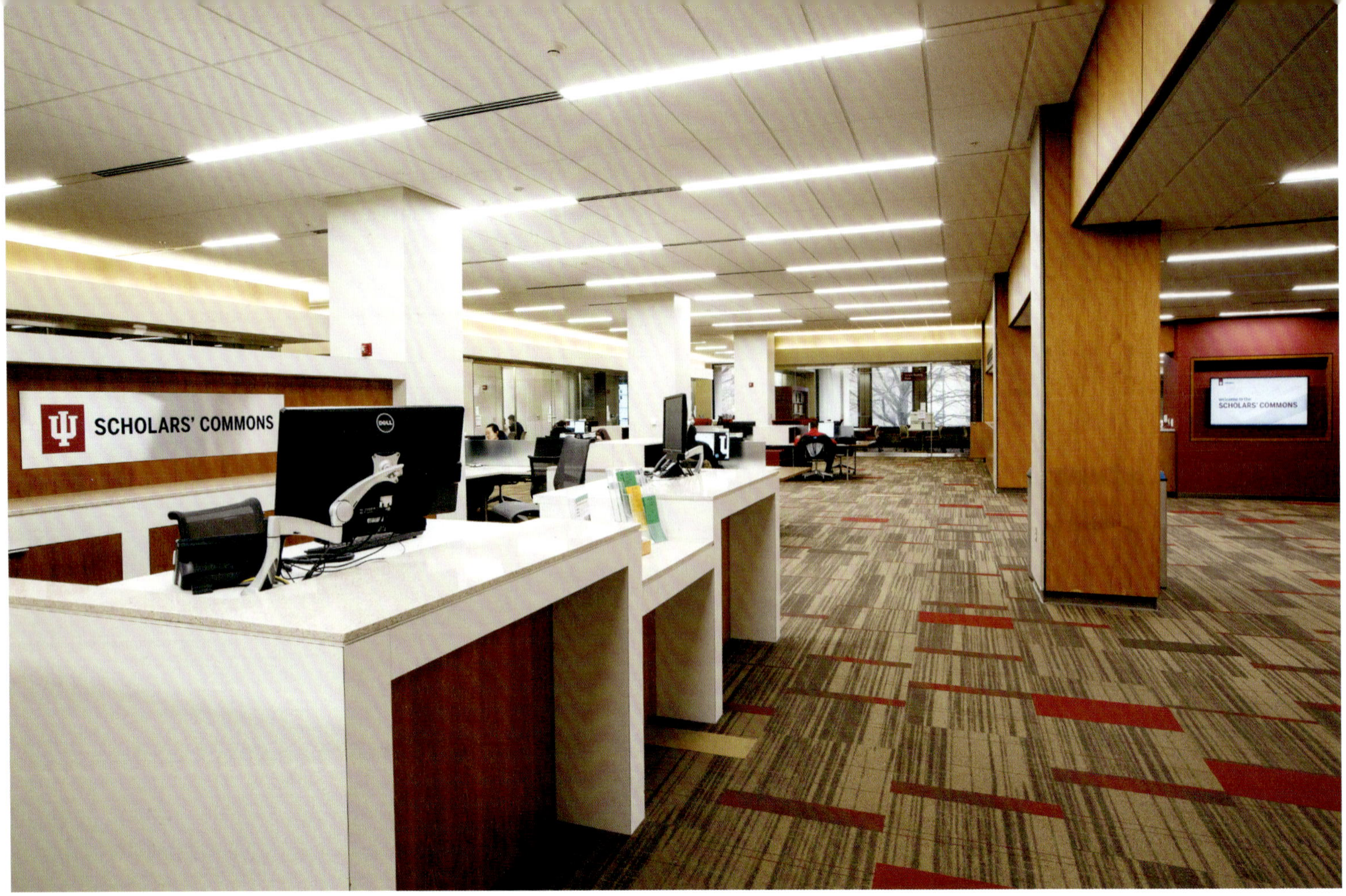

Scholars' Commons in Herman B Wells Library, 2017. Photo Credit: Tyagan Miller.

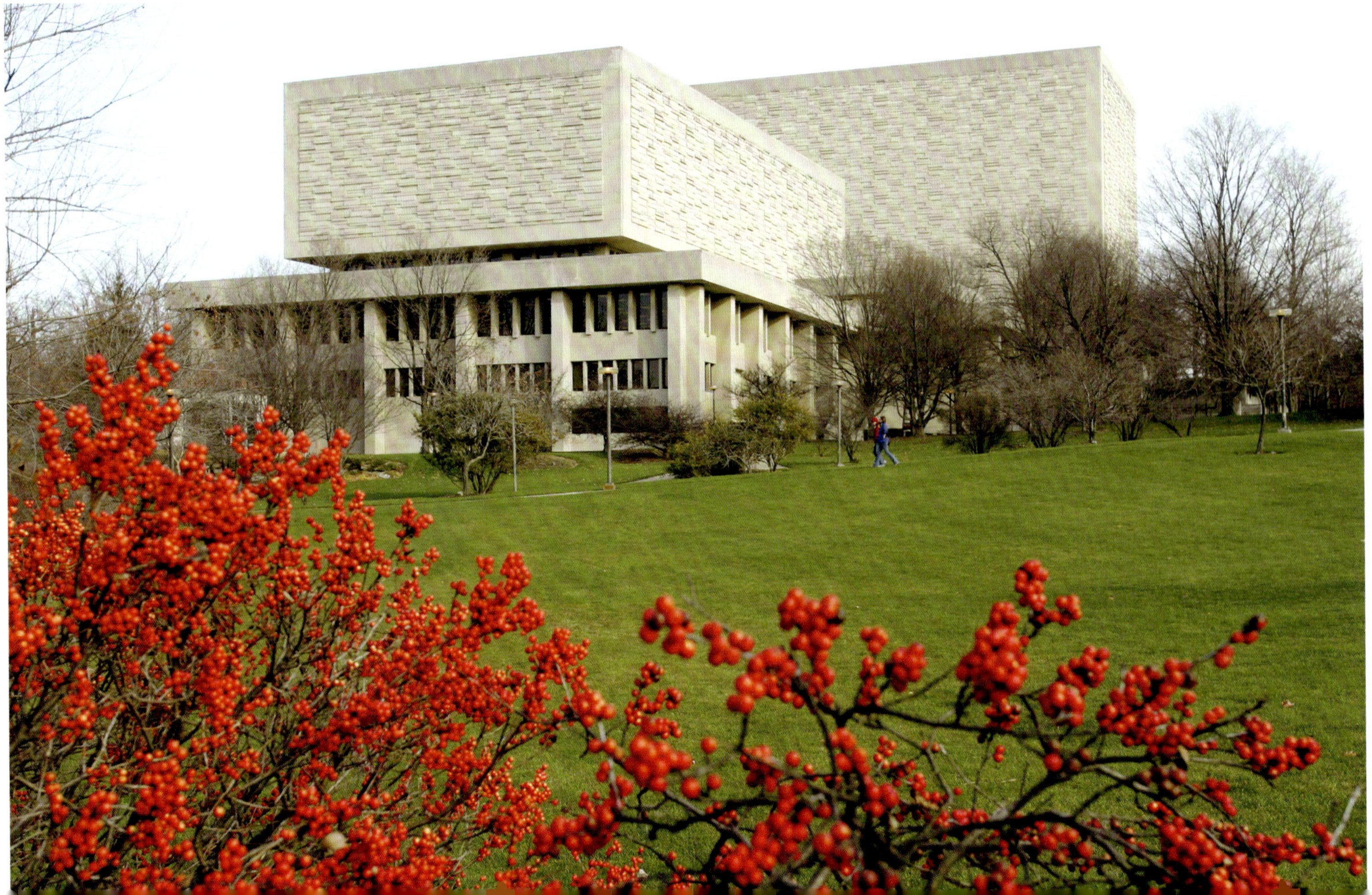

Early spring view of Herman B Wells Library from the Arboretum, 2003. Photo credit: Indiana University.

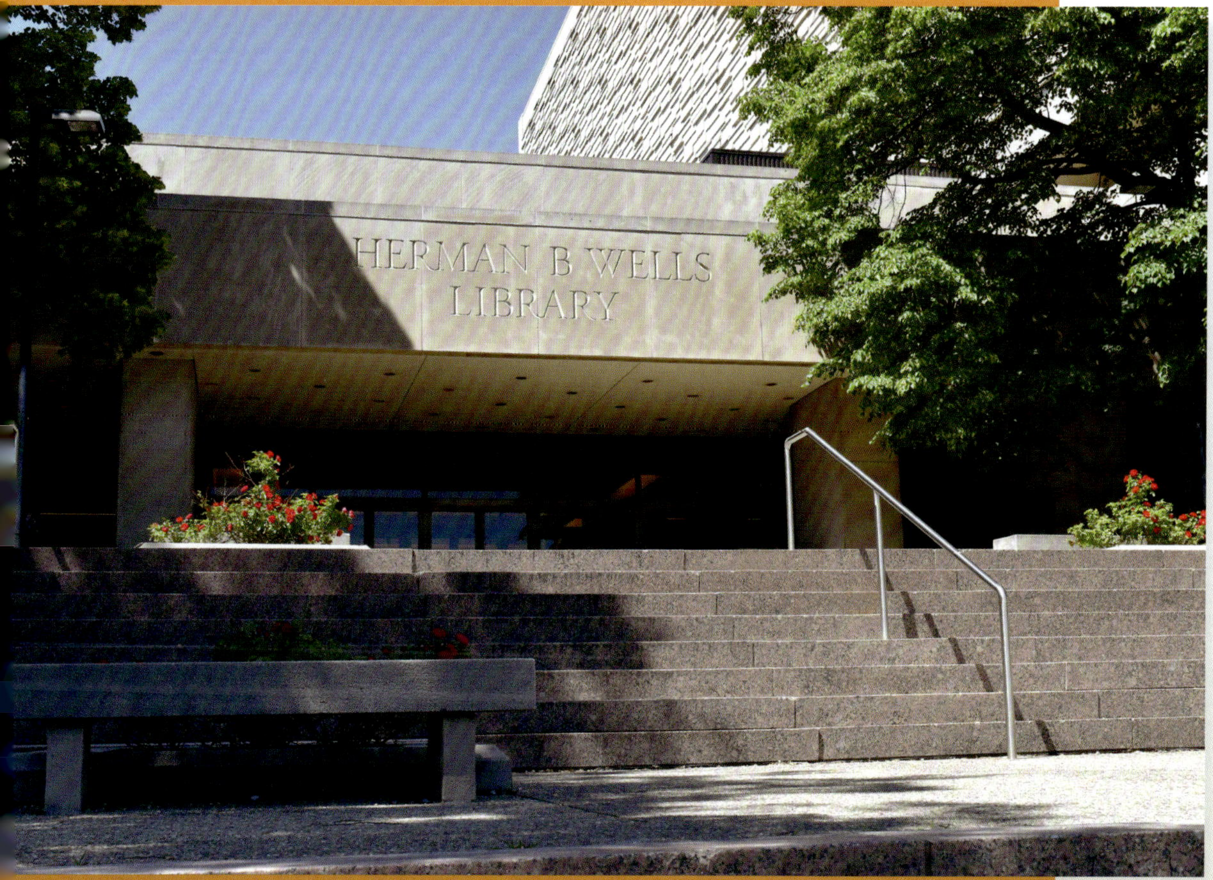

South entrance to Herman B Wells Library, 2017. Photo credit: Indiana University.

Sinking Library?

One of the most perpetually circulated rumors of university lore relates to the notion that when designing the building, the structural engineer failed to factor in the weight of the books, and thus, the library is slowly sinking. Even before the building was occupied in March of 1968, the *Indiana Daily Student* quoted library project director Joseph Hawkins of Huber, Hunt and Nichols: "I heard a rumor last week that the New Library was supposed to be sinking into the ground. It's impossible. The building is sitting on solid rock. Last summer about 14,000 cubic yards of stone were removed so we could start construction."[1]

1. Joseph Hawkins quoted in Dan Mills, "Building Not Sinking—It's Going Up," *Indiana Daily Student*, March 9, 1968, 4.

Showalter House 1974

ARCHITECT James Associates

ADDITION 2000, Ratio Architects

ARCHITECTURAL STYLE Collegiate Gothic

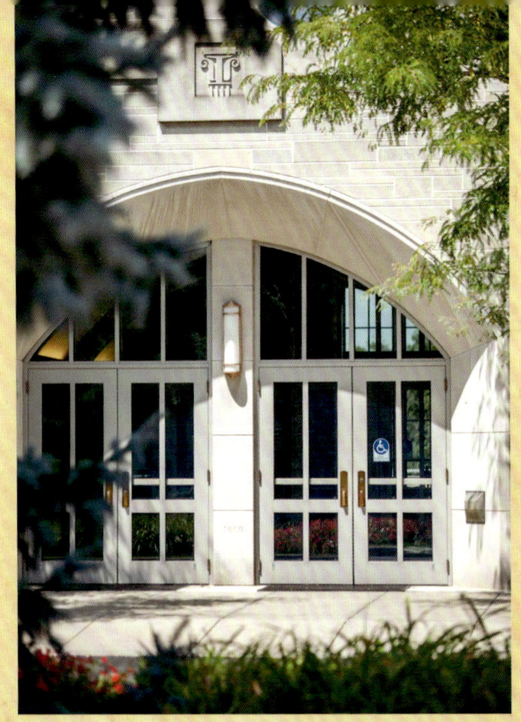

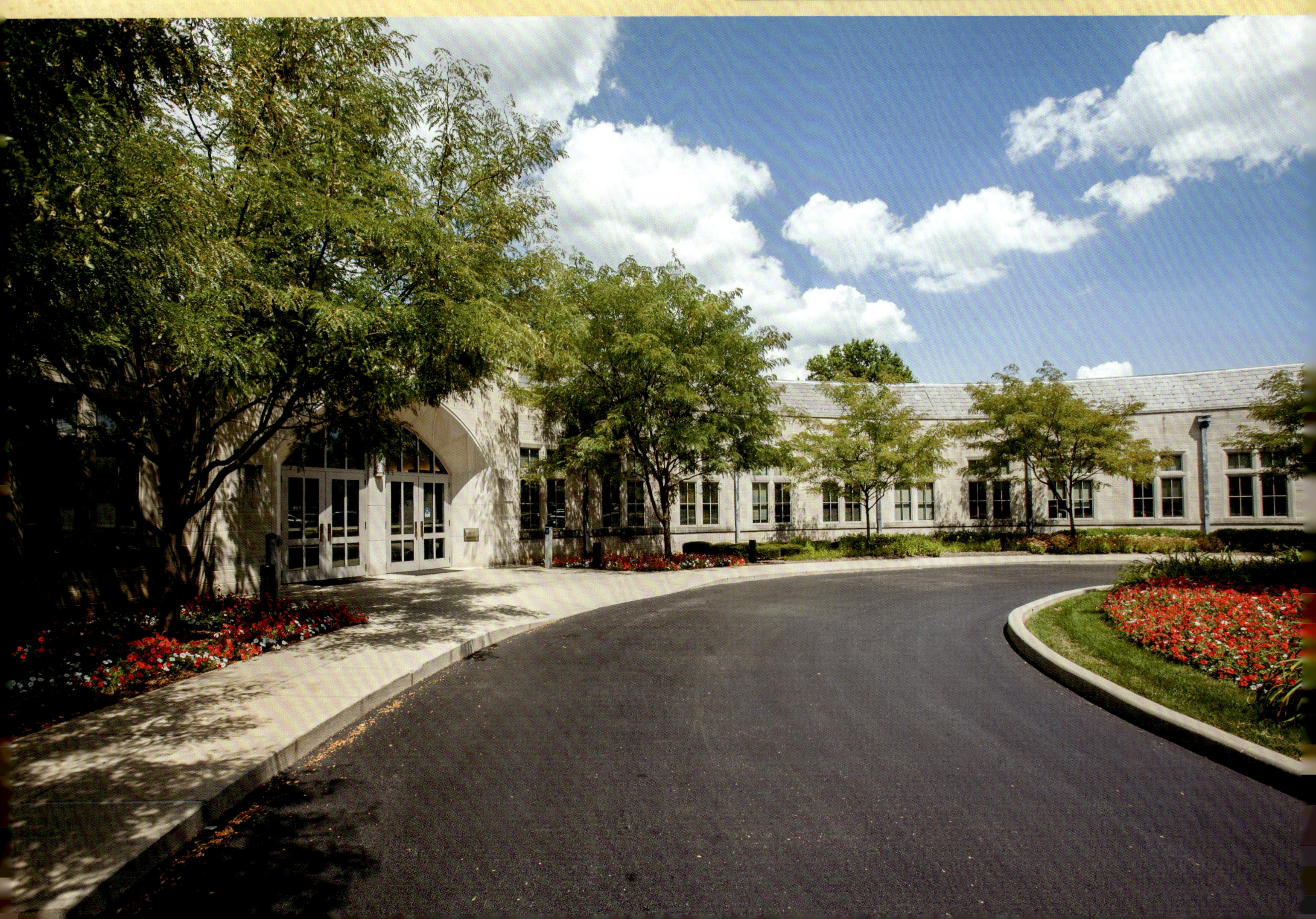

Showalter House

Philanthropy's Home

A gift to a state university paves and widens a path to higher planes of achievement and usefulness, provides a permanent agency for prompting the vital needs of education, and establishes one of the safest depositories for funds with which to advance great philanthropic enterprises.

—Indiana University Quarterly

INCORPORATED IN 1936 DURING THE PRESIDENCY of William Lowe Bryan, the Indiana University Foundation (IUF) was formed "to stimulate alumni and other friends of education to make gifts and bequests to aid Indiana University over a broad field: to finance research, to subsidize publications, to establish scholarships and fellowships, to hold patents and other property, and in general to aid the university in any undertaking for which funds were not otherwise available."[1]

Evolving from one part-time staff member and a few volunteers in the early years, foundation offices by 1972 were scattered across the campus in the Indiana Memorial Union, Owen Hall, and a vacated fraternity house on Third Street. Wanting to consolidate the IUF under one roof and to give it a permanent location, philanthropist Grace Showalter bequeathed $1.2 million for the construction of a new building. Showalter graduated with honors from Indiana University in 1915. She was the first woman on the IUF Board of Directors and a benefactor to IU through many generous gifts, including funding for Showalter Fountain.

Showalter's gift was supplemented by a grant from the Krannert Charitable Trust as well as a gift of land along the Indiana 45/46 Bypass near the IU Golf Course from the Board of Trustees, allowing construction of Showalter House, designed by James and Associates of Indianapolis, to begin in July 1973. The structure was a modern two-story building set on the side of a hill with a curving drive to the front door. It featured a facade of weathered brick and specially milled Indiana limestone. The interior included large open-concept office spaces, multipurpose meeting rooms with portable partitions, a large workroom, a student center with food service area, locker rooms, dark room, record room, data-processing equipment room, mail room, and storage areas.

Foundation staff moved into their new space in the fall of 1974, with the official dedication festivities postponed until April 1975 to coincide with the twenty-fifth-anniversary celebration of the Little 500 bicycle race. Called the Festival Fortnight and planned to demonstrate the versatility of Showalter House, the event began on April 14 with two Little 500–style shows, and continued with daily "afternoon salons" and "evening galas." These included symposia on sports with IU's famed swimming coach, Doc Counsilman, and IU's legendary men's basketball coach, Bob Knight, as well as on poetry and art with Mary Ellen Solt and Rudy Pozzatti. The celebration culminated on April 26 with the official building dedication in the morning, followed by the twenty-fifth running of the Little 500, and the variety show in the evening featuring Bob Hope, who appeared for the fourth time as the master of ceremonies of this annual event.

By the 1990s, private giving through the foundation had grown to more than $100 million a year, major fund-raising campaigns were more frequent, and additional programs

Facing top, Front entrance to Showalter House, 2016. Photo Credit: Tyagan Miller.

Facing bottom, Showalter House in Spring, 2016. Photo Credit: Tyagan Miller.

and services such as the IU Telefund were in place. As IUF programs expanded, so did the staff, many of whom were relegated to satellite offices around Bloomington. In 1997 the IUF Board of Directors, led by foundation president Curt Simic, initiated plans to enlarge Showalter House to once again accommodate all staff. The renovation and expansion was done in three phases over two years and completed in October 2000.

Concentrated primarily to the west and north sides of the existing structure, the additions designed by Ratio Architects of Indianapolis would more than double the gross square footage of the building and blend its architectural style with the rest of the campus. As Simic said, "the use of local limestone and the look of the building are designed to bring it into harmony with the architecture of the campus." The result was a Collegiate Gothic–style building featuring a limestone cladding facade, slate roof, and copper flashing. A curving central court represents the arms of the foundation "embracing the alumni."[2] The newly renovated building included a presidential suite, resource rooms, administrative offices, conference and training space, and a Grand Hall reception area. Elevators were added to comply with the Americans with Disabilities Act, the air-conditioning and heating systems were upgraded, parking expanded, and landscaping updated.

The central arched entryway leads into a reception hall with views to the rear terrace and offices on either side. The interior features a number of rooms named in honor of several of the foundation's most valued patrons, including John W. Anderson, Bert W. Elwert, Cecil and Inez Harlos, Robert A. Lucas, Dr. Arthur R. Metz, J. Dwight Peterson, John and Esther Reese, and Herman B Wells. Myles Brand, IU's sixteenth president, said at the Showalter House rededication ceremony on October 20, 2000, "This structure is built not just of limestone and mortar, but also on the vision and hopes and values of the people who first thought about what Indiana University could be and then set about making those dreams reality. . . . May all who work, meet, and pass within these walls bring still greater contributions to the advancement of knowledge, reflecting the ideals and principles of Indiana University."[3]

Over the decades the foundation accepted patents for the drunkometer (a predecessor to the Breathalyzer) by Dr. Rolla N. Harger of the Indiana University School of Medicine and for Joseph Muhler's Crest toothpaste. It received research funding from government agencies and foundations, such as the Ford Foundation, Lilly Endowment, and Krannert Charitable

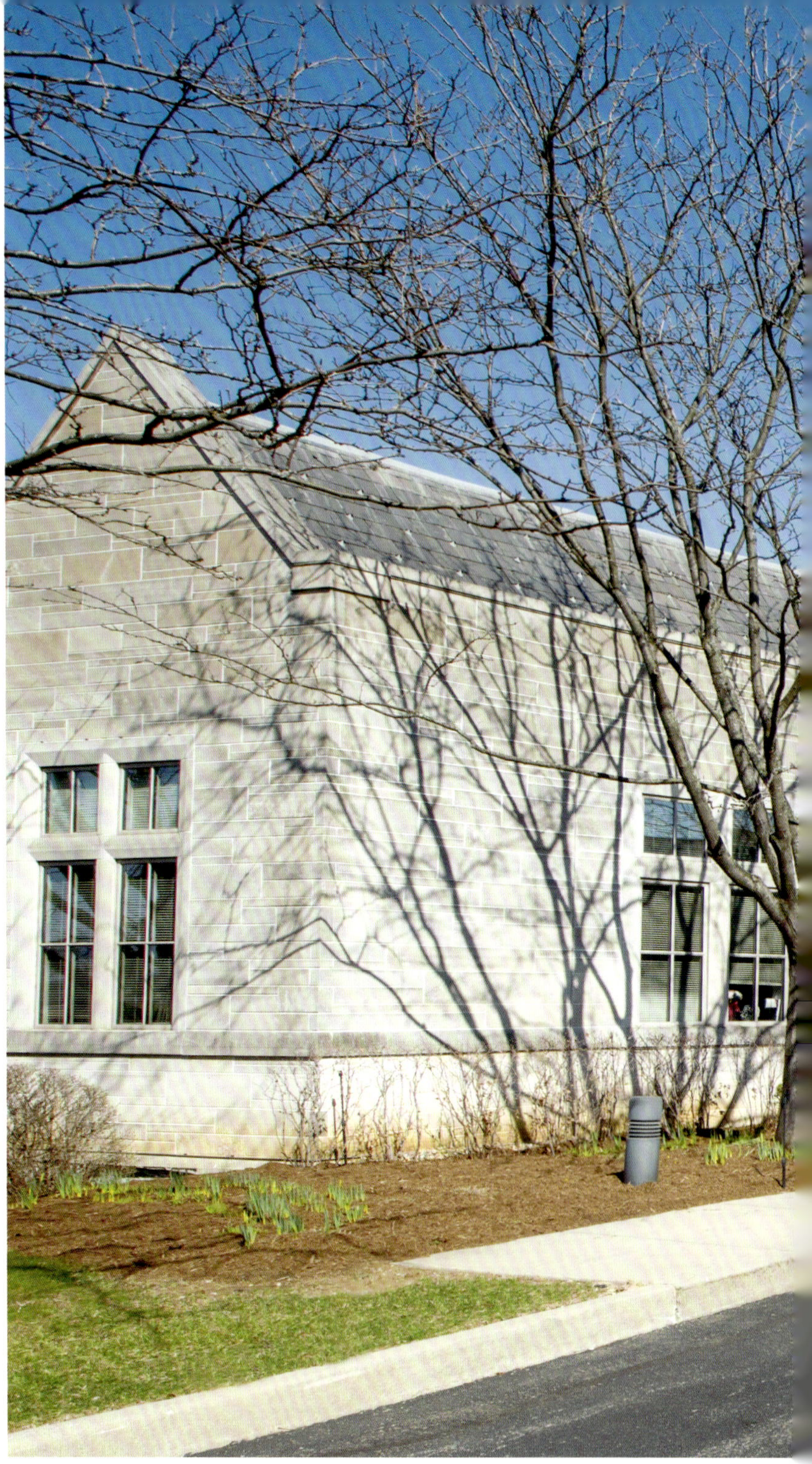

Panoramic view of Showalter House, 2017.
Photo credit: Tyagan Miller.

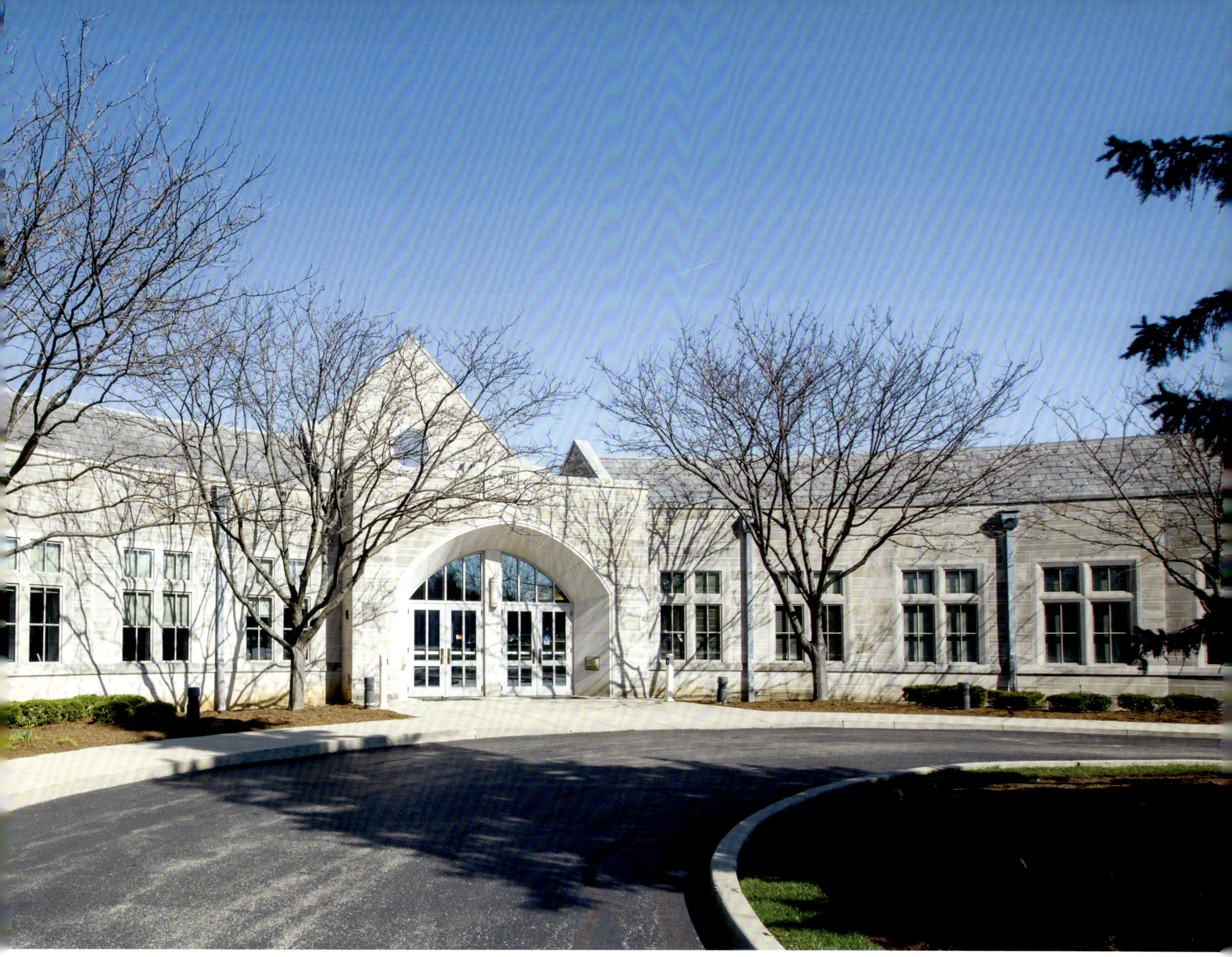

Trust, for endeavors such as the university's Russian and East European Studies Program and several overseas programs. The Rockefeller Foundation funded the addition of geneticist Herman Muller to the IU faculty in 1945; in 1946 Muller won the Nobel Prize for his research. It also provided the initial funding for Alfred Kinsey's Institute for Sex Research and initiated a successful campaign for the IU Sesquicentennial. The latter resulted in the construction of the Musical Arts Center, Assembly Hall, Hoosier Heritage Hall (which now houses the Glenn A. Black laboratory and Mathers Museum), and the Sidney and Lois Eskenazi Museum of Art. Finally, and for some most notably, in 1950 the IU Foundation created the IU Student Foundation, which raises money for scholarships through the nationally renowned annual Little 500 bicycle race.

Student Recreational Sports Center 1995

ARCHITECT Edward Larrabee Barnes / Browning Day Mullins Deardorf

ARCHITECTURAL STYLE Modern / Minimalist

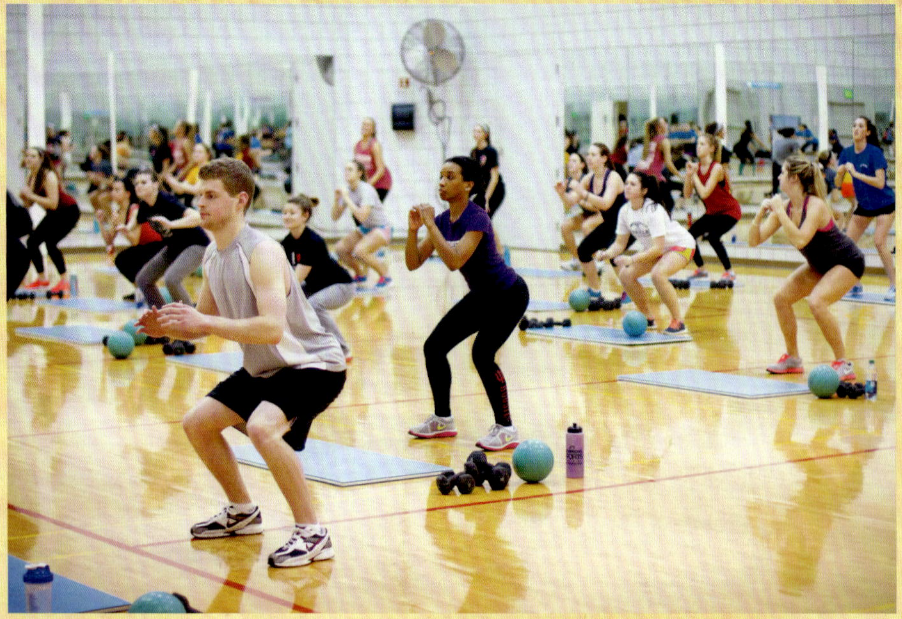

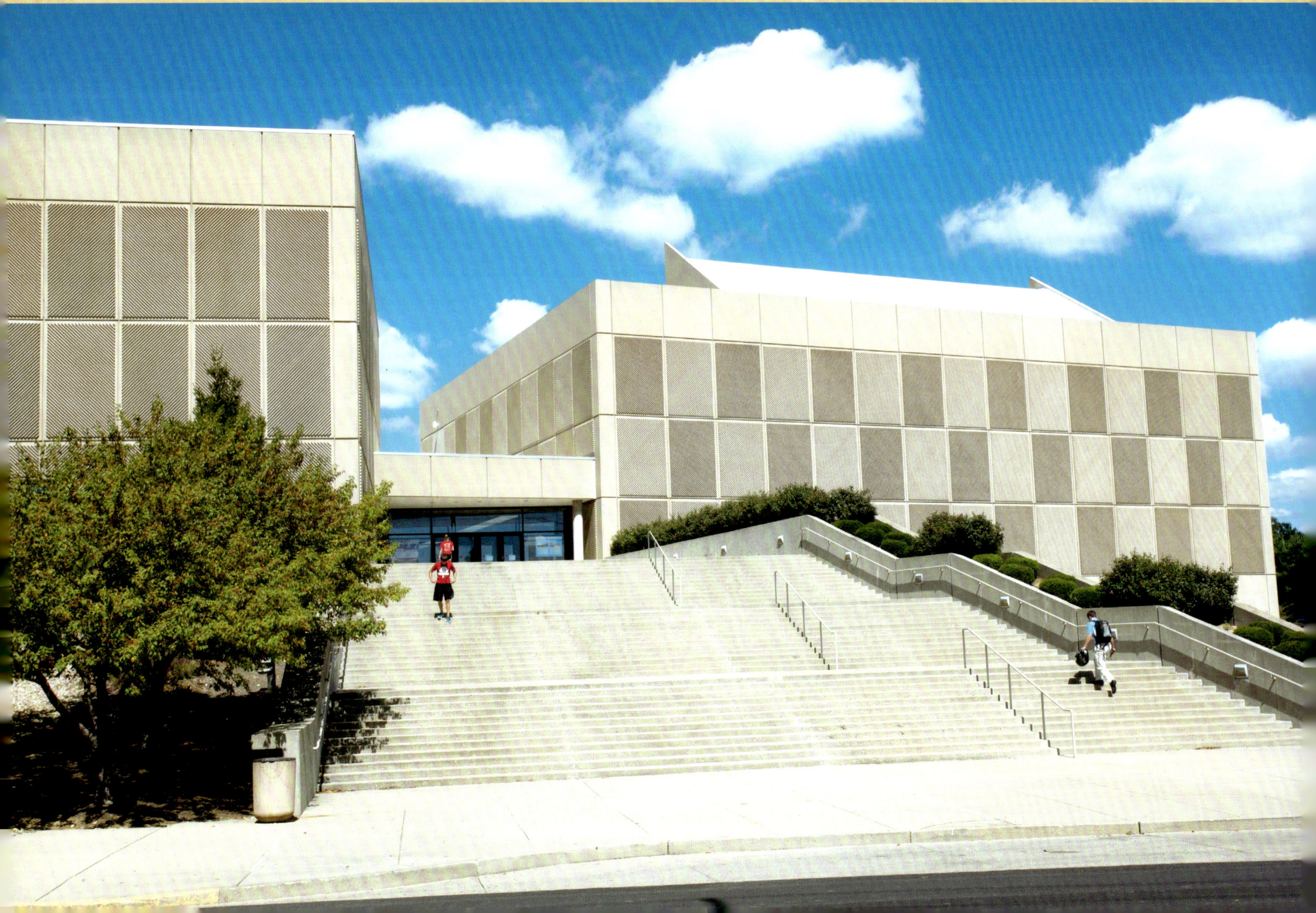

Student Recreational Sports Center

May this building be a creative environment
for the vitality of the mind and body
and a place of friendship.

—Indiana University President Myles Brand
at dedication ceremony

At the dedication ceremony in September 1995 for the Student Recreational Sports Center (SRSC) marked the opening of the first new indoor student activity space on the Indiana University Bloomington campus in thirty-five years. In the intervening years, student enrollment had soared from 14,487 to 35,063. Interest in recreational activity and intramurals had also skyrocketed, along with a national culture change that made the inclusion of women in sports part of the campus demographic. Title IX, legislation sponsored by IU alumnus Senator Birch Bayh, had a lot to do with this surge in women's participation in sports, both intramural and varsity. By the 1980s, the already-scarce indoor recreational space at IUB was at an unprecedented premium.

During the same period, IU athletics, particularly the men's and women's swimming and diving teams, had been without a regulation swimming and diving pool. The success achieved by iconic head coaches Doc Counsilman (swimming) and Hobie Billingsley (diving), which included winning six consecutive national championships from 1968 to 1973, was an extraordinary feat, even more so considering the lack of facility support. Although the construction of the state-of-the-art Natatorium on the Indiana University–Purdue University Indianapolis (IUPUI) campus in 1982 provided some relief for larger swimming and diving competitions, it did little for day-to-day practice and training or on-campus competitions. The time was right for the two interest groups not always prone to working together in a common cause—Recreational Sports and IU Athletics—to come together to plan a new facility. The unlikely coalition was a success, and a funding plan was identified that worked for both. Bonds issued by the university in 1960 to build the Health, Physical Education, and Recreation Building were maturing, and debt service was transferred to support the proposed SRSC. Those funds satisfied approximately 90 percent of the building cost. When IU students agreed to a fifty cents per credit hour increase (on average, an additional $15 each year per student), the funding gap vanished, allowing plans to proceed.

Internationally acclaimed architect Edward Larrabee Barnes of New York had been the master planner for Indiana University since 1974 and had reshaped the IUPUI campus and provided master plans for the rest of IU's campuses. He had been the architect on the celebrated IUPUI Natatorium, which at the time it was built was the only aquatic center in the world housing two indoor Olympic-size swimming pools. The Barnes firm had not been commissioned to do a new building project on the Bloomington campus, however, until the SRSC design opportunity occurred. Teamed with Browning Day Mullins Dierdorf of Indianapolis, the Barnes firm proceeded to give IU a significant building that would serve the student and varsity swimming and diving needs of Indiana University Bloomington for years to come.

The first order of business was to select a site. The SRSC needed to be within convenient walking distance for students

Facing top, Students enjoying aerobics class in a Student Recreational Sports Center (SRSC) exercise studio, undated. Photo credit: Indiana University.

Facing bottom, Steps leading to the entrance of the SRSC, undated. Photo credit: Indiana University.

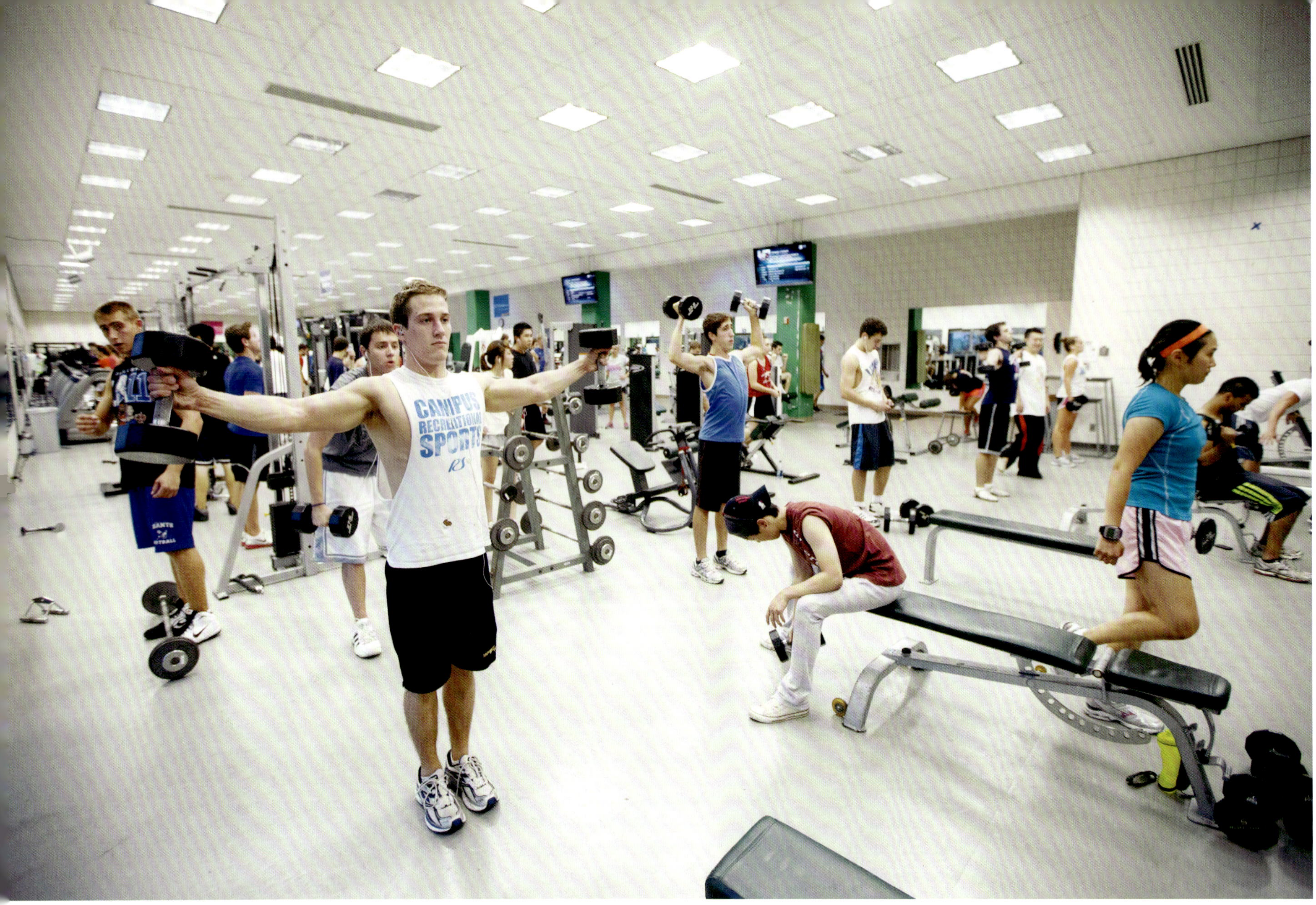

Students utilizing strength and conditioning space in the SRSC, 2012. Photo credit: Indiana University.

but away from the center of campus, which was already congested. Some parking for students who resided off campus would be included in the site plan. Potential building locations were considered, and finally a site convenient to student housing both north and south of Tenth Street, Greek houses, and married student housing was chosen: the northwest corner of Union Street and Law Lane. An existing parking lot on Tenth Street would serve the facility as needed.

When Edward Barnes visited the site, he immediately observed how the topography of the area would complement his building schematic, with a natural swale that would relieve the need to remove a vast quantity of limestone for the aquatic center. Architecturally, the building would be in a minimalist style and would reflect the design Barnes had used in many other significant projects he had completed around the country: a collection of simple geometric shapes assembled to fit together in an uncomplicated form. The steel skeletal frame was clad in precast concrete that blended well with the limestone residence halls located in the immediate neighborhood. Neither the university nor the architect wanted the SRSC to stand out, instead preferring it to be a reserved presence on campus. They especially did not want this new structure to distract from the nearby Metz Carillon Tower, which also guided the tone and texture of the building.

When the SRSC opened in 1996, it was one of the largest student recreational sports complexes in the United States. Barnes designed the 137,852-square-foot building in two distinctive parts: a 44,651-square-foot aquatic facility and a connecting building for all other recreational needs. In keeping with many Barnes designs, generous natural light poured in throughout the building via skylights. The interior spaces continued the simplistic themes, but with bold color used as a focal point in many rooms to generate emphasis by contrast. Five full basketball-volleyball courts, multiple strength and cardio areas, seven racquetball-wallyball courts, two squash courts, group exercise studios, and several multipurpose gymnasiums were newly available to support the recreational needs of IU students. On an upper level around one of the gymnasium areas, an indoor synthetic surface walking-jogging track was constructed.

The long-awaited aquatics center fulfilled the needs of IU's renowned swimming and diving teams and gave them a home worthy of their long history of Big Ten and NCAA excellence. The Counsilman-Billingsley Aquatic Center, which is also the home for the women's varsity water polo team, features an eight-lane Olympic size swimming pool and one of the few diving wells of its kind in the nation. It features two 1-meter and 3-meter springboards each and 1-, 3-, 5-, 7-, and 10-meter platforms, plus a full-service dryland facility. The interior decor is truly a showcase, designed to document the illustrious history of IU swimming and diving—and to intimidate the competition. With a seating capacity of 3,500, the aquatic center has played host to many national competitions including multiple Big Ten Championship events.

The Student Recreational Sports Center was the only project on the IU Bloomington campus and the last Indiana University commission undertaken by Edward Larrabee Barnes. Barnes was known for his architectural leaning toward clarity and functionality, and was the winner of the profession's two most prestigious awards—the Thomas Jefferson Medal in Architecture and the AIA Gold Medal. He retired before the SRSC was completed, but his Indiana partner in the project, Browning Day Mullins Dierdorf of Indianapolis, and Barnes's longtime associate, Gajinder Singh, saw the project to completion.

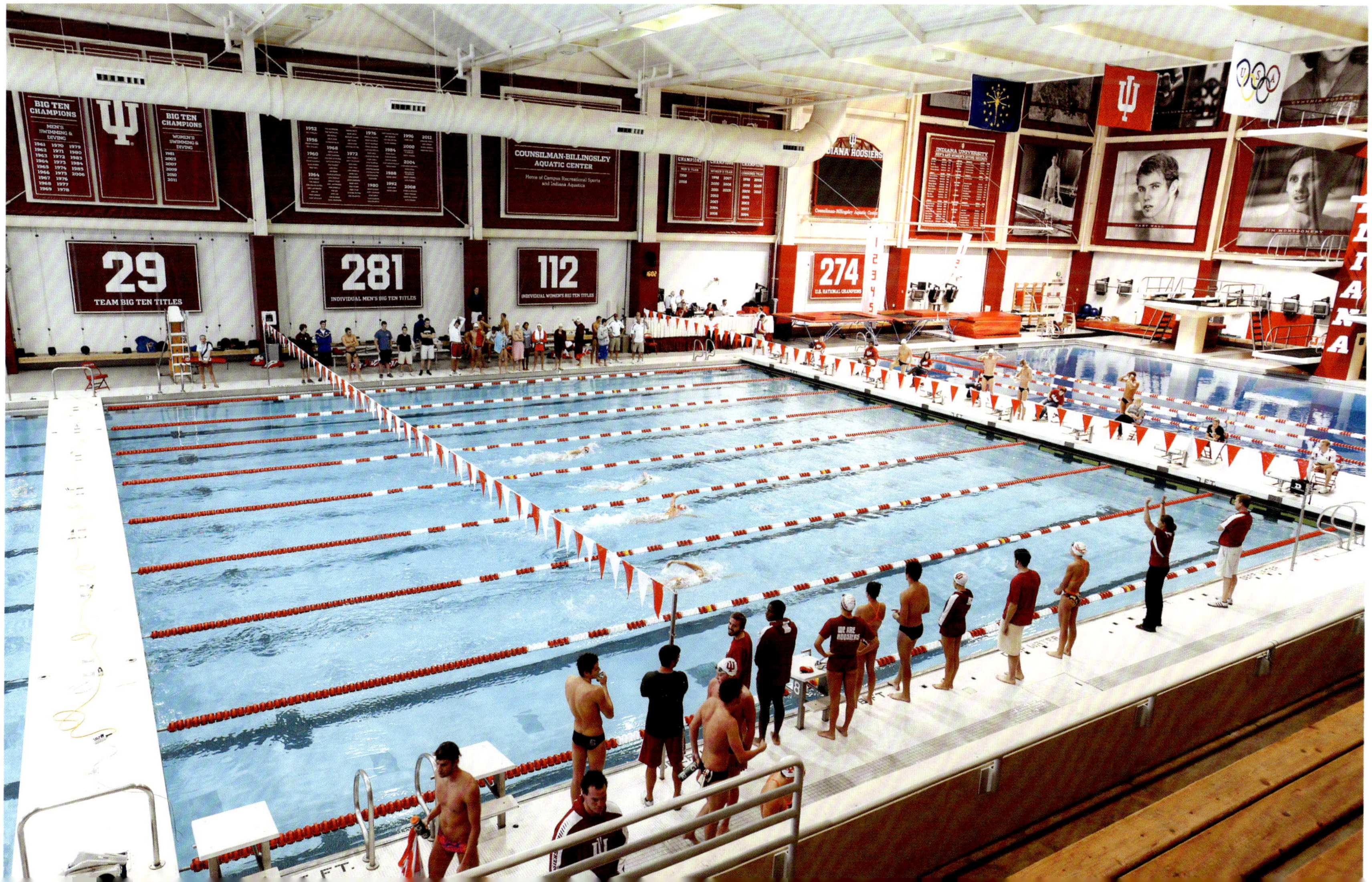

Below, Counsilman-Billingsley Aquatic Center in the SRSC, undated. Photo credit: Indiana University.

Edward L. Hutton Honors College 2008

ARCHITECT WDI Architecture / BSA LifeStructures

ARCHITECTURAL STYLE Residential Collegiate Gothic

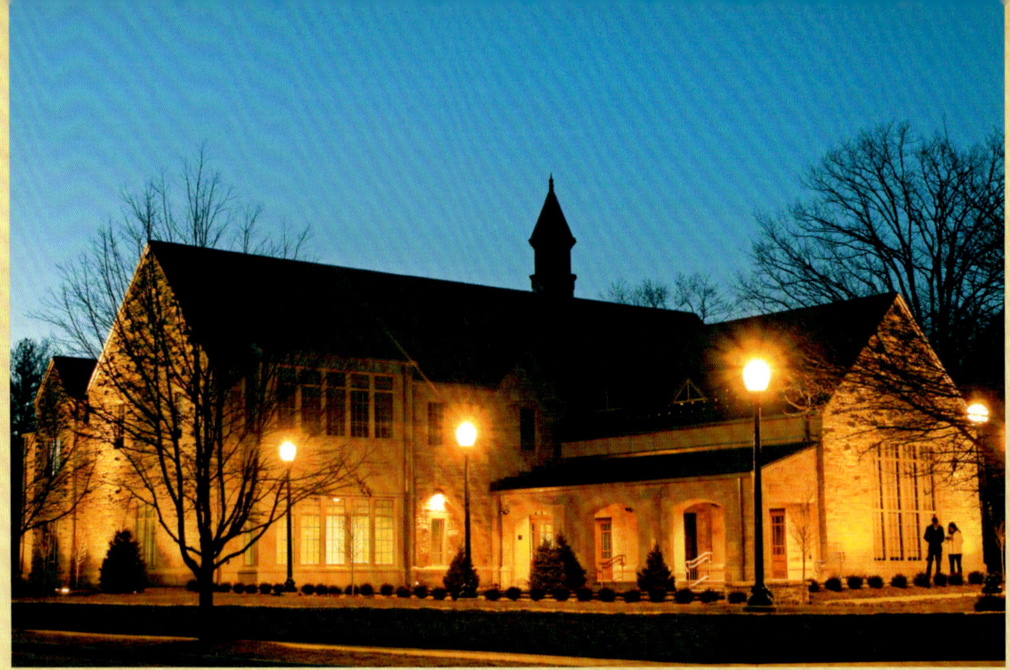

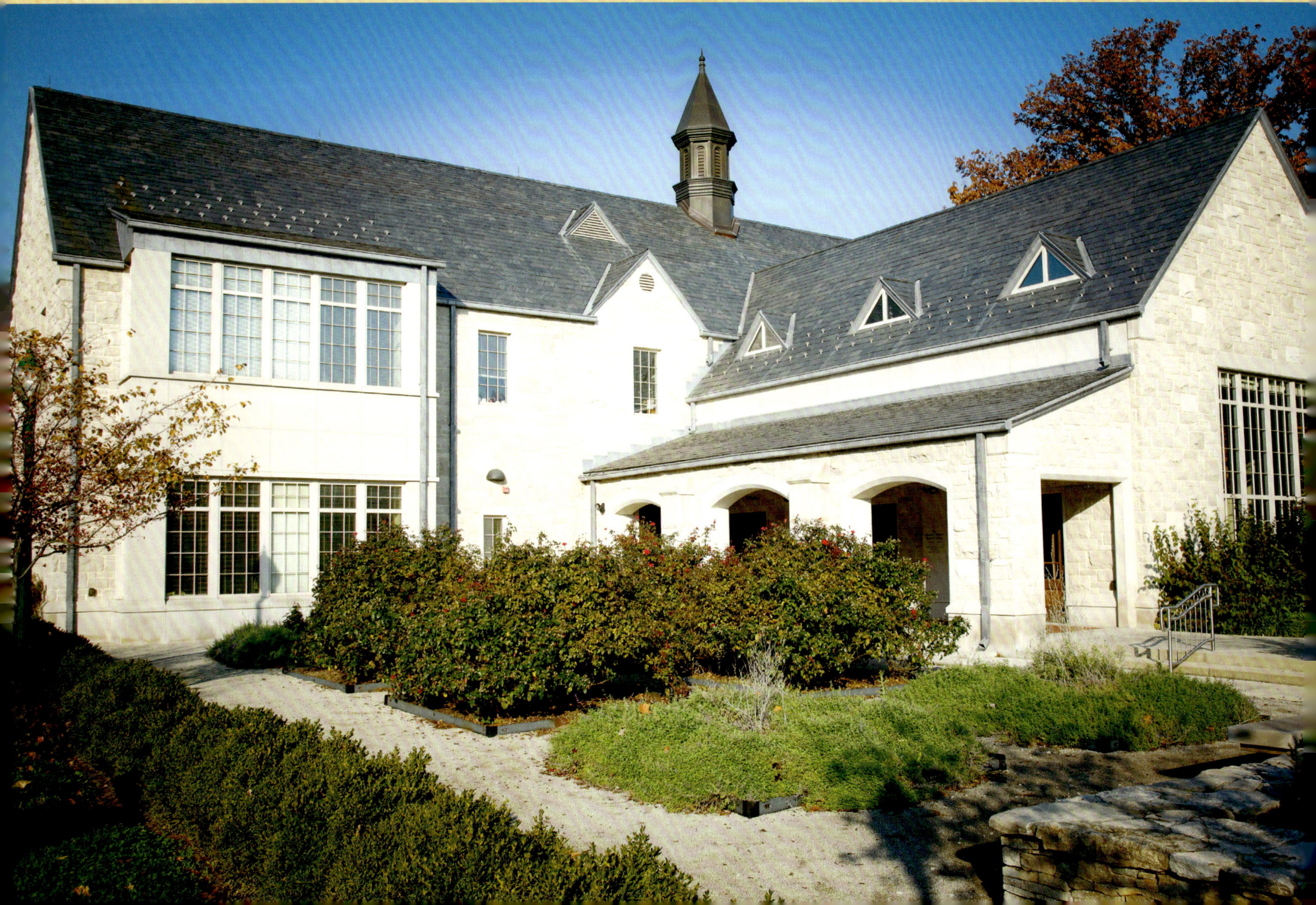

Edward L. Hutton Honors College

Home to IU Honors Students

Whenever you take a group of people and give them a place that they can call "home," it always brings them closer together. I appreciate the fact that the university built such a nice building exclusively for honors students. It shows that IU is dedicated to its honors program—which in turn makes me more dedicated to IU.

—IU honors student Caitlin Daley

A 1930 EDITORIAL IN THE INDIANA UNIVERSITY student–produced publication the *Vagabond* describes IU's then recently implemented honors reading program as a challenge to those students "who are seriously interested in the thousand and one good things in life, not the least of which are self-development, and that which follows self-development very closely, a knowledge of the worlds of both reality and intellect."[1] A young boy living just south of Bloomington would soon enter Indiana University and based on his university experiences, adopt a strikingly similar perspective.

With the support of an Indiana University scholarship, Bedford native Edward L. Hutton set forth on the Bloomington campus in 1936. After earning both his bachelor's and master's degrees with distinction, Hutton served in the military before moving on to a long and successful career in business. Always mindful of the monetary and personal support he received from his alma mater, Hutton generously repaid the university with both his time and money once that was possible. In 2003 Hutton gave the university $9 million to establish the International Experiences Program, which provides grants that enable IU students to study, work, or engage in service abroad; and the Edward L. Hutton Honors College is among the leaders in making the international experience a focal point of its mission and goals.

In 2004 Hutton donated funds to build a new home for the honors college that now bears his name. Previously, the honors college had been lodged in various campus locations, from Kirkwood Hall to the Student Building to houses on Jordan Avenue. Its new, permanent dwelling is an elegant structure located at the corner of Seventh Street and Woodlawn Avenue on the outer edge of the historic University Courts district. The architect of record was Daryl Williams-Dotson of WDI Architecture of Indianapolis. She was the first woman and first African American architect ever selected to design a Bloomington campus building. With the site in mind, Williams-Dotson designed Hutton Honors College to stand as a transition between the campus and the residential district. The result is a sophisticated two-story Collegiate Gothic building that resembles an upscale residence but maintains harmony with the limestone architecture of the old campus and nestles naturally into the surrounding neighborhood. The honors college home features a rubble limestone veneer; long, rectangular paned windows; and a slate stone roof with a charming copper cupola.

Matthew Auer, dean of the Hutton Honors College, said that by creating a permanent home for Hutton Honors students, Edward Hutton "wanted a public space similar to what students have at places like Oxford and Cambridge."[2] In keeping with his wishes, the library, which serves as a quiet study

Facing top, Edward L. Hutton Honors College at night, 2009. Photo credit: Indiana University.

Facing bottom, Hutton Honors College, 2016. Photo credit: Tyagan Miller.

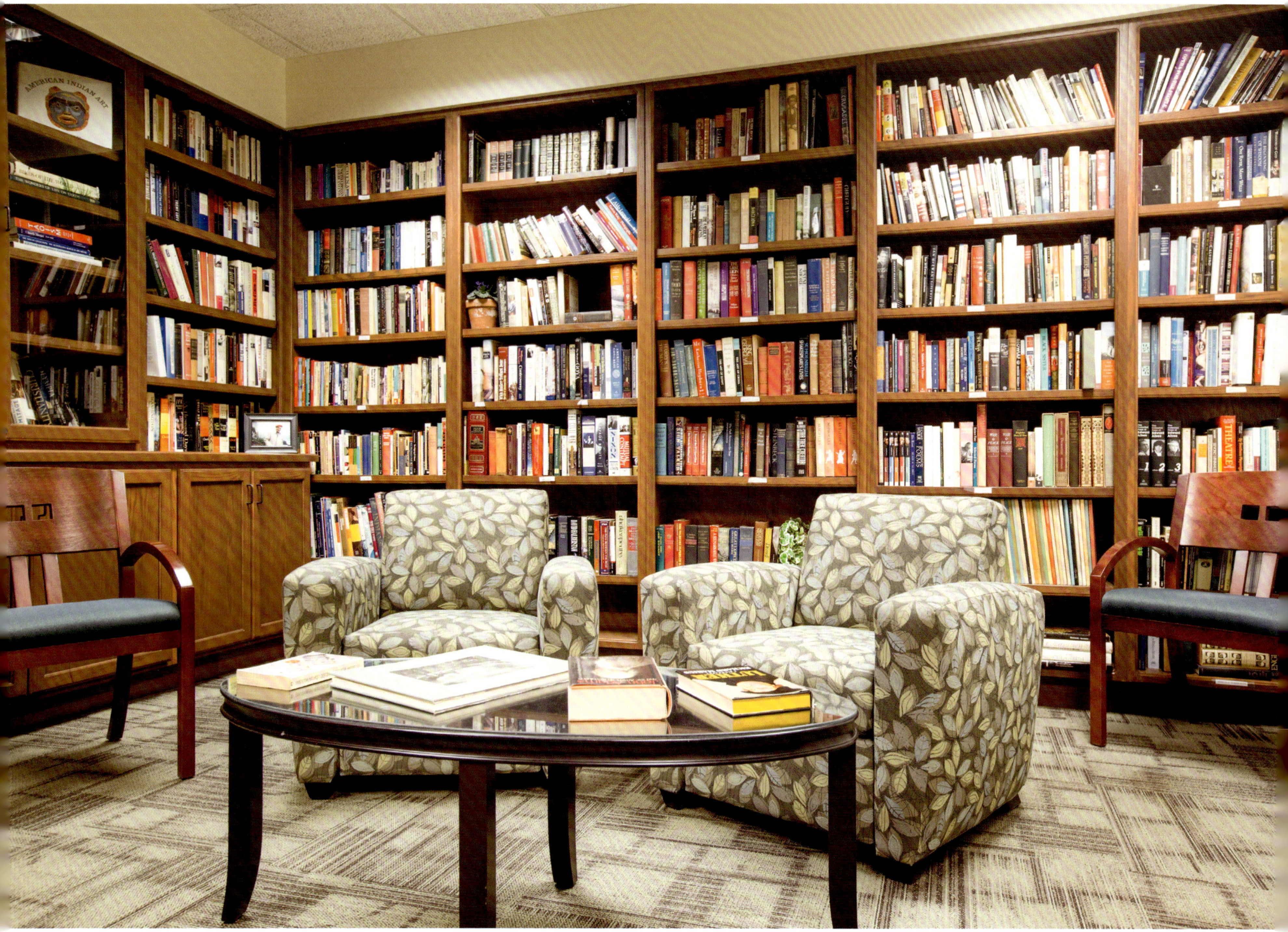

Comfortable library in Hutton Honors College, 2017. Photo credit: Tyagan Miller.

space for students, offers plush overstuffed chairs, floor-to-ceiling oak bookcases on three walls, and red oak paneling. Elsewhere in the house are a seminar room, collaborative workspace, and office space for honors student organizations, honors staff, and administrative personnel. A great room, used for extracurricular events, faces east with large windows that look toward the historic Ora L. Wildermuth Intramural Center and Indiana Memorial Union.

Students in the Hutton Honors College program come from around the nation and beyond. They are exposed to innovative coursework, work with top IU faculty, and meet one-on-one with distinguished campus visitors. These students also study

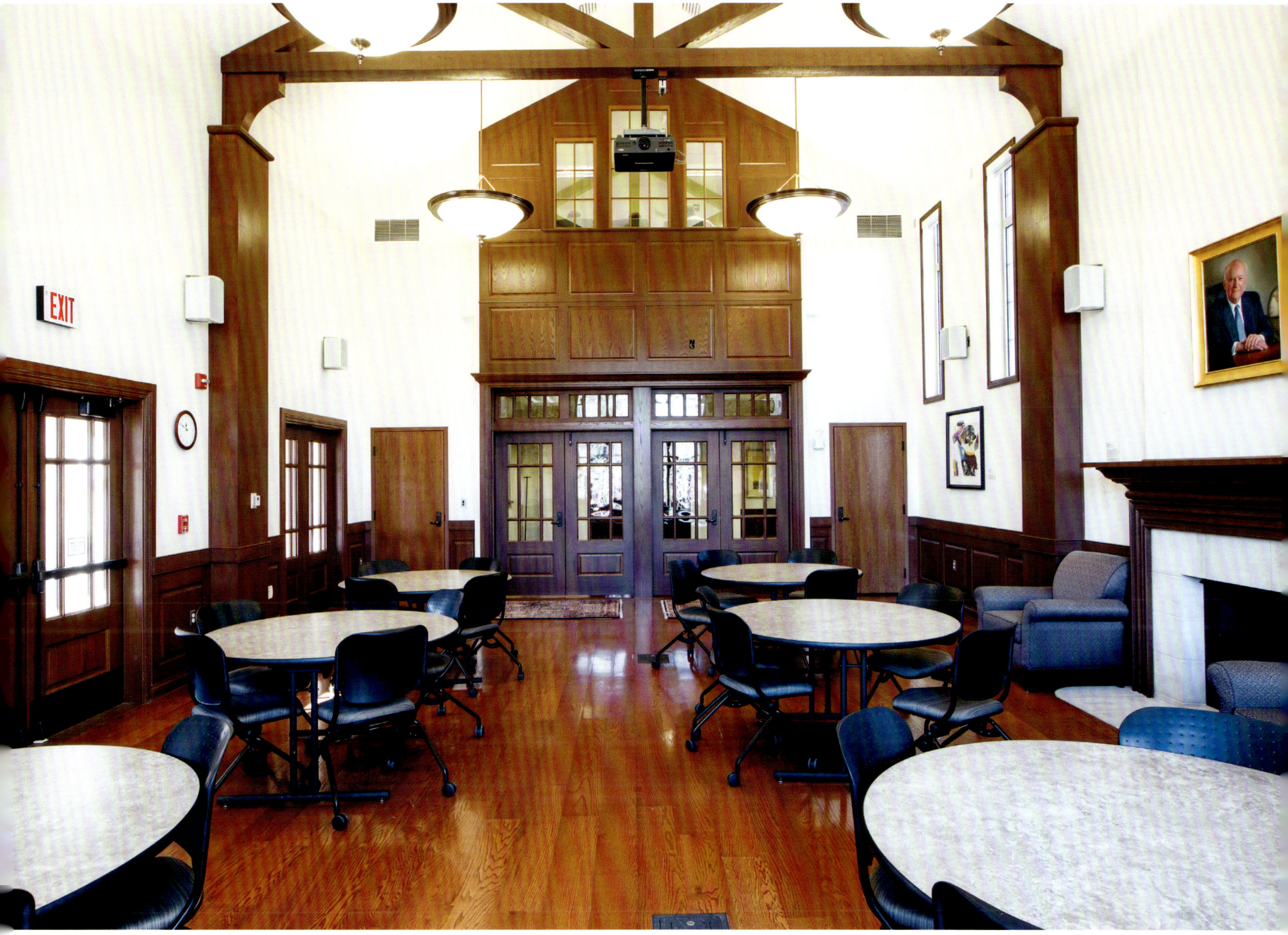

the world by experiencing the world. They do not receive a diploma from the college, but they do graduate with a General Honors Notation in combination with their academic degree.

Edward L. Hutton Honors College was dedicated April 8, 2009, a month after the man it honors passed away. In remembrance of the alumnus, businessman, and philanthropist, dedication attendees donned blue and gold pins featuring the bluebird, Edward Hutton's favorite bird. Despite his physical absence then and now, Hutton's thoughts are preserved in the building cornerstone:

> Let's make the world a better place.
>
> —Edward L. Hutton

Gathering space in Hutton Honors College, 2017. Photo credit: Tyagan Miller.

Data Center 2009
ARCHITECT SmithGroup / Ratio Architects
ARCHITECTURAL STYLE Technical Modern

Innovation Center 2009
ARCHITECT BSA LifeStructures / Messer Construction Co.
ARCHITECTURAL STYLE Technical Modern

Cyberinfrastructure Building 2011
ARCHITECT SmithGroup / Ratio Architects
ARCHITECTURAL STYLE Technical Modern

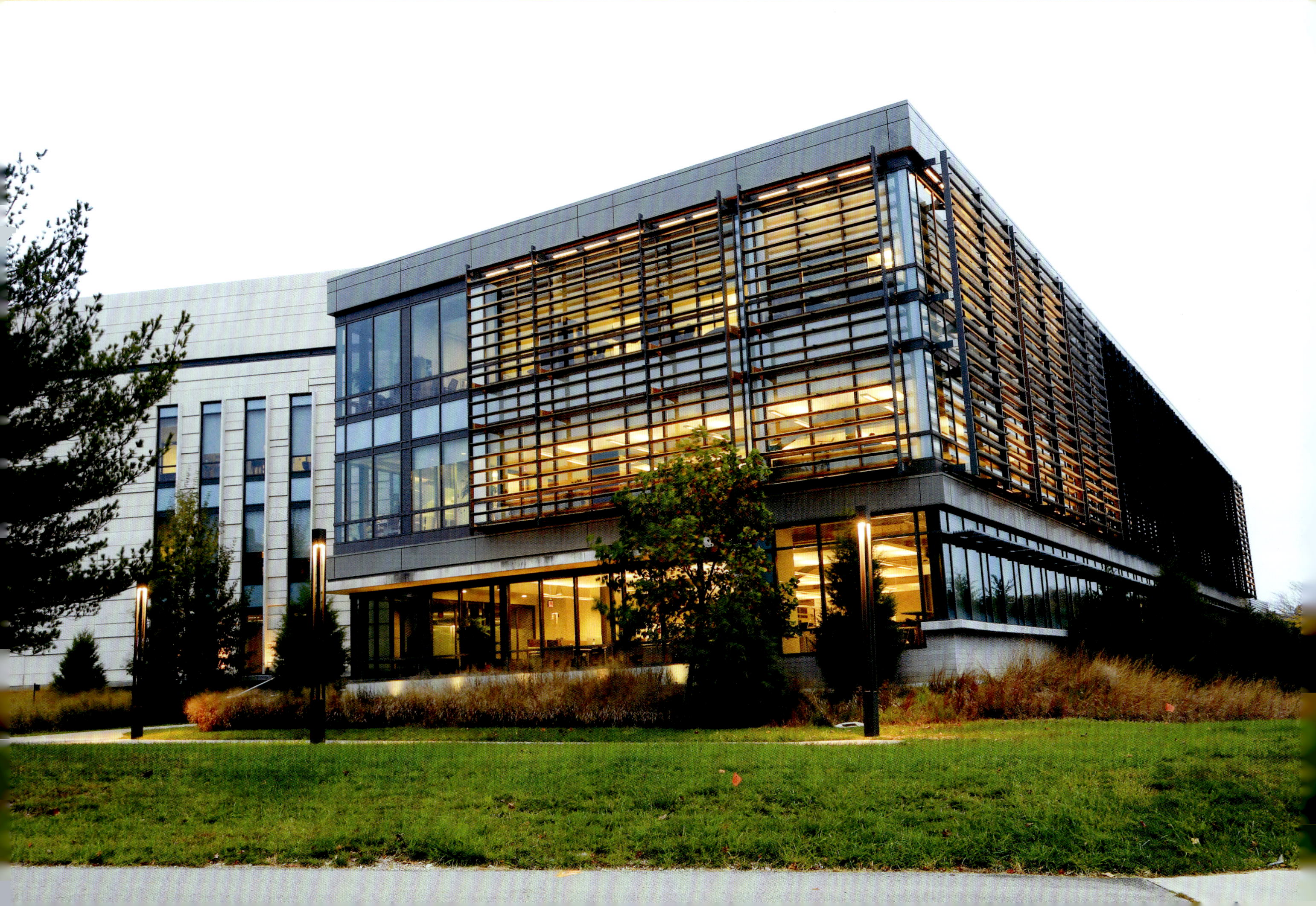

Technology Park

Research and Discovery Focused on the Future

A unique technology corridor at Indiana University Bloomington is cutting a fresh path for economic development and growth in Indiana. The corridor proves that IU is agile, nimble, and ready to respond quickly to economic opportunities and attract private sector development.

—Innovate Indiana

As Indiana University turned in the new millennium toward a strategy of creating public-private partnerships, the need became apparent to identify an area on or adjacent to campus where buildings designed for a shorter life cycle could be constructed. Financial models formulated jointly with potential outside business affiliates normally didn't allow for buildings clad in limestone and constructed to last a century or more. Flexibility, reuse, and eventual removal became key considerations for Indiana University administrators in discussions with David King of the SmithGroup, the architectural firm appointed as Indiana University's master planner in 2008. King provided IU with planning guidelines for new standards of construction that would allow for more affordable, environmentally sustainable buildings that would remain in harmony with the stone palette of the main Bloomington campus.

For many years the university had owned the property on the corner of the Indiana 45/46 Bypass and Tenth Street. The grounds had been home to University School since the late 1960s, but the school was decommissioned when other public schools were built in Bloomington. The remaining structures on the site served an assortment of services and were in poor physical condition. The entire area called for an imaginative reuse plan that would better serve the university's space needs. It proved to be the perfect location for the beginnings of a proposed technology park devoted to promoting joint ventures with private-sector partners as well as solving IU's technology space needs.

Data Center

Before substantial entrepreneurial efforts could be advanced, major infrastructure investment was necessary to maximize use of the site, and reliance on technology was an emerging requirement for every new initiative. Indiana University's machine rooms had long been viewed as at risk and were in need of a new home that would provide protection against natural disasters. SmithGroup of Washington, DC, and Ratio Architects of Indianapolis were asked to design a facility to provide the university with adequate security and protection and offer sufficient space to accommodate growth in technology and data management. David King, project architect for the SmithGroup, developed plans for an 81,186-square-foot, one-story building with a bunkered profile. Completed in May 2009, the structure is clad in concrete with a flat roof. The earth barrier provides mandatory safeguards and helps conceal the building's massive footprint. Research, enterprise, and future research pods constitute the core of the new Data Center and house IU's supercomputers. The building's substantial storage for all the information systems, including thousands of virtual servers, makes Indiana University one of the nation's leading universities in the area of technology.

Facing, Cyberinfrastructure Building, 2016. Photo credit: Indiana University.

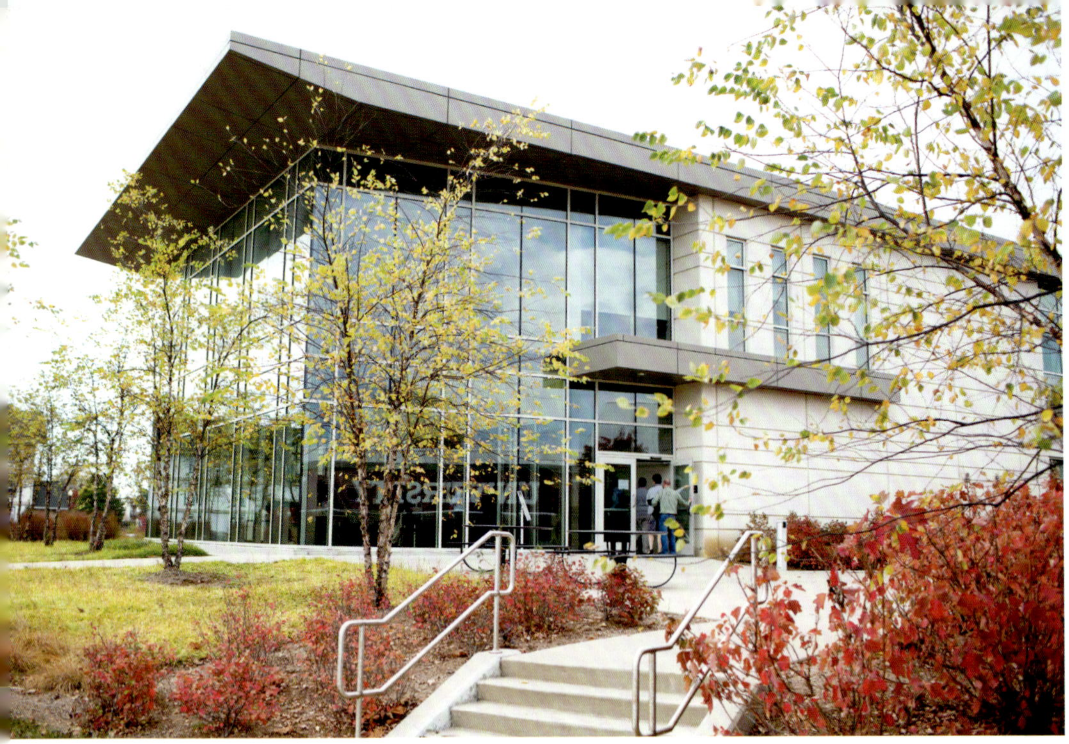

Innovation Center, 2015. Photo credit: Indiana University.

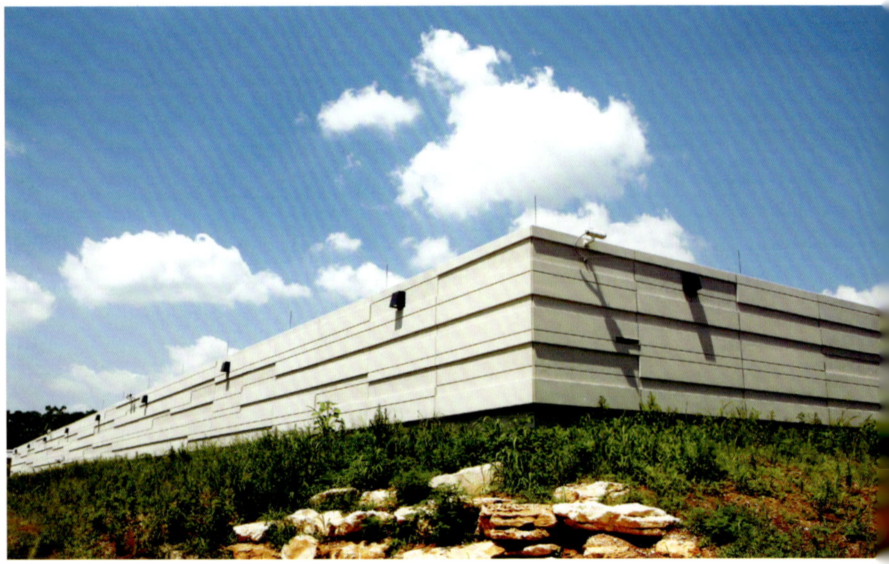

Data Center's bunkered profile, 2009.
Photo credit: Indiana University.

INNOVATION CENTER

Under the umbrella of the Indiana University Research and Technology Corporation, IU chose a new method for contracting building construction. The design-build (D-B) approach had recently been enabled by the Indiana General Assembly, and the university's desire to include basic "incubator space" in the new Technology Park could be more efficiently solved through this new methodology. Design-build is a project delivery system used in the construction industry whereby design and construction services are commissioned through a single entity known as the design-build contractor. In 2008, BSA LifeStructures and Messer Construction Co., both of Indianapolis, collaborated on a D-B proposal for the Innovation Center. It was accepted by the university, and the partnership was soon at work constructing a two-story, 39,871-square-foot building that would provide modular laboratories and office space in the university's new discovery-focused precinct. The BSA LifeStructures–Messer team integrated the building into the landscape using a precast concrete envelope; its buff color links the structure to the aesthetics of the core Indiana University campus. Generous glass curtain walls also help the overall scale of the building blend in. Completed in December 2009, the Innovation Center has a central circulation core that anchors the north and south wings. The main entry on the northeast corner features ground-to-roof glass windows and includes a canopy over the entrance.

CYBERINFRASTRUCTURE BUILDING

Completed in 2011 and designed by Ratio Architects and SmithGroup, the Cyberinfrastructure Building (CIB) provides work space for more than seven hundred personnel who support Indiana University's Information Technology platform. Inspired by plans used by tech firms in the Silicon Valley, the CIB design departs from the usual IU Bloomington exterior building presentation, utilizing a light frame structural system, prominent glass window walls, and an exterior aesthetic approach that highlights aluminum and glass sunshades to shield the interior from excessive heat gain. The facade is clad in precast concrete formed in an articulated banding pattern with limestone accents. The 131,868 square feet deliver four levels of work space, offer a central location for collaboration and resource sharing, and provide the central hub of activity for the proposed research park. The ample open community space promotes a team-oriented, mobile workforce for the new millennium. In 2013 CIB earned the first Gold LEED certification for IUB.[1]

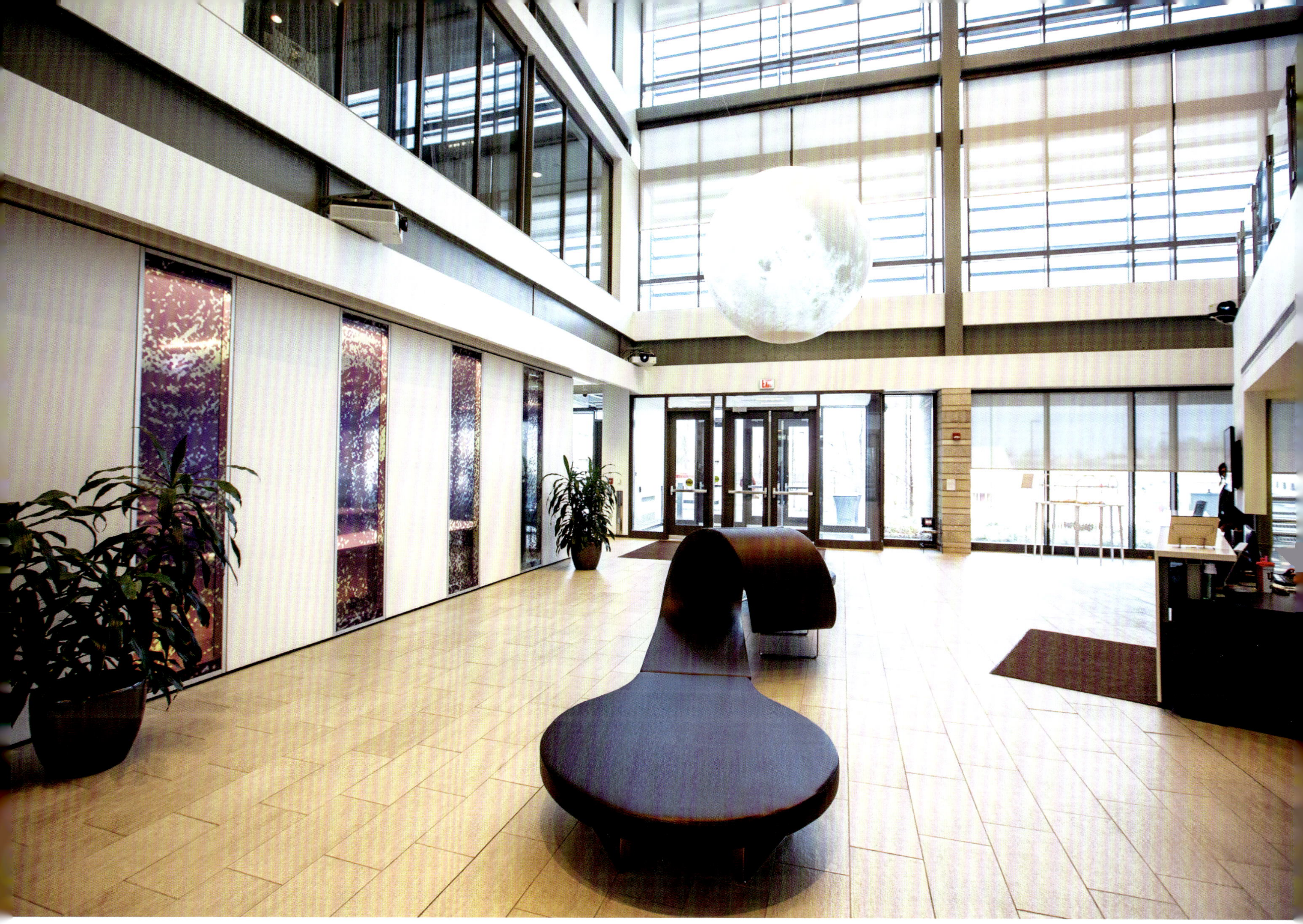

Lobby of the CIB; note globe suspended from the ceiling, 2017. Photo credit: Tyagan Miller.

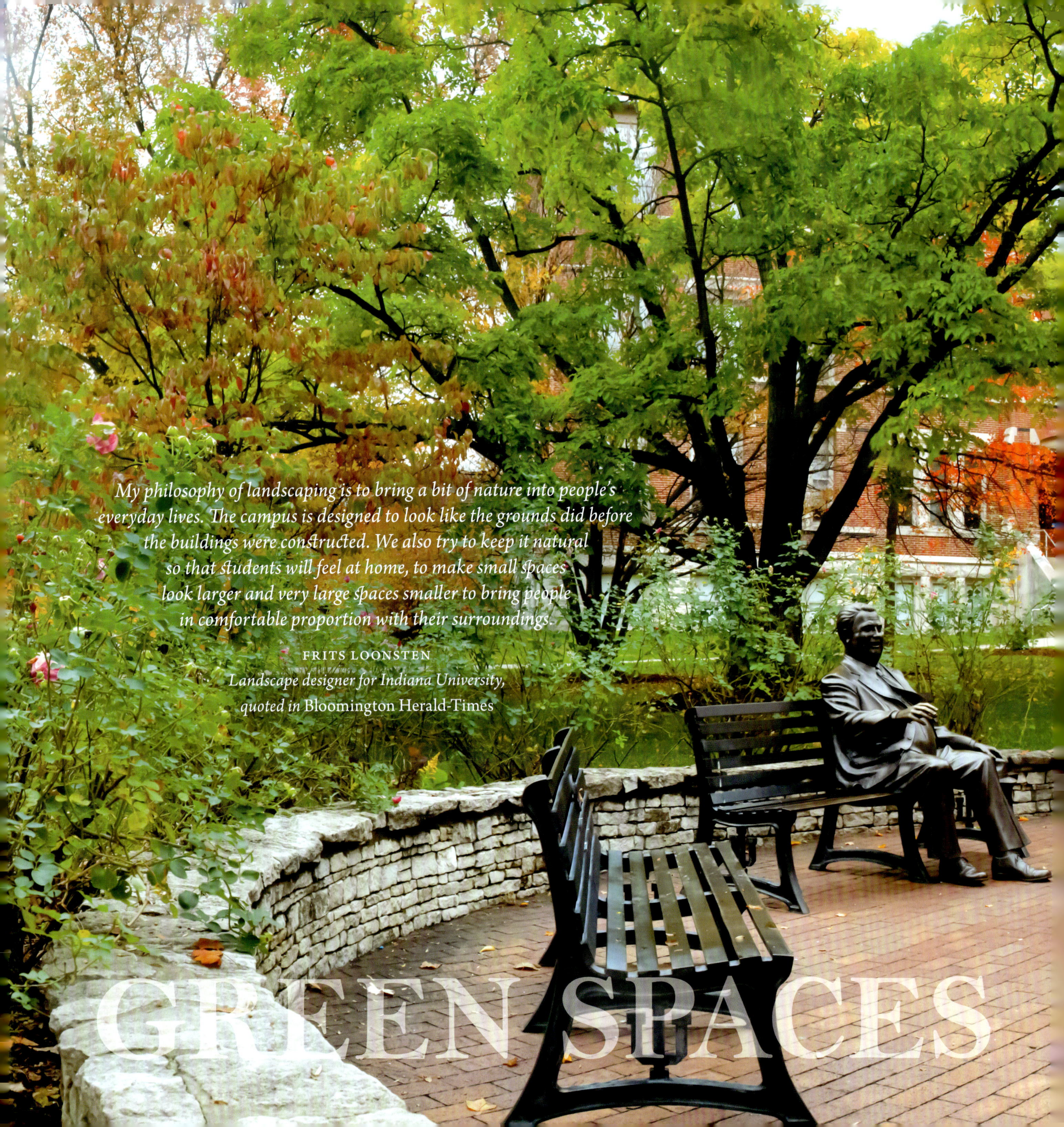

My philosophy of landscaping is to bring a bit of nature into people's everyday lives. The campus is designed to look like the grounds did before the buildings were constructed. We also try to keep it natural so that students will feel at home, to make small spaces look larger and very large spaces smaller to bring people in comfortable proportion with their surroundings.

FRITS LOONSTEN
Landscape designer for Indiana University, quoted in Bloomington Herald-Times

GREEN SPACES

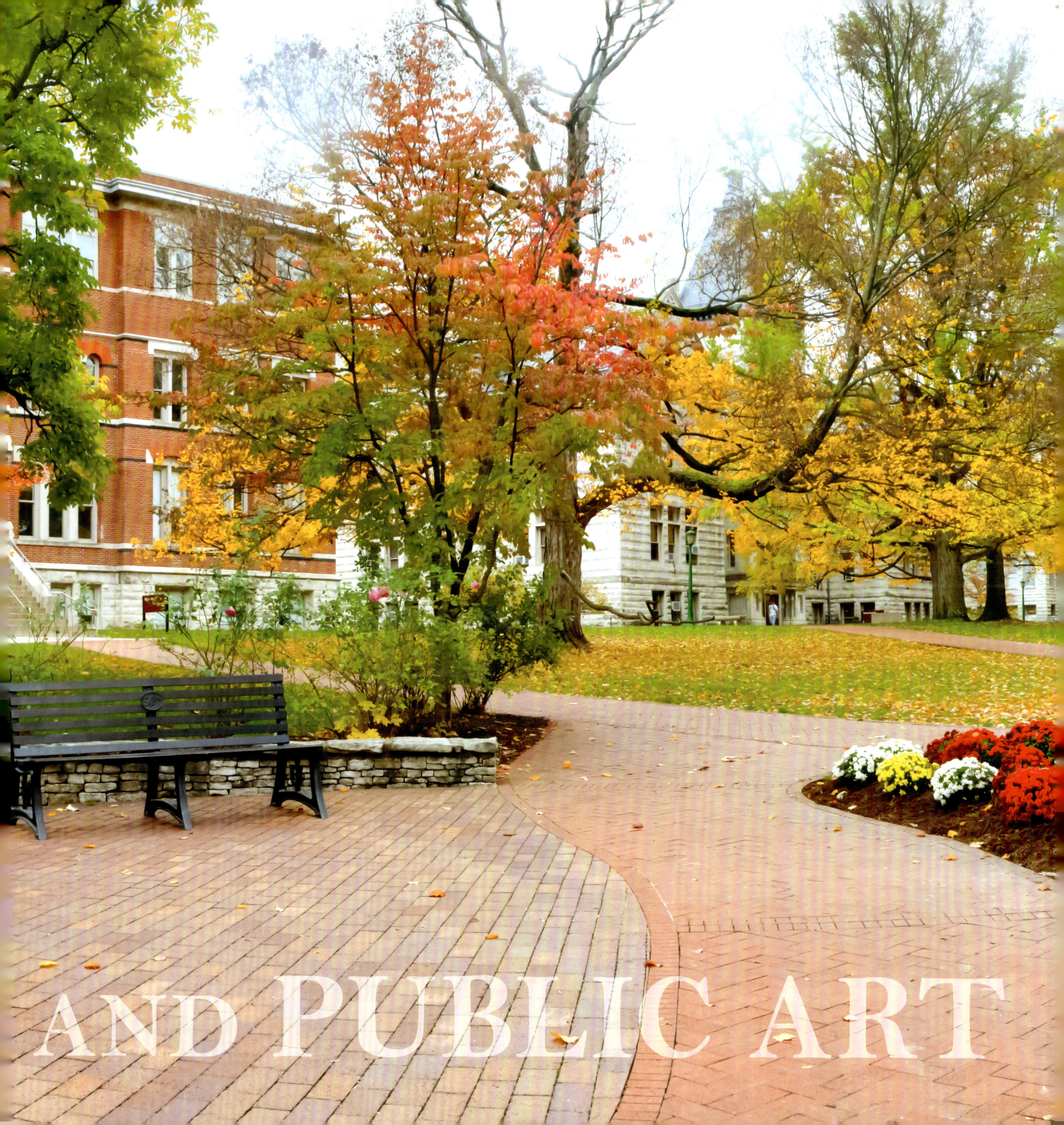
AND PUBLIC ART

Dunn Cemetery and Rogers Cemetery

Sacred Grounds

Courtyards, woodland, green sanctuaries, and limestone quadrangles all forge the memories of graduates who find their roles throughout the world. This is a place informed by its heritage, set apart for the individuality and the community of learning yet profoundly a part of the world and the realities of the present: an environment for the dreams and ideals through which we build the future.

—*Juliet Frey,* Islands of Green and Serenity

INDIANA UNIVERSITY HOLDS THE UNIQUE DIStinction among U.S. campuses as the home to a cemetery in which three Revolutionary War heroines are buried. Today, nestled between Indiana Memorial Union and Beck Chapel, Dunn Cemetery sits on hallowed ground surrounded by a low stone wall with access through a wrought-iron gate. Near the western corner, a chiseled stone pillar bears the inscription "This ground was deeded by Geo. (George) G. Dunn for perpetual use as a cemetery." With these words, Dunn permanently set aside this clearing in the trees, making it legally impossible to condemn or appropriate the land for public property.

Dated November 21, 1855, the deed further specifies that the plots remain for the descendants of three sisters—George G. Dunn's grandmother Ellenor (Brewster) Dunn (1754–1841) and her two sisters, Agnes (Brewster) Alexander (1763–1830) and Jennet (Brewster) Irwin (1761–1839)—to serve "forever as a place of private burial where they shall repose together as one family in the long night of death and rise up together as from one bed at the last day."[1] Legend has it that, when living in Virginia, the Brewster sisters served as aides in General George Washington's Revolutionary Army, working side by side with the general's men, sewing on buttons, bandaging wounds, and even melting their own pewter plates and other metals into bullets. The trio, who share the oldest gravestone near the western corner of the cemetery, eventually settled in the then tiny community of Bloomington, where Ellenor's son, Samuel Dunn Jr. purchased 160 acres of farmland from the government and built a home near what is today the Wildermuth Intramural Center. In accordance with the practice of early settlers, Samuel established a family burial plot on the property. His oldest son, George G. Dunn, inherited the land, and he in turn willed the family estate to his son Moses.

Following the fire of 1883, which destroyed the principal Indiana University building on the old Seminary Square campus, the IU Trustees purchased 20 acres known as Dunn's Woods from Moses Dunn on which to establish a new site for the university. The family burial plot, or God's Acre as it was called by Bloomington residents, was reserved from the sale—protected by George G. Dunn's foresight. In 2004 Marilyn Seward Warden was buried in Dunn Cemetery; few burial plots remain.

The second cemetery on IU's campus is Rogers Cemetery, one of the oldest in Monroe County, with grave markers dating back to 1818, two years prior to the founding of the university itself. The cemetery was established by one of Bloomington's earliest pioneer families, and named for their relative, Henry Rogers, a Revolutionary War soldier (circa 1750–1832). The Rogers family declined to move the cemetery when Foster Residence Center was built, and it permanently remains safely tucked under the trees in front of this dormitory on Fee Lane. Along with Henry Rogers, descendants of both the

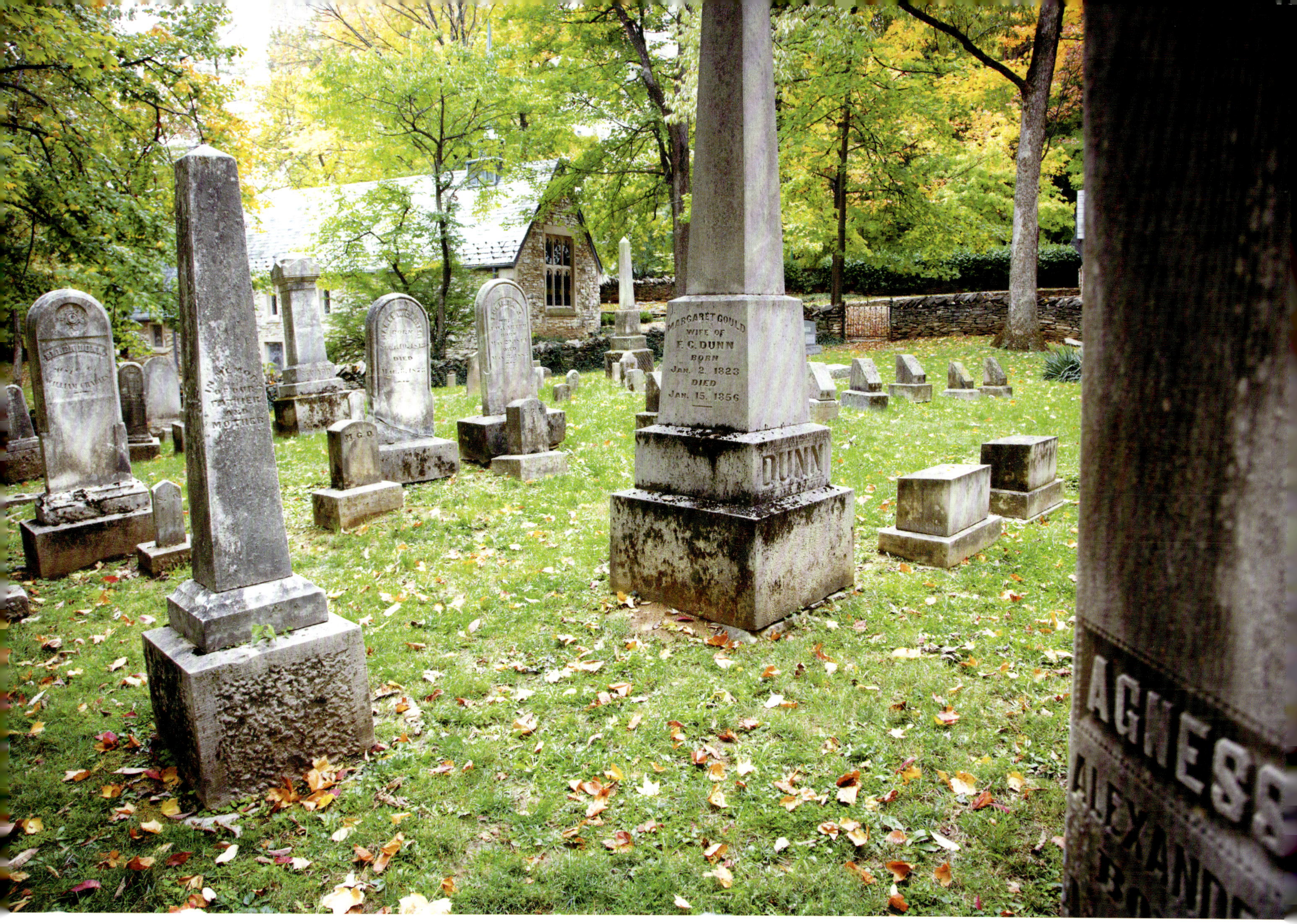

Dunn Cemetery, between Beck Chapel and Indiana Memorial Union, 2016. Photo credit: Tyagan Miller.

Rogers families and the Baugh families are buried here. James F. Baugh, the infant son of Joseph R. Baugh (1789–1856) and Martha Anderson Baugh (1793–1879), was buried in 1818 in the oldest known grave in Rogers Cemetery. James Baugh's grave is only one of several tombstones for infants and small children, symbolic of how difficult life was for the early settlers.

In addition, two plaques on campus indicate where ashes were once scattered: one outside Beck Chapel, where the ashes of Frank and Daisy Beck were spread beneath a tree, and the other at the base of the Sundial outside Maxwell Hall, around which the ashes of Otto and Mathilda Klopsch were scattered.

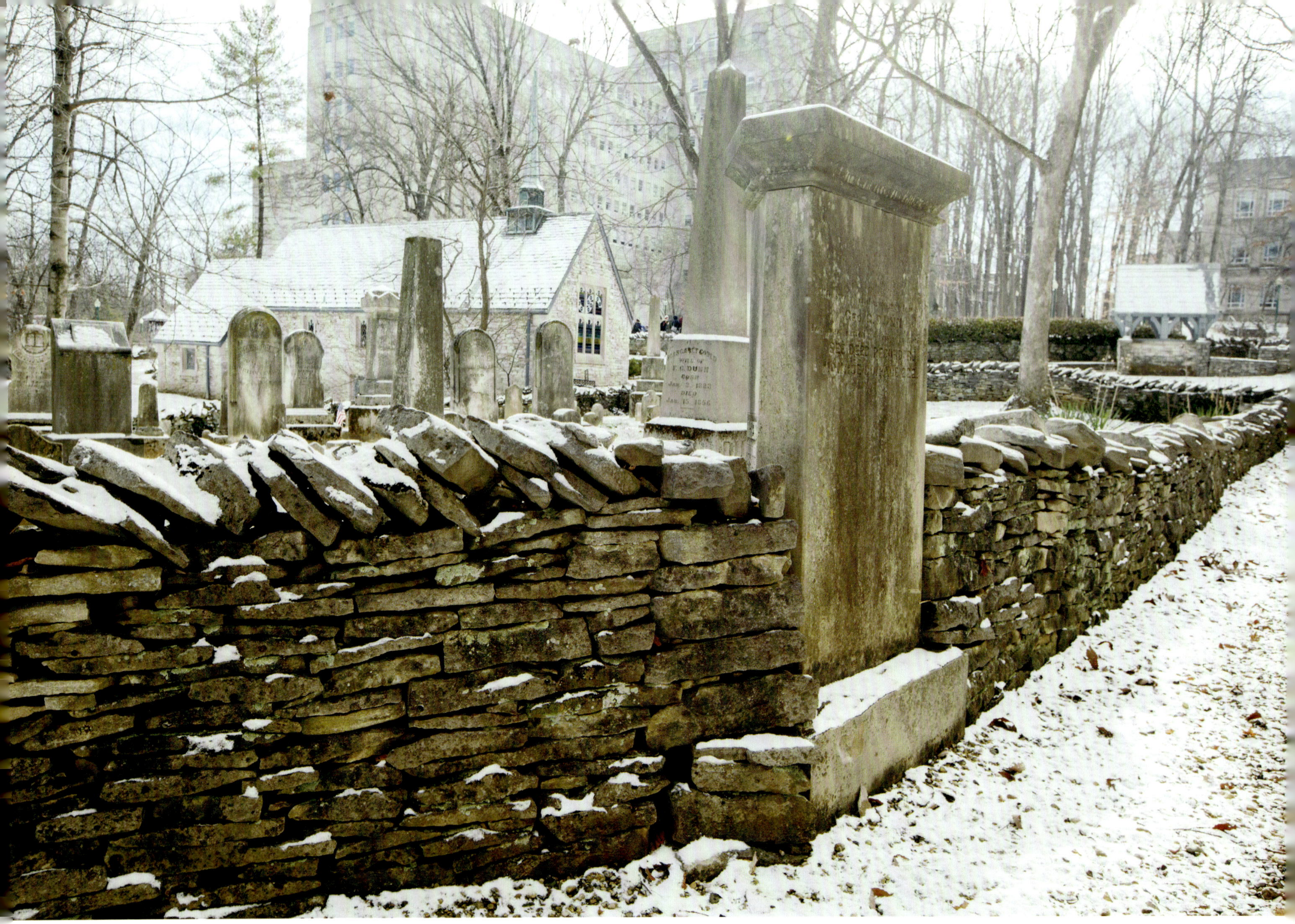

Above, Dunn Cemetery enclosed by stone wall; note the tallest gravestone shared by three Dunn family Revolutionary War heroines, 2016. Photo credit: Tyagan Miller.

Facing, Permanently protected ground, Rogers Cemetery in front of Foster Quadrangle on Fee Lane, 2016. Photo credit: Tyagan Miller.

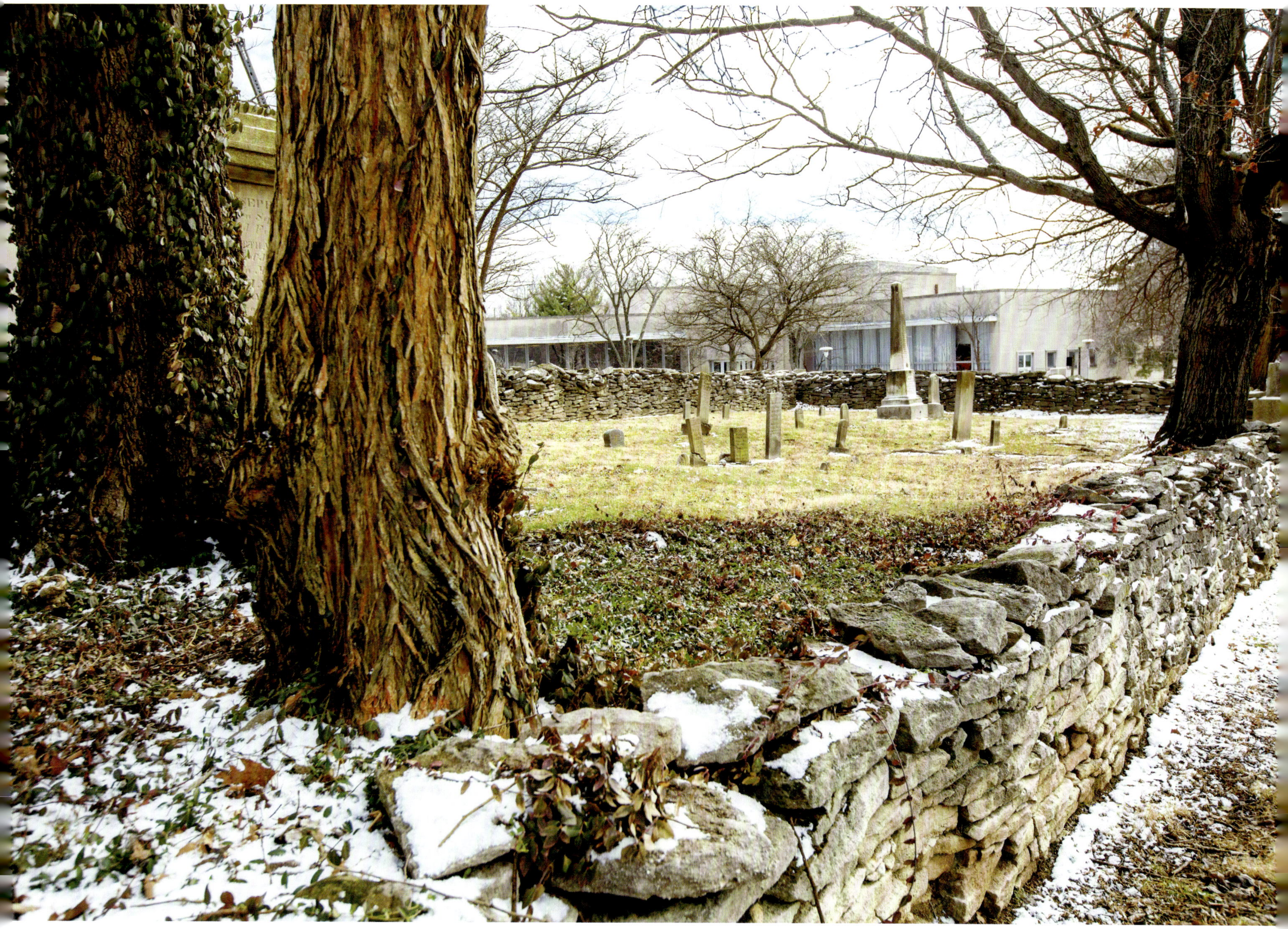

Sundial

A Timepiece from the Past

A beautiful and substantial sun dial has been erected in the campus by the contributions of the students, which is both useful and ornamental. By it the time of the University is regulated.

—Annual Report of Indiana University

IN THE OLD CRESCENT BETWEEN MAXWELL Hall and the Student Building resides a sundial from the first Indiana University campus at Seminary Square. It was originally erected in 1868 to stand at the "main walk leading to the college entrance" near College Avenue and Second Street. Often said to be a gift to the university from the class of 1868, it was more likely the result of the contributions from the whole student body. In 1906 the *Daily Student* interviewed two men who were students when the sundial was installed. They recalled that "the sun-dial was a point of central interest for a long time." The article stated that Dr. Theophilus Wylie, then a professor of chemistry, initiated the idea, and his students took up the cause. "The sun-dial was to cost about $150 and fifty cents, no more, no less" and "every student in college at the time had an equal opportunity to become one of the donors."[1]

Despite the fire of 1883 and the subsequent move of the university to the Dunn's Woods campus, the sundial stayed at Seminary Square until 1896, since the Old College building (1855) remained the "largest assembly room in the University" and "the hall of the various Literary Societies." In spring 1896, the sundial was moved to its new home in the Old Crescent. According to an 1896 article in the *Student*, the move was "instigated by the department of physics in order that the bells might be better regulated"—the bells being those in the college buildings that signaled the beginning and end of classes.[2]

Today, the iconic sundial is encircled by a wrought-iron fence, and its original limestone face with weathered Roman numerals is still visible. While it no longer serves the role as the students' timepiece, the campus landmark continued as a communal meeting place for decades. In the early 1930s, the student newspaper was peppered with notices from various groups: "the Drum Corps and all candidates are requested to appear at the sun dial in front of Maxwell Hall this evening at 6:30" and "Automobile Party Will Leave Dial at 8 O'clock for Oolitic Quarries."[3]

In 1935 the grounds around the sundial accepted the ashes of Otto Paul Klopsch (AB 1896, AM 1909) and Matilda Zwicker Klopsch (AB 1896), who first met there while students at the Seminary Square campus. They married in 1896, the year the sundial was moved to the new campus. Their son returned to campus to ask President William Lowe Bryan permission, which was granted, to scatter their remains around the base of the sundial. A plaque at its base commemorates their romance, which was inextricably linked to this historic timepiece.

Mathilda Zwicker Klopsch
Otto Paul Klopsch
Class of 1896
They met at this sundial
when classmates.
Their ashes rest here
together until eternity.

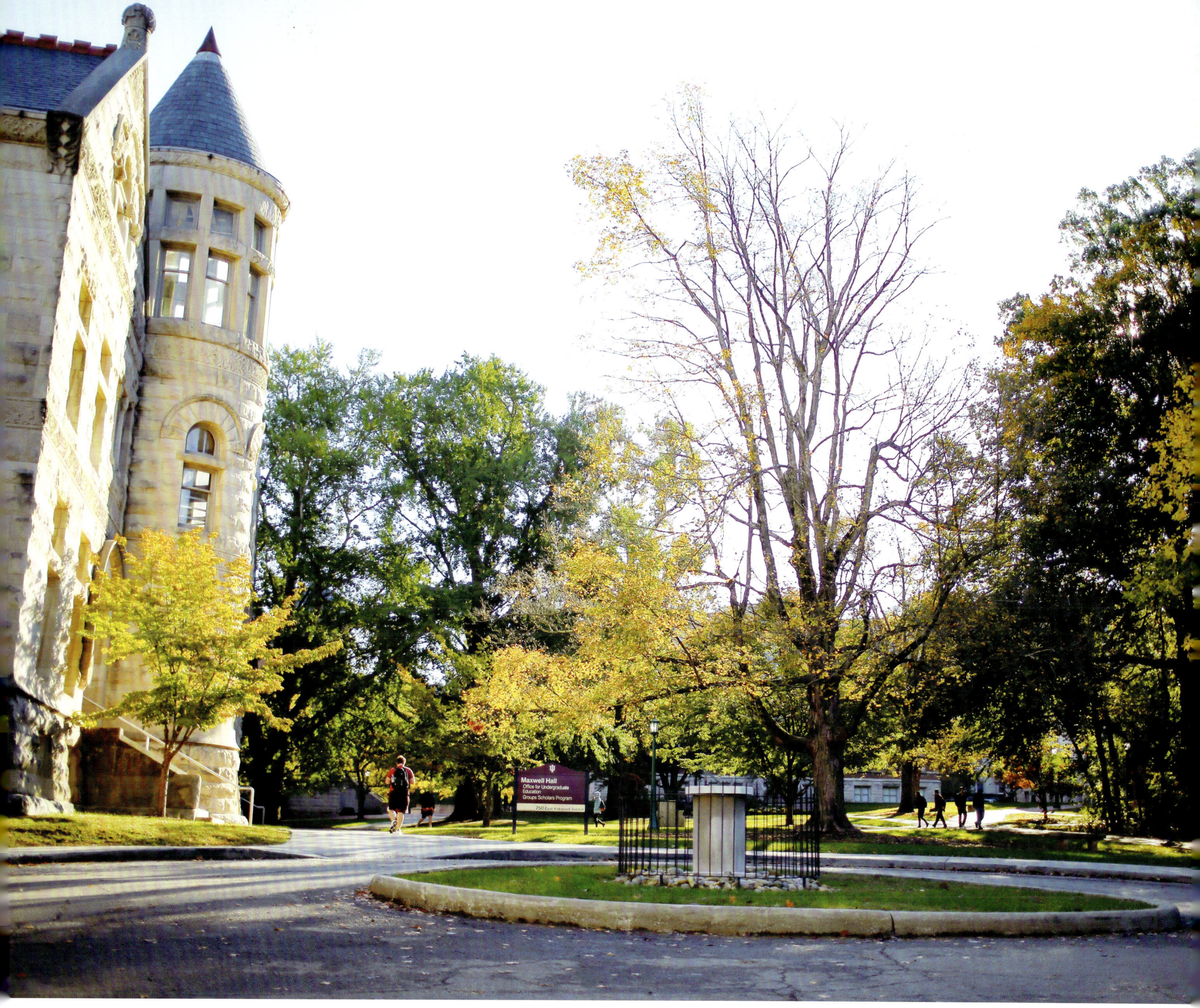

The sundial in traffic circle outside Maxwell Hall, a relic from the original Seminary Square campus, 2016. Photo credit: Indiana University.

Dunn's Woods

Our forest trees are your link with the past. May you find on the campus, especially in the old quadrangle, the beauty and sanctuary which will inspire you to dream long dreams of future usefulness to society.

— Indiana University Chancellor Herman B Wells

Perhaps no place on the IU Bloomington campus embodies the distinctive character of the university as well as Dunn's Woods. One could say it is the soul of the campus for no other spot embodies the essence of IU as distinctively and profoundly as Dunn's Woods. The woods were part of the first parcel of ground purchased from Moses Dunn in 1883, following a disastrous fire that consumed the Science Building at the original Seminary Square site. The old campus was landlocked by the town of Bloomington, and the adjacent Louisville, New Albany, and Salem Railroad was noisy and polluted the area with coal dust. University trustees wanted both room to grow and a better environment. The Dunn farm, a mile to the east of the original campus, provided a suitable location. The first 20 acres were purchased with insurance proceeds from the fire and gift funds from Monroe County residents. Additional parcels were purchased from the Dunn family over the next several years, allowing the campus to expand to the east and north. The land acquired, including Dunn's Woods, was a diverse mix of open farmland, forest, and brush. The tract's many beeches and maples created a parklike setting. Locals used the grounds for Sunday picnics and referred to the new campus as University Park.

Between 1884 and 1896, five buildings were constructed around the higher east edge of the new campus, forming a crescent shaped layout. That campus district today, which now includes nine structures, is still known as the Old Crescent and has been placed on the National Register of Historic Places. Dunn's Woods, also on the register, sits to the west and south of the Old Crescent and is bordered by Rawles Hall and Swain Hall to the south, Lowell E. Baier Hall on the southwest corner, and Bryan Hall on the west. Kirkwood Observatory has been nestled among the trees of Dunn's Woods since 1900.

Considerable care and protection are given to maintaining Dunn's Woods. Generally, no trees are removed except as the result of storm damage, and even then, every effort is made to clear the brick pathways through the interior while leaving fallen materials to provide homes for wildlife. This practice has been in place from the very earliest days of IU ownership. When then faculty member and future university president David Starr Jordan heard about the proposed site for the new campus in 1883, he wrote to President Lemuel Moss, "I am glad to hear of the general brightness of the prospects of the institution . . . the location is certainly better among those great maples. I hope that you will let none be cut down, except

Facing top, Bloomington in distance beyond Dunn's Woods, with Kirkwood Avenue to left of center and tower of the old Monroe County courthouse to the right, 1890. P0022323, IU Archives. Photo credit: Stratford and Jones.

Facing bottom, Aerial of campus, October 1998. P0025783, IU Archives.

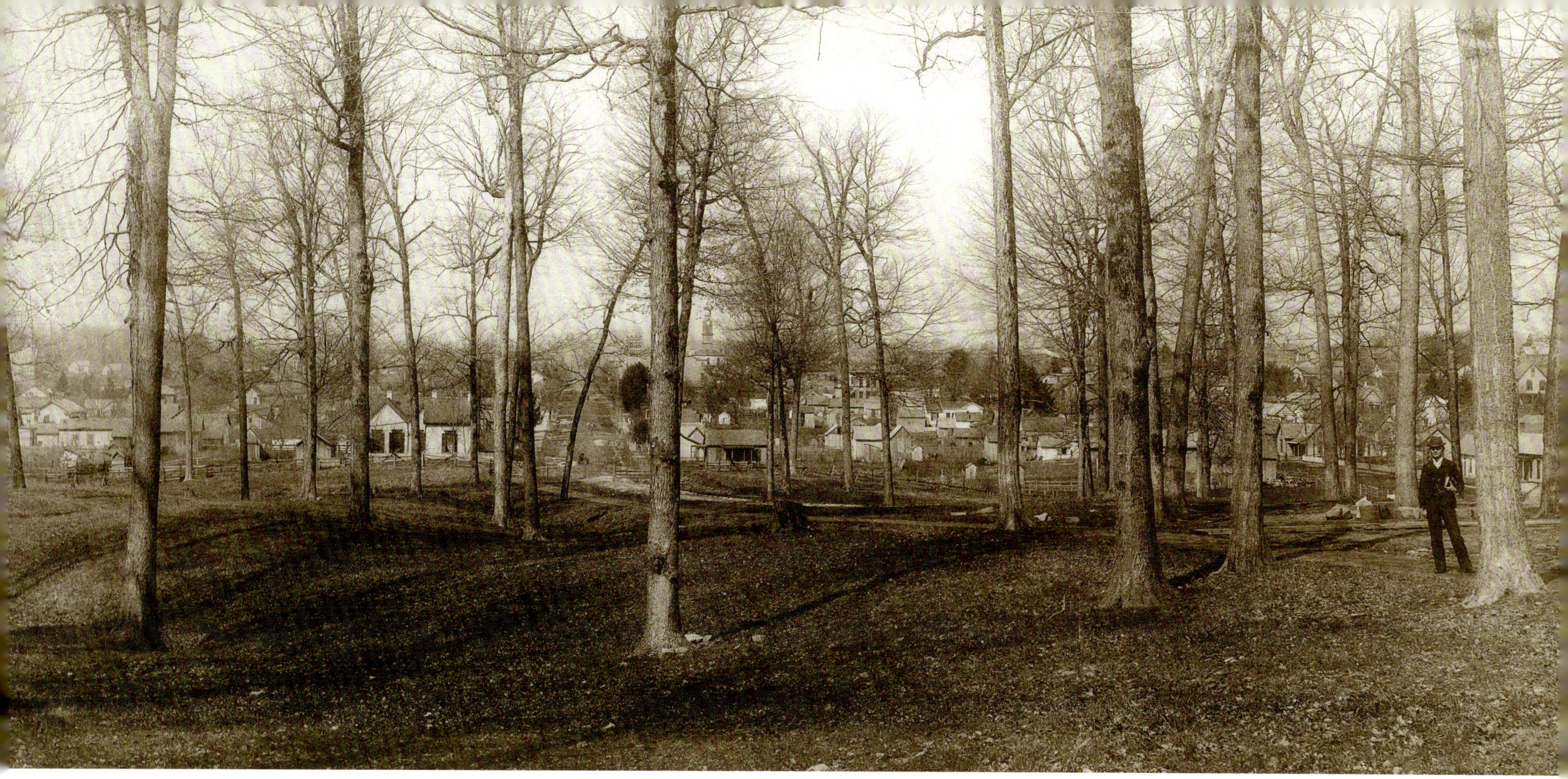

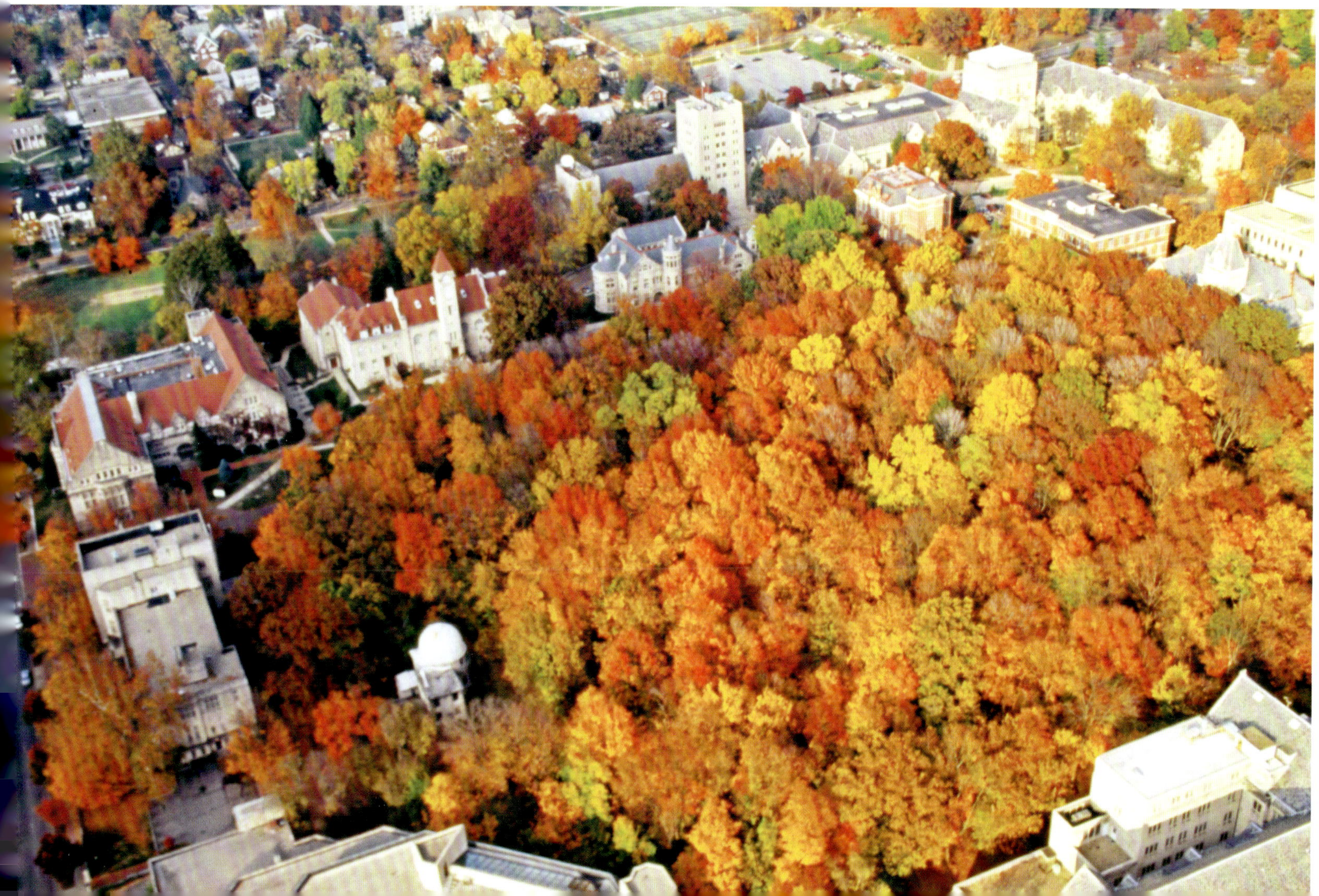

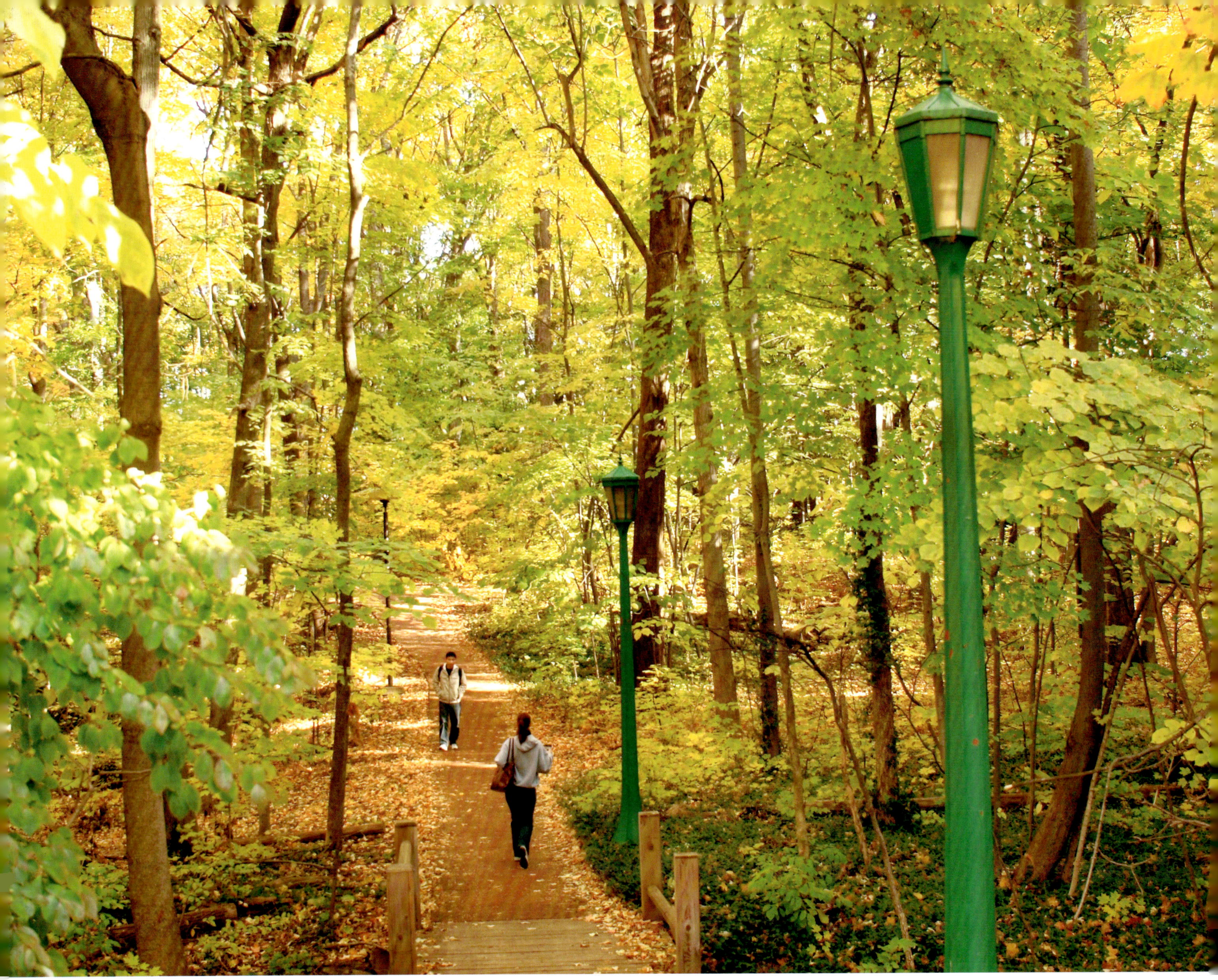

when their removal is absolutely necessary," and that has been the university way ever since.[1]

Today, Dunn's Woods is approximately 10 acres and includes several herringbone brick paths that carry students, faculty, and visitors through the densely forested grounds. The Sample Gates, at the historic entrance to the campus, is a welcoming portal, connecting IU to the town of Bloomington via Kirkwood Avenue. Sitting gracefully on the northeast edge of Dunn's Woods is Wells Plaza, with its sculpture of Herman B Wells sitting on a park bench, hand extended to greet students, a fitting host for this celebrated area. Meandering among the tall maples, beeches, and sycamores in Dunn's Woods evokes the sense of having traveled back to a time when IU was a fledgling university on the western edge of a young nation.

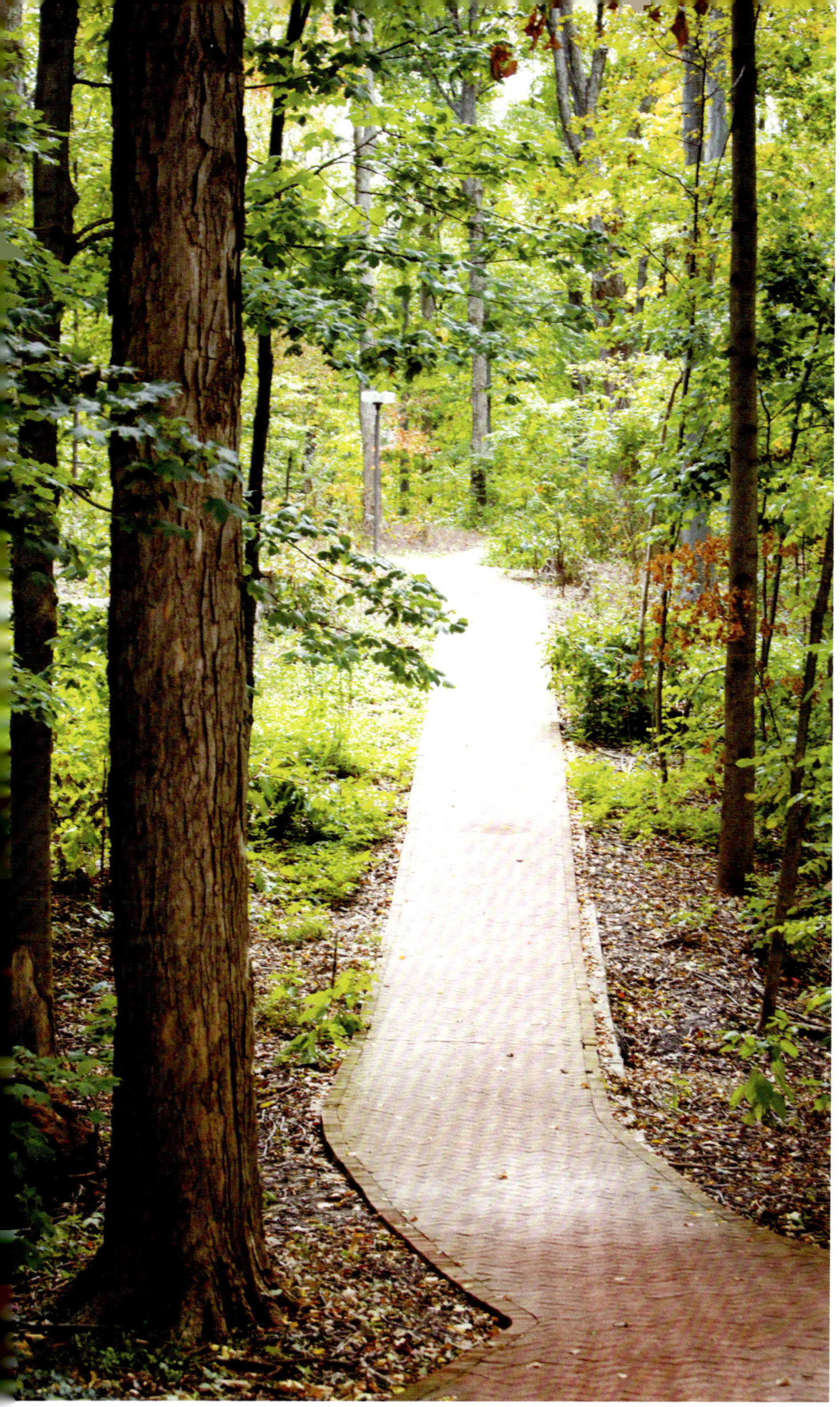

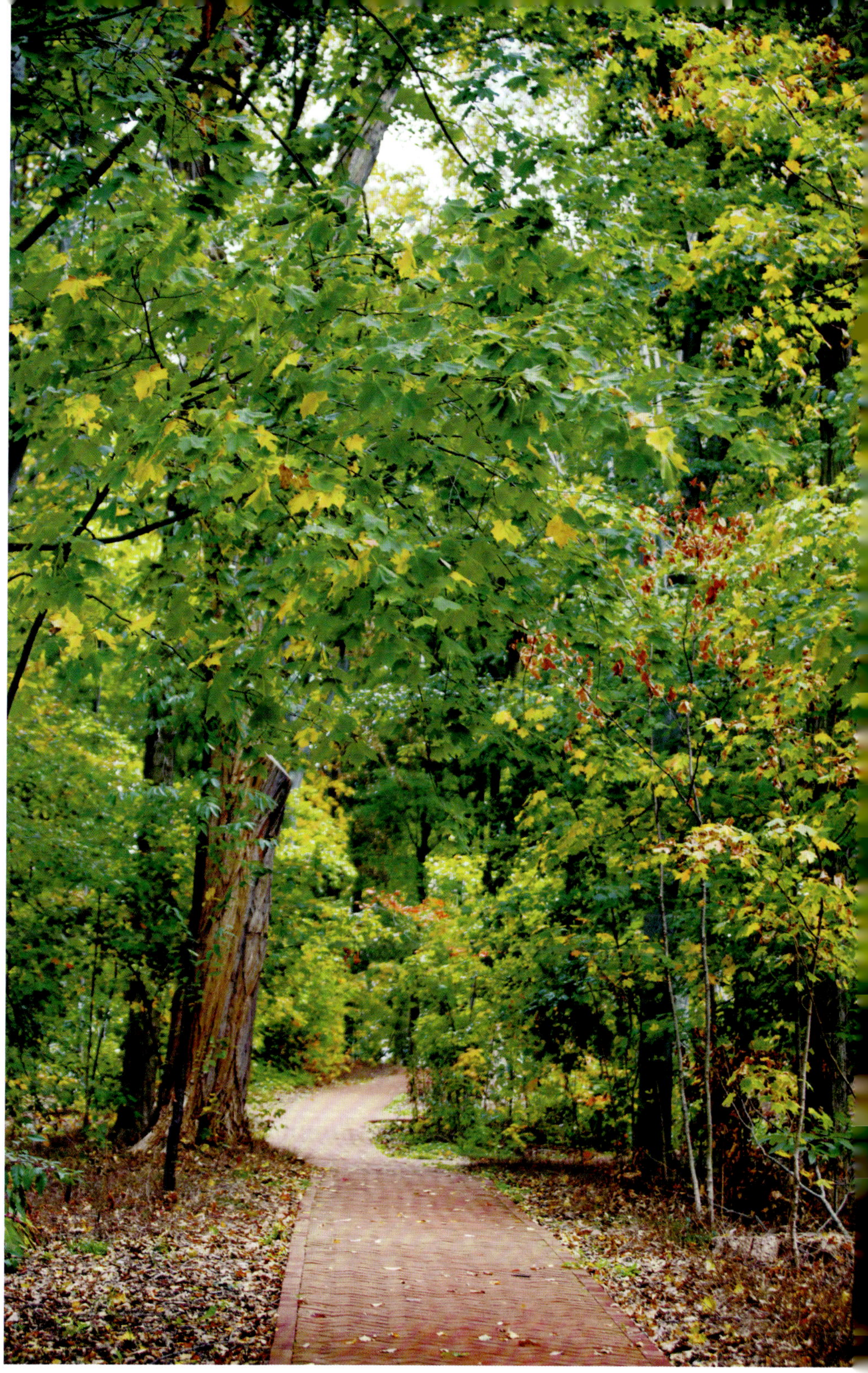

Above, Brick pathways through Dunn's Woods, 2016. Photo credit: Tyagan Miller.

Facing, A fall day in Dunn's Woods, 2014. Photo credit: Indiana University.

Dunn Meadow

A Gathering Place

The campus landscape is full of visual echoes of generations past that have left their mark upon and among the plantings.

—Moya Andrews, "The IU Campus in Spring"

THOSE WHO KNOW THE INDIANA UNIVERSITY Bloomington campus would be surprised to learn that Dunn Meadow was once the site of the Dunn Meadow Golf Club. In fact, these approximately 4 acres just north of the Indiana Memorial Union (IMU) have also been used as an airfield, a military marching ground, a stage for pageants, and a space for tent cities providing shelter for hundreds of protestors who camped out for weeks at a time to make visible their views on both national and local issues. Even an impromptu circus was assembled on Dunn Meadow in support of a student candidate running for president of the Indiana University Student Association.

Dunn Meadow derives its basic shape from Indiana Avenue on the west and Seventh Street on the north, which form two legs of a right-angle triangle. The Jordan River is the hypotenuse that completes the triangle. A monumental limestone bridge crossing the Jordan River connects Dunn Meadow to the IMU, while two other less imposing bridges span the Jordan and provide access to the IMU from Dunn Meadow as well. This area was not part of the original Dunn's Woods purchase from the Dunn family in 1883. It was acquired when the university procured three additional parcels of land from Moses Dunn in 1897, adding 29 acres to the original 20 acres.

No place on campus has a more interesting history than Dunn Meadow. In 1899 a group of twelve golf enthusiasts met and formed the Dunn Meadow Golf Club. Nine golf holes ranging in length from 125 to 400 yards were laid out over a total course length of 2,105 yards. As the field was muddy, the grass unkempt, and the ground rough and bordered by a stream, the club did not feel the need to create artificial golf hazards as it was clear nature had done enough of that. Although the golf club was short-lived, another golf course materialized in 1916 at Tenth Street and Woodlawn Avenue on what is now Woodlawn Field.

In October 1911, a crowd of five thousand gathered in Dunn Meadow to watch Horace Kearney, a Curtis Company barnstormer, take off in his biplane. Unfortunately, Kearney crashed at take-off, striking the top of a tree and falling into what was then known as Spanker's Branch—today the Jordan River. The pilot's pride was hurt more than his body, but he was taken by stretcher to the local clinic for examination.

In June 1920 a Centennial Pageant was held in Dunn Meadow celebrating the progress of Indiana University over its first one hundred years. It also sought to bring attention to the educational environment in 1920 as it affected Indiana University and the other universities in the nation. Pageants apparently were in vogue during the 1920s, and Dunn Meadow was the setting for the annual IU May Day celebration, called the May Festival, each year until 1930. These were spectacular events, with the May Day queen on her throne, a throng of female students costumed and dancing in a choreographed drama, and a concluding maypole dance.

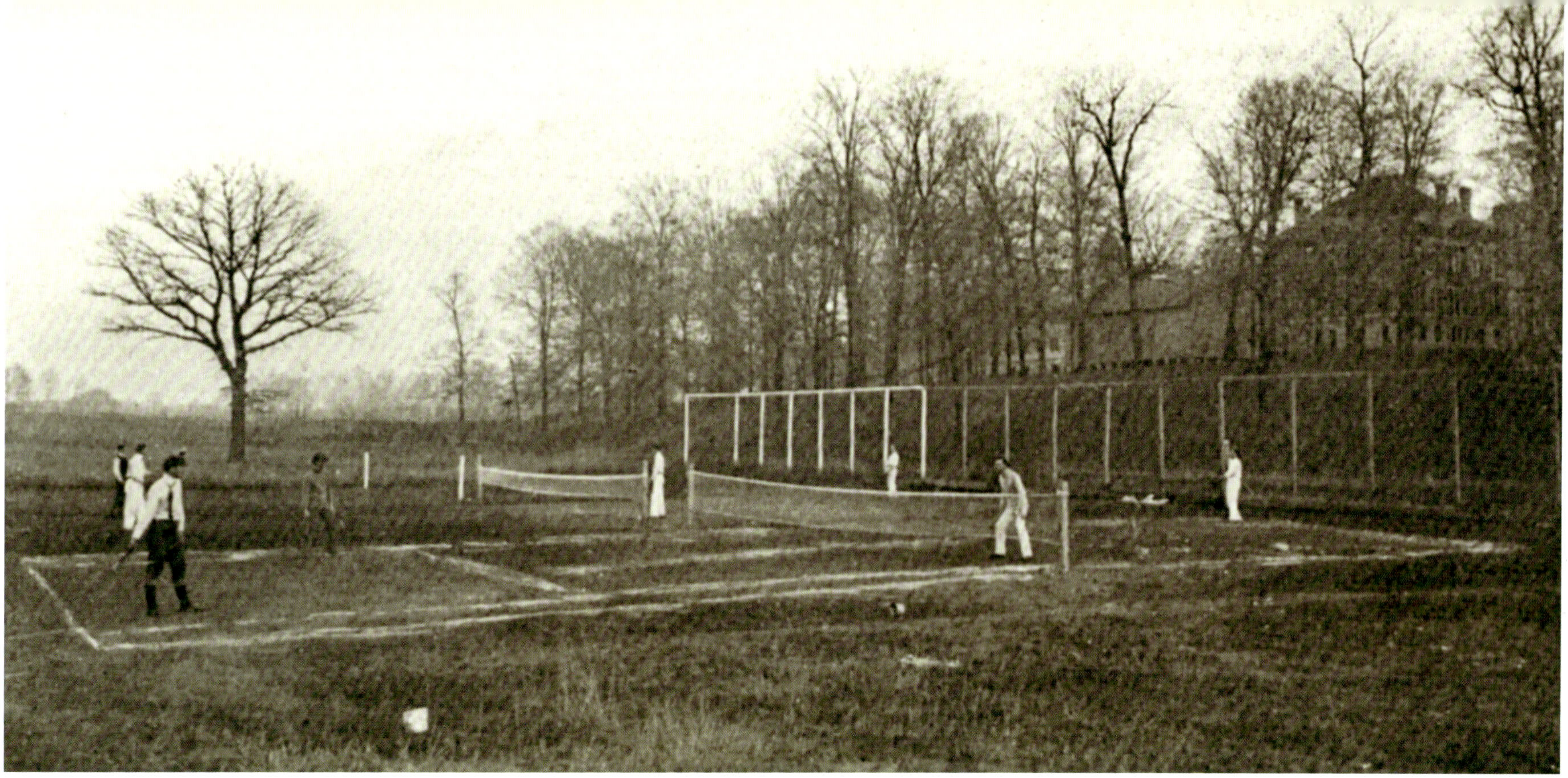

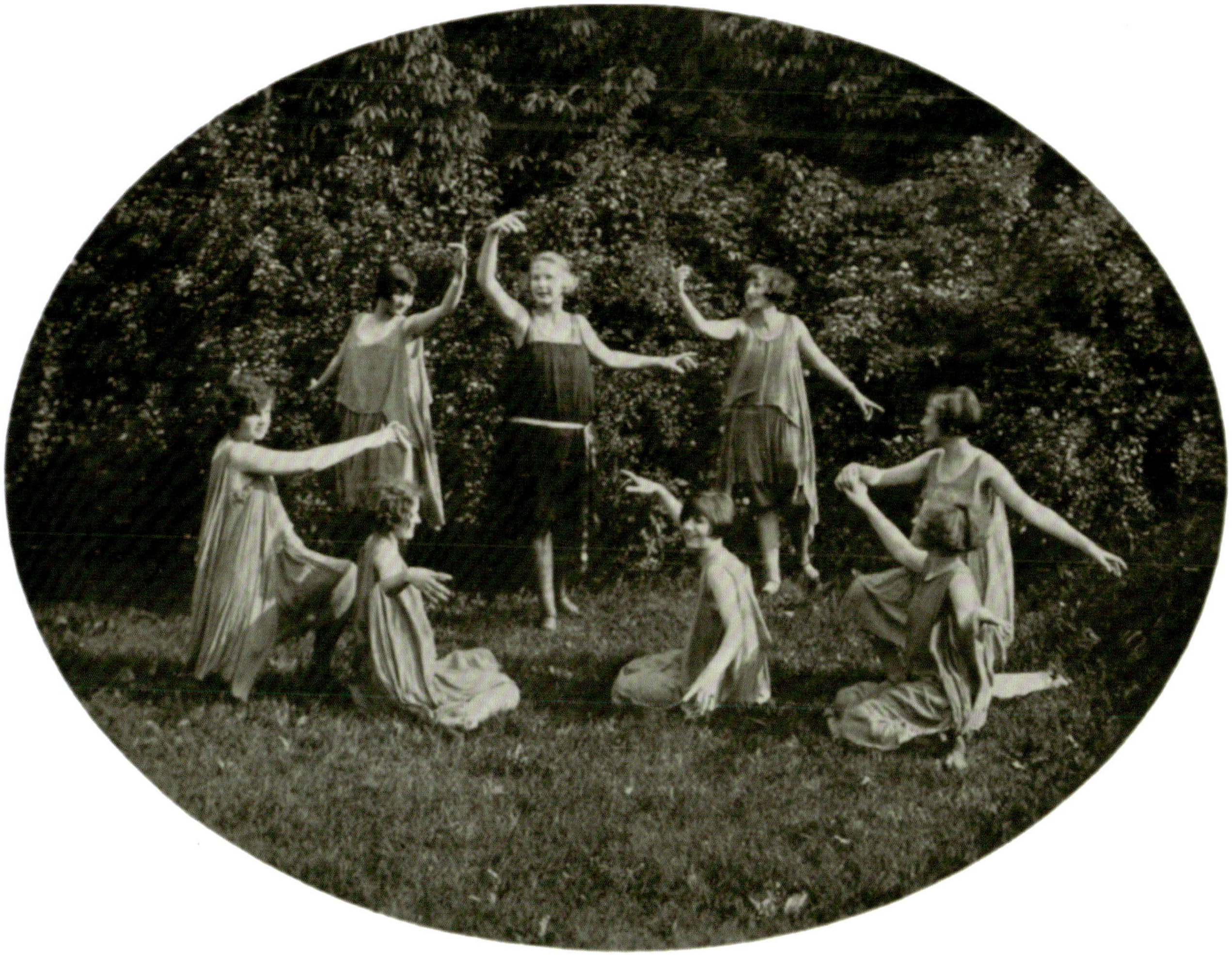

Above, Dunn Meadow tennis courts north of the Student Building, with Owen Hall in background, circa 1899. P0049307, IU Archives.

Left, Dancers at annual May Day Festival in Dunn Meadow, 1924. P0026270, IU Archives.

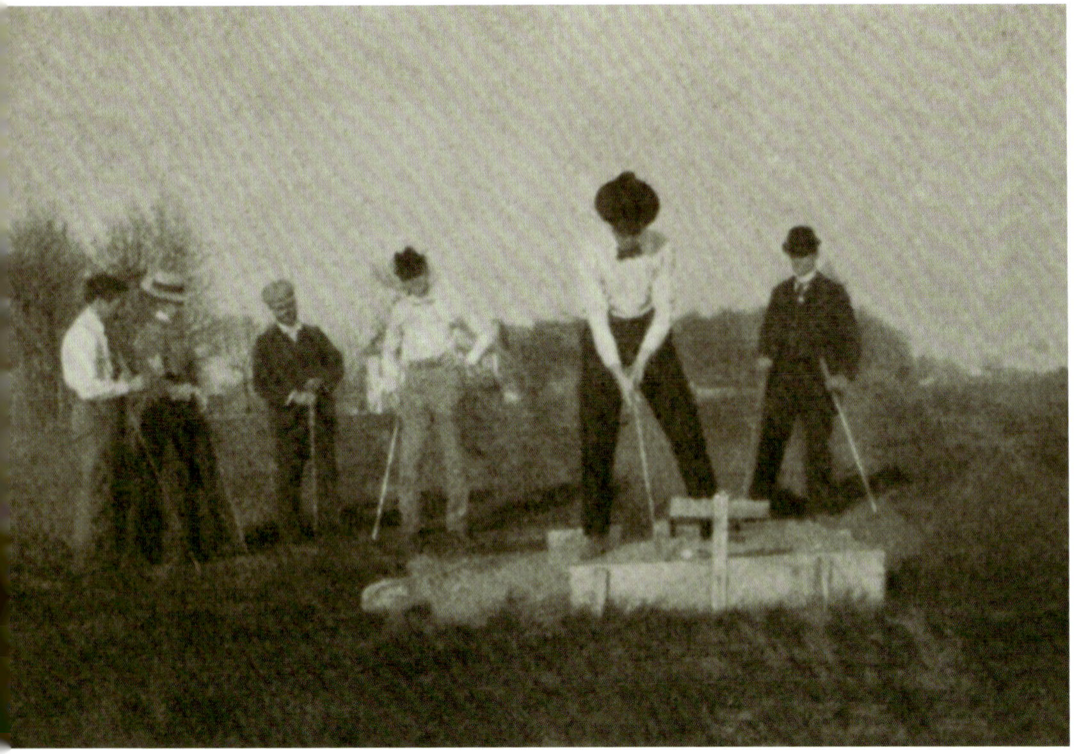

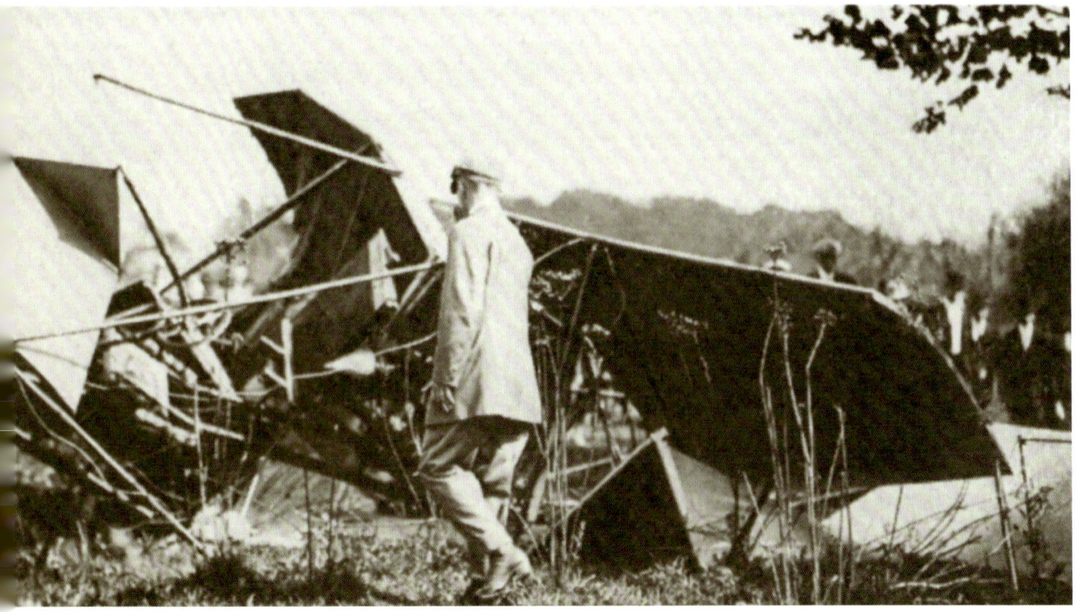

Top, Golfers at Dunn Meadow Golf Club, 1899 or 1900. P0049306, IU Archives.

Bottom, After Horace Kearney's plane crash on Dunn Meadow, 1911. P0022444, IU Archives; image from 1912 *Arbutus.*

Moving forward forty years, in 1962 the Indiana University Board of Trustees officially set aside Dunn Meadow as a place on campus for spontaneous free speech, and since then this field has been used as a staging area for protest. The Vietnam War era, beginning in 1965, brought thousands of students to Dunn Meadow almost weekly to vent their opinions on the county's involvement in the war. Early demonstrations were supportive of the war effort, but as draft quotas increased and the war crept closer to home, student opinions became negative. By 1967, antiwar rallies were continuous. A typical student protest occurred in that year when 3,500 students blocked Seventh Street as they marched toward Dunn Meadow chanting "Ho Ho Ho Chi Minh, the Viet Cong is going to win." Further student protests ranged from demanding that Dow Chemical Company representatives be banned from campus employment recruiting because of Dow's role in manufacturing napalm, to insisting that IU terminate its ROTC programs on campus. Tuition hikes also prompted student protests. More than eight thousand students marched in Dunn Meadow in the spring of 1969 to voice their anger over an unprecedented increase in the cost of attending college.

Probably the most publicized recent protest took place on September 13, 2000, when six thousand people showed up in Dunn Meadow to hear Coach Bob Knight's farewell speech. After twenty-nine years as the men's basketball coach at Indiana University, Knight had been terminated in what some saw as a controversial decision by the IU administration. As the crowd dispersed after Knight thanked them for their longtime support, some protesters headed for Bryan House, home of University President Myles Brand, causing minor damage to the grounds before campus police restored order.

Today, at least for the moment, Dunn Meadow is a welcoming place—even a playground—for students to gather and toss a Frisbee, sunbathe, or simply spread a blanket to nap or study. A low stone wall has been added along the Seventh Street and Indiana Avenue boundaries, the grassy surface reconditioned, and ornamental trees added for shade and aesthetic appeal.

Facing top, Student protest in Dunn Meadow, 1969. P0020532, IU Archives. Photo Credit: Elwood Martin "Barney" Cowherd.

Facing bottom, Earth Day in Dunn Meadow featuring a geodesic dome, exhibits, and many attendees, 1970. P0030724, IU Archives. Photo Credit: Jerry Mitchell.

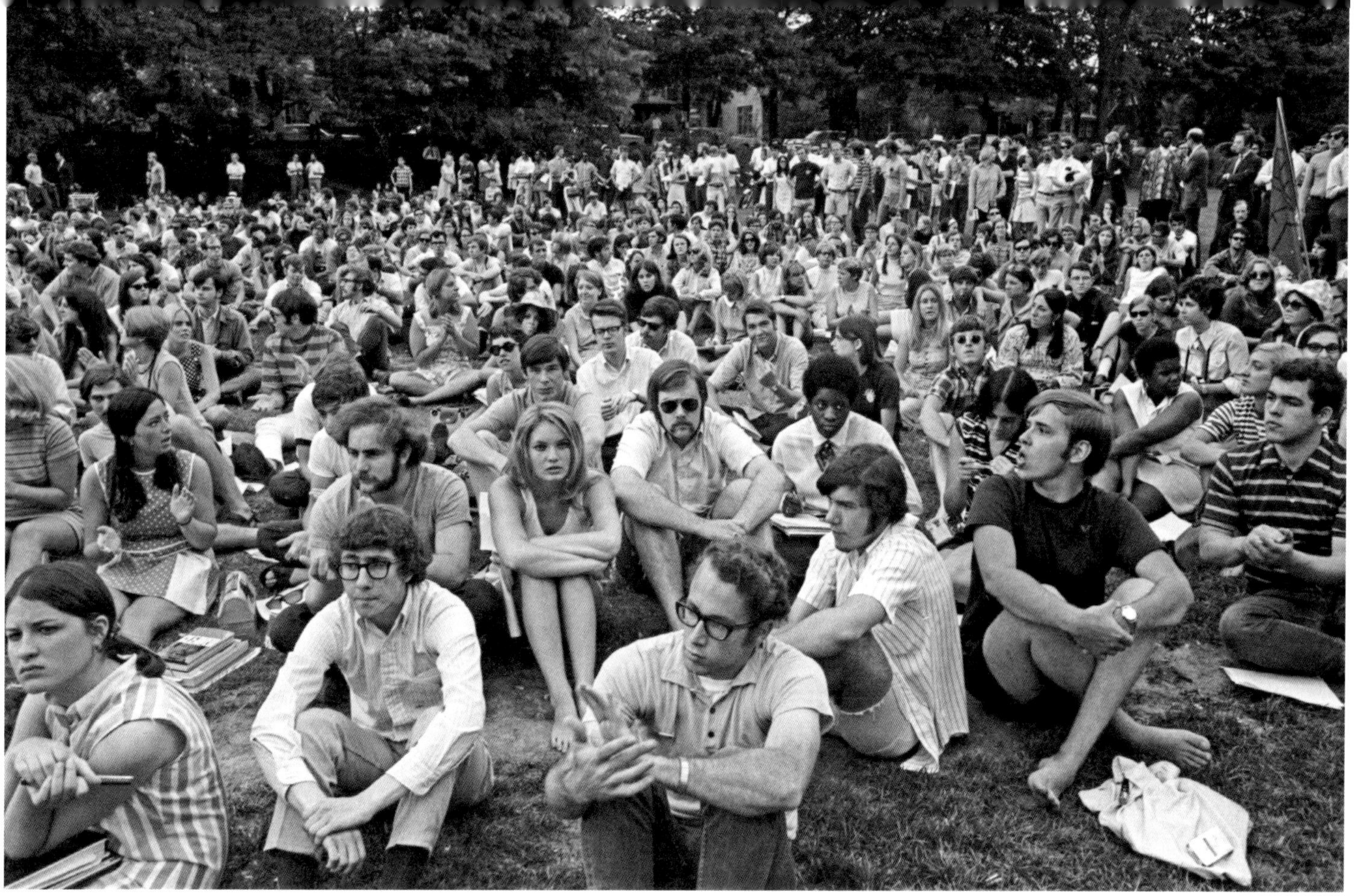

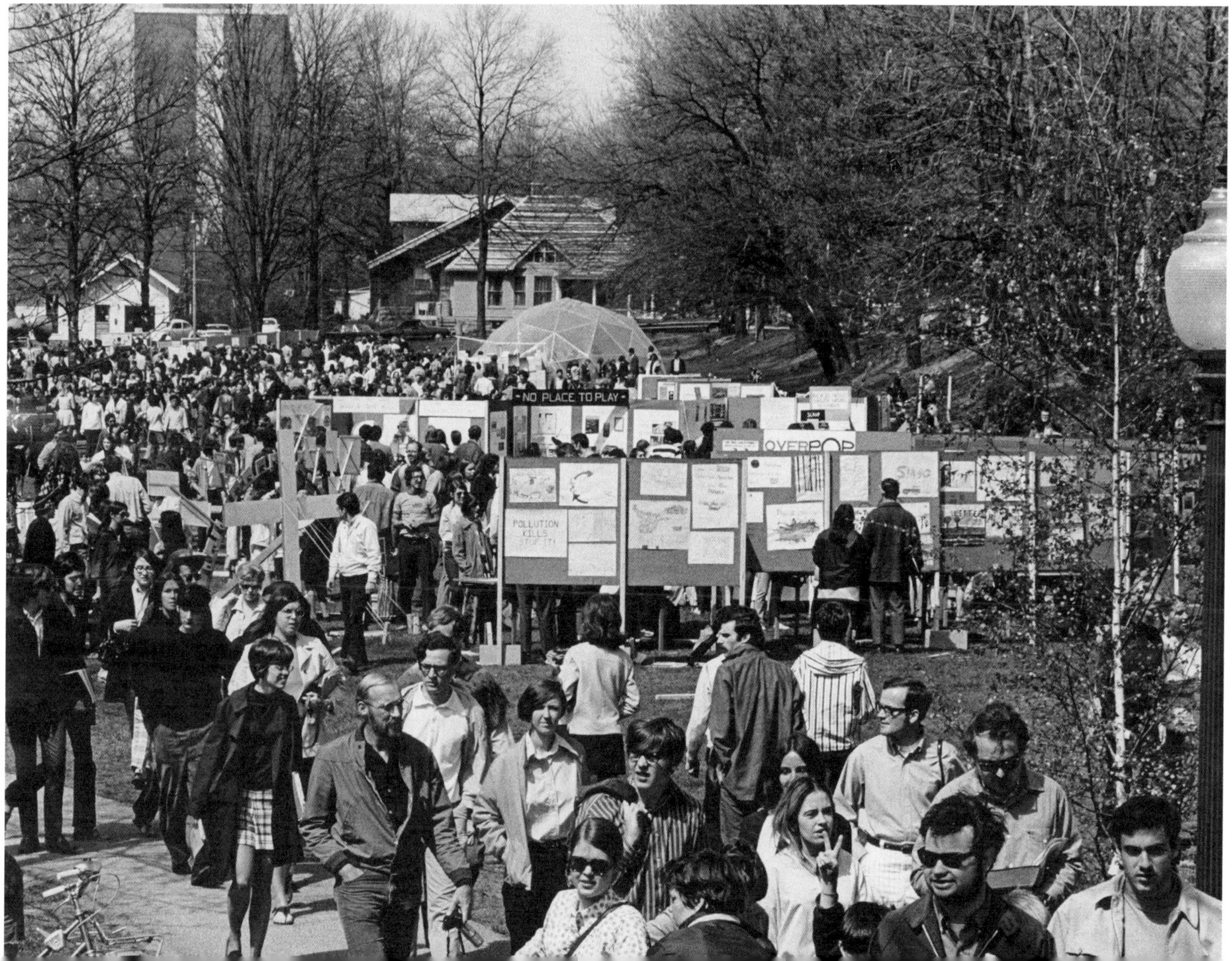
NO PLACE TO PLAY
OVERPOP
POLLUTION KILLS

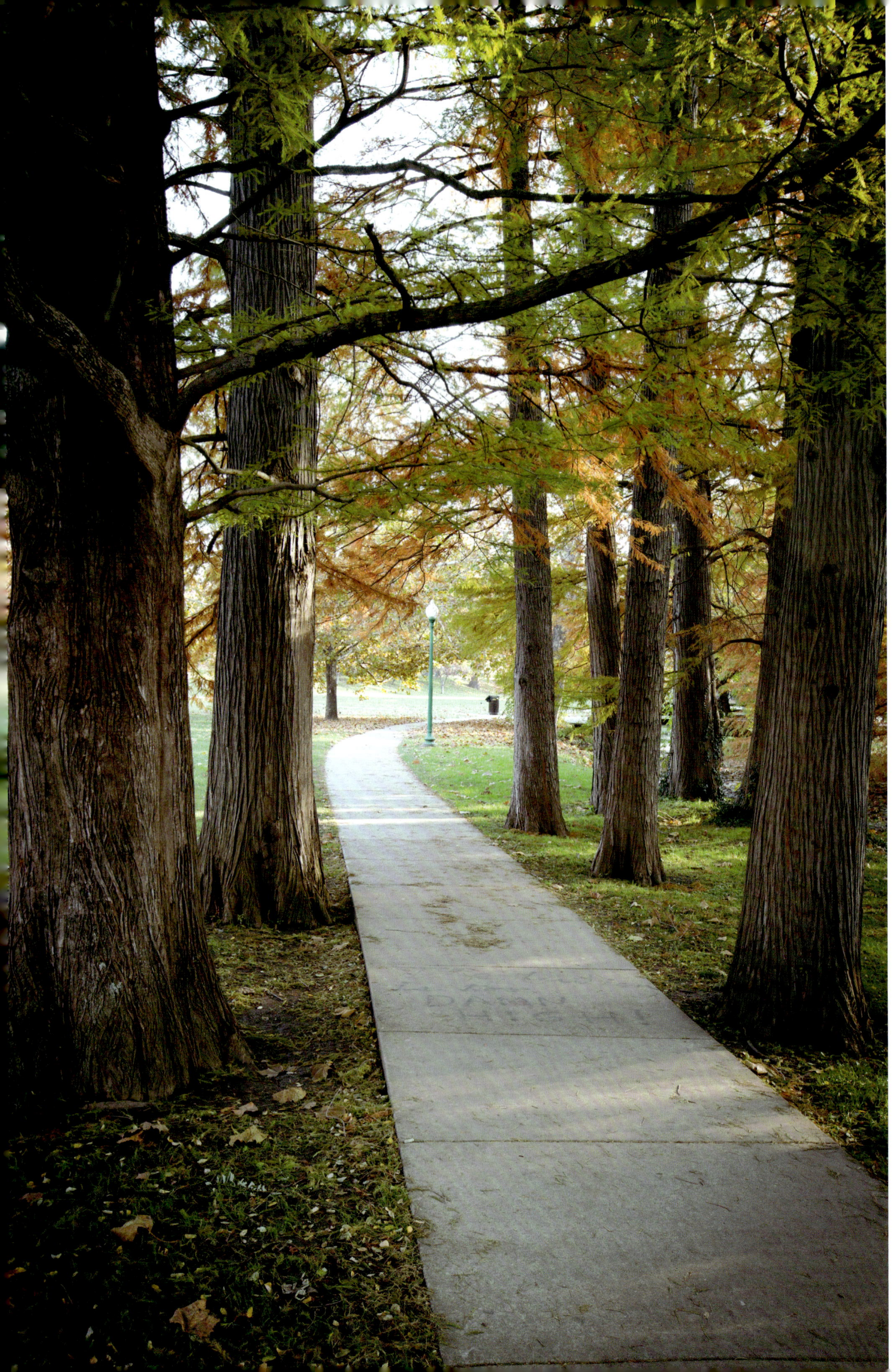

Left, Walkway through Dunn Meadow, 2016. Photo credit: Tyagan Miller.

Facing top, Jordan River and spring foliage in Dunn Meadow, undated. Photo credit: Indiana University.

Facing bottom, Stone bridge framed by fall leaves in Dunn Meadow, 2016. Photo credit: Tyagan Miller.

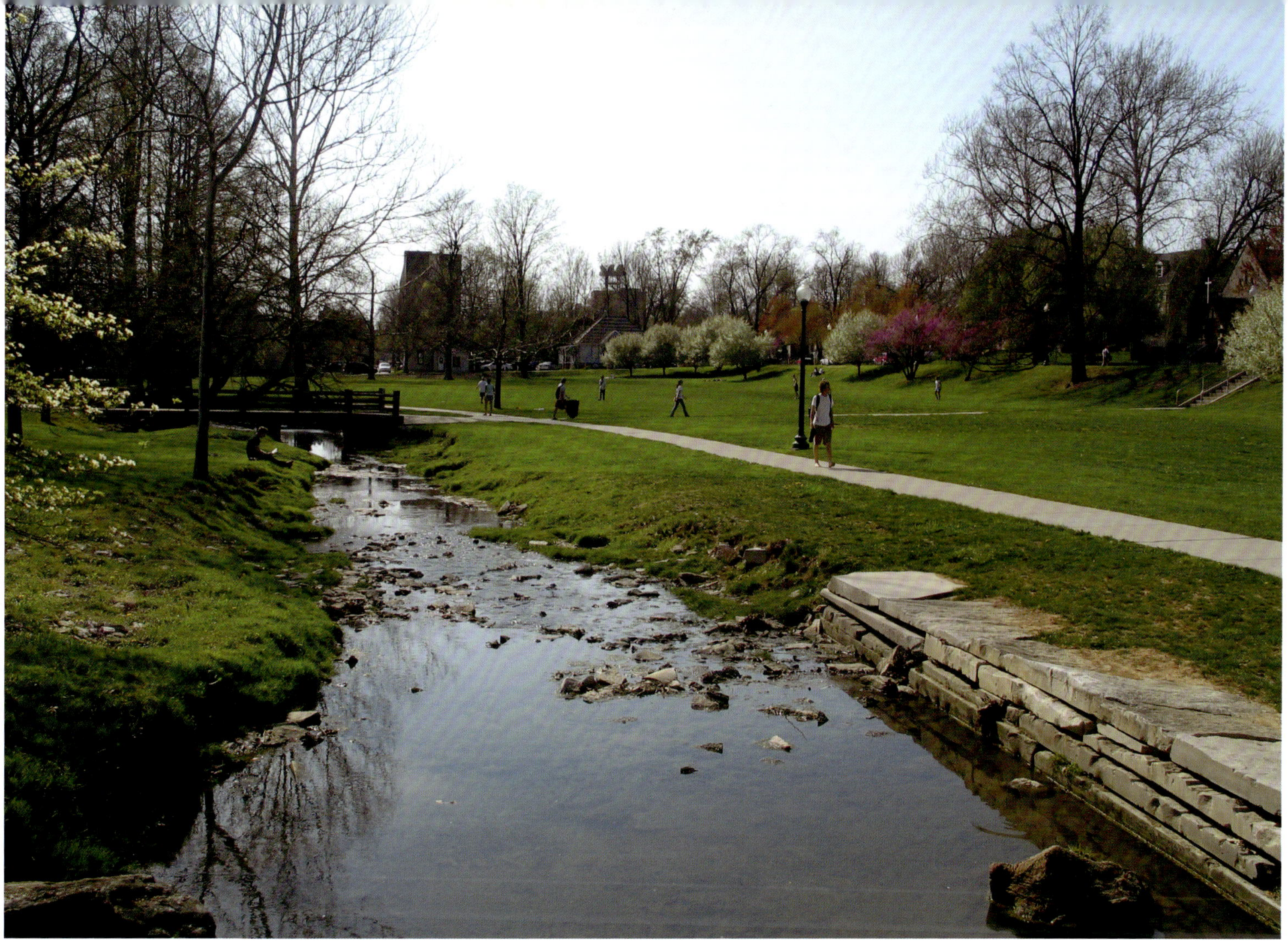

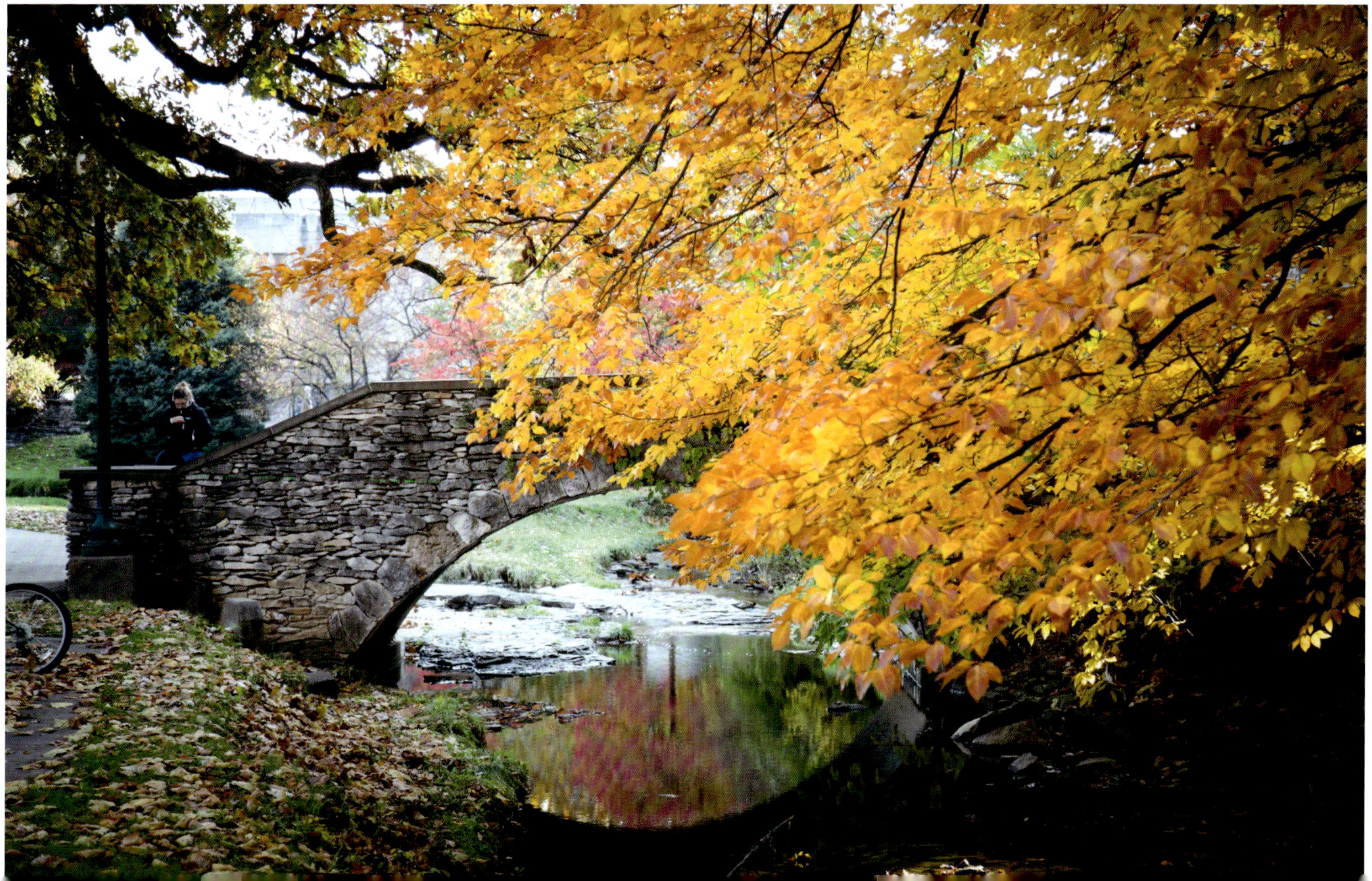

Benton Murals

Cultural and Industrial History of Indiana

On these walls the story of our state is told
How to our crude frontier culture came and knowledge spread
How this Hoosier soil was brought to bear our bread and meat
How men learned skill and craftsmanship
Took from the earth of its abundant wealth
So wrought and gave this state commanding place
In that material advance that builds the record of our nation.

—*Thomas Hibben*

The twenty-two-mural cycle titled *Cultural and Industrial History of Indiana* (the Benton Murals, also called the Indiana Murals) was completed in 1933 for the Indiana exhibit at the Century of Progress International Exposition in Chicago (better known as the Chicago World's Fair). Thomas Hart Benton, a U.S. artist and muralist from Missouri, was commissioned to paint a "cultural and material history of Indiana" at the suggestion of Indianapolis architect Thomas Hibben. Typical of the art movement known as American regionalism, Benton's subject matter focused on rural and small-town scenes, which he saw as symbolic of the entire country. In his own words, "the recorded parts of conventional history were, in my conception, subordinated to the more tremendous facts of common existence where man and his tools, under the constant pressure of every-day need, changed the face of a continent and became themselves something different in the process."[1]

Described by Benton as "a dream fulfilled," the original mural installation in Chicago, laid out by Thomas Hibben, ringed the room at 12 feet high and over 200 linear feet. About the murals, then director of the Indiana Commission for the Exposition Richard Lieber noted that "no one may deny that the fragrance of the unbroken soil, the tang of the burned clearing, the sweat of the face, that the flight of soaring ambitions, that depth of pain and despair as well as exultation of success are not contained in his earnest presentation of the growth and power of our state."[2]

With the close of the exposition, the murals returned to Indiana and were stored in the Manufacturers' Building at the Indiana State Fairgrounds awaiting construction of a proposed new state house. When these plans failed to come to fruition in 1938, then interim Indiana University president Herman B Wells, who had admired the murals at the exposition, began to search the Bloomington campus for a possible site. Possibilities included the new lounge addition of the Indiana Memorial Union, the University School, Alpha Hall, the main reading room of the library, the auditorium of the Student Building, and the original Assembly Hall (1896) at the suggestion of Fine Arts Professor Harry Engel. On May 10, 1938, the Board of Trustees "ordered that the President be authorized to secure the Benton Murals and to properly accommodate them in Assembly Hall, having such alterations made to the building as he may deem necessary."[3] As plans progressed to install the murals in Assembly Hall, so did plans for a new auditorium for the IU Bloomington campus. Ultimately, the trustees placed the murals in the proposed auditorium, and Assembly Hall was razed in 1938.

Benton was pleased at the prospect of his murals coming to Indiana University; after they were moved to Bloomington, he worked with the architect A. M. Strauss of Indianapolis to determine the final arrangement of the panels in three campus locations. In December 1939, what would become known at IU as the Benton Murals were transported from Indianapolis to Bloomington in five crates. The majority of the series (sixteen

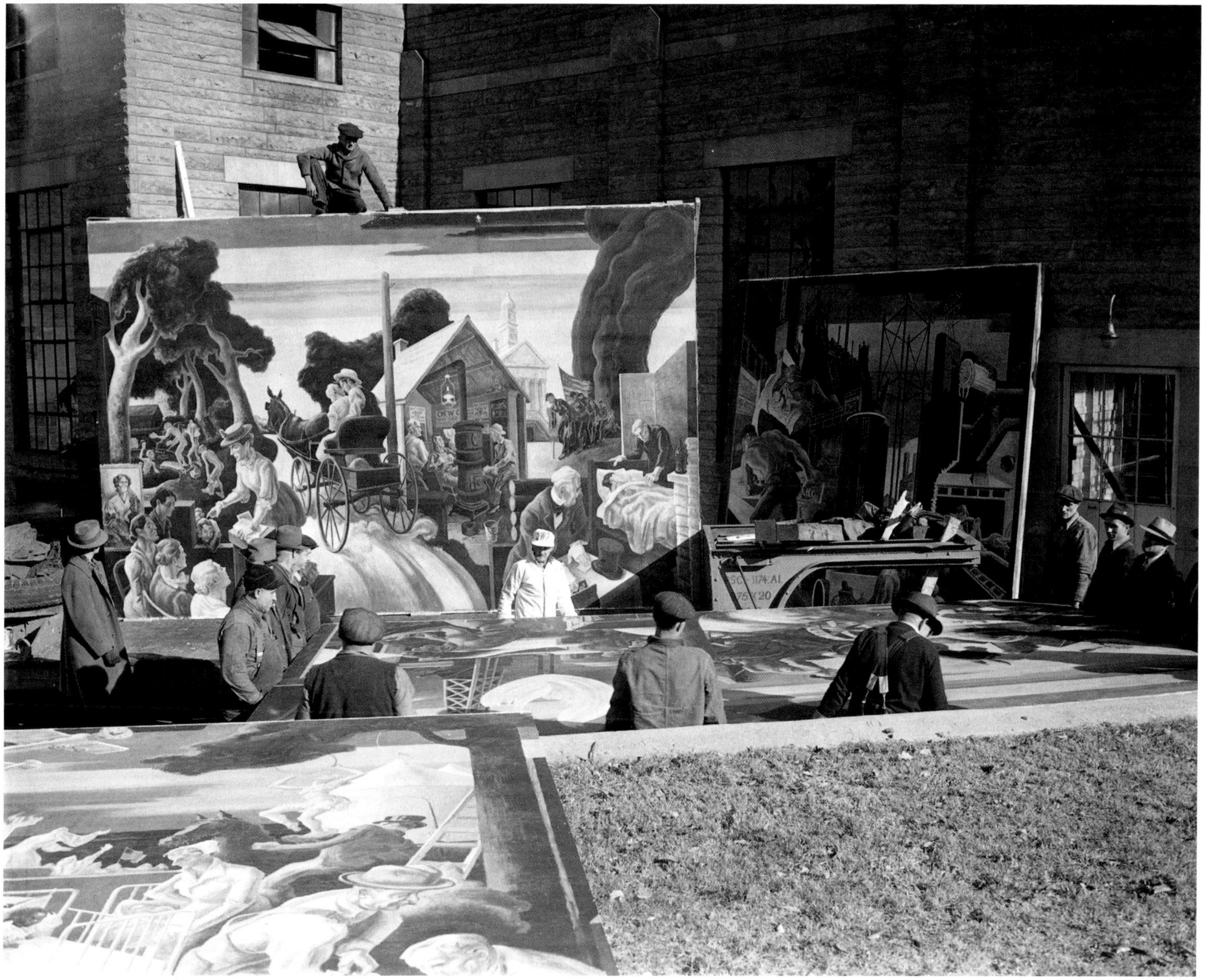

Unloading *The Old Time Doctor and the Grange* and *A Woman's Place*, two of Thomas Hart Benton's Indiana Murals, outside Indiana University Auditorium, 1939. P0031293, IU Archives.

panels) were positioned in the Indiana University Auditorium (a space now called the Hall of Murals), four were placed in what was then the Little Theatre (today the IU Cinema), and two panels were hung in Woodburn Hall. The murals graced the walls of the Auditorium in time for its dedication in March 1941.

The Cultural and Industrial History of Indiana murals were organized for the Chicago exposition into two parallel and chronological themes focusing on the industrial and cultural development of Indiana. Today, the first panel of each series is displayed in the IU Cinema. The first industrial panel, *The Indians*, touches on the foundations of hunting, farming, and craft; the first of the cultural panels, the *Mound Builders*, relates to the afterlife and worship. The two series resume in the auditorium. On the south and west walls, the industrial panels continue the story, moving from *The Fur Traders* and the *Pioneers* to *Home Industry, Internal Improvements, Civil War, Expansion, The Farmer Up and Down*, and *Coal, Gas Oil, Brick*. Each offers visual representations of improvements in agriculture, the home, infrastructure, or energy production,

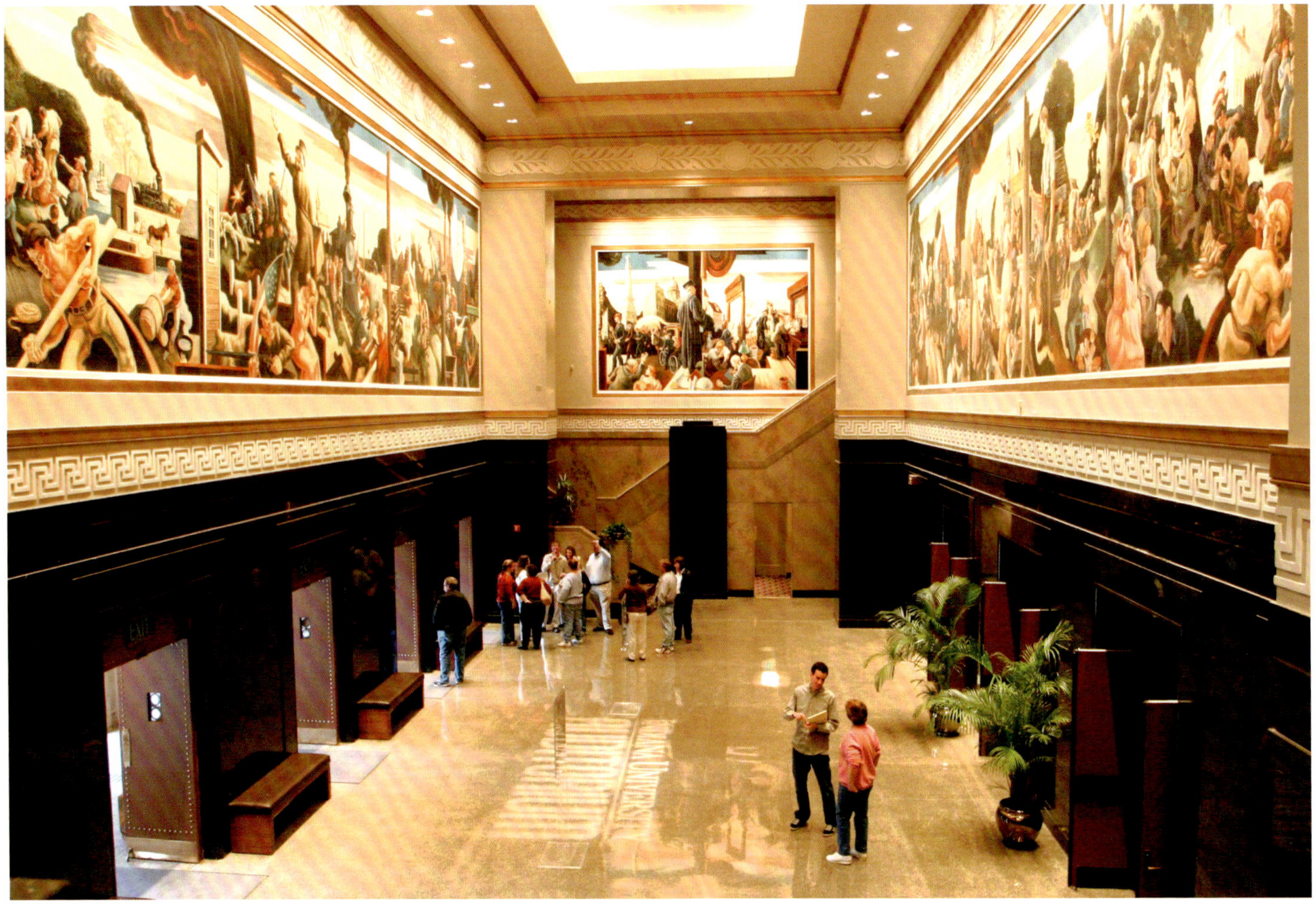

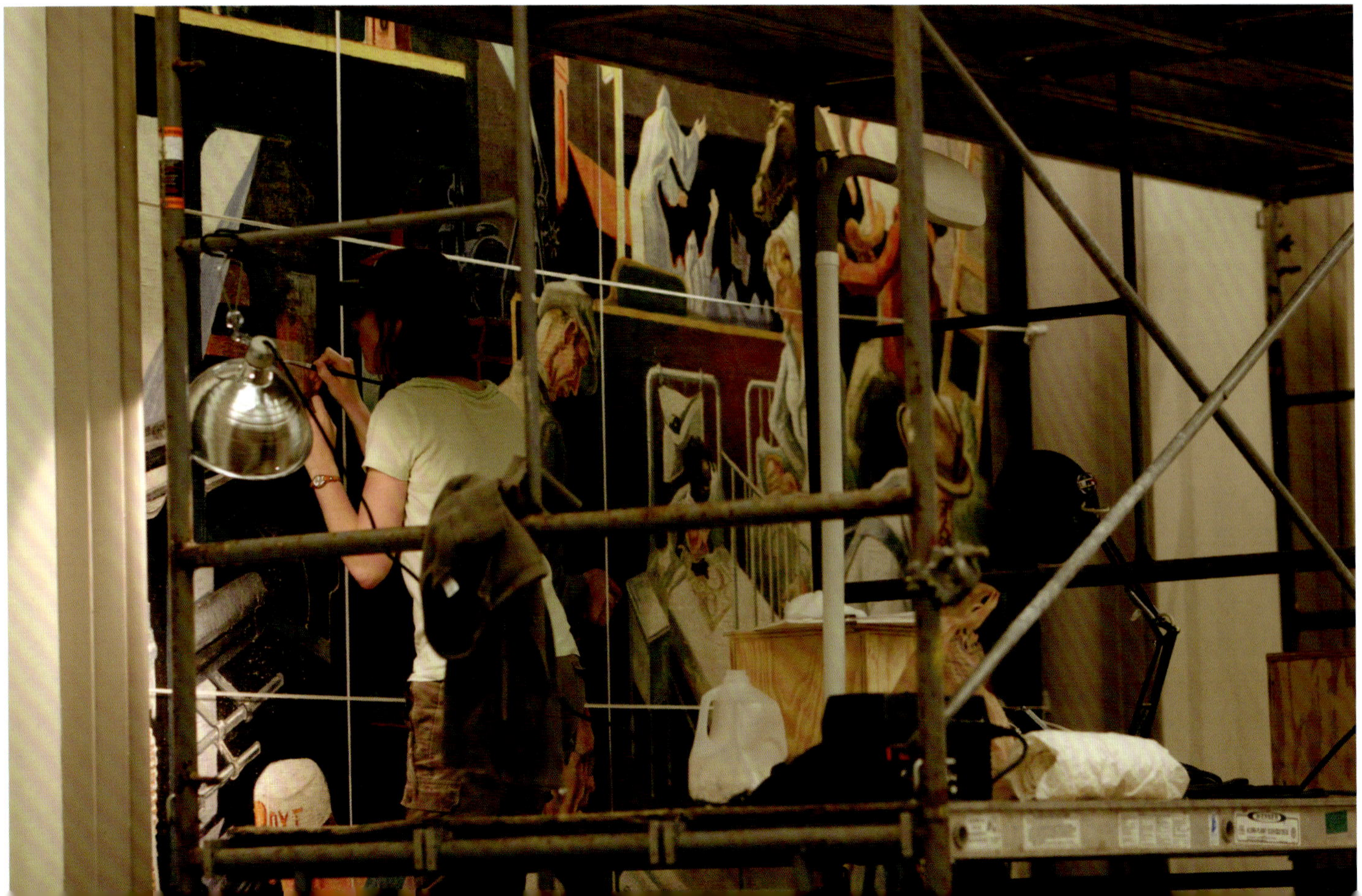

and all interrupted by the trauma of the Civil War. On the north and east walls, the cultural panels illustrate a historical progression—*The French* (traders), *Frontier Life, Early Schools . . . Communities, Reformers and Squatters, The Old Time Doctor and the Grange, A Woman's Place, Leisure and Literature,* and *Colleges and City Life*—touching on advances in education, social movements, medicine, and the arts.

The murals resume in Woodburn Hall—the industrial panel, *Electric Power, Motor Cars, Steel,* represents advances in manufacturing, and the cultural panel, *Parks, the Circus, the Klan, the Press,* references the state's darker side while offering hope by foregrounding the power of the free press. The two parallel mural cycles end where they began, at the IU Cinema, with a final set of forward-thinking panels, *Indiana Puts Her Trust in Work* and *Indiana Puts Her Trust in Thought.*[4]

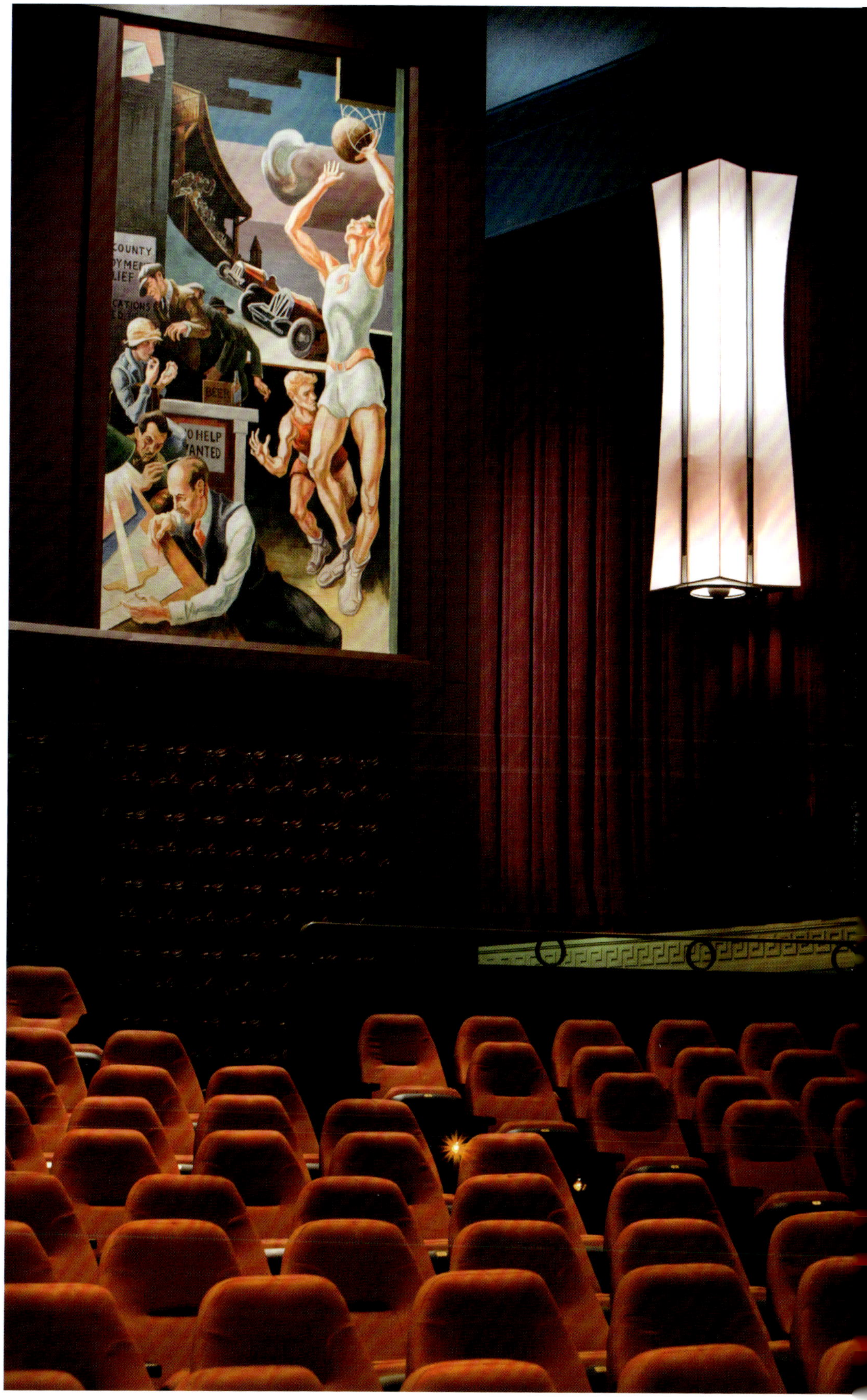

Facing top, The Hall of Murals in the Indiana University Auditorium features sixteen panels of Thomas Hart Benton's murals, undated. Photo credit: Indiana University.

Facing bottom, Conservators work on *Parks, the Circus, the Klan, the Press* panel in the main lecture hall of Woodburn Hall, 2010. Photo credit: Indiana University.

Right, Thomas Hart Benton's *Indiana Puts Her Trust in Thought* panel in IU Cinema, 2010. Photo credit: Tyagan Miller.

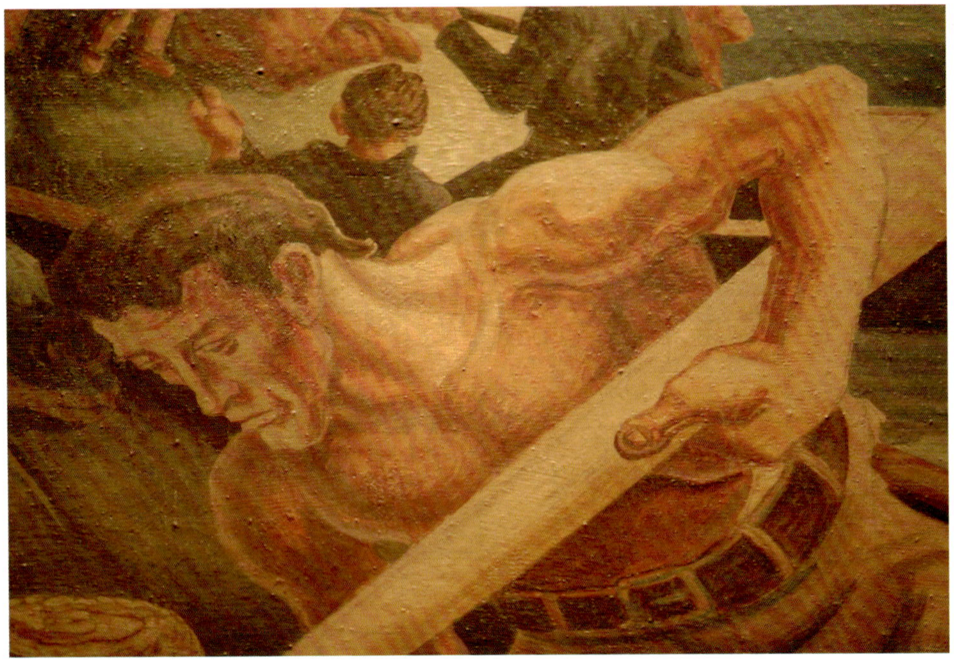

Detail from *Internal Improvements* panel in the Indiana University Auditorium, undated. Photo credit: Indiana University.

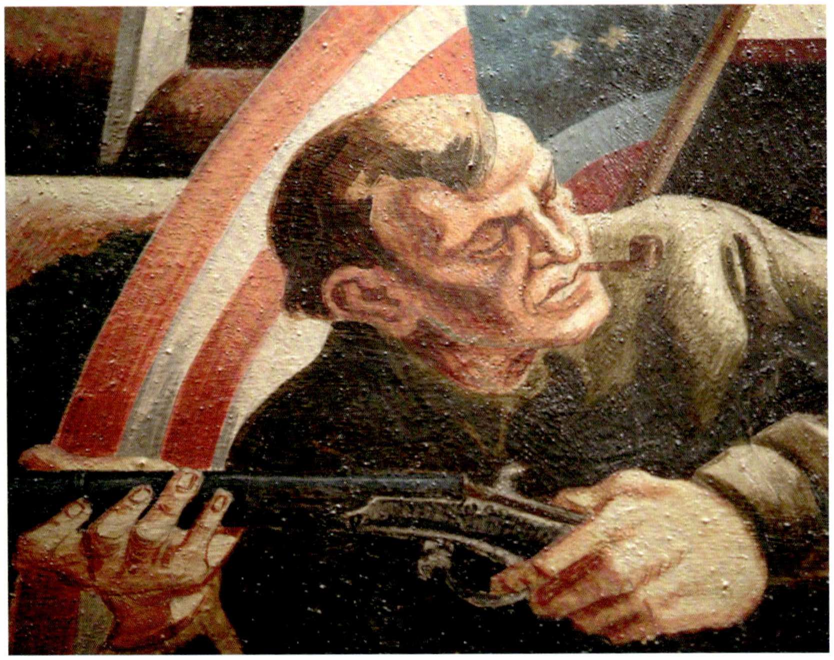

Detail of a solder from *Civil War* panel in the Indiana University Auditorium, undated. Photo credit: Indiana University.

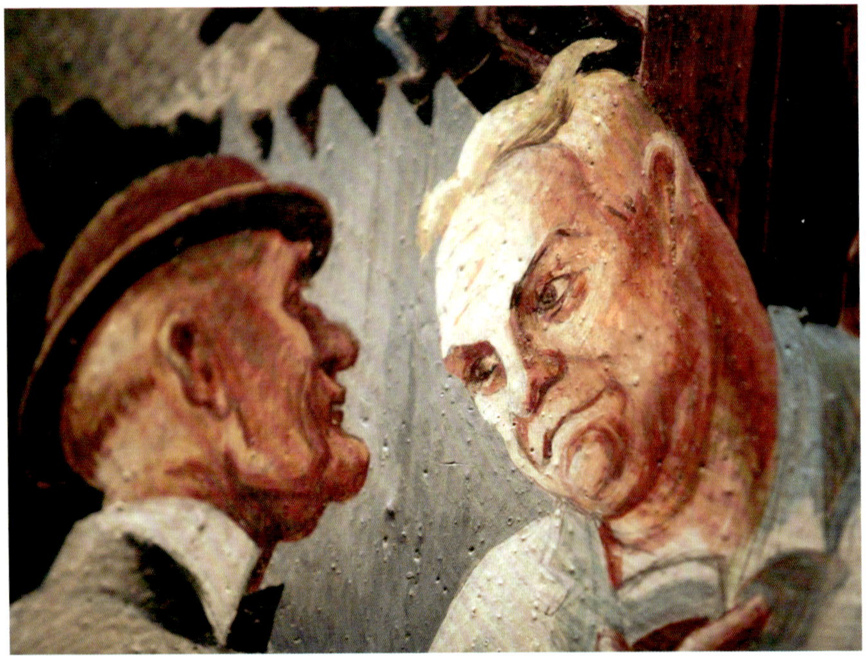

Detail of saloon bartender from *Leisure and Literature* panel in the Indiana University Auditorium, undated. Photo credit: Indiana University.

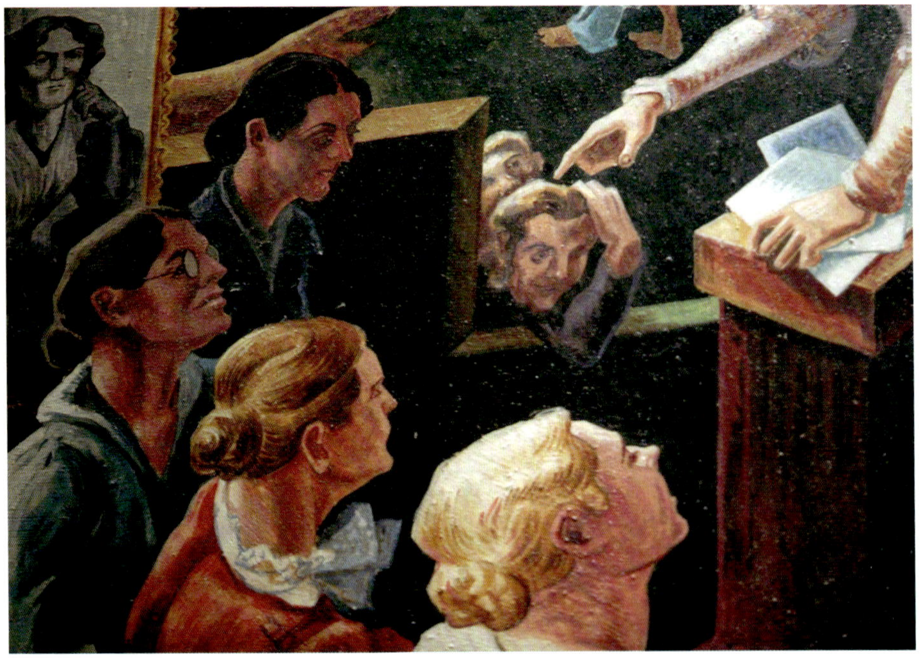

Detail of members of the Minerva Society, who believed men and women should be equal under the law, from *A Woman's Place* panel in the Indiana University Auditorium, undated. Photo credit: Indiana University.

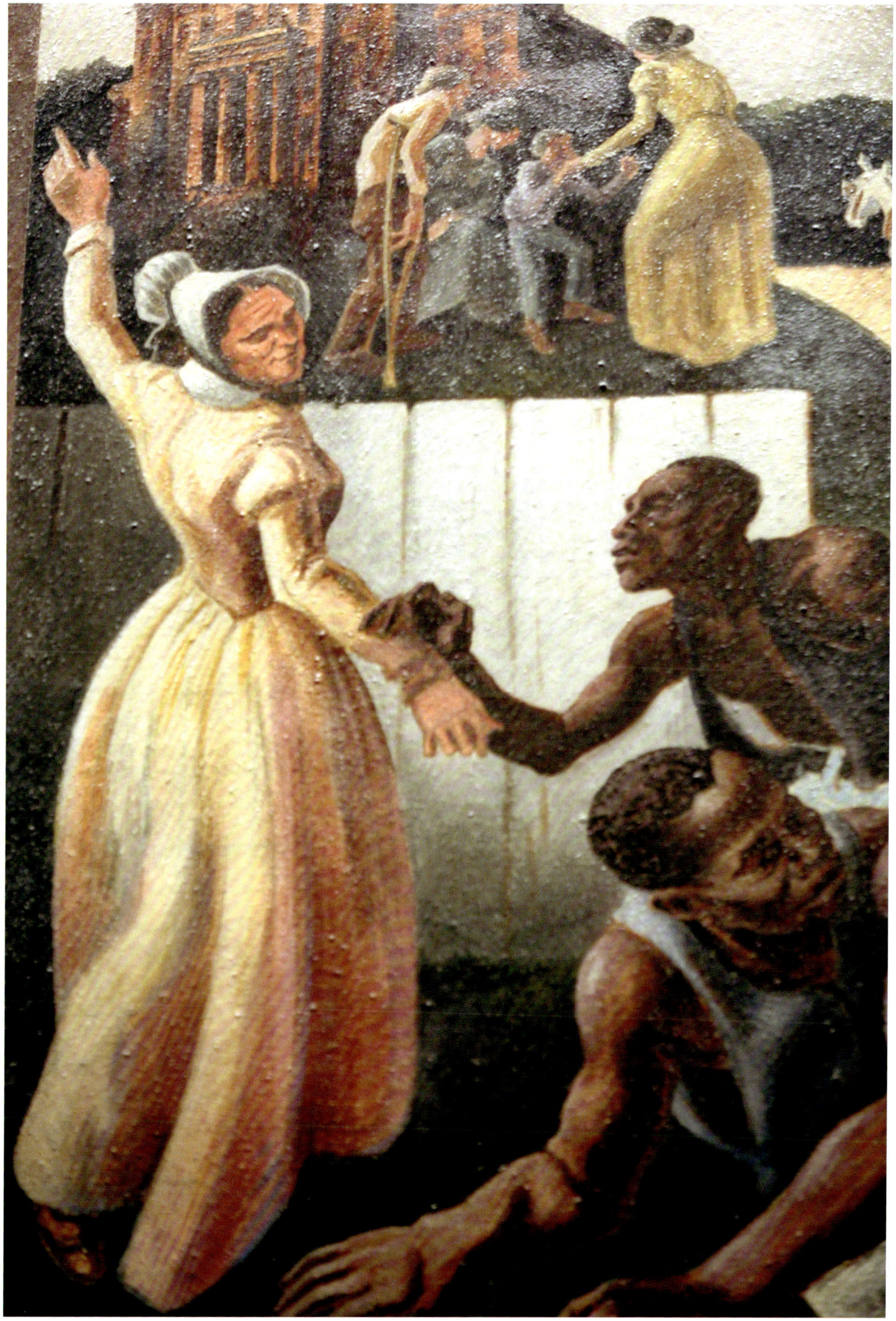

Detail representing the Underground Railroad from *Reformers and Squatters* panel in Indiana University Auditorium, undated. Photo credit: Indiana University.

Showalter Fountain

Centerpiece of the Fine Arts Plaza

This afternoon is a culmination of a dream long ago. . . . Indiana University has long been outstanding in the sciences and in the professions. Yet it remembers its ancient foundation upon the classics. Today in dedicating this magnificent Fountain with its central figure the goddess of love, truth, and beauty, we proudly reaffirm our belief in the importance of the arts and the life of the spirit.

— Indiana University President Herman B Wells at dedication ceremony

As early as 1939 architectural drawings from the architectural firm Eggers and Higgins of New York, proposed what was then referred to as a Fine Arts Group (the Indiana University Auditorium, Lilly Library, and the Fine Arts Building) with a fountain to be located in the central plaza enclosed by these buildings. With the completion of the Auditorium in 1941, the firm began submitting multiple concepts for a memorial fountain; however, it was nearly another ten years before progress was made.

While Eggers and Higgins continued to serve as the supervising architects for the project and conceptualized most of the overall design for the fountain itself, in 1952 Robert Laurent (professor of Fine Arts 1942–60) was selected to design a sculpture to serve as the centerpiece of the fountain basin. Born in Concarneau, France, Robert Laurent immigrated to the United States at the age of twenty to study under American Modernist painter, Hamilton Easter Field, and was later inspired by the bronze fountain groups created by Carl Milles at Cranbrook and in St. Louis. In 1954 Laurent began to visualize his design for the fountain while on sabbatical leave from IU as an artist-in-residence at the American Academy in Rome. With the original intention to create the sculpture in marble, Laurent was influenced by the essence of the Roman fountains and ultimately chose to utilize the lost-wax process for his figures, a traditional Italian technique of bronze casting. His design culminated in the imposing bronze, water-spouting rendition of the mythological story of the birth of Venus that we see today.

The bronze casts for the sculpture were completed by the Nicci Foundry in Rome in the summer of 1958 and shipped to Bloomington the following winter. In July 1960, while Laurent was still in Rome, the contract for the building of the fountain was authorized, with construction commencing in the spring of 1961. Eggers and Higgins supervised the completion of the fountain: design of the fountain basin, installation of the dolphins, the jets of water, mosaic floor, and the lighting. The result was the stunning 15-foot Venus reclining in a clamshell, surrounded by four 6-foot, swimming dolphins and one smaller dolphin (originally a fish, which was quickly deemed incompatible with the rest of the sculpture and replaced).

Funded by a major contribution from Grace Montgomery Showalter (for many years the only woman on the IU Foundation Board of Directors) in memory of her late husband, Ralph W. Showalter, the fountain was dedicated on Sunday, October 22, 1961, to great fanfare.

Today, the fountain lies at the heart of the fine arts quadrant of campus—a tranquil respite on the students' daily commute. It also has been the center of student revelry, protests, and sometimes vandalism following major campus events, such as NCAA basketball championships. Bubbles and colored additives have been put in the water, IU basketball coach Bob Knight's firing was protested here, and multiple times a dol-

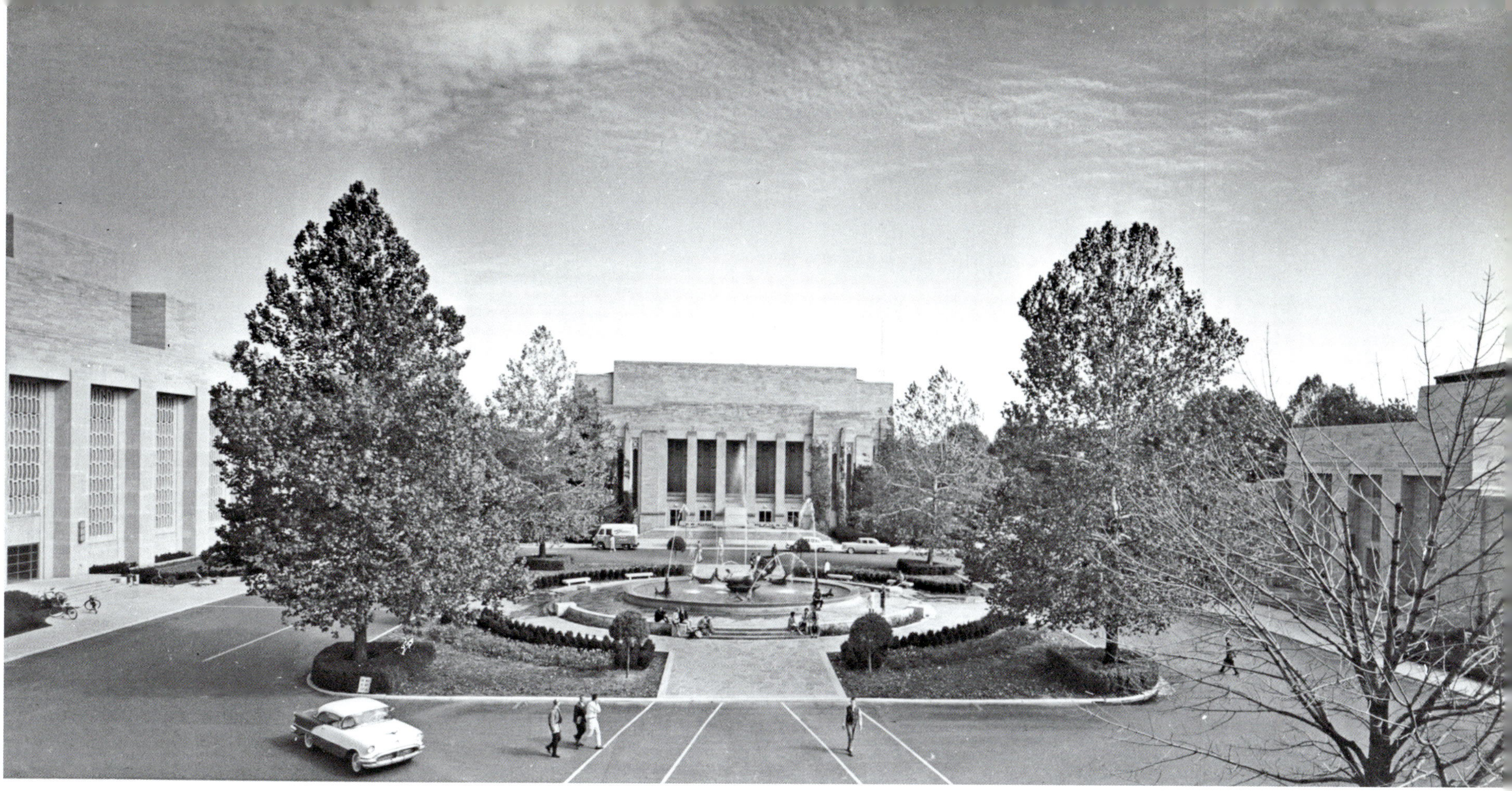

phin has mysteriously disappeared from the fountain, only to be recovered and restored to its place.

Two other Laurent sculptures grace the university campus: his limestone figures *Music* and *Dance* (1949) can be seen in the north and south niches of the Indiana University Auditorium foyer, and his large limestone bas-relief *Veritas Filia Temporis* (Truth Is the Daughter of Time; 1959) adorns the exterior wall of Ballantine Hall.

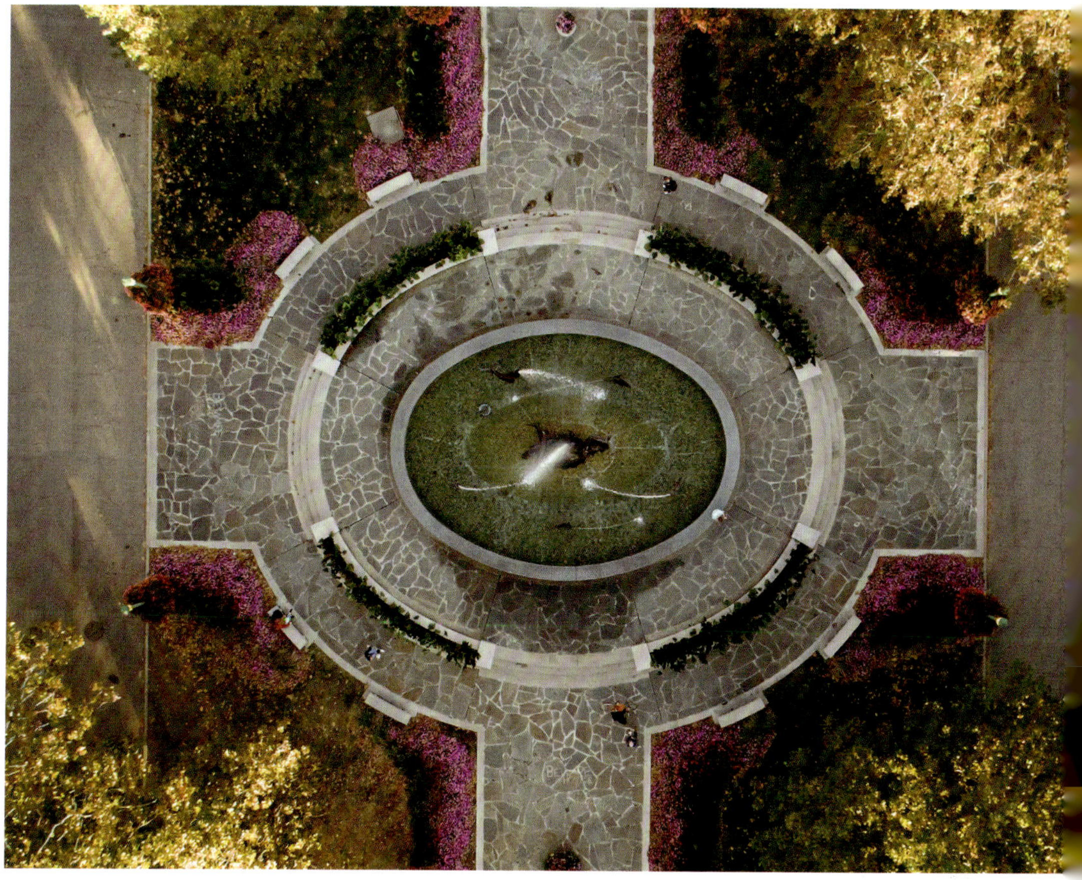

Above, Fine Arts Plaza, including the Fine Arts Building (*left*), Indiana University Auditorium (*center*), and Lilly Library (*right*), 1965. P0025887, IU Archives.

Right, Overhead view of Showalter Fountain with mosaic plaza, 2016. Photo credit: Indiana University.

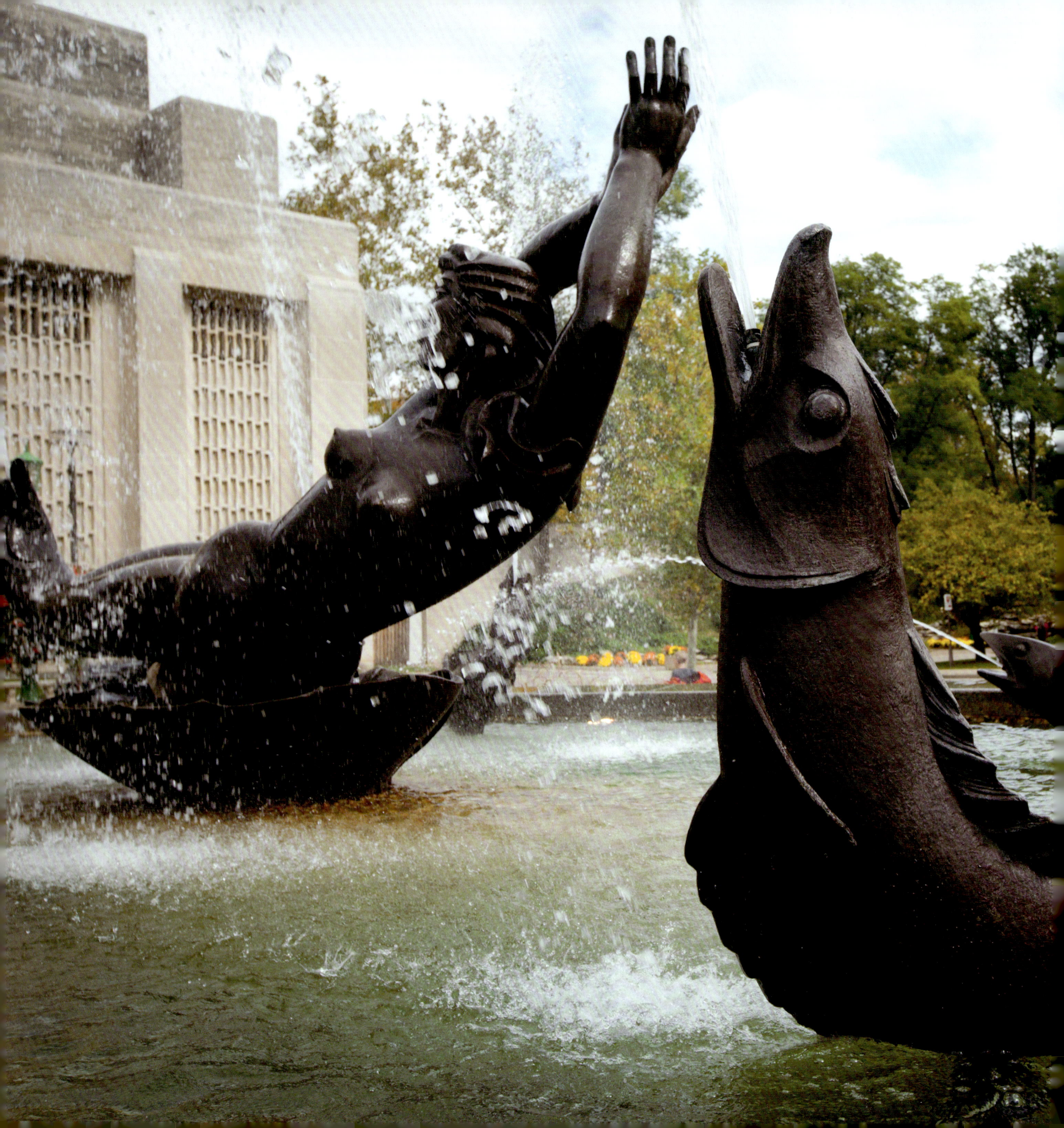

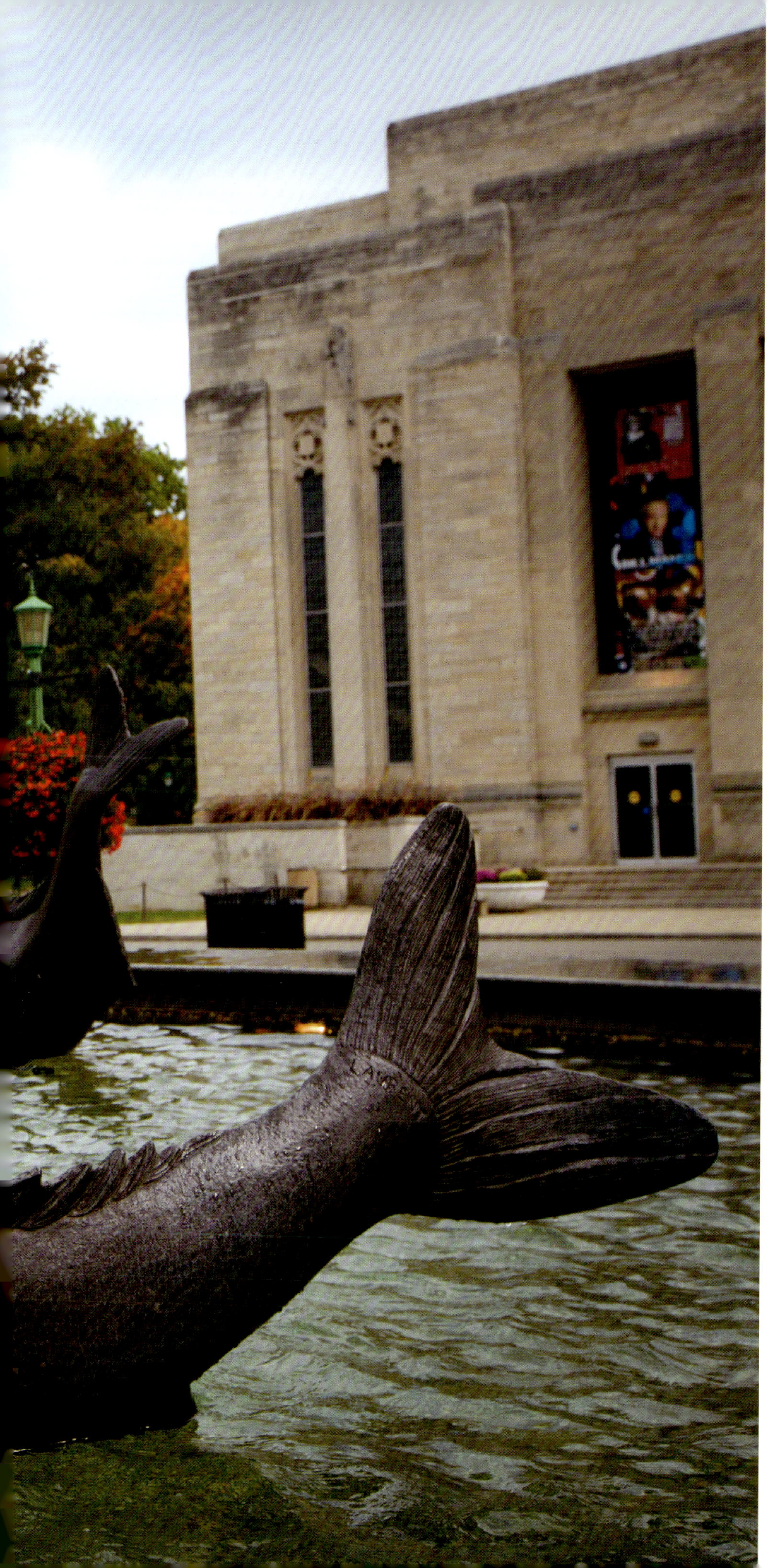

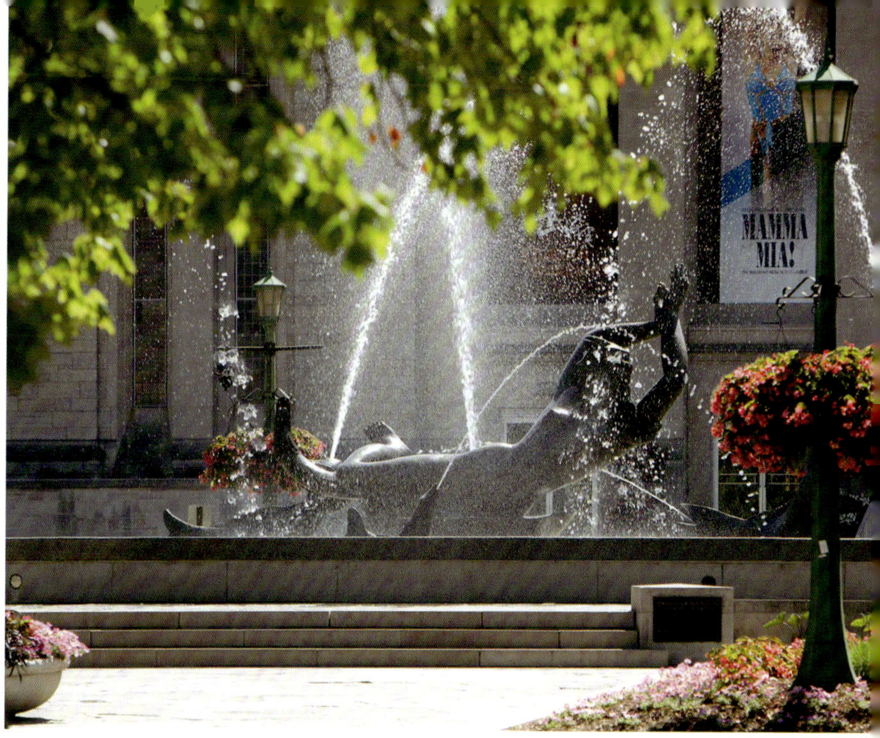

Looking east through Showalter Fountain, undated.
Photo credit: Indiana University.

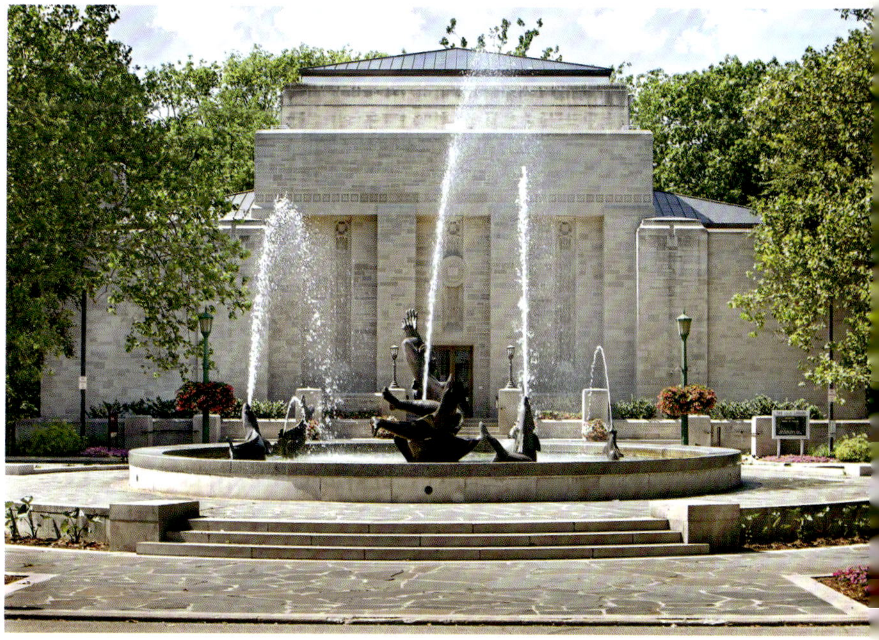

Above, Lilly Library through Showalter Fountain, undated.
Photo credit: Indiana University.

Facing, Robert Laurent's Modernist sculpture, *The Birth of Venus*, featuring Venus surrounded by five dolphins, 2016.
Photo credit: Tyagan Miller.

The Space Between: Adam and Eve

by Jean-Paul Darriau

Adam and Eve is the oldest idea we have of first man and first woman in our history, if we begin with the Hebrews first and the Greeks second (from which two, Christianity gets its beginning). But my interest here was in reminding myself and others of a need that life today often aggravates in us—the one of making a fresh start—from scratch; at least once in our life, to strip things down as bare as the statues.

—Jean-Paul Darriau

ON THE EASTERN EDGE OF DUNN'S WOODS, across from Kirkwood Hall, rests the bronze statue, *The Space Between: Adam and Eve*. The sculpture was created by IU professor and sculptor Jean-Paul Darriau (1929–2006), whose work has been shown in prestigious venues, including at the Guggenheim Museum, the Hirshhorn Museum and Sculpture Garden in Washington, DC, and the Galleria Schneider in Rome.

Darriau's career at IU spanned thirty-five years. A beloved teacher, he was voted one of Indiana University's top twenty-five professors in a 1995 campus-wide survey. His work was often symbolic, such as his *Red, Blond, Black and Olive*, in downtown Bloomington, which represents the world's four major races. Another of Darriau's Eves greets visitors at the entrance to the Fine Arts Building.

The Space Between: Adam and Eve has welcomed visitors to Dunn's Woods since its completion in 1968. It is believed that the artist used his children as models for the sculpture. Sharing a common concrete base, both figures are approximately 5 feet tall, with Eve about 2 inches shorter than Adam. The poses are serene, but the two seem to be in quiet movement forward, with their arms reaching toward each other. According to Sherry Rouse, the university's curator of campus art, it seems likely that the artist wanted us to think of Adam and Eve separately, rather than as a couple, with the space between them representing the differences between man and woman. However, the observer also could see Adam and Eve as representing every man and every woman, differing, but held together by the bonds of love.[1]

The sculpture has been damaged twice. The first time, Adam's penis was sawed off; it took Darriau many attempts to perfectly sculpt a second one. The second time, a severe storm in August 2012 felled trees in Dunn's Woods and throughout the campus, with Adam taking a direct hit from a falling tree, and Eve and the pedestal being knocked askew. This incident required removing the statues for the first time so repairs could be made. For decades IU students have enjoyed dressing Adam and Eve, the styles changing with fashion trends or fancy over the years.

Facing, Robert Laurent's *The Space Between: Adam and Eve* in Dunn's Woods, 2012. Photo credit: Tyagan Miller.

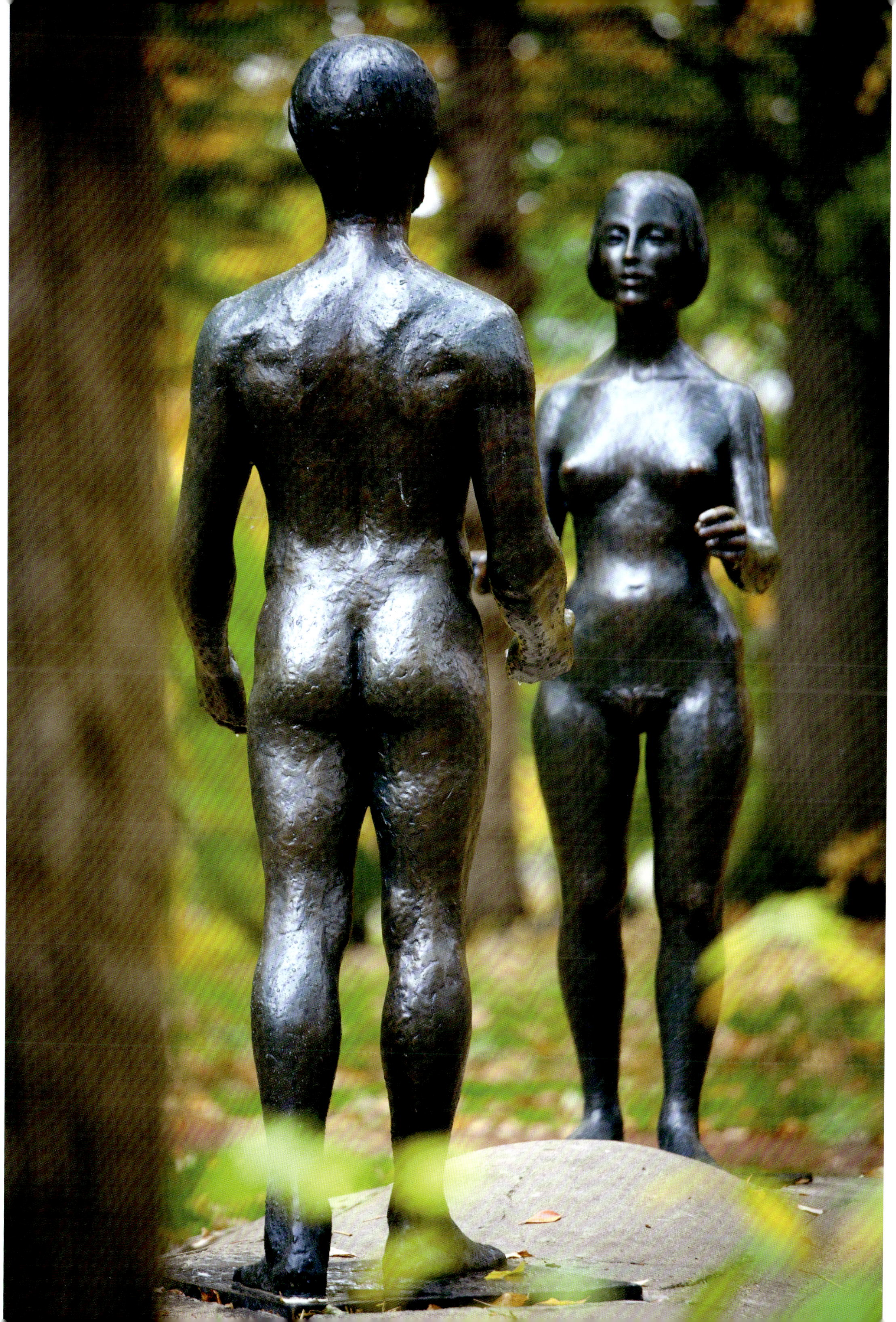

Arthur R. Metz Memorial Carillon

Music must take rank as the highest of the fine arts—as the one which, more than any other, ministers to human welfare.

—bell inscription

A Grand Bell Tower

STANDING PROUDLY ON ITS LOFTY PERCH NEAR Seventeenth Street and Jordan Avenue, the highest elevation on the IU Bloomington campus, is the Arthur R. Metz Memorial Carillon tower. In 1970, the Arthur R. Metz Foundation made a gift of the bell tower to the university in memory of its founder and namesake (1887–1963). Created by Dr. Metz in 1948, the foundation's original mission was to help medical students. In 1955, Metz established a scholarship program at IU to reward one outstanding senior male student. In 1963 this was doubled to include an exceptional senior female student. The number of scholarships has grown since his death, and the foundation continues to honor students who exhibit excellence in scholarship, leadership, and character and show "evidence of promise and future usefulness."[1]

The Metz Carillon was designed by Alfred John Porteous, senior partner with the Wright Porteous and Lowe firm of Indianapolis. It is Brutalist Modern in style and is constructed of poured concrete panels, which are smooth but with grooves that add textural interest. Standing nearly 93 feet tall, the carillon is an imposing structure, the top of which can be seen from afar. The freestanding tower houses an instrument room and, with sixty-one bells, is the larger of two carillons on the campus (the smaller carillon atop the Music Building Addition has forty-two bells). The bells were crafted at the Royal Eijsbouts bell foundry in Asten, the Netherlands, and installed by their technicians. Each bell in the Metz Carillon is engraved with an inscription. Following are several of the inscriptions on carillon bells:

> Sing these chimes of Indiana,
> Hail to the crimson hue;
> Sing her praise to Gloriana,
> Hail to our old IU.
>
> —Hoagy Carmichael, "Chimes of Indiana"

> Music is the universal language of mankind—poetry their universal pastime and delight.
>
> —Henry Wadsworth Longfellow, "Outre-Mer"

> Those evening bells! Those evening bells!
> How many a tale their music tells,
> Of youth, and home, and that sweet time,
> When last I heard their soothing chime.
>
> —Thomas Moore, "Those Evening Bells"

> The man that hath no music in himself,
> Nor is not moved with concord of sweet sounds,
> Is fit for treasons, stratagems, and spoils.
>
> —William Shakespeare, *The Merchant of Venice*

> Music resembles poetry; in each
> Are nameless graces which no methods teach,
> And which a master-hand alone can reach.
>
> —Alexander Pope, "Essay on Criticism"

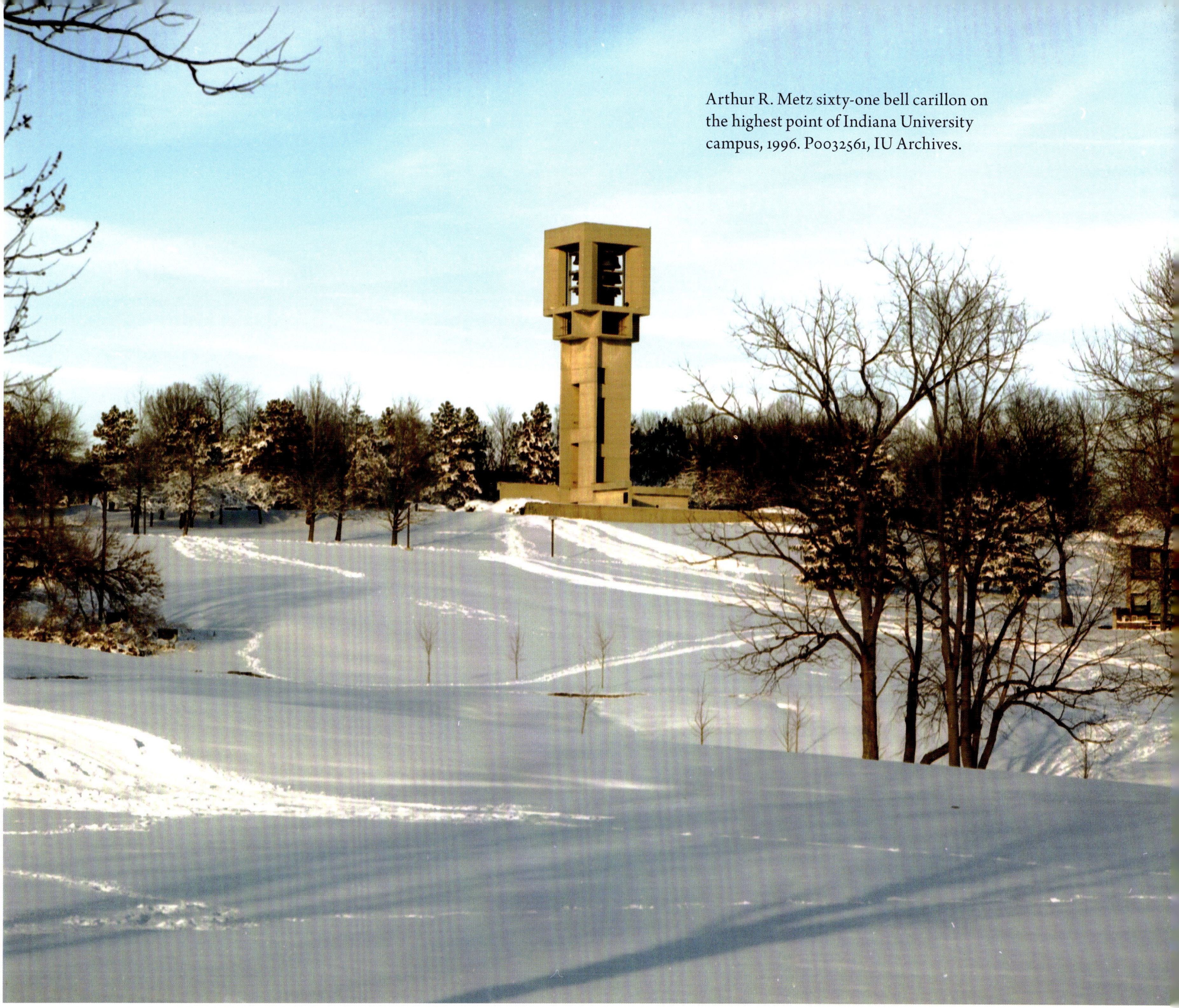

Arthur R. Metz sixty-one bell carillon on the highest point of Indiana University campus, 1996. P0032561, IU Archives.

A carillon is the heaviest musical instrument, and each note is produced by an individual bell, the musical range determined by the number of bells—with its unusually large number of bells, the Arthur R. Metz Memorial Carillon has an impressive range. Its sixty-one bells range in weight from 27 pounds to over 3 tons. The Jacobs School of Music maintains the carillon although it is rarely played.

In 2017 the university announced plans to move the carillon to a more central site on campus adjoining the Jesse H. and Beulah Chanley Cox Arboretum. Here larger audiences will be able to enjoy regular concerts performed by faculty from the Jacobs School of Music. Four new bells will be added, making the Arthur R. Metz Carillon a "grand carillon," one of only thirty worldwide.

Peau Rouge Indiana

by Alexander Calder

Grasping the heart of the situation he was asked to design for, Calder made a piece that is inseparable from the building it introduces. In the vital, upward thrust of its form and the brightness of its color, the stabile provides an emphatic accent to the sturdy façade of the Musical Arts Center.

—Dedication Week Festival

THE *PEAU ROUGE INDIANA* IS A MONUMENTAL stabile created in 1970 by the acclaimed U.S. sculptor Alexander Calder; it stands on the front lawn of the Musical Arts Center (MAC). The upward thrust of the inherently abstract stabile's form and its bold red-orange color, known as Calder Red, are in bold juxtaposition to the Brutalist Modern concrete-and-glass facade of the MAC. Generously funded by 1910 IU alumnus, attorney, and politician Oscar J. (Jack) Ewing of Greensburg, Indiana, the stabile was created at Calder's studio in Saché, France. After casting, it was erected at a foundry in Tours, France, then disassembled for shipment to Bloomington, where it was reerected in accordance with Calder's instructions.

Calder is well known for his whimsical toys, vibrant mobiles, and stationary sculptures known as stabiles. His *Peau Rouge Indiana*, literally Indiana Red Skin, stands 40 feet high and is constructed of steel plates held together with square-headed steel bolts. Its color, size, and originality draw the viewers' eyes to the sculpture as well as to the entrance of the Musical Arts Center: "Calder's stabile stands as if guarding the MAC and perpetuates the vibrant spirit of fantasy, introducing all to the intriguing world of music and dance hidden inside the MAC's walls."[1]

Peau Rogue Indiana was just one of Calder's best-known stabiles to make its debut in 1970–71: the second, *Bent Propeller*, was installed at the World Trade Center in New York. That hauntingly named stabile was lost amid the collapsing rubble of September 11, 2011, but *Peau Rogue Indiana* continues to greet thousands of students, faculty, and Indiana University campus visitors every day.

Peau Rouge Indiana, the bold red-orange creation of American sculptor Alexander Calder, 2016. Photo credit: Indiana University.

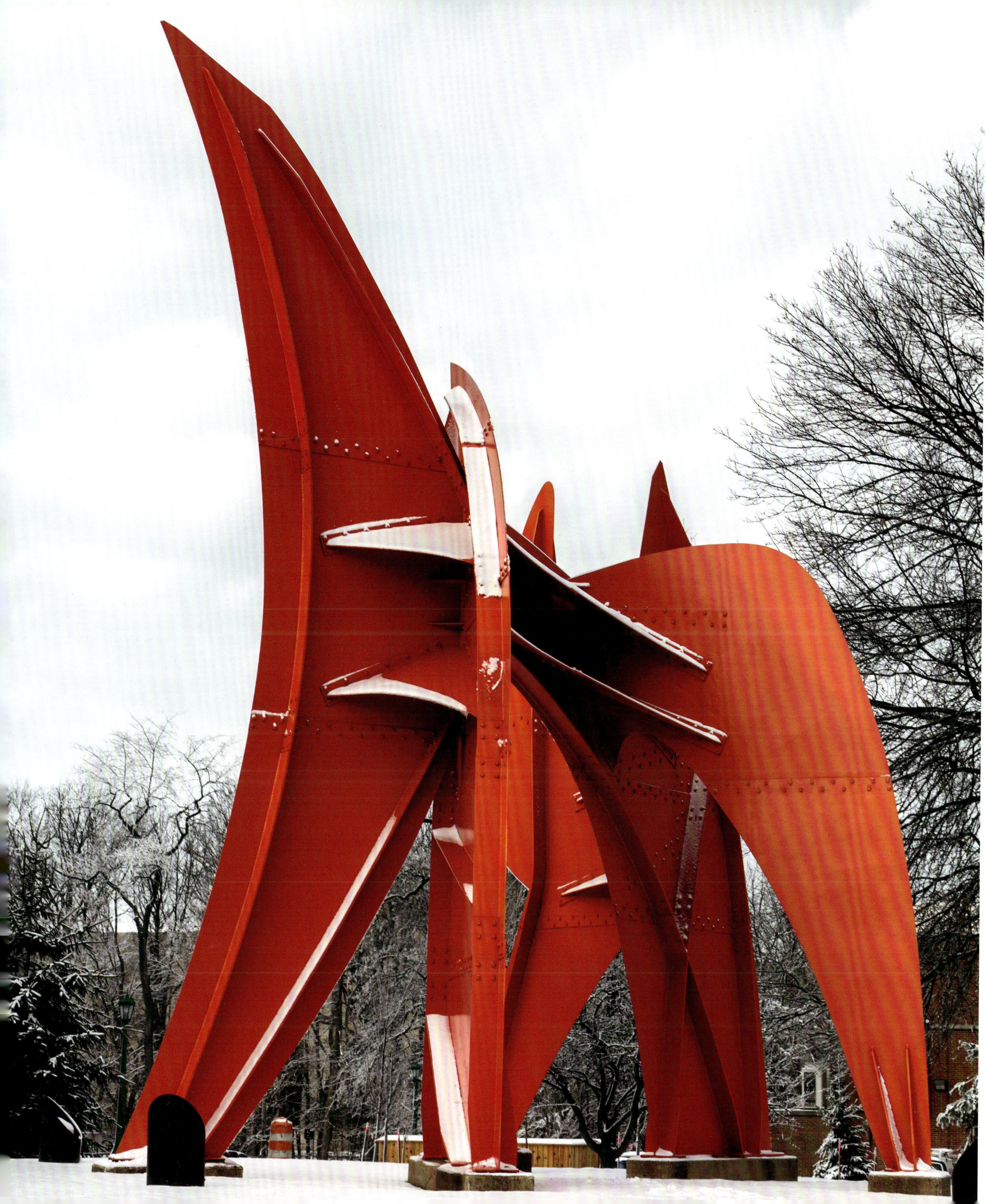

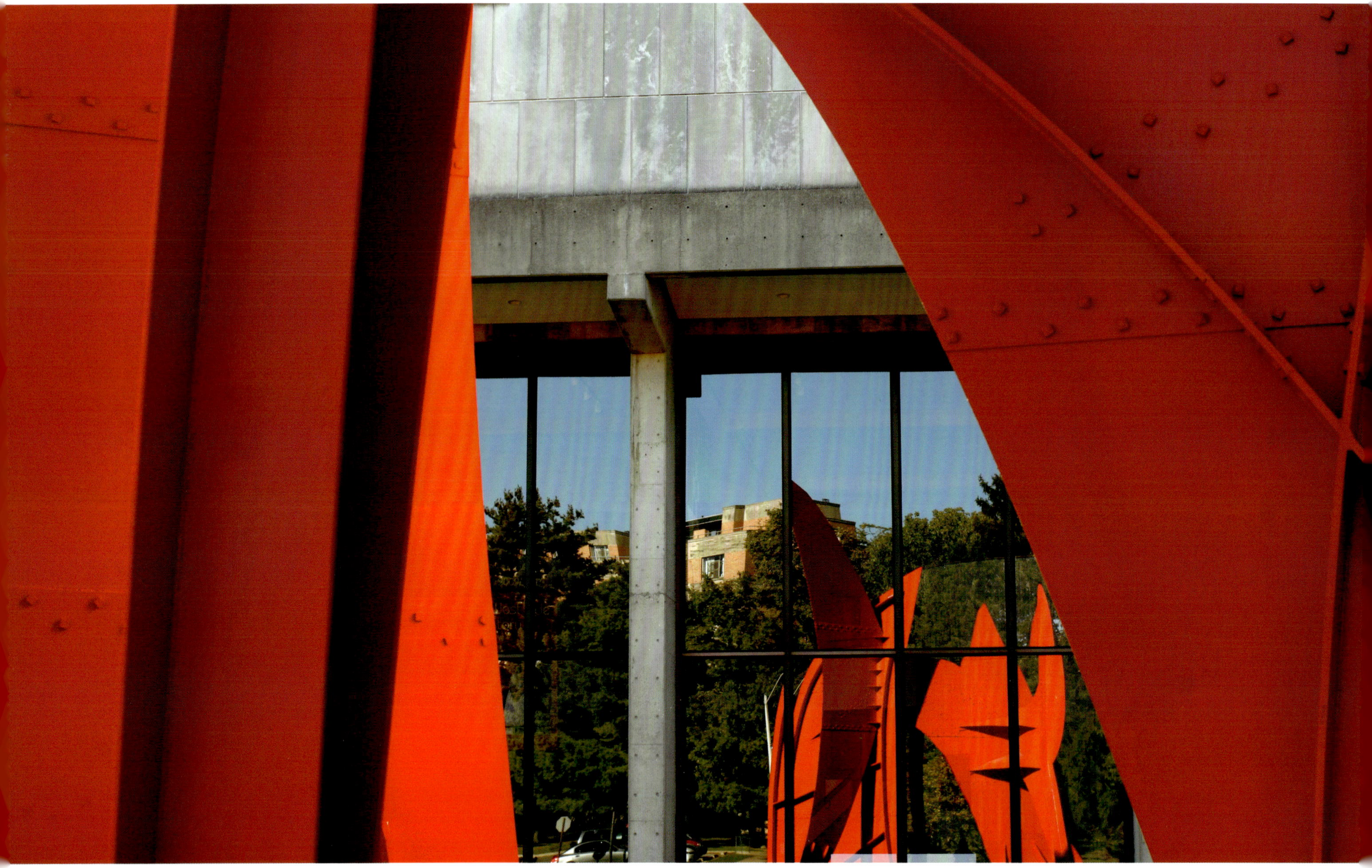

Above, Peau Rouge reflected in Musical Arts Center window, 2009. Photo credit: Indiana University.

Facing, Peau Rouge from inside Musical Arts Center, undated. Photo credit: Indiana University.

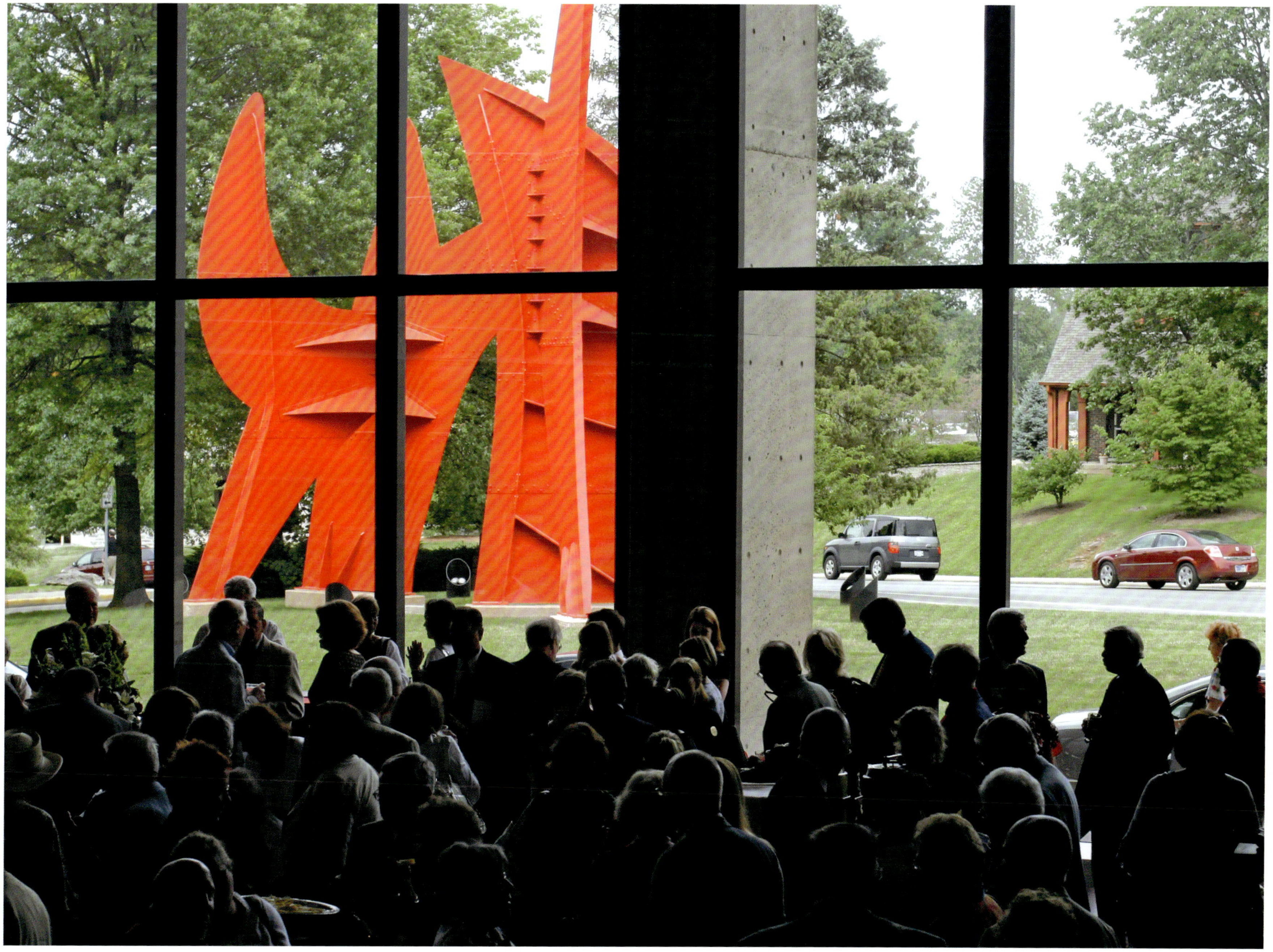

Jesse H. and Beulah Chanley Cox Arboretum

A Campus Botanical Garden and Park

The Hoosier Arboretum, to be created on the historic site of the Tenth Street Stadium, will be adorned with trees and shrubs and wildflowers from every county in the state, every state of our nation, and every nation of our globe, limited only by natural restrictions of climate and soil. It will be a place where students can find wooded tranquility and where alumni can recapture the "sense of something dear gone by," a place of serenity and beauty that will refresh the spirits of those who come to us seeking knowledge.

—President John W. Ryan

The original Memorial Stadium constructed in 1925 was sited along Tenth Street, then the northern campus boundary. Ensuing years brought growth that extended to the north and east, and by the time a new Memorial Stadium was completed on Seventeenth Street in 1960, the old site was in the midst of the campus academic core. Although the old stadium had become an impediment to campus traffic flow, both pedestrian and vehicular, there was reluctance to remove the structure because of its central location and venue for large events. Thus, it continued to be used for such functions as the Little 500 bicycle race, varsity track and field, and ROTC for the next twenty-two years, but under a new name: the Tenth Street Stadium. It was also the location for the race scenes in the 1979 film *Breaking Away*.

In the early 1980s it became clear that deterioration had taken its toll, with razing the old stadium the only option. The question became what to do with the centrally located and highly visible site itself. Supplemental parking quickly became a popular suggestion, and a strong case was presented that the programs in surrounding buildings needed a convenient place for their students, faculty, and visitors to park.

A keen observer of campus history, Indiana University president John W. Ryan had other ideas. He understood that one of the key principals of IU's planning success had been the way courtyards, large and small, threaded throughout the campus. He considered the Tenth Street Stadium site to be the next logical location for campus green space development, as it would extend the string of green jewels created by Dunn's Woods, Dunn Meadow, the grounds around Bryan House, and Woodlawn Field.

With a Board of Trustees meeting imminent, Ryan knew that disposition of this parcel of land would be discussed. He asked the university architect's office to create a land-use plan based on his vision for further campus courtyard and green space expansion. Working quickly, the staff of IU architects and landscape designers developed a proposal that dedicated the area as an arboretum, which would contain ponds, green lawns, walkways, and specimen trees indigenous to Indiana. The trees would be planted in groupings according to variety, and the walkways would be wide enough to carry the large number of students moving through the Arboretum each day on their way to class in the heart of campus.

The Board of Trustees embraced the Arboretum concept and granted approval to move forward with detailed planning. A design team was formed, led by J. Terry Clapacs, university director of facilities. He was joined by Amy Applegate, university landscape architect and Frits Loonsten, a landscape architect from Indianapolis who was commissioned to design the general arboretum site plan, most specifically a pond and recirculating stream.

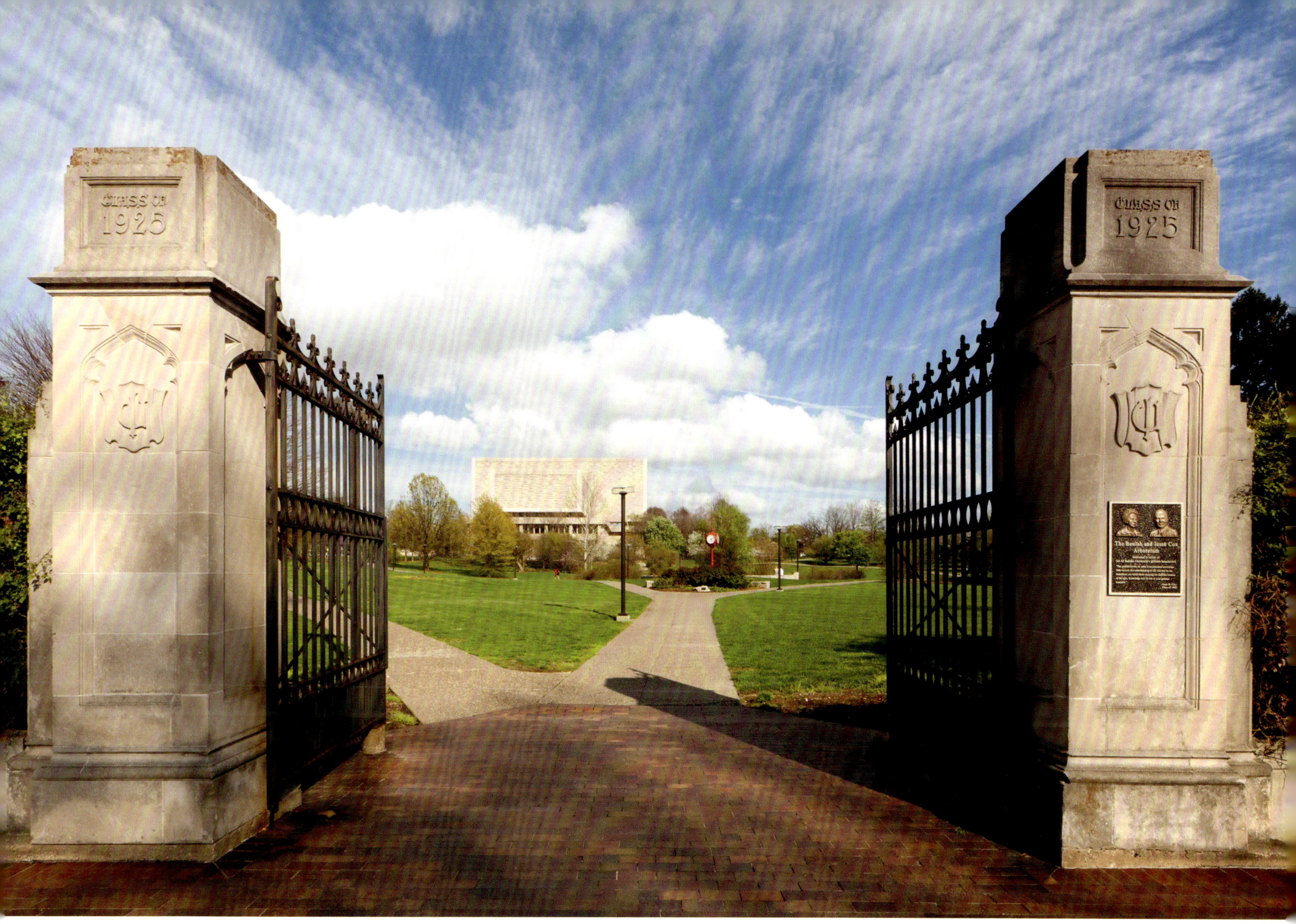

Looking east through Class of 1925 gates into Jesse H. and Beulah Chanley Cox Arboretum, 2016. Photo credit: Tyagan Miller.

Professor Charles Hagen of the Biology Department was retained to develop an accession list of plant materials and to identify possible research opportunities the Arboretum might engender; he envisioned an outdoor laboratory and research area for the study of plant sciences. The Arboretum would be developed so as to extend the "woodland campus" theme of Indiana University by selecting larger trees and woody plants that would augment the extensive collection already growing on the university grounds. The Arboretum was to serve as an instructional facility, not only for biologists, but also as a place to learn appreciation for aesthetics in public spaces. The resulting plan was presented and approved by the trustees in 1983, and demolition of the fifty-year-old stadium was soon underway.

The ramshackle Tenth Street Stadium practically fell to the ground on its own, and the site was swiftly cleared. The most unusual problem encountered during demolition was the large number of rats released from under the concrete structure.

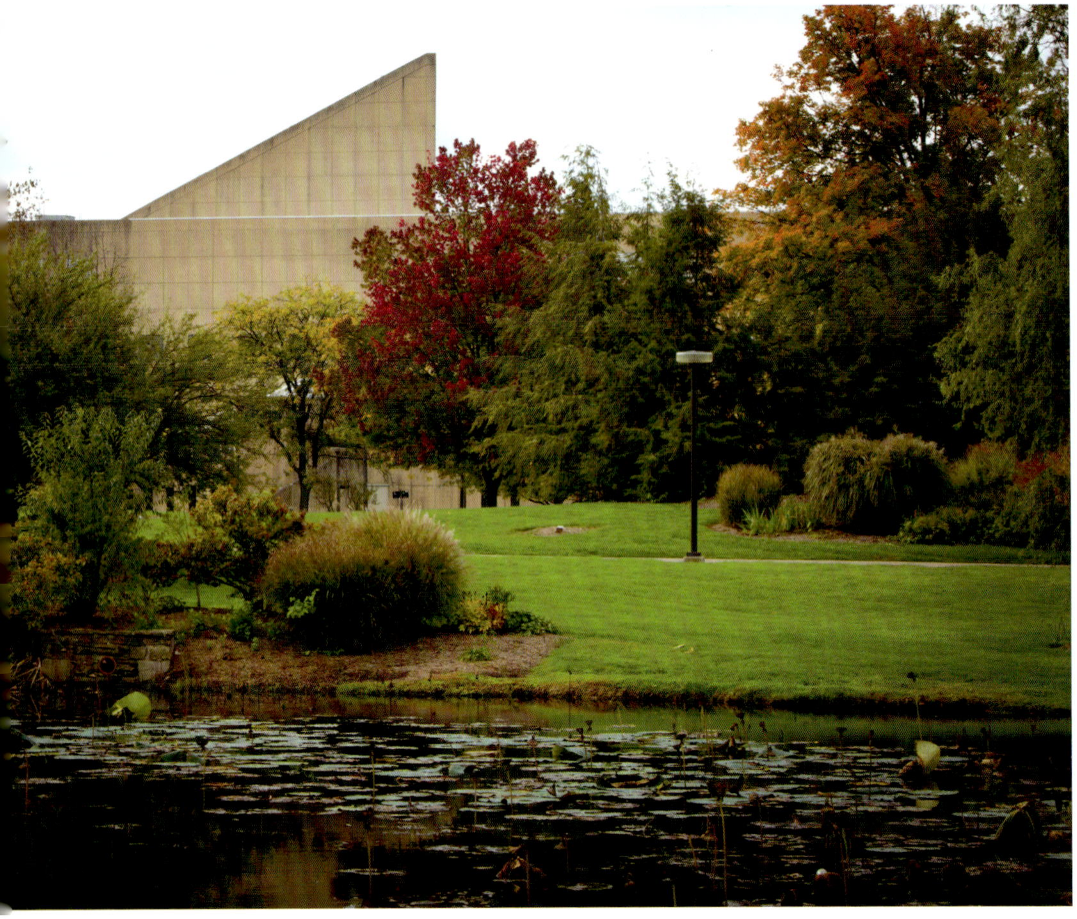

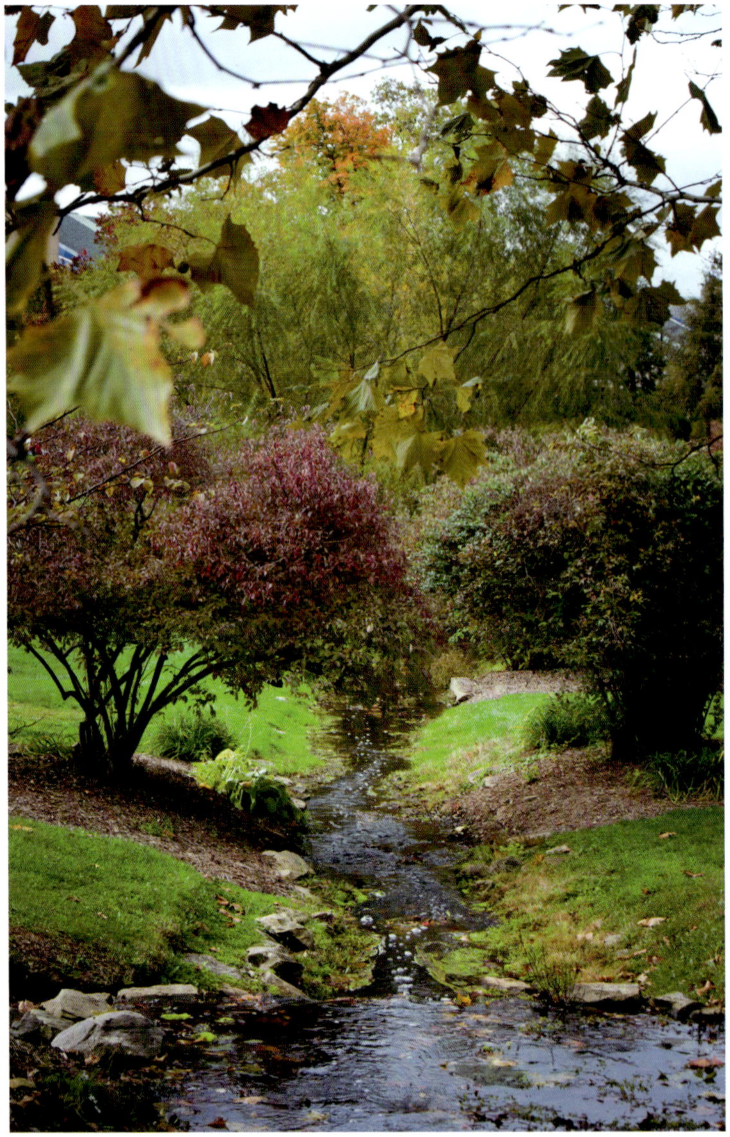

The rats scattered toward the campus, causing frenetic student reactions, but an emergency extermination plan quickly allayed concerns. Several historic elements from the old stadium were saved in place and subsequently incorporated into the Arboretum, including two flag towers from the grandstands, various limestone ticket booths, and the wrought-iron fence that formed the western boundary of the stadium site, a gift from the class of 1925. The largest of the ticket booths was taken apart stone by stone and reerected at the corner of Tenth Street and Fee Lane, now serving as a portico for hundreds of students who pass through the Arboretum each day.

The development of the Arboretum began when the Tenth Street Stadium was removed, and structural site work was completed in 1984. The Arboretum, however, continues to evolve today. It is now a mature, 11-acre park bounded by the Herman B Wells Library and the Global and International Studies Building to the east, Tenth Street to the north, Woodlawn Field to the west, and the Radio and Television Building and the Sidney and Lois Eskenazi Museum of Art to the south. Most of President John W. Ryan's hopes for the Arboretum have been fulfilled, including the planting of more than 450 trees and hundreds of varieties of shrubs and flowers from around the world. Broad walkways, expansive lawns, and a kidney-shaped pond fed by a recirculating stream and brimming with lily pads provide an inspirational setting for

Left, Looking south across the Arboretum with the triangular roofline of the Sidney and Lois Eskenazi Museum of Art in the background, 2016. Photo credit: Tyagan Miller.

Above, Recirculating stream flanked by lush foliage in the Arboretum, 2016. Photo credit: Tyagan Miller.

Facing, Arboretum gazebo looking over waterfall and stream, 2002. P0025015, IU Archives. Photo Credit: Paul Riley.

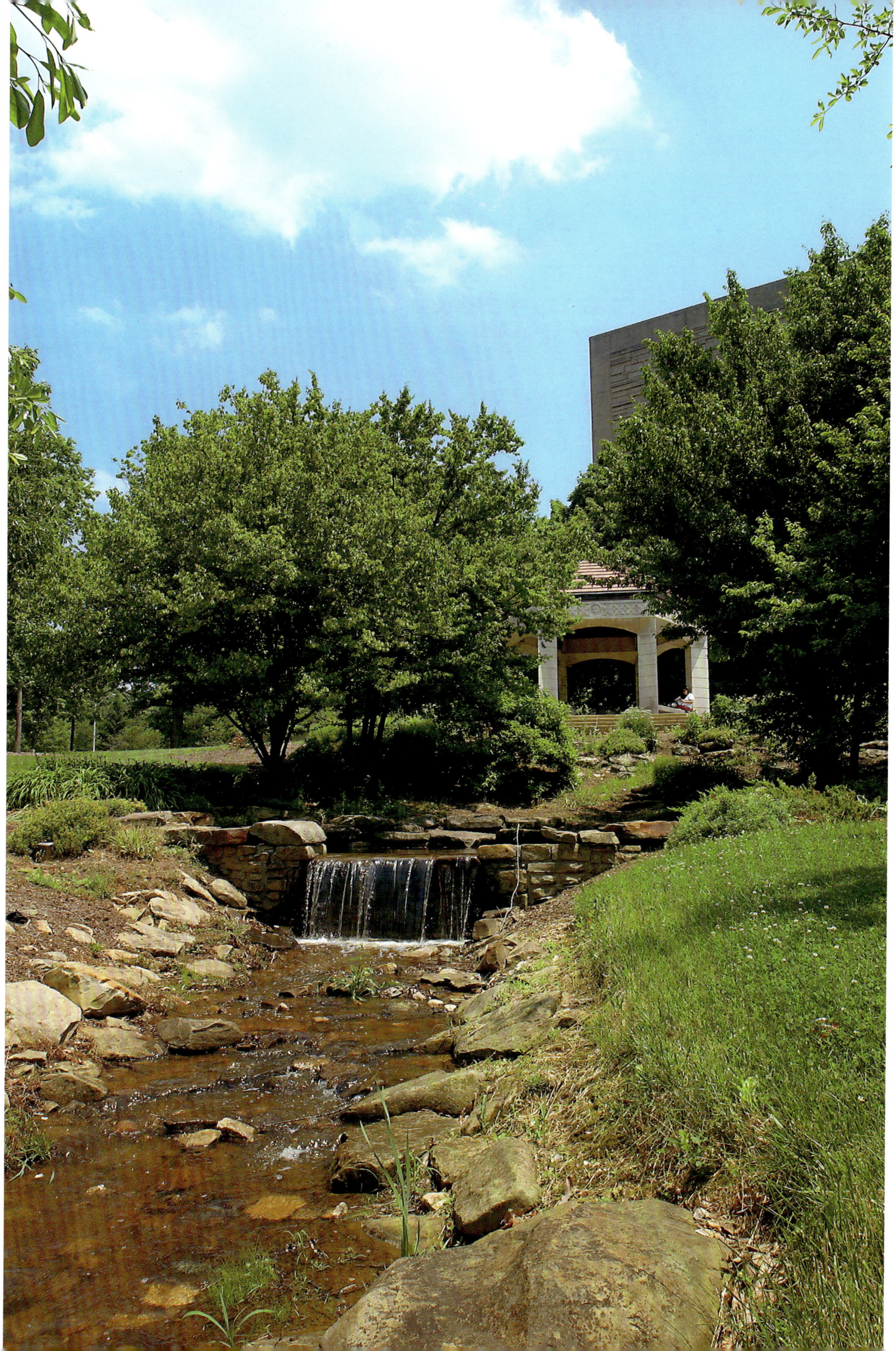

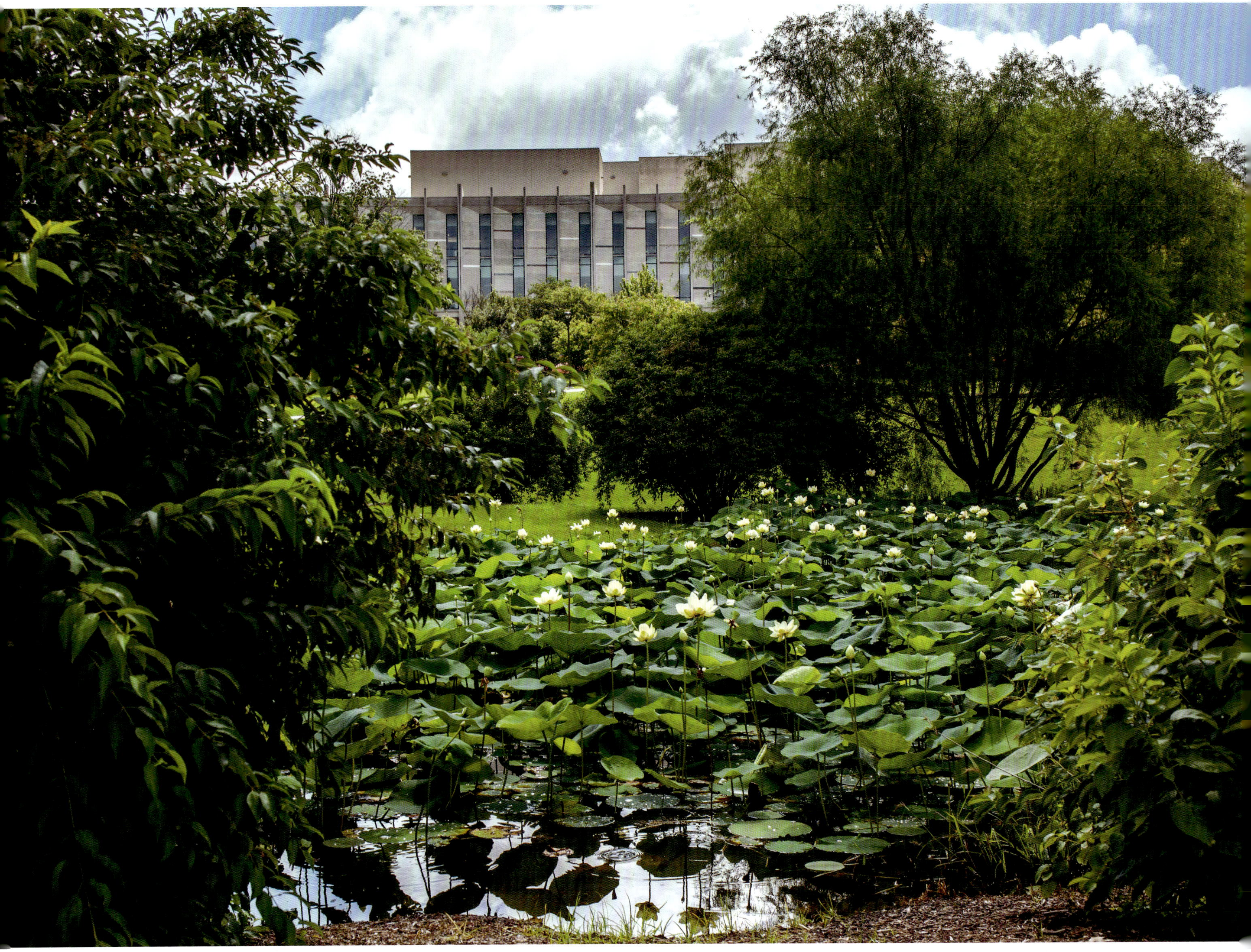

Above, The Arboretum's kidney-shaped pond brims with lily pads; Global and International Studies Building in background, 2015. Photo credit: Indiana University.

Facing, Looking east across the Arboretum toward Wells Library and Global and International Studies Building, 2016. Photo credit: Indiana University.

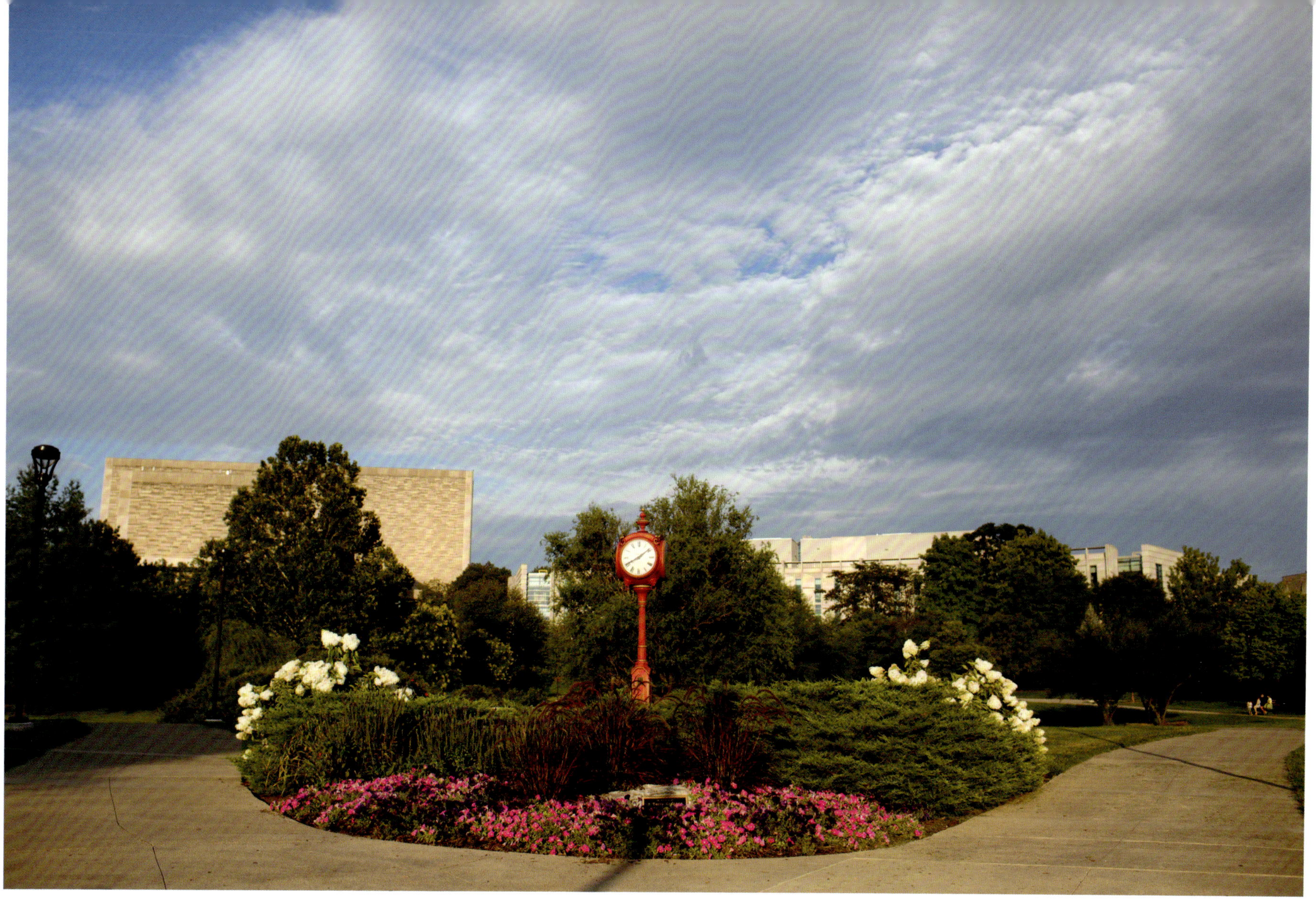

students as they stop for a respite from the day's rush or walk through the park to and from classes. The installation of the numerous trees, shrubs, flowers, and benches have been supported by gifts made to the university by donors to commemorate persons or events. Small placards placed at the base of each planting identify the flora variety and the donor.

At the east end of the Arboretum is an elegant, stone gazebo designed by Associate University Architect Robert W. Pond. The gazebo was named the Cox Pavilion for Jesse and Beulah Cox, and in 1997 the Arboretum was named for the couple as well. The Cox family funded the building of the gazebo and established an endowment fund for the continual care of the Arboretum grounds. They further enriched IU with their service and generosity by establishing the Cox Research Scholars program with their gift of $92 million, one of the largest philanthropic programs in the history of the university.

When the Arboretum was first planned, it was assumed the area would allow for development on a fifty-year continuum. The donor program of commemorative trees and other plants became so popular however, that university administrators were forced to consider alternate possibilities for such gifts. Today the entire Bloomington campus has been declared an arboretum, with the Jesse H. and Beulah Chanley Cox Arboretum at its center. Small placards scattered across campus mark a gift tree, bench, or shrub. These donor programs provide popular opportunities for alumni and friends of IU to participate in preserving Indiana University Bloomington as one of the nation's most beautiful college campuses.

Sample Gates

Celebrated Gateway to Indiana University

The grounds which all of us enter today through these gates are hallowed we think by an echo of the footsteps of thousands of members of the Indiana University community who came here throughout one hundred and two years, in their search for greater knowledge and understanding. . . . The gates stand as a monument to those who have gone before us, to the work and vision of all who've helped to bring this university to greatness.

—President John W. Ryan at dedication ceremony

BECAUSE THEIR DESIGN BLENDS SEAMLESSLY with the adjacent, much older campus architecture, many are often surprised to learn that the Sample Gates were not constructed until 1987. The vision for a campus entryway at Kirkwood Avenue, however, predates many of the early campus buildings. A mere fifteen years after the move to the present-day campus, members of the classes of 1899 through 1902 established a university arch fund for the construction of an arch over the Kirkwood Avenue entrance to the campus.[1]

The students, however, learned that Theodore F. Rose, IU alumnus (AB 1875) and trustee, was already pursuing the acquisition of two porticos from the University Building at Seminary Square for a similar purpose.[2] Thus, the funds were diverted toward the purchase of chimes for the Student Building, which was then under construction and dedicated on June 19, 1905. According to IU historian Thomas Clark, it became apparent that the narrow Gothic Seminary Square arches "would only serve further to block entrance to the campus, not even pedestrians could use the side entries with comfort. A less practical use had to be found for this cherished memento."[3] Instead, the porticos became the backbone for a new well house on the site of the campus cistern. The Rose Well House, a gift from Theodore Rose, was a memorial to the class of 1875. It was completed in time for graduation on June 2, 1908.

In the ensuing decades, several designs were proposed for the Kirkwood entrance to the campus, including a blocky, unadorned iteration from Newell Sanders (alumnus and U.S. senator 1912–13) in 1932, and in the same year four alternative designs more in keeping with the architectural style of the Old Crescent from Chicago architectural firm Granger, Lowe and Bollenbacher. Almost thirty years later, in 1961, university architect Eggers and Higgins presented a scheme for a "Fifth Street Gateway," which included plans to close the road that then ran through campus and replace it with a grassy mall. Their proposals ranged from Gothic to sleek, linear, and modernistic. The more traditional submission—quite similar to the structure that we have today—was chosen and was to be completed for the university's sesquicentennial.

Following the official announcement of its imminent construction in March 1972, opposition arose to what some students, faculty, and members of the community considered "wasteful alumni spending," and the project again was postponed. Finally, in the 1980s, when the majority of the opposition to the proposal had quieted, longtime university director of scholarships and financial aid Edson Sample stepped forward to fund a design by then associate university architect Robert W. Pond. The gates honor Sample's parents, Louise Waite Sample and Kimsey Ownbey Sample Sr. The completion of the Sample Gates coincided with a larger plan for the west side of campus that included permanently closing off traffic from Indiana Avenue east through campus and adding landscaping, brick paving, and benches in the area between the sundial and Indiana Avenue. Nearly a century in the

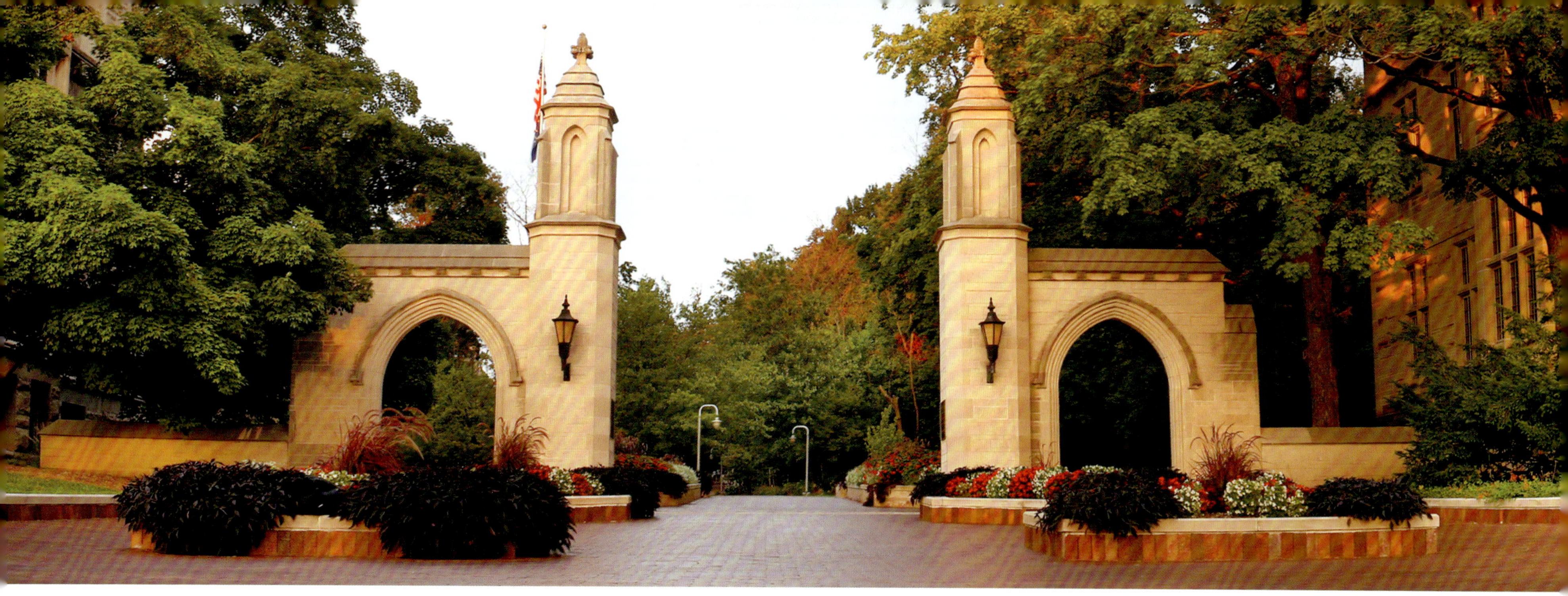

Above, Summertime at Sample Gates; note Gothic towers and pointed arches, 2016. Photo credit: Indiana University.

Below, Looking west through Sample Gates down Kirkwood Avenue, 2015. Photo credit: Indiana University.

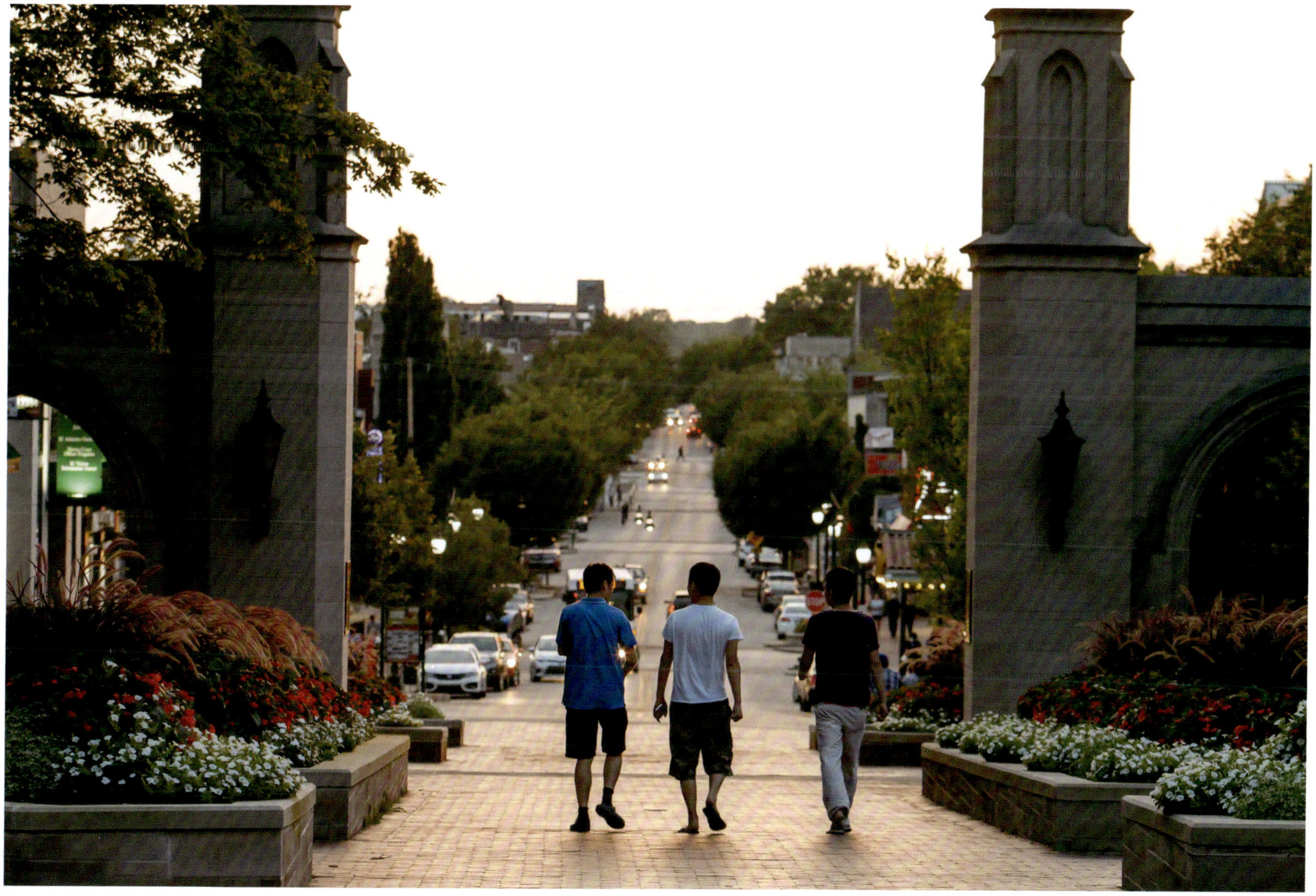

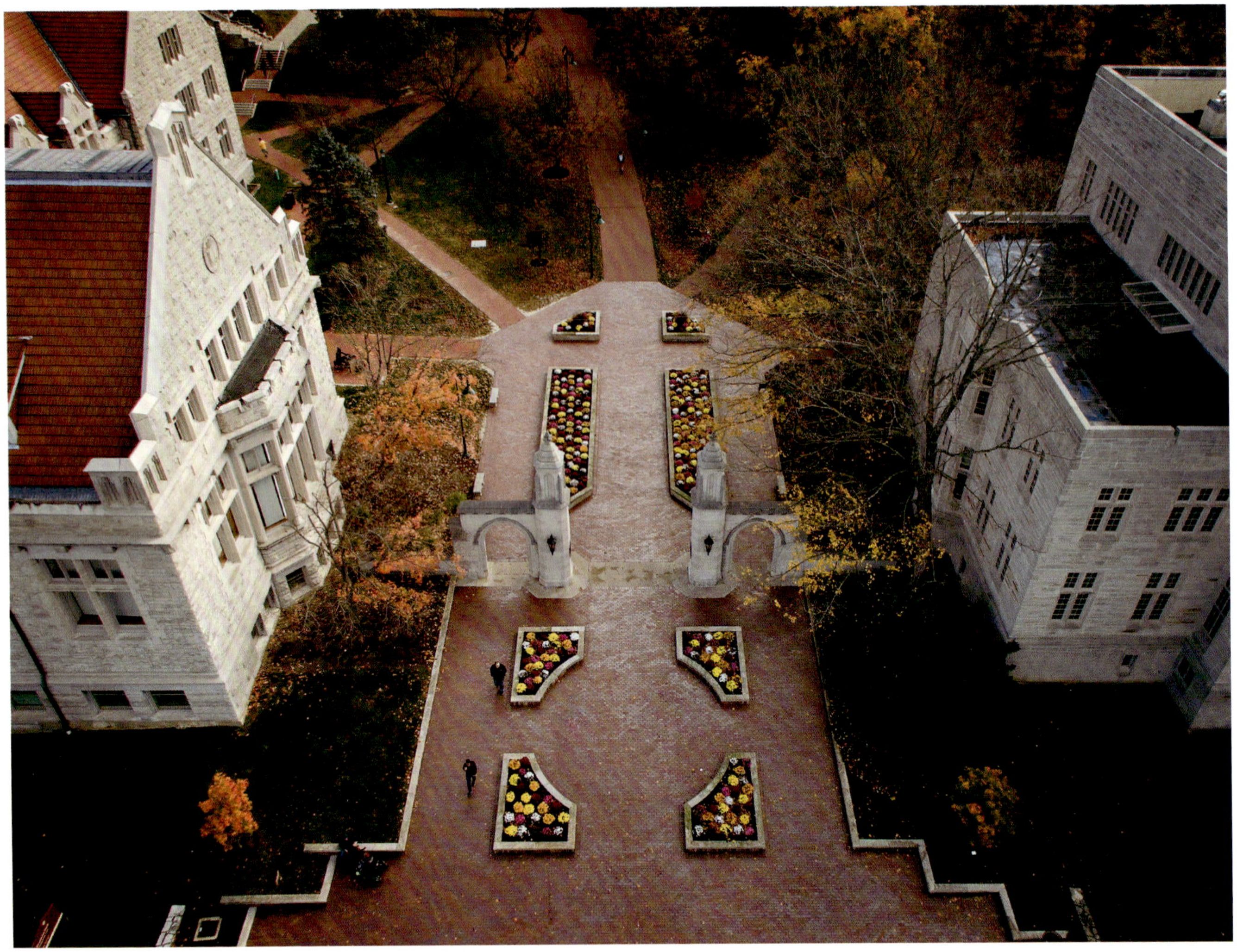

Aerial view of Sample Gates plaza with Franklin Hall on left and Bryan Hall on right, 2016. Photo credit: Indiana University.

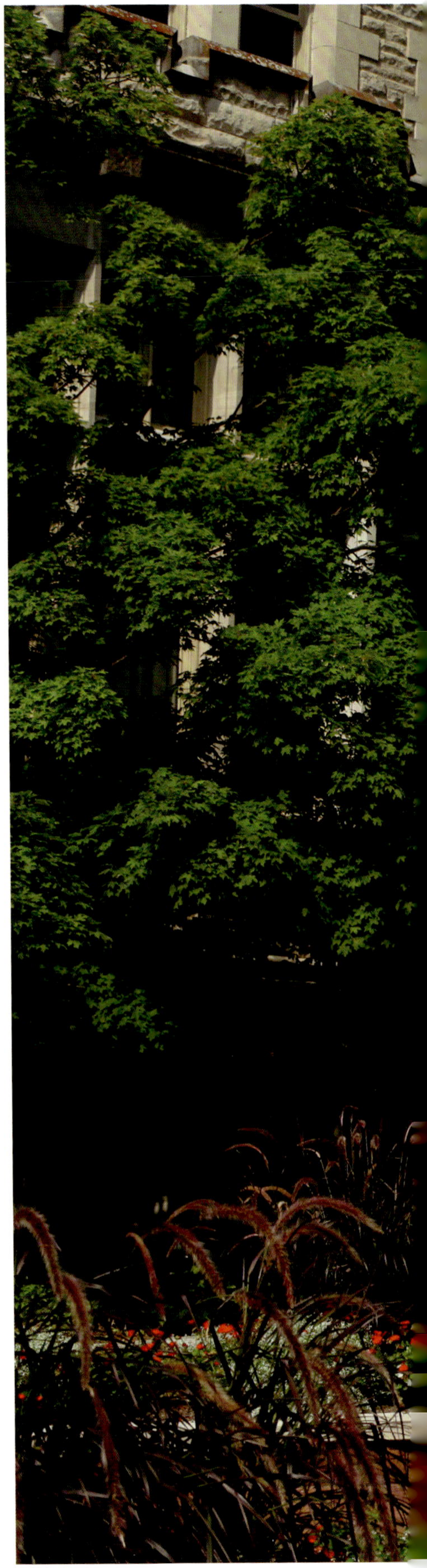

making, the Sample Gates were finally dedicated on June 13, 1987, and serve as an iconic landmark at the original entrance to Indiana University.

The Sample Gates are built of Indiana limestone in a smooth ashlar pattern. Gothic style features include the towers that frame the entrance. Each is embellished with four recessed, blind arches and a pitched roof topped by a finial. The towers are connected to short walls that include an open, pointed arch and a roof with a decorative cornice. This frequently photographed and painted gateway to the university changes from season to season: in the fall surrounded by the brilliant foliage of southern Indiana, in the winter snow covered and adorned with evergreen wreaths, and in the spring and summer overlooking a kaleidoscope of blooming flowers. Regardless of the season, the Sample Gates offer a memorable view.

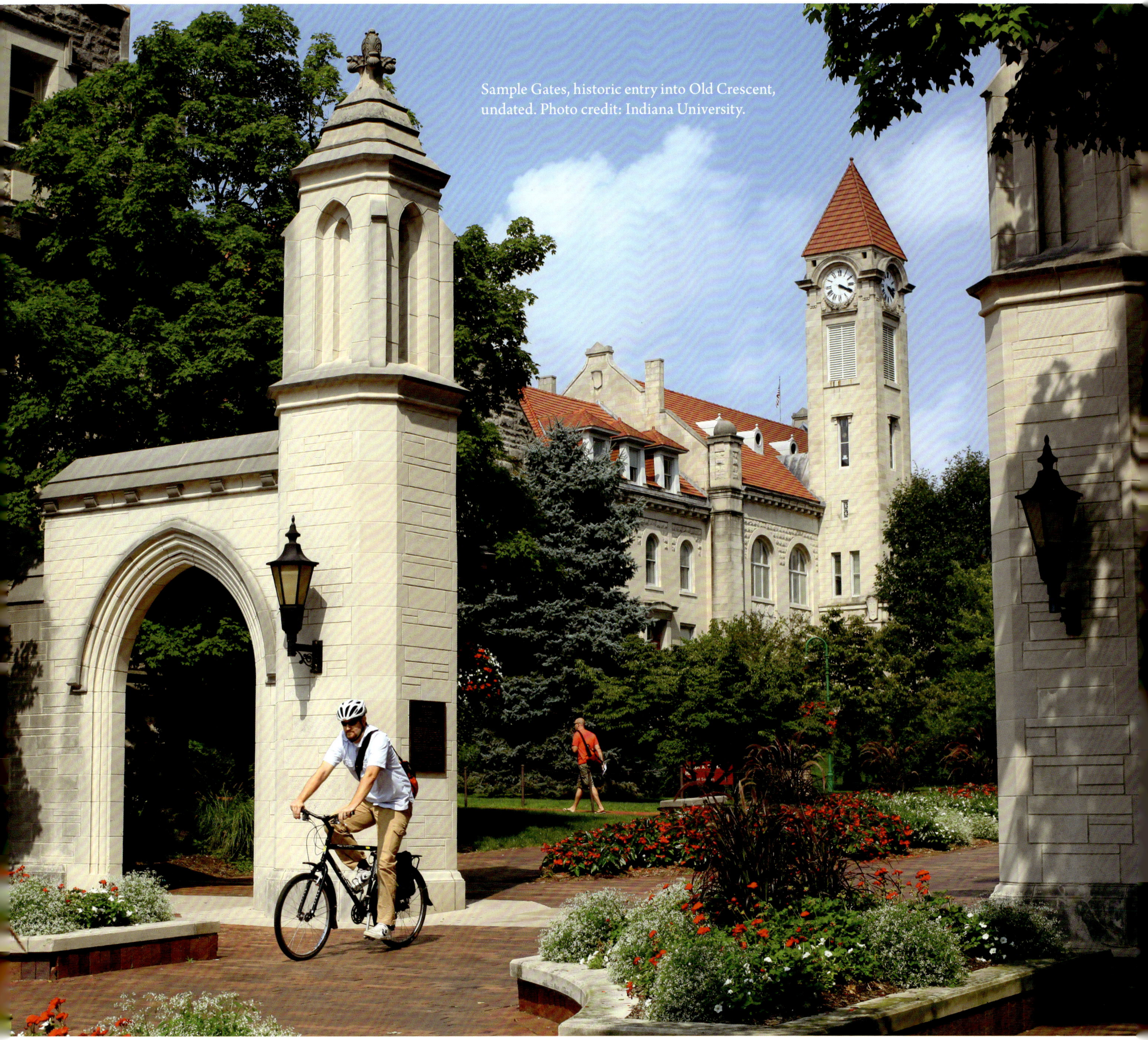

Sample Gates, historic entry into Old Crescent, undated. Photo credit: Indiana University.

Indiana Arc

by Charles Perry

The Charles Perry work was chosen for its visualization of timeless mathematical qualities, which make it so compatible with the mathematical and geometric aspects of our I. M. Pei Building.

—Director Emerita Adelheid M. Gealt

THE *INDIANA ARC*, IN ITS PLACE OF HONOR IN front of the Sidney and Lois Eskenazi Museum of Art, was commissioned to honor the presidency of Thomas Ehrlich and his wife, Ellen, at the time of their retirement from the university in 1994. IU's fifteenth president took office in 1987 and quickly made the performing and visual arts a key element of his administrative agenda. The Ehrlich years were also marked by support for artistic scholarship, and President Ehrlich elevated the university's standing among institutions delivering student opportunity for study in the arts.

The forecourt of the art museum, purposely left vacant by the architect, I. M. Pei, for a future piece of public art, provided an ideal space to recognize the Ehrlich presidency. Pei's buff-tinted concrete fashioned in straight lines and triangular pattern on the building's exterior was the perfect counterpoint for a large sculpture with vibrant color and contrasting shape to complement the massive museum.

With this goal in place, university administrators set out to find the appropriate artist with outstanding credentials. Charles O. Perry was selected. Perry trained as an architect and practiced with Skidmore, Owings, and Merrill, one of the nation's largest architectural firms, before launching his career as an artist. He was known for his large-scale sculptures located in public places nationally and abroad. Perry produced over a hundred major commissions, including work in the United States, Australia, Singapore, Saudi Arabia, and Japan. His

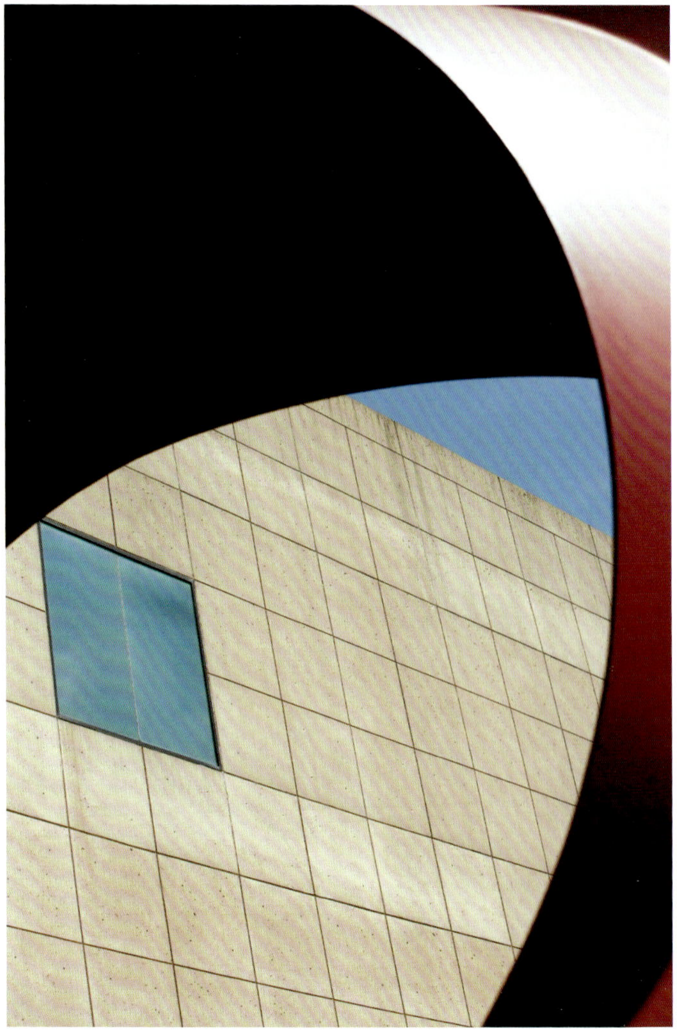

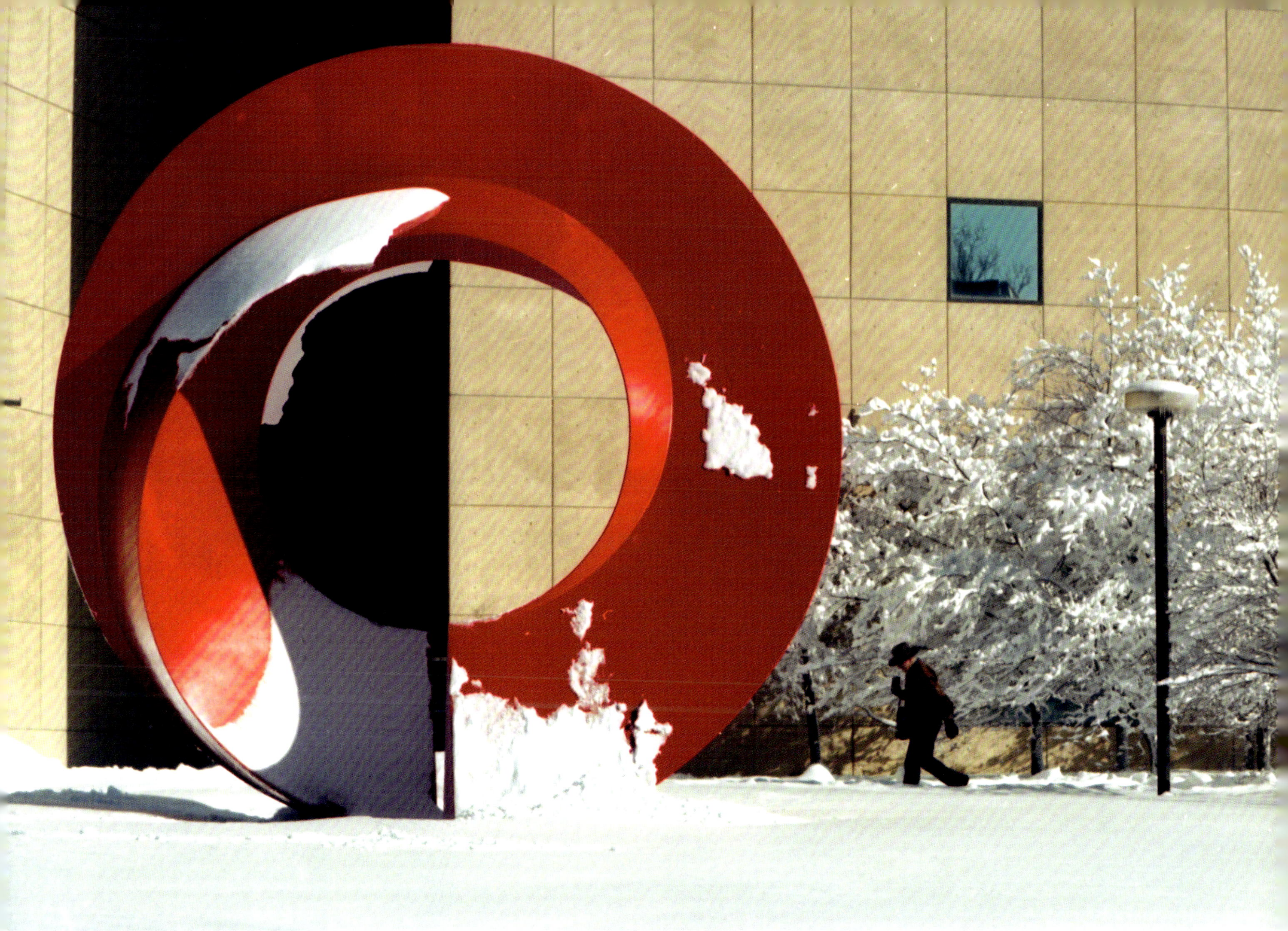

Facing, Red curves of Charles O. Perry's *Indiana Arc* contrast with angles of I. M. Pei's art museum, 2016. Photo credit: Tyagan Miller.

Above, Snow-covered *Indiana Arc* juxtaposed against Sidney and Lois Eskenazi Museum of Art, undated. P0056997, IU Archives. Photo credit: Ira Wilmer "Will" Counts Jr.

sculpture *Continuum*, which stands in front of the National Air and Space Museum in Washington, DC, is one of his most visible pieces of public art. He was a master at integrating building design with public art and blending the complexities of mathematics with the aesthetic qualities of sculpture.

Indiana Arc, the 21-foot-tall, massive red sculpture, has become an integral part of the charm of IU's campus. It is constructed of aluminum and uses an equilateral triangle as the basis for its shape, the same shape that I. M. Pei used as a building block for the art museum. According to Perry, the arc represents a question he often asked himself: "What does it all mean?"[1] The *Indiana Arc* was dedicated to the Ehrlichs' service to the university in 1995.

Frank E. McKinney Jr. Fountain

Art expands our vision of what is possible, calls us to account for our treatment of others, adds beauty to our existence, and elevates the soul.

—Cary Bryce, Lasting Legacies

An Artistic Blend of Two Passions

The Frank E. McKinney Jr. Fountain enlivens the grounds in front of the Bess Meshulam Simon Music Library and Recital Center. Marianne McKinney Tobias gifted and dedicated the fountain in memory of her late husband, Indiana University alumnus and former trustee, Frank E. McKinney Jr., who perished in a small-plane accident in 1992. Frank led the swim team to its first Big Ten Championship in 1961 and helped to inaugurate the IU swimming dynasty under Doc Cousilman, the university's iconic swimming coach from 1958 to 1991. McKinney held six world backstroke records, also winning a bronze medal at the Melbourne Olympic Games in 1956 and gold and silver medals at the 1960 Olympic Games in Rome. He later became a prominent Indiana banker.

The McKinney Fountain was designed by Environmental Design of Pittsburgh, Pennsylvania, to blend the two passions held by Marianne and Frank McKinney. Marianne's interest was in music; she was an accomplished pianist and performed professionally. She worked closely with the university architect and the Pittsburgh firm to design a fountain that included elements of music and competitive swimming. The desired result was achieved.

The slight horseshoe-shaped fountain, topped with fifty-two water jets, represents a seated orchestra, while the separate 12-foot limestone pedestal positioned between the fountain and the music center signifies the conductor. The length of the fountain equals an Olympic-sized swimming pool, and the water speaks for itself. The end result is a spectacular visual and aural display from dozens of plumes, water cascading down a series of steps, and the brilliant column and rotating arc in the middle that are the conductor and orchestra.

Dedicated in 1997, the fountain is one of the most intricate pieces of machinery on campus. The molded concrete fountain construction complements in both texture and color the limestone exterior of the neighboring Bess Meshulam Simon Music Library and Recital Center. The fountain pump room is located in the basement of the music center and includes water treatment equipment and sand-filtering devices. A computerized control box keeps the fountain on a regular schedule. Water flows through the McKinney Fountain beginning each day at 8:00 a.m. and stops at precisely 10:30 p.m. A wind sensor located near the fountain directs the mechanism to stop the flow for fifteen minutes if the wind exceeds 15 mph, both a conservation effort and to keep passersby from getting wet.

Swimming and diving has been a strong sports program at Indiana University for many decades, and multiple NCAA Championships have been won thanks to a long line of outstanding individual competitors. The aesthetically pleasing and creative Frank E. McKinney Jr. Fountain proudly honors one of IU's early champions.

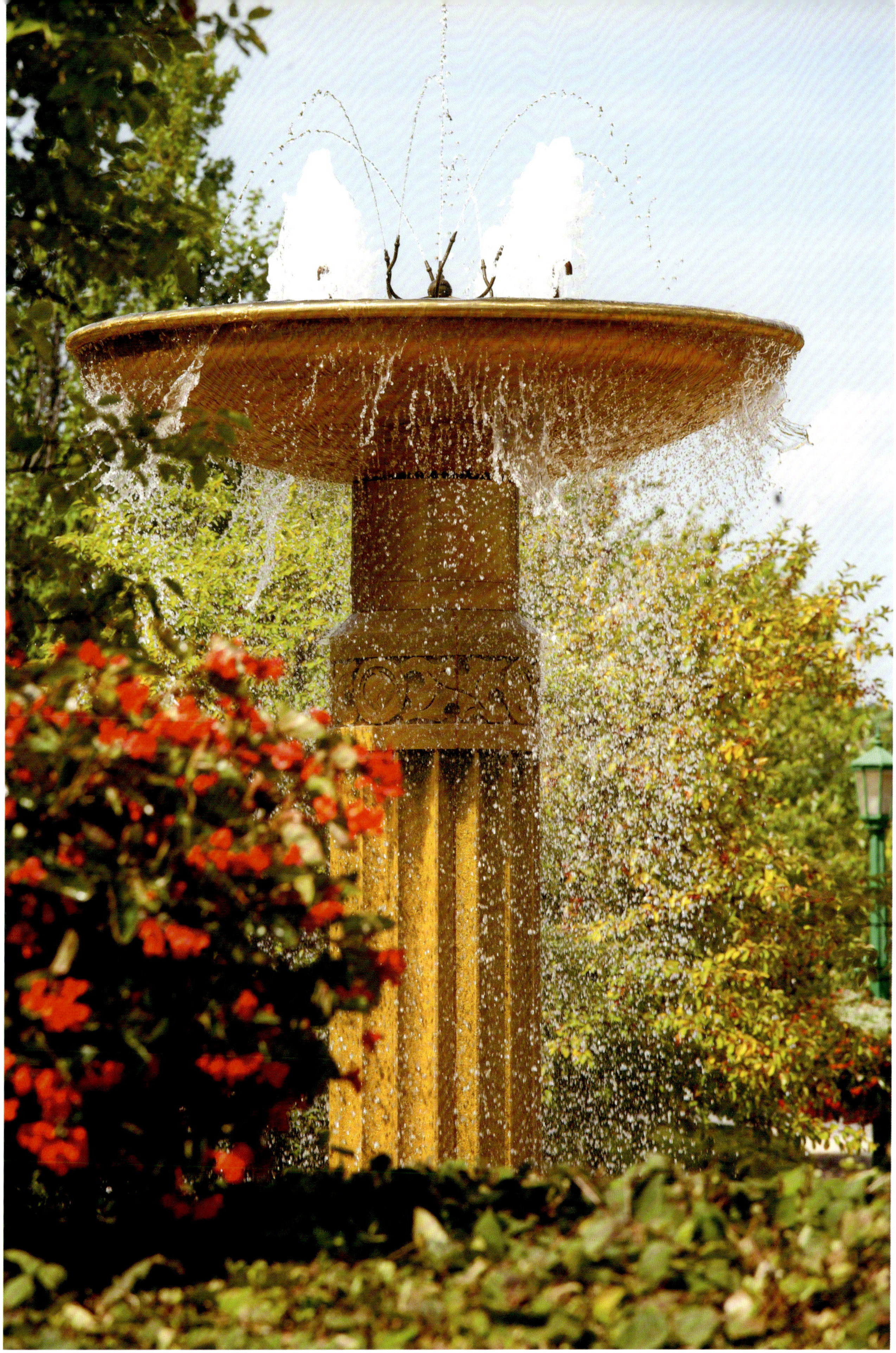

Limestone pedestal of McKinney Fountain symbolizing an orchestra conductor, 2016. Photo credit: Tyagan Miller.

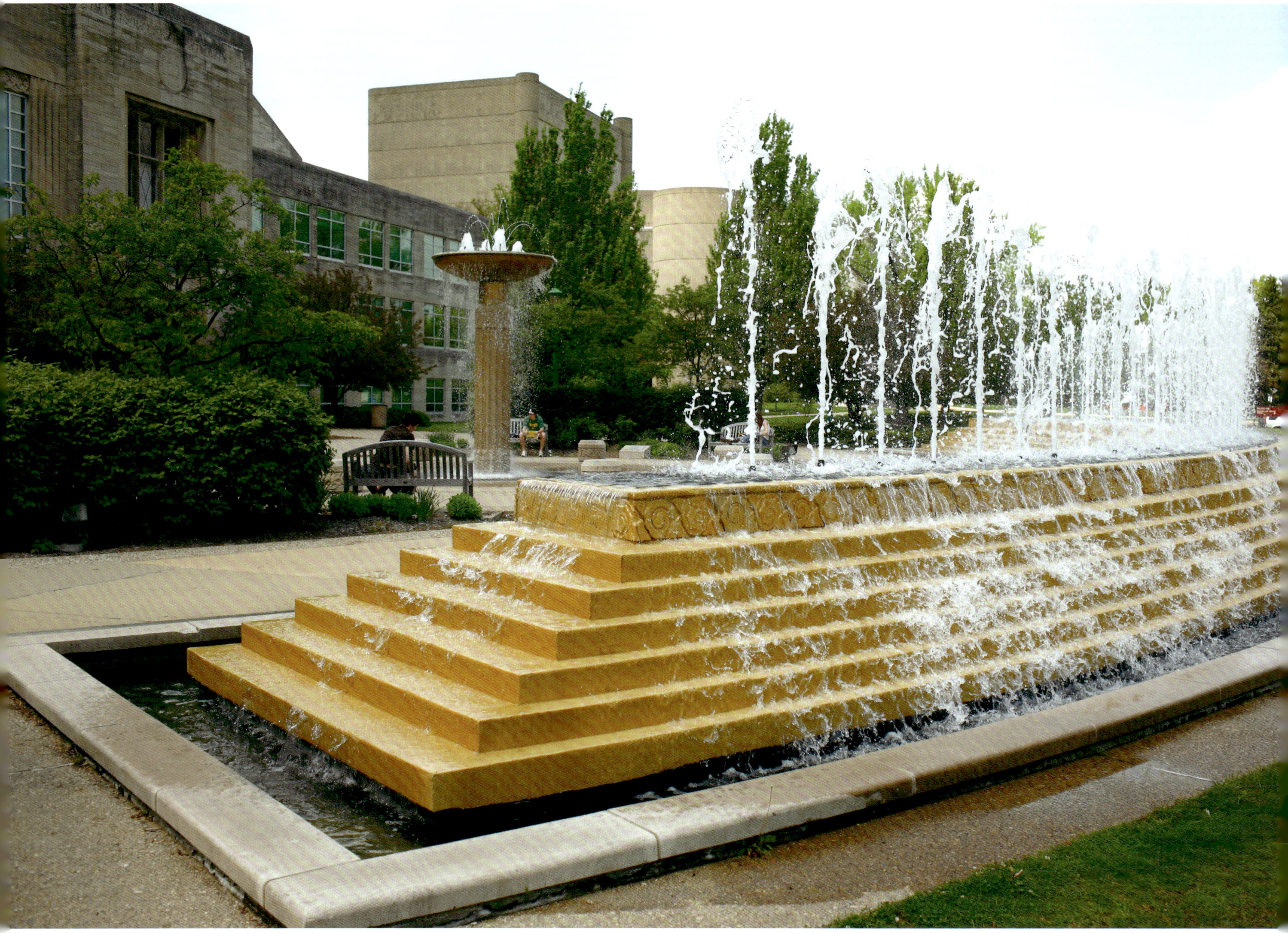

Frank E. McKinney Jr. Fountain in front of Bess Meshulam Simon Music Library and Recital Center, 1999. Photo credt: Indiana University.

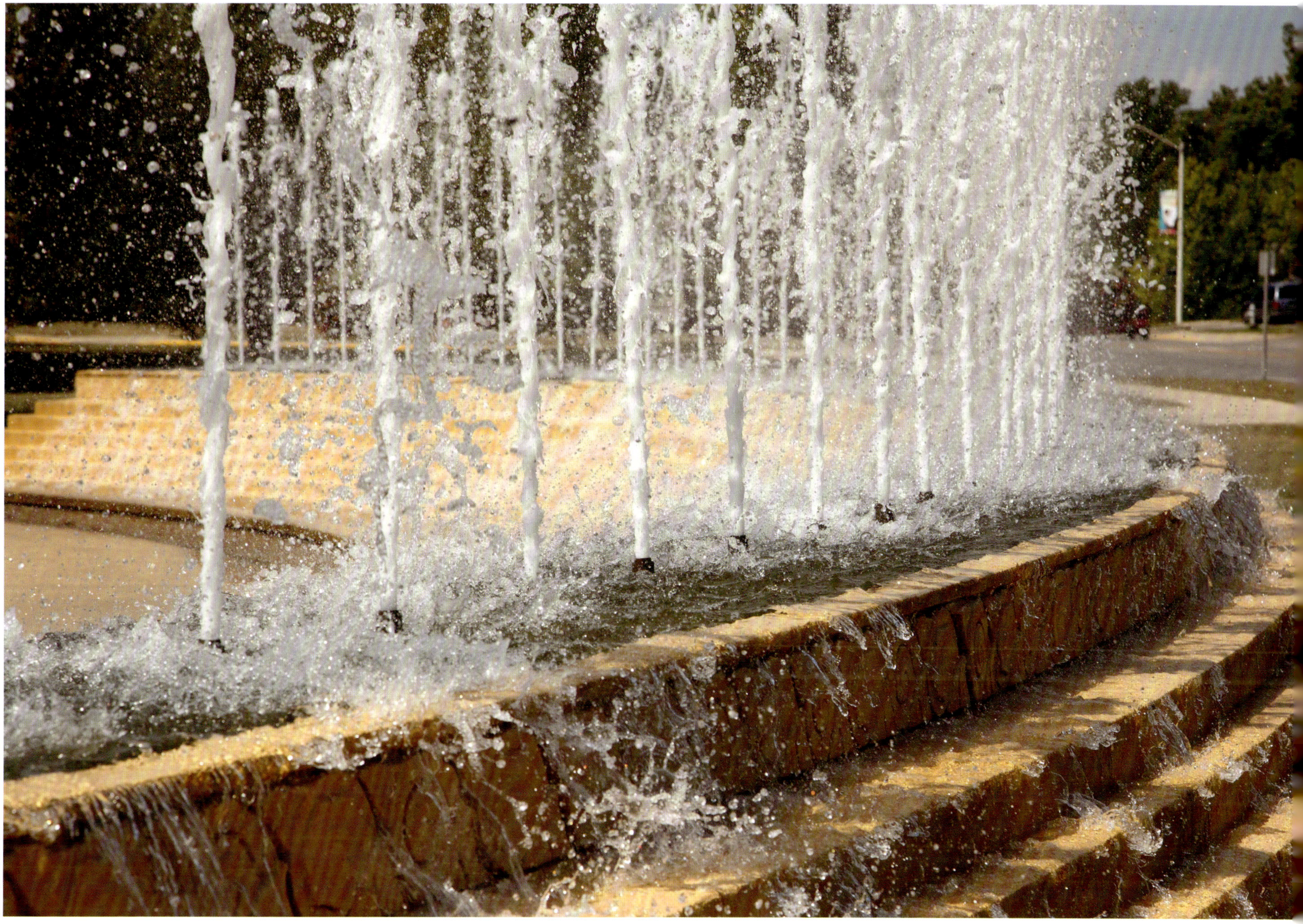

Horseshoe-shaped section of McKinney Fountain, topped with fifty-two water jets representing a seated orchestra, 2016. Photo credit: Tyagan Miller.

Herman B Wells Plaza

Where Wells Is Forever Immortalized

This statue, fittingly placed in the center of campus, will serve as a reminder of the fact that Chancellor Wells transformed a small Midwestern college into a major research university of international renown without sacrificing the friendly, hometown atmosphere that makes this campus such a special place to be.

—President Myles Brand at dedication ceremony

A STROLL THROUGH INDIANA UNIVERSITY'S OLD Crescent should include a stop at the Herman B Wells Plaza, between Owen Hall and Dunn's Woods. There, one can sit on a bench alongside the likeness of Herman B Wells, who, for many, embodies the spirit of the university.

A native of Boone County, Indiana, former president Herman B Wells began his association with IU as a transfer student from the University of Illinois in the early 1920s. He earned his undergraduate degree in business administration in 1924 and a master's degree in economics in 1927. By 1930, Wells was again in Bloomington as a member of the faculty in the Department of Economics and Sociology, and his rapid ascension followed. By 1935 President William Lowe Bryan had appointed him dean of the School of Business Administration, and when President Bryan retired in 1937, the IU Board of Trustees asked Wells to serve as interim president. Then in 1938, at the age of thirty-five, Herman B Wells became IU's eleventh president, also becoming the nation's youngest state university president. He remained in this role until his retirement in 1962, whereupon the trustees created the position of university chancellor, which allowed Wells to serve his beloved alma mater until his death in 2000.

In the late 1990s, IU alumnus and benefactor Bob LeBien was attending a home basketball game. When he glanced across Assembly Hall and saw Chancellor Wells sitting in his customary seat, it struck him that inevitably one day Hoosiers would no longer be able to enjoy Herman Wells's company at campus events. Thus began LeBien's efforts to develop a fitting and lasting tribute that would ensure Wells's presence on campus for all time. Working with the University Architect's Office, LeBien advanced the idea of a sculpture of Wells as part of a plaza in the midst of the Old Crescent, close to the office in Owen Hall that Chancellor Wells had occupied for the last three decades. All but the man himself thought this was a good idea, who, the story goes, remarked, "Can't you find something better to do with your money?"

Nonetheless, planning moved forward. Indiana University South Bend professor of fine arts Harold "Tuck" Langland was commissioned to create the sculpture. Langland met with Chancellor Wells several times, but rather than ask the nonagenarian to sit for long periods, the artist worked from archival photographs and with Wells's closest friends to ensure that the final product was a true representation of the man. Over the winter months from 1999 to 2000, Langland and his students sculpted the full-sized clay form in his South Bend studio. The completed clay sculpture was shipped to Beacon, New York, to be cast in bronze by the Polich Tallix Fine Art Foundry.

The finished sculpture was transported to Bloomington in the fall of 2000 for placement on the plaza, which featured a circular redbrick courtyard bordered by a low limestone wall. Two bronze park benches flanked the space reserved for Wells's homecoming. The sculpture of Dr. Wells and his

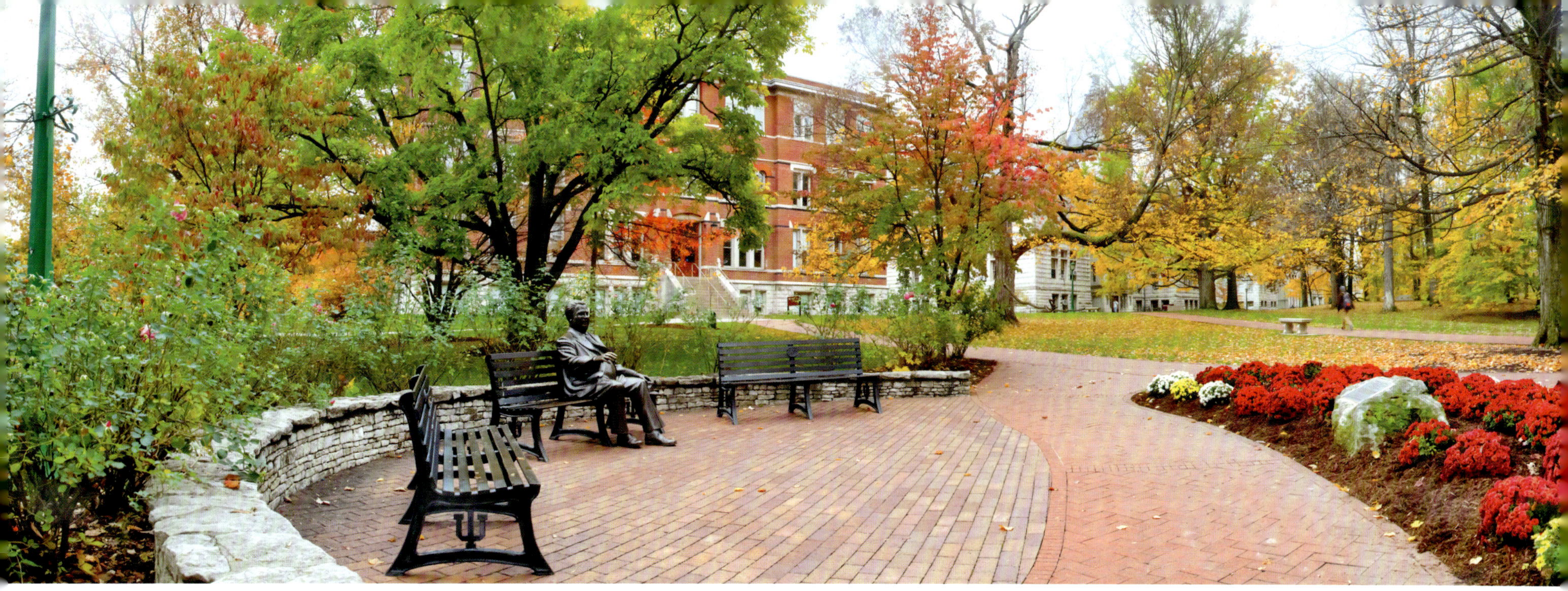

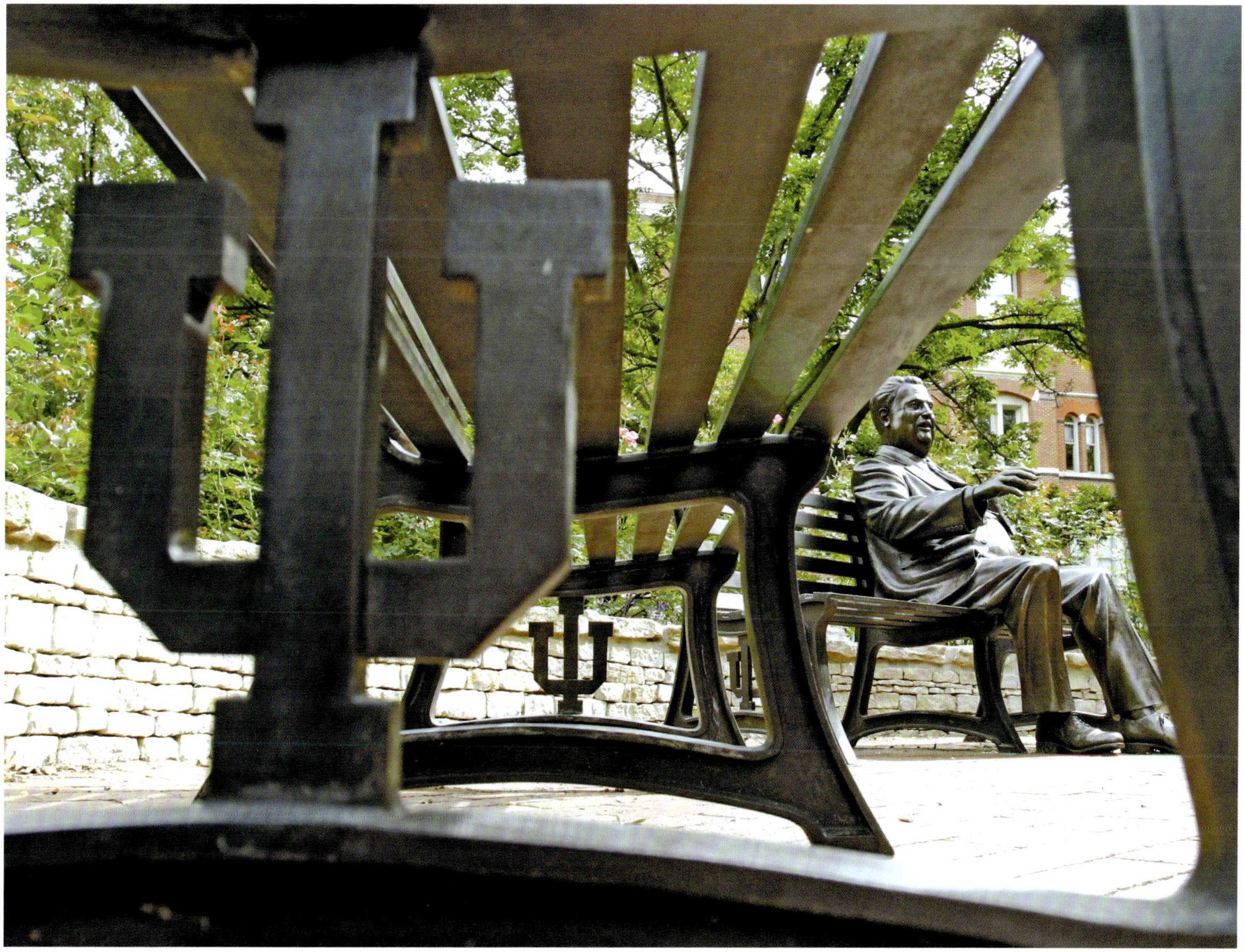

Above, Wide-angle view of Herman B Wells Plaza with Owen, Wylie, and Kirkwood Halls in background, undated. Photo credit: Indiana University.

Left, Wells sculpture bench detail, undated. Photo credit: Indiana University.

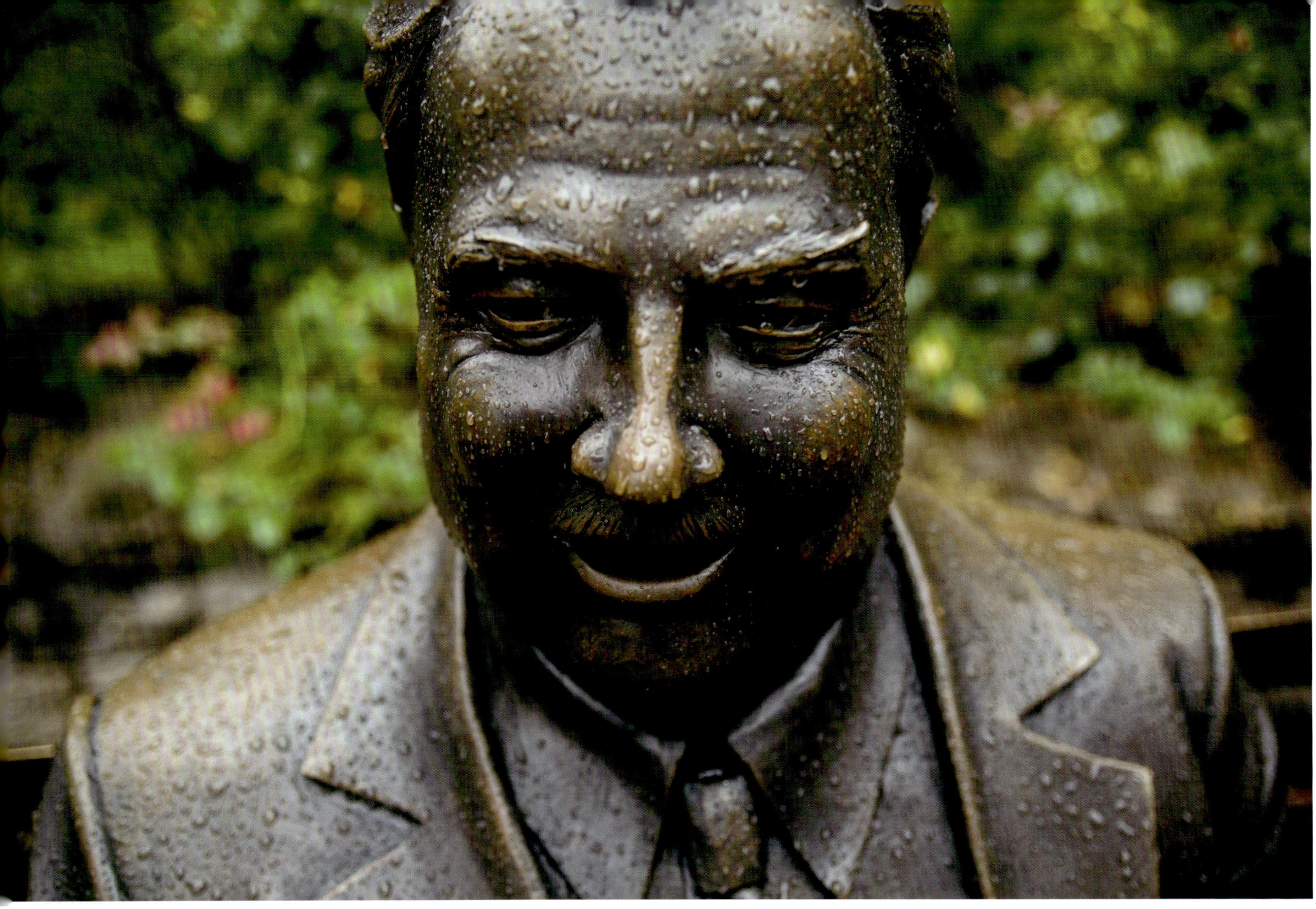

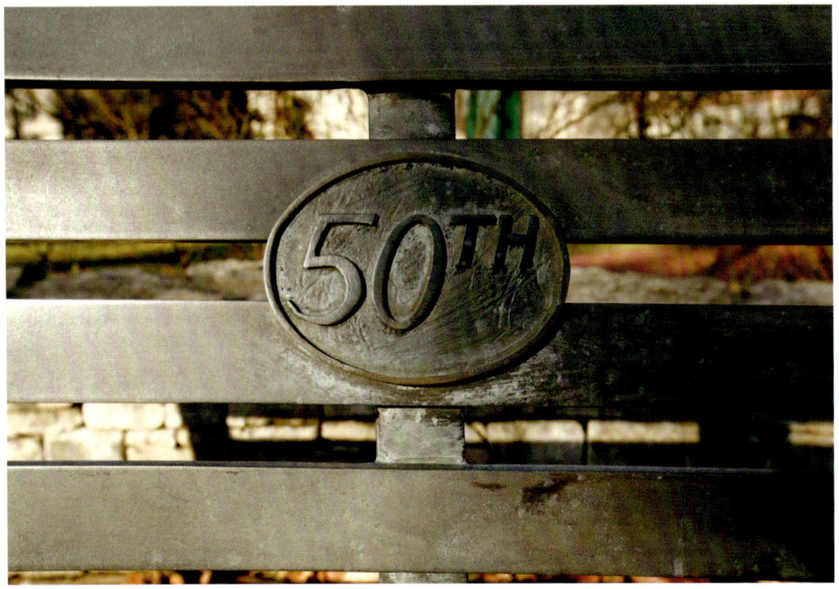
50TH

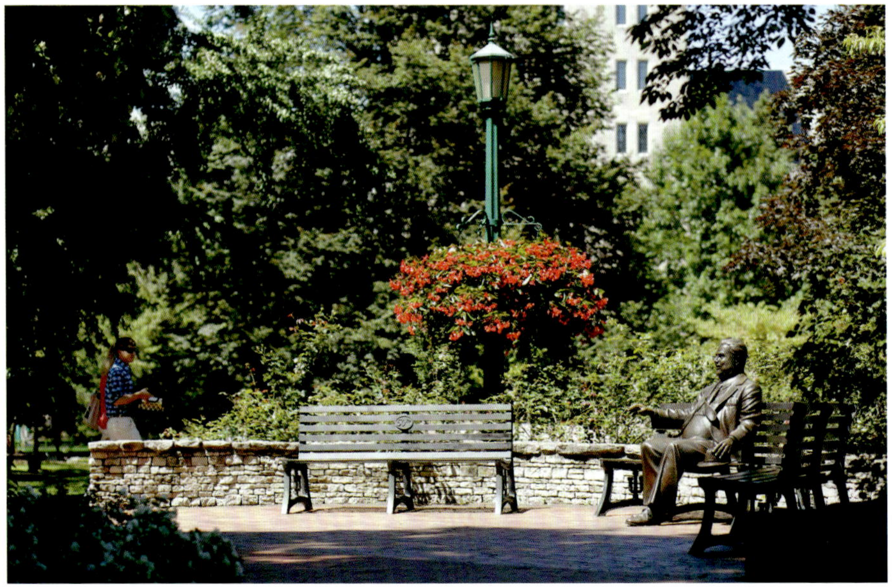

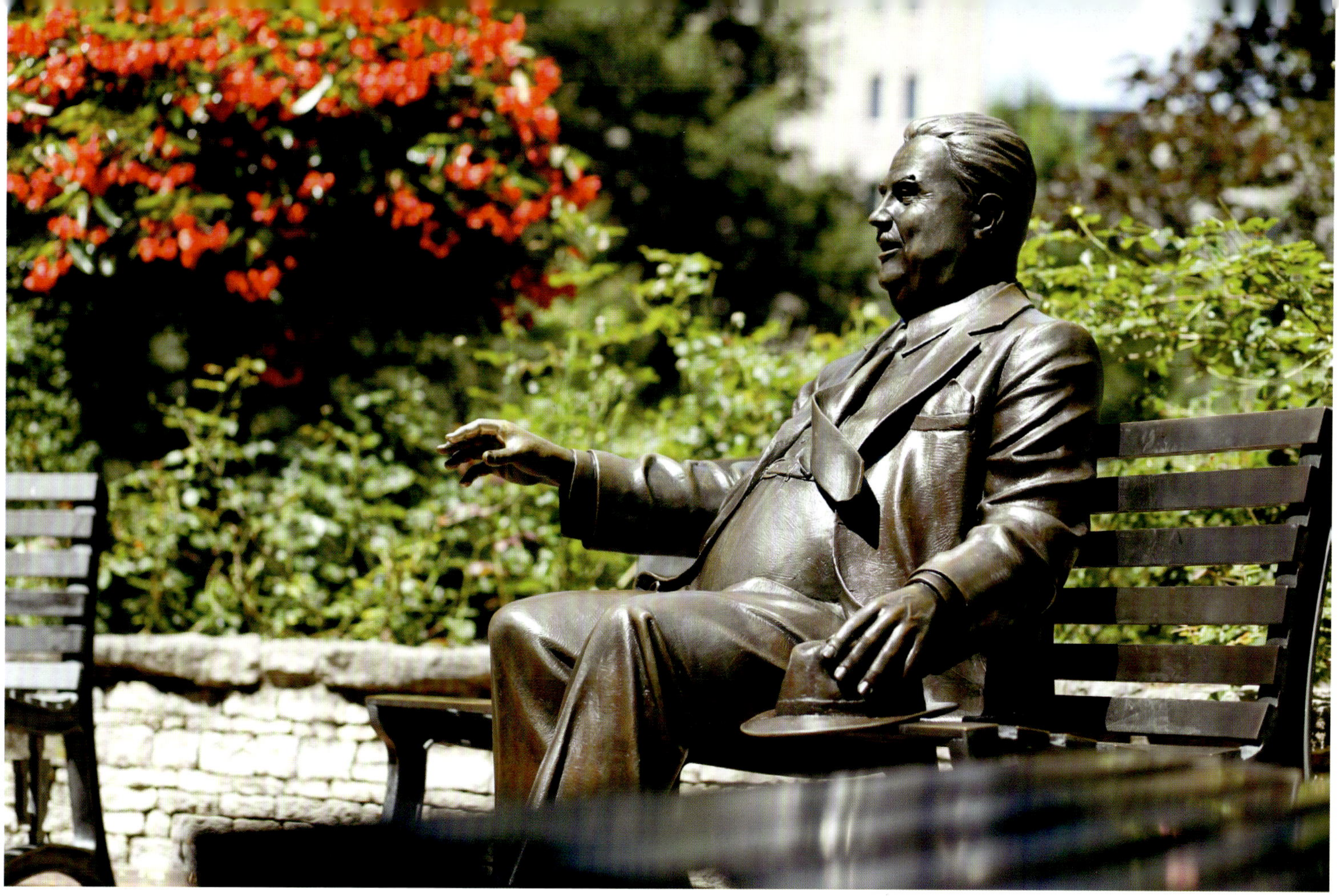

Above, Wells's right hand outstretched, inviting visitors to join him on his bench, 2015. Photo credit: Indiana University.

Facing top, Herman B Wells smiling through the rain, 2015. Photo credit: Indiana University.

Facing bottom left, Bench detail commemorating the fiftieth wedding anniversary of alumni Harriet and Richard Inskeep, 2017. Photo credit: Indiana University.

Facing bottom right, Herman B Wells Plaza in summer, 2015. Photo credit: Indiana University.

bronze park bench were lowered into place. The result, said LeBien, "represents Dr. Wells not as bigger than life but as part of life. It shows Dr. Wells as we all knew him—as one of us."[1]

This statue portrays Wells in his late sixties or early seventies, relaxed and comfortably seated on a park bench with his favorite soft hat beside him, his tie loosened for comfort and slightly flipped from a gust of wind, and his suit jacket open. Close inspection reveals the initialed cufflinks, cast from a pair in Wells's collection, fastening his French cuffs. His legs are uncrossed, and his right hand is raised and extended, ever ready to greet passersby. Touching his hand quickly became a tradition for students looking for a little extra luck on their way to exams, so much so that the curator of campus art Sherry Rouse remarked, "It keeps me busy keeping his finger re-patinated."[2]

The bronze statue and plaza were dedicated during Homecoming Weekend in 2000, just months after the passing of Dr. Wells. His statue was a gift from the estate of Virgil DeVault, and the plaza was funded by the children of Richard and Harriet Inskeep in honor of their parents' fiftieth wedding anniversary. The number "50" can be seen on the backs of two of the plaza benches.

Next time you find yourself in the Old Crescent, do join Herman Wells on the plaza and look for the sculptor's "Easter egg": Under the brim of Dr. Wells's hat, Langland, a University of Minnesota alum, carved: "IU vs Minnesota Oct 12 2000. Go Gophers." The artist assumed Dr. Wells would find that touch amusing, and he was probably correct.

Campus Clocks

Our Place in Time

Right, One of four IU red clocks located near Swain Hall, Woodburn Hall, Neal-Marshall Black Culture Center, and the Arboretum, 2014. Photo credit: Indiana University.

Facing, One of iconic campus red clocks near James Albert Woodburn Hall, 2016. Photo credit: Tyagan Miller.

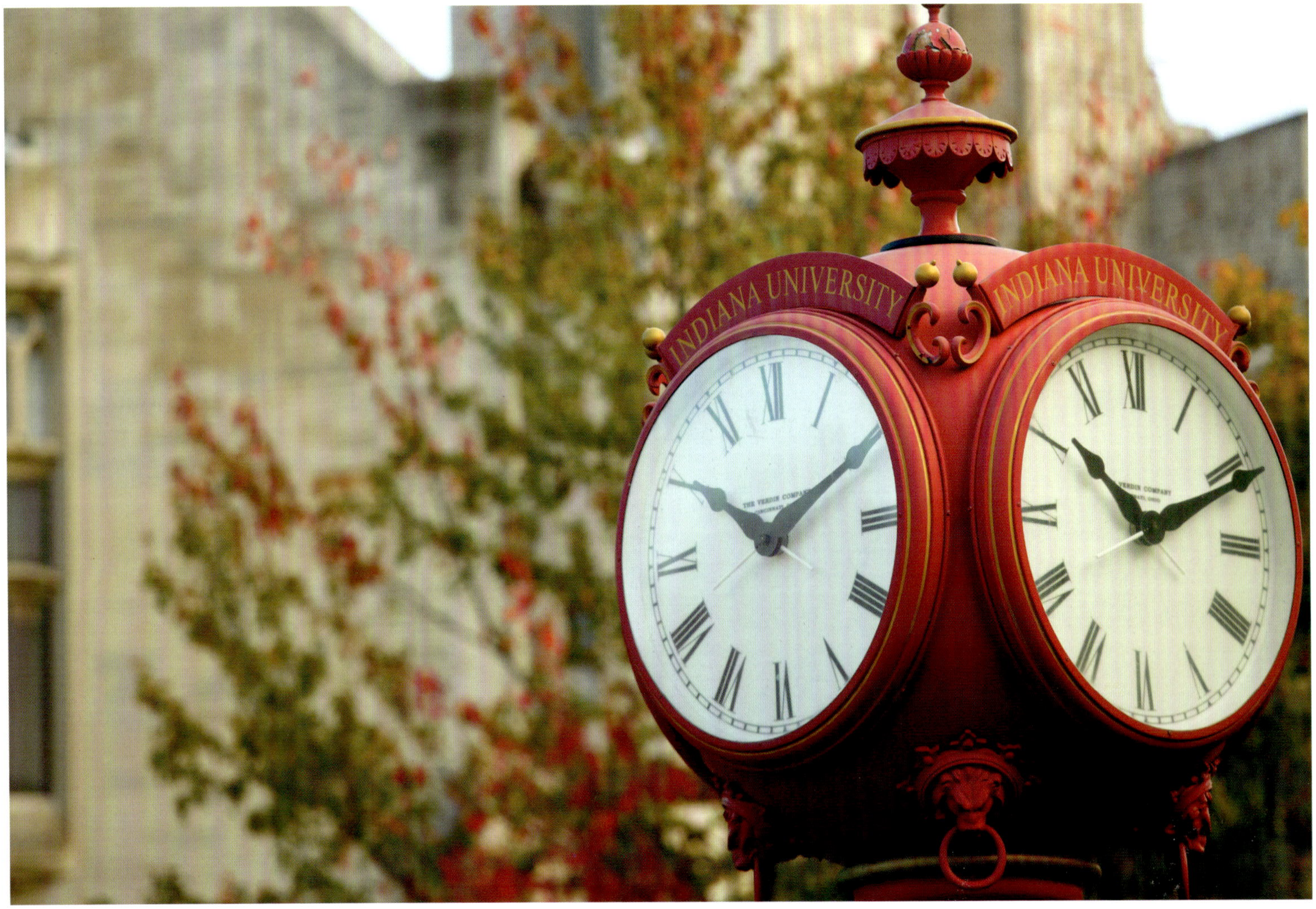

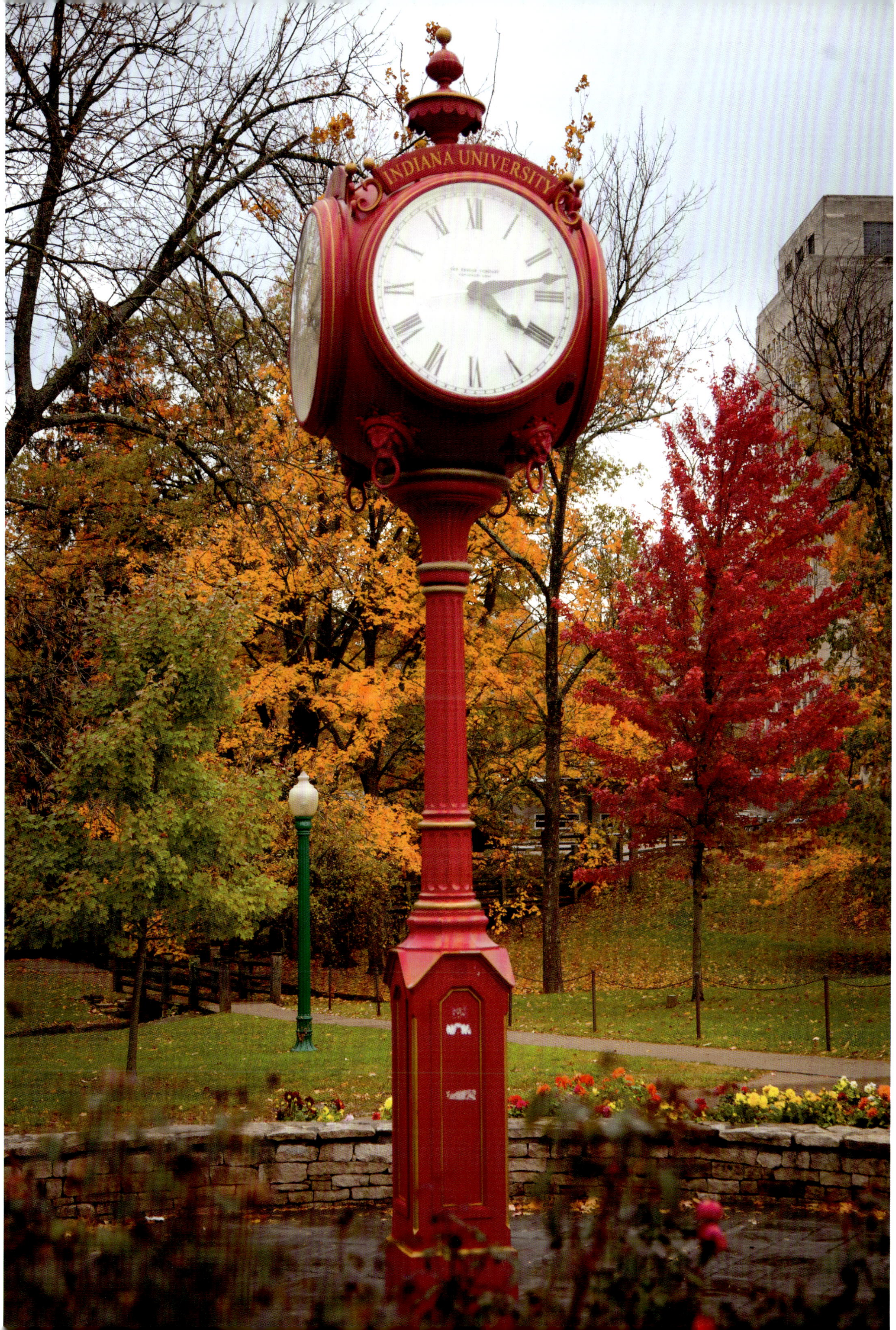
INDIANA UNIVERSITY

Hoagy Carmichael Sculpture

by Michael McAuley

A Tribute to the Man and His Music

Have you ever seen the big maples? The trunk are sometimes three feet in diameter and they shoot straight up, barren of branches, for some forty or fifty feet and then they spread out into a huge umbrella of limbs and foliage. Hundreds of these and an equal number of large beech trees shade the Indiana campus. For many years there were no walks—just natural paths winding among the trees.

—*Hoagy Carmichael,* The Stardust Road

Snuggled in a garden along a pathway on the northeast side of the Indiana University Auditorium, a life-size statue of Hoagy Carmichael at his grand piano serenades passersby as they leave the IU Cinema or simply stroll through the campus. The sculpture was initiated and created by Bloomington-born IU alumnus Michael McAuley (BS 1978, MS 1982) to bring attention and pay tribute to Carmichael, who like himself was also born in Bloomington and graduated from IU.

First conceived as an art piece to be placed in People's Park along Kirkwood Avenue, the artist turned to the university after members of the Carmichael family expressed interest in placing the sculpture on campus. In cooperation with the Indiana University Foundation, funding was provided and the artist proceeded to complete the sculpture, working nearly a year to bring the sculpture to life. He created a stunning, 800-pound likeness of Hoagy Carmichael sitting at a Steinway piano. As McAuley describes the work:

> Hoagy is seated at a grand piano, jacket off and tossed over the side of the grand, his long-sleeves rolled up, pencil in one ear, and fedora on and tilted back. His left hand is on a folder of his past compositions while his right is positioned hovering above the keyboard ready for a down-stroke. He is working on a composition—"Memphis in June."
>
> Hoagy is rather disheveled in appearance, having spent a long night of composing as he worked out the tune in his head, which also is translated unconsciously in him physically mouthing the words. A final touch is a bit of change—small change—has rolled out of his slacks' left pocket and lies on the piano bench. The coins symbolize that his passion for creating music, not money, is his main motivator. [1]

With plenty of space remaining on the bench alongside Hoagy, the sculpture invites his audience to participate, either to stop and sit with him or to leave a flower in his hand as with an old familiar friend. The Hoagy Carmichael sculpture was unveiled at the Indy Jazz Fest in Indianapolis on June 15, 2007, commencing a summer tour of the artwork across the state of Indiana, finally coming to rest on the IU Bloomington campus with its dedication at a public ceremony on September 18, 2007.

Hoagy Carmichael is an American music icon, but more specifically, he is a treasure belonging to Bloomington and Indiana University. He was born in Bloomington in 1899 and buried in his hometown's Rose Hill Cemetery in 1981. He earned his law degree from IU in 1926 and while going to school began to compose songs and perform. Over the years, Hoagy wrote such classics as "Georgia on My Mind," "Heart and Soul," and the 1952 Oscar-winning "In the Cool, Cool, Cool of the Evening." His "Chimes of Indiana" was inspired by the ringing bells of the Student Building. As Vice President Emeritus J. Terry Clapacs said, "Hoagy was an important figure in the new jazz era of this country and someone who

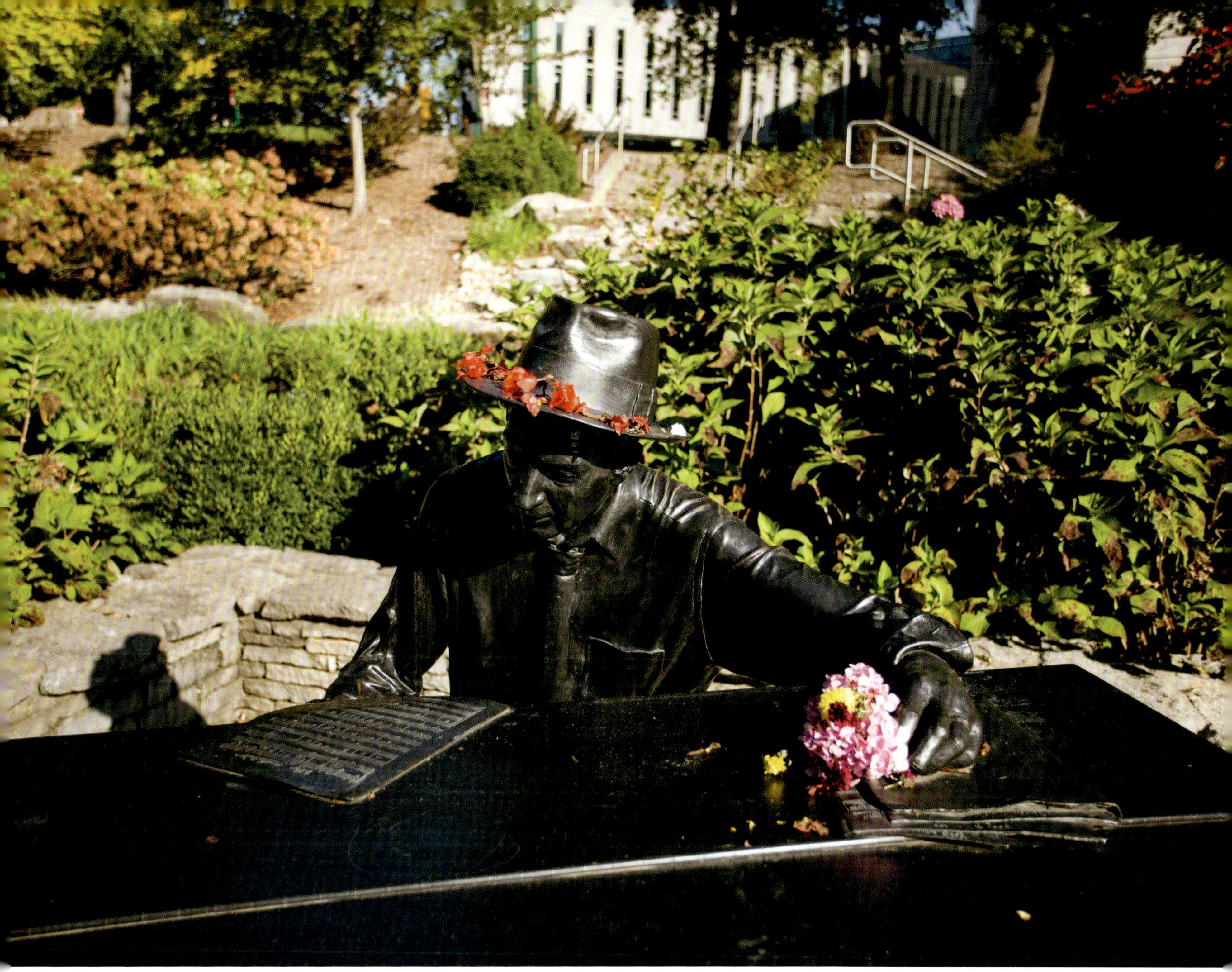

was breaking new ground on the music scene. His writing and recording of the song 'Stardust'—which at one time was the most recorded song in the history of the world—is a remarkable achievement, considering it was written right here, across Indiana Avenue, where the Gables building sits. I think the statue captures the spirit of Hoagy Carmichael in a way that Indiana University likes to remember him."[2]

Above, Hoagy Carmichael sculpture inviting audience to join the famed composer on the piano bench or to leave a flower, 2016. Photo credit: Indiana University.

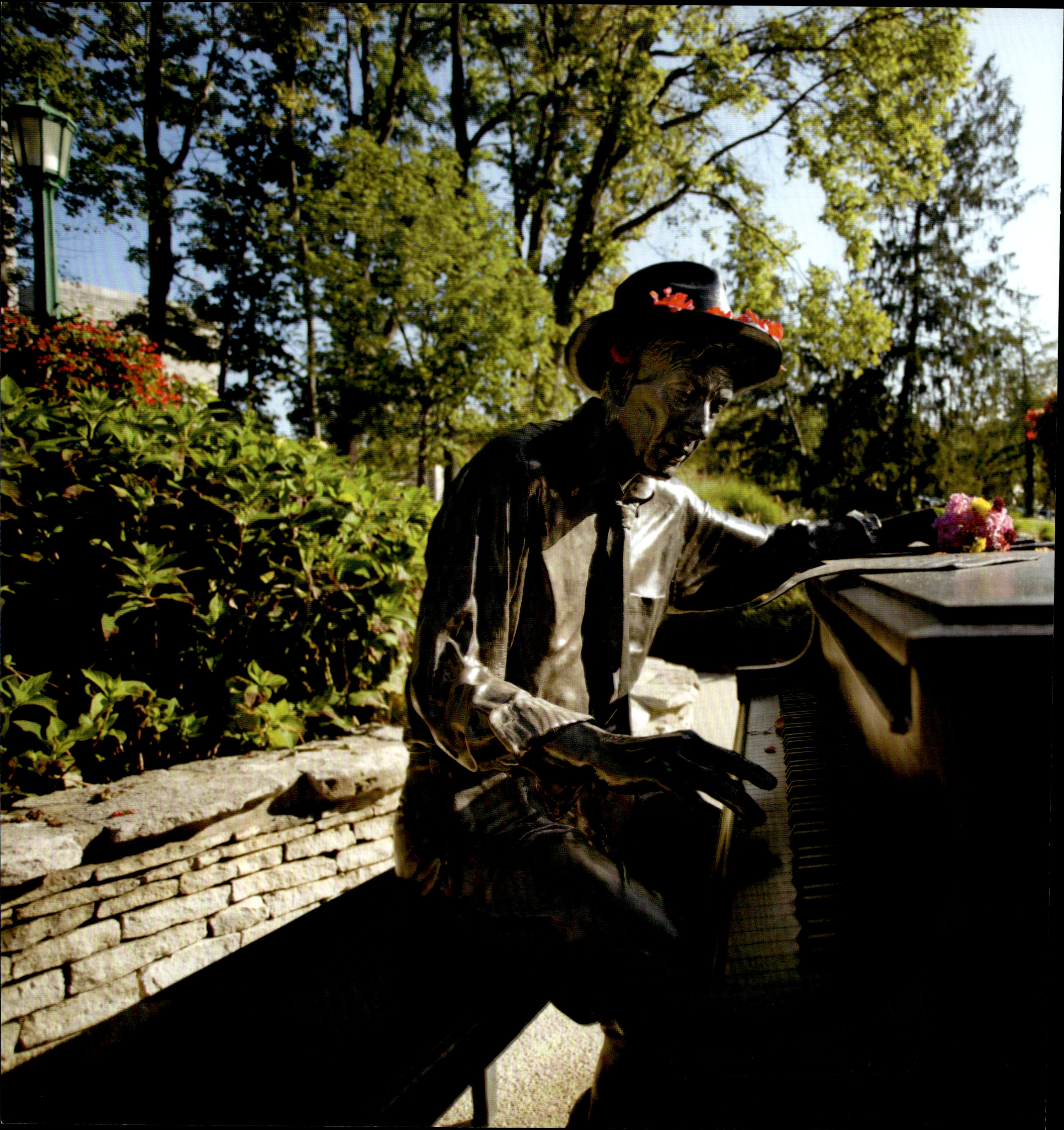

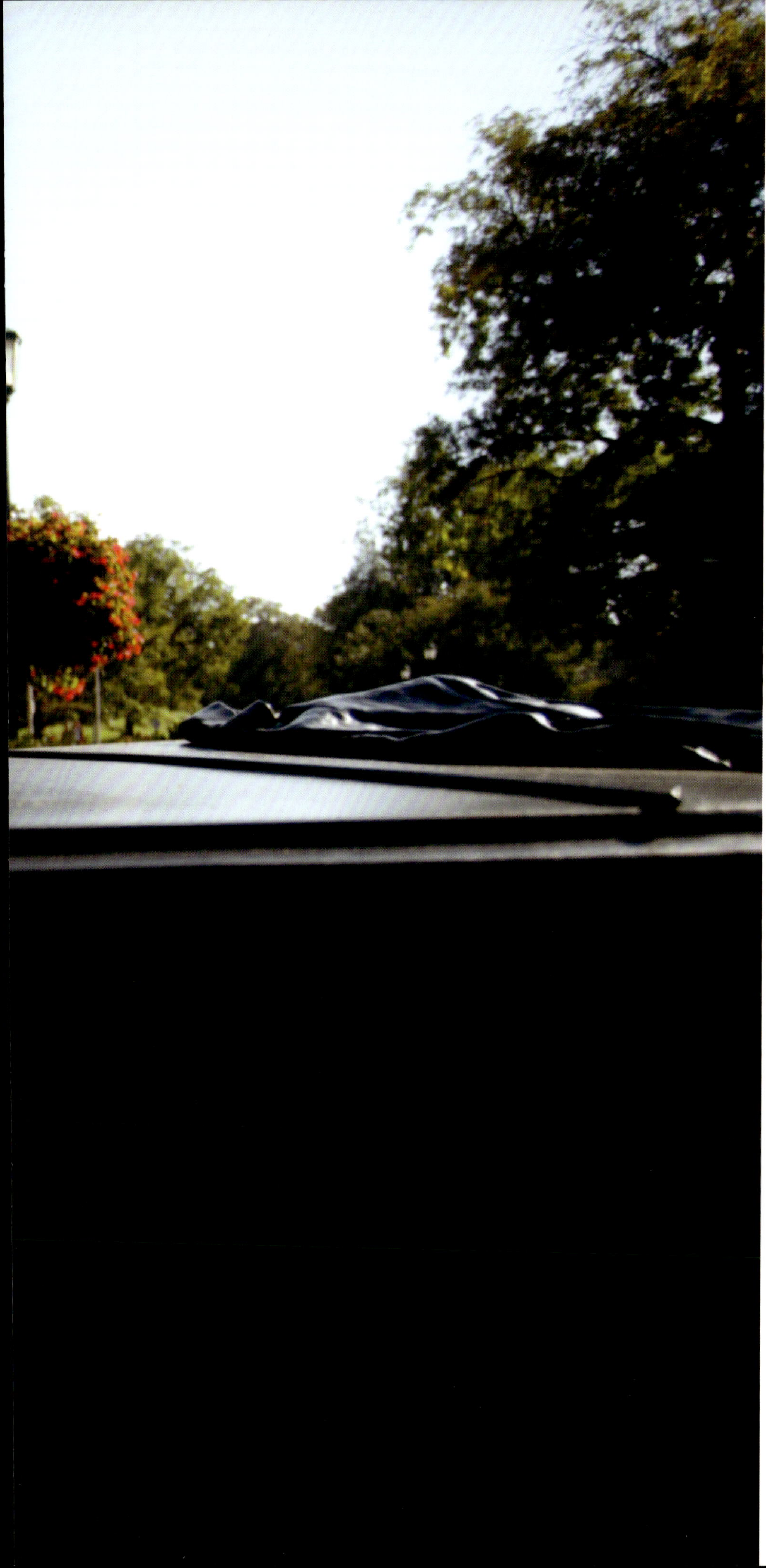

Hoagy Carmichael sculpture in garden outside IU Cinema, 2016. Photo credit: Indiana University.

Ernie Pyle Sculpture

by Harold Langland

IU's Revered Journalist and Storyteller

Positioning Pyle near a school devoted to storytelling through new technologies is fitting. . . . Pyle was embedded with the troops, where he relied on several forms of technology to transmit his columns from the field. But it was his stories about the soldiers' experiences that drew his devoted fans not the way the columns made it to print. This is our focus: to prepare students to tell great stories using the best technology at hand.

—Associate Dean Lesa Hatley Major

WITH THE INAUGURATION OF THE NEW MEDIA School at Indiana University Bloomington, journalism, communications and culture, and telecommunications merged, and Franklin Hall, located in the Old Crescent, became their new home. This move meant that Ernie Pyle Hall would no longer house the journalism program, which caused public concern that Ernie Pyle, one of IU's most distinguished alumni, might lose the recognition he deserves.

In answer to the growing concern, the university commissioned Harold "Tuck" Langland, IU South Bend professor emeritus and award-winning sculptor, to create a statue of the journalist for placement outside of Franklin Hall (Langland also sculpted the Herman B Wells statue on Wells Plaza). The clay model for the Ernie Pyle sculpture was created over some ten months in Langland's studio in South Bend. He worked from a photograph of Pyle along with one of his typewriters, which is kept at the university. The molding was cast in bronze in Oklahoma and then moved to Bloomington, where it was dedicated on homecoming weekend, October 2014, along with the new Media School.

Today, when you walk through the Sample Gates, you are greeted by an impressive bronze, life-size composition of Ernest Taylor Pyle at work. Tuck Langland portrayed Pyle sitting on an ammunition box at a warped table (details include what look like cigarette burns on the table's edges). He is wearing a bomber jacket, helmet, and goggles. On the table are his broken Underwood typewriter, notes, and a coffee cup. Across from the table is another ammunition box, welcoming passers-by to stop and sit with the journalist; or, as Langland suggested, "put their laptop right on the table and type with him."[1] The entire piece was meant to convey how Pyle worked alongside foot soldiers at the front during the World War II.

Harold "Tuck" Langland finishing details on Erie Pyle sculpture, 2015. Photo credit: Indiana University.

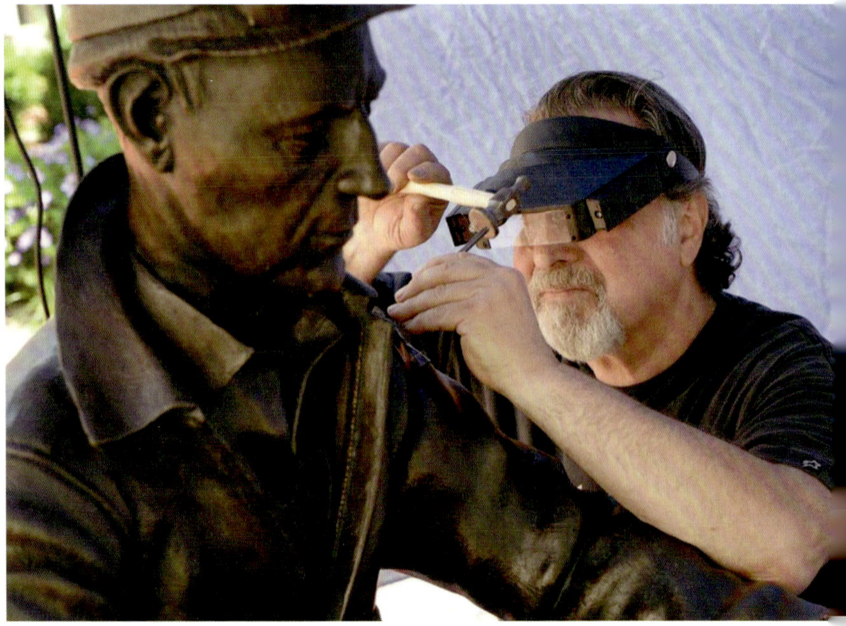

Ernie Pyle (1900–1945) was born in Dana, Indiana. He attended IU in the 1920s, where he majored in journalism and was an editor and columnist for the *Indiana Daily Student*. Pyle left the university in 1923, just shy of finishing his degree, to pursue a career in journalism. He became a reporter and from 1935 through 1941 traveled the country, writing about rural towns and their people. After the United States entered World War II, he became a war correspondent, first from the home front, and later from the European and Pacific theaters. He won the Pulitzer Prize in 1944 for his poignant stories, told from a first-person perspective, about the infantry soldiers. He was killed by a sniper on Iejima (then known as Ie Shima) during the Battle of Okinawa. President Harry Truman said about Pyle: "No man in this war has so well told the story of the American fighting man as American fighting men wanted it told. . . . He deserves the gratitude of all his countrymen."[2] Ernie Pyle is buried at the National Memorial Cemetery of the Pacific at Punchbowl Crater, Honolulu, Hawaii, but his spirit lives on at Indiana University.

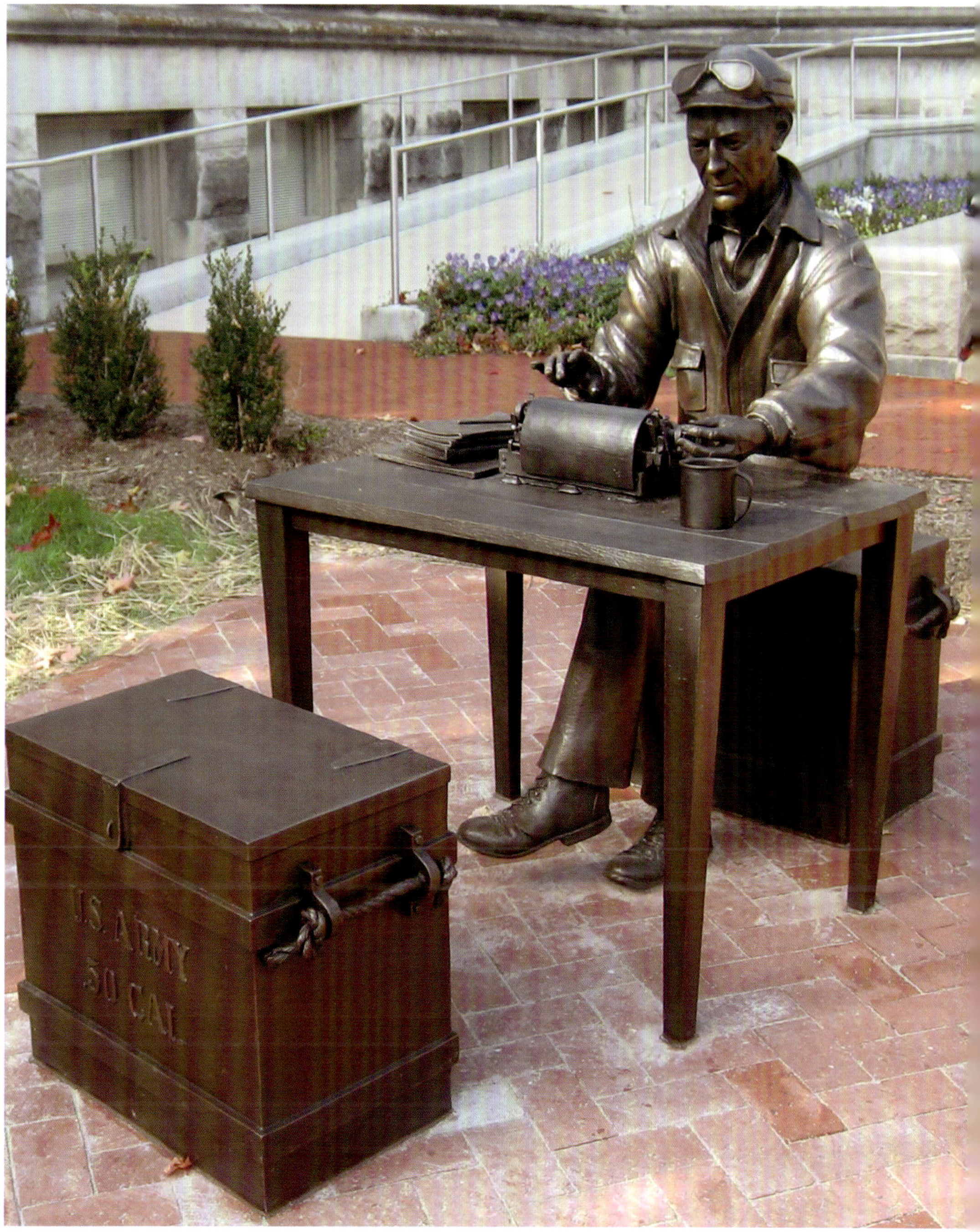

Ernie Pyle sculpture outside entrance to Joseph Amos Franklin Hall, 2015.
Photo credit: Indiana University.

CREAM AND CRIMSON SPIRIT

When the cares of life make us falter,
When we feel all the world is vain,
Still memories dear of the days passed here
Will come back to allay our pain.
When the joys of life make us thankful,
When our cup flows full to the brim,
A prayer and a blessing for old I. U.
We breathe as our eyes grow dim.

RUPERT REDIC
1910 Arbutus

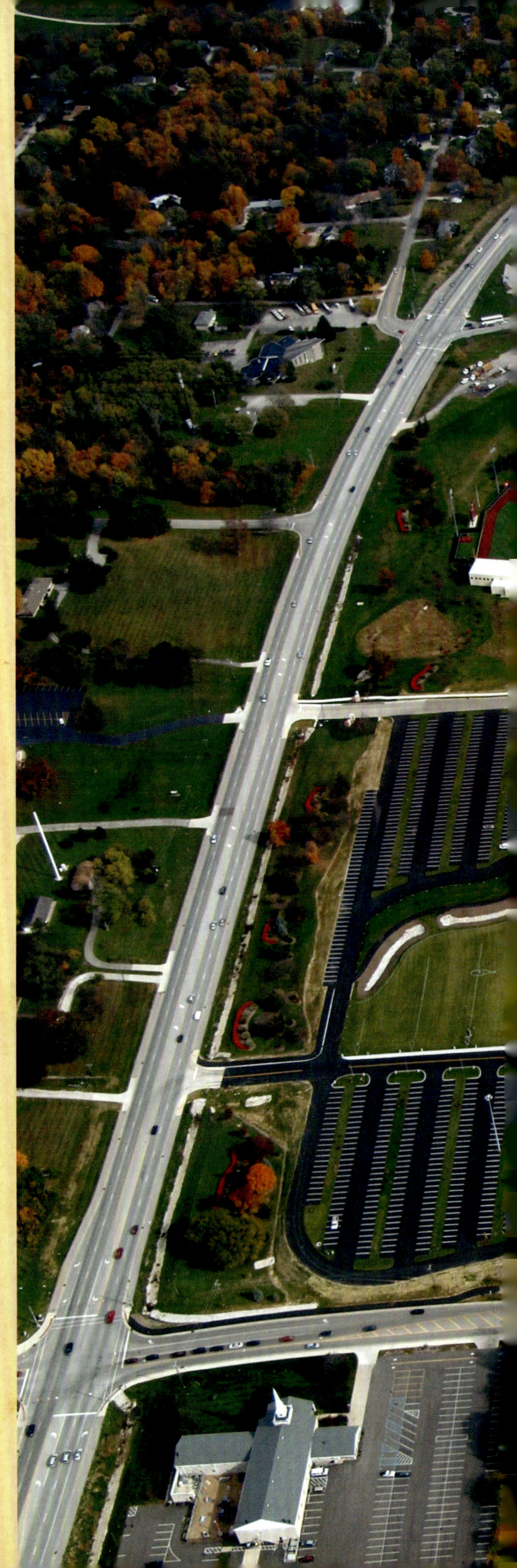

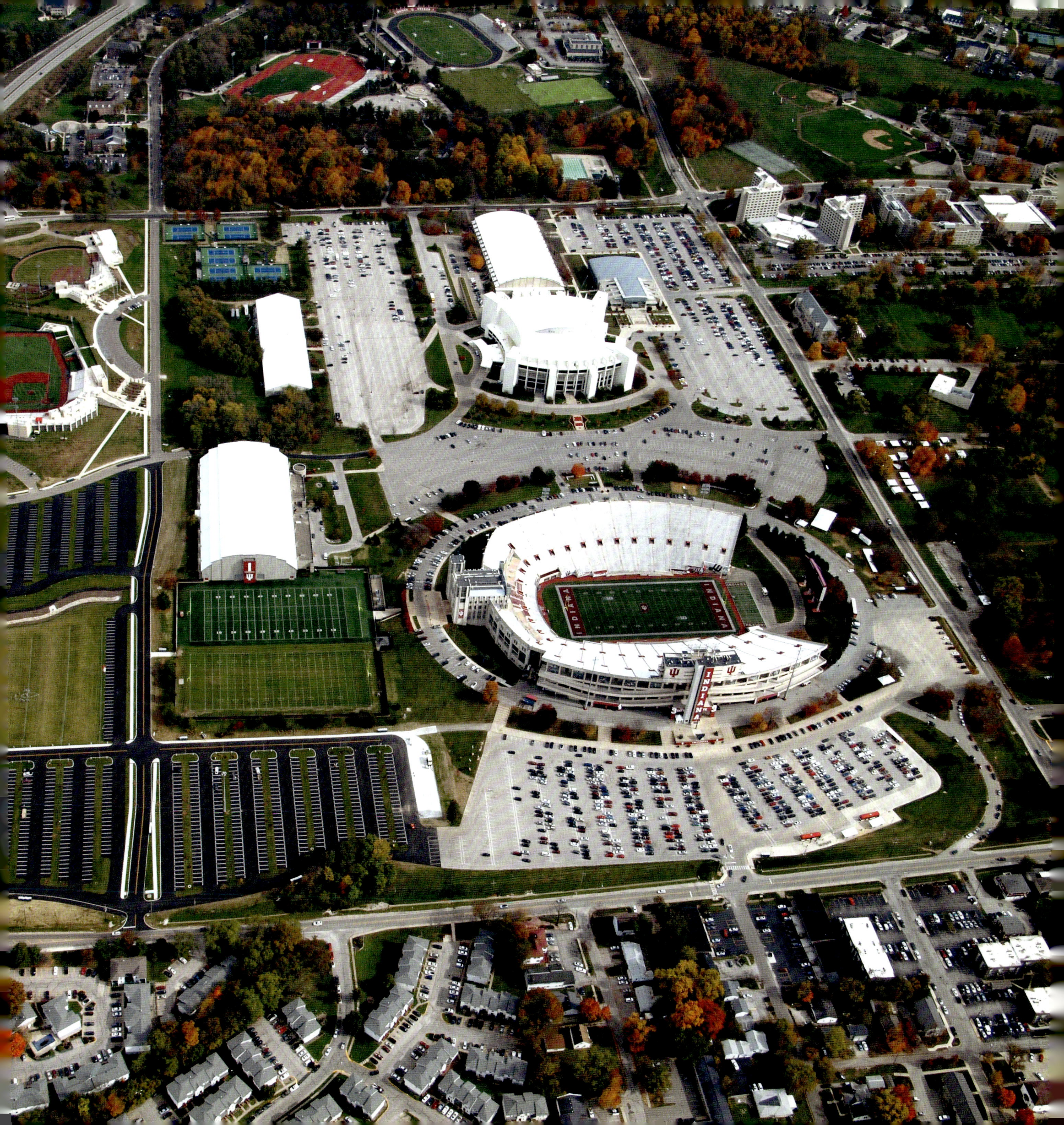
INDIANA

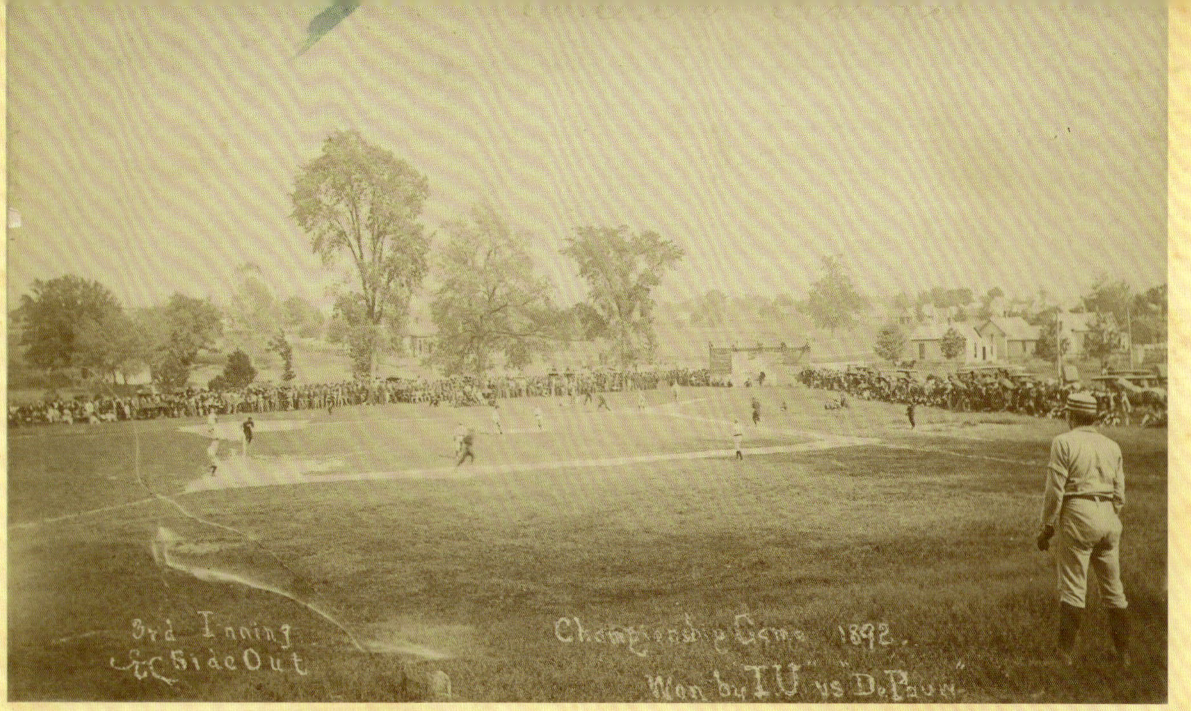
3rd Inning
Side Out
Championship Game 1892.
Won by "I.U." vs "DePauw"

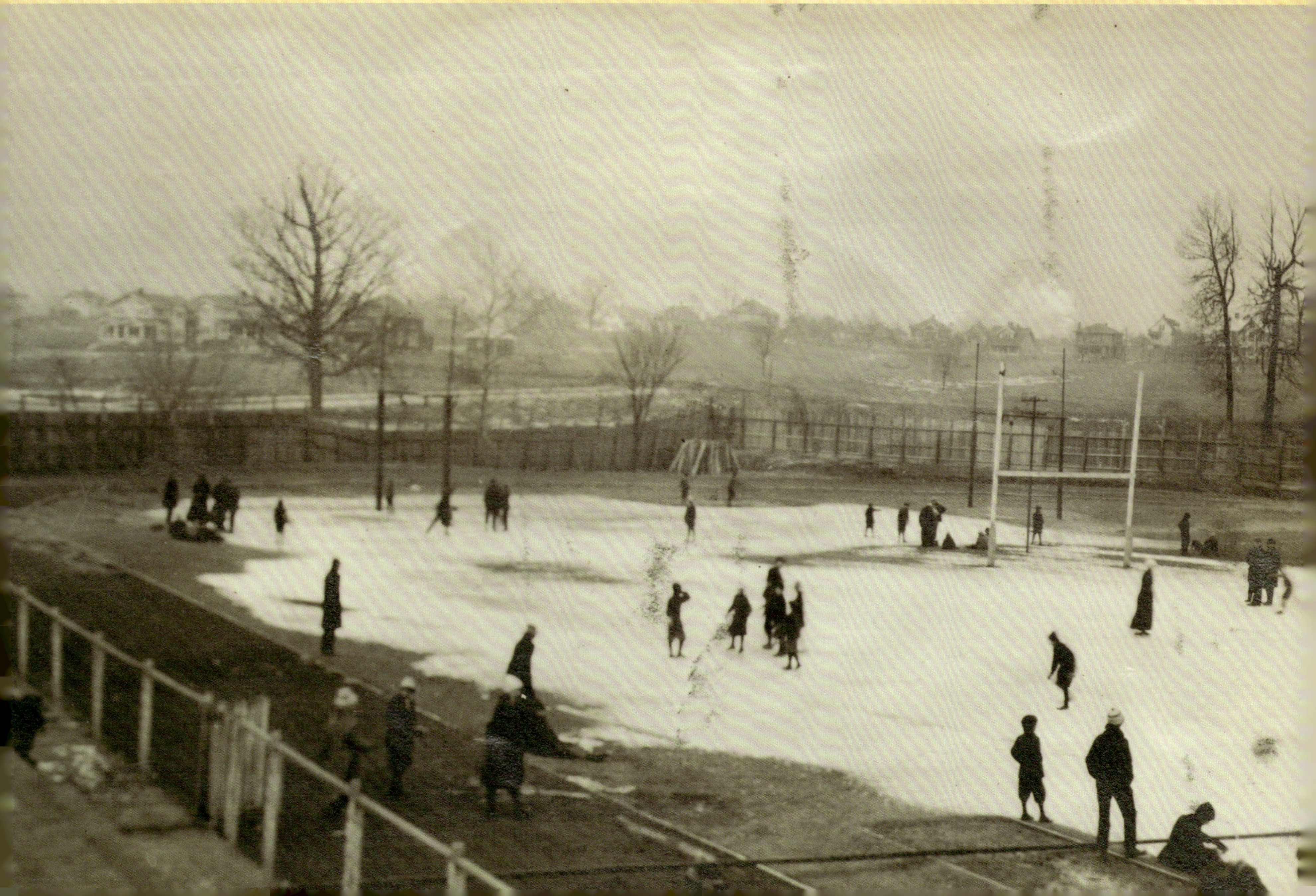

Jordan Field

A Swampy Beginning

We have passed over the Great Divide which, all these years, has separated us from the victories which our great university merits. Before us lie the paths of victory and Indiana will not—shall not—falter.

—Arbutus

OBSERVANT STUDENTS AND VISITORS DRIVING into the Indiana Memorial Union parking lot notice the plaque next to the electronic sign at the corner of the circle drive and Ernie Pyle Hall. If they took a moment to read the plaque, they would learn that, from 1897 through 1959, this lot for automobiles once served as the "field of dreams" for Indiana University athletes. It was called Jordan Field, named for David Starr Jordan, IU's seventh president.

After the devastating fire of 1883 at Seminary Square and the subsequent campus move to the Dunn's Wood site, athletes and spectators continued to walk the mile to the athletics field on the old campus for practices and contests. This continued for fourteen years until the summer of 1897, when the university purchased additional property from Moses Dunn adjacent to the new campus. With this addition, the decision was made to abandon the old field and make a new field on the new grounds. The site identified was next to a creek known as Spanker's Branch, today the Jordan River. Before it could become a viable athletics facility, however, the site needed a substantial amount of work, namely grading and creek diversion; Professor John W. Newsom, Department of Geology, was charged with building the field. In the fall of 1897, the IU football team played its first game on Jordan Field. When the spring of 1898 came and the baseball team began training, it became obvious that drainage at the site had not been addressed when the creek was diverted. As a result, with the

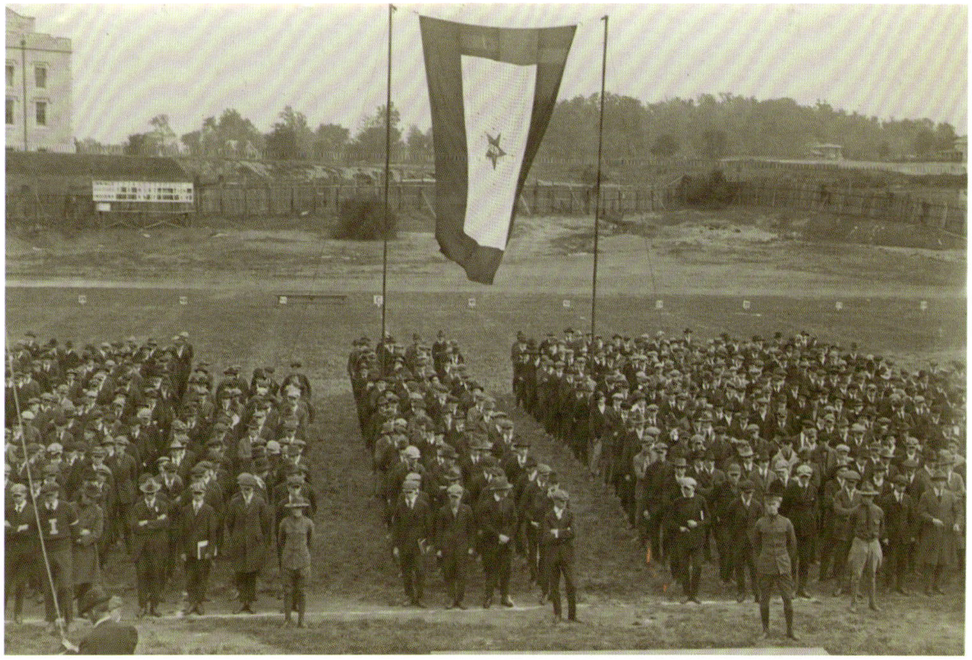

Above, Student Army Training Corps induction ceremony, 1918. P0047359, IU Archives. Photo credit: Henry Thew Stephenson.

Facing top left, IU versus DePauw baseball game at Athletic Park in Seminary Square, precursor to Jordan Field, 1892. P0032101, IU Archives.

Facing bottom left, Temporary ice rink on Jordan Field, winter of 1915–16; from student scrapbook of Ward G. Biddle, and the only known photograph of this usage of the field. P0056314, IU Archives.

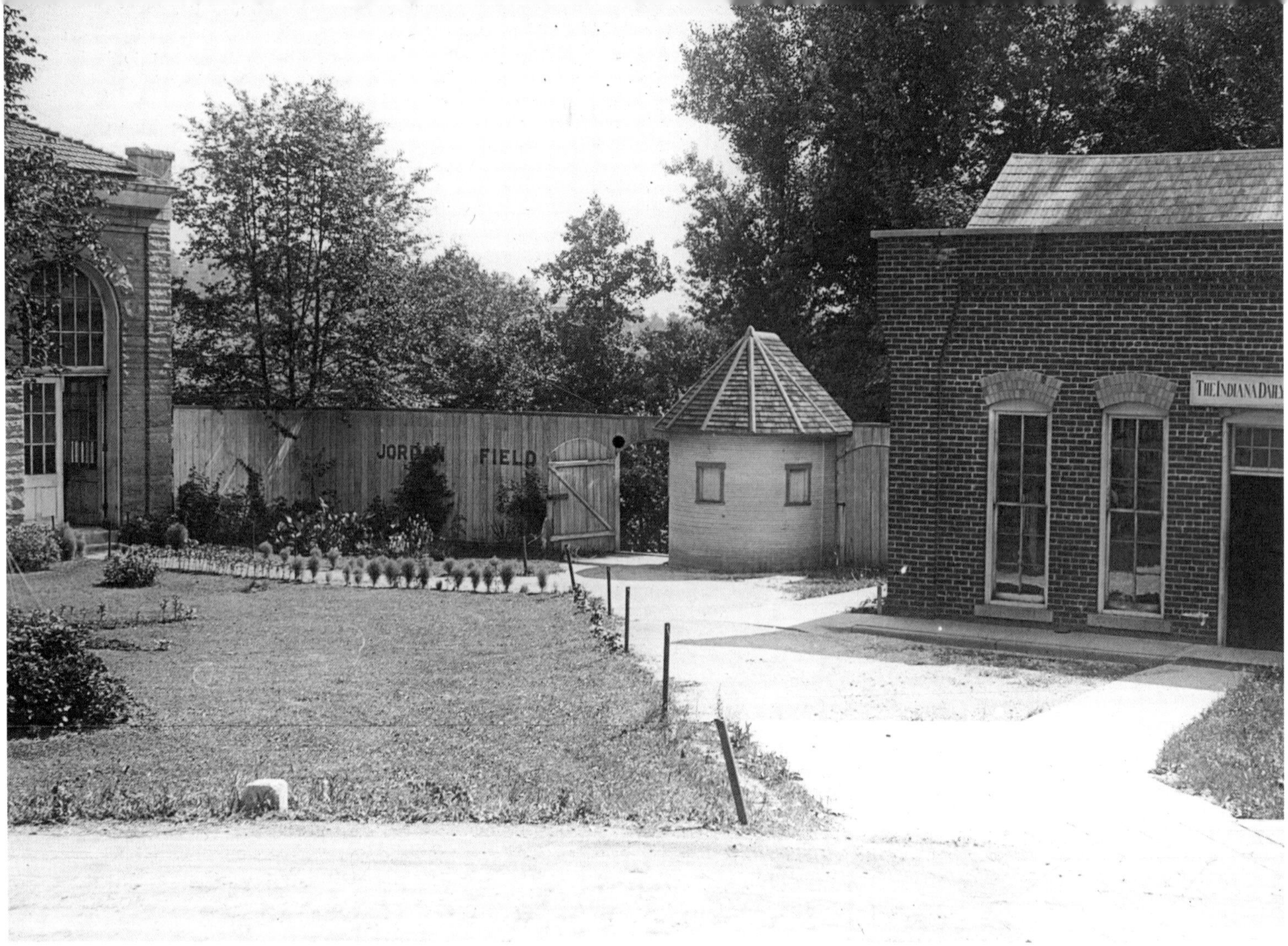

Entrance and ticket booth for Jordan Field, between the *Indiana Daily Student* office and the University Printing Plant, circa 1919. P0045533, IU Archives.

heavy spring rains, water from the creek overflowed onto the field, creating a muddy mess.[1] The springtime condition of Jordan Field continued to be a thorn in the university's side throughout its long life as an athletic field.

The university made small improvements to Jordan Field as funds allowed. In 1901, the Board of Trustees appropriated $500 for bleachers, with additional funds allocated the following year for additional grading and drainage work, as well as a 10-foot-tall fence—alas, no amount of work succeeded in improving the drainage. Over the years, thousands of spectators spent time on the beleaguered multipurpose turf cheering on baseball and football, the track and field team, intramural sports, class scraps, horse races, and polo matches; even the induction of the Student Army Training Corps during World War I took place here.

During the winter of 1908, athletics director James Sheldon decided it was time to take advantage of the land's swampy character. For years there had been talk of turning the field into a skating rink during its unused winter months, and after receiving the go-ahead from the administration, Sheldon supervised the flooding of Jordan Field to create an ice rink. Hydrants were directed at the ground until it was sufficiently covered and ready for the next freeze. To the delight of the students, this practice was repeated over the next several winters.

By 1915 the *Indiana Daily Student* began to issue reports about the impending demise of the "old field" and the university's plans for a new football arena. The accounts were more than a bit premature, however: it wasn't until the early 1920s that football departed. This move should have been to the 1925 Memorial Stadium, but its opening was delayed a year when structural issues forced the stadium to be scrapped and rebuilt. As a result, much of the 1924 football season was played on Indiana Field (a practice field). The final football game, however, was played on Jordan Field between Wabash College and IU

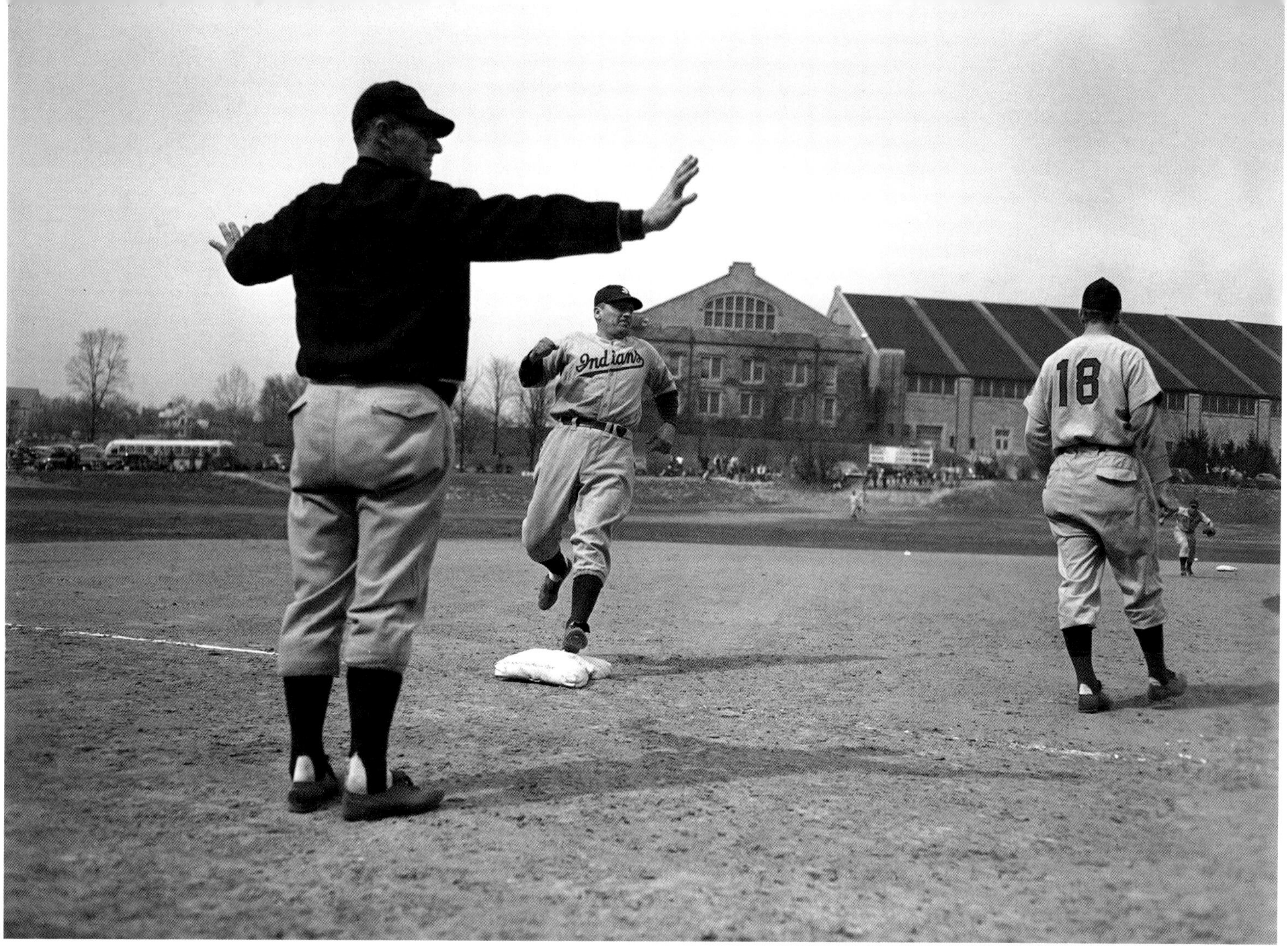

Exhibition game between Indianapolis Indians and Cincinnati Reds on Jordan Field, 1943. P0033647, IU Archives. Photo credit: Allen Graham.

on November 15, 1924. Without the gridiron games, Jordan Field continued to see a great deal of sports action for many years.

In the latter half of the 1930s, there was a movement afoot to finally repair or abandon Jordan Field altogether. In 1936, the IDS published an editorial titled "What a Diamond!" It read that Jordan Field was "still in use as the varsity baseball diamond despite the fact that the part designated as right field resembles a rock pile. Only the other day an Indiana outfielder fell headlong when he tripped over one of the rocks and luckily escaped serious injury. Visiting athletes frequently joke about the condition of the field. 'Hit the ball to me out here in this rock pile,' one was heard to remark."[2]

The cry fell on deaf ears. Several years later, in 1948, the Athletic Department asked the Board of Trustees to consider building a new baseball field on Fee Lane, arguing that Jordan was no longer adequate for baseball due to garages on the south side and overhead power lines near home plate. But the board wanted to investigate further, so baseball continued at Jordan, where minor improvements such as lighting were made to somewhat improve conditions.

The move finally came when the university initiated plans to expand the Indiana Memorial Union, and it became clear that the field would need to be commandeered for a parking area to serve the IMU hotel. In 1959 Jordan Field was paved over. In 1980, the I-Men's Association coordinated the laying of the historic marker by the IMU lot to commemorate Jordan Field and those hearty athletes who slogged their way through the mud and water to play for the "glory of old IU."

America's Pastime Travels to Bloomington

During World War II, Indiana University, like other universities, underwent changes in nearly every aspect of its operations. The number of males on campus dropped considerably due to the wartime effort and many of those who were on campus were in uniform. But during the springs of 1943 and 1944, men in another uniform appeared—baseball uniforms.

At the January 11, 1943, Athletics Committee meeting, IU Athletics Director Zora Clevenger reported that seven professional baseball "clubs" as well as the president of the American Association had contacted him inquiring about the use of the Fieldhouse (now the Ora L. Wildermuth Intramural Center) for spring training because wartime travel restrictions meant the major league teams couldn't go to warmer climes. The committee recommended that Clevenger and IU baseball coach Paul "Pooch" Harrell lead the way to reach an agreement with the Indianapolis Indians and one other team. Within the week, President Herman B Wells reported that the members of the executive committee had approved the proposal for the Indianapolis Indians and Cincinnati Reds to come to campus.

The *Indiana Daily Student* was all atwitter about this development, printing daily reports regarding both teams' arrivals, preparations, practices, and exhibition games. The student reporters were not alone—there was elevated excitement in the small town of Bloomington and across the IU campus. With the war wearing on, everyone longed for uplifting news and events.

In late winter, the Reds' groundskeeper came to campus in order to prep Jordan Field, though the team planned to begin training in the Fieldhouse until weather improved. The Reds, who began arriving March 15, were billeted at the Graham Hotel in town (now the Graham Plaza at 205 N. College). From there they walked to the 1925 Memorial Stadium (named Tenth Street Stadium in 1971, on the site that is now the Arboretum) to use the locker facilities before heading over to the Fieldhouse for four hours of daily practice. The first members of the Indianapolis Indians arrived on March 27, with the entire team due to follow by April 1 or shortly thereafter.

On April 8, 1943, the *Indiana Daily Student* wrote about the first exhibition game between the Reds and Indians on Jordan Field. The Reds triumphed over the Indians 8–6 before a capacity crowd of two thousand students, townspeople, visitors, and members of the armed forces. As those familiar with springtime in southern Indiana can guess, before long the weather became the biggest hurdle facing the two squads—wind, rain, and even snow. Another exhibition game between the Reds and Chicago Cubs, who traveled from their spring

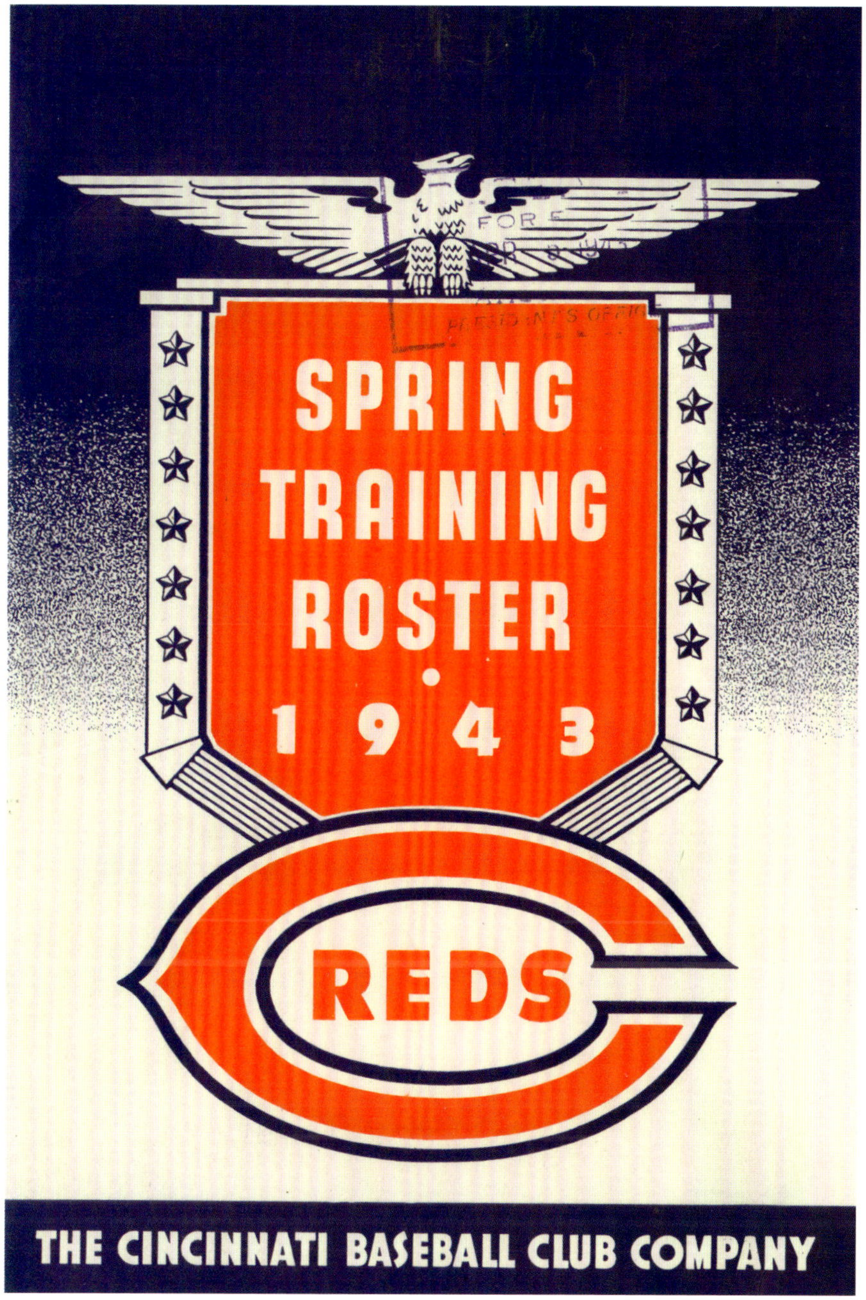

Spring training brochure for Cincinnati Reds, 1943. "Cincinnati Reds, 1943" folder, collection C213.121, IU Archives.

training home at French Lick, Indiana, was canceled due to the pouring rain. With that sad note, the Reds training camp came to a close and the Indians were left with added space in the Fieldhouse for their next few weeks of conditioning before they, too, left Bloomington.

Before the Indians left, they scheduled an exhibition game with the "Harrellmen" on April 13, an experience that would have been an absolute thrill for the IU team. But once again, the weather interfered: it snowed. The game was rescheduled for April 15, and again it snowed. Unfortunately, there was not enough time to reschedule; but the following year the game did take place and IU defeated the Indians, 5–3.

Adapted from "The Boys of Summer at IU," blog post, Indiana University Archives, September 1, 2011, https://blogs.libraries.iub.edu/iubarchives/2011/09/01/the-boys-of-summer-at-iu/.

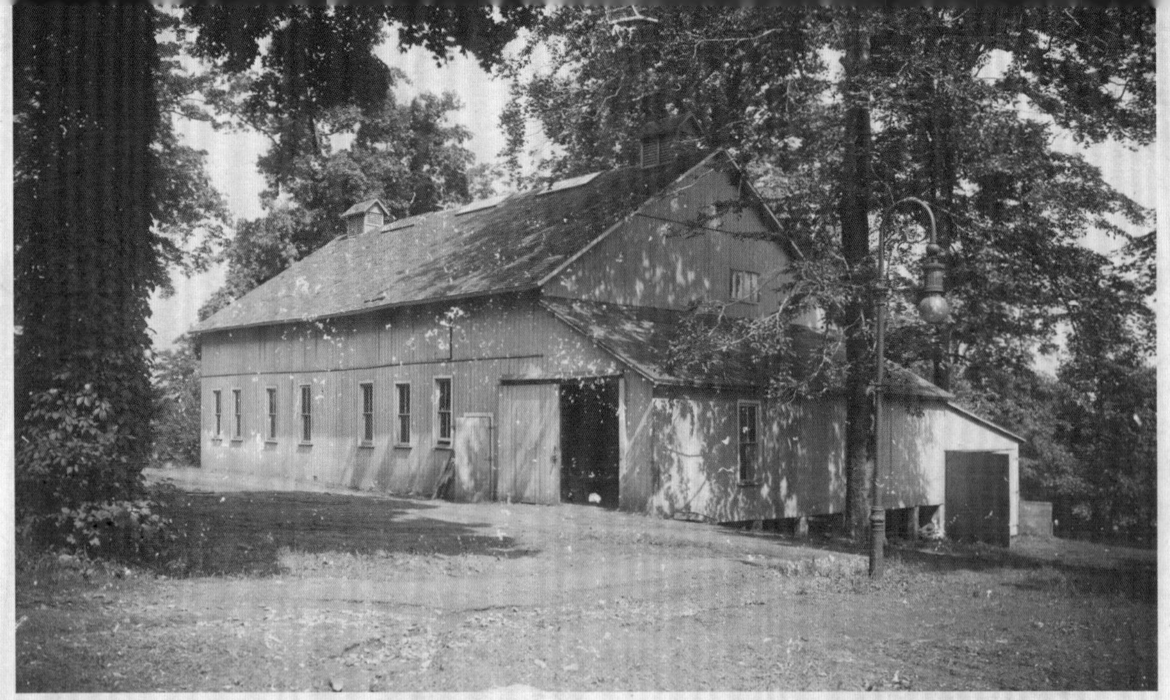

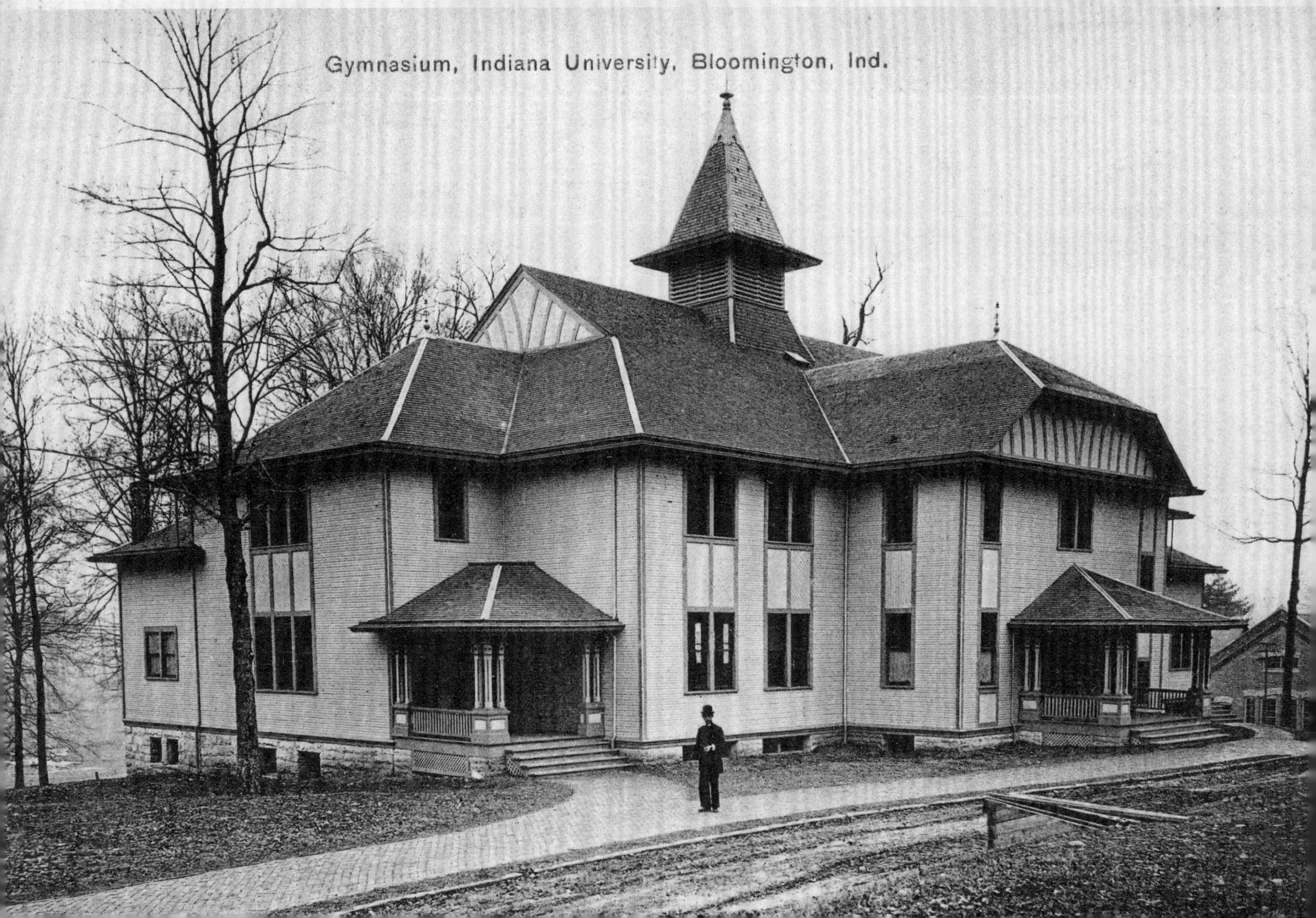
Gymnasium, Indiana University, Bloomington, Ind.

Early Men's Gymnasiums

A "Barn" and IU's Original Assembly Hall

Time and again pitiful wails have gone up from students and patrons of I.U. that that which was of prime importance in an education was kept almost wholly in the background—physical culture.

—Indiana Student *editorial*

In the late nineteenth century, the *Indiana Student*, as the IU student paper was then called, was full of editorial pleas for university administration to heed the needs and desires of students for more physical activity. Civil War veterans brought the new sport of baseball to campus and shortly thereafter came football, track, and other athletic endeavors. The young Hoosiers, however, were displeased that all of their physical activity revolved around the whims of Indiana weather and greatly desired a campus gymnasium that would allow them to train and practice year-round. In November 1889 the *Indiana Student* exclaimed: "Of the many things which I.U. is lacking and which might be used to the greatest advantage, none transcend in importance a good gymnasium. . . . While too much cannot be said in favor of mental and moral training, yet this should not be affected at the expense of physical culture. Too often do we see strong, robust students reduced to mere skeletons after swallowing the curriculum of a college course, intellectual giants but physical weaklings, dyspeptics and consumptives." IU Trustee James D. Maxwell then wrote to the renowned Dudley Allen Sargent of Harvard College about the practicality of building a gymnasium on the campus. Sargent responded with a rough sketch along with a detailed description of the "best plan of building a large, serviceable, yet cheaply constructed gymnasium." He suggested it would cost $15,000 to construct it of brick, a mere $1,500 if built of wood.[1]

Early in 1890 the students took it upon themselves to establish a gym off campus in a hall above the city post office. The students thought if the state could see how heavily the facility was used, it couldn't ignore the need for a campus facility. Despite these undertakings, building a campus gymnasium didn't gain traction within the university. Over the next year, the basement in Wylie Hall was fitted as a gymnasium for female students, and in the spring of 1891, the trustees appropriated $400 to equip a gymnasium for the men in the basement of Owen Hall (it is not clear if that plan ever materialized). By late 1891, the Board of Trustees finally approved funds not to exceed $1,000 to construct a gymnasium for the men. Although the small sum was below Sargent's recommended rock-bottom price of $1,500, the students nonetheless rejoiced: "One thousand dollars for a gymnasium to be erected and equipped immediately! We throw up our hats in appreciation of this promising act of the Board, and acknowledge with pleasure the faculty spirit that made the initiative [*sic*] step possible this year. I.U.! Rah!!"[2] Construction for the simple facility began immediately, and the building was ready for dedication by Foundation Day on January 22, 1892.

This first gymnasium was built so as to easily accommodate additions. Located 4 feet west and 71 feet north of Owen Hall, the simple wooden structure resembled a barn—it was 50 feet wide, 66 feet long, and had an 18-foot ceiling. The 1891 university catalog described it as "a new and spacious building

Facing top, First campus gymnasium, behind Owen Hall, later used as carpentry shop and barn, 1918. P0022843, IU Archives. Photo credit: Henry Thew Stephenson.

Facing bottom, Assembly Hall (the Second Men's Gymnasium), east of Owen Hall, 1912. P0020434, IU Archives.

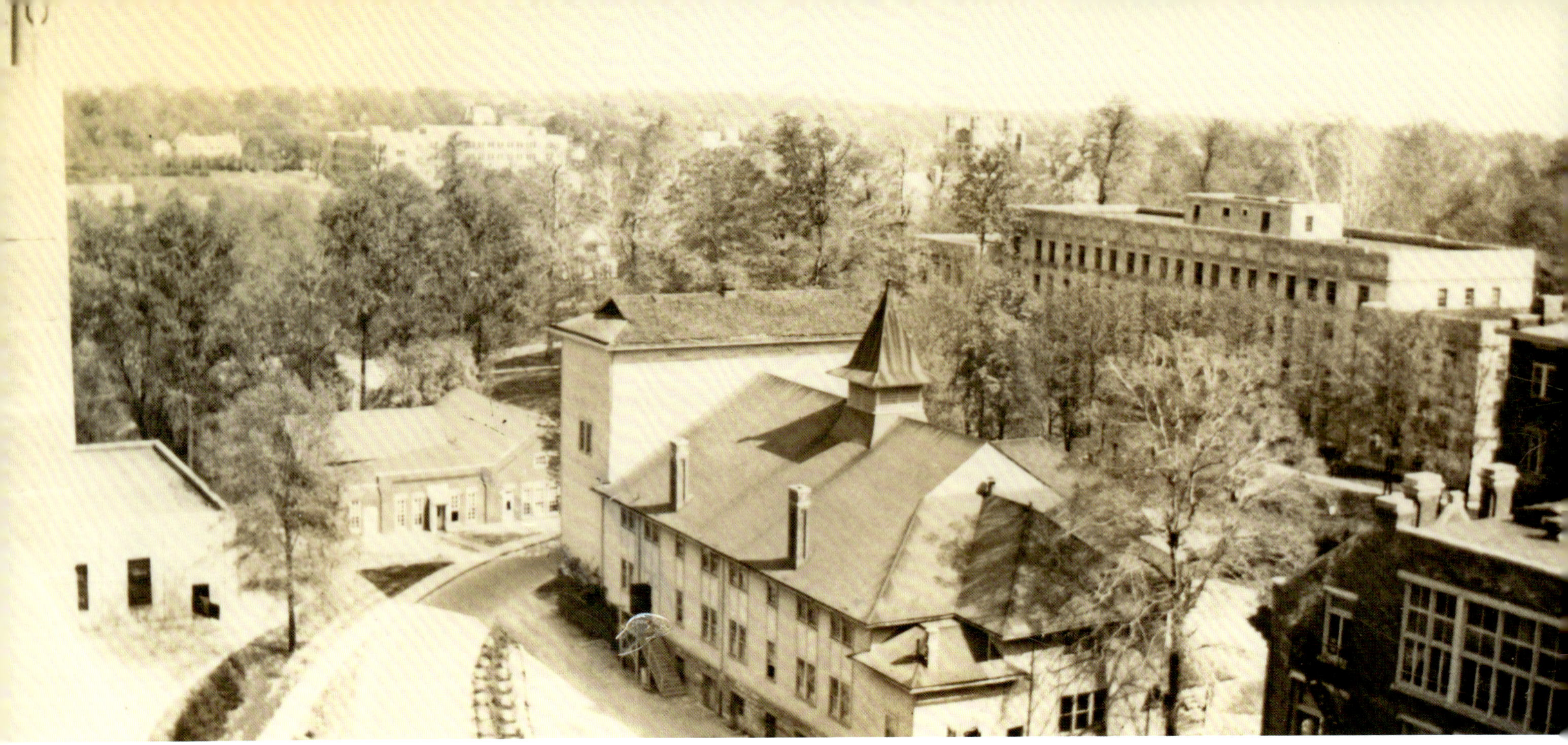

Assembly Hall and its surroundings, a photo by IU student George T. Engelman Jr. from atop IMU, 1938. P0025148, IU Archives.

and while not a pretentious building it is well adapted to the purpose for which it is intended."[3] The $1.00 charge per term for students to use the facility served a dual purpose: to raise funds for additional apparatus and to keep the gawkers away. As the students had predicted, the gymnasium was heavily utilized, and by December the trustees approved funds for more equipment and a 12-by-30-foot locker room. Still, the popularity, coupled with the growing student population and the lack of space to assemble the students as a body, revealed quickly that the hastily built gymnasium just wasn't large enough. By 1896, the university administration decided that a much larger, multipurpose building was needed. The First Men's Gymnasium was added to over the years and finally was repurposed as a carpentry shop and stable. It was razed in 1932 to make way for a road between Owen Hall and the newly constructed Indiana Memorial Union.

On August 10, 1896, the trustees awarded the architectural contract for the Second Men's Gymnasium, later known as Assembly Hall, to Philip Jeckel of Anderson. While it, too, was built of wood, the exterior was much more elaborate than the former gymnasium and was 125 feet long and 65 feet wide. It was a one-story structure with a basement constructed in an asymmetrical design, with bands of narrow, long windows, all topped with a jaunty cupola on its shingled roof. Craftsman style was reflected in the low-pitched gabled roofs, broad eaves, exposed wooden elements, and the two large, open porches. Located just east of Owen Hall, the gymnasium could seat sixteen hundred people unless the floor was being used for a sporting event; then only the galleries above, with room for four hundred, could be used for seating. The main floor was 90 feet long, and the galleries were along the north, south, and west ends. Because it was a multipurpose structure, a stage was built at the east end, complete with a dirt-floor dressing room.[4] The Second Men's Gymnasium was dedicated December 18, 1896.

Throughout its lifetime, Assembly Hall witnessed many athletic events, speakers, dramatic performances, weekly convocations, and even stood in as an infirmary for ailing soldiers during the 1918 influenza epidemic. The state's first high school basketball tournament was held within its walls on March 10 and 11, 1911, with twelve teams contending (Crawfordsville won the state championship over Lebanon, 24–17). IU's tenth and longest-serving president, William Lowe Bryan, was installed here on January 21, 1903. The first professional stars of music and theater ever to come to IU's campus, such as the Chicago Symphony Orchestra and Otis Skinner, performed here. Other luminaries who appeared in Assembly Hall were Carl Sandburg, James Whitcomb Riley, William Butler Yeats, and Helen Keller.

In 1914, the university made significant changes to enlarge the stage for The Legend of Leonora with US actress Maude Adams. As it was already difficult to effectively utilize Assembly Hall as a gymnasium due to the danger of running into one of the posts used to support the galleries, these additional renovations to enhance the theatrical facilities of the building sealed the fate of its future as an athletic facility. In 1915, the Board of Trustees authorized construction of a new gymnasium as soon as funds could be made available. After the new gymnasium opened in 1917, the Second Men's Gymnasium became known as Assembly Hall.

The university continued to use Assembly Hall for theatrical events, commencements, and other like occasions, but it was finally razed in late 1938 to make way for a parking lot. In 2015, a historical marker was placed on the site of the first Assembly Hall to mark the birthplace of Hoosier hysteria, an early stage for the creative arts, and the setting of the final send-off for thousands of graduating seniors.

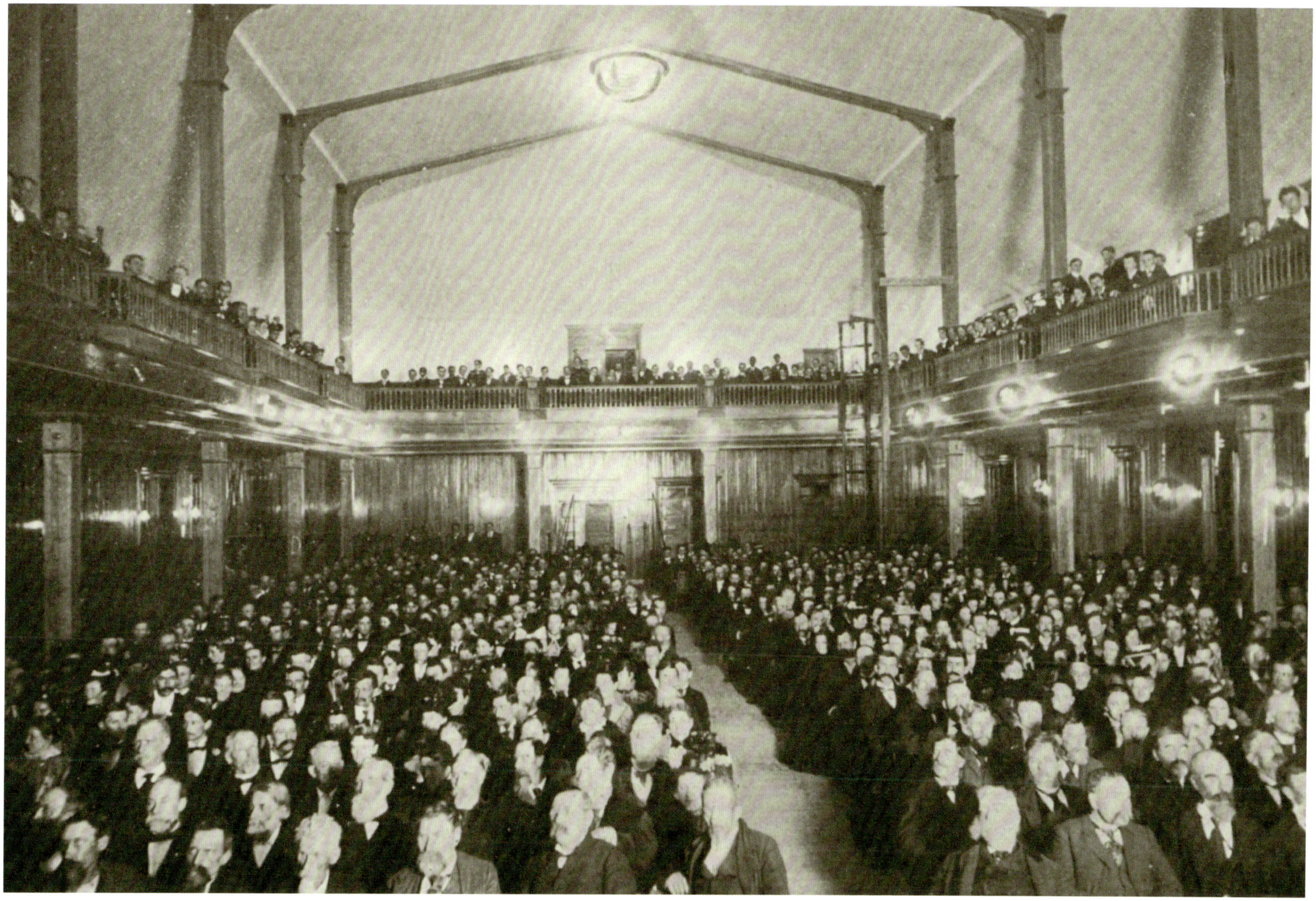

University community in Assembly Hall for lecture by former Confederate general John Brown Gordon, 1897. P0020439, IU Archives.

Tenth Street Stadium 1925

ARCHITECT Robert Frost Daggett

ARCHITECTURAL STYLE Collegiate Gothic

ORIGINAL NAME Memorial Stadium

RAZED 1982

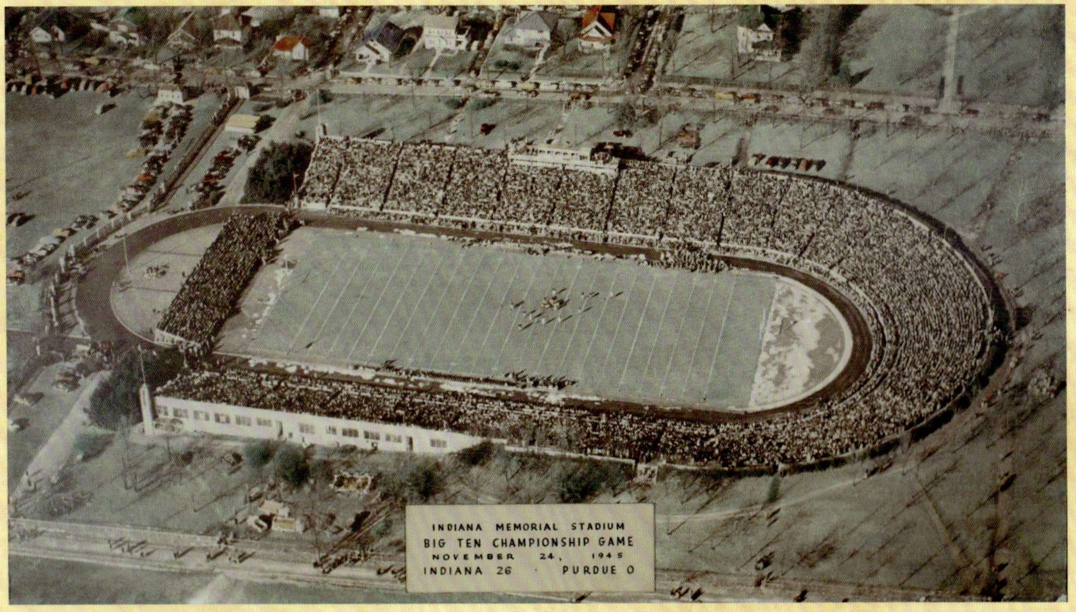

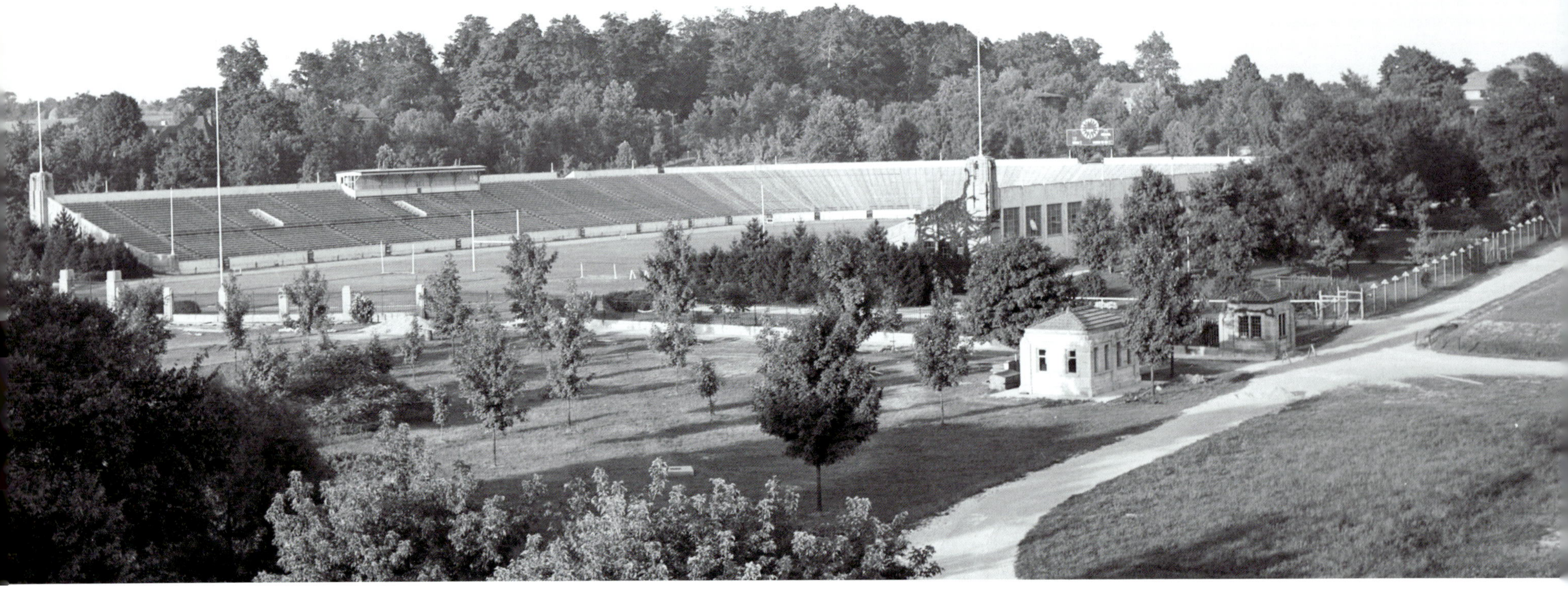

Tenth Street Stadium

"The Giant"

College without athletics would be like greens without bacon. Everyone makes room for an athlete and a monogram is more to be prized than much Greek and fine learning. Being able to demolish the ribs of a gridiron opponent, to appropriate hotel and Pullman towels to throw the bull make college worthwhile. A University is known by the athletes it keeps.

—Arbutus

THE UNIVERSITY'S FIRST STADIUM WAS ORIGINALLY named Memorial Stadium but renamed the Tenth Street Stadium in 1971. The structure was demolished in 1982 to make way for the Jesse H. and Beulah Chanley Cox Arboretum and now often is referred to as the First Memorial Stadium. Its history began in 1899, when Indiana University joined Purdue, Wisconsin, Michigan, Northwestern, Minnesota, Illinois, the University of Chicago, and Iowa as a member of the Western Conference (now the Big Ten): the modern era of IU athletics began then, setting the stage for a major expansion of both programs and facilities. Jordan Field, located approximately where the Indiana Memorial Union parking lot lies today, served as home venue for almost all of IU's athletic events and contained a gridiron, two baseball diamonds, and a cinder running path. The Jordan River, which ran to the immediate south, often flooded, spilling over on the playing areas, causing—it was said—more football games to be lost due to field conditions than lack of talent. The moment was right for Indiana University athletics to assume new prominence.

College football gained substantial popularity during the first decade of the twentieth century, and by 1915 it was clear to IU trustees and school officials, including President William Lowe Bryan, that something needed to be done if IU was to keep pace with its new conference rivals. A men's gymnasium had been completed in 1917, and planning efforts then turned to football. But the first of several disruptions and delays occurred: World War I. Interest in planning a new stadium was temporarily placed on the shelf to wait for peacetime. Four years later with the Great War ended, Indiana University launched a Memorial Fund drive that would provide support for a new women's dormitory, football stadium, and student union. The women's dormitory became Memorial Hall and the football stadium Memorial Stadium, each dedicated to those students who lost their lives serving in the war. The student union would become the Indiana Memorial Union but would not be completed until 1932.

Distinguished Indianapolis architect Robert Frost Daggett was hired to design what was first programmed to be a 40,000-seat football stadium. This lofty goal would increase the Jordan Field spectator capacity fivefold. Eventually the proposed size of the stadium was reduced to a more feasible 22,000 seats, which was still a comfortable capacity given the population of Bloomington and surrounding counties. Daggett delivered a horseshoe-shaped design that opened to the main campus,

Facing top, Full stadium for 1945 Big Ten Championship game between IU and Purdue. P0023502, IU Archives.

Facing bottom, Tenth Street Stadium (First Memorial Stadium), 1939. P0022466, IU Archives. Photo credit: Lloyd Evans, Indiana University.

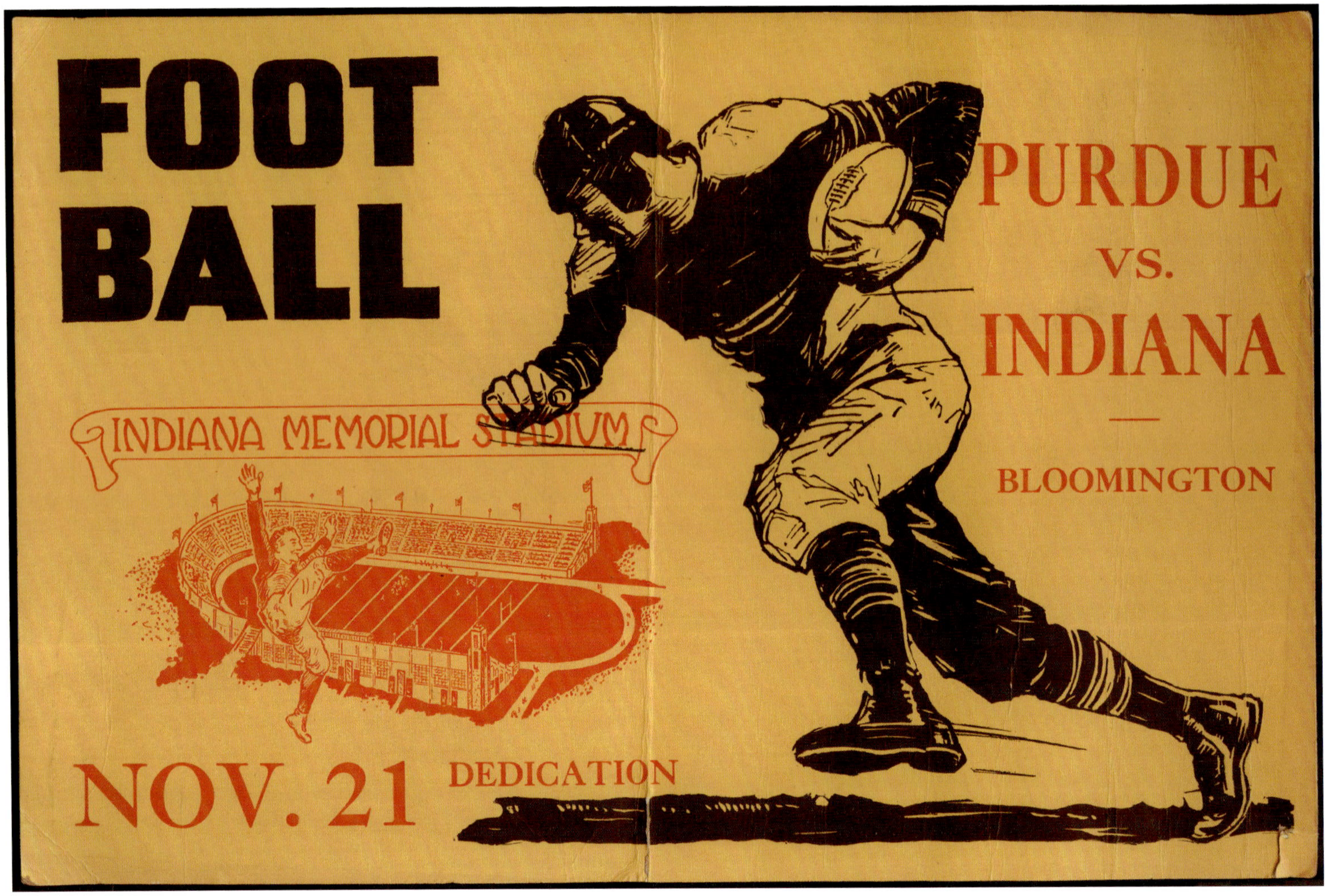

Stadium dedication and inaugural Old Oaken Bucket game poster, 1925. P0044700, IU Archives.

with two dominant towers to be built on the ends of the grandstands that ran on parallel east–west lines. The design concept carried a rich Collegiate Gothic theme that played well next to the new gymnasium, which was closely located south and west of the stadium. Daggett's design proposal was in full compliance with the university's master plan created by urban planner and landscape architect George Kessler a decade earlier.

Construction of the football stadium was a comedy of errors. As soon as site work was underway, it was discovered that the limestone excavation allowance would cover only 10 percent of the actual stone removal required to allow for pouring concrete. Poor construction weather then set in, again jeopardizing the scheduled completion date, which was established in hopes of accommodating a full football schedule in the fall of 1924. Additional incentive to finish work by 1924 was provided by Purdue University's plan to open Ross-Ade Stadium that same fall, and IU officials naturally didn't want to finish in second place behind the Boilermakers. Despite these setbacks, it still looked like the original completion date would be met. A ruinous disaster then struck: as the project was nearing completion, the newly poured concrete exhibited severe structural deficiencies. The entire structure was condemned and demolished. The 1924 football season would be impossible to host at the new stadium. Legal proceedings attendant to the concrete problem went on well into the 1930s; however, work on building a replacement stadium commenced immediately under a contract with a new builder. The home football schedule was transferred for one year to Indiana Field, which had been a football practice area located just east of the Men's Gymnasium, now the site of the Sidney and Lois Eskenazi Museum of Art.

Finally, as the 1925 school year approached, the new stadium was ready for use. Played on October 3, 1925, the first game resulted in a 31–0 win over Indiana State Normal. Additional victories over Miami of Ohio and Rose Polytechnic hyped the excitement of playing in the new campus "Giant," as it was frequently called by students. The first loss in the new venue occurred against Syracuse on October 17, but all eyes were on the Dedication Game to be played against Purdue on November 21. That game, in a brand-new football era, would require a new symbol—a trophy to be claimed by the winning team.

THE OLD OAKEN BUCKET

Many rumors cling to the origination story of the Old Oaken Bucket to this day. Some believe it was discovered in southern Indiana in an old well that was once a source of water for Morgan's Raiders during the Civil War. However, the truth is that Chicago area alumni of IU and Purdue came up with the idea, and Dr. Clarence Jones of IU and Russell Gray of Purdue procured the bucket from the Bruner family farm in southeastern Indiana. Fittingly, the first Old Oaken Bucket game ended in a scoreless tie and side-by-side block letters I and P were placed on the bucket. The tradition of placing an I for Indiana or a P for Purdue continues to this day, depending on which team wins the game. The Old Oaken Bucket is now the second oldest game trophy contested in college football. Only the Little Brown Jug, played for by Michigan and Minnesota, is older.

LITTLE 500

In 1951 the first official Little 500 bicycle race was run on the Indiana University campus and its home was the 1925 stadium on Tenth Street. There had been a smaller version of the Little 500 run the previous year around streets circling the auditorium, but when Howdy Wilcox, president of the Indiana University Foundation, created the modern-day race a better venue was needed. The stadium fit the bill perfectly. Like the renowned Indianapolis 500, thirty-three entrants won a race spot through qualification runs. Two hundred laps around a track measuring 440 yards resulted in a total race distance of approximately 50 miles. Very quickly the Little 500 gained national fame as the "World's Greatest College Weekend." Altogether thirty Little 500 races were run at the stadium on Tenth Street until the event moved to the newly constructed Bill Armstrong Stadium for the 1981 race. When the movie *Breaking Away*—written by alumnus Steve Tesich, a Little 500 bicycle rider in the early 1960s—was filmed in 1978, this stadium served as the location for the race scenes. The movie continues to be part of IU and Little 500 tradition.

By the late 1970s, the stadium was showing considerable wear and decline. Engineering studies were performed, and in a repeat of history, it was condemned to demolition. Disposition of the site became a major campus discussion topic. Some wanted parking; others thought it would be a good location for a classroom building. Close study of the university's land use plan however pointed to a more obvious use: green space. On the recommendation of President John Ryan, the university trustees adopted a plan created by the Indiana University Architect's Office to develop an arboretum. The plan incorporated the protection and preservation of many of the stadium's architectural features, including the end columns, ticket booths, and wrought-iron fence bordering the west side of the site, all of which have been incorporated in the Jesse H. and Beulah Chanley Cox Arboretum.

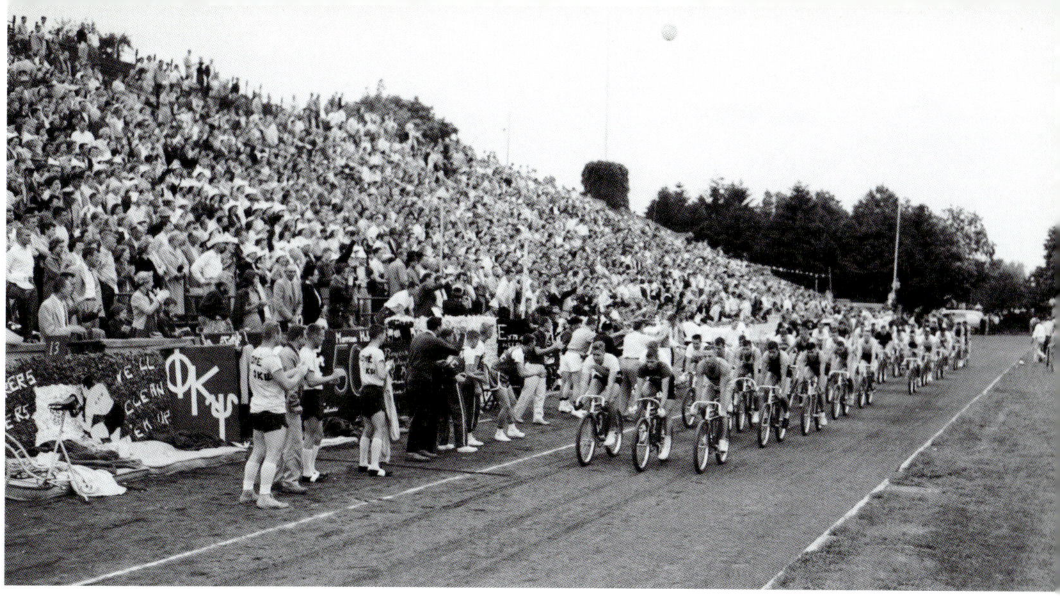

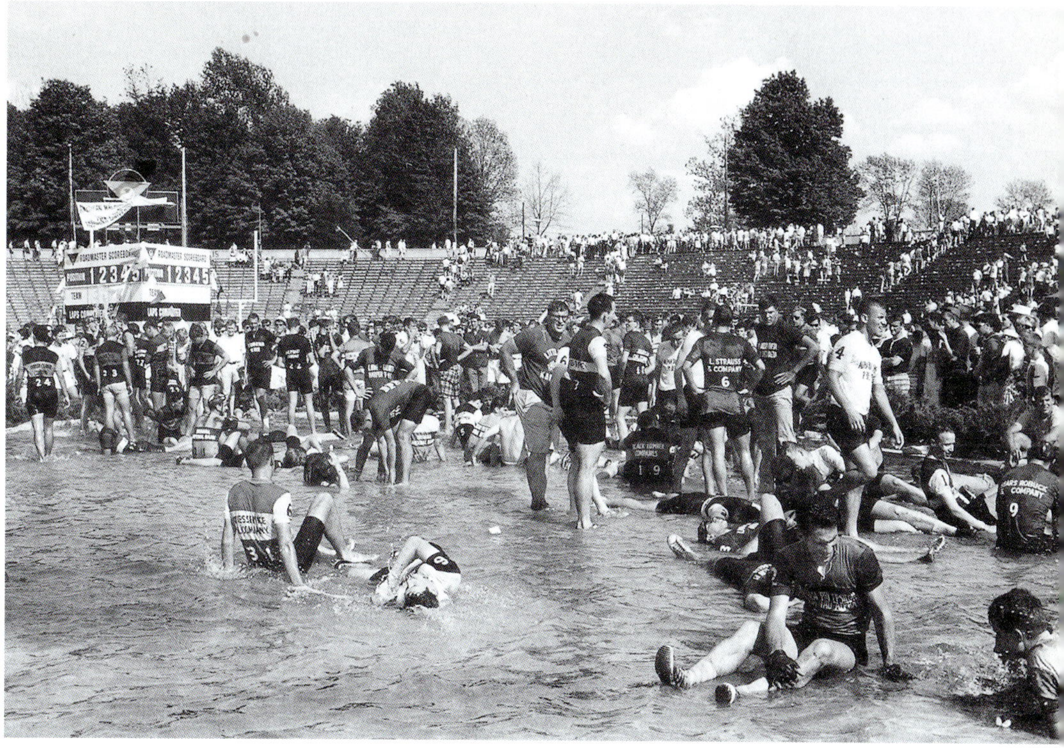

Top, Running of 1955 Little 500 bicycle race at the 1925 stadium. P0023774, IU Archives.

Above, Tradition of tired Little 500 riders cooling off in a makeshift infield pool after the race, circa 1965. Photo credit: Indiana University Student Foundation.

Ora L. Wildermuth Intramural Center 1928

ARCHITECT Robert Frost Daggett

ARCHITECTURAL STYLE Collegiate Gothic

ORIGINAL NAME Fieldhouse

Men's Gymnasium 1917

ARCHITECT R. P. Daggett and Co.

ARCHITECTURAL STYLE Collegiate Gothic

School of Public Health 1961

ARCHITECT Eggers and Higgins

ARCHITECTURAL STYLE Modern

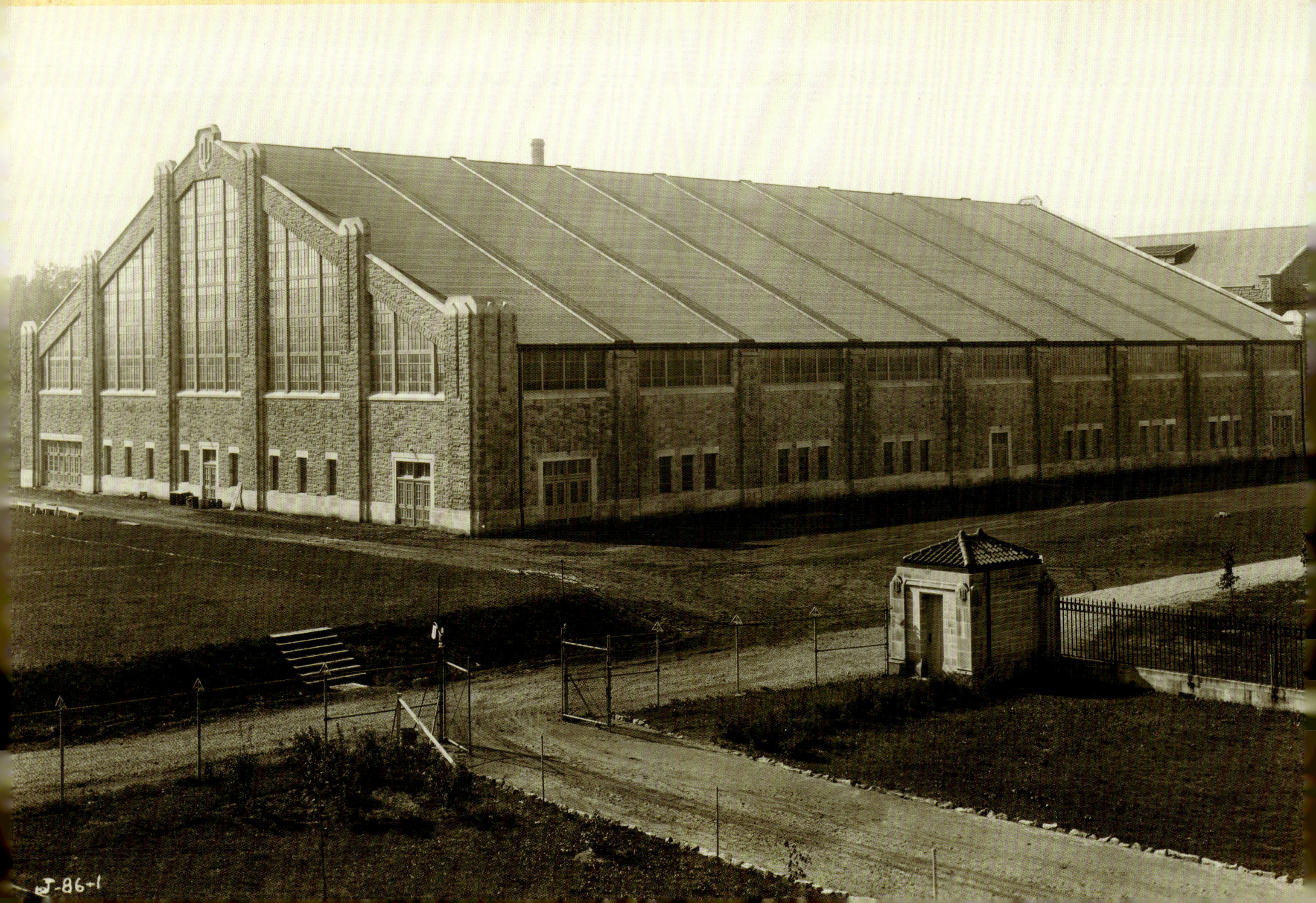

Ora L. Wildermuth Intramural Center

A Tableau of IU Sports and Leisure

The Gymnasium is a symbol of the University's creed. It stands for health, that is, for the whole man. A student who has trained his intellect and neglected his body is not a whole man. He is not ready for battle. The University stands for the whole man, the well man, and this great gymnasium is a part of the means of securing that end.

—Indiana University President William Lowe Bryan

SITTING HIGH ABOVE THE CENTER OF CAMPUS directly across Seventh Street from the Indiana Memorial Union stands one landmark structure made up of a trio of buildings. The first two constructed were the Men's Gymnasium and the Fieldhouse (the latter is now the Ora L. Wildermuth Intramural Center)—two campus historic structures built almost a hundred years ago. Attached to the northeast side of the two-building complex is the School of Public Health Building. Constructed in 1917, 1927, and 1961, respectively, the three edifices now serve as one large venue that supports student recreational life at Indiana University. At any hour scores of students are entering to take part in intramural sports or more casual physical activity at one of the numerous basketball courts, handball and racquetball courts, or a myriad of other spaces devoted to play. The complex touches the life of every single IU student at one time or another.

MEN'S GYMNASIUM (1917)

The Men's Gymnasium, the oldest of the three, was designed by R. P. Daggett and Co. of Indianapolis and was occupied in January 1917. To prepare the area for the new building, approximately two hundred apple trees had to be removed. More than five hundred male students answered the call, wielding axes as they marched to the site. Two hundred coeds provided an audience, offering the boys their moral support and water as the mad scene unfolded. Even President William Lowe Bryan pitched in with his own ax and helped cut down the orchard.[1] By the end of the day, the site was ready for excavation.

The new gymnasium was a quintessential American field house and was constructed of Indiana limestone in Collegiate Gothic style. The sprawling building has a west orientation, with two large main entrances facing what is now the Indiana Memorial Union parking lot and outdoor tennis courts. The entrances feature tall arched doorways with ornate stone carvings of early IU symbols. Monumental stairways carry students and faculty to wide hallways strung with offices and athletic courts. The architect designed a colonnade of arched windows along the second level of the west elevation of the gymnasium, allowing natural light to pour into the main basketball playing area.

When first opened, the Men's Gymnasium was home for IU athletics, including the athletic director and staff, and boasted a seating capacity of 2,500 for basketball games. The university's athletic programs grew substantially once the Men's Gymnasium was available for use. The men's swimming pool led to the debut of the first Indiana University varsity swimming program, and an IU boxing team was soon competing against other colleges in the Midwest. The IU baseball teams, track and field teams, and wrestling team benefited from the new availability of indoor practice space. The bowling alley in the basement allowed students to enjoy a sport not often found in small Indiana towns.

Facing, Wildermuth Fieldhouse, 1929. P0026774, IU Archives.

The first basketball game in the new gymnasium was played on January 19, 1917, the Hoosiers prevailing against the University of Iowa, 12–7. The varsity basketball team's record that year was 3–3 (the season record was 13–6).[2] The swimming pool in the gymnasium was one of the first common spaces ever racially integrated in Bloomington. We know that President Herman B Wells was the catalyst for this change. Wells later reported that he asked then athletic director Zora Clevenger to ask popular IU African American football lineman J. C. "Rooster" Coffee to jump into the pool and swim at the busiest hour.[3]

One feature in the hallways and stairways of the Men's Gymnasium requires particular explanation. The Greek crosses, or backward swastikas, were installed as graphic design tiles years before their use by Nazi Germany. At the time the gymnasium was built, the symbol represented luck, light, love, and life, as evidenced by the four L shapes forming the symbol.

Within ten years, the student body and Indiana University athletics had outgrown the Men's Gymnasium and plans were underway to build a new field house that would add considerably to the space available for varsity sports and student recreational activity.

THE FIELDHOUSE (ORA L. WILDERMUTH INTRAMURAL CENTER)

Completed in 1928, the building was originally called just the Fieldhouse but in 1971 was renamed for Ora L. Wildermuth of Gary, Indiana, an Indiana University alumnus, lawyer and judge, and an IU trustee for twenty-seven years. The Ora L. Wildermuth Intramural Center served as the home of Indiana University athletics from 1928 to 1960.

The Wildermuth Intramural Center was designed by Robert Frost Daggett of Indianapolis and was considered to be the best facility of its type in the nation when it opened. The lack of sight line–obstructing columns lends a feel of openness throughout the building. It is so architecturally compatible with the Men's Gymnasium that one has to look hard to find where the two structures are connected. Wildermuth was constructed of Indiana limestone, brick, and steel and features a sizable pitched roof. The limestone facade is stacked in a rough-faced, random ashlar pattern and is unpretentious in detail.

Two national championship basketball teams, 1940 and 1953, played home games in the Fieldhouse. The Hoosiers compiled an overall record of 234–74 in thirty-two seasons, including five Big Ten Conference Championships and six perfect home seasons in this venue. As men's basketball became more popular, the seating capacity for eight thousand patrons was deemed insufficient and plans were made to move to a larger facility. After a short stay of eleven years in Gladstein Fieldhouse, built in 1960, the Hoosiers found a permanent home in today's Assembly Hall.

The Wildermuth Intramural Center functions as one of two major hot spots for student recreational sports on the IU Bloomington campus. Coupled with the newer Student Recreational Sports Center on the north side of campus, Wildermuth Intramural Center plays host to thousands of students each day, adding to the quality of their lives, possibly more than any other two buildings on campus. The Indiana University recreational sports program is a national model for well-managed intramural sports.

SCHOOL OF PUBLIC HEALTH

By the late 1950s, student enrollment on the IU Bloomington campus had increased to fifteen thousand students, and programs in the School of Health, Physical Education, and Recreation were expanding rapidly as leisure time was becoming a greater dynamic in U.S. life. The architectural firm Eggers and Higgins of New York was commissioned to design a major addition to the Ora L. Wildermuth Intramural Center that would accomplish dual results: create space for the School of Health, Physical Education, and Recreation programs, and provide additional space for recreational sports sponsored by the school.

Eggers and Higgins designed a modest structure that blended with, rather than intruded on, the Men's Gymnasium and the Fieldhouse. The Health, Physical Education, and Recreation Building (HPER) opened in 1961 and expanded the previous, two-building footprint to the north. It was clad in Indiana limestone and designed as a rectangle with a spacious, open courtyard in the middle. The courtyard was closed in during a major renovation in 2010, adding 24,000 square feet to the facility.

Facing, William and Charlotte Lowe Bryan among IU faculty and students clearing an apple orchard to make room for new gymnasium, 1915. P0020482, IU Archives.

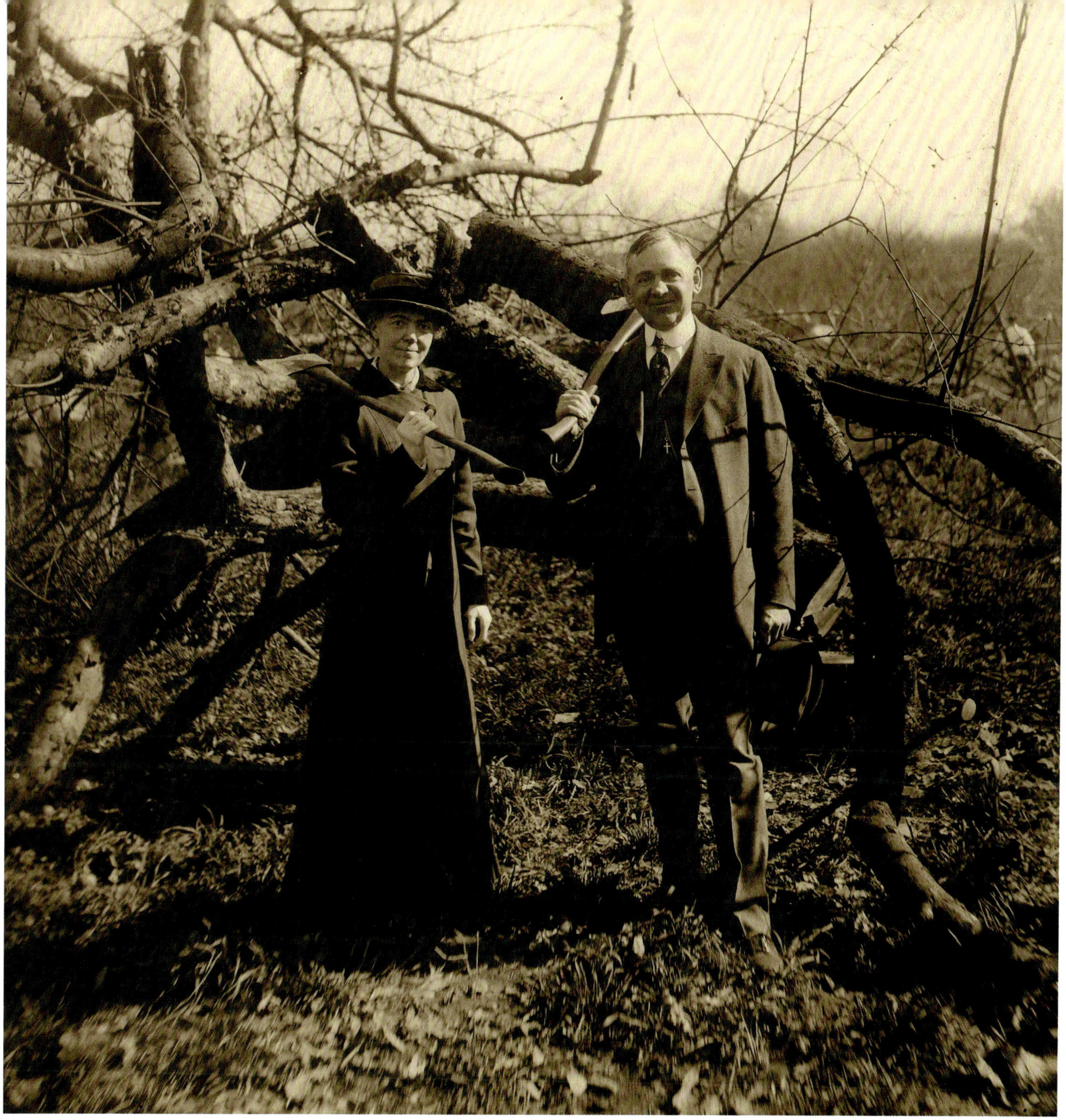

The 1961 School of Public Health included classrooms, faculty offices, a library, racquetball courts, and small, multipurpose gyms. But the true showcase of this new building was its new 25-yard, six-lane Royer Pool, named after Robert (Bob) Royer, IU men's swim coach from 1931 to 1943. Under the tutelage of Royer's successor, James "Doc" Counsilman, along with diving coach Hobie Billingsley, a dynasty began in Royer Pool. The record books are filled with the names of numerous Indiana University world-class swimmers, including many Olympic medal winners. The Indiana University men's swim team won twenty consecutive Big Ten titles (24 in all) and six consecutive NCAA Championships (1968–73).

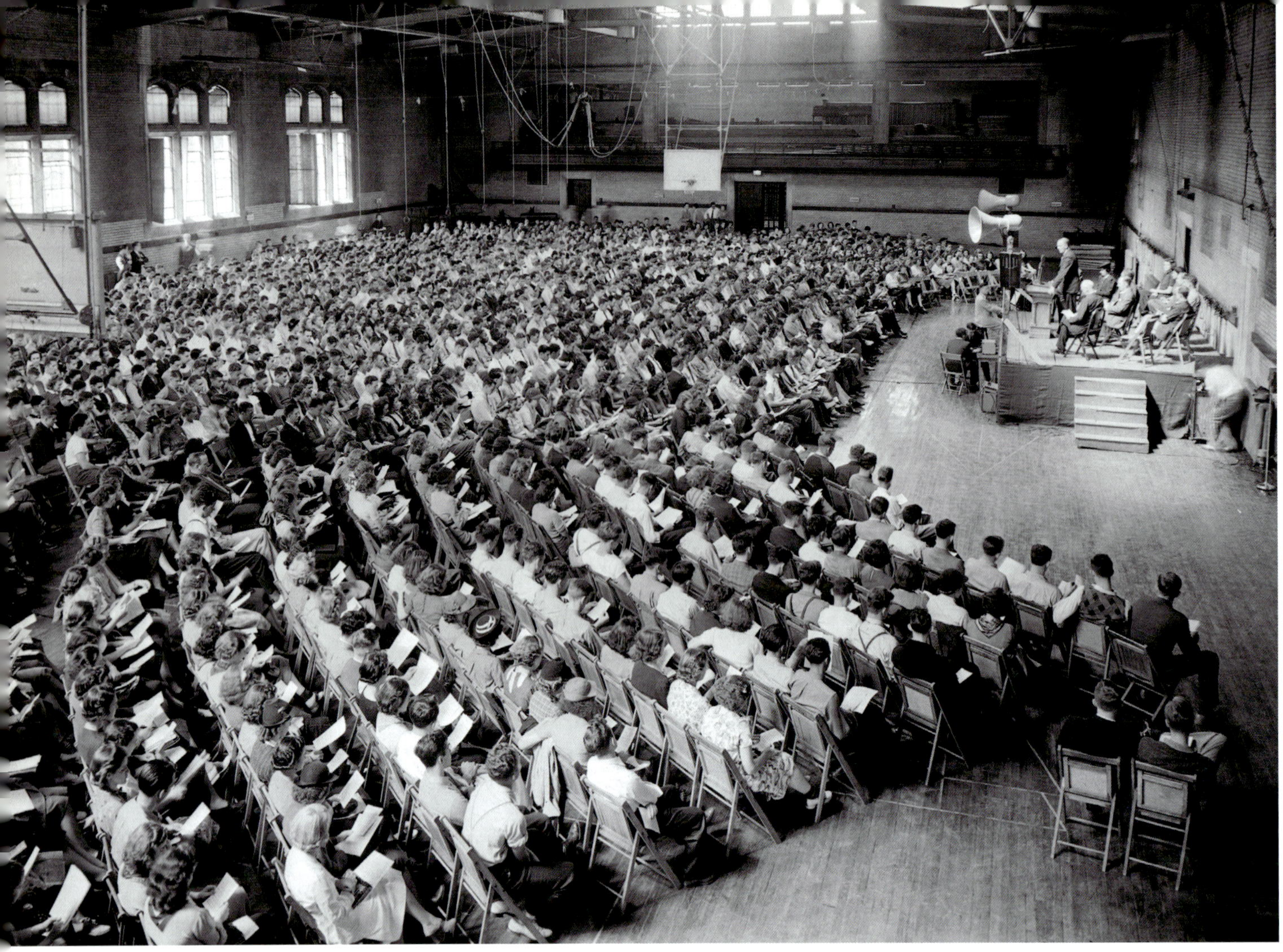

First freshman convocation in the Fieldhouse, in the second-floor gymnasium, 1938. P0031218, IU Archives.

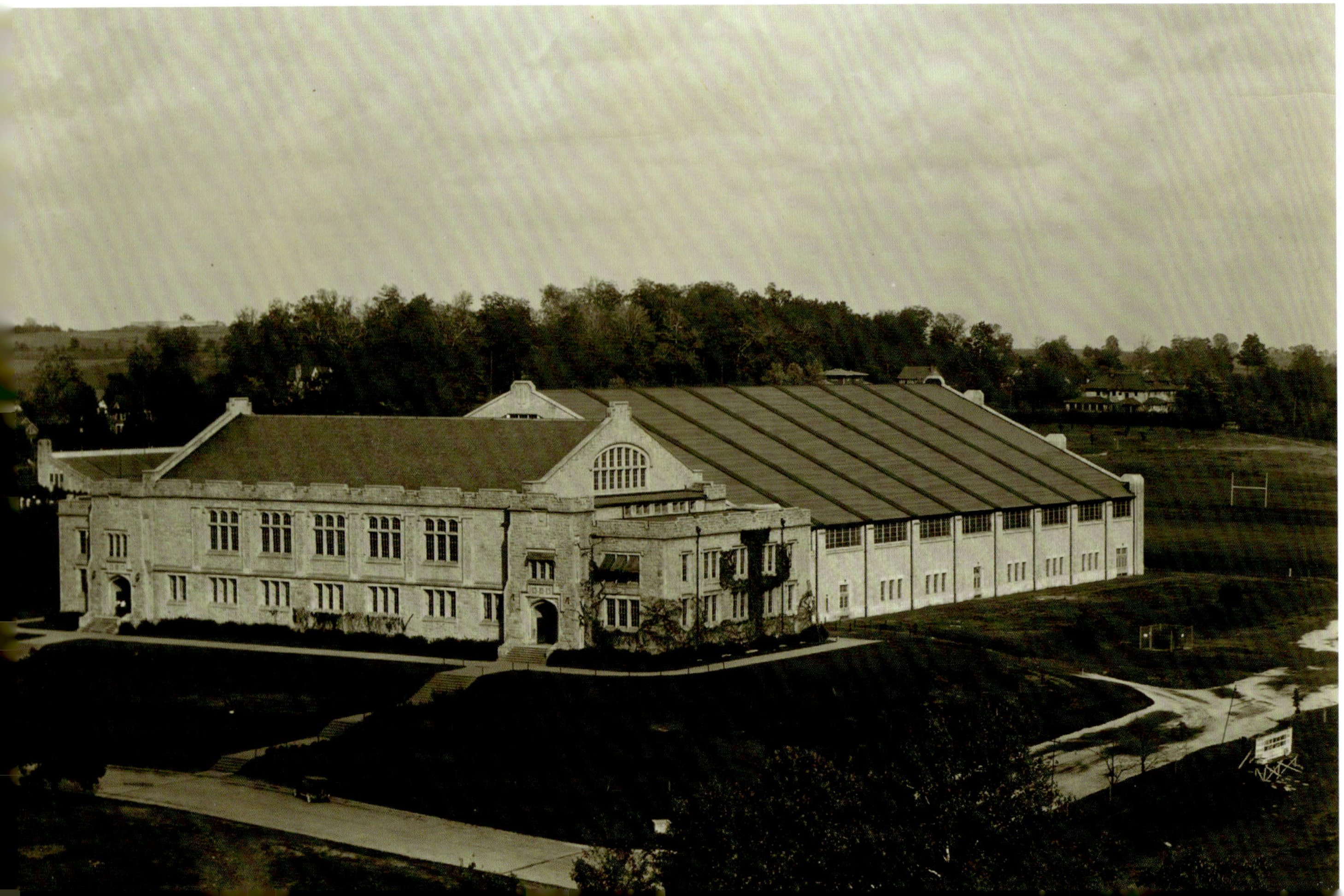

Men's Gymnasium with Fieldhouse addition; circa 1939. P0026800, IU Archives. Photo credit: Charles Gilbert Shaw.

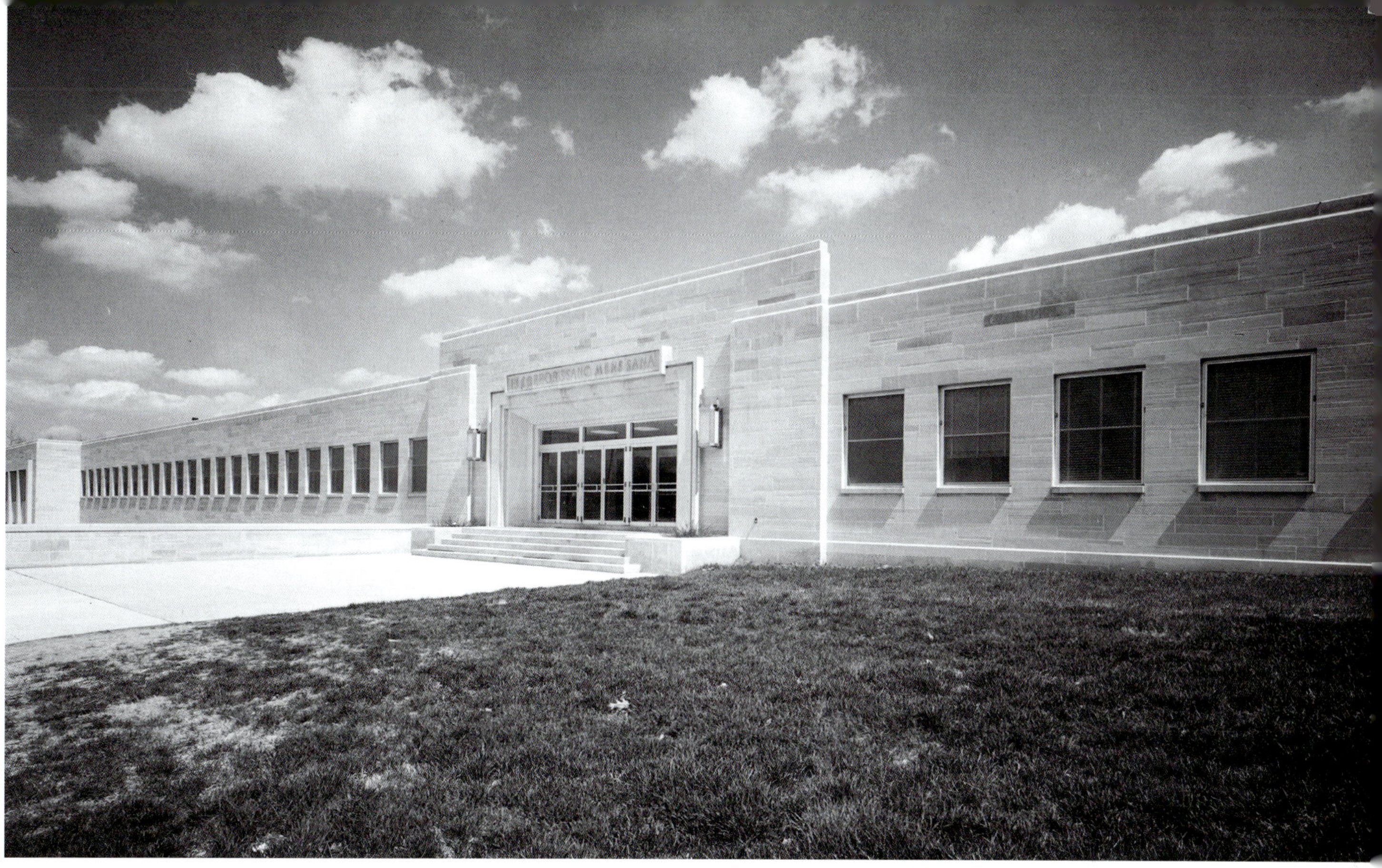

School of Public Health (HPER), 1962. P0042368, IU Archives. Photo credit: Ralph "Porky" Veal, Indiana University.

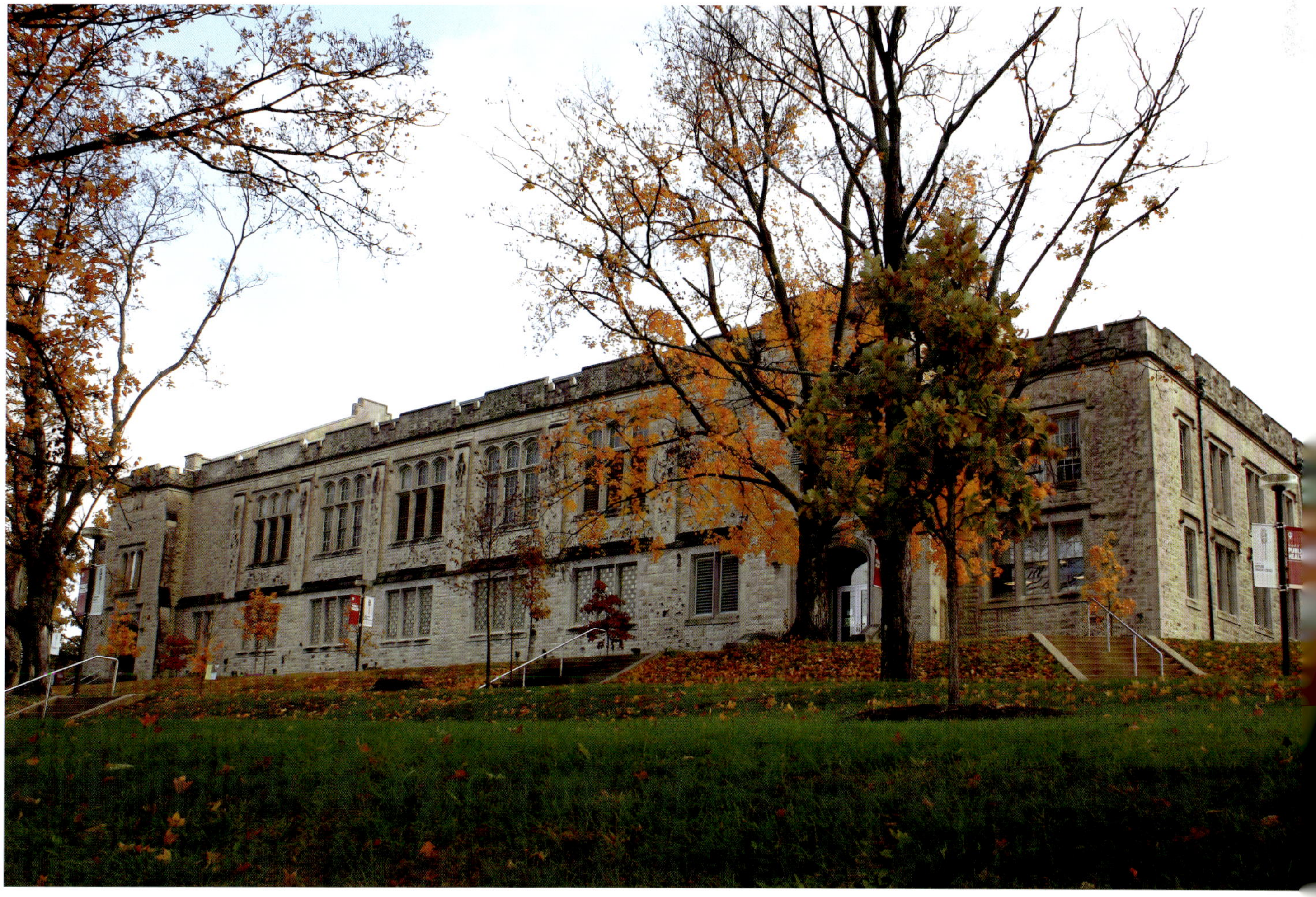

The 1917 Men's Gymnasium, undated. Photo credit: Indiana University.

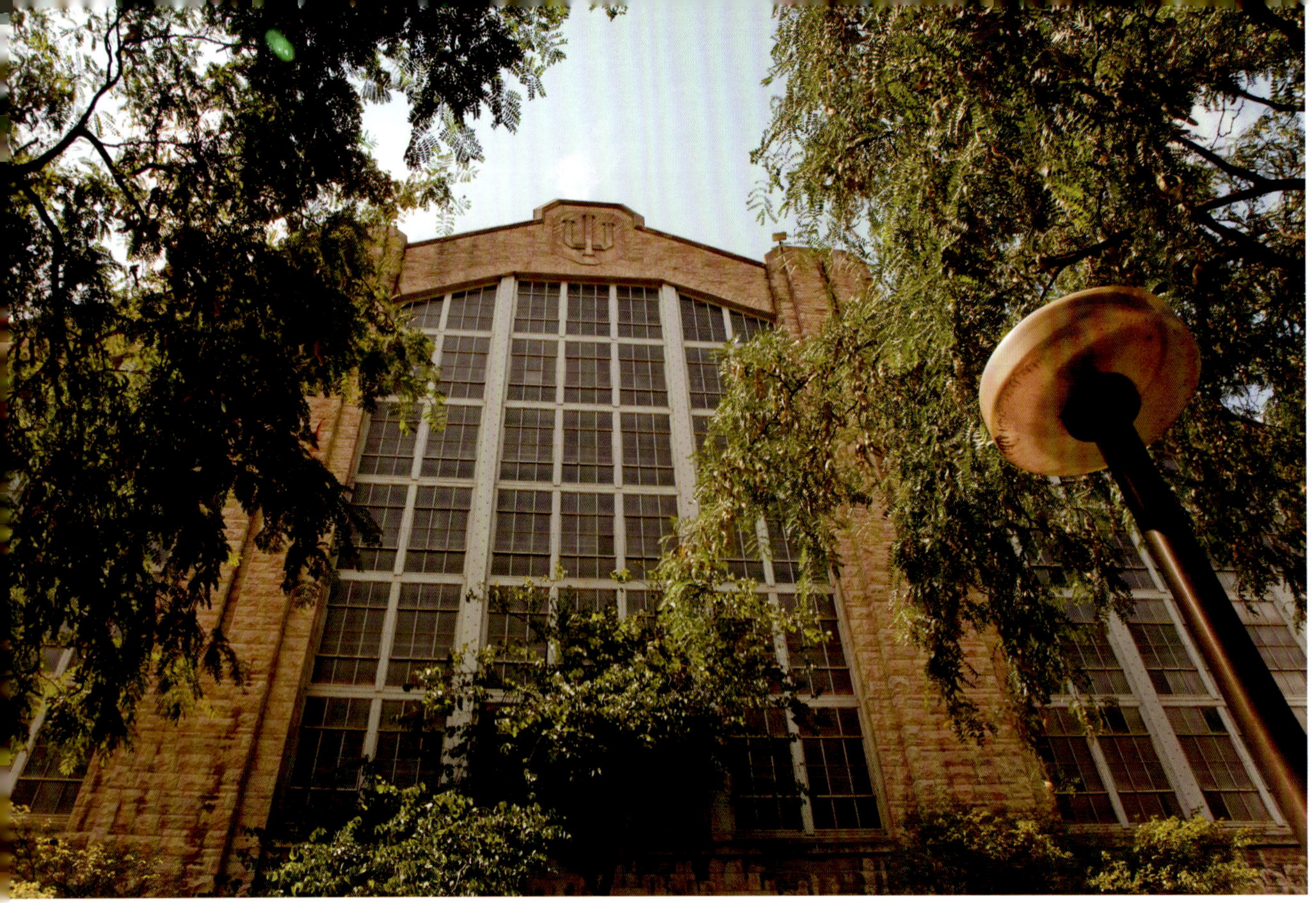

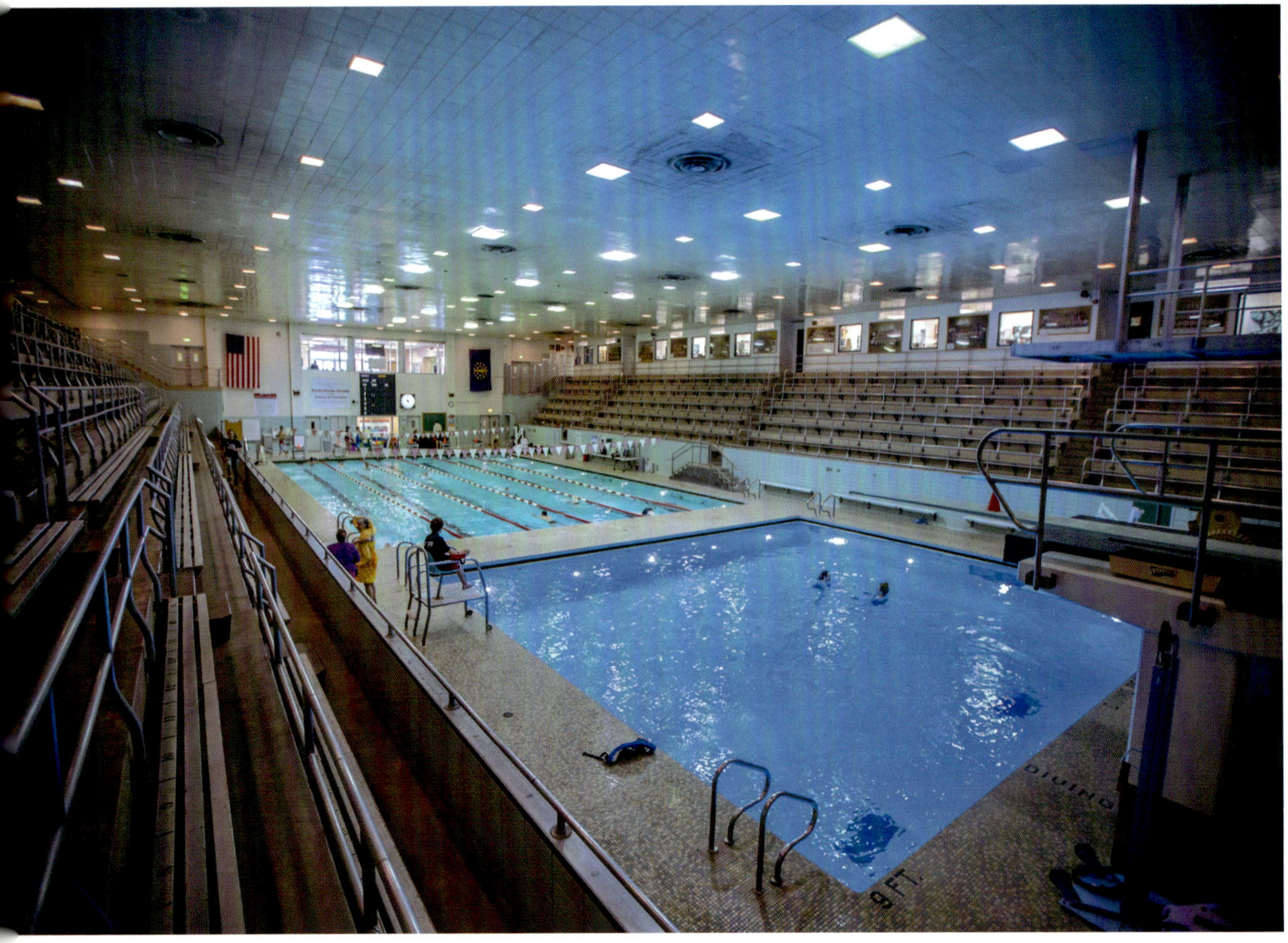

Above, East elevation of Ora L. Wildermuth Intramural Center, 2016. Photo Credit: Tyagan Miller.

Left, Royer Pool in old HPER Building (now School of Public Health Building), where Doc Counsilman's and Hobie Billingsley's championship era began, undated. Photo credit: Indiana University.

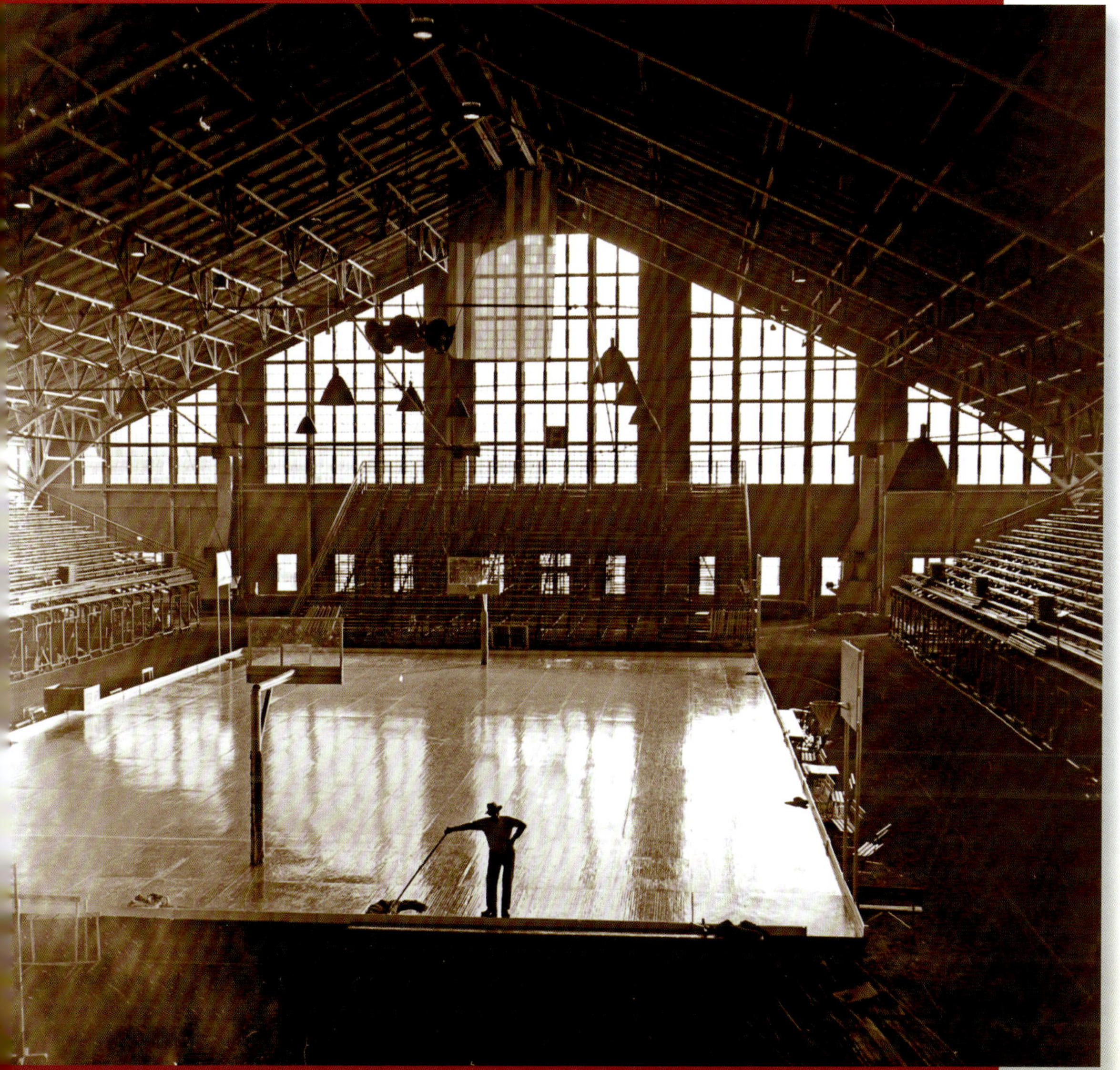

Well-polished floor and glass backboards set the stage for an upcoming IU men's basketball game in the Fieldhouse, 1952. These backboards are a legacy of the first glass backboards constructed for the Men's Gymnasium in the early 1900s. P0034702, IU Archives. Photo credit: Indiana University *Arbutus*.

The Move from Wood to Glass

The use of the basketball glass backboard in the United States was popularized when Indiana University removed the old wooden backboards in the newly constructed Men's Gymnasium and replaced them with glass (ca. 1917–19). Following the first few basketball games played in the new facility, spectators began complaining about obstructed views resulting from the opaque wooden backboards. Athletic Department administrators contacted the Nurre Mirror Plate Company in Bloomington about the possibility of creating a glass backboard, one that the fans could see through. In response, the Nurre Company crafted a backboard made of 1.5-inch-thick glass, strong enough to withstand court play.[1] Thus, IU can claim the impetus that led to the now universal use of the glass backboard in basketball today.

1. Jason Hiner, *Indiana University Basketball Encyclopedia* (n.p.: Sports Publishing, 2004), 447.

Memorial Stadium 1960

ARCHITECT Eggers and Higgins

ARCHITECTURAL STYLE 1960s Functional Modern

ORIGINAL NAME Seventeenth Street Football Stadium

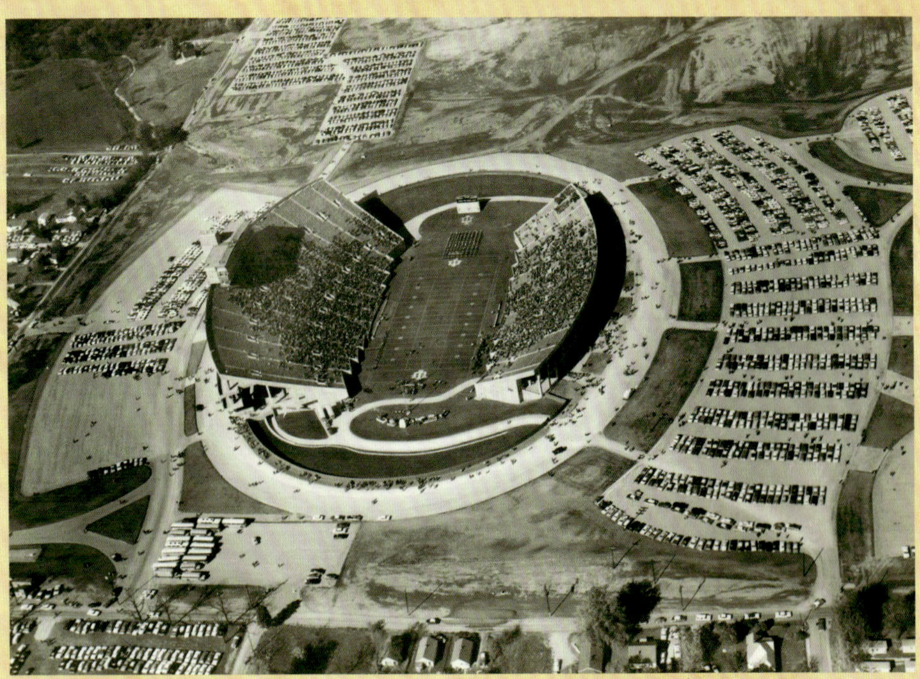

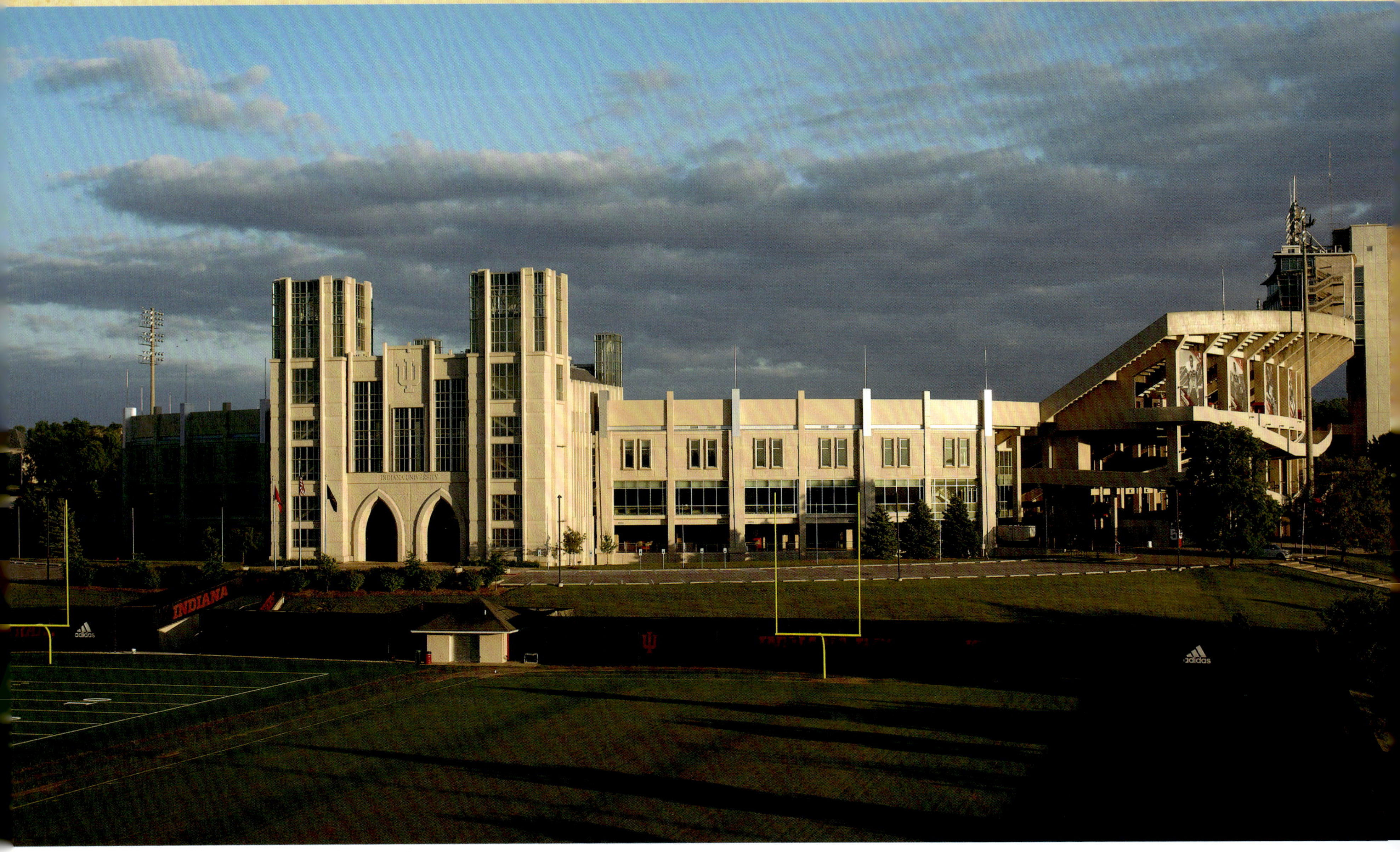

Memorial Stadium

Centerpiece of IU Athletics

Come and join in song together, Shout with might and main;
Our beloved Alma Mater, Sound her praise again.
Gloriana Frangipana, E'er to her be true.
She's the pride of Indiana,
Hail to Old IU!

—*"Hail to Old IU"*

AT THE END OF WORLD WAR II, THE CONDITION of the Indiana University Athletic Department physical plant was generally described as deplorable. With the war, all plans for improving various athletic venues had been set aside, and the large number of returning veterans after the war under the GI Bill placed pressure on the university to devote available resources to additional classrooms and living accommodations. A significant step forward occurred, however, in 1955 when President Herman B Wells quietly completed the purchase of the Faris family farm a half mile north of the then existing campus boundaries. The addition of the 160-acre Faris Farm, which included all of the area north of what is today Seventeenth Street to the Indiana 46/45 Bypass and between Dunn Street and Fee Lane, allowed IU master planners to lay out a new district on the campus to serve as an integrated athletic complex that offered sufficient space for both competition and parking.

Planning efforts to replace the existing 1925 stadium on Tenth Street had begun in 1950. Parking at the old football stadium located in the middle of campus was not adequate to handle the growing crowds attending football games. It was also clear that the old stadium would soon experience major structural problems, as concrete flaws were becoming visible at various locations around the stadium walls. A site for a new stadium was not obvious, however, until the Faris land became available.

Indiana University administrators turned to familiar partner Eggers and Higgins of New York to begin laying out the future home of IU athletics. The architects were charged with moving the entire center of athletic activity to the newly acquired property. Eggers and Higgins, under the leadership of firm partners, Theodore Young and R. Jackson Smith, created a site plan that placed a new football stadium, basketball arena, and field house in the middle of the available expanse and surrounded the proposed facilities with parking spaces for thirteen thousand cars. The parking areas were planned to be grass and would double as football practice fields. With an improved Indiana State Road 37 recently completed, additional attendance was anticipated as fans from Indianapolis to the north and Louisville to the south would find travel easier and travel times dramatically shortened. In addition, the Eggers and Higgins site plan made access to the stadium convenient from every direction.

Interested contractors submitted bids for the construction of the football stadium, basketball arena, and field house in 1958. With the aggregate cost of building all three venues far

Facing top, Memorial Stadium, 1960. P0043083, IU Archives.

Facing bottom, Memorial Stadium north end zone addition, at left, 2009. Photo credit: Indiana University.

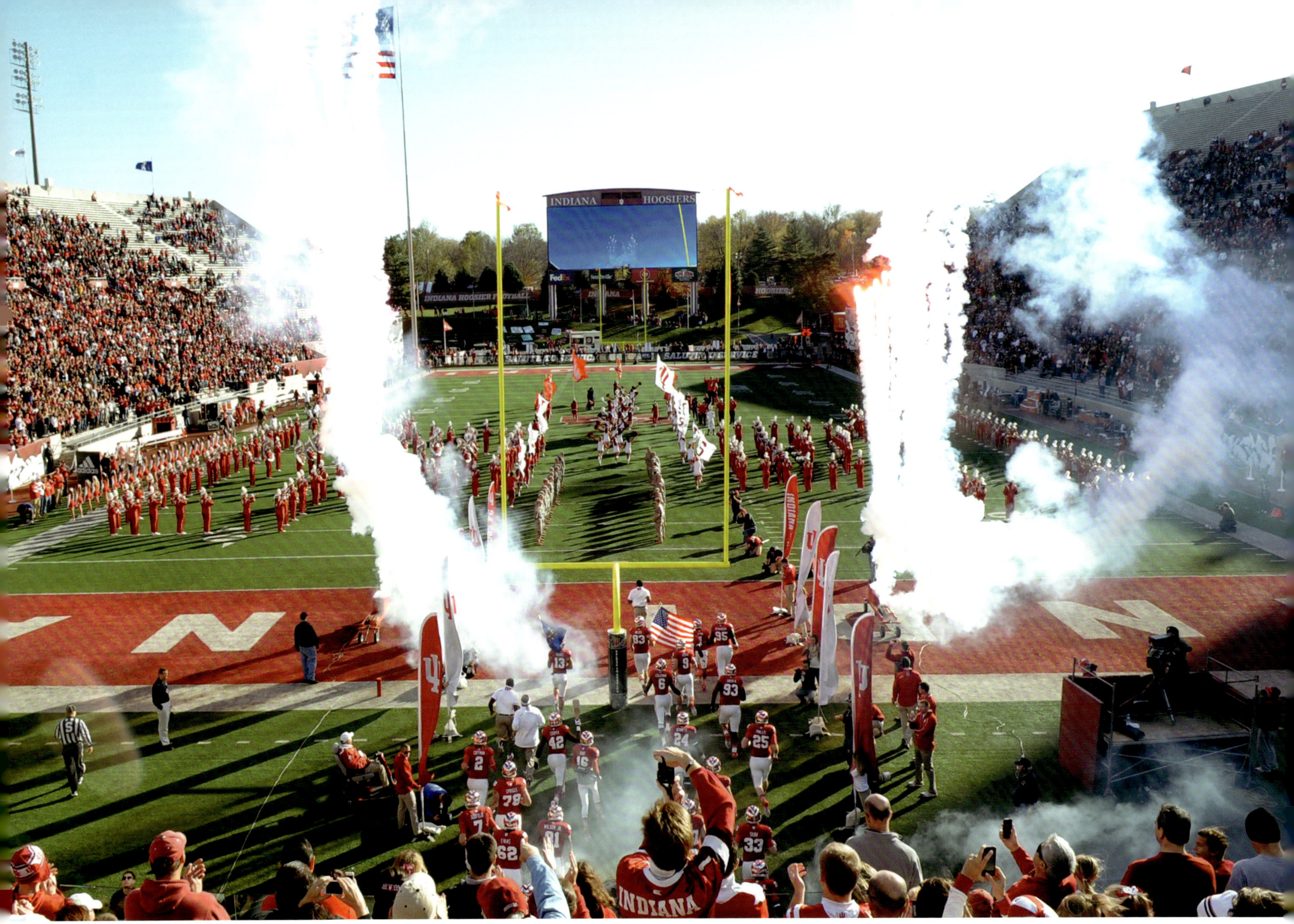

Pomp, pyrotechnics, and music as IU takes the field at Memorial Stadium, 2013. Photo credit: Indiana University.

exceeding available funds, the university was faced with tough decisions. The basketball arena was shelved, and it would be a decade before that project, Assembly Hall, would be undertaken again. Construction of the Harry Gladstein Fieldhouse did proceed as planned and it served as the new home for the IU basketball program until 1971, when Assembly Hall was completed.

The Seventeenth Street Football Stadium, as it was initially called, was constructed from 1958 through October 1960. It wasn't officially named Memorial Stadium until October 1971, when the first Memorial Stadium relinquished its name (the old stadium was henceforth known as the Tenth Street Stadium until its demolition in 1982). The name honors all Indiana University students who have served in the nation's armed forces.

The Eggers and Higgins plan for Memorial Stadium was to create a bowl effect, described by the firm as "the two curved stands fac[ing] each other like cupped hands."[1] The stands also

Windows, arches, and limestone cladding adorn north end zone main entry, 2009. Photo credit: Indiana University.

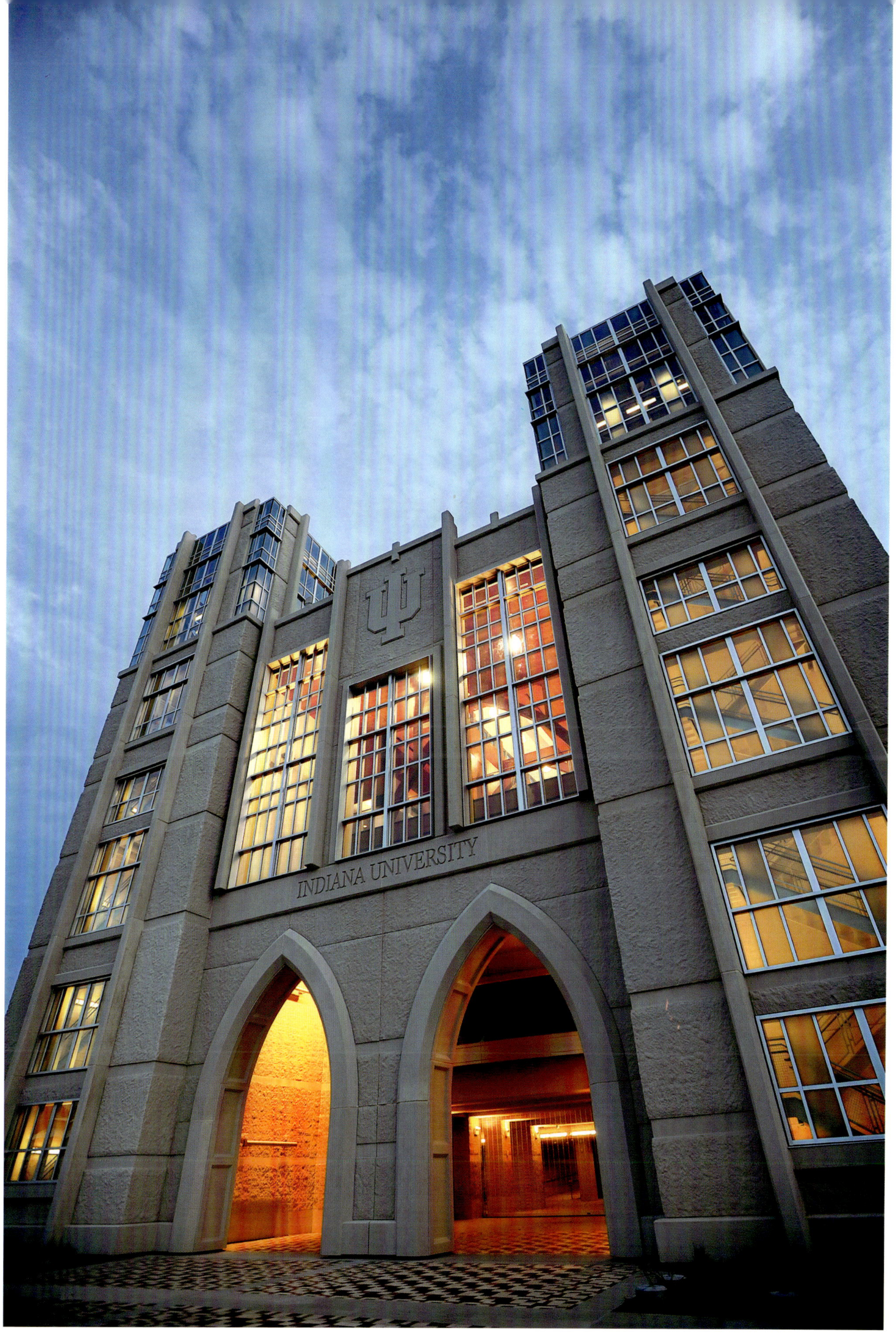

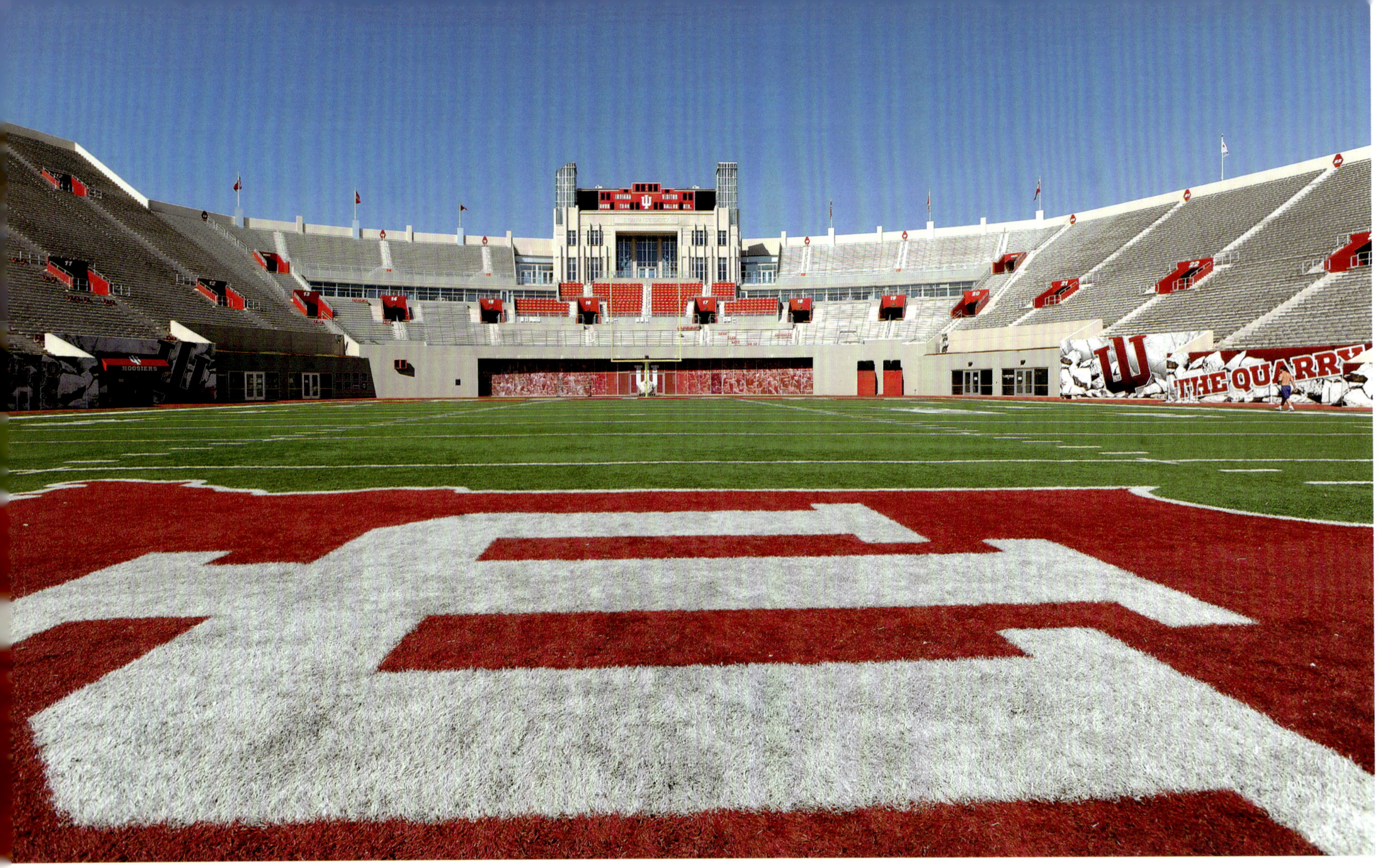

Memorial Stadium's synthetic surface, 2011. Photo credit: Indiana University.

were designed with an elliptical curve to improve sightlines: each seat faced the 50-yard line rather than the traditional seating parallel to the field, which forced fans to strain to see up or down the field. Looking toward the future as football became more successful, it was anticipated that the seating capacity would increase by completing the bowl and thus achieving a total stadium capacity of one hundred thousand spectators. To save money at the time, however, the east stands were cut back by thirty-five rows (ten thousand seats), causing the west side of the stadium to rise higher than the east. The three-level press box was cantilevered over the top rows of the west stands and curved to match the shape of the stadium. One elevator was installed to service the press box, but eventually a second elevator was added as club boxes were constructed to provide luxury seating in 2001. This new stadium was designed to enable a capacity crowd to exit in about twenty minutes, an innovation that served as a model for years to come.

The remarkable aspect of the Eggers and Higgins plan was the openness of the stands, so the whole complex seemed to be completely visible. The totality of Memorial Stadium was intended to be seen—both the interior and exterior offer views of the whole structure from most locations. As spectators walk up the outside ramps, parking lots are visible below. As fans move up or down the stairs on the inside, the playing field is always in view. The architect managed to make a massive stack of concrete appear light and inviting.

Although the stadium may look like it is constructed of Indiana limestone, it actually is cast-in-place concrete. The finished surface is periodically treated with sealers, and the resulting color complements the limestone found elsewhere on the campus. The playing surface, 25 feet below the main concourse level of the stadium, was natural turf until the late 1970s, when Head Football Coach Lee Corso asked that an artificial surface be installed. Later the field was returned to natural turf, and then back again to artificial turf. When this stadium was completed in 1960, the seating capacity was 48,344, or more than double that of the old stadium on Tenth Street. In 2016, the total seating capacity of Memorial Stadium, including the west and east stands, the north end zone, the Stadium Club and Suites, and the North End Zone Club seats was 52,929.

At the dedication ceremony on October 22, 1960, President Herman B Wells said, "We see in this Stadium the fulfillment of the dreams of years. . . . This is America's most modern structure of its kind. Though not the largest, none with it today can compare. We have built not for the present, but for the future."[2] How prophetic he was. Sixty years later, Memorial Stadium continues to be one of the most up-to-date football stadiums in the country.

Henke Hall of Champions in north end zone facility, 2010. Photo credit: Indiana University.

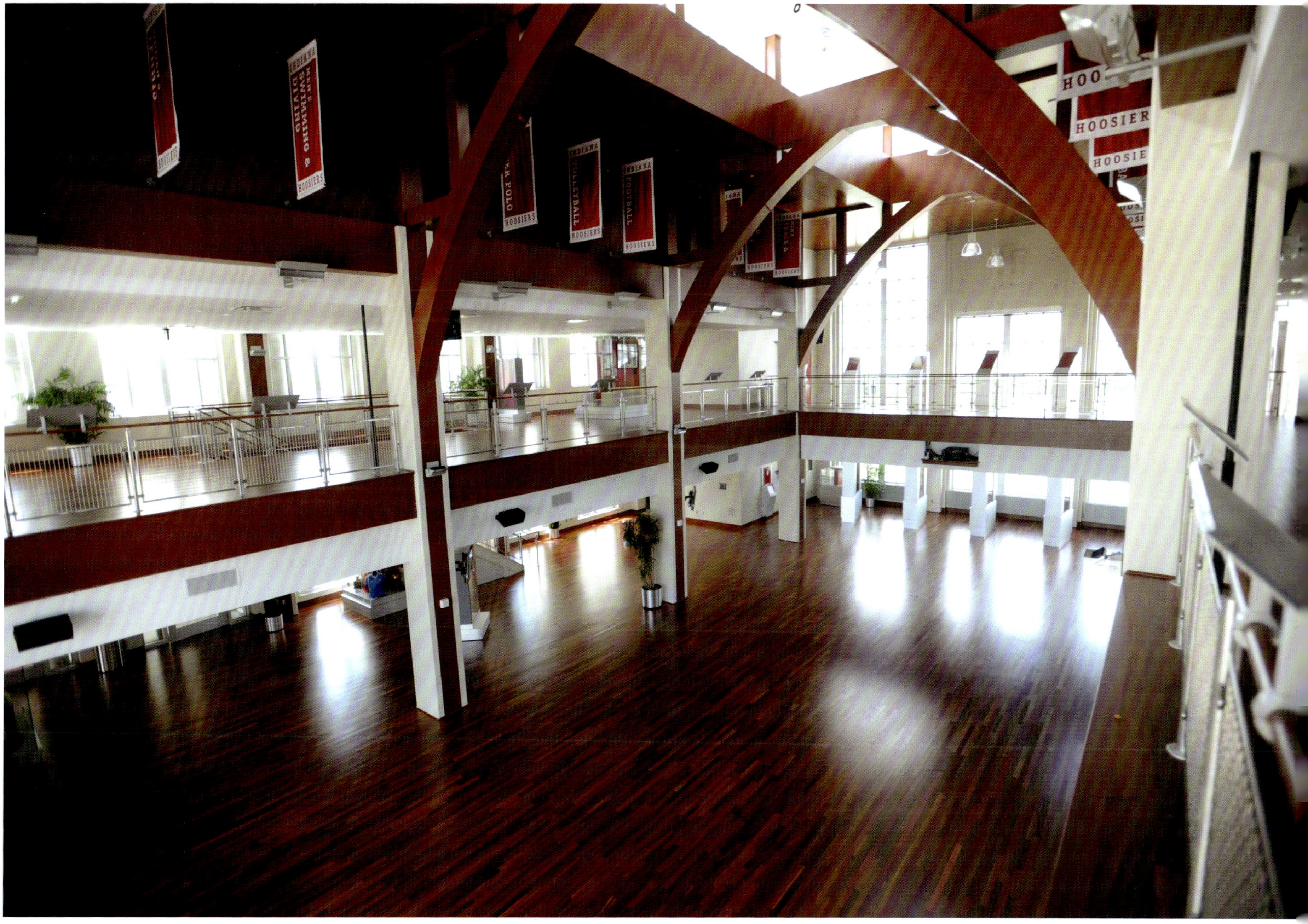

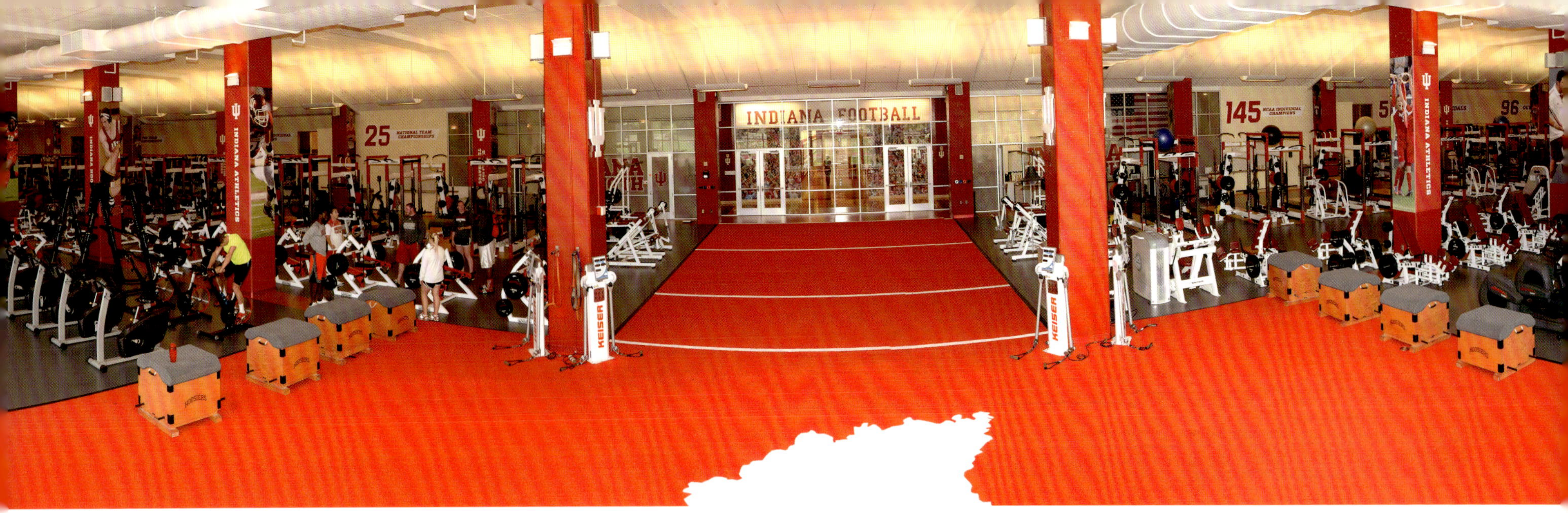

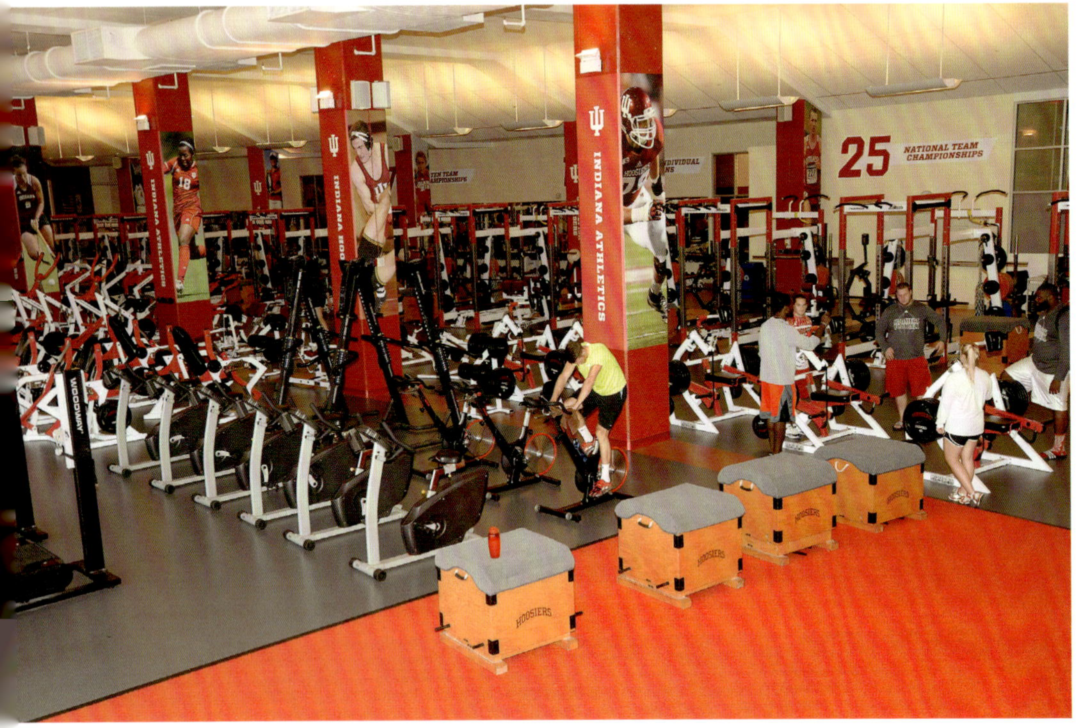

Top, Panoramic view of the 25,000-square-foot W. Jay and Nancy Wilkinson Performance Center, 2015. Photo credit: Indiana University.

Above, Student-athletes training in Wilkinson Performance Center, 2015. Photo credit: Indiana University.

In 1985, a 25,000-square-foot addition was completed under the east stands, providing new offices, training facilities, and an academic space for football. In 1988, through the generosity of IU benefactor Bill Cook, lights were added around the stadium. In 2009, a 138,000-square-foot north end zone (NEZ) addition was completed by Ratio Architects of Indianapolis, affording IU Athletics a home for its administrative offices and a new space for all things football. The project was designed in the modified Gothic tradition of the main campus buildings with stunning towers and an extensive seating bowl. The beautiful limestone cladding on the facade connects the structure to the architectural building palette of the university and quickly became an IU landmark. This addition converted Memorial Stadium into a horseshoe, connecting the east and west stands. The NEZ has five accessible levels. The ground floor includes the vast, state-of-the-art W. Jay and Nancy Wilkinson Performance Center for all the student-athletes, which ranks among the largest and finest strength and conditioning centers in the nation. Also on this level are football team position rooms, meeting rooms, and memorial galleries. The first floor is the entrance to the building, and the second level houses both the administrative and football offices. The NEZ's crowning jewel, the Henke Hall of Champions, is on the third and fourth floors. Here the IU faithful can gather for a multitude of occasions in the beautifully finished, two-story grand hall. A fifth floor can only be accessed by certain personnel. Glory Plaza, outside the main entrance to the NEZ, is filled with brick pavers personalized by IU alumni and friends. In 2010, the old football space beneath Memorial Stadium was repurposed to become a much-anticipated D. Ames Shuel Academic Center, also designed by Ratio Architects.

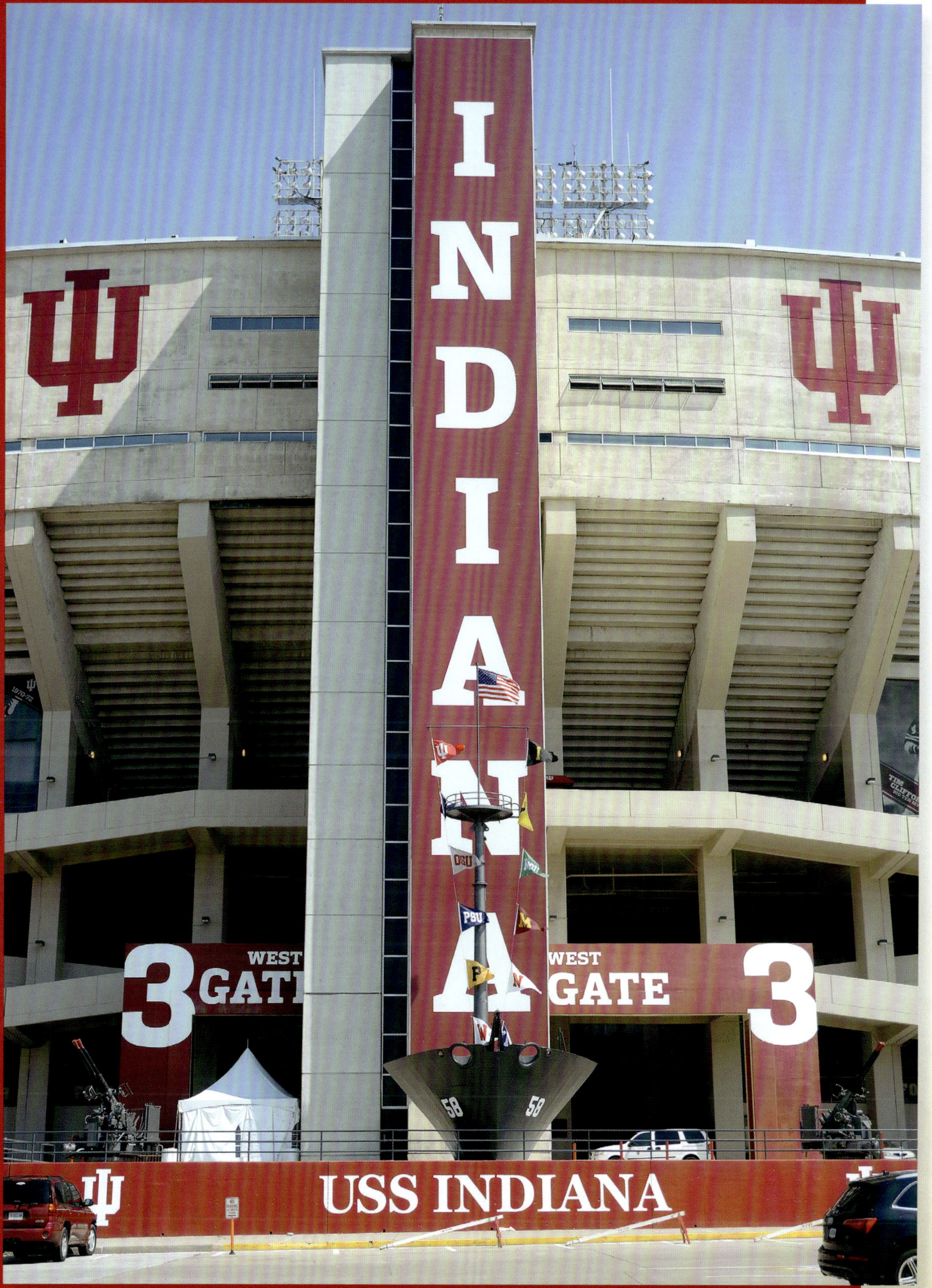

Mainmast, gun mounts, and prow from the USS *Indiana*, west side of Memorial Stadium, 2013. Photo credit: Indiana University.

USS Indiana

On the west side of the stadium, a World War II battleship mast, accompanied by armament, was a gift from the U.S. Navy, possibly encouraged by then president Elvis Stahr, who had been the U.S. Secretary of the Army. Both came from the battleship, the USS *Indiana*. On May 14, 1966, a ceremony was held to recognize the gift and a plaque was placed that reads "It stands as a memorial to the sons and daughters of the state of Indiana who have so gallantly served in the armed forces of the nation." In 2013, the original prow of the USS *Indiana* was reunited with its mainmast and two gun mounts at the stadium.

Simon Skjodt Assembly Hall 1971

ARCHITECT Eggers and Higgins

ARCHITECTURAL STYLE 1960s Modern

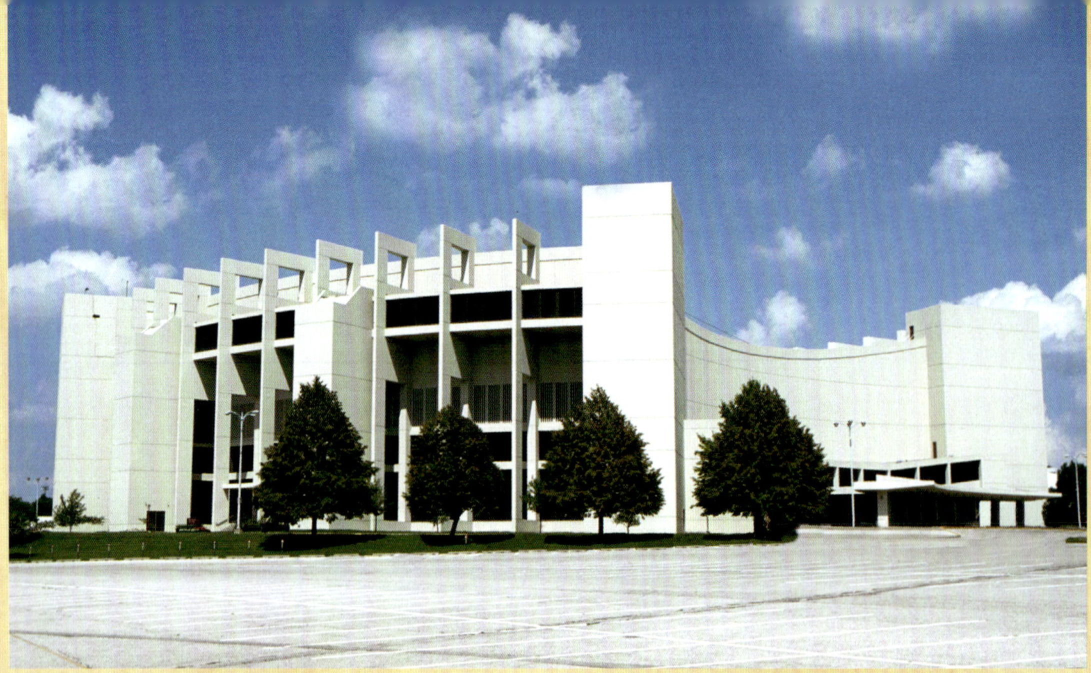

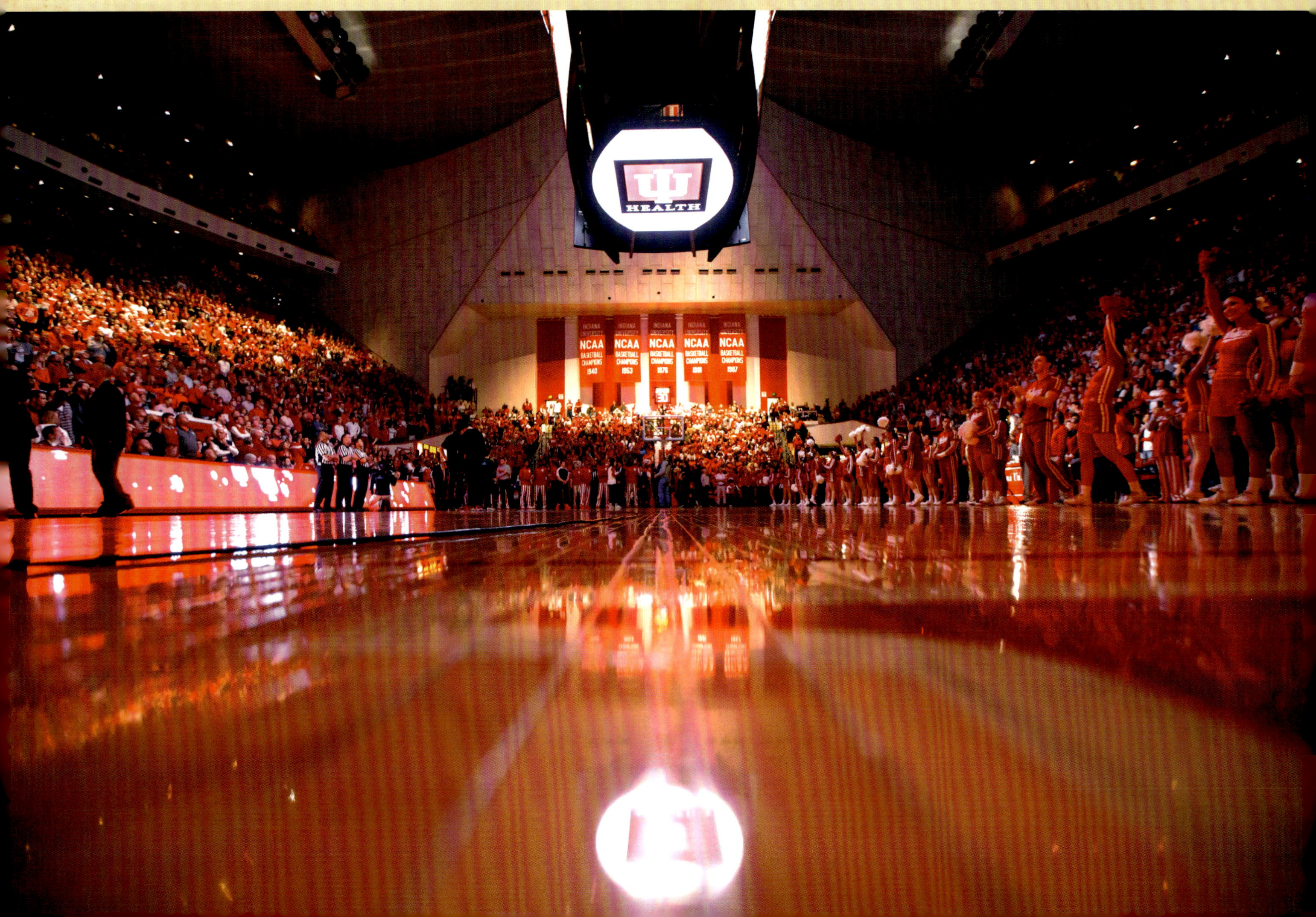

Simon Skjodt Assembly Hall

Basketball really had its origin in Indiana, which remains the center of the sport.

—James Naismith

Home Court Advantage

IN 1971 A NEW ERA OF BASKETBALL AT INDIANA University arrived with the much-anticipated completion of Assembly Hall and the hiring of Coach Robert Montgomery Knight. The basketball program, which already had claimed two National Championships in 1940 and 1953, would win three more NCAA titles (1976, 1981, 1987), and eleven Big Ten Championships during his twenty-nine-year coaching career. Coach Knight's arrival coincided with the opening of Assembly Hall, and he would be IU's only coach until 2000, a period of unprecedented basketball success.

When Assembly Hall was completed, it was already a fifteen-year-old building (at least on paper). Designed in the mid-1950s by the New York architects Eggers and Higgins at the same time that the firm designed Memorial Stadium, the basketball arena was shelved when construction bids for the two projects came in too high to proceed. Football was considered to be in greater need of a new facility than basketball. It was played in what was later known as the Tenth Street Stadium—a small, cramped, and deteriorating stadium completed in the mid-1920s. The university decided to move forward with a new football stadium and defer the basketball arena to a later date. That decision would prove to be costly in many respects, as the building in its original design contained an ice hockey rink, racquetball courts, and other athletic spaces that would be lost when the project was rebid in 1967. Harsh winters and substantial subgrade limestone removal helped drag out the construction process for nearly four years.

With athletic facilities ineligible for state funding support, the university struggled with financial options for the construction of Assembly Hall. The administration and Board of Trustees finally decided to use dedicated student fees, which meant that student tuition would be the funding source. Students immediately questioned the value they would receive from an increase in tuition and challenged the university on how much they would be able to use the proposed facility. The discussions went back and forth, with the administration pointing out that the Indiana University All-Events Building, as it was called then, would be a venue for large audience events such as commencement, touring artists, and stage productions.

The site selected for Assembly Hall was on Seventeenth Street between Fee Lane and Dunn Street. Eggers and Higgins assembled a strong design team that included Severud Associates of New York, a multinational consulting engineering firm founded in 1928 and used by many signature architectural firms. Severud Associates could point to the Gateway Arch in St. Louis and Madison Square Garden in New York as prime examples of their work. The Eggers and Higgins–Severud Associates team basically continued the structural scheme used in Memorial Stadium. Indeed, it can be said that Assembly

Facing top, Simon Skjodt Assembly Hall with flying-buttress design, 1992. Photo credit: Indiana University.

Facing bottom, Player introductions during Indiana University versus Purdue University men's basketball game, February 9, 2017. Photo Credit: Indiana University.

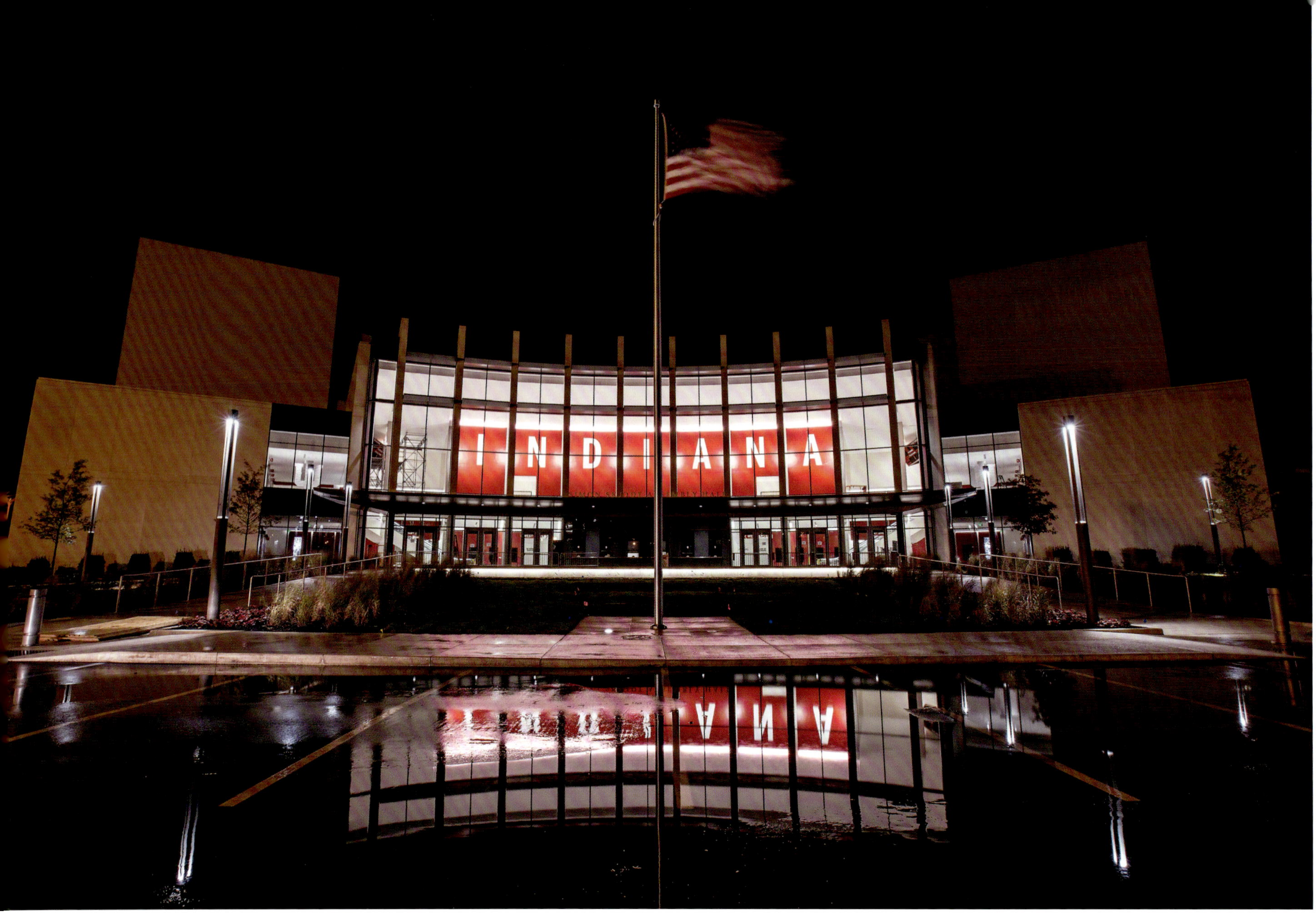

Skjodt Assembly Hall glowing at night, 2016.
Photo credit: Indiana University.

Hall *is* Memorial Stadium, compressed from every direction and then covered by a saddle-type suspension roof. The interior rake of the stands, aisle openings, and general feel mirror the football stadium. The design achieved the goal of placing all of the seating on the sides of the basketball floor. Only later did the success of the program demand the addition of seats behind the baskets and pull-out bleachers along the sides of the floor. Initial capacity was 15,300, and the additional seating pushed the capacity to 17,400.

The structural design of Assembly Hall is similar to a suspension bridge system and embodies two intersecting curved steel arches placed at 45 degrees from the horizontal plane. These arches spring from immense concrete buttress foundations located at the four corners of the arena floor. Suspended cables extending from the steel arches to vertical pylons at the west walls support the roof deck. The tension load of the roof cables transferred to the walls makes the entire structural system interlocking. That system, which is inherently inflexible, has constrained planners through the years in their attempts to upgrade Assembly Hall and increase seating capacity.

Ted Young, of Eggers and Higgins, was the project architect for the arena and made many site visits during the construction period. Young describes the architectural style as "an expressive design." Likely he was referring to the fact that

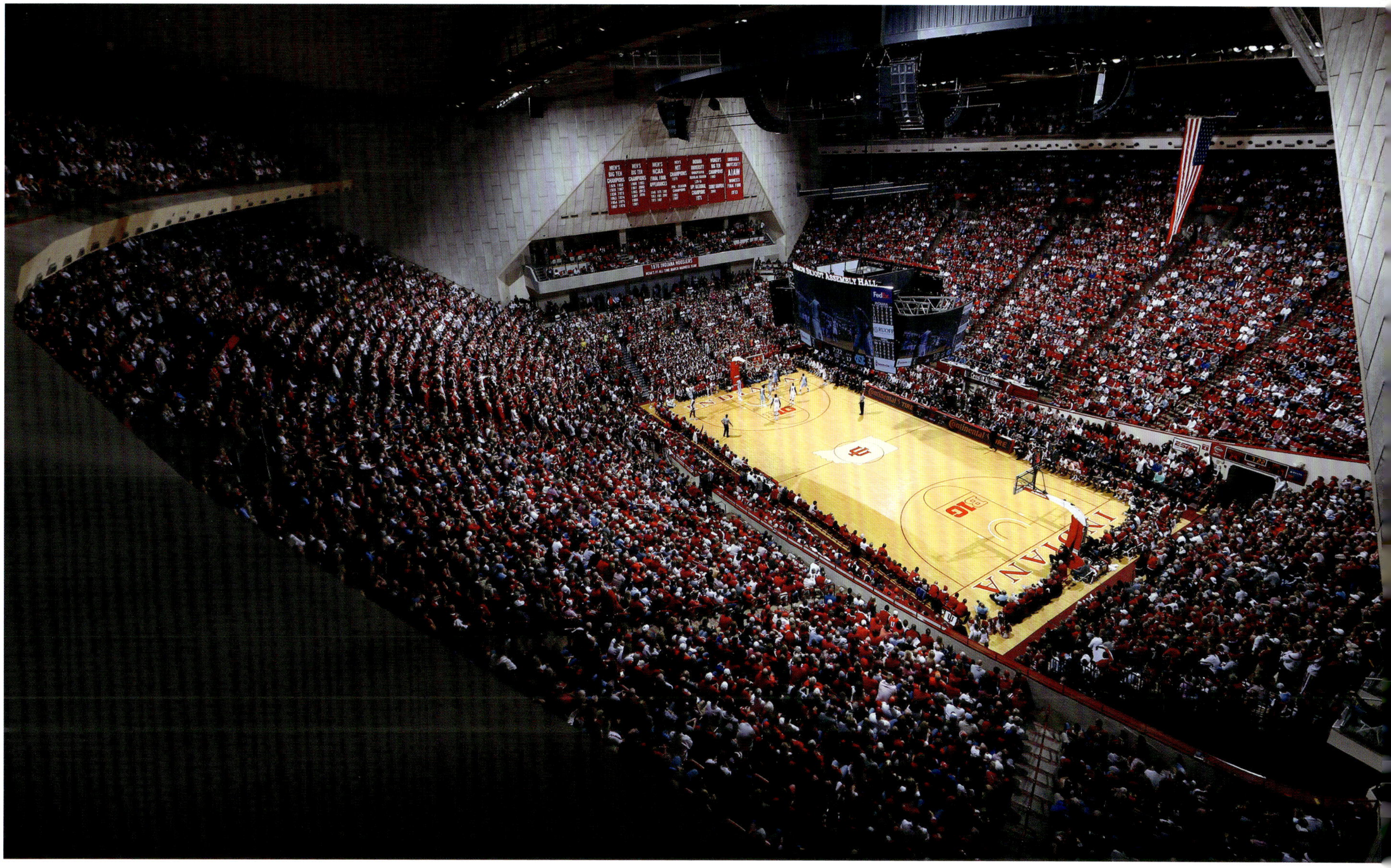

Packed to the rafters during IU-UNC basketball game, 2016.
Photo credit: Indiana University.

all of the component parts of the building are exposed to view, including the flying buttresses, main stairways, and the suspension roof. Spatial suspension structures are generally used for large-span roofs on public buildings and are fairly simple to erect but add a dramatic flair to the architectural product. On Assembly Hall, the roof covering over the cabling is a rubberized material. The exterior building material of Assembly Hall is primarily cast-in-place concrete. Flying buttresses are located along the north and south elevations. The flying buttress is inherited from Gothic architecture, where it was used primarily on churches. It bears the thrust away from the main structure of the building, as from a vaulted ceiling or wind-loading roof, to an outer buttress. The interior of Assembly Hall flows in open, graceful harmony, free of columns or other load-bearing elements that could obstruct the site lines. The resulting architectural style of the Hall can be characterized as mid-1960s Modern.

The all-purpose-use argument used by university officials held true, at least in the first few years, as Assembly Hall hosted grandiose events such as circuses and concerts never before possible. The homecoming show in 1971 featured Bob Hope and Petula Clark. Other performers to play in the hall included Bob Dylan, the Rolling Stones, Elvis Presley, the Jackson Five, the Grateful Dead, Elton John, and the Eagles. Former president Bill Clinton and then presidential candidate Barack Obama spoke in Assembly Hall during the 2008 presidential campaign. Along with men's and women's basketball games, the hall continues to host commencement ceremonies during inclement weather, touring artists, holiday shows, and a few other large-scale events.

As Assembly Hall has aged and new sports arenas have been constructed around the country, considerable discussions have ensued about the historic basketball facility's future. Substantial pressure was applied by university trustees as well as by the fan base in general to begin fund-raising for a new basketball complex commensurate with the program's elite image. In the fall of 2013, Indiana University and IU Athletics announced plans for the first major renovation of Assembly Hall since its opening in 1971. The work included replacing and upgrading major heating, cooling, and infrastructure throughout the complex; adding luxury seating above the south basket to accommodate an additional two hundred fans; and replacing the ramps with escalators to carry patrons to the upper levels of the building. The fan experience in the balconies was improved by the installation of a jumbotron, allowing all those in the nosebleed seats a close-up view of the floor action and providing game information to those in seats without a view of the scoreboard. Additional restrooms, restroom renovations, and improvements to the concession areas further improved the game-day experience. The Simon family, one of IU's most generous benefactors, made this extensive project possible. IU alumna Cindy Simon Skjodt pledged $40 million to support the renovation of the facility, which reopened in October 2016 under its new name, the Simon Skjodt Assembly Hall.

The newly renovated Simon Skjodt Assembly Hall will continue to be known as one of the greatest college basketball venues of all time and, for visiting teams, one of the most difficult in which to win. Current and future generations of fans will gain a new appreciation for the unique basketball home that serves Indiana University's men's and women's storied programs. Hoosier fans nationwide agree with Gus Johnson, sportscaster, that Assembly Hall truly is "the Carnegie Hall of Basketball."[1]

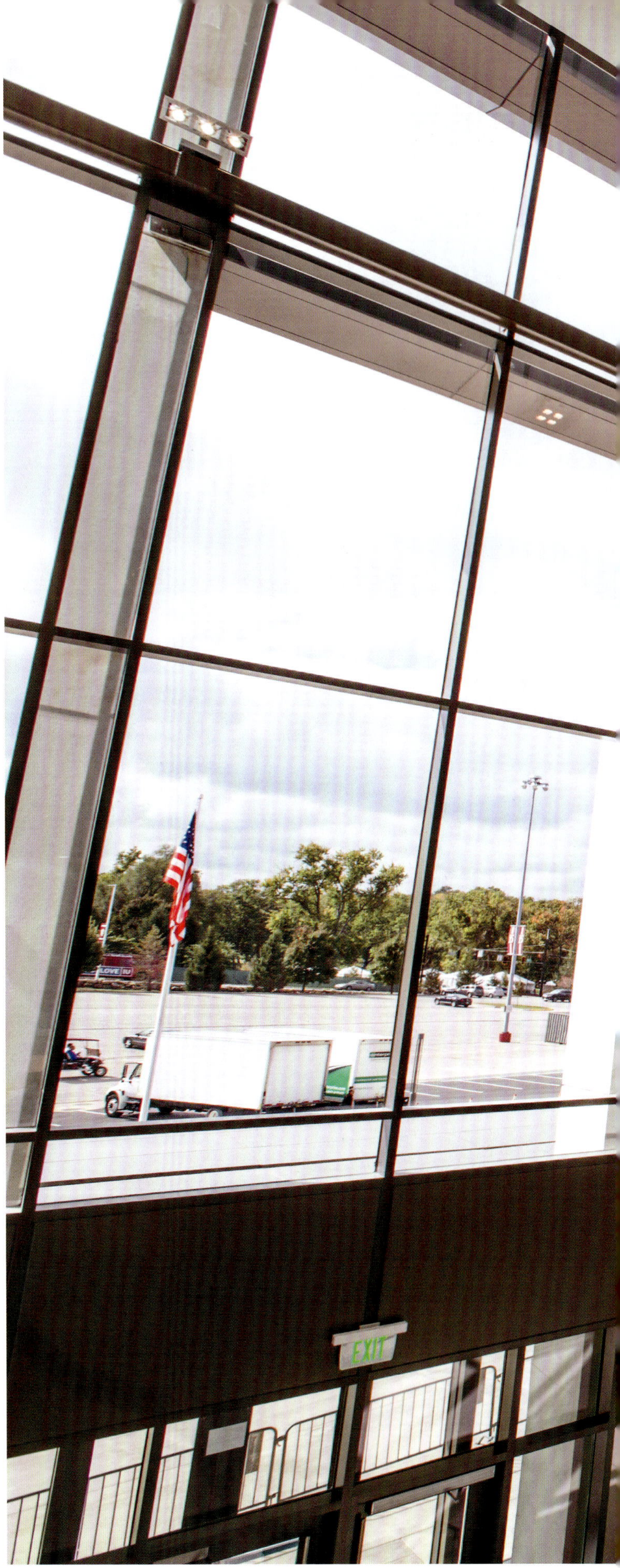

Facing, Interior promenade on south side, second level of Skjodt Assembly Hall, 2016. Photo credit: Indiana University.

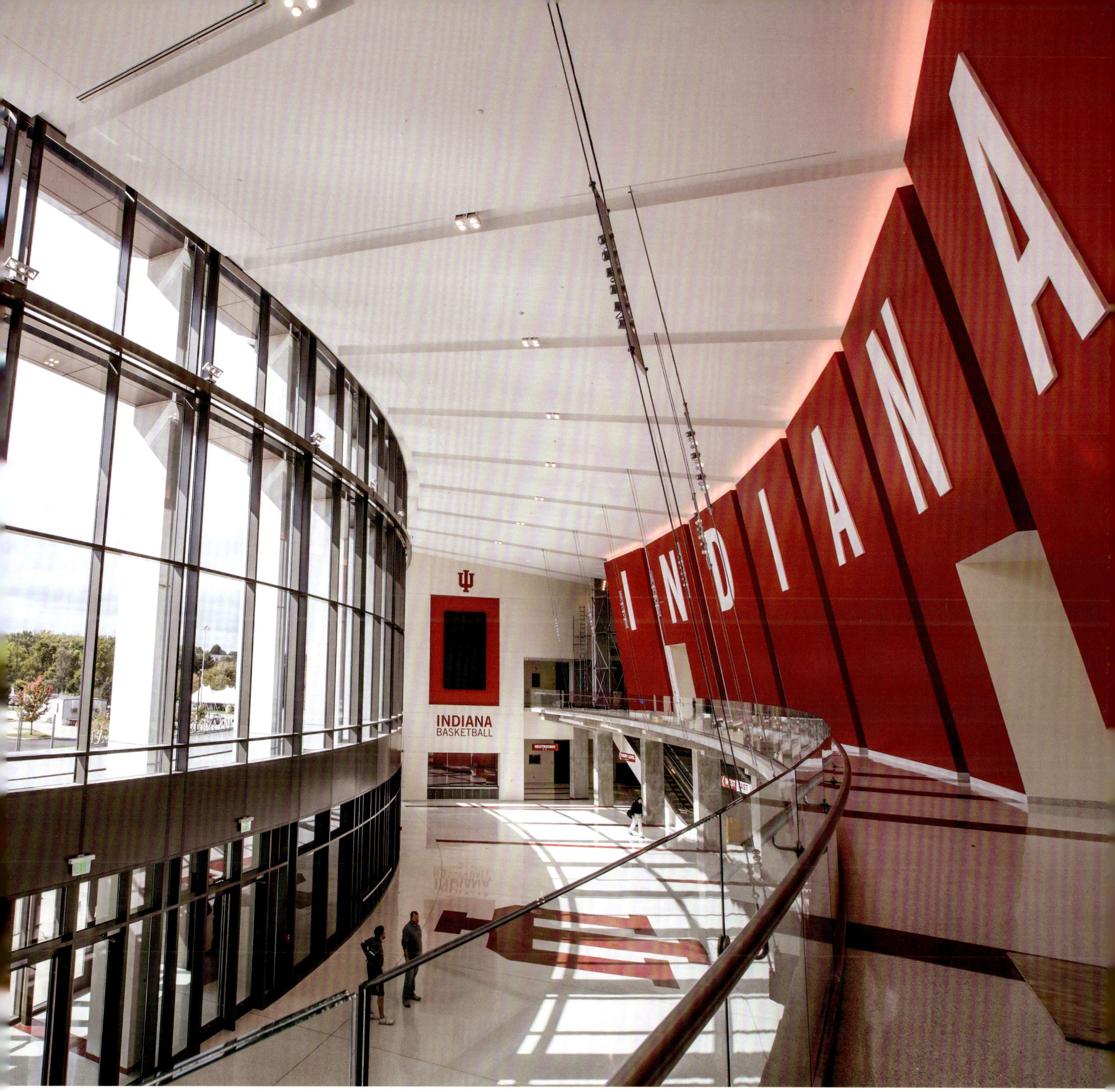
INDIANA
INDIANA
BASKETBALL
RESTROOMS

Cook Hall 2010

ARCHITECT Populous (HOK Sports) / Moody-Nolan

ARCHITECTURAL STYLE Contextual Modern

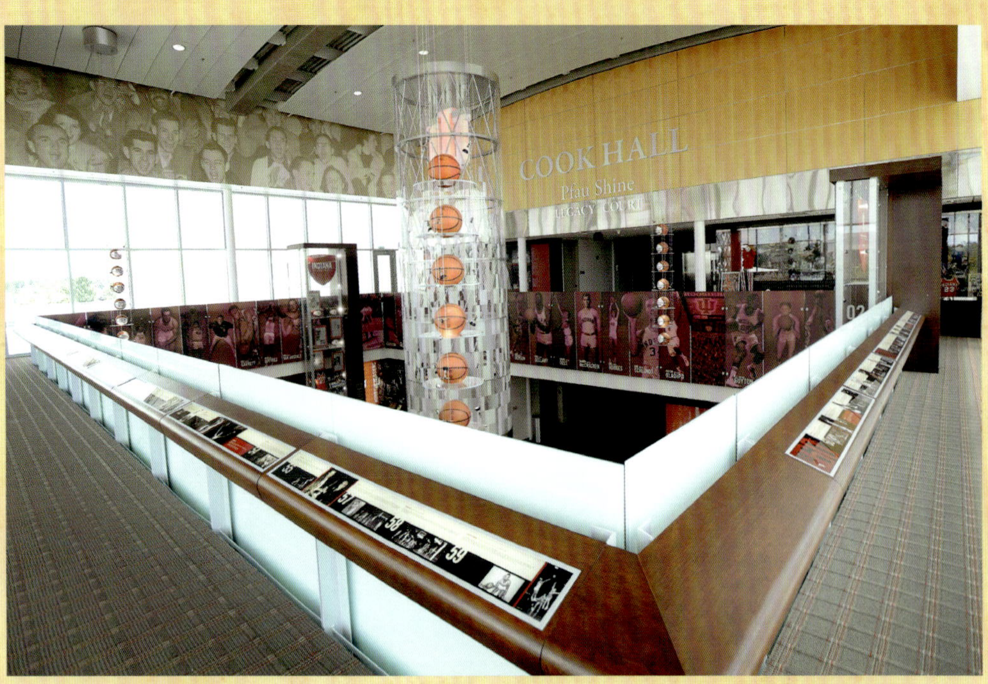

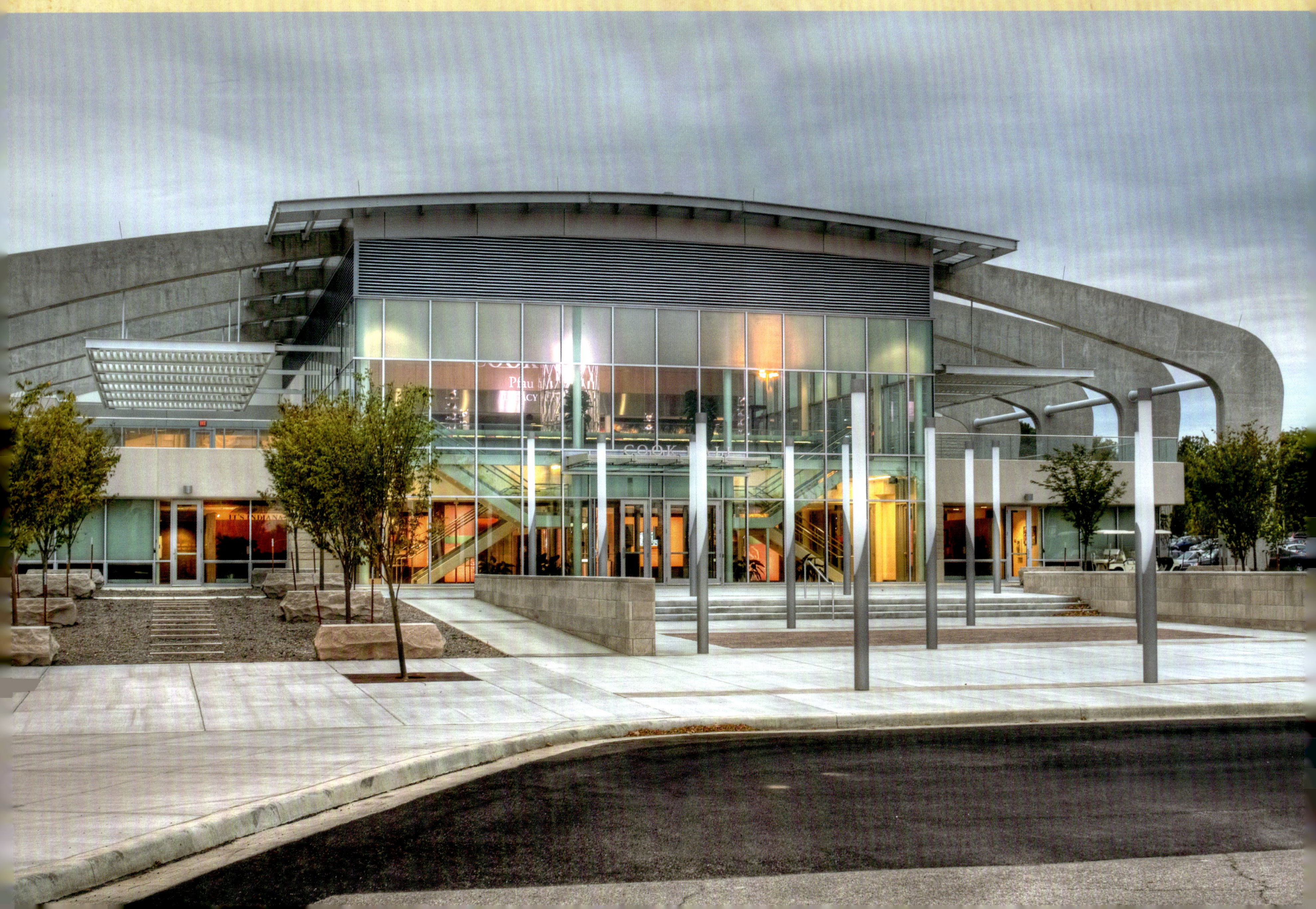

Cook Hall

A Place of Preparation

The key is not the "will to win" . . . everybody has that. It is the will to prepare to win that is important. The goal is to make practice more difficult, physically/mentally, than anything your players will face during a game. The single most important aspect of coaching is running effective practices.

—Coach Bob Knight

THE DEDICATION OF COOK HALL IN APRIL 2010 represented the culmination of university planning that had started well over a decade earlier. Basketball, a passion shared by most Hoosiers, had been underserved in the facility area for many years. The men's and women's programs had long been handicapped by the lack of practice courts, offices, and training/strength development space. Dreams of solving the problem by replacing Assembly Hall, the home of IU basketball since the 1970–71 season, had stalled due to high cost estimates and lack of an obvious site location. Indiana University officials turned to HOK Sports of Kansas City, Kansas, to help solve the dilemma. A new IU athletics precinct master plan was created that included a temporary solution to the problem—a practice facility that would allow the university time to consider either replacing Assembly Hall or renovating the storied venue. The cost estimate for a practice facility was a fraction of the estimate to replace Assembly Hall and carried the added feature of a short construction timeline.

After finalizing the athletics precinct master plan, the architectural firm HOK Sports was asked to design Cook Hall. The firm had successfully completed many significant sports facilities around the world such as Wembley Stadium in London, Yankee Stadium in New York, and Busch Stadium in St. Louis, and had designed London's 2012 Olympic Stadium. The university believed the international name recognition of HOK would aid in raising the needed funds to fully support the construction of the new facility. The firm was given the assignment to design a complex that would provide the university men's and women's basketball programs equal space for practice courts, coaches' offices, locker rooms, weight rooms, and video facilities. HOK began work on Cook Hall in 2007 and completed it in 2010.[1]

The building is named for Bill and Gayle Cook, principals of the Cook Group, founded in Bloomington in 1963 by William Cook. The late Bill Cook and his wife have given generously to Indiana University over the years, and their gift to IU athletics in response to the Glory of Old IU Capital Campaign was used primarily toward the development of Cook Hall. As IU team doctor and cochairman of the campaign, Dr. Larry Rink said, "Beyond the critical resources it provides, this gift is symbolic beyond measure. The Cook Group is a respected industry leader known for integrity, success and commitment to excellence. Indiana Basketball strives to embody these qualities that Cook has long valued and represented."[2] As requested by the Cooks, the names of ten thousand past and present Cook employees were placed on permanent plaques in the Cook Hall lobby area. It is not uncommon to see Cook employees and family members touring the facility attempting to find their names on the recognition wall.

The architectural design challenge was how to integrate Cook Hall with Assembly Hall, Memorial Stadium, and Gladstein Fieldhouse. The architect incorporated design fea-

Facing top, "Reader rail" in Cook Hall tracing history of IU basketball from 1901 to the present, 2013. Photo credit: Indiana University.

Facing bottom, West elevation of Cook Hall and the Trevor and Edna Gray Entry Plaza, 2014. Photo credit: Indiana University.

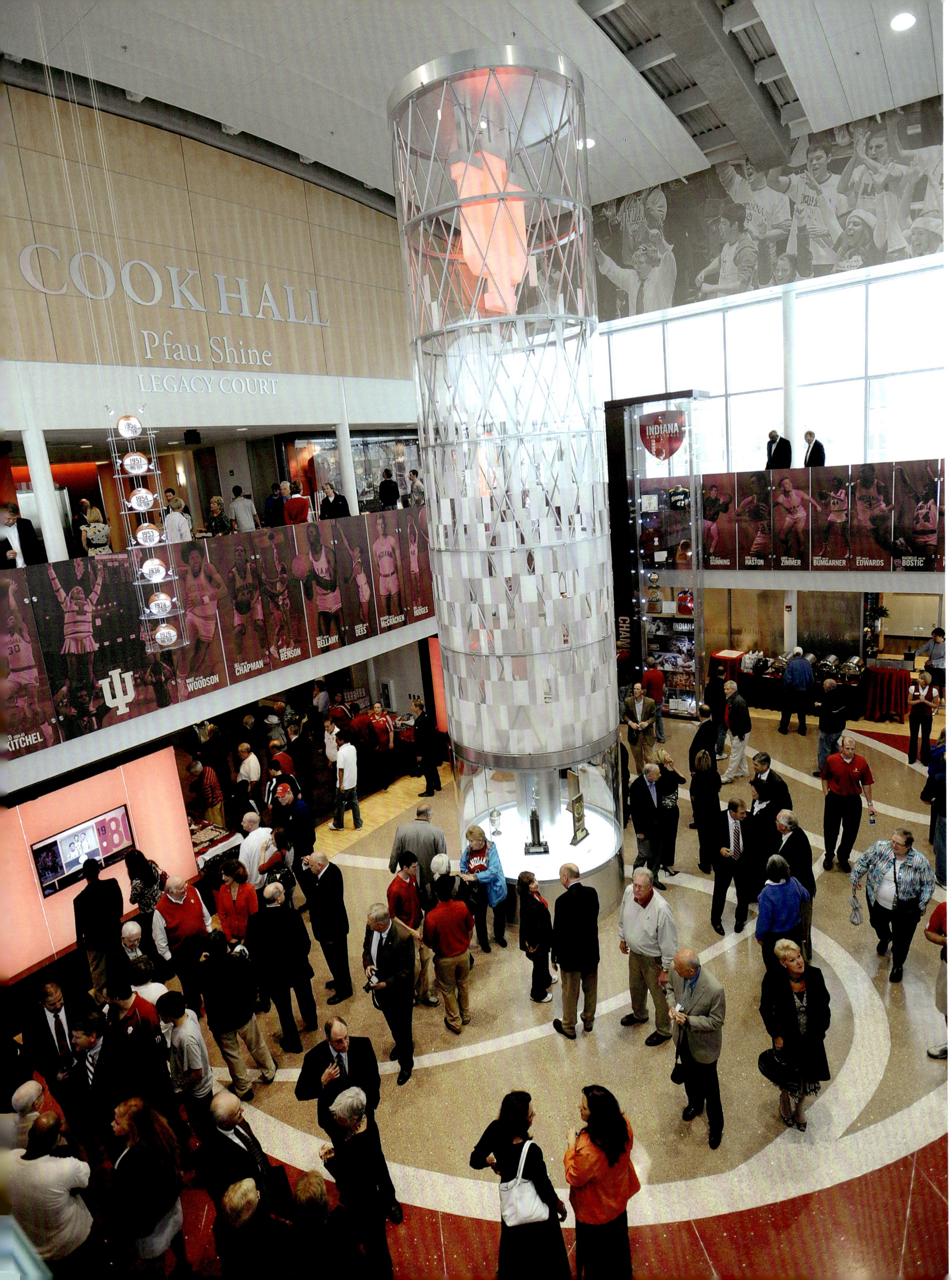

Two-story illuminated tower honoring IU's NCAA basketball championships in Legacy Court, 2013. Photo credit: Indiana University.

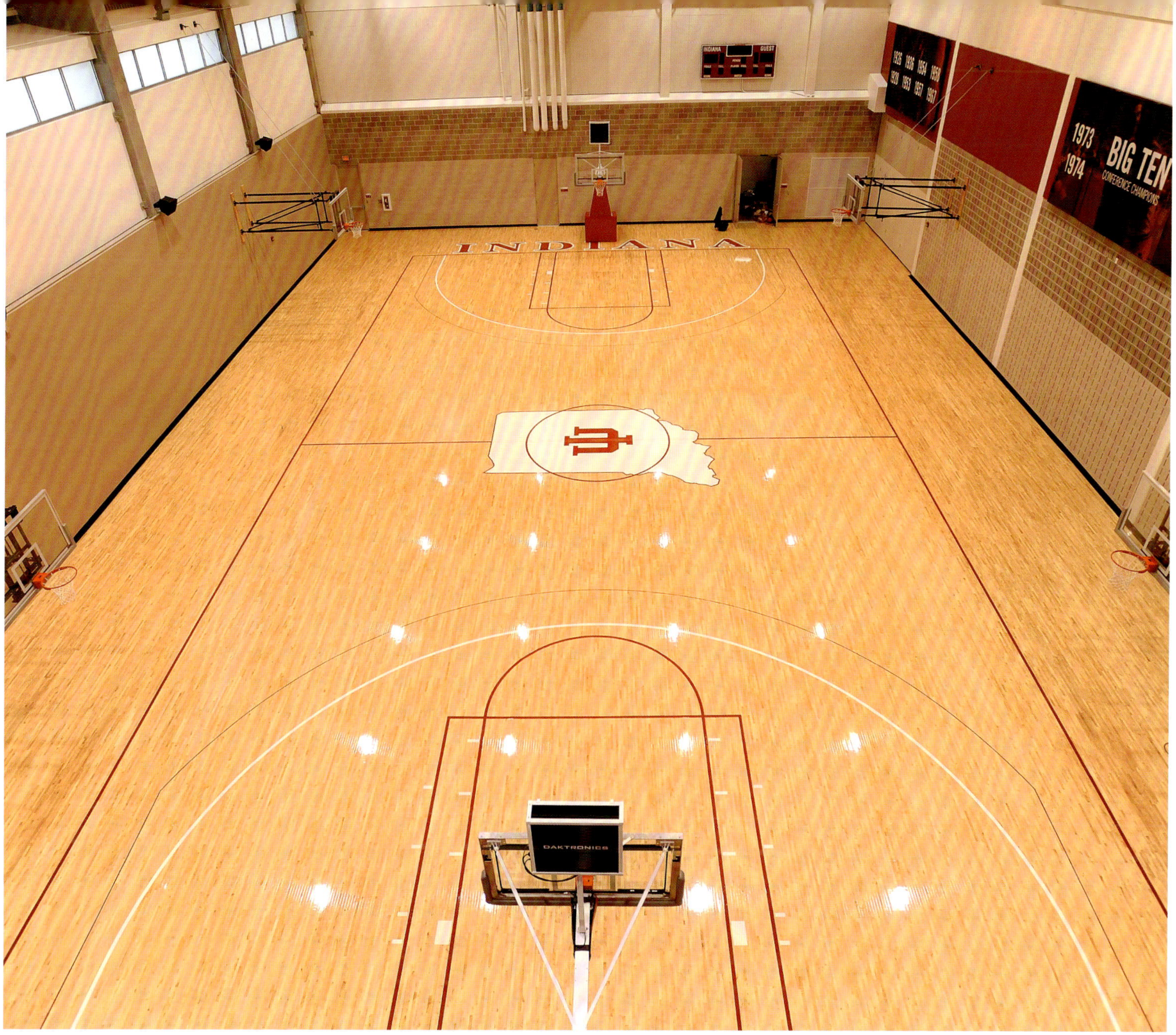

One of two practice courts in Cook Hall, 2017. Photo credit: Tyagan Miller.

tures from all three: the barrel-shaped roofline of Gladstein Fieldhouse, the flying buttresses of Assembly Hall, and the concrete exterior of Memorial Stadium. Cook Hall is massive, with 67,000 square feet and three serviceable levels, and is connected to Assembly Hall by an underground tunnel. Despite its size, Cook Hall has an imaginative and graceful architectural design.

Inside, the history of the renowned IU basketball program is displayed in the stunning two-story entry lobby, the Pfau Shine Legacy Court, a museum and exhibit space. Visitors will be awed by photographs, memorabilia in illuminated display cases, interactive kiosks, and particularly the two-story illuminated tower that honors IU's NCAA basketball championships. On the second floor, the reader rail traces the celebrated history of the IU basketball program from 1901 to the present. Offices on the main level welcome alums, recruits, and fans. Cook Hall houses two practice courts, one for each varsity basketball team. The courts can be configured as two regulation-size courts or four half courts. The structure also includes coaches' offices, locker rooms, and training and strength development rooms. Each team has its own suite, with player lounges and meeting/video rooms. In front of Cook Hall, the Trevor and Edna Gray Entry Plaza welcomes the hall's many visitors. It is especially lovely at night when the sixteen posts are set aglow.

Harry Gladstein Fieldhouse

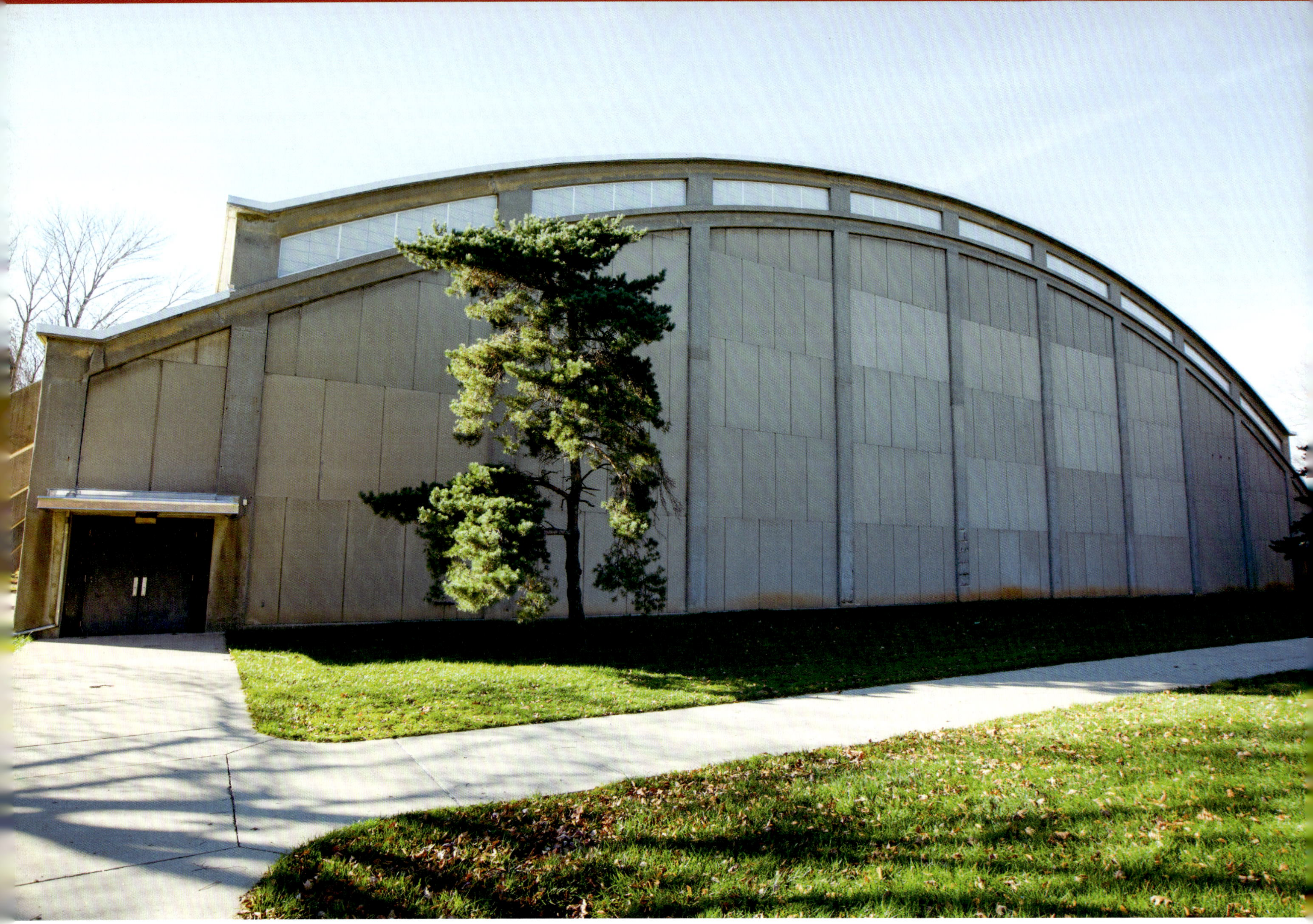

Above, East elevation of Harry Gladstein Fieldhouse, 2016. Photo credit: Tyagan Miller.

Facing top, Two-hundred-meter Mondo-surfaced banked track in Gladstein Fieldhouse, 2016. Photo credit: Tyagan Miller.

Facing bottom, Robert C. Haugh Track and Field Complex, 1997. Photo credit: Indiana University.

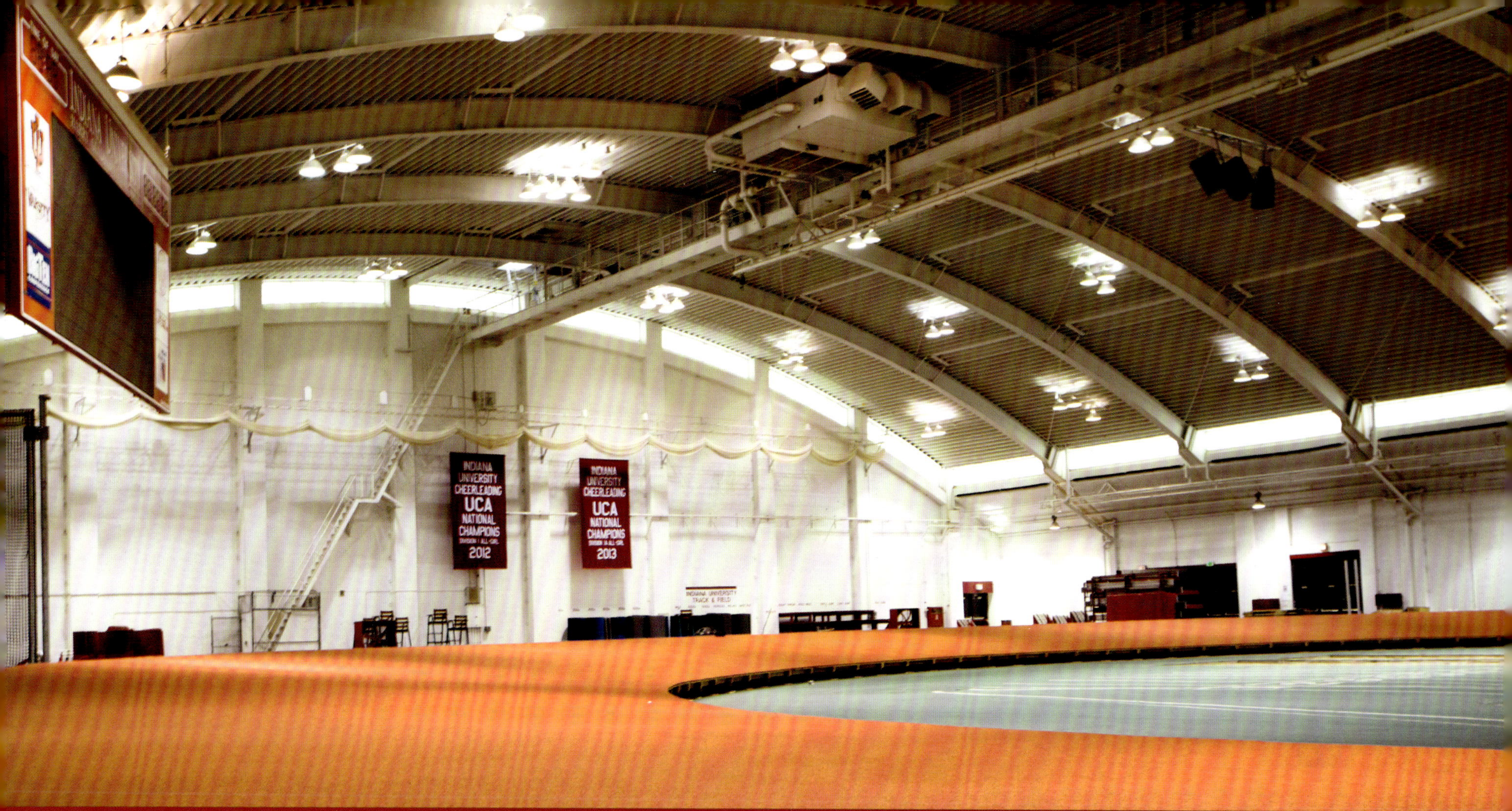

Robert C. Haugh Track and Field Complex

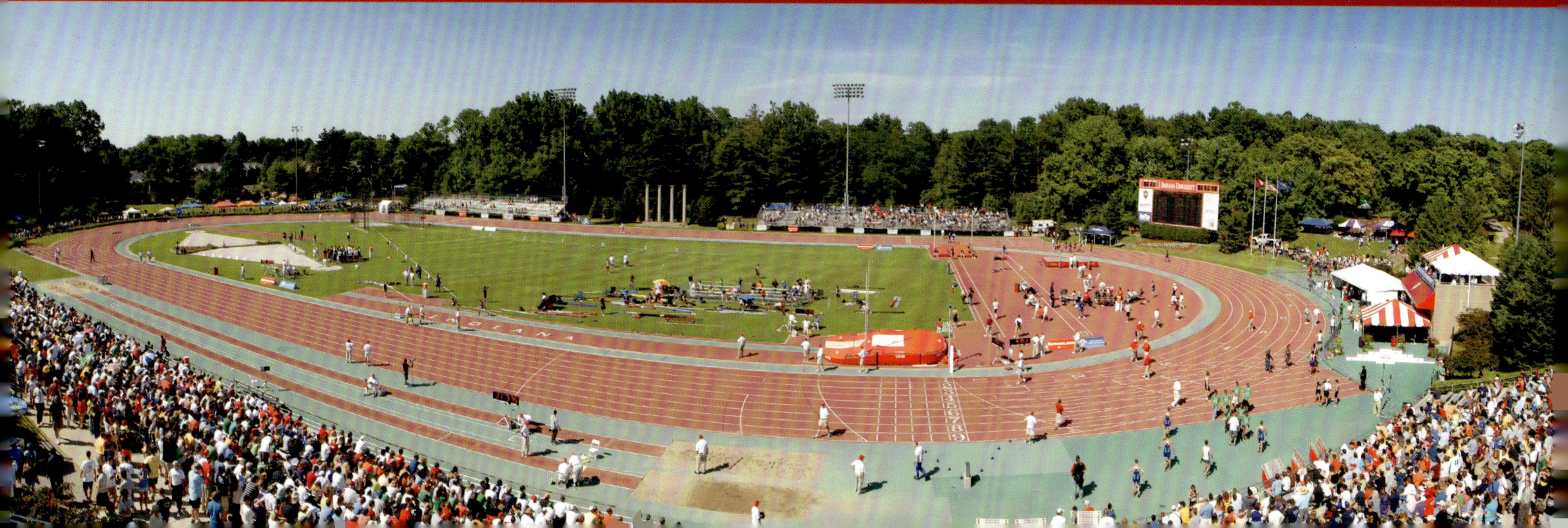

Bill Armstrong Stadium

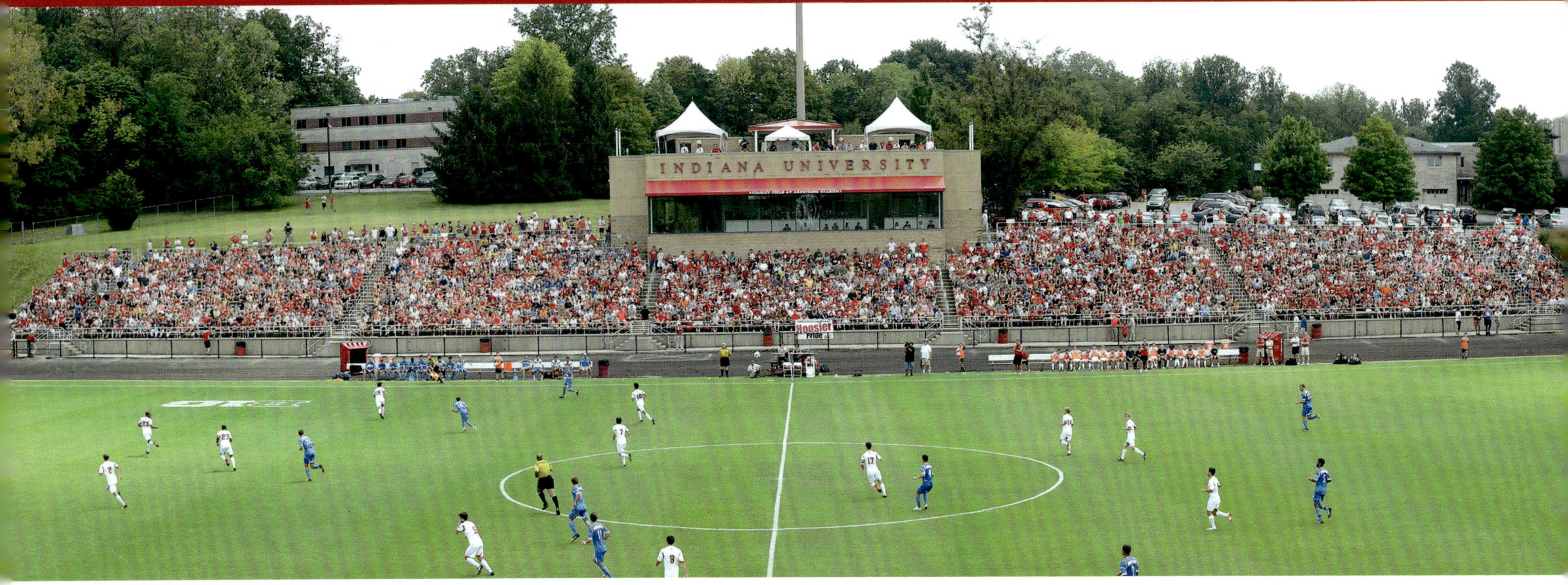

Above, Varsity soccer game on Yeagley Field in Bill Armstrong Stadium, 2013. Photo credit: Indiana University.

Right, Women's 2015 Little 500 bicycle race. Photo credit: Indiana University Student Foundation.

Facing, Men's 2016 Little 500 bicycle race. Photo credit: Indiana University Student Foundation.

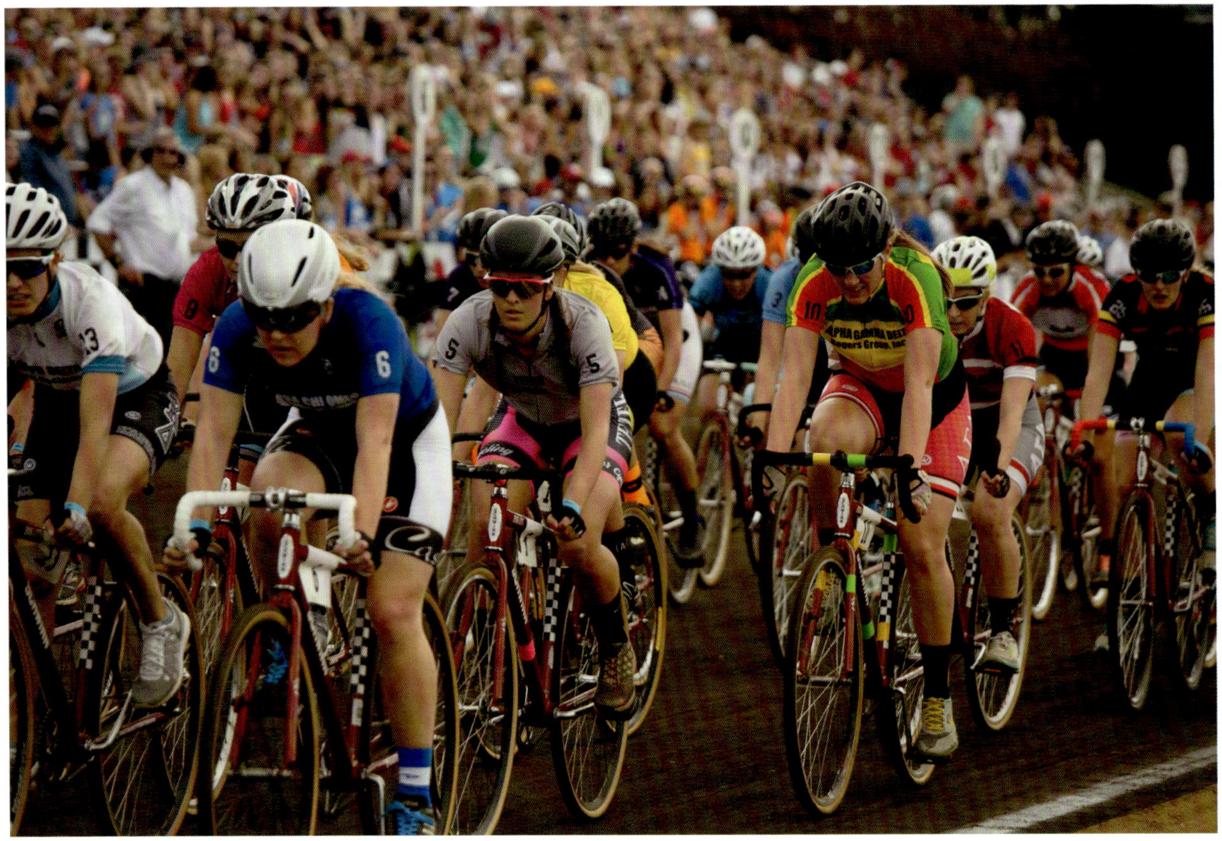

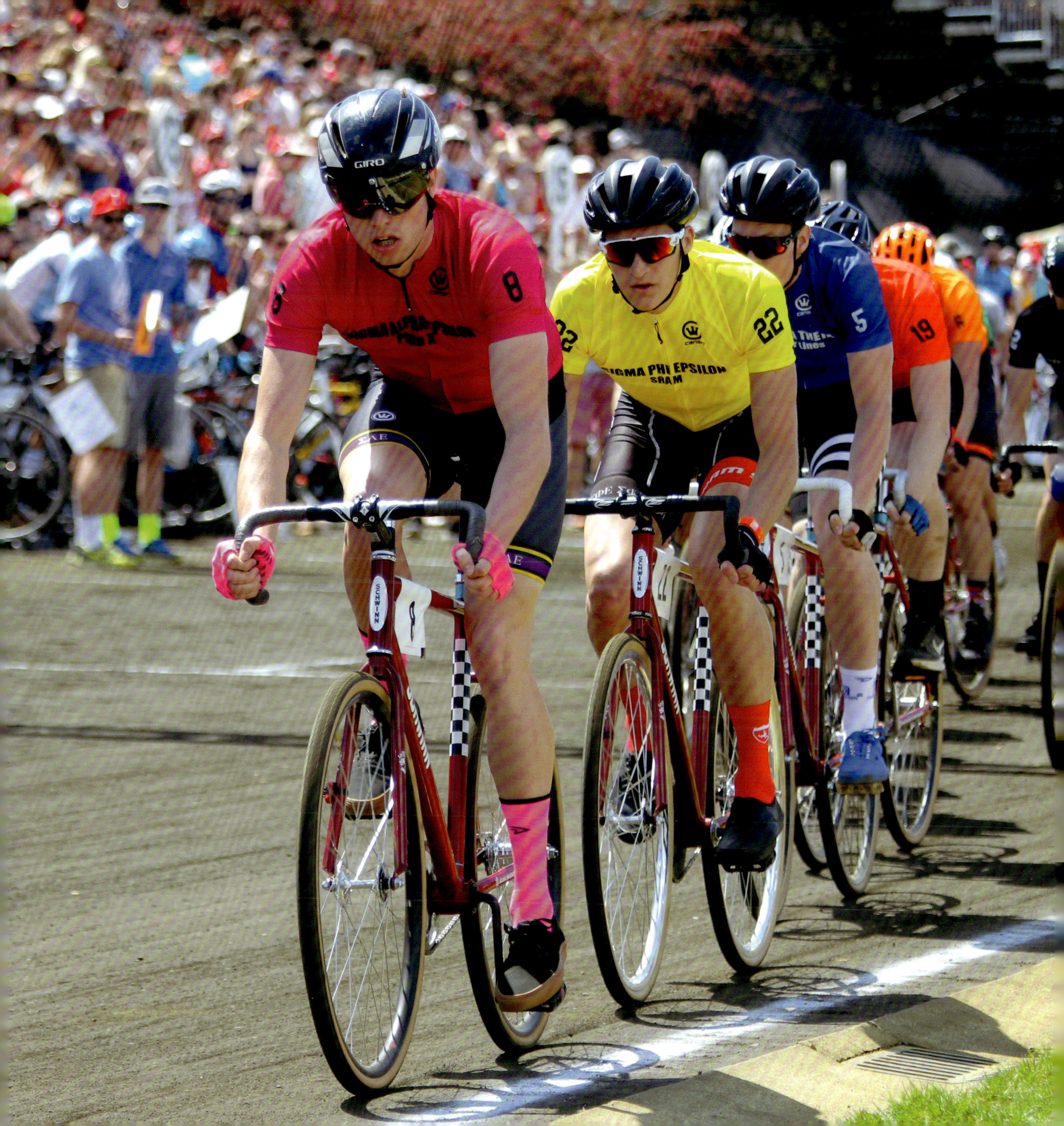
GIRO
8
22
SRAM
5
19

John Mellencamp Pavilion

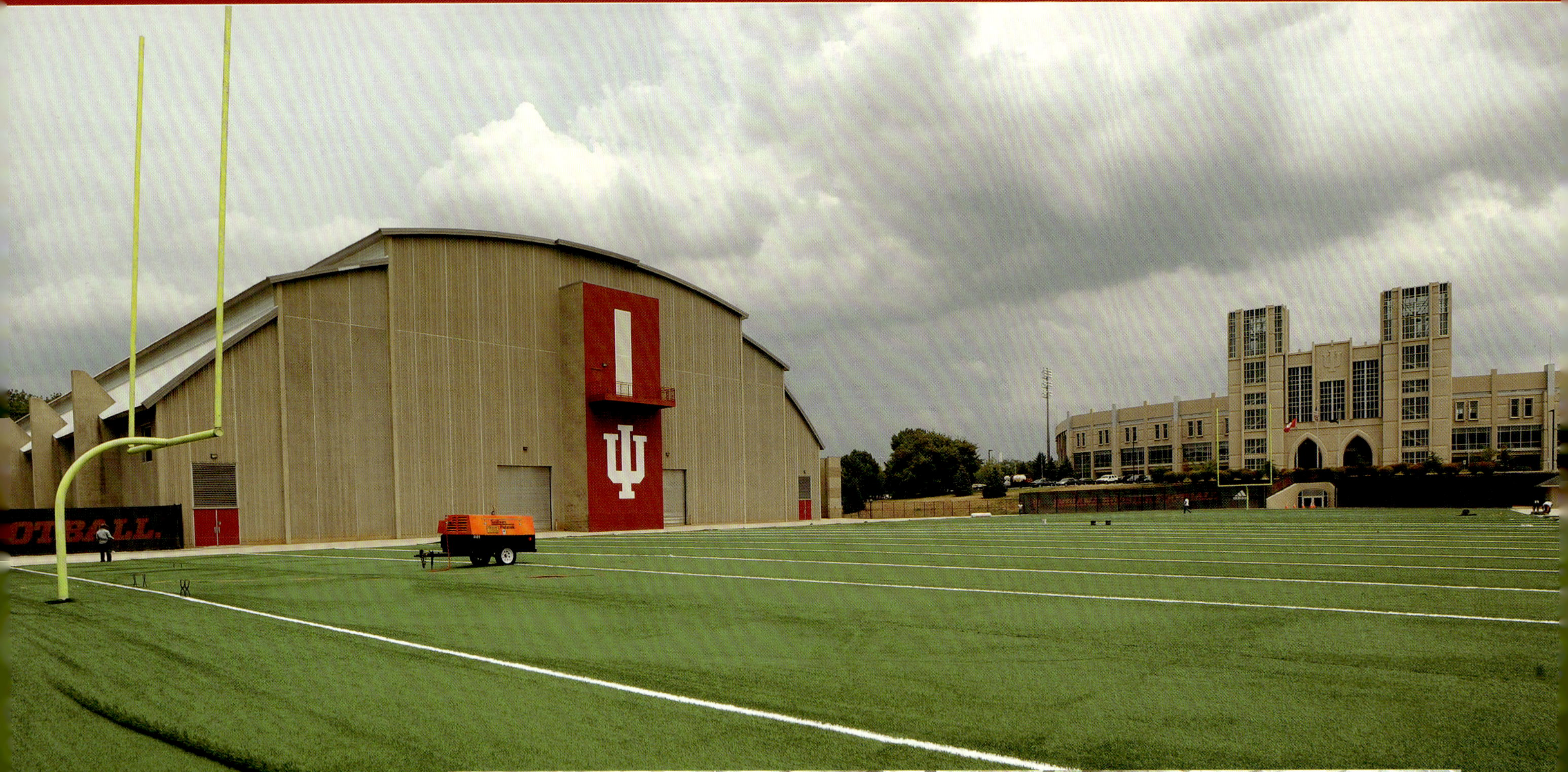

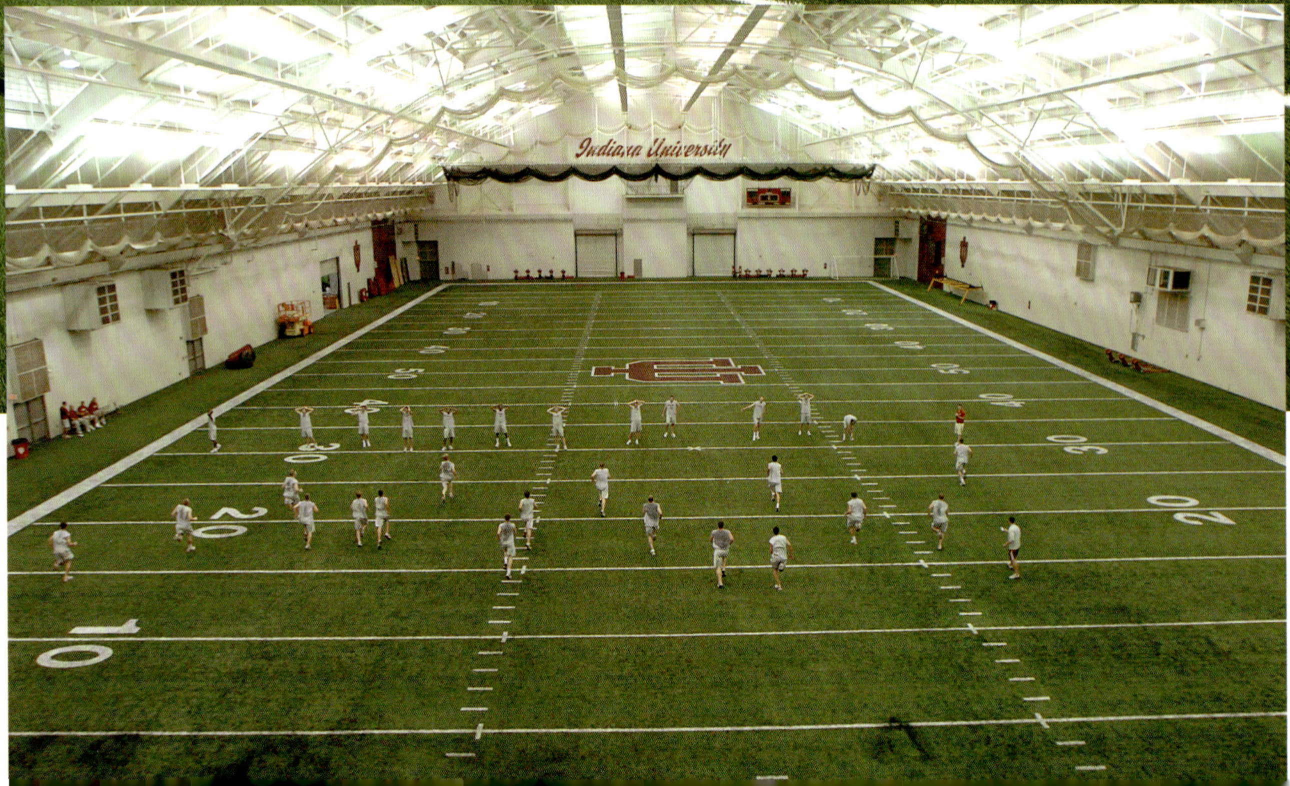

Above, John Mellencamp Pavilion beyond football practice field, 2008. Photo credit: Indiana University.

Indiana University Tennis Center

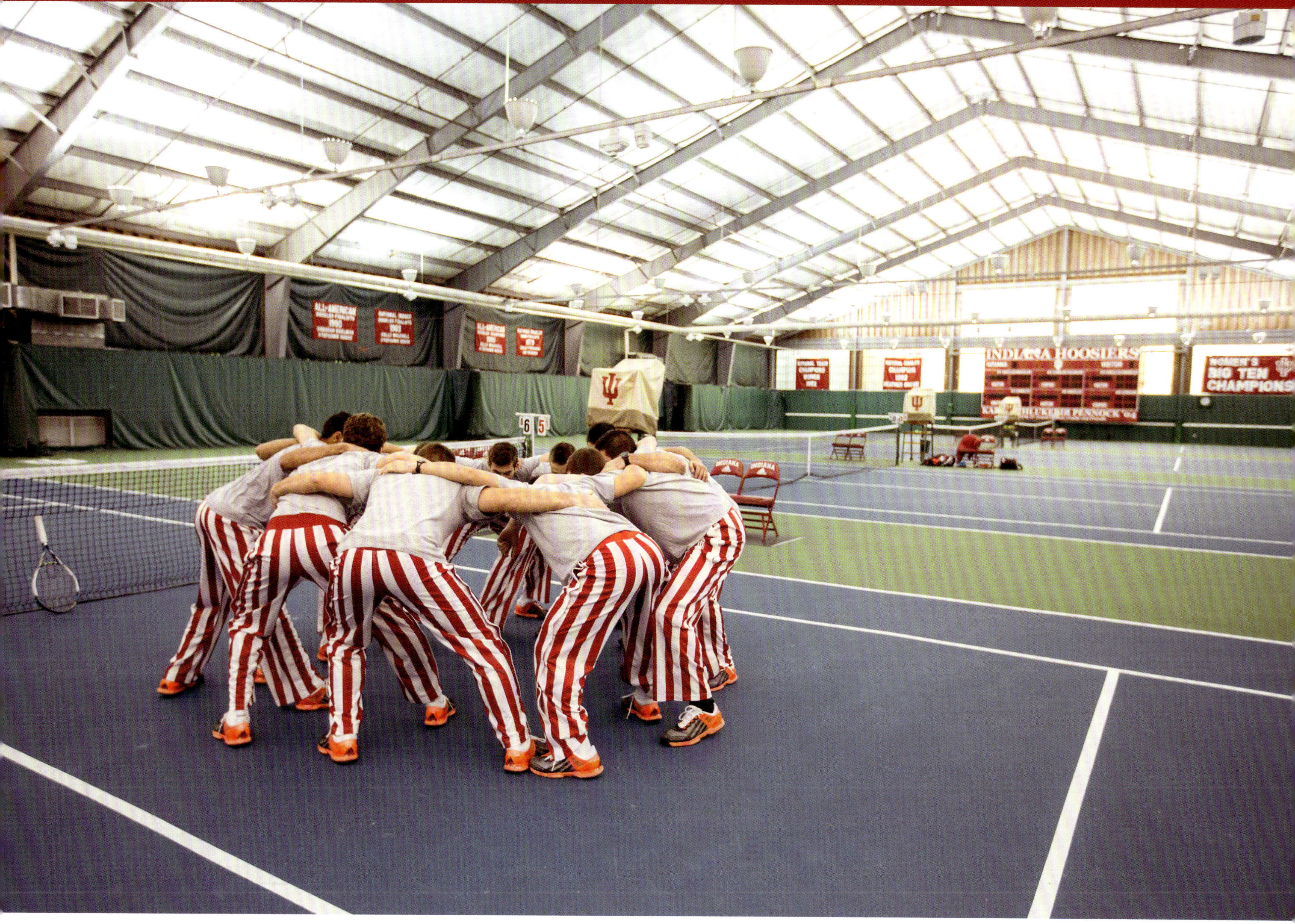

Facing bottom, Student-athletes warming up inside Mellencamp Pavilion, 2014. Photo credit: Indiana University.

Above, Varsity men's team huddling up before a match inside Tennis Center, 2016. Photo credit: Indiana University.

Bart Kaufman Field

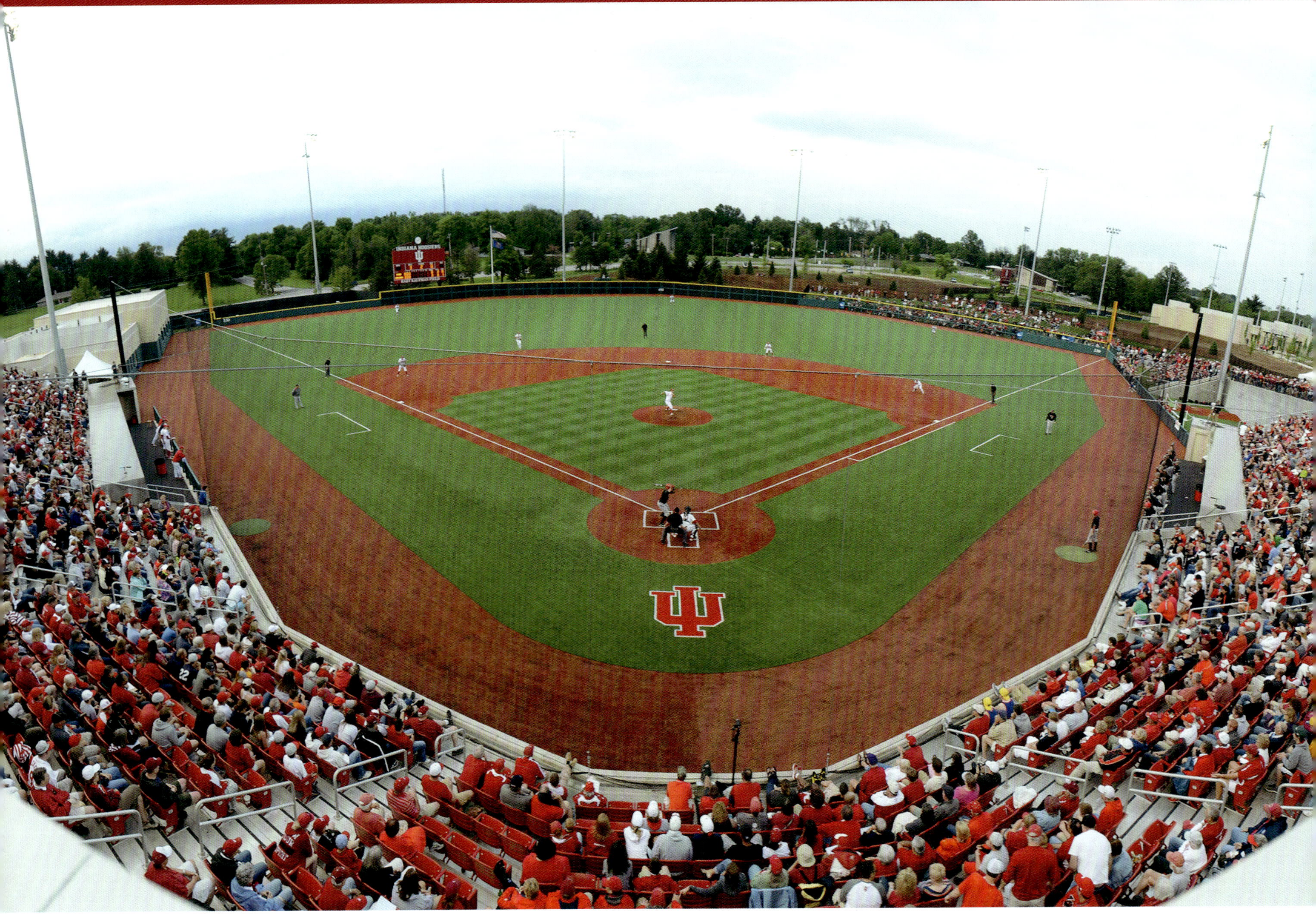

Varsity baseball game in progress at Bart Kaufman Field, 2013. Photo credit: Indiana University.

Andy Mohr Field

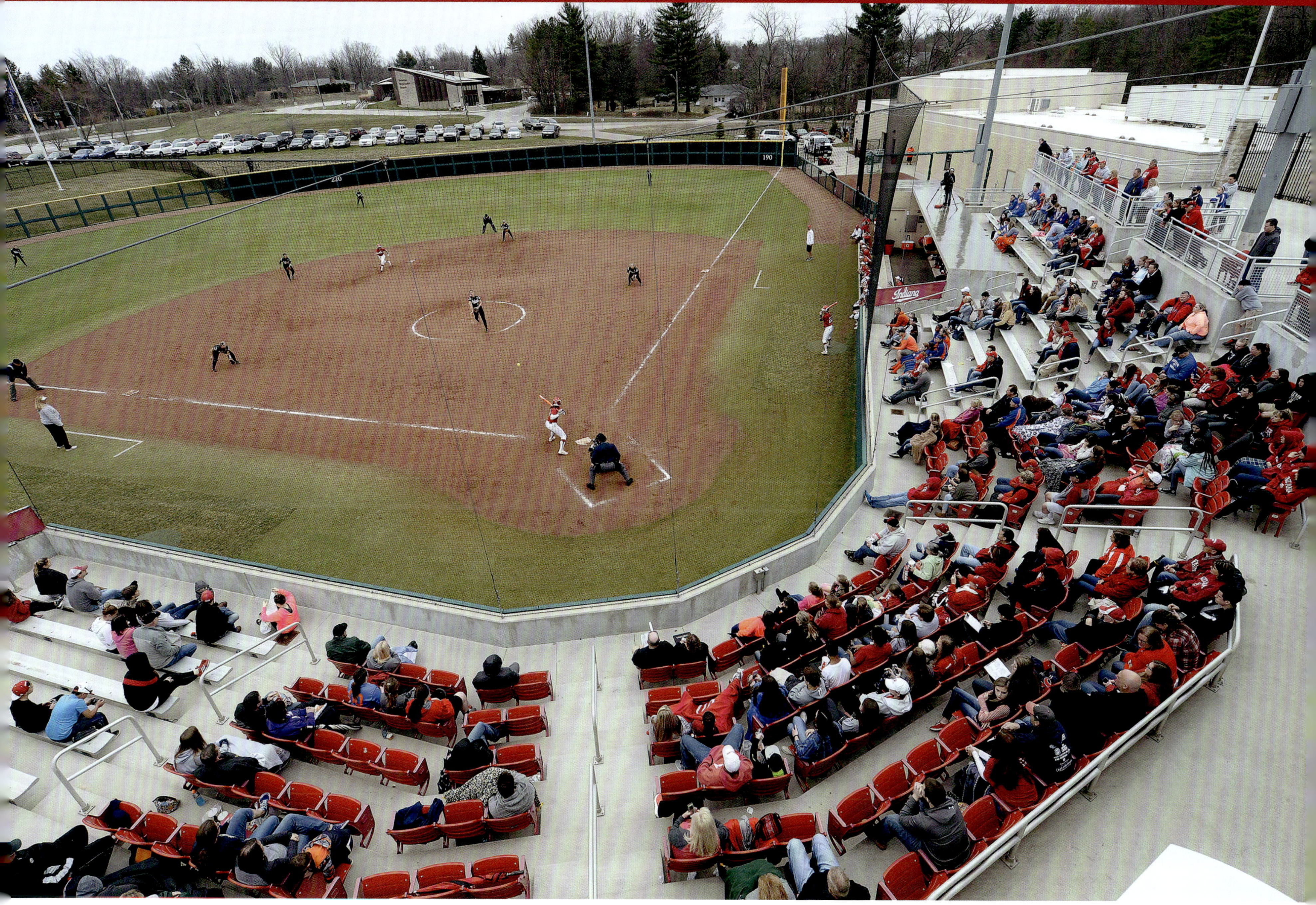

Varsity softball game in progress at Andy Mohr Field, 2016. Photo credit: Indiana University.

Indiana University Golf Course

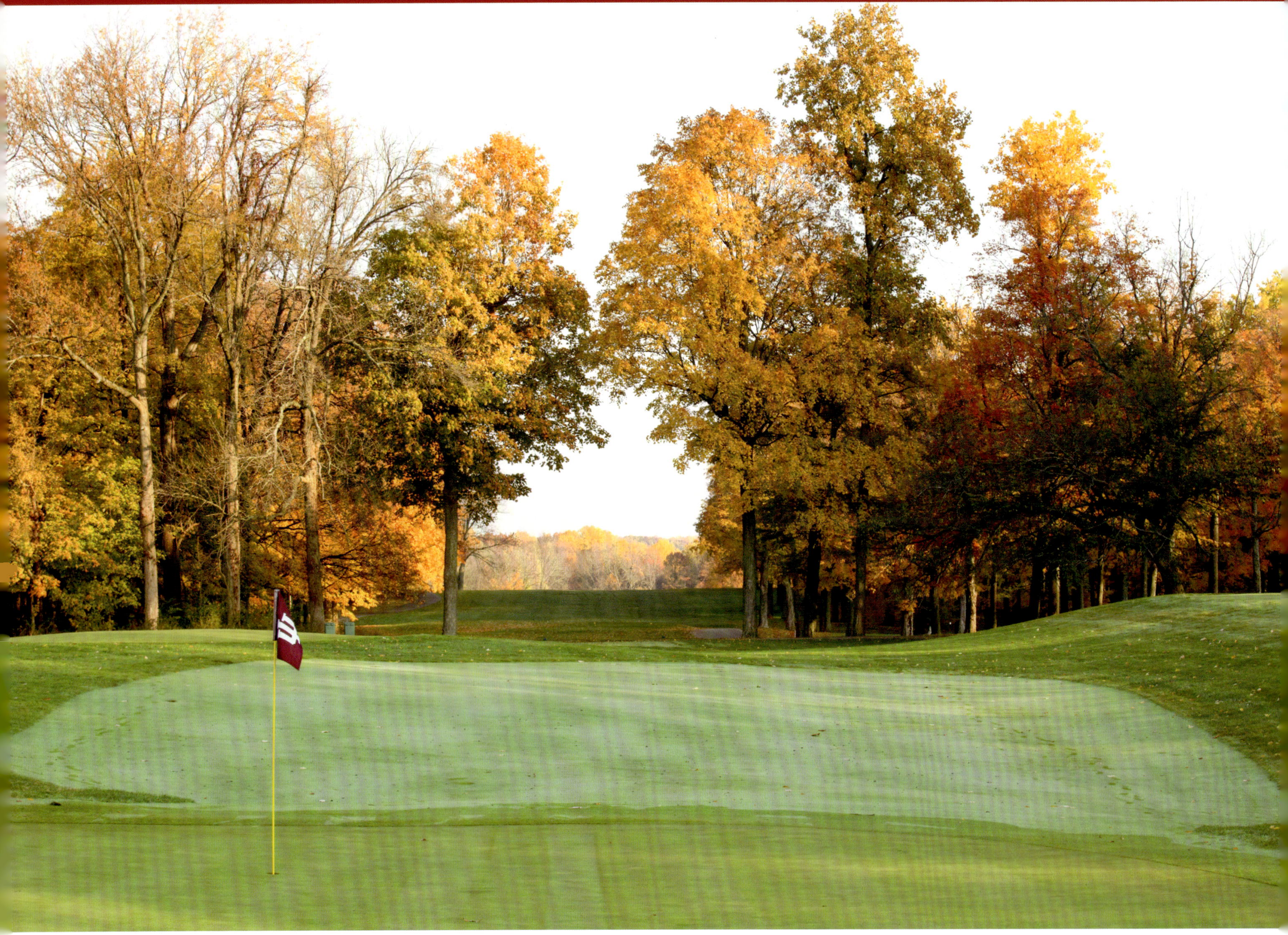

View from putting green on golf course, 2016. Photo credit: Tyagan Miller.

Indiana University Field Hockey Complex

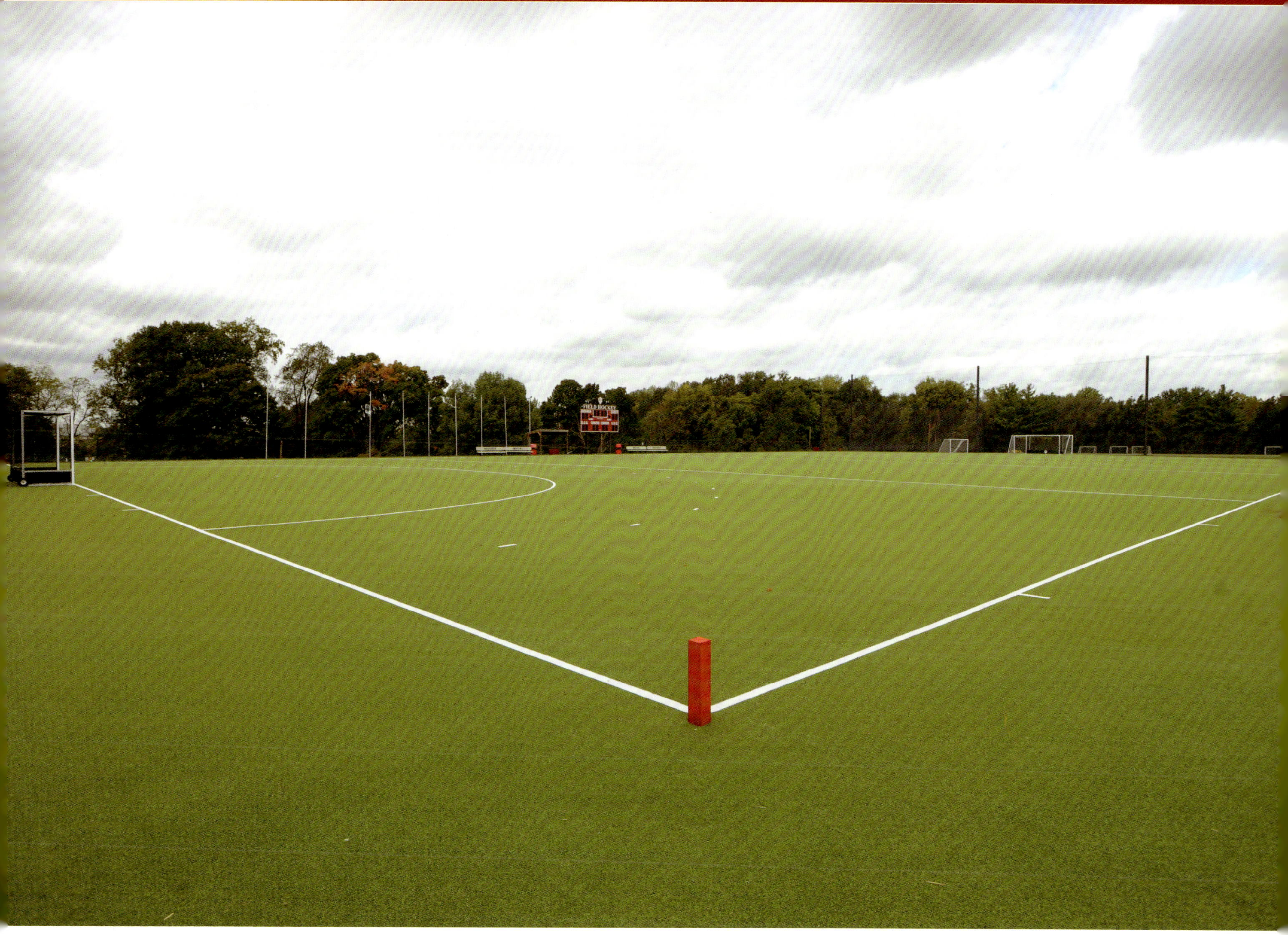

PolyTan playing surface at Field Hockey Complex, 2014. Photo credit: Indiana University.

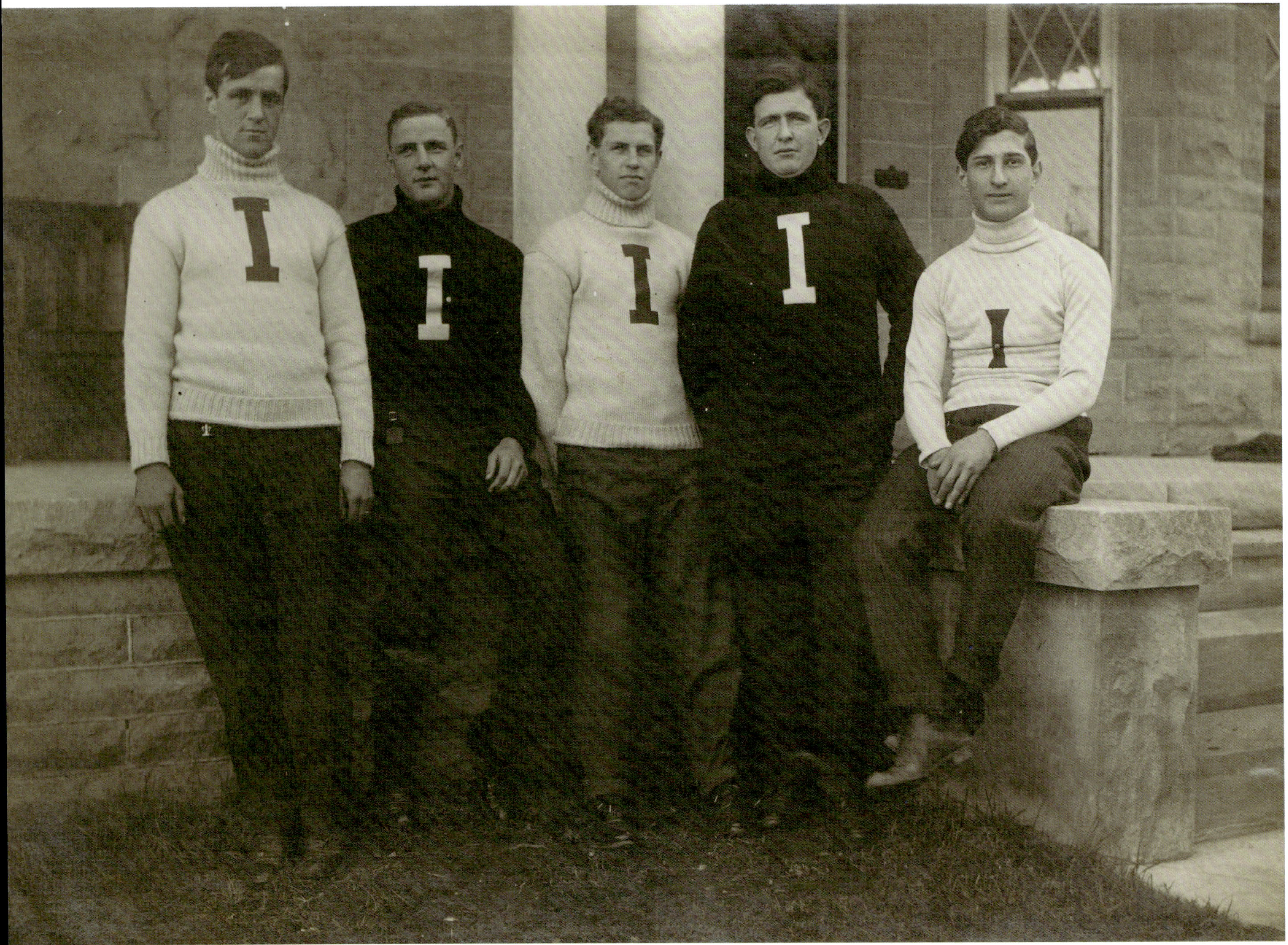

I-Men from scrapbook of IU alumnus Harry A. Hoffman, circa 1905. P0025136, IU Archives.

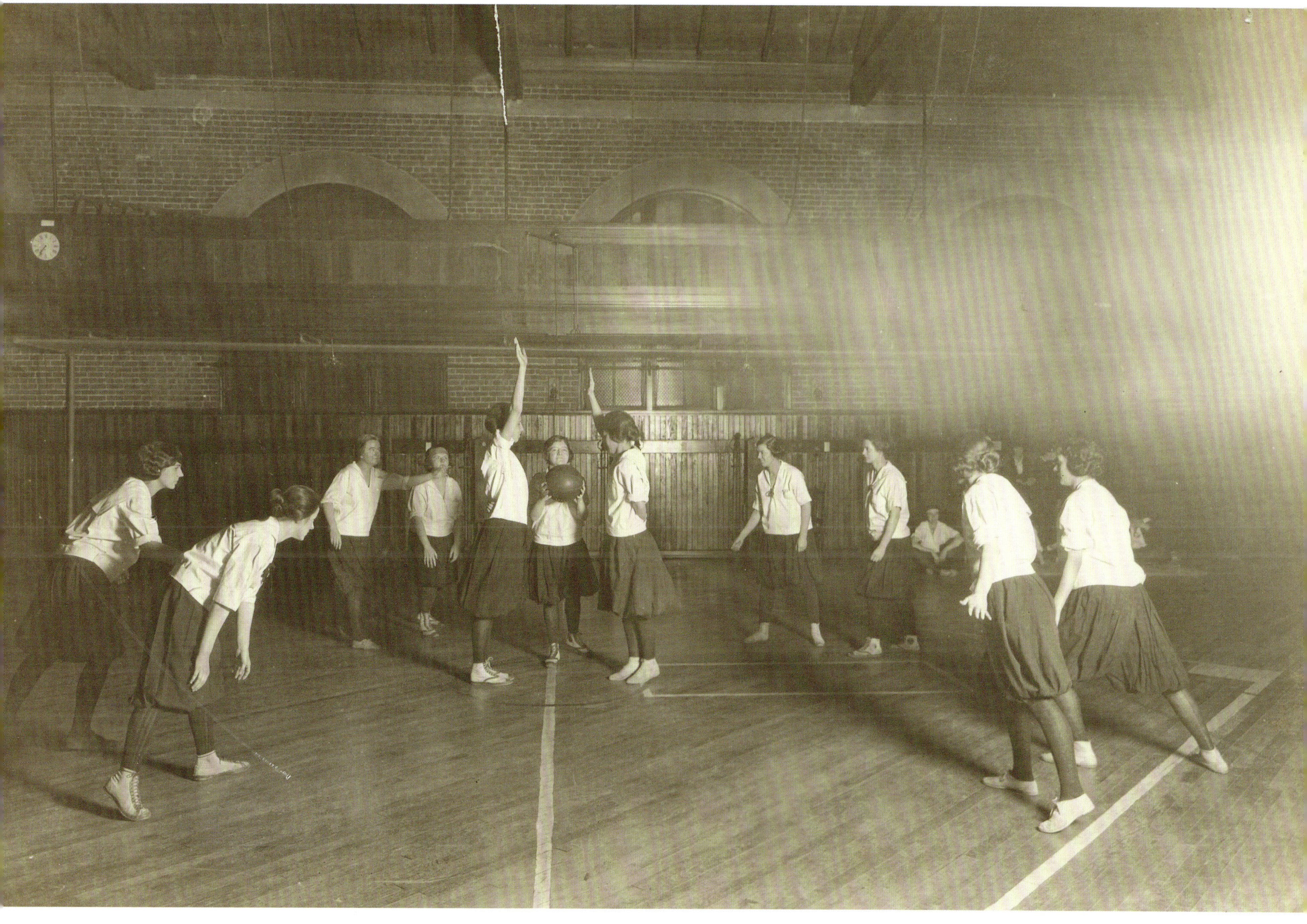

Intramural women's basketball championship game, in west wing of Student Building, 1922. P0027261, IU Archives.

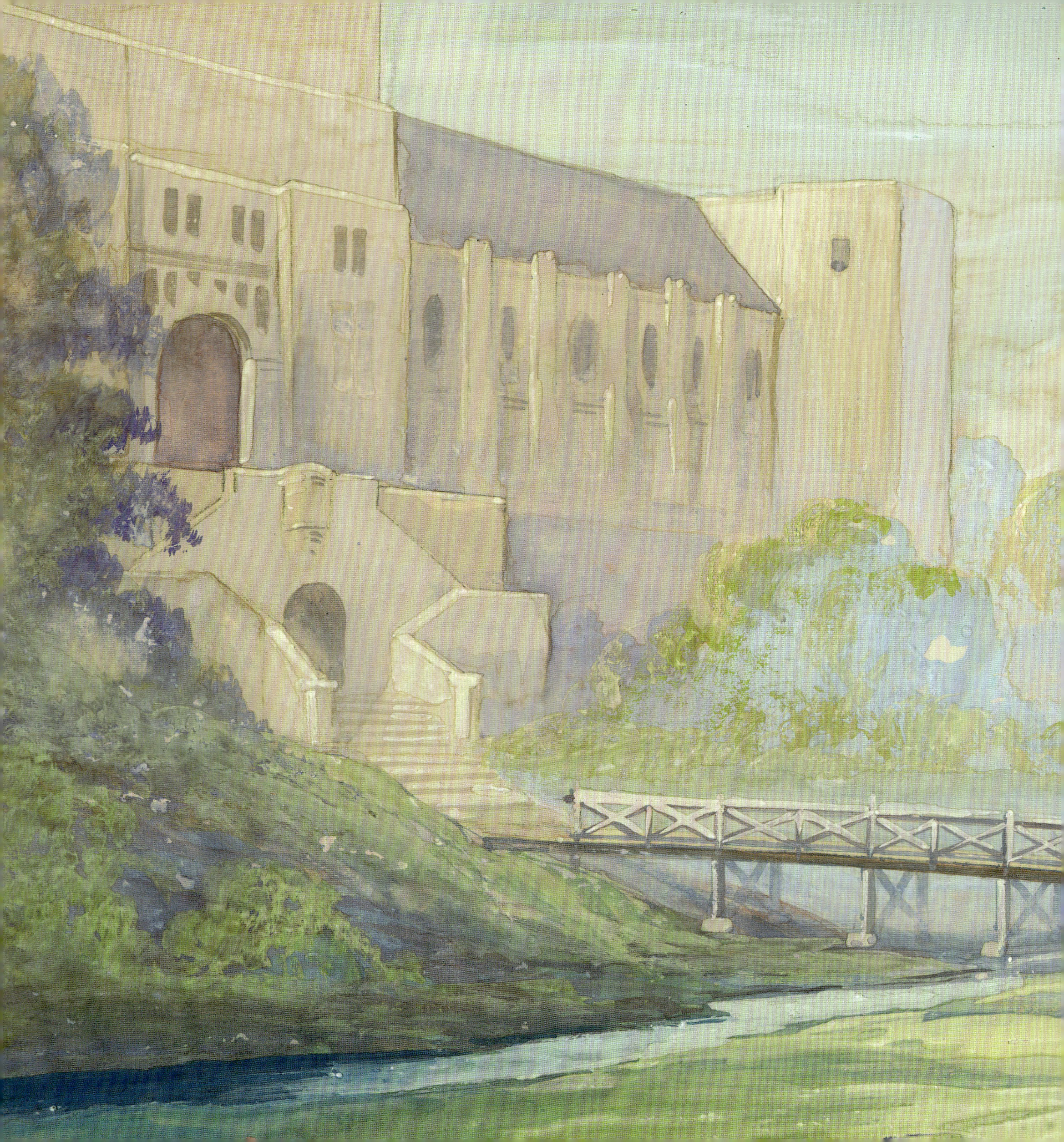

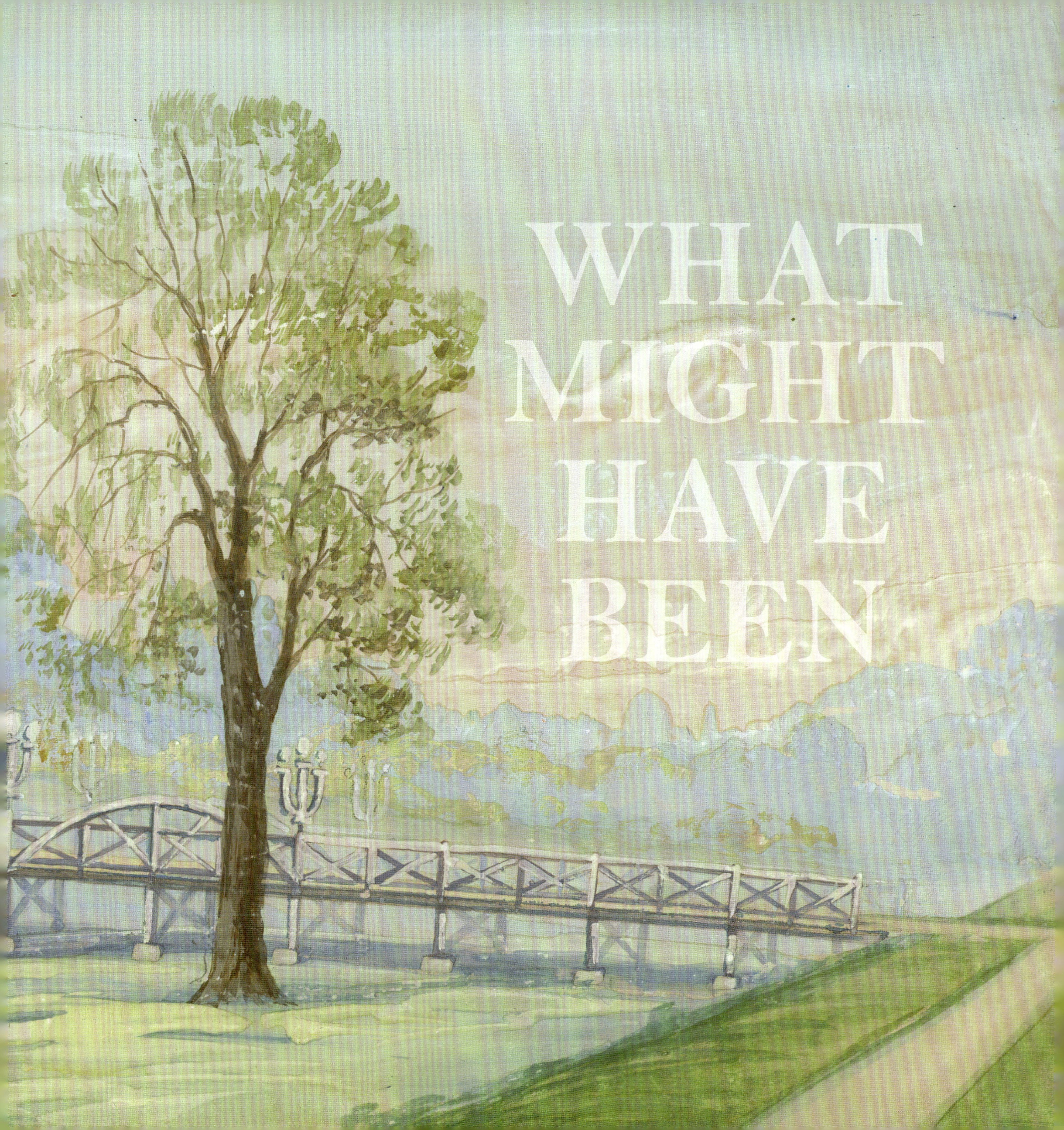
WHAT
MIGHT
HAVE
BEEN

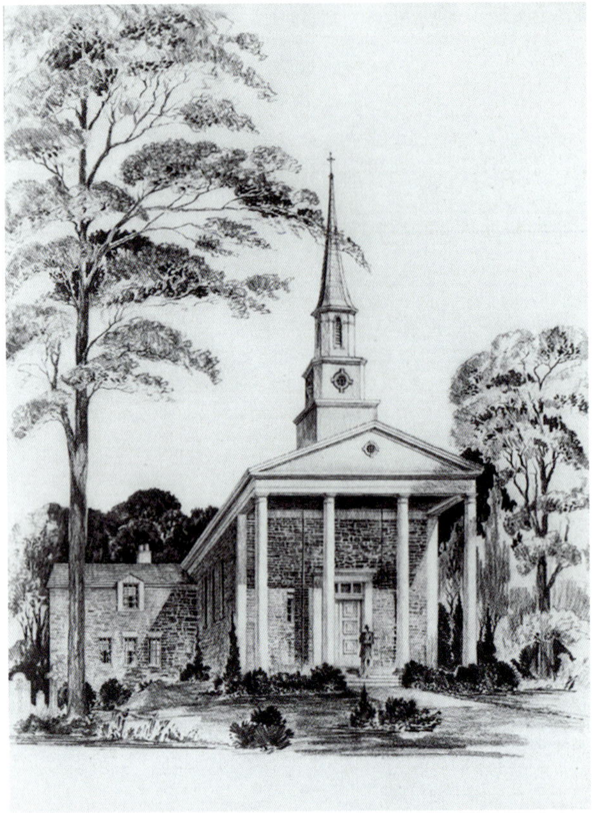

Beck Chapel. On January 29, 1941, following a banquet in Alumni Hall sponsored by the Committee on Religion and the Student Religious Cabinet, University President Herman B Wells stood before more than four hundred members of the faculty, student body, and public to announce a generous gift from Frank and Daisy Beck to construct a chapel for all faiths on the campus. Shortly thereafter, Indianapolis architect Edward D. James presented the conceptual drawing for the proposed structure shown here. The Georgian style design on the exterior featured a stone facade fronted by a massive portico supported by columns below. Interior plans included a seating capacity of 150, lounge, and study. Due to wartime scarcity of building materials, construction of the chapel was delayed until 1954, and this initial design was redesigned by the same architects in the Tudor style we know today. P0051706, IU Archives. Photo credit: Edward D. James, architect.

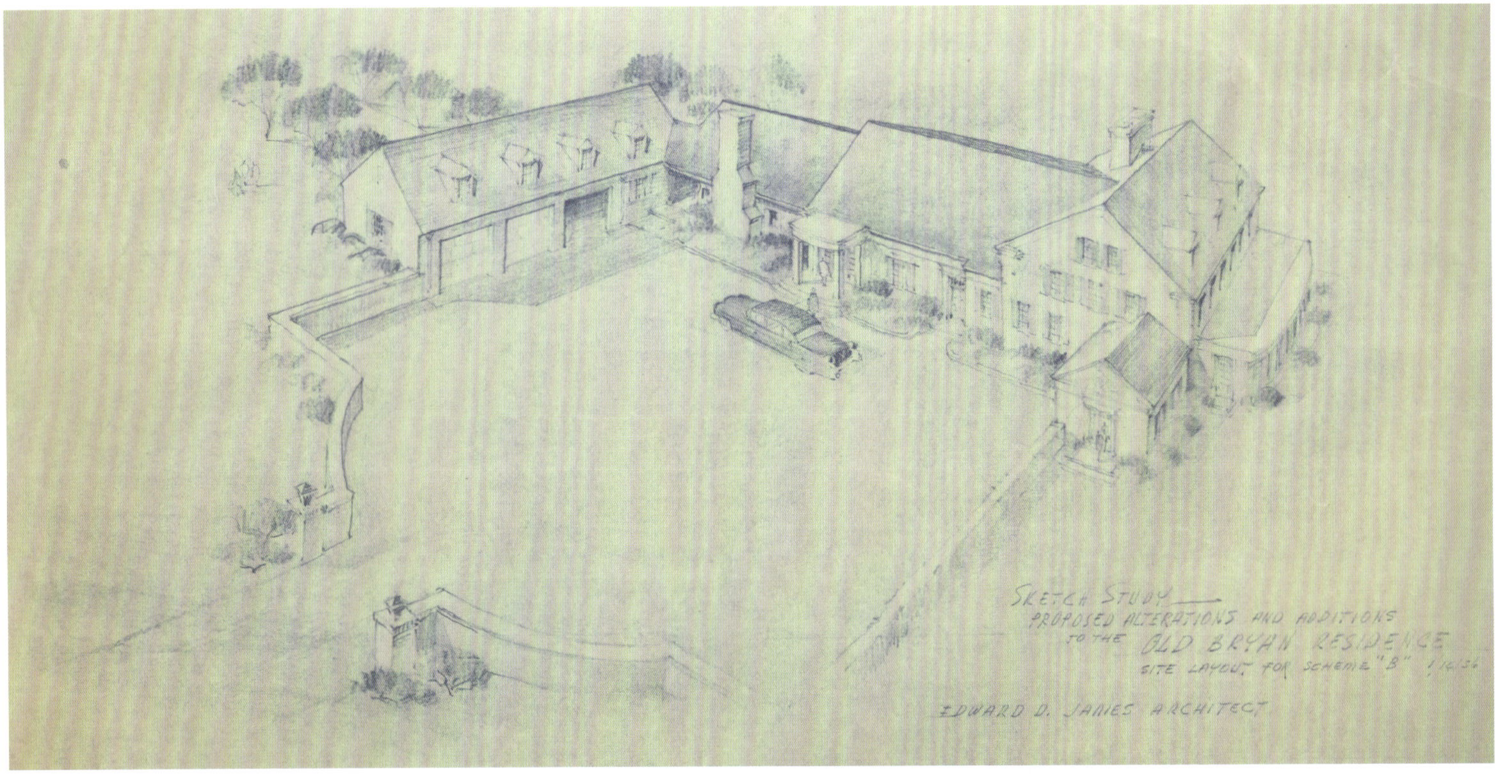

William and Charlotte Lowe Bryan House. Prior to President Herman B Wells's occupancy in 1957, the President's House, as the William and Charlotte Lowe Bryan House was then known, underwent extensive renovation. Ultimately, the plans shown here from early 1956 from Edward D. James were simplified to eliminate the large addition to the east side of the house, including a three-car garage. P0058434, IU Archives. Photo credit: Edward D. James, architect.

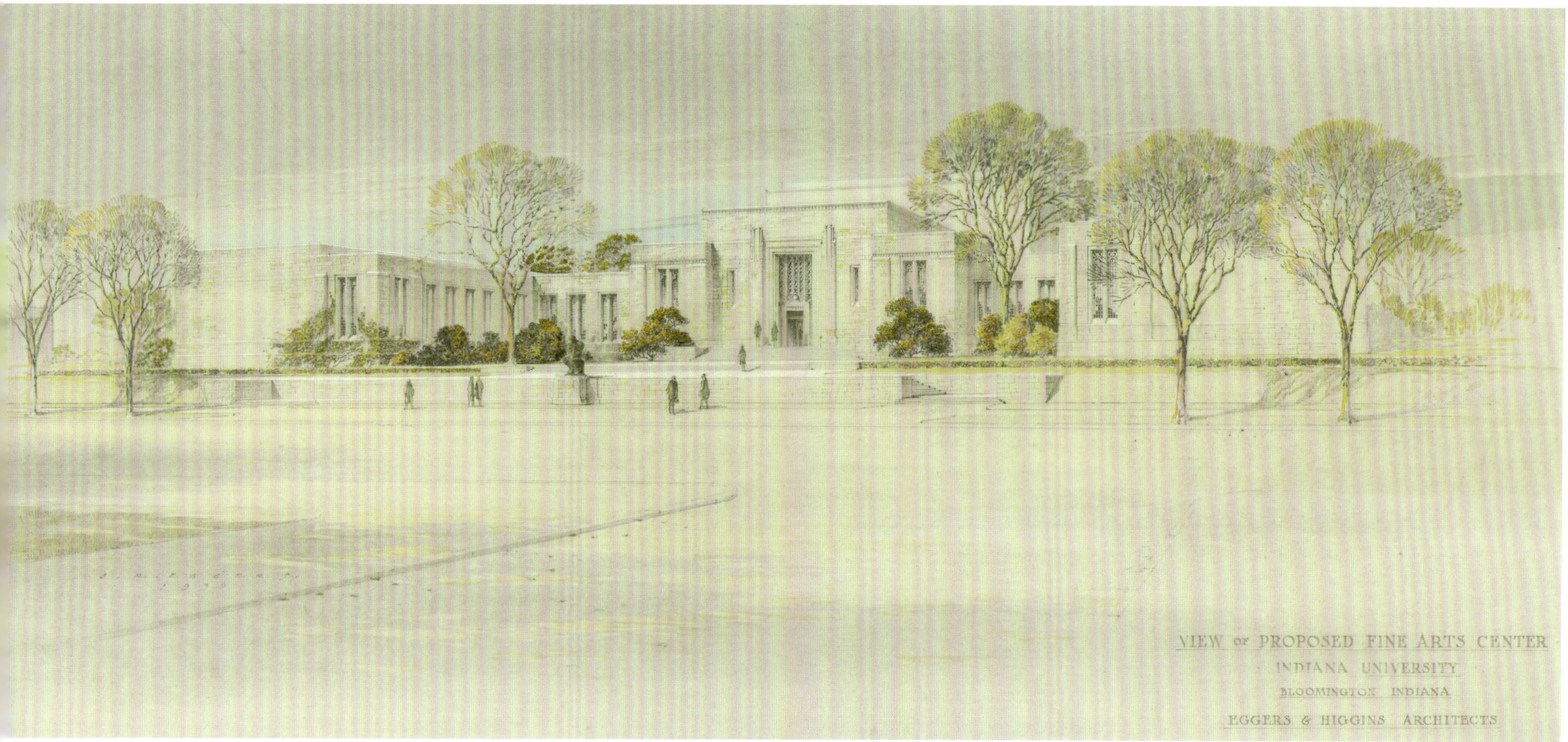

Fine Arts Building. In May 1941, during Henry Radford Hope's on-campus interview for chairman of the Fine Arts Department, President Herman B Wells unveiled this 1939 Eggers and Higgins watercolor rendering for a new fine arts center to complete the north side of a plaza dedicated to the arts. The Art Deco external facade featured a U-shaped orientation with a monumental arcade to the east and west and a central entryway flanked by massive flattened vertical columns. This design was altered dramatically to a more simplified rectilinear footprint completed in 1962. P0058445, IU Archives. Photo credit: Eggers and Higgins, architects.

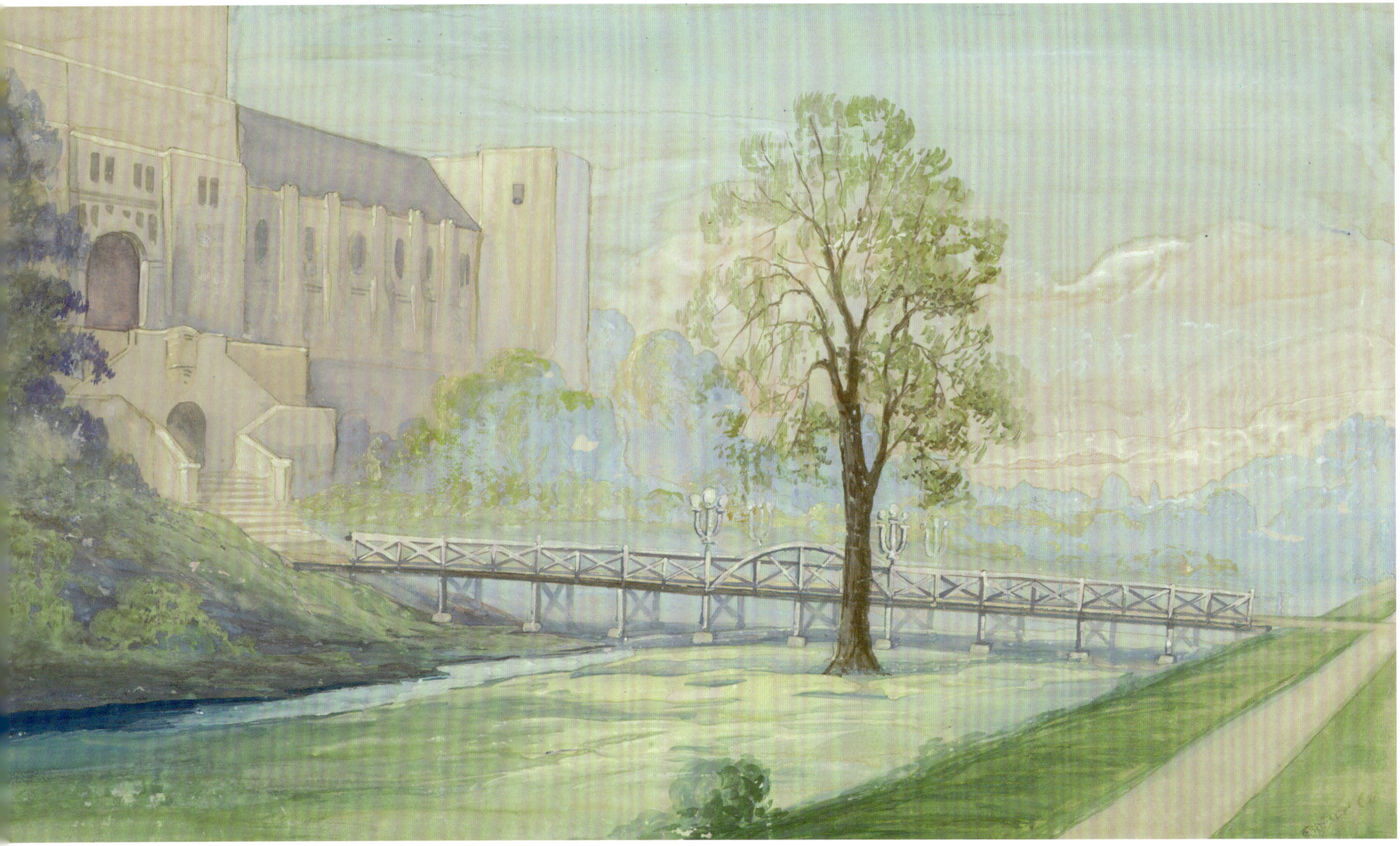

Jordan River Bridge. This drawing is a whimsical rendering of a bridge over Jordan River from Dunn Meadow into the main south entry to Indiana Memorial Union, undated. P0058442, IU Archives.

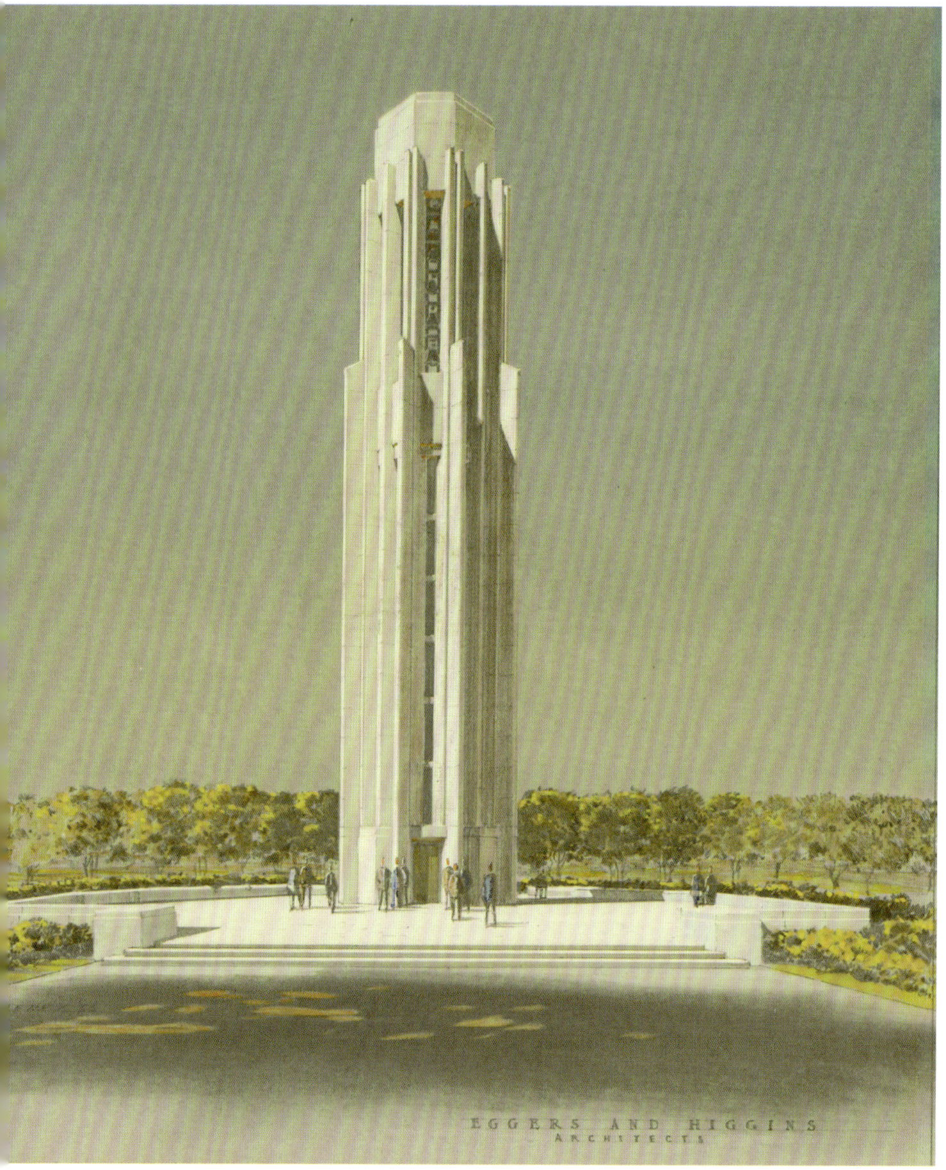

Arthur R. Metz Memorial Carillon. This 1963 design from the Eggers and Higgins architectural firm was the first of six known proposals for the Arthur R. Metz Memorial Carillon. This design accommodated a thirty-five-bell carillon; the executed carillon has sixty-one bells. P0058449, IU Archives. Photo credit: Eggers and Higgins, architects.

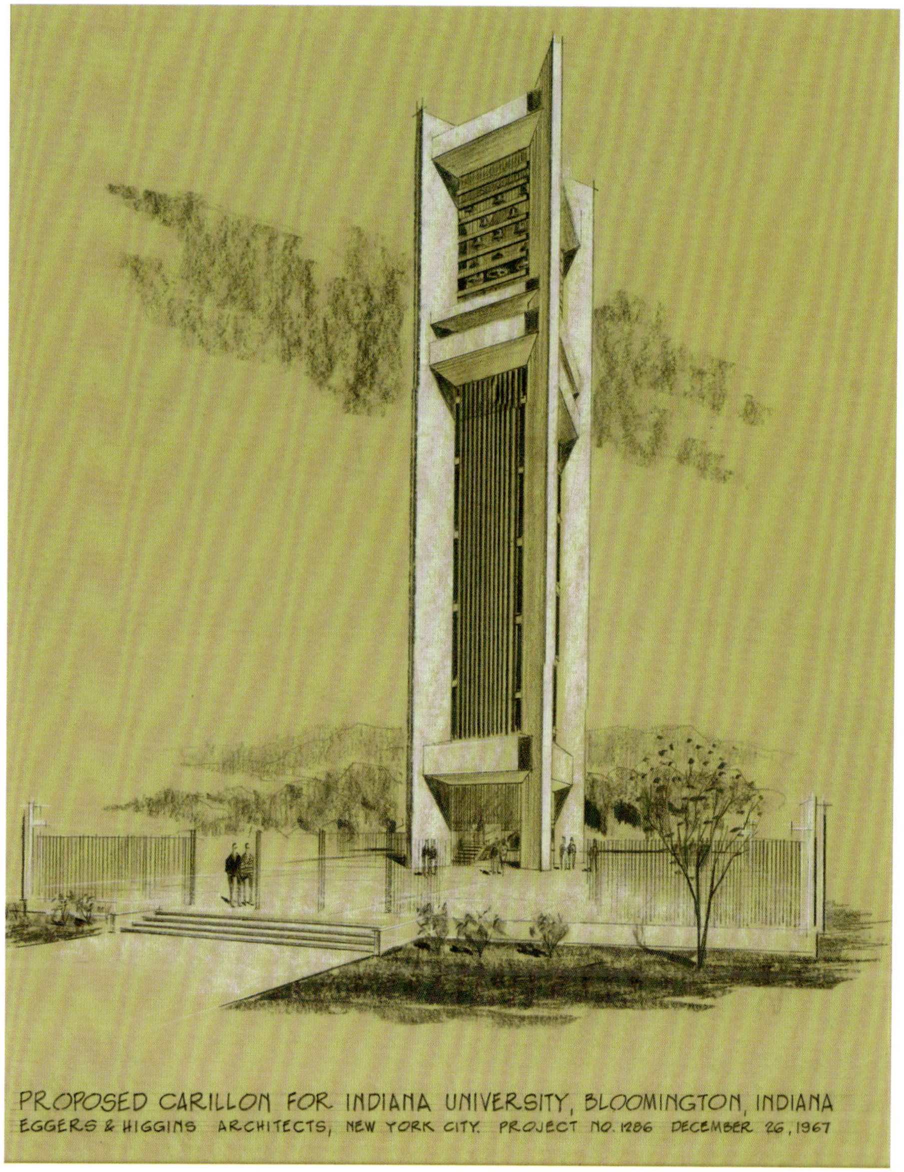

Arthur R. Metz Memorial Carillon. Preceded by another three designs in late 1966, this proposal from December 1967, again by Eggers and Higgins, offered a more simplified contemporary style so as not to block the sound of the bells with unnecessary ornamentation. Eventually deemed too modern by the donor and university chancellor Herman B Wells, a more traditional design was approved in 1969. P0058443, IU Archives. Photo credit: Eggers and Higgins, architects.

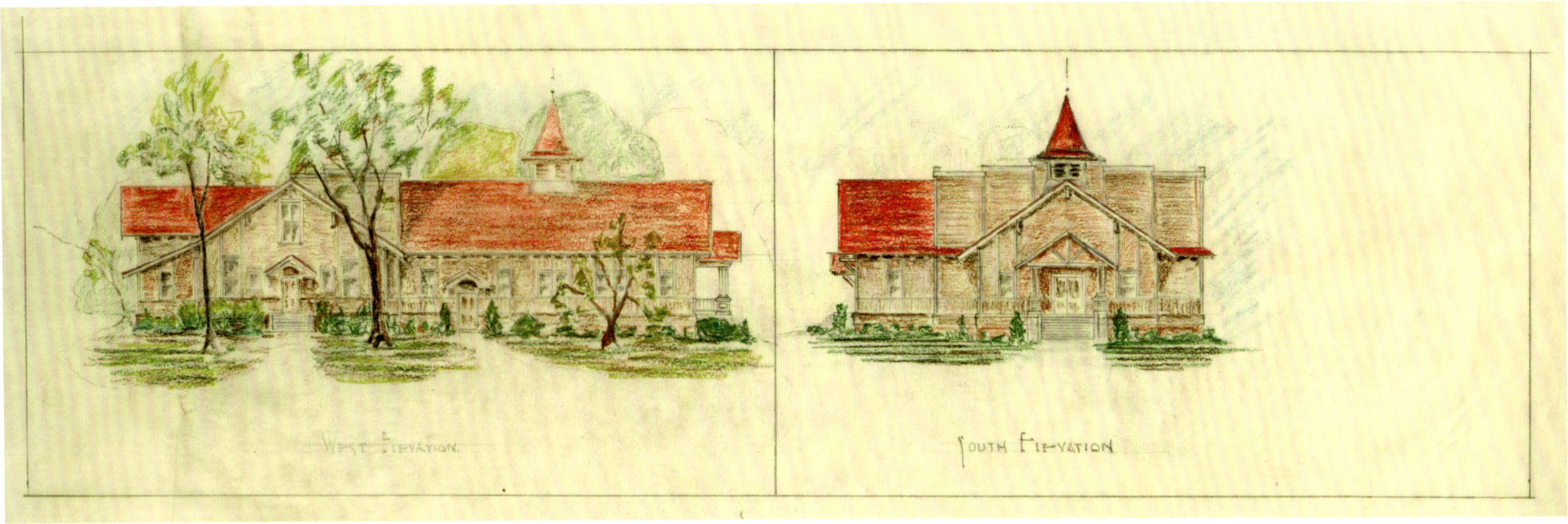

Mitchell Hall. Shortly before plans for the Little Theatre (today the IU Cinema) were added to the design proposals for the IU Auditorium, in 1938 Professors Lee Norvelle and H. H. Carter from the English Department advocated for the construction of an addition to Mitchell Hall to house a theater. Most campus theatrical performances were held in Alumni Hall in Indiana Memorial Union, with the sets and stage equipment being built in the old Assembly Hall. With Assembly Hall imminently on the docket for the wrecking ball, the English Department proposed using the salvaged materials to construct a small auditorium and storage space in Mitchell Hall. South and west elevations of a proposed addition to Mitchell Hall, 1938. P0024996, IU Archives.

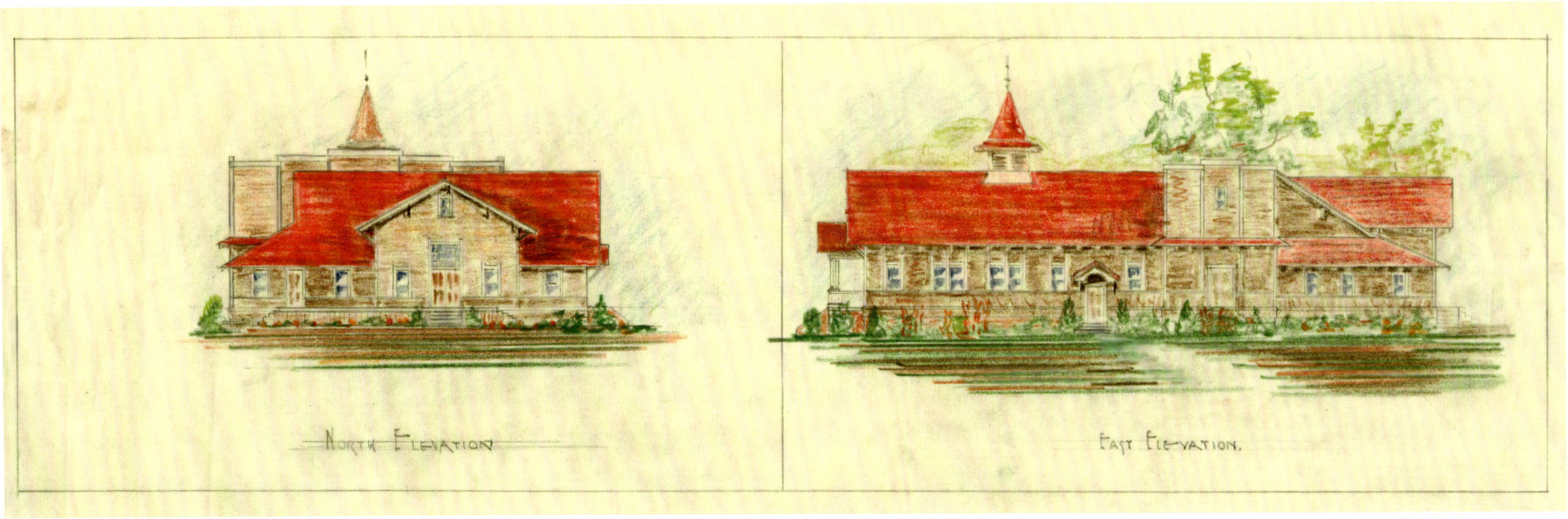

Mitchell Hall. In May 1938 Henry Pearson, superintendent of Buildings and Grounds, and Vergil Smith of the Speech Division, prepared and presented two design proposals, "one for extending the building to the east, and the other for extending it to the south" (Ward G. Biddle to President Herman B Wells, May 4, 1938, President Office Records, Little Theatre folder, collection C213, IU Archives). The latter addition to the south is shown here. When a space for the Little Theatre was added to the auditorium project (completed in 1941), the addition was scrapped. North and east elevations of a proposed addition to Mitchell Hall, 1938. P0024997, IU Archives.

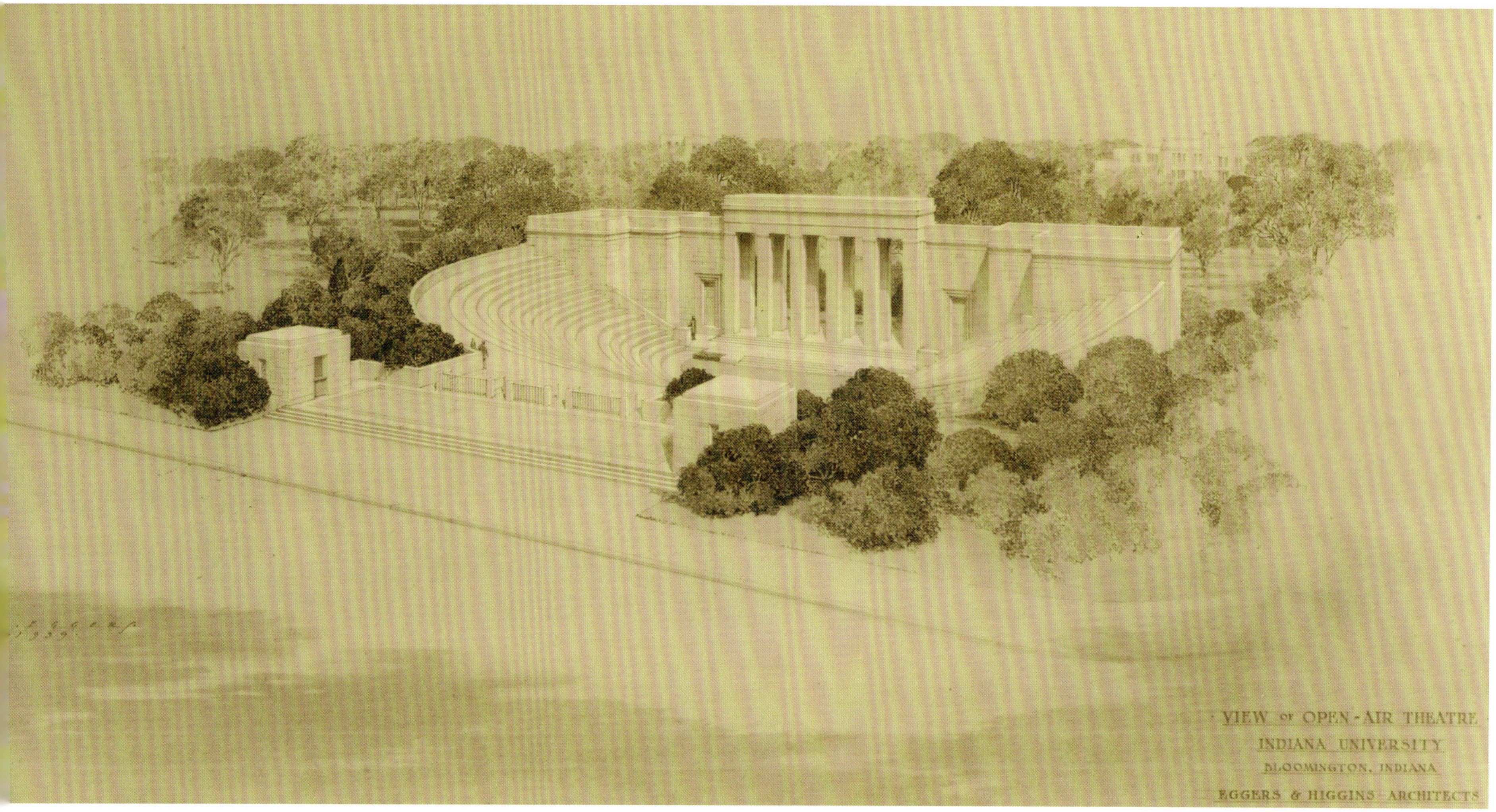

Proposed Open Air Theatre. In support of his goal to establish Indiana University as a cultural crossroads, president Herman B Wells asked Eggers and Higgins of New York to design a cultural arts plaza to be located in the center of campus. The firm responded with a proposed plan in 1939. The design called for an auditorium to serve as the focal point to the east, a fine arts building to the north, a sculptural fountain as the centerpiece, and on the sloping site to the south, an open-air Greek theater reminiscent of those on the Athenian Acropolis. Those plans remained in place until 1954, when the need to house J. K. Lilly Jr.'s rare books and manuscript donation to Indiana University necessitated another approach. According to Herman B Wells, "By the time we were ready to build the theater, the public had become so accustomed to air-conditioning that there was little desire for outdoor performances and assemblages. It seemed appropriate to use that site for the Lilly Library since it would contribute its share to the fine arts" (Herman B Wells, *Being Lucky: Reminiscences and Reflections*, 200). P0058454, IU Archives. Image credit: Eggers and Higgins, architects.

Sample Gates. In 1931, IU alumnus and U.S. senator Newell Sanders proposed a gateway to the university campus from Kirkwood Avenue in honor of the class of 1873. Responding to concerns from architects Robert Frost Daggett and Granger and Bollenbacher (who submitted alternate designs for consideration more in keeping with the surrounding architectural style of campus), the Board of Trustees and President William Lowe Bryan favored a design more in harmony with the surrounding Gothic-style buildings, Sanders continued to present the board with other slightly revised versions of his original proposal, including one designed in collaboration with the Indiana Limestone Company. Ultimately, because a consensus could not be reached on a design for the gateway, Sanders withdrew his proposals. Proposed memorial gateway in honor of 1873 class, 1931. P0058487, IU Archives. Image credit: Newell Sanders, architect.

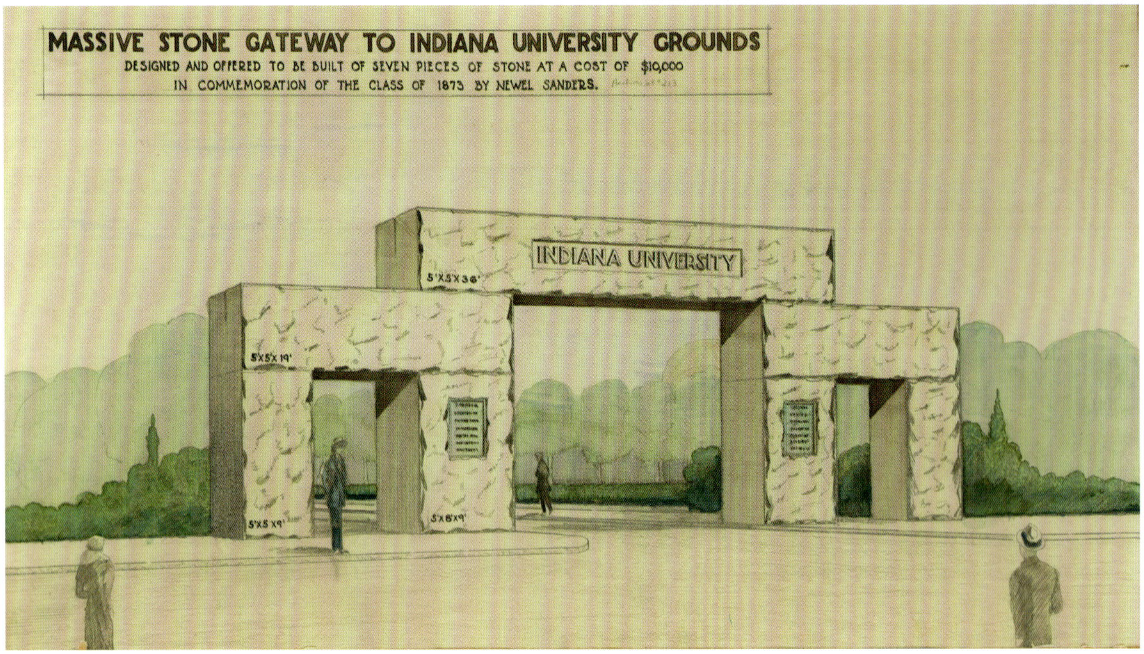

Sample Gates. In 1935 the prospect of building a gateway for the Kirkwood entrance to campus resurfaced when Theodore Skinner from the Indiana Works Progress Administration suggested to President Bryan that federal funds might be available for the completion of the project. It seems the proposal was short-lived, as correspondence only exists from early in the fall of 1935. The sketch shown here is probably the plan from the "stone man" that President Bryan refers to in his September 7, 1935, letter to Alfred Granger. Note the likeness of President Bryan's face in one of the stone carvings. Proposed WPA Project for Indiana University. P0050027, IU Archives.

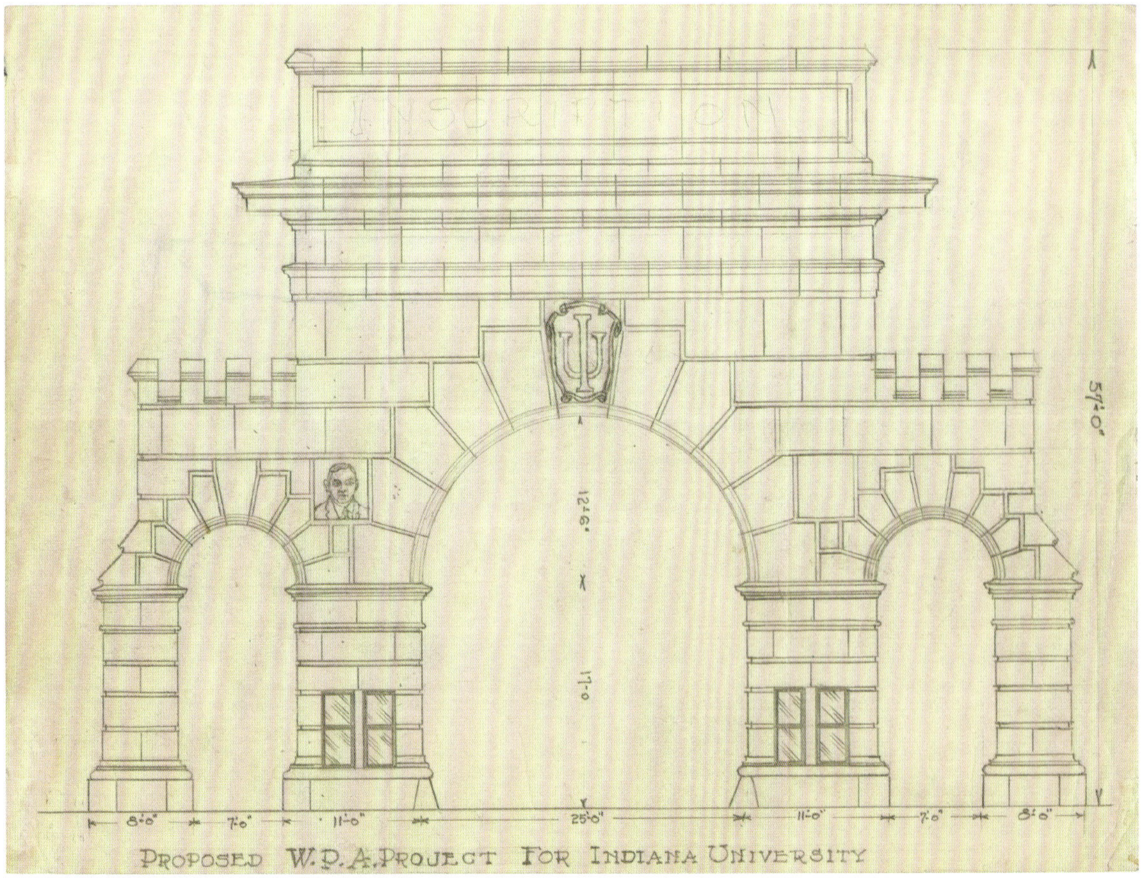

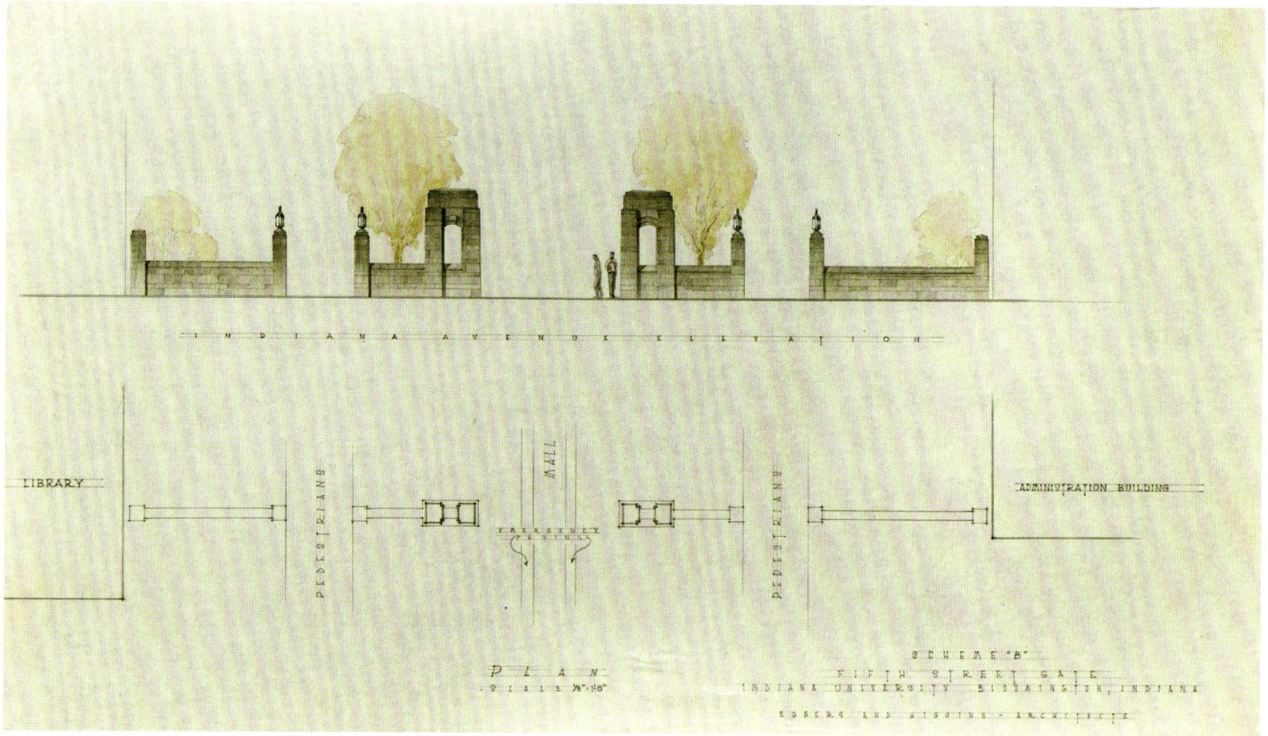

Sample Gates. By the 1960s, plans were again underway by consulting architects Eggers and Higgins for the construction of a Fifth Street gateway that included closing the road running through campus and replacing it with a grassy mall. An additional option called for a pull-off from Fifth Street "for staff being delivered or picked up at the Administration Building and the Library [Bryan and Franklin Halls] by car and taxi since now this creates a traffic problem on Indiana Avenue" (Joseph A. Franklin to Ted. J. Young, May 24, 1961, President's Office records, collection C213, IU Archives). Proposed designs included the one shown here as well as another with stronger Gothic stylistic influences quite similar to the design we have today. Proposed Fifth Street Gate, ca 1960. P0024991, IU Archives. Image credit: Eggers and Higgins, architects.

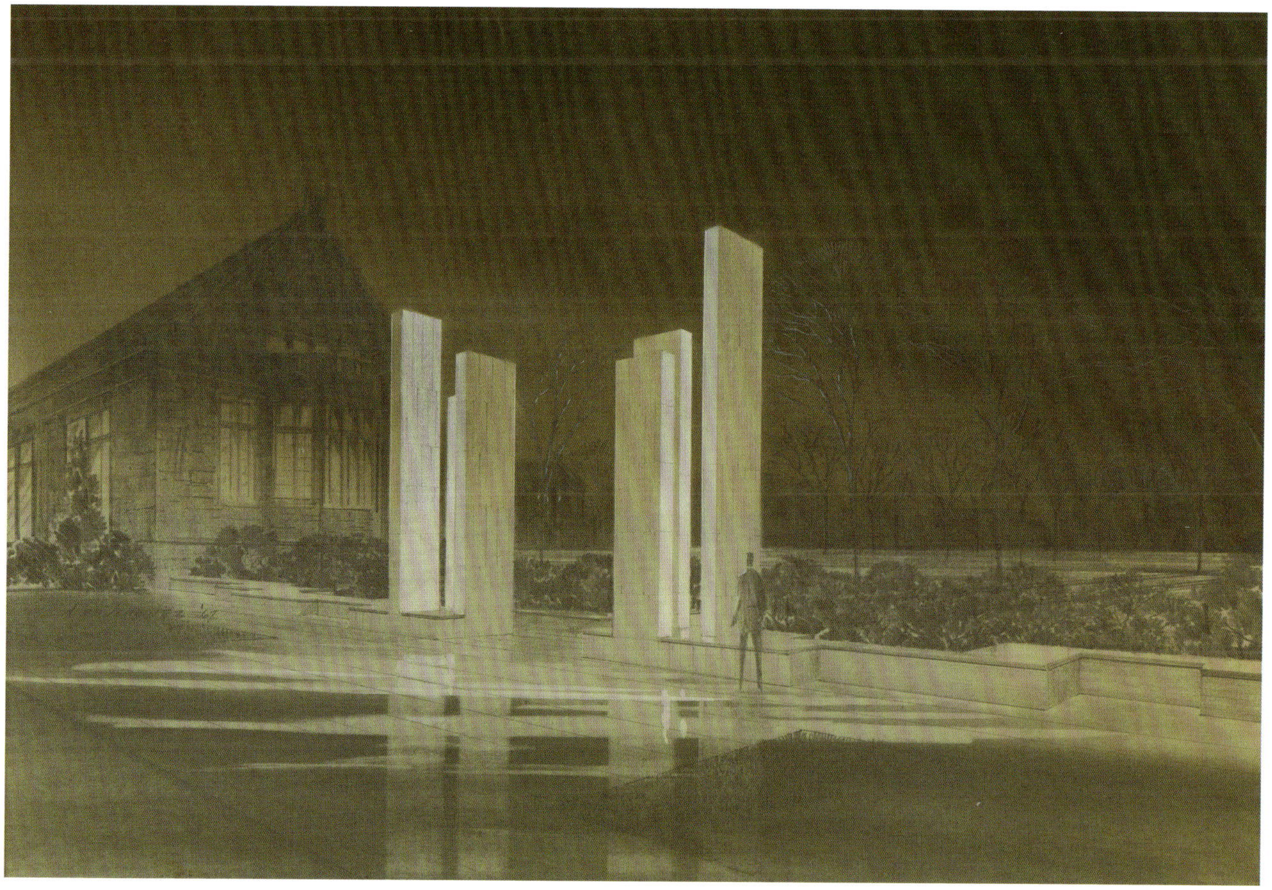

Sample Gates. With plans underway for the celebration of Indiana University's sesquicentennial in 1966, IU alumnus Benjamin H. Long conveyed his interest in erecting a gateway in memory of his parents, Benjamin F. and Lucy Nichols Long, both IU graduates. Eggers and Higgins had previously presented a Gothic design for the gates several years earlier, but stated in a 1967 report that "it is felt that a new approach to the design should be made." The resulting design (shown here) presented a more modern approach. The drastic change in design drew criticism from Benjamin Long and the trustees as well as Chancellor Wells. Concept drawing, 1967. P0031775, IU Archives. Image credit: Eggers and Higgins, architects; A. R. Jimenez, artist.

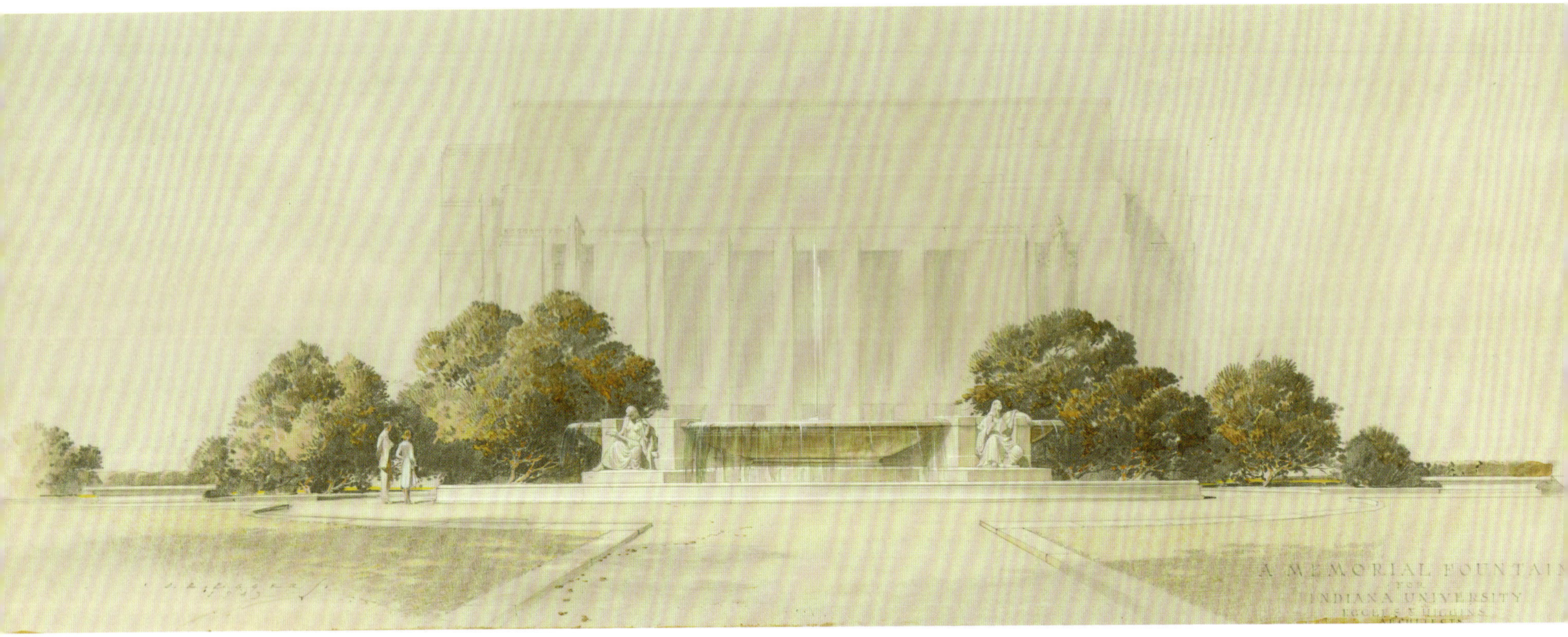

Showalter Fountain (*above*). Following the completion of the Indiana University Auditorium in 1941, President Herman B Wells and Ward Biddle, director of the Indiana Memorial Union, began advocating for the construction of a monumental fountain for the Fine Arts Plaza. The first detailed proposal from Eggers and Higgins for a memorial fountain shown here dates from 1943. Featuring native Indiana limestone and four seated figures representing music, sculpture, painting, and drama, corresponding to each of the proposed adjacent buildings, the concept was much more Neoclassical in style than the Modernist Showalter fountain we have today. P0058444, IU Archives. Image credit: Eggers and Higgins, architects.

Showalter Fountain (*facing*). While Eggers and Higgins continued to serve as supervising architects for the project and outlined most of the overall design for the fountain itself, in 1952 Robert Laurent (professor of Fine Arts 1942–60) was selected to design a sculpture to serve as the centerpiece of the fountain basin. The proposal shown here includes a vertically oriented Venus kneeling in a square cross-shaped basin. P0024999, IU Archives. Photo credit: Eggers and Higgins, architects; and Robert Laurent, artist.

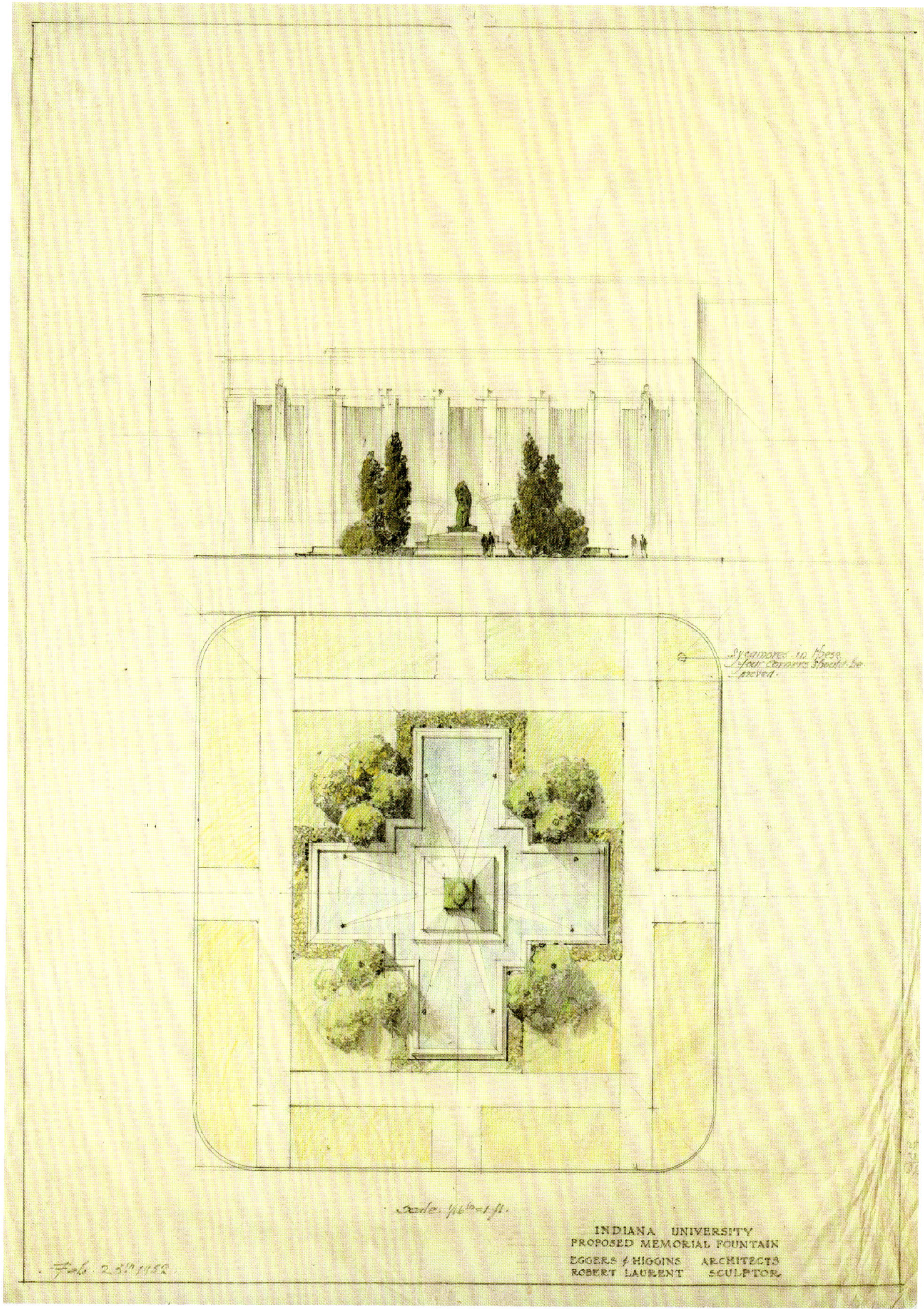
Sycamores in these four corners should be paved.
Scale 1/16th = 1 ft.
INDIANA UNIVERSITY
PROPOSED MEMORIAL FOUNTAIN
EGGERS & HIGGINS ARCHITECTS
ROBERT LAURENT SCULPTOR
Feb. 25th 1952

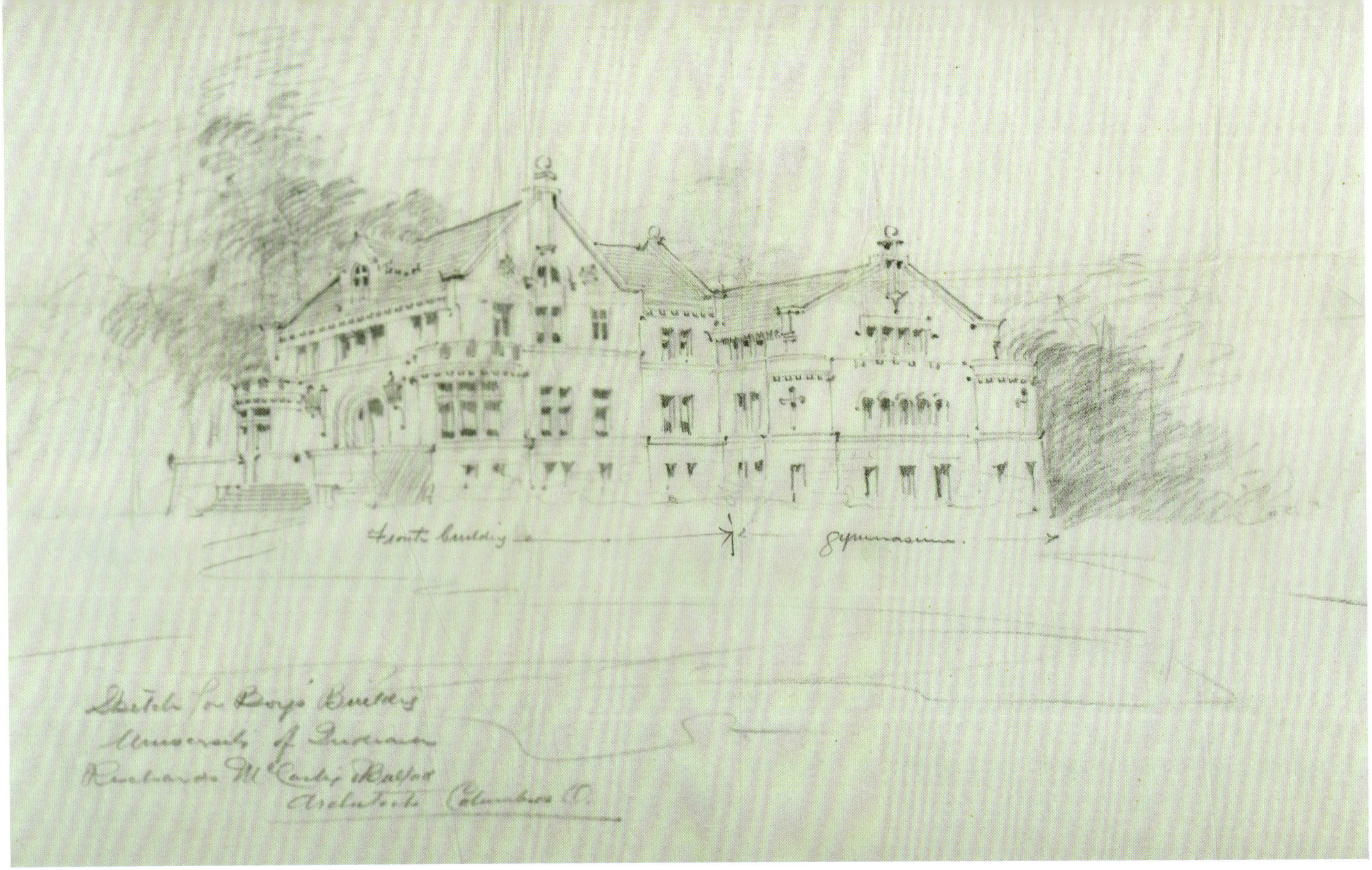
front building
gymnasium
Sketch for Boys' Building
University of Indiana
Richards McCarty & Bulford
Architects Columbus O.

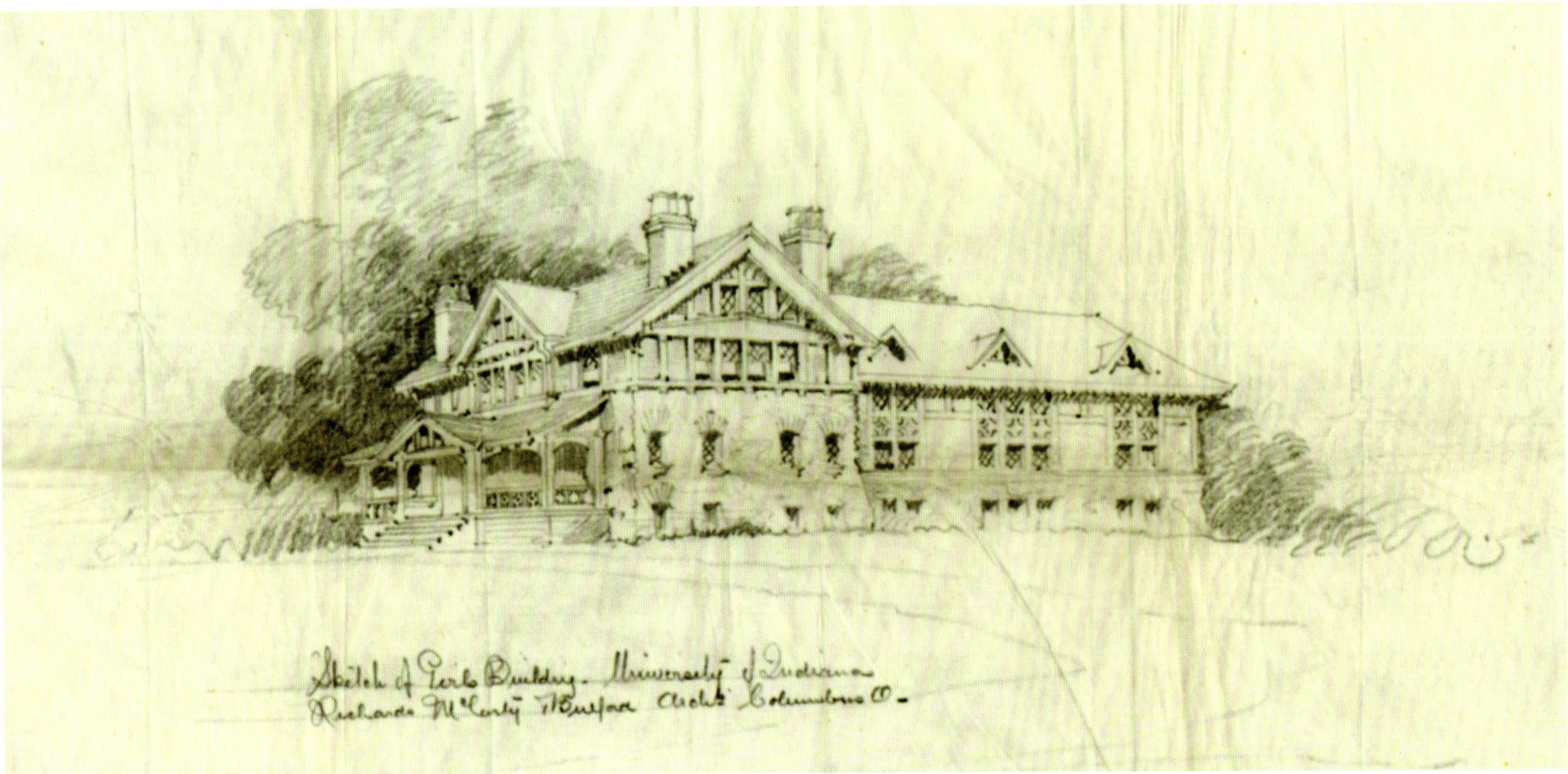
Sketch of Girls Building - University of Indiana
Richards McCarty & Bulford Archts Columbus O -

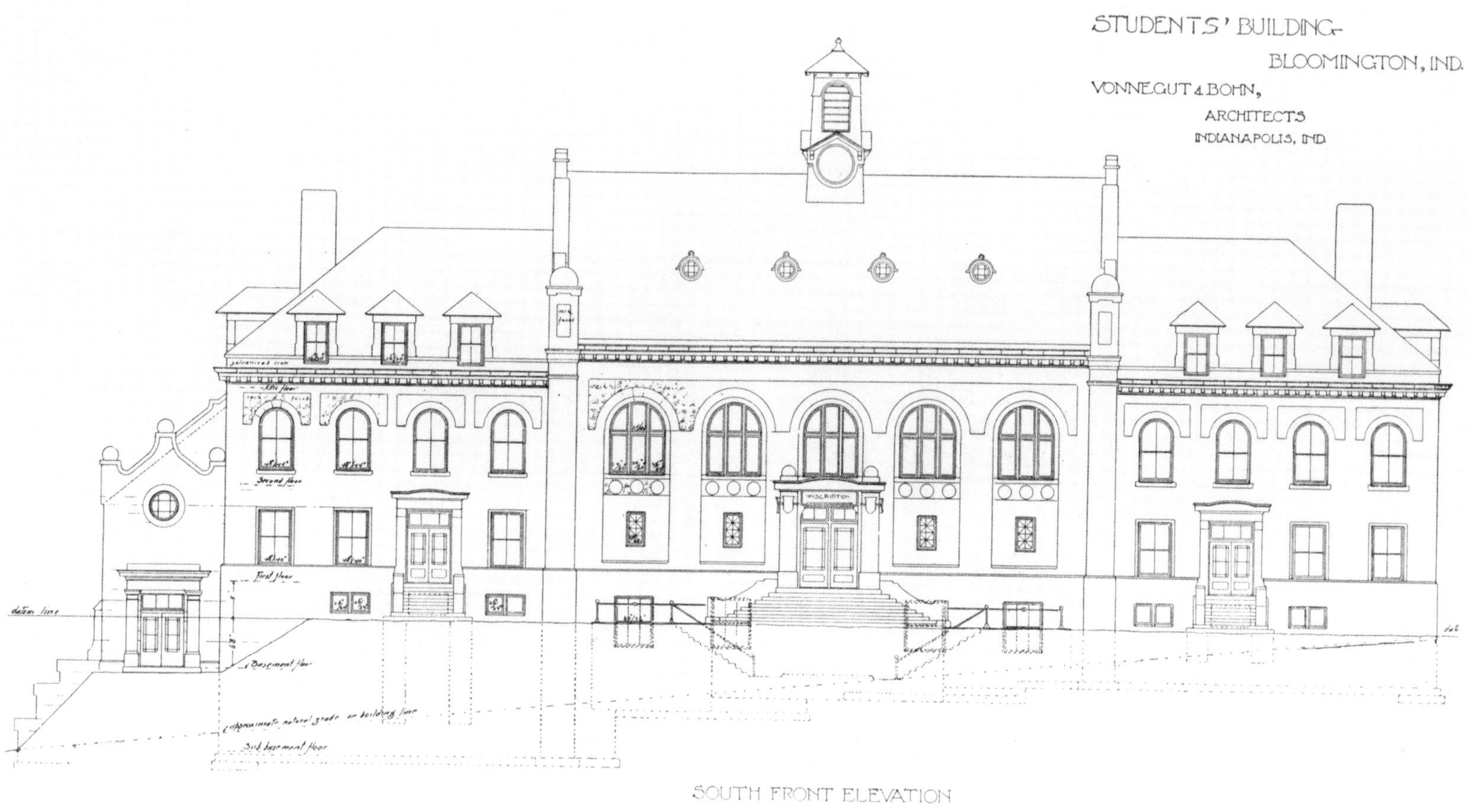

Student Building (*facing top*). In late 1902 President William Lowe Bryan invited several leading architects to submit preliminary sketches for two student buildings, one for women and one for men. While most architects declined, noting a lack of compensation, C. E. Richards of Columbus, Ohio, presented two designs. For the women's building, Richards suggested "something after the English country gothic type, constructed of a combination of rough stone, half-timber work and cement" on the exterior, with space inside for parlors, study rooms, a large banquet room and assembly hall, a gymnasium with running track, locker rooms, and a swimming pool (C. E. Richards [Richards, McCarty, and Bulford Architects], to President William Lowe Bryan, November 5, 1902, President's Office records, collection C270, IU Archives). P0058751, IU Archives. Photo credit: C. E. Richards, architect.

Student Building (*facing bottom*). C. E. Richards envisioned the men's building as having a bowling alley but otherwise with most of the same features as the women's building, "except on a more extensive scale" (C. E. Richards [Richards, McCarty, and Bulford Architects], to President William Lowe Bryan, November 5, 1902, President's Office records, collection C270, IU Archives). P0058750, IU Archives. Photo credit: C. E. Richards, architect.

Student Building (*above*). At the urging of John D. Rockefeller in 1902, the two proposed buildings were redesigned by Indianapolis architects Vonnegut and Bohn as one building to serve both men and women. Quite similar to the end product, this version lacks the iconic clock tower that was added to the design in 1905 after construction was already underway. P0030009, IU Archives. Photo credit: Vonnegut and Bohn, architects.

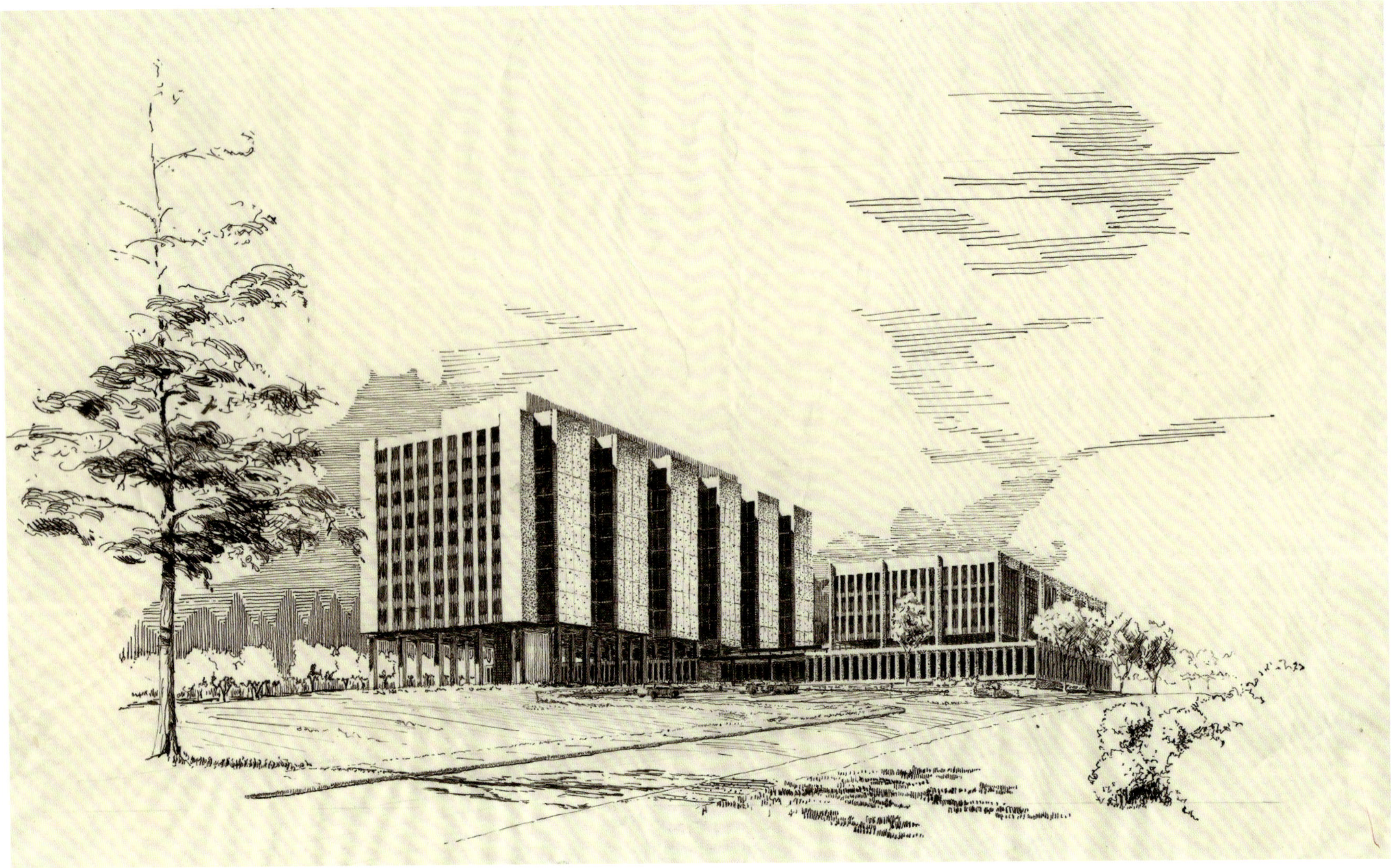

Herman B Wells Library. Design proposals for Herman B Wells Library evolved in the years prior to its construction. This July 1962 rendering from New York–based Eggers and Higgins architectural firm consists of two towers supported by small pillars or columns with a smooth facade containing windows in a grid-like pattern to the east and west, while in rows to the north and south. Other plans took into consideration future expansion with proposals for a tower that would span Jordan Avenue to the east, allowing traffic to flow underneath. P0053497, IU Archives. Photo credit: Eggers and Higgins, architects.

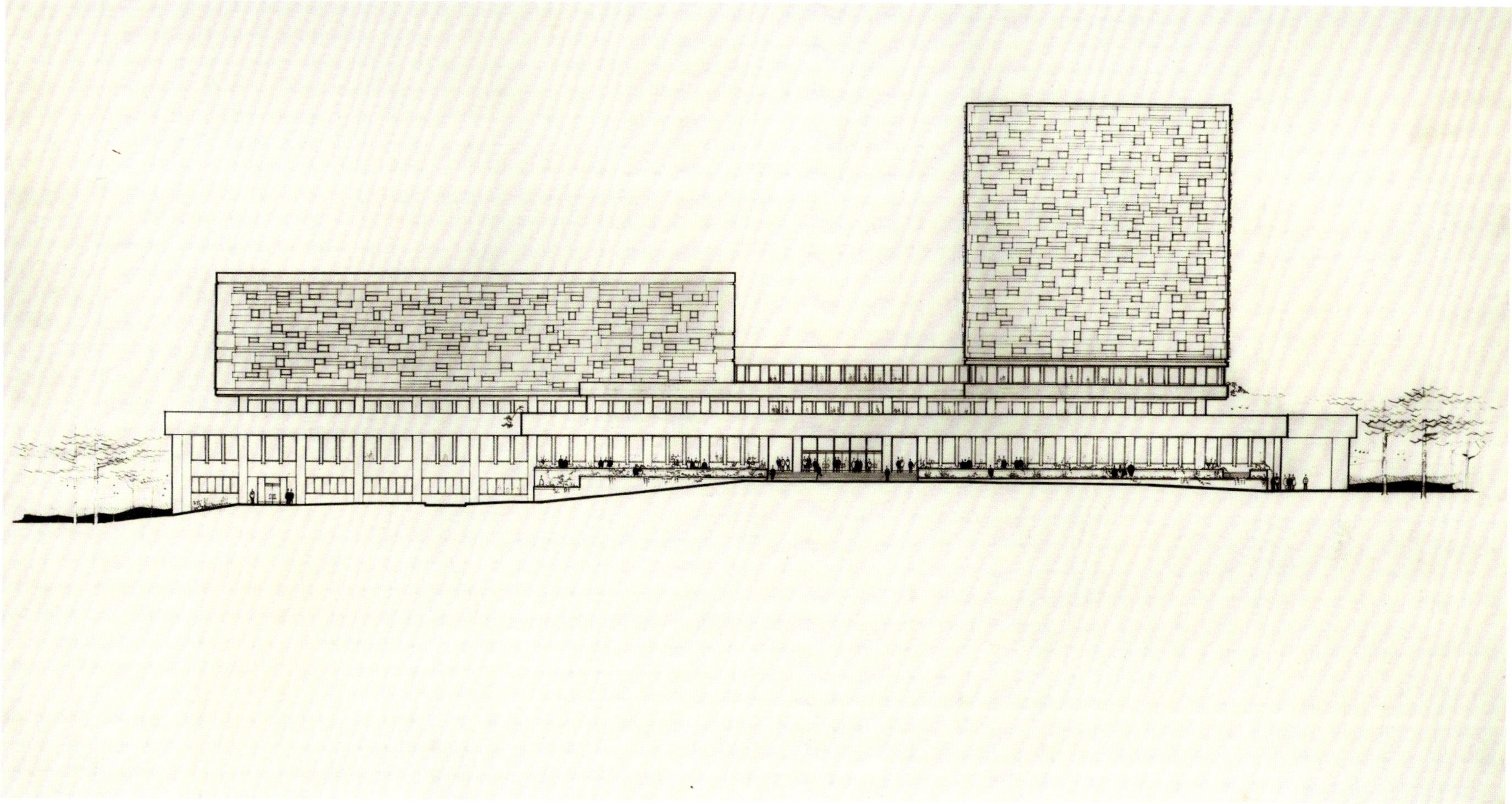

Herman B Wells Library. This design created in 1964 features an irregular limestone block cladding similar to the current facade, but with three-foot-square windows (the darker squares on this drawing) placed at random heights on each floor. In July 1964, under pressure to move forward with finalizing plans for the new library, the Board of Trustees reported that "complete ventilation and interior lighting makes the use of windows a matter of decorative rather than utilitarian consideration" (Indiana University Board of Trustees minutes, July 1, 1964, http://purl.dlib.indiana.edu/iudl/archives/iubot/1964-07-01). The board unanimously voted to eliminate windows, and the later Eggers and Higgins's design known informally as the "Towers of Silence," was approved. P0053498, IU Archives. Photo credit: Eggers and Higgins, architects.

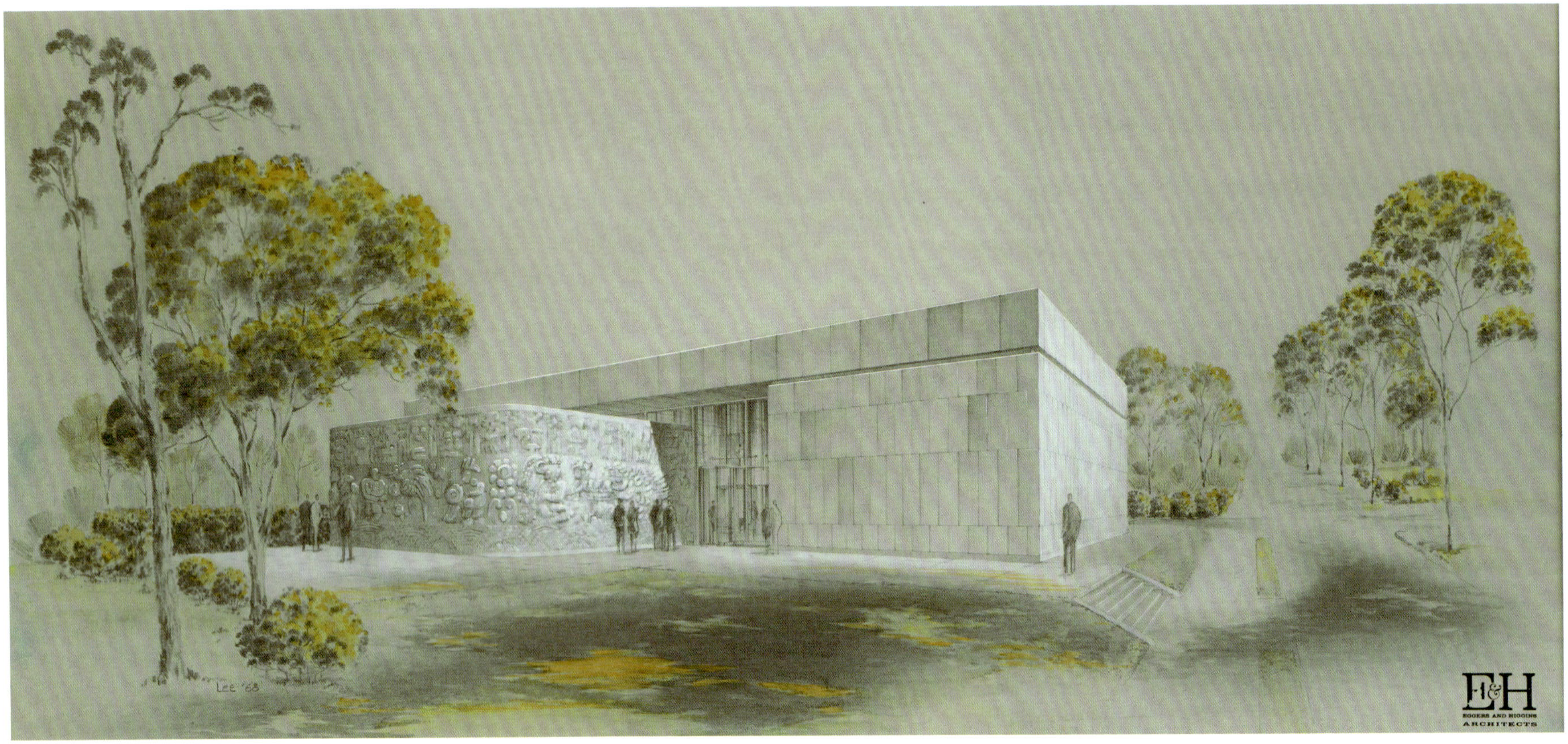

Glenn A. Black Laboratory. Two preliminary renderings for the Glenn A. Black Laboratory were initially considered, one from Eggers and Higgins of New York (shown here), and the second by James Associates of Indianapolis. Emphasizing the importance of the museum wing of the building, the Eggers and Higgins plan contrasted the more interesting rounded corners and bas-relief sculpture covering the facade of the museum portion of the structure with an unadorned smooth limestone, rectangular structure for the remainder of the building. However the donor, Eli Lilly, "was not satisfied with the design, that it was too cubistic and modern, and that something more simple and classic with a visible roof was desired" (Eggers and Higgins—Report of meeting at the IU Physical Plant, November 1, 1968, Chancellor's Office records, Glenn Black Archaeological Museum folder, collection C145, IU Archives). A second design from James Associates that included a precast stone exterior was perceived to be a more flexible in terms of connecting to the proposed Hoosier Heritage Hall (today the Mathers Museum). P0058484, IU Archives. Photo credit: Eggers and Higgins, architects.

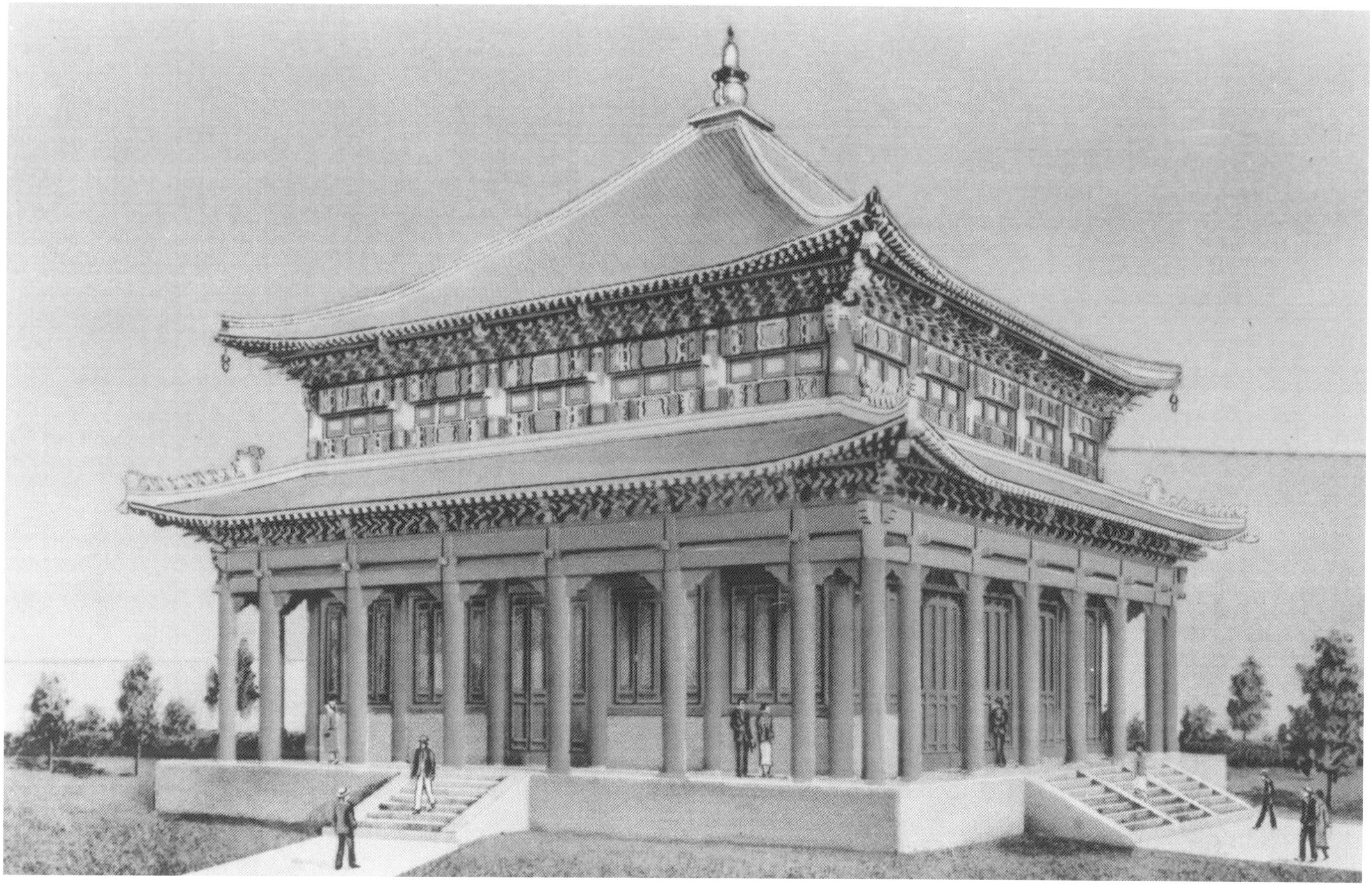

Lama Temple of Jehol. Commissioned by Swedish American industrialist Vincent Benddix, the Lama Temple of Jehol was constructed in 1932 under the direction of Sven Hedin by Chinese architect W. H. Liang in China for the Century of Progress Exhibition in Chicago. It was a replica of a 1771 Jehol temple in Inner Mongolia, China. After the exhibition closed, the temple was dismantled by a WPA crew in 1938 and transferred by the Archaeological Trust of Chicago to Oberlin College in Ohio, where it remained in storage in a warehouse. In 1969, Indiana University acquired the deed with the intention of restoring the structure and reerecting it on the Bloomington campus, either as additional space for fine arts or as an Asian Studies Research Center on the east side of Jordan Avenue. The project, however, was plagued both by a lack of funds and by a change in university presidents, and never materialized. Sometime in the 1980s, the temple was transferred to Sweden for possible reconstruction near Stockholm. P0025802, IU Archives.

INDIANA UNIVERSITY BLOOMINGTON
CAMPUS MAPS

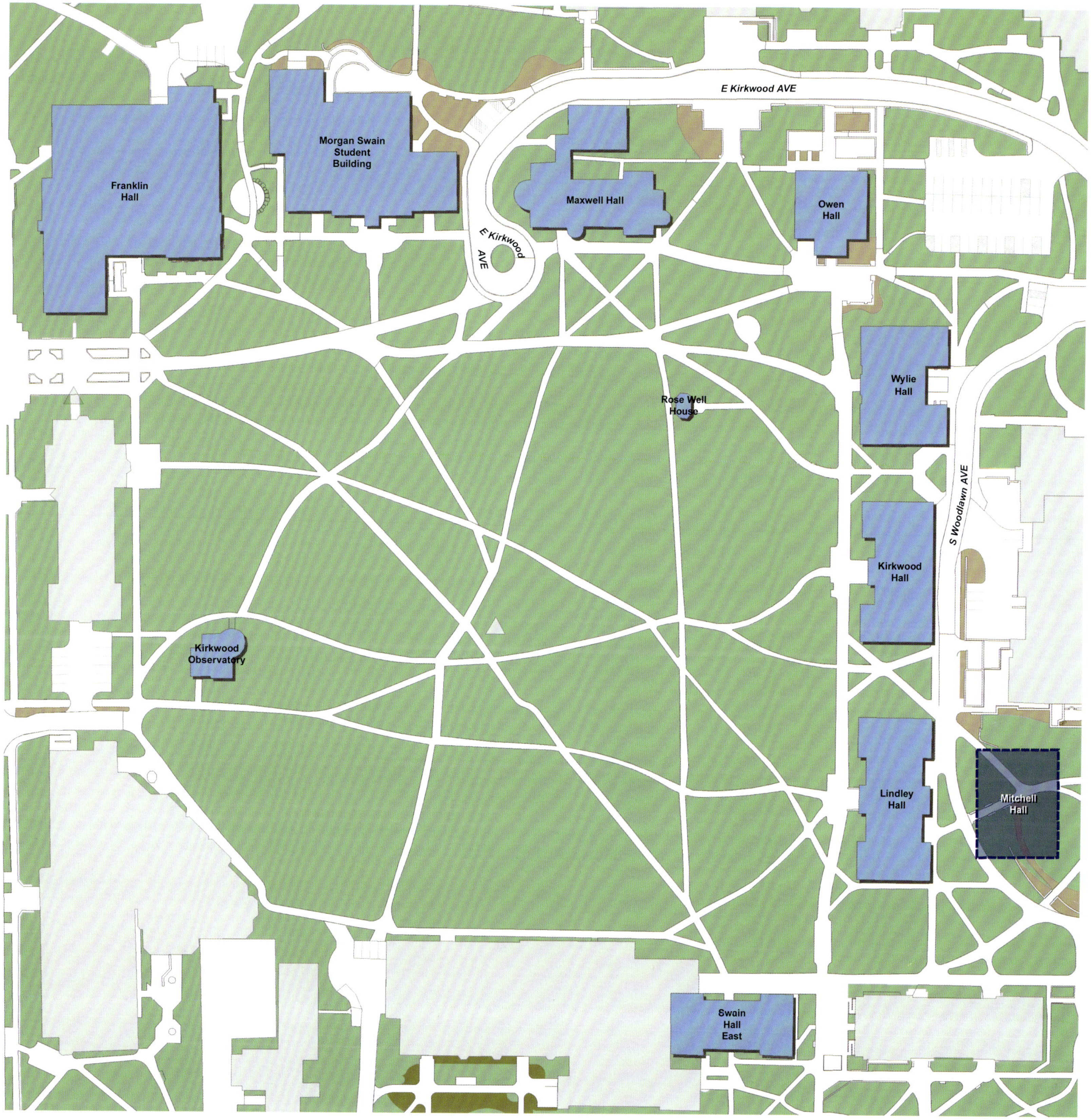

The Old Crescent. Map credit: Indiana University, 2017.

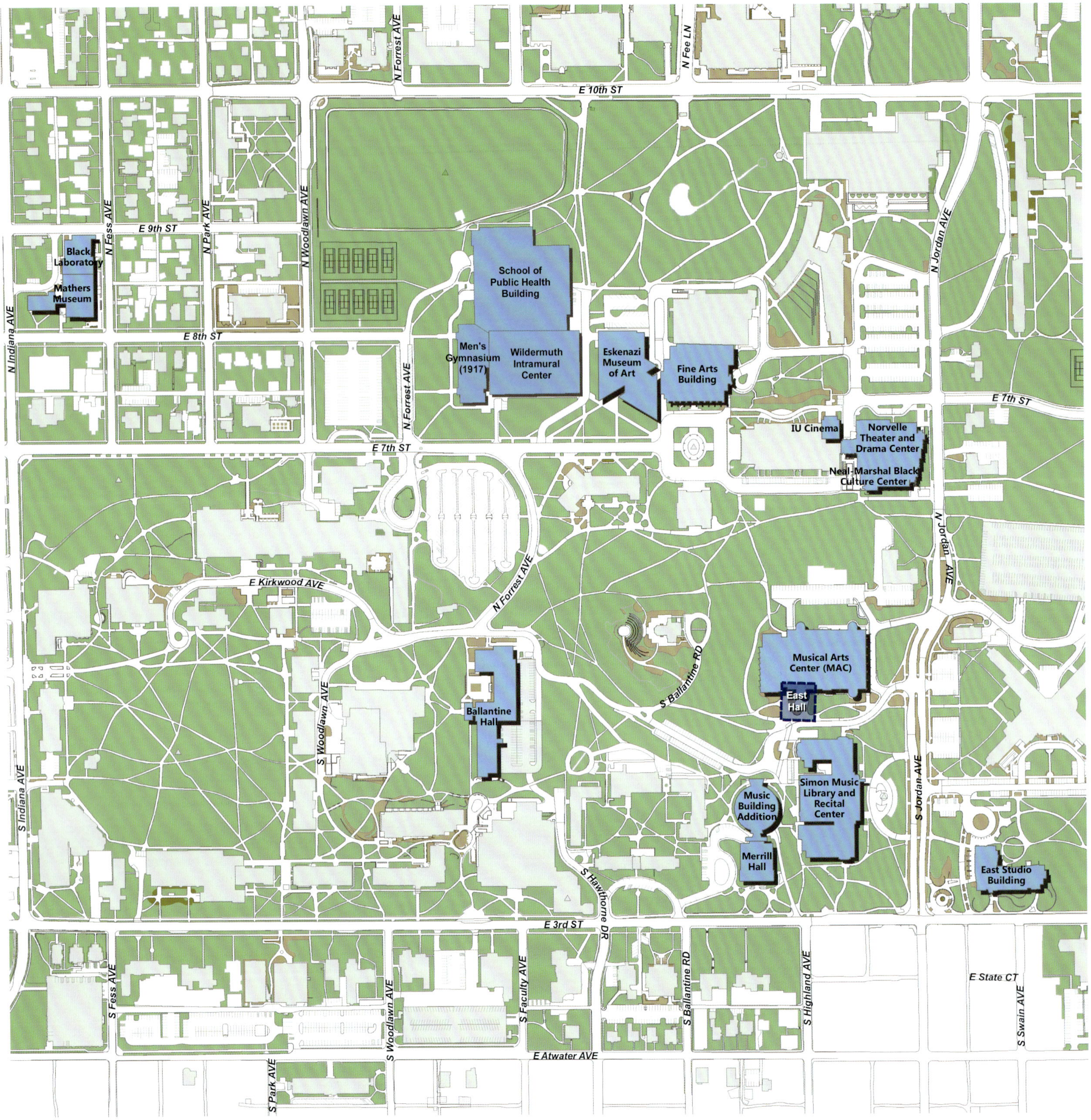

The Arts and Humanities. Map credit: Indiana University, 2017.

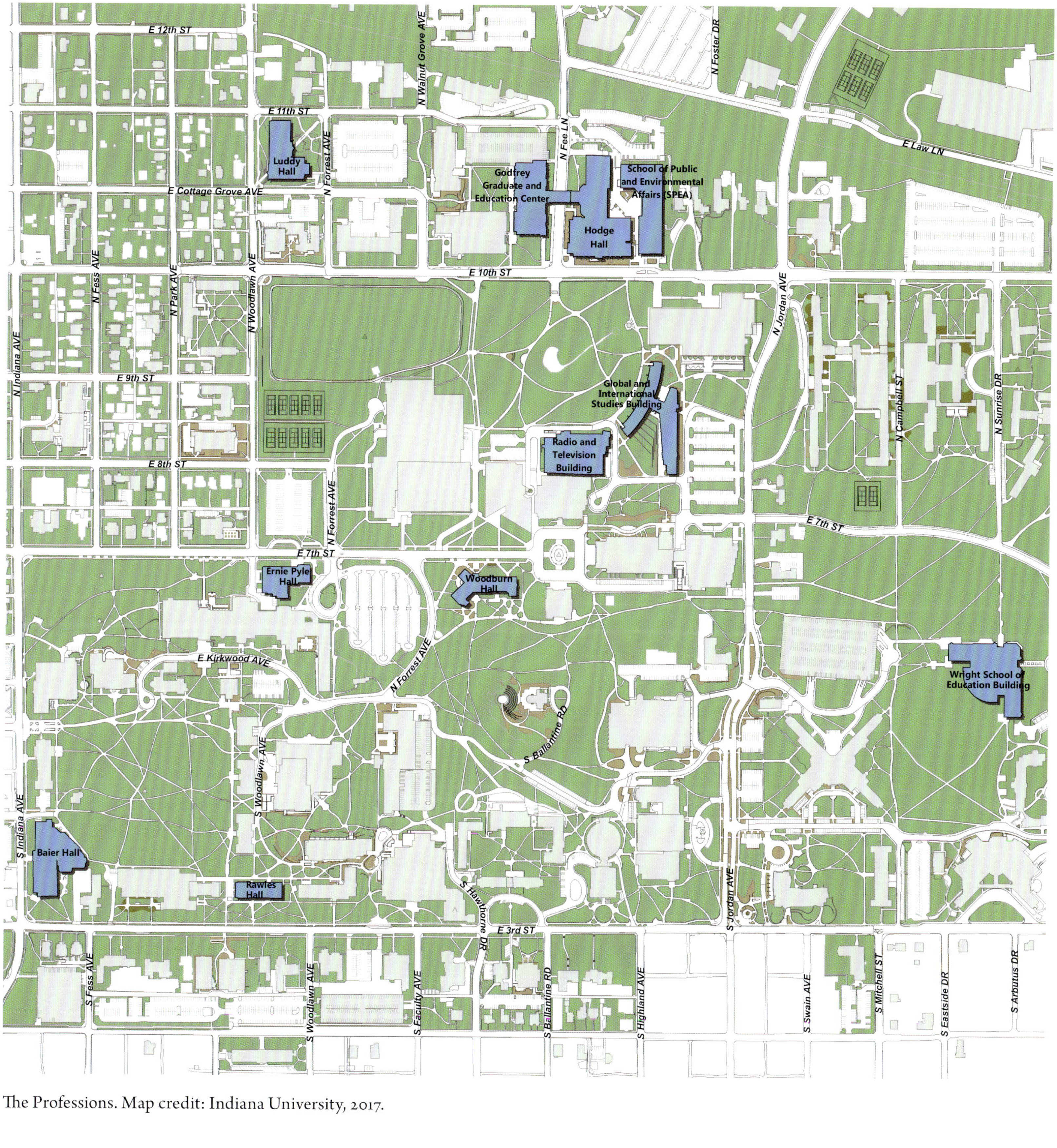

The Professions. Map credit: Indiana University, 2017.

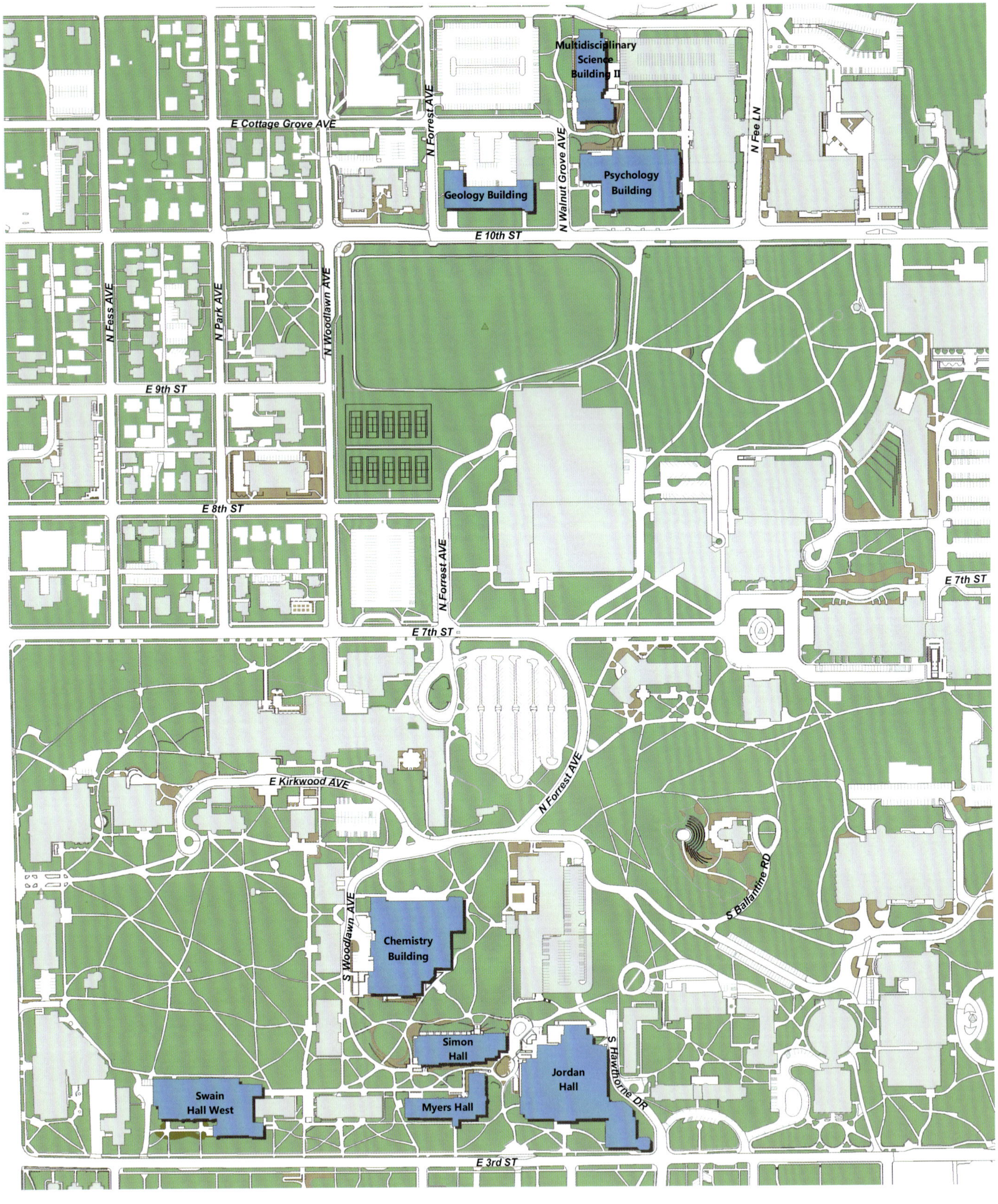

The Sciences. Map credit: Indiana University, 2017.

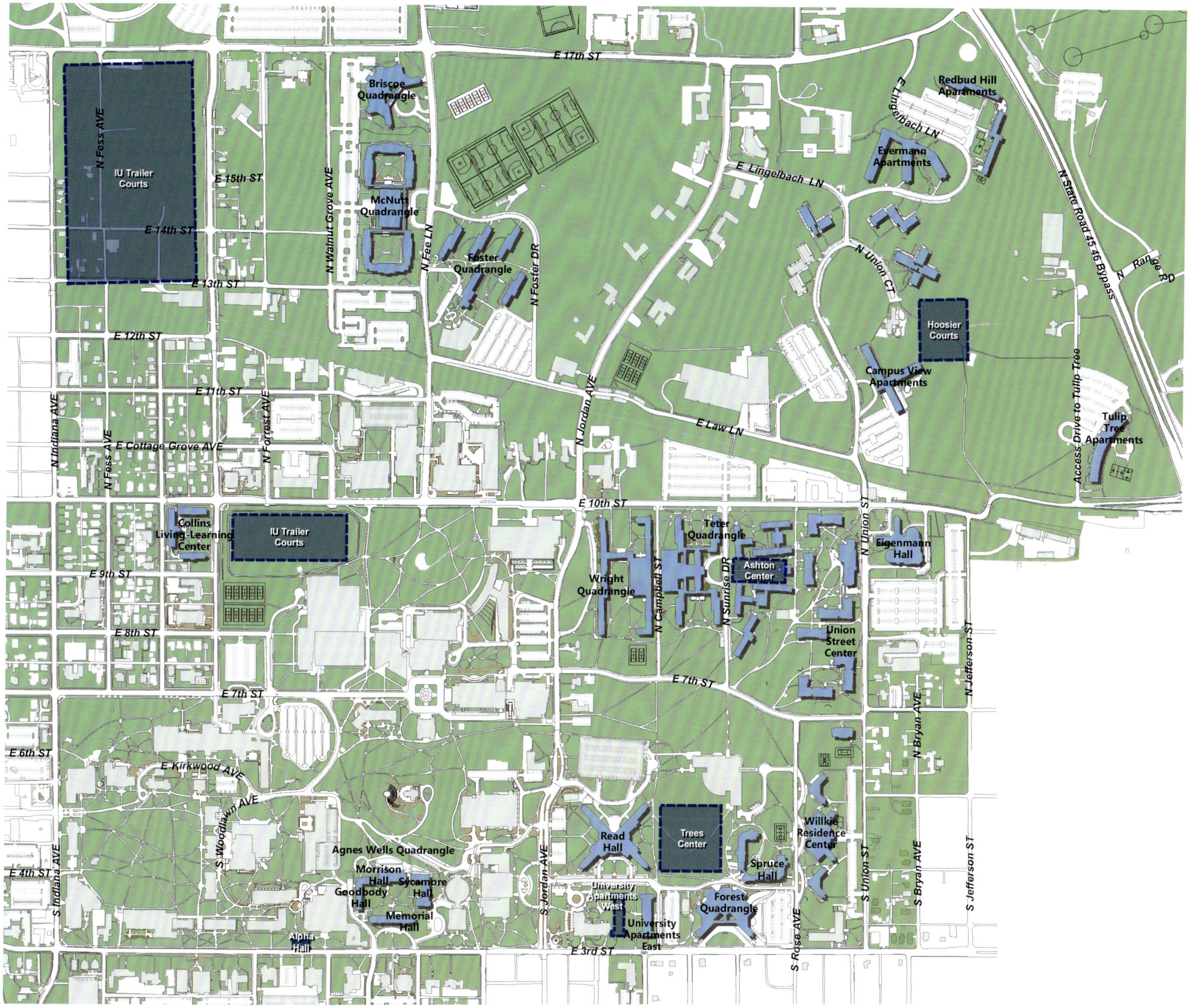

Student Housing. Map credit: Indiana University, 2017.

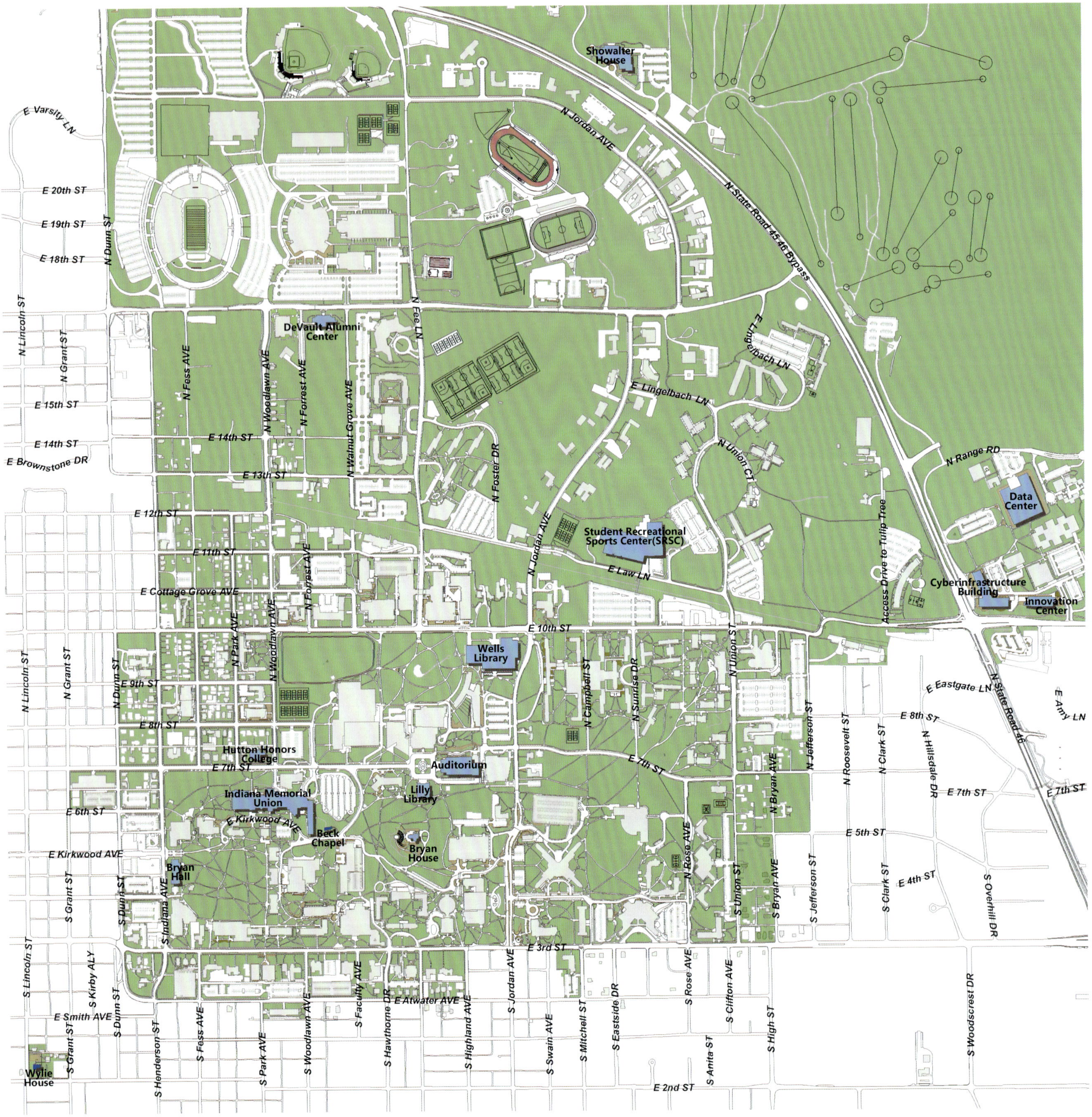

Common Facilities. Map credit: Indiana University, 2017.

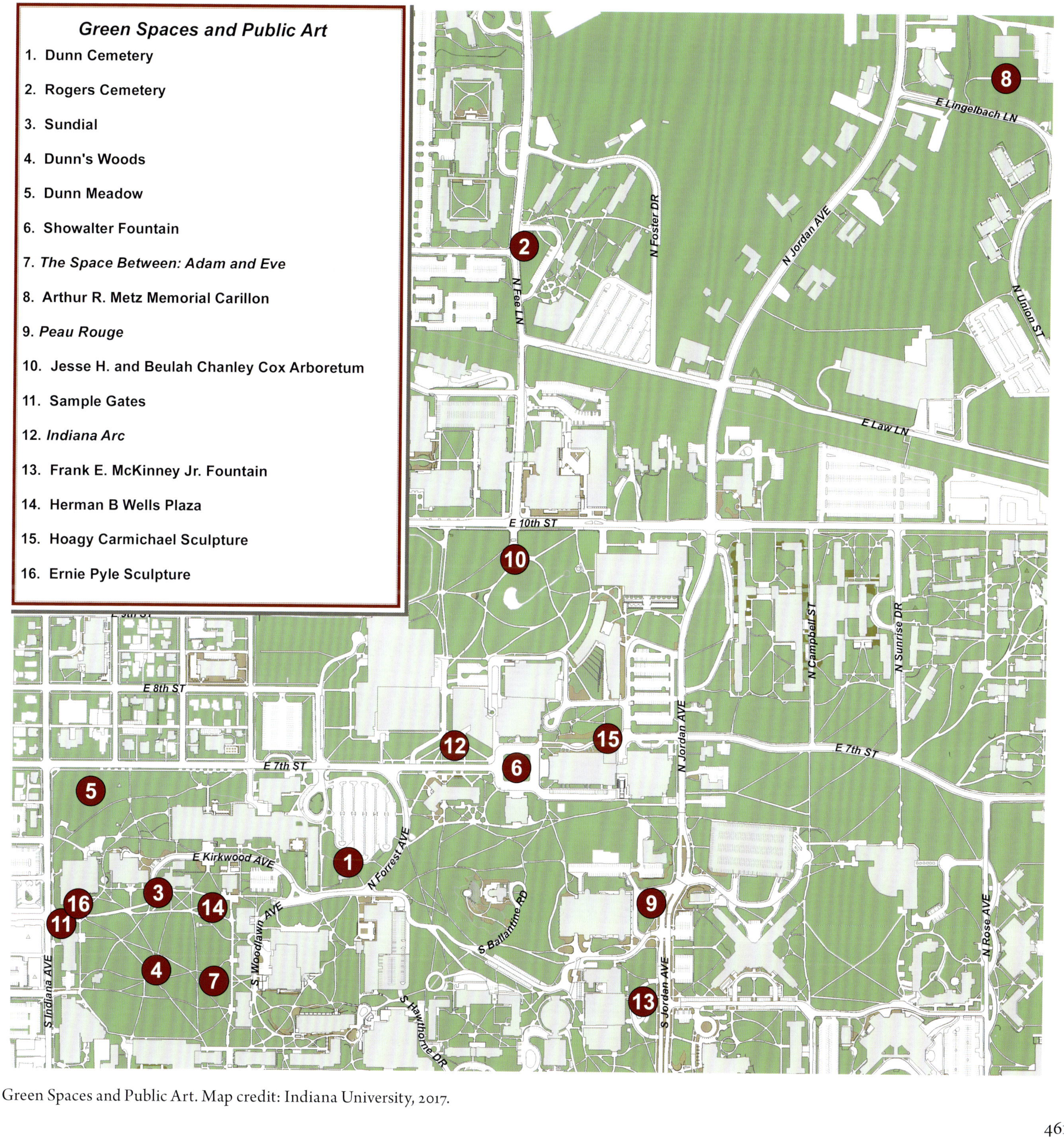

Green Spaces and Public Art. Map credit: Indiana University, 2017.

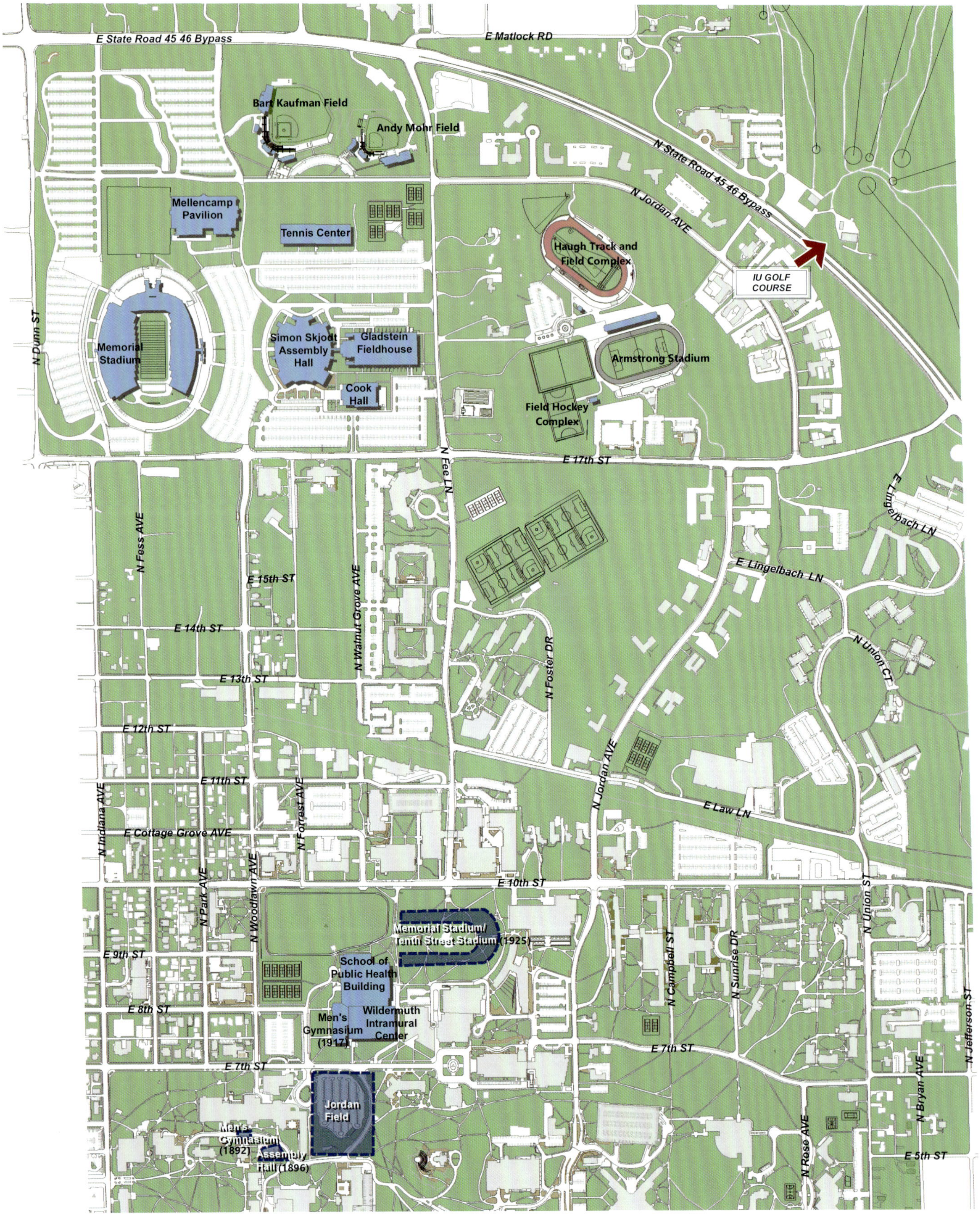

Cream and Crimson. Map credit: Indiana University, 2017.

MASTER PLANNERS AT INDIANA UNIVERSITY BLOOMINGTON

George Edward Kessler (1862–1923)

One of the most renowned city planners and landscape architects of his time, George E. Kessler successfully completed more than two hundred commissions worldwide during his forty-one-year career. His work can be found in a hundred cities around the world, including New York City, Mexico City, and Shanghai. Kessler based his approach on the concept that all planning should be comprehensive and every improvement or incremental step should contribute to the ultimate goal. In 1915 President William Lowe Bryan authorized George Kessler to undertake Indiana University's first wide-ranging master plan. Kessler's plan was used to guide university development over the next fifteen years and galvanized the bond between the university's bold architectural style found in the Old Crescent buildings and Bloomington's beautiful naturalistic environment.

Following his work at IU, Kessler was hired by the city of Indianapolis to plan an east–west boulevard on the north side of the city. He died before his work was completed, but the roadway was named Kessler Boulevard in his memory. George Kessler was an original member of the U.S. Commission on Fine Arts.

Olmsted Brothers
John Charles Olmsted (1852–1920)
Frederick Law Olmsted Jr. (1870–1957)

At the death of Frederick Law Olmsted in 1903, his two sons, John Charles Olmsted and Frederick Law Olmsted Jr., inherited their father's landscape architecture design firm. The senior Olmsted, known as the father of U.S. landscape architecture, had developed a national reputation as a result of his large-scale landscape design work that included Central Park in New York City and Golden Gate Park in San Francisco. His two sons not only continued to successfully operate the firm but pushed the firm's accomplishments to a new level of excellence with award-winning designs that helped create the Great Smoky Mountains National Park, Acadia National Park, Yosemite Valley, and a host of other equally prestigious commissions. The Olmsted Brothers firm also served as campus planners for thirty-three major universities around the country in addition to Indiana University Bloomington.

The work of the Olmsted Brothers at IU built on the master plan of George Kessler but extended Kessler's traditional design principles to new acreage that had been acquired to support university growth. The Olmsted master plan, completed in 1929, identified locations for future buildings and green spaces and routing for walkways and drives. Siting for residential housing, including Agnes E. Wells Quadrangle, as well as the establishment of Third Street as the campus southern boundary are the result of concepts developed by the Olmsted Brothers.

Eggers and Higgins
Otto Reinhold Eggers (1882–1964)
Daniel Paul Higgins (1886–1953)

Otto Eggers and Daniel Higgins were longtime associates of renowned U.S. architect John Russell Pope and acted as Pope's most trusted partners until his death in 1937. The pair then assumed operation of the Pope business and changed the name to Eggers and Higgins while continuing to manage Pope's unfinished projects, including the construction phase of the Jefferson Memorial in Washington, DC. The Eggers and Higgins firm soon established its own reputation for strong design and gained prestigious commissions, such as the Brooklyn War Memorial, Vanderbilt Hall at New York University School of Law, the Herbert Hoover Presidential Library-Museum, and Dirksen Senate Office Building.

In 1939, Indiana University President Herman B Wells contracted with Eggers and Higgins to design the auditorium, the first new structure of the Wells administration. The project was so well received that the Eggers and Higgins architectural firm was retained to provide master planning and building design services on campus for the next thirty years. IU was expanding to the north and Eggers and Higgins provided the university with a plan for the athletic precinct north of Seventeenth Street, including building sites for a new football stadium, field house, and basketball arena. When the firm of Eggers and Higgins was named architect of record for new building projects, the customary arrangement authorized Eggers and Higgins to complete the schematic design phase and then transfer planning to an Indiana-based architect who would finish design development, prepare construction documents, and provide construction administration.

Edward Larrabee Barnes (1915–2004)

Over the nearly sixty years that Edward Larrabee Barnes practiced architecture, he earned a reputation for understated architectural style and design. Barnes insisted that his buildings contribute to their surroundings rather than make an independent statement. He preferred improving the neighborhood to building a memorial to himself or his client. Barnes's best-known works include IBM Corporate Headquarters and the Walker Art Center in New York City, the Dallas Museum of Art, the Christian Theological Seminary in Indianapolis, and the Thurgood Marshall Federal Judiciary Building in Washington, DC. Barnes was retained as a master planner at Yale University, the National University of Singapore, Colonial Williamsburg, the State University of New York at both Purchase and Potsdam, and Indiana University.

In their search for a new master planner, IU trustees and administrators interviewed twenty-four architectural firms from around the country in 1974. Edward Larrabee Barnes was chosen and given the title master architect for the Indiana University eight-campus system. While the most pressing need was a blueprint for the development of Indiana University–Purdue University Indianapolis (IUPUI), Barnes also afforded attention to the Bloomington campus. He developed a functional zone plan for IUB and reexamined and reworked planning principles including future building sites and green spaces and appropriate campus density. As a follow up to his successful Natatorium project on the IUPUI campus, Barnes was asked to design the long-anticipated Student Recreational Sports Center (SRSC) on the Bloomington campus. Both won national design awards.

Edward Larrabee Barnes was honored with the American Institute of Architects highest award, the AIA Gold Medal, the Thomas Jefferson Medal in Architecture, and the Harvard University 350th Anniversary Medal.

John Belle (1932–2016)

A founding partner of Beyer Blinder Belle of New York City, one of the country's most highly respected architectural firms, John Belle believed strongly that proper professional architectural practice commanded a responsibility to social and cultural values. He was often quoted as saying that preservation was the highest form of good stewardship, and he practiced what he preached. A native of Cardiff, Wales, Belle emigrated to the United States in 1959 and quickly moved to the forefront of preservation-oriented architecture. He led the renovation and restoration effort of the then abandoned Ellis Island immigration station, converting the site and buildings to what is now the Ellis Island Museum of Immigration, now part of the Statue of Liberty National Monument. John Belle was the project architect on the restoration at New York Botanical Garden of the Enid A. Haupt Conservatory, the nation's largest glasshouse. The crown jewel in John Belle's lifetime of work was saving and restoring Grand Central Station, which had fallen into deplorable condition. He also served as a master planner for many universities, including Princeton and Indiana University.

John Belle was chosen to lead IU's master planning in 2005. He focused on defining new areas within the Bloomington campus to accommodate needed expansion of the science disciplines. New building sites were identified north of Tenth Street that placed proposed structures in a second campus science quad that integrated the existing classrooms and laboratories of the Geology Building and Psychology Building. The inner campus was also the object of Belle's work, and the successful assimilation of Simon Hall into a campus area of high density is a credit to his skill.

John Belle was the recipient of three Presidential Design Awards—the nation's highest design award for public architecture—and the Time Magazine Design Award.

David King (1953–)

David King, longtime chairman of the board and director of design for SmithGroupJJR architects, has practiced his profession for more than forty years. His firm is the oldest and one of the largest in the United States, founded in 1853 by Sheldon Smith, and now employs more than eight hundred people in ten cities throughout North America and in Shanghai, China. The SmithGroup merger with Johnson, Johnson and Roy of Ann Arbor, Michigan, in 2011 provided the joint firm with comprehensive campus master planning experience to complement an already strong building design component.

David King has been lead designer for SmithGroupJJR for more than ninety major projects and his work has earned him 130 national design awards. His portfolio includes professional schools, libraries, hospitals, research laboratories, athletic facilities, and master plans for public and private educational institutions. King was inducted into the AIA Academy of Fellows in 1993.

When Indiana University sought a new master planner in 2008, ten nationally recognized architectural firms were interviewed. The immediate challenge was to undertake the creation of a new comprehensive master plan for the Indiana University Bloomington campus and the IUPUI campus. King and SmithGroupJJR had successfully completed major projects on both campuses, and King was selected to be IU's new master planner. David King delivered a visionary plan to university trustees in 2009; his plan continues to be implemented today.

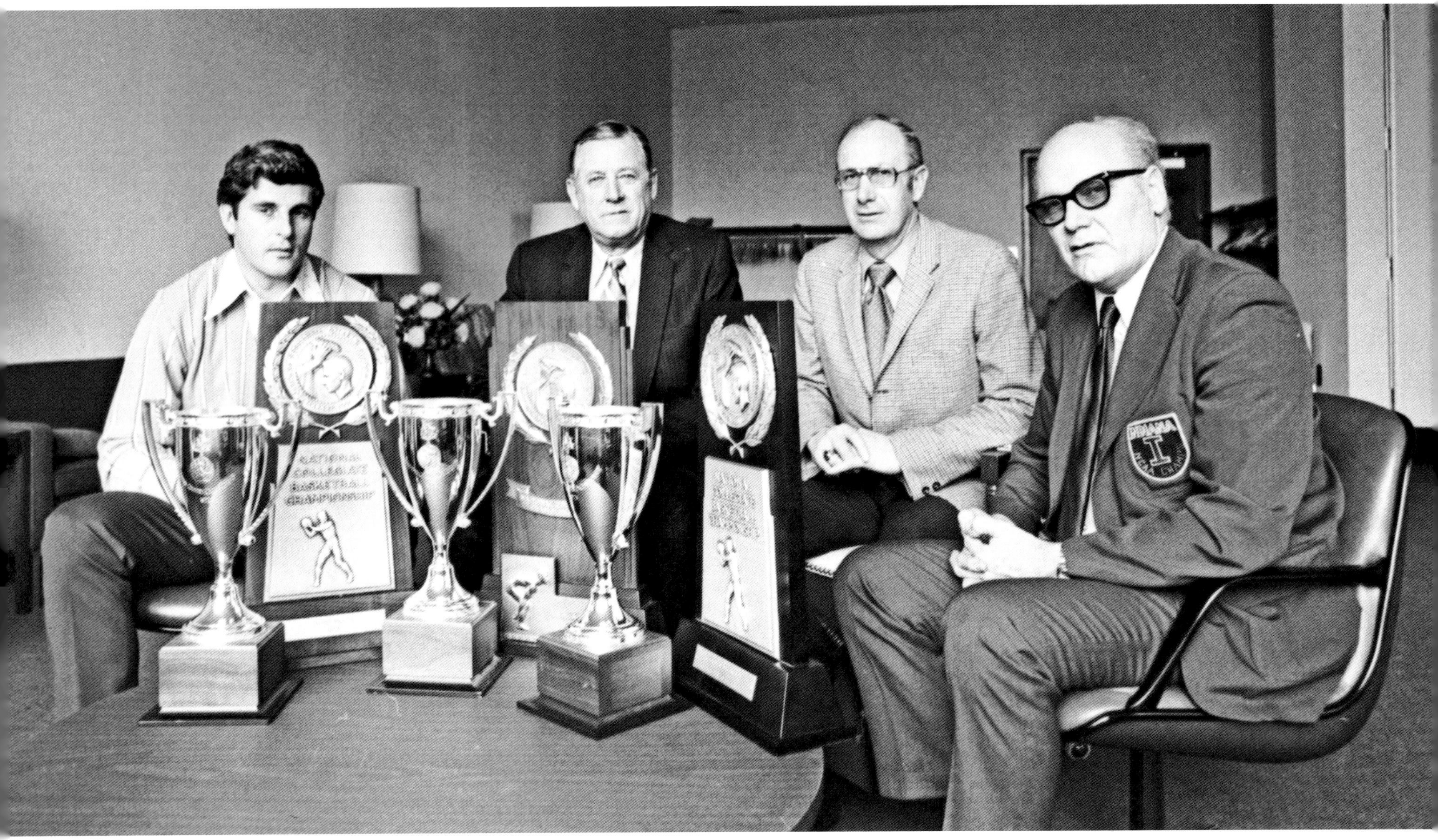

Above, The athletic director and Indiana University championship coaches with their teams' trophies (from left): IU men's basketball coach Bob Knight, athletic director Bill Orwig, men's track and field coach Sam Bell, and men's swimming coach Doc Counsilman, 1973. IU Archives.

Facing top, Delta Upsilon fraternity's firetruck as transport to an IU basketball game, circa 1963. P0026255, IU Archives; image from 1963 Arbutus.

Facing bottom, George Raffert, roommate of photographer Harry A. Hoffman, at desk, probably in Phi Kappa Psi House, circa 1905. Photo credit: P0025138, IU Archives.

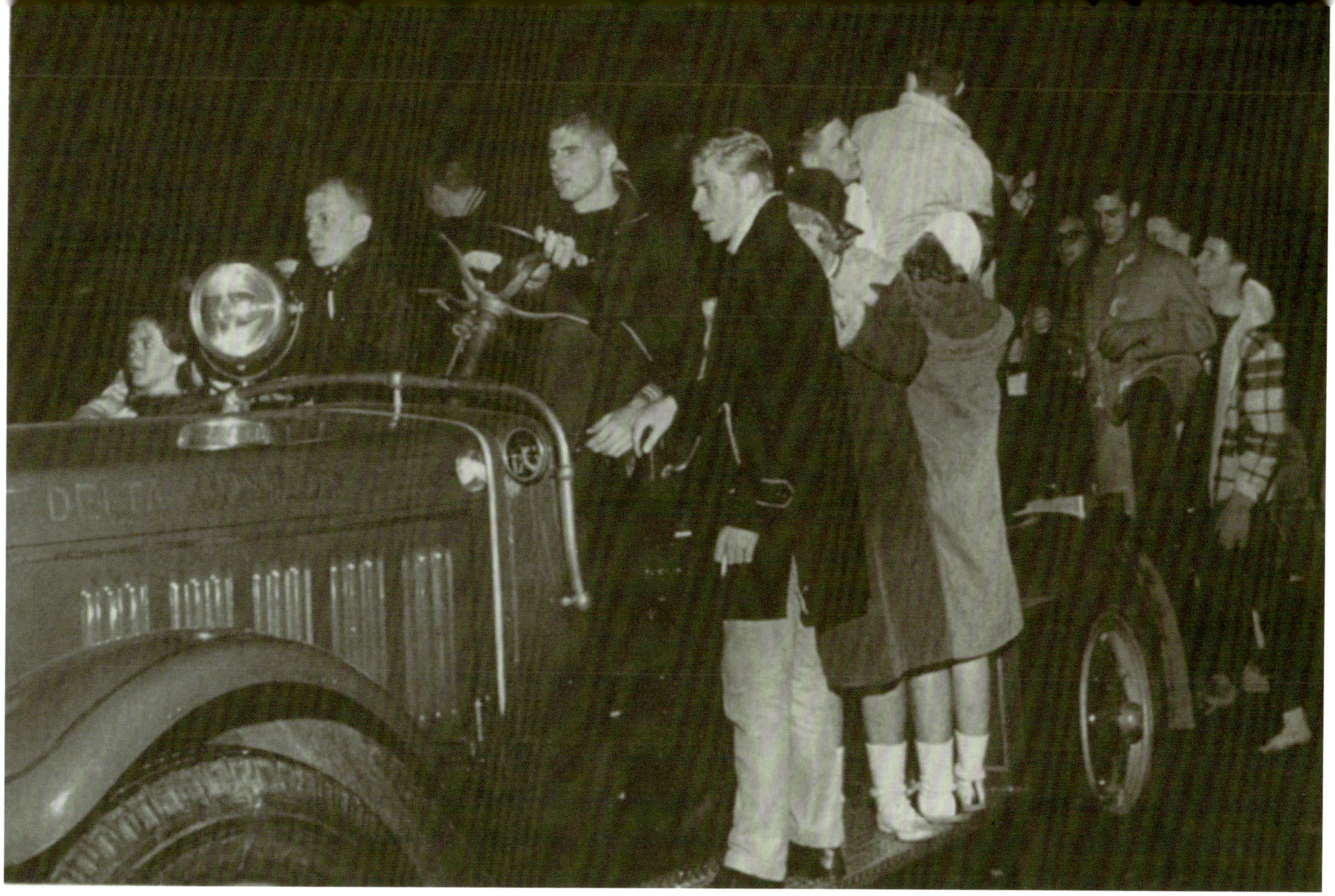
DELTA

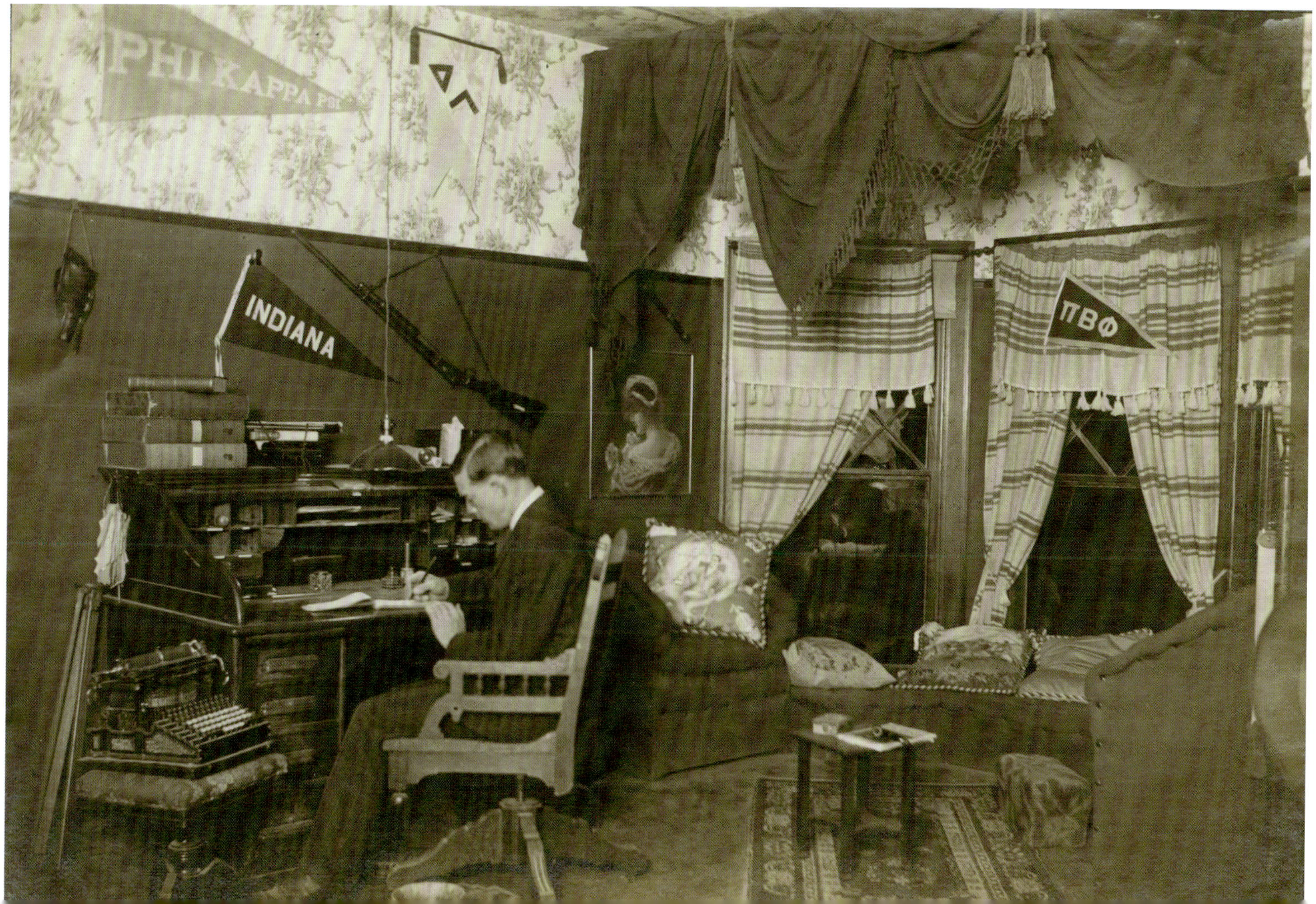
PHI KAPPA PSI
INDIANA
ΠΒΦ

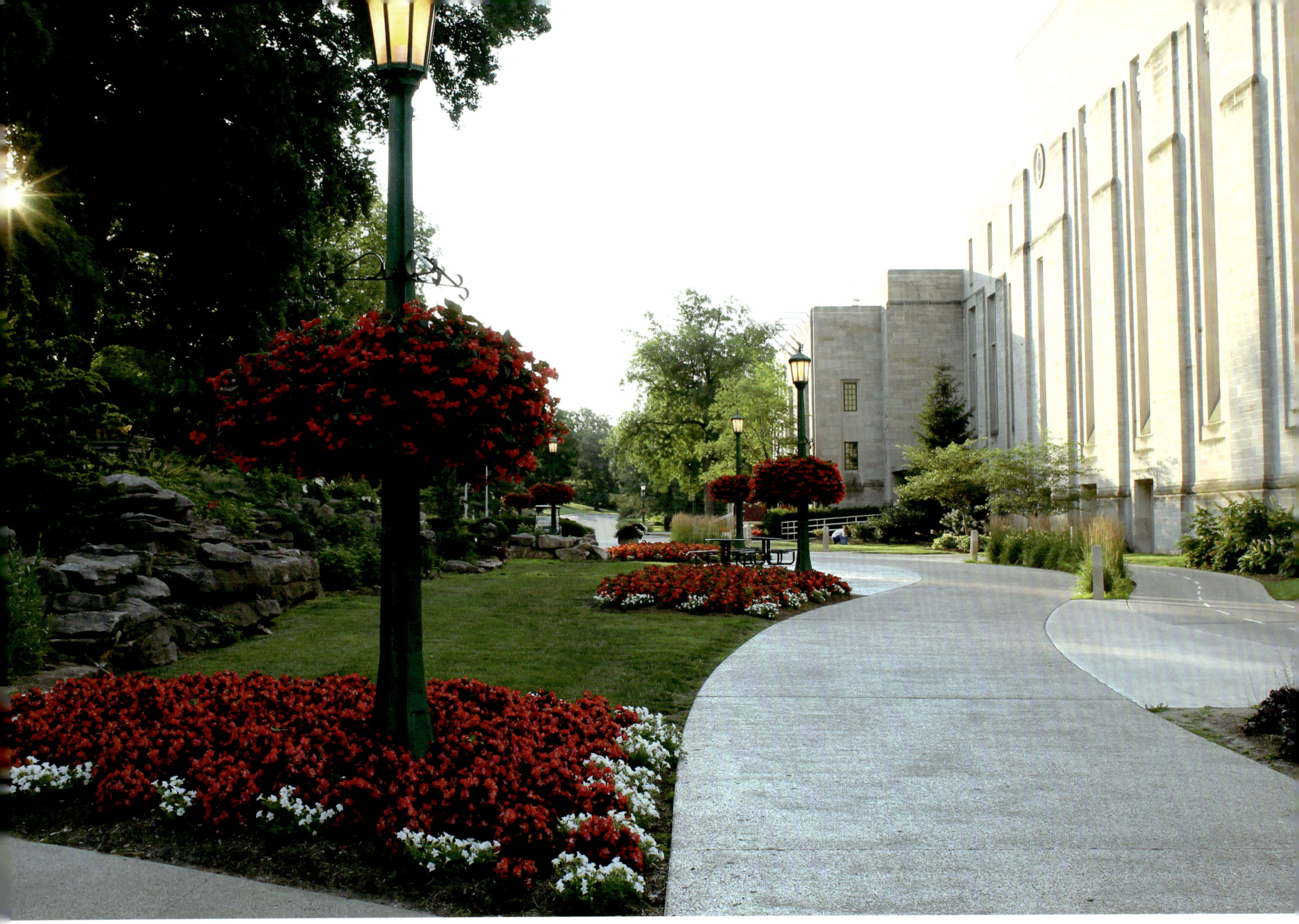

Bright red and white flowers adorn a campus path next to the Indiana University Auditorium on a sunny summer morning, 2017. Photo credit: Indiana University.

CHRONOLOGY OF ARCHITECTURE, ART, AND GREEN SPACES

1800s	Dunn Cemetery and Rogers Cemetery
1835	Wylie House
1868	Sundial (moved to Old Crescent in 1896)
1883	Dunn's Woods
1883	Dunn Meadow
1884	Wylie Hall
1884	Owen Hall
1885	Mitchell Hall (originally Maxwell Hall)
1890	Maxwell Hall (originally Library Hall)
1892	First Men's Gymnasium
1894	Kirkwood Hall
1896	Second Men's Gymnasium (later Assembly Hall)
1897	Jordan Field
1900	Kirkwood Observatory
1902	Ernest H. Lindley Hall (originally Science Hall)
1906	Frances Morgan Swain Student Building
1906	Alpha Hall
1907	Joseph Amos Franklin Hall (originally Library Building; Student Services Building)
1908	Rose Well House
1910	Swain Hall East (originally Biology Hall)
1917	Men's Gymnasium
1923	William A. Rawles Hall (originally Commerce Hall, later Business Administration Building, and Social Science Building)
1924	William and Charlotte Lowe Bryan House (originally the President's House)
1924	Ralph L. Collins Living-Learning Center (Men's Residence Center)
1925	Tenth Street Stadium (originally Memorial Stadium)
1925	Memorial Hall
1928	Ora L. Wildermuth Intramural Center (originally the Fieldhouse)
1931	Chemistry Building
1932	Indiana Memorial Union
1936	B. Winfred Merrill Hall (originally School of Music Building)
1936	Louise A. Goodbody Hall (originally Forest Hall)
1936	William Lowe Bryan Hall (originally the Administration Building)
1937	Burton Dorr Myers Hall (originally the Medical Building)
1938	Bess Meshulam Simon Music Library and Recital Center (originally University School; Wendell W. Wright School of Education)

1938	Ernie Pyle Hall (originally Stores and Services Building)
1940	Sycamore Hall
1940	Morrison Hall (originally Beech Hall)
1940	Swain Hall West (originally the Physical Sciences Building)
1940	James Albert Woodburn Hall (originally Business and Economics Building)
1941	IU Auditorium
1945	Woodlawn Courts trailers
1946	John W. Ashton Center (originally Rogers II)
1946	Hoosier Courts Apartments
1946	Trees Center
1948	East Hall (Opera House)
1949	University Apartments
1949	Joseph A. Wright Quadrangle (originally Men's Quadrangle)
1955	Charles M. Hepburn, Cyrus Nutt, Ernest P. Bicknell, and David D. Banta Apartments (originally Married Housing II)
1955	Daniel Read Hall (originally Smithwood Hall)
1955	Jordan Hall
1956	Beck Chapel
1956	Lowell E. Baier Hall (originally Law School Building)
1957	Evermann Apartment Center
1957	IU Golf Course
1959	Elisha Ballantine Hall
1959	Nellie S. Teter Quadrangle (originally Tower Quadrangle)
1959	Ward G. Biddle Hotel and Conference Center (originally Ward Gray Biddle Continuing Education Center)
1960	Harry Gladstein Fieldhouse
1960	Music Building Addition
1960	Lilly Library
1960	Redbud Hill Apartments (originally Married Student Housing Complex)
1960	Indiana Memorial Stadium
1961	Showalter Fountain
1961	School of Public Health Building (HPER)
1962	Campus View Apartments
1962	Geology Building
1962	Fine Arts Building
1963	Psychology Building
1963	Radio and Television Building
1963	John W. Foster Quadrangle
1963	Virgil T. DeVault Alumni Center (originally Administrative Services Building)
1964	Paul V. McNutt Quadrangle
1965	Herman T. Briscoe Quadrangle
1965	Tulip Tree Apartments
1965	IU Outdoor Pool
1965	Wendell L. Willkie Residence Center
1966	Forest Quadrangle
1966	Hodge Hall (originally School of Business)
1968	Eigenmann Hall
1968	*The Space Between: Adam and Eve* (Dunn's Woods)
1969	Herman B Wells Library (originally Library Building)
1970	Arthur R. Metz Memorial Carillon
1970	*Peau Rouge* (MAC)
1971	Simon Skjodt Assembly Hall
1971	Musical Arts Center (MAC)
1971	Glenn A. Black Laboratory of Archaeology
1974	Showalter House
1981	Sidney and Lois Eskenazi Museum of Art
1981	Bill Armstrong Stadium
1982	William Hammond Mathers Museum of World Cultures
1982	School of Public and Environmental Affairs (SPEA)
1984	Jesse H. and Beulah Chanley Cox Arboretum
1987	Sample Gates
1987	IU Tennis Center
1992	Wendell W. Wright Education Building
1995	Student Recreational Sports Center (SRSC)
1995	*Indiana Arc* (art museum)
1996	John Mellencamp Pavilion
1997	Frank E. McKinney Jr. Fountain

1997 Robert C. Haugh Track and Field Complex
2000 Herman B Wells Plaza
2002 Lee Norvelle Theatre and Drama Center
2002 Neal-Marshall Black Culture Center
2003 William Godfrey Graduate and Executive Education Center
2007 Simon Hall
2008 Hoagy Carmichael Sculpture
2008 Edward L. Hutton Honors College
2009 Multidisciplinary Science Building II
2009 North End Zone Facility
2009 Innovation Center
2009 Data Center
2010 Cook Hall
2010 Union Street Center
2010 IU Cinema
2011 Cyberinfrastructure Building
2013 Spruce Hall
2013 East Studio Building
2013 Andy Mohr Field
2013 Bart Kaufman Field
2015 Ernie Pyle Sculpture
2015 Global and International Studies Building
2018 Luddy Hall (School of Informatics and Computing)

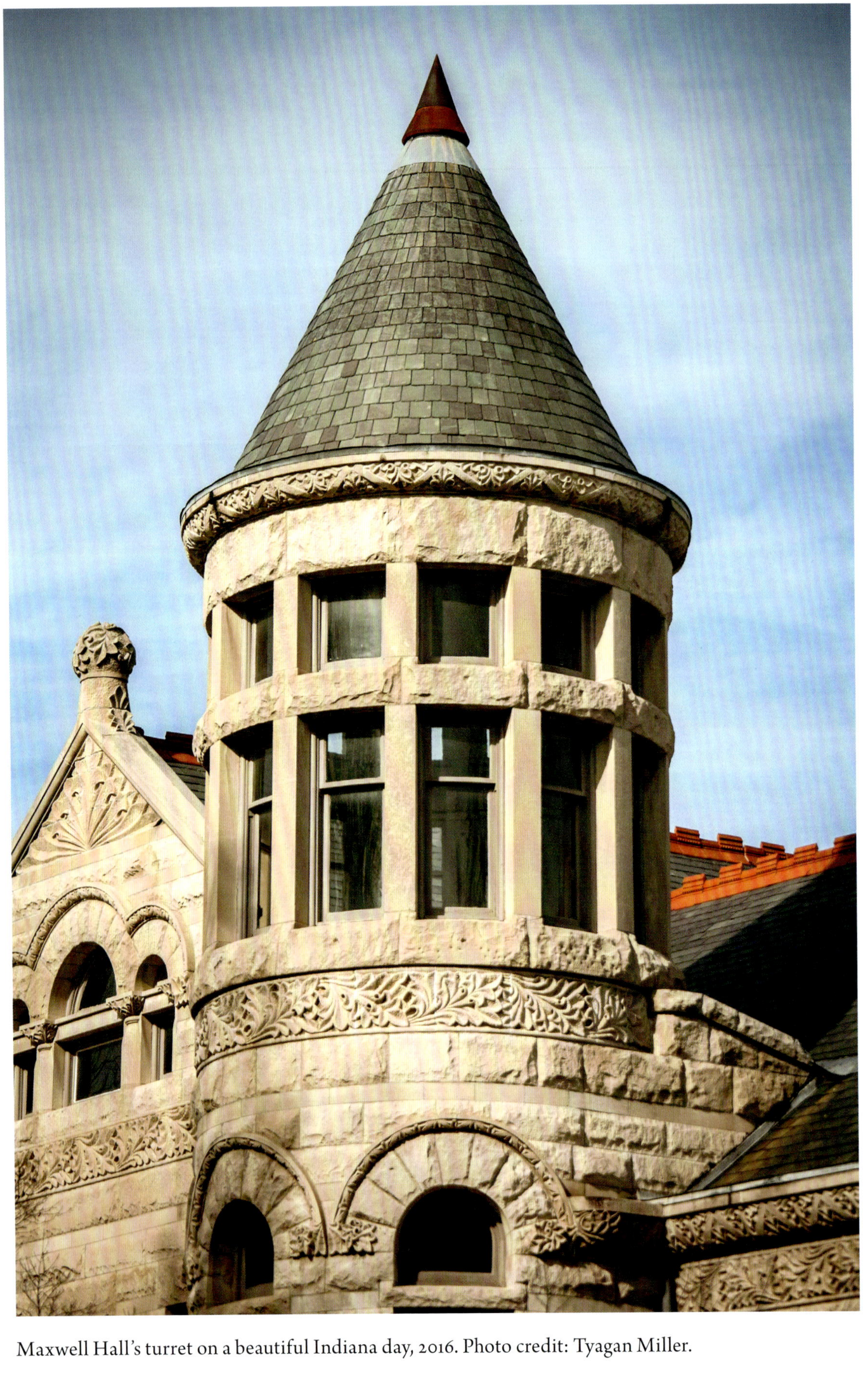

Maxwell Hall's turret on a beautiful Indiana day, 2016. Photo credit: Tyagan Miller.

GLOSSARY OF ARCHITECTURAL TERMS

Arcade A succession of consecutive arches supported by columns or piers.

Arch A curved structure spanning an opening and serving as support (round, pointed, Tudor, etc.).

Architrave A formalized lintel, the lowest member of classical entablature; molded frame around a door or window.

Arc-light chandelier A chandelier in which the light source is a high-intensity electric arc, either between carbon rods in air or between metal electrodes in a xenon gas atmosphere enclosed in a quartz bulb.

Arris The sharp edge or angle formed by the meeting of two surfaces (molding, stone).

Art Deco A popular design style of the 1920s and 1930s characterized especially by bold lines and sleek, streamlined, linear, symmetrical elements.

Art Moderne A late type of Art Deco architecture and design that emerged in the 1930s. Its architectural style emphasized curving forms, long horizontal lines, and sometimes nautical elements.

Articulation The manner of joining parts with each part remaining distinct in relation of the other parts.

Ashlar A thin, dressed stone cut in square or rectangular shapes, typically used as a wall facing in a pattern of varying shapes and sizes.

Atrium A top-lit, covered court rising through all stories of a building.

Axis A straight line laid down as a guide on either side of which elements of the plan are symmetrically or systematically disposed.

Baluster A small pillar or column supporting a parapet or handrail. Can be made of stone, wood, or metal.

Balustrade A horizontal railing composed of short posts (balusters) used for decoration, to enclose a space, or to support a handrail.

Bas-relief A sculpture that extends slightly from the adjoining surface.

Batter A receding upward slope of a wall or column, or other structure.

Battlement A parapet in which rectangular gaps or indentations occur at intervals, used for defense or decoration.

Bay window A window of one of more stories projecting from the face of a building.

Belfry A chamber in a tower where bells are hung.

Belt course A continuous horizontal band, separating the plane of a wall surface in a facade.

Blind arch An arch that has no actual opening and is applied to the surface of a wall as a decorative element.

Brackets A small decorative piece protruding from a wall and supporting another element, such as a door or window.

Butler-type A pre-engineered building system conceived by Butler Manufacturing. The structural framework is metal, but the exterior surface can be wood, stucco, stone, brick, or masonry.

Buttress The vertical member projecting from a wall to stabilize it or resist lateral thrust from a roof, arch, or vault. A *flying buttress* transmits the thrust to a heavy abutment by means of an arch or half-arch.

Canopy A projecting roof structure that shelters an entrance.

Cant An external angle, as of a building; an oblique or slanting surface.

Cantilever A projecting beam or member supported at only one end.

Capital The upper architectural, decorative element that crowns a column.

Cast-in-place concrete A mixture of sand, stone, and cement used as building material and poured in place during construction.

Chat-sawn limestone (sawed face) A finish obtained from the process used in producing units of building stone. It varies in texture from smooth to rough, and is typically named for the type of material used in sawing, for example, diamond sawn, sand sawn, chat sawn, and shot sawn.

Chimera A mythical, grotesque, or fantastic figure used for decorative purpose.

Cladding A visible, nonstructural, external finish of a building.

Clerestory An outside wall that rises above an adjoining roof and contains windows; the upper story of the nave of a church, containing windows.

Coffer A recessed panel in the shape of a square, rectangle, or octagon that serves as a decorative device, usually in a ceiling or vault.

Coffered ceiling A deep panel sunk in a ceiling, dome, soffit, or vault, often decorated in the center with a stylized flower or similar embellishment. A ceiling, etc., with coffer is said to be coffered.

Collegiate Gothic An architectural style also known as secular Gothic or Tudor Gothic, such as that of Oxford and Cambridge Colleges. The term *Collegiate Gothic* derives from Gothic Revival, an architectural style inspired by medieval Gothic architecture. Gothic Revival became a leading building style during the nineteenth century and was often employed because of its moral overtones for academic, political, and religious buildings. It is characterized by the use of pointed arches, external buttresses, finials, crenellation, parapets, a plaque set in the front, relief sculpture, and tracery.

Colonial Revival The most traditional home style of the twentieth century, and is a mix of all uniquely American styles, with generally a symmetrical and stately facade.

Colonnade A row of columns supporting entablature.

Contextual architecture A style that responds to its surroundings by respecting what is already there (contextualism).

Corbel A projecting element on a wall bearing a weight, such as a balcony.

Cornice A horizontal, projecting decorative molding along the top of a wall, building, or entablature.

Coursing A continuous, horizontal layer of material.

Crenellation A series of square indentations in a parapet giving a castle-like appearance.

Cresting A repetitive metal ornament finishing a roof ridge or parapet.

Cupola A small domed structure on top of a roof.

Dentils A series of small projecting rectangular blocks forming a molding, as under a cornice.

Diaper pattern A decorative pattern on a plain, flat, unbroken surface consisting of the constant repetition of simple figures (e.g., squares, lozenges, or polygons) closely connected with each other, sometimes with embellishments in the form of stylized flowers.

Dormer A window projecting from the sloping side of a roof.

Dutch gable A tall gable with sweeping curved sides, often ogees with volutes, crowned by a triangular pediment.

English Gothic The architectural style that flourished in England from about 1180 until about 1520. As with Gothic architecture, it is defined by its pointed arches, vaulted roofs, buttresses, large windows, and spires.

Entablature The upper horizontal part of a classical order, consisting of a cornice, frieze, and architrave.

Facade The exterior face or presentable front of a building.

Federal The style of architecture and decoration prevalent in the United States from the Declaration of Independence (1776) to circa 1830, evolving from Georgian. Typically, a Federal-style house is a simple square or rectangular box, two or three stories high, and two rooms deep.

Fenestration The pattern formed by or arrangement of windows in a building facade.

Fielded wood paneling A raised or recessed panel with a wide flat surface surrounded by moldings.

Finial An ornament at the top of a roof gable, spire, or other part of a building.

Flat arch An architectural element spanning an opening and serving as support. Arch shapes range from flat to semicircular to semielliptical to pointed.

Fleur-de-lis An ornament consisting of three leaflike pointed members above and one or three below a horizontal crossbar. It is essentially a stylized lily, often found in late Gothic tracery.

Fluting The shallow, concave, parallel grooves running vertically on a column or pilaster.

Footings The projecting courses at the bottom of a wall, wider than the walls.

Fossiliferous Containing fossils.

Frieze The central band in an entablature, above the architrave and below the cornice; a sculptured or ornamented band, as on a building.

Gable The triangular upper portion of a wall formed by the slopes of a pitched roof; the end wall of a building.

Gabled roof A roof with two sloping sides and a gable at each end.

Gargoyle A carved stone grotesque with a spout designed to convey water from a roof gutter.

Gazebo A freestanding pavilion often found in parks and gardens.

Georgian An architectural style commonly associated with the reigns of England's King George I through King George III. However, it is actually directly tied to the work of English architect Sir Christopher Wren. The dominant architectural trend in the colonies between 1700 and the Revolutionary War, it is symmetrical in design, with classic proportions, and decorative elements.

Gothic A style of architecture that flourished during the high and late medieval period. It evolved from Romanesque architecture and was succeeded by Renaissance architecture. Its characteristics include the pointed arch, the ribbed vault, and the flying buttress.

Gothic arch A pointed arch, especially one with a joint instead of a keystone at its apex.

Greek orders of architecture The three orders or organizational systems of Ancient Greek architecture, each composed of a column, with a base, shaft, capital, and entablature with frieze and cornice. (Corinthian, Doric, and Ionic)

Grill, grille A lattice or screen of open work, usually metal.

Grotesque A capricious classical ornament consisting of animals, figures, flowers, foliage, fruits, and sphinxes, all connected together (properly *grottesque*).

Hip roof A roof where the gables slope back toward the ridge instead of extending vertically.

Hood mold A projection from a cornice or sill designed to protect the area below from rainwater (as over a window or doorway).

Italianate A style of architecture that was a distinct nineteenth-century phase in the history of classical architecture, with nearly flat roofs, wide eaves, and massive brackets, suggested by the romantic villas of Renaissance Italy.

Italian Renaissance An architectural style during the Renaissance, and a later style inspired by the highly symmetrical and carefully proportioned buildings of classical Greece and Rome, with columns, arches, domes, sculpture, etc.

Keystone The central or pinnacle stone of an arch, sometimes embellished.

Latticework An ornamental lattice framework with a crisscrossed pattern, usually made of wood or metal.

LEED Certification A green building certification program administered by the U.S. Green Building Council, Leadership in Energy and Environmental Design (LEED) recognizes best building strategies and practices. LEED rating levels: Certified, Silver, Gold, and Platinum.

Limestone A common sedimentary rock consisting mostly of calcium carbonate, used as a building stone and in the manufacture of lime, carbon dioxide, and cement. Salem limestone is from a geological formation quarried primarily in south-central Indiana between Bloomington and Bedford.

Lintel The horizontal beam above a door or window.

Lozenge A diamond- or rhomboid-shaped equilateral parallelogram with two opposite angles more acute than the other two, occurring in moldings, as small lights over Gothic lancet lights in tracery, in net-vaults, and in other uses.

Lunette A crescent-shaped space, often above a door, used as a space for murals, sculpture, or mosaics, or used alone as a decorative element.

Mansard A roof having two slopes on all sides, with the lower slope steeper than the upper slope.

Massing The general shape, form, and size of a building.

Medallion A tablet or panel, resembling a medal, in a wall bearing a portrait or decorative element in relief.

Minimalist A style inspired by severe modern architecture, traditional Japanese architecture, and Zen Buddhist gardens. Minimalism seeks to avoid clutter, ornament, and even color. It has sometimes been adopted to suggest exclusiveness and luxury. A feature of the modern movement since the 1920s, it reemerged in the 1960s and 1980s.

Modernism An architectural movement utilizing ideas and methods that significantly differ from those used in the past.

Modernist Architectural style of the 1920s and 1930s incorporating decorative devices, influenced by Art Deco, Aztec, and Ancient Egyptian styles, and prompted by the

1925 Paris Exhibition. Among the more common motifs were chevrons, canted and corbelled arches, medallions, wave scrolls, flutings, moldings stepped over surfaces, and geometrical patterns. Modernistic buildings also incorporated streamlining and curved walls.

Molding A decorative recessed or relieved element.

Motif A theme or predominant feature of a design.

Mullion A slender vertical member that forms a division between units of a window, door, or screen or is used decoratively or for support.

Neo-colonial Buildings constructed after 1950 with allusions of the Colonial Revival architectural style.

Oriel window Large bay window projecting from a wall on an upper story, supported by brackets, corbels, a pier, or an engaged column.

Overburden The rock or soil overlying a mineral deposit, archaeological site, or other underground feature.

Palladian A Neoclassical architectural design, in imitation of the Italian architect, Andrea Palladio.

Parapet The portion of an exterior wall that projects above the edge of the roof; low wall around a balcony or similar structure.

Pavilion A freestanding structure near a main building or an end structure on building wings.

Pediment A triangular-shaped gable crowning a portico, door, or window.

Pier A freestanding vertical element supporting a structure above. A solid support between door or window openings, supporting a bridge.

Pilaster A slightly projecting column built into or applied to the face of a wall.

Plinth The base upon which a column, pedestal, or monument rests.

Portico A covered ambulatory consisting of a series of columns placed at regular intervals supporting a roof, normally attached as a colonnaded porch to a building, but sometimes forming a separate structure.

Prairie An architectural style with roots in the U.S. Midwest, emphasizing the relationship of the building to the site, used natural materials, and stressed horizontality.

Precast concrete Concrete that is cast in the form of a structural element (as a panel or beam) before being placed in final position.

Proportion The relationship between individual elements of a building and their size within the total building.

Public Works Administration (PWA) A public works construction agency established in response to the Great Depression and part of the 1933 New Deal. PWA built large-scale public works such as dams, bridges, hospitals, and schools.

Punched window A square or rectangular window having one or more pieces of glass surrounded by window framing; it can be quite large.

Pylon A usually massive gateway; an ancient Egyptian gateway building in a truncated pyramidal form; a monumental mass flanking an entranceway or an approach to a bridge.

Quadrangle A four-sided courtyard.

Quoins The stones or bricks used at the corners of a building, for emphasis or decoration, and differentiated from adjoining walls by size, color, projection, or texture.

Rake The inclination or slope of anything, such as the top of a triangular pediment or a pitched roof. Raked seating slopes upward away from the stage, in order to give those at the back a better view.

Random ashlar Masonry of ashlars not laid in continuous regular courses, but formed of dressed stones of different heights and widths fitted closely together.

Rectilinear buttress A buttress characterized by straight lines.

Return The receding edge of a flat face. Any part of an architectural feature that forms an angle with the main part.

Romanesque A revival style of architecture that borrowed heavily from the medieval Romanesque that often included round arches, heavy walls, arcades, ornamentation, and small windows. In the United States, the leading Romanesque architect was Henry Hobson Richardson (*Richardsonian Romanesque*).

Rosette A small circular stylized ornament, with floral enrichment, associated with Classical architecture, and usually in bas-relief.

Rose window A large ornamental window filled with ornamental tracery (ornamental stone work in window openings).

Rotunda A large and high circular room or hall in a building, usually topped by a dome.

Rough-sawn (sawed face) A finish obtained from the process used in producing units of building stone. It varies in texture from smooth to rough, and is typically named for the type of material used in sawing, for example, diamond sawn, sand sawn, chat sawn, and shot sawn.

Rusticated Stonework with roughly cut block faces.

Rustication Stonework emphasized by roughly cut block faces.

Saddle-type suspension roof A suspension roof that usually consists of systems of intersecting concave and convex wires that form either a grid or an envelope in the form of a hyperbolic paraboloid.

Sash Any framework of a window, moveable or fixed.

Sill A lower horizontal projecting element below an aperture (e.g., doorway or window), to throw water off of the wall below.

Spandrel The nearly triangular space between the left or right exterior curve of an arch and the rectangular framework surrounding it. The space between the shoulders of adjoining arches and the ceiling or molding above.

Spire A tall, tapering roof element with a steep point.

Split-face Stone that has been broken or split to expose a rougher surface; a rough-faced, building stone cut from stratified rock so that the split face exposes the bedding.

Stabile An abstract sculpture or construction similar in appearance to a mobile but made to be stationary.

Stringcourse A horizontal band in a building forming part of the design.

Suspension roof A roof system supported by cables attached to a frame. Suspension structures may be either plane or spatial. Spatial suspension structures are generally used for large-span roofs of public and industrial buildings.

Swale A low-lying or depressed and often wet stretch of land.

Terra-cotta A fired clay cast in molds, often used in decorative elements or to clad a building exterior.

Tracery A pattern of interlocking mullions in the upper part of a Gothic window, such as in a rose window.

Transom A window or other element above a door, but within its vertical frame.

Trapezoid Referring to symmetrical doors, windows, and buildings built wider at the base, tapering toward the top, in Egyptian style.

Travertine A form of limestone commonly used as a building material, particularly as a flooring tile. Usually pit marked and appears porous or worn and comes in a variety of colors.

Tripartite window treatment A window divided into or composed of three parts.

Truss A framework of straight timbers that is used to support a roof.

Tudor A style popular during the reign of the Tudors, 1485–1603, and covers the last phase of the Gothic style and the beginning of the Renaissance. Primarily associated with late-Perpendicular Gothic, flat four-centered or Tudor arches, domestic architecture of brick with diaper patterns, elaborate chimneys of carved and molded brick, and square-headed mullioned windows with hood molds and label-stops.

Tudor Revival A term descriptive of a mode of domestic architecture in the early twentieth century, emulating its Tudor architecture prototype. A revival of Tudor architecture in educational buildings (Collegiate Gothic). Often with diaper patterns, small casement windows with leaded lights, molded-brick chimneys, and even partially timber-framed structures.

Tumbled stone A weathered, aging finish created when stone is tumbled with sand, pebbles, or steel bearings.

Turret A small, often slender tower projecting from the corner of a building.

Veneer A thin decorative finish, usually brick, stone, or stucco.

Victorian Gothic An architectural style belonging to the later Gothic Revival of Victoria's reign and combining French, Italian, and English elements with a free use of parti-color materials.

Water table A stringcourse or similar element that projects so to dispel water.

Widow's walk A walkway or narrow platform on a roof, especially on early New England homes with a view of the sea.

NOTES

Foreword

1. Speech by Winston Churchill in the House of Commons, October 28, 1944.
2. John Ruskin, *The Stones of Venice: The Foundations* (1886; New York: CosimoClassics, 2007).
3. Marcus Vitruvius Pollio, *De architectura* (On Architecture), ca. 15 BCE.

Introduction

1. David Starr Jordan to Lemuel Moss, letter 7 October 1883, collection C73, Indiana University Archives, Indiana University, Bloomington.
2. Theodore A. Brown and Lyle W. Dorestt, *K.C.: A History of Kansas City, Missouri* (Boulder, CO: Pruett, 1978), 163–64.

In the Beginning

1. Abraham Lincoln Papers [letter to Jesse W. Fell], December 20, 1859, Library of Congress. Quoted in Roy P. Basler, ed., *Collected Works of Abraham Lincoln* (New Brunswick, NJ: Rutgers University Press, 1953–55), 3:511.
2. Theophilus Adam Wylie, diary entry November 1, 1891, Theophilus A. Wylie Papers, collection C202, Indiana University Archives, Indiana University, Bloomington.

THE OLD CRESCENT

The Emergence of a Modern University

1. Fassett Allen Cotton, *Education in Indiana*, Indiana Dept. of Public Instruction (W. B. Burford, contractor for state printing, 1904), 508; digitized Nov. 17, 2008.
2. "Indiana University Bloomington: 2010 Campus Master Plan," SmithGroup JJR, 2010.
3. Ibid.
4. National Register of Historic Places Nomination Form, Trustees of Indiana University, Bloomington, March 1978, "Buildings, Bloomington—Seminary Square Park, National Register of Historic Places designation" reference folder, Indiana University Archives, Indiana University, Bloomington.

Wylie Hall

Epigraph is from *Bloomington Telephone*, March 1884.

1. David Starr Jordan, *The Days of a Man, Being Memories of a Naturalist, Teacher, and Minor Prophet of Democracy* (Yonkers-on-Hudson, NY: World Book, 1922), 1:290.
2. Leland M. Roth, *American Architecture: A History* (Boulder, CO: Westview, 2001).
3. James A. Woodburn, *History of Indiana University*, vol. 1, *1820–1902* (Bloomington: Indiana University Press, 1940).

Owen Hall

Epigraph is from Indiana University Board of Trustees meeting minutes, *The University Buildings: The Indiana University Catalogue . . . Register . . . Announcements*, Board of Trustees, Bloomington, April 10, 1882, 52.

1. Diary entry, September 6, 1885, Theophilus A. Wylie papers, collection C202, Indiana University Archives, Indiana University, Bloomington.

2. Richard Bishop (retired IU Foundation officer), personal communication with the author, 2012.

Mitchell Hall

Epigraph is from *Indiana Student*, 12, no. 2 (February 1886): 114, "Buildings—Bloomington Campus, Mitchell" folder, Indiana University Archives, Indiana University, Bloomington.

Maxwell Hall

Epigraph is from David Starr Jordan, "Unpublished History of IU" (1892), "Buildings—Bloomington Campus, Maxwell Hall" folder, Indiana University Archives, Indiana University, Bloomington.

1. Thomas D. Clark, *Indiana University, Midwestern Pioneer*, vol. 3, *Years of Fulfillment* (Bloomington: Indiana University Press, 1977), 185–86.

2. *Indiana Daily Student*, Nov. 1, 1957.

Kirkwood Hall

Epigraph is from Herman B Wells, *Being Lucky: Reminiscences and Reflections* (Bloomington: Indiana University Press, 1980), 146.

1. "A Glorious Friday: Kirkwood Hall Dedicated," *Bloomington World* 1, no. 16 (January 26, 1895).

Kirkwood Observatory

Epigraph is from Joseph Swain, "Daniel Kirkwood," *Publications of the Astronomical Society of the Pacific* 13, no. 80 (October 1, 1901): 147.

1. Robert J. Aley, "Daniel Kirkwood," *Indiana School Journal* 41, no. 3 (March 1896): 177.

2. John A. Miller, "The Kirkwood Observatory of Indiana University," *Publications of the Astronomical Society of the Pacific* 13, no. 80 (October 1, 1901): 139.

3. Thomas D. Clark, *Indiana University, Midwestern Pioneer*, vol. 1, *The Early Years* (Bloomington: Indiana University Press, 1970), 293–94.

Ernest H. Lindley Hall

Epigraph is from *Arbutus*, 1906, 390.

1. "Lindley Hall Rededication," April 24, 1992, Kenneth R. Gros Louis speeches, collection C202, Indiana University Archives, Indiana University, Bloomington.

Frances Morgan Swain Student Building

Epigraph is from President Thomas Ehrlich, Student Building rededication ceremony, October 11, 1991, President Thomas Ehrlich speeches, collection C64, Indiana University Archives, Indiana University, Bloomington.

1. "The Women's Building," *Arbutus*, 1901.

2. "Notable Programme on Alumni Day—Student Building Dedicated under Most Favorable Auspices," *Daily Student*, June 23, 1906.

3. "Thanks Expressed—By President Bryan to Citizens, Friends of University, Students and Workers," *Daily Student*, June 23, 1906.

4. Student Building Re-dedication Ceremony Script, October 11, 1991, collection C29, University Relations and External Affairs Records, Indiana University Archives, Indiana University, Bloomington. "Will Play Chimes for Five Years to Pay Pledge to Indiana Memorial Fund," *Indiana Alumnus*, September 9, 1922, 6.

5. Herman B Wells, "The Student Building," *Bloomington Monthly Magazine*, September 1991.

6. Student Building Re-dedication Script.

Joseph Amos Franklin Hall

Epigraph is from a speech by Purdue University President W. E. Stone at the dedication of Franklin Hall (the Library Building), June 23, 1908, reprinted in "Seventy-Ninth Annual Commencement of Indiana University," *Indiana Medical Journal: A Monthly Journal of Medicine* 27, no. 1 (1908): 24–25.

1. Burton Door Myers, *History of Indiana University*, vol. 2, 1902–1937 (Bloomington: Indiana University Press, 1952), 33.

2. Ibid., 46.

3. Ibid., 47.

4. "IU Operations Threatened," *Indiana University Alumni Magazine*, April 1969. "These Smoke-Ups Are Coming in Agonizing Pairs," *Indiana Alumni Magazine*, June 1969, 15.

Rose Well House

Epigraph is from "Well-House Innovation: Old Graduate Stands Expense for Beautiful Addition to Campus," *Daily Student*, October 15, 1907.

1. John C. Robinson, class of 1861, "The University in the Later Fifties," address read before the Historical Society September 22, 1906, by Judge John C. Robinson, unpublished manuscript, "Students, Early—Robinson, John C., 1850s" reference folder, Indiana University Archives, Indiana University, Bloomington.

2. Burton Dorr Myers, Trustees and Officers of Indiana University, 1820–1950, ed. Ivy L. Chamness and Burton D. Myers (Bloomington: Indiana University, 1951), 355. Both Trustees and Officers (356) and Myers's History (2:52) claim that this committee was appointed in spring 1907, whereas the BOT minutes of June 20, 1904, contain the formation of and charge to the committee.

3. In acknowledging a holiday card with an image of the Well House, Hoagy Carmichael wrote to Herman B Wells: "I bet you didn't know that my own grandfather (Alex Robinson) built it." Donor file, "Carmichael, Hoagy, 1964–1970," accession 2006/011, box 8 (restricted access), Indiana University Archives, Indiana University, Bloomington.

4. "The National Order of the Tin Cup Bacteria Will Hold Its Convention at the Well House This Summer," Arbutus, 1912, 230.

Swain Hall East

Epigraph is from the "National Register of Historic Places Inventory Nomination Form," September 8, 1980, http://focus.nps.gov (accessed January 28, 2016).

1. President William Lowe Bryan quoted in Burton Dorr Myers, *History of Indiana University*, vol. 2, *1902–1934* (Bloomington: Indiana University Press, 1952), 76.

2. Ibid.

3. James Watson quoted in Evelyn Ellison, "Nobel Prize Winner Speaks," *Indiana Daily Student*, February 28, 1992.

4. Indiana University Board of Trustees minutes, June 1–5, 1939, http://purl.dlib.indiana.edu/iudl/archives/iubot/1939-06-01 (accessed January 27, 2016).

THE ARTS AND HUMANITIES

Music

B. Winfred Merrill Hall

Epigraph is from School of Music dean B. Winfred Merrill at Music Building dedication, June 13, 1937, quoted in "The 1937 Commencement," *Indiana University Alumni Quarterly* 24 (summer 1937): 306, "Buildings—Bloomington Campus, School of Music Building" folder, Indiana University Archives, Indiana University, Bloomington.

1. George M. Logan, *The Indiana University School of Music: A History* (Bloomington: Indiana University Press, 2000), 26–27.

2. Winifred Merrill Warren, "Home at Last," *Indiana Alumni*, July/August 1987.

3. "New Music Building of Indiana University," *Indiana Daily Student*, September 8, 1936.

4. Constance A. Mayer, review of *The Indiana University School of Music: A History* by George M. Logan, *Notes* 58, no. 4 (2002): 848–50.

Bess Meshulam Simon Music Library and Recital Center

Epigraph is from Charles Webb in dedication speech, November 17, 1995, "Bess Meshulam Simon Music Library and Recital Center Dedication Ceremony" script, President Myles Brand speeches, collection C263, Indiana University Archives, Indiana University, Bloomington.

1. Olmsted Brothers Campus Plan to President William Lowe Bryan, January 31, 1936, collection C286, Indiana University Archives, Indiana University, Bloomington.

2. Address at the dedication of the University School, June 13, 1938, Herman B Wells Speeches, collection C137, Indiana University Archives, Indiana University, Bloomington.

East Hall

Epigraph is from Hans Busch, "Farewell to East Hall," July 15, 1967, accession 2001/031, School of Music—Publicity Office records (unprocessed collection), accession 2001/031, Indiana University Archives, Indiana University, Bloomington.

1. Ruthie Given, "Superb Cast Gives Brilliant *La Bohème*," *Indiana Daily Student*, March 4, 1950, 1. Annual Report for the School of Music, 1949–50, President's Office records—Herman B Wells, collection C213, Indiana University Archives, Indiana University, Bloomington.

2. Hans Busch to Dean Wilfred Bain, May 1, 1964, "School of Music—Opera Theatre" folder, President's Office records—Elvis Stahr, collection C304, Indiana University Archives, Indiana University, Bloomington.

3. Busch, "Farewell to East Hall."

4. George M. Logan, *The Indiana University School of Music: A History* (Bloomington: Indiana University Press, 2000), 159.

Music Building Addition

Epigraph is from music critic Paul Hume at Music Building Addition dedication, April 15, 1962, quoted in "Hume Stresses Arts at Music Dedication," *Indiana Daily Student*, April 17, 1962.

1. "Addition to Music Building to Get Under Way in Fall," *Indiana Daily Student*, July 13, 1956.

2. School of Music annual report, 1957–1958, collection C213.404, Indiana University Archives, Indiana University, Bloomington.

3. "School of Music Addition Dedication," President Herman B Wells's speeches, collection C137.20, Indiana University Archives, Indiana University, Bloomington.

4. "Music School Addition Construction Progresses," *Indiana Daily Student*, March 12, 1959.

5. George M. Logan, *The Indiana University School of Music: A History* (Bloomington: Indiana University Press, 2000), 217.

Musical Arts Center

Epigraph is from President John W. Ryan, April 16, 1972, "Dedication of the Musical Arts Center" speech, "Buildings—Bloomington, Musical Arts Center, 1972 Dedication" reference file, Indiana University Archives, Indiana University, Bloomington.

1. Evan Woollen to Chancellor Wells, July 2, 1965, MAC—Correspondence folder, Chancellors records, collection C145, Indiana University Archives, Indiana University, Bloomington.

2. Evans Woollen quoted in "Recent Work of Evans Woolen," *Architectural Record*, May 1967, 139.

3. Harold C. Schonberg, "Music: Eaton's Dedicatory 'Heracles' Premiere Opens Fete at Indiana U. Center," *New York Times*, April 17, 1972; William Mootz, "A Complex 'Heracles' Opens IU's Music Arts Center," *Louisville Courier-Journal*, April 17, 1972; John Ardoin, "Opera in Review: Indiana U. Inaugurates 'Fort Bain,'" *Dallas Morning News*, April 18, 1972; Thomas Willis, "Opera: I.U.'s 'Most Ambitious' School, the Fruit of Herculean Labors," *Chicago Tribune*, April 23, 1972.

East Studio Building

Epigraph is from Menahem Pressler, Distinguished Professor of Piano, quoted in "Statements on Lilly Endowment Gift by IU Music, Law Faculty," news release, *IU News Room*, Indiana University, December 11, 2007, http://newsinfo.iu.edu/news/page/normal/7027.html (accessed April 10, 2017).

1. "IU Jacobs School Announces Architects for New $44,000,000 Building," news release, *IU News Room*, August 29, 2008, http://newsinfo.iu.edu/web/page/normal/8733.html (accessed January 29, 2015).

2. Latonya Yarbo, "Jacobs School's East Studio Building Nearing Completion," Campus Life, *Inside IU Bloomington*, June 13, 2013, http://archive.inside.indiana.edu/editors-picks/campus-life/2013-06-13-iniub-JacobsSchool-EastStudio.shtml (accessed April 14, 2017).

The Humanities

Elisha Ballantine Hall

Epigraph is from a speech by Professor of French and Italian Hulet H. Cook to faculty and staff about Ballantine Hall, May 6, 1960, Herman Wells Presidential papers, "Ballantine Hall" folder, collection C213, Indiana University Archives, Indiana University, Bloomington.

1. President's Report 1948–49, President's Office records, collection C213, Indiana University Archives, Indiana University, Bloomington.

2. Hulet H. Cook to faculty and staff in regards to Ballantine Hall, May 6, 1960, Herman Wells Presidential papers, "Ballantine Hall" folder, collection C213, Indiana University Archives, Indiana University, Bloomington.

3. Herman B Wells, *Being Lucky: Reminiscences and Reflections* (Bloomington: Indiana University Press, 1980), 200.

4. State of the University speech, March 30, 1960, Herman B Wells Presidential speeches, collection C137, Indiana University Archives, Indiana University, Bloomington.

5. Charles E. Harrell quoted in "Ballantine Hall," Indiana University News Bureau, November 1, 1960.

6. "'New White Giant' to Open Monday," *Indiana Daily Student*, September 16, 1959.

7. "Ballantine Hall," Indiana University News Bureau, November 1, 1960.

8. Newton Stallknecht quoted in "Work Begun on Sculpture for Ballantine," *Indiana Daily Student*, May 12, 1959.

9. "Ballantine Hall Named in Honor of Greek 'Prof,'" *Indiana Alumni Magazine*, October 1964, 15.

10. "Dedication of the Geo-Physical Globe" program, June 2, 1961, "Ballantine Hall, 1960–1962" folder, collection C213, Indiana University Archives, Indiana University, Bloomington.

11. Walter Laves quoted in Patricia Brogneaux, "Wilsons Present Globe to I.U.," *Indiana Daily Student*, June 3, 1961, 1.

Glenn A. Black Laboratory of Archaeology / William Hammond Mathers Museum of World Cultures

The epigraph is from "Remarks of Chancellor Herman B Wells, Dedication of Glenn A. Black Laboratory," April 21, 1971, Speeches of University Chancellor Herman B Wells, collection C548.5, Indiana University Archives, Indiana University, Bloomington.

1. Brian Keith, e-mail to the author, May 27, 2016.

2. Jason Baird Jackson quoted in Liz Leslie, "Mathers Museum Celebrates 50th Anniversary," *Bloomington Herald-Times*, October 27, 2013.

The Fine Arts

Fine Arts Building

Epigraph is from Elvis J. Stahr Jr., Fine Arts Building dedication, October 21, 1962, collection C48, Indiana University Archives, Indiana University, Bloomington.

1. Henry R. Hope to Herman B Wells, March 13, 1962, Fine Arts Building folder 1959–62, collection C213, Indiana University Archives, Indiana University, Bloomington.

2. Henry R. Hope, "Statement Concerning Needs for Fine Arts Center," Post-War Building Program 1944–45 folder, collection C213, Indiana University Archives, Indiana University, Bloomington.

3. Henry R. Hope, "The Indiana University Art Museum," *Art Journal* 30, no. 2 (winter 1970–71): 170.

4. Theodore J. Young from Eggers and Higgins to Joseph A. Franklin, March 13, 1958, Fine Arts Reference Files,Indiana University Archives, Indiana University, Bloomington.

5. Henry Radford Hope School of Fine Arts Naming Ceremony remarks, April 28, 1990, President Thomas Ehrlich speeches, collection C64, Indiana University Archives, Indiana University, Bloomington.

Sidney and Lois Eskenazi Museum of Art

Epigraph is from I. M. Pei, quoted in Andy Graham, "Building of Art: IU Art Museum Celebrates 25 Years in Its I. M. Pei–Designed Structure," Herald Times Online, June 10, 2007.

1. I. M. Pei, quoted in Russell C. Tornabene, "A New Home for the Arts," *Indiana Alumni*, March 1981.

2. Pei, quoted in Graham, "Building of Art."

Lee Norvelle Theatre and Drama Center

Epigraph is from Daniel O. Kelley, dedication speech for the Neal-Marshall Black Culture Center and Theatre and Drama Center, January 18, 2002, University Ceremonies event files, accession 2007/154, Indiana University Archives, Indiana University, Bloomington.

1. Lee Norvelle, *The Road Taken* (n.p.: Indiana University Foundation, 1980).

2. Report of a Team Appointed by the National Association of Schools of Theatre to Evaluate the Program in Theatre at Indiana University, April 1989, collection C177, Office of State Relations Assistant Director's records, Indiana University Archives, Indiana University, Bloomington.

3. Renovation and New Construction for an Arts Complex Housing the Theatre and Drama Center and the Neal-Marshall Black Culture Center, October 4, 1989, Neal-Marshall Black Culture Center 1989 folder, collection C234, Indiana University Archives, Indiana University, Bloomington.

4. MGA Partners Architects, Theater and Drama Center/Neal Marshall Center Project Description, n.d., "Theater and Drama Center Reference" file, Indiana University Archives, Indiana University, Bloomington.

5. Leon I. Brauner, Neal-Marshall Black Culture Center—Theatre and Drama Center Dedication Ceremony program, January 18, 2002, University Ceremonies, accession 2008/001, Indiana University Archives, Indiana University, Bloomington.

Neal-Marshall Black Culture Center

Epigraph is from Herman B Wells, "Remarks on Layman Sunday at the First Methodist Church: The Church at Its Best," March 5, 1944, Herman B Wells Presidential speeches, collection C137, Indiana University Archives, Indiana University, Bloomington.

1. Faculty Council Circular 55—Consolidation of Afro-American Programs, ca. January 21, 1969, Faculty Council records, collection C181, Indiana University Archives, Indiana University, Bloomington.

2. Herman Hudson to Herman B Wells, May 9, 1972, Black Culture Center file, collection C459, Indiana University Archives, Indiana University, Bloomington.

3. Black Culture Center Annual Report, 1979–80, collection C176, Indiana University Archives, Indiana University, Bloomington.

4. Board of Trustees minutes, June 2, 1984.

5. "New Black Culture Center closer to realization," *Neal-Marshall Alumni Club Newsletter* 12, no. 2 (summer 1994).

6. Myles Brand, "Diversity at IU: A Vision Realized," Remarks at the Dedication of the Marcellus Neal and Frances Marshall Black Culture and Theatre and Drama Center, January 18, 2002, Neal Marshall Archives reference file, Indiana University Archives, Indiana University, Bloomington.

Indiana University Cinema

Epigraph is from President Michael McRobbie, "The Difference the Big Screen Makes: The Dedication of the IU Cinema," Office of the President, January 27, 2011, https://archive.president.iu.edu/speeches/archive/2011/20110127-02.shtml (accessed September 12, 2014).

1. "Union Is Ready for Series and 'Movies,'" *Indiana Daily Student*, October 28, 1914.

2. "Union Movie Show First of Its Kind," *Indiana Daily Student*, December 1, 1914.

3. "The Straight Road: Union Movie Show Has Powerful Photoplay for Tonight," *Indiana Daily Student*, March 5, 1915.

4. Board of Trustees minutes, September 19, 1997, http://purl.dlib.indiana.edu/iudl/archives/iubot/1997-09-19 (accessed September 12, 2014).

5. "Building on a Glorious IU Tradition: Breaking New Ground in the Arts and Humanities," President Michael McRobbie, IU Cinema Groundbreaking/Theatre and Drama Building Renovation, October 17, 2009, http://pres.iu.edu/speeches/2009/20091017-01.shtml (accessed April 2, 2013).

6. "Grand Opening of IU Cinema Scheduled for January 2011," press release, *IU News Room*, September 14, 2010, http://newsinfo.iu.edu/news-archive/15336.html (accessed September 14, 2010). According to the official THX site, "The goal of THX cinema certification is to reproduce the acoustics and ambience of the movie studio, allowing audiences to enjoy a movie's sound effects, score, dialogue and visual presentation with the clarity and detail of the final mastering session." It provides "standards for acoustic performance, background noise, sound isolation, and image quality." http://www.thx.com/professional/cinema-certification/thx-certified-cinemas/ (accessed September 17, 2014).

THE PROFESSIONS

William A. Rawles Hall

Epigraph is from Charles A. Lippincott of the Studebaker Corporation, quoted in "Dedication of Commerce Hall," *Indiana University Alumni Quarterly* 10, no. 3 (July 1923): 484.

1. William A. Rawles to the Indiana University President and the Board of Trustees, October 8, 1920, "Rawles, William A., 1914–1922" file, collection C286.217, Indiana University Archives, Indiana University, Bloomington.

2. "Will Start Work on Commerce Building Early Next Month," *Indiana Daily Student*, April 12, 1922.

3. Harry L. Onstott, "Commerce Building Contains Auditorium that Seats 350, 22 Lecture Rooms, Offices," *Indiana Daily Student*, January 17, 1923.

Ernie Pyle Hall

Epigraph is from "The Right to Knowledge," An Address by J. R. Wiggins at the Dedication of Ernie Pyle Hall, October 10, 1954, Ernie Pyle Hall dedication folder, collection C213, Indiana University Archives, Indiana University, Bloomington. Wiggins was the managing editor of the *Washington Post* and *Times Herald*.

1. "Salutatory," *Indiana Student*, February 22, 1867.

2. "'The Shack' Still Lives in Our Hearts," *Indiana Daily Student*, October 9, 1954.

3. Marjorie (Smith) Blewett, "Reminisce with Marge: Ernie Pyle Hall—The Fanciest Tool Shed in the Big Ten," *Newswire* 39, no. 1 (spring/summer 2014): 41.

4. Indiana University News Bureau Release, September 16, 1954, "Ernie Pyle Dedication" folder, President's Office records, collection C213, Indiana University Archives, Indiana University, Bloomington.

5. "War Correspondent Returning to His Alma Mater to Receive Honorary Degree, Revisits Scenes of His Newspaper Beginnings," *Publisher*, November 25, 1944.

James Albert Woodburn Hall

Epigraph is from "The President's Report for 1937–1942," *Indiana University Bulletin* 16, no. 10 (May 31, 1943): 44.

1. Dean Burton D. Myers to Herman B Wells, May 17, 1938, "Buildings 1938–1939" folder, President's Office records, collection C213, Indiana University Archives, Indiana University, Bloomington. Herman B Wells to Public Works Administration, July 20, 1938, "Addition to Physical Plant 1937–1938" folder, ibid.

2. D. R. Kennicott to W. G. Biddle, July 26, 1938, "PWA Telegram" folder, ibid.

3. A. M. Strauss to Eggers and Higgins, September 17, 1938, "Strauss 1938–1939" folder, ibid.

4. Thomas Clark, *Indiana University Midwestern Pioneer*, vol. 3, *Years of Fulfillment* (Bloomington: Indiana University Press, 1977), 175.

5. "Plans for New Gothic Building Announced: Work Already Started on Modern University Limestone Structure," *Indiana Daily Student*, December 9, 1938.

6. A. M. Strauss to Dean Barker, February 14, 1939, "Strauss 1938–1939" folder.

7. Plaque at Woodburn Hall.

Lowell E. Baier Hall

Epigraph is from "Dedication Convocation of School of Law Building," November 2, 1937, Herman B Wells speeches, collection C137, Indiana University Archives, Indiana University, Bloomington.

1. Ibid.

2. Robert G. Miller, "Indiana University School of Law: Notes and material gathered for the preparation of a history of the Law School of Indiana University," unpublished manuscript, August 1950, typescript, "Law School History-Book by Robert G. Miller" reference file, Indiana University Archives, Indiana University, Bloomington.

3. Indiana University Board of Trustees minutes, 20 March 1889, collection C218, Indiana University Archives, Indiana University, Bloomington.

4. J. Terry Clapacs quoted in "IU Will Save the Woods—and Build Law Library Addition," *Indiana University Alumni Magazine*, May/June 1982, 14.

5. "Indiana University Maurer School of Law Announces $20 Million Gift," press release, *IU Newsroom*, March 25, 2015, http://news.iu.edu/releases/iu/2015/03/baier-law-naming-gift.shtml (accessed May 6, 2016).

Radio and Television Building

"Department of Radio and Television Expected to Expand in All Directions," Indiana Daily Student, December 16, 1961.

1. "Opera by Wireless Entertains I.U. Audience for the First Time," *Indiana Daily Student*, January 6, 1922.

2. Post-War Planning Committee, Report of Graduate School and College of Arts and Sciences, 1946, collection C213, Indiana University Archives, Indiana University, Bloomington.

3. Elmer Sulzer quoted in "Department of Radio and Television Expected to Expand in All Directions," *Indiana Daily Student*, December 16, 1961.

4. Ray Casati quoted in Marijke Rowland, "Radio and TV Building Will Be Expanded," *Indiana Daily Student*, June 26, 1995.

Hodge Hall Undergraduate Center / William Godfrey Graduate and Executive Education Center

Epigraph is from Remarks of Elvis J. Stahr, Dedication of the School of Business Building, November 18, 1966, Speeches of President Elvis J. Stahr, collection C48.4, Indiana University Archives, Indiana University, Bloomington.

1. Ibid.

2. 2015 Indiana Design Awards, AIA Indiana (Indiana Chapter of the American Institute of Architects), http://aiaindiana.org/member-services/awards/2015-aia-indiana-design-awards (accessed September 6, 2016).

School of Public and Environmental Affairs (SPEA)

Epigraph is from Thomas D. Clark, *Indiana University, Midwestern Pioneer*, vol. 3, *Years of Fulfillment* (Bloomington: Indiana University Press, 1977), 195.

1. Dedication Ceremony, School of Business/SPEA building, October 7, 1982, President John W. Ryan speeches, collection C45, Indiana University Archives, Indiana University, Bloomington.

Wendell W. Wright Education Building

Epigraph is from dedication remarks by Howard Mehlinger, March 26, 1993, "New Building Dedication" folder, School of Education, Office of Communications and Public Relations records, accession 2011/127, Indiana University Archives, Indiana University, Bloomington.

1. "The Center for Excellence in Education, Indiana University: A Prospectus," September 1983, "School of Education, 1967–89" folder, Chancellor's Office records, accession 2006/010, Indiana University Archives, Indiana University, Bloomington.

2. Howard Mehlinger, ground-breaking remarks, June 15, 1989, reprinted in *Chalkboard: Indiana University School of Education Alumni Association* (fall/winter 1989): 2.

3. *American School and University Architectural Profile*, November 1989.

4. "Partnership with AT&T to Benefit Center for Excellence," *Chalkboard: Indiana University School of Education Alumni Association* (winter 1987).

Global and International Studies Building

Epigraph is from Dean Lee Feinstein, Global and International Studies Building dedication speech, October 14, 2015, copy of speech provided to the author by Lee Feinstein.

1. Julie Masterson, "IU Has Dedication Ceremony for New Global [and] International Studies Building," *Indiana Daily Student*, October 14, 2015.

2. Susan T. Rodriguez, speech at the GISB dedication, October 14, 2015, copy of the speech provided to the author by Susan Rodriquez.

3. Ibid.

Luddy Hall

The epigraph is by Bobby Schnabel, dean of the IU School of Informatics and Computing, quoted in "IU School of Informatics and Computing Breaks Ground on New Building, Announces $8 Million Gift," press release, *IU Bloomington Newsroom*, October 2, 2015, http://news.indiana

.edu/releases/iu/2015/10/luddy-groundbreaking.shtml (accessed May 6, 2016).

1. "IU Trustees Approve Merger of Schools of Informatics, Library Science," press release, *IU News Room*, October 12, 2012, http://newsinfo.iu.edu/news-archive/23284.html (accessed September 6, 2016).

2. Jim Shea and Bill Butler, "Building the Future," *Innovations* 12, no. 1 (summer 2015): 10–13.

3. "IU School of Informatics and Computing Breaks Ground on New Building." Fred Luddy quoted in "Fred Luddy: Naming Donor," Alumni & Giving, School of Informatics and Computing, IU Bloomington, n.d., http://www.soic.indiana.edu/alumni-giving/luddy-hall/Fred-Luddy-Bio.html (accessed September 14, 2016).

THE SCIENCES

Chemistry Building

Epigraph is from Theodore Roosevelt's 1918 commencement speech in the outdoor amphitheater where the Chemistry Building would later be sited, http://theodore-roosevelt.com/images/research/txtspeeches/889.pdf.

Burton Dorr Myers Hall

Epigraph is from "Remarks at Dedication of the School of Medicine Building, November 21, 1937," President Herman B Wells speeches, collection C137, Indiana University Archives, Indiana University, Bloomington.

1. Burton D. Myers to William Lowe Bryan, April 15, 1926, "Myers, B. D., 1924–1926," collection C286.188, Indiana University Archives, Indiana University, Bloomington.

2. A. M. Strauss to Olmsted Brothers, February 24, 1936, "Strauss, A. M., 1935–1936," collection C286.257, Indiana University Archives, Indiana University, Bloomington.

3. Myers Hall Rededication Ceremony script, University Ceremonies, Accession 2007/154, Indiana University Archives.

Swain Hall West

Epigraph is from Thomas D. Clark, *Indiana University: Midwestern Pioneer*, vol. 3, *Years of Fulfillment* (Bloomington: Indiana University Press, 1977), 172.

1. Allan C. G. Mitchell to Herman B. Wells, February 15, 1938, "Mitchell" folder, collection C213, Indiana University Archives, Indiana University, Bloomington.

2. Indiana University Board of Trustees minutes, May 18-21, 1957, http://purl.dlib.indiana.edu/iudl/archives/iubot/1957-05-18.

3. "Swain Hall to Honor I.U.'s Ninth President," *Indiana Daily Student*, August 1, 1939.

4. Allan C. G. Mitchell to Herman B Wells, August 23, 1945, President's Office records, "Mitchell 1945–46" folder, collection C213, Indiana University Archives, Indiana University, Bloomington.

5. "Building Program to End Next Semester: Five Years Work on 13 Structures Nears Completion," *Indiana Daily Student*, June 3, 1940.

6. "Huge New Cyclotron Turned on at I.U.: Job Is to Disintegrate Atom's Nucleus," *Indianapolis Star*, April 15, 1941.

7. The Manhattan Project refers to the U.S.-led research and development of the first atomic bombs during World War II (1942–45). During the fall of 1942, a team of scientists from the University of Chicago traveled to Bloomington to use IU's cyclotron, as it was superior to the one in Chicago. Just a few months later, scientists succeeded in creating the first chain reaction in uranium, which led to the development of the atomic bomb.

8. Notes for Remarks on the Occasion of the V-J Day Celebration—City Park, August 15, 1945, Herman B Wells Speeches, Indiana University Archives, Indiana University, Bloomington.

Jordan Hall

Epigraph is from "Biology at Indiana University," speech delivered by Fernandus Payne at the dedication dinner for Jordan Hall, June 8, 1956, Fernandus Payne papers, collection C188, Indiana University Archives, Indiana University, Bloomington.

1. "Dedication of Biology Hall," June 8, 1956,collection C137, Herman B Wells President's speeches, Indiana University Archives, Indiana University, Bloomington.

2. Theodore J. Young, "Life Science Building, Indiana University," *American School and University*, 1948–49.

3. Ibid.

4. "Dedication of Jordan Hall," IU News Bureau, June 8, 1956.

5. Indiana University Construction Planning Report, September 1959, collection C213, President's Office records, Indiana University Archives, Indiana University, Bloomington.

6. "Jordan Hall Addition: An Ingeniously Well-Made Puzzle Piece," *Arts & Sciences* 8, no. 1 (fall 1984).

Geology Building

Epigraph is John B. Patton quoted in "Geology Building Dedicated," *Indiana Alumni Magazine*, June–July 1964, 27.

1. "Request for Changes in Geology Building Construction, Indiana University Board of Trustees minutes, July 15, 1960," http://purl.dlib.indiana.edu/iudl/archives/iubot/1960-07-15 (accessed April 14, 2017).

2. Richard K. Leininger quoted in "New Geology Building Will House All Units," *Indiana Daily Student*, December 1, 1961.

Psychology Building

Epigraph is from IU Bloomington chancellor Sharon Stephens Brehm at Psychology Building Addition dedication, March 26, 2003, "Psychology Building Dedication Ceremony script," accession 2008/001 (unprocessed collection), Indiana University Archives, Indiana University, Bloomington.

1. Roger W. Russell to Lynne L. Merritt Jr., undated memo (circa 1965), "Department of Psychology, 1962–1963" file, collection C304.131, Indiana University Archives, Indiana University, Bloomington.

2. James H. Capshew, *The Legacy of the Laboratory: Psychological and Brain Sciences at Indiana University, 1888–2013* (Bloomington: IU Department of Psychological and Brain Sciences, 2014), 110.

3. "Unveiling of IU PBS Brain Sculpture," YouTube Video, 16:23, posted by IUB Psychological & Brain Sciences, February 17, 2014, https://www.youtube.com/watch?v=lZfhKxZn7WQ.

Simon Hall

Epigraph is from Provost Karen Hanson, quoted in "Simon Opens, and IU Bloomington Celebrates the Wonders of Science," press release, *IU News Room*, October 15, 2007, http://newsinfo.iu.edu/news/page/normal/6561.html (accessed November 24, 2015).

Multidisciplinary Science Building II

Epigraph is from President Michael McRobbie's speech at the MSBII dedication, October 22, 2009, quoted in "The Unfolding of Great Possibility: Dedicating a New Space for Science at Indiana University," Office of the President, https://archive.president.iu.edu/speeches/archive/2009/20091022–01.shtml (accessed April 14, 2017).

1. David Black, quoted in Alyson Brodsy, "New structures planned to fit with campus style," *Indiana Daily Student*, January 31,2005. http://www.idsnews.com/article/2005/01/new-structures-planned-to-fit-with-campus-style (accessed June 5, 2017).

2. Ibid.

3. Blackburn Architects Inc., "Multidisciplinary Science Building: Phase II, Indiana University," Facebook page, https://www.facebook.com (accessed December 7, 2015).

STUDENT HOUSING

Alpha Hall

Epigraph is from oral history interview with Mrs. Stuart Wilson by Barbara E. Benson and D. Scott Peterson, June 12, 1971, accession 2000/054.36, Indiana University Archives, Indiana University, Bloomington.

1. Louden memoir, 1954, "Alpha Hall" reference file, Indiana University Archives, Indiana University, Bloomington.

2. "Report of Sanitary Survey of Girls Dormitory at Indiana University, Bloomington, Indiana," 1912, "Alpha Hall" reference file, Indiana University Archives, Indiana University, Bloomington.

3. "Oral History Interview with Mrs. Alice Nelson by Thomas D. Clark," April 28, 1969, call number 69–004, Indiana University Center for the Study of History and Memory.

4. "Dean Wells' Specifications for the Repairs on Alpha Hall," circa 1919, accession 0463.1, "Papers concerning reconditioning Alpha Hall for leasing to Univ. for Girls Dormitory" file, collection 0463.1, Indiana University Archives, Indiana University, Bloomington.

5. Bond resolution and receipt, "Forest Realty Bonds, 1936–1943," collection C255, Indiana University Archives, Indiana University, Bloomington.

Ralph L. Collins Living-Learning Center

Epigraph is from Patricia Montgomery, IU parent, to IU Board of Trustees re 1971 threat to close MRC, April 30, 1971, quoted in Tate Holt, "Don't Just Think About It: Do It," Collins Living-Learning Center reference file, Indiana University Archives, Indiana University, Bloomington.

1. Petition to IU Board of Trustees Executive Committee, April 18, 1925, "South Hall" file, collection C286.246, Indiana University Archives, Indiana University, Bloomington.

2. Alice McDonald to William Lowe Bryan, September 25, 1924, "McDonald, Alice, 1920–1926," collection C286.173, Indiana University Archives, Indiana University, Bloomington.

3. Halls of Residence Committee minutes, March 19, 1970, collection C310.2, Indiana University Archives, Indiana University, Bloomington.

4. Notes from phone call with E. James, September 29, 1938, "Burns & James, 1938–1939" file, collection C213.101, Indiana University Archives, Indiana University, Bloomington.

5. Nolan Eller, "United States Naval Training School and the U.S.S. Indiana University," *Blogging Hoosier History* (blog), January 7, 2013, Indiana University Archives, https://blogs.libraries.iub.edu/iubarchives/2013/01/07/uss-iu/.

Agnes E. Wells Quadrangle

Epigraph is from Charlotte Lowe Bryan at Memorial Hall cornerstone laying ceremony, quoted in "Corner Stone Ceremonies for Memorial Buildings," *Indiana University News-Letter* 13, no. 2 (February 1925): 9.

1. "E. A. Carson to U. H. Smith," September 19, 1924, "Carson, E.A. Company, 1924–1926" file, collection C286.50, Indiana University Archives, Indiana University, Bloomington.

2. Dean of Women Agnes E. Wells quoted in "Corner Stone Ceremonies for Memorial Building," 10.

3. Lowe & Bollenbacher to William Lowe Bryan, "Lowe and Bollenbacher, January–June 1923" file, collection C286.164, Indiana University Archives, Indiana University, Bloomington.

4. "Morrison Hall," *Indiana Alumni Magazine*, June 1942, 26.

5. Notes from telephone call with Burns and James, September 29, 1938, "Burns & James, 1938–1939" file, collection C213.101, Indiana University Archives, Indiana University, Bloomington.

6. Kate H. Mueller, "New Dormitories to Be Decorated in Varied Styles," *Indiana Daily Student*, December 8, 1939.

7. Janie Renn, "Memorial Hall Shows Signs of Old Age," *Indiana Daily Student*, March 15, 1977.

Post–World War II Housing

Epigraph is from Men's Residence Center Association, *Corridor* 6, no. 1 (October 10, 1946).

1. James H. Capshew, *Herman B Wells: The Promise of the American University* (Bloomington: Indiana University Press and Indianapolis: Indiana Historical Society Press, 2012), 181–84.

2. Suzanne Mettler, "How the G.I. Bill Built the Middle Class and Enhanced Democracy," Scholars Strategy Network, January 2012, www.scholars strategynetwork.org (accessed November 11, 2013).

3. "The GI Bill's History: Born of Controversy: The GI Bill of Rights," U.S. Department of Veterans Affairs, http://web.archive.org/web/20131114015716/http://www.gibill.va.gov/Benefits/history_timeline/index.html (accessed April 18, 2015).

4. "Facts Concerning the Expansion of Dormitory Facilities on the Campus of Indiana University at Bloomington," July 1946, prepared by the Office of the Treasurer Indiana University, "Financing of Dormitory Facilities, 1946–1947" file, collection C213.278, Indiana University Archives, Indiana University, Bloomington.

5. Men's Residence Center Association.

6. "Agreement to Furnish Temporary Housing for Students and Faculty of Indiana University at McCormick's Creek State Park," contract, "Temporary Housing—Canyon Inn, 1946" file, collection C178.6, Indiana University Archives, Indiana University, Bloomington.

7. Halls of Residence Report, 1946–1947, "Halls, Housing Reports and Correspondence, 1947–1948" file, collection C178.7, Indiana University Archives, Indiana University, Bloomington.

8. Hoosier Courts Scrapbook website, http://hoosiercourts.com/ (accessed November 11, 2013; defunct site).

9. "Housing, Nelson, 1946–1947" file, collection C178.6, Indiana University Archives, Indiana University, Bloomington.

10. Clarence Arbuckle to Ed James, April 8, 1948, "Smithwood Alterations, 1947–1948" file, collection C178.7, Indiana University Archives, Indiana University, Bloomington.

11. "Facts Concerning the Expansion of Dormitory Facilities on the Campus of Indiana University at Bloomington," prepared by the Office of the Treasurer, Indiana University, July 1946, "Financing of Dormitory Facilities, 1946–1947," file, collection C213.27, Indiana University Archives, Indiana University, Bloomington.

12. Oscar O. Winther to Herman B Wells, May 20, 1946, "Housing for Faculty, 1945–1946" file, collection C213.277, Indiana University Archives, Indiana University, Bloomington. B. F. Skinner to Herman B Wells, January 26, 1946, ibid.

Joseph A. Wright Quadrangle

Epigraph is from Herman B Wells, *At Home at Indiana* housing brochure, circa 1948, "Buildings–Bloomington–Wright Quad" reference file, Indiana University Archives, Indiana University, Bloomington.

1. "Conference on Building Problems of Urban Universities, Hotel Cleveland, Cleveland, Ohio, May 19–20, 1947. Brief notes on the principal topics of discussion," "Eggers and Higgins, 1946–1947" file, collection C213.179, Indiana University Archives, Indiana University, Bloomington.

2. Alice Nelson to Edward D. James, March 29, 1949, "Halls of Residence—New Men's Dorms, 1948–1949" file, collection C178.9, Indiana University Archives, Indiana University, Bloomington.

Daniel Read Hall

Epigraph is from oral history interview with Barbara Gordon Grande, June 18, 2010, for Indiana University Bicentennial Oral History Project, page 3. IU Archives Accession 2013/031.

Nellie S. Teter Quadrangle

Epigraph is from Nellie S. Teter in a note to Herman Wells (November 11, 1941?), "Teter, Nellie S., 1941–1942" folder, Indiana University President's Office records, collection C213, Indiana University Archives, Indiana University, Bloomington.

Married Student Housing

Epigraph is from Peggy Fletcher Stack, "Marriage: What's Love Got to Do with It?," *Salt Lake Tribune*, February 12, 2014.

1. *Vital Statistics of the United States 1961*, vol. 1, *Natality* ([Washington, DC]: U.S. Department of Health, Education, and Welfare, 1961), 1–18.

2. Indiana University Board of Trustees minutes, November 2–3, 1945, http://purl.dlib.indiana.edu/iudl/archives/iubot/1945-11-02 (accessed March 3, 2014).

3. "Apartment Open House Comments Turned In on Cards," "Halls, Row Housing, 1950–1951," collection C178.11, Indiana University Archives, Indiana University, Bloomington.

4. "Survey of Comments and Criticism on Livability of Hoosier Courts Expansion," circa 1951, "Hall, Survey of Livability of Row Housing, 1951" file, collection C178.12, Indiana University Archives, Indiana University, Bloomington.

5. "Tenants Move into New Hoosier Court Apartments," *Indiana Daily Student*, July 6, 1955.

Fee Lane Dormitories

Epigraph is from Thomas A Gaines, *The Campus as a Work of Art* (Westport, CT: Praeger, 1991), 135.

1. Indiana University Foster Quad Student Government records, 1961–2004, bulk 1986–1992, prepared by Elia Van Lith, Indiana University Archives, Indiana University, Bloomington.

Wendell L. Willkie Residence Center

Epigraph is from Wendell L. Willkie, "Why I Believe in America," *North American Review* 248, no. 2 (winter 1939–40).

Forest Quadrangle

Epigraph is from Thomas D. Clark, *Indiana University Midwestern Pioneer*, vol. 3, *Years of Fulfillment* (Bloomington: Indiana University Press, 1977), 195.

1. Megan Warmouth, "The Restaurants at Woodland, Indiana University, Bloomington," February 7, 2014, http://www.foodservicedirector.com/ideas-innovation/design-portfolio/snapshot/restaurants-woodland-indiana-university-bloomington (accessed November 16, 2015).

Eigenmann Hall

Epigraph is from John W. Ryan, "The Investiture of John W. Ryan as Fourteenth President of Indiana University, January 20, 1972," President John W. Ryan speeches, collection C45, Indiana University Archives, Indiana University, Bloomington.

Union Street Center

Epigraph is from Moya Andrews, "The Campus in Spring," *Bloom*, April/May 2009, 80.

1. "Student Life: Design for the 21st Century Student Experience," Ratio Architects, http://www.ratiodesign.com/student-life-0 (accessed September 3, 2015).

Spruce Hall

Epigraph is from Paul Weatherwax, *The Woodland Campus of Indiana University* (Bloomington: Indiana University Foundation, 1974), n. p.

1. Mackey Mitchell Architects, http://www.mackeymitchell.com/projects/rose-avenue-residence-hall/ (accessed August 14, 2015).

COMMON FACILITIES

Wylie House Museum

Epigraph is from agreement regarding the building of a house between Andrew Wylie and George L. Troop and John McDonald, January 26, 1835, Andrew Wylie papers, collection C1, Indiana University Archives, Indiana University, Bloomington.

1. Carrol Krause, "Life in 1800s Bloomington: Wylie House," *Houses and Books Blog*, October 16, 2011, http://housesandbooks.wordpress.com/2011/10/16/life-in-1800s-bloomington-wylie-house/ (accessed October 24, 2013).
2. Theophilus A. Wylie diaries, Theophilus A. Wylie papers, collection C202, Indiana University Archives, Indiana University, Bloomington.
3. Rebecca Wylie (Bloomington, IN) to Miss Lou Wylie (Care of Professor Ballantine, Walnut Hills, near Cincinnati, OH), July 25, 1867; T. A. Wylie (Bloomington, IN) to Miss E. L. M. Wylie (Princeton, IN), August 16, 1867; and Mary O. Ballantine (Marion, IN) to Miss Louise E. Wylie (Bloomington, IN), September 1867. All in Theophilus Wylie Family Correspondence collection, Wylie House Museum, Indiana University Libraries, Bloomington, IN.

William and Charlotte Lowe Bryan House

Epigraph is from "Dedication Ceremony Program," April 11, 1925, cited in Bryan House brochure, ca. 1990, Bryan House Reference File, Indiana University Archives, Indiana University, Bloomington.

1. "President's Residence Is Planned for Campus: Building to Be Erected on East Side of Campus by Dr. Bryan," *Indiana Daily Student*, September 22, 1915, 1.
2. Indianapolis architect Edward D. James, who supervised the 1957 renovation, recalled being in the office of architect Robert F. Daggett when the Bryans came in with a photograph of the townhouse of Woodrow Wilson. News Bureau Press Release September 1957, President's House Reference file, Indiana University Archives, Indiana University, Bloomington.
3. William Lowe Bryan quoted in Carolyn Lucas and Mary O'Connor, "Dr. William Lowe Bryan's House Reflects Long Work of Wife," *Indiana Daily Student*, April 25, 1950, 1.

Indiana Memorial Union / Ward G. Biddle Hotel and Conference Center

Epigraph is from Herman B Wells, "Indiana Memorial Union Building Dedication," President Herman B Wells speeches, collection C137, Indiana University Archives, Indiana University, Bloomington.

1. "Final Chapter of University 'Golden Book' Being Written Today; Sacred Tome Will Honor I.U. War Heroes, Donors for Memorial Buildings," *Indiana Daily Student*, June 13, 1932.

William Lowe Bryan Hall

Epigraph is from address of President W. L. Bryan, June 15, 1936, Exercises for the New Administration Building, June 15, 1936, President William Lowe Bryan speeches, collection C71, Indiana University Archives, Indiana University, Bloomington.

1. William Lowe Bryan to J. C. Bollenbacher, February 5, 1935, President's Office Records, collection C286, Indiana University Archives, Indiana University, Bloomington.
2. "Romantic Lovers Lane at Indiana U. Is Threatened by Building Program," *Indianapolis Times*, March 12, 1935. William Lowe Bryan to Judge Ora Wildermuth, February 7, 1935, President's Office Records, collection C286, Indiana University Archives, Indiana University, Bloomington. Board of Trustees minutes, March 4, 1935, http://purl.dlib.indiana.edu/iudl/archives/iubot/1935-03-04 (accessed April 17, 2017). Alfred Kinsey to President W. L. Bryan, April 4, 1935, President's Office Records, collection C286, Indiana University Archives, Indiana University, Bloomington. Albert S. Kuntz to President W. L. Bryan, April 4, 1935, ibid.
3. President William Lowe Bryan to Granger and Bollenbacher, December 24, 1938, President's Office Records, collection C286, Indiana University Archives, Indiana University, Bloomington.

Indiana University Auditorium

Epigraph is from William Lowe Bryan, quoted in "Auditorium Praised," *Indiana Daily Student*, March 22, 1941, 1.

1. "Remarks at the Dedication of the Music Auditorium," March 22, 1941, Herman B Wells President's speeches, collection C137, Indiana University Archives, Indiana University, Bloomington. Quoted in James H. Capshew, "The Campus as a Pedagogical Agent: Herman B Wells, Cultural Entrepreneurship, and the Benton Murals," *Indiana Magazine of History* 105, no. 2 (June 2009): 196.
2. "Indiana University Auditorium Organ," Indiana University Auditorium, http://www.iuauditorium.com/about-us/indiana-university-auditorium-organ (accessed March 26, 2014).

Beck Chapel

Epigraph is from Frank Beck, "The Indiana University Chapel: It's [*sic*] Location," Chapel Paper 2, ca. 1954, Frank O. and Daisy Beck papers, collection C168, Indiana University Archives, Indiana University, Bloomington.

1. *Indiana University Catalogue*, 1830–1831, 3, Indiana University Archives, Indiana University, Bloomington.

2. Frank Beck, "The Indiana University Chapel: It's [*sic*] Purpose," Chapel Paper 4, ca. 1957, Frank O. and Daisy Beck papers.

3. Report to the Beck Chapel Committee from Polly LaRoche, April 13, 1988, accession 2006/010, Indiana University Chancellor's Records, Indiana University Archives, Indiana University, Bloomington.

Lilly Library

Epigraph is from Herman B Wells, dedication convocation of the Lilly Library, October 3, 1960, President Herman B Wells speeches, collection C137, Indiana University Archives, Indiana University, Bloomington.

1. Thomas D. Clark, *Indiana University: Midwestern Pioneer*, vol. 3, *Years of Fulfillment* (Bloomington: Indiana University Press, 1977), 515. "Gift of Rare Book Collection," Board of Trustees minutes, December 4, 1954, http://purl.dlib.indiana.edu/iudl/archives/iubot/1954-12-04 (accessed April 14, 2017). Report on the Libraries of Indiana University, July 1955–June 1956, President's Office Records, collection C213, Indiana University Archives, Indiana University, Bloomington.

2. Herman B Wells, *Being Lucky: Reminiscences and Reflections* (Bloomington: Indiana University Press, 1980), 200.

3. Frederick B. Adams Jr., "Dedication Address—Lilly Library." *Antiquarian Bookman: The Specialist Book Trade Weekly*, October 24, 1960, 1427.

4. Herman B Wells, dedication convocation.

5. Thomas D. Clark, *Indiana University: Midwestern Pioneer*, vol. 3, *Years of Fulfillment* (Bloomington: Indiana University Press, 1977), 524.

Virgil T. DeVault Alumni Center

Epigraph is from President Myles Brand's dedication ceremony remarks, June 14, 1997, President Myles Brand speeches, collection C263, Indiana University Archives, Indiana University, Bloomington.

1. Report to the Board of Trustees—Administrative Service Building: Need for Space, ca. July 1961, Board of Trustees working papers, July 14, 1961, meeting folder, collection C44, Indiana University Archives, Indiana University, Bloomington.

2. Letter from Joseph A. Franklin to President Wells, July 11, 1961, ibid. Letter from Joseph A. Franklin to President Wells, July 6, 1961, ibid.

3. Anne Kibbler, "A Home for Indiana Alumni," *Indiana Alumni Magazine*, November/December 1991, 36.

4. Wayne S. Schmidt quoted in DeVault Alumni Center Naming Ceremony program, June 14, 1997, DeVault Alumni Center reference file, Indiana University Archives, Indiana University, Bloomington. J. Terry Clapacs quoted in "IU Alumni Association to Get New Home," *Indiana Daily Student*, December 5, 1994, 2.

Herman B Wells Library

Epigraph is from Report of the Section Committee on the University Library, January 25, 1968, collection C181, Indiana University Archives, Indiana University, Bloomington.

1. Board of Trustees minutes, June 9, 1950, http://purl.dlib.indiana.edu/iudl/archives/iubot/1950-06-09 (accessed April 18, 2017).

2. Robert F. Byrnes quoted in Thomas Clark, *Indiana University: Midwestern Pioneer*, vol. 3, *Years of Fulfillment* (Bloomington: Indiana University Press, 1977), 194.

3. Library Review and Planning Committee Interim Report, February 1962, Faculty Council records, collection C286, Indiana University Archives, Indiana University, Bloomington.

4. Library Review and Planning Committee Interim Report II, November 1962, Faculty Council records, collection C181, Indiana University Archives, Indiana University, Bloomington.

5. Thomas A. Gaines, *The Campus as a Work of Art*, 1st ed. (Westport, CT: Praeger, 1991), 101.

6. Gordon N. Ray, "Indiana University Dedication Address," Papers Delivered at the Indiana University Library Dedication, October 9–10, 1970, 9, "Committee on Dedications—Library Dedication" folder, Indiana University President's Office records, collection C268, Indiana University Archives, Indiana University, Bloomington.

Showalter House

Epigraph is from "Indiana University Foundation," *Indiana University Alumni Quarterly*, fall 1937, 504.

1. Herman B Wells, *Being Lucky: Reminiscences and Reflections* (Bloomington: Indiana University Press, 1980), 165–66.

2. Curt Simic quoted in "IU Foundation to Rededicate Its Home Friday," press release, Office of Communications and Marketing, Indiana University, October 18, 2000, https://web.archive.org/web/20110311113819/http://newsinfo.iu.edu/OCM/releases/showhouse.htm (accessed April 18, 2017). Holly Johnson, "Ceremony Honors IU Foundation," *Indiana Daily Student*, October 23, 2000.

3. Showalter House Re-dedication Ceremony, October 20, 2000, University Ceremony records, collection C222, Indiana University Archives, Indiana University, Bloomington.

Student Recreational Sports Center

Epigraph is from Myles Brand, SRSC dedication speech, September 15, 1995, President Myles Brand speeches, collection C286, Indiana University Archives, Indiana University, Bloomington.

Edward L. Hutton Honors College

Epigraph is from Caitlin Daley, IU honors student, quoted in "IU Hutton Honors College April Dedication a 'Celebration of Life' for Ed Hutton," Indiana University, press release, March 24, 2009.

1. "About the Honors Courses," *Vagabond* 4 (May 1930): 35–36.

2. Matthew Auer quoted in "HHC, IU Mourn Friend and Benefactor Edward L. Hutton (1919–2009)," Hutton Honors College, Indiana University. http://www.indiana.edu/~iubhonor/hutton/elh.php (accessed September 9, 2016).

Technology Park

Epigraph is from "Technology Park," Innovate Indiana, Indiana University, http://innovateindiana.iu.edu/initiatives/tech-park.shtml (accessed March 23, 2017).

1. "Cyberinfrastructure Building Earns Top Marks for Energy Efficiency," IT News and Events, September 5, 2013, https://itnews.iu.edu/articles/2013/from-green-to-gold-ius-cyberinfrastructure-building-earns-top-marks-for-energy-efficiency.php.

GREEN SPACES AND PUBLIC ART

Dunn Cemetery and Rogers Cemetery

Epigraph is from Juliet Fry, *Islands of Green and Serenity: The Courtyards of Indiana University* (Bloomington: University Relations, n.d.).

1. "Deed to Cemetery," 1855, collection C97, Indiana University Archives, Indiana University, Bloomington.

Sundial

Epigraph is from *Annual Report of Indiana University including the Catalogue for the Academic Year 1868–1869* (Indianapolis, 1869), 30.

1. Gil R. Stormont, "Stormont: Indiana University," *Alumni Quarterly* 7, no. 4 (October 1920): 540. "Old Students Recall Placing of Sun-Dial," *Daily Student*, May 4, 1906.

2. *The Indiana University Catalogue, 1895–1986* (Bloomington, April 1896), 19. "Local," *Student* 12, no. 29 (May 26, 1896).

3. "Drum Corps Will Be Reorganized," *Indiana Student*, October 3, 1912; "Excursions Arranged for Students Tomorrow," *Indiana Summer Student*, June 16, 1922.

Dunn's Woods

Epigraph is from Herman B Wells to students, quoted in "Wells' Vision for Greenspace—Taking IU from 20 Acres to 2100 Acres," *Physical Plant Perspective*, spring 2000.

1. David Starr Jordan to Lemuel Moss, October 7, 1882, President's Office records, 1880–1884, collection C73, Indiana University Archives, Indiana University, Bloomington.

Dunn Meadow

Epigraph is from Moya Andrews, "The IU Campus in Spring," *Bloom*, April/May 2009, 80.

Benton Murals

Epigraph is from Thomas Hibben, "Dedication," in David Laurance Chambers and Thomas Hart Benton, *Indiana, a Hoosier History* (Indianapolis: Bobbs-Merrill, 1933).

1. Richard Lieber, foreword to ibid, 3. Thomas Hart Benton, "A Dream Fulfilled," in ibid.

2. Lieber, foreword.

3. Board of Trustees minutes, May 10, 1938, http://purl.dlib.indiana.edu/iudl/archives/iubot/1938-05-09 (accessed September 2, 2016).

4. See Kathleen A. Foster, Nanette Esseck Brewer, and Margaret Contompasis, *Thomas Hart Benton and the Indiana Murals* (Bloomington: Indiana University Art Museum in association with Indiana University Press, 2008).

Showalter Fountain

Epigraph is from Herman B Wells, Showalter Fountain dedication speech, October 22, 1961, President Herman B Wells speeches, collection C137, Indiana University Archives, Indiana University, Bloomington.

***The Space Between: Adam and Eve* by Jean-Paul Darriau**

Epigraph is from Jean-Paul Darriau, open letter about the Adam and Eve Project, August 26, 1969, Chancellor's Records, Herman B Wells, collection C145, Indiana University Archives, Indiana University, Bloomington.

1. Sherry Rouse, IU curator of campus art, communication with the author, 2016.

Arthur R. Metz Memorial Carillon

Epigraph is from an inscription on one of the Metz carillon bells, quoting Herbert Spencer, "On the Origin and Function of Music."

1. "Record Number of IU Bloomington Students Receive Arthur R. Metz Scholarship Support," press release, *IU Newsroom*, January 14, 2014, rev. January 18, 2011, http://newsinfo.iu.edu/news/page/normal/16929.html (accessed October 16, 2015).

***Peau Rouge Indiana* by Alexander Calder**

Epigraph is from *Dedication Week Festival* pamphlet, Musical Arts Center, April 15–21, 1972, Musical Arts Center—Calder Stabile reference file, Indiana University Archives, Indiana University, Bloomington.

1. Claire Bletz, "Art All Around: Statues, Fountains throughout Campus Carry Rich Histories," *Indiana Daily Student*, October 7, 2004.

Jesse H. and Beulah Chanley Cox Arboretum

Epigraph is from a speech by President John W. Ryan at an alumni luncheon, June 19, 1982, John W. Ryan Speeches 1971–1987, collection C45, Indiana University Archives, Indiana University, Bloomington.

Sample Gates

Epigraph is from President John W. Ryan's Dedication Speech, Sample Gates and Plaza—President John Ryan, June 13, 1987, President John W. Ryan speeches, collection C45, Indiana University Archives, Indiana University, Bloomington.

1. "Committee to the Members of the Classes for 1899, 1900, 1901 and 1902, June 5, 1905," Arch Fund folder, President's Office records—Joseph Swain, collection C174, Indiana University Archives, Indiana University, Bloomington.

2. Board of Trustees minutes, June 20, 1904, collection C218, Indiana University Archives, Indiana University, Bloomington.

3. Thomas D. Clark, *Indiana University, Midwestern Pioneer*, vol. 2, *In Mid-Passage* (Bloomington: Indiana University Press, 1973), 15.

Indiana Arc by Charles Perry

Epigraph is from Adelheid M. Gealt, director emerita of the art museum, quoted in Claire Bletz, "Art All Around: Statues, Fountains throughout Campus Carry Rich Histories," *Indiana Daily Student*, October 7, 2004.

1. Indiana Arch dedication ceremony program, November 18, 1995, "Buildings and Grounds-Indiana Arc" reference file, Indiana University Archives, Indiana University, Bloomington.

Frank E. McKinney Jr. Fountain

Epigraph is from the Indiana Arch dedication ceremony program, November 18, 1995, "Buildings and Grounds-Indiana Arc" reference file, Indiana University Archives, Indiana University Bloomington.

Herman B Wells Plaza

Epigraph is from President Myles Brand, Wells Plaza dedication, October 21, 2000, "Herman B Wells Sculpture and Plaza Dedication" script, accession 2002/050 (unprocessed collection), Indiana University Archives, Indiana University, Bloomington.

1. "Committee Member Reflects on Story behind Wells Sculpture," press release, *IU Newsroom*, October 21, 2000.
2. Sherry Rouse quoted in Danielle Rindler, "Revealing the Stories behind IU's Iconic Art," *Indiana Daily Student*, April 14, 2010.

Hoagy Carmichael Sculpture by Michael McAuley

Epigraph is from Hoagy Carmichael, *The Stardust Road* (Bloomington: Indiana University Press, 1946), 33–34.

1. "Hoagy on His Mind," press release, Live at IU, July 5, 2007.
2. J. Terry Clapacs quoted in "Hoagy Carmichael Sculpture Finds Permanent Home at IU," press release, *IU News Room*, September 5, 2008, http://newsinfo.iu.edu/news-archive/8766.html (accessed April 19, 2017).

Ernie Pyle Sculpture by Harold Langland

Epigraph is from Associate Dean of the Media School Lesa Hatley Major, quoted in "IU to Inaugurate Media School and Dedicate Ernie Pyle Sculpture," press release, *IU Bloomington Newsroom*, October 13, 2014, http://news.indiana.edu/releases/iu/2014/10/media-school-inauguration-announcement.shtml (accessed April 13, 2016).

1. Elizabeth Andrews, "Take a Seat Next to a Legend at New Ernie Pyle Sculpture," *Bloom Magazine*, June/July 2014.
2. Statement by the President on the Death of Ernie Pyle, April 18, 1945, Public Papers of the Presidents, Harry S. Truman Library and Museum, Independence, MO, https://trumanlibrary.org/publicpapers/index.php?pid=14&st=&st1= (accessed April 19, 2017).

Jordan Field

Epigraph is from "Up from the Doormat," *Arbutus*, 1920, 53.

1. Ken Bikoff, "Field of Dreams," *Inside Indiana* 19, no. 8 (October 31, 2009).
2. "What a Diamond!," *Indiana Daily Student*, editorial, April 19, 1936.

Early Men's Gymnasiums

Epigraph is from editorial, *Indiana Student*, February 1890.

1. Editorial, *Indiana Student*, November 1, 1889. Dudley Allen Sargent to James D. Maxwell, 22 May 1889, "Men's Gymnasium" reference file, Indiana University Archives, Indiana University, Bloomington.
2. Editorial, *Indiana Student*, November 1, 1891.
3. John W. Cravens, "Buildings on the Old and New Campuses of Indiana University," *Indiana University Alumni Quarterly* 9, no. 3 (July 1922).
4. Ken Bikoff, "The Birthplace of Hoosier Hysteria," *Inside Indiana* 19, no. 6 (October 17, 2009).

Tenth Street Stadium

Epigraph is from 1914 Arbutus, 164.

Ora L. Wildermuth Intramural Center

Epigraph is from William Lowe Bryan, "President William Lowe Bryan's Address at Ground-Breaking Ceremonies," *Indiana Daily Student*, December 8, 1915.

1. "Break Ground for New Gym Tomorrow," *Indiana Daily Student* 41, no. 28 (October 22, 1915); "Tree Cutting on New Gym Ground Success." *Indiana Daily Student* 41, no. 30 (October 25, 1915).
2. "Indiana Opens Gym with Win over Iowa," *Indiana Daily Student*, January 20, 1917.
3. Herman B Wells, *Being Lucky: Reminiscences and Reflections* (Bloomington: Indiana University Press, 1980), 216–17.

Memorial Stadium

Epigraph is from Indiana University alma mater, "Hail to Old IU," lyrics by J. T. Giles.

1. Supplementary descriptive material on Memorial Stadium from Eggers and Higgins to Ross Bartley, director of IU Public Relations, October 13, 1960, Memorial Stadium (17th Street) reference files, Indiana University Archives, Indiana University, Bloomington.
2. Speech by Herman B Wells at the dedication of Memorial Stadium, October 22, 1960, Stadium Dedication remarks, October 22, 1960, collection C137, President Herman B Wells speeches, Indiana University Archives, Indiana University, Bloomington.

Simon Skjodt Assembly Hall

Epigraph is from James Naismith, quoted in "The 'Hoosier State' of Basketball," Hidden Gyms, blog, April 27, 2011, http://hiddengyms.blogspot.com/2011/04/hoosier-state-of-basketball.html (accessed November 10, 2015).

1. "Assembly Hall Renovations to Preserve Greatest Home Court Advantage in College Basketball," IU Athletics, April 7, 2015, http://iuhoosiers.com/news/2015/4/7/Assembly_Hall_Renovations_to_Preserve_Greatest_Home_Court_Advantage_in_College_Basketball.aspx (accessed April 24, 2017).

Cook Hall

Epigraph is from Bob Knight, IU Basketball Coach (1971–2000), private communications with the author, 1995–2000.

1. HOK Sports rebranded itself as Populous in 2009.

2. Larry Rink quoted in Alex Bozich, "New Basketball Practice Facility Named Cook Hall," IU press release, February 21, 2010, reposted at Inside the Hall, http://www.insidethehall.com/2010/02/21/new-basketball-practice-facility-named-cook-hall/ (accessed January 13, 2015).

FOR FURTHER READING

Carmony, Donald F. "Indiana University: From Seminary Square to Dunn's Woods, 1820–1885." Indiana University Publications: Indiana University Printing Services, n.d.

Clark, Thomas D. *Indiana University: Midwestern Pioneer.* Vol. 1, *The Early Years.* Bloomington: Indiana University Press, 1970.

———. *Indiana University: Midwestern Pioneer.* Vol. 2, *In Mid-Passage.* Bloomington: Indiana University Press, 1973.

———. *Indiana University: Midwestern Pioneer.* Vol. 3, *Years of Fulfillment.* Bloomington: Indiana University Press, 1977.

———. *Indiana University: Midwestern Pioneer.* Vol. 4, *Historical Documents since 1816.* Bloomington: Indiana University Press, 1977.

Collins, Dorothy C., and Cecil K. Byrd. *Indiana University: A Pictorial History.* Bloomington: Indiana University Press, 1992.

Foster, Kathleen A., Nanette Esseck Brewer, and Margaret Contompasis. *Thomas Hart Benton and the Indiana Murals.* Bloomington: Indiana University Art Museum / Indiana University Press. 2000.

Gaines, Thomas A. *The Campus as a Work of Art.* New York: Praeger, 1991.

Glancy, Jonathan. *Architecture.* Eyewitness Companions. New York: DK, 2006.

Hennessy, Mildred J. *Herman B Wells: Memories of a Colleague.* Bloomington: Indiana University Press, 2003.

"Indiana University Bloomington: 2010 Campus Master Plan." SmithGroup, JJR, 2010.

Jordan, David Starr. *The Days of a Man, Being Memories of a Naturalist, Teacher, and Minor Prophet of Democracy.* Yonkers-on-Hudson, NY: World Book, 1922.

Keith, Brian D. "A Walking Tour of Building Stone and Architecture on the Central Campus of Indiana University Bloomington." Indiana Geological Survey, 2006.

———. "Follow the Limestone: A Walking Tour of Indiana University." Indiana Geological Survey and the Bloomington/Monroe County Convention and Visitors Bureau, 2009.

Kostof, Spiro, and Greg Castillo. *A History of Architecture: Settings and Rituals.* 2nd ed. New York: Oxford University Press, 1995.

McDonald, William H. "A Short History of Indiana Limestone." Bedford, IN: Lawrence County Tourism Commission, 1995.

Myers, Burton D. *History of Indiana University.* Vol. 2, *1902–1937.* Edited by Ivy L. Chamness and Burton D. Myers. Bloomington: Indiana University Press, 1952.

Roth, Leland, M. *American Architecture: A History.* Boulder, CO: Westview Press, 2001.

Sanders, Scott R. *Stone Country.* Photographs by Jeffrey A. Wolin. Bloomington: Indiana University Press, 1985.

Turner, Paul Venable. *Campus: An American Planning Tradition.* New York: Architectural History Foundation; Cambridge, MA: MIT Press, 1984.

Wells, Herman B. *Being Lucky: Reminiscences and Reflections.* Bloomington: Indiana University Press, 1980.

Woodburn, James A. *History of Indiana University.* Vol. 1, *1820–1902.* Bloomington: Indiana University Press, 1940.

"The Woodland Campus: Indiana University–Bloomington: A Historic Walking Tour." School of Public and Environmental Affairs, Indiana University–Bloomington, 1974.

DIRECTOR	*Gary Dunham*
ASSISTANT ACQUISITIONS EDITOR	*Peggy Solic*
PROJECT MANAGER	*Nancy Lightfoot*
BOOK AND JACKET DESIGNER	*Pamela Rude*
COMPOSITION COORDINATOR	*Tony Brewer*
TYPEFACES	*Arno, Bell, Bickham*

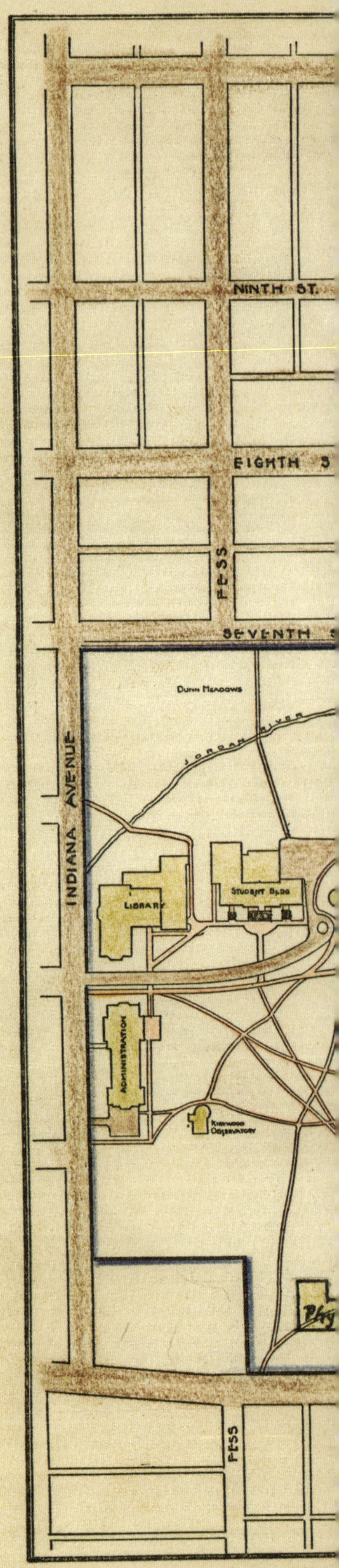
NINTH ST.
EIGHTH S
FESS
SEVENTH S
DUNN MEADOWS
JORDAN RIVER
INDIANA AVENUE
LIBRARY
STUDENT BLDG
ADMINISTRATION
KIRKWOOD OBSERVATORY
FESS